AF398660

# IIT-JEE
## SOLVED PAPERS
### (JEE Main & Advanced)

# Chemistry

## 2020-2002

✓ *Includes Latest Question Papers with Solutions*

# Contents


| | | |
|---|---|---|
| Preface | | 3 |
| How to Handle your Enterances and Boards Like a Pro | | 4 |
| 1. | Some Basic Concepts in Chemistry | 5 |
| 2. | States of Matter | 21 |
| 3. | The Solid State | 32 |
| 4. | Solutions | 40 |
| 5. | Atomic Structure | 58 |
| 6. | Nuclear Chemistry | 73 |
| 7. | Chemical Bonding and Molecular Structure | 77 |
| 8. | Thermodynamics | 92 |
| 9. | Equilibrium | 109 |
| 10. | Redox Reactions | 131 |
| 11. | Electrochemistry | 136 |
| 12. | Chemical Kinetics | 153 |
| 13. | Surface Chemistry | 172 |
| 14. | Classification of Elements and Periodicity in Properties | 181 |
| 15. | General Principles and Processes of Isolation of Elements | 188 |
| 16. | Hydrogen | 196 |
| 17. | The s-Block Elements | 199 |
| 18. | The p-Block Elements | 203 |
| 19. | The d- and f-Block Elements | 231 |
| 20. | Co-ordination Compounds | 240 |
| 21. | Environmental Chemistry | 269 |
| 22. | Organic Chemistry–Some Basic Principles and Techniques | 273 |
| 23. | Hydrocarbons | 278 |
| 24. | Haloalkanes and Haloarenes | 302 |
| 25. | Alcohols, Phenols and Ethers | 324 |
| 26. | Aldehydes, Ketones and Carboxylic Acids | 344 |
| 27. | Nitrogen Containing Compounds | 380 |
| 28. | Polymers | 405 |
| 29. | Biomolecules | 412 |
| 30. | Chemistry in Everyday Life | 425 |



**Edition :** 2021

**Price :** ₹549

**ISBN :** 978-93-90278-59-6

## OSWAL PUBLISHERS

**Head Office** : 1/12, Sahitya Kunj, M.G. Road Agra-282 002
**Phone** : (0562) 2527771-4, 7534077222
**E-mail** : contact@oswalpublishers.com, sales@oswalpublishers.com
**Website** : www.oswalpublishers.com
**Printed at** : Upkar Printing Unit, Agra
The cover of this book has been designed using resources from Freepik.com

# Preface

We feel immense pleasure in introducing the first edition of IIT JEE Solved Papers for JEE aspirants. This edition strictly adheres to the latest syllabus prescribed by the National Testing Agency (NTA), New Delhi.

The book has been carefully designed so as to be useful for JEE aspirants. The solutions have been fully explained so that each reader can acquire the relevant knowledge as per their requirements.

**Special features of the book include:**

- a number of solved question papers, conducted in previous years, are incorporated for practice to enhance the ability of a student to understand the concept clearly and develop the skills to answer accurately.

- last 19 years' (Main & Advanced) questions, i.e. from 2020-2002.

- questions arranged 'Chapter-wise' for students to prepare the section that requires more attention.

- simple and lucid question-solving method for the students to prepare perfectly.

All endeavors have been made to make this book student-friendly by simplifying the graphs and tables.

In spite of our best efforts, the possibilities of some errors of omission cannot be ruled out. Constructive suggestions will be appreciated and thankfully acknowledged.

**–Publisher**

# HOW TO HANDLE YOUR ENTRANCES AND BOARDS LIKE A PRO

Entrance tests and board exams have always been a worrisome affair for the students, for they have always posed a tough task before them. Getting your preparation right is important as these tests can be a Launchpad for your career.

It becomes difficult to balance between the highly competitive entrance exams like NEET, IIT-JEE, and board exams. This raises the performance pressure and anxiety among students. Hence, it is essential to have a proper plan and execute it effectively.

## Valuable tips to prepare well for the entrances and boards:

» **Understanding the basic concepts** : You should always follow the right CBSE solutions/ICSE Solution books to prepare for 10th or 12th board exams as they can help you to identify these areas easily.

» **Optimising your Preparation** : IIT-JEE is a highly competitive entrance exam which is taken to get admissions into specialisations like engineering in the IIT colleges of India. Oswal textbooks and question banks for IIT-JEE completely corresponds with the prescribed NCERT syllabus. You can use these as a reference and prepare well for both the entrance test as well as the main board exams.

» **Simplifying and Prioritising** : Always utilise your time efficiently as these exams are very important for your career. By referring to IIT-JEE books and other subject books, you can prioritise the topics that are important. This will help you prepare in a hassle-free manner.

» **Studying and Revising** : Revising the same chapters can be monotonous but having a quick glance at Oswal IIT-JEE exam books will surely boost your preparation. Divide the syllabus in an organised manner and finish the complete course at a normal pace, leaving adequate time to revise as well.

» **Mock Analysis** : In order to use time optimally, try to do the mock analysis for self-assessment regarding your preparation. Practising mock tests saves your time and efforts from being wasted on chapters that don't need too much attention.

» **Wise Planning and Taking a Break** : Preparing for both entrance and board exams can be quite frustrating at times. So, don't forget to set aside some time for relaxation by taking small breaks, a short nap, having your favourite snack, meditating or going for a walk.

# Some Basic Concepts in Chemistry

## ⓠ QUESTIONS

1. The IUPAC name for the following compound is : **[2020, Main]**

$$CHO$$

(structure: $H_3C$ ... $CH_3$, $COOH$)

(1) 2, 5-dimethyl-6-carboxy-hex-3-enal
(2) 6-formyl-2-methyl-hex-3-enoic acid
(3) 2, 5-dimethyl-5-carboxy-hex-3-enal
(4) 2, 5-dimethyl-6-oxo-hex-3-enoic acid

2. The mole fraction of glucose $(C_6H_{12}O_6)$ in an aqueous binary solution is 0.1. The mass percentage of water in it, to the nearest integer, is ............ . **[2020, Main]**

3. Complex A has a composition of $H_{12}O_6Cl_3Cr$. If the complex on treatment with conc. $H_2SO_4$ loses 13.5% of its original mass, the correct molecular formula of A is : **[2020, Main]**
   [Given : atomic mass of $Cr = 52$ amu and $Cl = 35$ amu]
   (1) $[Cr(H_2O)_5Cl]Cl_2.H_2O$
   (2) $[Cr(H_2O)_3Cl_3].3H_2O$
   (3) $[Cr(H_2O)_4Cl_2]Cl.2H_2O$
   (4) $[Cr(H_2O)_6]Cl_3$

4. The volume (in mL) of 0.1 N NaOH required to neutralise 10 mL of 0.1 N phosphinic acid is ...... .

5. The mass of ammonia in grams produced when 2.8 kg of dinitrogen quantitatively reacts with 1 kg of dihydrogen is .............. . **[2020, Main]**

6. A 20.0 mL solution containing 0.2 g impure $H_2O_2$ reacts completely with 0.316 g of $KMnO_4$ in acid solution. The purity of $H_2O_2$ (in %) is ............ (mol. wt. of $H_2O_2 = 34$; mol. wt of $KMnO_4 = 158$) **[2020, Main]**

7. The average molar mass of chlorine is 35.5 g mol$^{-1}$. The ratio of $^{35}$Cl to $^{37}$Cl in naturally occurring chlorine is close to : **[2020, Main]**
   (1) 4 : 1          (2) 1 : 1
   (3) 2 : 1          (4) 3 : 1

8. In an estimation of bromine by Carius method, 1.6 g of an organic compound gave 1.88 g of AgBr. The mass percentage of bromine in the compound is .............. . **[2020, Main]**
   (Atomic mass, Ag = 108, Br = 80 g mol$^{-1}$)

9. Consider the following equations :
$$2Fe^{2+} + H_2O_2 \rightarrow xA + yB$$
   (in basic medium)
$$2MnO_4^- + 6H^+ + 5H_2O_2 \rightarrow x'C + y'D + z'E$$
   (in acidic medium)
   The sum of the stoichiometric coefficients $x$, $y$, $x'$, $y'$ and $z'$ for products A, B, C, D and E, respectively, is .............. . **[2020, Main]**

10. In the chemical reaction between stoichiometric quantities of $KMnO_4$ and KI in weakly basic solution, what is the number of moles of $I_2$ released for 4 moles of $KMnO_4$ consumed ? **[2020, Main]**

11. Arrange the following labelled hydrogens in decreasing order of acidity : **[2020, Main]**

   $NO_2$   $C \equiv C - Ⓗ_a$  (structure with $Ⓗ_d - O$, $O - Ⓗ_c$, $COOⒽ_b$)

   (1) b > c > d > a          (2) c > b > a > d
   (3) b > a > c > d          (4) c > b > d > a

12. Consider the following molecules and statements related to them : **[2020, Main]**

   (A) (structure)
   (B) (structure)

   (a) (B) is more likely to be crystalline than (A)
   (b) (B) has higher boiling point than (A)
   (c) (B) dissolves more readily than (A) in water
   Identify the correct option from below :
   (1) only (a) is true
   (2) (a) and (c) are true
   (3) (b) and (c) are true
   (4) (a) and (b) are true

**13.** The IUPAC name of the following compound is :

**[2020, Main]**

(1) 4-Bromo-2-methylcyclopentane carboxylic acid

(2) 5-Bromo-3-methylcyclopentanoic acid

(3) 3-Bromo-5-methylcyclopentane carboxylic acid

(4) 3-Bromo-5-methylcyclopentanoic acid

**14.** The IUPAC name of the following compound is :

**[2020, Main]**

(1) 3-amino-4-hydroxymethyl-5-nitrobenzaldehyde

(2) 2-nitro-4-hydroxymethyl-5-amino-benzaldehyde

(3) 4-amino-2-formyl-5-hydroxymethylnitrobenzene

(4) 5-amino-4-hydroxymethyl-2-nitrobenzaldehyde

**15.** Which one of the following structures has the IUPAC name 3-ethynyl-2-hydroxy-4-methylhex-3-en-5-ynoic acid ? **[2020, Advanced]**

**16.** In the following reaction, compound Q is obtained from compound P via an ionic intermediate

(A coloured compound)

What is the degree of unsaturation of Q ?

**[2020, Main]**

**17.** An organic compound ($C_8H_{10}O_2$) rotates plane-polarized light. It produces pink colour with neutral $FeCl_3$ solution. What is the total number of all the possible isomers for this compound ?

**18.** Consider the following four compounds I, II, III and IV. **[2020, Advanced]**

Choose the correct statement(s).

(1) The order of basicity is II > I > III > IV

(2) The magnitude of $pK_b$ difference between I and II is more than that between III and IV

(3) Resonance effect is more in III than in IV

(4) Steric effect makes compound IV more basic than III

**19.** Consider the following transformations of a compound P. **[2020, Advanced]**

Choose the correct option(s).

(1) P is

(2) X is Pd-C/quinoline/$H_2$

(3) P is

(4) R is

**20.** While titrating dilute HCl solution with aqueous NaOH, which of the following will not be required ? **[2020, Main]**

(1) Clamp and phenolphthalein

(2) Pipette and distilled water

(3) Burette and porcelain tile

(4) Bunsen burner and measuring cylinder

**21.** Amongst the following statements, that which was not proposed by Dalton was : **[2020, Main]**

(1) all the atoms of a given element have identical properties including identical mass. Atoms of different elements differ in mass.

(2) chemical reactions involve reorganisation of atoms. These are neither created nor destroyed in a chemical reaction.

(3) when gases combine or reproduced in a chemical reaction they do so in a simple ratio by volume provided all gases are at the same 'I' and 'P'.

(4) matter consists of indivisible atoms.

**22.** The increasing order of basicity for the following intermediates is (from weak to strong) : **[2020, Main]**

(i) $H_3C - \overset{\overset{\displaystyle CH_3}{|}}{\underset{\underset{\displaystyle CH_3}{|}}{C}}{}^{\ominus}$  (ii) $H_2C = CH - \overset{\ominus}{C}H_2$

(iii) $HC \equiv \overset{\ominus}{C}$  (iv) $\overset{\ominus}{C}H_3$

(v) $\overset{\ominus}{C}N$

(1) (iv) < (i) < (iv) < (ii) < (iii)

(2) (iii) < (i) < (ii) < (iv) < (v)

(3) (v) < (iii) < (ii) < (iv) < (i)

(4) (iii) < (iv) < (ii) < (i) < (v)

**23.** 100 mL of a water sample contains 0.81 g of calcium bicarbonate and 0.73 g of magnesium bicarbonate. The hardness of this water sample expressed in terms of equivalents of $CaCO_3$ is :

(molar mass of calcium bicarbonate is 162 g mol$^{-1}$ and magnesium bicarbuonate is 146 g mol$^{-1}$)

**[2019, Main]**

(1) 5,000 ppm  (2) 1,000 ppm

(3) 100 ppm  (4) 10,000 ppm

**24.** Polysubstitution is a major drawback in : **[2019, Main]**

(1) Friedel Craft's alkylation

(2) Remer Tiemanin reaction

(3) Acetylation of aniline

(4) Friedel Craft's acylation

**25.** 0.27 g of a long chain fatty acid was dissolved in 100 cm$^3$ of hexane. 10 mL of this solution was added dropwise to the surface of water in a round watch glass. Hexane evaporates and a monolayer is formed. The distance from edge to centre of the watch glass is 10 cm. What is the height of the monolayer ? **[2019, Main]**

[Density of fatty acid = 0.9 g cm$^{-3}$; $\pi = 3$]

(1) $10^{-6}$ m  (2) $10^{-8}$ m

(3) $10^{-2}$ m  (4) $10^{-4}$ m

**26.** The strength of 11.2 volume solution of $H_2O_2$ is : **[2019, Main]**

[Give that molar mass of H = 1 g mol$^{-1}$ and O = 16 g mol$^{-1}$]

(1) 13.6%  (2) 3.4%

(3) 34%  (4) 1.7%

**27.** For a reaction,

$$N_2(g) + 3H_2(g) \longrightarrow 2NH_3(g);$$

identify dihydrogen ($H_2$) as a limiting reagent in the following reaction mixtures. **[2019, Main]**

(1) 56 g of $N_2$ + 10 g of $H_2$

(2) 35 g of $N_2$ + 8 g of $H_2$

(3) 28 g of $N_2$ + 6 g + $H_2$

(4) 14 g of $N_2$ + 4 g of $H_2$

**28.** What would be the molality of 20% (mass/mass) aqueous solution of KI ? **[2019, Main]**

(molar mass of KI = 166 g mol$^{-1}$)

(1) 1.08  (2) 1.35

(3) 1.48  (4) 1.51

**29.** The minimum amount of $O_2(g)$ consumed per gram of reactant is for the reaction : **[2019, Main]**

(Given atomic mass : Fe = 56, O = 16, Mg = 24, P = 31, C = 12, H = 1)

(1) $4Fe(s) + 3O_2(g) \rightarrow 2Fe_2O_3(s)$

(2) $P_4(s) + 5O_2(g) \rightarrow P_4O_{10}(s)$

(3) $C_3H_8(g) + 5O_2(g) \rightarrow 3CO_2(g) + 4H_2O(l)$

(4) $2Mg(s) + O_2(g) \rightarrow 2MgO(s)$

**30.** The mole fraction of a solvent in aqueous solution of a solute is 0.8. The molality (in mol kg$^{-1}$) of the aqueous` is ....... **[2019, Main]**

(Given data : Molar masses of urea and water are 60 g mol$^{-1}$ and 18 g mol$^{-1}$, respectively)

**34.** The ammonia prepared by treating ammonim sulphate with calcium hydroxide is completely used by $NiCl_2.6H_2O$ to form a stable coordination compound. Assume that both the reactions are 100% complete. If 1584 g of ammonium sulphate and 952 g of $NiCl_2.6H_2O$ are used in the preparation, the combined weight (in grams) of gypsum and the nickel-ammonia coordination compound thus produced is ......... .

**[2018, Advanced]**

(Atomic weights in g mol$^{-1}$ : H = 1, N = 14, O = 16, S = 32, Cl = 35.5, Ca = 40, Ni = 59)

**35.** Galena (an ore) is partially oxidised by passing air through it at high temperature. After some time, the passage of air is stopped, but the heating is continued in a closed furnace such that the contents undergo self-reduction. The weight (in kg) of Pb produced per kg of $O_2$ consumed is .....

(Atomic weights in g mol$^{-1}$ : O = 16, S = 32, Pb = 207) **[2018, Advanced]**

**36.** The ratio of mass percent of C and H of an organic compound ($C_XH_YO_Z$) is 6 : 1. If one molecule of the above compound ($C_XH_YO_Z$) contains half as much oxygen as required to burn one molecule of compound $C_XH_Y$ completely to $CO_2$ and $H_2O$. The empirical formula of compound $C_XH_YO_Z$ is :

**[2018, Main]**

(1) $C_3H_6O_3$       (2) $C_2H_4O$

(3) $C_3H_4O_2$       (4) $C_2H_4O_3$

**37.** A sample of $NaClO_3$ is converted by heat to NaCl with a loss of 0.16 g of oxygen. The residue is dissolved in water and precipitated as AgCl. The mass of AgCl (in g) obtained will be : (Given : Molar mass of AgCl = 143.5 g $mol^{-1}$)

**[2018, Main]**

(1) 0.35       (2) 0.41

(3) 0.48       (4) 0.54

**38.** An unknown chlorohydrocarbon has 3.55% of chlorine. If each molecule of the hydrocarbon has one chlorine atom only; chlorine atoms present in 1 g of chlorohydrocarbon are : **[2018, Main]**

(Atomic wt. of Cl = 35.5 u;

Avogadro constant = $6.023 \times 10^{23}$ $mol^{-1}$)

(1) $6.023 \times 10^{20}$       (2) $6.023 \times 10^9$

(3) $6.023 \times 10^{21}$       (4) $6.023 \times 10^{23}$

**39.** 1 gram of a carbonate ($M_2CO_3$) on treatment with excess HCl produces 0.01186 mole of $CO_2$. The molar mass of $M_2CO_3$ in g $mol^{-1}$ is : **[2017, Main]**

(1) 118.6       (2) 11.86

(3) 1186       (4) 84.3

**40.** The most abundant elements by mass in the body of a healthy human adult are :

Oxygen (61.4%); Carbon (22.9%); Hydrogen (10.0%); and Nitrogen (2.6%).

The weight which a 75 kg person would gain, if all $^1H$ atoms are replaced by $^2H$ atoms is :

**[2017, Main]**

(1) 7.5 kg       (2) 10 kg

(3) 15 kg       (4) 37.5 kg

**41.** Excess of NaOH (aq) was added to 100 mL of $FeCl_3$ (aq) resulting into 2.14 g of $Fe(OH)_3$. The molarity of $FeCl_3$ (aq) is : **[2017, Main]**

(Given molar mass of Fe = 56 g $mol^{-1}$ and molar mass of Cl = 35.5 g $mol^{-1}$)

(1) 0.2 M       (2) 0.3 M

(3) 0.6 M       (4) 1.8 M

**42.** At 300 K, the density of a certain gaseous molecule at 2 bar is double to that of dinitrogen ($N_2$) at 4 bar. The molar mass of gaseous molecule is :

**[2017, Main]**

(1) 28 g $mol^{-1}$       (2) 56 g $mol^{-1}$

(3) 112 g $mol^{-1}$       (4) 224 g $mol^{-1}$

**43.** What quantity (in mL) of a 45% acid solution of a mono-protic strong acid must be mixed with a 20% solution of the same acid to produce 800 mL of a 29.875% acid solution ? **[2017, Main]**

**44.** The mole fraction of a solute in a solution is 0.1. At 298 K, molarity of this solution is the same as its molality. Density of this solution at 298 K is 2.0 g $cm^{-3}$. The ratio of the molecular weights of the solute and solvent, $\left( \dfrac{MW_{solute}}{MW_{solvent}} \right)$, is.

**[2016, Advanced]**

**45.** The amount of arsenic pentasulphide that can be obtained when 35.5 g arsenic acid is treated with excess $H_2S$ in the presence of conc. HCl (assuming 100% conversion) is : **[2016, Main]**

(1) 0.50 mol       (2) 0.25 mol

(3) 0.125 mol       (4) 0.333 mol

**46.** An organic compound contains C, H and S. The minimum molecular weight of the compound containing 8% sulphur is : **[2016, Main]**

(atomic weight of S = 32 amu)

(1) 200 g $mol^{-1}$       (2) 400 g $mol^{-1}$

(3) 600 g $mol^{-1}$       (4) 300 g $mol^{-1}$

**47.** 5 L of an alkane requires 25 L of oxygen for its complete combustion. If all volumes are measured at constant temperature and pressure, the alkane is : **[2016, Main]**

(1) Ethane       (2) Propane

(3) Butane       (4) Isobutane

**48.** At 300 K and 1 atm, 15 mL of a gaseous hydrocarbon requires 375 mL air containing 20% $O_2$ by volume for complete combustion. After combustion the gases occupy 330 mL. Assuming that the water formed is in liquid form and the volumes were measured at the same temperature and pressure, the formula of the hydrocarbon is :

**[2016, Main]**

(1) $C_3H_6$       (2) $C_2H_{12}$

(3) $C_4H_8$       (4) $C_4H_{10}$

**49.** The molecular formula of commercial resin used for exchanging ions in water softening is $C_8H_7SO_3Na$ (Mol. wt. 206). What would be the maximum uptake of $Ca^{2+}$ ions by the resin when expressed in mole per gram resin ? **[2015, Main]**

(1) $\dfrac{1}{103}$       (2) $\dfrac{1}{206}$

(3) $\dfrac{2}{309}$       (4) $\dfrac{1}{412}$

**50.** In Carius method of estmation of halogens, 250 mg of an organic compound gave 141 mg of AgBr. The percentage of bromine in the compound is : (at mass Ag = 108; Br = 80) **[2015, Main]**

(1) 24       (2) 36

(3) 48       (4) 60

**51.** A sample of a hydrate of barium chloride weighing 61 g was heated until all the water of hydration is removed. The dried sample weighed 52 g. The formula of the hydrated salt is : (atomic mass, Ba = 137 amu, Cl = 35.5 amu) **[2015, Main]**
(1) $BaCl_2.H_2O$      (2) $BaCl_2.2H_2O$
(3) $BaCl_2.3H_2O$      (4) $BaCl_2.4H_2O$

**52.** $A + 2B + 2C \rightleftharpoons AB_2C_3$
Reaction of 6.0 g of A, $6.0 \times 10^{23}$ atoms of B, and 0.036 mol of C yields 4.8 g of compound $AB_2C_3$. If the atomic mass of A and C are 60 and 80 amu, respectively, the atomic mass of B is (Avogadro no. $= 6 \times 10^{23}$) : **[2015, Main]**
(1) 70 amu      (2) 60 amu
(3) 50 amu      (4) 40 amu

**53.** Choose the incorrect formula out of the four compounds for an element X below : **[2015, Main]**
(1) $X_2Cl_3$      (2) $X_2O_3$
(3) $X_2(SO_4)_3$      (4) $XPO_4$

**54.** A compound $H_2X$ with molar weight of 80 g is dissolved in a solvent having density of 0.4 g ml$^{-1}$. Assuming no change in volume upon dissolution, the molality of a 3.2 molar solution is. **[2014, Advanced]**

**55.** The ratio of masses of oxygen and nitrogen in a particular gaseous mixture is 1 : 4. The ratio of number of their molecule is : **[2014, Main]**
(1) 1 : 4      (2) 7 : 32
(3) 1 : 8      (4) 3 : 16

**56.** Dissolving 120 g of a compound of (mol. wt. 60) in 1000 g of water gave a solution of density 1.12 g/mL. The molarity of the solution is : **[2014, Main]**
(1) 1.00 M      (2) 2.00 M
(3) 2.50 M      (4) 4.00 M

**57.** The amount of oxygen in 3.6 moles of water is : **[2014, Main]**
(1) 115.2 g      (2) 57.6 g
(3) 28.8 g      (4) 18.4 g

**58.** A gaseous compound of nitrogen and hydrogen contains 12.5% (by mass) of hydrogen. The density of the compound relative to hydrogen is 16. The molecular formula of the compound is : **[2014, Main]**
(1) $NH_2$      (2) $N_3H$
(3) $NH_3$      (4) $N_2H_4$

**59.** The amount of $BaSO_4$ formed upon mixing 100 mL of 20.8% $BaCl_2$ solution with 50 mL of 9.8% $H_2SO_4$ solution will be : **[2014, Main]**
(Ba = 137, Cl = 35.5, S = 32, H = 1 and O = 16)
(1) 23.3 g      (2) 11.65 g

(3) 30.6 g      (4) 33.2 g

**60.** 29.2% (w/w) HCl stock solution has a density of 1.25 g mL$^{-1}$. The molecular weight of HCl is 36.5 g mol$^{-1}$. The volume (mL) of stock solution required to prepare a 200 mL solution of 0.4 M HCl is. **[2012, Advanced]**

**61.** Dissolving 120 g of urea (mol. wt. 60) in 1000 g of water gave a solution of density 1.15 g/mL. The molarity of the solution is : **[2011, Advanced]**
(1) 1.78 M      (2) 2.00 M
(3) 2.05 M      (4) 2.22 M

**62.** Reaction of $Br_2$ with $Na_2CO_3$ in aqueous solution gives sodium bromide and sodium bromate with evolution of $CO_2$ gas. The number of sodium bromide molecules involved in the balanced chemical equation is. **[2011, Advanced]**

**63.** The volume (in mL) of 0.1 M $AgNO_3$ required for complete precipitation of chloride ions present in 30 mL of 0.01 M solution of $[Cr(H_2O)_5Cl]Cl_2$, as silver chloride is close to. **[2011, Advanced]**

**64.** A student performs a titration with different burettes and finds titre values of 25.2 mL, 25.25 mL and 25.0 mL. The number of significant figures in the average titre value is. **[2010, Advanced]**

**65.** Silver (atomic weight = 108 g mol$^{-1}$) has a density of 10.5 g cm$^{-3}$. The number of silver atoms on a surface of area $10^{-12}$ m$^2$ can be expressed in scientific notation as $y \times 10^x$. The value of $x$ is. **[2010, Advanced]**

**66.** (a) Calculate the amount of Calcium oxide required when it reacts with 852 gm of $P_4O_{10}$.
(b) Write the structure of $P_4O_{10}$. **[2005, Main]**

**67.** Calculate the molarity of water if its density is 1000 kg/m$^3$. **[2003, Main]**

**68.** Which has maximum number of atoms ? **[2003, Screening]**
(1) 24g of C (12)      (2) 56g of Fe (56)
(3) 27g of Al (27)      (4) 108g of Ag(108)

**69.** How many moles of electron weigh one kilogram : **[2002, Screening]**
(1) $6.023 \times 10^{23}$
(2) $\dfrac{1}{9.108} \times 10^{31}$
(3) $\dfrac{6.023}{9.108} \times 10^{54}$
(4) $\dfrac{1}{9.108 \times 6.023} \times 10^8$

## ANSWER KEY

| 1. (4) | 2. (*) | 3. (3) | 4. (*) | 5. (*) | 6. (*) | 7. (4) | 8. (*) | 9. (*) | 10. (*) |
|---|---|---|---|---|---|---|---|---|---|
| 11. (1) | 12. (3) | 13. (1) | 14. (4) | 15. (4) | 16. (*) | 17. (*) | 18. (3,4) | 19. (2,3) | 20. (4) |
| 21. (3) | 22. (3) | 23. (4) | 24. (4) | 25. (1) | 26. (2) | 27. (1) | 28. (4) | 29. (1) | 30. (3) |
| 31. (4) | 32. (*) | 33. (*) | 34. (*) | 35. (*) | 36. (4) | 37. (3) | 38. (1) | 39. (4) | 40. (1) |
| 41. (1) | 42. (3) | 43. (3) | 44. (*) | 45. (3) | 46. (2) | 47. (2) | 48. (*) | 49. (4) | 50. (1) |
| 51. (2) | 52. (3) | 53. (1) | 54. (*) | 55. (2) | 56. (2) | 57. (2) | 58. (4) | 59. (1) | 60. (*) |
| 61. (3) | 62. (*) | 63. (*) | 64. (3) | 65. (*) | 66. (*) | 67. (*) | 68. (1) | 69. (4) | |

## ANSWERS WITH EXPLANATIONS

**1. (4)**

$$\overset{6}{C}HO,\ H_3C\overset{5}{\phantom{}}\overset{4}{\phantom{}}\overset{3}{=}\overset{2}{\phantom{}}CH_3,\ COOH$$

IUPAC name

2, 5-dimethyl-6-oxo-hex-3-enoic acid

**2.** $X_{C_6H_{12}O_6} = 0.1$

Let total mole is 1 mol then mole of glucose will be 0.1 and mole of water will be 0.9, so mass % of water

$$= \frac{0.9 \times 18}{0.1 \times 180 + 0.9 \times 18} \times 100$$

$$= 47.36$$

**3. (3)** % mass of water

$$= \frac{x \times 18}{(12 + 6 \times 16 + 35 \times 3 + 52)} \times 100 = 13.5$$

$$\Rightarrow \quad x = \frac{265 \times 13.5}{18 \times 100} = 2$$

**4.** $H_3PO_2 + NaOH \rightarrow NaH_2PO_2 + H_2O$

$$\frac{n_{H_3PO_2}\text{ reacted}}{1} = \frac{n_{NaOH}\text{ reacted}}{1}$$

$$\Rightarrow \quad \frac{0.1 \times 10}{1} = 0.1 \times V_{NaOH}$$

$$\Rightarrow \quad V_{NaOH} = 10 \text{ ml.}$$

**5.**

$$N_2 \quad + \quad 3H_2 \quad \rightarrow \quad 2NH_3$$

$$\frac{2.8}{28} \text{ K mol} \quad \frac{1}{2} \text{ K mol}$$

$$= 0.1 \text{ K mol} \quad 0.5 \text{ K mol} \quad —$$

$$= 0.2 \text{ K mol} \quad 0.2 \text{ K mol} \quad —$$

$$\text{mass }(NH_3) = 0.2 \times 17 \text{ kg}$$

$$= 3.4 \text{ Kg}$$

$$= 3400 \text{ gm}$$

**6.**

$$M_{eq} \text{ of } H_2O_2 = M_{eq} \text{ of } KMnO_4$$

$$x \times 2 = \frac{0.316}{158} \times 5$$

$$x = 5 \times 10^{-3} \text{ mol}$$

$$m_{H_2O_2} = 5 \times 10^{-3} \times 34 = 0.17 \text{ gm}$$

$$\%H_2O_2 = \frac{0.17}{0.2} \times 100 = 85$$

**7. (4)**

| | $^{35}Cl$ | $^{37}Cl$ | Av. molar |
|---|---|---|---|
| let | $x$ | 1 | mass = 35.5 |

mole ratio

$$\text{Av. molar mass} = \frac{n_1 M_1 + n_2 M_2}{(n_1 + n_2)}$$

$$35.5 = \frac{x \times 35 + 1 \times 37}{x + 1}$$

$$x = 3$$

**8.** Given,

Mass of organic compound = 1.6 g

Mass of AgBr = 1.88 g

Moles of Br = Moles of AgBr = $\frac{1.88}{188} = 0.01$

Mass of Br = 0.01 × 80 = 0.80 g

% of Br = $\frac{0.80 \times 100}{1.60} = 50\%$

**9.** $[Fe^{2+} \rightarrow Fe^{3+} + e^-] \times 2$

$$\frac{H_2O_2 + 2e^- \rightarrow 2HO^-}{2Fe^{2+} + H_2O_2 \rightarrow 2Fe^{3+} + 2HO^-_{(q\omega)}}$$

$x = 2 \quad y = 2$

$[8H^+ + MnO_4^- + 5e^- \rightarrow Mn^{2+} + 4H_2O] \times 2$

$[H_2O_2 \rightarrow O_{2(g)} + 2H^+ + 2e^-] \times 5$

$\Rightarrow 16H^+ + 2MnO_4^- + 5H_2O_2$
$\quad \rightarrow 2Mn^{2+} + 8H_2O + 5O_{2(g)} + 10H^+$

$\Rightarrow 6H^+ + 2MnO_4^- + 5H_2O_2$
$\quad \rightarrow 2Mn^{2+} + 8H_2O + 5O_{2(g)}$

So $x' = 2 \quad y' = 8 \quad z' = 5$

so $x + y + x' + y' + z'$

$\Rightarrow 2 + 2 + 2 + 8 + 5$

$\Rightarrow 19$

**10.** $KMnO_4 + KI \rightarrow MnO_2 + I_2$

$$\text{Eq. of } KMNO_4 = \text{Eq. of } I_2$$

$$4 \times 3 = n \times 2$$

$$n = 6$$

**11. (1)** Acidic strength order :

$$\underset{\substack{\| \\ O}}{R - C} - OH > R - OH > R - C \equiv CH$$

Reason : $R - \overset{O}{\underset{\|}{C}} - O^-$ stable by equivalent resonance.

Stable :

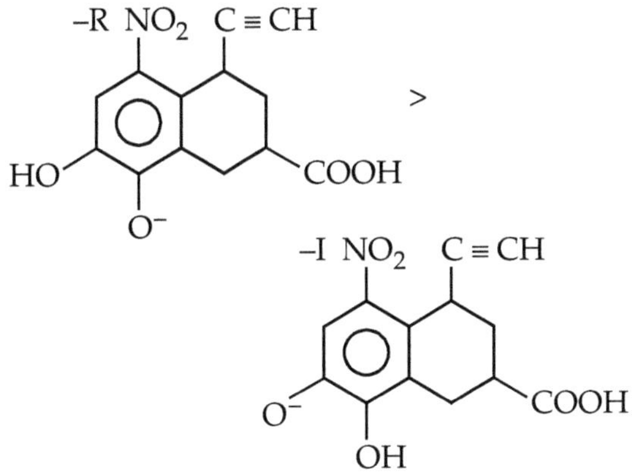

So answer is b > c > d > a.

**12. (3)**

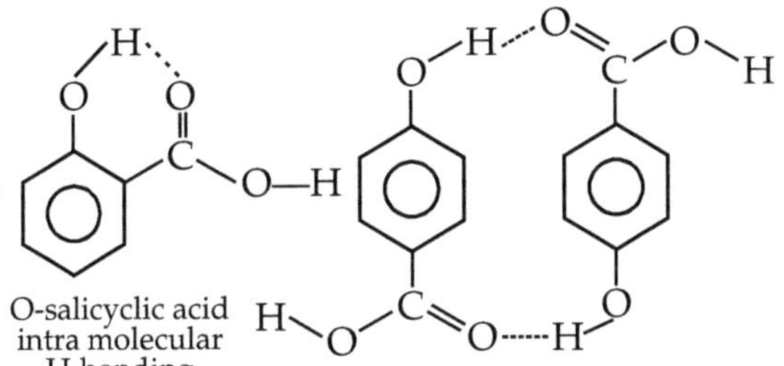

O-salicyclic acid
intra molecular
H-bonding

*p*-salicyclic acid
inter molecular H-bonding

(a) B will be more crystalline due to more inter molecular interactions hence more efficient packing.

(b) B will have higher boiling point due to higher intermolecular interactions.

(c) B will be more soluble in water than A as B will have more extent of H-bonding in water.

So all three statements are correct.

{Solubility date $\Rightarrow$ O-salicylic acid = 2g/L

P-salicylic acid = 5 g/L

**13. (1)**

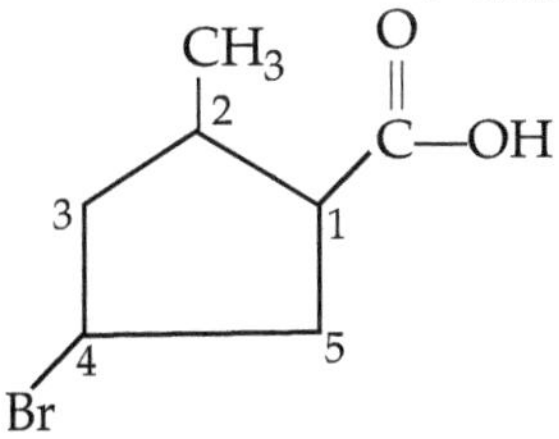

4-bromo-2-methyl cyclopentane carboxylic acid.

**14. (4)**

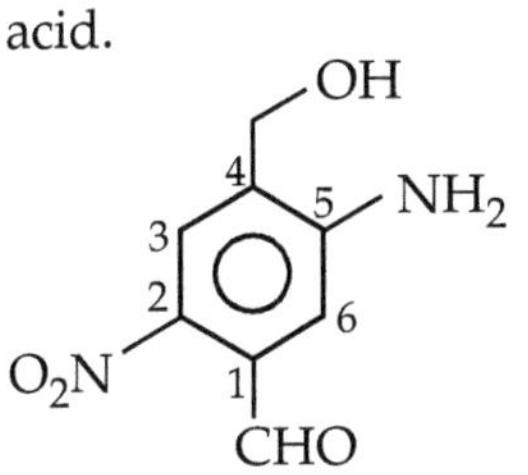

5-amino-4-hydroxymethyl-2-nitrobenzalde-hyde.

**15. (4)**

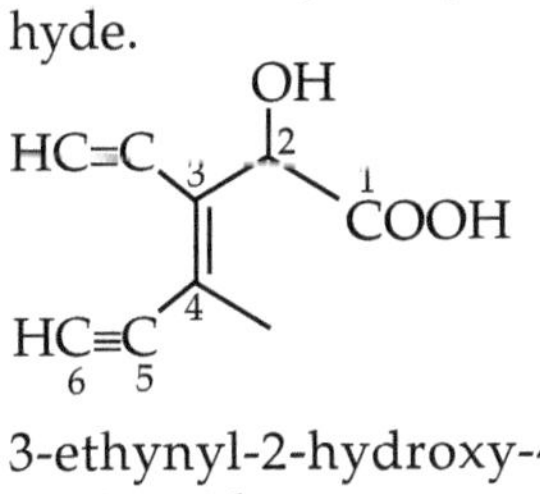

3-ethynyl-2-hydroxy-4-methyl-hex-3-en-5-ynoic acid.

**16.**

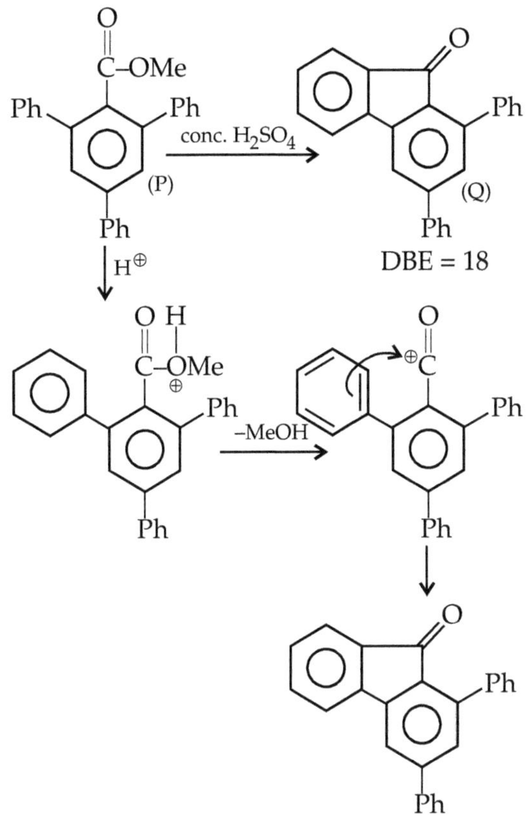

conc. $H_2SO_4$

(P)

(Q)

DBE = 18

$H^{\oplus}$

$-MeOH$

**17.** $C_8H_{10}O_2 \rightarrow$ Gives $FeCl_3$ test means Phenol derivative

$\downarrow$

Rotate plane polarized light means optically active

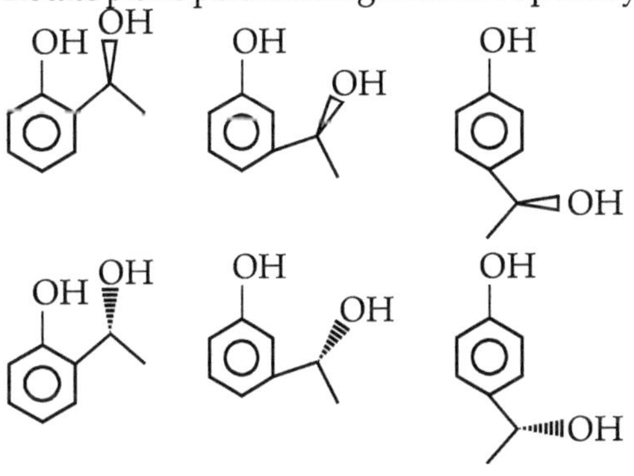

Hence, total optically active isomers wil be 6.

**18. (3,4)**

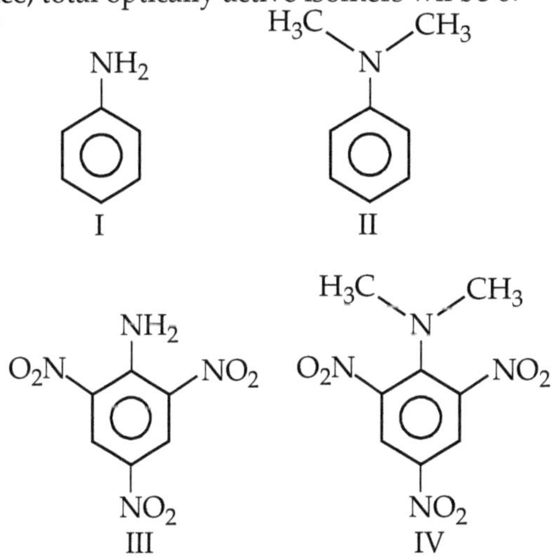

I

II

III

IV

$pK_b$ different between I and II is 0.53 and that of III and IV is 4.6.

So option (B) is incorrect

Correct statement (C), (D).

The most basic compound in the given option is (II) and least basic compound is (III).

In 2,4,6-trinitro aniline (III) due to strong –R effect of $-NO_2$ groups, the l.p. of $-NH_2$ is more involved with benzene ring hence it has least basic strength.

Whereas (IV) N,N-Dimethyl 2, 4, 6-trinitro aniline, due to steric inhibition to resonance (SIR) effect; the lone pair of nitrogen is not in the plane of benzene, hence make it (l.p.) more free to protonate.

more effective resonance

L.P. is not in conjugation

**19. (2,3)**

**20. (4)** In this acid base titration, there is no use of Bunsen burner and measuring cylinder other laboratory equipments will be required for getting the end point of tiration.

**21. (3)** Option (3) is according to Gaylussac's law of volume combination.

**22. (3)**

(i)

(ii)

(iii)

(iv)

(v)

Basic strength order : (i) > (iv) > (ii) > (iii) > (v)

**23. (4)** The number of equivalents of $CaCO_3$ will be equal to the sum of the number of equivalents of $Ca(HNO_3)_2$ and $Mg(HCO_3)_2$ as shown below :

$$n_{eq}(CaCO_3) = n_{eq}(Ca(HCO_3)_2)$$
$$+ n_{eq}(Mg(HCO_3)_2)$$

$$\frac{m}{100} \times 2 = \frac{0.81}{162} \times 2 + \frac{0.73}{146} \times 2$$

$$m = \frac{1}{50} \times 50$$

$$m = 1 \text{ g}$$

The hardness of water is calculated as shown below :

$$\text{Hardness} = \frac{1}{100} \times 10^6 = 10,000 \text{ ppm}$$

**24. (4)** The percent composition by mole is calculated as shown below :

Percent composition by mole of C

$$= \frac{\text{Number of moles of carbon}}{\left(\begin{array}{c}\text{Total number of moles of} \\ \text{all the elements in } CH_4\end{array}\right)} \times 100\%$$

$$= \frac{1 \text{ mol}}{5 \text{ mol}} \times 100\%$$

$$= 20\%$$

**25. (1)** The radius of watch glass is 10 cm. The surface area is calculated as shown below :

$$\text{Surface area} = \pi r^2$$
$$= 3 \times (10)^2$$
$$= 300 \text{ cm}^2$$

In 10 mL solution, the mass of fatty acid is

$$= \frac{10 \times 0.27}{100}$$
$$= 0.027 \text{ g}$$

$$\text{The volume of fatty acid is} = \frac{\text{Mass}}{\text{Density}}$$

$$= \frac{0.027 \text{ g}}{0.9 \text{ g/cm}^3}$$

$$= 0.03 \text{ cm}^3$$

The height of the monolayer can be calculated as shown below :

$$\text{Height} = \frac{\text{Volume of fatty acid}}{\text{Surface area of watch glass}}$$

$$= \frac{0.03 \text{ cm}^3}{300 \text{ cm}^2}$$

$$= 0.0001 \text{ cm}$$

$$= 10^{-6} \text{ m}$$

**26. (2)** The molarity is calculated as shown below :

$$\text{Volume strength} = 11.2 \times \text{Molarity}$$
$$11.2 = 11.2 \times \text{Molarity}$$
$$\text{Molarity} = 1 \text{ M}$$

The molar mass of $H_2O_2$ is 34 g/mol, therefore, the strength of solution is 34 g/L.

$$\text{Strength (\% w/w)} = \frac{34}{1000} \times 1000$$

$$= 0.34\%$$

**27. (1)** The chemical equation for the reaction between nitrogen and oxygen gas is shown below :

$$N_2(g) + 3H_2(g) \rightarrow 2NH_3(g)$$

One mole of nitrogen gas reacts with three moles of hydrogen gas.

The calculation for number of moles in each case is shown below :

| | Mass of $N_2$ | Mass of $H_2$ | Number of moles of $N_2$ | Number of moles of $H_2$ |
|---|---|---|---|---|
| Case I | 56 g | 10 g | $\dfrac{56 \text{ g}}{28 \text{ g/mol}}$ $= 2$ mol | $\dfrac{10 \text{ g}}{2 \text{ g/mol}}$ $= 5$ mol |
| Case II | 35 g | 8 g | $\dfrac{35 \text{ g}}{28 \text{ g/mol}}$ $= 1.25$ mol | $\dfrac{8 \text{ g}}{2 \text{ g/mol}}$ $= 4$ mol |
| Case III | 28 g | 6 g | $\dfrac{28 \text{ g}}{28 \text{ g/mol}}$ $= 1$ mol | $\dfrac{6 \text{ g}}{2 \text{ g/mol}}$ $= 3$ mol |
| Case IV | 14 g | 4 g | $\dfrac{14 \text{ g}}{28 \text{ g/mol}}$ $= 2$ mol | $\dfrac{4 \text{ g}}{2 \text{ g/mol}}$ $= 2$ mol |

Therefore, the combination in which dihydrogen is limiting reagent is 56 g of $N_2$ and 10 g of $H_2$.

**28. (4)** The 100 g of aqueous solution of KI contains 80 g of water and 20 g of KI.

The molar mass of KI is 166 g/mol.

Molality can be calculated using the equation given below :

$$m_{\text{solute}} = \frac{m_{\text{KI}}}{m_{\text{solvent}} M_{\text{KI}}}$$

$$= \frac{(20 \text{ g})}{(80 \text{ g})\left(\dfrac{1 \text{ kg}}{1000 \text{ g}}\right)(166 \text{ g/mol})}$$

$$= 1.5060 \text{ mol/kg}$$

$$\approx 1.51 \text{ mol/kg}$$

**29. (1)** Consider the reaction of propane with oxygen.

$$C_3H_8 + 5O_2 \rightarrow 3CO_2 + 4H_2O$$

For 44 g $C_3H_8$, 160 g $O_2$ is required. Therefore, for 1 g $C_3H_8$, $= \dfrac{160}{44}$ g $O_2 = 3.63$ g $O_2$ is required.

Consider the reaction of phosphorous with oxygen.

$$P_4 + 5O_2 \rightarrow P_4O_{10}$$

For 124 g $P_4$, 160 g $O_2$ is required. Therefore, for 1 g $P_4$, $= \dfrac{160}{124}$ g $O_2 = 1.29$ g $O_2$ is required.

Consider the reaction of iron with oxygen.

$$4Fe + 3O_2 \rightarrow 2Fe_2O_3$$

For 223.2 g Fe, 96 g $O_2$ is required. Therefore, for 1 g Fe, $= \dfrac{96}{223.2}$ g $O_2 = 0.43$ g $O_2$ is required.

Consider the reaction of magnesium with oxygen.

$$2Mg + O_2 \rightarrow 2MgO$$

For 48 g Mg, 32 g $O_2$ is required. Therefore, for 1 g Mg, $= \dfrac{32}{48}$ g $O_2 = 0.67$ g $O_2$ is required.

Therefore, the least amount of oxygen is required by Fe.

**30. (3)** The molar mass of water is 18 g/mol.

The molar fraction of water is 0.8.

The molar fraction of solute is $(1 - 0.8) = 0.2$.

Molality can be calculated using the equation given below :

$$m_{\text{solute}} = \frac{100 x_{\text{solute}}}{x_{\text{solvent}} M_{\text{solvent}}}$$

Substitute the values of $x_{\text{solute}}$, $x_{\text{solvent}}$ and $M_{\text{solvent}}$ in the above equation.

$$m_{\text{solute}} = \frac{1000(0.2)}{(0.8)(18 \text{ g/mol})}$$

$$= 1.388 \text{ mol}$$

**31. (4)** The molar mass of A is $M_A$.

The molar mass of B is $M_B$.

The mass of 5 mol of $AB_2$ is calculated as shown below :

$$5(M_A + 2M_B) = 125 \times 10^{-3} \text{ kg} \qquad ...(1)$$

The mass of 10 mol of $A_2B_2$ is calculated as shown below :

$$5(2M_A + 2M_B) = 300 \times 10^{-3} \text{ kg} \qquad ...(2)$$

The value of $M_A$ and $M_B$ obtained after solving the equation (1) and (2) are $5 \times 10^{-3}$ and $10 \times 10^{-3}$ respectively.

**32.** The chemical reaction between $S_8$ and nitric acid is shown below :

$$S_8 + 48HNO_3 \rightarrow 8H_2SO_4 + 48NO_2 + 16H_2O$$

One mole of $S_8$ produces 16 moles of water.

The mass of 16 mol of water is calculated as shown below :

$$m = nM$$
$$= (16 \text{ mol})(18 \text{ g/mol})$$
$$= 288.00 \text{ g}$$

**33.** The number of moles of water is calculated as shown below :

$$n = \frac{900 \text{ g}}{18 \text{ g/mol}}$$
$$= 50 \text{ mol}$$

The mole of fraction of the urea is calculated as shown below :

$$x_U = \frac{n_U}{n_U + n_W}$$

$$0.5 = \frac{n_U}{n_U + 50 \text{ mol}}$$

Rearrange the above equation for the value of $n_U$.

$$19\, n_U = 50 \text{ mol}$$
$$n_U = \frac{50}{19} \text{ mol}$$
$$= 2.63 \text{ mol}$$

The mass of the urea is calculates as shown below :

$$m = (2.63 \text{ mol})(60 \text{ g/mol})$$
$$= 157.8 \text{ g}$$

The volume of the solution is calculated as shown below :

$$V = \frac{(157.8 + 900) \text{ g}}{1.2 \text{ g/mL}}$$
$$= 881.5 \text{ mL}$$

The molarity fo the solution is shown below :

$$\text{Molarity} = \frac{2.63 \times 1000}{881.5}$$
$$= 2.98 \text{ M}$$

**34.** The given reactions are shown below.

$$(NH_4)_2SO_4 + Ca(OH)_2 \rightarrow CaSO_4.2H_2O + 2NH_3$$
$$NiCl_2.6H_2O + 6NH_3 \rightarrow [Ni(NH_3)_6]Cl_2 + 6H_2O$$

$$\text{Number of moles of } (NH_4)_2SO_4 = \frac{1584 \text{ g}}{132 \text{ g/mol}}$$
$$= 12 \text{ mol}$$

Number of moles of $CaSO_4.2H_2O = 12$ mol

$$\text{Mass of gypsum} = 12 \times 172$$
$$= 2064 \text{ g}$$

Number of moles of $NH_3$ that is released $= 24$ mol

$$\text{Number of moles of } NiCl_2.6H_2O = \frac{952 \text{ g}}{238 \text{ g/mol}}$$
$$= 4 \text{ mol}$$

Number of moles of $[Ni(NH_3)_6]Cl_2 = 4$ mol

$$\text{Mass of } [Ni(NH_3)_6] = 4 \times 232$$
$$= 928 \text{ g}$$

$$\text{Total mass} = (2064 + 928) \text{ g}$$
$$= 2992 \text{ g}$$

**35.** The given reactions are shown below :

$$2PbS + 3O_2 \rightarrow 2PbO + 2SO_2$$
$$2PbO + PbS \rightarrow 3Pb + SO_2$$

The number of moles of lead produced by 3 moles of oxygen = 3

Mass of 1 mole of oxygen = 16 g

Mass of 3 moles of oxygen = 3 × 16 g
$$= 96 \text{ g}$$

Mass of 1 mole of lead = 207.2 g

Mass of 3 moles of lead = 3 ×207.2 g
$$= 621.6 \text{ g}$$

Mass of lead produced by 96g oxygen = 621.6 g

$$\text{Mass of lead produced by 1 g oxygen} = \frac{621.6\text{g}}{96}$$
$$= 6.475 \text{ g}$$

Mass of lead produced by 1000 g oxygen

$$= \frac{621.6}{96} \times 1000\text{g}$$
$$= 6475 \text{ g}$$

Mass of lead produced by 1 kg oxygen = 6.475 kg

**36. (4)** The number of atoms of carbon present in the given compound is considered to be X, the number of atoms of hydrogen be Y and the number of atoms of oxygen in the given compound Z is.

The balanced chemical equation for the combustion of $C_XH_Y$ is,

$$C_XH_Y + \left(X + \frac{Y}{4}\right)O_2 \rightarrow XCO_2 + \frac{Y}{2}H_2O$$

The number of atoms of oxygen required in the combustion of $C_XH_Y$ is

Number of oxygen atoms required

$$= 2\left(X + \frac{Y}{4}\right)$$
$$= \left(2X + \frac{Y}{2}\right)$$

The relation between the mass of carbon and hydrogen atoms in the given compound is,

$$\frac{12X}{Y} = \frac{6}{1} \qquad \qquad ...(1)$$
$$2X = Y$$

The relation between the mass of oxygen and carbon in the given compound is,

$$Z = \frac{1}{2}\left(2X + \frac{Y}{2}\right)$$

Substitute the value of Y in terms of X from equation (1) in the above equation.

$$Z = \frac{1}{2}\left(2X + \frac{2X}{2}\right)$$

$$= \frac{3X}{2}$$

The ratio of carbon hydrogen and oxygen in the given compound is calculated as,

$$X : 2X : \frac{3X}{2} = 2X : 4X : 3X$$

$$= 2 : 4 : 3$$

Hence, the empirical formula of the given compound is $C_2H_4O_3$.

**37. (3)** The molar mass of $O_2$ is 32 g/mol.

The formula to calculate number of moles is,

$$n = \frac{m}{M_w}$$

$$= \frac{0.16g}{32 \text{ g/mol}}$$

$$= 0.005 \text{ mol}$$

The reaction for the formation of NaCl with a loss of oxygen from $NaClO_3$ is shown below :

$$2NaClO_3 \rightarrow 2NaCl + 3O_2$$

Therefore,

$$3 \text{ moles of } O_2 = 2 \text{ moles of NaCl}$$
$$= 2 \text{ moles of AgCl}$$

$$0.005 \text{ moles of } O_2 = 0.005 \times \frac{2}{3} \text{ moles of AgCl}$$

$$= 0.00333 \text{ moles of AgCl}$$

The molar mass of AgCl is 143.5 g/mol. Therefore, mass of AgCl obtained is

$$n = \frac{m}{M_w}$$

$$m = n \times M_w$$
$$= 143.5 \text{ g/mol} \times 0.00333 \text{ mol}$$
$$= 0.48 \text{ g}$$

**38. (1)** The percentage of chlorine in an unknown chlorohydrocarboin is 3.55%

It means 100 g of chlorohydrocarbon contains 3.55 g Cl.

Therefore,

1 g of chlorohydrocarbon

$$= 3.55\frac{1}{100} \text{ of chlorine}$$

$$= 0.355 \text{ g Cl}$$

The atomic weight of chlorine is 35.5 g/mol. The formula to calculate the number of moles is,

$$n = \frac{m}{M_w}$$

$$= \frac{0.355g}{35.5 \text{ g/mol}}$$

$$= 0.001 \text{ mol}$$

The formula to calculate the number of atoms of chlorine is,

number of atoms of Cl = mole × $N_A$
$$= (0.001 \text{ mol}) \times (6.023 \times 10^{23} \text{ mol}^{-1})$$
$$= 6.023 \times 10^{20}$$

**39. (4)** The reaction of $M_2CO_3$ with excess of HCl is,

$$M_2CO_3 + 2HCl \rightarrow 2MCl + H_2O + CO_2$$

Mass (m) of $M_2CO_3$ is 1 gram.

Molar mass of $M_2CO_3$ is assumed to be M.

Therefore, $n_{M_2CO_3} = n_{CO_2}$.

The number of moles of $M_2CO_3$ is expressed by the formula,

$$n = \frac{m}{M}$$

Thus,

$$\frac{1\,g}{M} = 0.01186 \text{ mol}$$

$$M = \frac{1\,g}{0.01186 \text{ mol}}$$

$$M = 84.3 \text{ g/mol}$$

**40. (1)** Mass of hydrogen in 75 kg of a person is calculated as,

$$\text{Mass of hydrogen} = \frac{10}{100} \times 75 \text{ kg}$$

$$= 7.5 \text{ kg}$$

Now, $^1H$ atoms are replaced by $^2H$ atoms. Therefore, replacing $^1H$ atoms by $^2H$ atoms would replace 7.5 kg with 2 × 7.5 kg = 15 kg. Hence, net gain is 7.5 kg.

**41. (1)** The reaction of NaOH with $FeCl_3$ is given below.

$$3NaOH \text{ (excess)(aq)} + FeCl_3(aq)$$
$$100 \text{ mL}$$
$$\rightarrow Fe(OH)_3(s) + 3NaCl(aq)$$
$$2.14 \text{ g}$$

$$\text{Moles of } Fe(OH)_3 = \frac{2.14 \text{ g}}{107 \text{ g/mol}}$$

$$= 2 \times 10^{-2} \text{ mol}$$

If one mole of $FeCl_3$ gives one mole of $Fe(OH)_3$, then,

$2 \times 10^{-2}$ mole of $Fe(OH)_3$ will be formed by $2 \times 10^{-2}$ mole of $FeCl_3$.

$$\text{Thus, Molarity of } FeCl_3 = \frac{0.02 \text{ mol}}{100} \times 1000$$

$$= 0.2 \text{ M}$$

**42. (3)** The density of gaseous molecule at 2 bar is double to $N_2$ at 4 bar

Thus, the molar mass (x) of gas is calculated as shown below :

$$\frac{2 \times 0.987 \text{ atm} \times x}{R \times 300 \text{ K}} = \frac{4 \times 0.987 \text{ atm} \times 28 \text{ g/mol}}{R \times 300 \text{ K}} \times 2$$

$$= 112 \text{ g/mol}$$

**43. (3)** The required quantity of a 45% acid solution is calculated by the formula,

$$V_1 \times A_1 + V_2 \times A_2 = V_f \times A_f$$

Substitute the values of $V_1$, $A_1$, $V_2$, $A_2$, $V_f$ and $A_f$ in the above expression.

$$V_1 \times \frac{45}{100} + (800 - V_1) \times \frac{20}{100} = 800 \times \frac{29.875}{100}$$

$$\frac{9V_1}{20} + 160 - \frac{V_1}{5} = 239$$

$$V_1 = 316 \text{ mL}$$

**44.** The ratio of mole fraction of solute and solution is,

$$\frac{X_{\text{solute}}}{X_{\text{solvent}}} = \frac{0.1}{0.9} = \frac{1}{9}$$

So,

$$\frac{W_{\text{solute}}}{W_{\text{solvent}}} \times \frac{MW_{\text{solvent}}}{MW_{\text{solute}}} = \frac{1}{9} \qquad \ldots(1)$$

$$W_{\text{solute}} + W_{\text{solvent}} = W_{\text{solution}}$$

$$W_{\text{solution}} = \text{density} \times \text{volume}$$

$$= 2 \times V \qquad \ldots(2)$$

Molality and molarity of this solution is same. So,

$$\frac{n_{\text{solute}}}{V_{\text{solution}}} = \frac{n_{\text{solute}}}{W_{\text{solvent}}}$$

$$W_{\text{solvent}} = V_{\text{solution}}$$

$$V_{\text{solution}} = \frac{W_{\text{solute}} + W_{\text{solvent}}}{2}$$

$$W_{\text{solvent}} = \frac{W_{\text{solute}} + W_{\text{solvent}}}{2}$$

$$2W_{\text{solvent}} = W_{\text{solute}} + W_{\text{solvent}}$$

$$W_{\text{solute}} = W_{\text{solvent}} \qquad \ldots(3)$$

Using equation (1) and (3),

$$\frac{MW_{\text{solvent}}}{MW_{\text{solute}}} = 9$$

**45. (3)** The reaction of arsenic acid with excess of $H_2S$ in the presence of HCl is given as follows.

$$2H_3AsO_4 + 5H_2S \xrightarrow{\text{Conc. HCl}} As_2S_5 + 8H_2O$$

Two moles of arsenic acid forms one mole of arsenic pentasulphide.

Therefore, one moles of arsenic acid forms half mole of arsenic pentasulphide.

1 mole of arsenic acid $\rightarrow$ 1/2 mole of arsenic pentasulphide

The molar mass of $H_3AsO_4$ is 142 g/mol.

Thus, the total number of moles of $H_3AsO_4$ is

$$\frac{35.5}{142} = 0.25 \text{ mol.}$$

The total number of moles of $As_2S_5$ is,

$$\frac{0.25}{2} = 0.125 \text{ mol.}$$

**46. (2)** The percentage of sulfur in the organic compound is 8% that is 8g of sulfur is present in the compound.

If 8g of sulfur is present in 100g of compound, then,

$$32 \text{ g of sulfur is present in} = \frac{100}{8} \times 32$$

$$= 400 \text{ g of organic compound}$$

Thus, the molecular weight of the compound is 400g/mol.

**47. (2)** The common reaction for the combustion of an alkane is shown as follows :

$$\underset{5L}{C_nH_{2n+2}} + \underset{25L}{\left(\frac{3n+1}{2}\right)O_2} \rightarrow nCO_2 + (n+1)H_2O$$

As, the volume is always calculated at constant temperature and pressure, thus, volume $\propto$ mole.

$$n_{\text{alkane}} = \left(\frac{2}{3n+1}\right) \times n_{O_2}$$

Therefore,

$$5 = \left(\frac{2}{3n+1}\right) \times 25$$

$$n = 3$$

Hence, $n = 3$ that satisfies by propane with molecular formula $C_3H_8$.

**48.** Volume of oxygen that is used $= \dfrac{20}{100} \times 375$

$$= 75 \text{ mL}$$

The volume of air that is left $= (375 - 75)$ mL

$$= 300 \text{ mL}$$

Volume occupied by $CO_2 = (330 - 300)$ mL

$$= 30 \text{ mL}$$

The general combustion reaction is shown below :

$$C_xH_y + \left(x + \frac{y}{4}\right)O_2 \rightarrow xCO_2 + \frac{y}{2}H_2O$$

Thus,

$$15x = 30$$

$$x = 2$$

The amount of oxygen used is given as shown below :

$$15\left(x + \frac{y}{4}\right) = 75$$

$$2 + \frac{y}{4} = 5$$

$$y = 12$$

Thus, the hydrocarbon is $C_2H_{12}$.

**49. (4)** The exchanging of ions is,

$$Ca^{2+} + 2C_8H_7SO_3Na \rightarrow Ca(C_8H_7SO_3)_2 + 2Na^+$$

1 mol        2 mol

Thus, the maximum uptake of $Ca^{2+}$ ions by the resin is

$$= \frac{1}{206 \times 2}$$

$$= \frac{1}{412} \text{ mol/g}$$

**50. (1)** The percentage of bromine in the compound is calculated by the formula,

$$= \frac{W_{AgBr}}{M_{AgBr}} \times \frac{M_{Br}}{W_{O.C.}} \times 100$$

Where,

$W_{O.C.}$ is the weight of organic compound.

Substitute the given values in above equation.

$$= \frac{141}{188} \times \frac{80}{250} \times 100$$

$$= 24$$

**51. (2)** The initial weight of salt is 61 g.

The weight of salt after dehydration is 52 g.

The mass of water is,

$$m_{H_2O} = 61 \text{ g} - 52 \text{ g}$$

$$= 9 \text{ g}$$

The number of moles of salt $BaCl_2$ is,

$$n_{BaCl_2} = \frac{52 \text{ g}}{208 \text{ g/mol}}$$

$$= \frac{1}{4} \text{ mol}$$

The number of moles of water is,

$$n_{H_2O} = \frac{9 \text{ g}}{18 \text{ g/mol}}$$

$$= \frac{1}{2} \text{ mol}$$

Hence, the ratio of $BaCl_2$ and $H_2O$ is 2 : 4 or 1 : 2. Thus, the formula of hydrated salt is $BaCl_2.2H_2O$.

**52. (3)** The number of moles of A is calculated as shown below :

$$\text{Moles of A} = \frac{6.0}{60}$$

$$= 0.1$$

The number of moles of B is calculated as shown below :

$$\text{Moles of B} = \frac{6.023 \times 10^{23}}{6.023 \times 10^{23}}$$

$$= 1$$

The number of moles of C is 0.036 mole. Thus, C is the limiting reagent.

The number of moles of product formed is calculated as shown below :

$$\text{Number of moles of product formed} = \frac{0.036}{3}$$

$$= 0.012$$

The molar mass of product is calculated as shown below :

$$\text{Molar mass} = \frac{\text{Given mass}}{\text{Mole of product}}$$

$$60 \times 2x + 80 \times 3 = \frac{4.8}{0.012}$$

$$x = 50 \text{ amu}$$

**53. (1)** The incorrect formula is $X_2Cl_3$. The valency of X in $X_2O_3$, $X_2(SO_4)_3$ and $XPO_4$ is + 3. Thus, the frmula for chloride is $XCl_3$.

**54.** The volume of solution is considered to be 1 litre = 1000 ml.

The density of the solvent is 0.4 g ml$^{-1}$

Therefore, weight of solvent is calculated as,

$$\text{Weight} = \text{Volume} \times \text{Density}$$

$$= 1000 \text{ ml} \times 0.4 \text{ g ml}^{-1}$$

$$= 0.4 \text{ kg}$$

The molar weight of solute is 80 g/mol.

The number of moles of solute is 3.2 mol.

Thus, the molality of solution is,

$$\text{Molality} = \frac{3.2}{0.4}$$

$$= 8.$$

**55. (2)** Assume the mass of oxygen in a particular gaseous mixture to be $x$. Hence, mass of nitrogen in that gaseous mixture will be $4x$.

Number of moles of $O_2$ is calculated as,

$$n_{O_2} = \frac{x}{32}$$

Number of moles of $N_2$ is calculated as,

$$n_{N_2} = \frac{4x}{28}$$

The ratio of number of their molecules will be,

$$\frac{n_{O_2}}{n_{N_2}} = \frac{\dfrac{x}{32}}{\dfrac{4x}{28}}$$

$$= \frac{7}{32}$$

**56. (2)** The molarity of the solution is calculated as follows :

$$\text{Molarity} = \frac{\left(\dfrac{120}{60}\right)}{\dfrac{1120}{1.12} \times \dfrac{1}{1000}}$$

$$= 2M$$

Thus, the molarity of the solution is 2M.

**57. (2)** The amount of oxygen in 3.6 moles of water is calculated as follows :

$$3.6 \text{ moles of water} = 3.6 \text{ moles of oxygen}$$
$$= 3.6 \times 16g \text{ of oxygen}$$
$$= 57.6 \text{ g}$$

Thus, the amount of oxygen is 3.6 moles of water is 57.6 g.

**58. (4)** The empirical formula of the gaseous compound is calculated by the help of following table.

| | Nitrogen | Hydrogen |
|---|---|---|
| Mass % | 87.5 | 12.5 |
| Number of moles | $\dfrac{87.5}{14} = 6.25$ | $\dfrac{12.5}{1} = 12.5$ |

The ratio of moles of nitrogen and hydrogen is 1 : 2.. Therefore, empirical formula will be $NH_2$. Hence, formula mass will be $14 + (2 \times 1) = 16$.

The density of compound relative to hydrogen is 16. Therefore, molecular mass will be,

$$\text{Molar mass} = 2 \times \text{Density}$$
$$= 2 \times 16$$
$$= 32$$

$$n = \frac{\text{Molecular mass}}{\text{Formula mass}}$$

$$= \frac{32}{16}$$

$$= 2$$

Molecular formula is calculated as,

$$\text{Molecular formula} = (\text{Empirical formula})_n$$
$$= (NH_2)_2$$
$$= N_2H_4$$

**59. (1)** The number of moles $BaCl_2$ is calcualted as,

$$\text{Moles of } BaCl_2 = \frac{2.08 \text{ g}}{137 \text{ g/mol} + 2 \times 35.5 \text{ g/mol}}$$

$$= 0.01 \text{ mol}$$

The molarity of the given $BaCl_2$ solution is calculated as,

$$\text{Molarity of } BaCl_2 = \frac{0.01 \text{ mol}}{0.1 \text{ L}}$$

$$= 0.1 \text{ M}$$

The number of moles of $H_2SO_4$ is as,

Moles of $H_2SO_4$

$$= \frac{0.98 \text{ g}}{2 \times 1 \text{ g/mol} + 32 \text{ g/mol} + 4 \times 16 \text{ g/mol}}$$

$$= 0.01 \text{ mol}$$

The molarity of the given $H_2SO_4$ solution is calculated as,

$$\text{Molarity of } H_2SO_4 = \frac{0.01 \text{ mol}}{0.05 \text{ L}}$$

$$= 0.2 \text{ M}$$

The number of moles of $BaSO_4$ formed from $BaCl_2$ and $H_2SO_4$ solution is 0.1 mol because the number of moles of barium is limited. The mass of $BaSO_4$ formed in the given system is calculaed by multiplying its moles with the molar mass.

$$\text{Mass of } BaSO_4 = 0.1 \text{ mol} \times (137 \text{ g/mol} + 32 \text{ g/mol} + 4 \times 16 \text{ g/mol})$$

$$= 23.3 \text{ g}$$

**60.** The number of moles of $HCl = 0.4 \text{ mol.L}^{-1} \times 0.2 \text{ L}$

$$= 0.08 \text{ mol}$$

Let $v$ is the volume of original HCl solution.

Mass of HCl solution $= 1.25 \times v$

$$\frac{\text{weight}}{\text{weight}}\% = \frac{\text{weight of solute}}{\text{weight of solution}} \times 100$$

$$29.2 = \frac{\text{weight of solute}}{1.25v} \times 100$$

$$\text{weight of solute} = \frac{29.2 \times 1.25v}{100}$$

The volume is calculated as,

$$0.08 = \frac{\dfrac{29.2 \times 1.25v}{100}}{36.5}$$

$$v = 8 \text{ mL}$$

**61. (3)** Molarity calculated by the formula,

$$\text{Molarity} = \frac{\text{Number of solutes}}{\text{Volume of solution in liter}}$$

$$\text{Moles of urea (solute)} = \frac{120 \text{ g}}{60 \text{ g/mol}}$$

$$= 2 \text{ mol}$$

$$\text{Volume of solution} = \frac{1120 \text{ g}}{1.15 \text{ g/mL}}$$

$$= 973.91 \text{ mL}$$

$$= 973.91 \times 10^{-3} \text{ L}$$

$$= 0.973 \text{ L}$$

$$\text{Molarity} = \frac{2 \text{ mol}}{0.973 \text{ L}}$$

$$= 0.05 \text{ mol/L}$$

$$= 2.05 \text{ M}$$

**62.** The balanced reaction between bromine and carbonate ion is given as,

$$3Br_2 + 2Na_2CO_3 \rightarrow 5NaBr + NaBrO_3 + 3CO_2$$

Therefore, the number of sodium bromide molecules involved in the balanced chemical equation is five.

**63.** The reaction between $AgNO_3$ and given complex is as follows :

$$2AgNO_3 + [Cr(H_2O)_5Cl]Cl_2 \rightarrow 2AgCl$$
$$+ Cr(H_2O)_5Cl](NO_3)_2$$

Above reaction is a balanced reaction. Therefore, milli equivalent of both the reactants will be same. It is shown as,

$$(M \times n \times V)_{AgNO_3} = (M \times n \times V)_{[Cr(H_2O)_5Cl]Cl_2}$$

$$0.01 \times 1 \times V = 0.01 \times 2 \times 30$$

$$V = 6 \text{ ml}$$

**64. (3)** The average of three titration values is,

$$\text{Average Titre value} = \frac{25.2 + 25.25 + 25}{3}$$

$$= \frac{75.4}{3}$$

$$= 25.1$$

So, there are three significant figures in the average titre value.

**65.** Volume of one mole of Ag atoms is

$$\text{Volume} = \frac{108}{10.5} \text{ cm}^3/\text{mole}$$

The volume of one silver atom is,

$$\text{Volume} = \frac{108}{10.5} \text{ cm}^3/\text{mole} \times \frac{1}{N_A}$$

$$= \frac{108}{10.5} \text{ cm}^3/\text{mole} \times \frac{1}{6.023 \times 10^{-23}}$$

$$= 1.708 \times 10^{23}$$

So, the volume is

$$V = \frac{4}{3}\pi r^3$$

$$1.708 \times 10^{23} = \frac{4}{3}\pi r^3$$

$$r^3 = 0.407 \times 10^{29} \text{ m}^3$$

Area of each silver atom is,

$$A = \pi r^2$$

$$= \pi (0.407 \times 10^{29} \text{ m}^3)^{2/3}$$

Thus, the number of silver atoms in the given area is,

$$\text{Number of Ag atoms} = \frac{10^{-12}}{(0.407 \times 10^{29} \text{ m}^3)^{2/3}}$$

$$= 1.5 \times 10^7$$

So, $y = 1.5$ and $x = 7$.

**66.** The reaction of CaO with $P_4O_{10}$ is as follows :

$$6CaO + P_4O_{10} \rightarrow 2Ca_3(PO_4)_2$$

The number of moles of $P_4O_{10}$ is,

$$= \frac{\text{Given mass}}{\text{Molar mass}}$$

$$= \frac{852}{284}$$

$$= 3 \text{ mol}$$

According to the above equation, 1 mol of $P_4O_{10}$ reacts with 6 mol of CaO.

Therefore, the number of moles of CaO required to react with 3 mol of $P_4O_{10}$ is = $6 \times 3 = 18$ mol.

The amount of CaO required is calculated as,

$$\text{Mass of CaO} = \text{Number of moles} \times \text{Molar mass}$$

$$= 18 \times 56$$

$$= 1008 \text{ g}$$

(b) The structure of $P_4O_{10}$ consists of 4 oxygen atoms doubly bonded to each P atom.

Six P – O – P bonds are also present in the compound. The structure is given below.

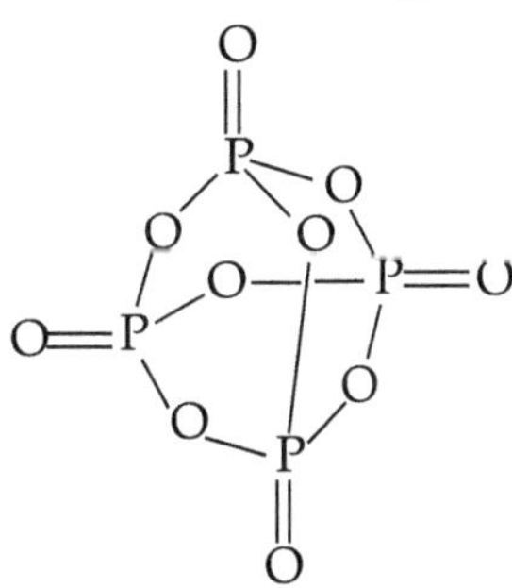

**67.** The molecular weight of water is 18 g/mol.

The formula to calculate density is

$$d = \frac{m}{V} \qquad ...(1)$$

The formula to calculate molarity is,

$$\text{Molarity} = \frac{m}{M_w \times V}$$

Substitute the value of $\frac{m}{V}$ from equation (1) in the above formula.

$$\text{Mo,arity} = \frac{d}{M_w}$$

Therefore, the molarity of water is,

$$\text{Molarity} = \frac{1000}{18}$$

$$= 55.55 \text{ M of } H_2O$$

**68. (1)** Number of atoms of an element present in the given sample is directly proportional to its number of moles.

The number of moles present in the sample containing 24 g of carbon is calculated as,

$$\text{Moles of C} = \frac{24 \text{ g}}{12.0 \text{ g}}$$

$$= 2.0 \text{ mol}$$

The number of moles present in the sample containing 56 g of iron is calculated as,

$$\text{Moles of Fe} = \frac{56 \text{ g}}{55.85 \text{ g/mol}}$$

$$= 1.0 \text{ mol}$$

The number of moles present in the sample containing 27 g of aluminium is calculated as,

$$\text{Moles of Al} = \frac{27 \text{ g}}{27.0 \text{ g}}$$

$$= 1.0 \text{ mol}$$

The number of moles present in the sample containing 108 g of silver is calculated as,

$$\text{Moles of Ag} = \frac{108 \text{ g}}{107.86 \text{ g}}$$

$$= 1.0 \text{ mol}$$

The number of moles of 24 g of C is greater than number of moles of A, Ag and iron. Therefore, the sample given in the option (1) has maximum number of atoms

**69. (4)** The number of moles of electron in 1 kg is calculated by the formula,

Number of moles of electron in 1 kg

$$= \frac{1}{\text{Moles of electron} \times \text{Avogadro number}}$$

$$= \frac{1}{9.108 \times 10^{-31} \times 6.023 \times 10^{23}}$$

$$= \frac{1}{9.108 \times 6.023} \times 10^{8}$$

## ⌑ QUESTIONS

1. For one mole of an ideal gas, which of these statements must be true ? **[2020, Main]**
   (a) U and H each depends only on temperature
   (b) Compressibility factor $z$ is not equal to 1
   (c) $C_{P,m} - C_{V,m} = R$
   (d) $dU = C_V dT$ for any process
   
   (1) (a), (c) and (d)   (2) (b), (c) and (d)
   (3) (c) and (d)   (4) (a) and (c)

2. A spherical balloon of radius 3 cm containing helium gas has a pressure of $48 \times 10^{-3}$ bar. At the same temperature, the pressure, of a spherical balloon of radius 12 cm containing the same amount of gas will be .......... $\times 10^{-6}$ bar.
   **[2020, Main]**

3. If the distribution of molecular speeds of a gas is as per the figure shown below, then the ratio of the most probable, the average and the roots mean square speeds, respectively, is :
   **[2020, Advanced]**

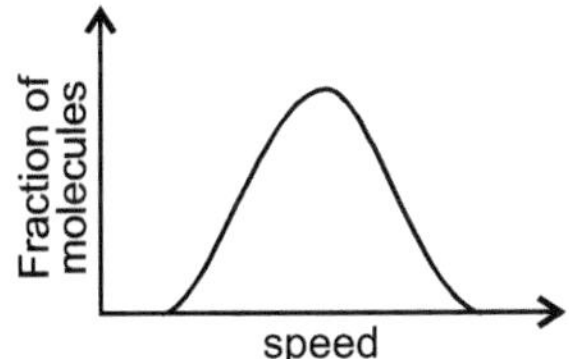


   (1) $1:1:1$   (2) $1:1:1.224$
   (3) $1:1.128:1.224$   (4) $1:1.128:1$

4. The figure below is the plot of potential energy versus internuclear distance ($d$) of $H_2$ molecule in the electronic ground state. What is the value of the net potential energy $E_0$ (as indicated in the figure) in kJ mol$^{-1}$, for $d = d_0$ at which the electron-electron repulsion and the nucleus-nucleus repulsion energies are absent ? As reference, the potential energy of H atom is taken as zero when its electron and the nucleus are infinitely far apart. Use Avogadro constant as $6.023 \times 10^{23}$ mol$^{-1}$.
   **[2020, Advanced]**

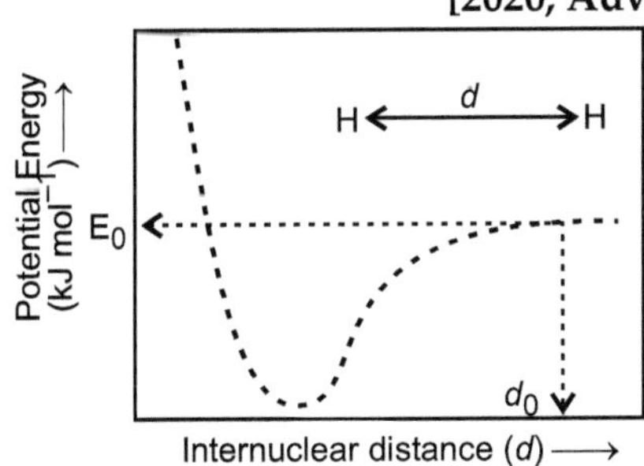


5. Consider the reaction sequence from P to Q shown below. The overall yield of the major product Q from P is 75%. What is the amount in grams of Q obtained from 9.3 mL of P? (Use density of P = 1.00 g mL$^{-1}$, Molar mass of C = 12.0, H = 1.0, O = 16.0 and N = 14.0 g mol$^{-1}$)
   **[2020, Advanced]**

$$P \xrightarrow[\substack{(ii)\ \text{naphthol} + NaOH \\ (iii)\ CH_3CO_2H/H_2O}]{(i)\ NaNO_2 + HCl/0\text{–}5°C} Q$$

6. 'X' melts at low temperature and is a bad conductor of electricity in both liquid and solid state. X is : **[2020, Main]**
   (1) Carbon tetrachloride   (2) Mercury
   (3) Silicon carbide   (4) Zinc sulphide

7. Consider the vander Waal's constants, $a$ and $b$, for the following gases.

| Gas | Ar | Ne | Kr | Xe |
|---|---|---|---|---|
| $a/(\text{atm dm}^6 \text{ mol}^{-2})$ | 1.3 | 0.2 | 5.1 | 4.1 |
| $b/(10^{-2} \text{ dm}^3 \text{ mol}^{-1})$ | 3.2 | 1.7 | 1.0 | 5.0 |

   Which gas is expected to have the highest critical temperature ? **[2020, Main]**
   (1) Kr   (2) Ne
   (3) Xe   (4) Ar

8. At a given temperature T, gases Ne, Ar, Xe and Kr are found to deviate from ideal gas behaviour. Their equation of state is given as $p = \dfrac{RT}{V-b}$ at P.

   Here, $b$ is the van der Waal's constant. Which gas will exhibit steepest increase in the plot of Z (compression factor) vs $p$ ? **[2019, Main]**
   (1) Xe   (2) Kr
   (3) Ne   (4) Ar

9. Consider the following table :

| Gas | $a/(k \text{ Pa dm}^6 \text{ mol}^{-1})$ | $b/(\text{dm}^3 \text{ mol}^{-1})$ |
|---|---|---|
| A | 642.32 | 0.05196 |
| B | 155.21 | 0.04136 |
| C | 431.91 | 0.05196 |
| D | 155.21 | 0.4382 |

   $a$ and $b$ are van der Waal's constants. The correct statement about the gases is : **[2019, Main]**

   (1) Gas C will occupy more volume than gas. A, gas B will be more compressible than gas D

   (2) Gas C will occupy lesser volume than gas A; gas B will be lesser compressible than gas D

   (3) Gas C will occupy more volume than gas A; gas B will be lesser compressible than gas D

   (4) Gas C will occupy lesser volume than gas A; gas B will be more compressible than gas D

**10.** Assuming ideal gas behaviour, the ratio of density of ammonia to that of hydrogen chloride at same temperature and pressure is : (Atomic wt. of Cl = 35.5 u) **[2018, Main]**

   (1) 1.46      (2) 0.46

   (3) 1.64      (4) 0.64

**11.** Among the following, the incorrect statement is : **[2017, Main]**

   (1) At low pressure, real gases show ideal behaviour.

   (2) At very low temperature, real gases show ideal behaviour.

   (3) At very large volume, real gases show ideal behaviour.

   (4) At Boyle's temperature, real gases show ideal behaviour.

**12.** The diffusion coefficient of an ideal gas is proportional to its mean free path and mean speed. The absolute temperature of an ideal gas is increased 4 times and its pressure is increased 2 times. As a result, the diffusion coefficient of this gas increases $x$ times. The value of $x$ is. **[2016, Advanced]**

**13.** The qualitative sketches of I, II and III is given below show the variation of surface tension with molar concentration of three different aqueous solutions of KCl, $CH_3OH$ and $CH_3(CH_2)_{11}OS_3^-$ $Na^+$ at room temperature. The correct assignment of the sketches is **[2016, Advanced]**

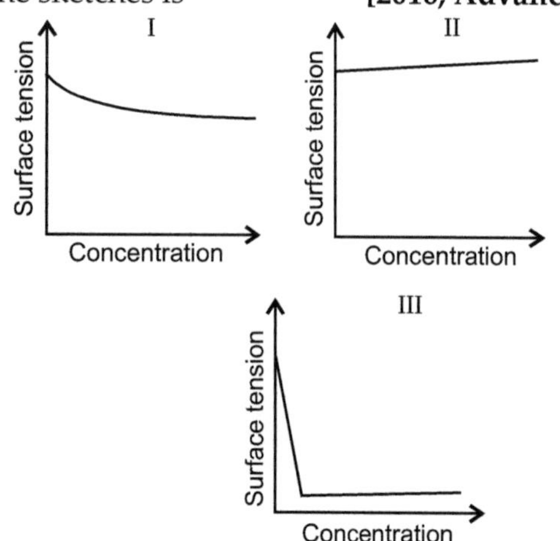


   (1) I : KCl       II : $CH_3OH$
     III : $CH_3(CH_2)_{11}OSO_3^-Na^+$

   (2) I : $CH_3(CH_2)_{11}OSO_3^-Na^+$    II : $CH_3OH$
     III : KCl

   (3) I : KCl
     II : $CH_3(CH_2)_{11}OSO_3^-Na^+$

     III : $CH_3OH$

   (4) I : $CH_3OH$       II : KCl
     III : $CH_3(CH_2)_{11}OSO_3^-Na^+$

**14.** At very high pressures, the compressibility factor of one mole of a gas is given by : **[2016, Main]**

   (1) $\dfrac{pb}{RT}$      (2) $1+\dfrac{pb}{RT}$

   (3) $1-\dfrac{pb}{RT}$      (4) $1-\dfrac{b}{(VRT)}$

**15.** Which intermolecular force is most responsible in allowing xenon gas to liquefy ? **[2016, Main]**

   (1) Dipole-dipole

   (2) Ion-dipole

   (3) Instantaneous dipole-induced dipole

   (4) Ionic

**16.** Initially, the *root mean square (rms)* velocity of $N_2$ molecules at certain temperature is $u$. If this temperature is doubled and all the nitrogen molecules dissociate into nitrogen atoms, then the new *rms* velocity will be : **[2016, Main]**

   (1) $u/2$      (2) $2u$

   (3) $4u$      (4) $14u$

**17.** Oxidation of succinate ion produces ethylene and carbon dioxide gases. On passing 0.2 Faraday electricity through an aqueous solution of potassium succinate, the total volume of gases (at both cathode and anode) at STP (1 atm and 273 K) is : **[2016, Main]**

   (1) 2.24 L      (2) 4.48 L

   (3) 6.72 L      (4) 8.96 L

**18.** Two closed bulbs of equal volume (V) containing an ideal gas initially at pressure $p_i$ and temperature $T_1$ are connected through a narrow tube of negligible volume as shown in the figure below. The temperature of one of the bulbs is then raised to $T_2$. The final pressure $p_f$ is : **[2016, Main]**

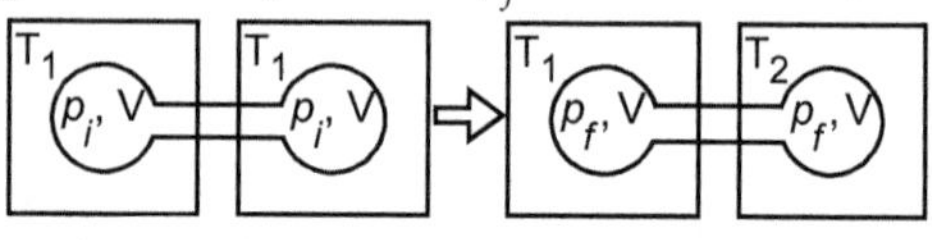


   (1) $p_i\left(\dfrac{T_1T_2}{T_1+T_2}\right)$      (2) $2p_i\left(\dfrac{T_1}{T_1+T_2}\right)$

   (3) $2p_i\left(\dfrac{T_2}{T_1+T_2}\right)$      (4) $2p_i\left(\dfrac{T_1T_2}{T_1+T_2}\right)$

**19.** One mole of a monoatomic real gas satisfies the equation $p(V-b)=RT$, where, $b$ is a constant. The relationship of interatomic potential $V(r)$ and interatomic distance $r$ for the gas is given by : **[2015, Advanced]**

   (1) 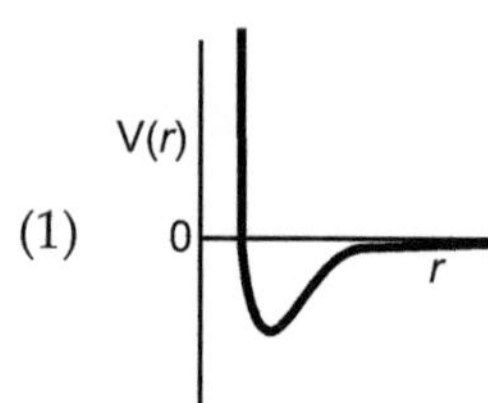

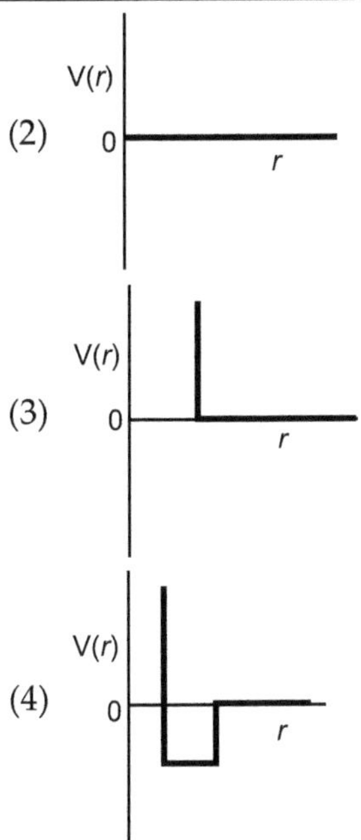



**20.** Which of the following is not an assumption of the kinetic theory of gases ?  **[2015, Main]**

(1) A gas consists of many identical particles which are in continual motion

(2) Gas particles have negligible volume

(3) At high pressure, gas particles are difficult to compress

(4) Collisions of gas particles are perfectly elastic

**21.** When does a gas deviate the most from its ideal behaviour ?  **[2015, Main]**

(1) At low pressure and low temperature

(2) At low pressure and high temperature

(3) At high pressure and low temperature

(4) At high pressure and high temperature

**22.** If the value of Avogadro number is $6.023 \times 10^{23}$ mol$^{-1}$ and the value of Boltzmann constant is $1.380 \times 10^{-23}$ J K$^{-1}$, then the number of significant digits in the calculated value of the universal gas constant is.  **[2014, Advanced]**

**Paragraph for Question 23 and 24**

**X** and **Y** are two volatile liquids with molar weights of 10 g mol$^{-1}$ and 40 g mol$^{-1}$ respectively. Two cotton plugs, one soaked in **X** and the other soaked in **Y**, are simultaneously placed at the ends of a tube of length **L** = 24 cm, as shown in the figure. The tube is filled with an inert gas at 1 atmosphere pressure and a temperature of 300 K. Vapours of **X** and **Y** react to form a product which is first observed at a distance **d** cm from the plut soaked in **X**. Take **X** and **Y** to have equal molecular diameters and assume ideal behaviour for the inert gas and the two vapours.

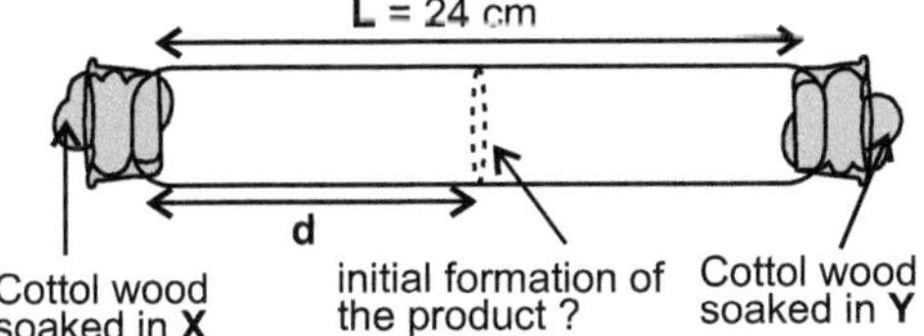



**23.** The value of **d** in cm (shown in the figure), as estimated from Graham's law, is :  **[2014, Advanced]**

(1) 8

(2) 12

(3) 16

(4) 20

**24.** The experimental value of **d** is found to be smaller than the estimate obtained using Graham's law. This is due to :  **[2014, Advanced]**

(1) larger mean free path for **X** as compared to that of **Y**.

(2) larger mean free path for **Y** as compared to that of **X**.

(3) increased collision frequency of **Y** with the inert gas as compared to that of **X** with the inert gas

(4) increased collision frequency of **X** with the inert gas as compared to that of **Y** with the inert gas

**25.** CsCl crystallises in body centered cubic lattice. If `a' is its edge length then which of the following expressions is correct ?  **[2014, Main]**

(1) $r_{Cs^+} + r_{Cl^-} = 3a$

(2) $r_{Cs^+} + r_{Cl^-} = \dfrac{3a}{2}$

(3) $r_{Cs^+} + r_{Cl^-} = \dfrac{\sqrt{3}}{2}a$

(4) $r_{Cs^+} + r_{Cl^-} = \sqrt{3}a$

**26.** Van der Waal's equation for a gas is stated as,

$$p = \frac{nRT}{V - nb} - a\left(\frac{n}{V}\right)^2 .$$

This equation reduces to the perfect gas equation, $p = \dfrac{nRT}{V}$ when,  **[2014, Main]**

(1) temperature is sufficiently high and pressure is low

(2) temperature is sufficiently low and pressure is high

(3) both temperature and pressure are very high

(4) both temperature and pressure are very low

**27.** The temperature at which oxygen molecules have the same root mean square speed as helium atoms have at 300 K is :  **[2014, Main]**

(Atomic masses : He = 4 u, O = 16 u)

(1) 300 K

(2) 600 K

(3) 1200 K

(4) 2400 K

**28.** The initial volume of a gas cylinder is 750.0 mL. If the pressure of gas inside the cylinder changes from 840.0 mm Hg to 360.0 mm Hg, the final volume the gas will be :  **[2014, Main]**

(1) 1.750 L

(2) 3.60 L

(3) 4.032 L

(4) 7.50 L

**29.** Sulphur dioxide and oxygen were allowed to diffuse through a porous partition. 20 dm$^3$ of $SO_2$ diffuses through the porous partition in 60 seconds. The volume of $O_2$ in dm$^3$ which diffuses under the similar condition in 30 seconds will be (atomic mass of sulphur = 32 u) :  **[2014, Main]**

(1)  7.09
(2)  14.1
(3)  10.0
(4)  28.2

**30.** For one mole of a van der Waals gas when $b = 0$ and T = 300 K, the PV vs. 1/V plot is shown below. The value of the van der Waals constant $a$ (atm.liter$^2$ mol$^{-2}$) is : **[2012, Advanced]**

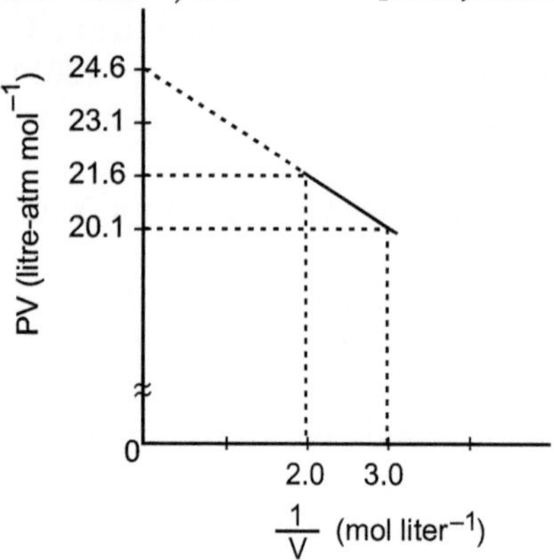

(1)  1.0
(2)  4.5
(3)  1.5
(4)  3.0

**31.** According to kinetic theory of gases :
**[2011, Advanced]**
(1)  collisions are always elastic.
(2)  heavier molecules transfer more momentum to the wall of the container.
(3)  only a small number of molecules have very high velocity.
(4)  between collisions, the molecules move in straight lines with constant velocities.

**32.** A decapeptide (Mol. wt. 796) on complete hydrolysis gives glycine (Mol. Wt. 75), alanine and phenylalanine. Glycine contributes 47.0% to the total weight of the hydrolysed products. The number of glycine units present in the decapeptide is. **[2011, Advanced]**

**33.** The term that corrects for the attractive forces present in a real gas in the van der Waals equation is : **[2009, Advanced]**

(1)  $nb$
(2)  $\dfrac{an^2}{V^2}$

(3)  $-\dfrac{an^2}{V^2}$
(4)  $-nb$

**34.** At 400 K, the root mean square (rms) speed of a gas **X** (molecular weight = 40) is equal to the most probable speed of gas **Y** at 60 K. The molecular weight of the gas **Y** is. **[2009, Advanced]**

**35.** A gas described by van der Waals equation
(1)  behaves similar to an ideal gas in the limit of large molar volumes
(2)  behaves similar to an ideal gas in the limit of large pressures
(3)  is characterised by van der Waals coefficients that are dependent on the identity of the gas but are independent of the temperature
(4)  has the pressure that is lower than the pressure exerted by the same gas behaving ideally

**36.** Match the gases under specified conditions listed in **Column I** with their properties/laws in **Column II**. Indicate your answer by darkening the appropriate bubbles of the 4 × 4 matrix given in the ORS. **[2007, Advanced]**

| Column I | | Column II | |
|---|---|---|---|
| (A) | hydrogen gas (P = 200 atm, T = 273 K) | (p) | compressibility factor $\neq 1$ |
| (B) | hydrogen gas (P ~ 0, T = 273 K) | (q) | attractive forces are dominant |
| (C) | $CO_2$ (P = 1 atm, T = 273 K) | (r) | PV = $n$RT |
| (D) | real gas with very large molar volume | (s) | P(V − $n$b) = $n$RT |

**37.** The given graph represents the variation of Z (compressibility factor $= \dfrac{PV}{nRT}$) versus P, for three real gases A, B and C. Identify the only incorrect statement. **[2006, Main]**

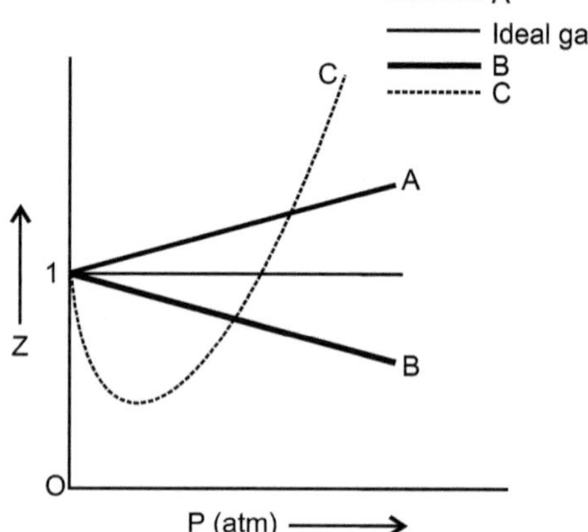


(1)  For the gas A, $a = 0$ and its dependence on P is linear at all pressure
(2)  For the gas B, $b = 0$ and its dependence on P is linear at all pressure
(3)  For the gas C, which is typical real gas for which neither a nor $b = 0$. By knowing the minima and the point of intersection, with Z = 1, $a$ and $b$ can be calculated
(4)  At high pressure, the slope is positive for all real gases

**38.** 20% surface sites have adsorbed $N_2$. On heating $N_2$ gas evolved from sites and were collected at 0.001 atm and 298 K in a container of volume is 2.46 cm$^3$. Density of surface sites is 6.023 × 10$^{14}$/cm$^2$ and surface area is 1000 cm$^2$, find out the no. of surface sites occupied per molecule of $N_2$.
**[2005, Main]**

**39.** If helium and methane are allowed to diffuse out of the container under the similar conditons of temperature and pressure, then the ratio of rate of diffusion of helium to methane is :
**[2005, Screening]**

(1)  2.0
(2)  1.0
(3)  0.5
(4)  4.0

**40.** For a monoatomic gas kinetic energy = E. The relation with rms velocity is : **[2004, Screening]**

(1) $u = \left(\dfrac{2E}{m}\right)^{1/2}$

(2) $u = \left(\dfrac{3E}{2m}\right)^{1/2}$

(3) $u = \left(\dfrac{E}{2m}\right)^{1/2}$

(4) $u = \left(\dfrac{E}{3m}\right)^{1/2}$

**41.** The average velocity of gas molecules is 400 m/sec. Calculate its rms velocity at the same temperature. **[2003, Main]**

**42.** The density of the vapour of a substance at 1 atm pressure and 500 K is 0.36 kg m$^{-3}$. The vapour effuses through a small hole at a rate of 1.33 times faster than oxygen under the same condition. **[2002, Main]**

(1) Determine (i) molecular weight, (ii) molar volume, (iii) compression factor (Z) of the vapour and (iv) which forces among the gas molecules are dominating, the attractive or the repulsive ?

(b) If the vapour behaves ideally at 1000K, determine the average transtational kinetic energy of a molecule.

**43.** Which of the following volume (V)–temperature (T) plots represents the behaviour of one mole of an ideal gas gas at one atmospheric pressure ? **[2002, Screening]**

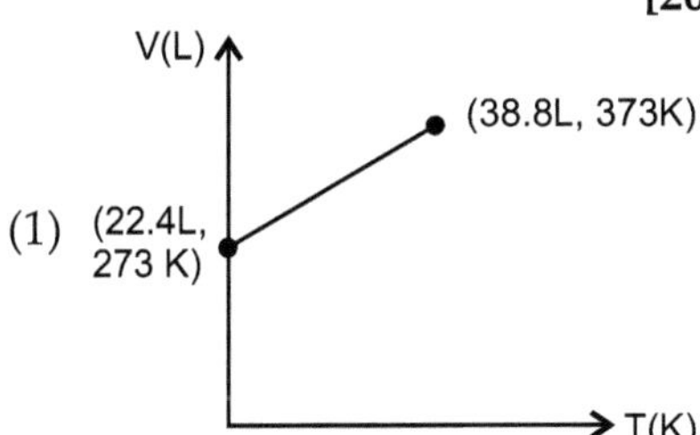

(1) (22.4L, 273 K) — (38.8L, 373K)

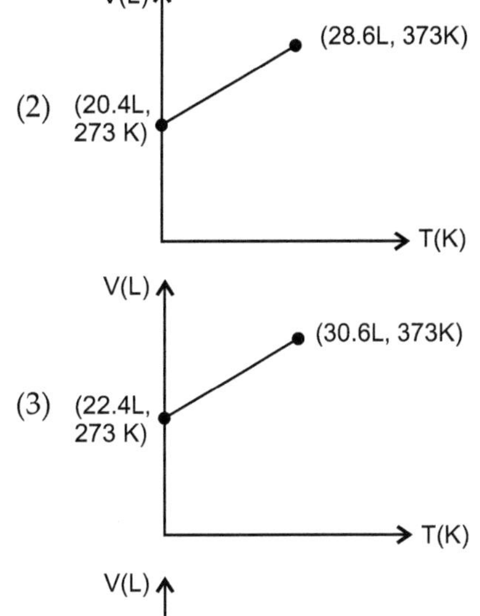

(2) (20.4L, 273 K) — (28.6L, 373K)

(3) (22.4L, 273 K) — (30.6L, 373K)

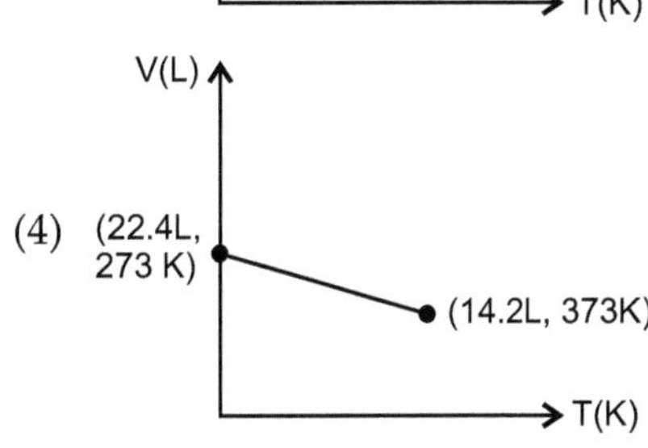

(4) (22.4L, 273 K) — (14.2L, 373K)

**44.** When the temperature is increased, surface tension of water : **[2002, Screening]**

(1) increases

(2) decreases

(3) remains constant

(4) shows irregular behaviour

# ANSWER KEY

| | | | | | | | | | |
|---|---|---|---|---|---|---|---|---|---|
| **1.** (1) | **2.** (*) | **3.** (2) | **4.** (*) | **5.** (*) | **6.** (1) | **7.** (1) | **8.** (1) | **9.** (1) | **10.** (2) |
| **11.** (2) | **12.** (4) | **13.** (4) | **14.** (2) | **15.** (3) | **16.** (2) | **17.** (4) | **18.** (3) | **19.** (3) | **20.** (3) |
| **21.** (3) | **22.** (4) | **23.** (3) | **24.** (4) | **25.** (2) | **26.** (1) | **27.** (4) | **28.** (1) | **29.** (2) | **30.** (3) |
| **31.** (1,2,3,4) | **32.** (*) | **33.** (2) | **34.** (4) | **35.** (1,3,4) | **36.** (*) | **37.** (2) | **38.** (2) | **39.** (1) | **40.** (1) |
| **41.** (*) | **42.** (*) | **43.** (3) | **44.** (2) | | | | | | |

# ANSWERS WITH EXPLANATIONS

**1. (1)** $\left.\dfrac{\delta v}{\delta v}\right|_T = 0$ and $\left.\dfrac{\delta H}{\delta v}\right|_T = 0$

(a) Hence function of temp. only.

(b) Compressibility factor $(z) = 1$

(c) $C_{p,m} - C_{v,m} = R$

(d) $dv = nC_{v,m}\,dT$ for all process.

**2.** If volume of 3 cm radius balloon is = V

Volume of 12 cm radius balloon = 64V

So pressure will become 1/64 times = $1/64 \times 48 \times 10^{-3}$ bar = $750 \times 10^{-3}$ bar

**3. (2)** Graph represents symmetrical distribution of speed and hence, the most probable and the average speed should be same. But the root mean square speed must be greater than the average speed.

**4.** At $d = d_0$, nucleus-nucleus & electron-electron repulsion is absent.

Hence potential energy will be calculated for 2 H atoms. (P.E. due to attraction of proton and electron)

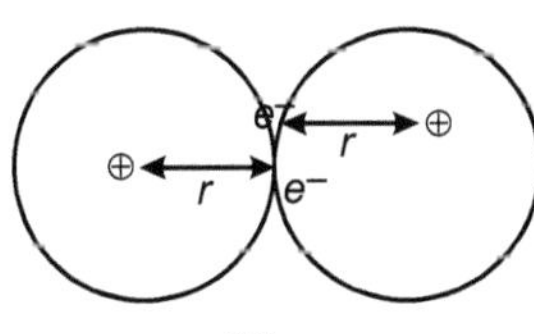

$$\text{P.E.} = \dfrac{-Kq_1q_2}{r}$$

(Bohr radius)

$$= \frac{(9\times10^9)(1.6\times10^{-19})^2}{0.529\times10^{-10}}$$

$$= -4.355 \times 10^{-21} \text{ kJ}$$

For 1 mol $= -4.355 \times 10^{-21} \times 6.023 \times 10^{23}$

$$= -2623.249 \text{ kJ/mol}$$

For 2 H atoms $= -5246.49 \text{ kJ/mol}$

**5.**

Molecular weight of aniline

$$= \text{M. wt. of } C_6NH_7$$

$$= 72 + 7 + 14 = 93$$

density of P $= 1 \text{ gm ml}^{-1}$

9.3 ml of P = 9. 3 gm P $= \dfrac{9.3}{9.3} = 0.1$ mole P

The mole ratio: $PhN_2^+ : PhN_2^+ :$

$$= 1 : 1 : 1$$

so, the mole of Q formed will be 0.1 mole and extent of reaction is 100% but if it is 75% yield.

Then amount of Q $= 0.1 \times \dfrac{75}{100} = 0.075$ mol

The molecualr formula of Q $= C_{16}H_{12}ON_2$

so, M. wt. of Q $= 16 \times 12 + 12 \times 1 + 16 + 2 \times 14$

$$= 192 + 12 + 16 + 28$$

$$= 248 \text{ gm}$$

so, amount of Q $= 248 \times 0.075$

$$= 18.6 \text{ gm}$$

**6. (1)** $CCl_4$ is molecular solid so does not conduct electricity in liquid & solid state.

**7. (1)** The foluma of critical temperarture is shown below :

$$T_c = \frac{8}{27Rb}$$

Therefore, the value of critical temperature depends on $a/b$ ratio.

The data table is shown below :

| Gas | a/(atm dm$^6$ mol$^{-2}$) | b/($10^{-2}$ dm$^{-3}$ mol$^{-1}$) | a/b |
|---|---|---|---|
| Ar | 1.3 | 3.2 | 0.40625 |
| Ne | 0.2 | 1.7 | 0.1176 |
| Kr | 5.1 | 1.0 | 4.1 |
| Xe | 4.1 | 5.0 | 0.82 |

Therefore, Kr has highest critical temperature.

**8. (1)** The slope of Z vs $p$ graph is given expression as shown below :

$$\text{Slope} = \frac{b}{RT}$$

The plot become steeper when value of $b$ increases. The value of $b$ for Xe is the highest. Therefore, the plot of Z vs $p$ graph for Xe is steepest.

**9. (1)** From the table, the value of 'b' for gases A and C are the same, whereas, A has a higher value of 'a'. The gas that has a higher value of 'a' possesses higher force of attraction between the molecules, and hence, possessing lesser volume. Therefore, gas C will occupy more volume than gas A.

From the table, the value of 'a' for gases B and D are the same, whereas B has a lower value of 'b'. The gas that has a lower value of 'b' is more compressible. Therefore, gas B is more compressible than gas D.

**10. (2)** The ideal gas equation is

$$PV = nRT \qquad \text{...(1)}$$

The formula to calculate the number of moles is,

$$n = \frac{m}{M}$$

Therefore,

$$PV = \frac{m}{M}RT \qquad \text{...(2)}$$

The formula to calculate density is,

$$d = \frac{m}{V}$$

The equation (2) can be written as,

$$P = \frac{dRT}{M} \qquad \text{...(3)}$$

When temperature and pressure become constant than equation (3) can be written as

$$d \propto M$$

$$\frac{d_1}{d_2} = \frac{M_1}{M_2}$$

Therefore, the ratio of the density of $NH_3$ : HCl is

$$\frac{d_1}{d_2} = \frac{M_1}{M_2}$$

$$= \frac{17}{36.5}$$

$$= 0.46$$

**11. (2)** The real gases do not show ideal behavior at very low temperature because real gases show their deviation from ideal behavior at low temperature, high pressure and low volume. Hence, at very low temperature they cannot show ideal behavior.

Therefore, the statement that at very low temperature, real gases show ideal behavior is incorrect.

**12. (4)** Diffusion coefficient $\propto$ Mean free path $\times$ mean speed

$$D \propto \lambda \times v_{mean}$$

$$D \propto \left(\frac{T}{P} \times \sqrt{T}\right) \qquad ...(1)$$

So, ratio of initial and final diffraction is,

$$\frac{D_i}{D_f} = \frac{\left(\dfrac{T\sqrt{T}}{P}\right)}{\left(\dfrac{4T\sqrt{4T}}{2P}\right)}$$

$$\frac{D_i}{D_f} = \frac{2}{4 \times 2}$$

$$\frac{D_f}{D_i} = 4$$

Diffusion coefficient of this gas increases four times.

**13. (4)** Surface tension is affected by the impurities. Substances like $CH_3(CH_2)_{11}OSO_3^-Na^+$, that is, soap reduces the surface tension.

Alcohol has small dielectric constant. Dielectric constant is directly proportional to surface tension. So, $CH_3OH$ in water will decrease the overall dielectric constant and thus reduces the surface tension of water.

Inorganic impurities like KCl, if present in greater amount will increase the surface tension of water.

Thus, the correct assignment of the sketches is as follows :

I is $CH_3OH$, II is KCl and III is $CH_3(CH_2)_{11}OSO_3^-Na^+$

**14. (2)** According to van der Waals equations, for one mole of gas,

$$\left(p + \frac{a}{V^2}\right)(V - b) = RT$$

At very high pressure, $p > \dfrac{a}{V^2}$.

Thus,

$$p(V - b) = RT$$

$$pV - pb = RT$$
$$pV = RT + pb$$

On division by RT, the above equation becomes,

$$Z(\text{compressibility factor}) = 1 + \frac{pb}{RT}$$

**15. (3)** Instantaneous dipole-induced dipole force, also known as London dispersion force, is responsible for allowing xenon gas to liquefy.

**16. (2)** The initial root mean square velocity for nitrogen is

$$\text{rms}(N_2) = \sqrt{\frac{3RT}{M_{N_2}}}$$

$$= \sqrt{\frac{3RT}{28}}$$

$$= u$$

After dissociation of all the nitrogen molecules into nitrogen atoms, the new roots mean square velocity becomes,

$$\text{rms}(N) = \sqrt{\frac{3R(2T)}{M_N}}$$

$$= \sqrt{\frac{3R(2T)}{14}}$$

$$= 2u$$

**17. (4)** The oxidation of succinate ion produces ethylene and carbon dioxide gases.

An ideal gas equation is,
$$PV = nRT$$

The above formula can be written as,

$$V = \frac{nRT}{P}$$

$$= \frac{0.4 \times 0.0821 \times 273}{1}$$

$$= 8.96 \text{ L}$$

**18. (3)** The number of initial moles is equal to the number of final moles.

$$\frac{P_i V}{RT_1} + \frac{P_i V}{RT_1} = \frac{P_f V}{RT_1} + \frac{P_f V}{RT_2}$$

$$\frac{P_i}{T_1} + \frac{P_i}{T_1} = \frac{P_f}{T_1} + \frac{P_f}{T_2}$$

$$2\frac{P_i}{T_1} = P_f\left(\frac{1}{T_1} + \frac{1}{T_2}\right)$$

$$P_f = 2P_i\left(\frac{T_2}{T_1 + T_1}\right)$$

**19. (3)** The given equation is,
$$p(V - b) = RT$$

When only repulsive force act,

$V(r) = \infty$ then $r < \sigma$, and when $V(r) = 0$ then $r > \sigma$.

**20. (3)** Gas particles are compressible at high pressure. The given statement that gas particles are difficult to compress at high pressure is not an assumption of kinetic theory of gases.

**21. (3)** At high pressure and low temperature, a gas deviate the most from its ideal behavior because at low temperature, kinetic energy decreases and at high pressure, more intermolecular forces occur.

**22. (4)** The value of Boltzmann constant is $1.380 \times 10^{-23}$ JK$^{-1}$. It has four significant digits. The value of Avogadro number is $6.023 \times 10^{23}$ mol$^{-1}$. It also has four significant digits.

The value of universal gas constant is calculated by the formula,
$$R = KN_A$$
Therefore,
$$R = 1.380 \times 10^{-23} \text{ JK}^{-1} \times 6.023 \times 10^{23} \text{ mol}^{-1}$$
$$= 8.312 \text{ JK}^{-1} \text{ mol}^{-1}$$

Hence, the calculated value of universal gas constant is $8.312$ JK$^{-1}$ mol$^{-1}$ has four significant digits.

**23. (3)** Graham's law is given by the formula,
$$\frac{\text{Rate}_1}{\text{Rate}_2} = \sqrt{\frac{M_2}{M_1}}$$

Molar weight of X is $M_1 = 10$ g mol$^{-1}$.
Molar weight of Y is $M_2 = 40$ g mol$^{-1}$.
The value of $d$ is calculated as,
$$\frac{d}{24-d} = \sqrt{\frac{40}{10}}$$
$$\frac{d}{24-d} = \frac{2}{1}$$
$$d = 16$$

**24. (4)** The collision frequency ($z$) is given by the formula,
$$z = \frac{\pi n^2 \sigma^2 \mu_{av}}{\sqrt{2}}$$

The mean free path ($\lambda$) is given by the formula,
$$\lambda = \frac{1}{\sqrt{2} n \sigma^2}$$

Where,

$n$ is the number of molecules per unit molar volume.

$\sigma$ is the collision diameter.

If the size of the molecules is large; its mean free path is small. The experimental value of $d$ is smaller than the one which is obtained by Graham's law because the collision frequency of **X** is larger than that of **Y**.

**25. (2)** The van der Waals equation is represented as,
$$\left( P + \frac{n^2 a}{V^2} \right)(V - nb) = nRT$$

If the value of $n = 1$, then
$$\left( P + \frac{a}{V^2} \right)(V - b) = RT$$

At low pressure, $V - b \approx V$. Therefore,
$$PV + \frac{a}{V} = RT$$
$$PV = RT - \frac{a}{V}$$
$$Z = 1 - \frac{a}{RTV}$$

**26. (1)** The van der Waals equation for a gas reduces to the perfect gas equation that is $p = \dfrac{nRT}{V}$ when, the temperature is sufficiently high and pressure is low.

**27. (4)** The relation between root mean square velocity of oxygen and helium is as follows :
$$(U_{rms})_{O_2} = (U_{rms})_{He}$$

Here, $U_{rms}$ is the root mean square velocity.
$$(U_{rms})_{O_2} = (U_{rms})_{He}$$
$$\frac{3RT_{O_2}}{32} = \frac{3RT_{He}}{4}$$
$$T_{O_2} = 8 \times 300 = 2400 \text{ K}$$

**28. (1)** The final volume is calculated by the formula,
$$P_1 V_1 = P_2 V_2$$
$$840 \times 750 = 360 \times V_2$$
$$V_2 = 1750 \text{ mL}$$
$$= 1.75 \text{ L}$$

**29. (2)** The volume of $O_2$ which diffuses under given condition is calculated by the formula,
$$\frac{r_{SO_2}}{r_{O_2}} = \sqrt{\frac{M_{O_2}}{M_{SO_2}}}$$
$$\frac{V_{SO_2} / t_{SO_2}}{V_{O_2} / t_{O_2}} = \sqrt{\frac{M_{O_2}}{M_{SO_2}}}$$

Substitute the given values in above equation.
$$\frac{20 / 60}{V_{O_2} / 30} = \sqrt{\frac{32}{65}}$$
$$\frac{10}{V_{O_2}} = \sqrt{\frac{1}{2}}$$
$$V_{O_2} = 14.1$$

**30. (3)** The van der Waals equations corresponding to the given situation is shown below :

$$\left(P+\frac{a}{V^2}\right)(V) = RT$$

$$PV+\frac{a}{V} = RT$$

The straight line equation is $y = mx + c$

$$PV = RT-\frac{a}{V}$$

The slope of the equation is a.
The slope is calculated as shown below :

$$\text{slope} = a = \frac{y_2 - y_1}{x_2 - x_1}$$

$$= \frac{21.6 - 20.1}{3 - 2}$$

$$= 1.5$$

**21. (1,2,3,4)** All the given statements are postulates of kinetic theory of gases. These are as follows :

Collisions are always elastic.

Heavier molecules transfer more momentum to the wall of the container because momentum is directly proportional to the mass and velocity.

All the molecules cannot have very high velocity.

Between collisions, the molecules move in straight line with constant velocities because collisions are directional in nature.

**32.** The partial pressure of helium gas is calculated as,

$$p_{He} = p_{Total} - p_x$$
$$= (1 - 0.68) \text{ atm}$$
$$= 0.32 \text{ atm}$$

The total volume of the gases is calculated as,

$$V = n_{He}\frac{RT}{p_{He}}$$

$$= \frac{0.1 \times 0.082 \times 273}{0.32}$$

$$= 7 \text{ L}$$

**33. (2)** The intermolecular forces of attraction of gases are function of pressure. Therefore, the term corresponding to the correction of pressure involves the correction of attractive forces in the molecules of real gases. Hence, the correction of intermolecular forces in the van der Waals equation is $\frac{an^2}{V^2}$.

**34. (4)** The molecular weight of the gas Y is calculated by the formula,

$$V_{rms(X)} = V_{mp(Y)}$$

$$\sqrt{\frac{3RT_X}{M_X}} = \sqrt{\frac{2RT_Y}{M_Y}}$$

Substitute the values of $T_X$, $M_x$ and $T_Y$ in the above equation,

$$\sqrt{\frac{3R \times 400}{40}} = \sqrt{\frac{2R \times 60}{M_Y}}$$

Simplify the above equation to calculate the molar mass of gas Y,

$$\frac{400 \times 3}{40} = \frac{2 \times 60}{M_Y}$$

$$M_Y = \frac{120}{30}$$

$$= 4 \text{ g/mol}$$

**35. (1,3,4)** The van der Waals equation is

$$\left(P+\frac{n^2a}{V^2}\right)(V - nb) = nRT$$

(1) According to van der Waals equation, large volume is occupied by the gas when the pressure is very low. The intermolecular interactions between gas molecules are negligible at large molar volumes and it behaves as an ideal gas.

(2) At large pressure, the molecules of gas come close to each other; hence it deviates from the ideal behaviour at high pressure.

(3) The van der Waals coefficient $a$ and $b$ depend upon the type of gas whereas they are independent of the temperature.

(4) In van der Waals equation, the whole term $\left(P+\frac{n^2a}{V^2}\right)$ represents the pressure due to ideal gas and P represents the pressure due to real gas. The value of pressure of ideal gas increases with increase in pressure of real gas. Hence, the value of pressure of gas described by van der Waals equation is lower that the gas that behaves ideally.

**36. (A)** At low temperature and high pressure the compressibility factor, Z is,

$$Z = \frac{PV_m}{RT}$$

The van der Waals equation at above condition reduces to,

$$P(V - nb) = nRT$$

**(B)** At P ~ 0, the value of Z is equal to one for hydrogen gas. Thus, the ideal gas equation becomes,

$$PV = nRT$$

(C) At given conditions (P = 1 atm, T = 273 K or 0°C), carbon dioxide gas possesses stronger attractive forces and compressibility factor is not equal to zero.

(D) At large $V_m$ of gases,
$$Z \neq 1$$
The van der Waals equation at above condition is,
$$P(V - nb) = nRT$$

**37. (2)** The option (2) is incorrect because at high pressure slope changes from negative to positive.

**38. (2)** The ideal gas equation is given as follows :
$$pV = nRT$$
The number of moles of $N_2$ is calculated as
$$n = \frac{PV}{RT}$$
$$= \frac{0.001 \text{ atm} \times 2.46 \times 10^{-3} L}{0.0821 \text{ L.atm.mol}^{-1}K^{-1} \times 298 K}$$
$$= 1 \times 10^{-7} \text{ mol}$$
The number of molecules of $N_2$ is = $1 \times 10^{-7} \times 6.022 \times 10^{23}$ = $6.022 \times 10^{16}$ molecules
The total number of surface sites is,
$$= \text{density} \times \text{surface area}$$
$$= 6.022 \times 10^{14} \times 1000$$
$$= 6.022 \times 10^{17}$$
It is given that 20% surface sites have absorbed $N_2$, that is
$$= 20\% \text{ of } 6.022 \times 10^{17}$$
$$= \frac{20}{100} \times 6.022 \times 10^{17}$$
$$= 12.04 \times 10^{16}$$
Therefore, the sites occupied by nitrogen gas is calculated as
$$\text{Sites occupied} = \frac{\text{Total number of sites}}{\text{Total number of molecules}}$$
$$= \frac{12.04 \times 10^{16}}{6.022 \times 10^{16}}$$
$$= 2$$

**39. (1)** The molar mass of helium is 4.
The molar mass of methane is 16.
The ratio of rate of diffusion of helium is given by the expression,
$$\frac{r_{He}}{r_{CH_4}} = \sqrt{\frac{M_{CH_4}}{M_{He}}}$$
Substitute the value of molar mass of helium and methane in the above expression.
$$\frac{r_{He}}{r_{CH_4}} = \sqrt{\frac{16}{4}}$$
$$= 2:1$$

Thus, the ratio of rate of rate of diffusion of helium to methane is 2.0
Hence, the correct option is a.

**40. (1)** For one molecule, PV = KT
$$\text{Root mean square velocity} = \sqrt{\frac{3PV}{m}}$$
$$= \sqrt{\frac{3 \times KT}{m}}$$
$$\text{Kinetic energy} = \frac{3}{2}KT$$
Therefore, 2KE = 3KT.
$$\text{Root mean square velocity} = \sqrt{\frac{3 \times KT}{m}}$$
$$= \sqrt{\frac{2KE}{m}}$$
$$= \sqrt{\frac{2E}{m}}$$

**41.** The formula to calculate rms velocity of a gas is,
$$C_{rms} = \sqrt{\frac{3RT}{M_w}}$$
The formula to calculate average velocity of a gas is,
$$C_{avg} = \sqrt{\frac{8RT}{\pi M_w}}$$
The ratio of $C_{rms}$ and $C_{avg}$ is as follows :
$$\frac{C_{rms}}{C_{avg}} = \frac{\sqrt{\frac{3RT}{M_w}}}{\sqrt{\frac{8RT}{\pi M_w}}}$$
$$= \sqrt{\frac{3\pi}{8}}$$
$$= 1.085$$
The rms velocity at the same temperature is,
$$C_{rms} = 1.085 \times C_{avg}$$
$$= 1.085 \times 400$$
$$= 434 \text{ ms}^{-1}$$

**42. (a) (I)** According to Graham's law of diffusion,
$$\frac{r_{vapour}}{r_{O_2}} = \sqrt{\frac{M_{O_2}}{M_V}}$$
Substitute all the given values in the above formula.
$$1.33 = \sqrt{\frac{32}{M_V}}$$
$$M_V = \frac{32}{(1.33)^2}$$
$$= 18.09$$

Thus, the molecular weight of the vapour is 18.09 gm/mol.

(II) The formula to calculate density is,

$$\text{Density} = \frac{\text{Mass}}{\text{Volume}}$$

Substitute the given values in the above formula

$$0.35 \text{ g/L} = \left(\frac{18.09 \times 10^{-3}}{0.36}\right) m^3$$

$$= 50.25 \text{ L}$$

(III) The compression factor (Z) of the vapour is as follows :

$$Z = \frac{(PV)_{observed}}{(PV)_{ideal}}$$

$$= \frac{1 \times 50.25}{1 \times 41.025}$$

$$= 1.224$$

(IV) The value of Z is more than 1. Thus, the repulsive forces among the gas molecules will dominate.

(b) The average translational kinetic energy of a molecule is

$$\text{K.E.} = \frac{3}{2}kT$$

$$= \frac{3}{2} \times 1.38 \times 10^{-23} \times 1000$$

$$= 2.07 \times 10^{-20} \text{ J}$$

**43. (3)** The volume of gas at 373 K and 1 atm is calculated as shown below.

$$V = \frac{RT}{P}$$

$$= \frac{0.082 \times 373 \text{K}}{1 \text{ atm}}$$

$$= 30.586 \text{ L}$$

The correct value of volume is shown in graph (3).

**44. (2)** The surface tension decreases, if inter-molecular forces are weak. Thus, the increase in temperature results in decrease of surface tension of water due to decrease in intermolecular forces.

●●

# Chapter 3 — The Solid State

## QUESTIONS

1. An element with molar mass $2.7 \times 10^{-2}$ kg mol$^{-1}$ forms a cubic unit cell with edge length 405 pm. If its density is $2.7 \times 10^3$ kgm$^{-3}$, the radius of the element is approximately ......... $\times 10^{-12}$ m (to the nearest integer). **[2020, Main]**

2. A diatomic molecule $X_2$ has a body-centred cubic (bcc) structure with a cell edge of 300 pm. The density of the moleculer is 6.17 g cm$^{-3}$. The number of molecules present in 200 g of $X_2$ is (Avogadro constant $(N_A) = 6 \times 10^{23}$ mol$^{-1}$

   **[2020, Main]**

   (1) $8\,N_A$      (2) $40\,N_A$
   (3) $4\,N_A$      (4) $2\,N_A$

3. An element crystallises in a face-centered cubic (fcc) unit cell with cell edge a. The distance between the centres of two nearest octahedral voids in the crystal lattice is : **[2020, Main]**

   (1) $a$      (2) $\sqrt{2}a$

   (3) $\dfrac{a}{\sqrt{2}}$      (4) $\dfrac{a}{2}$

4. The cubic unit cell structure of a compound containing cation M and anion X is shown below. When compared to the anion, the cation has smaller ionic radius. Choose the correct statement(s). **[2020, Advanced]**

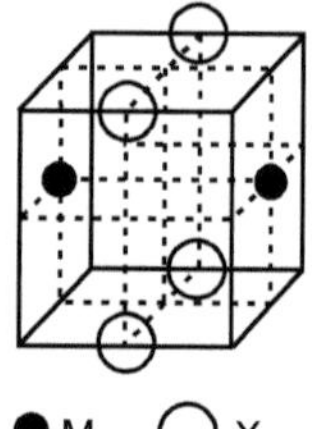


   (1) The empirical formula of the compound is MX.
   (2) The cation M and anion X have different coordination geometries.
   (3) The ratio of M-X bond length to the cubic unit cell edge length is 0.866.
   (4) The ratio of the ionic radii of cation M to anion X is 0.414.

5. Which of the following compounds is likely to show both Frenkel and Schottky defects in its crystalline form ? **[2020, Main]**

   (1) AgBr      (2) ZnS
   (3) KBr      (4) CsCl

6. Consider an ionic solid MX with NaCl structure. Construct a new structure (Z) whose unit cell is constructed from the unit cell of MX following the sequential instructions given below. Neglect the charge balance. **[2018, Advanced]**

   (i) Remove all the anions (**X**) except the central one
   (ii) Replace all the face centered cations (**M**) by anions (**X**)
   (iii) Remove all the corner cations (**M**)
   (iv) Replace the central anion (**X**) with cation (**M**)

   The value of $\left(\dfrac{\text{number of anions}}{\text{number of cations}}\right)$ in Z is .......... .

7. Which type of 'defect' has the presence of cations in the interstitial sites ? **[2018, Main]**

   (1) Schottky defect
   (2) Vacancy defect
   (3) Frenkel defect
   (4) Metal deficiency defect

8. All of the following share the same crystal structure except : **[2018, Main]**

   (1) LiCl      (2) NaCl
   (3) RbCl      (4) CsCl

9. Which of the following arrangements shows the schematic alignment of magnetic moments of antiferromagnetic substance ? **[2018, Main]**

   (1) ○ ○ ○ ○ ○ ○
   (2) ○ ⇩ ⇩ ⇩ ⇩ ○
   (3) ○ ⇩ ○ ⇩ ○ ⇩
   (4) ○ ○ ⇩ ○ ○ ⇩

10. A crystalline solid of a pure substance has a face-centered cubic structure with a cell edge of 400 pm. If the density of the susbtance in the crystal is 8 g cm$^{-3}$, then the number of atoms present in 256 g of the crystal is N $\times 10^{24}$. The value of N is.

    **[2017, Advanced]**

11. A meal crystallises in a face centered cubic structure. If the edge length of its unit cell is `a`, the closest approach between two atoms in metallic cyrstal will be : **[2017, Main]**

(1) $\sqrt{2}a$

(2) $\dfrac{a}{\sqrt{2}}$

(3) $2a$

(4) $2\sqrt{2}a$

**12.** The **correct** statements for cubic close packed (ccp) three dimensional structure is/are : **[2016, Advanced]**

(1) The number of the nearest neighbours of an atom present in the topmost layer is 12

(2) The efficiency of atom packing is 74%

(3) The number of octahedral and tetrahedral voids per atom are 1 and 2, respectively

(4) The unit cell edge length is $2\sqrt{2}$ times the radius of the atom

**13.** If the unit cell of a mineral has cubic close packed (ccp) array of oxygen atoms with m fraction of octahedral holes occupied by a luminium ions and n fraction of tetrahedral holes occupied by magnesium ions, m and n, respectively, are : **[2015, Advanced]**

(1) $\dfrac{1}{2}, \dfrac{1}{8}$

(2) $1, \dfrac{1}{4}$

(3) $\dfrac{1}{2}, \dfrac{1}{2}$

(4) $\dfrac{1}{4}, \dfrac{1}{8}$

**14.** Sodium metal crystallizes in a body centred cubic lattice with a unit cell edge of 4.29 Å. The radius of sodium atom is approximately : **[2015, Main]**

(1) 1.86 Å

(2) 3.22 Å

(3) 5.72 Å

(4) 0.93 Å

**15.** CsCl crystallises in body centred cubic lattice. If `a' is its edge length then which of the following expressions is correct ? **[2014, Main]**

(1) $r_{Cs^+} + r_{Cl^-} = 3a$

(2) $r_{Cs^+} + r_{Cl^-} = \dfrac{3a}{2}$

(3) $r_{Cs^+} + r_{Cl^-} = \dfrac{\sqrt{3}}{2}a$

(4) $r_{Cs^+} + r_{Cl^-} = \sqrt{3}a$

**16.** The correct statement for the molecule, $CsI_3$, is : **[2014, Main]**

(1) it is a covalent molecule.

(2) it contains $Cs^+$ and $I_3^-$ ions.

(3) it contains $Cs^{3+}$ and $I^-$ ions.

(4) it contains $Cs^+$, $I^-$ and lattice $I_2$ molecule.

**17.** In a face centered cubic lattice atoms A are at the corner points and atoms B at the face centered points. If atom B is missing from one of the face centered points, the formula of the ionic compound is : **[2014, Main]**

(1) $AB_2$

(2) $A_5B_2$

(3) $A_2B_3$

(4) $A_2B_5$

**18.** The appearance of colour in solid alkali metal halides is generally due to : **[2014, Main]**

(1) Schottky defect

(2) Frenkel defect

(3) Interstitial position

(4) F-centres

**19.** In a monoclinic unit cell, the relation of sides and angles are respectively : **[2014, Main]**

(1) $a = b \neq c$ and $\alpha = \beta = \gamma = 90°$

(2) $a \neq b \neq c$ and $\alpha = \beta = \gamma = 90°$

(3) $a \neq b \neq c$ and $\beta = \gamma = 90° \neq \alpha$

(4) $a \neq b \neq c$ and $\alpha \neq \beta \neq \gamma \neq 90°$

**20.** The total number of octahedral void(s) per atom present in a cubic close packed structure is : **[2014, Main]**

(1) 2

(2) 4

(3) 1

(4) 3

**21.** The arrangement of $X^-$ ions around $A^+$ ion in solid AX is given in the figure (not drawn to scale). If the radius of $X^-$ is 250 pm, the radius of $A^+$ is : **[2013, Advanced]**

(1) 104 pm

(2) 125 pm

(3) 183 pm

(4) 57 pm

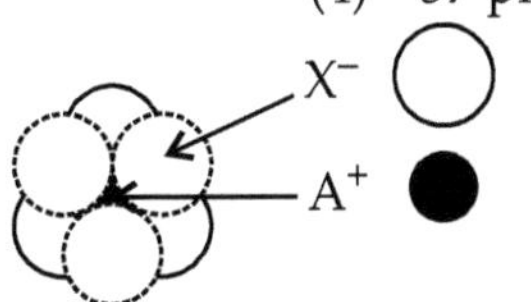


**22.** A compound $M_pX_q$ has cubic close packing (ccp) arrangement of X. Its unit cell structure is shown below. The empirical formula of the compound is : **[2012, Advanced]**

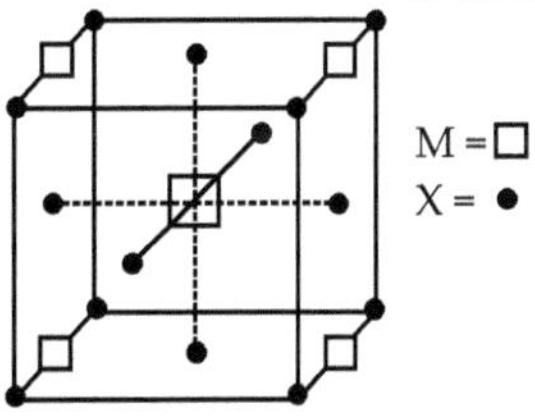


(1) MX

(2) $MX_2$

(3) $M_2X$

(4) $M_5X_{14}$

**23.** The number of hexagonal faces that are present in a truncated octahedron is. **[2011, Advanced]**

**24.** The packing efficiency of the two-dimensional square unit cell shown below is : **[2010, Advanced]**

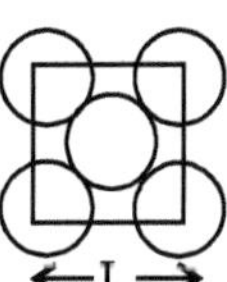


(1) 39.27%

(2) 68.02%

(3) 74.05%

(4) 78.54%

**25.** The correct statements regarding defects in solids is/are : **[2009, Advanced]**

(1) Frenkel defect is usually favoured by a very small difference in the sizes of cation and anion

(2) Frenkel defect is a dislocation defect

(3) Trapping of an electron in the lattice leads to the formation of F-center

(4) Schottky defects have no effect on the physical properties of solids

**26.** The coordination number of Al in the crystalline state of $AlCl_3$ is. **[2009, Advanced]**

**Paragraph to Questio 27 to 29**

In hexagonal systems of crystals, a frequently encountered arrangement of atoms is described as a hexagonal prism. Here, the top and bottom of the cell are regular hexagons and three atoms are sandwiched in between them. A space-filling modelof this structure, called hexagonal close-packed (HCP), is constituted of a sphere on a flat surface surrounded in the same plane by six identical spheres as closely as possible. Three spheres are then placed over the first layer so that they touch each other and represent the second layer. Each one of these three spheres touches three spheres of the bottom layer. Fianlly, the second layer is covered with a third layer that is identical to the bottom layer in relative position. Assume radius of every sphere to be '$r$'.

**27.** The number of atoms in this **HCP** unit is :

**[2008, Advanced]**

(1) 4  (2) 6

(3) 12  (4) 17

**28.** The volume of this **HCP** unit cell is :

**[2008, Advanced]**

(1) $24\sqrt{2}\,r^3$  (2) $16\sqrt{2}\,r^3$

(3) $12\sqrt{2}\,r^3$  (4) $\dfrac{64}{3\sqrt{3}}r^3$

**29.** The empty space in this **HCP** unit cell is :

**[2008, Advanced]**

(1) 74%  (2) 47.6%

(3) 32%  (4) 26%

**30. Statement-1 :** Band gap in germanium is small. because

**Statement-2 :** The energy spread of each germanium atomic energy level is infinitesimally small.

**[2007, Advanced]**

(1) Statement-1 is True, Statement-2 is True; Statement-2 is a correct explanation for Statement-1

(2) Statement-1 is True, Statement-2 is True; Statement-2 is not a correct explanation for Statement-1

(3) Statement-1 is True, Statement-2 is False

(4) Statement-1 is False, Statement-2 is True

**31.** Match the crystal system/unit cells mentioned in Column I with their characteristic features mentioned in Column II. Indicate your answer by darkening the appropriate bubbles of the 4 × 4 matrix given in the ORS. **[2007, Advanced]**

| | **Column I** | | **Column II** |
|---|---|---|---|
| (1) | simple cubic and face-centered cubic | (p) | have these cell parameters $a = b = c$ and $\alpha = \beta = \gamma$ |
| (2) | cubic and rhombo-hedral | (q) | are two crystal systems |
| (3) | cubic and tetrago-nal | (r) | have only two crystallographic angles of 90° |
| (4) | hexagonal and monoclinic | (s) | belong to same cyrstal system |

**32.** The edge length of unit cell of a metal having molecular weight 75 g/mol is 5Å which crystallises in cubic lattice. If the density is 2 g/cc then find the radius of metal atom. ($N_A = 6 \times 10^{23}$) . Give the answer in pm. **[2006, Main]**

**33.** An element crystallizes in fcc lattice having edge length 400 pm. Calculate the maximum diameter of atom which can be placed in interstitial site without distorting the structure. **[2005, Main]**

**34.** Which of the following FCC structure contains cations in alternate tetrahedral voids ?

**[2004, Main]**

(1) NaCl  (2) ZnS

(3) $Na_2O$  (4) $CaF_2$

**35.** The crystal AB (rock salt structure) has molecular weight 6.023 y amu, where $y$ is an arbitrary number in amu. If the maximum distance between cation and anion is $y^{1/3}$ nm and the observed density is 20 kg/m³. Find the :

(a) density in Kg/m³ and

(b) type of defect **[2004, Main]**

**36.** (a) You are given marbles of diameter 10 mm. They are to be placed such that their centres are lying in a square bound by four lines each of length 40 mm. What will be the arrangements of marbles in a plane so that maximum number of marbles can be placed inside the area ? Sketch the diagram and derive expression for the number of molecules per unit area.

(b) 1 gm of charcoal adsorbs 100 ml 0.5 M $CH_3COOH$ to form a monolayer, and thereby the molarity of $CH_3COOH$ reduces to 0.49. Calculate the surface area of the charcoal adsorbed by each molecule of acetic acid. Surface area of charcoal = $3.01 \times 10^2$ m²/gm. **[2003, Main]**

**37.** A substance $A_XB_Y$ crystallizes in a face centered cubic (FCC) lattice in which atoms 'A' occupy each corner of the cube and atoms 'B' occupy the centres of each face of the cube. Identify the correct composition of the substance $A_XB_Y$. **[2002, Screening]**

(1) $AB_3$

(2) $A_4B_3$

(3) $A_3B$

(4) Composition cannot be specified

# ANSWER KEY

| | | | | | | | | | |
|---|---|---|---|---|---|---|---|---|---|
| **1.** (*) | **2.** (3) | **3.** (3) | **4.** (1,3) | **5.** (1) | **6.** (3) | **7.** (3) | **8.** (1) | **9.** (3) | **10.** (2) |
| **11.** (2) | **12.** (2,3,4) | **13.** (1) | **14.** (1) | **15.** (3) | **16.** (2) | **17.** (4) | **18.** (4) | **19.** (3) | **20.** (3) |
| **21.** (1) | **22.** (2) | **23.** (*) | **24.** (4) | **25.** (2, 3) | **26.** (*) | **27.** (2) | **28.** (1) | **29.** (4) | **30.** (3) |
| **31.** (*) | **32.** (*) | **33.** (*) | **34.** (2) | **35.** (*) | **36.** (*) | **37.** (1) | | | |

# ANSWERS WITH EXPLANATIONS

**1.**
$$d = \frac{z\left(\dfrac{M}{N_A}\right)}{a^3}$$

$$2.7 \times 10^3 = z\frac{2.7\times10^{-2}}{6\times10^{23}(4.05\times10^{-10})^3}$$

$$2.7 \times 10^3 = z\frac{\left(\dfrac{2.7\times10^{-2}}{}\right)}{6\times10^{23}(4.05\times10)^{10}}$$

$$2.7 \times 10^3 = z\frac{(2.7\times10^{-2})}{6\times10^{23}\times66.43\times10^{-30}}$$

$$3.98 = z$$

$z \approx 4$ structure is fcc

$$\frac{a}{\sqrt{2}} = 2r$$

$$r = \frac{a}{2\sqrt{2}} = \frac{\sqrt{2}a}{4}$$

$$= \frac{1.414\times405\times10^{-12}}{4}$$

$$r = 143.16 \times 10^{-12}$$

**2. (3)**
$$p = \frac{2\times\dfrac{M}{N_A}}{a^3}$$

$$\Rightarrow \quad 6.17 = \frac{2\times\dfrac{M}{N_A}}{(3\times10^{-8}\ \text{cm})^3}$$

$$\Rightarrow \quad M = 50\ \text{gm/mol}$$

$$N_o = \frac{w}{M}\times N_A$$

$$= \frac{200}{50}\times N_A = 4N_A$$

**3. (3)**

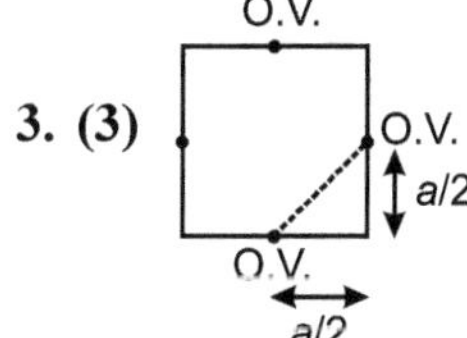


Distance between nearest Octahedral Voids (O.V.)

$$= \sqrt{\left(\frac{a}{2}\right)^2 + \left(\frac{a}{2}\right)^2}$$

$$= \frac{a}{\sqrt{2}}$$

**4. (1,3)** (1)
$$Z_M = 2\times\frac{1}{2} = 1$$

$$Z_X = 4\times\frac{1}{4} = 1$$

$\therefore$ Empirical formula is MX.

(2) Coordination numbers of both M and X is 8. Therefore option 2 is incorrect.

(3) Bond length of M – X bond

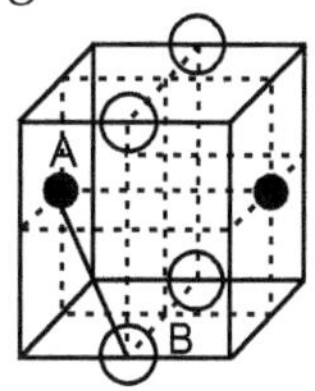


$$= AB = \sqrt{3}\cdot\frac{a}{2}$$

$$= 0.866\ ba$$

(4)
$$r_M : r_X = (\sqrt{3} - 1) : 1$$

$$= 0.732 : 1.000$$

Therefore option 4 is incorrect.

**5. (1)** Since AgBr has intermediate radius ratio.
$\therefore$ It shows both schottky and Frenkel defects
ZnS $\rightarrow$ Frenkel defects
KBr, CsSl $\rightarrow$ Schottky defects

**6. (3)** (i) Number of cations is 4 and number of anions is 1.
(ii) Number of cations is 1 and number of anions is 4.
(iii) Number of cations is 1 and number of anions is 4.
(iv) Number of cations is 1 and number of anions is 3.

**7. (3)** Frenkel defect is the defect in which cations get displaced from their position and occupy the interstitial site. Therefore, the type of defect which has the presence of cations in the interstitial sites is the Frenkel defects.

**8. (1)** All compounds have same type of crystal structure but in case of LiCl, it forms hydrated crystal with two molecules of water.

Thus, LiCl has different crystal structure

**9. (3)** The schematic alignment of magnetic moment of anti-ferromagnetic substance is shown below.

The alignment of magnetic moment in anti ferromagnetic substance is in anti-parallel manner with neighboring spin.

**10. (2)** For face centered cubic structure, the molar mass of the pure substance is calculated as,

$$M = \frac{d \times a^3 \times N_A}{Z}$$

$$= \frac{8 g/cm^{-3} \times 64 \times 10^{-24} cm^3 \times 6.022 \times 10^{23}\, mol^{-1}}{4}$$

$$= 77.082\ g/mol$$

The number of atoms present in given mass is calculated as,

$$N = \frac{\text{Given mass}}{\text{Molar mass}}$$

$$N \times 10^{24} = \frac{256 g \times 6.022 \times 10^{23}\ mol^{-1}}{77.08 g/mol}$$

$$= 20.00 \times 10^{23}$$

$$N = 2.0$$

**11. (2)** One of the faces of FCC crystal lattice is shown below :

In $\triangle ABC$, by applying Pytha-goras theorem,

$$a^2 + a^2 = (4r)^2$$
$$2a^2 = 16r^2$$
$$r = \frac{1}{2\sqrt{2}}a$$

Therefore, the closest approach, that is, the distance between two atoms is,

$$2r = \frac{a}{\sqrt{2}}$$

**12. (2,3,4)** (A) Coordination number is not 12 for any atom in the top most layers as there is no layer above top layer. So, statement (1) is incorrect.
(B) The packing efficiency of atoms for ccp is 74%. So, statement (2) is correct.
(C) The number of voids in octahedral and tetrahedral is 1 and 2 respectively. So, statement (3) is correct.
(D) The relation between edge length and radius of atom is,

$$\sqrt{2}a = 4r$$
$$a = 2\sqrt{2}r$$

Thus, statement (4) is correct.
Thus, correct statements are (2), (3) and (4).

**13. (1)** In ccp, $O^{2-}$ ions are 4. Thus, total charge is

$$= 4\,(-2)$$
$$= -8$$

Number of octahedral voids per unit cell is $4(Al^{3+})$.

Number of tetrahedral voids per unit cell is $8(Mg^{2+})$.

Let m is $Al^{3+}$ and n is $Mg^{2+}$.

Therefore, due to charge neutrality,

$$4(-2) + 4m\,(+3) + 8n\,(+2) = 0$$

$$m = \frac{1}{2}, n = \frac{1}{8}$$

**14. (1)** The edge length of a BCC lattice is calculated by the formula,

$$a = \frac{4}{\sqrt{3}}r$$

Substitute the value of $a$ in above equation.

$$4.29 = \frac{4}{\sqrt{3}}r$$

$$r \approx 1.86\,\text{Å}$$

**15. (3)** CsCl crystallizes in a body centered cubic lattice. Therefore, edge length (a) will be,

$$a = \frac{2}{\sqrt{3}}(r_{Cs^+} + r_{Cl^-})$$

$$r_{Cs^+} + r_{Cl^-} = \frac{\sqrt{3}}{2}a$$

**16. (2)** The molecule $CsI_3$ contains $Cs^+$ and $I_3^-$ ions.

$$CsI_3 \rightarrow Cs^+ + I_3^-$$

**17. (4)**

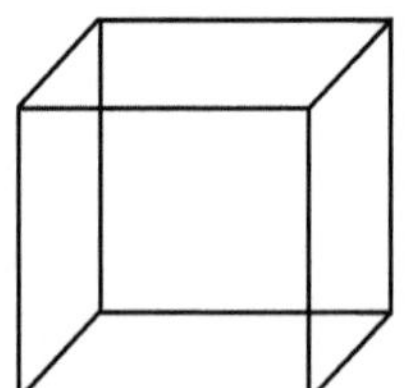

$$\text{Atom A at corners of a cube} = 8 \times \frac{1}{8}$$
$$= 1$$

$$\text{Atom B at the face centers of a cube} = 6 \times \frac{1}{2} - 1 \times \frac{1}{2}$$
$$= \frac{5}{2}$$

Thus, the ration of atoms is

$$A : B = 1 : \frac{5}{2}$$
$$= 2 : 5$$

Therefore, the formula of the ionic compound is $\mathbf{A_2B_5}$.

**18. (4)** Solid alkali metal halides are generally colored due to F-centres. The F-centres are paramagnetic due to the presence of one or more unpaired electrons. Coloration is observed when these electrons absorb light in visible region.

**19. (3)** The relation between sides of a monoclinic unit cell is $a \neq b \neq c$, and the relationship between angles of monoclinic unit cell is $\gamma = \beta = 90°$ and $\alpha \neq 90°$.

**20. (3)** In CCP structure the total number of octahedral vois is four.

$$= \left(12 \times \frac{1}{4}\right) + 1$$
$$= 4$$

Therefore, the total number of octahedral voids per atom is one.

**21. (1)** The given figure shows that $A^+$ ion is surrounded by six $X^-$ ions. Thus, the positive ion is placed in octahedral void.

The radius of $A^+$ ion in octahedral void is calculated by the formula,

$$\text{Radius of } A^+ = 0.414 \times \text{Radius of } X^-$$

Substitute the values of radius of $A^+$ and $X^-$ in the above expression.

$$\text{Radius of } A^+ = 0.414 \times 250 \text{ pm}$$
$$= 103.5 \text{ pm}$$

Thus, the value of radius of anion is approximately equal to 104 pm.

**22. (2)** The number of atoms of M $= \left(\frac{1}{4} \times 4\right) + 1$

$$= 2$$

The number of atoms of X $= \left(\frac{1}{8} \times 8\right) + \left(\frac{1}{2} \times 6\right)$

$$= 4$$

The formula of given compound is $M_2X_4$.

Its empirical formula is $MX_2$.

**23.** The shape of truncated tetrahedron is given as,

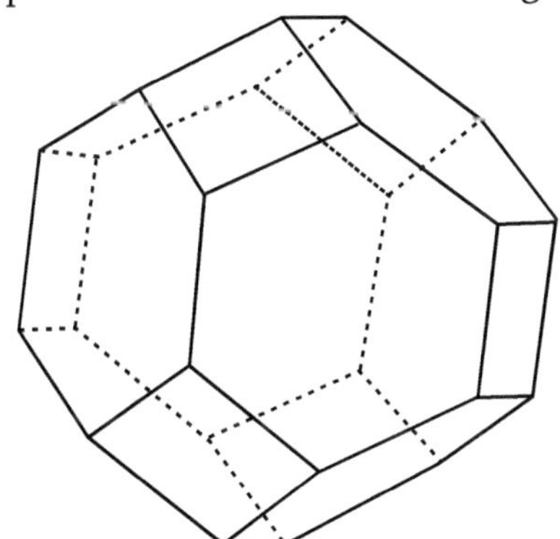

It has total fourteen faces. Eight faces are hexagonal and rest six faces are square shaped.

**24. (4)** As from the given figure,

$$L = 2\sqrt{2}r$$

Area of a square unit cell is,

$$A = (2\sqrt{2}r)^2$$
$$= 8r^2$$

Area of atoms present in one unit cell is,

Area of atoms in one unit cell $= 2\pi r^2$

The packing efficiency is calculated as,

$$\text{Packing efficiency} = \frac{\text{Area of atoms per unit cell}}{\text{Area of square unit cell}}$$

$$= \frac{2\pi r^2}{8r^2} \times 100$$

$$= \frac{\pi}{4} \times 100$$
$$= 78.54\%$$

**25. (2, 3)** Frenkel defect involves the displacement of an atom from its original position to the interstitial site. Therefore, it is known as dislocation defect. The increase in the difference of size of cation and anion favors the frenkel defect.

F-centers are created in the solids when an anionic vacancy is filled by one or more number of unpaired electrons which is generally known as trapping of electrons. Schottky defects affect the physical properties of solid as density of the solid decreases with increase in the Schottky defects.

**26.** In the crystalline state, $AlCl_3$ exists in the cubic close packed structure. The coordination number of the atoms present in the cubic close packed structure is six. Therefore, the coordination number of aluminium in crystalline state of is $AlCl_3$ is 6.

**27. (2)** The number of atoms present in HCP unit cell is,

$$\text{atoms in HCP} = \left(12 \times \frac{1}{6}\right) + \left(2 \times \frac{1}{2}\right) + 3$$
$$= 6$$

**28. (1)** The volume of HCP unit cell is,

$$\text{Volume} = \text{height} \times \text{base area}$$

The height of unit cell is given as,

$$\text{Height} = 4r\sqrt{\frac{2}{3}}$$

The base area is given as,

$$\text{Base area} = 6 \times \frac{\sqrt{3}}{r}(2r)^2$$

Substitute the value of height and base area in the above formula,

$$\text{Volume} = 4r\sqrt{\frac{2}{3}} \times 6 \times \frac{\sqrt{3}}{4}(2r)^2$$
$$= 24\sqrt{2}r^3$$

**29. (4)** The packing fraction of HCP is 74%.

The empty space present in HCP is,

$$\text{empty space} = 100 - 74$$
$$= 26\%$$

**30. (3)** Band gap in germanium is small. It is due to sufficiently small energy gap between each germanium atomic energy levels.

**31.** (A)-(p), (s); (B)-(p)-(q); (C)-(q); (D)-(q),(r.

(A) Both simple cubic and FCC (face-centered cubic) belong to cubic crystal system and possess the following features.

$$a = b = c \text{ and}$$
$$\alpha = \beta = \gamma$$

(B) Both cubic and rhombohedral possess the following features.

$$a = b = c \text{ and}$$
$$\alpha = \beta = \gamma$$

However, they are two different classes of crystal systems.

(C) Cubic and tetragonal are two different classes of crystal systems.

**32.** The formula to calcuate density is,

$$d = \frac{Zm}{N_A \times a^3}$$

The above formula can be written as,

$$d = \frac{Zm}{N_A \times a^3}$$

$$Z = \frac{d \times N_A \times a^3}{m}$$

Substitute all the values in the above formula :

$$d = \frac{Zm}{N_A \times a^3}$$

$$Z = \frac{2 \times 6 \times 10^{23} \times (5)^3}{75}$$

$$= 20 \times 10^{-1}$$

$$= 2$$

The cubic lattice is a body centered.

The relation between $a$ and $r$ for BCC is as follows :

$$\sqrt{3}a = 4r$$

$$r = \frac{\sqrt{3}}{r}a$$

Therefore, the radius of the atom is,

$$r = \frac{1.732 \times 5 \times 10^2}{4}$$

$$= 2.165 \times 10^2$$

$$= 217 \,\text{pm}$$

**33.** The two types of voids present in a crystal system are octahedral voids and tetrahedral voids. These voids correspond to the interstitial sites in a crystal lattice. If $r_1$ and $r_2$ represent the radius of atom present in interstitial site and radius of atom present in the face centered cubic lattice then the radius ratios are given as follows :

$$\left(\frac{r_1}{r_2}\right)_{\text{oct}} = 0.414$$

$$\left(\frac{r_1}{r_2}\right)_{\text{tetra}} = 0.225$$

Since, the value of $\left(\dfrac{r_1}{r_2}\right)_{\text{oct}}$ is greater than $\left(\dfrac{r_1}{r_2}\right)_{\text{tetra}}$, octahedral voids have larger radius than tetrahedral voids. Hence, octahedral voids would be considered for maximum diameter of an atom in the interstitial sites. Therefore, the diameter required is calculated as shown below :

$$\left(\frac{r_1}{r_2}\right)_{\text{oct}} = 0.414$$

$$\left(\frac{2r_1}{2r_2}\right)_{\text{oct}} = 0.414$$

$$(2r_1) = (2r_2) \times 0.414$$

$$= \frac{2 \times 400 \times 0.414}{2\sqrt{2}}$$

$$= 117.1 \,\text{pm}$$

**34. (2)** The FCC structure that possess the cations in alternate tetrahedral voids is ZnS. In the structure of ZnS, the anion $S^{2-}$ are positioned as FCC and $Zn^{2+}$ cations are positioned in the alternate tetrahedral voids as shown below :

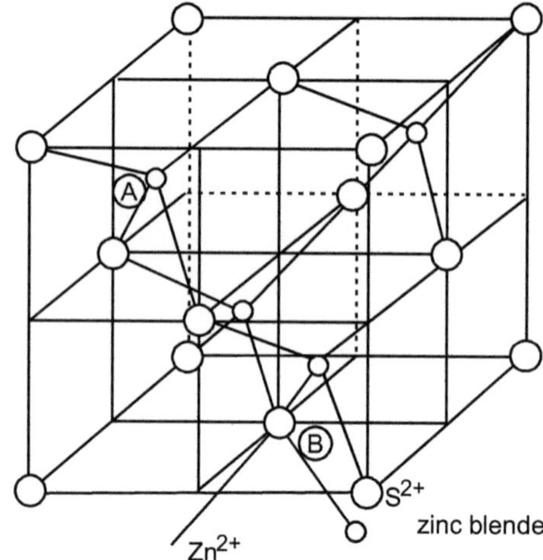


Thus, the correct option is (2).

**35. (a)** The formula to calculate density is,

$$\text{Density} = \frac{Z \times M}{N_A \times V}$$

The value of Z for NaCl is 4. The value of $a$ is $2y^{1/3}$.

The given molecular weight of crystal AB is 6.023 y amu.

Substitute all the values in the above formula.

$$\text{Density} = \frac{4 \times 6.023 \times y}{6.023 \times 10^{23} \times 8 \times y \times 10^{-27}}$$

$$= 5 \,\text{kg/m}^3$$

(b) The observed density is 20 kg/m³, whereas the calculated density is 5 kg/m³. It shows that the observed density is higher than the calculated density due to which the defect present in the solid is non-stoichiometric defect that is metal excess defect.

**36.** (a) The side of a square is 40 mm.

The diameter of a marbles is 10 mm.

The conversion of mm into cm is,

$$1 \text{ cm} = 100 \text{ mm}$$

The side of square is 4 cm.

Thus, the area of square is,

$$= 4 \text{ cm} \times 4 \text{ cm}$$
$$= 16 \text{ cm}^2$$

The packing must be *hcp* to have the maximum number of spheres as shown below :

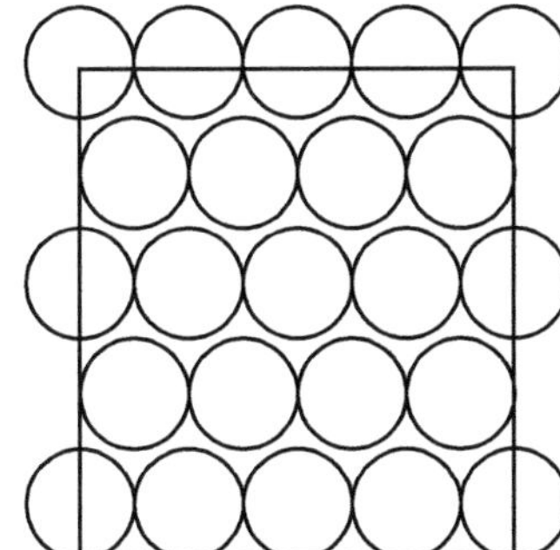

Thus, maximum number of spheres are 18.

Therefore, the number of spheres per $cm^2$ is,

$$= \frac{18}{16}$$
$$= 1.125$$

(b) The number of moles taken for $CH_3COOH$ initially is,

$$= 100 \times 0.5$$
$$= 2$$

Since, it is given that the concentration reduces to 0.49 M. Therefore, the final number of moles of $CH_3COOH$ is,

$$= 100 \times 0.49$$
$$= 49$$

Therefore, the number of moles of $CH_3COOH$ get absorbed is,

$$= 50 - 49$$
$$= 1$$

The number of molecules of $CH_3COOH$ gets adsorbed is $6.02 \times 10^{23}$.

The given surface area of one gram of charcoal is $3.01 \times 10^2 \text{ m}^2$.

Therefore, one molecule of acetic acid gets adsorbed is,

$$= \frac{3.01 \times 10^2}{6.02 \times 10^{23}}$$
$$= 5 \times 10^{-18} \text{ m}^2$$

**37. (1)** The effective number of atom A present in corners is calculated as shown below :

$$A = 8 \times \frac{1}{8}$$
$$= 1$$

The effective number of atom B present in centers of each face is calculated as shown below :

$$B = 6 \times \frac{1}{2}$$
$$= 3$$

Therefore, the correct composition of the substance is $AB_3$.

●●

# Solutions

## QUESTIONS

1. Liquids A and B form ideal solution for all compositions of A and B at 25°C. Two such solutions with 0.25 and 0.50 mole fractions of A have the total vapour pressures of 0.3 and 0.4 bar, respectively. What is the vapour pressure of pure liquid B in bar ? **[2020, Advanced]**

2. An open beaker of water in equilibrium with water vapour is in a sealed container. When a few grams of glucose are added to the beaker of water, the rate at which water molecules : **[2020, Main]**
   (1) leaves the vapour increases
   (2) leaves the solution increases
   (3) leaves the solution decreases
   (4) leaves the vapour decreases

3. Which one of the following graphs is not correct for ideal gas ? **[2020, Main]**

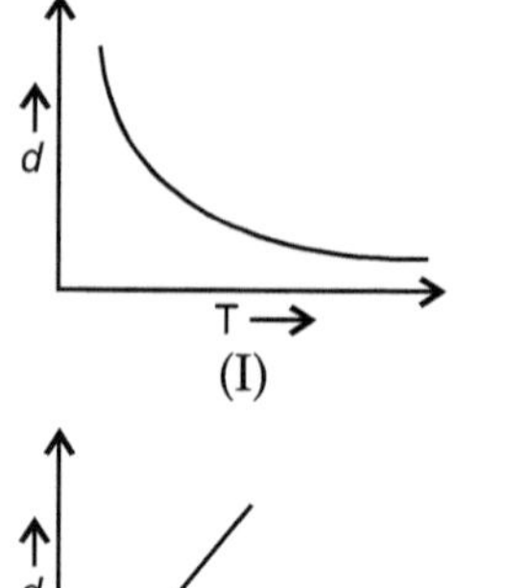

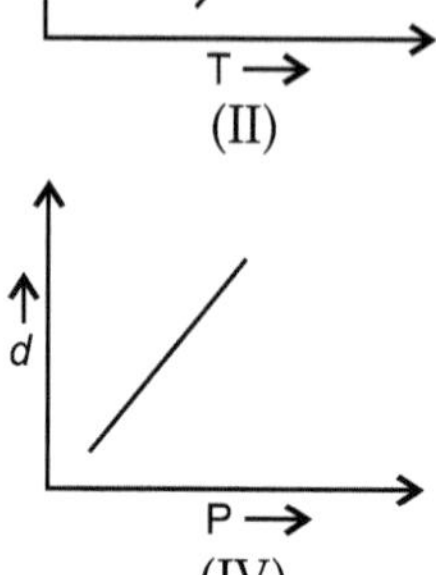

$d$ = Density, P = Pressure, T = Temperature
   (1) II
   (2) III
   (3) I
   (4) IV

4. The size of a raw mango shrinks to a much smaller size when kept in a concentrated salt solution. Which one of the following processes can explain this ? **[2020, Main]**
   (1) Diffusion
   (2) Dialysis
   (3) Osmosis
   (4) Reverse osmosis

5. If the boiling point of $H_2O$ is 373 K, the boiling pont of $H_2S$ will be : **[2020, Main]**
   (1) Greater than 300 K but less than 373 K
   (2) Less than 300 K
   (3) Equal to 373 K
   (4) More than 373 K

6. Glycerol is separated in soap industries by : **[2020, Main]**
   (1) Steam distillation
   (2) Differential extraction
   (3) Distillation under reduced pressure
   (4) Fractional distillation

7. The volume strength of 8.9 M $H_2O_2$ solution calculated at 273 K and 1 atm is ....... .
   (R = 0.0821 L atm $K^{-1}$ $mol^{-1}$) (rounded off to the nearest integer) **[2020, Main]**

8. The strengths of 5.6 volume hydrogen peroxide (of density 1 g/mL) in terms of mass percentage and molarity (M), respectively, are :
   (Take molar mass of hydrogen peroxide as 34 g/mol) **[2020, Main]**
   (1) 1.7 and 0.25
   (2) 1.7 and 0.5
   (3) 0.85 and 0.5
   (4) 0.85 and 0.25

9. A mixture of one mole each of $H_2$, He and $O_2$ each are enclosed in a cylinder of volume V at temperature T. If the partial pressure of $H_2$ is 2 atm, the total pressure of the gases in the cylinder is : **[2020, Main]**
   (1) 14 atm
   (2) 22 atm
   (3) 6 atm
   (4) 38 atm

10. $6.023 \times 10^{22}$ molecules are present in 10 g of a substance '$x$'. The molarity of a solution containing 5 g of substance '$x$' in 2 L solution is ........... $\times 10^{-3}$. **[2020, Main]**

11. If 250 $cm^3$ of an aqueous solution containing 0.73 g of a protein A is isotonic with one litre of another aqueous solution containing 1.65 g of a protein B, at 298 K, the ratio of the molecular masses of A and B is ............. $\times 10^{-2}$ (to the nearest integer). **[2020, Main]**

12. At 300 K, the vapour pressure of a solution containing 1 mole of $n$-hexane and 3 moles of $n$-heptane is 550 mm of Hg. At the same temperatuer, if one more mole of $n$-heptane is added to this solution, the vapour pressure of the solution increases by 10 mm of Hg. What is the vapour pressure in mm Hg of $n$-heptane in its pure state ................. ?
   **[2020, Main]**

13. A set of solutions is prepared using 180 g of water as a solvent and 10 g of different non-volatile

solutes A, B and C. The relative lowering of vapour pressure in the presence of these solutes are in the order [Given, molar mass of A = 100 g mol$^{-1}$; B = 200 g mol$^{-1}$; C = 10,000 g mol$^{-1}$]

**[2020, Main]**

(1) A > B > C     (2) A > C > B
(3) C > B > A     (4) B > C > A

**14.** A soft drink was bottled with a partial pressure of $CO_2$ of 3 bar over the liquid at room temperature. The partial pressure of $CO_2$ over the solution approaches a value of 30 bar when 44 g of $CO_2$ is dissolved in 1 kg of water at room temperature. The approximate pH of the soft drink is ................ × 10$^{-1}$.

(First dissociation constant of $H_2CO_3 = 4.0 / 10^{-7}$; log 2 = 0.3; density of the soft drink = 1 g mL$^{-1}$)

**[2020, Main]**

**15.** A solution of two components containing $n_1$ moles of the 1$^{st}$ component and $n_2$ moles of the 2$^{nd}$ component is prepared. $M_1$ and $M_2$ are the molecular weights of component 1 and 2 respectively. If $d$ is the density of the solution in g mL$^{-1}$, $C_2$ is the molarity and $x_2$ is the mole fraction of the 2$^{nd}$ component, then $C_2$ can be expressed as : **[2020, Main]**

(1) $C_2 = \dfrac{1000 x_2}{M_1 + x_2(M_2 - M_1)}$

(2) $C_2 = \dfrac{d x_2}{M_2 + x_2(M_2 - M_1)}$

(3) $C_2 = \dfrac{d x_1}{M_2 + x_2(M_2 - M_1)}$

(4) $C_2 = \dfrac{1000 d x_2}{M_1 + x_2(M_2 - M_1)}$

**16.** The elevation of boiling point of 0.10 m aqueous $CrCl_3.xNH_3$ solution is two times that of 0.05 m aqueous $CaCl_2$ solution. The value of $x$ is ....... .
[Assume 100% ionisation of the complex and $CaCl_2$, coordination number of Cr as 6 and that all $NH_3$ molecules are present inside the coordination sphere] **[2020, Main]**

**17.** A 100 mL solution was made by adding 1.43 g of $Na_2CO_3.xH_2O$. The normality of the solution is 0.1 N. The value of $x$ is ....... .
(The atomic mass of Na is 23 g/mol).

**[2020, Main]**

**18.** The osmotic pressure of a solution of NaCl is 0.10 atm and that of a glucose solution is 0.20 atm. The osmotic pressure of a solution formed by mixing 1 L of the sodium chloride solution with 2 L of the glucose solution is $x \times 10^{-3}$ atm. $x$ is ...... . (nearest integer) **[2020, Main]**

**19.** The volume, in mL, of 0.02 M $K_2Cr_2O_7$ solution required to react with 0.288 g of ferrous oxalate in acidic medium is ............. .
(Molar mass of Fe = 56 g mol$^{-1}$) **[2020, Main]**

**20.** 5.00 mL of 0.10 M oxalic acid solution taken in a conical flask is titrated against NaOH from a burette using phenolphthalein indicator. The volume of NaOH required for the appearance of permanent faint pink colour is tabulated below for five experiments. What is the concentration, in molarity, of the NaOH solution ?

| Exp. No. | Vol. of NaOH (mL) |
|---|---|
| 1 | 12.5 |
| 2 | 10.5 |
| 3 | 9.0 |
| 4 | 9.0 |
| 5 | 9.0 |

**[2020, Advanced]**

**21.** Aluminium reacts with sulphuric acid to form aluminium sulphate and hydrogen. What is the volume of hydrogen gas in litres (L) produced at 300 K and 1.0 atm pressure, when 5.4 g of aluminium and 50.0 mL of 5.0 M sulphuric acid are combined for the reaction ?
(Use molar mass of aluminium as 27.0 g mol$^{-1}$, R = 0.082 atm L mol$^{-1}$ K$^{-1}$) **[2020, Advanced]**

**22.** A solution of 0.1 M weak base (B) is titrated with 0.1 M of a strong acid (HA). The variation of pH of the solution with the volume of HA added is shown in the figure below. What is the $pK_b$ of the base ? The neutralization reaction is given by $B + HA \rightarrow BH^+ + A^-$.

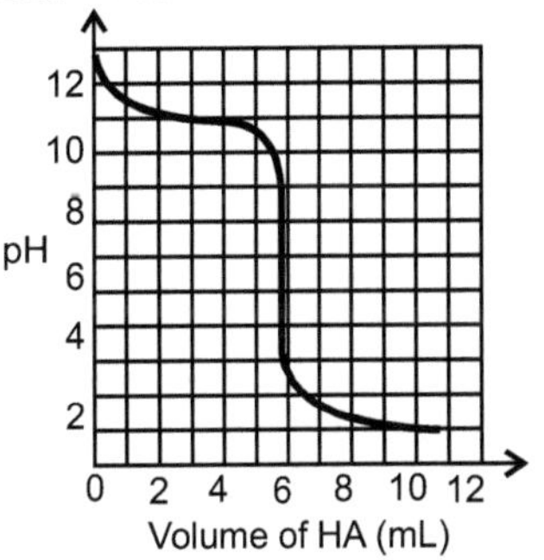


**[2020, Advanced]**

**23.** An acidified solution of 0.05 M $Zn^{2+}$ is saturated with 0.1 M $H_2S$. What is the minimum molar concentration (M) of $H^+$ required to prevent the precipitation of ZnS ?
Use $K_{sp}$ (ZnS) = 1.25 × 10$^{-22}$ and Overall dissociation constant of $H_2S$, $K_{NET} = K_1K_2$ = 1 × 10$^{-21}$.

**24.** The $K_{sp}$ for the following dissociation is 1.6 × 10$^{-5}$

$$PbCl_{2(s)} \rightleftharpoons Pb^{2+}_{(aq)} + 2Cl^-_{(aq)}$$

Which of the following choices is correct for a mixture of 300 mL 0.134 M $Pb(NO_3)_2$ and 100 mL 0.4 M NaCl ? **[2020, Main]**

(1) $Q < K_{sp}$
(2) $Q > K_{sp}$
(3) $Q = K_{sp}$
(4) Not enough data provided

**25.** The Molarity of $HNO_3$ in a sample which has density 1.4 g/mL and mass percentage of 63% is ........... . (Molecular Weight of $HNO_3 = 63$)

**[2020, Main]**

**26.** How much amount of NaCl should be added to 600 g of water ($\rho = 1.00$ g/mL) to decrease the freezing point of water to $-0.2\ °C$ ? ........ . (The freezing point depression constant for water = 2K kg mol$^{-1}$) **[2020, Main]**

**27.** A flask contains a mixture of isohexane and 3-methylpentane. One of the liquids boils at 63°C while the other boils at 60°C. What is the best way to separate the two liquids and which one will be distilled out first ? **[2020, Main]**

(1) simple distillation, 3-methylpentane
(2) simple distillation, isohexane
(3) fractional distillation, isohexane
(4) fractional distillation, 3 methylpentane

**28.** The stoichiometry and solubility product of a salt with the solubility curve given below is, respectively : **[2020, Main]**

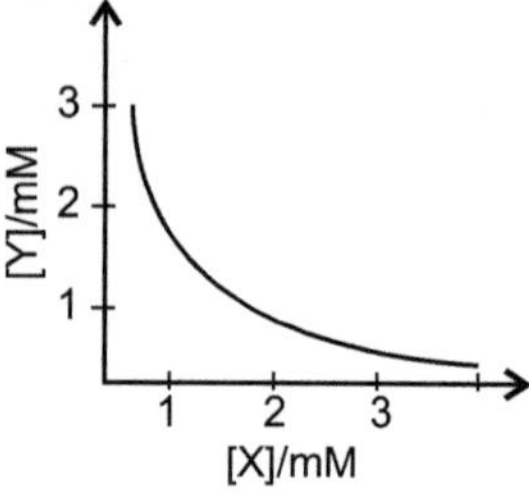

(1) $X_2Y$, $2 \times 10^{-9}\,M^3$
(2) $XY_2$, $1 \times 10^{-9}\,M^3$
(3) $XY_2$, $4 \times 10^{-9}\,M^3$
(4) $XY$, $2 \times 10^{-6}\,M^3$

**29.** The strength of an aqueous NaOH solution is most accurately determined by titrating : **[2020, Main]**

(Note : consider that an appropriate indicator is used)

(1) Aq. NaOH in a volumetric flask and concentrated $H_2SO_4$ in a conical flask.
(2) Aq. NaOH in a pipette and aqueous oxalic acid in a burette
(3) Aq. NaOH in a burette and concentrated $H_2SO_4$ in a conical flask
(4) Aq. NaOH in a burette and aqueous oxalic acid in a conical flask

**30.** A graph of vapour pressure and temperature for three different liquids X, Y and Z is shown below :

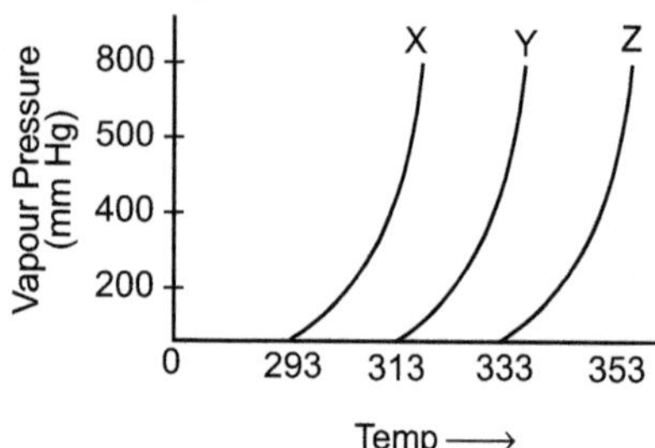

The following inferences are made :

**[2020, Main]**

(A) X has higher intermolecular interactions compared to Y.
(B) X has lower intermolecular interactions compared to Y.
(C) Z has lower intermolecular interactions compared to Y.

The correct inference(s) is/are :

(1) A      (2) (C)
(3) (B)     (4) (A) and (C)

**31.** At 35°C, the vapour pressure of $CS_2$ is 512 mm Hg and that of acetone is 344 mm Hg. A solution of $CS_2$ in acetone has a total vapour pressure of 600 mm Hg. The false statement amongst the following is : **[2020, Main]**

(1) heat msut be absorbed in order to produce the solution at 35°C
(2) Raoult's law is not obeyed by this system
(3) a mixture of 100 mL $CS_2$ and 100 mL acetone has a volume $< 200$ mL
(4) $CS_2$ and acetone are less attracted to each other than to themselves

**32.** Amongst the following, the form of water with the lowest ionic conductance at 298 K is : **[2020, Main]**

(1) distilled water
(2) water from a well
(3) saline water used for intravenous injection
(4) sea water

**33.** A cylinder containing an ideal gas (0.1 mol of 1.0 dm$^3$) is in thermal equilibrium with a large volume of 0.5 molal aqueous solution of ethylene glycol at its freezing point. If the stoppers $S_1$ and $S_2$ (as shown in the figure) are suddenly withdrawn, the volume of the gas in litres after equilibrium is achieved will be ........... .

(Given, $K_f$ (water) = 2.0 K kg mol$^{-1}$), R = 0.08 dm$^3$ atm K$^{-1}$ mol$^{-1}$) **[2020, Main]**

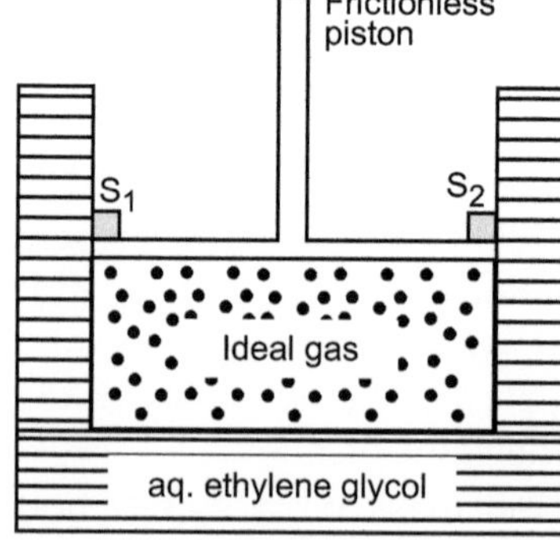


**34.** 10.30 mg of $O_2$ is dissolved into a liter of sea water of density 1.03 g/mL. The concentration of $O_2$ in ppm is ................ . **[2020, Main]**

**35.** The ammonia ($NH_3$) released on quantitative reaction of 0.6 g ures ($NH_2CONH_2$) with sodium hydroxide (NaOH) can be neutralized by : **[2020, Main]**

(1) 200 ml of 0.2 N HCl
(2) 200 mL of 0.4 N HCl
(3) 100 mL of 0.1 N HCl
(4) 100 mL of 0.2 N HCl

**36.** A chromatography column, packed with silica gel as stationary phase, was used to separate a mixture of compounds consisting of (A) benzanilide (B) aniline and (C) acetophenone. When the column is eluted with a mixture of solvents, hexane : ethyl acetate 920 : 80), the sequence of obtained compounds is :

**[2020, Main]**

(1) (B), (A) and (C)    (2) (C), (A) and (B)
(3) (B), (C) and (A)    (4) (A), (B) and (C)

**37.** Which of the following statements is correct ?

**[2020, Main]**

(1) Gluconic acid can form cyclic (acetal/hemiacetal) structure)
(2) Gluconic acid is a dicarboxylic acid
(3) Gluconic acid is obtained by oxidation of glucose with $HNO_3$
(4) Gluconic acid is a partial oxidation product of glucose

**38.** The vapour pressures of pure liquids A and B are 400 and 600 mmHg, respectively at 298 K. On mixing the two liquids, the sum of their initial volumes is equal to the volume of the final mixture. The mole fraction of liquid B is 0.5 in the mixture. The vapour pressure of the final solution, the mole fractions of components A and B in vapour phase, respectively are :

**[2019, Main]**

(1) 450 mmHg, 0.4, 0.6
(2) 500 mmHg, 0.5, 0.5
(3) 450 mm/Hg, 0.5, 0.5
(4) 500 mMHg, 0.4, 0.6

**39.** For the solution of the gases $w$, $x$, $y$ and $z$ in water at 298 K, the Henry's law constants ($K_H$) are 0.5, 2, 35 and 40 k bar, respectively. The correct plot for the given data is :     **[2019, Main]**

(1)
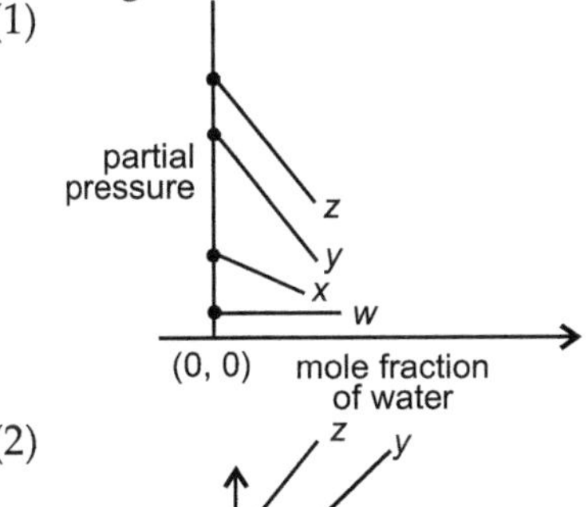


(2)


(3)
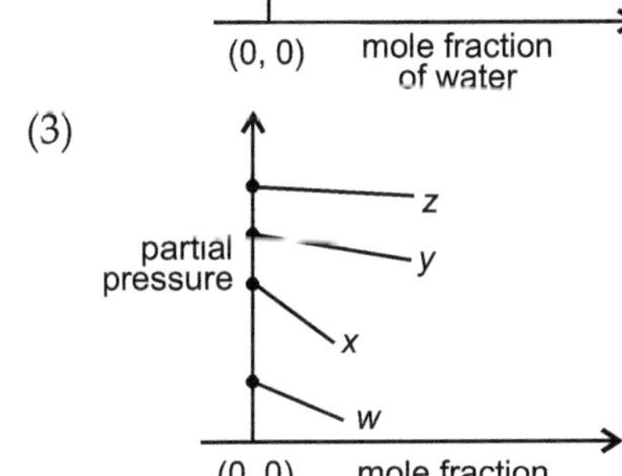


(4)
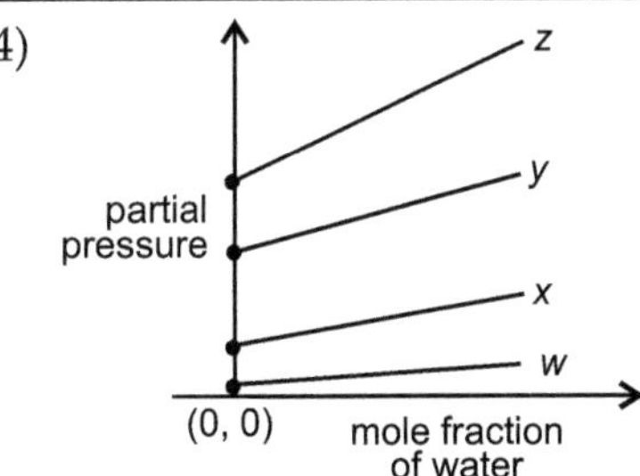


**40.** Liquid 'M' and liquid 'N' form an ideal solution. The vapour pressures of pure liquids 'M' and 'N' are 450 and 700 mmHg, respectively, at the same temperature. Then correct statement is :

**[2019, Main]**

($x_M$ = Mole fraction of 'M' in solution;
$x_N$ = Mole fraction of 'N' in solution;
$y_M$ = Mole fraction of 'M' in vapour phase;
$y_N$ = Mole fraction of 'N' in vapour phase;

(1) $\dfrac{x_M}{x_N} = \dfrac{y_M}{y_N}$

(2) $(x_M - y_M) < (x_N - y_N)$

(3) $\dfrac{x_M}{x_N} < \dfrac{y_M}{y_N}$

(4) $\dfrac{x_M}{x_N} > \dfrac{y_M}{y_N}$

**41.** The osmotic pressure of a dilute solution of an ionic compound XY in water is four times that of a solution of 0.01 M $BaCl_2$ in water. Assuming complete dissociation of the given ionic compounds in water, the concentration oif XY (in mol L$^{-1}$) in solution is :     **[2019, Main]**

(1) $4 \times 10^{-2}$    (2) $6 \times 10^{-2}$
(3) $4 \times 10^{-4}$    (4) $16 \times 10^{-4}$

**42.** Molal depression constant for a solvent is 4.0 K kg mol$^{-1}$. The depression in the freezing point of the solvent for 0.03 mol kg$^{-1}$ solution of $K_2SO_4$ is : (Assume complete dissociation of the electrolyte)

**[2019, Main]**

(1) 0.18 K    (2) 0.24 K
(3) 0.12 K    (4) 0.36 K

**43.** At room temperature, a dilute solution of urea is prepared by dissolving 0.60 of urea in 360 g of water. If the vapour pressure of pure water at this temperature is 35 mmHg, lowering of vapour pressure will be :     **[2019, Main]**

(molar mass of urea = 60 g mol$^{-1}$)

(1) 0.027 mmHg    (2) 0.028 mmHg
(3) 0.017 mmHg    (4) 0.031 mmHg

**44.** 1 g of a non-volatile non-electrolyte solute is dissolved in 100 g of two different solvents A and B whose ebullioscopic constants are in the ratio of 1 : 5. The ratio of the elevation in their boiling points, $\dfrac{\Delta T_b(A)}{\Delta T_b(B)}$, is :     **[2019, Main]**

(1)  5 : 1          (2)  10 : 1

(3)  1 : 5          (4)  1 : 0.2

**45.** A solution is prepared by dissolving 0.6 g of urea (molar mass = 60 g mol$^{-1}$) and 1.8 g of glucose (molar mass = 180 g mol$^{-1}$) in 100 mL of water at 27°C. The osmotic pressure of the solution is : **[2019, Main]**

($R$ = 0.08206 L atm K$^{-1}$ mol$^{-1}$)

(1)  8.2 atm          (2)  2.46 atm

(3)  4.92 atm        (4)  1.64 atm

**46.** On dissolving 0.5 g iof a non-volatile non-ionic solute to 39 g of benzene, its vapour pressure decreases from 650 mmHg to 640 mmHg. The depression of freezing point of benzene (in K) upon addition of the solute is :    **[2019, Main]** (Given data : Molar mass and the molal freezing point depression constant of benzene are 78 g mol$^{-1}$ and 5.12 K kg mol$^{-1}$, respectively).

**47.** Liquid A and B form ideal solution over the entire range of composition. At temperature T, equimolar binary solution of liquids A and B has vapour pressure 45 Torr. At the same temperature, a new solution of A and B having mole fractions $x_A$ and $x_B$ respectively, has vapour pressure of 22.5 Torr. The value of $x_A/x_B$ in the new solution is ........

(given that the vapour pressure of pure liquid A is 20 Torr is temperature T)  **[2018, Advanced]**

**48.** The plot given below shows P – T curves (where P is the pressure and T is the temperature) for two solvents X and Y and isomolal solutions of NaCl in these solvents. NaCl completely dissociates in both the solvents. **[2018, Advanced]**

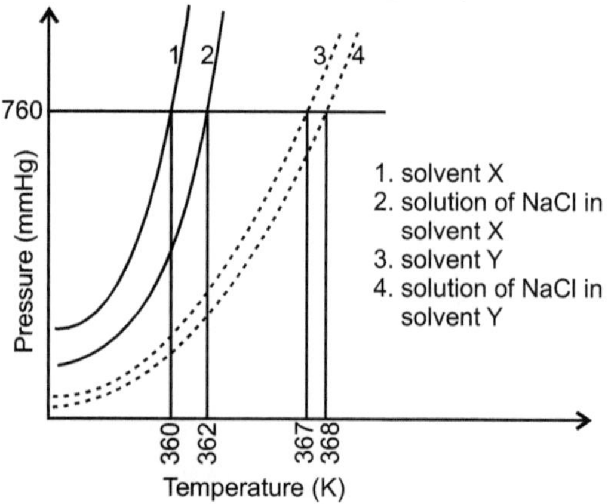


On addition of equal number of moles of a non-volatile solute S in equal amount (in kg) of these solvents, the elevation of boiling point of solvent X is three times that of solvent Y. Solute S is known to undergo dimerisation in these solvents. If the degree of dimerisation is 0.7 in solvent Y, the degree of dimerisation in solvent X is ............. .

**49.** For 1 molal aqueous solution of the following compounds, which one will show the highest freezing point ?    **[2018, Main]**

(1)  $[Co(H_2O)_6]Cl_3$

(2)  $[Co(H_2O)_5Cl]Cl_2 \cdot H_2O$

(3)  $[Co(H_2O)_4Cl_2]Cl.2H_2O$

(4)  $[Co(H_2O)_3Cl_3].3H_2O$

**50.** Two 5 molal solutions are prepared by dissolving a non-electrolyte non-volatile solute separately in the solvents X and Y. The molecular weights of the solvents are $M_X$ and $M_Y$, respectively where $M_X = \dfrac{3}{4}M_Y$. The relative lowering of vapour pressure of the solution in X is ``m" times that of the solution in Y. Given that the number of moles of solute is very small in comparison to that of solvent, the value of ``m" is :    **[2018, Main]**

(1)  $\dfrac{4}{3}$          (2)  $\dfrac{3}{4}$

(3)  $\dfrac{1}{2}$          (4)  $\dfrac{1}{4}$

**51.** The mass of non-volatile, non-electrolyte solute (molar mass = 50 g mol$^{-1}$) needed to be dissolved in 114 g octane to reduce its vapour pressure by 75%, is :    **[2018, Main]**

(1)  37.5 g          (2)  75 g

(3)  150 g          (4)  50 g

**52.** For a solution formed by mixing liquids L and M, the vapour pressure of L plotted against the mole fraction of M in solution is shown in the following figure. Here $x_L$ and $x_M$ represent mole fractions of L and M, respectively, in the solution. The correct statements applicable to this system is/are :    **[2017, Advanced]**

(1)  The point Z represents vapour pressure of pure liquid M and Raoult's law is obeyed from $x_L$ = 0 to $x_L$ = 1

(2)  The point Z represents vapour pressure of pure liquid L and Raoult's law is obeyed from $x_L \rightarrow 1$

(3)  The point Z represents vapour pressure of pure liquid M and Raoult's law is obeyed when $x_L \rightarrow 0$

(4)  Attractive intermolecular interactions between L-L in pure liquid L and M-M in pure liquid M are stronger than those between L-M when mixed in solution

**53.** Pure water freezes at 273 K and 1 bar. The addition of 34.5 g of ethanol to 500 g of water changes the freezing point of the solution. Use the freezing point depression constant of water as 2 K kg mol$^{-1}$. The figures shown below represent plots of vapour pressure (V.P.) versus temperature (T). [molecular weight of ethanol is 46 g mol⁻¹]

Among the following, the option representing change in the freezing point is : **[2017, Advanced]**

(1) 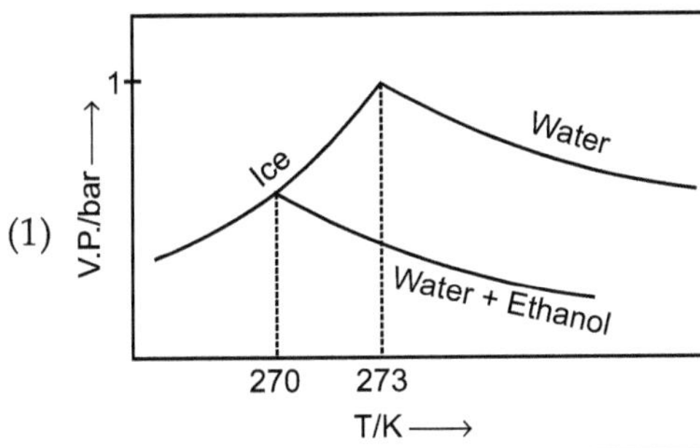

(2) 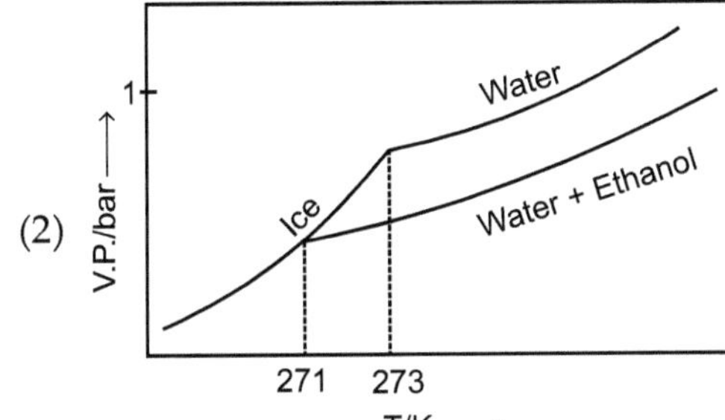

(3) 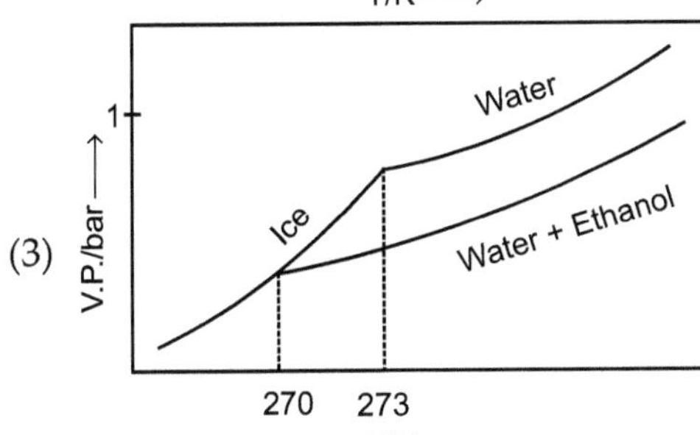

(4) 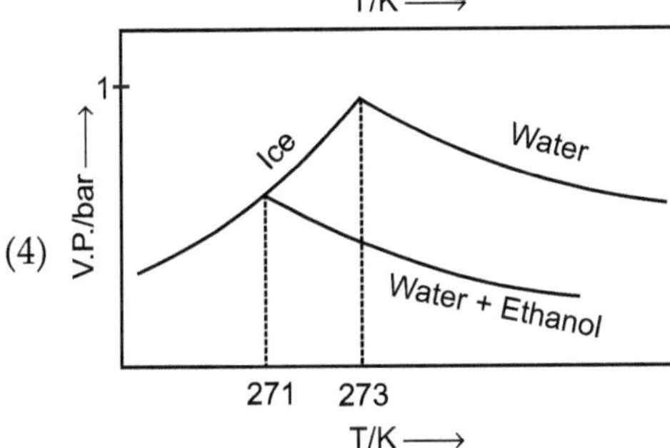

54. The freezing point of benzene decreases by 0.45°C when 0.2 g of acetic acid is added to 20 g of benzene. If acetic acid associates to form a dimer in benzene, percentage association of acetic acid in benzene will be **[2017, Main]**
($K_f$ for benzene = 5.12 K kg mol⁻¹)
(1) 74.6%  (2) 94.6%
(3) 64.6%  (4) 80.4%

55. 5 g of $Na_2SO_4$ was dissolved in $x$ g of $H_2O$. The change in freezing point was found to be 3.82°C. If $Na_2SO_4$ is 81.5% ionised, the value of $x$
($K_f$ for water = 1.86°C kg mol⁻¹) is approximately :
(molar mass of S = 32 g mol⁻¹ and that of Na = 23 g mol⁻¹) **[2017, Main]**
(1) 15 g  (2) 25 g
(3) 45 g  (4) 65 g

56. A solution is prepared by mixing 8.5 g of $CH_2Cl_2$ and 11.95 g of $CHCl_3$. If vapour pressure of $CH_2Cl_2$ and $CHCl_3$ at 298 K are 415 and 200 mmHg respectively, the mole fraction of $CHCl_3$ in vapour form is : **[2017, Main]**
(Molar mass of Cl = 35.5 g mol⁻¹)
(1) 0.162  (2) 0.675
(3) 0.325  (4) 0.486

57. Mixtures showing positive deviation from Raoult's law at 35°C is/are : **[2016, Advanced]**
(1) carbon tetrachloride + methanol
(2) carbon disulphide + acetone
(3) benzene + toluene
(4) phenol + aniline

58. The solubility of $N_2$ in water at 300 K and 500 torr partial pressure is 0.01 g L⁻¹. The solubility (in g L⁻¹) at 750 torr partial pressure is : **[2016, Main]**
(1) 0.0075  (2) 0.015
(3) 0.02  (4) 0.005

59. An aqueous solution of a salt $MX_2$ at certain temperature has a van't Hoff factor of 2. The degree of dissociation for this solution of the salt is : **[2016, Main]**
(1) 0.33  (2) 0.50
(3) 0.67  (4) 0.80

60. 18 g glucose ($C_6H_{12}O_6$) is added to 178.2 g water. The vapour pressure of water (in torr) for this aqueous solution is : **[2016, Main]**
(1) 7.6  (2) 76.0
(3) 752.4  (4) 759.0

61. If the freezing point of a 0.01 molal aqueous solution of a cobalt(III) chloride-ammonia complex (which behaves as a strong electrolyte) is − 0.0558 °C, the number of chlorides in the coordination sphere of the complex is

**[2015, Advanced]**

[$K_f$ of water = 1.86 K kg mol⁻¹]

62. The vapour pressure of acetone at 20°C is 185 torr. When 1.2 g of a non-volatile substance was dissolved in 100 g of acetone at 20°C, its vapour pressure was 183 torr. The molar mass (g mol⁻¹) of the substance is : **[2015, Main]**
(1) 32  (2) 64
(3) 128  (4) 488

63. A solution at 20°C is composed of 1.5 mol of benzene and 3.5 mol of toluene. If the vapour pressure of pure benzene and pure toluene at this temperature are 74.7 torr and 22.3 torr, respectively, then the total vapour pressure of the solution and the benzene mole fraction in equilibrium with it will be, respectively :

**[2015, Main]**

(1) 35.0 torr and 0.480  (2) 38.0 torr and 0.589
(3) 30.5 torr and 0.389  (4) 35.8 torr and 0.280

**64.** Determination of the molar mass of acetic acid in benzene using freezing point depression is affected by : **[2015, Main]**
(1) dissociation
(2) association
(3) partial ionisation
(4) complex formation

**65.** $MX_2$ dissociates into $M^{2+}$ and $X^-$ ions in an aqueous solution, with a degree of dissociation ($\alpha$) of 0.5. The ratio of the observed depression of freezing point of the aqueous solution to the value of the depression of freezing point in the absence of ionic dissociation is. **[2014, Advanced]**

**66.** Consider separate solutions of 0.500 M $C_2H_5OH$(aq), 0.100 M $Mg_3(PO_4)_2$(aq), 0.250 M KBr(aq) and 0.125 M $Na_3PO_4$(aq) at 25°C. Which statement is true about these solutions, assuming all the salts to be strong electrolytes ?
**[2014, Main]**
(1) They all have the same osmotic pressure.
(2) 0.100 M $Mg_3(PO_4)_2$ (aq) has the highest osmotic pressure.
(3) 0.125 M $Na_3PO_4$(aq) has the highest osmotic pressure.
(4) 0.500 M $C_2H_5OH$(aq) has the highest osmotic pressure.

**67.** Choose the correct statement with respect to the vapour pressure of a liquid among the following :
**[2014, Main]**
(1) Increases linearly with increasing temperature
(2) Increases non-linearly with increasing temperature
(3) Decreases linearly with increasing temperature
(4) Decreases non-linearly with increasing tempetature

**68.** The observed osmotic pressure for a 0.10 M solution of $Fe(NH_4)_2(SO_4)_2$ at 25°C is 10.8 atm. The expected and experimental (observed) values of Van't Hoff factor (i) will be respectively :
**[2014, Main]**
($R = 0.082$ L atm $K^{-1}$ $mol^{-1}$)
(1) 5 and 4.42
(2) 4 and 4.00
(3) 5 and 3.42
(4) 3 and 5.42

**69.** For an ideal solution of two components A and B, which of the following is true ? **[2014, Main]**
(1) $\Delta H_{mixing} < 0$ (zero)
(2) $\Delta H_{mixing} > 0$ (zero)
(3) A–B interaction is stronger than A–A and B–B interactions
(4) A–A, B–B and A–B interactions are identical

**70.** For a dilute solution containing 2.5 g of a non-volatile non-electrolyte solute in 100 g of water, the elevation in boiling point at 1 atm pressure is 2°C. Assuming concentration of solute is much lower than the concentration of solvent, the vapour pressure (mm of Hg) of the solution is (take $K_b = 0.76$ K kg $mol^{-1}$) **[2012, Advanced]**
(1) 724
(2) 740
(3) 736
(4) 718

**71.** The freezing point (in °C) of a solution containing 0.1 g of $K_3[Fe(CN)_6]$ (Mol. Wt. 329) in 100 g of water ($K_f = 1.86$ K kg $mol^{-1}$) is :**[2011, Advanced]**
(1) $-2.3 \times 10^{-2}$
(2) $-5.7 \times 10^{-2}$
(3) $-5.7 \times 10^{-3}$
(4) $-1.2 \times 10^{-2}$

**72.** The Henry's law constant for the solubility of $N_2$ gas in water at 298 K is $1.0 \times 10^5$ atm. The mole fraction of $N_2$ in air is 0.8. The number of moles of $N_2$ from air dissolved in 10 moles of water at 298 K and 5 atm pressure is : **[2009, Advanced]**
(1) $4.0 \times 10^{-4}$
(2) $4.0 \times 10^{-5}$
(3) $5.0 \times 10^{-4}$
(4) $4.0 \times 10^{-6}$

**73.** The freezing point of the solution M is :
**[2008, Advanced]**
(1) 268.7 K
(2) 268.5 K
(3) 234.2 K
(4) 150.9 K

**74.** The vapour pressure of the solution M is :
**[2008, Advanced]**
(1) 39.3 mm Hg
(2) 36.0 mm Hg
(3) 29.5 mm Hg
(4) 28.8 mm Hg

**75.** Water is added to the solution M such that the mole fraction of water in the solution becomes 0.9. The boiling point of this solution is :
**[2008, Advanced]**
(1) 380.4 K
(2) 376.2 K
(3) 375.5 K
(4) 354.7 K

**76.** When 20 g of naphthoic acid ($C_{11}H_8O_2$) is dissolved in 50 g of benzene ($K_f = 1.72$ K kg $mol^{-1}$), a freezing point depression of 2K is observed. The van't Hoff factor ($i$) is : **[2007, Advanced]**
(1) 0.5
(2) 1
(3) 2
(4) 3

**77.** 75.2 g of $C_6H_5OH$ (phenol) is dissolved in a solvent of $K_f = 14$ K kg $mol^{-1}$. If the depression in freezing point is 7 K then find the % of phenol that dimerises. **[2006, Main]**

**78.** The elevation in boiling point, when 13.44 g of freshly prepared $CuCl_2$ are added to one kilogram of water, is. **[2005, Screening]**
[Some useful data, $K_b = 0.52$ kg K $mol^{-1}$, molecular weight of $CuCl_2 = 134.4$ gm].
(1) 0.05
(2) 0.1
(3) 0.16
(4) 0.21

**79.** (a) 1.22 g $C_6H_5$ COOH is added into two solvent and data of $\Delta T_b$ and $K_b$ are given as :
**[2004, Main]**
(i) In 100 g $CH_3COCH_3$, $\Delta T_b = 0.17$
$K_b = 1.7$ Kg Kelvin/mol
(ii) In 100 g benzene, $\Delta T_b = 0.13$ and $K_b = 2.6$ Kg Kelvin/mol

Find out the molecular weight of $C_6H_5COOH$ in both the cases the interpret the result.

(b) 0.1 M of HA is titrated with 0.1 M NaOH, calculate the pH at end point. Given Ka(HA) $= 5 \times 10^{-6}$ and $\alpha \ll 1$.

**80.** 0.004 M $Na_2SO_4$ is isotonic with 0.01 M Glucose. Degree of dissociation of $Na_2SO_4$ is :

**[2004, Screening]**

(1) 75%      (2) 50%

(3) 25%      (4) 85%

**81.** During depression of freezing point in a solution the following are in equilibrium :

**[2003, Screening]**

(1) liquid solvent, solid solvent

(2) liquid solvent, solid solute

(3) liquid solute, solid solute

(4) liquid solute, solid solvent

**82.** Positive deviation from ideal behaviour takes place because of : **[2003, Screening]**

(1) Molecular interaction between atoms and $PV/nRT > 1$

(2) Molecular interaction between atoms and $PV/nRT < 1$

(3) Finite size of atoms and $PV/nRT > 1$

(4) Finite size of atoms and $PV/nRT < 1$

## ANSWER KEY

| | | | | | | | | | |
|---|---|---|---|---|---|---|---|---|---|
| 1. (*) | 2. (1) | 3. (1) | 4. (3) | 5. (2) | 6. (3) | 7. (*) | 8. (2) | 9. (3) | 10. (*) |
| 11. (*) | 12. (*) | 13. (1) | 14. (*) | 15. (4) | 16. (*) | 17. (*) | 18. (*) | 19. (*) | 20. (*) |
| 21. (*) | 22. (*) | 23. (*) | 24. (2) | 25. (*) | 26. (*) | 27. (3) | 28. (3) | 29. (4) | 30. (3) |
| 31. (3) | 32. (1) | 33. (*) | 34. (*) | 35. (4) | 36. (2) | 37. (4) | 38. (4) | 39. (1) | 40. (4) |
| 41. (2) | 42. (4) | 43. (3) | 44. (3) | 45. (3) | 46. (*) | 47. (*) | 48. (*) | 49. (4) | 50. (2) |
| 51. (3) | 52. (2, 4) | 53. (3) | 54. (2) | 55. (3) | 56. (3) | 57. (1, 2) | 58. (2) | 59. (2) | 60 (3) |
| 61. (1) | 62. (2) | 63. (2) | 64. (2) | 65. (2) | 66. (1) | 67. (2) | 68. (1) | 69. (4) | 70 (1) |
| 71. (1) | 72. (1) | 73. (4) | 74. (2) | 75. (2) | 76. (1) | 77. (*) | 78. (3) | 79. (*) | 80 (1) |
| 81. (1) | 82. (1) | | | | | | | | |

## ANSWERS WITH EXPLANATIONS

**1.**
$$P_T = P_A^\circ X_A + P_B^\circ X_B$$
$$0.3 = P_A^\circ \times 0.25 + P_B^\circ \times 0.75 \quad ...(i)$$
$$0.4 = P_A^\circ \times 0.5 + P_B^\circ \times 0.5$$
$$0.8 = P_A^\circ + P_B^\circ \quad ...(ii)$$
On solving eqn (i) and (ii)
$P_A^\circ = 0.6$, $P_B^\circ = 0.2$

**2. (1)** With addition of solute in solvent, surface area for vapourisation decreases causes lowering in vapour pressure. As the vapour pressure of solution will be less than vapour pressure of pure solvent, so some vapour molecules will get condensed to maintain new equilibrium.

**3. (1)** $PM = dRT \Rightarrow d \propto \dfrac{1}{T}$

So graph between $d$ Vs T is not a straight line.

**4. (3)** Raw mango shrink in salt solution due to net transfer of water molecules from mango to salt solution due to phenomenon of osmosis.

**5. (2)** Boiling point of $H_2S$ < Boiling point of $H_2O$
(213 K)        (373 K)

**6. (3)** Glycerol is separated by reduced pressure distillation in soap industries.

**7.** Volume strength of $H_2O_2$ at 1 atm 273 kelvin = M × 11.2 = 8.9 × 11.2 = 99.68

**8. (2)** Volume strength = 11.2 × molarity

$$\Rightarrow \quad molarity = \frac{5.6}{11.2} = 0.5$$

Assuming 1 litre solution;

$$mass\ of\ solution = 1000\ ml \times 1\ g/ml$$
$$= 1000\ g$$
$$mass\ of\ solute = moles \times molar\ mass$$
$$= 0.5\ mol \times 34\ g/mol$$
$$= 17\ gm.$$

$$\Rightarrow \quad mass\% = \frac{17}{1000} \times 100 = 1.7\%$$

**9. (3)** According to Dalton's law of partial pressure

$$p_i = x_i \times P_T$$

$p_i$ = partial pressure of the $i^{th}$ component

$x_i$ = mole fraction of the $i^{th}$ component

$p_T$ = total pressure of mixture

$$\Rightarrow \quad 2\ atm = \left(\frac{n_{H_2}}{n_{H_2} + n_{H_e} + n_{O_2}}\right) \times p_T$$

$$\Rightarrow \quad p_1 = 2\ atm \times \frac{3}{1} = 6\ atm$$

**10.**
$$Moles = \frac{number\ of\ molecules}{6 \times 10^{23}}$$
$$= \frac{given\ mass}{molar\ mass}$$

$$\Rightarrow \text{molar mass} = \frac{10 \times 6.023 \times 10^{23}}{6.023 \times 10^{22}} = 100 \, \text{g/mol}$$

$$\Rightarrow \quad \text{molarity} = \frac{\text{moles of solute}}{\text{volume of solution } (l)}$$

$$= \frac{(5/100)}{2} = 0.025$$

**11.** Let molar mass of protein A = $x$ g/mol

Let molar mass of protein B = $y$ g/mol

$\pi_A$ = osmotic pressure of protein A

$$= \frac{\left(\dfrac{0.73}{x}\right)}{0.25} RT$$

$\pi_B$ = osmotic pressure of protein B

$$= \frac{\left(\dfrac{1.65}{y}\right)}{1} RT$$

$$\pi_A = \pi_B$$

$$\Rightarrow \quad \left(\frac{0.73}{x \times 0.25}\right) RT = \left(\frac{1.65}{y}\right) RT$$

$$\Rightarrow \quad \left(\frac{x}{y}\right) = \frac{0.73}{0.25 \times 1.65}$$

$$= 1.769 \cong 1.77$$

**12.**

$$550 = P_A^o \times \frac{1}{4} + P_B^o \times \frac{3}{4}$$

$$2200 = P_A^o + 3P_B^o \qquad \text{...(i)}$$

$$2800 = P_A^o + 4P_B^o \qquad \text{...(ii)}$$

$$560 = P_A^o \times \frac{1}{5} + P_B^o \times \frac{4}{5}$$

$$P_B^o = 600, \ P_A^o = 400$$

**13. (1)** Relative lowering of V.P. $= \dfrac{\Delta P}{P^0} = x_{\text{solute}}$

$$\left(\frac{\Delta P}{P^0}\right)_A = \frac{\dfrac{10}{100}}{\dfrac{10}{100} + \dfrac{180}{18}};$$

$$\left(\frac{\Delta P}{P^0}\right)_B = \frac{\dfrac{10}{200}}{\dfrac{10}{200} + \dfrac{180}{18}}$$

$$\left(\frac{\Delta P}{P^0}\right)_C = \frac{\dfrac{10}{10,000}}{\dfrac{10}{10,000} + \dfrac{180}{18}} ; \left(\frac{\Delta P}{P^0}\right)_A > \left(\frac{\Delta P}{P^0}\right)_B$$

$$> \left(\frac{\Delta P}{P^0}\right)_C$$

**14.**

$$P_{CO_2} = K_H \times CO_2$$

$$\frac{3}{30} = \frac{K_H \cdot n_{CO_2}}{K_H 1} \Rightarrow n_{CO_2 = 0.1} \text{ mol}$$

$$pH = \frac{1}{2}(pka_1 - \log c)$$

$$= \frac{1}{2}(6.4 \times 1) = 3.7$$

$$pH = 37 \times 10^{-1}$$

**15. (4)** $\quad C_2 = \dfrac{1000 d x_2}{M_1 + x_2(M_2 - M_1)}$

**16.** 5.00.

**17.** Molar mass of $Na_2CO_3 \cdot xH_2O$

$$\Rightarrow \quad 23 \times 2 + 12 + 48 + 18x$$

$$\Rightarrow \quad 46 + 12 + 48 + 18x$$

$$\Rightarrow \quad (106 + 18x)$$

$$\text{Eqwt} = \frac{M}{2} = (53 + 9x)$$

As $n_{\text{factor}}$ in dissolution will be determined from net cationic or anionic charge; which is 2 so

$$\text{Eqwt} = \frac{M}{2} = 53 + 9x$$

$$\text{Gmeq} = \frac{\text{wt}}{\text{Eqwt}} = \frac{1.43}{53 + 9x}$$

$$\text{Normality} = \frac{\text{Gmeq}}{V_{\text{litre}}}$$

$$\text{Normality} = 0.1 = \frac{\dfrac{1.43}{53 + 9x}}{0.1}$$

As volume = 100 ml

$$= 0.1 \text{ Litre}$$

So, $\quad 10^{-2} = \dfrac{1.43}{53 + 9x}$

$$53 + 9x = 143$$

$$9x = 90$$

$$x = 10.00$$

**18.** Osmotic pressure $= \pi = i \times C \times RT$

For NaCl $i = 2$ so,

$$\pi_{NaCl} = i \times C_{NaCl} \times RT$$

$$C_{NaCl} = \text{conc. of NaCl}$$

$$0.1 = 2 \times C_{NaCl} \times RT$$

$$C_{NaCl} = \frac{0.05}{RT}$$

$$C_{\text{glucose}} = \text{conc. of glucose}$$

For glucose $i = 1$ so,

$$\pi_{\text{glucose}} = i \times C_{\text{glucose}} \times RT$$

$$0.2 = 1 \times C_{glucose} \times RT$$

$$C_{glucose} = \frac{0.2}{RT}$$

$$\eta_{NaCl} = \text{No. of moles of NaCl}$$

$$\eta_{NaCl} \text{ in 1 L} = C_{NaCl} \times V_{Litre}$$

$$= \frac{0.05}{RT}$$

$$\eta_{glucose} = \text{No. of moles of glucose}$$

$$\eta_{glucose} \text{ in 2 L} = C_{glucose} \times V_{Litre}$$

$$= \frac{0.4}{RT}$$

$$V_{Total} = 1 + 2 = 3L$$

so, final conc. NaCl $= \dfrac{0.05}{3RT}$

Final conc. glucose $= \dfrac{0.4}{3RT}$

$$\pi_{Total} = \pi_{NaCl} + \pi_{glucose}$$
$$= [i \times C_{NaCl} + C_{glucose}] \times RT$$
$$= \left( \frac{2\times0.05}{3RT} + \frac{0.4}{3RT} \right) \times RT$$
$$= \frac{0.5}{3} \text{ atm}$$
$$= 0.1666 \text{ atm}$$
$$= 166.6 \times 10^{-3} \text{ atm}$$
$$\Rightarrow 167.00 \times 10^{-3} \text{ atm}$$

so, $x = 167.00$

**19.** $K_2Cr_2O_7 + FeC_2O_4 \longrightarrow Cr^{+3} + Fe^{+3} + CO_2$

$\quad n = 6 \qquad n = 3$

$$\frac{0.02\times6\times V(mL)}{1000} = \frac{0.288}{144}\times3$$

$$\Rightarrow V = 50 \text{ mL}$$

**20.** No. of eq. of oxalic acid = No. of eq. of NaOH

or $\quad \dfrac{5.00\times0.10}{1000}\times2 = \dfrac{9.0\times M}{1000}\times1$

$\therefore$ Molarity of NaOH solution $= \dfrac{1}{9} = 0.11M$

**21.** $2Al + 3H_2SO_4 \longrightarrow Al_2(SO_4)_3 + 3H_2$

Moles of Al taken $= \dfrac{5.4}{27} = 0.2$

Moles of $H_2SO_4$ taken $= \dfrac{50\times5.0}{1000} = 0.25$

As $\dfrac{0.2}{2} > \dfrac{0.25}{3}$, $H_2SO_4$ is limiting reagent

as 0.2 moles of Al reacts with 0.3 moles of sulphuric acid.

Now, moles of $H_2$ formed $= 3/3 \times 0.25 = 0.25$
[as 3 moles of sulphuric acid form 3 moles of $H_2$ gas.]

volume of $H_2$ gas formed $= nRT/P$

[from gas equation]

$= (0.25 \times 0.082 \times 300)/1 = 6.15$ L

Therefore, the volume of Hydrogen gas in litres is 6.15 L.

**22.** Equivalence point

$$\text{B} \quad + \quad \text{HA} \longrightarrow \text{BH}^+ \quad + \quad \text{A}^-$$

$\quad 0.1 \times 6 \qquad\quad 0.1 \times 6$

$\quad = 0.6 \text{ m mol} \quad = 0.6 \text{ m mol}$

Therefore, total volume $= 12$ ml

Concentration of salt $= \dfrac{0.6}{12}$

$$pH = 6 = \sqrt{\frac{k_w}{k_b}\times c}$$

$$= \sqrt{\frac{10^{-14}\times0.6}{k_b \times 12}}$$

$\{pH = 0.6, [H^+] = 10^{-6}\}$

$$\Rightarrow \quad [H^+] = 10^{-6} = \sqrt{\frac{k_w}{k_b}\times\frac{0.1\times6}{12}}$$

$$10^{-12} = \frac{10^{-14}\times10^{-1}}{K_b}\times\frac{1}{2}$$

$$k_b = 5 \times 10{-4}$$

$$pk_b = -\log k_b = -\log(5 \times 10^{-4})$$

$$= -\log 5 + 4 \log 10$$

$$pk_b = 4 - 0.7$$

$$pk_b = 3.3$$

**23.** For ppt, $\quad [Zn^{+2}][S^{-2}] = K_{sp}$

$$[S^{-2}] = \frac{1.25\times10^{-22}}{0.05}$$

$$= 2.5 \times 10^{-21} \text{ M}$$

$$H_2S \rightleftharpoons 2H^+ + S^{-2}$$

$$K_{Net} = 10^{-21} = \frac{[H^+]^2\times2.5\times10^{-21}}{0.1}$$

$$[H^+]^2 = \frac{1}{25}$$

$$[H^+] = \frac{1}{5}M = 0.2 \text{ M}$$

**24. (2)** $\quad [Pb^{+2}] = \dfrac{300\times0.134}{400}$

$$= 1.005 \times 10^{-1} \text{ M}$$

$$[Cl^-] = \frac{100\times0.4}{400}$$

$$= 10^{-1} \text{ M}$$

$$PbCl_{2(s)} \rightleftharpoons Pb^{+2}_{(aq)} + 2Cl^-_{(aq)}$$

$$Q = [Pb^{2+}] \times [Cl^-]^2$$
$$= 1.005 \times 10^{-3} > k_{sp}$$

**25.** 100 gm soln $\rightarrow$ 63 gm $HNO_3$

$$\frac{100}{1.4} \text{ mL} \rightarrow 1 \text{ mole } HNO_3$$

$$\text{Molarity} = \frac{1}{\dfrac{100}{1.4} \times \dfrac{1}{1000}} = 14M$$

**26.**
$$\Delta T_f = i \times m \, K_f$$
$$0.2 = 2 \times 2 \times \frac{w/58.5}{600/1000}$$
$$w = 1.755 \text{ gm}$$

**27. (3)** Liquid which have less difference in boiling point can be isolated by fractional distillation and liquid with less boiling will be isolated first.

**28. (3)** From the graph and dimensions salt is : $XY_2$

$[X] = 1 \times 10^{-3}$ M

$[Y] = 2 \times 10^{-3}$ M

$$XY_2(s) \rightleftharpoons X^{2+}_{(aq.)} + 2Y^-_{(aq.)}$$

$$k_{sp} = [X^{2+}][Y^-]^2$$
$$= (10^{-3}) (2 \times 10^{-3})^2$$
$$= 4 \times 10^{-9} \text{ M}^3$$

**29. (4)**

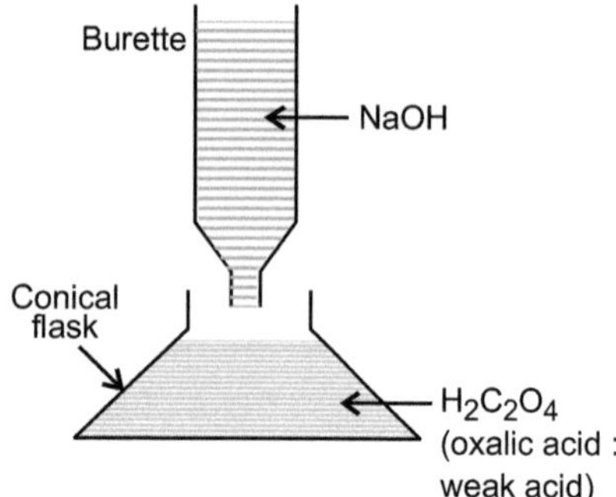


**30. (3)** Order of B.P. is : $Z > Y > X$
Order of vapour pressure : $Z < Y < X$
Order of intermolecular interaction : $Z > Y > X$.

**31. (3)** The vapour pressure of mixture ($= 600$ mm Hg) is greater than the individual vapour pressure of its constitutents (Vapour pressure of $CS_2 = 512$ mm Hg, acetone $= 344$ mm Hg). hence, the solution formed shows positive deviation from Raoult's law.
$\Rightarrow$ (1) $D_{Sol}H > 0$, (2) Raoult's law is not obeyed (3) $D_{sol.}$ Volume $> 0$
(4) $CS_2$ and Acetone are less attracted to each ether than to themselves.

**32. (1)** Distilled water have lowest ionic conductance.

**33.** 2.17 or 2.18

$$\text{For gas P} = \frac{0.1 \times 0.08 \times 272}{1}$$

$$P = 2.176 \text{ atm}$$
$$P_1V_1 = P_2V_2$$
$$2.176 \times 1 = 1 \times V_2$$
$$V_2 = 2.176 \text{ litre}$$

**34.** $\text{ppm} = \dfrac{10.3 \times 10^{-3}}{1030} \times 10^6 = 10.$

**35. (4)** 100 ml of 0.2 NHCl.
$$2 \times \text{mole of urea} = \text{mole} = NH_3 \quad \text{...(1)}$$
$$\text{Mole of } NH_3 = \text{mole of HCl} \quad \text{...(2)}$$
$$\therefore \quad \text{Mole of HCl} = 0.02 \text{ mole}$$

**36. (2)** More polar compound will comes out first.

**37. (4)** Gluconic acid

$$\begin{bmatrix} CH_2 - CH - CH - CH - CH - COOH \\ | \quad\quad | \quad\quad | \quad\quad | \quad\quad | \\ OH \quad OH \quad OH \quad OH \quad OH \end{bmatrix}$$

is obtained by partial oxidation of glucose by Tollen's reagent or Fehling solution or $Br_2$, $H_2O$.
Gluconic acid cannot form hemiacetal or acetal.

**38. (4)** The vapour pressure of the final solution is calculated as shown below :

$$p_{total} = x_A p_A{}^\circ + x_B p_B{}^\circ$$
$$= (0.5 \times 400) + (0.5 \times 600)$$
$$= (200 + 300) \text{ mm Hg}$$
$$= 500 \text{ mm Hg}$$

The mole fraction of A in vapour phase is calculated as shown below :

$$y_A = \frac{p_A}{p_{total}}$$
$$= \frac{0.5 \times 400}{500}$$
$$= 0.4$$

The mole fraction of B in vapour phase is calculated as shown below :

$$y_B = 1 - 0.4$$
$$= 0.6$$

**39. (1)** The value of partial pressure can be calculated by the formula as shown below :

$$p = k_H \times \frac{n_{gas}}{n_{water} + n_{gas}}$$

$$= K_H \times \left( 1 - \frac{n_{water}}{n_{water} + n_{gas}} \right)$$

$$= K_H \times (1 - x_{water})$$
$$= K_H - k_H x_{water}$$

As the value of $K_H$ increases, the deviation of the plot also increases. Therefore, the correct plot is shown below :

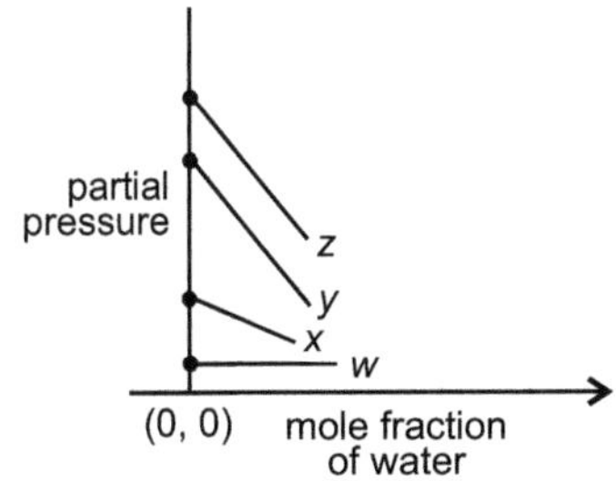


**40. (4)** The vapour pressure pure liquid M is less than the vapour pressure of pure liquid N.

Therefore, the mole fraction of M in solution will be higher than the mole fraction of M in vapour phase.

$$x_M > y_M \qquad \text{...(1)}$$

Similarly, the mole fraction of N in solution will be lower than the mole fraction of N in vapour phase.

$$y_N > x_N \qquad \text{...(2)}$$

Multiply equation (1) and (2).

$$x_M y_N > x_N y_M$$

$$\frac{x_M}{x_N} > \frac{y_M}{y_N}$$

**41. (2)** The value of $i$ for ionic compound (XY) is 2. The value of $i$ for $BaCl_2$ is 3.

The relation between the osmatic pressure of ionic compound (XY) and $BaCl_2$ is shown below :

$$\pi(XY) = 4\pi(BaCl_2)$$

$$i_{XY}[XY]RT = 4i_{BaCl_2}[BaCl_2]RT$$

$$i_{XY}[XY] = 4i_{BaCl_2}[BaCl_2]$$

Substitute the values of concentration of $BaCl_2$, $i_{XY}$ and $i_{BaCl2}$ in the above expression.

$$[XY] = (4)(3)(0.01\ M)$$

$$[XY] = \frac{(4)(3)(0.01\ M)}{2}$$

$$= 6 \times 10^{-2}\ M$$

**42. (4)** The value of $i$ for $K_2SO_4$ is 3.

The depression in freezing point is calculated as shown below :

$$\Delta T_f = iK_f m$$
$$= (3)\ (4\ K\ kg\ mol^{-1})(0.03\ mol\ kg^{-1})$$
$$= 0.36\ K$$

**43. (3)** The lowering of vapour pressure is calculated as shown below :

$$\Delta p = p^\circ - p = p^\circ . x_{solute}$$

$$= 35 \times \frac{0.6/60}{\dfrac{0.6}{60} + \dfrac{360}{18}}$$

$$= 35 \times \frac{0.01}{0.01 + 20}$$

$$= 0.017\ mm\ Hg$$

**44. (3)** The ratio of elevation in boiling points is shown below :

$$\Delta T_b = K_b \times m$$

$$\frac{\Delta T_b(A)}{\Delta T_b(B)} = \frac{K_b(A)}{K_b(B)}(m_A = m_B)$$

$$\frac{\Delta T_b(A)}{\Delta T_b(B)} = \frac{1}{5}$$

**45. (3)** The number of moles of urea is calculated as shown below :

$$n_{urea} = \frac{0.6\ g}{60\ g/mol}$$

$$= 0.01\ mol$$

The number of moles of glucose is calculated as shown below :

$$n_{glucose} = \frac{1.8\ g}{180\ g/mol}$$

$$= 0.01\ mol$$

The osmotic pressure of the solution is shown below :

$$\pi = \left(\frac{(0.01\ mol + 0.01\ mol)\ 1000}{100}\right)(0.08206)(300)$$

$$= 4.9236\ atm$$

**46.** The number of moles of solute is calculated as shown below :

$$\frac{p^\circ - p}{p} = \frac{n_{solute}}{n_{solute} + n_{solvent}}$$

$$\frac{650 - 640}{650} = \frac{n_{solute}}{n_{solute} + n_{solvent}}$$

$$n_{solute} = \frac{5}{640}$$

The depression in freezing point is calculated as shown below :

$$\Delta T_f = \frac{K_f \times n_{solute} \times 1000}{w_1}$$

$$= \frac{5.12 \times 5 \times 1000}{640 \times 39}$$

$$= 1.03$$

**47.** The total vapor pressure is given as shown below.

$$p_T = p^\circ_A x_A + p^\circ_B x_B$$

$$45 = 20\left(\frac{1}{2}\right) + p^\circ_B\left(\frac{1}{2}\right)$$

$$p^\circ_B = 70$$

The new total vapor pressure is given as shown below.

$$p_T = p^\circ_A x_A + p^\circ_B x_B$$

$$22.5 = 20x_A + 70(1 - x_A)$$

$$22.5 = 20x_A + 70 - 70x_A$$

$$x_A = 0.95$$

As it is known that $x_A + x_B = 1$, therefore, $x_B = 0.05$.

Thus,    $\dfrac{x_A}{x_B} = \dfrac{0.95}{0.05}$

$= 19$

**48.** The solution for solvent X is done as shown below.

$$(\Delta T_b)_X = i \times (K_b)_X \times m$$
$$2 = 2(K_b)_X \times m \qquad \ldots(1)$$

The solution for solvent Y is done as shown below.

$$(\Delta T_b)_Y = i \times (K_b)_Y \times m$$
$$1 = 2(K_b)_Y \times m \qquad \ldots(2)$$

On dividing the above two equations,

$$\dfrac{(K_b)_X}{(K_b)_Y} = 2$$

The van't Hoff factor $(i) = 1 - \dfrac{\alpha}{2}$

The value of van't Hoff factor $(i)$ for $Y = 1 - \dfrac{0.7}{2}$

$$= 0.65$$

According to the given information,

$$(\Delta T_b)_X = 3(\Delta T_b)_Y$$
$$i_X \times (K_b)_X \times m = 3i_Y \times (K_b)_Y \times m$$
$$\left(1 - \dfrac{\alpha_X}{2}\right)(K_b)_X = 3 \times 0.65(K_b)_Y$$
$$\left(1 - \dfrac{\alpha_X}{2}\right)2 = 3 \times 0.65$$
$$\alpha_X = 0.05$$

**49. (4)** The freezing point of the given solution is inversely proportional to its van't Hoff factor. The van't Hoff factor for the complex $[Co(H_2O)_3Cl_3].3H_2O$ is lowest due to minimum number of solute particles. Therefore, the freezing point of the solution containing this complex is highest among the given solutions.

**50. (2)** The relationship between molar masses of two solvents is,

$$M_x = \dfrac{3}{4}M_y \qquad \ldots(1)$$

The relative lowering of vapor pressure of two solutions is,

$$\left(\dfrac{\Delta P}{P}\right)_x = m\left(\dfrac{\Delta P}{P}\right)_y$$

The relative lowering of vapor pressure of solution is directly proportional to mole fraction of solute.

$$M_x \times \dfrac{5}{1000} = m \times M_y \times \dfrac{5}{1000} \qquad \ldots(2)$$

Substitute the equation (1) in equation (2).

$$\dfrac{3}{4}M_y \times \dfrac{5}{1000} = m \times M_y \times \dfrac{5}{1000}$$

$$m = \dfrac{3}{4}$$

So value of $m = \dfrac{3}{4}$.

**51. (3)** Let the vapour pressure of pure octane is $p_1^0$.

Therefore, the vapour pressure of pure octane after dissolving the non-volatile solute is $0.75\, p_1^0$.

The molar mass of solute is 50 g/mol.
The given mass of octane is 114 g.
The molar mass of octane is 114 g/mol.
The required mass of solute is calculated by the formula.

$$(p_1^0 - p_1)/p_1^0 = \dfrac{n_1}{n_1 + n_2}$$

Substitute all the values in the above formula.

$$(p_1^0 - p_1)/p_1^0 = \dfrac{n_1}{n_1 + n_2}$$

$$0.75 = \dfrac{\dfrac{w_2}{50}}{\dfrac{w_2}{50} + \dfrac{114}{114}}$$

$$0.75 = \dfrac{1}{1 + \dfrac{50}{w_2}}$$

$$w_2 = 150\text{g}$$

**52. (2, 4)** For the given condition of a mixture solution, the graph of vapor pressure against mole fraction is given as,

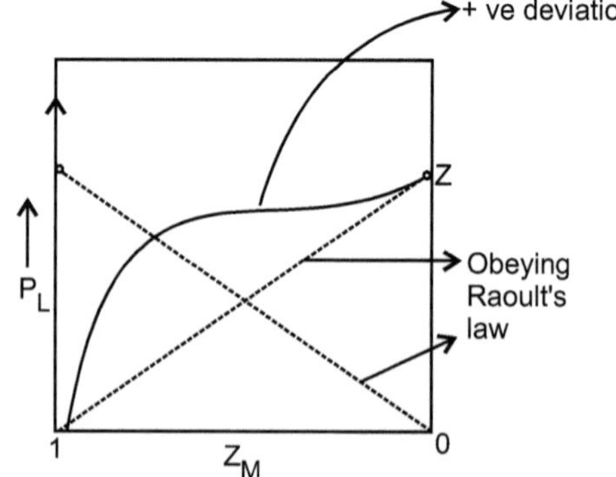


From the above figure it is clear that the point Z represents the vapor pressure of pure liquid L not the liquid M. Raoult's law is not obeyed from $x_L = 0$ to $x_L = 1$. It is obeyed when $x_L \to 1$.

In the above graph, positive deviation is observed. Therefore, condition given in 4th statement is valid.

**53. (3)** Change in freezing point is calculated by the formula,

$$\Delta T_f = K_f \times m$$

$$= 2\,K\,kg\,mol^{-1} \times \frac{(34.5/46)\,mol}{0.500\,kg}$$

$$= 3\,K$$

From the calculated value of change in freezing point, freezing point of mixture is calculated as,

Freezing point of mixture $= (273 - 3)\,K$

$$= 270\,K$$

The vapor pressure of mixture of water and ethanol will increase with temperature. Third figure (option C) represents the same.

**54. (2)** The depression in freezing point is given by the formula,

$$\Delta T_f = i \frac{K_f \times w_2}{w_1 \times M_2} \times 1000$$

Therefore,

$$0.45 = i\left(\frac{5.12 \times 0.2}{20 \times 60}\right) \times 1000$$

$$i = 0.527$$

The reaction for the association of acetic acid is shown as,

$$2CH_3COOH \rightleftharpoons (CH_3COOH)_2$$

$$1 - \alpha \qquad\qquad \frac{\alpha}{2}$$

$$i = 1 - \frac{\alpha}{2}$$

$$0.527 = 1 - \frac{\alpha}{2}$$

$$\frac{\alpha}{2} = 0.473$$

$$\alpha = 0.946$$

Therefore, the percentage association of acetic acid is,

$$0.946 \times 100 = 94.6\%$$

**55. (3)**

$$\text{Molality(experimental)} = \frac{\Delta T_f}{K_f}$$

$$= \frac{3.82}{1.86}$$

$$= 2.054\,mol/1000\,g\,solvent$$

$$\text{Molality(theoretical)} = \frac{\text{moles of solute}}{\text{weight of solvent}} \times 1000$$

$$= \frac{5g/142g/mol}{x} \times 1000$$

$$= \frac{0.0352}{x} \times 1000$$

$$Na_2SO_4 \rightarrow 2Na^+ + SO_4^{2-}$$

| | | | |
|---|---|---|---|
| Moles before dissociation | 1 | 0 | 0 |
| Moles after dissociation | $1-x$ | $2x$ | $x$ |

Thus,

$$\text{Van't Hoff factor } (i) = \frac{\text{Moles after dissocation}}{\text{Moles before dissocation}}$$

$$= \frac{(1-x) + 2x + x}{1}$$

The compound $Na_2SO_4$ is 81.5% $= 0.815$ dissociated. Thus, $x = 0.815$

Substitute the value of $x$ in the above equation.

$$i = \frac{(1 - 0.815) + 2(0.815) + 0.815}{1}$$

$$= 2.63$$

Therefore,

$$i = \frac{\text{Observed molality}}{\text{Calculated molality}}$$

$$2.63 = \frac{2.054}{\dfrac{0.0352}{x} \times 1000}$$

$$= 45.07\,g \approx 45g$$

**56. (3)** The vapour pressure of above solution is calculated by the formula,

$$P = \begin{pmatrix} \text{Mole fraction of } CHCl_3 \times \\ \text{Vapour pressure of } CHCl_3 + \\ \text{Mole fraction of } CH_2Cl_2 \times \\ \text{Vapour pressure of } CH_2Cl_2 \end{pmatrix}$$

$$= \frac{11.95}{119.5 \times 0.2} \times 0.263 + \frac{8.5}{85 \times 0.2} \times 0.546$$

$$= 0.5 \times 0.263 + 0.5 \times 0.546$$

$$= 0.4045$$

The mole fraction of    is calculated by the formula,

$$P_i = y_i P_{Total}$$

$$\text{Mole fraction of } CHCl_3 = \frac{0.5 \times 0.263}{0.4045}$$

$$= 0.325$$

**57. (1, 2)** (A) The mixture of carbon tetrachloride and methanol will show positive deviation from Raoult's law as the intermolecular force of attraction between the solute and the solvent are weaker than that of solute-solute and solvent-solvent molecules.

(B) The mixture of carbon disulfide and acetone will show positive deviation from Raoult's law as the intermolecular force of attraction between the solute and the solvent are weaker than that of solute-solute and solvent-solvent molecules.

(C) The mixture of benzene and toluene will form an ideal solution.

(D) The mixture of phenol and aniline will show negative deviation from Raoult's law as the intermolecular force of attraction between the solute and the solvent are stronger than that of solute-solute and solvent-solvent molecules.

Thus, mixtures in option (A) and (B) will show positive deviation from Raoult's law.

**58. (2)** Partial pressure $(p)$ = mole fraction
$$\times \text{ solubility}(s)$$

If the solubility of $N_2$ at 750 torr is $x$ then,
Therefore,
$$\frac{p_1}{s_1} = \frac{p_2}{s_2}$$
$$\frac{500}{0.01} = \frac{750}{x}$$
$$x = 0.015 \text{g/L}$$

**59. (2)** The decomposition of $MX_2$ is as follows :
$$MX_2(s) \rightleftharpoons M^{2+} + 2X^-$$
$$\text{At eq.} \quad 1-\alpha \qquad \alpha \qquad 2\alpha$$

Thus, the total number of particles after dissociation is,
$$= 1 - \alpha + \alpha + 2\alpha$$
$$= 1 + 2\alpha$$

The number of particles before dissociation is 1.

The formula to calculate the Van't Hoff factor is,
$$i = \frac{\text{No. of particles after dissociation}}{\text{No. of particles before dissociation}}$$

Therefore, the degree of dissociation for the given solution is,
$$i = \frac{1 + 2\alpha}{1}$$
$$\alpha = 0.50$$

**60. (3)** The relative lowering of vapour pressure is calculated as shown below.
$$\frac{P° - P_s}{P°} = \frac{n_2}{n_1}$$
$$\frac{760 - P_s}{760} = \frac{w_2}{M_2} \times \frac{M_1}{w_1}$$
$$\frac{760 - P_s}{760} = \frac{18}{180} \times \frac{18}{178.2}$$
$$P_s = 752.32 \text{ torr}$$

**61.** The formula to calculate freezing point is
$$\Delta T_f = K_f \times i \times m$$
$$0.0558 = 1.86 \times i \times 0.01$$
$$i = 3$$

It is given that the complex behaves as a strong electrolyte.

Thus, one molecule of complex gives   ions in water.

The given complex is $[Co(NH_3)_5Cl]Cl_2$.

Therefore, the number of $Cl^-$ ion in the coordination sphere is 1.

**62. (2)** The molar mass of non-volatile substance $(M_B)$ is calculated by the formula,
$$\frac{P_A^o - P_S}{P_S} = \frac{W_B}{M_B} \times \frac{M_A}{W_A}$$

Substitute the given values in above equation.
$$\frac{185 - 183}{183} = \frac{1.2}{M_B} \times \frac{58}{100}$$
$$M_B = \frac{1.2}{2} \times \frac{58}{100} \times 183$$
$$\approx 64 \text{g/mol}$$

**63. (2)** The mole fraction of benzene is,
$$x_{\text{benzene}} = \frac{1.5}{3.5 + 1.5}$$
$$= 0.3$$

Mole fraction of toluene is,
$$x_{\text{toluene}} = 1 - 0.3$$
$$= 0.7$$

The total pressure of solution is,
$$P_T = (74.7 \times 0.3) + (22.3 \times 0.7)$$
$$= 22.41 + 15.61$$
$$= 38.02 \text{ torr}$$

The mole fraction of benzene in equilibrium is,
$$y_{\text{benzene}} = \frac{74.7 \times 0.3}{38.02}$$
$$= \frac{22.41}{38.0}$$
$$= 0.589$$

**64. (2)** Acetic acid and benzene are polar and non-polar solvents respectively. Due to non-polar nature of benzene, the molecules of acetic acid stick to each other to form dimer as shown below :

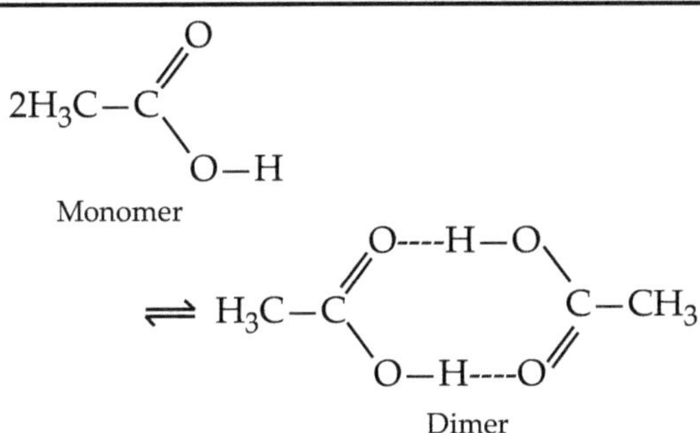



**65. (2)** The dissociation of $MX_2$ into $M^{2+}$ and $X^-$ ions is shown below.

$$MX_2 \rightarrow M^{2+} + 2X^-$$

$$\begin{array}{ccc} 1 & 0 & 0 \\ 1-\alpha & \alpha & 2\alpha \end{array}$$

A degree of dissociation ($\alpha$) is 0.5.

Therefore, the value of $i$ is,

$$i = 1 + 2\alpha$$
$$= 1 + 2(0.5)$$
$$= 2$$

The ratio of the observed depression of freezing point of the aqueous solution to the value of the depression of freezing point in the absence of ionic dissociation is,

$$\frac{(\Delta T_f)_{obs}}{(\Delta T_f)_{th}} = i = 2$$

**66. (1)** All the given electrolytes are strong electrolytes. They will dissociate completely. Their osmotic pressures are,

For 0.500 M $C_2H_5OH$, $\pi = 1 \times 0.5 \times RT$
$$= 0.5 \times RT$$

For 0.100 M $Mg_3(PO_4)_2$, $\pi = 5 \times 0.1 \times RT$
$$= 0.5 \times RT$$

For 0.250 M KBr, $\pi = 2 \times 0.25 \times RT = 0.5 \times RT$

For 0.125 M $Na_3PO_4$, $\pi = 4 \times 0.125 \times RT$
$$= 0.5 \times RT$$

All the solutions have same osmotic pressure. Therefore, all are isotonic solutions.

**67. (2)** The vapor pressure of a liquid increases non-linearly with increase in temperature.

**68. (1)** The observed value of Van't Hoff factor ($i$) is calculated by the formula,

$$i = \frac{\pi}{CRT}$$

Substitute the given values in above equation.

$$i = \frac{10.8}{0.1 \times 0.0821 \times 298}$$

$$i = 4.42$$

The expected value of Van't Hoff factor is 5. The option that corresponds to the above value is (1).

**69. (4)** For an ideal solution of two components A and B, following interactions are identical.

$$A-A$$
$$B-B$$
$$A-B$$

**70. (1)** The relative lowering of vapor pressure is given as shown below.

$$\frac{p^\circ - p_s}{p^\circ} = X_B = \frac{n_B}{n_B + n_A}$$

$$\frac{p^\circ - p_s}{p^\circ} = \frac{n_B}{n_A}$$

$$\frac{760 - p_s}{760} = \frac{2.5}{M_B} \times \frac{M_A}{18 \times \dfrac{1000}{1000}}$$

$$\frac{760 - p_s}{760} = m \times M \times 10^{-3}$$

The value of $\Delta T_b$ is,

$$\Delta T_b = K_b \times m$$

$$2 = 0.76 \, K \, Kg \, mol^{-1} \times m$$

Substitute in the above equation.

$$\frac{760 - p_s}{760} = \frac{2}{0.76} \times 18 \times 10^{-3}$$

$$p_s = 724$$

**71. (1)** The depression in freezing point of a solution containing 0.1 g of potassium cyanate in 100 g of water is calculated by the formula,

$$\Delta T_f = m \times K_f \times i$$

$$= \frac{0.1 \times 1000}{329 \times 100} \times 1.86 \times 4$$

$$= 0.023$$

The freezing point is calculated as,

$$T_f = 0 - \Delta T_f$$
$$= 0 - 0.023$$
$$= -2.3 \times 10^{-3}$$

**72. (1)** The mole fraction of nitrogen gas in the solution is calculated by the formula,

$$P = K_H X_{N_2}$$

Substitute the values of P and $K_H$ in the above equation.

$$0.8 \times 5.0 \, atm = 1.0 \times 10^5 \times X_{N_2}$$

$$X_{N_2} = \frac{4.0 \, atm}{1.0 \times 10^5 \, atm}$$

$$= 4.0 \times 10^{-5}$$

The number of moles of nitrogen gas in the solution is calculated by the formula,

$$X_{N_2} = \frac{n_{N_2}}{n_{N_2} + n_{H_2O}}$$

$$4.0 \times 10^{-5} = \frac{n_{N_2}}{n_{N_2} + 10\,mol}$$

$$n_{N_2} = \frac{4.0 \times 10^{-5} \times 10\,mol}{(1 - 4.0 \times 10^{-5})}$$

$$= 4.0 \times 10^{-4}\,mol$$

**73. (4)** The depression in freezing point is given as,

$$\Delta T_f = K_f \times m$$

The total number of moles are assumed to be 1. Hence, the number of moles of ethanol is 0.9 and the number of moles of water is 0.1. The depression in freezing point is,

$$\Delta T_f = 2.0\,K\,kg\,mol^{-1} \times \frac{0.1}{0.9 \times 46} \times 1000$$

$$= 2.0\,K\,kg\,mol^{-1} \times 2.4\,kg^{-1}\,mol$$

$$= 4.8\,K$$

The freezing point of solution M is,

$$T_f = 155.7 - 4.8$$

$$= 150.9\,K$$

**74. (2)** The vapour pressure of solution M is,

$$P = 0.9 \times 40\,mm\,Hg$$

$$= 36\,mm\,Hg$$

**75. (2)** The elevation in boiling point is given as,

$$\Delta T_b = K_b \times m$$

Substitute the value of molar mass of water, mole fraction of water and boiling point elevation constant of water in the above equation.

$$\Delta T_b = 0.52\,K\,kg\,mol^{-1} \times \frac{0.1}{0.9 \times 18} \times 1000$$

$$= 0.52\,K\,kg\,mol^{-1} \times 6.173\,kg^{-1}\,mol$$

$$= 3.2\,K$$

The boiling point of solution is,

$$T_b = 373\,K + 3.2\,K$$

$$= 376.2\,K$$

**76. (1)** The van't Hoff factor ($i$) of given acid is calculated as,

$$\Delta T_f = K_f \times m \times i$$

The molecular weight of naphthoic acid is 172 g mol$^{-1}$.
The molality of naphthoic acid is calculated as,

$$m = \frac{20}{172} \times \frac{1000}{50}$$

Substitute the above value of $m$ and given values of $\Delta T_f$ and $K_f$ in above equation.

$$2 = 1.72 \times \frac{20}{172} \times \frac{1000}{50} \times i$$

$$i = 0.5$$

**77.** The dimerization of phenol is as follows :

$$2C_6H_5OH \rightleftharpoons (C_6H_5OH)_2$$

$$\begin{array}{cc} 1 & 0 \\ 1-\alpha & \alpha/2 \end{array}$$

The formula to calculate $\Delta T_f$ is,

$$\Delta T_f = i \times k_f \times m$$

The molecular weight of phenol is 94 g/mol.
The formula to calculate molality is,

$$m = \frac{moles\ of\ solute}{kg\ of\ solvent}$$

Therefore, the value of $m$ is,

$$m = \frac{75.2}{1 \times 94}$$

$$= 0.8$$

Substitute all the values in equation (1).

$$7 = 14 \times 0.8 \left( \frac{2-\alpha}{2} \right)$$

$$\alpha = 0.75$$

$$= 75\%$$

**78. (3)** The given mass of $CuCl_2$ is 13.44 g.
The molecular weight of $CuCl_2$ is 134.4 g.
The given mass of water is 1 kg.
The given value of boiling constant, $K_b$ is 0.52 kg mol$^{-1}$.
The value of Vant Hoff's factor is 3.
The molality of the solution is calculated as,

$$Molality = \frac{n_{CuCl_2}}{n_{Water}}$$

Substitute the value of number of moles of and water in the above expression.

$$Molality = \frac{13.44g/134.4g}{1000/1000}$$

$$= 0.1$$

The formula to calculte the elevation in boiling point is,

$$\Delta T_b = i \times K_b \times m$$

Substitute the value of vanthoff'd factor, boiling constant and molality in the above expression.

$$\Delta T_b = 3 \times 0.52\,kg\,K\,mol^{-1} \times 0.1$$

$$\approx 0.16$$

Therefore, the elevation in boiling point if freshly preapared 13.44 g $CuCl_2$ is added in one kilogram water is $\approx 0.16$.
Thus, the correct option is (C).

**79.** (a)  (i) The formula to calculate $\Delta T_b$ is,
$$\Delta T_b = K_b \times m$$
Where,

$m$ is the molality.

Substitute all the given values in the above formula.
$$\Delta T_b = K_b \times m$$
$$0.17 = 1.7 \times \frac{1.22}{M \times 100 \times 10^{-3}}$$
$$M = 122 \text{ g}$$

(ii)  Similarly, the molecular weight of $C_6H_5COOH$ in second case is,
$$\Delta T_b = K_b \times m$$
$$0.13 = 2.6 \times \frac{1.22}{M \times 100 \times 10^{-3}}$$
$$M = 244$$

(b)  The reaction involved in this process is as follows :
$$HA + NaOH \rightleftharpoons Na^+A^- + H_2O$$

NaA is a salt of weak acid and strong base. The concentration of NaA is 0.05 M.

The value of $[H^+]$ is calculated as follows :
$$[H^+] = \sqrt{\frac{10^{-14} \times 5.6 \times 10^{-6}}{0.05}}$$
$$= 10^{-9} \times \sqrt{1.12}$$

The value of pH at end point is calculated as follows :
$$pH = 9 - \frac{1}{2}\log 1.12$$
$$= 8.97$$

**80. (1)**  The osmotic pressure of  0.004 M $Na_2SO_4$ solution is equal to 0.01 M glucose solution.

$$\pi_{Na_2SO_4} = \pi_{glucose}$$
$$i \times 0.004 \times RT = 0.01 \times RT$$
$$i = 2.5$$

The dissociation of $Na_2SO_4$ is expressed as,
$$Na_2SO_4 \rightleftharpoons 2Na^+ + SO_4^{2-}$$
$$1 - \alpha \qquad 2\alpha \qquad \alpha$$

The degree of dissociation of  $Na_2SO_4$ is,
$$\alpha = \frac{i-1}{2}$$
$$= \frac{2.5-1}{2}$$
$$= 0.75$$
$$= 75\%$$

**81. (1)**  Liquid and solid remain in equilibrium at the freezing point. If non-volatile solute solution is cooled to a temperature that is below the freezing point of solution then some liquid solvent will separate as a solid solvent and due to which there is an increase in the concentration of solution.

**82. (1)**  In positive deviation, partial vapour pressure of each component of solution is higher than the vapour pressure calculated from Raoult's law.

For positive deviation,
$$PV = nRT + nPb$$

This equation shows that the factor $nPb$ is directly related to PV. $b$ is the effective volume of molecule. So it is the finite size of molecules that leads to the origin of  $b$ and hence positive deviation at high pressure.

●●

## QUESTIONS

**1.** The number of subshells associated with $n = 4$ and $m = -2$ quantum numbers is : **[2020, Main]**
(1) 4      (2) 8
(3) 16      (4) 2

**2.** Of the species, $NO$, $NO^+$, $NO^{2+}$, $NO^-$, the one with minimum bond strength is : **[2020, Main]**
(1) $NO^{2+}$      (2) $NO^+$
(3) $NO$      (4) $NO^-$

**3.** Consider the hypothetical situation where the azimuthal quantum number, $l$, takes values 0, 1, 2, ...... $n + 1$, where $n$ is the principal quantum number. Then, the element with atomic number : **[2020, Main]**
(1) 13 has a half-filled valence subshell
(2) 9 is the first alkali metal
(3) 8 is the first noble gas
(4) 6 has a $2p$-valence subshell

**4.** The region in the electromagnetic spectrum where the Balmer series lines appear is : **[2020, Main]**
(1) Visible      (2) Microwave
(3) Ultraviolet      (4) Infrared

**5.** The difference between the radii of $3^{rd}$ and $4^{th}$ orbits of $Li^{2+}$ is $\Delta R_1$. The difference between the radii of $3^{rd}$ and $4^{th}$ orbits of $He^+$ is $\Delta R_2$. Ratio $\Delta R_1 : \Delta R_2$ is : **[2020, Main]**
(1) $8 : 3$      (2) $3 : 2$
(3) $3 : 8$      (4) $2 : 3$

**6.** The correct electronic configuration and spinonly magnetic moment (BM) of $Gd^{3+}$ ($Z = 64$), respectively, are : **[2020, Main]**
(1) $[Xe]5f^7$ and 8.9      (2) $[Xe]4f^7$ and 7.9
(3) $[Xe]5f^7$ and 7.9      (4) $[Xe]4f^7$ and 8.9

**7.** The set that contains atomic number of only transition element is : **[2020, Main]**
(1) 21, 32, 53, 64      (2) 21, 25, 42, 72
(3) 9, 17, 34, 38      (4) 37, 42, 50, 64

**8.** The shortest wavelength of H atom is the Lyman series is $\lambda_1$. The longest wavelength in the Balmer series of $He^+$ is : **[2020, Main]**
(1) $\dfrac{5\lambda_1}{9}$      (2) $\dfrac{27\lambda_1}{5}$
(3) $\dfrac{9\lambda_1}{5}$      (4) $\dfrac{36\lambda_1}{5}$

**9.** The correct statement about probability density (except at infinite distance from nucleus) is : **[2020, Main]**
(1) It can be negative for $2p$ orbital.
(2) It can be zero for $3p$ orbital.
(3) It can be zero for $1s$ orbital.
(4) It can never be zero for $2s$ orbital.

**10.** The $1^{st}$, $2^{nd}$ and the $3^{rd}$ ionization enthalpies $I_1$, $I_2$ and $I_3$ of four atoms with atomic numbers $n$, $n + 1$, $n + 2$ and $n + 3$, where $n < 10$ are tabulated below. What is the value of $n$ ?

| Atomic number | Ionization Enthalpy (kJ/mol) | | |
|---|---|---|---|
| | $I_1$ | $I_2$ | $I_3$ |
| $n$ | 1681 | 3374 | 6050 |
| $n + 1$ | 2081 | 3952 | 6122 |
| $n + 2$ | 496 | 4562 | 6910 |
| $n + 3$ | 738 | 1451 | 7733 |

**[2020, Advanced]**

**11.** The number of orbitals associated with quantum numbers $n = 5$, $m_s = +\dfrac{1}{2}$ is : **[2020, Main]**
(1) 11      (2) 25
(3) 15      (4) 50

**12.** For the Balmer series in the spectrum of H atom, $\bar{v} = R_H \left\{ \dfrac{1}{n_1^2} - \dfrac{1}{n_2^2} \right\}$, the correct statements among (I) and (IV) are : **[2020, Main]**
(I) As wavelength decreases, the lines in the series converge
(II) The integer $n_1$ is equal to 2
(III) The lines of longest wavelength corresponds to $n_2 = 3$
(IV) The ionisation energy of hydrogen can be calculated from wave number of these lines
(1) (II), (III), (IV)      (2) (I), (II), (III)
(3) (I), (III), (IV)      (4) (I), (II), (IV)

**13.** The radius of the second Bohr orbit, in terms of the Bohr radius, $a_0$, in $Li^{2+}$ is : **[2020, Main]**
(1) $\dfrac{4a_0}{9}$      (2) $\dfrac{2a_0}{9}$
(3) $\dfrac{2a_0}{3}$      (4) $\dfrac{4a_0}{3}$

14. The size of the iso-electronic species $Cl^-$, Ar and $Ca^{2+}$ is affected by : **[2019, Main]**
    (1) azimuthal quantum number of valence shell
    (2) electron-electron interaction in the outer orbitals
    (3) Principal quantum number of valence shell
    (4) a nuclear charge

15. The quantum number of four electrons are given below :
    I. $n = 4, l = 2, m_l = -2, m_s = -1/2$
    II. $n = 3, l = 2, m_l = 1, m_s = +1/2$
    III. $n = 4, l = 1, m_l = 0, m_s = +1/2$
    IV. $n = 3, l = 1, m_l = 0, m_s = -1/2$
    The correct order of their increasing energies will be : **[2019, Main]**
    (1) IV < III < II < I     (2) I < II < III < IV
    (3) IV < II < III < I     (4) I < III < II < IV

16. If $p$ is the momentum of the fastest electron ejected from a metal surface after the irradiation of light having wavelength l, then for 1.5 p momentum of the photoelectron, the wavelength of the light should be : **[2019, Main]**
    (Assume kinetic energy of ejected photoelectron to be very high in comparison to work function) :
    (1) $\dfrac{3}{4}\lambda$     (2) $\dfrac{1}{2}\lambda$
    (3) $\dfrac{2}{3}\lambda$     (4) $\dfrac{4}{9}\lambda$

17. For any given series of spectral lines of atomic hydrogen, let $\Delta\bar{v} = \bar{v}_{max} - \bar{v}_{min}$ be the difference in maximum and minimum frequencies in $cm^{-1}$. The ratio $\Delta\bar{v}_{Lyman} / \Delta\bar{v}_{Balmer}$ is : **[2019, Main]**
    (1) 4 : 1     (2) 9 : 4
    (3) 5 : 4     (4) 27 : 5

18. Which one of the following about an electron occupying the $1s$ orbital in a hydrogen atom is incorrect ? (The Bohr radius is represented by $a_0$). **[2019, Main]**
    (1) The probability density of finding the electron is maximum at the nucleus.
    (2) The electron density fo finding the distance $2a_0$ from the nucleus.
    (3) The magnitude of the potential energy is double that oif its kinetic energy of an average.
    (4) The total energy of the electron is maximum when it is at a distance $a_0$ from the nucleus.

19. The graph between $|\psi|^2$ and $r$(radial distance) is shown below. This represents : **[2019, Main]**

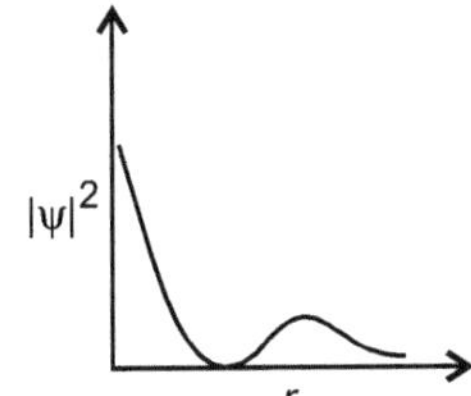

(1) $3s$ orbital     (2) $2s$ orbital
(3) $1s$ orbital     (4) $2p$ orbital

20. The ratio of the shortest wavelength of two spectral series of hydrogen spectrum is found to be about 9. The spectral series are : **[2019, Main]**
    (1) Lyman and Paschen
    (2) Balmer and Brackett
    (3) Brackett and Pfund
    (4) Paschen and Pfund

21. The electrons are more like to be found : **[2019, Main]**

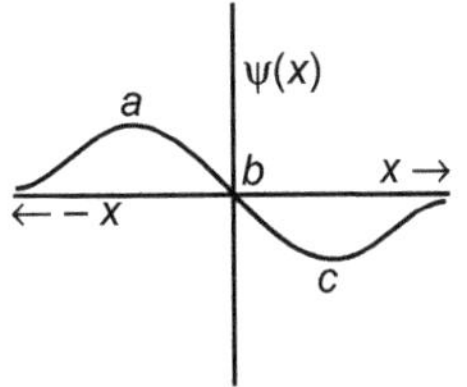

(1) in the region $a$ and $c$
(2) in the region $a$ and $b$
(3) only in the region $a$
(4) only in the region $c$

22. The ground state energy of hydrogen atom is – 13.6 eV. Consider an electronic state $\psi$ of $He^+$ whose energy, azimuthal quantum number and magnetic quantum number are – 3.4 eV, 2 and 0, respectively. Which of the following statement(s) is(are) true for the state $\psi'$ ? **[2019, Main]**
    (1) It is a $4d$ state
    (2) It has 2 angular nodes
    (3) It has 3 radial nodes
    (4) The nuclear charge experienced by the electron in this state is less than $2e$, where $e$ is the magnitude of the electronic charge

**Paragraph for Question 23 and 24**

Consdier the Bohr's model of a one-electron atom where the electron moves around the nucleus. In the following, List-I contains some quantities for the $n^{th}$ orbit of the atom and List-II contains options showing how they depend on $n$.

| List–I | List–II |
|---|---|
| (I) Radius of the $n^{th}$ orbit | (P) $\propto n^{-2}$ |
| (II) Angular momentum of the electron in the $n^{th}$ orbit | (Q) $\propto n^{-1}$ |
| (III) Kinetic energy of the electron in the $n^{th}$ orbit | (R) $\propto n^{0}$ |
| (iv) Potential energy of the electron in the $n^{th}$ orbit | (S) $\propto n^{1}$ |
| | (T) $\propto n^{2}$ |
| | (L) $\propto n^{1/2}$ |

23. Which of the following options has the correct combination considering List-I and List-II ? **[2019, Main]**
    (1) (I), (P)     (2) (I), (T)
    (3) (II), (Q)     (4) (II), (R)

**24.** Which of the following options has the correct combination considering List-I and List-II ? **[2019, Main]**

(1) (III), (P) (2) (III), (S)
(3) (IV), (Q) (4) (IV), (U)

**25.** The de-Broglie's wavelength of electron present in first Bohr orbit of 'H' atom is : **[2018, Main]**

(1) 0.529 Å (2) $2\pi \times 0.529$ Å
(3) $\frac{0.529}{2\pi}$ Å (4) $4 \times 0.529$ Å

**26.** Ejection of the photoelectron from metal in the photoelectric effect experiment can be stopped by applying 0.5 V when the radiation of 250 nm is used. The work function of the metal is : **[2018, Main]**

(1) 4 eV (2) 4.5 eV
(3) 5 eV (4) 5.5 eV

**27.** Which of the following statements is **false** ?

(1) Photon has momentum as well as wavelength.
(2) Splitting of spectral lines in electrical field is called Stark effect.
(3) Rydberg cosntant has unit of energy.
(4) Frequency of emitted radiation from a black body goes from a lower wavelength to higher wavelength as the temperature increases.

**Paragraph for Question 28, 29, and 30**

Answer 4, 5 and 6 by approximately matching the information given in the three columns of the following table :

The wave funnction $\psi_{n,l,m_l}$ is a mathematical function whose value depends upon spherical polar coordinates $(r, \theta, \phi)$ of the electron and characterised by the quantum numbers $n$, $l$ and $m_l$. Here $r$ is distance from nucleus, $\theta$ is colatitude and $\phi$ is azimuth. In the mathematical functions given in the Table, Z is atomic number and $a_o$ is Bohr radius.

| Column 1 | Column 2 | Column 3 |
|---|---|---|
| (I) 1$s$ orbital | (i) $\psi_{n,l,m_l} \propto \left(\frac{Z}{a_o}\right)^{\frac{3}{2}} e^{-\left(\frac{Zr}{a_o}\right)}$ | 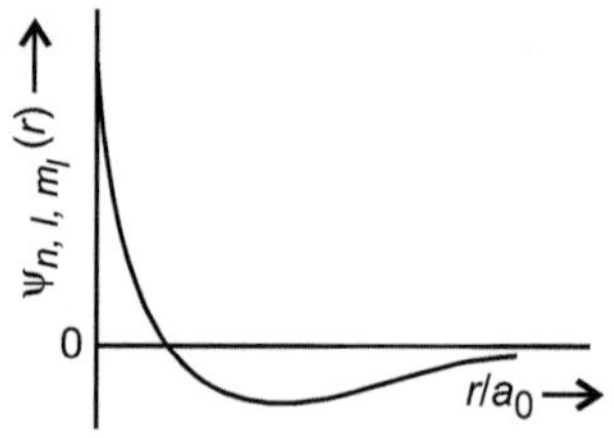 |
| (II) 2$s$ orbital | (ii) One radial node | (Q) Probability density at nucleus $\propto \frac{1}{a_o^3}$ |
| (III) 2$p_z$ orbital | (iii) $\psi_{n,l,m_l} \propto \left(\frac{Z}{a_o}\right)^{\frac{5}{2}} re^{-\left(\frac{Zr}{2a_o}\right)} \cos\theta$ | (R) Probability density is maximum at nucelus |
| (IV) 3$d_z^2$ orbital | (iv) $xy$-plane is a nodal plane | (S) Energy needed to excite electro from $n = 2$ state to $n = 4$ state is $\frac{27}{32}$ times the energy needed to excite electron from $n = 2$ state to $n = 6$ state |

**28.** For the given orbital in Column 1, the only **CORRECT** combination for any hydrogen-like species is : **[2017, Advanced]**

(1) (I) (ii) (S) (2) (IV) (iv) (R)
(3) (II) (ii) (P) (4) (III) (iiii) (P)

**29.** For hydrogen atom, the only **CORRECT** combination is : **[2017, Advanced]**

(1) (I) (i) (S) (2) (II) (i) (Q)
(3) (I) (i) (P) (4) (I) (iv) (R)

**30.** For He⁺ ion, the only **INCORRECT** combination is : **[2017, Advanced]**

(1) (I) (i) (R) (2) (II) (ii) (Q)
(3) (I) (iii) (R) (4) (I) (i) (S)

**31.** The radius of the second Bohr orbit for hydrogen atom is : **[2017, Main]**

(Planck's Const. $h = 6.6262 \times 10^{-34}$ Js;
mass of electron $= 9.1091 \times 10^{-31}$ kg;
charge of electron $e = 1.60210 \times 10^{-19}$ C;
permittivity of vacuum
$e_0 = 8.854185 \times 10^{-12}$ kg$^{-1}$ m$^{-3}$A$^2$)

(1) 0.529 Å (2) 2.12 Å
(3) 1.65 Å (4) 4.76 Å

**32.** If the shortest wavelength in Lyman series of hydrogen atom is A, then the longest wavelength in Paschen series of He⁺ is : **[2017, Main]**

   (1) $\dfrac{5A}{9}$       (2) $\dfrac{9A}{5}$

   (3) $\dfrac{36A}{5}$       (4) $\dfrac{36A}{7}$

**33.** The electron in the hydrogen atom undergoes transition from higher orbitals to orbital of radius 211.6 pm. This transition is associated with :

**[2017, Main]**

   (1) Lyman series       (2) Balmer series

   (3) Paschen series       (4) Brackett series

**34.** P is the probability of finding the 1$s$ electron of hydrogen atom in a spherical shell of infinitesimal thickness, $dr$, at a distance $r$ from the nucleus. The volume of this shell is $4\pi r^2 dr$. The qualitative sketch of the dependence of P on $r$ is :

**[2016, Advanced]**

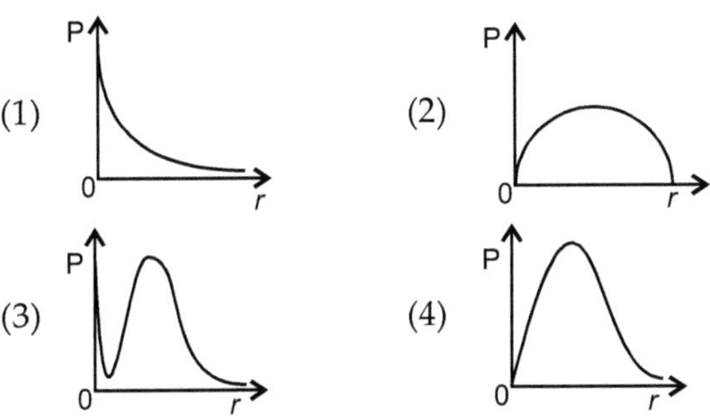

**35.** The total number of orbitals associated with the principal quantum number 5 is :    **[2016, Main]**

   (1) 5       (2) 10

   (3) 20       (4) 25

**36.** A stream of electrons from a heated filament was passed between two charged plates kept at a potential difference V esu. If $e$ and $m$ are charge and mass of an electron, respectively, then the value of $h/\lambda$ (where $\lambda$ is wavelength associated with electron wave) is given by :    **[2016, Main]**

   (1) $meV$       (2) $2meV$

   (3) $\sqrt{meV}$       (4) $\sqrt{2meV}$

**37.** Not considering the electronic spin, the degeneracy of the second excited state ($n = 3$) of H atom is 9, while the degeneracy of the second excited state of H$^-$ is :    **[2015, Advanced]**

**38.** Which of the following is the energy of a possible excited state of hydrogen ?    **[2015, Main]**

   (1) $+13.6$ eV       (2) $-6.8$ eV

   (3) $-3.4$ eV       (4) $+6.8$ eV

**39.** If the principal quantum number $n = 6$, the correct sequence of filling of electrons will be :

**[2015, Main]**

   (1) $ns \rightarrow np \rightarrow (n-1)d \rightarrow (n-2)f$
   (2) $ns \rightarrow (n-2)f \rightarrow (n-1)d \rightarrow np$
   (3) $ns \rightarrow (n-1)d \rightarrow (n-2)f \rightarrow np$
   (4) $ns \rightarrow (n-2)f \rightarrow np \rightarrow (n-1)d$

**40.** The heat of atomisation of methane and ethane are 360 kJ/mol and 620 kJ/mol, respectively. The longest wavelength of light capable of breaking the C-C bond is (Avogadro number = $6.02 \times 10^{23}$, $h = 6.62 \times 10^{-34}$ J s) :    **[2015, Main]**

   (1) $1.49 \times 10^3$ nm       (2) $2.48 \times 10^3$ nm

   (3) $2.48 \times 10^4$ nm       (4) $1.49 \times 10^4$ nm

**41.** At temperature T, the average kinetic energy of any particle is $\dfrac{3}{2}$ kT. The de Broglie wavelength follows the order :    **[2015, Main]**

   (1) Thermal proton > Visible photon > Thermal electron

   (2) Thermal proton > Thermal electron > Visible photon

   (3) Visible photon > Thermal electron > Thermal neutron

   (4) Visible photon > Thermal neutron > Thermal electron

**42.** In an atom, the total number of electrons having quantum numbers $n = 4$, $|m_l| = 1$ and $m_s = -\dfrac{1}{2}$ is :    **[2014, Advanced]**

**43.** The correct set of four quantum numbers for the valence electrons of rubidium atom (Z = 37) is :

**[2014, Main]**

   (1) $5, 0, 0, +\dfrac{1}{2}$       (2) $5, 1, 0, +\dfrac{1}{2}$

   (3) $5, 1, 1, +\dfrac{1}{2}$       (4) $5, 0, 1, +\dfrac{1}{2}$

**44.** The energy of an electron in first Bohr orbit of H-atom is $-13.6$ eV. The energy value of electron in the excited state of Li$^{2+}$ is :    **[2014, Main]**

   (1) $-27.2$ eV       (2) $30.6$ eV

   (3) $-30.6$ eV       (4) $27.2$ eV

**45.** If $\lambda_0$ and $\lambda$ be the threshold wavelength and wavelength of incident light, the velocity of photoelectron ejected from the metal surface is :

**[2014, Main]**

   (1) $\sqrt{\dfrac{2h}{m}(\lambda_0 - \lambda)}$       (2) $\sqrt{\dfrac{2hc}{m}(\lambda_0 - \lambda)}$

   (3) $\sqrt{\dfrac{2hc}{m}\left(\dfrac{\lambda_0 - \lambda}{\lambda\lambda_0}\right)}$       (4) $\sqrt{\dfrac{2h}{m}\left(\dfrac{1}{\lambda_0} - \dfrac{1}{\lambda}\right)}$

**46.** Based on the equation :    **[2014, Main]**

$$\Delta E = -2.0 \times 10^{-18} J \left(\dfrac{1}{n_2^2} - \dfrac{1}{n_1^2}\right)$$

the wavelength of the light that must be absorbed to excite hydrogen electron from level $n = 1$ to level $n = 2$ will be :

($h = 6.625 \times 10^{-34}$ Js, C = $3 \times 10^8$ ms$^{-1}$)

   (1) $1.325 \times 10^{-7}$ m       (2) $1.325 \times 10^{-10}$ m

   (3) $2.650 \times 10^{-7}$ m       (4) $5.300 \times 10^{-10}$ m

**47.** If $m$ and $e$ are the mass and charge of the revolving electron in the orbit of radius $r$ for hydrogen atom, the total energy of the revolving electron will be : **[2014, Main]**

(1) $\dfrac{1}{2}\dfrac{e^2}{r}$

(2) $-\dfrac{e^2}{r}$

(3) $\dfrac{me^2}{r}$

(4) $-\dfrac{1}{2}\dfrac{e^2}{r}$

**48.** The de-Broglie wavelength of a particle of mass 6.63 g moving with a velocity of 100 ms$^{-1}$ is : **[2014, Main]**

(1) $10^{-33}$ m

(2) $10^{-35}$ m

(3) $10^{-31}$ m

(4) $10^{-25}$ m

**49.** Excited hydrogen atom emits light in the ultraviolet region at $2.47 \times 10^{15}$ Hz. With this frequency, the energy of a single photon is : ($h = 6.63 \times 10^{-34}$ Js) **[2014, Main]**

(1) $8.041 \times 10^{-40}$ J

(2) $2.680 \times 10^{-19}$ J

(3) $1.640 \times 10^{-18}$ J

(4) $6.111 \times 10^{-17}$ J

**50.** Ionisation energy of gaseous Na atoms is 495.5 kJmol$^{-1}$. The lowest possible frequency of light that ionizes a sodium atom is ($h = 6.626 \times 10^{-34}$ Js, $N_A = 6.022 \times 10^{23}$ mol$^{-1}$) **[2014, Main]**

(1) $7.50 \times 10^4$ s$^{-1}$

(2) $4.76 \times 10^{14}$ s$^{-1}$

(3) $3.15 \times 10^{15}$ s$^{-1}$

(4) $1.24 \times 10^{15}$ s$^{-1}$

**51.** The atomic masses of He and Ne are 4 and 20 a.m.u., respectvely. The value of the de Broglie wavelength of He gas at $-73\,°C$ is "M" times that of the de Broglie wavelength of Ne at 727 °C. M is : **[2013, Advanced]**

**52.** The kinetic energy of an electron in the second Bohr orbit of a hydrogen atom is [$a_0$ is Bohr radius] **[2012, Advanced]**

(1) $\dfrac{h^2}{4\pi^2 ma_0^2}$

(2) $\dfrac{h^2}{16\pi^2 ma_0^2}$

(3) $\dfrac{h^2}{32\pi^2 ma_0^2}$

(4) $\dfrac{h^2}{64\pi^2 ma_0^2}$

**53.** The maximum number of electrons that can have principal quantum number, $n = 3$ and spin quantum number, $m_s = -\dfrac{1}{2}$, is : **[2011, Advanced]**

**54.** The work function ($\phi$) of some metals is listed below. The number of metals which will show photoelectric effect when light of 300 nm wavelength falls on the metal is : **[2011, Advanced]**

| Metal | Li | Na | K | Mg | Cu | Ag | Fe | Pt | W |
|---|---|---|---|---|---|---|---|---|---|
| $\phi$(eV) | 2.4 | 2.3 | 2.2 | 3.7 | 4.8 | 4.3 | 4.7 | 6.3 | 4.75 |

### Paragraph for Questions 55 to 57

The hydrogen-like species Li$^{2+}$ is in a spherically symmetric state $S_1$ with one radial node. Upon absorbing light the ion undergoes transition to a state $S_2$. The state $S_2$ has one radial node and its energy si equal tothe ground state energy of the hydrogen atom.

**55.** The state $S_1$ is : **[2010, Advanced]**

(1) $1s$

(2) $2s$

(3) $2p$

(4) $3s$

**56.** Energy of the state $S_1$ in units of the hydrogen atom ground state energy is : **[2010, Advanced]**

(1) 0.75

(2) 1.50

(3) 2.25

(4) 4.50

**57.** The orbital angular momentum quantum number of the state $S_2$ is : **[2010, Advanced]**

(1) 0

(2) 1

(3) 2

(4) 3

**58.** **Statement-1 :** The plot of atomic number ($y$-axis) versus number of neutrons ($x$-axis) for stable nuclei shows a curvature towards $x$-axis from the line of 45° slope as the atomic number is increased.

and

**Statement-2 :** Proton-proton electrostatic repulsions begin to overcome attractive forces involving protons and neutrons in heavier nuclides. **[2008, Advanced]**

(1) **Statement-1** is True, **Statement-2** is True; **Statement-2** is a correct explanation for **Statement-1**

(2) **Statement-1** is True, **Statement-2** is True; **Statement-2** is not a correct explanation for **Statement-1**

(3) **Statement-1** is True, **Statement-2** is False

(4) **Statement-1** is False, **Statement-2** is True

**59.** Match the entries in **Column I** with the correctly related quantum numbers in **Column II**. Indicate your answer by darkening the appropriate bubbles of the $4 \times 4$ matrix given in the ORS.

**[2008, Advanced]**

| Column I | | Column II |
|---|---|---|
| (A) | Orbital angular momentum of the electron in a hydrogen-like atomic orbital | (p) Principal quantum number |
| (B) | A hydrogen-like one-electron wave function obeying Pauli principle | (q) Azimuthal quantum number |
| (C) | Shape, size and orientation of hydrogen-like atomic orbitals | (r) Magnetic quantum number |
| (D) | Probability density of electron at the nucleus in hydrogen-like atom | (s) Electron spin quantum number |

**60.** According to Bohr's theory,

$E_n$ = Total energy

$K_n$ = Kinetic energy

$V_n$ = Potential enegy

$r_n$ = Radius of $n^{th}$ orbit

Match the following : **[2006, Main]**

| Column I | Column II |
|---|---|
| (A) $V_n/K_n = ?$ | (P)   0 |
| (B) If radius of $n^{th}$ orbit $\propto$ $E_n^x$, $x = ?$ | (Q)   $-1$ |
| (C) Angular momentum in lowest orbital | (R)   $-2$ |
| (D) $\dfrac{1}{r^n} \propto Z^y$, $y = ?$ | (S)   $1$ |

**61.** (a) Calculate velocity of electron in first Bohr orbit of hydrogen atom (Given $r = a_0$).

**[2005, Main]**

(b) Find de-Broglie wavelength of the electron in first Bohr orbit.

(c) Find the orbital angular momentum of $2p$ orbital in terms of $h/2\pi$ units.

**62.** The number of radial nodes in $3s$ and $2p$ respectively are : **[2005, Screening]**

(1) 2 and 0  (2) 1 and 2

(3) 0 and 2  (4) 2 and 1

**63.** (a) The Schrodinger wave equation for hydrogen atom is : **[2004, Screening]**

$$\psi_{2s} = \frac{1}{4(2\pi)^{1/2}}\left(\frac{1}{a_0}\right)^{3/2}\left(2 - \frac{r}{a_0}\right)e^{-r/u}$$

Where $a_0$ is Bohr's radius. Let the radius node in $2s$ be at $r_0$. Then find $r$ in terms of $a_0$.

(b) A base ball having mass 100 g moves with velocity 100 m/sec. Find out the value of wave length of base ball.

(c) $_{92}X^{234} \xrightarrow[-6\beta]{-7\alpha} Y$. Find out atomic number, mass number of Y and identify it.

**64.** Which Hydrogen like species will have same radius as that of Bohr orbit of Hydrogen atom ? **[2004, Screening]**

(1) $n = 2$, $Li^{+2}$  (2) $n = 2$, $Be^{3+}$

(3) $n = 2$, $He^+$  (4) $n = 3$, $Li^{2+}$

**65.** Wavelength of high energy transition of H-atoms is 91.2 nm. Calculate the corresponding wavelength of He atoms. **[2003, Main]**

**66.** Rutherford's experiment, which established the nuclear model of the atom, used a beam of : **[2002, Screening]**

(1) β-particles, which impinged on a metal foil and got absorbed

(2) γ-rays, which impinged on a metal foil and ejected electrons

(3) helium atoms, which impinged on a metal foil and got scattered

(4) helium nuclei, which impinged on a metal foil and got scattered

**67.** If the Nitrogen atom had electronic configuration $1s^7$, it would have energy lower than that of the normal ground state configuration $1s^2 2s^2 2p^3$, because the electrons would be closer to the nucleus. Yet $1s^7$ is not observed because it violates. **[2002, Screening]**

(1) Heisenberg uncertainty principle

(2) Hund's rule

(3) Pauli exclusion Principle

(4) Bohr postulate of stationary orbits

## ANSWER KEY

| | | | | | | | | | |
|---|---|---|---|---|---|---|---|---|---|
| **1.** (4) | **2.** (4) | **3.** (1) | **4.** (1) | **5.** (4) | **6.** (2) | **7.** (2) | **8.** (3) | **9.** (2) | **10.** (*) |
| **11.** (2) | **12.** (2) | **13.** (4) | **14.** (4) | **15.** (3) | **16.** (4) | **17.** (2) | **18.** (2) | **19.** (2) | **20.** (1) |
| **21.** (1) | **22.** (1, 2) | **23.** (2) | **24.** (1) | **25.** (2) | **26.** (2) | **27.** (1) | **28.** (3) | **29.** (1) | **30.** (3) |
| **31.** (2) | **32.** (4) | **33.** (2) | **34.** (4) | **35.** (4) | **36.** (4) | **37.** (3) | **38.** (3) | **39.** (2) | **40.** (1) |
| **41.** (3) | **42.** (*) | **43.** (1) | **44.** (3) | **45.** (3) | **46.** (1) | **47.** (4) | **48.** (1) | **49.** (3) | **50.** (4) |
| **51.** (*) | **52.** (3) | **53.** (*) | **54.** (4) | **55.** (2) | **56.** (3) | **57.** (2) | **58.** (1) | **59.** (*) | **60.** (*) |
| **61.** (4) | **62.** (1) | **63.** (*) | **64.** (2) | **65.** (*) | **66.** (4) | **67.** (3) | | | |

## ANSWERS WITH EXPLANATIONS

**1. (4)** For $n = 4$

$l = 0, 1, 2, 3$

$\therefore$ $4d$ and $4f$ subshell associated with $n = 4$, $m = -2$

**2. (4)** Bond order of $NO^{2+}$ = 2.5

Bond order of $NO^+$ = 3

Bond order of NO = 2.5

Bond order of $NO^-$ = 2

As bond order is inversely proportional to bond strength, therefore, the species with minimum bond order is $NO^-$.

**3. (1)** $l = 0$ to $(n + 1)$

$n = 1$  $\qquad n = 2$

$l = 0, 1, 2$  $\qquad l = 0, 1, 2, 3$

$(n + l) \Rightarrow \frac{1s}{1}\frac{1p}{2}\frac{1d}{3}$ $\frac{2s}{2}\frac{2p}{3}\frac{2d}{4}\frac{2f}{5}$

$n = 3$

$l = 0, 1, 2, 3, 4$

$\frac{3s}{3}\frac{3p}{4}\frac{3d}{5}\frac{3f}{6}\frac{3g}{7}$

Now, in order to write electronic configuration, we need to apply $(n + l)$ rule

Energy order : $1s < 1p < 2s < 1d < 2p < 3s < 2d$..

Option 1) 13 : $1s^2 1p^6 2s^2 1d^3$ is not half filled

Option 2) 9 : $1s^2 1p^6 2s^1$ is the first alkali metal because after losing one electron, it will achieve first noble gas configuration

Option 3) 8: $1s^2 1p^6$ is the first noble gas because after $1p^6$ $e^-$ will enter 2s hence new period

Option 4) 6 : $1s^2 1p^4$ has 1p valence subshell.

**4. (1)** Balmer series give visible lines for H-atom.

**5. (4)**

$$\frac{\Delta R_1}{\Delta R_2} = \frac{(r_4 - r_3)_{4^{2+}}}{(r_4 - r_3)_{He^+}}$$

$$= \frac{\frac{4^2}{3} - \frac{3^2}{3}}{\frac{4^2}{2} - \frac{3^2}{2}}$$

$$= \frac{7/3}{7/2} = \frac{2}{3} \text{ or } 2:3$$

**6. (2)** Electronic configuration of $Gd^{3+}$ is

${}_{64}Gd^{3+} = [Xe]4f^7$

[Xe] ↿ ↿ ↿ ↿ ↿ ↿ ↿

$Gd^{3+}$ having 7 unpaired electrons.

$$\text{Magnetic moment } (\mu) = \sqrt{n(n+2)} \text{ B.M.}$$

$$\mu = \sqrt{7(7+2)} \text{ B.M.}$$

$$= 7.9 \text{ B.M.}$$

$n \Rightarrow$ Number of unpaired electrons.

**7. (2)** 21, 25, 42, 72

**8. (3)** As we know $\Delta E = \frac{hc}{\lambda}$

So, $\lambda = \frac{hc}{\Delta E}$ for $\lambda$ minimum i.e.,

shortest : $\Delta E$ = maximum

For Lyman series $n = 1$ and for $\Delta E_{max}$

Transition must be form $n = \infty$ to $n = 1$

So, $\frac{1}{\lambda} = R_H Z^2 \left(\frac{1}{n_1^2} - \frac{1}{n_2^2}\right)$

$$\frac{1}{\lambda} = R_H Z^2 (1 - 0)$$

$$\frac{1}{\lambda} = R \times (1)^2$$

$$\Rightarrow \quad \lambda_1 = \frac{1}{R}$$

For longest wavelength $\Delta E$ = minimum for Balmer series $n = 3$ to $n = 2$ will have $\Delta E$ minimum

for $He^+$ $Z = 2$

So, $\frac{1}{\lambda_2} = R_H \times Z^2 \left(\frac{1}{n_1^2} - \frac{1}{n_2^2}\right)$

$$\frac{1}{\lambda_2} = R_H \times 4\left(\frac{1}{4} - \frac{1}{9}\right)$$

$$\frac{1}{\lambda_2} = R_H \times \frac{5}{9}$$

$$\lambda_2 = \lambda_1 \times \frac{9}{5}$$

**9. (2)** $[R(r)]^2$

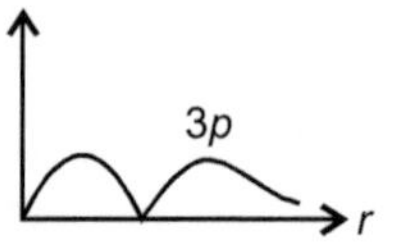


**10.** By observing the values of $I_1$, $I_2$ and $I_3$ for atomic number $(n + 2)$, it is observed that $I_2 >> I_1$.

This indicates that number of valence shell electrons is 1 and atomic number $(n + 2)$ should be an alkali metal.

Also for atomic number $(n + 3)$, $I_3 >> I_2$.

This indicates that it will be an alkaline earth metal which suggests that atomic number $(n + 1)$ should be a noble gas and atomic number $(n)$ should belong to halogen family. Since $n < 10$; hence $n = 9$ (F atom)

**Note :** $n = 1$ (H atom) cannot be the answer because it does not have $I_2$ and $I_3$ values.

**11. (2)** No. of orbitals $= n^2 = 5^2 = 25$

For $n = 5$, no. of orbitals $= n^2 = 25$

Total number of orbitals is equal to no. of electrons having $m_s = \frac{1}{2}$

**12. (2)** For balmer : $n_1 = 2$, $n_2 = 3, 4, 5, \ldots\ldots \infty$

$$\bar{v} = \frac{1}{\lambda} = R_H\left[\frac{1}{2^2} - \frac{1}{n_2^2}\right]$$

$$\frac{1}{\lambda_{longest}} = R_H\left[\frac{1}{2^2} - \frac{1}{3^2}\right]$$

**13. (4)**

$$r_n = \frac{n^2 \times a_0}{z}$$

For 2nd Bohr orbit of $Li^{+2}$

$n = 2$

$z = 3$

$$\Rightarrow \quad r_n = \frac{2^2 \times a_0}{3} = \frac{4a_0}{3}$$

**14. (4)** The species in which the number of electrons is the same is known as isoelectronic species. The size of an ion depends on the force of attraction between the outermost valence shell and the nucleus. Therefore, the size of isoeletronic species depends on the nuclear charge.

**15. (3)** The values of $(n + l)$ for the four elements as shown below :

I : $(n + l) = 4 + 2 = 6$

II : $(n + l) = 3 + 2 = 5$

III : $(n + l) = 4 + 1 = 5$

IV : $(n + l) = 3 + 1 = 4$

Ax the value of $(n + l)$ increases, the energy of an electron also increases. If the value of $(n + l)$ is the same for two electrons, then the electron with the higher value of $n$ will have more energy. Therefore, the correct order of increasing energy is IV < II < III < I.

**16. (4)** The kinetic energy of ejected electron is calculated as shown below :

$$h\upsilon - \phi = \text{K.E.}$$

$$\left(\frac{hc}{\lambda}\right)_{\text{incident}} = \text{K.E.} + \phi$$

$$\left(\frac{hc}{\lambda}\right)_{\text{incident}} = \text{K.E.}$$

The kinetic energy is related to the momentum $(p)$ as shown below :

$$\text{K.E.} = \frac{p^2}{2m} = \left(\frac{hc}{\lambda}\right)_{\text{incident}} = \frac{hc}{\lambda} \quad \text{...(1)}$$

The kinetic energy is related to the momentum $(1.5p)$ as shown below :

$$\text{K.E.} = \frac{(1.5\,p)^2}{2m} = \frac{hc}{\lambda'} \quad \text{...(2)}$$

Divide equation (1) by equation (2),

$$\frac{p^2}{2m} \times \frac{2m}{2.25p^2} = \frac{hc}{\lambda} \times \frac{\lambda'}{hc}$$

$$\lambda' = \frac{1}{2.25}\lambda$$

$$\lambda' = \frac{4}{9}\lambda$$

**17. (2)** The Rydberg equation for the hydrogen atom is represented as shown below :

$$\overline{\upsilon} = R_H\left(\frac{1}{n_f^2} - \frac{1}{n_i^2}\right)$$

The final level for Lyman series is 1.
The final level for Balmer series is 2.

The value of $\overline{\upsilon}_{\max}$ for Lyman series is calculated as shown below :

$$\overline{\upsilon} = R_H\left(\frac{1}{1^2} - \frac{1}{(\infty)^2}\right)$$

$$= R_H$$

The value of $\overline{\upsilon}_{\min}$ for Lyman series is calculated as shown below :

$$\overline{\upsilon} = R_H\left(\frac{1}{1^2} - \frac{1}{(2)^2}\right)$$

$$= \frac{3}{4}R_H$$

The value of $\Delta\overline{\upsilon}$ for Lyman series is calculated as shown below :

$$\Delta\overline{\upsilon} = \overline{\upsilon}_{\max} - \overline{\upsilon}_{\min}$$

$$= R_H - \frac{3}{4}R_H$$

$$= \frac{1}{4}R_H$$

The value of $\overline{\upsilon}_{\max}$ for Balmer series is calculated as shown below :

$$\overline{\upsilon} = R_H\left(\frac{1}{2^2} - \frac{1}{(\infty)^2}\right)$$

$$= \frac{R_H}{4}$$

The value of $\overline{\upsilon}_{\min}$ for Balmer series is calculated as shown below :

$$\overline{\upsilon} = R_H\left(\frac{1}{(2)^2} - \frac{1}{(3)^2}\right)$$

$$= \frac{5}{36}R_H$$

The value of $\Delta\overline{\upsilon}$ for Balmer series is calculated as shown below :

$$\Delta\overline{\upsilon} = \overline{\upsilon}_{\max} - \overline{\upsilon}_{\min}$$

$$= \frac{R_H}{4} - \frac{5}{36}R_H$$

$$= \frac{4}{36}R_H$$

$$= \frac{1}{9}R_H$$

The ratio $\Delta\overline{\upsilon}_{\text{Lyman}} / \Delta\overline{\upsilon}_{\text{Balmer}}$ is calculated as shown below :

$$\frac{\Delta\overline{\upsilon}_{\text{Lyman}}}{\Delta\overline{\upsilon}_{\text{Balmer}}} = \frac{\frac{1}{4}R_H}{\frac{1}{9}R_H}$$

$$= \frac{9}{4}$$

**18. (2)** The wavefunction ($\psi$) contains all the information about the state of electron in atom. The square of the probability function, $|\psi|^2$, relates to the probability density. The radial probability graph is shown below :

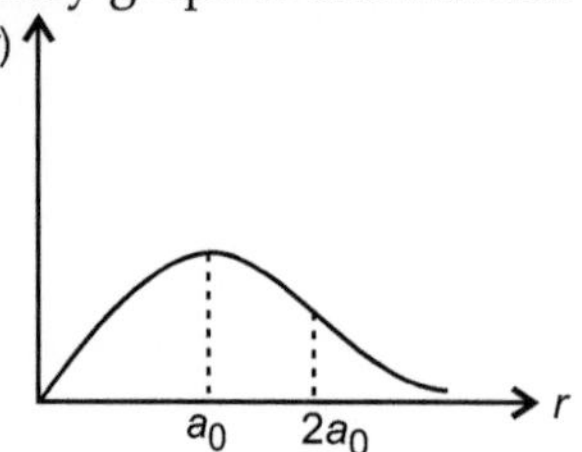


Therefore, the electron can be found at a distance $2a_0$ from the nucleus.

**19. (2)** In the graph, one radial node is present. At $r = 0$, $|\psi|^2$ has some value. Therefore, the graph represents an $s$ orbital. The value of $n$ can be calculated as shown below :

$$n - l - 1 = 1$$
$$n - 0 - 1 = 1$$
$$n = 2$$

Therefore, the graph represents a $2s$ orbital.

**20. (1)** The ratio of wavelength of two spectral series can be calculated as shown below :

$$\frac{\dfrac{1}{\lambda_2} = R_H\left(\dfrac{1}{n_1^2} - \dfrac{1}{n_2^2}\right)Z^2}{\dfrac{1}{\lambda_1} = R_H\left(\dfrac{1}{m_1^2} - \dfrac{1}{m_2^2}\right)Z^2}$$

The shortest wavelenghts the value of $m_2$ and $n_2$ are equal to infinity.

$$\frac{\lambda_1}{\lambda_2} = \frac{9}{1} = \frac{m_1^2}{n_1^2} = \frac{3^2}{1^2}$$

Therefore, $m_1 = 3$ and $n_1 = 1$, that is, the spectral series are Lyman and Paschen.

**21. (1)** The wavefunction ($y$) contains all the information about the size of electron in atom. The square of the probability function, $|\psi|^2$, relates to the probability density. The maximum of $\psi$ and $|\psi|^2$ will be present on the same region. Therefore, the electrons are most likely to found in region $a$ and $c$.

**22. (1,2)** The energy of a energy level of atom is calcualted by the formula as shown below :

$$E_n = -\frac{(13.6)Z^2}{n^2}$$

$$3.4 = \frac{(13.6)(2)^2}{n^2}$$

Rearrange the above expression for the value of $n$.

$$n = \left(\frac{13.6 \times 4}{3.4}\right)^{1/2}$$

$$n = 4$$

This state has $4d$ orbital.

The number of angular nodes will be $l = 2$.

The number of radial nodes will be $(n - l - 1) = 1$.

**23. (2)** The corrects matches are shown below in the table :

| (I) Radius of the $n^{th}$ orbit | $r = \dfrac{0.529 n^2}{Z}$ | (T) $r \propto n^2$ |
|---|---|---|
| (II) Angular momentum of the electron in the $n^{th}$ orbit | $L = \dfrac{nh}{2\pi}$ | (S) $L \propto n^1$ |
| (III) Kinetic energy of the electron in the $n^{th}$ orbit | $KE = \dfrac{13.6 Z^2}{n^2}$ | (P) $KE \propto \dfrac{1}{n^2}$ $\propto n^{-2}$ |
| (IV) Potential energy of the electron in the $n^{th}$ orbit | $PE = -2 \times \dfrac{13.6 Z^2}{n^2}$ | (P) $PE \propto \dfrac{1}{n^2}$ $\propto n^{-2}$ |

Therefore, the correct combination is (I)(T).

**24. (2)** The corrects matches are shown below in the table :

| (I) Radius of the $n^{th}$ orbit | $r = \dfrac{0.529 n^2}{Z}$ | (T) $r \propto n^2$ |
|---|---|---|
| (II) Angular momentum of the electron in the $n^{th}$ orbit | $L = \dfrac{nh}{2\pi}$ | (S) $L \propto n^1$ |
| (III) Kinetic energy of the electron in the $n^{th}$ orbit | $KE = \dfrac{13.6 Z^2}{n^2}$ | (P) $KE \propto \dfrac{1}{n^2}$ $\propto n^{-2}$ |
| (IV) Potential energy of the electron in the $n^{th}$ orbit | $PE = -2 \times \dfrac{13.6 Z^2}{n^2}$ | (P) $PE \propto \dfrac{1}{n^2}$ $\propto n^{-2}$ |

Therefore, the correct combination is (III)(P).

**25. (2)** First Bohr's orbit of hydrogen atom has radius $r = 0.529$ Å and angular momentum is also quantized.

$$mvr = \frac{h}{2\pi}$$

$$2\pi r = \frac{h}{mv} = \lambda \qquad ...(1)$$

So,
$$\lambda = 2\pi r$$
$$= 2\pi \times 0.529 \text{ Å}$$

So, de-Broglie's wavelength of electron present in first Bohr's orbit of hydrogen atom is $2\pi \times 0.529$ Å.

**26. (2)** The given wavelength is 250 nm. The value of wavelength in Å is 2500 Å.

The formula to calculate energy is,

$$E = \frac{hC}{\lambda}$$

$$= \frac{(6.6 \times 10^{-34}) \times (3 \times 10^8)}{2500}$$

$$= 4.96 \text{ eV}$$

The value of stopping potential is equal to kinetic energy.

The relation between energy and kinetic energy is,

$$E = W_o + K.E.$$
$$4.96 = W_o = 0.5$$
$$W_o = 4.5 \text{ eV}$$

Thus, the value of work function is 4.5 eV.

**27. (1)** The option (3) is wrong because the unit of Rydberg is *m*.

**28. (3)** For the given orbital in column I, the only correct combination for any hydrogen like species is C,

For 2s orbital, wave equation is given as,

$$2s\psi_{2,0,0} = \frac{1}{4\sqrt{2\pi}} \left( \frac{Z}{a_0} \right)^{3/2} \left( 2 - \frac{Z_r}{a_0} \right) e^{\frac{-Zr}{2a_0}}$$

The radial node is calculated as,

$$\text{Radial node} = n - 1 - 0$$
$$= 2 - 1 - 0$$
$$= 1$$

Figure P has only one node.

**29. (1)** For hydrogen atom, the wave equation is given as

$$\psi_{n,l,m_l} \propto \left( \frac{Z}{a_0} \right)^{3/2} e^{-\left( \frac{Zr}{2a_0} \right)}$$

It has only s orbital. Therefore, its principal quantum number is one and azimuthal quantum number is zero. The number of radial node is calculated by the formula,

$$\text{Radial node} = n - 1 - 1$$
$$= 1 - 0 - 1$$
$$= 0$$

It also has the following relation according to the column 3 (S),

$$E_4 - E_2 = \frac{3}{16}$$

$$E_6 - E_2 = \frac{2}{9}$$

From the above equations, the new relation is generated as,

$$(E_6 - E_2) \times \frac{27}{32} = (E_4 - E_2)$$

**30. (3)** Helium in unipositive ionic form behaves hydrogen like species. Therefore, the entire wave like properties of this ion will be similar to hydrogen. In hydrogen only 1s orbital is involved and it is non-directional in nature. Therefore, $\psi$ will not depend upon cos $\theta$.

**31. (2)** The radius of Bohr orbit of hydrogen atom is expressed by the formula,

$$r = \frac{n^2 h^2 \varepsilon_0}{\pi m_e e^2}$$

Therefore,

$$r = \frac{(2)^2 \times (6.6262 \times 10^{-34})^2 \times 8.854185 \times 10^{-12}}{3.14 \times 9.1091 \times 10^{-31} \times (1.60210 \times 10^{-19})^2}$$

$$= 2.12 \text{ Å}$$

**32. (4)** In Lyman series, for shortest wavelength, $n_1 = 1$, $n_2 = \infty$.

$$\frac{1}{\lambda} = Rz^2 \left( \frac{1}{n_1^2} - \frac{1}{n_2^2} \right)$$

$$\frac{1}{A} = 1^2 R \left( \frac{1}{1} - \frac{1}{\infty} \right)$$

$$= R$$

For the longest wavelength, $n_1 = 3$, $n_2 = 4$.

$$\frac{1}{\lambda} = Rz^2 \left( \frac{1}{3^2} - \frac{1}{4^2} \right)$$

$$\frac{1}{\lambda} = \frac{R7}{36}$$

If $R = \frac{1}{A}$, then,

$$\frac{1}{\lambda} = \frac{\frac{1}{A} \times 7}{36}$$

$$\lambda = \frac{36A}{7}$$

**33. (2)** The conversion of units of radius into Å is shown below :

$$211.6 \text{ pm} = 2.11 \text{ Å}$$

The value of $n^2$ is calculated by the formula,

$$n^2 = \frac{R \times Z}{0.529}$$

$$= \frac{2.11 \times 1}{0.529}$$

$$= 3.99 \ 4$$

$$n = 2$$

The above formula of $n$ corresponds to Balmer series.

**34. (4)** For 1s electron in hydrogen atom, the plot of radial probability function $(4\pi r^2 R^2)$ V/s r is shown below :

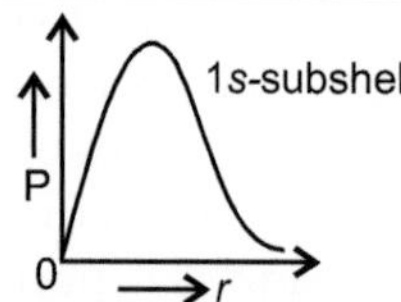



**35. (4)** The total number of orbitals associated with principal quantum number $n = 5$ is,

$$n^2 = (5)^2$$
$$= 25$$

**36. (4)** The value of kinetic energy = eV

The wavelength of electron $\lambda = \dfrac{h}{\sqrt{2m\ KE}}$

$$\lambda = \dfrac{h}{\sqrt{2m\ eV}}$$

$$\dfrac{h}{\lambda} = \sqrt{2m\ eV}$$

**37. (3)** Multi-electron species follows $(n + l)$ rule, whereas single electron species do not.

The ground state of $H^-$ is $1s^2 2s^0 2p^0$.

The second excited state of $H^-$ is $2p$.

Thus, the degenercy of $H^-$ is 3.

**38. (3)** For excited state,

$$E_{\text{excited state}} < 0$$
$$n > 1$$

For hydrogen, the excited state is equal to two $(n = 2)$.

The energy of excited state of hydrogen is calculated by the formula,

$$n = \sqrt{\dfrac{-13.6}{E_{\text{excited state}}}}$$

Substitute the value of $n$ in above equation.

$$2 = \sqrt{\dfrac{-13.6}{E_{\text{excited state}}}}$$

$$4 = \dfrac{-13.6}{E_{\text{excited state}}}$$

$$E_{\text{excited state}} = -3.4$$

**39. (2)** The filling of electron in the atomic orbital takes place according to Aufbau principle. The principal quantum number is $n = 6$, hence the filling of electron will take place in the order $6s\ 4f\ 5d\ 6p$. Hence, the correct sequence is $ns \rightarrow (n-2)f \rightarrow (n-1)d \rightarrow np$.

**40. (1)** The energy required to break four $C - H$ bond in methane is 360 kJ/mol.

The energy required to break one $C - H$ bond is,

$$E_{C-H} = \dfrac{360}{4}\ \text{kJ/mol}$$

$$= 90\ \text{kJ/mol}$$

The energy required to break six $C - H$ bond in methane is 540 kJ/mol.

The energy required to break $C - C$ bond in ethane is,

$$E_{C-C} = 620\ \text{kJ/mol} - 540\ \text{kJ/mol}$$
$$= 80\ \text{kJ/mol}$$

The wavelength is calculated by,

$$\lambda = \dfrac{N_A \times hc}{E_{C-C}}$$

The wavelength of light is,

$$\lambda = \dfrac{6.02 \times 10^{23} \times 6.62 \times 10^{-34} \times 3 \times 10^8}{80 \times 1000\ \text{J}}$$

$$= \dfrac{119.56 \times 10^{-6}}{80}$$

$$= 1.49 \times 10^3\ \text{nm}$$

**41. (3)** De Broglie wavelength is calculated by the formula,

$$\lambda \propto \dfrac{1}{\sqrt{m}}$$

Thus, the order of De Broglie wavelength is Visible photon < Thermal electron > Thermal neutron

**42.** The principal quantum number is 4. Therefore,

$$l = n - 1$$
$$l = 4 - 1$$
$$l = 3$$
$$l = 0, 1, 2\ \text{and}\ 3$$

Magnetic quantum number $|m_l| = 1$, only in $p$, $d$ and $f$-orbitals

Spin quantum number is $m_s = -\dfrac{1}{2}$. Therefore,

total numbers of electrons are calculated as,

$$4p = 2e^-$$
$$4d = 2e^-$$
$$4f = 2e^-$$

**43. (1)** The electronic cofiguration of rubidium atom is $[Kr]5s^1$. Therefore, the values of four quantum numbers for valence electrons of rubidium atom are :

$$n = 5, l = 0, m = 0, s = +\dfrac{1}{2}.$$

**44. (3)** In the excited state of $Li^+$, the energy of $e^-$ is calculated as follows.

$$E = -13.6 \times \dfrac{Z^2}{n^2}$$

$$= -13.6 \times \dfrac{3^2}{2^2}\ \text{eV}$$

$$= -13.6 \times \dfrac{9}{4}\ \text{eV}$$

$$= -30.6\ \text{eV}$$

Thus, the energy of the electron is $-30.6$ eV.

**45. (3)** The velocity of photoelectron ejected from the metal surface is calculated by using Einstein's theory of photoelectric effect. The formula to calculate velocity of photoelectron is,

$$E = W + \frac{1}{2}mv^2$$

$$\frac{hc}{\lambda} = \frac{hc}{\lambda_o} + \frac{1}{2}mv^2$$

$$v^2 = \frac{2hc}{m}\left[\frac{1}{\lambda} - \frac{1}{\lambda_o}\right]$$

$$v = \sqrt{\frac{2hc}{m}\left(\frac{\lambda_o - \lambda}{\lambda\lambda_o}\right)}$$

**46. (1)** The wavelength of the light is calculated by the formula,

$$\Delta E = -2\times 10^{-18}\,J\left[\frac{1}{n_2^2} - \frac{1}{n_1^2}\right]$$

$$\frac{1}{\lambda} = \frac{2\times 10^{-18}}{hc}\left[\frac{1}{(1)^2} - \frac{1}{(2)^2}\right]$$

$$= \frac{2\times 10^{-18}\times 3}{6.625\times 10^{-34}\times 3\times 10^8 \times 4}$$

$$\lambda = 13.25 \times 10^{-8}$$
$$= 1.325 \times 10^{-7}\,m$$

**47. (4)** The total energy of a revolving electron in the hydrogen atom is calculated by adding the potential energy and kinetic energy of the electron.

$$TE = PE + KE$$

$$= \frac{Ze^2}{r} + \frac{Ze^2}{2r}$$

$$= -\frac{Ze^2}{2r}$$

The value of Z for hydrogen atom is 1.

$$E = -\frac{(1)e^2}{2r}$$

$$= -\frac{e^2}{2r}$$

**48. (1)** The momentum of the particle is calculated by the formula,

$$p = m.v$$
$$= 6.63 \times 10^{-3}\,kg \times 100\,m/s$$
$$= 0.663\,kg.m/s$$

The de Broglie wavelength of the given particle is calculated by the formula,

$$p = \frac{h}{\lambda}$$

$$\lambda = \frac{6.626\times 10^{-34}\,J.s}{0.663\,kg.m/s}$$

$$= 10.00 \times 10^{-34}\,m\ (= 10^{-33}\,m)$$

**49. (3)** The energy of a photon is calculated by the formula,

$$E = h\nu$$
$$= 6.63 \times 10^{-34}\,J\,s \times 2.47 \times 10^{15}\,Hz$$
$$= 1.640 \times 10^{-18}\,J$$

**50. (4)** The lowest frequency of light by which ionisation of sodium atom takes place is calculated by the formula,

$$v = \frac{\Delta E}{h} \times \frac{1}{N_A}$$

Substitute the given values in above equation.

$$v = \frac{495.5\times 10^3}{5.626\times 10^{-34}} \times \frac{1}{6.023\times 10^{23}}$$

$$= 1.24\times 10^{15}\,s^{-1}$$

**51.** The ratio of wavelength of He and Ne is shown below :

$$\frac{\lambda_{He}}{\lambda_{Ne}} = \frac{m_{He}V_{He}}{m_{Ne}V_{Ne}}$$

The value of M is calculated as shown below :

$$M = \frac{20}{4} \times \frac{\sqrt{1000/20}}{\sqrt{200/4}}$$

$$= 5\times\sqrt{\frac{50}{50}}$$

$$= 5$$

**52. (3)** The radius of second orbit $= \dfrac{a_0 \times n^2}{Z}$

$$= \frac{a_0 \times 2^2}{Z}$$

$$= \frac{a_0 \times 4}{1}$$

$$= 4a_0$$

The existence of electrons occur in those orbits only in which angular momentum is an integral multiple of $\dfrac{h}{2\pi}$.

$$mvr = \frac{nh}{2\pi}$$

$$v = \frac{2h}{2\pi mr}$$

$$= \frac{h}{\pi m(4a_0)}$$

The kinetic energy equation of electron in second Bohr orbit of hydrogen atom

$$= \frac{1}{2}mv^2$$

$$= \frac{1}{2}m\left(\frac{h}{4\pi ma_0}\right)^2$$

$$= \frac{h}{32\pi ma_0{}^2}$$

**53.** For any value of principal quantum number "$n$", the number of orbitals is always equal to square of "$n$".

$$\text{Number of orbitals} = n^2$$
$$= 3^2$$
$$= 9$$

Each orbital contains two electrons with spin quantum number $\pm\frac{1}{2}$. It means there are total eighteen electrons with the value of $m_s \pm\frac{1}{2}$.

Therefore, only nine electrons would have $m_s$ value $-\frac{1}{2}$.

**54. (4)** Energy of incident photons is calculated by the formula,

$$E = \frac{6.6\times10^{-34}\,\text{J.s}\times 3\times10^8\,\text{m.s}^{-1}}{300\times10^{-9}\,\text{m}}$$
$$= 4.125\,\text{eV}$$

All those metals whose value of work function is equal or less than the calculated value of energy will show photoelectric effect.

Therefore, lithium, sodium, potassium and magnesium metal will show photoelectric effect.

**55. (2)** For a spherical symmetrical state ($S_1$), Number of radial nodes = 1
Therefore,

$$n - 1 = 1$$
$$n = 2$$

For ($S_2$),
Number of radial nodes = 1

$$E_{S_2} = -\frac{13.6\times z^2}{n^2}$$

$E_H$ in ground state = $-13.6$

$$E = -\frac{13.6\times 9}{n^2}$$

$$n = 3$$

So, state $S_1$ is $2s$ and $S_2$ is $3p$.

**56. (3)** Energy of state $S_1$ is,

$$E_{S_1} = -\frac{13.6\times z^2}{n^2}$$

$$E_{S_1} = -\frac{13.6\times 9}{2^2}\,\text{eV/atom}$$

Energy of state $S_1$ in units of hydrogen atom ground state energy is,

$$\frac{E_{S_1}}{E_H} = -\frac{13.6\times 9}{2^2\times -13.6}$$
$$= 2.25$$

So, energy of state $S_1$ in units of hydrogen atom ground state energy is 2.25.

**57. (2)** For ($S_2$),
Number of radial nodes = 1

$$= -\frac{13.6\times z^2}{n^2}$$

$E_H$ for ground state $\overset{E_{S_2}}{=} -13.6$

$$E = -\frac{13.6\times 9}{n^2}$$

$$n = 3$$

Number of radial nodes = 1
Therefore,

$$n - l - 1 = 1$$
$$3 - l - 1 = 1$$
$$l = 1$$

For ($S_2$), the orbital agular momentum quantum number is 1.

**58. (1)** The number of neutrons increases with increase in atomic number and shows curvature towards $x$-axis, which represents the number of neutrons.

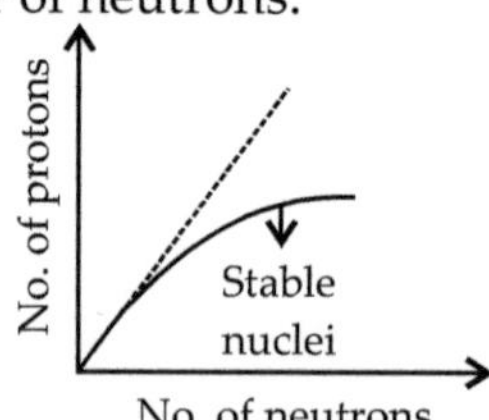


The electrostatic repulsion between two protons increases in heavier nuclides and this repulsion overcomes the force of attraction between protons and neutrons

**59. (A)** (q) (r); **(B)** (p), (q), (r), (s); **(C)** (p) (q) (r); **(D)** (p), (q)

**(A)** In hydrogen like atomic orbital, the orbital angular momentum of an electron is related to Azimuthal quantum number and magnetic quantum number.

**(B)** A wave function that follows Pauli's exclusion principle is related to principal quantum number, Azimuthal quantum number, magnetic quantum number and electron spin quantum number.

**(C)** The shape, size and orientation of hydrogen like orbitals is related to principal quantum number, Azimuthal quantum number and magnetic quantum number.

**(D)** Principal quantum number and Azimuthal quantum number are related to the probability density of an electron in the hydrogen like atom present in the nucleus.

**60.** The formula to calculate U is as follows :

$$U = \frac{V_n}{K_n}$$

The value of $V_n$ is,

$$V_n = -\frac{kze^2}{2r}$$

The value of $K_n$ is,

$$K_n = \frac{kze^2}{2r}$$

Substitute the value of $K_n$ and $V_n$ in the above formula.

$$U = \frac{-kze^2/r}{kze^2/2r}$$

$$= -2$$

It is given that the radius of $n^{th}$ orbit is proportional to $E_n{}^x$. Thus, the value of $x$ is $-1$.

The value of angular momentum in lowest orbital is,

$$\text{Angular momentum of electron} = \sqrt{1(1+1)}\,\frac{h}{2\pi}$$

$$= \sqrt{0(0+1)}\,\frac{h}{2\pi}$$

$$= 0$$

It is given that the radius of $n^{th}$ orbit is inversely proportional to $Z^y$. Thus, the value of $y$ is 1.

**61. (4)** (a) The given value of $r$ is $a_0$ that is equal to $0.529\ \text{Å}$ or $5.29 \times 10^{-11}$ m

The value of $n$ is 1.

The mass of hydrogen atom is $9.1 \times 10^{-31}$ g.

The value of Planck's constant is $6.63 \times 10^{-34}$ J.sec.

The expression for the velocity of first Bohr orbit of hydrogen atom is given as,

$$mvr = \frac{nh}{2\pi}$$

$$v = \frac{nh}{2\pi mr}$$

Substitute the value of mass, Planck's constant, $n$ and $\pi$ in the above expression.

$$v = \frac{1 \times 6.63 \times 10^{-34}}{2 \times 3.14 \times 9.1 \times 10^{-31} \times 5.29 \times 10^{-11}}$$

$$= 2.18 \text{ m/sec}$$

Thus, the value of velocity of electron in first Bohr orbit of hydrogen is 2.18 m/sec.

(b) The expression to calculate the de-Broglie wavelength of the electron in first Bohr model orbit is,

$$\lambda = \frac{h}{mv}$$

Substitute the value of mass, Planck's constant, and velocity in the above expression.

$$\lambda = \frac{6.63 \times 10^{-34}}{9.1 \times 10^{-31} \times 2.18}$$

$$= 0.33 \times 10^{-9} \text{ m}$$

Thus, the value de-Broglie wavelength of the electron in first Bohr model orbit is $0.33 \times 10^{-9}$ m.

(c) The value of angular momentum quantum number for $2p$ orbital is $l = 1$.

The formula of orbital angular quantum momentum is,

$$\text{Orbital angular momentum} = \sqrt{l(l+1)}\,\frac{h}{2\pi}$$

Substitute the value $l = 1$ in the above expression.

$$\text{Orbital angular momentum} = \sqrt{1(1+1)}\,\frac{h}{2\pi}$$

$$= \sqrt{2}\,\frac{h}{2\pi}$$

Thus, the orbital angular quantum momentum $2p$ orbital is for $\sqrt{2}\,\dfrac{h}{2\pi}$.

**62. (1)** The value of principal quantum number, $n$ for $3s$ orbital is 3.

The value of principal quantum number, $n$ for $2p$ orbital is 2.

The value of angular momentum quantum number, $l$ for $3s$ orbital is 0.

The value of angular momentum quantum number, $l$ for $2p$ orbital is 1.

The expression to calculate the radial nodes is,

$$\text{Number of radial nodes} = n - l - 1 \quad \dots(1)$$

Substitute the value of $n$ and $l$ for $3s$ orbital in equation (1).

$$\text{Number of radial nodes} = 3 - 0 - 1$$

$$= 2$$

Substitute the value of $n$ and $l$ for $2p$ orbital in equation (1).

$$\text{Number of radial nodes} = 2 - 1 - 1$$

$$= 0$$

Thus, the radial nodes for $3s$ and $2p$ are 2 and 0 respectively.

Hence, the correct option is (1).

**63.** (a) The Schrodinger wave equation for hydrogen atom is given.

Where,

$\psi_{2s}{}^2$ is the probability of finding electrons at any place.

$\psi^2$ at anode is zero.

Substitute all the values in the given formula.

$$\psi^2 = 0 = \frac{1}{4\sqrt{2\pi}}\left[\frac{1}{a^\circ}\right]^3\left(2 - \frac{r}{a_0}\right)$$

$$\left(2 - \frac{r}{a_0}\right) = 0$$

$$2 = \frac{r}{a_0}$$

$$r = 2a_0$$

(b) The wavelength is calculated by the formula,

$$\lambda = \frac{h}{mv}$$

Substitute all the values in the above formula.

$$\lambda = \frac{h}{mv}$$

$$= \frac{6.626 \times 10^{-34}}{100 \times 10^{-3} \times 100}$$

$$= 6.626 \times 10^{-25}$$

(c) The Y formed for the given reaction is,

$$_{92}X^{234} \xrightarrow[-6\beta]{-7\alpha} {}_{84}Po^{206}$$

Thus, the atomic number of Y is 84. The mass number of Y is 206.

**64. (2)** The radius of Bohr orbit of the hydrogen atom is expressed as,

$$r = \frac{n^2 r_{1(H^+)}}{z}$$

For the hydrogen atom, radius of Bohr orbit is,

$$r = r_{1(H^+)}$$

For $n = 2$, $Be^{3+}$, radius of Bohr orbit is,

$$r_{1(H^+)} = \frac{(2)^2 r_{2(Be^{3+})}}{4}$$

$$= r_{2(Be^{3+})}$$

**65.** The given wavelength of H-atoms is 91.2 nm. The value of $n_1$ and $n_2$ for maximum energy are 1 and $\infty$.

The wavelength of hydrogen atom is calculated as follow :

$$\frac{1}{\lambda_H} = R_H Z^2\left(\frac{1}{1^2} - \frac{1}{\infty^2}\right) \quad ...(1)$$

$$= R_H Z_H^2$$

Similarly, the wavelength of helium ion is calculated as follows :

$$\frac{1}{\lambda_{He^+}} = R_{He} Z_{He}^2 \quad ...(2)$$

From equation (1) and (2)

$$\frac{\lambda_{He^+}}{\lambda_{He}} = \frac{R_H Z_H^2}{R_{He} Z_{He^+}^2}$$

$$\lambda_{He^+} = \frac{\lambda_H}{4}$$

$$= 22.8 \text{ nm}$$

**66. (4)** Rutherford used a beam of $\alpha$-particles. These particles are positively charged and similar to helium nuclei.

**67. (3)** According to Pauli Exclusion Principle, one orbital can occupy only two electrons in opposite spins. $s$ orbital cannot accommodate more than two electrons.

●●

# Nuclear Chemistry

## ❓ QUESTIONS

1. During the nuclear explosion, one of the products is $^{90}$Sr with half life of 6.93 years. If 1 mg of $^{90}$Sr was absorbed in thebones of a newly born baby in place of Ca, how much time, in years, is required to reduce it by 90% if it is not lost metabolically ........... : **[2020, Main]**

2. A plot of the number of neutrons (N) against the number of protons (P) of stable nuclei exhibits upward deviation from linearity for atomic number, Z > 20. For an unstable nucleus having N/P ratio less than 1, the possible mode(s) of decay is/are : **[2016, Advanced]**
   (1) β⁻-decay (β emission)
   (2) orbital or K-electron capture
   (3) neutron emission
   (4) β⁺-decay (positron emission)

3. A closed vessel with rigid walls contains 1 mol of $^{238}_{92}$U and 1 mol of air at 298 K. Considering complete decay of $^{238}_{92}$U to $^{206}_{82}$Pb, the ratio of the final pressure to the initial pressure of the system at 298 K is. **[2015, Advanced]**

4. In the nuclear transmutation **[2013, Advanced]**
$$^{9}_{4}Be + X \longrightarrow ^{8}_{4}Be + Y$$
   (X, Y) is/are :
   (1) (γ, n)          (2) (p, D)
   (3) (n, D)          (4) (γ, p)

5. The periodic table consists of 18 groups. An isotope of copper, on bombardment with protons, undergoes a nuclear reaction yielding element **X** as shown below. To which group, element **X** belongs in the periodic table ? **[2012, Advanced]**
$$^{63}_{29}Cu + ^{1}_{1}H \rightarrow 6^{1}_{0}n + \alpha + 2^{1}_{1}H + \mathbf{X}$$

6. Bombardment of aluminium by α-particle leads to its artificial disintegration in two ways, (i) and (ii) as shown. Products **X**, **Y** and **Z** respectively are : **[2011, Advanced]**

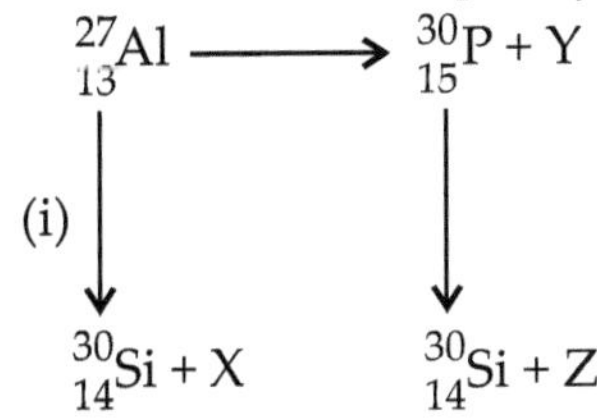

7. (1) proton, neutron, positron
   (2) neutron, positron, proton
   (3) proton, positron, neutron
   (4) positron, proton, neutron

7. The number of neutrons emitted when $^{235}_{92}$U undergoes controlled nuclear fission to $^{142}_{54}$Xe and $^{90}_{38}$Sr is. **[2010, Advanced]**

8. Given that the abundances of isotopes $^{54}$Fe, $^{56}$Fe and $^{57}$Fe are 5%, 90% and 5%, respectively, the atomic mass of Fe is : **[2009, Advanced]**
   (1) 55.85          (2) 55.95
   (3) 55.75          (4) 56.05

9. The total number of α and β particles emitted in the nuclear reaction $^{238}_{92}$U $\rightarrow$ $^{214}_{82}$Pb is.

**[2009, Advanced]**

10. A positron is emitted from $^{23}_{11}$Na. The ratio of the atomic mass and atomic number of the resulting nuclide is. **[2007, Advanced]**
   (1) 22/10          (2) 22/11
   (3) 23/10          (4) 23/12

11. Which of the following option is correct ?

**[2006, Main]**
   (1) In living organisms, circulation of $^{14}$C from atmosphere is high so the carbon content is constat in organism.
   (2) Carbon dating can be used to find out the age of earth crust and rocks.
   (3) Radioactive absorption due to cosmic radiation is equal to the rate of radioactive decay, hence the carbon content remains constant in living organism.
   (4) Carbon dating can not be used to determine concentration of $^{14}$C in dead beings.

12. What should be the age of fossil for meaningful determination of its age ? **[2006, Main]**
   (1) 6 years
   (2) 6000 years
   (3) 60,000 years
   (4) It can be used to calculate any age

13. A nuclear explosion has taken place leading to increase in concentration of $C^{14}$ in nearby area. $C^{14}$ concentration is $C_1$ in nearby areas and $C_2$ in areas far away. If the age of the fossil is determined to be $T_1$ and $T_2$ at the places respectively then :

**[2006, Main]**

(1) The age of the fossil will increase at the place where explosion has taken place and $T_1 - T_2$

$$= \frac{1}{\lambda} \ln \frac{C_1}{C_2}$$

(2) The age of the fossil will decrease at the place where explosion has taken place and $T_1 - T_2$

$$= \frac{1}{\lambda} \ln \frac{C_1}{C_2}$$

(3) The age of fossil will be determined to be same

(4) $\dfrac{T_1}{T_2} = \dfrac{C_1}{C_2}$

14. Fill in the blanks : **[2005, Main]**

(a) $^{235}U_{92} + {}_0n^1 \longrightarrow {}^{137}A_{52} + {}^{97}B_{40} + \ldots\ldots$

(b) $^{82}Se_{34} \longrightarrow 2\,{}_{-1}e^0 + \ldots\ldots$

15. $^{23}$Na is the more stable isotope of Na. Find out the process by which $^{24}_{11}$Na can undergo radioactive decay : **[2003, Screening]**

(1) $\beta^-$ emission      (2) $\alpha$ emission

(3) $\beta^+$ emission      (4) K electron caputre

16. $^{64}$Cu (half-life = 12.8 h) decays by $\beta^-$ emission (38%), $\beta^+$ emission (19%) and electron capture (43%). Write the decay products and calculate partial half-lives for each of the decay processes.

**[2002, Main]**

## ANSWER KEY

1. (*)    2. (2, 4)    3. (*)    4. (1, 2)    5. (*)    6. (1)    7. (4)    8. (2)    9. (*)    10. (3)

11. (3)    12. (2)    13. (1)    14. (*)    15. (1)    16. (*)

## ANSWERS WITH EXPLANATIONS

1. All nuclear decays follow first order kinetics

$$t = \frac{1}{k} \ln \frac{[A_0]}{[A]}$$

$$= \frac{(t_{1/2})}{0.693} \times 2.303 \log_{10} 10$$

$$= 10 \times 2.303 \times 1$$

$$= 23.03 \text{ years}$$

2. **(2, 4)** (1) There will no Beta-emission.

     In N/P should increase.

(2) Possible mode of decays are,

$$_0e^{-1} + {}_1^1P \rightarrow {}_1^0n$$

K-electron is captured.

(3) There will be no neutron emission.

(4) There will be $\beta^+$-decay (positron emission).

$$+{}_1^1P \rightarrow {}_1^0n + {}_{+1}^0\beta$$

So, the correct options are (2) and (4).

3. The initial mole ($n_i$) of gas is 1.

The complete decay of $^{238}_{92}U$ is :

$$^{238}_{92}U \rightarrow {}_{82}Pb^{206} + 8\,{}_2^4He + 6\,{}_{-1}e^0$$

Since, 1 mol of $^{238}_{92}U$ gives 8 moles of $^4_2$He.

Therefore, the final moles ($n_f$) of gases is,

$$= 8 + 1$$

$$= 9$$

At constant temperature and pressure,

$$p \propto n$$

Therefore, the ratio of the final pressure to the initial pressure of the system at 298 K is,

$$\frac{P_f}{P_i} = \frac{n_f}{n_i} = \frac{9}{1}$$

4. **(1, 2)** The complete nuclear transmutation reaction is shown as follows :

$$^9_4Be + \gamma \rightarrow {}^8_4Be + {}^1_0n$$

$$^9_4Be + {}^1_1P \rightarrow {}^8_4Be + {}^2_1H$$

5. The sum of mass number at the left hand side must be equal to the mass number at the right hand side. The mass number of **X** is calculated as shown below :

$$63 + 1 = 6 + 4 + 2 + A$$

$$A = 52$$

The sum of atomic number at the left hand side must be equal to the atomic number at the right hand side. The atomic number of **X** is calculated as shown below :

$$29 + 1 = 0 + 2 + 2 + Z$$

$$A = 26$$

Element with atomic number 26 is iron and it belongs to group 8.

6. **(1)** The complete nuclear reactions are shown below :

$$_2He^4 + _{13}Al^{27} \rightarrow _{14}Si^{30} + _1p^1 \text{ (proton)}$$
$$_2He^4 + _{13}Al^{27} \rightarrow _{15}Si^{30} + _0n^1 \text{ (neutron)}$$
$$_{15}P^{30} \rightarrow _{14}Si^{30} + _{+1}e^0 \text{ (positron)}$$

From the above equations it is clear that **X, Y** and **Z** respectively are proton, neutron and positron.

7. **(4)** The following reaction takes place when $_{92}^{235}U$ undergoes nuclear fission to $_{54}^{142}Xe$ and $_{38}^{90}Sr$.

$$_{92}^{235}U + _0^1n \rightarrow _{54}^{142}Xe + _{38}^{90}Sr + Y_0^1n$$

The total mass of reactants is equal to total mass of product.

$$235 + 1 = 142 + 90 + y$$
$$236 = 232 + y$$
$$y = 4$$

8. **(2)** The atomic mass of iron is calculated by the formula,

$$\bar{A} = \frac{\Sigma A_i x_i}{\Sigma x_i}$$

Substitute the values of atomic mass of isotopes and their percentage in the above equation.

$$\text{Atomic mass of Fe} = 54 \text{g/mol} \times \frac{5}{100}$$
$$+ 56 \text{g/mol} \times \frac{90}{100}$$
$$+ 57 \text{g/mol} \times \frac{5}{100}$$
$$= 55.95 \text{ g/mol}$$

9. The balanced chemical equation for the given nuclear reaction is,

$$_{92}U^{238} \rightarrow _{82}Pb^{214} + 6\,_2He^4 + 2\,_{-1}e^0$$

Therefore, six alpha particles and two beta particles are emitted in the given nuclear reaction. Hence, the total number of particles emitted is $(6 + 2) = 8$.

10. **(3)** The emission of a positron from $_{11}^{23}Na$ is,

$$_{11}^{23}Na \rightarrow _{10}^{23}Na + e^+ + v_e$$

Thus, the ratio of atomic mass of the atomic number is 23/10.

11. **(3)** Carbon dating can be used to determine concentration of $^{14}C$ in dead being, but it cannot be used to find out the age of earth crust and rocks.

Thus, the correct statement from the given option is (3).

12. **(2)** Carbon dating can be used to determine concentration of $^{14}C$ in dead being. The 6000 year old fossil can be used in the process of C-dating.

13. **(1)** It is given that $C_1$ is the concentration of $C^{14}$ in the sample taken near nuclear site, whereas, $C_2$ is the concentration of $C^{14}$ in the sample taken away from nuclear site.

The age of the fossil fuel will increase at the place where explosion has taken place and the relation is as follows :

$$T_1 - T_2 = \frac{1}{\lambda}\ln\frac{C_1}{C_2}.$$

14. **(a)** The nuclear fission of Uranium-235 takes place by the absorption of a neutron. The atom of Uranium-235 splits into two fragments along with the release of neutrons. The corresponding reaction is shown below :

$$^{235}U_{92} + _0n^1 \rightarrow ^{137}A_{52} + ^{97}B_{40} + 2\,_0n^1$$

**(b)** The given reaction shows double beta decay of Selenium-82. The products of the decay are given below :

$$^{82}Se_{34} + \rightarrow 2\,_{-1}e^0 + ^{82}Kr_{36}$$

15. **(1)** The ratio of neutron and proton in $^{24}Na$ is 13 : 11. It is greater than unity. Thus, it is radioactive. To get the stability, it will tend to adjust its neutron and proton ratio equals to unity. This can be possible by breaking neutron into electron and proton.

The emission taking place is,

$$_0n^1 \rightarrow _{+1}p^1 + _{-1}e^0$$

The electron will be emitted out as β-ray.

Thus, the emission taking place is β⁻ decay.

16. The decay product formed by the β⁻ emission of $^{64}Cu$ is as follows :

$$_{29}^{64}Cu \xrightarrow[k_1]{\beta\text{-emission}} _{30}Zn^{64} + _{-1}e$$

The decay product formed by the electron capture of $^{64}Cu$ is as follows :

$$_{29}^{64}Cu \xrightarrow[k_2]{\beta\text{-emission}} _{28}Ni^{64} + _{+1}e$$

The decay product formed by the β+ emission of $^{64}Cu$ is as follows :

$$_{29}^{64}Cu \xrightarrow[k_3]{\beta\text{-emission}} _{28}Ni^{64}$$

The overall rate constant is,

$$= k_1 + k_2 + k_3$$

$$= \frac{0.693}{t_{1/2}}$$

$$= \frac{0.693}{12.8}\,h^{-1}$$

The $t_1$ for the first decay is,

$$t_1 = \frac{0.693 \times 12.8}{0.38 \times 0.693}$$

$$= 33.68\,h$$

The $t_2$ for the first decay is,

$$t_2 = \frac{0.693 \times 12.8}{0.19 \times 0.693}$$

$$= 67.36\,h$$

The $t_3$ for the first decay is,

$$t_3 = \frac{12.8}{0.43}$$

$$= 29.76\,h$$

●●

# Chemical Bonding and Molecular Structure

## 🗨 QUESTIONS

**1.** If $AB_4$ molecule is a polar molecule, a possible geometry of $AB_4$ is : **[2020, Main]**
(1) Square pyramidal
(2) Tetrahedral
(3) Square planar
(4) Rectangular planar

**2.** The shape/structure of $[XeF_5]^-$ and $XeO_3F_2$, respectively, are : **[2020, Main]**
(1) Pentagonal planar and trigonal bipyramidal
(2) Trigonal bipyramidal and pentagonal planar
(3) Octahedral and square pyramidal
(4) Trigonal bipyramidal and trigonal bipyramidal

**3.** The molecular geometry of $SF_6$ is octahedral. What is the geometry of $SF_4$ (including lone pair(s) of electrons, if any ) ? **[2020, Main]**
(1) Trigonal bipyramidal (2) Square planar
(3) Tetrahderal (4) Pyramidal

**4.** The structure of $PCl_5$ in the solid state is : **[2020, Main]**
(1) Square pyramidal
(2) Tetrahderal $[PCl_4]^+$ and octahedral $[PCl_6]^-$
(3) Square planar $[PCl_4]^+$ and octahedral $[PCl_6]^-$
(4) Trigonal bipyramidal

**5.** The reaction in which the hybridisation of the underlined atom is affected is : **[2020, Main]**
(1) $\underline{N}H_3 \xrightarrow{H^+}$
(2) $\underline{Xe}F_4 + SbF_5 \rightarrow$
(3) $H_2\underline{S}O_4 + NaCl \xrightarrow{420\ K}$
(4) $H_3\underline{P}O_2 \xrightarrow{Disproportionation}$

**6.** The molecule in which hybrid MOs involve only one $d$-orbital of the central atom is : **[2020, Main]**
(1) $[Ni(CN)_4]^{2-}$ (2) $[CrF_6]^{3-}$
(3) $BrF_5$ (4) $XeF_4$

**7.** Among the following compounds, which one has the shortest C—Cl bond ? **[2020, Main]**

(1) $H_3C$–$Cl$

(2) $\begin{array}{c} H_3C \\ H_3C \!-\!\!\!\!\!\diagup\!\!\!\!-Cl \\ CH_3 \end{array}$

(3) $\begin{array}{c} Cl \\ \diagup \\ CH \\ \| \\ CH_2 \end{array}$

(4) $\begin{array}{c} HC \diagdown Cl \\ \| \\ CH_2 \end{array}$

**8.** The incorrect statement(s) among (a)-(c) is (are) : **[2020, Main]**
(a) W(VI) is more stable than Cr(VI)
(b) in the presence of HCl, permanganate titrations provide statisfactory results
(c) some lanthanoid oxides can be used as phosphors.
(1) (a) and (b) only (2) (a) only
(3) (b) and (c) only (4) (b) only

**9.** The increasing order of boiling points of the following compounds is : **[2020, Main]**

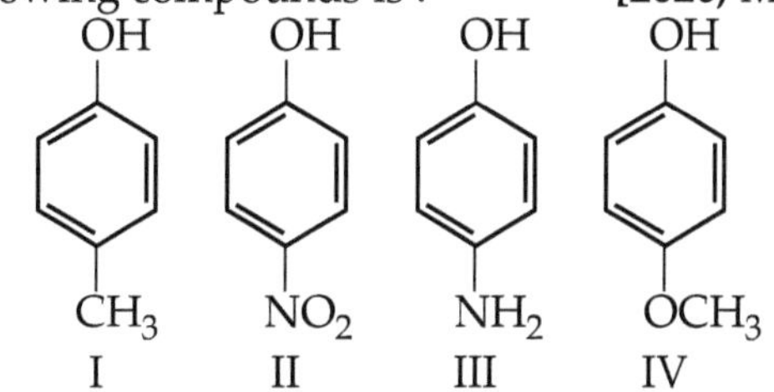


(1) I < IV < III < II (2) IV < I < II < III
(3) I < III < IV < II (4) III < I < II < IV

**10.** The compound that has the largest H–M–H bond angle (M = N, O, S, C), is : **[2020, Main]**
(1) $H_2O$ (2) $CH_4$
(3) $NH_3$ (4) $H_2S$

**11.** Hydrogen peroxide, in the pure state, is : **[2020, Main]**
(1) Non-planar and almost colourless.
(2) Linear and almost colourless.
(3) Planar and blue in colour.
(4) Linear and blue in colour.

**12.** Considering that $\Delta_0 > P$, the magnetic moment (in BM) of $[Ru(H_2O)_6]^{2+}$ would be ......... . **[2020, Main]**

**13.** Consider the following compounds in the liquid form :
$O_2$, HF, $H_2O$, $NH_3$, $H_2O_2$, $CCl_4$, $CHCl_3$, $C_6H_6$, $C_6H_5Cl$
When a charged comb is brought near their flowing stream, how many of them show deflection as per the following figure ?

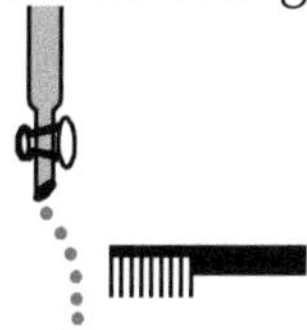

**[2020, Advanced]**

**14.** The potential energy curve for the $H_2$ molecule as a function of internuclear distance is :

**[2020, Main]**

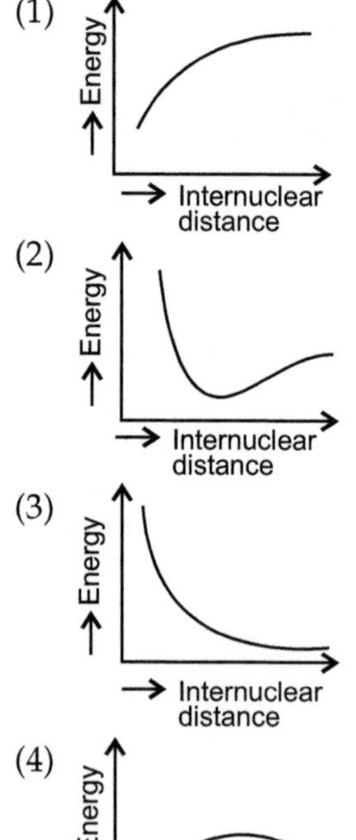

(1)

(2)

(3)

(4)

**15.** The dipole moments of $CCl_4$, $CHCl_3$ and $CH_4$ are in the order : **[2020, Main]**

(1) $CH_4 = CCl_4 < CHCl_3$

(2) $CH_4 < CCl_4 < CHCl_3$

(3) $CCl_4 < CH_4 < CHCl_3$

(4) $CHCl_3 < CH_4 = CCl_4$

**16.** The relative strength of interionic/intermolecular forces in decreasing order is : **[2020, Main]**

(a) ion-dipole > ion-ion > dipole-dipole

(b) dipole-dipole > ion-dipole > ion-ion

(c) ion-dipole > dipole-dipole > ion-ion

(d) ion-ion > ion-dipole > dipole-dipole

Which of the reaction(s) will not produce Saytzeff product ?

(1) (c) only

(2) (a), (c) and (d)

(3) (d) only

(4) (b) and (d)

**17.** Consider the following reactions : **[2020, Main]**

(a) $(CH_3)_3 CCH(OH)CH_3 \xrightarrow{\text{conc. } H_2SO_4}$

(b) $(CH_3)_2 CHCH(Br)CH_3 \xrightarrow{\text{alc. KOH}}$

(c)

$(CH_3)_2 CHCH(Br)CH_3 \xrightarrow[\text{It should be } (CH_3)_3CO^-K^+]{\text{given by NTA } (CH_3)_3O^-K^+}$

(d) $(CH_3)_2 \underset{\underset{OH}{|}}{C} - CH_2 - CHO \xrightarrow{\Delta}$

Which of the reaction(s) will not produce saytzeff product?

(1) (a) and (d)

(2) (a), (c) and (d)

(3) (d) only

(4) (c) only

**18.** Chlorine reacts with hot and concentrated NaOH and produces compounds (X) and (Y). Compound (X) gives white precipitate with silver nitrate solution. The average bond order between Cl and O atoms in (Y) is ................. . **[2020, Main]**

**19.** Arrange the following bonds according to their average bond energies in descending order : **[2020, Main]**

C–Cl, C–Br, C–F, C–I

(1) C–I > C–Br > C–Cl > C–F

(2) C–Br > C–I > C–Cl > C–F

(3) C–F > C–Cl > C–Br > C–I

(4) C–Cl > C–Br > C–I > C–F

**20.** If the magnetic moment of a dioxygen species is 1.73 B.M., it may be : **[2020, Main]**

(1) $O_2^-$ or $O_2^+$

(2) $O_2$ or $O_2^+$

(3) $O_2$ or $O_2^-$

(4) $O_2, O_2^-$ or $O_2^+$

**21.** The predominant intermolecular forces present in ethyl acetate, a liquid, are : **[2020, Main]**

(1) Hydrogen bonding and London dispersion

(2) Dipole-dipole and hydrogen bonding

(3) London dispersion and dipole-dipole

(4) London dispersion, dipole-dipole and hydrogen bonding

**22.** Which of the following has the shortest $C-Cl$ bond ? **[2020, Main]**

(1) $Cl–CH = CH–OCH_3$

(2) $Cl–CH=CH–CH_3$

(3) $Cl–CH=CH_2$

(4) $Cl–CH=CH–NO_2$

**23.** The number of $sp^2$ hybrid orbitals in a molecule of benzene is : **[2020, Main]**

(1) 24

(2) 6

(3) 12

(4) 18

**24.** The sum of the total number of bonds between chromium and oxygen atoms in chromate and dichromate ions is ............... . **[2020, Main]**

**25.** The bond order and the magnetic characteristics of CN– are : **[2020, Main]**

(1) 3, paramagnetic

(2) $2\frac{1}{2}$, diamagnetic

(3) 3, diamagnetic

(4) $2\frac{1}{2}$, paramagnetic

**26.** Among the following molecules/ions

$$C_2^{2-}, N_2^{2-}, O_2^{2-}, O_2$$

which one is diamagnetic and has the shortest bond length ? **[2019, Main]**

(1) $O_2$

(2) $N_2^{2-}$

(3) $O_2^{2-}$

(4) $C_2^{2-}$

**27.** The ion that has $sp^3d^2$ hybridisation for the central atom is : **[2019, Main]**

(1) $[ICl_4]^-$

(2) $[ICl_2]^-$

(3) $[IF_6]^-$

(4) $[BrF_2]^-$

**28.** Among the following, the molecule expected to be stabilised by anion formation is : $C_2, O_2, NO, F_2$ **[2019, Main]**

(1) $C_2$

(2) $F_2$

(3) $NO$

(4) $O_2$

**29.** HF has highest boiling point among hydrogen halides, because it has : **[2019, Main]**
(1) strongest van der Waals' interactions
(2) lowest ionic character
(3) strongest hydrogen bonding
(4) lowest dissociation enthalpy

**30.** Among the following species, the diamagnetic molecule is : **[2019, Main]**
(1) NO
(2) CO
(3) $B_2$
(4) $O_2$

**31.** During the change of $O_2$ to $O_2^-$, the incoming electron goes to the orbital : **[2019, Main]**
(1) $\pi\, 2p_y$
(2) $\sigma^*\, 2p_z$
(3) $\pi^*\, 2p_x$
(4) $\pi\, 2p_x$

**32.** Each of the following options contains a set of four molecules. Identify the option(s) where all four molecules possess permanent dipole moment at room temperature. **[2019, Main]**
(1) $BeCl_2$, $CO_2$, $BCl_3$, $CHCl_3$
(2) $NO_2$, $NH_3$, $POCl_3$, $CH_3Cl$
(3) $BF_3$, $O_3$, $SF_6$, $XeF_6$
(4) $SO_2$, $C_6H_5Cl$, $H_2Se$, $BrF_5$

**33.** According to molecular orbital theory, which of the following will not be a viable molecule ? **[2018, Main]**
(1) $He_2^{2+}$
(2) $He_2^+$
(3) $H_2^-$
(4) $H_2^{2-}$

**34.** Which of the following best describes the diagram below of a molecular orbital ? **[2018, Main]**

(1) A non-bonding orbital
(2) An antibonding $\sigma$ orbital
(3) A bonding $\pi$ orbital
(4) An antibonding $\pi$ orbital

**35.** In the molecular orbital diagram for the molecular ion, $N_2^+$, the number of electrons in the $\sigma_{2p}$ molecular orbital is : **[2018, Main]**
(1) 0
(2) 1
(3) 2
(4) 3

**36.** $H—N \overset{(I)}{------} N \overset{(II)}{------} N$

In hydrogen azide (above) the bond orders of bonds (I) and (II) are : **[2018, Main]**

Molecular orb

(1) (1) < 2, (II) > 2

(2) (1) > 2, (II) > 2

(3) (1) > 2, (II) < 2

(4) (1) < 2, (II) < 2

**37.** The decreasing order of bond angles in $BF_3$, $NH_3$, $PF_3$ and $I_3^-$ is : **[2018, Main]**
(1) $I_3^- > NH_3 > PF_3 > BF_3$
(2) $I_3^- > BF_3 > NH_3 > PF_3$
(3) $BF_3 > I_3^- > PF_3 > NH_3$
(4) $BF_3 > NH_3 > PF_3 > I_3^-$

**38.** The incorrect geometry is represented by : **[2018, Main]**
(1) $BF_3$-trigonal planar
(2) $H_2O$-bent
(3) $NF_3$-trigonal planar
(4) $AsF_5$-trigonal bipyramidal

**39.** Which of the following conversions involves change in both shape and hybridisation ? **[2018, Main]**
(1) $NH_3 \rightarrow NH_4^+$
(2) $CH_4 \rightarrow C_2H_6$
(3) $H_2O \rightarrow H_3O^+$
(4) $BF_3 \rightarrow BF_4^-$

**40.** The colour of the $X_2$ molecules of group 17 elements changes gradually from yellow to violet down the group. This is due to :**[2017, Advanced]**
(1) The physical state of $X_2$ at room temperature changes from gas to solid down the group
(2) decrease in ionization energy down the group
(3) decrease in $\pi^*$-$\sigma^*$ gap down the group
(4) decrease in HOMO-LUMO gap down the group

**41.** Among $H_2$, $He_2^+$, $Li_2$, $Be_2$, $B_2$, $C_2$, $N_2$, $O_2^-$, and $F_2$, the number of diamagnetic species is (Atomic numbers : H = 1, He = 2, Li = 3, Be = 4, B = 5, C = 6, N = 7, O = 8, F = 9) **[2017, Advanced]**

**42.** Which of the following species is not paramagnetic ? **[2017, Main]**
(1) $O_2$
(2) $B_2$
(3) NO
(4) CO

**43.** Which of the following is paramagnetic ? **[2017, Main]**
(1) $NO^+$
(2) CO
(3) $O_2^{2-}$
(4) $B_2$

**44.** $sp^3d^2$ hybridization is not displayed by : **[2017, Main]**
(1) $BrF_5$
(2) $SF_6$
(3) $[CrF_6]^{3-}$
(4) $PF_5$

**45.** The group having triangular planar structures is : **[2017, Main]**
(1) $BF_3$, $NF_3$, $CO_3^{2-}$
(2) $CO_3^{2-}$, $NO_3^-$, $SO_3$
(3) $NH_3$, $SO_3$, $CO_3^{2-}$
(4) $NCl_3$, $BCl_3$, $SO_3$

**46.** According to Molecular Orbital Theory : **[2016, Advanced]**
(1) $C_2^{2-}$ is expected to be diamagnetic
(2) $O_2^{2+}$ is expected to have a longer bond length than $O_2$
(3) $N_2^+$ and $N_2^-$ have the same bond order
(4) $He_2^+$ has the same energy as two isolated He atoms

**47.** The bond angle H-X-H is the greatest in the compound : **[2016, Main]**
(1) $CH_4$
(2) $NH_3$
(3) $H_2O$
(4) $PH_3$

**48.** Which of the following statements about water is False ? **[2016, Main]**
(1) Water is oxidized to oxygen during photosynthesis
(2) Water can act both as an acid and as a base
(3) There is extensive intramolecular hydrogen bonding in the condensed phase
(4) Ice formed by heavy water sinks in normal water

**49.** The total number of lone pairs of electrons in $N_2O_3$ is ? **[2015, Advanced]**

**50.** Among the triatomic molecules/ions, $BeCl_2$, $N_3^-$, $N_2O$, $NO_2^+$, $O_3$, $SCl_2$, $ICl_2^-$, $I_3^-$ and $XeF_2$, the total number of linear molecules/ions where the hybridisation of the central atom does not have contribution from the $d$-orbitals is :
[Atomic number : S = 16, Cl = 17, I = 53 and Xe = 54] **[2015, Advanced]**

**51.** The correct statements regarding, (i) HClO, (ii) $HClO_2$, (iii) $HClO_3$ and (iv) $HClO_4$, is/are : **[2015, Advanced]**
(1) The number of Cl = O bonds in (ii) and (iii) together is two
(2) The number of lone pairs of electrons on Cl in (ii) and (iii) together is three
(3) The hybridisation of Cl in (iv) is $sp^3$
(4) Amongst (i) to (iv), the strongest acid is (i)

**52.** The intermolecular interaction that is dependent on the inverse cube of distance between the molecules is : **[2015, Main]**
(1) Ion-ion interaction
(2) Ion-dipole interaction
(3) London force
(4) Hydrogen bond

**53.** After understanding the assertion and reason, choose the correct option. **[2015, Advanced]**
**Assertion :** In the bonding molecular orbital (MO) of $H_2$, electron density is increased between the nuclei.
**Reason :** The bonding MO is $\psi_A + \psi_B$, which shows destructive interference of the combining electron waves.
(1) Assertion and reason are correct and reason is the correct explanation for the assertion
(2) Assertion and reason are correct, but reason is not the correct explanation for the assertion
(3) Assertion is correct, reason is incorrect
(4) Assertion is incorrect, reason is correct

**54.** Molecule AB has a bond length of 1.617 Å and a dipole moment of 0.38 D. The fractional charge on each atom (absolute magnitude) is :
($e_0$ = 4.802 × 10⁻¹⁰ esu) **[2015, Main]**
(1) 0
(2) 0.05
(3) 0.5
(4) 1.0

**55.** Hydrogen bonding plays a central role in the following phenomena : **[2014, Advanced]**
(1) Ice floats in water
(2) Higher Lewis basicity of primary amines than tertiary amines in aqueous solutions
(3) Formic acid is more acidic than acetic acid
(4) Dimerisation of acetic acid in benzene

**56.** Assuming $2s$-$2p$ mixing is NOT operative, the paramagnetic species among the following is : **[2014, Advanced]**
(1) $Be_2$
(2) $B_2$
(3) $C_2$
(4) $N_2$

**57.** Match the orbital overlap figures shown in List-I with the description given in List-II and select the correct answer using the code given below the lists : **[2014, Advanced]**

| List-I | List-II |
|---|---|
| P.  | 1. $p$-$d$ antibonding |
| Q.  | 2. $d$-$d$ bonding |
| R.  | 3. $p$-$d$ bonding |
| S. 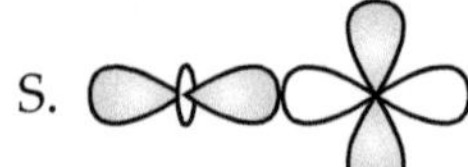 | 4. $d$-$d$ antibonding |

**Codes :**

| | P | Q | R | S |
|---|---|---|---|---|
| (1) | 2 | 1 | 3 | 4 |
| (2) | 4 | 3 | 1 | 2 |
| (3) | 2 | 3 | 1 | 4 |
| (4) | 4 | 1 | 3 | 2 |

**58.** Which of the following has unpaired electrons ? **[2014, Main]**
(1) $N_2$
(2) $O_2^-$
(3) $N_2^{2+}$
(4) $O_2^{2-}$

**59.** The number and type of bonds in $C_2^{2-}$ ion in $CaC_2$ are : **[2014, Main]**
(1) One σ bond and one π-bond
(2) One σ bond and two π-bonds
(3) Two σ bonds and two π-bonds
(4) Two σ bonds and one π-bond

**60.** The correct order of bond dissociation energy among $N_2$, $O_2$, $O_2^-$ is shown in which of the following arrangements ? **[2014, Main]**
(1) $N_2 > O_2^- > O_2$
(2) $O_2^- > O_2 > N_2$
(3) $N_2 > O_2 > O_2^-$
(4) $O_2 > O_2^- > N_2$

**61.** Which one of the following does not have a pyramidal shape ? **[2014, Main]**
(1) $(CH_3)_3N$
(2) $(SiH_3)_3N$
(3) $P(CH_3)_3$
(4) $P(SiH_3)_3$

**62.** In allene ($C_3H_4$), the types of hybridisation of the carbon atoms is/are : **[2014, Main]**
(1) $sp$ and $sp^3$ 　　(2) $sp^2$ and $sp$
(3) only $sp^2$ 　　(4) $sp^2$ and $sp^3$

**63.** Which one of the following molecules is paramagnetic ? **[2014, Main]**
(1) $N_2$ 　　(2) NO
(3) CO 　　(4) $O_3$

**64.** Amongst LiCl, RbCl, $BeCl_2$ and $MgCl_2$ the compounds with the greatest and the least ionic character, respectively are : **[2014, Main]**
(1) LiCl and RbCl 　　(2) RbCl and $BeCl_2$
(3) $MgCl_2$ and $BeCl_2$ 　　(4) RbCl and $MgCl_2$

**65.** The hyperconjugative stabilities of *tert*-butyl cation and 2-butene, respectively, are due to : **[2013, Advanced]**
(1) $\sigma \to \pi$ (empty) and $\sigma \to \pi^*$ electron delocalisations
(2) $\sigma \to \sigma^*$ and $\sigma \to \pi$ electron delocalisations
(3) $\sigma \to \pi$ (filled) and $\sigma \to \pi$ electron delocalisations
(4) $\pi$ (filled) $\to \sigma^*$ and $\sigma \to \pi^*$ electron delocalisations

**66.** Based on VSEPR theory, the number of 90 degree F-Br-F angles in $BrF_5$ is. **[2010, Advanced]**

**67.** The species having pyramidal shape is : **[2010, Advanced]**
(1) $SO_3$ 　　(2) $BrF_3$
(3) $SiO_3^{2-}$ 　　(4) $OSF_2$

**68.** Assuming that Hund's rule is violated, the bond order and magnetic nature of the diatomic molecule $B_2$ is : **[2010, Advanced]**
(1) 1 and diamagnetic 　　(2) 1 and paramagnetic
(3) 0 and diamagnetic 　　(4) 0 and paramagnetic

**69.** Match each of the diatomic molecules in Column I with its property/properties in Column II. **[2009, Advanced]**

| Column I | Column II |
|---|---|
| (1) $B_2$ | (p) Paramagnetic |
| (2) $N_2$ | (q) Undergoes oxidation |
| (3) $O_2^-$ | (r) Undergoes reduction |
| (4) $O_2$ | (s) Bond order $\geq 2$ |
|  | (t) Mixing of 's' and 'p' orbitals |

**70.** The species having bond order different from that in CO is : **[2007, Advanced]**
(1) $NO^-$ 　　(2) $NO^+$
(3) $CN^-$ 　　(4) $N_2$

**71.** Among the following, the paramagnetic compound is : **[2007, Advanced]**
(1) $Na_2O_4$ 　　(2) $O_3$
(3) $N_2O$ 　　(4) $KO_2$

**72.** **Statement-I** : Boron always forms covalent bond
because
**Statement-II** : The small size of $B^{3+}$ favours formation of covalent bond. **[2007, Advanced]**
(1) Statement-I is True, Statement-II is True, Statement-II is a correct explanation for Statement-I
(2) Statement-I is True, Statement-II is True, Statement-II is NOT a correct explanation for Statement-I
(3) Statement-I is True, Statement-II is False
(4) Statement-I is False, Statement-II is True

**73.** Predict whether the following molecules are iso-structural or not. Justify your answer. **[2005, Main]**
(1) $NMe_3$ 　　(2) $N(SiMe_3)_3$

**74.** Draw the shape of $XeF_4$ and $OSF_4$ according to VSEPR theory. Show the lone pair of electrons on the central atom. **[2004, Main]**

**75.** On the basis of ground state electronic configuration arrange the following molecules in increasing O-O bond length order.
$KO_2, O_2, O_2[AsF_6]$. **[2004, Main]**

**76.** According to MO theory : **[2004, Screening]**
(1) $O_2^+$ is paramagnetic and bond order is greater than $O_2$
(2) $O_2^+$ is paramagnetic and bond order is less than $O_2$
(3) $O_2^+$ is diamagnetic and bond order is less than $O_2$
(4) $O_2^+$ is diamagnetic and bond order is more than $O_2$

**77.** Using VSEPR theory. Draw the shape of $PCl_6$ and $BrF_5$. **[2003, Morning]**

**78.** Which of the following are isoelectronic and isostructural ?
$NO_3^-, CO_3^{2-}, ClO_3^-, SO_3$ **[2003, Screening]**
(1) $NO_3^-, CO_3^{2-}$ 　　(2) $SO_3, NO_3^-$
(3) $ClO_3^-, CO_3^{2-}$ 　　(4) $CO_3^{2-}, SO_3$

**79.** Which of the following represents the given mode of hybridisation $sp^2 - sp^2 - sp - sp$ from left to right ? **[2003, Screening]**
(1) $H_2C = CH - C \equiv N$ 　　(2) $H_2C = CH - CH = CH_2$
(3) $H_2C = C = C = CH_2$ 　　(4) $H_2C = C = CH - CH_3$

**80.** Specify the coordination geometry around and hybridisation of N and B atoms in a 1 : 1 complex $BF_3$ and $NH_3$. **[2002, Screening]**
(1) N : tetrahedral, $sp^3$, B : tetrahedral, $sp^3$
(2) N : pyramidal, $sp^3$, B : pyramidal, $sp^3$
(3) N : pyramidal, $sp^3$, B : planar, $sp^2$
(4) N : pyramidal, $sp^3$, B : tetrahedral, $sp^3$

**81.** Which of the following molecular species has unpaired electrons ? **[2002, Screening]**
(1) $N_2$ 　　(2) $F_2$
(3) $O_2^-$ 　　(4) $O_2^{2-}$

## ANSWER KEY

| | | | | | | | | | |
|---|---|---|---|---|---|---|---|---|---|
| **1.** (1) | **2.** (1) | **3.** (1) | **4.** (2) | **5.** (2) | **6.** (1) | **7.** (3) | **8.** (4) | **9.** (1) | **10.** (2) |
| **11.** (1) | **12.** (*) | **13.** (*) | **14.** (2) | **15.** (1) | **16.** (3) | **17.** (4) | **18.** (*) | **19.** (3) | **20.** (1) |
| **21.** (3) | **22.** (4) | **23.** (4) | **24.** (12) | **25.** (3) | **26.** (4) | **27.** (1) | **28.** (1) | **29.** (3) | **30.** (2) |
| **31.** (3) | **32.** (2, 4) | **33.** (4) | **34.** (4) | **35.** (2) | **36.** (1) | **37.** (2) | **38.** (3) | **39.** (4) | **40.** (3, 4) |
| **41.** (*) | **42.** (4) | **43.** (4) | **44.** (4) | **45.** (2) | **46.** (1, 3) | **47.** (1) | **48.** (3) | **49.** (*) | **50.** (*) |
| **51.** (2, 3) | **52.** (4) | **53.** (3) | **54.** (2) | **55.** (1,2,4) | **56.** (3) | **57.** (3) | **58.** (2) | **59.** (2) | **60.** (3) |
| **61.** (2) | **62.** (2) | **63.** (2) | **64.** (2) | **65.** (1) | **66.** (*) | **67.** (4) | **68.** (1) | **69.** (*) | **70.** (1) |
| **71.** (4) | **72.** (1) | **73.** (*) | **74.** (*) | **75.** (*) | **76.** (1) | **77.** (*) | **78.** (1) | **79.** (1) | **80.** (1) |
| **81.** (3) | | | | | | | | | |

## ANSWERS WITH EXPLANATIONS

**1. (1)** (1) If $AB_4$ molecule is a square pyramidal then it has one lone pair and their structure should be 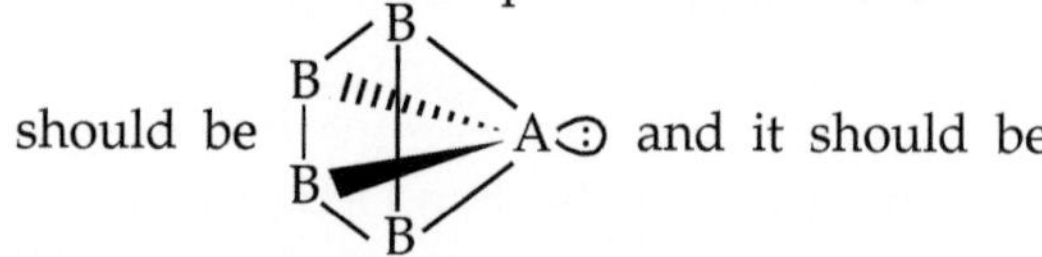 and it should be polar because dipole moment of lone pair of 'A' never be cancelled by others.

(2) If $AB_4$ molecule is a tetrahedral then it has no lone pair and their structure should be 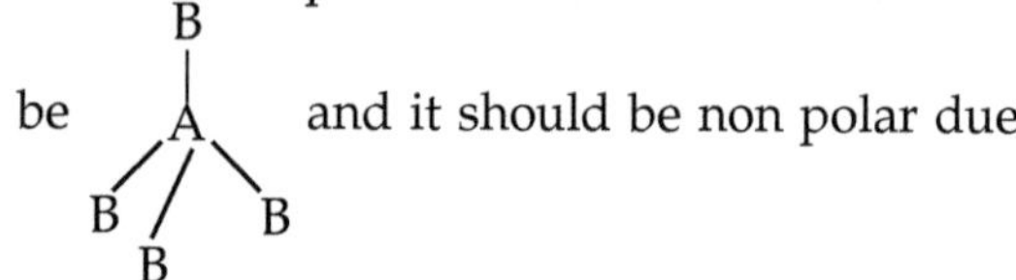 and it should be non polar due to perfect symmetry.

(3) If $AB_4$ molecule is a square planar then it should be non polar because vector sum of dipole moment is zero.

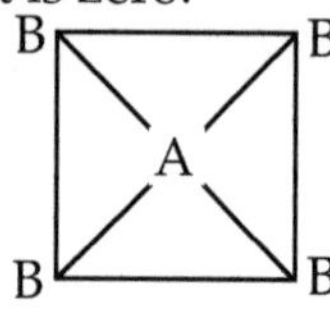

(4) If $AB_4$ molecule is a rectangular planar then it should be non polar because vector sum of dipole moment is zero.

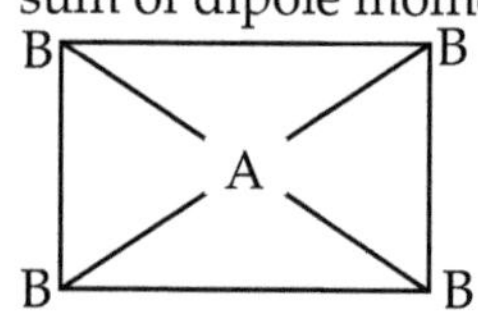

**2. (1)**

$XeF_5^-$
$sp^3d^3$
Pentagonal planar

$XeO_3F_2$
$sp^3d$
Trigonal bipyramidal

**3. (1)**

$4\sigma$ bonds + 1 lone pair
∴ Shape (including lone pair of electrons) is Trigonal bipyramidal.

**4. (2)** $PCl_{5(s)}$ exist as $[PCl_4]^+$ and $[PCl_6]^-$

$[PCl_4]^+ \Rightarrow$ ($sp^3$ hybridisation)
Tetrahedral

$[PCl_6]^- \Rightarrow$
octahedral
$sp^3d^2$ hybridization

**5. (2)** $XeF_4 + SbF_5 \rightarrow [XeF_3]^+ [SbF_6]^-$
$\quad\quad sp^3d^2 \quad sp^3d \quad\quad sp^3d \quad sp^3d^2$

**6. (1)** $[Ni(CN)_4]^{2-}$
$dsp^2$ hybridisation.

**7. (3)**

In option (3) C—Cl bond is shortest due to resonance of lone pair of —Cl.

Due to resonance C—Cl bond acquire partial double bond character.

Hence C—Cl bond length is least.

**8. (4)** $KMnO_4$ will not give satisfactory result when it is titrated by HCl.

**9. (1)**

I — CH₃, II — NO₂ (o=N<o), III — NH₂, IV — OCH₃ (all with OH)

BP value ≈ 202°C ≈ 279°C ≈ 284°C ≈ 243°C
from net

$BP \propto$ dipolement ($\mu$)

**Alternative Method :**

Increasing order of boiling point is :

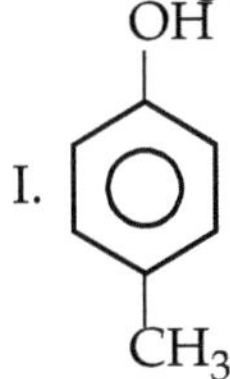

I.

Structure I shows hydrogen bonding from –O–H group only.

II.

Structure II shows strongest hydrogen bonding from both sides of –OH group as well as –NO₂ group.

III.

Structure III shows stronger hydrogen bonding from both side of –OH group as well as –NH₂ group.

IV.

Structure IV shows stronger hydrogen bonding from one side –OH–group and another side of –OCH₃ group shows only dipole-dipole interaction.

⇒ Hence correct order of boiling point is :

(I) < (IV) < (III) < (II)

**10. (2)** (1) $sp^3$, 104°5′

(2) $sp^3$, 109°28′

(3) $sp^3$, 107°

(4) 92°

**11. (1)**

Hydrogen peroxide, in the pure state, is non-planar and almost colourless (very pale blue) liquid.

**12.** Magnetic moment (in B.M.) of $[Ru(H_2O)_6]^{2+}$ would be; while considering that $\Delta_0 > P$,

$Ru_{(44)}$; $[Kr]4d^7 5s^1$(in ground state)

$\Rightarrow$ In $Ru^{2+} \Rightarrow 4d^6 \Rightarrow (t_2g)^6(eg)^0$

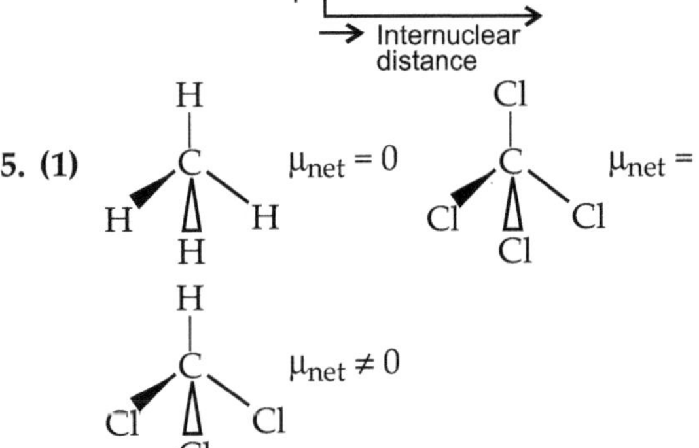

$\Rightarrow$ Here number of unpaired electrons in

$Ru^{2+} = (t_2g)^6 (eg)^0 = 0$ and Hence

$\mu_m = \sqrt{n(n+2)}$ B.M. $= 0$ B.M.

**13.** Only polar molecules in the liquid form will be attracted/deflected near charged comb.

**Polar molecules :** HF, $H_2O$, $NH_3$, $H_2O_2$, $CHCl_3$, $C_6H_5Cl$ (6-polar molecules)

**Non-polar molecules :** $O_2$, $CCl_4$, $C_6H_6$ so there are 6 polar molecules which show deflection.

**14. (2)** Potential energy curve for $H_2$ molecule is.

**15. (1)**

$\mu_{net} = 0$

$\mu_{net} = 0$

$\mu_{net} \neq 0$

**16. (3)** Interionic/intermolecular forces are directly proportional to the charge on the species. As ions are charged species and dipoles are partially charged, therefore, the correct order is :

ion – ion > ion – dipole > dipole – dipole

**17. (4)**

(a)

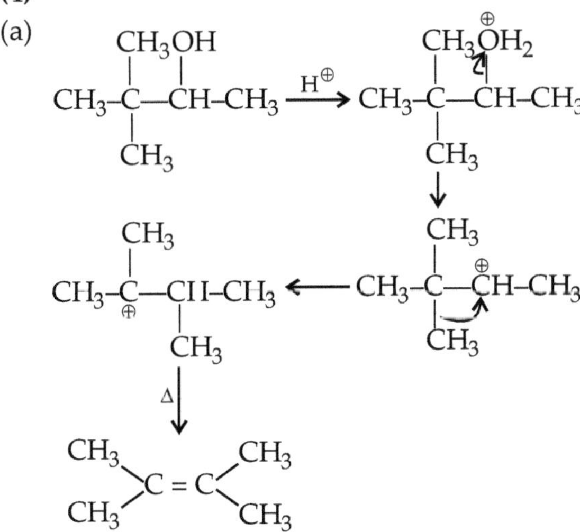

Saytzeff product

**(b)**

$$CH_3-\underset{\underset{CH_3Br}{|}}{CH}-\underset{\underset{CH_3}{|}}{CH}-CH_3 \xrightarrow[\Delta]{alc.\ KOH} CH_3-\underset{\underset{CH_3}{|}}{C}=CH-CH_3$$

(Saytzeff major)

**(c)**

Saytzeff product

$$CH_3-\underset{\underset{CH_3Br}{|}}{CH}-\overset{\beta}{\underset{}{CH}}-\overset{\alpha}{CH_3} \xrightarrow[\text{Bulky Base}]{t\text{-BuOK}^{\oplus}} CH_3-CH-CH-CH_2$$

$t$-BuO$^-$

$$\downarrow$$

$$CH_3-\underset{\underset{CH_3}{|}}{CH}-CH=CH_2$$

Non-Saytzeff product

**(d)**

$$CH_3-\underset{\underset{CH_3}{|}}{\overset{\overset{OH}{|}}{C}}-CH_2-\overset{\overset{O}{||}}{C}-H \xrightarrow{\Delta} \underset{CH_3}{\overset{CH_3}{>}}=CH-\overset{\overset{O}{||}}{C}-H$$

(Saytzeff major)

**18.** $3Cl_2 + 6NaOH \rightarrow 5NaCl + NaClO_3 + 3H_2O$

$\qquad\qquad\qquad\qquad\quad$ (X) $\qquad$ (Y)

$NaCl + AgNO_3 \rightarrow AgCl + NaNO_3$
(X) $\qquad\qquad$ (White ppt)

Y is $NaClO_3$

$$Na^+ \begin{bmatrix} \overset{\overset{\cdot\cdot}{Cl}}{} \\ O^- \overset{||}{O} O \end{bmatrix}$$

Bond order = Valency of the peripheral atom +(charge on acid radical/total number of peripheral atoms)

Bond order of Cl–O Bond $= 1 + \dfrac{2}{3} = \dfrac{5}{3}$

$\qquad\qquad\qquad\qquad = 1.66$ or $1.67$

**19. (3)** Bond length order in carbon halogen bonds are in the order of $C - F < C - Cl < C - Br < C - I$

Hence, Bond energy order
$C - F > C - Cl > C - Br > C - I$

**20. (1)**

| Number of unpaired electron | | Magnetic moment |
|---|---|---|
| $O_2^-$ | 1 | 1.73 B.M |
| $O_2^+$ | 1 | 1.73 B.M |
| $O_2$ | 2 | 2.83 B.M |

**21. (3)** Ethyl acetate $\left( H_5C-\overset{\overset{\parallel}{O}}{C}-O-CH_2-CH_3 \right)$

polar molecule. Hence, the predominant intermolecular forces present in it are dipole-dipole attraction and london dispersion forces.

**22. (4)** $:\overset{\frown}{\underset{\cdot\cdot}{Cl}} \overset{\curvearrowright}{} CH = CH \overset{\frown}{} N \overset{\overset{O}{\diagup}}{\diagdown O}$

Due to –m effect of –$NO_2$ and +m effect of Cl the double bond character between C – Cl bond is maximum and bond length is shortest.

The resonance form of Cl–CH=CH–$NO_2$ is given below :

$:\overset{\frown}{\underset{\cdot\cdot}{Cl}} CH=CH-\overset{\oplus}{N}\overset{\overset{O}{\diagup}}{\underset{O^{\ominus}}{}} \rightleftharpoons \overset{\oplus}{Cl}=CH-\overset{\ominus}{CH}-\overset{\oplus}{N}\overset{\overset{O}{\diagup}}{\underset{O^{\ominus}}{}}$

$\Updownarrow$

$\overset{\oplus}{Cl}=CH-CH=\overset{\oplus}{N}\overset{\overset{O^{\ominus}}{\diagup}}{\underset{O^{\ominus}}{}}$

**23. (4)**

Each carbon atom in benzene ring is $sp^2$ hybridized as it forms three sigma bonds and one pie bond.

Therefore each carbon has 3 $sp^2$ hybrid orbitals.

Hence, total $sp^2$ hybrid orbitals are 18.

**24.**

Chromate $\qquad\qquad$ Dichromate
$CrO_4^{2-}$ $\qquad\qquad\qquad$ $Cr_2O_7^{2-}$

Total Cr-O bonds = 6 $\quad$ Total Cr-O bonds = 12
$\quad$ ($4\sigma + 2\pi$) $\qquad\qquad$ ($8\sigma + 4\pi$)

Total number of bonds between chromium and oxygen in both structures are 18.

**Note :** But answer of NTA is 12. They consider only linkages between Chromium and Oxygen but in question total no. of bonds are asked so $\sigma$ and $\pi$ bonds must be considered separately.

**25. (3)** $CN^-$ has 14 electron.

$CN^- : \sigma_{1s}^2, \sigma_{1s}^{*2}, \sigma_{2s}^2, \sigma_{2s}^{*2}, \pi_{2p_x}^2 = \pi_{2p_y}^2, \sigma_{2p_z}^2$

Bond order $= \dfrac{N_b - N_a}{2} = 3 C^- \equiv N$

$CN^-$ is diamagnetic as all the electrons are paired.

**26. (4)** The electronic configuration of $C_2^{2-}$ is shown below :

$(\sigma_{1s})^2 (\sigma_{1s}^*)^2 (\sigma_{2s})^2 (\sigma_{2s}^*)^2 (\pi_{2p_x}^2 \pi_{2p_y}^2)(\sigma_{2p_z})^2$

The ion $C_2^{2-}$ does not possess any unpaired electron, therefore, it is diamagnetic.

The bond order is calculated as shown below :

$$\text{B.O.} = \frac{N_b - N_a}{2}$$
$$= \frac{10 - 4}{2}$$
$$= 3$$

The electronic configuration of $N_2^{2-}$ is shown below :

$$(\sigma_{1s})^2(\sigma_{1s}^*)^2(\sigma_{2s})^2(\sigma_{2s}^*)^2(\pi_{2p_x}^2\,\pi_{2p_y}^2)(\sigma_{2p_z})^2$$
$$(\pi_{2p_x}^{*1}\,\pi_{2p_y}^{*1})$$

The ion $N_2^{2-}$ possesses two unpaired electrons, therefore, it is paramagnetic.
The bond order is calculated as shown below :

$$\text{B.O.} = \frac{N_b - N_a}{2}$$
$$= \frac{10 - 6}{2}$$
$$= 2$$

The electronic configuration of $O_2$ is shown below :

$$(\sigma_{1s})^2(\sigma_{1s}^*)^2(\sigma_{2s})^2(\sigma_{2s}^*)^2(\sigma_{2p_z})^2(\pi_{2p_x}^2\,\pi_{2p_y}^2)$$
$$(\pi_{2p_x}^{*1}\,\pi_{2p_y}^{*1})$$

The molecule $O_2$ possesses two unpaired electrons, therefore, it is paramagnetic.
The bond order is calculated as shown below :

$$\text{B.O.} = \frac{N_b - N_a}{2}$$
$$= \frac{10 - 6}{2}$$
$$= 2$$

The electronic configuration of $O_2^{2-}$ is shown below :

$$(\sigma_{1s})^2(\sigma_{1s}^*)^2(\sigma_{2s})^2(\sigma_{2s}^*)^2(\sigma_{2p_z})^2(\pi_{2p_x}^2\,\pi_{2p_y}^2)$$
$$(\pi_{2p_x}^{*2}\,\pi_{2p_y}^{*2})$$

The ion $O_2^{2-}$ does not possess any unpaired electron, therefore, it is diamagnetic.
The bond order is calculated as shown below :

$$\text{B.O.} = \frac{N_b - N_a}{2}$$
$$= \frac{10 - 8}{2}$$
$$= 1$$

The bond order is inversely proportional to bond length. Therefore, the ion that is diamagnetic and possesses the shortest bond length is $C_2^{2-}$.

**27. (1)** Hybridization is a process that determines the shape and geometry of a molecule. The steric number is one of the way to determine the hybridization of a molecule. It can be calculated using the formula given below :

$$X = 1/2\,(V + M - C + A)$$

Where, V = number of valence electron s of the central atom

M = number of monovalent groups
C = number of positive charges
A = number of negative charges
The steric number of $[ICl_4]^-$ is calculated as

$$= \frac{1}{2} \times (7 + 4 + 0 + 1)$$

$$= 6$$

The steric number of $[ICl_4]^-$ is 6, hence, the hybridisation is $sp^3d^2$.

**28. (1)** The electronic configuration of $C_2$ is shown below :

$$(\sigma_{1s})^2(\sigma_{1s}^*)^2(\sigma_{2s})^2(\sigma_{2s}^*)^2(\pi_{2p_x}^2\,\pi_{2p_y}^2)(\sigma_{2p_z})^0$$

The extra electron will enter in bonding orbital. Therefore, the stability of the molecule will not change. In case of $O_2$, NO and $F_2$ extra electron will enter in antibonding orbital and the anion will not be stable. Therefore, $C_2$ will make a stablised anion.

**29. (3)** There is a high electronegativity difference between H and F in HF molecule due to which they are connected to each other through strong intermolecular hydrogen bonding.
The hydrogen bonding between the atoms of HF is shown below :

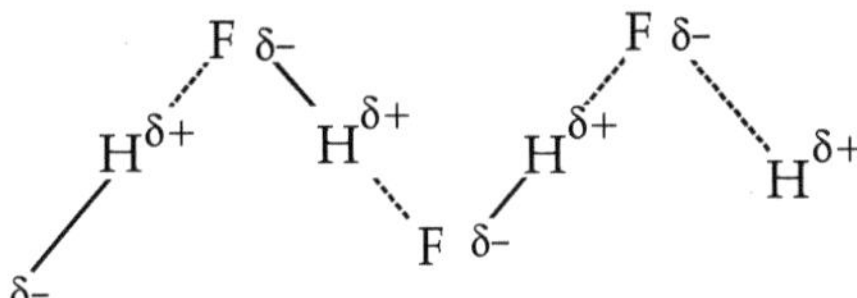

Due to the strong intermolecular hydrogen bonding the boiling point of HF is higher than other hydrogen halides because it forms strong hydrogen bond and other hydrogen halides does not form hydrogen bonds.

**30. (2)** The electronic configuration of NO is shown below :

$$(\sigma_{1s})^2(\sigma_{1s}^*)^2(\sigma_{2s})^2(\sigma_{2s}^*)^2(\sigma_{2p_z})^2(\pi_{2p_x}^2\,\pi_{2p_y}^2)$$
$$(\pi_{2p_x}^*\,\pi_{2p_y}^*)$$

The electronic configuration of CO is shown below :

$$(\sigma_{1s})^2(\sigma_{1s}^*)^2(\sigma_{2s})^2(\sigma_{2s}^*)^2(\sigma_{2p_z})^2(\pi_{2p_x}^2\,\pi_{2p_y}^2)$$

The electronic configuration of $B_2$ is shown below :

$$(\sigma_{1s})^2(\sigma_{1s}^*)^2(\sigma_{2s})^2(\sigma_{2s}^*)^2(\pi_{2p_x}^1\,\pi_{2p_y}^1)(\sigma_{2p_z})^0$$

The electronic configuration of $O_2$ is shown below :

$$(\sigma_{1s})^2(\sigma_{1s}^*)^2(\sigma_{2s})^2(\sigma_{2s}^*)^2(\sigma_{2p_z})^2(\pi_{2p_x}^2\,\pi_{2p_y}^2)$$
$$(\pi_{2p_x}^{*1}\,\pi_{2p_y}^{*1})$$

Carbon monoxide does not have any unpaired electron in its molecular orbital. Therefore, CO is a diamagnetic compound.

**31. (3)** The molecular orbital diagram of $O_2$ is given below :

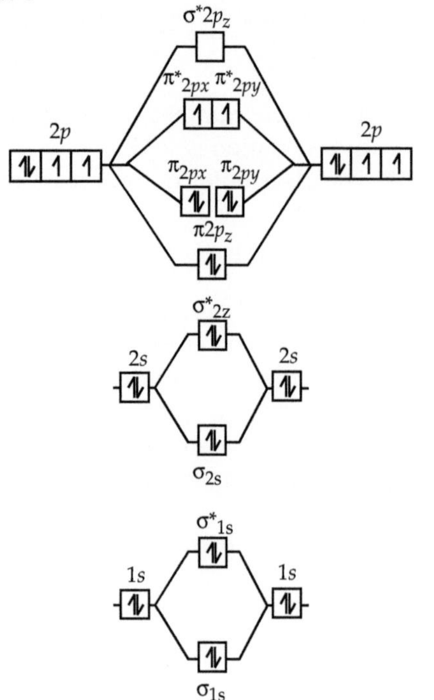

During the change of $O_2$ to $O_2^-$, the incoming electron will enter $\pi^*2p_x$ orbital.

**32. (2, 4)**

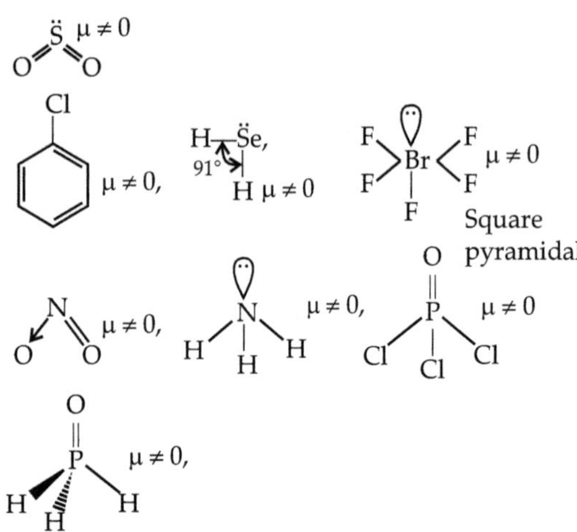

**33. (4)** The electronic configuration of $H_2^{2-}$ is

$$H_2^{2-} = \sigma_{1s^2}\sigma^*_{1s_2}$$

The bond order of $H_2^{2-}$ molecule is calculated as,

$$\text{Bond order of } H_2^{2-} = \frac{1}{2}(2-2)$$
$$= 0$$

According to the molecular orbital diagram of $H_2^{2-}$, the bond order of $H_2^{2-}$ molecule is

zero. Therefore, this molecule is too unstable and is not viable according to molecular orbital theory.

**34. (4)** An antibonding pi orbital describes the diagram of molecular orbital in which two orbitals overlap sideways to form pi bond.

The given combination of these two $p$-orbitals, give $\pi^*$ molecular orbital.

So, diagram describes an antibonding pi orbital.

**35. (2)** The molecular orbital diagram of $N_2^+$ is shown below :

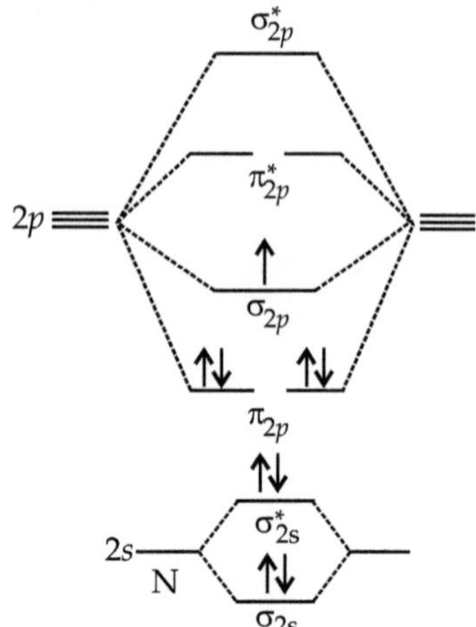

The number electrons in the $\sigma_{2p}$ is 1.

**36. (1)** The resonance structure of hydrogen azide is shown below :

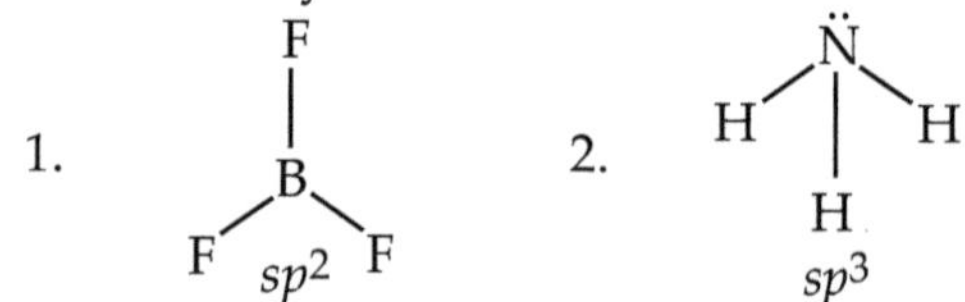

The bond orders of (I) is $< 2$ and of (II) is $> 2$ as shown in the above figure.

**37. (2)** The bond angles of $BF_3$, $NH_3$, $PF_3$ and $I_3^-$ and with their hybridization are shown below :

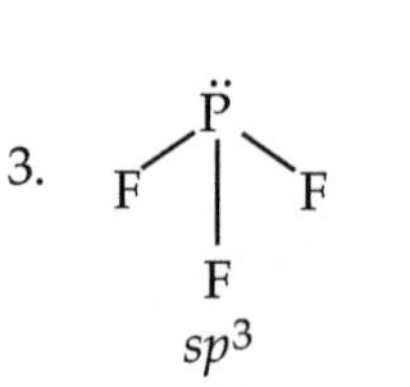

Between $NH_3$ and $PF_3$, bond angle of $NH_3$ is greater because when the size of the central atom increases, its bond angle decreases. Therefore, the decreasing order of bond angle is,

$$I_3^- > BF_3 > NH_3 > PF_3$$

**38. (3)** In $NF_3$ molecule, nitrogen atom has alone pair and three bond pairs of electrons. Thus, $NF_3$ is $sp^3$ hybridised and possesses trigonal pyramidal geometry, not trigonal planar.

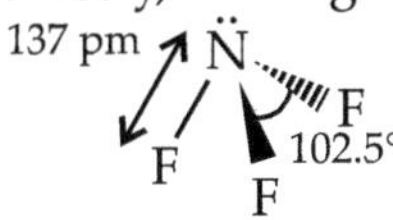


**39. (4)** The conversion of BF3 ® $BF_4^-$ involves change in both shape and hybridisation. BF3 is trigonal planar with $sp^2$ hybridisation whereas $BF_4^-$ is tetrahedral with $sp^3$ hybridisation. Their geometry can be represented as :

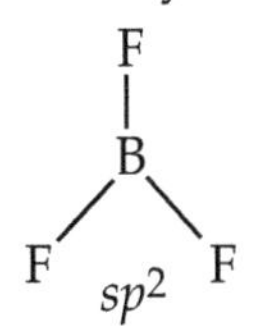
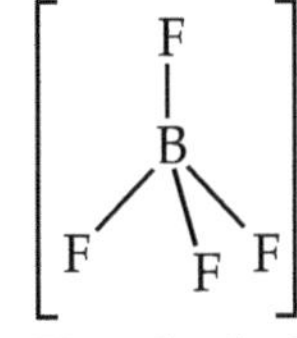


Trigonal planar          Tetrahedral

**40. (3, 4)** Physical state of $X_2$ molecules of group 17 elements changes from gas to solid at room temperature on moving down the group but this is not responsible for change in the color. Similarly, their ionization energy also decreases down the group but again this is not responsible for change in their color.

Pi antibonding orbital to sigma antibonding orbital gap decreases down the group. This is responsible for the change in color. In other words, highest occupied molecular orbital (HOMO) to lowest unoccupied molecular orbital (LUMO) gap decreases down the group and it is responsible for the color change. It is shown as for $F_2$,

$$[Ne]\pi 2p_x^2 = \pi 2p_y^2 (\pi^* 2p_x^2 = \pi^* 2p_y^2)$$

$$(HOMO), \ \sigma^* 2p_z^0 (LUMO)$$

From the above configuration it is clear that the transition from HOMO to LUMO are responsible for color change in halogen molecules.

**41.** Molecular electronic configuration of all the species is given as,

$$H_2 = \sigma 1s^2$$

$$He_2^+ = \sigma 1s^2, \sigma^* 1s^1$$

$$Li_2 = \sigma 1s^2, \sigma^* 1s^2, \sigma 2s^2$$

$$Be_2 = \sigma 1s^2, \sigma^* 1s^2, \sigma 2s^2, \sigma^* 2s^2$$

$$B_2 = \sigma 1s^2, \sigma^* 1s^2, \sigma 2s^2, \sigma^* 2s^2, \pi 2p_x^1, \pi 2p_y^1$$

$$C_2 = \sigma 1s^2, \sigma^* 1s^2, \sigma 2s^2, \sigma^* 2s^2, \pi 2p_x^2, \pi 2p_y^2$$

$$N_2 = \sigma 1s^2, \sigma^* 1s^2, \sigma 2s^2, \sigma^* 2s^2, \pi 2p_x^2, \pi 2p_y^2, \sigma 2p_z^2$$

$$O_2^- : \sigma 1s^2, \sigma^* 1s^2, \sigma 2s^2, \sigma^* 2s^2, \pi 2p_z^2, \pi 2p_x^2,$$
$$\pi 2p_y^2, \pi^* 2p_x^2, \pi^* 2p_y^1$$

$$F_2 = \sigma 1s^2, \sigma^* 1s^2, \sigma 2s^2, \sigma^* 2s^2, \sigma 2p_z^2, \pi 2p_x^2,$$
$$\pi 2p_y^2, \pi^* 2p_x^2, \pi^* 2p_y^2$$

With help of above configuration bond order is to be calculated by the given formula,

$$\text{Bond order} = \frac{\text{Bonding orbital} - \text{antibonding orbital}}{2}$$

If the value of bond order is even then the molecule is diamagnetic otherwise paramagnetic. Therefore, out of the given species, only $B_2$, $He_2^+$ and $O_2^-$ are paramagnetic in nature whereas rest are diamagnetic in nature.

**42. (4)** (1) The total number of electrons in $O_2$ is 16 (even), but it is paramagnetic because it consists of two unpaired electrons in molecular orbitals $\pi^* 2p_x$ and $\pi^* 2p_y$.
(2) The total number of electrons in $B_2$ is (even), but it is paramagnetic because it consists of two unpaired electrons in molecular orbitals $\pi 2p_x$ and $\pi 2p_y$.
(3) The total number of electrons in NO is 15 (odd). It is paramagnetic because it has one unpaired electron in $\pi^* 2p$ molecular orbital.
(4) The total number of electrons in CO is 14 (even). It is diamagnetic.

**43. (4)** According to molecular orbital theory, the electronic configuration of the given species is shown below.
$$B_2 = 10$$
$$= \sigma(1s)^2 \ \sigma^*(1s)^2 \ \sigma(2s)^2 \ \sigma^*(2s)^2 \ (\pi 2p_x)^1 \ (\pi 2p_y)^1$$
The molecule $B_2$ contains two unpaired electrons. Thus, it is paramagnetic.

**44. (4)** The compound $PF_5$ shows $sp^3 d$ hybridisation instead of $sp^3 d^2$ hybridisation . The central P atom has 5 sets of bonding electron pairs which corresponds to sp3d hybridisation. Its structure is shown below :

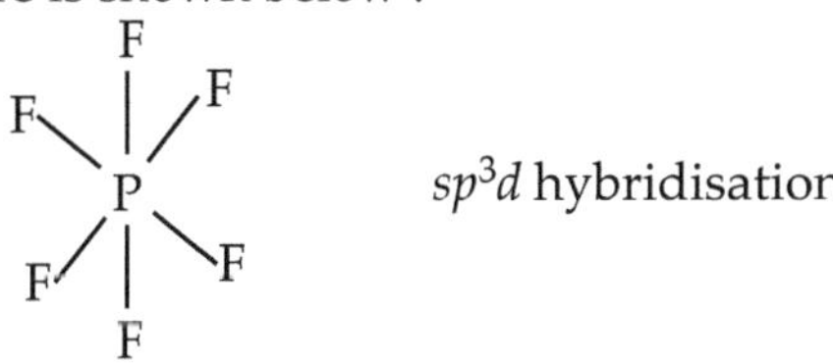


**45. (2)** The central atoms in $CO_3^{2-}$, $NO_3^-$ and $SO_3$ are $sp^2$ hybridised with triangular planar molecular geometry.

The molecular geometries of $CO_3^{2-}$, $NO_3^-$ and $SO_3$ are shown below.

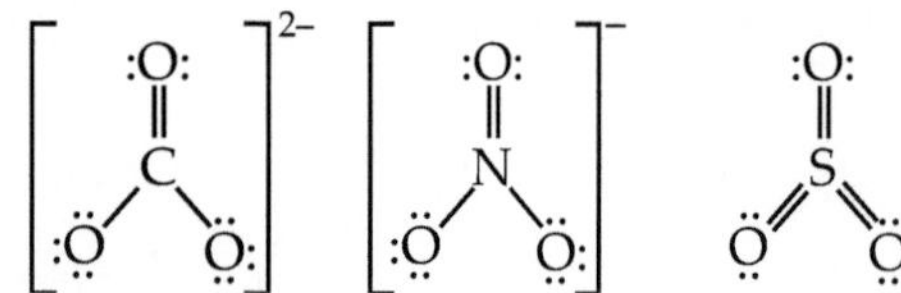

**46. (1, 3)** (1) In $C_2^{2-}$, total number of electrons is 14 and all are paired. So, it is diamagnetic.

(2) In $O_2^{2+}$, bond order is 3 and in $O_2$ bond order is 2.

Therefore, bond length in $O_2^{2+}$ is less than the bond length in $O_2$.

(3) Bond order of $N_2^{2+}$ and $N_2^{2-}$ is 2.5. So, both have same bond order.

(4) Energy is released during the formation of $He_2^{2+}$ from two isolated helium atoms. So $He_2^{2+}$ does not have same energy as two isolated helium atoms.

Thus, the correct statements are (1) and (3).

**47. (1)** The bond angle value of $CH_4$ is 109°28, whereas for $PH_3$, $NH_3$ and $H_2O$ are 98°, 107° and 104.5° respectively.

**48. (3)** Water possess intermolecular hydrogen bonding in the condensed phase.

**49.** The total number of lone pairs of electrons present in $N_2O_3$ is 8 as shown below :

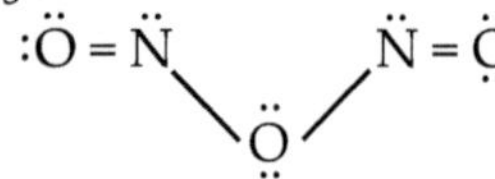

**50.** The linear molecules/ions that does not involve *d*-orbital in their hybdridization are $BeCl_2$, $N_3^-$, $N_2O$ and $NO_2^+$. The hybridisation of these molecules/ions is *sp*. Thus, among the given molecules/ions, only 4 molecules/ions does not have contribution from *d*-orbital. Among the remaining molecules/ions, $SCl_2$ is V shaped with $sp^3$ hybridization, $O_3$ is bent, $ICl_2^-$, $I_3^-$ and $XeF_2$, are linear with $sp^3d$ hybridization.

**51. (2, 3)** The number of lone pairs in $HClO_2$ and $HClO_3$ is

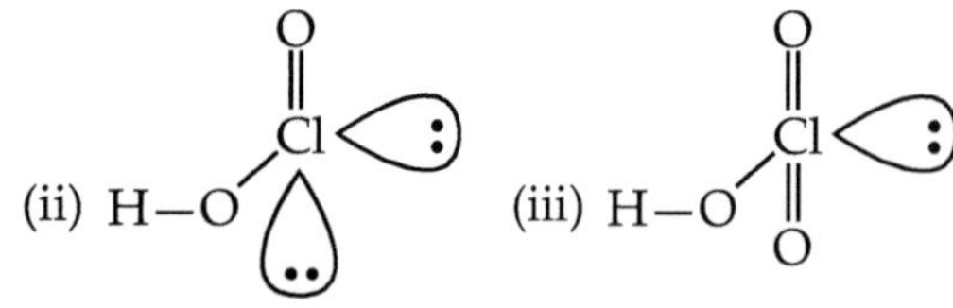

The total lone pairs on chlorine in $HClO_2$ and $HClO_3$ together is $2 + 1 = 3$.

The hybridisation of Cl in $HClO_4$ is $sp^3$ which means that there are four bonding domains and zero lone pair of electrons.

**52. (4)** Hydrogen bond comes in the category of dipole-dipole interaction. It is dependent on the inverse cube of distance between molecules.

**53. (3)** The electron density between the nuclei, in the bonding molecular orbital of $H_2$, is increased due to constructive interference of the combining electron waves.

**54. (2)** The conversion of units of bond length is shown below :

$$1.617 \text{ Å} = 1.617 \times 10^{-8} \text{ cm}$$

The conversion of units of dipole moment is shown below :

$$0.38 \times 10^{-18} \text{ D} = 0.38 \times 10^{-18} \text{ esu cm}$$

The fractional charge on each atom is calculated by the formula,

$$\delta = \frac{\text{dipole moment}}{\text{Bond length} \times e_0}$$

$$= \frac{0.38 \times 10^{-18} \text{ esu cm}}{1.617 \times 10^{-8} \text{ cm} \times 4.802 \times 10^{-10} \text{ esu}}$$

$$= \frac{0.38 \times 10^{-18}}{7.765 \times 10^{-18}}$$

$$= 0.0489 \approx 0.05$$

**55. (1,2,4)** (A) Ice floats in water due to the presence of intermolecular hydrogen bonding that results in the formation of cage like structure. In this cage like structure, each water molecule is surrounded tetrahedrally by four other water molecules through hydrogen bonding. The effective volume increases and ice floats in water.

(B) In aqueous solution, primary amines show higher Lewis basicity than tertiary amines because they undergo more hydration as compared to tertiary amines.

(C) Formic acid is stronger acid than acetic acid due to the presence of electron donating methyl group in acetic acid. Methyl group shows +I effect.

(D) Dimerisation of acetic acid results through intermolecular hydrogen bonding.

**56. (3)** The molecular orbital configuration of $C_2$ is

$$\sigma_{1s}^2 \, \sigma_{1s}^{*2} \, \sigma_{2s}^2 \, \sigma_{2s}^{*2} \, \sigma_{2s}^{*2} \, \sigma_{2pz}^2 \, \pi_{2px}^1 \, \pi_{2py}^1$$

There are two unpaired electrons in $\pi_{2px}$ and $\pi_{2py}$ orbitals. Therefore, it is paramagnetic.

**57. (3)** The correct match is shown below :

P = 2, Due to linear combination of atomic orbitals of *d-d* σ bonding.

Q = 3, Due to linear combination of atomic orbitals of *p-d* π bonding.

R = 1, Due to linear combination of atomic orbitals of *p-d* π antibonding.

S = 4, Due to linear combination of atomic orbitals of *d-d* σ antibonding.

**58. (2)** The molecule of $O_2^-$ possesses one unpaired electron in $\pi^*$ molecular orbital as shown below :

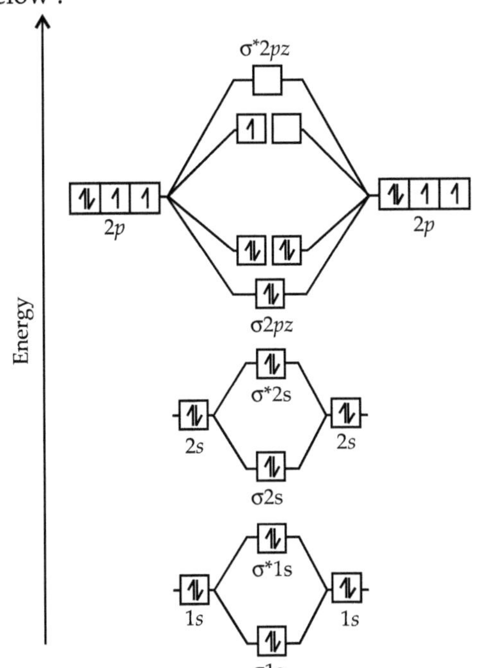


**59. (2)** The dicarbide ion, $C_2^{2-}$ in $CaC_2$ contains one $\sigma$ bond and two $\pi$ bonds as shown below :

$$Ca^{2+} \, [C \equiv C]^{-2}$$

**60. (3)** The bond dissociation energy is directly proportional to bond order. The value of bond order for the given species is :

$N_2 \to 3$

$O_2 \to 2$

$O_2^- \to 1.5$

Therefore, the correct order of bond dissociation energy is $N_2 > O_2 > O_2^-$.

**61. (2)** $(SiH_3)_3N$ does not have a pyramidal shape. It possesses trigonal planar shape. This is due to the presence of vacant $d$ orbitals in silicon which allows $p\pi$–$d\pi$ bonding in $(SiH_3)_3N$. Hybridisation of nitrogen is sp$^2$ in $(SiH_3)_3N$.

**62. (2)** In allene $(C_3H_4)$, the terminal carbon atoms are $sp^2$ hybridised while central carbon atom is sp hybridised. Its structure is shown below :

$$\overset{H}{\underset{H}{\diagdown}} \overset{sp^2}{C} = \overset{sp}{C} = \overset{sp^2}{C} \overset{H}{\underset{H}{\diagup}}$$

**63. (2)** The electronic configuration of NO molecule is :

$$(\sigma_{1s^2})(\sigma^*_{1s^2})(\sigma_{2s^2})(\sigma^*_{2s^2})(\pi_{2p_x^2})(\pi_{2p_y^2})(\pi_{2p_z^2})(\pi^*_{2p_x^1})$$

The NO molecule contains one unpaired electron. Thus, it is paramagnetic.

**64. (2)** In $BeCl_2$ beryllium exists as $Be^{2+}$ and in $RbCl$ rubidium exist as $Rb^+$. $Be^{2+}$ is a cation that is small in size and has large charge. On the contrary, $Rb^+$ is large in size and has small charge. According to Fajan's rule,

A cation with small size and large charge possesses greater covalent character.

A cation with large size and small charge possesses greater ionic character.

Thus, RbCl is most ionic in nature wheras $BeCl_2$ is least ionic.

**65. (1)** The hyperconjugative stabilities of tert-butyl cation and 2-butene are due to σ to π and σ to $\pi^*$ delocalisation of electrons respectively.

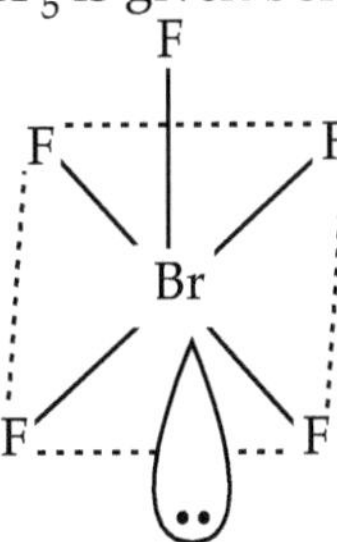


**66.** According to VSPER theory, there are total six electron pairs around bromine atom. Five are bond pairs and one is lone pair.

The structure of $BrF_5$ is given below.

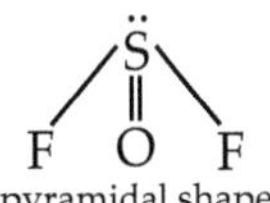


There are bond pair-lone pair repulsion present in $BrF_5$, due to which F–Br–F bond angle is reduced from 90° to 84.8°.

**67. (4)** Pyramidal shape arises due to $sp^3$ hybridisation.

In $OSF_2$, sulphur has a lone pair of electrons on top, three downward legs of the pyramid are bonded to each flourine with a single bond and to the oxygen atom with a double bond.



**68. (1)** According to the Hund's rule, if two or more orbitals of equal energy are available, electrons will occupy them singly before filling them in pairs. The total number of electrons in $B_2$ is 10.

If Hund's rule is violated then the electronic configuration of $B_2$ according to the given condition is,

$$(\sigma 1s^2),\ (\sigma^* 1s^2),\ (\sigma 2s^2)(\sigma^* 2s^2),\ \pi 2p_x^2 = \pi 2p_y^0$$

Bond order is calculated as :

$$= \frac{\begin{pmatrix} \text{No. of electrons} \\ \text{in bonding} \\ \text{orbitals} \end{pmatrix} - \begin{pmatrix} \text{No. of electrons} \\ \text{in anti-bonding} \\ \text{orbitals} \end{pmatrix}}{2}$$

$$= \frac{6-4}{2}$$

$$= 1$$

As there are no unpaired electrons, it is dimagnetic, and bond order is 1.

**69.** (1)-(p), (r), (t); (2)-(s), (t); (3)-(p), (q); and (4)-(p), (q), (s).

The electronic configuration of the given compounds is,

$$B_2 = (\sigma_{2s}^2)(\sigma_{2s}^{*2})(\pi_{2p_x}^1)(\pi_{2p_y}^1)$$

$$N_2 = (\sigma_{2s}^2)(\sigma_{2s}^{*2})(\pi_{2p_x}^2)(\pi_{2p_y}^2)(\sigma_{2p_x}^2)$$

$$O_2 = (\sigma_{2s}^2)(\sigma_{2s}^{*2})(\pi_{2p_x}^2)(\pi_{2p_y}^2)(\sigma_{2p_z}^2)(\pi_{2p_x}^{*1})(\pi_{2p_y}^{*1})$$

$$O_2^- = (\sigma_{2s}^2)(\sigma_{2s}^{*2})(\pi_{2p_x}^2)(\pi_{2p_y}^2)(\sigma_{2p_z}^2)(\pi_{2p_x}^{*1})(\pi_{2p_x}^{*1})$$

The unpaired electrons present in the compounds $B_2$, $O_2$ and $O_2^-$. Therefore, they are paramagnetic. $B_2$ undergoes reduction due to the presence of unpaired electrons in its outermost shell. $N_2$ neither undergoes oxidation nor reduction because it has fully filled electronic configuration. $O_2$ and $O_2^-$ undergo oxidation due to the presence of two unpaired electrons in antibonding pi orbital.

The bond order is equal to or more than 2 in case of $N_2$ and $O_2$ because triple bond is present in $N_2$ and double bond in $O_2$. On the other hand only single bond is present in the diatomic molecules and $B_2$ and $O_2^-$.

The mixing of $s$ and $p$ orbitals is possible in the $B_2$ and $N_2$ because they have less effective nuclear charge as compared to $O_2$ and $O_2^-$.

**70.** **(1)** The bond order of a species is calculated by the formula,

$$\text{Bond order} = \frac{N_b - N_a}{2}$$

The electronic configuration of $NO^-$ is,

$$\sigma_{1s}^2 \sigma_{1s}^{*2} \sigma_{2s}^2 \sigma_{2s}^{*2} \sigma_{2p_z}^2 \sigma_{2p_x}^2 \sigma_{2p_y}^2 \sigma_{2p_x}^{*2} \pi_{2p_y}^1$$

In $NO^-$ there are 10 bonding electrons ($N_b$) and 6 antibonding electrons ($N_a$).
Thus, the bond order of $NO^-$ is :

$$\text{Bond order} = \frac{10-6}{2}$$

$$= 2$$

The electronic configuration of CO is :

$$\sigma_{1s}^2 \sigma_{1s}^{*2} \sigma_{2s}^2 \sigma_{2s}^{*2} \pi_{2p_x}^2 \pi_{2p_y}^2 \sigma_{2p_z}^2$$

In CO there are 10 bonding electrrons ($N_b$) and 4 antibonding electrons ($N_b$). Thus, the bond order of CO is,

$$\text{Bond order} = \frac{10-4}{2}$$

$$= 3$$

Hence, the species that has different bond order from that in CO is $NO^-$.

**71.** **(4)** In $KO_2$ compound, $O_2$ exist as $O_2^-$. The electronic configuration of $O_2^-$ is,

$$\sigma_{1s}^2 \sigma_{1s}^{*2} \sigma_{2s}^2 \sigma_{2s}^{*2} \sigma_{2p_z}^2 \pi_{2p_x}^2 \pi_{2p_y}^2 \pi_{2px}^{*2} \pi_{2p_y}^{*1}$$

There is one unpaired electron in $O_2^-$. Therefore, it is paramagnetic.
Hence, the paramagnetic compound is $KO_2$.

**72.** **(1)** The $B^{3+}$ ion is a cation and has high charge. Its size is also small.
According to Fajan's rule, a cation that contains high charge and small size possesses large polarization power and large covalent character. So, boron forms covalent bond.

**73.** The structures of given molecules are shown below :
The two molecules are not iso-structural as $N(Me)_3$ is trigonal planar whereas $N(SiMe_3)_3$ is trigonal pyramidal. The difference in structures is due to the presence of back bonding in $N(SiMe_3)_3$.

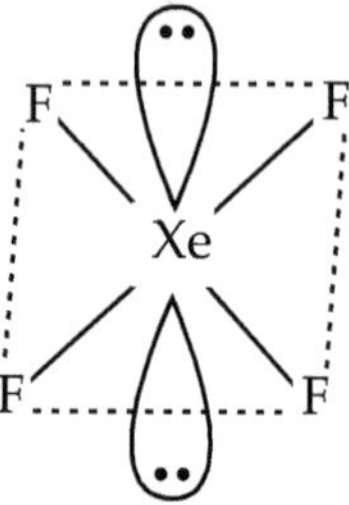

**74.** According to VSEPR theory, the hybridisation of $XeF_4$ is $sp^3d^2$, whereas the hybridisation of $OsF_4$ is $sp^3d$. The geometry of $XeF_4$ is square planar as shown below :

The geometry of $OsF_4$ is trigonal bipyramidal as shown below :

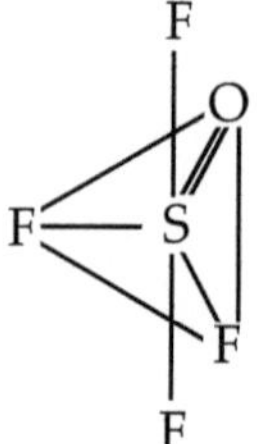

**75.** The formula to calculate bond order is,

$$\text{Bond order} = \frac{\text{Bonding electrons} - \text{antibonding electrons}}{2}$$

The number of bonding and antibonding electrons present in $O_2$ are 10 and 6.

Thus, the bond order for $O_2$ is,

$$\text{Bond order} = \frac{10-6}{2}$$

$$= 2$$

In $KO_2$ compound, $O_2$ exist as $O_2^-$. The number of bonding and antibonding electrons present in $O_2^-$ are 10 and 7. Thus, the bond order for $O_2^-$ is 1.5.

In $AsF_6$ compound, $O_2$ exist as $O_2^+$. The number of bonding and antibonding electrons present in $O_2^+$ are 10 and 5. Thus, the bond order for $O_2^+$ is 2.5.

The relationship between bond order and bond length is as follows :

$$\text{Bond order} \propto \frac{1}{\text{Bond length}}$$

Therefore, the increasing order of bond length will be,

$$O_2^+ < O_2 < O_2^-$$

**76. (1)** The bond order is calculated by the formula

$$\text{Bond order} = \frac{1}{2}\ [\text{number of bonding}$$

electrons – number of antibonding electrons]

The number of bonding electrons and antibonding electrons in $O_2^+$ are 10 and 5, respectively.

The bond order of $O_2^+$ is :

$$\text{Bond order} = \frac{1}{2}[10-5]$$

$$= 2.5$$

The number of bonding electrons and antibonding electrons in $O_2$ are 10 and 6, respectively.

The bond order of $O_2$ is

$$\text{Bond order} = \frac{1}{2}[10-6]$$

$$= 2$$

In a $O_2^+$ molecule, there are total 15 electrons. The moleculr orbital configuration $O_2^+$ is as follows :

$$\sigma_{1s^2}\overset{*}{\sigma}_{1s^2}\sigma_{2s^2}\overset{*}{\sigma}_{2s^2}\sigma_{2p_x^2}\pi_{2p_x^2}\pi_{2p_y^2}\overset{*}{\pi}_{2p_x^1}\overset{*}{\pi}_{2p_y^0}$$

The electronic configuration of $O_2^+$ shows that it contains one unpaired electron in antibonding orbital, hence, it is paramagnetic.

**77.** According to VSEPR theory, the hybridisation of $PCl_5$ is $sp^3d$, whereas the hybridisation of

$BrF_5$ is $sp^3d_2$. The geometry of $PCl_5$ is trigonal bipyramidal as shown below :

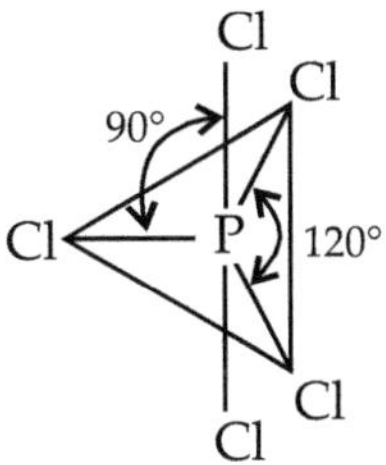


The geometry of $BrF_5$ is square pyramidal as shown below :

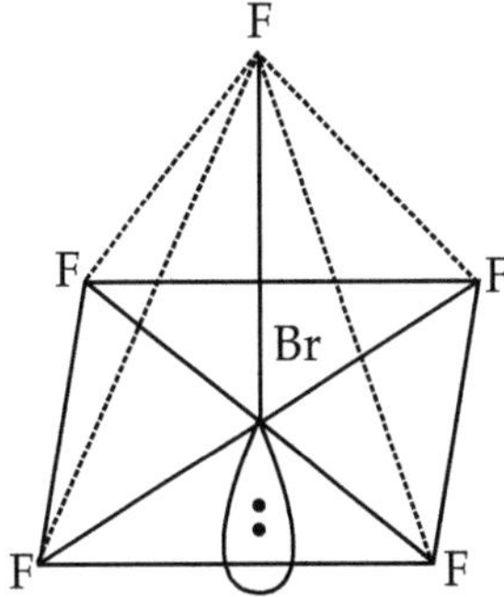


**78. (1)** The species $CO_3^{2-}$ and $NO_3^-$ are isoelectronic species among the given species because both of them have equal total number of electrons in their structure i.e., 32 electrons. Both these species contains three oxygen atoms around the central metal ion and possess trigonal planar geometry.

**79. (1)** In the compound $H_2C = CH - C \equiv N$,

The hybridisation of carbon atom in $CH_2$ is $sp^2$.

The hybridisation of carbon atom in $CH$ is $sp^2$.

The hybridisation of carbon atom in C is $sp$.

The hybridisation of carbon atom in N is $sp$.

**80. (1)** The compounds, $NH_3$ and $BF_3$ behave as Lewis base and Lewis acid respectively due to which they form tetrahedral complex as shown below :



The above complex shows that both have tetrahedral geometry and $sp^3$ hybridization

**81. (3)** Out of all the given species unpaired electrons are present in antibonding molecular orbital of $O_2^-$.

It has 17 electrons and its molecular orbital configuration is :

$$\sigma_{1s^2}\overset{*}{\sigma}_{1s^2}, \sigma_{2s}^2\overset{*}{\sigma}_{2s^2}, \sigma_{2p_x^2}, \pi_{2p_y^2}, \pi_{2p_z^2}, \overset{''}{\pi}_{2p_y^2}, \overset{*}{\pi}_{2p_z^1}$$

●●

# | 8 | Thermodynamics

## ❓ QUESTIONS

1. The intermolecular potential energy for the molecules A, B, C and D given below suggests that : **[2020, Main]**

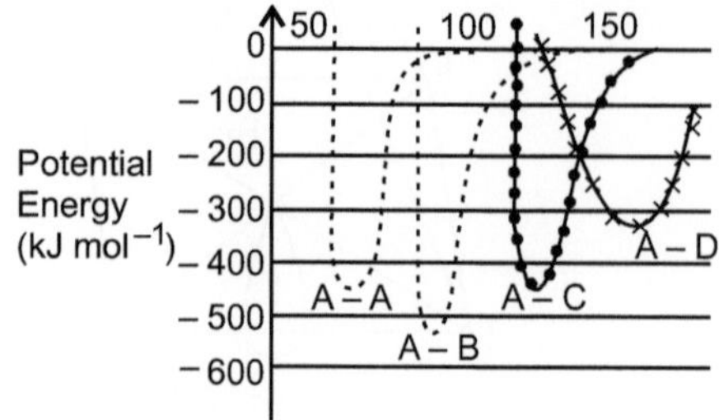



   (1) D is more electronegative than other atoms
   (2) A-D has the shortest bond length
   (3) A-B has the stiffest bond
   (4) A-A has the largest bond enthalpy

2. The internal energy change (in J) when 90 g of water undergoes complete evaporation at $100°C$ is ............... .
   (Given : $\Delta H_{vap}$ for water at 373 K = 41 kJ/mol, R = 8.314 $JK^{-1}mol^{-1}$) **[2020, Main]**

3. The heat of combustion of ethanol into carbon dioxide and water is − 327 kcal at constant pressure. The heat evolved (in cal) at constant volume and $27°C$ (if all gases behave ideally) is......
   (R = 2 cal $mol^{-1}$ $K^{-1}$) **[2020, Main]**

4. For the given cell :
   Cu(s) | $Cu^{2+}$ $(C_1M)$ | | $Cu^{2+}$ $(C_2M)$ | Cu(s) change in Gibbs energy $(\Delta G)$ is negative, if :
   **[2020, Main]**

   (1) $C_1 = 2C_2$
   (2) $C_2 = \dfrac{C_1}{\sqrt{2}}$
   (3) $C_1 = C_2$
   (4) $C_2 = \sqrt{2}C_1$

5. For a reaction,
   $$4M(s) + nO_2(g) \rightarrow 2M_2O_n(s),$$
   the free energy change is plotted as a function of temperature. The temperature below which the oxide is stable could be inferred from the plot as the point at which : **[2020, Main]**

   (1) the slope changes from positive to zero.
   (2) the free energy change shows a change from negative to positive value.
   (3) the slope changes from negative to positive.
   (4) the slope changes from positive to negative.

6. An Ellingham diagram provides information about : **[2020, Main]**
   (1) the pressure dependence of the standard electrode potentials of reduction reactions involved in the extraction of metals
   (2) the kinetics of the reduction process
   (3) the temperature dependence of the standard Gibbs energies of formation of some metal oxides
   (4) the conditions of pH and potential under which a species is thermodynamically stable

7. Five moles of an ideal gas at 1 bar and 298 K is expanded into vacuum to double the volume. The work done is : **[2020, Main]**
   (1) $C_V (T_2 - T_1)$
   (2) $- RT \ln V_2/V_1$
   (3) $- RT (V_2 - V_1)$
   (4) Zero

8. The process that is NOT endothermic in nature is : **[2020, Advanced]**
   (1) $Ar_{(g)} + e^- \rightarrow Ar_{(g)}^-$
   (2) $H_{(g)} + e^- \rightarrow H_{(g)}^-$
   (3) $Na_{(g)} \rightarrow Na_{(g)}^+ + e^-$
   (4) $O_{(g)}^- + e^- \rightarrow O_{(g)}^{2-}$

9. Lattice enthalpy and enthalpy of solution of NaCl are 788 kJ $mol^{-1}$ and 4 kJ $mol^{-1}$, respectively. The hydration enthalpy of NaCl is : **[2020, Main]**
   (1) − 780 kJ $mol^{-1}$
   (2) − 784 kJ $mol^{-1}$
   (3) 780 kJ $mol^{-1}$
   (4) 784 kJ $mol^{-1}$

10. For a dimerization reaction,
    $2A(g) \rightarrow A_2(g)$
    at 298 K, $\Delta U^{\ominus}$, = − 20 kJ $mol^{-1}$, $\Delta S^{\ominus}$ = − 30 J $K^{-1}$ $mol^{-1}$, then the $\Delta G^{\ominus}$ will be .............. J.
    **[2020, Main]**

11. In thermodynamics the P-V work done is given by
    $$w = -\int dV P_{ext}$$
    For a system undergoing a particular process, the work done is,
    $$w = -\int dV \left( \frac{RT}{V-b} - \frac{a}{V^2} \right)$$
    This equation is applicable to a **[2020, Advanced]**
    (1) System that satisfies the van der Waals equation of state.
    (2) Process that is reversible and isothermal.
    (3) Process that is reversible and adiabatic.
    (4) Process that is irreversible and at constant isothermal.

**12.** Consider the reaction $A \rightleftharpoons B$ at 1000 K. At time $t'$, the temperature of the system was increased to 2000 K and the system was allowed to reach equilibrium. Throughout this experiment the partial pressure of A was maintained at 1 bar. Given below is the plot of the partial pressure of B with time. What is the ratio of the standard Gibbs energy of the reaction at 1000 K to that at 2000 K ? **[2020, Advanced]**

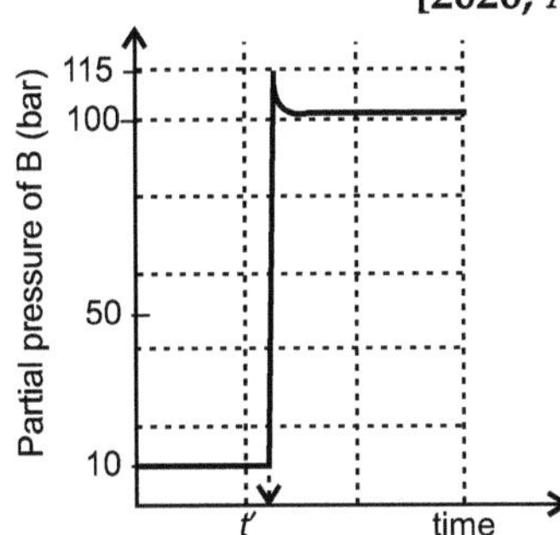



**13.** Consider a 70% efficient hydrogen-oxygen fuel cell working under standard conditions at 1 bar and 298 K. Its cell reaction is :

$$H_2(g) + \frac{1}{2}O_2(g) \rightarrow H_2O(l)$$

The work derived from the cell on the consumption of $1.0 \times 10^{-3}$ mol of $H_2(g)$ is used to compress 1.00 mol of a monoatomic ideal gas in a thermally insulated container. What is the change in the temperature (in K) of the ideal gas ?

The standard reduction potentials for the two half-cells are given below :

$O_2(g) + 4H^+ (aq.) + 4e^- \rightarrow 2H_2O\ (l)$, E° = 1.23 V,
$\quad\quad 2H^+ (aq.) + 2e^- \rightarrow H_2(g)$, E° = 0.00V
Use F = 96500 C mol$^{-1}$, R = 8.314 mol$^{-1}$ K$^{-1}$.

**[2020, Advanced]**

**14.** Tin is obtained from cassiterite by reduction with coke. Use the data given below to determine the minimum temperature (in K) at which the reduction of cassiterite by coke would take place.
At 298 K : $\Delta_f H°(SnO_2(s)) = -581.0$ kJ mol$^{-1}$,
$\Delta_f H°(CO_2(g)) = -394.0$ kJ mol$^{-1}$
$S° (SnO_2(s)) = 56.0$ J K$^{-1}$ mol$^{-1}$, S° (Sn(s)) = 52.0 J K$^{-1}$ mol$^{-1}$
$S° (C (s)) = 6.0$ J K$^{-1}$ mol$^{-1}$, S°(CO$_2$(g)) = 210.0 J K$^{-1}$ mol$^{-1}$.
Assume that the enthalpies and the entropies are temperature independent. **[2020, Advanced]**

**15.** Consider the reaction sequence given below :

$$\rightarrow\!-Br \xrightarrow[H_2O]{OH^\ominus} \rightarrow\!- OH + Br^\ominus \quad\quad ...(i)$$

$$rate = k[t\text{-BuBr}]$$

$$\xrightarrow[C_2H_5OH]{OH^\ominus} H_2C \!\!\diagup\!\!\!\!\diagdown \!\! CH_3 \overset{CH_3}{} + HOH + Br^\ominus \quad ...(ii)$$

$$rate = k[t\text{-BuBr}][OH^-] \quad \textbf{[2020, Main]}$$

Which of the following statements is true :
(1) Changing the concentration of base will have no effect on reaction (1)
(2) Changing the concentration of base will have no effect on reaction (2)
(3) Changing the base from $OH^\ominus$ to $^\ominus OR$ will have no effect on reaction(2)
(4) Doubling the concentration of base will double the rate of both the reactions

**16.** According to the following diagram, A reduces $BO_2$ when the temperature is : **[2020, Main]**

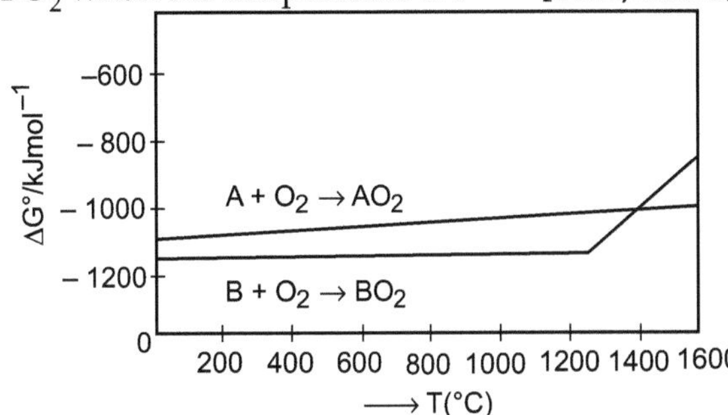



(1) < 1400 °C
(2) > 1400 °C
(3) < 1200 °C
(4) > 1200 °C but < 1400 °C

**17.** If enthalpy of atomisation for $Br_{2(l)}$ is $x$ kJ/mol and bond enthalpy for $Br_2$ is $y$ kj/mo, the relation between them : **[2020, Main]**
(1) is $x = y$       (2) is $x < y$
(3) does not exist     (4) is $x > y$

**18.** The true statement amongst the following is : **[2020, Main]**
(1) Both $\Delta S$ and S are functions of temperature.
(2) S is not a function of temperature but $\Delta S$ is a function of temperature.
(3) Both S and $\Delta S$ are not functions of temperature.
(4) S is a function of temperature but $\Delta S$ is not a function of temperature.

**19.** At constant volume, 4 mol of an ideal gas when heated from 300 K to 500 K changes it internal energy by 5000 J. The molar heat capacity at constant volume is ........... . **[2020, Main]**

**20.** The standard heat of formation $(\Delta_f H^0_{298})$ of ethane (in kJ/mol), if the heat of combustion of ethane, hydrogen and graphite are $-1560, -393.5$ and $-286$ kJ/mol, respectively is ........... . **[2020, Main]**

**21.** 3 g of acetic acid is added to 250 mL of 0.1 M HCl and the solution made up to 500 mL. To 20 mL of this solution $\frac{1}{2}$ mL of 5 M NaOH is added. The pH of the solution is : **[2020, Main]**
[Given : pKa of acetic acid = 4.75, molar mass of acetic acid = 60 g/mol, log 3 = 0.4771]
Neglect any changes in volume.

**22.** A reversible cyclic process for an ideal gas is shown below. Here, P, V and T are pressure, volume and temperature, respectively. The thermodynamic parameters $q$, $w$, H and U are heat, work, enthalpy and internal energy, respectively.

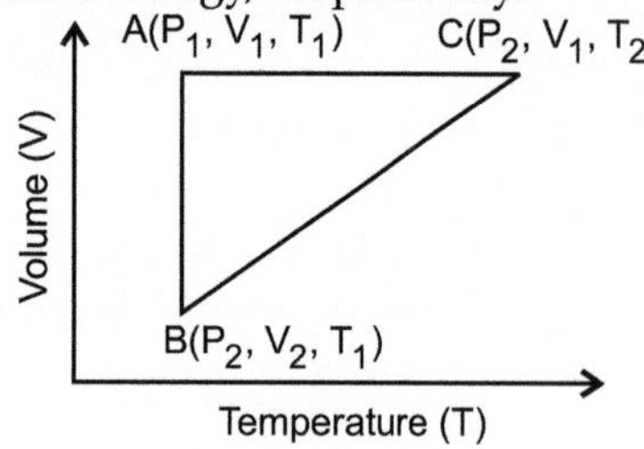


The correct options is/are : **[2018, Advanced]**

(1) $q_{AC} = \Delta U_{BC}$ and $w_{AB} = P_2(V_2 - V_1)$

(2) $w_{BC} = P_2(V_2 - V_1)$ and $q_{BC} = \Delta H_{AC}$

(3) $\Delta H_{CA} < \Delta U_{CA}$ and $q_{AC} = \Delta U_{BC}$

(4) $q_{BC} = \Delta H_{AC}$ and $\Delta H_{CA} > \Delta U_{CA}$

**23.** A closed tank has two compartments A and B, both filled with oxygen (assumed to be ideal gas). The partition separating the two compartments is fixed and is a perfect heat insulator (Figure 1.) If the old partition is replaced by a new partition which can slide and conduct heat but does **Not** allow the gas to leak across (figure 2), the volume (in $m^3$) of the compartment **A** after the system attains equilibrium is ............... .

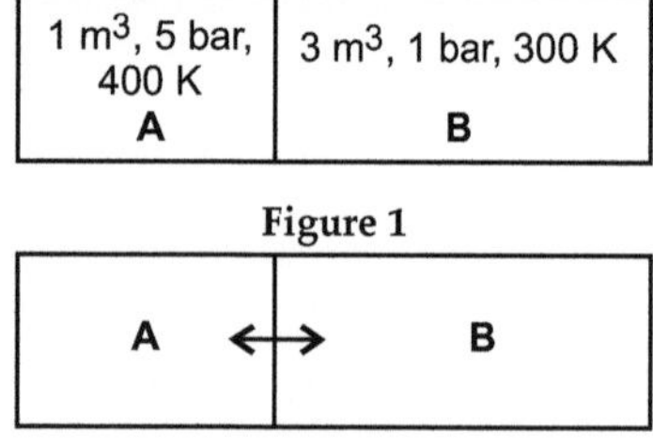

| 1 m³, 5 bar, 400 K | 3 m³, 1 bar, 300 K |
|---|---|
| **A** | **B** |

**Figure 1**

| A | $\leftrightarrow$ | B |
|---|---|---|

**Figure 2**

**24.** The combustion of benzene (l) gives $CO_2(g)$ and $H_2O(l)$. Given that heat of combustion of benzene at constant volume is $-3263.9$ kJ $mol^{-1}$ at 25°C; heat of combustion (in kJ $mol^{-1}$) of benzene at constant pressure will be : **[2018, Main]**
($R = 8.314$ $JK^{-1}$ $mol^{-1}$)

(1) 4152.6          (2) $-452.46$

(3) 3260          (4) $-3267.6$

**25.** $\Delta_f G°$ at 500 K for substance `S' in liquid state and gaseous state are $+100.7$ kcal $mol^{-1}$ and $+103$ kcal $mol^{-1}$, respectively. Vapour pressure of liquid `S' at 500 K is approximately equal to :
($R = 2$ cal $K^{-1}$ $mol^{-1}$) **[2018, Main]**

(1) 0.1 atm          (2) 1 atm

(3) 10 atm          (4) 100 atm

**26.** Given

(i) $2Fe_2O_3(s) \rightarrow 4Fe(s) + 3O_2(g)$; $\Delta_r G° = +1487.0$ kJ $mol^{-1}$

(ii) $2CO(g) + O_2(g) \rightarrow 2CO_2(g)$; $\Delta_r G° = -514.4$ kJ $mol^{-1}$

Free energy change, $\Delta_r G°$ for the reaction $2Fe_2O_3(s) + 6CO(g) \rightarrow 4Fe(s) + 6CO_2(g)$ will be : **[2018, Main]**

(1) $-112.4$ kJ $mol^{-1}$

(2) $-56.2$ kJ $mol^{-1}$

(3) $-168.2$ kJ $mol^{-1}$

(4) $-208.0$ kJ $mol^{-1}$

**27.** For which of the following reactions, $\Delta H$ is equal to $\Delta U$ ? **[2018, Main]**

(1) $N_2(g) + 3H_2(g) \rightarrow 2NH_3(g)$

(2) $2HI(g) \rightarrow H_2(g) + I_2(g)$

(3) $2NO_2(g) \rightarrow N_2O_4(g)$

(4) $2SO_2(g) + O_2(g) \rightarrow 2SO_3(g)$

**28.** An ideal gas undergoes a cyclic process as shown in figure.

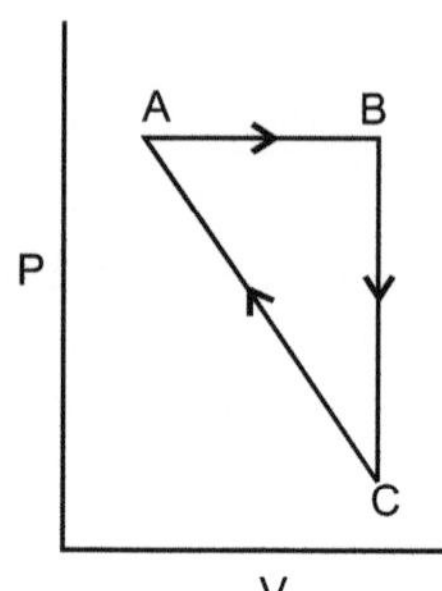


$\Delta U_{BC} = -5$ kJ $mol^{-1}$, $q_{AB} = 2$ kJ $mol^{-1}$
$W_{AB} = -5$ kJ $mol^{-1}$, $W_{CA} = 3$ kJ $mol^{-1}$
Heat absorbed by the system during process CA is : **[2018, Main]**

(1) $-5$ kJ $mol^{-1}$          (2) $+5$ kJ $mol^{-1}$

(3) 18 kJ $mol^{-1}$          (4) $-18$ kJ $mol^{-1}$

**29.** For which of the following processes, $\Delta S$ is negative ? **[2018, Main]**

(1) $H_2(g) \rightarrow 2H(g)$

(2) $N_2(g, 1$ atm$) \rightarrow N_2(g, 5$ atm$)$

(3) $C(\text{diamond}) \rightarrow C(\text{graphite})$

(4) $N_2(g, 273$ K$) \rightarrow N_2(g, 300$ K$)$

**30.** An ideal gas is expanded from $(p_1, V_1, T_1)$ to $(p_2, V_2, T_2)$ under different conditions. The correct statement(s) among the following is/are : **[2017, Advanced]**

(1) The work done on the gas is maximum when it is compressed irreversibly from $(p_2, V_2)$ to $(p_1, V_1)$ against constant pressure $p_1$

(2) If the expansion is carried out freely, it is simultaneously both isothermal as well as adiabatic

(3) The work done by the gas is less when it is expanded reversibly from $V_1$ to $V_2$ under adiabatic conditions as compared to that when expanded reversibly from $V_1$ to $V_2$ under isothermal conditions

(4) The change in internal energy of the gas is (i) zero, if it is expanded reversibly with $T_1 = T_2$, and (ii) positive, if it is expanded reversibly under adiabatic conditions with $T_1 \neq T_2$

**31.** Given
$$C_{(graphite)} + O_2(g) \rightarrow CO_2(g);$$
$$\Delta_r H^\circ = -393.5 \text{ kJ mol}^{-1}$$

$$H_2(g) + \frac{1}{2}O_2(g) \rightarrow H_2O(l);$$

$$CO_2(g) + 2H_2O(l) \rightarrow CH_4(g) + 2O_2(g);$$
$$\Delta_r H^\circ = -285.8 \text{ kJ mol}^{-1}$$
$$\Delta_r H^\circ = +890.3 \text{ kJ mol}^{-1}$$
Based on the above thermochemical equations, the value of $\Delta_r H^\circ$ at 298 K for the reaction $C_{(graphite)} + 2H_2(g) \rightarrow CH_4(g)$ will be
**[2017, Main]**
(1)  $-74.8 \text{ kJ mol}^{-1}$   (2)  $-144.0 \text{ kJ mol}^{-1}$
(3)  $+74.8 \text{ kJ mol}^{-1}$   (4)  $+144.0 \text{ kJ mol}^{-1}$

**32.** $\Delta U$ is equal to :   **[2017, Main]**
(1)  Adiabatic work   (2)  Isothermal work
(3)  Isochoric work   (4)  Isobaric work

**33.** For a reaction, $A(g) \rightarrow A(l); \Delta H = -3RT$. The correct statement for the reaction is :   **[2017, Main]**
(1)  $\Delta H = \Delta U \neq O$   (2)  $\Delta H = \Delta U = O$
(3)  $|\Delta H| < |\Delta U|$   (4)  $|\Delta H| > |\Delta U|$

**34.** The enthalpy change on freezing of 1 mol of water at 5°C to ice at $-5$°C is :   **[2017, Main]**
(Given $\Delta_{fus}H = 6 \text{ kJ mol}^{-1}$ at 0°C,
$C_p(H_2O, l) = 75.3 \text{ J mol}^{-1} \text{ K}^{-1}$,
$C_p(H_2O, s) = 36.8 \text{ J mol}^{-1} \text{ K}^{-1}$)
(1)  $5.44 \text{ kJ mol}^{-1}$   (2)  $5.81 \text{ kJ mol}^{-1}$
(3)  $6.56 \text{ kJ mol}^{-1}$   (4)  $6.00 \text{ kJ mol}^{-1}$

**35.** An ideal gas undergoes isothermal expansion at constant pressure. During the process :
**[2017, Main]**
(1)  enthalpy increases but entropy decreases
(2)  enthalpy remains constant but entropy increases
(3)  enthalpy decreases but entropy increases
(4)  Both enthalpy and entropy remain constant

**36.** A gas undergoes change from state A to state B. In this process, the heat absorbed and work done by the gas is 5 J and 8 J, respectively. Now gas is brought back to A by another process during which 3 J of heat is evolved. In this reverse process of B to A :   **[2017, Main]**
(1)  10 J of the work will be done by the gas
(2)  6 J of the work will be done by the gas
(3)  10 J of the work will be done by the surrouding on gas
(4)  6 J of the work will be done by the surrouding on gas

**37.** One mole of an ideal gas at 300 K in thermal contact with surroundings expands isothermally from 1.0 L to 2.0 L against a constant pressure of 3.0 atm. In this process, the change in entropy of surroundings ($\Delta S_{surr}$) in J K$^{-1}$ is :
(1 L atm = 101.3 J)   **[2016, Advanced]**
(1)  5.763   (2)  1.013
(3)  $-1.013$   (4)  $-5.763$

**38.** A reaction at 1 bar is non-spontaneous at low temperature but becomes spontaneous at high temperature. Identify the correct statement about the reaction among the following : **[2016, Main]**
(1)  Both $\Delta H$ and $\Delta S$ are negative
(2)  Both $\Delta H$ and $\Delta S$ are positive
(3)  $\Delta H$ is positive while $\Delta S$ is negative
(4)  $\Delta H$ is negative while $\Delta S$ is positive

**39.** For the reaction,
$A(g) + B(g) \rightarrow C(g) + D(g)$, $\Delta H^\circ$ and $\Delta S^\circ$ are respectively, $-29.8 \text{ kJ mol}^{-1}$ and $-0.100 \text{ kJ}$ $K^{-1} \text{ mol}^{-1}$ at 298 K. The equilibrium constant for the reaciton at 298 K is :   **[2016, Main]**
(1)  $1.0 \times 10^{-10}$   (2)  $1.0 \times 10^{10}$
(3)  10   (4)  1

**40.** If 100 mole of $H_2O_2$ decompose at 1 bar and 300 K, the work done (kJ) by one mole of $O_2(g)$ as it expands against 1 bar pressure is :
**[2016, Main]**
$$2H_2O_2(l) \rightleftharpoons 2H_2O(l) + O_2(g)$$
$(R = 8.3 \text{ J K}^{-1} \text{ mol}^{-1})$
(1)  62.25   (2)  124.50
(3)  249.00   (4)  498.00

**41.** The heats of combustion of carbon and carbon monoxide are $-393.5$ and $-283.5 \text{ kJ mol}^{-1}$, respectively. The heat of formation (in kJ) of carbon monoxide per mole is :   **[2016, Main]**
(1)  110.5   (2)  676.5
(3)  $-676.5$   (4)  $-110.5$

**42.** Match the thermodynamic processes given under Column I with the expression given under Column II.   **[2015, Advanced]**

| Column I | Column II |
|---|---|
| (A)  Freezing of water at 273 K and 1 atm | (P)  $q = 0$ |
| (B)  Expansion of 1 mol of an ideal gas into a vacuum under isolated conditions | (Q)  $w = 0$ |
| (C)  Mixing of equal volumes of two ideal gases at constant temperature and pressure in an isolated container | (R)  $\Delta S_{sys} < 0$ |
| (D)  Reversible heating of $H_2(g)$ at 1 atm from 300 K to 600 K, followed by reversible cooling to 300 K at 1 atm | (S)  $\Delta U = 0$ |
|  | (T)  $\Delta G = 0$ |

**43.** An ideal gas in a thermally insulated vessel at internal pressure = $P_1$, volume = $V_1$ and absolute temperature = $T_1$ expands irreversibly against zero external pressure, as shown in the diagram. The final internal pressure, volume and absolute temperature of the gas are $P_2$, $V_2$ and $T_2$, respectively. For this expansion :

**[2014, Advanced]**

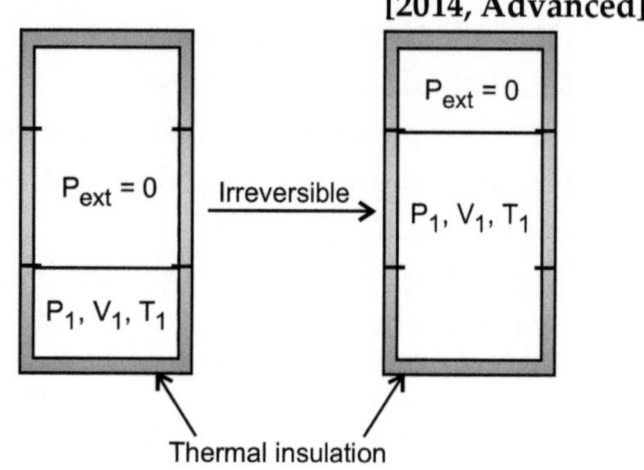


(1) $q = 0$
(2) $T_2 = T_1$
(3) $P_2V_2 = P_1V_1$
(4) $P_2V_2^\gamma = P_1V_1^\gamma$

**44.** For the process

$$H_2O(l) \rightarrow H_2O(g)$$

at $T = 100°C$ and 1 atmosphere pressure the correct choise is : **[2014, Advanced]**

(1) $\Delta S_{system} > 0$ and $\Delta S_{surroundings} > 0$
(2) $\Delta S_{system} > 0$ and $\Delta S_{surroundings} < 0$
(3) $\Delta S_{system} < 0$ and $\Delta S_{surroundings} > 0$
(4) $\Delta S_{system} < 0$ and $\Delta S_{surroundings} < 0$

**45.** For complete combustion of ethanol

$$C_2H_5OH(l) + 3O_2(g) \rightarrow 2CO_2(g) + 3H_2O(l),$$

the amount of heat produced as measured in bomb calorimeter, is 1364.47 kJ mol$^{-1}$ at 25°C. Assuming ideality the Enthalpy of combustion, $\Delta_C H$, for the reaction will be : **[2014, Main]**

$(R = 8.314 \text{ kJ mol}^{-1})$

(1) $-1366.95$ kJ mol$^{-1}$
(2) $-1361.95$ kJ mol$^{-1}$
(3) $-1460.50$ kJ mol$^{-1}$
(4) $-1350.50$ kJ mol$^{-1}$

**46.** The standard enthalpy of formation of $NH_3$ is $-46.0$ kJ/mol. If the enthalpy of formation of $H_2$ from its atoms is $-436$ kJ/mol and that of $N_2$ is $-712$ kJ/mol, the average bond enthalpy of $N-H$ bond in $NH_3$ is : **[2014, Main]**

(1) $-1102$ kJ/mol
(2) $-964$ kJ/mol
(3) $+352$ kJ/mol
(4) $+1056$ kJ/mol

**47.** The molar heat capacity $(C_p)$ of $CD_2O$ is 10 cals at 1000 K. The change in entropy associated with cooling of 32 g of $CD_2O$ vapour from 1000 K to 100 K at constant pressure will be :

$(D = $ deuterium, at. mass $= 2u)$ **[2014, Main]**

(1) $23.03$ cal deg$^{-1}$
(2) $-23.03$ cal deg$^{-1}$
(3) $2.303$ cal deg$^{-1}$
(4) $-2.303$ cal deg$^{-1}$

**48.** The entropy $(S°)$ of the following substances are :

$CH_4(g)$    186.2 J K$^{-1}$ mol$^{-1}$
$O_2(g)$    205.0 J K$^{-1}$ mol$^{-1}$
$CO_2(g)$    213.6 J K$^{-1}$ mol$^{-1}$
$H_2O(l)$    69.6 J K$^{-1}$ mol$^{-1}$

The entropy change $(\Delta S°)$ for the reaction
$$CH_4(g) + 2O_2(g) \rightarrow CO_2(g) + 2H_2O(l) \text{ is :}$$

(1) $-312.5$ J K$^{-1}$ mol$^{-1}$
(2) $-242.8$ J K$^{-1}$ mol$^{-1}$
(3) $-108.1$ J K$^{-1}$ mol$^{-1}$
(4) $-37.6$ J K$^{-1}$ mol$^{-1}$

**49.** The standard enthalpy of formation $(\Delta_f H°_{298})$ for methane, $CH_4$ is $-74.9$ kJ mol$^{-1}$. In order to calculate the average energy given out in the formation of a $C-H$ bond from this it is necessary to know which one of the following ?

**[2014, Main]**

(1) the dissociation energy of the hydrogen molecule, $H_2$

(2) the first four ionisation energeis of carbon

(3) the dissociation energy of $H_2$ and enthalpy of sublimation of carbon (graphite).

(4) the first four ionisation energies of carbon and electron affinity of hydrogen

**50.** The standard enthalpies of formation of $CO_2(g)$, $H_2O(l)$ and glucose(s) at 25 °C are $-400$ kJ/mol, $-300$ kJ/mol and $-1300$ kJ/mol, respectively. The standard enthalpy of combustion per gram of glucose at 25 °C is : **[2013, Advanced]**

(1) $+2900$ kJ
(2) $-2900$ kJ
(3) $-16.11$ kJ
(4) $+16.11$ kJ

**51.** Benzene and naphthalene form an ideal solution at room temperature. For this process, the true statements is/are : **[2013, Advanced]**

(1) $\Delta G$ is positive
(2) $\Delta S_{system}$ is positive
(3) $\Delta S_{surroundings} = 0$
(4) $\Delta H = 0$

**Paragraph for Question 52 and 53**

A fixed mass '$m$' of a gas is subjected to transformation of states from K to L to M to N and back to K as shown in the figure.

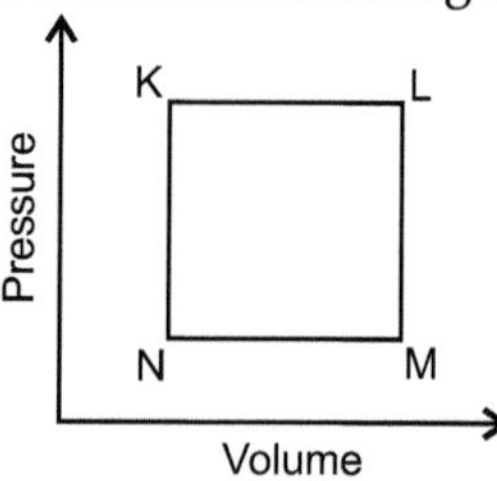


**52.** The succeeding operations that enable this transformation of states are : **[2013, Advanced]**
(1) Heating, cooling, heating, cooling
(2) Cooling, heating, cooling, heating
(3) Heating, cooling, cooling, heating
(4) Cooling, heating, heating, cooling

**53.** The pair of isochoric processes among the transformation of states is : **[2013, Advanced]**
(1) K to L and L to M
(2) L to M and N to K
(3) L to M and M to N
(4) M to N and N to K

**54.** For an ideal gas, consider only P-V work in going from an initial state X to the final state Z. The final state Z can be reached by either of the two paths shown in the figure. Which of the following choices is/are correct ? [Take $\Delta S$ as change in entropy and $w$ as work done] **[2012, Advanced]**

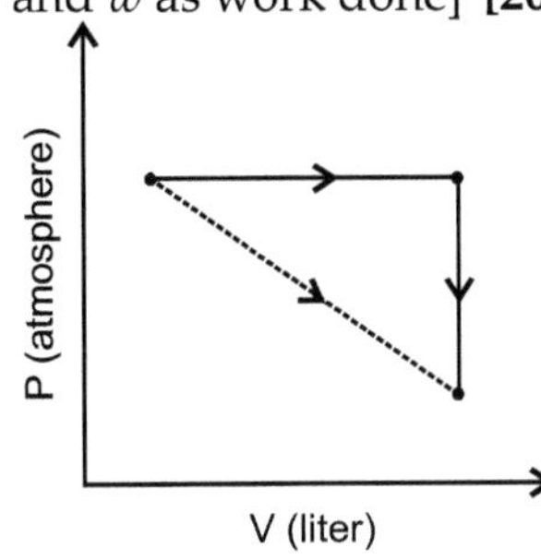

(1) $\Delta S_{x \to z} = \Delta S_{x \to y} + \Delta S_{y \to z}$
(2) $w_{x \to z} = w_{x \to y} + w_{y \to z}$
(3) $w_{x \to y \to z} = w_{x \to y}$
(4) $\Delta S_{x \to y \to z} = \Delta S_{x \to y}$

**55.** Using the data provided, calculate the multiple bond energy (kJ mol$^{-1}$) of a $C \equiv C$ bond in $C_2H_2$. That energy is (take the bond energy of a C–H bond as 350 kJ mol$^{-1}$.) **[2012, Advanced]**

$$2C(s) + H_2(g) \to C_2H_2(g) \qquad \Delta H = 225 \text{ kJ mol}^{-1}$$
$$2C(s) \to 2C(g) \qquad \Delta H = 1410 \text{ kJ mol}^{-1}$$
$$H_2(g) \to 2H(g) \qquad \Delta H = 330 \text{ kJ mol}^{-1}$$

(1) 1165  (2) 837
(3) 865  (4) 815

**56.** The reversible expansion of an ideal gas under adiabatic and isothermal conditions is shown in the figure. Which of the following statements is/are correct ? **[2012, Advanced]**

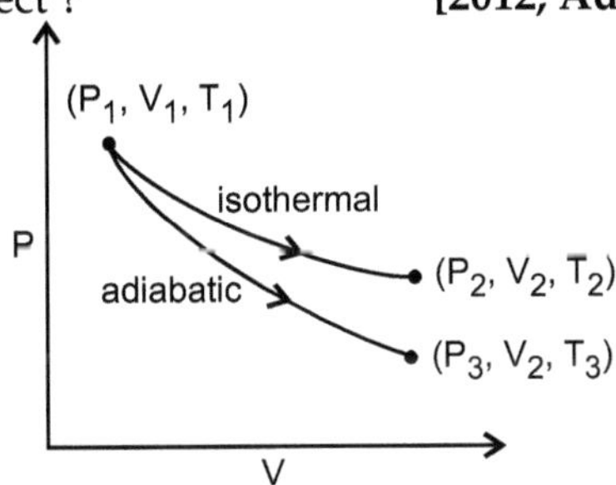

(1) $T_1 = T_2$
(2) $T_3 > T_1$
(3) $w_{\text{isothermal}} > w_{\text{adiabatic}}$
(4) $\Delta U_{\text{isothermal}} > \Delta U_{\text{adiabatic}}$

**57.** Match the transformation in **column I** with appropriate options in **column II** :

**[2011, Advanced]**

| Column I | Column II |
| --- | --- |
| (1) $CO_2(s) \to CO_2(g)$ | (p) phase transition |
| (2) $CaCO_3(s) \to CaO(s) + CO_2(g)$ | (q) allotropic change |
| (3) $2H\bullet \to H_2(g)$ | (r) $\Delta H$ is positive |
| (4) $P_{(\text{white, solid})} \to P_{(\text{red, solid})}$ | (s) $\Delta S$ is positive |
| | (t) $\Delta S$ is negative |

**58.** The species which by definition has **ZERO** standard molar enthalpy of formation at 298 K is : **[2010, Advanced]**

(1) $Br_2$ (g)  (2) $Cl_2$ (g)
(3) $H_2O$ (g)  (4) $CH_4$ (g)

**59.** The bond energy (in **kcal mol$^{-1}$**) of a C – C single bond is approximately : **[2010, Advanced]**

(1) 1  (2) 10
(3) 100  (4) 1000

**60.** One mole of an ideal gas is taken from $a$ to $b$ along two paths denoted by the solid and the dashed lines as shown in the graph below. If the work done along the solid line path is $w_S$ and that along the dotted line path is $w_d$, then the integer closest to the ratio $w_d/w_s$ is : **[2010, Advanced]**

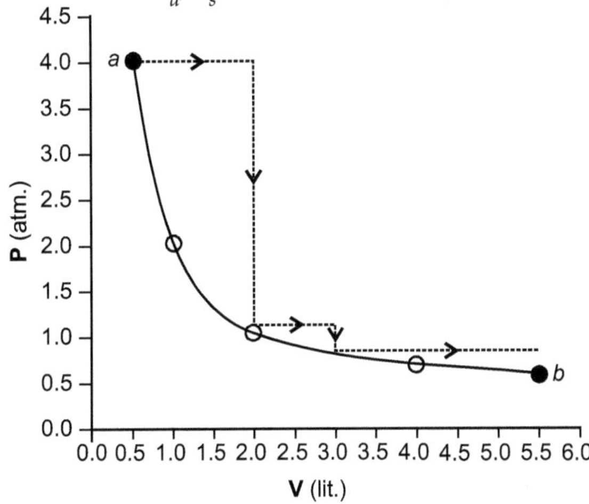

**61.** Among the following, the state functions is/are : **[2009, Advanced]**

(1) Internal energy
(2) Irreversible expansion work
(3) Reversible expansion work
(4) Molar enthalpy

**62.** In a constant volume calorimeter, 3.5 g of a gas with molecular weight 28 was burnt in excess oxygen at 298.0 K. The temperature of the calorimeter was found to increase from 298.0 K to 298.45 K due to the combustion process. Given that the heat capacity of the calorimeter is 2.5 kJ K$^{-1}$, the numerical value for the enthalpy of combustion of the gas in kJ mol$^{-1}$ is. **[2009, Advanced]**

**63. Statement-1 :** For every chemical reaction at equilibrium, standard Gibbs energy of reaction is zero.

and

**Statement-2 :** At constant temperature and pressure, chemical reactions are spontaneous n the direction of decreasing Gibbs energy. **[2008, Advanced]**

(1) **Statement-1** is True, **Statement-2** is True; **Statement-2** is a correct explanation for **Statement-1**

(2) **Statement-1** is True, **Statement-2** is True; **Statement-2** is **NOT** a correct explanation for **Statement-1**

(3) **Statement-1** is True, **Statement-2** is False

(4) **Statement-1** is False, **Statement-2** is True

**64. Statement-1 :** There is a ntural asymmetry between converting work to heat and converting heat to work.

and

**Statement-2 :** No process is possible in which the sole result is the absorption of heat from a reservoir and its complete conversion into work **[2008, Advanced]**

(1) **Statement-1** is True, **Statement-2** is True; **Statement-2** is a correct explanation for **Statement-1**

(2) **Statement-1** is True, **Statement-2** is True; **Statement-2** is **NOT** a correct explanation for **Statement-1**

(3) **Statement-1** is True, **Statement-2** is False

(4) **Statement-1** is False, **Statement-2** is True

**65.** The value of $\log_{10} K$ for a reaction $A \rightleftharpoons B$ is (Given : $\Delta_r H^\circ_{298K} = -54.07$ kJ mol$^{-1}$, $\Delta_r S^\circ_{298K} = 10$ JK$^{-1}$ mol$^{-1}$ and R = 8.314 JK$^{-1}$ mol$^{-1}$; $2.303 \times 8.314 \times 298 = 5705$) **[2007, Advanced]**

(1) 5        (2) 10

(3) 95       (4) 100

**66.** For the process $H_2O(l)$ (1 bar, 373 K) $\rightarrow H_2O(g)$ (1 bar, 373 K), the correct set of thermodynamic parameters is : **[2007, Advanced]**

(1) $\Delta G = 0, \Delta S = +$ ve    (2) $\Delta G = 0, \Delta S = -$ ve

(3) $\Delta G = +$ve, $\Delta S = 0$    (4) $\Delta G = -$ve, $\Delta S = +$ve

**67.** A monatomic ideal gas undergoes a process in which the ratio of P to V at any instant is constant and equals to 1. What is the molar heat capacity of the gas ? **[2006, Main]**

(1) $\dfrac{4R}{2}$        (2) $\dfrac{3R}{2}$

(3) $\dfrac{5R}{2}$        (4) 0

**68.** The direct conversion of A to B is difficult, hence it is required out by the following shown path :

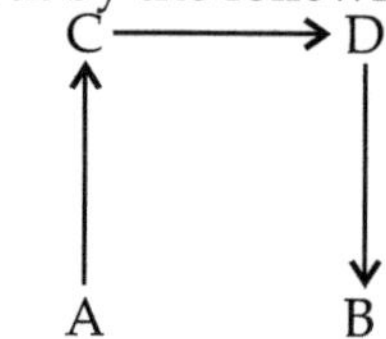


Given : $\Delta S_{(A \rightarrow C)} = 50$ e.u.
$\Delta S_{(C \rightarrow D)} = 30$ e.u.
$\Delta S_{(B \rightarrow D)} = 20$ e.u.

where, e.u. is entropy unit then $\Delta S_{(A \rightarrow B)}$ is : **[2006, Main]**

(1) $+100$ e.u.     (2) $+60$ e.u.

(3) $-100$ e.u.     (4) $-60$ e.u.

**69.** For the reaction, $2CO + O_2 \rightarrow 2CO_2$; $\Delta H = -560$ kJ. Two moles of CO and one mole of $O_2$ are taken in a container of volume 1 L. They completely form two moles of $CO_2$, the gases deviate appreciably from ideal behaviour. If the pressure in the vessel changes from 70 to 40 atm, find the magnitude (absolute value) of $\Delta U$ at 500 K. (1 L atm = 0.1 kL) **[2006, Main]**

**70.** One mole of monoatomic ideal gas expands adiabatically at initial temperature T against a constant external pressure of 1 atm. from one litre to two litre. Find out the final temperature (R = 0.0821 lt. atm K$^{-1}$ mole$^{-1}$) **[2005, Screening]**

(1) T        (2) $\dfrac{T}{(2)^{\frac{5}{3}-1}}$

(3) $T - \dfrac{2}{3 \times 0.0821}$    (4) $T + \dfrac{2}{3 \times 0.0821}$

**71.** 100 ml of a liquid contained in an isolated container at a pressure of 1 bar. The pressure is steeply increased to 100 bar. The volume of the liquid is decreased by 1 ml at this constant pressure. Find the $\Delta H$ and $\Delta U$. **[2004, Main]**

**72. (a)** In the following equilibrium
$$N_2O_4(g) \rightleftharpoons 2NO_2(g)$$ **[2004, Main]**
when 5 moles of each are taken, the temperature is kept at 298 K the total pressure was found to be 20 bar. Given that
$\Delta G_f^0(N_2O_4) = 100$ KJ
$\Delta G_f^0(NO_2) = 50$ KJ
(i) Find $\Delta G$ of the reaction
(ii) The direction of the reaction in which the equilibrium shifts

**(b)** A graph is plotted for a real gas which follows Vander Waal's equation with $PV_m$ taken on Y-axis and P on X-axis. Find the intercept of the line where $V_m$ is molar volume.

**73.** $\Delta H_{vap} = 30$ KJ/mole and $\Delta S_{vap.} = 75$ mol Jmol$^{-1}$K$^{-1}$. Find temperature of vapour, at one atmosphere . **[2004, Screening]**

(1) 400 K      (2) 350 K

(3) 298 K      (4) 250 K

**74.** 2 mol of an ideal gas expanded isothermally and reversibly from 1 litre to 10 litres at 300 K. What is the enthalpy change ? **[2004, Screening]**

(1) 4.98 KJ      (2) 11.47 KJ

(3) $-11.47$ KJ    (4) 0 KJ

**75. (a)** Match the following if the molecular weights of X, Y and Z are same. **[2003, Main]**

| | **Boiling Point** | $K_b$ |
|---|---|---|
| X | 100 | 0.68 |
| Y | 27 | 0.53 |
| Z | 253 | 0.98 |

**(b)** $C_v$ value of He is always 3R/2 but $C_v$ value of $H_2$ is 3R/2 at low temperature and 5R/2 at moderate temperature and more than 5R/2 at higher temperature explain in two to three lines.

**76.** Which of the reaction defines $\Delta H_f^0$

[2003, Screening]

(1) $C_{(diamond)} + O_{2(g)} \rightarrow CO_{2(g)}$

(2) $\dfrac{1}{2}H_{2(g)} + \dfrac{1}{2}F_{2(g)} \rightarrow HF_{(g)}$

(3) $N_{2(g)} + 3H_{2(g)} \rightarrow 2NH_{3(g)}$

(4) $CO_{(g)} + \dfrac{1}{2}O_{2(g)} \rightarrow CO_{2(g)}$

**77.** Two moles of a perfect gas undergo the following processes : [2002, Main]

(1) a reversible isobaric expansion from (1.0 atm, 20.0 L) to (1.0 atm, 40.0 L);

(2) a reversible isochoric charge of state from (1.0 atm, 40.0 L) to (0.5 atm, 40.0 L);

(3) a reversible isothermal compression from (0.5 atm, 40.0 L) to (1.0 atm, 20.0 L)

(i) Sketch with lables each of the processes on the same P-V diagram

(ii) Calculate the total work (w) and the total heat change (q) involved in the above processes.

(iii) What will be the values of $\Delta U$, $\Delta H$ and $\Delta S$ for the overall process ?

**78.** One mole of a non-ideal gas undergoes a change of state (2.0 atm, 3.0 L, 95(K) $\rightarrow$ (4.0 atm, 5.0 L, 245 K) with a change in internal energy, $\Delta U = 30.0$ L atm. The change in enthalpy ($\Delta H$) of the processes in L atm is : [2002, Screening]

(1) 40.0

(2) 42.3

(3) 44.0

(4) not defined, because pressure is not constant

## ANSWER KEY

| | | | | | | | | | |
|---|---|---|---|---|---|---|---|---|---|
| **1.** (3) | **2.** (*) | **3.** (*) | **4.** (4) | **5.** (2) | **6.** (3) | **7.** (4) | **8.** (2) | **9.** (2) | **10.** (*) |
| **11.** (1,2,3) | **12.** (*) | **13.** (*) | **14.** (*) | **15.** (1) | **16.** (2) | **17.** (4) | **18.** (1) | **19.** (*) | **20.** (*) |
| **21.** (*) | **22.** (2,3) | **23.** (*) | **24.** (4) | **25.** (3) | **26.** (2) | **27.** (2) | **28.** (2) | **29.** (2) | **30.** (1,2,3) |
| **31.** (1) | **32.** (1) | **33.** (4) | **34.** (3) | **35.** (2) | **36.** (2) | **37.** (3) | **38.** (2) | **39.** (4) | **40.** (2) |
| **41.** (4) | **42.** (*) | **43.** (1,2,3) | **44.** (2) | **45.** (1) | **46.** (3) | **47.** (2) | **48.** (2) | **49.** (3) | **50.** (3) |
| **51.** (2,3,4) | **52.** (3) | **53.** (2) | **54.** (1, 3) | **55.** (4) | **56.** (1,3,4) | **57.** (*) | **58.** (2) | **59.** (3) | **60.** (2) |
| **61.** (1, 4) | **62.** (*) | **63.** (4) | **64.** (1) | **65.** (2) | **66.** (1) | **67.** (1) | **68.** (2) | **69.** (*) | **70.** (3) |
| **71.** (*) | **72.** (*) | **73.** (1) | **74.** (4) | **75.** (*) | **76.** (1) | **77.** (*) | **78.** (3) | | |

## ANSWERS WITH EXPLANATIONS

**1. (3)** From the given graph, potential energy of A-B molecule is minimum.

Thus A-B bond is most stable and have strongest bond amongst these

B $\rightarrow$ Most electronegative

D $\rightarrow$ Least electronegative

A-B $\rightarrow$ Shortest bond length

A-B $\rightarrow$ Largest bond enthalpy

Therefore correct option is (3).

**2.** $H_2O(l) \rightleftharpoons H_2O(g)$     90 gm of $H_2O$

$\Delta H = \Delta U + \Delta n_g RT$     $\Rightarrow 5$ moles of $H_2O$

$5 \times 41000\,J = \Delta U + 1 \times 8.314 \times 373 \times 5$

$\Delta U = 189494.39$ Joule

**3.** $C_2H_5OH_{(l)} + 3O_{2(g)} \rightarrow 2CO_{2(g)} + 3H_2O_{(l)}$

$$\Delta n_g = 2 - 3 = -1$$
$$\Delta_c H = \Delta_c U + (\Delta n_g)RT$$
$$\Delta_c H = \Delta_c U - RT$$
$$\Delta_c U = \Delta_c H + RT$$
$$= -327 \times 10^3 + 2 \times 300$$
$$= -326400 \text{ cal.}$$

$\therefore$ Heat evolved $= -326400$ cal.

**4. (4)** $\Delta G = -n\,F\,E_{cell}$

$\Delta G$ is negative, if $E_{cell}$ is positive

Anode : $Cu(s) \longrightarrow Cu^{+2}\,(C_1) + 2e^- : E^\circ$

Cathode : $Cu^{+2}(C_2) + 2e^- \longrightarrow Cu(S) : -E^\circ$

Cell reaction : $Cu^{+2}(C_2) \longrightarrow Cu^{+2}(C_1)\ E^\circ_{cell} = 0$

$$E_{cell} = E^o_{cell} - \frac{2.303RT}{nF}\log Q$$

$$E_{cell} = 0 - \frac{2.303Rt}{nF}\log\left(\frac{C_1}{C_2}\right)$$

$$E_{cell} > 0 : \text{if } \frac{C_1}{C_2} < 1 \Rightarrow C_1 < C_2$$

**5. (2)** The free energy change shows a change from negative to positive value. This is because for an oxide to be stable its free energy change value should be negative.

**6. (3)** Ellingham diagram provides information about temperature dependence of the standard gibbs energies of formation of some metal oxides.

**7. (4)** As the expansion is done in vaccum that is in absence of $p_{ext}$ so , work done is zero.

$$W = zero$$

**8. (2)** The reaction $H_{(g)} + e^- \rightarrow H^-$ is exothermic in nature rest of all are endothermic process.

**9. (2)**

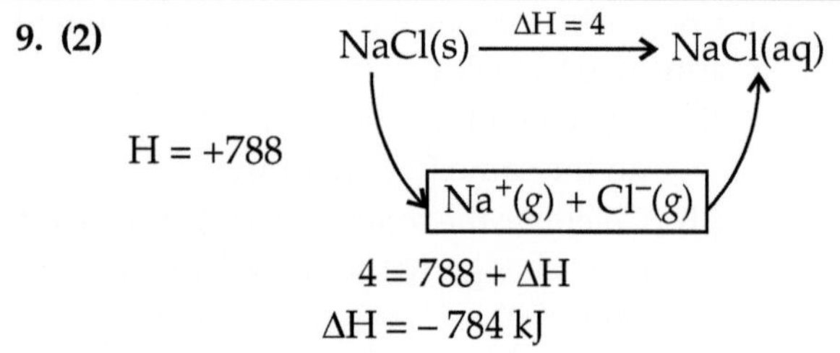

$$H = +788$$

$$4 = 788 + \Delta H$$
$$\Delta H = -784 \text{ kJ}$$

**10.** $-13537.57$

$$\Delta G^{\ominus} = \Delta H^{\ominus} - T\Delta S^{\ominus}$$
$$= (\Delta U^{\ominus} + \Delta n_g RT) - T\Delta S^{\ominus}$$
$$= \left[\left\{-20 + (-1)\frac{8.314}{1000} \times 298\right\} - \frac{298}{1000} \times (-30)\right] kJ$$
$$= -13.537572 \text{ kJ}$$
$$= -13537.57 \text{ Joule}$$

**11. (1,2,3)** For 1 mole Vander Waal's gas

$$\left(P + \frac{a}{V^2}\right)(V - b) = RT$$

$$P = \frac{RT}{V - b} - \frac{a}{V^2}$$

If $P_{ext} = P$, means process is reversible. For Van der Waal's gas, expression is correct for all reversible process.

**12.**

$$K_{eq.} = \frac{[B]}{[A]}$$

$$K_{1000} = \frac{10}{1} = 10$$

and $\quad K_{2000} = \frac{100}{1} = 100$

Now, $\dfrac{\Delta G^0_{1000}}{\Delta G^0_{2000}} = \dfrac{(-RT\,l\,n\,K_{eq})_{1000}}{(-RT\,l\,n\,K_{eq})_{2000}}$

$$= \frac{1000 \times l\,n\,10}{2000 \times l\,n\,100} = 0.25$$

**13.** For given reaction :

$$H_2(g) + \frac{1}{2}O_2(g) \xrightarrow{2e^-} H_2O(l) \quad E° = 1.23 \text{ V}$$

$$\Delta G° = -nFE°_{cell} = [-2 \times 96500 \times 1.23]\,1 \times 10^{-3}$$
$$\times 0.7 = -166.173 \text{ J}$$

$$W = 166.173 \text{ J}$$

$$W = \frac{nR\Delta T}{\gamma - 1}$$

$$166.173 = \frac{1 \times 8.314 \times \Delta T}{\left(\frac{5}{3} - 1\right)}$$

$$= \frac{8.314 \times 3}{2} \Delta T$$

$$\Delta T = \frac{166.173 \times 2}{8.314 \times 3} = 13.32$$

**14.**

$$SnO_{2(S)} + C_{(S)} \longrightarrow Sn_{(S)} + CO_{2(g)}$$
$$\Delta H°_{rxn} = [-394] - [-58] = 187 \text{ kJ/mole}$$
$$\Delta S°_{rxn} = [52 + 210] - [56 + 6]$$
$$= 200 \text{ J/k-mole}$$
$$T = \frac{\Delta H°}{\Delta S°} = \frac{187 \times 1000}{200}$$
$$= 935 \text{ K}$$

**15. (1)** Reaction 1 : $SN_1$

Reaction 2 : $E_2$

$SN_1$ is independent of concentration of nucleophile/base.

**16. (2)** A reduces $BO_2$ when temperature is above 1400 °C because above 1400 °C A has more $-ve$ $\Delta G°$ for $AO_2$ formation than B to $BO_2$ formation.

**17. (4)** Enthalpy of atomisation of $Br_2(l)$

$$Br_2(l) \xrightarrow{\Delta H_{vap}} Br_2(g) \xrightarrow{\Delta H_{BE}} 2Br(g)$$
$$\Delta H_{atom}$$

$$\Delta H_{atom} = \Delta H_{vap} + \Delta H_{BE}$$
$$x = \Delta H_{vap} + y$$

So, $x > y$.

**18. (1)**

$$ds = \int \frac{q_{rev.}}{T}$$

**19.** For ideal gas :

$$\Delta U = nC_V[T_2 - T_1]$$
$$\Rightarrow \quad 5000 = 4 \times C_V[500 - 300]$$
$$\Rightarrow \quad C_V = \frac{5000}{800}$$
$$= 6.25 \text{ J mole}^{-1}\text{ K}^{-1}$$

**20.** 192.5

$$2C(\text{graphite}) + 3H_{2(g)} \to 1C_2H_6 \quad \Delta H_4(C_2H_6)$$

(1) $\quad C_2H_6 + \frac{7}{2}O_2 \to 2CO_2 + 3H_2O \quad \Delta H_C = -1560$

(2) $\quad H_2 + \frac{1}{2}O_2 \to H_2O \quad\quad\quad\quad \Delta H_C = -393.5$

(3) $\quad C(\text{graphite}) + O_2 \to CO_2 \quad \Delta H_C = -286 \text{ kJ/mol}$

$$\Delta H_f(C_2H_6) = 3(-393.5) + 2(-286) + 1560$$
$$= -1180.5 + (-572) + 1560$$
$$= 192.5$$

**21.** $m$ mol of acetic acid in 20 ml = 2

$m$ mol of HCl in 20 ml = 1

$m$ mol of NaOH in 20 ml = 2.5

$$NaOH + CH_3COOH \to CH_3COONa + H_2O$$
(left)

| 1.5 | 2 | 0 | 0 |
|---|---|---|---|
| 0 | 0.5 | 1.5 | |

$$pH = pK_a + \log\frac{3/2}{2}$$

$$= 4.74 + \log 3$$
$$= 5.22$$

**22. (2,3)** (1) Process is isochoric from A to C. Thus, $q_{AC} = \Delta U_{AC} = nC_{V,\,m}(T_2 - T_1) = \Delta U_{BC}$. The work done is given as

$$w_{AB} = -nRT \ln \frac{V_2}{V_1}. \text{ Thus, 1 is}$$

incorrect.

(2) As, $w_{BC} = -P_2(V_1 - V_2)$ and $q_{BC} = \Delta H_{BC} = nC_{P,\,m}(T_2 - T_1) = \Delta H_{AC}$. Thus, it is $= P_2(V_2 - V_1)$ correct.

(3) As, $\Delta H_{CA} = nC_{P,\,m}(T_1 - T_2)$ and $\Delta U_{CA} = nC_{V,\,m}(T_1 - T_2)$. The final solution for each is negative. Thus, $\Delta H_{CA} < \Delta U_{CA}$. Thus, it is correct.

(4) As $q_{BC} = \Delta H_{BC} = nC_{P,\,m}(T_2 - T_1) = \Delta H_{AC}$ but $\Delta H_{AC} < \Delta U_{AA}$. Thus, it is incorrect.

**23.** Number of moles in system **A** $= \dfrac{PV_A}{RT}$

$$= \frac{5\,\text{bar} \times 1\,\text{m}^3}{R \times 400\,\text{K}}$$

Number of moles in system **B** $= \dfrac{PV_B}{RT}$

$$= \frac{1\,\text{bar} \times 3\,\text{m}^3}{R \times 300\,\text{K}}$$

The conditions after attaining the equilibrium is,

$$P_A = P_B$$

$$\frac{5}{400\,RV_A} = \frac{1}{100\,RV_B}$$

$$4V_A = 5V_B$$

Volume of system **A** is given as,

$$4 = V_A + V_B$$

$$4 = V_A + \frac{4V_A}{5}$$

$$V_A = 2.22\,\text{m}^3$$

**24. (4)** The balanced chemical equation for the combustion of benzene is,

$$C_6H_6(l) + \frac{15}{2}O_2(g) \rightarrow 6CO_2(g) + 3H_2O(l)$$

The change in the number of gaseous molecules in the given reaction is $-1.5$. The heat of combustion of benzene is calculated by the formula,

$$\Delta H = \Delta E + \Delta n_g RT$$
$$= -3263.9\,\text{kJ/mol} + (-1.5) \times 8.314$$
$$\times 10^{-3}\,\text{kJ/mol K} \times 298\,\text{K}$$
$$= -3267.62\,\text{kJ/mol}$$

**25. (3)** $\Delta G^{\circ}_{rxn} = \Delta G^{\circ}_{vapour} - \Delta G^{\circ}_{liquid}$

$$\Delta G^{\circ}_{rxn} = 103 - 100.7$$
$$= 2.3\,\text{Kcal/mol}$$
$$= 2300\,\text{cal/mol}$$

$$\Delta G^{\circ}_{rxn} = -RT\ln K$$
$$2300\,\text{cal/mol} = -2\,\text{cal/mol/K} \times 500\,\text{K} \times \ln K$$
$$\ln K = 2.3$$
$$K = 10\,\text{atm}$$

So, vapour pressure of liquid 'S' at 500 K is approximately equal to 10 atm.

**26. (2)** The value of $\Delta G^{\circ}_{rxn}$ for first reaction is $+1487.0$ kJ/mol.

The value of $\Delta G^{\circ}_{rxn}$ for second reaction is $-514.4$ kJ/mol.
$$2CO(g) + O_2(g) \rightarrow 2CO_2(g)$$
The free energy change for third reaction,
$$2Fe_2O_3(s) + 6CO(g) \rightarrow 4Fe(s) + 6CO_2(g)$$
$$\Delta G^{\circ}_{rxn} = +1487.0\,\text{kJ/mol} - 3 \times (514.4\,\text{kJ/mol})$$
$$\Delta G^{\circ}_{rxn} = +1487.0\,\text{kJ/mol} - 1543.2\,\text{kJ/mol}$$
$$= -56.2\,\text{kJ/mol}$$

The free energy change for reaction is $-56.2$ kJ/mol.

**27. (2)** The relation between $\Delta H$ and $\Delta U$ is,
$$\Delta H = \Delta U + \Delta n_g RT$$
The value of $\Delta n$ is,
$$\Delta n = 1 + 1 - 2$$
$$= 0$$
Substitute the value of $\Delta n$ in the above formula
$$\Delta H = \Delta U + \Delta n_g RT$$
$$\Delta H = \Delta U + (0)RT$$
$$\Delta H = \Delta U$$
Therefore, for the reaction
$$2HI(g) \rightarrow H_2(g) + I_2(g),$$
$$\Delta H = \Delta U$$

**28. (2)** The given cyclic process is shown below.

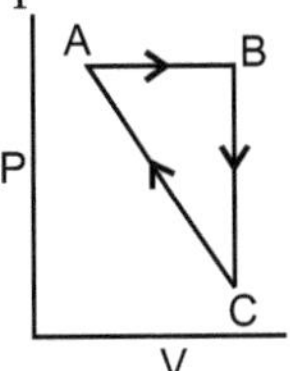


The relation between $\Delta U$ and W is,
$$\Delta U = q + W$$
The value of $\Delta U_{AB}$ is,
$$\Delta U_{AB} = q + W$$
$$= 2 - 5$$
$$= -3$$

For $\Delta U_{ABC}$
$$\Delta U_{ABC} = \Delta U_{AB} + \Delta U_{BC}$$
$$= -3 - 5$$

$$= -8 \text{ kJ}$$

Similarly, for $\Delta U_{CBA} = +8 \text{ kJ}$

$$\Delta U = q + W$$
$$8 = q + 3$$
$$q = +5 \text{ kJ}$$

**29. (2)** The process in which $\Delta S$ is negative is,

$$N_2 \text{ (g, 1 atm)} \rightarrow N_2 \text{ (g, 5 atm)}$$

Molecules of gas come closer when pressure increases due to which intermolecular distance decreases. Hence, entropy also decrease $\Delta S < 0$.

**30. (1,2,3)** When an ideal gas is compressed irreversibly from $(p_2, V_2)$ to $(p_1, V_1)$ to against constant pressure, then work done will on the gas will be maximum. This is correct statement.

Both in isothermal and adiabatic free expansion, work done will be zero due to the absence of external pressure.

In adiabatic condition the work done is lesser than the isothermal conditions when gas is expended reversibly. This is shown by the following figure,

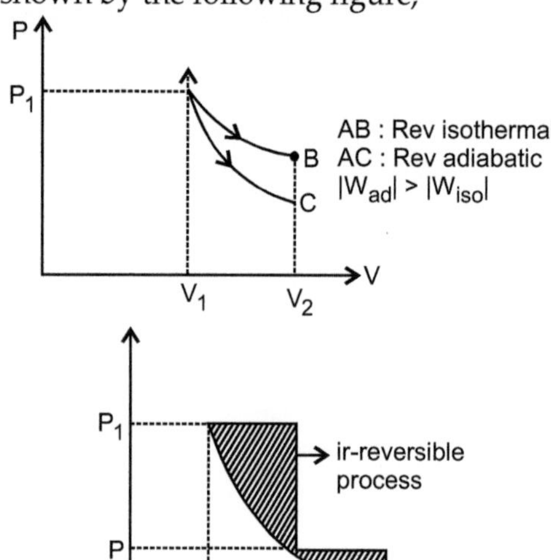


In both the conditions internal energy change will be zero.

**31. (1)** The given equations are,

$$C_{(graphite)} + O_2(g) \rightarrow CO_2(g); \qquad ...(1)$$
$$\Delta_r H^\circ = -393.5 \text{ kJ mol}^{-1}$$

$$H_2(g) + \frac{1}{2} O_2(g) \rightarrow H_2O(l); \qquad ...(2)$$
$$\Delta_r H^\circ = -285.8 \text{ kJ mol}^{-1}$$

$$CO_2(g) + 2H_2O(l) \rightarrow CH_4(g) + 2O_2(g); \quad ...(3)$$
$$\Delta_r H^\circ = +890.3 \text{ kJ mol}^{-1}$$

Multiply equation (2) by 2.

$$2H_2(g) + O_2(g) \rightarrow 2H_2O(l); \qquad ...(4)$$
$$\Delta_r H^\circ = -571.6 \text{ kJ mol}^{-1}$$

On adding equations (1), (3) and (4) the final equation is,

$$C_{(graphite)} + 2H_2(g) \rightarrow CH_4(g); \qquad ...(5)$$
$$\Delta_r H^\circ = (-393.5 - 571.6 + 890.3) \text{ kJ mol}^{-1}$$
$$\Delta_r H^\circ = -74.8 \text{ kJ mol}^{-1}$$

Hence, the value of $\Delta_r H^\circ$ is $-74.8$ kJ mol$^{-1}$.

**32. (1)** The first law of thermodynamics is expressed as,

$$\Delta U = q + w$$

For an adiabatic process, $q = 0$.
Therefore,

$$\Delta U = w$$

**33. (4)** For the given reaction, $A(g) \rightarrow A(l)$

$\Delta H = -3RT$, the enthalpy is given as follows.

$$\Delta H = \Delta U + \Delta n_g RT$$
$$\Delta n_g = n_p - n_r$$

As,
$$= 0 - 1$$
$$= -1$$

Thus, the above enthalpy equation becomes,

$$\Delta H = \Delta U - RT$$
$$-3RT = \Delta U - RT$$
$$-2RT = \Delta U$$

Thus, $|\Delta H| > |\Delta U|$.

**34. (3)** The enthalpy changes from 5°C to $-5$ °C as shown as follows.

$$\text{Total } \Delta H = C_P [H_2O(l)]\Delta T + \Delta H_{freezing} + C_p[H_2O(s)]\Delta T$$
$$= (75.3 \text{ Jmol}^{-1}\text{K}^{-1})(-5) \text{ K}$$
$$+ (-6 \times 10^3 \text{ Jmol}^{-1}\text{K}^{-1})$$
$$+ (36.8 \text{ Jmol}^{-1}\text{K}^{-1})(-5)\text{K}$$
$$= -6.56 \text{ kJ mol}^{-1}$$

The negative value indicates that the enthalpy change to exothermic.

**35. (2)** The expression for enthalpy is shown below. As the pressure and temperature are constant, thus $\Delta H = 0$.

The expression for entropy is shown below.

$$\Delta S = n R \ln\left(\frac{V_f}{V_i}\right)$$

The expansion is accompanied by increase in volume. Thus, entropy will increase.

**36. (2)** The process of change from A to B state and B to A state is shown below.



The value of change in internal energy from A to B is calculated as shown below.

$$\Delta U = q + W$$

Work done from B to A state is calculated as shown below :

$$W = \Delta Y_{BA} - q$$
$$= 3 - (-3)$$
$$= +6 \text{ J}$$

**37. (3)** The process is isothermal so, $\Delta E = 0$.

$$\Delta E = q + w$$
$$0 = q + \left(-P_{ext}\Delta V\right)$$
$$q = P_{ext}\Delta V$$

Substitute the external pressure and change in volume in the equation.

$$q = 3\,atm \times (2-1)L$$
$$= 3\,atm\,L$$

The change in entropy of surroundings is calculated as,

$$\Delta S_{surr} = -\frac{q}{T}$$
$$= -\frac{3 \times 101.3\,J}{300}$$
$$= -1.013\,J/K$$

**38. (2)** If the value of $\Delta H > 0$ and $\Delta S > 0$, only then the reaction is feasible at high temperature and non-feasible at low temperature.

**39. (4)** $\Delta G° = \Delta H° - T\Delta S°$

$$\Delta G° = -29.8\,kJ/mol + \left(0.1 \times 298\,kJ/mol\right)$$
$$= 0$$

The equilibrium constant is calculated by the equation,

$$\Delta G° = -2.303\,RT\,\log K$$
$$0 = -2.303\,RT\,\log K$$
$$\log K = 0$$
$$K = 1$$

**40. (2)** The decomposition of $H_2O_2$ is as follows :

$$2H_2O_2(l) \rightleftharpoons 2H_2O(l) + O_2(g)$$

It is given that 100 mol of $H_2O_2$ on decomposition gives 50 mol $O_2$.

Therefore, the work done by one mole of oxygen is calculated as follows :

$$W = -P_{ext}(\Delta V)$$
$$= -(n_{O_2})RT$$
$$= -(50)(8.3)(300)$$
$$= -124500\,J$$

Thus, the word done by oxygen gas is 124.5 kJ.

**41. (4)** The reactions involved in the given combustion process are shown below :

$$C(s) + O_2(g) \rightarrow CO_2(g)$$
$$\Delta H_1 = -393.5\ kJ.mol^{-1}$$

$$CO(g) + \frac{1}{2}O_2(g) \rightarrow CO_2(g)$$
$$\Delta H_2 = -283.5\ kJ.mol^{-1}$$

Subtract second equation from first

$$C(s) + \frac{1}{2}O_2(g) \rightarrow CO(g)\ \Delta H_3 = ?$$

Thus, the final heat of combustion is given as shown below.

$$\Delta H_3 = -393.5\,kJ.mol^{-1} - \left(-283.5\,kJ.mol^{-1}\right)$$
$$= -110\,kJ.mol^{-1}$$

**42.** (A)-(R), (T); (B)-(P, (Q), (S); (C)-(P), (Q), (S); (D)-(P), (S), (T)

(A) At $0°C$ and 1 atm,
$$H_2O(l) \rightarrow H_2O(s)$$
Randomness decreases which means $\Delta S_{syst} < 0$ $\Delta H = -ve$ and thus, $\Delta G = 0$

(B) In expansion of 1 mol an ideal gas into a vacuum under isolated conditions
$$q = 0\ \text{as it is a isolated system}$$
$$w = 0\ \text{as}\ P_{external} = 0$$
$$\Delta H = 0\ \text{as}\ q + w = 0$$

(C) When equal volume of two ideal gases are mixed at constant T and P,
$$q = 0\ \text{as it is a isolated system.}$$
$$\Delta U = 0\ \text{as it is a isothermal process.}$$
$$w = 0$$

(D) Reversible heating of $H_2$ at 1 atm, then cooling by the same path.
$q = 0$ because heat absorbed is equal to heat released.
$w = 0$ because work done by the system is equal to the work done on the system.
$$\Delta U = 0\ \text{and}\ \Delta G = 0$$

**43. (1,2,3)** (1) External pressure is zero. Therefore, W = 0.
An ideal gas is thermally insulated. So, $q = 0$.

(2) From first law of thermodynamics,
$$\Delta U = q + w$$
Therefore, $\Delta U = 0$. Hence, $T_2 = T_1$.

(3) Also, $n$ and T are constant. Therefore, $P_2V_2 = P_1V_1$.

(4) $P_2V_2^\gamma = P_1V_1^\gamma$, this expression is applicable for an ideal gas in reversible adiabatic process.

**44. (2)** The reaction is,
$$H_2O(l) \rightarrow H_2O(g)$$
For a thermodynamic process,
$$\Delta S_{system} + \Delta S_{surrounding} = 0$$
$$\Delta S_{system} = -\Delta S_{surrounding}$$

Thus, $\Delta S_{system} > 0$ and $\Delta S_{surrounding} < 0$.

**45. (1)** The chemical equation for combustion of ethanol is,
$$C_2H_5OH(l) + 3O_2(g) \rightarrow 2CO_2(g) + 3H_2O(l)$$
The formula to calculate enthalpy of combustion is,
$$\Delta H = \Delta E + \Delta nRT$$
The change in the number of moles of gaseous species is $-1$. Therefore,

$$q_p = q_v + \Delta nRT$$

$$= -1364.47 - \frac{1 \times 8.314 \times 298}{1000}$$

$$= -1364.47 - 2.477$$

$$= -1366.95 \text{ kJ mol}^{-1}$$

**46. (3)** According to the question,

$$\frac{1}{2}N_{2(g)} + \frac{3}{2}H_{2(g)} \rightarrow NH_{3(g)}, \Delta H_g^\circ = -46$$

$$\frac{1}{2} \times 712 \qquad \frac{3}{2} \times 436$$

$$N_{(g)} + 3H_{(g)}$$

Thus, the bond enthalpy is calculated as follows :

$$\text{Bond enthalpy} = \frac{1}{2} \times (-712) + \frac{3}{2}(-436) + (-46)$$

$$= -1056 \text{kJ/mol}$$

The average bond enthalpy for the three $N - H$ bonds in $NH_3$ is,

$$\frac{1056 \text{kJ/mol}}{3} = -352 \text{kJ/mol}$$

The sign of the bond enthalpy (bond-dissociation) will be reversed as +352 kJ/mol because it is calculated from the bond formation that is reverse of bond-dissociation.

**47. (2)** The change in entropy is calculated by the formula,

$$\Delta S = nC_p \ln\left(\frac{T_2}{T_1}\right)$$

$$= 2.303 \times n \times C_p \log\left(\frac{T_2}{T_1}\right)$$

$$= 2.303 \times 1 \times 10 \times \log\left(\frac{100}{1000}\right)$$

$$= -23.03 \text{ Cal deg}^{-1}$$

**48. (2)** The standard entropy change of the given reaction is calculated by the formula,

$$\Delta S^\circ = \Sigma nS^\circ \text{ (products)} - \Sigma mS^\circ \text{ (reactants)}$$

$$= \left(S^\circ_{CO_2(g)} + 2S^\circ_{H_2O(l)}\right) - \left(S^\circ_{CH_4(g)} + 2S^\circ_{O_2(g)}\right)$$

$$= (1 \text{ mol} \times 213.6 \text{ J/mol.K} + 2 \text{ mol}$$
$$\times 69.9 \text{ J/mol.K}) - (1 \text{ mol} \times 186.2 \text{ J/mol.K}$$
$$+ 2 \text{ mol} \times 205.0 \text{ J/mol.K})$$

$$= -242.8 \text{ J/mol.K}$$

**49. (3)** The balanced chemical equation for the formation of methane is,

$$C(s) + H_2(g) \rightarrow CH_4(g)$$
$$\Delta_f H^\circ_{298} = -74.9 \text{ kJ/mol}$$

The average energy released in the given reaction can be calculated if the values of enthalpy of sublimation of carbon and bond dissociation energy of $H_2$ are known.

**50. (3)** The combustion reaction of glucose is shown below.

$$C_6H_{12}O_6(s) + 6O_2(g) \rightarrow 6CO_2(g) + 6H_2O(l)$$

The standard enthalpy of combustion of glucose per mole at given temperature is calculated by the formula,

$$\Delta H^\circ = \left(nH^\circ_{CO_2} + nH^\circ_{H_2O}\right) - nH^\circ_{C_6H_{12}O_6}$$

Substitute the values of standard enthalpies of carbon dioxide, water and glucose in the above expression.

$$\Delta H^\circ = (6 \times (-400) + 6 \times (-300)) - 1$$
$$\times (-1300) \text{ kJ/mol}$$

$$= -2400 - 1800 + 1300 \text{ kJ/mol}$$

$$= -4200 + 1300 \text{ kJ/mol}$$

$$= -2900 \text{ kJ/mol}$$

The standard enthalpy of combustion per gram of glucose is calculated by the formula,

$$\Delta H^\circ = \frac{\text{Standard enthalpy of combustion of glucose}}{\text{Molar mass of glucose}}$$

$$= \frac{-2900 \text{ kJ/mol}}{180 \text{g/mol}}$$

$$= -16.1 \text{kJ/g}$$

**51. (2,3,4)** In ideal solution, there is no exchange of heat which results in zero value of $\Delta H$, positive value of $\Delta S_{\text{system}}$ of system, zero value of $\Delta S_{\text{surrounding}}$.

**52. (3)** The change from K to L shows the increase in volume, V at constant pressure, P. Therefore, it shows increase in temperature that is heating. The change from L to M shows the decrease in P at constant V. Therefore, it shows decrease in temperature that is cooling. The change from M to N also shows decrease in V at constant P. Therefore, it shows decrease in temperature that is cooling. The change from N to K shows the increase in P at constant volume, V. Therefore, it shows increase in temperature that is heating.

The succeeding operations that enable the given transformation of states are heating, cooling, cooling and then again heating.

**53. (2)** The pair of isochoric processes among the transformation of states is L to M and N to K because these changes occur at constant volume.

**54. (1, 3)** (1) Entropy is a state function and is therefore, additive in nature. Thus, $\Delta S_{x \rightarrow z} = \Delta S_{x \rightarrow y} + \Delta S_{y \rightarrow z}$ is correct.

(2) The work done is zero when system shifts from state $y$ to $z$ as it is an isochoric process, that is, there is no

change in volume. Thus, $w_{x \to z} = w_{x \to y} + w_{y \to z}$ is incorrect.

(3) The work done is zero when system shifts from state $y$ to $z$ as it is an isochoric process, that is, there is no change in volume. Thus, $w_{x \to y \to z} = w_{x \to y}$ correct.

(4) Entropy is a state function and is therefore, additive in nature. Thus, $\Delta S_{x \to y \to z} = \Delta S_{x \to y}$ is incorrect.

**55. (4)** The value of $\Delta H$ is calculated as shown below.

$$\Delta H = \begin{pmatrix} (\Delta H_{C(s) \to C(g)} + 1 \times BE_{H-H}) \\ -(2 \times BE_{C-H} + 1 \times BE_{C \equiv C}) \end{pmatrix}$$

$$225\,kJ \cdot mol^{-1} = (1410 + 330 - 2 \times 350$$
$$- BE_{C \equiv C})\,kJ \cdot mol^{-1}$$

$$BE_{C \equiv C} = 815\,kJ \cdot mol^{-1}$$

**56. (1,3,4)** (1) As isothermal condition is given; therefore, $T_1 = T_2$.

(2) Adiabatic cooling occurs; therefore, $T_3 < T_1$.

(3) Area under the isothermal curve is more in comparison to area under the adiabatic curve. Thus, $w_{isothermal} > w_{adiabatic}$.

(4) Internal energy decreases in case of adiabatic process and it leads to cooling. Thus, $\Delta U$ is negative. There is no change in internal energy in isothermal process. Thus, $\Delta U$ is zero. Thus, $\Delta U_{isothermal} > \Delta U_{adiabatic}$.

**57.** (A)-(p), (r), (s); (B)-(r), (s); (C)-(t); (D)-(p), (q), (t)

The reactions for all transformation processes are shown below.

(A) $CO_2(s) + Q \to CO_2(g)$

Here, enthalpy change will be positive because heat is required for the reaction. Solid is converted to gas, therefore, entropy increases here.

(B) $CaCO_3(s) + Q \to CaO(s) + CO_2(g)$
$$\Delta H = + ve$$
$$\Delta S = + ve$$

(C) $\qquad 2H^{\bullet} \to H_2(g)$
$$\Delta S = - ve$$

(D) $\qquad P_{white,\,solid} \to P_{red,\,solid}$
$$\Delta S = - ve$$

This is an allotropic change which involves phase transition.

**58. (2)** The element that exists in its standard or elemental state will have zero standard molar enthalpy of formation at 298 K. The standard state of $Cl^2$ is gas and that of $Br_2$ is liquid at 298 K. So, $Cl_2(g)$ will have zero standard molar enthalpy of formation at 298 K.

**69. (3)** The bond energy of $C - C$ bond is 348 kJ/mol. The value of 1 kcal/mol = 4.2 kJ/mol Thus, the value of bond energy of $C - C$ bond is,

$$Bond\ energy\ of\ C - C\,(kcal/mol) = \frac{348}{4.2}$$
$$= 82.85\,kcal/mol$$
$$\approx 100\,kcal/mol$$

Thus, the value of bond energy of $C - C$ bond is 100 kcal/mol.

**60. (2)** The reversible isothermal process is shown by solid line. So, the work done is,

$$W_s = -4 \times 0.5 \ln\left(\frac{5.5}{0.5}\right)$$
$$= -2 \ln 11\ L.atm$$

The work done by the dotted process (irreversible and three step) is,

$$W_d = -\left[(4 \times 1.5) + (1 \times 1) + \left(\frac{2}{3} \times 2.5\right)\right]L \cdot atm$$
$$= -\frac{26}{3}L \cdot atm$$

So,

$$\frac{W_d}{W_s} = \frac{-26}{3 \times (-2 \ln 11)}$$
$$= 2$$

**61. (1, 4)** State functions are the functions which depend only upon the initial and final state of the system. Internal energy and molar enthalpy are the functions which depend only upon the initial and final states of the system. Therefore, they are state functions. The functions such as irreversible expansion work and reversible expansion work depends upon the path of the reaction but not only upon the initial and final states of the system. Therefore, they are not state functions.

Hence, the option (1) and (4) are correct.

**62.** The number of moles of gas present in the calorimeter is calculated by dividing its mass by the molar mass.

$$Moles\ of\ gas = \frac{3.5g}{28g/mol}$$
$$= 0.125\,mol$$

The enthalpy of combustion for the given reaction is calculated by using the formula,

$$\Delta H_{comb} = \frac{-C_{cal}(T_2 - T_1)}{n}$$

Substitute the values of $C_{cal}$, $T_1$, $T_2$ and $n$ in the above equation.

$$\Delta H_{comb} = \frac{-2.5\,kJ/K \times (298.5 - 298)\,K}{0.125\,mol}$$
$$= -9.0\,kJ/mol$$

**63. (4)** At equilibrium, Gibbs energy is zero, however, standard Gibbs energy is not equal to zero.

$$\Delta G = 0, \Delta G^\circ \neq 0$$

The value of Gibbs energy is negative or less than zero for spontaneous reactions. Hence, chemical reactions are spontaneous in the direction of decreasing Gibbs energy.

**64. (1)** The second statement corresponds to the second law of thermodynamics which states that all heat absorbed cannot be converted into work; there is always a loss of heat during the process.

**65. (2)** The $\Delta_r G^\circ_{298K}$ of given reaction is calculated by the formula,

$$\Delta_r G^\circ_{298K} = \Delta_r H^\circ_{298K} - T\Delta_r S^\circ_{298K}$$
$$= -54.07 \times 1000 - 298 \times 10$$
$$= -57050$$

The relation between $\Delta_r G^\circ_{298K}$ and $\log_{10} K$ is,

$$\Delta_r G^\circ_{298K} = -2.303 RT \log_{10} K$$

The given value of 2.303RT is 5705.
Substitute the values of 2.303 RT and $\Delta_r G^\circ_{298K}$ in above equation.

$$-57050 = -5705 \log_{10} K$$
$$\log_{10} K = 10$$

**66. (1)** The given process is an equilibrium reaction as both phases of water are possible. At equilibrium the value of $\Delta G = 0$.
$\Delta S = +ve$ as liquid molecules are converting into gaseous molecules at 373 K or 100°C.

**67. (1)** An ideal gas equation is,
$$PV = nRT \qquad ...(1)$$
The value of specific heat for monoatomic gas is,

$$C_v = \frac{3}{2}R$$

It is given that the ratio of pressure and volume is equal to one. Therefore,

$$\frac{P}{V} = 1$$

The relationship between specific heat and internal energy is as follows :
$$dq = C_v dT + pdV \qquad ...(2)$$
For one mole of gas, the equation (1) can be written as,

$$PV = RT$$

On differentiation, the above formula becomes,
$$PdV + VdP = RdT \qquad ...(3)$$
The equation (3) can be written as,
$$2PdV = RdT$$
$$PdV = \frac{RdT}{2}$$

Substitute the value of equation (4) in equation (2).

$$dq = C_v dT + \frac{RdT}{2}$$
$$= \frac{3}{2}R + \frac{RdT}{2}$$
$$= \frac{4}{2}R$$

Thus, the molar heat capacity of the gas is $\frac{4}{2}R$.

**68. (2)** The $\Delta S$ for the conversion of A to C is 50 e.u.
The $\Delta S$ for the conversion of C to D is 30 e.u.
The $\Delta S$ for the conversion of B to D is 20 e.u.
The $\Delta S$ for the conversion of A to B is calculated by the formula,
$$S_{(A \to B)} = \Delta S_{(A \to C)} + \Delta S_{(C \to D)} - \Delta S_{(B \to D)}$$

Substitute the values of $\Delta S$ in the above formula.
$$\Delta S_{(A \to B)} = \Delta S_{(A \to C)} + \Delta S_{(C \to D)} - \Delta S_{(B \to D)}$$
$$= 50 + 30 - 20$$
$$= 60\ e.u$$

**69.** The relation between $\Delta H$ and $\Delta U$ is as follows :
$$\Delta H = \Delta U + \Delta(PV)$$
The above formula can be written as,
$$\Delta H = \Delta U + \Delta(PV)$$
$$\Delta H = \Delta U + V\Delta P$$
$$\Delta U = \Delta H - V\Delta P$$
Substitute all the values in the above formula.
$$= -560 + 1 \times 30 \times 0.1$$
$$= -557\ kJ$$

**70. (3)** The expression for work done that is opposing the constant external pressure is,
$$W = P_{ext}(V_2 - V_1)$$
In case of adiabatic situation, the value of $\Delta q$ is zero, thus, $W = \Delta u$.

The value of universal gas constant is 0.0821 atm.L/mol.K.

The given value of initial volume of the ideal gas is 1L.

The given final volume of the ideal gas is 2L.

The given pressure is 1 atm.

For the negative expansion of work, the expression is given as,

$$-P_{ext}(V_2 - V_1) = \frac{3}{2}R(T_2 - T_1)$$

Substitute the value of pressure, universal gas constant, initial and final volumes in the above expression.

**71.** The relation between $\Delta U$ and $q$ is as follows :

$$\Delta U = q + W$$

The value of $q$ for adiabatic process is 0.

Therefore, equation (1) becomes,

$$\Delta U = W \qquad \qquad ...(1)$$

The formula to calculate W is,

$$W = PdV$$
$$= P(V_2 - V_1) \qquad \qquad ...(2)$$

Substitute the given values in equation (2).

$$W = P(V_2 - V_1)$$
$$= -100(99 - 100)$$
$$= 100 \text{ bar mL}$$

Therefore, the value of $\Delta U$ is 100 bar mL.

The value of $\Delta H$ is calculated as follows :

$$\Delta H = \Delta U + \Delta(PV)$$
$$= \Delta U + (P_2V_2 - P_1V_1)$$
$$= 100 + (100 \times 99 - 1 \times 100)$$
$$= 9900 \text{ bar mL}$$

**72. (a) (i)** The given reaction is,

$$N_2O_4(g) \rightarrow 2NO_2(g)$$

The reaction quotient for the given reaction is,

$$= \frac{P^2_{NO_2}}{P_{N_2O_4}}$$
$$= \frac{100}{10}$$
$$= 10 \text{ atm}$$

The Gibbs free energy of formation is calculated by the formula,

$$\Delta G° = 2\Delta G_f°(NO_2) - \Delta G_f°(N_2O_4)$$

Substitute all the values in the above formula.

$$\Delta G° = 2\Delta G_f°(NO_2) - \Delta G_f°(N_2O_4)$$
$$= 100 - 100$$
$$= 0$$

The $\Delta G$ for the given reaction is calculated as follows :

$$\Delta G = \Delta G° + RT \ln k$$
$$RT \ln k = \Delta G° + RT \ln k$$
$$= 2.303 \times 0.82 \times 298 \times \log 9.9$$
$$= 56.03 \text{ Lit atm}$$

**(ii)** The value of $K_p$ is less than $Q_p$. Therefore, the reaction proceed in the backward direction.

The Van der Waal's equation for one mole of a real gas is,

$$\left[P + \frac{a}{V_m^2}\right](V_m - b) = RT$$

$$\left[P + \frac{a}{PV^2}\right]\left(\frac{PV}{P} - b\right) = RT$$

The above equation can be written as,

$$[(PV)^2 P + aP^2][(PV) - b] = P(PV)^2 RT$$

$$P[(PV)^2 + aP](PV - bP) = P(PV)^2 RT$$

After putting $P = 0$, the above equation becomes,

$$(PV)^3 = (PV)^2 RT$$

Therefore, the intercept is RT.

**73. (1)** The Gibbs free energy is given as,

$$\Delta G = \Delta H - T\Delta S$$

The value of $\Delta G$ at equilibrium is 0.

Hence, the temperature is,

$$T = \frac{\Delta H}{\Delta S}$$
$$= \frac{30 \times 10^3 \text{ J/mol}}{75 \text{ J mol}^{-1} \text{K}^{-1}}$$
$$= 400 \text{ K}$$

**74. (4)** According to the first law of thermodynamics, enthalpy change is expressed as,

$$\Delta H = \Delta U + nR\Delta T$$

The change in internal change and change in temperature during isothermal expansion of gas is,

$$\Delta U = 0$$
$$\Delta T = 0$$

Hence, the change in enthalpy is $\Delta H = 0$.

**75. (a)** The polarity of solvent molecules depends upon the value of $K_b$. If value of $K_b$ is high, the polarity of solvent molecules is larger. Therefore, correct order of $K_b$ for the given solvents is given below :

| Solvents | $K_b$ |
| --- | --- |
| X | 0.63 |
| Y | 0.53 |
| Z | 0.92 |

**(b)** The degree of freedom in helium molecule is three which corresponds to the three translational motion. Thus, the value of $C_v$ is always 3/2 R.

In case of hydrogen molecule, translational as well as rotational and vibrational motion is present due to which the value of $C_v$ increases with increase in temperature.

**76. (1)** $\Delta H°_f$ is the change in heat when 1 mol of a substance is formed from its composite elements at standard room temperature and pressure. Thus, the reaction that defines $\Delta H°_f$ is,

$$C_{(Diamond)} + O_2(g) \rightarrow CO_2(g)$$

**77.** (i) The diagram that shows all the process is shown below :

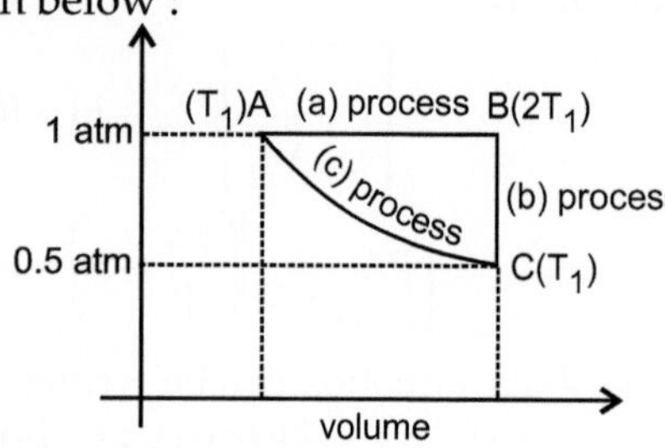


In this figure, $T_1$ and $T_2$ are temperature when gas is at A and B.

(ii) The total work in the above process is calculated as follows :

$$W = W_1 + W_2 + W_3$$

$$= -P\Delta V + 0 + 2.303 n RT \log \frac{V_1}{V_2}$$

$$= -1 \times 20 + 2.303 \times 2 \times 0.082 \times 121.95 \log 2$$

$$= -6.13 \, L\, atm$$

The given process is cyclic. Thus, the value of $\Delta U$ is 0. Therefore, $\Delta Q$ for the above process is,

$$\Delta U = q + W$$

$$q = -W$$

$$= 6.13 \, L.atm$$

$$= 6.13 \times 10^3 \, J$$

(iii) Since, the process is cyclic, the value of $\Delta U$ is zero because entropy is a state function. Similarly, the value of $\Delta H$ and $\Delta U$ is zero.

**78. (3)** The change in enthalpy is calculated by the formula,

$$\Delta H = \Delta U + (P_2 V_2 - P_1 V_1)$$

$$= 30 L\, atm + (4\, atm \times 5L - 2 atm \times 3L)$$

$$= 30 + (20 - 6) L\, atm$$

$$= 44 L\, atm$$

●●

## QUESTIONS

1. For the following Assertion and Reason, the correct option is :

   **Assertion (A) :** When Cu (II) and sulphide ions are mixed, they react together extremely quickly to give a solid.

   **Reason (R) :** The equilibrium constant of $Cu^{2+}$ (aq) $+ S^{2-}$ (aq) $\rightleftharpoons$ CuS(s) is high because the solubility product is low.

   **[2020, Main]**

   (1) Both (A) and (R) are true and (R) is the explanation for (A)

   (2) Both (A) and (R) are false

   (3) (A) is false and (R) is true

   (4) Both (A) and (R) are true but (R) is not the explanation for (A)

2. Henry's constant (in kbar) for four gases $\alpha$, $\beta$, $\gamma$ and $\delta$ in water at 298 K is given below :

   |  | $\alpha$ | $\beta$ | $\gamma$ | $\delta$ |
   |---|---|---|---|---|
   | $K_H$ | 50 | 2 | $2\times10^{-5}$ | 0.5 |

   (density of water = $10^3$ kg m$^{-3}$ at 298 K)
   This table implies that :　　　**[2020, Main]**

   (1) The pressure of a 55.5 molal solution of $\gamma$ is 1 bar

   (2) The pressure of a 55.5 molal solution of $\delta$ is 250 bar

   (3) Solubility of $\gamma$ at 308 K is lower than at 298 K

   (4) A has the highest solubility in water at a given pressure

3. An acetic buffer is obtained on mixing :

   **[2020, Main]**

   (1) 100 mL of 0.1 M $CH_3COOH$ and 200 mL of 0.1 M NaOH

   (2) 100 mL of 0.1 M $CH_3COOH$ and 100 mL of 0.1 M NaOH

   (3) 100 mL of 0.1 M HCl and 200 mL of 0.1 M $CH_3COONa$

   (4) 100 mL of 0.1 M HCl and 200 mL of 0.1 M NaCl

4. 100 mL of 0.1 M HCl is taken in a beaker and to it 100 mL of 0.1 M NaOH is added in steps of 2 mL and the pH is continuously measured. Which of the following graphs correctly depicts the change in pH ?　　　**[2020, Main]**

(1) 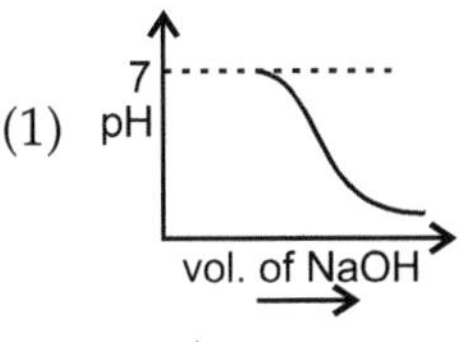

(2) 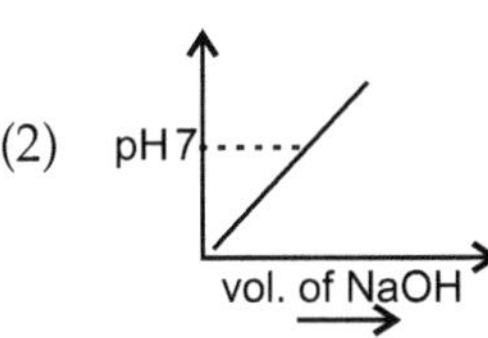

(3) 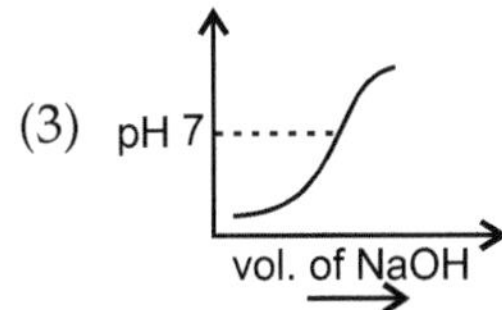

(4) 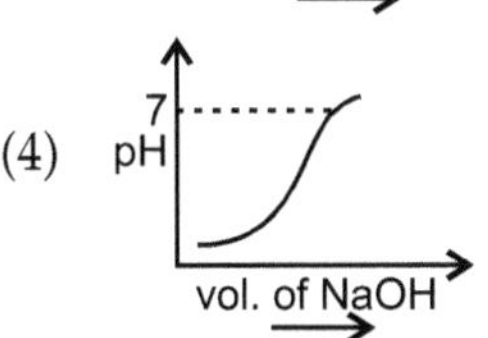

5. The value of $K_C$ is 64 at 800 K for the reaction

   $$N_2(g) + 3H_2(g) \rightleftharpoons 2NH_3(g)$$

   The value of $K_C$ for the following reaction is :

   $$NH_3(g) \rightleftharpoons \frac{1}{2}N_2(g) + \frac{3}{2}H_2(g)$$

   **[2020, Main]**

   (1) $\dfrac{1}{4}$　　　　　　(2) $\dfrac{1}{8}$

   (3) 8　　　　　　(4) $\dfrac{1}{64}$

6. If the solubility product of $AB_2$ is $3.20 \times 10^{-11}$ M$^3$, then the solubility of $AB_2$ in pure water is ...... × $10^{-4}$ mol L$^{-1}$. [Assuming that neither kind of ion reacts with water]　　　**[2020, Main]**

7. Consider the following reaction :

   $$N_2O_4(g) \rightleftharpoons 2NO_2(g); \Delta H^0 = +58 \text{ kJ}$$

   For each of the following cases (a, b) the direction in which the equilibrium shifts is :

   **[2020, Main]**

   (a) Temperature is decreased.

   (b) Pressure is increased by adding $N_2$ at constant T.

   (1) (a) towards reactant, (b) no change

   (2) (a) towards product, (b) towards reactant

   (3) (a) towards product, (b) no change

   (4) (a) towards reactant, (b) towards product

8. For the reaction :

   $$Fe_2N(s) + \frac{3}{2}H_2(g) \rightleftharpoons 2Fe(s) + NH_3(g)$$

   **[2020, Main]**

   (1) $K_C = K_P(RT)$　　　(2) $K_C = K_P(RT)^{-1/2}$

   (3) $K_C = K_P(RT)^{-3/2}$　　　(4) $K_C = K_P(RT)^{1/2}$

**9.** Arrange the following solutions in the decreasing order of pOH : **[2020, Main]**
(A) 0.01 M HCl
(B) 0.01 M NaOH
(C) 0.01 M $CH_3COONa$
(D) 0.01 M NaCl
(1) (B) > (C) > (D) > (A)
(2) (A) > (C) > (D) > (B)
(3) (B) > (D) > (C) > (A)
(4) (A) > (D) > (C) > (B)

**10.** The increasing order of $pK_b$ values of the following compounds is : **[2020, Main]**

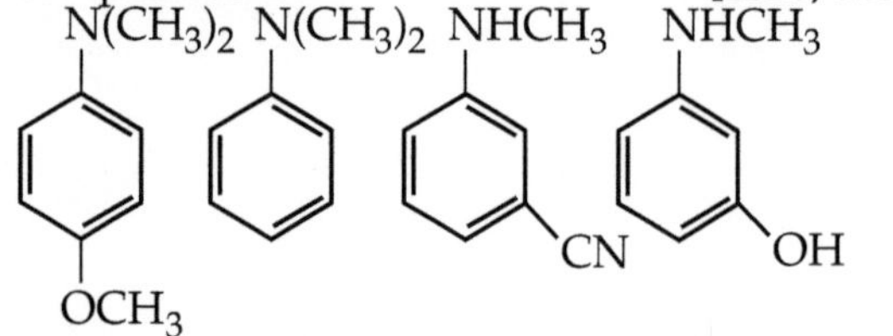

I          II          III          IV
(1) I < II < IV < III
(2) II < IV < III < I
(3) II < I < III < IV
(4) I < II < III < IV

**11.** The variation of equilibrium constant with temperature is given below :

| Temperature | Equilibrium constant |
| --- | --- |
| $T_1 = 25°C$ | $K_1 = 100$ |
| $T_2 = 100°C$ | $K_2 = 100$ |

The values of $\Delta H°$, $\Delta G°$ at $T_1$ and $\Delta G°$ at $T_2$ (in kJ mol$^{-1}$) respectively, are close to :
[Use R = 8.314 JK$^{-1}$mol$^{-1}$)

**[2020, Main]**

(1) 0.64, – 5.71 and – 14.29
(2) 28.4, – 7.14 and – 5.71
(3) 28.4, – 5.71 and – 14.29
(4) 0.64, – 7.14 and – 5.71

**12.** If the equilibrium constant for A $\rightleftharpoons$ B + C is $K_{eq}^{(1)}$ and that of B + C $\rightleftharpoons$ P is $K_{eq}^{(2)}$, the equilibrium constant for A $\rightleftharpoons$ P is : **[2020, Main]**
(1) $K_{eq}^{(2)} - K_{eq}^{(1)}$
(2) $K_{eq}^{(1)}K_{eq}^{(2)}$
(3) $K_{eq}^{(1)} / K_{eq}^{(2)}$
(4) $K_{eq}^{(1)} + K_{eq}^{(2)}$

**13.** For a reaction X + Y $\rightleftharpoons$ 2Z, 1.0 mol of X, 1.5 mol of Y and 0.5 mol of Z were taken in a 1 L vessel and allowed to react. At equilibrium, the concentration of Z was 1.0 mol L$^{-1}$. The equilibrium constant of the reaction is ...... $\dfrac{x}{15}$.

The value of $x$ is ................. . **[2020, Main]**

**14.** In the figure shown below reactant A (represented by square) is in equilibrium with product B (represented by circle). The equilibrium constant is : **[2020, Main]**

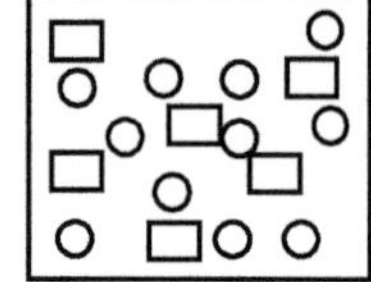

**(1)** 2
**(2)** 1
**(3)** 8
**(4)** 4

**15.** The hardness of a water sample containing $10^{-3}$ M $MgSO_4$ expressed as $CaCO_3$ equivalents (in ppm) is ............. . **[2020, Main]**
(molar mass of $MgSO_4$ is 120.37 g/mol)
(1) R
(2) A
(3) A
(4) A

**16.** Ferrous sulphate heptahydrate is used to fortify foods with iron. The amount (in grams) of the salt required to achieve 10 ppm of iron in 100 kg of wheat is .............. . **[2020, Main]**
Atomic weight : Fe = 55.85; S = 32.0; O = 16.00

**17.** The increasing order of $pK_b$ for the following compounds will be : **[2020, Main]**
$NH_2 - CH = NH$,
(A)

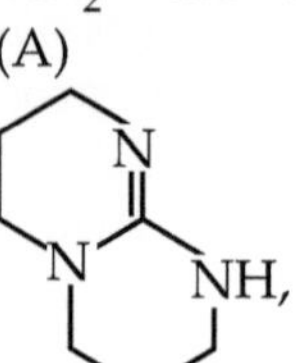

(B)
$CH_3NHCH_3$
(C)
(1) (A) < (B) < (C)
(2) (C) < (A) < (B)
(3) (B) < (A) < (C)
(4) (B) < (C) < (A)

**18.** $NaClO_3$ is used, even in spacecrafts, to produce $O_2$. The daily consumption of pure $O_2$ by a person is 492L at 1 atm, 300 K. How much amount of $NaClO_3$, in grams, is required to produce $O_2$ for the daily consumption of a person at 1 atm, 300 K ? **[2020, Main]**
$NaClO_3(s) + Fe(s) \rightarrow O_2(g) + NaCl(s) + FeO(s)$
R = 0.082 L atm mol$^{-1}$ K$^{-1}$

**19.** Identify the correct labels of A, B and C in the following graph from the options given below :

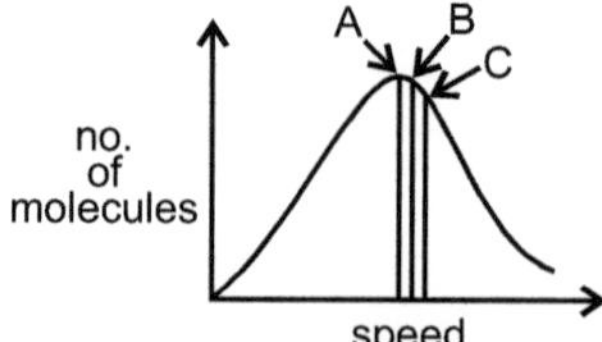


Root mean square speed (V$_{rms}$); most probable speed (V$_{mp}$); Average speed (V$_{av}$).
(1) A - V$_{mp}$; B - C$_{av}$; C - V$_{rms}$
(2) A - V$_{mp}$; B - C$_{rms}$; C - V$_{av}$
(3) A - V$_{av}$; B - C$_{rms}$; C - V$_{mp}$
(4) A - V$_{rms}$; B - C$_{mp}$; C - V$_{av}$

**20.** For the reaction
$$2H_2(g) + 2NO(g) \rightarrow N_2(g) + 2H_2O(g)$$
the observed rate expression is, rate $= k_f[NO_2][H_2]$. The rate expression for the reverse reaction is : **[2020, Main]**

(1) $k_b[N_2][H_2O]^2$
(2) $k_b[N_2][H_2O]$
(3) $k_b[N_2][H_2O]^2/H_2O$
(4) $k_b[N_2][H_2O]^2/[NO]$

**21.** The equation that is incorrect is : **[2020, Main]**

(1) $(\lambda_m^0)_{NaBr} - (\lambda_m^0)_{NaI} = (\lambda_m^0)_{KBr} - (\lambda_m^0)_{NaBr}$

(2) $(\lambda_m^0)_{NaBr} - (\lambda_m^0)_{NaCl} = (\lambda_m^0)_{KBr} - (\lambda_m^0)_{KCl}$

(3) $(\lambda_m^0)_{KCl} - (\lambda_m^0)_{NaCl} = (\lambda_m^0)_{KBr} - (\lambda_m^0)_{NaBr}$

(4) $(\lambda_m^0)_{H_2O} = (\lambda_m^0)_{HCl} + (\lambda_m^0)_{NaOH} - (\lambda_m^0)_{NaCl}$

**22.** If solubility product of $Zr_3(PO_4)$ is denoted by $K_{sp}$ and its molar solubility is denoted by S, then which of the following relation between S and $K_{sp}$ is correct ? **[2019, Main]**

(1) $S = \left(\dfrac{K_{sp}}{144}\right)^{1/6}$ 
(2) $S = \left(\dfrac{K_{sp}}{6912}\right)^{1/7}$

(3) $S = \left(\dfrac{K_{sp}}{929}\right)^{1/9}$ 
(4) $S = \left(\dfrac{K_{sp}}{216}\right)^{1/7}$

**23.** For the following reactions, equilibrium constants are given :

$S(s) + O_2(g) \rightleftharpoons SO_2(g); K_1 = 10^{52}$
$2S(s) + 3O_2(g) \rightleftharpoons 2SO_3(g); K_2 = 10^{129}$

The equilibrium constant for the reaction,
$2SO_2(g) + O_2(g) \rightleftharpoons 2SO_3(g)$ is : **[2019, Main]**

(1) $10^{154}$ 
(2) $10^{181}$
(3) $10^{25}$ 
(4) $10^{77}$

**24.** Consider the following statements
(a) The pH of a mixture containing 400 mL of 0.1 M H2SO4 and 400 mL of 0.1 M NaOH will be approximately 1.3.
(b) Ionic product oif water is temperature dependent
(c) A monobasic acid with $K_a = 10^{-5}$ has a pH = 5. The degree of dissociation of this acid is 50%.
(d) The Le Chatelier's principle is not applicable to common-ion effect.

The correct statements are : **[2019, Main]**

(1) (a), (b) and (d) 
(2) (a), (b) and (c)
(3) (b) and (c) 
(4) (a) and (b)

**25.** The pH of a 0.02 M $NH_4Cl$ solution will be [given $K_b$ $(NH_4OH) = 10^{-5}$ and log 2 = 0.301] **[2019, Main]**

(1) 2.65 
(2) 4.35
(3) 4.65 
(4) 5.35

**26.** For the reaction,
$2SO_2(g) + O_2(g) \rightleftharpoons 2SO_3(g)$,
$\Delta H = -57.2$ kJ mol$^{-1}$ and
$K_c = 1.7 \times 10^{16}$.
Which of the following statements is INCORRECT ? **[2019, Main]**

(1) The equilibrium constant is large suggestive of reaction going to completion and so on catalyst is required.
(2) The equilibrium will shift in forward direction as the pressure increases.
(3) The equilirbium constant decreases as the temperature increases.
(4) The addition of inert gas at constant volume will not affect the equilibrium constant.

**27.** What is the molar solubility of $Al(OH)_3$ in 0.2 M NaOH solution ? Given that, solubility product of $Al(OH)_3 = 2.4 \times 10^{-24}$. **[2019, Main]**

(1) $3 \times 10^{-19}$ 
(2) $12 \times 10^{-21}$
(3) $3 \times 10^{-22}$ 
(4) $12 \times 10^{-23}$

**28.** The molar solubility of $Cd(OH)_2$ is $1.84 \times 10^{-5}$ M in water. The expected solubility of $Cd(OH)_2$ in a buffer solution of pH = 12 is : **[2019, Main]**

(1) $1.84 \times 10^{-9}$ M 
(2) $\dfrac{21.49}{1.84} \times 10^{-9}$ M

(3) $6.23 \times 10^{-11}$ M 
(4) $2.49 \times 10^{-10}$ M

**29.** In which one of the following equilibria, $K_p \neq K_c$ ? **[2019, Main]**

(1) $2C(s) + O_2(g) \rightleftharpoons 2CO(g)$
(2) $2HI(g) \rightleftharpoons H_2(g) + I_2(g)$
(3) $NO_2(g) + SO_2(g) \rightleftharpoons NO(g) + SO_3(g)$
(4) $2NO(g) \rightleftharpoons N_2(g) + O_2(g)$

**30.** The INCORRECT match in the following is : **[2019, Main]**

(1) $\Delta G^0 < 0, K > 1$ 
(2) $\Delta G^0 = 0, K = 1$
(3) $\Delta G^0 > 0, K < 1$ 
(4) $\Delta G^0 < 0, K < 1$

**31.** The solubility of a salt of weak acid (AB) at pH 3 is $Y \times 10^{-3}$ mol L$^{-1}$. The value of Y is ............ .

**[2018, Advanced]**

(Given that the value of solubility product of AB $(K_{sp}) = 2 \times 10^{-10}$ and the value of ionisation constant of HB $(K_a) = 1 \times 10^{-8}$).

**32.** For a reaction, $A \rightleftharpoons P$, the plots of [A] and [P] with time at temperatures $T_1$ and $T_2$ are given below.

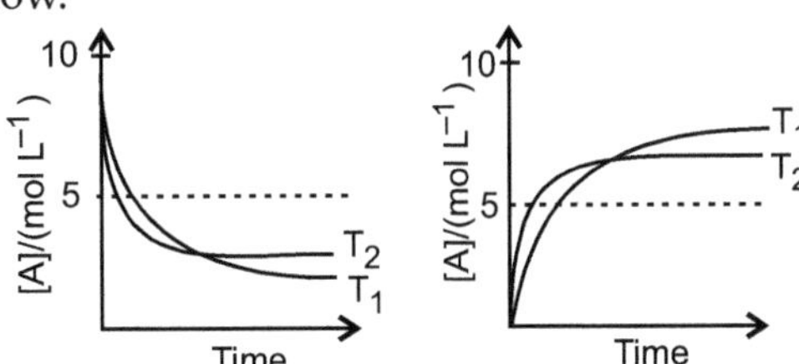


If $T_2 > T_1$, the correct statements is/are : (Assume $\Delta H^\theta$ and $\Delta S^\theta$ are independent of temperature and ratio of ln K at $T_1$ to ln K at $T_2$ is greater than $T_2/T_1$. Here H, S, G and K are enthalpy, entropy, Gibbs energy and equilibrium constant, respectively.) **[2018, Advanced]**

(1) $\Delta H^\theta < 0, \Delta S^\theta < 0$ 
(2) $\Delta G^\theta < 0, \Delta H^\theta < 0$
(3) $\Delta G^\theta < 0, \Delta S^\theta < 0$ 
(4) $\Delta G^\theta < 0, \Delta S^\theta > 0$

**33.** Dilution processes of different aqueous solutions, with water, are given in List-I. The effects of dilution of the solutions on $[H^+]$ are given in List-II. (Note : Degree of dissociation ($\alpha$) of weak acid and weak base is $\ll 1$; degree of hydrolysis of salt $\ll 1$; $[H^+]$ represents the concentration of $H^+$ ions)

| List-I | List-II |
|---|---|
| P. (10 mL of 0.1 M NaOH + 20 mL of 0.1 M acetic acid) diluted to 60 mL | 1. the value of $[H^+]$ does not change on dilution |
| Q. (20 mL of 0.1 M NaOH + 20 mL of 0.1 M acetic acid) diluted to 80 mL | 2. the value of $[H^+]$ changes to half of its initial value on dilution |
| R. (20 mL of 0.1 M HCl + 20 mL of 0.1 M ammonia solution) diluted to 80 mL | 3. the value of $[H^+]$ changes to two times of its initial value on dilution |
| S. 10 mL saturated solution of $Ni(OH)_2$ in equilibrium with excess solid $Ni(OH)_2$ is diluted to 20 mL (solid $Ni(OH)_2$ is still present after dilution). | 4. the value of $[H^+]$ changes to $\dfrac{1}{\sqrt{2}}$ times of its initial value on dilution |
| | the value of $[H^+]$ changes to $\sqrt{2}$ times of its initial value on dilution |

Match each process given in List-I with one or more effects in List-II. The correct option is : **[2018, Advanced]**

(1) $P \to 4; Q \to 2; R \to 3; S \to 1$
(2) $P \to 4; Q \to 3; R \to 2; S \to 3$
(3) $P \to 1; Q \to 4; R \to 5; S \to 3$
(4) $P \to 1; Q \to 5; R \to 4; S \to 1$

**34.** Which of the following lines correctly show the temperature dependence of equilibrium constant, K, for an exothermic reaction ? **[2018, Main]**

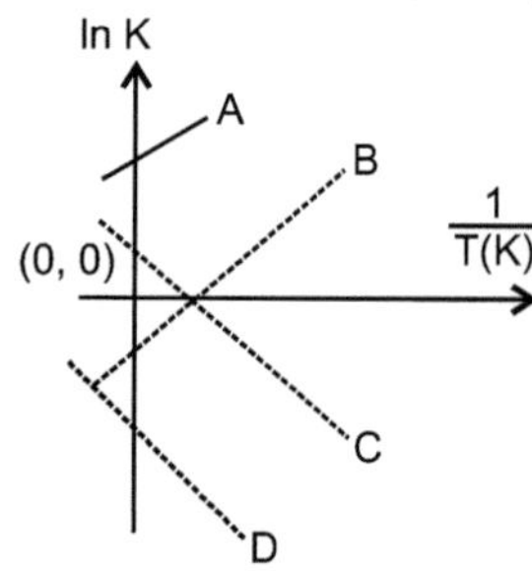


(1) A and B
(2) B and C
(3) C and D
(4) A and D

**35.** An aqueous solution contains 0.10 M $H_2S$ and 0.20 M HCl. If the equilibrium constants for the formation of $HS^-$ from $H_2S$ is $1.0 \times 10^{-7}$ and that of $S^{2-}$ from $HS^-$ ions is $1.2 \times 10^{-13}$ then the concentration of $S^{2-}$ ions in aqueous solution is : **[2018, Main]**

(1) $5 \times 10^{-8}$
(2) $3 \times 10^{-20}$
(3) $6 \times 10^{-21}$
(4) $5 \times 10^{-19}$

**36.** An aqueous solution contains an unknown concentration of $Ba^{2+}$. When 50 mL of a 1 M solution of $Na_2SO_4$ is added, $BaSO_4$ just begins to precipitate. The final volume is 500 mL. The solubility product of $BaSO_4$ is $1 \times 10^{-10}$. What is the original concentration of $Ba^{2+}$ ? **[2018, Main]**

(1) $5 \times 10^{-9}$ M
(2) $2 \times 10^{-9}$ M
(3) $1.1 \times 10^{-9}$ M
(4) $1.0 \times 10^{-10}$ M

**37.** Which of the following are Lewis acids ? **[2018, Main]**

(1) $PH_3$ and $BCl_3$
(2) $AlCl_3$ and $SiCl_4$
(3) $PH_3$ and $SiCl_4$
(4) $BCl_3$ and $AlCl_3$

**38.** Which of the following salts is the most basic in aqueous solution ? **[2018, Main]**

(1) $Al(CN)_3$
(2) $CH_3COOK$
(3) $FeCl_3$
(4) $Pb(CH_3COO)_2$

**39.** An alkali is titrated against an acid with methyl orange as indicator, which of the following is a correct combination ? **[2018, Main]**

| | Base | Acid | End point |
|---|---|---|---|
| (1) | Weak | Strong | Colourless to pink |
| (2) | Strong | Strong | Pinkish red to yellow |
| (3) | Weak | Strong | Yellow to pinkish red |
| (4) | Strong | Strong | Pink to colourless |

**40.** Following four solutions are prepared by mixing different volumes of NaOH and HCl of different concentrations, pH of which one of them will be equal to 1 ? **[2018, Main]**

(1) 100 mL $\dfrac{M}{10}$ HCl + 100 mL $\dfrac{M}{10}$ NaOH
(2) 75 mL $\dfrac{M}{5}$ HCl + 25 mL $\dfrac{M}{5}$ NaOH
(3) 60 mL $\dfrac{M}{10}$ HCl + 40 mL $\dfrac{M}{10}$ NaOH
(4) 55 mL $\dfrac{M}{10}$ HCl + 45 mL $\dfrac{M}{10}$ NaOH

**41.** At a certain temperature in a 5 L vessel, 2 moles of carbon monoxide and 3 moles of chlorine were allowed to reach equilibrium according to the reaction,

$$CO + Cl_2 \rightleftharpoons COCl_2$$

At equilibrium, if one mole of CO is present then equilibrium constant ($K_C$) for the reaction is : **[2018, Main]**

(1) 2
(2) 2.5
(3) 3
(4) 4

**42.** The minimum volume of water required to dissolve 0.1 g lead(II) chloride to get a saturated solution ($K_{sp}$ of $PbCl_2 = 3.2 \times 10^{-8}$; atomic mass of Pb = 207 u) is : **[2018, Main]**

(1) 0.36 L      (2) 17.98 L

(3) 0.18 L      (4) 1.798 L

**43.** Which of the following is a Lewis acid ?

**[2018, Main]**

(1) $PH_3$      (2) $B(CH_3)_3$

(3) $NaH$      (4) $NF_3$

**44.** A white sodium salt dissolves readily in water to give a solution which is neutral to litmus. When silver nitrate solution is added to the aforementioned solution, a white precipitate is obtained which does not dissolve in dil. nitric acid. The anion is : **[2018, Main]**

(1) $CO_3^{2-}$      (2) $SO_4^{2-}$

(3) $Cl^-$      (4) $S^{2-}$

**45.** The gas phase reaction $2NO_2(g) \rightarrow N_2O_2(g)$ is an exothermic reaction. The decomposition of $N_2O_4$, in equilibrium mixture of $NO_2(g)$ and $N_2O_4(g)$, can be increased by : **[2018, Main]**

(1) lowering the temperature

(2) increasing the pressure

(3) addition of an inert gas at constant volume

(4) addition of an inert gas at constant pressure

**46.** At 320 K, a gas $A_2$ is 20% dissociated to $A(g)$. The standard free energy change at 320 K and 1 atm in J $mol^{-1}$ is approximately : $(R = 8.314\, JK^{-1}\, mol^{-1};$ $\ln 2 = 0.693;\ \ln 3 = 1.098)$ **[2018, Main]**

(1) 4763      (2) 2068

(3) 1844      (4) 4281

**47.** The incorrect statement is : **[2018, Main]**

(1) $Cu^{2+}$ salts give red coloured borax bead test in reducing flame

(2) $Cu^{2+}$ and $Ni^{2+}$ ions give black precipitate with $H_2S$ in presence of HCl solution

(3) Ferric ion gives blood red colour with potassium thiocyanate

(4) $Cu^{2+}$ ion gives chocolate coloured precipitate with potassium ferrocyanide solution

**48.** For standardising NaOH solution, which of the following is used as a primary standard ? **[2018, Main]**

(1) Ferrous Ammonium Sulfate

(2) dil. HCl

(3) Oxalic acid

(4) Sodium tetraborate

**49.** For a reaction taking place in a container in equilibrium with its surroundings, the effect of temperature on its equilibrium constant K in terms of change in entropy is described by : **[2017, Advanced]**

(1) With increase in temperature, the value of K for exothermic reaction decreases because the entropy change of the system is positive

(2) With increase in temperature, the value of K for endothermic reaction increases because unfavourable change in entropy of the surroundings decreases

(3) With increase in temperature, the value of K for endothermic reaction increases because the entropy change of the system is negative

(4) With increase in temperature, the value of K for exothermic reaction decreases because favourable change in entropy of the surroundings decreases

**50.** $pK_a$ of a weak acid (HA) and $pK_b$ of a weak base (BOH) are 3.2 and 3.4, respectively. The pH of their salt (AB) solution is : **[2017, Main]**

(1) 7.0      (2) 1.0

(3) 7.2      (4) 6.9

**51.** Addition of sodium hydroxide solution to a weak acid (HA) results in a buffer of pH 6. If ionisation constant of HA is $10^{-5}$, the ratio of salt to acid concentration in the buffer solution will be : **[2017, Main]**

(1) 4 : 5      (2) 1 : 10

(3) 10 : 1      (4) 5 : 4

**52.** 50 mL of 0.2 M ammonia solution is treated with 25 mL of 0.2 M HCl. If $pK_b$ of ammonia solution is 4.75, the pH of the mixture will be : **[2017, Main]**

(1) 3.75      (2) 4.75

(3) 8.25      (4) 9.25

**53.** The following reaction occurs in the Blast Furnace where iron ore is reduced to iron metal :

$$Fe_2O_3(s) + 3(CO)g \rightleftharpoons 2Fe(l) + 3CO_3(g)$$

Using the Le Chatelier's principle, predict which one of the following will not disturb the equilibrium ? **[2017, Main]**

(1) Removal of CO      (2) Removal of $CO_2$

(3) Addition of $CO_2$      (4) Addition of $Fe_2O_3$

**54.** The reagents that can selectively precipitate $S^{2-}$ from a mixture of $S^{2-}$ and $SO_4^{2-}$ in aqueous solution is/are : **[2017, Advanced]**

(1) $CuCl_2$      (2) $BaCl_2$

(3) $Pb(OOCCH_3)_2$      (4) $Na_2[Fe(CN)_5NO]$

**55.** The equilibrium constant $K_P$ for this reaction at 298 K, in terms of $\beta_{equilibrium}$, is : **[2016, Advanced]**

(1) $\dfrac{8\beta^2_{equilibrium}}{2 - \beta_{equilibrium}}$      (2) $\dfrac{8\beta^2_{equilibrium}}{4 - \beta^2_{equilibrium}}$

(3) $\dfrac{4\beta^2_{equilibrium}}{2 - \beta_{equilibrium}}$      (4) $\dfrac{4\beta^2_{equilibrium}}{4 - \beta^2_{equilibrium}}$

**56.** In incorrect statement among the following, for this reaction, is : **[2016, Advanced]**

(1) Decrease in the total pressure will result in formation of more moles of gaseous X

(2) At the start of the reaction, dissociation of gaseous $X_2$ takes place spontaneously

(3) $\beta_{equilibrium} = 0.7$

(4) $K_C < 1$

**57.** The amount of arsenic pentasulphide that can be obtained when 35.5 g arsenic acid is treated with excess $H_2S$ in the presence of conc. HCl (assuming 100% conversion) is : **[2016, Main]**

(1)  0.50 mol       (2)  0.25 mol

(3)  0.125 mol      (4)  0.333 mol

**58.** A solid XY kept in an evacuated sealed container undergoes decomposition to form a mixture of gases X and Y at temperature T. the equilibrium pressure is 10 bar in this vessel. $K_p$ for this reaction is : **[2016, Main]**

(1)  5          (2)  10

(3)  25        (4)  100

**59.** The equilibrium constant at 298 K for a reaction $A + B \rightleftharpoons C + D$ is 100. If the initial concentration of all the four species were 1 M each, then equilibrium concentration of D (in mol L$^{-1}$) will be : **[2016, Main]**

(1)  0.182      (2)  0.818

(3)  1.818      (4)  1.182

**60.** The % yield of ammonia as a function of time in the reaction

$$N_2(g) + 3H_2(g) \rightleftharpoons 2NH_3(g), \Delta H < 0$$

at $(P, T_1)$ is given below. **[2016, Advanced]**

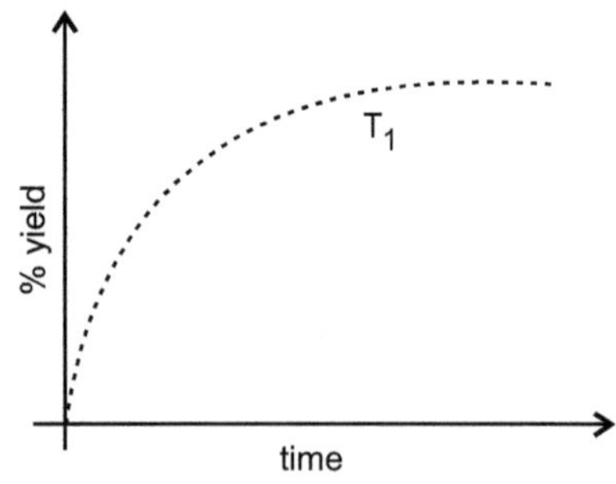

If this reaction is conducted at $(P, T_2)$, with $T_2 > T_1$, the % yield of ammonia as a function of time is represented by :

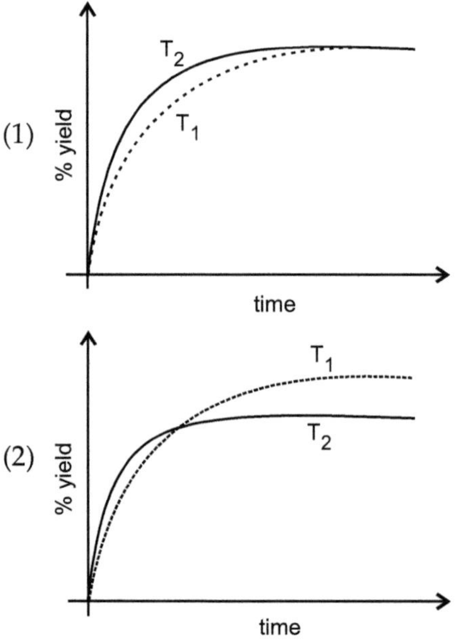

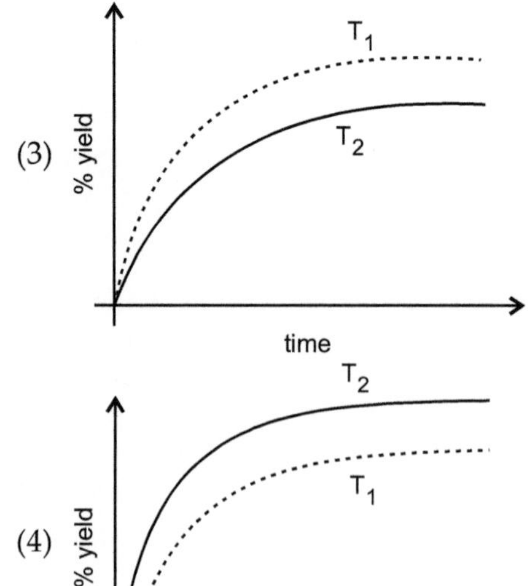

**61.** The molar conductivity of a solution of a weak acid HX (0.01 M) is 10 times smaller than the molar conductivity of a solution of a weak acid HY (0.10) M). If $\lambda^0_{X^-} \approx \lambda^0_{Y^-}$, the difference in their $pK_a$ values, $pK_a(HX) - pK_a(HY)$, is (consider degree of ionisation of both acids to be ≪ 1).

**[2015, Advanced]**

**62.** Enthalpy of dissociation (in kJ mol$^{-1}$) of acetic acid obtained from the Expt. 2 is : **[2015, Advanced]**

(1)  1.0        (2)  10.0

(3)  24.5      (4)  51.4

**63.** The pH of the solution after Expt. 2 is :

**[2015, Advanced]**

(1)  2.8        (2)  4.7

(3)  5.0        (4)  7.0

**64.** The following reaction is performed at 298 K.
$$2NO(g) + O_2(g) \rightleftharpoons 2NO_2(g)$$
The standard free energy of formation of NO(g) is 86.6 kJ/mol at 298 K. What is the standard free energy of formation of NO$_2$(g) at 298 K ? ($K_p = 1.6 \times 10^{12}$) **[2015, Main]**

(1)  $R(298) \ln(1.6 \times 10^{12}) - 86600$

(2)  $86600 + R(298) \ln(1.6 \times 10^{12})$

(3)  $86600 - \dfrac{\ln(1.6 \times 10^{12})}{R(298)}$

(4)  $0.5[2 \times 86{,}600 - R(298) \ln(1.6 \times 10^{12})]$

**65.** The standard Gibbs energy change at 300 K for the reaction $2A \rightleftharpoons B + C$ is 2494.2 J. At a given time, the composition of the reaction mixture is $[A] = \dfrac{1}{2}, [B] = 2$ and $C = \dfrac{1}{2}$. The reaction proceeds in the : [R = 8.314 J/K/mol, $e$ = 2.718] **[2015, Main]**

(1)  forward direction because $Q > K_C$

(2)  reverse direction because $Q > K_C$

(3)  forward direction because $Q < K_C$

(4)  reverse direction because $Q < K_C$

**66.** Gaseous $N_2O_4$ dissociates into gaseous $NO_2$ according to the reaction

$$N_2O_4(g) \rightleftharpoons 2NO_2(g)$$

At 300 K and 1 atm pressure, the degree of dissociation of $N_2O_4$ is 0.2. If one mole of $N_2O_4$ gas is contained in a vessel, then the density of the equilibrium mixture is : **[2015, Main]**

(1)  1.56 g/L        (2)  3.11 g/L
(3)  4.56 g/L        (4)  6.22 g/L

**67.** For the equilibrium, $A(g) \rightleftharpoons B(g)$, $\Delta H$ is $-40$ kJ/mol. If the ratio of the activation energies of the forward ($E_f$) and reverse ($E_b$) reactions is $\dfrac{2}{3}$ then :

**[2015, Main]**

(1)  $E_f = 60$ kJ/mol; $E_b = 100$ kJ/mol
(2)  $E_f = 30$ kJ/mol; $E_b = 70$ kJ/mol
(3)  $E_f = 80$ kJ/mol; $E_b = 120$ kJ/mol
(4)  $E_f = 70$ kJ/mol; $E_b = 30$ kJ/mol

**68.** The increase of pressure on ice $\rightleftharpoons$ water system at constant temperature will lead to :

**[2015, Main]**

(1)  no effect on the equilibrium
(2)  a decrease in the entropy of the system
(3)  a shift of the equilibrium in the forward direction
(4)  an increase in the Gibbs energy of the system

**69.** For the reaction $SO_{2(g)} + \dfrac{1}{2}O_{2(g)} \rightleftharpoons SO_{3(g)}$, if $K_P = K_C(RT)^x$ where the symbols have usual meaning then the value of $x$ is : **[2014, Main]** (assuming ideality)

(1)  $-1$        (2)  $-\dfrac{1}{2}$

(3)  $\dfrac{1}{2}$        (4)  $1$

**70.** At a certain temperature, only 50% HI is dissociated into $H_2$ and $I_2$ at equilibrium. The equilibrium constant is : **[2014, Main]**

(1)  1.0        (2)  3.0
(3)  0.5        (4)  0.25

**71.** Assuming that the degree of hydrolysis is small, the pH of 0.1 M solution of sodium acetate ($K_a = 1.0 \times 10^{-5}$) will be : **[2014, Main]**

(1)  5.0        (2)  6.0
(3)  8.0        (4)  9.0

**72.** In some solutions, the concentration of $H_3O^+$ remains constant even when small amounts of strong acid or strong base are added to them. These solutions are known as : **[2014, Main]**

(1)  Ideal solutions
(2)  Colloidal solutions
(3)  True solutions
(4)  Buffer solutions

**73.** Consider the following equilibrium

$$AgCl \downarrow 2NH_3 \rightleftharpoons [Ag(NH_3)_2]^+ + Cl^-$$

White precipitate of AgCl appears on adding which of the following ? **[2014, Main]**

(1)  $NH_3$        (2)  aqueous NaCl
(3)  aqueous $HNO_3$        (4)  aqueous $NH_4Cl$

**74.** What happens when an inert gas is added to an equilibrium keeping volume unchanged ?

**[2014, Main]**

(1)  More product will form
(2)  Less product will form
(3)  More reactant will form
(4)  Equilibrium will remain unchanged

**75.** The conjugate base of hydrazoic acid is :

**[2014, Main]**

(1)  $N^{-3}$        (2)  $N_3^-$
(3)  $N_2^-$        (4)  $HN_3^-$

**76.** Zirconium phosphate $[Zr_3(PO_4)_4]$ dissociates into three zirconium cations of charge $+4$ and four phosphate anions of charge $-3$. If molar solubility of zirconium phosphate is denoted by S and its solubility product by $K_{sp}$ then which of the following relationship between S and $K_{sp}$ is correct ? **[2014, Main]**

(1)  $S = \{K_{sp}/(6912)^{1/7}\}$    (2)  $S = \{K_{sp}/144\}^{1/7}$
(3)  $S = (K_{sp}/6912)^{1/7}$    (4)  $S = \{K_{sp}/6912\}^7$

**77.** For the decomposition of the compound represented as

$$NH_2COONH_4(s) \rightleftharpoons 2NH_3(g) + CO_2(g)$$

the $K_P = 2.9 \times 10^{-5}$ atm$^3$.

If the reaction is started with 1 mol of the compound, the total pressure at equilibrium would be : **[2014, Main]**

(1)  $1.94 \times 10^{-2}$ atm    (2)  $5.82 \times 10^{-2}$ atm
(3)  $7.66 \times 10^{-2}$ atm    (4)  $38.8 \times 10^{-2}$ atm

**78.** The initial rate of hydrolysis of methyl acetate (1M) by a weak acid (HA, 1M) is $1/100^{th}$ of that of a strong acid (HX, 1M), at 25°C. The $K_a$ of HA is : **[2013, Advanced]**

(1)  $1 \times 10^{-4}$        (2)  $1 \times 10^{-5}$
(3)  $1 \times 10^{-6}$        (4)  $1 \times 10^{-3}$

**79.** The thermal dissociation equilibrium of $CaCO_3(s)$ is studied under different conditions.

$$CaCO_3(s) \rightarrow CaO(s) + CO_2(g)$$

For this equilibrium, the correct statements is/are : **[2013, Advanced]**

(1)  $\Delta H$ is dependent on T
(2)  K is independent of the initial amount of $CaCO_3$
(3)  K is dependent on the pressure of $CO_2$ at a given T
(4)  $\Delta H$ is independent of the catalyst, if any

80. The $K_{sp}$ of $Ag_2CrO_4$ is $1.1 \times 10^{-12}$ at 298 K. The solubility (in mol/L) of $Ag_2CrO_4$ in a 0.1 M $AgNO_3$ solution is : **[2013, Advanced]**
    (1) $1.1 \times 10^{-11}$
    (2) $1.1 \times 10^{-10}$
    (3) $1.1 \times 10^{-12}$
    (4) $1.1 \times 10^{-9}$

81. $AgNO_3$(aq.) was added to an aqueous KCl solution gradually and the conductivity of the solution was measured. The plot of conductance ($\Lambda$) versus the volume of $AgNO_3$ is :

**[2011, Advanced]**

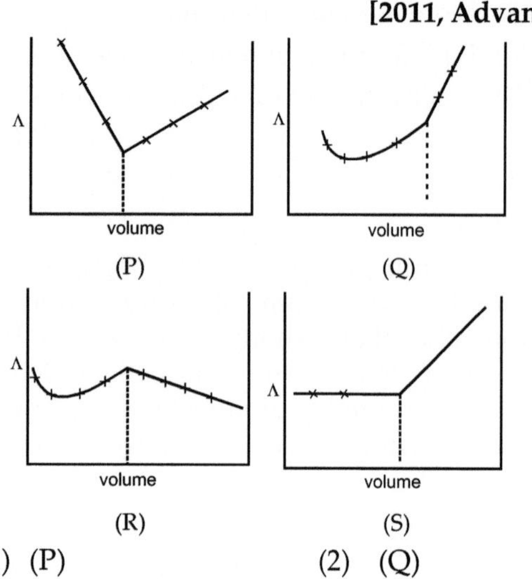

(1) (P)
(2) (Q)
(3) (R)
(4) (S)

82. The equilibrium

$$2Cu^I \rightleftharpoons Cu^O + Cu^{II}$$

in aqueous medium at 25°C shifts towards the left in the presence of : **[2011, Advanced]**
    (1) $NO_3^-$
    (2) $Cl^-$
    (3) $SCN^-$
    (4) $CN^-$

83. In 1 L saturated solution of AgCl $[K_{sp}(AgCl) = 1.6 \times 10^{-10}]$, 0.1 mol of CuCl $[K_{sp}(CuCl) = 1.0 \times 10^{-6}]$ is added. The resultant concentration of $Ag^+$ in the solution is $1.6 \times 10^{-x}$. The value of ``$x$'' is. **[2011, Advanced]**

84. Aqueous solutions of $HNO_3$, KOH, $CH_3COOH$, and $CH_3COONa$ of identical concentrations are provided. The pair(s) of solutions which form a buffer upon mixing is/are : **[2010, Advanced]**
    (1) $HNO_3$ and $CH_3COOH$
    (2) KOH and $CH_3COONa$
    (3) $HNO_3$ and $CH_3COONa$
    (4) $CH_3COOH$ and $CH_3COONa$

85. The total number of diprotic acids among the following is : **[2010, Advanced]**
$H_3PO_4$  $H_2SO_4$  $H_3PO_3$  $H_2CO_3$  $H_2S_2O_7$
$H_3BO_3$  $H_3PO_2$  $H_2CrO_4$  $H_2SO_3$

86. The dissociation constant of a substituted benzoic acid at 25°C is $1.0 \times 10^{-4}$. The pH of a 0.01 M solution of its sodium salt is : **[2009, Advanced]**

87. 2.5 mL of $\frac{2}{5}$ M weak monoacidic base ($K_b = 1 \times 10^{-12}$ at 25°C) is titrated with $\frac{2}{15}$ M HCl in water at 25°C. The concentration of $H^+$ at equivalence point is ($K_w = 1 \times 10^{-14}$ at 25°C) **[2008, Advanced]**
    (1) $3.7 \times 10^{-13}$ M
    (2) $3.2 \times 10^{-7}$ M
    (3) $3.2 \times 10^{-2}$ M
    (4) $2.7 \times 10^{-2}$ M

88. Solubility product constants ($K_{sp}$) of salts of types MX, $MX_2$ and $M_3X$ at temperature `T' are $4.0 \times 10^{-8}$, $3.2 \times 10^{-14}$ and $2.7 \times 10^{-15}$, respectively. Solubilities (mol $dm^{-3}$) of the salts at temperature `T' are in the order : **[2008, Advanced]**
    (1) $MX > MX_2 > M_3X$
    (2) $M_3X > MX_2 > MX$
    (3) $MX_2 > M_3X > MX$
    (4) $MX > M_3X > MX_2$

89. A solution of a metal ion when treated with KI gives a red precipitate which dissolves in excess KI to give a colourless solution. Moreover, the solution of metal ion on treatment with a solution of cobalt(II) thiocyanate gives rise to a deep blue crystalline precipitate. The metal ion is : **[2007, Advanced]**
    (1) $Pb^{2+}$
    (2) $Hg^{2+}$
    (3) $Cu^{2+}$
    (4) $Co^{2+}$

90. $Ag^+ + NH_3 \rightleftharpoons [Ag(NH_3)^+]$; $k_1 = 3.5 \times 10^{-3}$
$[Ag(NH_3)]^+ + NH_3 \rightleftharpoons [Ag(NH_3)_2]^+$; $k_2 = 1.7 \times 10^{-3}$
then the formation constant of $[Ag(NH_3)_2]^+$ is : **[2006, Main]**
    (1) $6.08 \times 10^{-6}$
    (2) $6.08 \times 10^6$
    (3) $6.08 \times 10^{-9}$
    (4) None

91. $N_2 + 3H_2 \rightleftharpoons 2NH_3$
Which is correct statement if $N_2$ is added at equilibrium condition ? **[2006, Main]**
    (1) The equilibrium will shift to forward direction because according to $II^{nd}$ Law of Thermodynamics the entropy must increases in the direction of spontaneous reaction
    (2) The condition for equilibrium is $G_{N_2} + 3G_{H_2}$ $= 2G_{NH_3}$, where, **G** is Gibbs free energy per mole of the gaseous species measured at that partial pressure. The condition of equilibrium is unaffected by the use of catalyst, which increases the rate of both the forward and backward reactions to the same extent
    (3) The catalyst will increase the rate of forward reaction by $\alpha$ and that of backward reaction by $\beta$
    (4) Catalyst will not alter the rate of either of the reaction

92. The species present in solution when $CO_2$ is dissolved in water are : **[2006, Main]**
    (1) $CO_2, H_2CO_3, HCO_3^-, CO_3^{2-}$
    (2) $H_2CO_3, CO_3^{2-}$
    (3) $CO_3^{2-}, HCO_3^-$
    (4) $CO_2, H_2CO_3$

**93.** We have taken a saturated solution of AgBr. $K_{sp}$ of AgBr is $12 \times 10^{-14}$. If $10^{-7}$ mole of $AgNO_3$ are added to 1 litre of this solution find conductivity (specific conductance) of this solution in terms of $10^{-7}$ S m$^{-1}$ units. **[2006, Main]**

Given, $\lambda^o_{(Ag^+)} = 6 \times 10^{-3}$ Sm$^2$ mol$^{-1}$, $\lambda^o_{(Br^-)} = 8 \times 10^{-3}$ Sm$^2$ mol$^{-1}$, $\lambda^o_{(NO_3^-)} = 7 \times 10^{-3}$ Sm$^2$ mol$^{-1}$.

**94.** $CH_3.NH_2$ (0.1 mole, $K_b = 5 \times 10^{-4}$) is added to 0.08 moles of HCl and the solution is diluted to one litre, resulting hydrogen ion concentration is : **[2005, Screening]**
(1) $1.6 \times 10^{-11}$
(2) $8 \times 10^{-11}$
(3) $5 \times 10^{-5}$
(4) $8 \times 10^{-2}$

**95.** Arrange the following oxides in the increasing order of Bronsted basicity. **[2004, Main]**
$Cl_2O_7$, $BaO$, $SO_3$, $CO_2$, $B_2O_3$

**96.** $AlF_3$ is insoluble in anhydrous HF but when little KF is added to the compound it becomes soluble. On addition of $BF_3$, $AlF_3$ is precipitated. Write the balanced chemical equations. **[2004, Main]**

**97.** HX is a weak acid ($K_a = 10^{-5}$). It forms a salt NaX (0.1M) on reacting with caustic soda. The degree of hydrolysis of NaX is : **[2004, Screening]**
(1) 0.01%
(2) 0.0001%
(3) 0.1%
(4) 0.5%

**98.** Match the $K_a$ values **[2003, Main]**

$$K_a$$

(a) Benzoic acid — $3.3 \times 10^{-5}$

(b) $O_2N$—⟨⟩—COOH — $6.3 \times 10^{-5}$

(c) $Cl$—⟨⟩—COOH — $30.6 \times 10^{-5}$

(d) $H_2CO$—⟨⟩—COOH — $6.4 \times 10^{-5}$

(e) $H_2C$—⟨⟩—COOH — $4.2 \times 10^{-5}$

**99.** A solution which is $10^{-3}$ M each in $Mn^{2+}$, $Fe^{2+}$, $Zn^{2+}$ and $Hg^{2+}$ is treated with $10^{-16}$ M sulphide ion. If $K_{sp}$ of MnS, FeS, ZnS and HgS are $10^{-15}$, $10^{-23}$, $10^{-20}$ and $10^{-54}$ respectively, which one will precipitate first ? **[2003, Screening]**
(1) FeS
(2) MgS
(3) HgS
(4) ZnS

**100.** 500 mL of 0.02 M aqueous solution of acetic acid is mixed with 500 mL of 0.2 M HCl at 25°C. **[2002, Main]**
(i) Calculate the degree of dissociation of acetic acid in the resulting solution and pH of the solution
(ii) If 6 g of NaOH is added to the above solution, determine the final pH. [Assume there is no change in volume on mixing; Ka of acetic acid is $1.75 \times 10^{-5}$ mol L$^{-1}$]

**101.** Consider the following equilibrium in a closed container :

$$N_2O_4(g) \rightleftharpoons 2NO_2(g)$$

At a fixed temperature, the volume of the reaction container is halved. For this change, which of the following statements holds true regarding the equilibrium constant ($K_p$) and degree of dissociation ($\alpha$) ? **[2002, Screening]**
(1) neither $K_p$ nor $\alpha$ changes
(2) both $K_p$ and $\alpha$ change
(3) $K_p$ changes, but $\alpha$ does not change
(4) $K_p$ does not change, but $\alpha$ changes

**102.** Identify the correct order of solubility of $Na_2S$, CuS and ZnS in aqueous medium : **[2002, Screening]**
(1) $CuS > ZnS > Na_2S$
(2) $ZnS > Na_2S > CuS$
(3) $Na_2S > CuS > ZnS$
(4) $Na_2S > ZnS > CuS$

**103.** Which of the following acids has the smallest dissociation constant ? **[2002, Screening]**
(1) $CH_3CHFCOOH$
(2) $FCH_2CH_2COOH$
(3) $BrCH_2CH_2COOH$
(4) $CH_3CHBrCOOH$

## ANSWER KEY

| | | | | | | | | | |
|---|---|---|---|---|---|---|---|---|---|
| **1.** (4) | **2.** (2) | **3.** (3) | **4.** (3) | **5.** (2) | **6.** (*) | **7.** (1) | **8.** (4) | **9.** (4) | **10.** (1) |
| **11.** (3) | **12.** (2) | **13.** (*) | **14.** (1) | **15.** (*) | **16.** (*) | **17.** (3) | **18.** (*) | **19.** (1) | **20.** (1) |
| **21.** (1) | **22.** (2) | **23.** (3) | **24.** (2) | **25.** (4) | **26.** (1) | **27.** (3) | **28.** (3) | **29.** (1) | **30.** (4) |
| **31.** (*) | **32.** (1,3) | **33.** (4) | **34.** (1) | **35.** (2) | **36.** (3) | **37.** (4) | **38.** (4) | **39.** (3) | **40.** (2) |
| **41.** (2) | **42.** (3) | **43.** (2) | **44.** (3) | **45.** (2) | **46.** (4) | **47.** (2) | **48.** (3) | **49.** (2,4) | **50.** (4) |
| **51.** (3) | **52.** (2) | **53.** (4) | **54.** (1,3) | **55.** (2) | **56.** (3) | **57.** (2) | **58.** (3) | **59.** (3) | **60.** (2) |
| **61.** (3) | **62.** (1) | **63.** (2) | **64.** (4) | **65.** (2) | **66.** (2) | **67.** (3) | **68.** (3) | **69.** (2) | **70.** (4) |
| **71.** (4) | **72.** (4) | **73.** (3) | **74.** (4) | **75.** (2) | **76.** (3) | **77.** (2) | **78.** (1) | **79.** (1,2,4) | **80.** (2) |
| **81.** (4) | **82.** (2,3,4) | **83.** (*) | **84.** (3,4) | **85.** (*) | **86.** (*) | **87.** (4) | **88.** (4) | **89.** (2) | **90.** (1) |
| **91.** (2) | **92.** (1) | **93.** (*) | **94.** (2) | **95.** (*) | **96.** (*) | **97.** (1) | **98.** (*) | **99.** (3) | **100.** (*) |
| **101.** (4) | **102.** (4) | **103.** (3) | | | | | | | |

## ANSWERS WITH EXPLANATIONS

1. **(4)** Both (A) and (R) are true but (R) is not the explanation for (A) because rate of chemical reaction does not determine the value of equilibrium constant.

2. **(2)** (1)
$$P_\gamma = K_H X_Y$$
$$P_\gamma = 2\times10^{-15}\times\dfrac{55.5}{55.5+\dfrac{1000}{18}}$$
$$= 2\times10^{-5}\text{ K bar}$$
$$= 2\times10^{-2}\text{ bar}$$

   (2)
$$P_\delta = K_H X_\delta$$
$$P_\delta = 0.5\times\dfrac{55.5}{55.5+\dfrac{1000}{18}}$$
$$= 0.249\text{ K bar} = 249\text{ bar}$$

   (3) On increasing temperature solubility of gases decreases.

   (4) $K_H \downarrow$ solubility $\uparrow$ and lowest $K_H$ is for $\gamma$.

3. **(3)**
$$\underset{\substack{10\text{ mili mol}\\-}}{HCl} + \underset{\substack{20\text{ mili mol}\\10\text{ mili mol}}}{CH_3COONa} \rightarrow \underset{10\text{ mili mol}}{CH_3COOH} + \underset{10\text{ mili mol}}{NaCl}$$

   So, finally we get mixture of $CH_3COOH$ and $CH_3COONa$ that will work like acidic buffer solution.

4. **(3)** Steep rise in pH around the equivalence point for titration of strong acid with strong base.

5. **(2)** $N_2 + 3H_2 \rightleftharpoons 2NH_3 \rightarrow K_C = 64$
$$2NH_3 \rightleftharpoons N_2 + 3H_2 \rightarrow K_C = \dfrac{1}{64}$$
$$NH_3 \rightleftharpoons \dfrac{1}{2}N_2 + \dfrac{3}{2}H_2 \rightarrow K_C = \left(\dfrac{1}{64}\right)^{1/2}$$
$$= \dfrac{1}{8}$$

6. $$AB_2(s) \rightleftharpoons \underset{s}{A^{+2}_{(aq.)}} + \underset{2s}{2B^-_{(aq.)}} : K_{sp}$$
$$K_{SP} = S^1 \times (2s)^2 = 4s^3$$
$$3.2\times10^{-11} = 4\times S^3$$
$$S = 2\times10^{-4}\text{ M/L}$$

7. **(1)** $\Delta H° > 0 \quad T\downarrow$ equation shifts backward.
   $N_2$ is treated as inert gas in this case hence no effect on equilibrium.

8. **(4)** $K_C = K_P(RT)^{1/20}$

9. **(4)** (A) $10^{-2}$ M HCl $= [H^+] = 10^{-2}$ M $=$ pH $= 2$
   (B) $10^{-2}$ M NaOH $= [OH^-] = 10^{-2}$ M $=$ pOH $= 2$
   (C) $10^{-2}$ M $CH_3COO^-Na^+ = [OH^+] > 10^{-7}$
   $= $ pOH $< 7$
   (D) $10^{-2}$ M NaCl $=$ Neutral pOH $= 7$
   Therefore, (A) > (D) > (C) > (B)

10. **(1)** I < II < IV < III

11. **(3)** $28.4, -5.71$ and $-14.29$

12. **(2)** $A \rightleftharpoons B + C \quad K_{eq}^{(1)} = \dfrac{[B][C]}{[A]}$ ...(i)
$$B + C \rightleftharpoons P \quad K_{eq}^{(2)} = \dfrac{[P]}{[B][C]}$$ ...(ii)
   For
$$A \rightleftharpoons P \qquad K_{eq} = \dfrac{[P]}{[A]}$$
   Multiplying equation (1) and (2), we get
$$K_{eq}^{(1)} \times K_{eq}^{(2)} = \dfrac{[P]}{[A]} = K_{eq}$$

13. 

|  | X | + | Y | = | 2Z |
|---|---|---|---|---|---|
| $t=0$ | 1 |  | 1.5 |  | 0.5 |
| At eq. | 0.75 |  | 1.25 |  | 1 |

$$K_{eq.} = \dfrac{1^2}{\dfrac{3}{4}\times\dfrac{5}{4}} = \dfrac{16}{15}$$

14. **(1)** Bonus (no reaction is given)
$$A \rightleftharpoons B \quad \text{(Assume reaction)}$$
$$K = \dfrac{[B]}{[A]} = \dfrac{11}{6} \simeq 2$$

15. 100
    1 Litre has 10–3 moles $MgSO_4$
    So, 1000 litre has 1 mole $MgSO_4$
$$= 1\text{ mole } CaCO_3$$
$$= 100\text{ ppm}$$

16. 4.97
    $FeSO_4.7H_2O$ (M = 277.85)
$$ppm = \dfrac{\text{wt. of Fe}}{\text{wt. of wheat}}\times10^6$$
    let the wt. of salt be $= w$ gm
$$\text{moles} = \dfrac{w}{277.85}$$
$$\text{wt. of Fe} = \left(\dfrac{W}{277.85}\times55.85\right)\text{gm}$$
$$10 = \dfrac{\dfrac{W}{277.85}\times55.85}{10^5}\times10^6$$
$$W = \dfrac{277.85}{55.85} = 4.97$$

17. **(3)** Base strength order

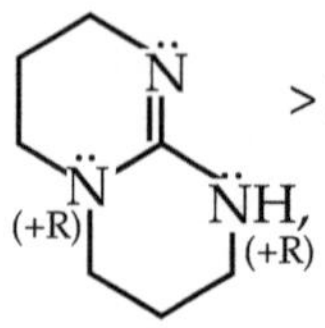

(B) [cyclic amidine structure with two N (+R) and NH (+R)] $> \ddot{N}H_2 - CH = \ddot{N}H > CH_3 - \ddot{N}H - CH_3$

(A) $\qquad$ (C)

**18.** 2130

Mole of $O_2$ comsumed $= \dfrac{1 \times 492}{0.082 \times 300} = 20$

Mole of $NaClO_3$ required = 20

Mass of $NaClO_3$ = 20 × 106.5 = 2130 gm

**19. (1)** A - $V_{mp}$; B - $C_{av}$; C - $V_{rms}$

**20. (3)** $k_b[N_2][H_2O]^2/H_2O$

$$2H_2(g) + 2NO(g) \rightleftharpoons N_2(g) + 2H_2O(g)$$

$$K_C = \frac{K_f}{K_b} = \frac{[N_2][H_2O]^2}{[H_2]^2[NO]^2}$$

Given, for forward reaction rate $= K_f[NO]^2[H_2]$

For reverse reaction rate $= K_b[N_2][H_2O]^2/[H_2]$

**21. (1)** $(\lambda_m^0)_{NaBr} - (\lambda_m^0)_{NaI} = (\lambda_m^0)_{KBr} - (\lambda_m^0)_{NaBr}$

$\Lambda_m^0 NaI - \Lambda_m^0 NaBr = \lambda_m^0 I - \Lambda_m^0 Br$

$\Lambda_m^0 NaBr - \Lambda_m^0 KBr = \lambda_m^0 Na - \Lambda_m^0 K$

**22. (2)** The dissociation of $Zr_3(PO_4)_4$ is shown below :

$$Zr_3(PO_4)_4(s) \rightleftharpoons 3Zr^{4+}(aq) + 4PO_4^{3-}(aq)$$
$$\quad\quad\quad\quad\quad\quad\quad 3S \quad\quad\quad 4S$$

Where S denotes the molar solubility.

The solubility product is calculated as shown below :

$$K_{sp} = [Zr^{4+}]^3 [PO_4^{3-}]^4$$
$$= [3S]^3 [4S]^4$$
$$= 25S^3 \times 256 \, S^4$$
$$= 6912 \, S^7$$

The value of S is calculated as shown below :

$$S = \left(\frac{K_{sp}}{6912}\right)^{1/7}$$

**23. (3)**

$$S(s) + O_2(g) \rightleftharpoons SO_2(g) \quad K_1 = 10^{52} \,...(1)$$
$$2S(s) + 3O_2(g) \rightleftharpoons 2SO_3(g) K_1 = 10^{129} \,...(2)$$

Multiply equation (1) by 2.

$$2S(s) + 2O_2(g) \rightleftharpoons 2SO_2(g) K_1 = 10^{104} \,....(3)$$

Subtract equation (3) from equation (2).

$$2SO_2(g) + O_2(g) \rightleftharpoons 2SO_3(g)$$
$$K_1 = 10^{129-104}$$
$$= 10^{25}$$

**24. (2)** (a) The neutralisation reaction is given below :

$$H_2SO_4 + 2NaOH \rightleftharpoons Na_2SO_4 + 2H_2O$$

$$400 \times 0.1 \quad\; 400 \times 0.1$$
$$= 40 \text{ mol} \quad = 40 \text{ mol}$$

The pH is calculated as shown below :

$$[H^+] = \frac{20 \times 2}{800} = \frac{1}{2}$$

$$pH = -\log\left(\frac{1}{20}\right)$$

$$= 1.3$$

Therefore, statement (a) is correct.

(b) Ionic product of water is temperature dependent as $\log\left(\dfrac{K_{w2}}{K_{w2}}\right) = \dfrac{\Delta H}{2.303R}\left[\dfrac{1}{T_1} - \dfrac{1}{T_2}\right]$.

Therefore, statement (b) is correct.

(c) If pH = 5, then $[H^+] = 10^{-pH} = 10^{-5}$.

The value of degree of dissociation is calculated as shown below :

$$K_a = \frac{c\alpha^2}{1-\alpha}$$

$$K_a = \frac{[H^+] \cdot \alpha}{1-\alpha}$$

$$10^{-5} = \frac{10^{-5} \cdot \alpha}{1-\alpha}$$

$$\alpha = \frac{1}{2} = 50\%$$

Therefore, statement (c) is correct.

(d) Statement (d) is incorrect as Le Chatelier's principle is applicable to common-ion effect.

**25. (4)** The pH is calculated as shown below :

$$[H^+] = \sqrt{\frac{K_w \times C}{K_b}}$$

$$= \sqrt{\frac{10^{-14} \times 0.02}{10^{-5}}}$$

$$-\log[H^+] = 6 - \frac{1}{2}\log 20$$

$$pH = 5.35$$

**26. (1)** The number of moles of reactants is more than the number of moles of product that is, the value of $\Delta n_g$ is negative. Therefore, as the pressure increases, the reaction would move in the forward reaction.

The given reaction is exothermic. Therefore, the value of equilibrium constant would decrease if the temperature increases.

At constant volume, addition of an inert gas would not affect the equilibrium constant.

Vanadium pentoxide is used as a catalyst for the preparation of $SO_3$ from $SO_2$.

**27. (3)** The chemical reaction for the dissociation of $Al(OH)_3$ is shown below :

$$Al(OH)_3 \rightleftharpoons Al^{3+} + 3OH^-$$

The molar solubility of $Al^{3+}$ will be S.

The molar solubility of $OH^-$ will be aproximately 0.2 M.

The molar solubility of $Al(OH)_3$ is calculated as shown below :

$$K_{sp} = (S)(0.2)^3$$

$$2.4 \times 10^{-24} = (S)(8 \times 10^{-3})$$

$$S = \frac{2.4 \times 10^{-24}}{8 \times 10^{-3}}$$

$$= 3 \times 10^{-22} \text{ M}$$

**28. (3)** The chemical equation for the dissociation of $Cd(OH)_2$ is shown below :

$$Cd(OH)_2 \rightleftharpoons Cd^{2+} + 2OH^-$$

The molar solubility of $Cd^{2+}$ and $^-OH$ is assumed to be S.

The value of $K_{sp}$ of $Cd(OH)_2$ is calculated as shown below :

$$K_{sp} = 4(S)^3$$
$$= 4(1.84 \times 10^{-5} \text{ M})^3$$
$$= 2.49 \times 10^{-14} \text{ M}$$

The formula of pH of a solution is given by the expression as shown below :

$$pH = -\log [H_3O^+] \qquad ...(1)$$

The relation between hydronium ion and hydroxide ios in the solution is given by the expression as shown below :

$$[HO^-] = \frac{10^{-14} \text{M}}{[H_3O^+]} \qquad ...(2)$$

Rearrange the equation (1) from the value of $[H_3O^+]$.

$$[H_3O^+] = \text{antilog} (-pH)$$

Substitute the value of pH of the neutral solution in the above equation.

$$[H_3O^+] = \text{antilog} (-12)$$
$$= 10^{-12} \text{ M}$$

Substitute the values of $[H_3O^+]$ in the equation (2).

$$[HO^-] = \frac{10^{-14} \text{ M}^2}{10^{-12} \text{ M}}$$

$$= 10^{-2} \text{ M}$$

The value of $K_{sp}$ of $Cd(OH)_2$ at pH = 12 is calculated as shown below :

$$K_{sp} = 4(S) [HO^-]^2$$
$$2.49 \times 10^{-14} \text{ M} = 4(S) \, 10^{-2} \text{ M}$$

$$\frac{2.49 \times 10^{-14} \text{ M}}{4 \times 10^{-2}} = S$$

$$6.23 \times 10^{-11} \text{ M} = S$$

**29. (1)** The relation between $K_p$ and $K_c$ is shown below :

$$K_p = K_c \, (RT)^{\Delta n_g}$$

For the condition $\Delta n_g \neq 0$, the value of $K_p$ and $K_c$ is not equal.

The reaction for the combustion of carbon is shown below :

$$2C(s) + O_2(g) \rightleftharpoons 2CO(g)$$

For the above reaction the value of $K_p$ and $K_c$ is not equal as it does not satisfies the condition of $\Delta n_g = 0$.

**30. (4)** The Gibbs free energy of the reaction can be given by the expression as shown below :

$$\Delta G° = -RT \ln K$$

The natural logarithm of a number that is less than one is always negative. The right-hand side of the equation will be positive.

**31.** The dissociation of salt AB is shown below :

$$\begin{array}{ccccc} AB & \rightleftharpoons & A^+ & + & B^- \\ & & x & & x-y \end{array}$$

The formation of HB occurs as shown below :

$$\begin{array}{ccccc} H^+ & + & B^- & \rightleftharpoons & HB \\ 10^{-3} & & x-y & & y \end{array}$$

Further equation is solved as shown below :

$$10^8 = \frac{y}{(x-y)(10^{-3})}$$

$$\frac{y}{(x-y)} = 10^5$$

$$y = 10^5 \, (x-y)$$

Now, the equation is solved as shown below :

$$x - (x-y) = 2 \times 10^{-10}$$
$$x^2 - xy - 2 \times 10^{-10} = 0$$
$$x^2 - 2 \times 10^{-5} = 0$$
$$x = 4.47 \times 10^{-3}$$

**32. (1,3)** As the temperature increases the concentration decreases. It means the given reaction is exothermic in nature. Therefore, $\Delta H^\ominus < 0$.

$$\frac{\ln K_{T_1}}{\ln K_{T_2}} > \frac{T_2}{T_1}$$

It is given that $T \ln K_{T_1} > T_2 \ln K_{T_2}$

$$-RT \ln K_{T_1} < -RT_2 \ln K_{T_2}$$

$$\Delta G^\ominus_{T_1} < \Delta G^\ominus_{T_2}$$

With increase in temperature, the value of change in Gibbs free energy increases, this occurs when $\Delta S^\ominus < 0$.

**33. (4)** (P) The millimoles of each species are found as shown below.

$$NaOH + CH_3COOH \rightarrow CH_3COONa + H_2O$$
millimoles  1          2

The given solution is a buffer, therefore, they occurs no change in the concentration of hydrogen ions.

(Q) The millimoles of each species are found as shown below :

$$NaOH + CH_3COOH \rightarrow CH_3COONa + H_2O$$
millimoles 2          2

The given solution consists of salt of weak acid and strong base. Thus hydrogen ion concentration is given as shown below.

$$[H^+]_i = \sqrt{\dfrac{K}{K_a \times c}}$$

After dilution the concentration decreases by half.

$$[H^+]_f = \sqrt{\dfrac{K_w}{K_a \times c/2}}$$

$$= [H^+]_i \times \sqrt{2}$$

(R) The millimoles of each species are found as shown below :

$$HCl + NH_3 \rightarrow NH_4Cl$$
millimoles     2     2

The given solution consists of salt of strong acid and weak base. Thus hydrogen ion concentration is given as shown below :

$$[H^+]_i = \sqrt{\dfrac{K_w \times c}{K_b}}$$

After dilution the concentration decreases by half.

$$[H^+]_f = \sqrt{\dfrac{K_w \times 2}{K_a}}$$

$$= \dfrac{[H^+]_i}{\sqrt{2}}$$

(S) The given salt is sparingly soluble. It means it occurs no change in hydroxide ion concentration and thus $[H^+]_i = [H^+]_f$.

**34. (1)** The dependence of equilibrium constant of the reaction on the enthalpy change is given as,

$$\ln K = \dfrac{-\Delta H^\circ}{RT} + \dfrac{-\Delta S^\circ}{R}$$

Since, the value of enthalpy change is negative in case of an exothermic reaction.

Therefore, the slope of the graph $\left(\dfrac{-\Delta H^\circ}{R}\right)$ is positive for an exothermic reaction. The line having positive slope out of the lines given on graph are the lines A and B. Hence, these lines show correct variation of equilibrium constant for an exothermic reaction.

**35. (2)** The equilibrium reactions for the dissociation of $H_2S$ are

$$H_2S \rightleftharpoons HS^- + H^+ \quad K_1 = 1.0 \times 10^{-7}$$

$$HS^- \rightleftharpoons S^{2-} + H^+ \quad K_2 = 1.2 \times 10^{-13}$$

The concentration of $S^{2-}$ ions in the given solution is calculated by the formula,

$$K_{eq} = \dfrac{[S^{2-}][H^+]^2}{[H_2S]}$$

Substitute the value of $K_{eq}$ in the above equation to calculate the concentration of $S^{2-}$ ions.

$$K_1 \times K_2 = \dfrac{[S^{2-}][H^+]^2}{[H_2S]}$$

$$[S^{2-}] = \dfrac{K_1 \times K_2 \times [H_2S]}{[H^+]^2}$$

Substitute the values of $K_1$, $K_2$, $[H_2S]$ and $[H^+]$ in the above equation.

$$[S^{2-}] = \dfrac{1.0 \times 10^{-7} \times 1.2 \times 10^{-13} \times 0.10 \text{ M}}{(0.20 \text{ M})^2}$$

$$= 3.0 \times 10^{-20} \text{ M}.$$

**36. (3)** The concentration of sulfate ions in the solution after mixing is calculated by the formula,

$$M_1V_1 = M_2V_2$$

Substitute the values of $M_1$, $V_1$ and $V_2$ in the above equation.

$$M_2 = \dfrac{1.0 \text{ M} \times 500 \text{ mL}}{(500) \text{ mL}}$$

$$= 0.1 \text{ M}$$

The concentration of barium ions after mixing is calculated by the formula,

$$[Ba^{2+}][SO_4^{2-}] = K_{sp}$$
$$[Ba^{2+}] \times 0.1 \text{ M} = 1.0 \times 10^{-10}$$
$$[Ba^{2+}] = 1.0 \times 10^{-9}$$

The concentration of barium ions in the original solution is calculated by the formula,

$$M_1V_1 = M_2V_2$$

$$= \dfrac{1.0 \times 10^{-9} \text{ M} \times 500 \text{ mL}}{(500 - 5) \text{ mL}}$$

$$= \dfrac{1.0 \times 10^{-9} \text{ M} \times 500 \text{ mL}}{450 \text{ mL}}$$

$$= 1.11 \times 10^{-9} \text{ M}$$

**37. (4)** The compounds which have tendency to accept a pair of electrons are known as Lewis acids. The compunds $AlCl_3$ and $BCl_3$ contains vacant $p$ orbitals in aluminium and boron respectively. Therefore, they have tendency to accept a pair of electrons and acts as Lewis acids.

**38. (4)** The salt $CH_3COOK$ is formed from acetic acid (weak acid) and potassium hydroxide (strong base). Therefore, it will be the most basic in its aqueous solution.

**39. (3)** Methyl orange is yellow in colour in the basic medium which becomes pinkish red in the acidic medium. Therefore, in the titration of an alkali against an acid, the colour of methyl orange changes from yellow to pinkish red.

**40. (2)** 25 mL $\dfrac{M}{5}$ NaOH will neutralize 75 mL $\dfrac{M}{5}$ HCl.

Amount of HCl that will remain

$$= 75 \text{ mL} - 25 \text{ mL}$$
$$= 50 \text{ mL}$$

So, 50 mL $\dfrac{M}{5}$ HCl will remain.

Total volume of solution is 75 mL + 25 mL
= 100 mL.

50 mL $\dfrac{M}{5}$ HCl will be diluted to 100 mL.

$$[H^+] = [HCl] = \dfrac{M}{5} \times \dfrac{50 \text{ mL}}{100 \text{ mL}}$$

$$= \dfrac{M}{10}$$

$$pH = -\log_{10}[H^+]$$
$$= -\log_{10} \dfrac{M}{10}$$

$$pH = 1$$

So, 75 mL $\dfrac{M}{5}$ HCl + 25 mL $\dfrac{M}{5}$ NaOH will have pH = 1.

**41. (2)** The following reaction is

$$CO + Cl_2 \rightleftharpoons COCl_2$$

Initial concentration of CO is 2 moles and that $Cl_2$ is 3 moles.

At equilibrium, number of moles of CO is 1 mole.

So, at equilibrium, concentration of $Cl_2$ is 2 moles and of $COCl_2$ is 1 mole.

$$V = 5L$$

Thus,

$$K_c = \dfrac{[COCl_2]}{[Cl_2][CO]}$$

$$= \dfrac{1 \text{ mol/5 L}}{(2 \text{ mol/5 L}) \times (1 \text{ mol/5 L})}$$

$$= \dfrac{5}{2}$$

$$= 2.5$$

Thus, $K_c = 2.5$.

**42. (3)** The $K_{sp}$ of $PbCl_2$ is $3.2 \times 10^{-8}$.

The reaction for the dissociation of $PbCl_2$ is shown below :

$$PbCl_2 \rightleftharpoons Pb^{2+} + 2Cl^-$$

The expression for $K_{sp}$ of $PbCl_2$ is shown below :

$$K_{sp} = [Pb^{2+}][Cl^-]^1$$

Make the ICE table for dissociation reaction of $PbCl_2$.

| | | $PbCl_2 \rightleftharpoons$ | $Pb^{2+}$ | $Cl^-$ |
|---|---|---|---|---|
| Initial (M) | : | 1 | 0 | 0 |
| Change (M) | : | $-S$ | $S$ | $2S$ |
| Equilibrium (M) | : | $1-S$ | $S$ | $2S$ |

Therefore, the expression becomes

$$K_{sp} = (S)(2S)^2$$
$$= 4S^3$$

$$S = \sqrt[3]{8 \times 10^{-9}}$$

$$= 2 \times 10^{-3} \text{ mol/L}$$

The molar mass of $PbCl_2$ is 278 amu. Thus, the solubility of $PbCl_2$ is,

$$= 2 \times 10^{-3} \text{ mol/L} \times 278$$
$$= 0.556 \text{ g/L}$$

It means that 0.556 g/L of $PbCl_2$ is dissolved in 1L water.

Therefore, 0.1 g $PbCl_2$ is dissolved in 0.18 L water.

**43. (2)** $B(CH_3)_3$ is a lewis acid. The octet of boron in $B(CH_3)_3$ is incomplete. It contains $6e^-$ and has empty orbital to accept electron pair.

**44. (3)** It is given that white sodium salt dissolves in water to give a solution which is neutral to litmus.

Silver nitrate reacts with sodium salt to give white colour ppt (AgCl) which are insoluble in $H_2O$ as well as in dil. $HNO_3$.

Therefore, the anion is chloride ion ($Cl^-$).

**45. (2)** The given reaction is an exothermic reaction. According to Le chatelier's principle, on increasing the pressure on the given reaction the position of equilibrium shifts towards the backward direction which leads to the formation of $N_2O_4$.

**46. (4)** At 320 K, the dissociation of $A_2$ gives,

$$A_2 \rightleftharpoons 2A$$

Let initially

$$[A_2] = 1 \text{ M}$$
$$[A] = 0 \text{ M}$$

It is given that the dissociation of $A_2$ is 20%. It means 80% of $A_2$ remains.

$$[A_2] = 1 \times \dfrac{80}{100}$$

$$= 0.8 \text{ M}$$

The equilibrium constant for the above reaction is,

$$K = \dfrac{[A]^2}{[A_2]}$$

$$= \dfrac{[0.4]^2}{[0.8]}$$

$$= 0.2$$

The relation between $\Delta G°$ and K is given below.

$$\Delta G° = -RT \ln K$$
$$= -8.314 \times 320 \times \ln 0.2$$
$$= 4281 \text{ J/mol}$$

**47. (2)** The incorrect option is (2).
Due to common ion effect, concentration of sulfide ion produce is insufficient. Thus, the precipitation of NiS is not possible because the product of $[Ni^{2+}]$ and $[S^{2-}]$ ion is less than the $K_{sp}$ of NiS.

**48. (3)** For standardizing NaOH solution, oxalic acid is used as a primary standard.

**49. (2,4)** With increases in temperature, the value of equilibrium constant increases for endothermic reaction. This is a true statement. Therefore, statement 1 is incorrect.

In other words, with increase in temperature the value of equilibrium constant decreases for exothermic reaction. Therefore, statement D is correct but statement 3 is incorrect.

**50. (4)** The pH of a salt solution (AB) is calculated by the formula,

$$pH = 7 + \frac{1}{2}(pK_a - pK_b)$$

Therefore,

$$pH = 7 + \frac{1}{2}(3.2 - 3.4)$$
$$= 7 - 0.1$$
$$= 6.9$$

**51. (3)** The reaction of weak acid and sodium hydroxide is given as follows :

$$Ha + NaOH \rightarrow NaA + H_2O$$

The ionized form of product is given below :

$$NaA \rightarrow Na^+ + A^-$$

The equilibrium constant for the above reaction is shown as follows,

$$K_a = \frac{[H^+][A^-]}{[HA]}$$

$$\frac{[K_a]}{[H^+]} = \frac{[HA]}{[A^-]}$$

$$\frac{[K_a]}{[H^+]} = \frac{10^{-5}}{10^{-6}}$$

$$= \frac{10}{1}$$

Thus, the ratio of salt to acid concentration is 10 : 1.

**52. (2)** The reaction is shown below.

$$NH_3 + HCl \rightarrow NH_4Cl$$

The number of moles of ammonia is calculated as shown below.

$$\text{Moles of } NH_3 = \frac{50 \times 0.2}{1000} = 5$$

The number of moles of hydrochloric acid is calculated as shown below.

$$\text{Moles of HCl} = \frac{25 \times 0.2}{1000} = 0.005$$

The value of $pOH$ is calculated by the formula,

$$pOH = pK_b (NH_3)$$

Substitute the value of $pK_b$ of ammonia in above expression.

$$pOH = 4.75.$$

**53. (4)** Addition of a solid compound does not disturb the equilibrium, while addition or removal of gaseous reactant disturbs the equilibrium.

**54. (1,3)** The following reactions will take place in the given compounds.

(A)  $Cu^{2+} + S^{2-} \rightarrow CuS\downarrow$
$\qquad\qquad$ Black ppt
$\qquad Cu^{2+} + SO_4^{2-} \rightarrow$ No. ppt

(B)  $Ba^{2+} + S^{2-} \rightarrow$ No. ppt
$\qquad Ba^{2+} + SO_4^{2-} \rightarrow BaSO_4\downarrow$
$\qquad\qquad$ White ppt

(C)  $Pb^{2+} + S^{2-} \rightarrow PbS\downarrow\ K_{sp}(PbS) = 10^{-28}$
$\qquad\qquad$ Black ppt
$\qquad Pb^{2+} + SO_4^{2-} \rightarrow PbSO_4\ K_{sp}(PbS) = 1.6 \times 10^{-8}$
$\qquad\qquad$ White ppt

(D) $Na_2[Fe(CN)_5NO]^{2-} + S^{-2} \rightarrow [Fe(CN)_5NO]$
$\qquad\qquad$ Purple colour
$\qquad Na_2[Fe(CN)_5NO] + S_4^{2-} \rightarrow$ No. ppt.

In $CuCl_2$ and $Pb(OOCCH_3)_2$, $S^{2-}$ can be selectively precipitated out from the mixture of $S^{2-}$ and $SO_4^{2-}$.

In option (C), there is a large difference in $K_{sp}$ of Pbs and $PbSO_4$. So, only PbS is selectively precipitated.

So, reagents are $CuCl_2$ and $Pb(OOCCH_3)_2$.

**55. (2)** The following equilibrium is,

$$X_2(g) \rightleftharpoons 2X(g)$$

At equilibrium,

$$X_2(g) \rightleftharpoons 2X(g)$$

$$\left(1 - \frac{\beta_{eq}}{2}\right) \qquad B_{eq}$$

Total number of moles at equilibrium is,
Number of moles at equilibrium is

$$= \left(1 - \frac{\beta_{eq}}{2}\right) + B_{eq}$$

Number of moles at equilibrium is $= 1 + \dfrac{B_{eq}}{2}$

The equilibrium constant in terms of $K_p$ is,

$$K_p = \frac{(p_x)^2}{p_{x_2}}$$

$$= \frac{\left(\dfrac{2\beta_{eq}}{2+\beta_{eq}} \times p_{total}\right)}{\left(\dfrac{2-\beta_{eq}}{2+\beta_{eq}} \times p_{total}\right)}$$

$$= \frac{4\beta_{eq}^2}{4-\beta_{eq}^2} \times 2$$

$$= \frac{8\beta_{eq}^2}{4-\beta_{eq}^2}$$

Thus, option (2) is correct.

**56. (3)** (1) When pressure decreases, the reaction will move in the direction where number of molecules of gas increases.

So, statement (A) is correct.

(2) At the starting of the reaction $Q_p < K_p$ so, dissociation of $X_2$ takes place spontaneously.

So, statement (2) is correct.

(3) The equilibrium constant in terms of $K_p$ is

$$K_p = \frac{8\beta_{eq}^2}{4-\beta_{eq}^2}$$

If $\beta_{eq} = 0.7$ then,

$$K_p = \frac{8(0.7)^2}{4-(0.7)^2}$$

$$K_p = \frac{3.92}{3.51} > 1$$

The value of $K_p$ cannot be greater than one, as $\Delta G° > 0$.

Therefore, $K_p < 1$.

Thus statement (3) is incorrect.

(4) As $\Delta G° > 0$ and $\Delta G° = -RT \ln K$

$$K_p < 1$$

So $\quad K = 1$

$$K_p = -K_c(RT)^{\Delta ng}$$

If $(RT > 1)$

$$K_c = \frac{K_p}{RT}$$

$$K_c < K_p$$
$$K_c < 1$$

Thus statement (4) is correct.

**57. (2)** According to law of equivalence, the equivalence of acid is equal to equivalence of base.

$$N_1V_1 = N_2V_2$$

Thus, the volume required is,

$$0.1 \times V_1 = 0.04 \times 1$$
$$V_1 = 0.4 \text{ L}$$

$$= 400 \text{ mL}.$$

**58. (3)** The decomposition of XY is as follows :

$$XY(s) \rightleftharpoons X(g) + Y(g)$$

At eq. $\qquad\qquad$ P $\qquad$ P

Thus, total pressure is,

$$= 2P$$
$$= 10 \text{ bar}$$

Therefore, the $K_p$ for the given reaction is,

$$K_p = (P_x)(P_y)$$
$$= P^2$$
$$= 25.$$

**59. (3)** The given reaction is shown below :

$$A+B \rightleftharpoons C+D$$

The value of Q is shown below :

$$Q = \frac{1\times1}{1\times1}$$

$$= 1$$

As $K > Q$; therefore, the reaction moves in the forward direction.

$$\begin{array}{cccccc} & A & + & B & \rightleftharpoons & C & + & D \\ \text{Initial} & 1 & & 1 & & 1 & & 1 \\ \text{Equilibrium} & 1-x & & 1-x & & 1+x & & 1+x \end{array}$$

The equilibrium constant is calculated as shown below.

$$K = \frac{(1+x)(1+x)}{(1-x)(1-x)}$$

$$100 = \frac{(1+x)^2}{(1-x)^2}$$

$$10 = \frac{1+x}{1-x}$$

$$x = \frac{9}{11}$$

The concentration of D is $1 + = \dfrac{9}{11}$

$$= 1.818 \text{ mol.L}^{-1}.$$

**60. (2)** As the temperature increases, the rate of reaction also increases. So with time % yield will also increase. But ammonia synthesis is exothermic. Thus; its yield will decrease on increasing the temperature. Therefore, at equilibrium % yield at $T_2$ would be less than at $T_1$. The correct graph for the % yield of ammonia as a function of time is

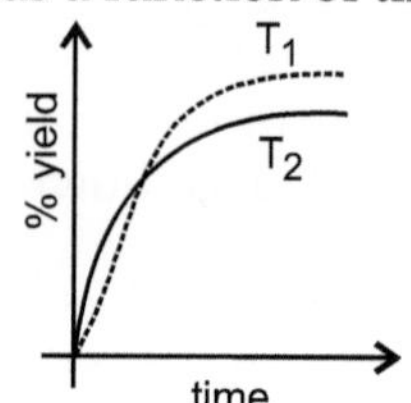


**61. (3)** Let assume HX is I.

Let HY is II.

The degree of ionisation of weak acid HX is,

$$\alpha_I = \frac{\wedge_I}{\wedge_o}$$

Similarly, the degree of ionisation of weak acid HY is,

$$\alpha_{II} = \frac{\wedge_{II}}{\wedge_o}$$

The ratio of $\alpha_1$ and $\alpha_2$ is as follows.

$$\frac{\alpha_I}{\alpha_{II}} = \frac{\wedge_I}{\wedge_{II}} = \frac{1}{10}$$

The realation between $K_a$ and $\alpha$ is,

$$K_a = \alpha^2 C$$

The ratio of $K_{a_I}$ and $K_{a_{II}}$ is as follows :

$$\frac{K_{a_I}}{K_{a_{II}}} = \frac{\alpha_I^2 C_I}{\alpha_{II}^2 C_{II}} = \frac{0.01}{0.1}\left(\frac{1}{10}\right)^2$$

$$= 10^{-3}$$

Thus,

The $pK_{a_I} - pK_{a_{II}} = 3$.

**62. (1)** The reaction is as follows :

$$HCl + NaOH \rightarrow NaCl + H_2O$$

The number of moles is 0.1 mole.

Energy involved due to neutralisation of HCl and NaOH is,

$$= 0.1 \times 57$$
$$= 5.7 \text{ kJ}$$
$$= 5700 \text{ Joule}$$

Energy used to increase temperature of solution is,

$$= 200 \times 4.2 \times 5.7$$
$$= 4788 \text{ Joule}$$

Thus, energy used to increase temperature of calorimeter is,

$$= 5700 - 4788$$
$$= 912 \text{ Joule}$$

Let C is the calorimetric constant.

The formula to calculate amount of heat is

$$Q = m.s.\Delta T + C.\Delta T$$

$$5.7 = \frac{200 \times 4.2 \times 5.7}{1000} + C \times 5.7$$

$$C = 0.16$$

After experiment 2,

The amount of heat is,

$$Q = m.s.\Delta T + C.\Delta T$$

$$\frac{x}{10} = \frac{200 \times 4.2 \times 5.6}{1000} + 0.16 \times 5.6$$

$$x = 56$$

Thus, the enthalpy of dissociation of acetic acid obtained from the experiment 2 is,

$$\Delta H_{N(WASB)} = \Delta H_{N(SASB)} + \Delta H_{\text{diss. of WA}}$$
$$57 = 56 + \Delta H_{\text{diss. of WA}}$$
$$\Delta H_{\text{diss. of WA}} = 1 \text{ kJ/mol}$$

**63. (2)** After experiment 2,

The reaction is

$$CH_3COOH + NaOH \rightleftharpoons CH_3COONa + H_2O$$

The initial concentration of acetic acid, NaOH and $CH_3COONa$ is 0.2, 0.1 and 0.

The final concentration of acetic acid, NaOH and $CH_3COONa$ is 0.1, 0 and 0.1.

The formula to calculate pH is,

$$pH = pK_a + \log\frac{[\text{conjugate base}]}{[\text{acid}]}$$

Substitute all the values in the above formula.

$$pH = pK_a + \log\frac{[\text{conjugate base}]}{[\text{acid}]}$$

$$= 5 - \log 2 + \log\frac{1/2}{1/2}$$

$$= 4.7.$$

**64. (4)** The $\Delta G^\circ_{f,NO_2}$ of given reaction is calculated by the formula,

$$\Delta G^\circ_{rxn.} = 2(\Delta G^\circ_{f,NO_2}) - 2(\Delta G^\circ_{f,NO})$$

$$-RT \ln K_p = 2(\Delta G^\circ_{f,NO_2}) - 2(\Delta G^\circ_{f,NO})$$

$$2(\Delta G^\circ_{f,NO}) - RT \ln K_p = 2(\Delta G^\circ_{f,NO_2})$$

$$\frac{2(\Delta G^\circ_{f,NO}) - RT \ln K_p}{2} = \Delta G^\circ_{f,NO_2}$$

Substitute the given values in above equation.

$$G^\circ_{f,NO_2} = \frac{2 \times 86600 - R(298) \ln(1.6 \times 10^{12})}{2}$$

$$= 0.5[2 \times 86600 - R(298) \ln (1.6 \times 10^{12})$$

**65. (2)** The $K_C$ of given reaction is calculated by the formula,

$$\Delta G^\circ = -2.303 RT \log K_C$$

Substitute the values of $\Delta G^\circ$, R and T in the above equation.

$$2494.2 = -2.303 \times 8.314 \times 300 \log K_C$$

$$-0.434 = \log K_C$$

$$K_C = 0.368$$

The Q of given reaction is calculated by the formula,

$$Q = \frac{[C][B]}{[A]^2}$$

Substitute the values of [C], [B] and [A] in above equation.

$$Q = \frac{\frac{1}{2} \times 2}{\left(\frac{1}{2}\right)^2}$$

$$Q = 4$$

Therefore,

$$Q > K_C$$

Reverse direction.

**66. (2)** The ratio of theoretical molecular mass and observed molecular mass is given as,

$$\frac{M_{Th}}{M_{Ob}} = 1 + (2-1)\alpha$$

The observed molecular mass is,

$$M_{Ob} = \frac{92}{1 + (2-1)0.2}$$

$$= \frac{92}{1.2}$$

$$= 76.67$$

The density is given as,

$$d = \frac{PM_{Ob}}{RT}$$

$$= \frac{1 \times 76.67}{0.082 \times 300}$$

$$= 3.11 \text{ g/L}$$

**67. (3)** The values of $E_f$ and $E_b$ are $2x$ and $3x$ respectively.

The value of $\Delta H$ is calculated by the formula,

$$\Delta H = E_f - E_b$$
$$-40 \text{ kJ/mol} = 2x - 3x$$
$$40 \text{ kJ/mol} = x$$

Thus,

$$E_f = 2 \times 40 \text{ kJ/mol}$$
$$= 80 \text{ kJ/mol}$$
$$E_b = 3 \times 40 \text{ kJ/mol}$$
$$= 120 \text{ kJ/mol}$$

**68. (3)** The density of ice is $0.9340 \text{ g/cm}^3$.

The density of water is $0.997 \text{ g/cm}^3$.

Thus, the above values indicate that density of ice is low as compared to water due to which reaction will shift in forward direction.

**69. (2)** The given chemical equation is,

$$SO_2(g) + \frac{1}{2}O_2 \rightarrow SO_3(g)$$

The change in the number of moles of gaseous species ($\Delta n$) is,

$$1 - \left(1 + \frac{1}{2}\right) = -\frac{1}{2}$$

The expression for relationship between $K_p$ and $K_c$ is,

$$K_P = K_C(RT)^{\Delta n}$$

The given expressions is,

$$K_P = K_C(RT)^x$$

Therefore, $\Delta n$ or $x$ is $-\dfrac{1}{2}$.

**70. (4)** The reaction of dissociation of HI is given as follows :

$$2HI \rightleftharpoons I_2 + H_2$$
$$1-a \qquad \frac{a}{2} \quad \frac{a}{2}$$

Here, $a$ is the concentration.

The equilibrium constant of the above reaction is given as follows :

$$K_{eq} = \frac{\left(\frac{a}{2}\right)^2}{(1-a)^2}$$

$$= \frac{a^2}{4(1-a)^2}$$

$$= \frac{\left(\frac{1}{2}\right)^2}{4(1/2)^2}$$

$$= \frac{1}{4}$$

Thus, the value of equilibrium constant is 0.25.

**71. (4)** The dissociation reaction of sodium acetate is,

$$CH_3COONa \rightleftharpoons CH_3COO^- + Na^+$$

Hydrolysis takes place in aqueous medium as shown below :

$$CH_3COO^- + H_2O \rightleftharpoons CH_3COOH + OH^-$$
$$C \qquad\qquad\qquad\qquad - \qquad\quad -$$
$$C(1-a) \qquad\qquad\qquad C\alpha \qquad C\alpha$$

The equilibrium constant for the above reaction is expressed as,

$$K_b = \frac{[CH_3COOH][OH^-]}{[CH_3COO^-]}$$

$$= \frac{K_w}{K_a} = \frac{C\alpha^2}{1-\alpha}$$

Substitute the value of $K_a$ and $K_w$ in the above expression.

$$\frac{10^{-14}}{10^{-5}} = \frac{C\alpha^2}{1-\alpha}$$

The degree of hydrolysis ($\alpha$) is very small. Therefore, $1 - \alpha \approx 1$.

$$\frac{10^{-14}}{10^{-5}} = C\alpha^2$$

$$\alpha = \sqrt{\frac{10^{-9}}{0.1}}$$
$$= 10^{-4}$$

Therefore, $[OH^-] = C\alpha$
$$= 0.1 \times 10^{-4}$$
$$= 10^{-5}$$
$$pOH = -\log [OH^-]$$
$$= 5$$
$$pH = 14 - pOH$$
$$= 14 - 5$$
$$= 9$$

**72. (4)** In buffer solutions, the concentration of $H_3O^+$ remains constant even when small quantity of strong acid or strong base is added to them.

**73. (3)** Silver chloride reacts with ammonia to form the complex $[Ag(NH_3)_2]^+$ and chloride ions. Addition of aqueous $HNO_3$ regenerates the silver ions which combine with chloride ions to form white precipitate of AgCl according to the following chemical equation.
$$2HNO_3 + [Ag(NH_3)_2]^+ \rightarrow 2NH_4^+ + Ag^+ + 2NO_3^-$$

**74. (4)** The addition of inert gas at constant volume does not change the molar concentration of reactants and products due to which the state of equilibrium remains unchanged. Therefore, the addition of an inert gas at constant volume does not affect the equilibrium.

**75. (2)** The dissociation of hydrazoic acid is given as
$$HN_3 \rightarrow H^+ + N_3^-$$
Therefore, the conjugate base of hydrazoic acid is $N_3^{-3}$.

**76. (3)** The dissociation of zirconium phosphate is,
$$[Zr_3(PO_4)_4] \rightarrow 3Zr^{4+} + PO_4^{3-}$$
The molar solubility of zirconium ion is $(3S)^3$. The molar solubility of phosphate ion is $(4S)^4$.

The solubility product of zirconium phosphate is expressed as,
$$K_{sp} = (3S)^3(4S)^4$$
$$S = (K_{sp}/6912)^{1/7}$$

**77. (2)** At equilibrium,
The partial pressure of $NH_3(g)$ is 2P.
The partial pressure of $CO_2(g)$ is P.
The $K_p$ of given reaction is calculated as,
$$K_p = (2P)^2(P)$$
$$K_p = 4P^3$$
Substitute the value of $K_p$ in above equation.
$$2.9 \times 10^{-5} = 4P^3$$
$$P = 1.94 \times 10^{-2} \text{ atm}$$

Total pressure,
$$= 2P + P$$
$$= 3P$$
$$= 3 \times 1.94 \times 10^{-2}$$
$$= 5.82 \times 10^{-2} \text{ atm}$$

**78. (1)** The ratio of rate of hydrolysis of methyl acetate by weak acid and strong acid is shown below :
$$\frac{R_1}{R_2} = \frac{[H^+]_{\text{weak acid}}}{[H^+]_{\text{Strong acid}}}$$

$$\frac{[H^+]_{\text{weak acid}}}{[H^+]_{\text{Strong acid}}} = \frac{1}{100}$$

Rearrange the above expression.
$$[H^+]_{\text{weak acid}} = \frac{[H^+]_{\text{Strong acid}}}{100} \quad ...(1)$$

Substitute the value of $[H^+]_{\text{Strong acid}}$ in equation (1).
$$[H^+]_{\text{weak acid}} = \frac{1}{100} M$$
$$= 0.01 \text{ M}$$
The value of $K_\alpha$ is calculated by the formula
$$K_\alpha = C.\alpha^2$$
$$= 1.(0.01)^2$$
$$= 1 \times 10^{-4}$$
$$K_\alpha = 1.(0.01)^2$$
$$= 1 \times 10^{-4}$$

**79. (1,2,4)** (1) The enthalpy, $\Delta H$ of the given equilibrium is dependent on the given temperature because the given equilibrium is totally dependent on the thermal conditions.
(2) The equilibrium constant, K is independent of the initial concentration of $CaCO_3$.
(3) The equilibrium constant, K is independenct of the pressure of $CO_2$.
(4) The enthalpy, $\Delta H$ of the given equilibrium is independent of the catalyst at the given temperature. Catalyst just change the activation energy of the reaction.

**80. (2)** $K_{sp}$ of $Ag_2CrO_4 = [Ag^+]^2[CrO_4^{2-}]$
$$= 1.1 \times 10^{-12}$$
$$1.1 \times 10^{-12} = [0.1]^2[s]$$
$$s = 1.1 \times 10^{-10}$$

**81. (4)** The aqueous form of $AgNO_3$ and KCl are ionic in nature. When $AgNO_3(aq)$ is added to KCl(aq), both dissociates in their respective ions. After complete ionisation, precipitate formation of AgCl is started. After complete precipitation, the conductance of the solution increases due to the more addition of $AgNO_3(aq)$ solution.

**82. (2,3,4)** For the given reaction, equilibrium shifts towards left in the presence of $Cl^-$, $SCN^-$ and $CN^-$ ions. In the presence of $NO_3^-$, it does not shift towards left due to the formation of stable compound that is nitrogen monoxide gas. It is a gas therefore, easily escaped out. In rest of three ions, three complexes are formed given as,

$$CuCl(ppt), [Cu(SCN)_4]^{3-} \text{ and } [Cu(CN)_4]^{3-}$$

**83.** Both siver chloride and copper chloride are sparingly soluble salts.

Therefore, the equilibrium reactions for both are as follows,

$$\begin{array}{ccccc} AgCl & \rightleftharpoons & Ag^+ & + & Cl^- \\ & & y & & y \\ CuCl & \rightleftharpoons & Cu^+ & + & Cl^- \\ & & z & & z \end{array}$$

Total chloride ion concentrations is $(y + z)$ solubility products for both is written as,

$$k_{sp(AgCl)} = [Ag^+][Cl^-]$$
$$1.6 \times 10^{-10} = y(y + z) \qquad ...(1)$$
$$k_{sp(CuCl)} = [Cu^+][Cl^-]$$
$$1.0 \times 10^{-6} = z(y + z) \qquad ...(2)$$

On dividing equation (1) by (2),

$$\frac{y}{z} = 1.6 \times 10^{-4}$$

$$z = \frac{10^4}{1.6}y$$

Substitute this value in (1).

$$1.6 \times 10^{-10} = y\left(y + \frac{10^4}{1.6}y\right)$$

(neglect $x$ inside bracket)

$$\frac{10^4}{1.6}y^2 = 1.6 \times 10^{-10}$$
$$y^2 = (1.6)^2 \times 10^{-14}$$
$$y = (1.6) \times 10^{-7}$$

The value of $x$ will be 7.

**84. (3,4)** If $HNO_3$ is added in a limited amount, then the mixture of $HNO_3$ and $CH_3COONa$ will act as a buffer.

The mixture of weak acid and its salt in strong base will act as acidic buffer solution.

In option (D), acetic acid is weak acid and $CH_3COONa$ is salt of its acid and $NaOH$. So, it will act as buffer solution.

**85.** Diprotic acids are those species which can donate two protons in an aqueous medium.

$$H_2SO_4, H_3PO_4, H_2CO_3, H_2S_2O_7, H_2SO_3, H_2CrO_4$$

These all species can donate two protons in an aqueous medium.

**86.** The balanced chemical equation for the dissociation of substituted benzoic acid is given as

$$C_6H_5COO^- + H_2O \rightleftharpoons C_6H_5COOH + OH^-$$

| | | | |
|---|---|---|---|
| Initial : | 0.01 | 0.0 | 0.0 |
| Final : | 0.01(1 − x) | 0.01x | 0.01x |

The dissociation constant of the benzoic acid is written as,

$$K_b = \frac{K_w}{K_a} = \frac{0.01x^2}{(1-x)}$$

The value of $(1 - x)$ is approximately equal to one because the value of $x$ is very less than one.

$$\frac{10^{-14}}{1 \times 10^{-4}} = \frac{0.01x^2}{1}$$

$$x^2 = \frac{10^{-10}}{0.01}$$

$$x = 10^{-6}$$

The pH of the solution is calculated by using the formula,

$$14 - pH = -\log[OH^-]$$

Substitute the value of $[OH^-]$ in the above equation.

$$14 - pH = -\log(10^{-6})$$
$$pH = 8.0$$

**87. (4)** The equation for reaction of weak monoacidic base with HCl is expressed as,

$$BOH + HCl \rightarrow BCl + H_2O$$

The concentration of salt (BCl) is C.

At equilibrium the reaction is,

$$\begin{array}{ccccccc} B^+ & + & H_2O & \rightleftharpoons & BOH & + & H^+ \\ C(1-h) & & & & Ch & & Ch \end{array}$$

The volume of HCl used during titration is,

$$V = \frac{2.5 \times \dfrac{2}{5}}{\dfrac{2}{15}}$$

$$= 7.5 \text{ mL}$$

The total volume is $= 7.5$ mL $+ 2.5$ mL
$$= 10 \text{ mL}$$

The concentration of salt is,

$$C = \frac{2.5 \times \dfrac{2}{5}}{10}$$

$$= 0.1 \text{ M}$$

The relationship between concentration at equilibrium and $\dfrac{K_w}{K_b}$ is,

$$\frac{K_w}{K_b} = \frac{Ch^2}{1-h}$$

$$\frac{1 \times 10^{-14}}{1 \times 10^{-12}} = \frac{0.1 \times h^2}{1-h}$$

Simplifying $h^2$, $h = 0.27$.
The concentration of $H^+$ is
$$[H^+] = Ch$$
$$= 0.1 \text{ M} \times 0.27$$
$$2.7 \times 10^{-2} \text{ M}.$$

**88. (4)** The solubility of salt type of MX is,
$$\text{Solubility} = \sqrt{4.0 \times 10^{-8}}$$
$$= 2 \times 10^{-4}$$
The solubility of salt type $MX_2$ is,
$$\text{Solubility} = \sqrt[3]{\frac{3.2 \times 10^{-14}}{4}}$$
$$= 2 \times 10^{-5}$$
The solubility of salt type $M_3X$ is,
$$\text{Solubility} = \sqrt[4]{\frac{2.7 \times 10^{-15}}{27}}$$
$$= 10^{-4}$$

**89. (2)** The solution of $Hg^{2+}$ gives red precipitate when it is treated with KI.
$$Hg^{2+} + KI \rightarrow HgI_2$$
(Red ppt.)

The precipitate dissolves in excess KI and gives a colourless solution.
$$HgI_2 + KI(\text{excess}) \rightarrow K_2HgI_4$$
The solution of $Hg^{2+}$ gives deep blue crystalline precipitate when it is treated with a solution of $Co(SCN)_2$.
$$Hg^{2+} + Co(SCN)_2 \rightarrow Hg(SCN)$$
(deep blue ppt.)

**90. (1)** The given reaction is,
$$Ag^+ + NH_3 \rightleftharpoons [Ag(NH_3)^+]$$
$$[Ag(NH_3)^+] + NH_3 \rightleftharpoons [Ag(NH_3)^+]$$
The $k_1$ and $k_2$ for the above reaction is $3.5 \times 10^{-3}$ and $1.7 \times 10^{-3}$.
The equilibrium constant for the given reaction is calculated by the formula.
$$k = k_1 \times k_2$$
Substitute the value of $k_1$ and $k_2$ in the above formula.
$$k = k_1 \times k_2$$
$$= 3.5 \times 10^{-3} \times 1.7 \times 10^{-3}$$
$$= 5.95 \times 10^{-6}$$
$$\approx 6 \times 10^{-6}$$
Thus, the value of equilibrium constant of $[Ag(NH_3)_2]^+$ is $6 \times 10^{-6}$.

**91. (2)** The given reaction is
$$N_2 + 3H_2 \rightleftharpoons 2NH_3$$
The given reaction is an example of Haber process in which synthesis of ammonia takes place. For any reaction, at equilibrium state $\Delta G$ is equal to zero that is $\Delta G = 0$.
At equilibrium,
$$\Delta G = G_P - G_R$$
Where,
$G_R$ is the Gibbs free energy of reactant.
$G_P$ is the Gibbs free energy of product.

Therefore, the condition for the given reaction at equilibrium is as follows.
$$\Delta G = G_P - G_R$$
$$0 = (G_{N_2} + 3G_{H_2}) - 2G_{NH_3}$$
$$2G_{NH_3} = G_{N_2} + 3G_{H_2}$$
Thus, the correct statement is (2).

**92. (1)** The reaction that takes place between $CO_2$ and $H_2O$ is as follows :
$$CO_2 + H_2O \rightleftharpoons H_2CO_3$$
This results in the formation of carbonic acid $(H_2CO_3)$.
The reaction for the dissociation of $H_2CO_3$ is as follows :
$$H_2CO_3 \rightleftharpoons HCO_3^- + H^+$$
$$HCO_3^- \rightleftharpoons H^+ + CO_3^{2-}$$
Therefore, the species that are present in a solution when carbon dioxide is dissolved in water are : $CO_2$, $H_2CO_3$, $HCO_3^-$ and $CO_3^{2-}$

**93.** The reaction involved in this process is as follows :
$$AgBr \rightarrow Ag^+ + Br^-$$
$$AgNO_3 \rightarrow Ag^+ + NO_3^-$$
The solubility of AgBr in the presence of $10^{-7}$ molar of $AgNO_3$ is $3 \times 10^{-7}$ M.
Therefore,
$[Br^-] = 3 \times 10^{-7} \text{ m}^3$,
$[Ag^+] = 4 \times 10^{-4} \text{ m}^3$,
$[NO_3^-] = 10^{-4} \text{ m}^3$.
Thus, the $k_{total}$ is
$$k_{total} = k_{Br^-} + k_{Ag^+} + k_{NO_3^-}$$
$$= 55 \text{ Sm}^{-1}$$

**94. (2)** The given concentration of $CH_3NH_2$ is 0.1 mole.
The given value of equilibrium constant, $K_b$ is $5 \times 10^4$.
The given concentration of HCl is 0.08 mole.
In the above reaction, the limiting reagent is HCl. Thus, the reaction of $CH_3NH_2$ with HCl is
$$CH_3NH_2 + HCl \rightarrow CH_3N^+H_3 + Cl^-$$
Initial conc. 0.1    0.08      0
Final conc. 0.02    0      0.08
The concentration of $[OH^-]$ ions is calculated by the formula,
$$[OH^-] = K_b \frac{[CH_3NH_2]}{[CH_3NH_3^+]}$$
Substitute the values of the concentration of $CH_3NH_2$, $CH_3NH_3^+$ and the value of $K_b$ in the above expression.
$$[OH^-] = 5 \times 10^{-4} \times \frac{0.02}{0.08}$$
$$= 1.25 \times 10^{-4}$$
The value of $K_W$ is $10^{-14}$.

The formula to calculate the hydrogen ion concentration is,

$$[H^+] = \frac{K_W}{[OH^-]}$$

Substitute the value of the concentration of $[OH^-]$ and the value of $K_W$ in the above expression.

$$[H^+] = \frac{10^{-14}}{1.25 \times 10^{-4}}$$

$$= 8 \times 10^{-11}$$

Thus, the resulting value of hydrogen ion concentration is $8 \times 10^{-11}$.

Hence, the correct option is (2).

**95.** In periodic table, on moving down the group, the basic nature of oxides increases, whereas on moving left to right the basic nature of oxides decreases.

Therefore, the increasing order of Bronsted basicity is as follows :

$$Cl_2O_7 < SO_3 < CO_2 < B_2O_3 < BaO$$

**96.** The balanced equation follows the law of conservation of mass. The unbalanced equation means that number of the atoms of elements present in the reactant is not equal to the product side.

The balanced chemical reaction for the given reaction is as follows :

$$3KF + AlF_3 \rightarrow K_3AlF_6$$
$$K_3AlF_6 + 3BF_3 \rightarrow AlF_3 + 3KBF_4$$

**97. (1)** The hydrolysis constant of salt of weak acid and strong base is given as shown below :

$$h = \sqrt{\frac{Kw}{Ka \times c}}$$

$$= \sqrt{\frac{10^{-14}}{10^{-5} \times 0.1}}$$

$$= 10^{-4}$$

Percentage hydrolysis $= 10^{-4} \times 100$

$$= 10^{-2}$$

$$= 0.01\%.$$

**98.** The acid that has larger $K_a$ value will be more acidic. Therefore, the correct increasing order of acidic strength for the given compounds is shown below.

COOH  COOH  COOH  COOH COOH

$$\bigcirc < \bigcirc < \bigcirc < \bigcirc < \bigcirc$$

OCH$_3$    CH$_3$              Cl        NO$_2$

Thus, the correct value of $K_a$ for benzoic acid is $6.4 \times 10^{-5}$, for *p*-nitrobenzoic acid is $36.2 \times 10^{-5}$, for *p*-chlorobenzoic acid is $10.2 \times 10^{-5}$, for *p*-methylbenzoic acid is $4.2 \times 10^{-5}$, for *p*-methyoxybenzoic acid is $3.3 \times 10^{-5}$.

**99. (3)** Precipitation depends upon the $K_{sp}$ value. The compound that has low $K_{sp}$ value will precipitate first. Therefore, among given compounds, HgS will precipitate first.

**100.** (I) The reaction for the dissociation of $CH_3COOH$ is as follows :

$$CH_3COOH \rightarrow CH_3COO^- + H^+$$
$$\quad C \qquad\qquad 0 \qquad\quad 0$$
$$C(1-\alpha) \qquad\quad C\alpha \qquad C\alpha + 0.1$$

The $K_a$ for the given reaction is as follows :

$$K_a = \frac{[CH_3COO^-][H^+]}{[CH_3COOH]}$$

$$= \frac{C\alpha^2 + 0.1\alpha}{1-\alpha}$$

$$\alpha = 1.75 \times 10^{-4}$$

The total concentration of $H^+$ is 0.1.

Therefore, the pH of the solution is 1.

(II) The number of moles for NaOH is

$$n = \frac{6}{40}$$

$$= 0.15 \text{ mole}$$

The reaction of sodium hydroxide with hydrochloric acid is as follows :

$$HCl + NaOH \rightarrow NaCl + H_2O$$

The reaction shows that 0.1 mole of sodium hydroxide is consumed by 0.1 mole of hydrochloric acid. Thus, the reaction of 0.05 mole of NaOH with 0.1 mole $CH_3COOH$ is as follows :

$$CH_3COOH + NaOH \rightarrow CH_3COONa + H_2O$$

| 0.1 mol | 0.05 mol | 0 | 0 |
| 0.05 mol | 0 | 0.05 mol | 0.05 mol |

Thus, the value of final pH is as follows :

$$pH = pK_a + \log\frac{[salt]}{[acid]}$$

$$= -\log(1.75 \times 10^{-5} + \log 1$$
$$= 4.75.$$

**101. (4)** The expression for $K_p$ is shown below.

$$K_p = K_c \times (RT)^{\Delta n}$$

The above expression indicates that the value of equilibrium constant $(K_p)$ will not change at fixed temperature. As the volume of the reaction container becomes half of its original value, the pressure will be doubled due to which degree of dissociation $(\alpha)$ decreases.

**102. (4)** The solubility of compounds relies upon the value of solubility product. The value of solubility product of copper is less as compared to zinc. Sodium ion is highly soluble due to small charge on its as compared to copper and zinc ions.

**103. (3)** The dissociation constant of $BrCH_2CH_2COOH$ is small because negative inductive effect of bromine is less than that of fluorine and it is also present away from carboxylic group.

●●

## QUESTIONS

1. The compound that cannot act both as oxidising and reducing agent is : **[2020, Main]**
   (1) $H_2O_2$
   (2) $H_2SO_3$
   (3) $HNO_2$
   (4) $H_3PO_4$

2. The redox reaction among the following is : **[2020, Main]**
   (1) formation of ozone from atmospheric oxygen in the presence of sunlight
   (2) reaction of $H_2SO_4$ with NaOH
   (3) combination of dinitrogen with dioxygen at 2000 K
   (4) reaction of $[Co(H_2O)_6]Cl_3$ with $AgNO_3$

3. In order to oxidise a mixture of one mole of each of $FeC_2O_4$, $Fe_2(C_2O_4)_3$, $FeSO_4$ and $Fe_2(SO_4)_3$ in acidic medium, the number of moles of $KMnO_4$ required is : **[2019, Main]**
   (1) 2
   (2) 1
   (3) 3
   (4) 1.5

4. An example of a disproportionation reaction is : **[2019, Main]**
   (1) $2MnO_4^- + 10I^- + 16H^+ \rightarrow 2Mn^{2+} + 5I_2 + 8H_2O$
   (2) $2NaBr + Cl_2 \rightarrow 2NaCl + Br_2$
   (3) $KMnO_4 \rightarrow K_2MnO_4 + MnO_2 + O_2$
   (4) $2CuBr \rightarrow CuBr_2 + Cu$

5. In $KO_2$, the nature of oxygen species and the oxidation state of oxygen atom are, respectively : **[2018, Main]**
   (1) Oxide and – 2
   (2) Superoxide and – 1/2
   (3) Peroxide and – 1/2
   (4) Superoxide and – 1

6. Lithium aluminium hydride reacts with silicon tetrachloride to form : **[2018, Main]**
   (1) $LiCl$, $AleH_3$ and $SiH_4$
   (2) $LiCl$, $AlCl_3$ and $SiH_4$
   (3) $LiH$, $AlCl_3$ and $SiCl_2$
   (4) $LiH$, $AlH_3$ and $SiH_4$

7. $Fe^{3+}$ is reduced to $Fe^{2+}$ by using : **[2015, Advanced]**
   (1) $H_2O_2$ in presence of NaOH
   (2) $Na_2O_2$ in water
   (3) $H_2O_2$ in presence of $H_2SO_4$
   (4) $Na_2O_2$ in presence of $H_2SO_4$

8. In a galvanic cell, the salt bridge : **[2014, Advanced]**
   (1) Does not participate chemically in the cell reaction
   (2) Stops the diffusion of ions from one electrode to another
   (3) Is necessary for the occurrence of the cell reaction
   (4) Ensures mixing of the two electrolytic solutions

9. For the reaction :
   $$I^- + ClO_3^- + H_2SO_4 \rightarrow Cl^- + HSO_4^- + I_2$$
   The correct statements in the balanced equation is/are : **[2014, Advanced]**
   (1) Stoichiometric coefficient of $HSO_4^-$ is 6
   (2) Iodide is oxidised
   (3) Sulphur is reduced
   (4) $H_2O$ is one of the products

10. Consider the following list of reagents : **[2014, Advanced]**
    Acidified $K_2Cr_2O_7$, alkaline $KMnO_4$, $CuSO_4$, $H_2O_2$, $Cl_2$, $O_3$, $FeCl_3$, $HNO_3$ and $Na_2S_2O_3$.
    The total number of reagents that can oxidise aqueous iodide to iodine is.

11. Which of the following statements about $Na_2O_2$ is not correct ? **[2014, Advanced]**
    (1) It is diamagnetic in nature
    (2) It is a derivative of $H_2O_2$
    (3) $Na_2O_2$ oxidises $Cr^{3+}$ to $CrO_4^{2-}$ in acid medium
    (4) It is the super oxide of sodium

12. Consider the reaction :
    $$H_2SO_{3(aq)} + Sn_{(aq)}^{4+} + H_2O_{(l)} \rightarrow Sn_{(aq)}^{2+} + HSO_{4(aq)}^- + 3H_{(aq)}^+$$
    Which of the following statement is correct ? **[2014, Main]**
    (1) $Sn^{4+}$ is the oxidising agent because it undergoes oxidation.
    (2) $Sn^{4+}$ is the reducing agent because it undergoes oxidation.
    (3) $H_2SO_3$ is the reducing agent because it undergoes oxidation.
    (4) $H_2SO_3$ is the reducing agent because it undergoes reduction.

**13.** How many electrons are involved in the following redox reaction ? **[2014, Main]**

$$Cr_2O_7^{2-} + Fe^{2+} + C_2O_4^{2-} \rightarrow Cr^{3+} + Fe^{3+} + CO_2$$

(Unbalanced)

(1) 3        (2) 4

(3) 6        (4) 5

**14.** Amongst the following, identify the species with an atom in +6 oxidation state : **[2014, Main]**

(1) $[MnO_4]^-$        (2) $[Cr(CN)_6]^{3-}$

(3) $Cr_2O_3$        (4) $CrO_2Cl_2$

**15.** Which ordering of compounds is according to the decreasing order of the oxidation state of nitrogen ? **[2012, Advanced]**

(1) $HNO_3$, NO, $NH_4Cl$, $N_2$

(2) $HNO_3$, NO, $N_2$, $NH_4Cl$

(3) $HNO_3$, $NH_4Cl$, NO, $N_2$

(4) NO, $HNO_3$, $NH_4Cl$, $N_2$

**16.** 25 mL of household bleach solution was mixed with 30 mL of 0.50 M KI and 10 mL of 4N acetic acid. In the titration of the liberated iodine, 48 mL of 0.25 N $Na_2S_2O_3$ was used to reach the end point. The molarity of the household bleach solution is : **[2012, Advanced]**

(1) 0.48 M        (2) 0.96 M

(3) 0.24 M        (4) 0.024 M

**17.** For the given aqueous reactions, which of the statements is/are true ? **[2012, Advanced]**

$$\text{excess KI} + K_3[Fe(CN)_6] \xrightarrow{\text{dilute } H_2SO_4}$$

↓

brownish-yellow solution

↓ $ZnSO_4$

white precipitate + brownish-yellow filtrate

↓ $Na_2S_2O_3$

colourless solution

(1) The first reaction is a redox reaction

(2) White precipitate is $Zn_3[Fe(CN)_6]_2$

(3) Addition of filtrate to starch solution gives blue colour

(4) White precipitate is soluble in NaOH solution

**18.** The difference in the oxidation number of the two types of sulphur atoms in $Na_2S_4O_6$ is. **[2011, Advanced]**

**19.** In self-reduction, the reducing species is : **[2011, Advanced]**

(1) S        (2) $O^{2-}$

(3) $S^{2-}$        (4) $SO_2$

**20.** Among the following, the number of elements showing only one non-zero oxidation state is : O, Cl, F, N, P, Sn, T1, Na, Ti **[2010, Advanced]**

**21.** Aqueous solution of $Na_2S_2O_3$ on reaction with $Cl_2$ gives : **[2008, Advanced]**

(1) $Na_2S_4O_6$        (2) $NaHSO_4$

(3) NaCl        (4) NaOH

**22.** Match the reaction in Column I with nature of the reactions/type of the products in Column II. Indicate your answer by darkening the appropriate bubbles of the 4 × 4 matrix gives in the ORS. **[2007, Advanced]**

| Column I | Column II |
|---|---|
| (1) $O_2^- \rightarrow O_2 + O_2^{2-}$ | (p) redox reaction |
| (2) $CrO_4^{2-} + H^+ \rightarrow$ | (q) one of the products has trigonal planar structure |
| (3) $MnO_4^- + NO_2^- + H^+ \rightarrow$ | (r) dimeric bridged tetrahedral metal ion |
| (4) $NO_3^- + H_2SO_4 + Fe^{2+} \rightarrow$ | (s) disproportionation |

**23.** Identify the following :

$$Na_2CO_3 \xrightarrow{SO_2} A \xrightarrow{Na_2CO_3} B \xrightarrow{\text{Elemental } 8} C \xrightarrow{I_2} D$$

Also mention the oxidation state of S in all the compounds. **[2003, Main]**

## ANSWER KEY

| 1. (4) | 2. (3) | 3. (1) | 4. (4) | 5. (2) | 6. (2) | 7. (1,2) | 8. (1,3) | 9. (1,2,4) | 10. (*) |
|---|---|---|---|---|---|---|---|---|---|
| 11. (4) | 12. (3) | 13. (3) | 14. (4) | 15. (2) | 16. (3) | 17. (1,3,4) | 18. (*) | 19. (3) | 20. (2) |
| 21. (3) | 22. (*) | 23. (*) | | | | | | | |

## ANSWERS WITH EXPLANATIONS

**1. (4)** (i) $H_2O_2$ act as oxidising agent as well as reducing agent depending on condition.

(ii) $H_2SO_3$ act as oxidising agent as well as reducing agent depending on condition.

(iii) $HNO_2$ act as oxidising agent as well as reducing agent depending on condition.

(iv) $H_3PO_4$ can not act both as oxidising and reducing agent.

$H_3PO_4$ can act as only oxidising agent.

$$H_3PO_4 \rightleftharpoons 3H^+ + PO_4^{3-}$$

**2. (3)** combination of dinitrogen with dioxygen at 2000 K.

(i) $3O_2 \xrightarrow{h\nu} 2O_3$ (Non-redox reaction)

(ii) $H_2SO_4 + 2NaOH \longrightarrow Na_2SO_4 + 2H_2O$

(neutralisation reaction)

(iii) $N_2 + O_2 \xrightarrow{2000\,K} 2NO$

(Redox reaction)

During the reaction, oxidation of nitrogen takes place from 0 to 2 and reduction of oxygen takes place from 0 to $-2$. It means this reaction is Redox reaction.

(iv) $[CO(H_2O)_6]Cl_3 + 3AgNO_3 \longrightarrow 3AgCl$

(white ppt.)

$+ [Co(H_2O)_6](NO_3)_3$

3. **(1)** The number of equivalents of $KMnO_4$ required to neutralise the mixture is given below :

$$n_{eq}(KMnO_4) = n_{eq}(FeC_2O_4 + Fe_2(C_2O_4)_3 \\ + FeSO_4)$$

$$n \times 5 = (1 \times 3) + (1 \times 6) + (1 \times 1)$$

$$n = 2$$

4. **(4)** In a disporportion reaction same element is oxidized an reduced. In the reaction of CuBr, the copper is reduced from +1 to 0 and oxidized from +1 to +2. The reaction of CuBr is shown below :

$$\overset{reduction}{\overbrace{\underset{+1}{2Cu}\ Br \to \underset{+2}{Cu}\ Br + \underset{0}{Cu}}}$$

Oxidation 2

5. **(2)** In $KO_2$, the nature of oxygen species is superoxide (the superoxide ion is $O_2^-$)

The oxidation state of oxygen is assumed to be $x$ and oxidation state of potassium is +1. So,

O.S of K + O.S of O = Net charge on $KO_2$

$$(+1) + 2(x) = 0$$

$$x = -\frac{1}{2}$$

So, oxidation state of oxygen in $KO_2 = -\frac{1}{2}$

6. **(2)** The following reaction will take place when lithium aluminium hydride reacts with $SiCl_4$.

$$SiCl_4 + LiAH_4 \to SiH_4 + LiCl + AlCl_3$$

7. **(1,2)** The reaction of $Fe^{3+}$ and $H_2O_2$ in presence of NaOH is

$$2Fe^{3+} + H_2O_2 + 2NaOH \to 2Fe^{2+} + 2H_2O + O_2$$

Thus, $Fe^{3+}$ is reduced to $Fe^{2+}$ in presence of base.

Similarly, it can be reduced by the reaction of $Fe^{3+}$ and $Na_2O_2$ in presence of water.

$$Na_2O_2 + H_2O \to H_2O_2 + NaOH$$

$$2Fe^{3+} + H_2O_2 + 2NaOH \to 2Fe^{2+} + 2H_2O + O_2$$

8. **(1,3)** (A) Salt bridge does not participate chemically in the reaction as it consists of ions that do not interfere with the ions involved in a chemical reaction.

(B) Salt bridge does not stop the diffusion of ions from one electrode to another.

(C) Salt bridge is necessary for the cell reaction to maintain electrical neutrality.

(D) It does not ensure mixing of the two electrolytic solutions.

9. **(1,2,4)** The balanced chemical reaction is,

$$6I^- + ClO_3^- + 6H_2SO_4 \to Cl^- + 6HSO_4^- \\ + 3I_2 + 3H_2O$$

(A) The stoichiometric coefficient of $HSO_4^-$ is 6 as shown in the above equation.

(B) Iodide is reducing agent and $ClO_3^-$ is oxidizing agent. Therefore, iodide is oxidized.

(C) In the above reaction, $ClO_3^-$ is oxidizing agent. Therefore, it is reduced.

(D) In the above reaction, three molecules of $H_2O$ are formed.

10. The total numbers of reagents that oxidize aqueous iodide to iodine are seven which are shown as

1. $K_2Cr_2O_7 + H_2SO_4 + KI \to K_2SO_4 + Cr_2(SO_4)_3 \\ + H_2O + I_2$

2. $KMnO_4 + KOH + KI \to KIO_3 + K_2MnO_4 + H_2O$
$IO_3^- + 5I^- + 6H^+ \to 3I_2 + 3H_2O$

3. $2CuSO_4 + 4KI \to 4CuI + I_2 + 2K_2SO_4$

4. $H_2O_2 + KI \to KOH + I_2 + H_2O$

5. $FeCl_3 + KI \to FeI_2 + I_2 + KCl$

6. $HNO_3 + KI \to KNO_3 + H_2O + I_2 + [NO]$

7. $2I^- + H_2O + O_3 \to 2OH^- + I_2 + O_2$

11. **(4)** $Na_2O_2$ is a peroxide of sodium. All the other statements are correct about $Na_2O_2$.

12. **(3)** A reducing agent undergoes oxidation and an oxidizing agent undergoes reduction. In the given reaction $H_2SO_4$ undergoes oxidation and forms $HSO_4^-$. It reduces $Sn^{4+}$ to $Sn^{2+}$.

13. **(3)** The reactions taking place at anode and cathode are,

Anode (Ox.) :

$$Fe^{2+} + C_2O_4^{2-} \to Fe^{3+} + 2CO_2 + 3e^-$$

Cathode (Red) :

$$Cr_2O_7^{2-} + 14H^+ + 6e^- \to 2Cr^{3+} + 7H_2O$$

To balance the number of electrons, multiply oxidation half reaction with two and add both the oxidation and reduction half reactions to get overall balanced reaction.

Anode (Ox.) :
$$2Fe^{2+} + 2C_2O_4^{2-} \rightarrow 2Fe^{3+} + 4CO_2 + 6e^-$$
Cathode (Red.) :
$$Cr_2O_7^{2-} + 14H^+ + 6e^- \rightarrow 2Cr^{3+} + 7H_2O$$
Overall :
$$2Fe^{2+} + Cr_2O_7^{2-} + 2C_2O_4^{2-} + 14H^+ \rightarrow 2Fe^{3+} + 2Cr^{3+} + 4CO_2 + 7H_2O$$

Thus, six electrons are involve in the given redox reaction.

**14. (4)** Chromium metal in $CrO_2Cl_2$ has oxidation state equal to +6.
$$x + 2(-2) + 2(-1) = 0$$
$$x - 6 = 0$$
$$x = +6$$

**15. (2)** The oxidation state of nitrogen in $HNO_3$ is +5.

The oxidation state of nitrogen in NO is +2. The oxidation state of nitrogen in $NH_4Cl$ is – 3.

The oxidation state of nitrogen in $N_2$ is zero. Therefore, the correct decreasing order for oxidation state of nitrogen is $HNO_3$, NO, $N_2$, $NH_4Cl$.

**16. (3)** The reactions involved in the given process are shown below.
$$Ca(OCl)Cl + 2CH_3COOH \rightarrow Cl_2 + (CH_3COO)_2Ca + H_2O$$
$$Cl_2 + 2KI \rightarrow 2KCl + I_2$$
$$I_2 + 2Na_2S_2O_3 \rightarrow 2NaI + 2Na_2S_3O_6$$
Normality of $Na_2S_2O_3$ is equal to its molarity.

Number of moles of $Na_2S_2O_3$
$$= 48 \times 0.001 \, L \times 0.25 \, \frac{mol}{L}$$
$$= 0.012 \, mol$$

Number of moles of $I_2$ is,
$$= \frac{\text{Moles of } Na_2S_2O_3}{2}$$
$$= 0.006 \, mol$$

Number of moles of Cl is 0.006 mol.

Number of moles of bleaching powder is 0.006 mol.

Assume the molarity of bleaching powder to be M.
$$25 \times 10^{-3} \times M = 0.006$$
$$M = 0.24$$

**17. (1,3,4)** (A) The reaction involved is shown below :
$$\text{excess } KI + K_3[Fe(CN)_6] \rightarrow KI_3 + K_4[Fe(CN)_6]$$

The oxidation state of iron in $K_3[Fe(CN)_6]$ is +3 while in $K_4[Fe(CN)_6]$ it is +2.

Thus, it is a redox reaction.

(B) The next reaction is shown below :
$$K_4[Fe(CN)_6] + ZnSO_4 \rightarrow K_2Zn_3[Fe(CN)_6]$$
The white precipitate is given by complex $K_2Zn_3[Fe(CN)_6]$.

(C) The given reaction is shown below :
$$I_3^- + Na_2S_2O_3 \rightarrow Na_2S_4O_6 + NaI + I^-$$
Triiodide (filtrate) reacts with starch to give blue coloured solution.

(D) The given reaction is shown below :
$$K_2Zn_3[Fe(CN)_6] + NaOH \rightarrow Na_2[Zn(OH)_4]$$
The complex that is formed is soluble.

**18.** The structure of $Na_2S_4O_6$ is given as,

$$\begin{array}{ccc} & O & O \\ & \| & \| \\ NaO{-}\overset{+}{S}{-}\overset{-}{S}{-}\overset{0}{S}{-}\overset{0}{S}{-}ONa \\ & \| & \| \\ & O & O \end{array}$$

The oxidation state of doubly bonded two sulfur atoms is five. Therefore, the difference between two types of sulfur atom is $5 - 0 = 5$.

**19. (3)** The reducing species are those species which itself gets oxidised.
$$Cu_2S + Cu_2O \rightarrow 6Cu + SO_2$$
In the following reaction, $S^{2-}$ is oxidised to $S^{4+}$. So, $S^{2-}$ is reducing species.

**20. (2)** Fluorine shows 0 and – 1 oxidation state and sodium shows 0 and + 1 oxidation state. So, only F and Na show only 1 non-zero oxidation state.

**21. (3)** Sodium thiosulphate is used to remove the extra chlorine, which is used for the bleaching of clothes. Sodium thiosulphate converts to sodium bisulphate on reaction with $Cl_2$. The reaction is expressed as,
$$Na_2S_2O_3 + 4Cl_2 + 5H_2O \rightarrow 2NaHSO_4 + 8HCl$$

**22.** (1)-(p), (s); (2)-(r); (3)-(p), (q); (4)-(p);

(1) The $O_2^- \rightarrow O_2$ is an oxidation reaction as oxidation number increases from $O_2^-$ to $O_2$. The $O_2^- \rightarrow O_2^{2-}$ is a reduction reaction as oxidation number increases from $O_2^-$ to $O_2^{2-}$.

Thus, it is a redox reaction as well as disproportionation reaction as one molecule gets converted into two different products through oxidation and reduction reaction

(2) The product of gien ionic reaction is,
$$2CrO_4^{2-} + H^+ \rightarrow Cr_2O_7^{2-}$$
The structure of $Cr_2O_7^{2-}$ is dimeric bridge in which chromium is a tetrahedral metal ion.

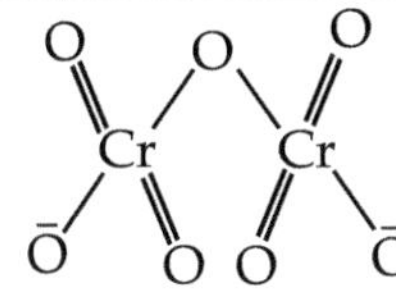

(3) The given reaction is a redox reaction.

$$MnO_2^- + NO_2^- + H^+ \rightarrow MN^{2+} + NO_3^- + H_2O$$

In the above reaction, $NO_3^-$ possesses trigonal planar structure.

(4) The given reaction is a redox reaction.

$$NO_3^- + H_2SO_4 + Fe^{2+} \rightarrow Fe^{2+} + SO_4^{2-} + NO + H_2O$$

Oxidation : $Fe^{2+} \rightarrow Fe^{3+}$

Reduction : $NO_3^- \rightarrow NO$

**23.** The reaction of $Na_2CO_3$ with $SO_2$ is as follows :

$$Na_2CO_3 + 2SO_2 + H_2O \rightarrow 2NaHSO_3 + CO_2$$

The compound A is $NaHSO_3$. The oxidation state of sulphur in $NaHSO_3$ is $+4$.

The reaction of $NaHSO_3$ with $Na_2CO_2$ is as follows :

$$NaHSO_3 + Na_2CO_3 \rightarrow 2Na_2SO_3 + H_2O + CO_2$$

The compound B is $Na_2SO_3$. The oxidation state of sulphur in $Na_2SO_3$ is $+4$.

The reaction of $Na_2SO_3$ with S is as follows :

$$Na_2SO_3 + S \rightarrow 2Na_2S_2O_3$$

The compound C is $Na_2S_2O_3$. The oxidation state of sulphur in $Na_2S_2O_3$ is $+2$.

The reaction of $Na_2S_2O_3$ with $I_2$ is as follows :

$$Na_2SO_3 + I_2 \rightarrow 2Na_2S_4O_6 + 2NaI$$

The compound D is $Na_2S_4O_6$. The oxidation state of sulphur in $Na_2S_4O_6$ is $+2.5$.

●●

## ⓩ QUESTIONS

**1.** The Gibbs energy change (in J) for the given reaction at $[Cu^{2+}] = [Sn^{2+}] = 1$ M and 298K is :
$Cu(s) + Sn^{2+}$ (aq.) $\rightarrow Cu^{2+}$ (aq.) $+ Sn(s)$;
$(E^0_{Sn^{2+}|Sn} = -0.16V, E^0_{Cu^{2+}|Cu} = 0.34V,$

Take F = 96500 C $mol^{-1}$) **[2020, Main]**

**2.** For the disproportionation reaction :
$2Cu^+(aq) \rightleftharpoons Cu(s) + Cu^{2+}$ (aq) at 298 K.
In K (where K is the equilibrium constant) is ...... $\times 10^{-1}$.
Given
$(E^0_{Cu^{2+}/Cu^+} = 0.16$ V

$E^0_{Cu^+/Cu} = 0.52$ V

$\dfrac{RT}{F} = 0.025)$ **[2020, Main]**

**3.** Let $C_{NaCl}$ and $C_{BaSO_4}$ be the conductances (in S) measured for saturated aqueous solutions of NaCl and $BaSO_4$, respectively, at a temperature T. Which of the following is false ?

**[2020, Main]**

(1) Ionic mobilities of ions from both salts increase with T.
(2) $C_{NaCl} >> C_{BaSO_4}$ at a given T
(3) $C_{NaCl} (T_2) > C_{NaCl} (T_1)$ for $T_2 > T_1$
(4) $C_{BaSO_4} (T_2) > C_{BaSO_4} (T_1)$ for $T_2 > T_1$

**4.** The photoelectric current from Na (work function, $w_0 = 2.3$ eV) is stopped by the output voltage of the cell
$Pt(s) | H_2(g, 1 bar) | HCl(aq., pH=1) | AgCl(s) | Ag(s)$
The pH of aq. HCl required to stop the photoelectric current from $K(w_0 = 2.25$ eV), all other conditions remaining the same, is .............. $\times 10^{-2}$ (to the nearest integer).

Given, $2.303 \dfrac{RT}{F} = 0.06V; E^0_{AgCl|Ag|Cl^-} = 0.22$ V

**[2020, Main]**

**5.** An acidic solution of dichromate is electrolyzed for 8 minutes using 2A current. As per the following equation
$Cr_7O_7^{2-} + 14H^+ + 6e^- \rightarrow 2Cr^{3+} + 7H_2O$
The amount of $Cr^{3+}$ obtained was 0.104 g. The efficiency of the process (in %) is
(Take : F =96000 C, At. mass of chromium = 52)

**[2020, Main]**

**6.**

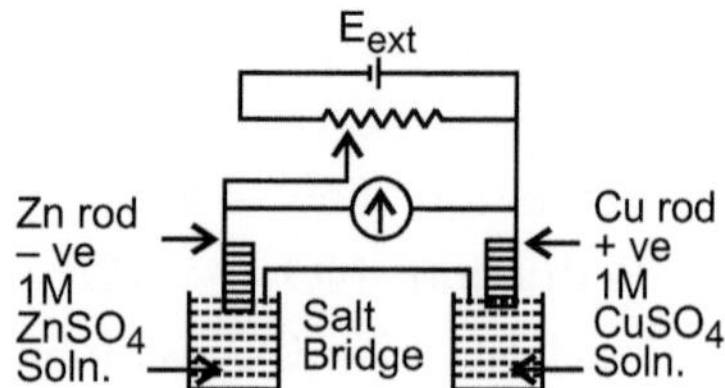


$E^0_{Cu^{2+}|Cu} = + 0.34V$

$E^0_{Zn^{2+}|Zn} = - 0.76V$

Identify the incorrect statement from the options below for the above cell : **[2020, Main]**

(1) If $E_{ext} > 1.1$ V, Zn dissovles at Zn electrode and Cu deposits at Cu electrode
(2) If $E_{ext} > 1.1$ V, $e^-$ flows from Cu to Zn
(3) If $E_{ext} = 1.1$ V, no flow of $e^-$ or current occurs
(4) If $E_{ext} < 1.1$ V, Zn dissolves at anode and Cu deposits at cathode

**7.** An oxidation-reduction reaction in which 3 electrons are transferred has a $\Delta G°$ of 17.37 kJ $mol^{-1}$ at 25°C. The value of $E°_{cell}$ (in V) is ...........
$\times 10^{-2}$.
(1 F = 96,500 C $mol^{-1}$) **[2020, Main]**

**8.** Potassium chlorate is prepared by the electrolysis of KCl in basic solution

$6OH^- + Cl^- \rightarrow ClO_3^- + 3H_2O + 6e^-$

If only 60% of the current is utilized in the reaction, the time (rounded to the nearest hour) required to produce 10 g of $KClO_3$ using a current of 2 A is .............. .

(Given : F = 96,500 C $mol^{-1}$ molar mass of $KClO_3$ = 122 $gmol^{-1}$) **[2020, Main]**

**9.** 250 mL of a waste solution obtained from the workshop of a goldsmith contains 0.1 M $AgNO_3$ and 0.1 M AuCl. The solution was electrolyzed at 2 V by passing current of 1 A for 15 minutes. The metal/metals electrodeposited will be :

$(E^0_{Ag^+/Ag} = 0.80$ V$, E^0_{Au^+/Au} = 1.69$ V$)$

**[2020, Main]**

(1) only silver
(2) only gold
(3) silver and gold in equal mass proportion
(4) silver and gold in proportion to their atomic weights

**10.** The variation of molar conductivity with concentration of an electrolyte (X) in aqueous solution is shown in the given figure.

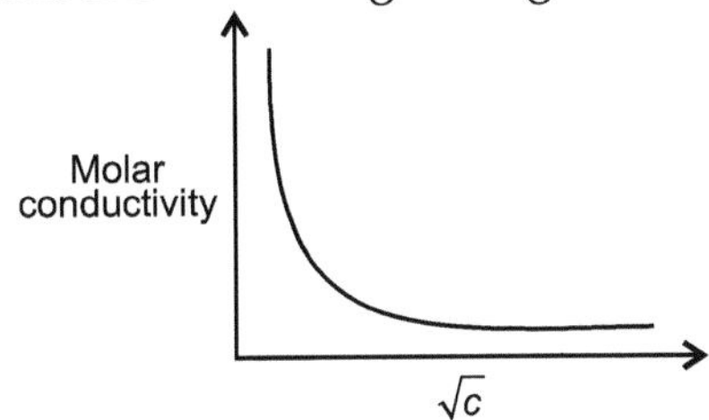

The electrolyte X is : **[2020, Main]**

(1) $CH_3COOH$  (2) $KNO_3$

(3) HCl  (4) NaCl

**11.** The solubility product of $Cr(OH)_3$ at 298 K is $6.0 \times 10^{-31}$. The concentration of hydroxide ions in a saturated solution of $Cr(OH)_3$ will be : **[2020, Main]**

(1) $(18 \times 10^{-31})^{1/4}$  (2) $(2.22 \times 10^{-31})^{1/4}$

(3) $(4.86 \times 10^{-29})^{1/4}$  (4) $(18 \times 10^{-31})^{1/2}$

**12.** 108 g of silver (molar mass 108 g $mol^{-1}$) is deposited at cathode from $AgNO_3$(aq) solution by a certain quantity of electricity. The volume (in L) of oxygen gas produced at 273 K and 1 bar pressure from water by the same quantity of electricity is ............... **[2020, Main]**

**13.** The volume (in mL) of 0.125 M $AgNO_3$ required to quantitatively precipitate chloride ions in 0.3 g of $[Co(NH_3)_6]Cl_3$ is ............ .

$^M[Co(NH_3)_6]Cl_3 = 267.46$ g/mol

$^MAgNO_3 = 169.87$ g/mol  **[2020, Main]**

**14.** What would be the electrode potential for the given half cell reaction at pH = 5 ? .........

**[2020, Main]**

$2H_2O \rightarrow O_2 + 4H^\oplus + 4e^-$; $E_{red}^0 = 1.23$ V

(R = 8.314 J $mol^{-1}$ $K^{-1}$; Temp = 298 K; oxygen under std. atm. pressure of 1 bar)

**15.** Given that the standard potentials (E°) of $Cu^{2+}/Cu$ and $Cu^+/Cu$ are 0.34 V and 0.522 V respectively, the E° of $Cu^{2+}/Cu^+$ is : **[2020, Main]**

(1) $+0.158$ V  (2) 0.182 V

(3) $-0.182$ V  (4) $-0.158$ V

**16.** In comparison to the zeolite process for the removal of permanent hardness, the synthetic resins method is : **[2020, Main]**

(1) less efficient as it exchanges only anions

(2) more efficient as it can exchange only cations

(3) less efficient as the resins cannot be regenerated

(4) more efficient as it can exchange both cations as well as anions

**17.** For an electrochemical cell

$Sn(s)\,|\,Sn^{2+}$ (aq, 1M) $\|$ $Pb^{2+}$ (aq, 1M) $|\,Pb(s)$ the ratio $\dfrac{[Sn^{2+}]}{[Pb^{2+}]}$ when this cell attains equilibrium is .........

(Given $E^0_{Su^+/Su} = -0.14$V.

$E^0_{Pb^+/Pb} = -0.13$V. $\dfrac{2.303RT}{F} = 0.06$) **[2020, Main]**

**18.** Given that $E^\ominus_{O_2/H_2O} = +1.23$V; **[2019, Main]**

$E^\ominus_{S_2O_8^{2-}/SO_4^{2-}} = 2.05$ V

$E^\ominus_{Br_2/Br^-} = +1.09$V;

$E^\ominus_{Au^{3+}/Au} = +1.4$V

The strongest oxidising agent is :

(1) $Au^{3+}$  (2) $O_2$

(3) $S_2O_8^{2-}$  (4) $Br_2$

**19.** Calculate the standard cell potential (in V) of the cell in which following reaction takes place :

**[2019, Main]**

$Fe^{2+}(aq) + Ag^+(aq) \rightarrow Fe^{3+}(aq) + Ag(s)$

$E^o_{Ag^+/Ag} = xV$

$E^o_{Fe^{2+}/Fe} = yV$

$E^o_{Fe^{3+}/Fe} = zV$

(1) $x - z$  (2) $x - y$

(3) $x + 2y - 3z$  (4) $x + y - z$

**20.** The standard Gibbs energy for the given cell reaction in kJ $mol^{-1}$ at 298 K is : **[2019, Main]**

$Zn(s) + Cu^{2+}(aq) \rightarrow Zn^{2+}(aq) + Cu(s)$,

$E° = 2$ V at 298 K

(Faraday's constant, F = 96000 C $mol^{-1}$)

(1) $-384$  (2) 384

(3) 192  (4) $-192$

**21.** A solution of $Ni(NO_3)_2$ is electrolysed between platinum electrodes using 0.1 Faraday electricity. How many mole of Ni will be deposited at the cathode ? **[2019, Main]**

(1) 0.05  (2) 0.20

(3) 0.15  (4) 0.10

**22.** Consider the statements S1 and S2 :

**[2019, Main]**

S1 : Conductivity always increases with decreases in the concentration of electrolyte.

S2 : Molar conductivity always increases with decrease in the concentration of electrolyte,

The correct option among the following is :

(1) Both S1 and S2 are wrong

(2) S1 is wrong and S2 is correct

(3) Both S1 and S2 are correct

(4) S1 is correct and S2 is wrong

**23.** Which of the following graphs between molar conductivity $(\Lambda_m)$ versus $\sqrt{C}$ is correct ?

**[2019, Main]**

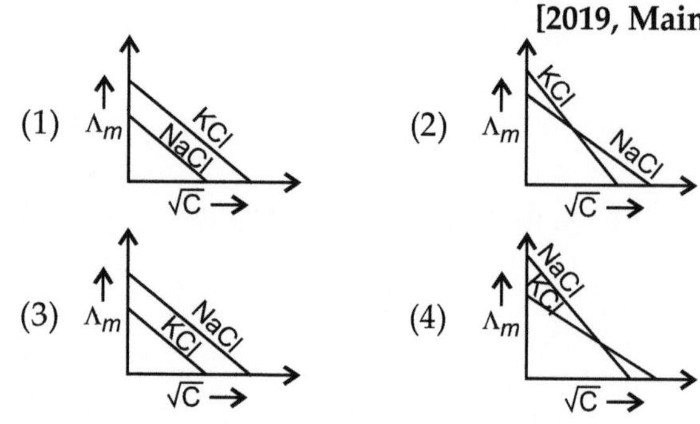

**24.** Given :
$Co^{3+} + e^- \rightarrow Co^{2+}$; $E° = + 1.81$ V
$Pb^{4+} + 2e^- \rightarrow Pb^{2+}$; $E° = + 1.67$ V
$Ce^{4+} + e^- \rightarrow Co^{3+}$; $E° = + 1.61$ V
$Bi^{3+} + 3e^- \rightarrow Bi$; $E° = + 0.20$ V
Oxidising power of the species will increase in the order : **[2019, Main]**
(1) $Ce^{4+} < Pb^{4+} < Bi^{3+} < Co^{3+}$
(2) $Bi^{3+} < Ce^{4+} < Pb^{4+} < Co^{3+}$
(3) $Co^{3+} < Ce^{4+} < Bi^{3+} < Pb^{4+}$
(4) $Co^{3+} < Pb^{4+} < Ce^{4+} < Bi^{3+}$

**25.** The decreasing order of electrical conductivity of the following aqueous solution is : **[2019, Main]**
0.1 M Formic acid (A),
0.1 M Formic acid (B),
0.1 M Formic acid (C),
(1) A > C > B      (2) C > B > A
(3) A > B > C      (4) C > A > B

**26.** Molar conductivity ($\Lambda_m$) of aqueous solution of sodium stearate, which behaves asa strong electrolyte, is recorded at varying concentrations (c) of sodium stearate. Which of the following plots provides the correct representation of micelle formation in the solution ?
(critical micelle concentration (CMC) is marked with an arrow in the figures) **[2019, Advanced]**

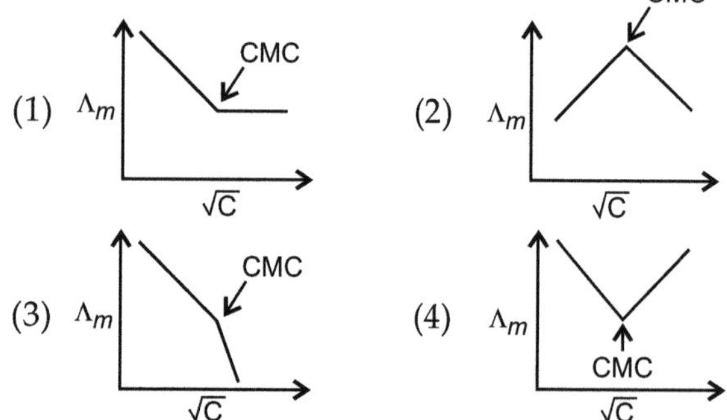

**27.** For the following reaction, the equilibrium constant $K_c$ at 298 K is $1.6 \times 10^{17}$.

$$Fe^{2+}(aq) + S^{2-}(aq) \rightleftharpoons FeS(s)$$

When equal volumes of 0.06 M $Fe^{21}$ (aq) and 0.2 M $S^2$ (aq) is found to be $Y \times 10^{-17}$ M. The value of Y is ........ **[2019, Advanced]**

**28.** For the electrochemical cell,
$$Mg(s) \mid Mg^{2+}(aq, 1 M) \parallel Cu^{2+}(aq, 1 M) \mid Cu(s)$$
the standard emf of the cell is 2.70 V at 300 K. When the concentration of $Mg^{2+}$ is changed to $x$ M, the cell potential changes to 2.67 V at 300 K. The value of $x$ is ............. . **[2018, Advanced]**

(Given : $\dfrac{F}{R} = 11500$ K V$^{-1}$, where F is the Faraday constant and R is the gas constant, ln(10) = 2.30)

**29.** Consider an electrochemical cell : A(s) | A$^{n+}$ (aq, 2 M) || B$^{2n+}$ (aq, 1 M) | B(s). The value of $\Delta H^\theta$ for the cell reaction is twice that of $\Delta G^\theta$ at 300 K. If the emf of the cell is zero, the $\Delta S^\theta$ (in JK$^{-1}$ mol$^{-1}$) of the cell reaction per mole of B formed at 300 K is ......... . **[2018, Advanced]**
(Given : ln(2) = 0.7, R (universal gas constant) = 8.3 J K$^{-1}$ mol$^{-1}$. H, S and G are enthalpy, entropy and Gibbs energy, respectively.)

**30.** How long (approximate) should water be electrolysed by passing through 100 amperes current so that the oxygen released can completely burn 27.66 g of diborane ? **[2018, Main]**
(Atomic weight of B = 10.8 u)
(1) 6.4 hours      (2) 0.8 hours
(3) 3.2 hours      (4) 1.6 hours

**31.** When an electric current is passed through acidified water, 112 mL of hydrogen gas at N.T.P. was collected at the cathode in 965 seconds. The current passed, in ampere, is : **[2018, Main]**
(1) 1.0      (2) 0.5
(3) 0.1      (4) 2.0

**32.** When 9.65 ampere current was passed for 1.0 hour into nitrobenzene in acidic medium, the amount of $p$-aminophenol produced is : **[2018, Main]**
(1) 9.81 g      (2) 10.9 g
(3) 98.1 g      (4) 109.0 g

**33.** The conductance of a 0.0015 M aqueous solution of a weak monobasic acid was determined by using a conductivity cell consisting of platinised Pt electrodes. The distance between the electrodes is 120 cm with an area of cross section of 1 cm$^2$. The conductance of this solution was found to be $5 \times 10^{-7}$ S. The pH of the solution is 4. The value of limiting molar conductivity ($\Lambda_m^0$) of this weak monobasic acid in aqueous solution is Z × 10$^2$ S cm$^{-1}$ mol$^{-1}$. The value of Z is. **[2017, Advanced]**

**34.** For the following cell,
$$Zn(s) \mid ZnSO_4(aq) \parallel CuSO_4(aq) \mid Cu(s)$$
when the concentration of $Zn^{2+}$ is 10 times the concentration of $Cu^{2+}$, the expression for $\Delta G$ (in J mol$^{-1}$) is
[F is Faraday constant; R is gas constant; T is temperature; E°(cell) = 1.1 V] **[2017, Advanced]**
(1) 1.1 F      (2) 2.303 RT – 2.2 F
(3) 2.303 RT + 1.1 F      (4) – 2.2 F

**35.** Which of the following combination will produce H$_2$ gas ? **[2017, Advanced]**
(1) Fe metal and conc. HNO$_3$
(2) Cu metal and conc. HNO$_3$
(3) Zn metal and NaOH(aq)
(4) Au metal and NaCN(aq) in the presence of air

**36.** Given                   **[2017, Main]**

$$E^o_{Cl_2/Cl^-} = 1.36\,V, E^o_{Cr^{3+}/Cr} = -0.74\,V$$

$$E^o_{Cr_2O_7^{2-}/Cr^{3+}} = 1.33\,V, E^o_{MnO_4^-/Mn^{2+}} = 1.51\,V$$

Among the following, the strongest reducing agent is :

(1) $Cr^{3+}$          (2) $Cl^-$
(3) $Cr$            (4) $Mn^{2+}$

**37.** What is the standard reduction potential (E°) for $Fe^{3+} \to Fe$ ?     **[2017, Main]**

Given that :

$$Fe^{2+} + 2e^0 \to Fe; E^o_{Fe^{2+}/Fe} = -0.47\,V$$

$$Fe^{3+} + e^\circledast \to Fe^{2+}; E^o_{Fe^{3+}/Fe^{2+}} = +0.77\,V$$

(1) $-0.057$ V       (2) $+0.057$ V
(3) $+0.30$ V        (4) $-0.30$ V

**38.** Consider the following standard electrode potentials (E° in volts) in aqueous solution :

| Element | $M^{3+}/M$ | $M^+/M$ |
|---------|-----------|---------|
| A1 | $-1.66$ | $+0.55$ |
| T1 | $+1.26$ | $-0.34$ |

Based on these data, which of the following statements is correct ?     **[2017, Main]**

(1) $T1^+$ is more stable than $Al^{3+}$
(2) $A1^+$ is more stable than $Al^{3+}$
(3) $T1^+$ is more stable than $Al^+$
(4) $T1^{3+}$ is more stable than $Al^{3+}$

**39.** To find the standard potential of $M^{3+}/M$ electrode, the following cell is constituted : Pt/M/ $M^{3+}$ (0.001 mol $L^{-1}$)/$Ag^+$ (0.01 mol $L^{-1}$)/Ag

The emf of the cell is found to be 0.421 volt at 298 K. The standard potential of half reaction $M^{3+} + 3e^- \to M$ at 298 K will be :     **[2017, Main]**

(Given $E^\ominus_{Ag^+/Ag}$ at 298 K = 0.80 Volt)

(1) 0.38 Volt      (2) 0.32 Volt
(3) 1.28 Volt      (4) 0.66 Volt

**40.** For the following electrochemical cell at 298 K,

$$Pt(s)|H_2(g, 1\,bar)|H^+(aq\,1M)\|M^{4+}(aq), M^{2+}(aq)|Pt(s)$$

$$E_{cell} = 0.092\,V \text{ when } \frac{[M^{2+}(aq)]}{[M^{4+}(aq)]} = 10^x.$$

Given : $E^o_{M^{4+}/M^{2+}} = 0.151\,V; 2.303\frac{RT}{F} = 0.059\,V$

The value of $x$ is :     **[2016, Advanced]**

(1) $-2$         (2) $-1$
(3) 1           (4) 2

**41.** What will occur if a block of copper metal is dropped into a beaker containing a solution of 1M $ZnSO_4$ ?     **[2016, Main]**

(1) The copper metal will dissolve and zinc metal will be deposited
(2) The copper metal will dissolve with evolution of hydrogen gas
(3) The copper metal will dissolve with evolution of oxygen gas
(4) No reaction will occur

**42.** Identify the correct statement :     **[2016, Main]**
(1) Iron corrodes in oxygen-free water
(2) Iron corrodes more rapidly in salt water because its electrochemical potential is higher
(3) Corrosion of iron can be minimized by forming a contact with another metal with a higher reduction potential
(4) Corrosion of iron can be minimized by forming an impermeable barrier at its surface

**43.** Galvanisation is applying a coating of :     **[2016, Main]**
(1) Pb         (2) Cr
(3) Cu         (4) Zn

**44.** All the energy released from the reaction $X \to Y$, $\Delta_r G^0 = -193$ kJ $mol^{-1}$ is used for oxidixing $M^+$ as $M^+ \to M^{3+} + 2e^-$, $E^\circ = -0.25$ V.
Under standard conditions, the number of moles of $M^+$ oxidised when one mole of X is coverted to Y is [F = 96500 C $mol^{-1}$]     **[2015, Advanced]**

**45.** Two Faraday of electricity is passed through a solution of $CuSO_4$. The mass of copper deposited at the cathode is :     **[2015, Main]**
(at. mass of Cu = 63.5 amu)
(1) 0 g         (2) 63.5 g
(3) 2 g         (4) 127 g

**46.** A variable, opposite external potential ($E_{ext}$) is applied to the cell $Zn | Zn^{2+}$ (1 M) $\| Cu^{2+}$ (1M) $| Cu$, of potential 1.1 V. When $E_{ext} < 1.1$ V and $E_{ext} > 1.1$ V, respectively electrons flow from :     **[2015, Main]**
(1) anode to cathode and cathode to anode
(2) cathode to anode and anode to cathode
(3) cathode to anode in both cases
(4) anode to cathode in both cases

**47.** At 298 K, the standard reduction potentials are 1.51 V for $MnO_4^-|Mn^{2+}$, 1.36 V for $Cl_2/Cl^-$, 1.07 V for $Br_2/Br^-$, and 0.54 V for $I_2/I^-$. At pH = 3, permanganate is expected to oxidize : $\left(\frac{RT}{F} = 0.059\,V\right)$     **[2015, Main]**
(1) $Cl^-$, $Br^-$ and $I^-$     (2) $Cl^-$ and $Br^-$
(3) $Br^-$ and $I^-$       (4) $I^-$ only

**48.** Resistance of 0.2 M solution of an electrolyte is 50 $\Omega$. The specific conductance of the solution is 1.4 S $m^{-1}$. The resistance of 0.5 M solution of the same electrolyte is 280 $\Omega$. The molar conductivity of 0.5 M solution of the electrolyte in S $m^2$ $mol^{-1}$ is :     **[2014, Main]**

(1) $5 \times 10^{-4}$      (2) $5 \times 10^{-3}$

(3) $5 \times 10^3$      (4) $5 \times 10^2$

**49.** The equivalent conductance of NaCl at concentration C and at infinite dilution are $\lambda_C$ and $\lambda_\infty$, respectively. The correct relationship between l C and li is given as : **[2014, Main]** (where the constant B is positive)

(1) $\lambda_C = \lambda_\infty + (B)C$

(2) $\lambda_C = \lambda_\infty - (B)C$

(3) $\lambda_C = \lambda_\infty - (B)\sqrt{C}$

(4) $\lambda_C = \lambda_\infty + (B)\sqrt{C}$

**50.** The metal that cannot be obtained by electrolysis of an aqueous solution of its salts is : **[2014, Main]**

(1) Ag      (2) Ca

(3) Cu      (4) Cr

**51.** Given below are the half-cell reactions :

$Mn^{2+} + 2e^- \rightarrow Mn;\ E° = -1.18\ V$

$2(Mn^{3+} + e^- \rightarrow Mn^{2+});\ E° = +1.51\ V$

The E° for $3Mn^{2+} \rightarrow Mn + 2Mn^{3+}$ will be : **[2014, Main]**

(1) $-2.69$ V; the reaction will not occur

(2) $-2.69$ V; the reaction will occur

(3) $-0.33$ V; the reaction will not occur

(4) $-0.33$ V; the reaction will occur

**52.** The standard electrode potentials $(ER°_{M^+/M})$ of four metals A, B, C and D are $-1.2$ V, 0.6 V, 0.85 V and $-0.76$ V, respectively. The sequence of deposition of metals on applying potential is : **[2014, Main]**

(1) A, C, B, D      (2) B, D, C, A

(3) C, B, D, A      (4) D, A, B, C

**53.** A current of 10.0 A flows for 2.00 h through an electrolytic cell containing a molten salt of metal X. This results in the decomposition of 0.250 mol of metal X at the cathode. The oxidation state of X in the molten salt is : (F = 96,500 C) **[2014, Main]**

(1) $1+$      (2) $2+$

(3) $3+$      (4) $4+$

**54.** Given

$Fe^{3+}(aq) + e^- \rightarrow Fe^{2+}(aq);\ E° = +0.77\ V$

$Al^{3+}(aq) + 3e^- \rightarrow Al(s);\ E° = -1.66\ V$

$Br_2(aq) + 2e^- \rightarrow 2Br^-;\ E° = +1.09\ V$

Considering the electrode potentials, which of the following represents the correct order of reducing power ? **[2014, Main]**

(1) $Fe^{2+} < Al < Br^-$      (2) $Br^- < Fe^{2+} < Al$

(3) $Al < Br^- < Fe^{2+}$      (4) $Al < Fe^{2+} < Br^-$

**55.** How many electrons would be required to deposit 6.35 g of copper at the cathode during the electrolysis of an aqueous solution of copper sulphate ? (Atomic mass of copper = 63.5 u, $N_A$ = Avogadro's constant) : **[2014, Main]**

(1) $\dfrac{N_A}{20}$      (2) $\dfrac{N_A}{10}$

(3) $\dfrac{N_A}{5}$      (4) $\dfrac{N_A}{2}$

**56.** The standard reduction potential data at 25°C is given below. **[2013, Advanced]**

$E°(Fe^{3+}, Fe^{2+}) = +0.77\ V;$

$E°(Fe^{2+}, Fe) = -0.44\ V;$

$E°(Cu^{2+}, Cu) = +0.34\ V;$

$E°(Cu^+, Cu) = +0.52\ V;$

$E°[O_2(g) + 4H^+ + 4e^- \rightarrow 2H_2O] = +1.23\ V;$

$E°[O_2(g) + 2H_2O + 4e^- \rightarrow 4OH^-] = +0.40\ V;$

$E°[Cr^{3+}, Cr] = -0.74\ V;$

$E°[Cr^{3+}, Cr] = -0.91\ V;$

Match E° of the redox pair in List I with the values given in List II and select the correct answer using the code given below the lists :

| | List I | | List II |
|---|---|---|---|
| P. | $E°(Fe^{3+}, Fe)$ | 1. | $-0.18$ V |
| Q. | $E°(4H_2O \rightleftharpoons 4H^+ + 4OH^-)$ | 2. | $-0.4$ V |
| R. | $E°(Cu^{2+} + Cu \rightarrow 2Cu^+)$ | 3. | $-0.04$ V |
| S. | $E°(Cr^{3+}, Cr^{2+})$ | 4. | $-0.18$ V |

**Codes :**

| | P | Q | R | S |
|---|---|---|---|---|
| (1) | 4 | 1 | 2 | 3 |
| (2) | 2 | 3 | 4 | 1 |
| (3) | 1 | 2 | 3 | 4 |
| (4) | 3 | 4 | 1 | 2 |

**57.** An aqueous solution of X is added slowly to an aqueous solution of Y as shown in List I. The variation in conductivity of these reactions is given in List II. Match List I with List II and select the correct answer using the code given below the lists : **[2013, Advanced]**

| | List I | | List II |
|---|---|---|---|
| P. | $(C_2H_5)_3N$   +   $CH_3COOH$<br>    X            Y | 1. | Conductivity decreases and then increases |
| Q. | $KI\ (0.1M)$ + $AgNO_3$<br>    X         Y<br>          (0.01M) | 2. | Conductivity decreases and then does not change much |
| R. | $CH_3COOH$ + $KOH$<br>    X         Y | 3. | Conductivity increases and then does not change much |
| S. | $NaOH$ + $HI$<br>    X     Y | 4. | Conductivity does not change much and then increases |

**Codes :**

| | P | Q | R | S |
|---|---|---|---|---|
| (1) | 3 | 4 | 2 | 1 |
| (2) | 4 | 3 | 2 | 1 |
| (3) | 2 | 3 | 4 | 1 |
| (4) | 1 | 4 | 3 | 2 |

**58.** The solubility product ($K_{sp}$; $mol_3\,dm^{-9}$) of $MX_2$ at 298 K based on the information available for the given concentration cell is (take $2.303 \times R \times 298/F = 0.059$ V) **[2012, Advanced]**
(1) $1 \times 10^{-15}$ (2) $4 \times 10^{-15}$
(3) $1 \times 10^{-12}$ (4) $4 \times 10^{-12}$

**59.** The value of $\Delta G$($kJ\,mol^{-1}$) for the given cell is (take $1F = 96500$ $C\,mol^{-1}$) **[2012, Advanced]**
(1) $-5.7$ (2) $5.7$
(3) $11.4$ (4) $-11.4$

**60.** The metal rod M is : **[2011, Advanced]**
(1) Fe (2) Cu
(3) Ni (4) Co

**61.** The compound N is : **[2011, Advanced]**
(1) $AgNO_3$ (2) $Zn(NO_3)_2$
(3) $Al(NO_3)_3$ (4) $Pb(NO_3)_2$

**62.** Consider the following cell reaction :
$$2Fe(s) + O_2(g) + 4H^+(aq) \to 2Fe^{2+}(aq) + 2H_2O(l)$$
$E° = 1.67$ V
At $[Fe^{2+}] = 10^{-3}$ M, $P(O_2) = 0.1$ atm and pH = 3, the cell potential at 25°C is : **[2011, Advanced]**
(1) 1.47 V (2) 1.77 V
(3) 1.87 V (4) 1.57 V

**63.** Among the following, the intensive property is (properties are) : **[2010, Advanced]**
(1) molar conductivity
(2) electromotive force
(3) resistance
(4) heat capacity

**64.** For the above cell : **[2010, Advanced]**
(1) $E_{cell} < 0;\ \Delta G > 0$ (2) $E_{cell} > 0;\ \Delta G < 0$
(3) $E_{cell} < 0;\ \Delta G° > 0$ (4) $E_{cell} > 0;\ \Delta G° < 0$

**65.** If the 0.05 molar solution of $M^+$ is replaced by a 0.0025 molar $M^+$ solution, then the magnitude of the cell potential would be : **[2010, Advanced]**
(1) 35 mV (2) 70 mV
(3) 140 mV (4) 700 mV

**66.** For the reduction of $NO_3^-$ ion in an aqueous solution, $E°$ is $+0.96$ V. Values of $E°$ for some metal ions are given below : **[2009, Advanced]**
$V^{2+}$ (aq) $+ 2e^- \to V$ $\quad E° = -1.19$ V
$Fe^{3+}$ (aq) $+ 3e^- \to Fe$ $\quad E° = -0.04$ V
$Au^{3+}$ (aq) $+ 3e^- \to Au$ $\quad E° = +1.40$ V
$Hg^{2+}$ (aq) $+ 2e^- \to Hg$ $\quad E° = +0.86$ V
The pairs of metals that is/are oxidised by $NO_3^-$ in aqueous solution is/are :
(1) V and Hg (2) Hg and Fe
(3) Fe and Au (4) Fe and V

**67.** Electrolysis of dilute aqueous NaCl solution was carried out by passing 10 milli ampere current. The time required to liberate 0.01 mol of $H_2$ gas at cathode is (1 Faraday = 96500 $C\,mol^{-1}$)
**[2008, Advanced]**
(1) $9.65 \times 10^4$ sec (2) $19.3 \times 10^4$ sec
(3) $28.95 \times 10^4$ sec (4) $38.6 \times 10^4$ sec

**68.** The total number of moles of chlorine gas evolved is : **[2007, Advanced]**
(1) 0.5 (2) 1.0
(3) 2.0 (4) 3.0

**69.** If the cathode is a Hg electrode, the maximum weight (g) of amalgam formed from this solution is : **[2007, Advanced]**
(1) 200 (2) 225
(3) 400 (4) 446

**70.** The total charge (coulombs) required for complete electrolysis is : **[2007, Advanced]**
(1) 24125 (2) 48250
(3) 96500 (4) 193000

**71.** Among the following, identify the correct statement. **[2007, Advanced]**
(1) Chloride ion is oxidised by $O_2$
(2) $Fe^{2+}$ is oxidised by iodine
(3) Iodide ion is oxidised by chlorine
(4) $Mn^{2+}$ is oxidised by chlorine

**72.** $2Ag^+ + C_6H_{12}O_6 + H_2O_2 \to Ag(s) + C_6H_{12}O_7 + 2H^+$
Find ln K of this reaction. **[2006, Main]**
(1) 66.13 (2) 58.38
(3) 28.30 (4) 46.29

**73.** When ammonia is added to the solution, pH is raised to 11. Which half-cell reaction is affected by pH and by how much ? **[2006, Main]**
(1) $E_{oxd}$ will increase by a factor of 0.65 from $E°_{oxd}$
(2) $E_{oxd}$ will decrease by a factor of 0.65 from $E°_{oxd}$
(3) $E_{red}$ will increase by a factor of 0.65 from $E°_{red}$
(4) $E_{red}$ will decrease by a factor of 0.65 from $E°_{red}$

**74.** Ammonia is always is added in this reaction. Which of the following must be incorrect ?
**[2006, Main]**
(1) $NH_3$ combines with $Ag^+$ to form a complex
(2) $Ag(NH_3)_2^+$ is a stronger oxidising reagent than $Ag^+$
(3) In absence of $NH_3$ silver salt of gluconic acid is formed
(4) $NH_3$ has affected the standard reduction potential of glucose/gluconic acid electrode

**75.** (a) Calculate $\Delta G_r^0$ of the following reaction :
$$Ag^+_{(aq)} + Cl^-_{(aq.)} \to AgCl_{(s)}$$
**[2005, Main]**
Given :
$\Delta G_f^0(AgCl)$ $\quad\quad -109$ kJ/mole
$\Delta G_f^0(Cl^-)$ $\quad\quad -129$ kJ/mole
$\Delta G_f^0(Ag^+)$ $\quad\quad -77$ kJ/mole

Represent the above reaction in form of a cell. Calculate $E°$ of the cell. Find $\log_{10}K_{sp}$ of AgCl.

(b) $6.539 \times 10^{-2}$ g of metallic Zn (amu = 65.39) was added to 100 mol of saturated solution of AgCl.

Calculate $\log_{10}\dfrac{[Zn^{2+}]}{[Ag^+]}$. Given that

$$Ag^+ + e^- \to Ag \qquad E° = 0.80 \text{ V}$$
$$Zn^{2+} + 2e^- \to Zn \qquad E° = -0.76 \text{ V}$$

Also find how many moles of Ag will be formed ?

**76.** The half cell reactions for rusting of iron are :

$$2H^+ + \frac{1}{2}O_2 + 2e^- \to H_2O; E° = +1.23V$$

$$Fe^{2+} + 2e^- \to Fe_{(s)}; E° = -0.44V$$

$\Delta G°$ (in kJ) for the reaction is : **[2005, Screening]**
(1) $-76$           (2) $-332$
(3) $-122$          (4) $-176$

**77.** Find the equilibrium constant for the reaction

$$Cu^{+2} + In^{+2} \rightleftharpoons Cu^+ + In^{+3}$$

Given that             **[2004, Main]**

$$E°_{Cu^{+2}/Cu^+} = 0.15V$$
$$E°_{In^{+2}/In^+} = -0.4V$$
$$E°_{In^{+3}/In^+} = -0.42V$$

**78.** Zn Palatino $Zn^{2+}$ $(a = 0.1M) \parallel Fe^{2+}$ $(a = 0.01M) \mid Fe$. The emf of the above cell is 0.2905 V. Equilibrium constant for the cell reaction is :

                     **[2004, Screening]**
(1) $10^{0.32/0.0591}$       (2) $10^{0.32/0.0295}$
(3) $10^{0.26/0.0295}$       (4) $10^{0.32/0.0295}$

**79.** (a) Will the pH of water be same at 4°C and 25°C ? Explain.

(b) Two students use same stock solution of $ZnSO_4$ and a solution of $CuSO_4$. The emf of one cell is 0.03 V higher than the other. The conc. of $CuSO_4$ in the cell with higher emf value is 0.5 M. Find out the conc. of $CuSO_4$ in the other cell (2.203 RT/F = 0.08).

                   **[2003, Main]**

**80.** In the electrolytic cell, flow of electrons is from :
                   **[2003, Screening]**
(1) Cathode to anode in solution
(2) Cathode to anode through internal supply
(3) Cathode to anode through internal supply
(4) Anode to cathode through internal supply

**81.** Standard electrode potential data are useful for understanding the suitability of an oxidant in a redox titration. Some half cell reactions and their standard potentials are given below :

$$MnO_4^-(aq.) + 8H^+(aq.) + 5e^- \to Mn^{2+}(aq.) + 4H_2O(l)$$
$$E° = 1.51 \text{ V}$$
$$Cr_2O_7^{2-}(aq.) + 14H^+(aq.) + 6e^- \to 2Cr^{3+}(aq.)$$
$$+ 7H_2O(l) \quad E° = 0.77 \text{ V}$$
$$Fe^{3+}(aq.) + e^- \to Fe^{2+}(aq.) \qquad E° = 0.77 \text{ V}$$
$$Cl_2(g) + 2e^- \to 2Cl^-(aq.) \qquad E° = 1.40 \text{ V}$$

Identify the only incorrect statement regarding the quantitative estimation of aqueous $Fe(NO_3)_2$ :

                   **[2002, Screening]**
(1) $MnO_4^-$ can be used in aqueous HCl
(2) $Cr_2O_7^{2-}$ can be used in aqueous HCl
(3) $MnO_4^-$ can be used in aqueous $H_2SO_4$
(4) $Cr_2O_7^{2-}$ can be used in aqueous $H_2SO_4$

## ANSWER KEY

| | | | | | | | | | |
|---|---|---|---|---|---|---|---|---|---|
| 1. (*) | 2. (*) | 3. (3) | 4. (*) | 5. (*) | 6. (1) | 7. (*) | 8. (*) | 9. (4) | 10. (1) |
| 11. (1) | 12. (*) | 13. (*) | 14. (*) | 15. (1) | 16. (4) | 17. (*) | 18. (3) | 19. (3) | 20. (1) |
| 21. (1) | 22. (2) | 23. (1) | 24. (2) | 25. (1) | 26. (3) | 27. (*) | 28. (*) | 29. (*) | 30. (3) |
| 31. (1) | 32. (1) | 33. (*) | 34. (2) | 35. (3) | 36. (3) | 37. (1) | 38. (3) | 39. (2) | 40. (4) |
| 41. (4) | 42. (4) | 43. (4) | 44. (4) | 45. (2) | 46. (4) | 47. (3) | 48. (1) | 49. (3) | 50. (2) |
| 51. (1) | 52. (3) | 53. (3) | 54. (4) | 55. (3) | 56. (4) | 57. (1) | 58. (2) | 59. (4) | 60. (2) |
| 61. (1) | 62. (4) | 63. (1, 2) | 64. (2) | 65. (3) | 66. (1,2,4) | 67. (2) | 68. (2) | 69. (4) | 70. (4) |
| 71. (3) | 72. (1) | 73. (1) | 74. (4) | 75. (*) | 76. (2) | 77. (*) | 78. (2) | 79. (*) | 80. (3) |
| 81. (1) | | | | | | | | | |

## ANSWERS WITH EXPLANATIONS

**1.**
$$\Delta G = \Delta G° + RT \ln\left[\frac{Sn^{+2}}{Cu^{+2}}\right]$$

$$= -2 \times 96500\,[(-0.16) - 0.34] + RT \ln\left(\frac{1}{1}\right)$$

$$= 96500 \text{ J}$$

**2.**
$$Cu^+ \longrightarrow Cu + e^-$$
$$\underline{Cu^+ + e^- \longrightarrow Cu(s)}$$
$$2Cu^+ \longrightarrow Cu^{2+} + Cu$$

$$E°_{cell} = E°_{Cu^+/Cu} - E°_{Cu^{2+}/Cu^+}$$

$$= 0.52 - 0.16$$

$$= 0.36 \text{ V}$$

At equilibrium $\rightarrow E_{cell} = 0$

$$E^o_{cell} = \frac{RT}{nF} \ln K$$

$$\ln K = \frac{E^o_{cell} \times nF}{RT}$$

$$\ln K = \frac{0.36 \times 1}{0.025}$$

$$= 14.4 = 144 \times 10^{-1}$$

**3. (3)** Dissolution of $BaSO_4$ is an endothermic reaction. On increasing temperature number of ions of $BaSO_4$ decrease so it's conduction also decrease.

**4.**

$$\frac{1}{2}H_2 \rightarrow H^+ + e^-$$

$$\underline{e^- + AgCl_{(s)} \rightarrow Ag_{(s)} + Cl^-}$$

$$\frac{1}{2}H_2 + AgCl_{(s)} \rightarrow H^+_{(aq)} + Ag_{(s)} + Cl^-_{(aq)}$$

$$E = \varepsilon^0 - \frac{.06}{1}\log\frac{[H^+][Cl^-]}{P_{H_2}^{\frac{1}{2}}}$$

$$E = 0.22 - .06\log\frac{(10^{-1})(10^{-1})}{1^{\frac{1}{2}}}$$

$$E = 0.22 + .12 = .34 \text{ volt}$$

$\Rightarrow$ total energy of photon will be (for Na)

$$= 2.3 + 0.34 = 2.64 \text{ eV}$$

$\Rightarrow$ stopping potential required for K

$$= 2.64 - 2.25 = 0.39 \text{ volt}$$

$$E = \varepsilon^0 - \frac{.06}{1}\log\frac{[H^+][Cl^-]}{P_{H_2}^{\frac{1}{2}}}$$

as $\quad [H^+] = [Cl^-]$ so

$$0.39 = 0.22 - .06\log\frac{[H^+]^2}{1^{\frac{1}{2}}}$$

$$0.17 = + .12 \text{ pH}$$

$$pH = 1.4166 \Rightarrow 1.42$$

**5.** $\qquad$ Moles of $e^- = \left(\dfrac{8 \times 60 \times 2}{96000}\right)$

Using stoichiometry; theoritically

$$\frac{n_{e^-}\text{used}}{6} = \frac{n_{er^{+3}}\text{ produced}}{2}$$

$$\Rightarrow n_{er^{+3}} \text{ produced} = \frac{2}{6} \times \frac{8 \times 60 \times 2}{96000}$$

$$= \frac{0.02}{6}$$

$\Rightarrow wt_{er^{+3}}$ theoretically produced

$$= \left(\frac{0.02}{6} \times 52\right) g$$

$\Rightarrow \quad$ % efficiency $= \dfrac{0.104g}{\left(\dfrac{0.02 \times 52}{6}\right)g} \times 100$

$$= 60\%$$

**6. (1)** $\qquad E^o_{cell} = 0.34 - (-0.76)$

$$= 1.10 \text{ volt}$$

If $E_{ext} > 1.10$ volt

$$Cu \rightarrow Anode$$
$$Zn \rightarrow Cathode$$

If $E_{ext} = 1.10$ volt

$$Zn \rightarrow Anode$$
$$Cu \rightarrow Cathode$$

**7.**

$$\Delta G^o = -AFE^o = -3 \times 96500 \times E^o$$

$$\Rightarrow \qquad E^o = -6 \times 10^{-2} \text{ V}$$

**8.** $\quad \dfrac{2 \times t \times 60 \times 60 \times 0.60 \times 122 \times 1}{96500} = \dfrac{10}{6}$

So, $t = 10.98$ hours or 11 hours

**9. (4)** As voltage is '2V' so both $Ag^+$ and $Au^+$ will reduce and their equal gm equivalent will reduce to

$$g_{meq} \, Ag = g_{meq} \text{ of Au}$$

$$\frac{Wt_{Ag}}{E_{qwt_{Ag}}} = \frac{Wt_{Au}}{E_{qwt_{Au}}}$$

So, $\qquad \dfrac{wt_{Ag}}{wt_{Au}} = \dfrac{E_{qwt_{Ag}}}{E_{qwt_{Au}}} = \dfrac{At.\,wt_{Ag}}{At.\,wt_{Au}}$

**10. (1)** Its a weak electrolyte hence : $CH_3COOH$.

**11. (1)** $Cr(OH)_3(s) \underset{(s)}{\rightleftharpoons} \underset{(3s)}{Cr^{3+}(aq.) + 3OH^-(aq.)}$

$$\Rightarrow \quad
\begin{aligned}
k_{sp} &= 27(s)^4 = 6 \times 10^{-31}\\
[3(s)]^4 &= 18 \times 10^{-31}\\
[OH^-] &= 3(s) = [18 \times 10^{-31}]^{1/4}
\end{aligned}$$

**12.** $\qquad$ gm eq. of Ag $= \dfrac{108}{108} = 1$

$$\text{gm eq. of } O_2(g) = 1$$

$$\text{Volume of } O_2(g) = 22.7 \times \frac{1}{4}$$

$$= 5.675 \text{ litre}$$

**13.** 26.92

Number of moles of $Cl^-$ precipitated in $[Co(NH_3)_6]$

$Cl_3$ is equal to number of moles of $AgNO_3$ used.

$$\frac{0.3}{267.46} \times 3 = \frac{0.125 \times V}{1000}$$

where V is volume of $AgNO_3$ (in mL) V = 26.92 mL.

**14.** – 0.935 V

$$2H_2O(l) \rightarrow O_2(g) + 4H^+ + 4e^- : E_{red}^0 = 1.23 \text{ V}$$

$$E_{cell} = E_{cell}^0 - \frac{RT}{nF} \ln Q$$

at 1 bar & 298 K

$$\frac{2.303RT}{F} = 0.059$$

$$pH = 5$$

$$\Rightarrow \qquad [H^+] = 10^{-5} \text{ M}$$

$$E_{oxidation}^o = 1.23 \text{ volt}$$

$$E_{cell} = -1.23 - \frac{0.059}{4} \log[H^+]^4$$

$$E_{cell} = -1.23 - \frac{0.059}{4} \log(10^{-5})^4$$

$$= -1.23 + 0.059 \times 5$$

$$= -0.935 \text{ V}$$

**15. (1)**

$$\begin{array}{llll} & & E^0 & \Delta G^0 \\ Cu^{2\oplus} + 2e^\oplus \rightarrow Cu & 0.34 & = -2F(0.34) \\ Cu^{2\oplus} + e^\oplus \rightarrow Cu & 0.522 & = -F(0.522) \\ Cu^{2\oplus} + e^\oplus \rightarrow Cu^+ & & \end{array}$$

$$\Delta G^0 = -2F(0.34) - (-F(0.522))$$

$$= -F(0.68 - 0.522)$$

$$= -F(0.158)$$

$$E^\circ = \frac{-F(0.158)}{-F} = 0.158 \text{V}$$

**16. (4)** (a) Zeolite method removes only cations ($Ca^{2+}$ and $Mg^{2+}$ ion) present in hard water

$$2NaZ + M^{2+} (aq) \rightarrow R_2M(s) + 2Na^+(aq)$$
$$(M \rightarrow Mg, Ca)$$

(b) Synthetic resin method removes cations ($Ca^{2+}$ and $Mg^{2+}$ ion) and anions (like $Cl^-$, $HCO_3^-$, $SO_4^{2-}$ etc.)

(i) $2RNa(s) + M^{2+}(aq) \rightarrow R_2M(s) + 2Na^+ (aq)$
 (Cation exchange $\qquad$ (M → Mg, Ca)
 resin)

(ii) $RNH_3^+ OH^-(s) + X^-(aq) \rightarrow RNH_3^+X^-(s)$
$$+ OH^-(aq)$$
 (Anion exchange) ($X^- = Cl^-$, $HCO_3^-$, $SO_4^{2-}$)

**17.** Cell reaction is :

$$Sn(s) + Pb^{+2}(aq) \rightarrow Sn^{+2}(aq) + Pb(s)$$

Apply Nernst equation :

$$E_{cell} = E_{cell}^0 0 - \frac{0.06}{2} \log \frac{[Sn^{+2}]}{[Pb^{+2}]} \qquad \qquad ...(1)$$

At equilibrium : $E_{cell} = 0$
Substituting in (1)

$$0 = 0.01 - \frac{0.06}{2} \log \frac{[Sn^{+2}]}{[Pb^{+2}]}$$

$$\Rightarrow \qquad \frac{1}{3} = \log \frac{[Sn^{+2}]}{[Pb^{+2}]}$$

$$\Rightarrow \qquad \frac{[Sn^{+2}]}{[Pb^{+2}]} = 2.15$$

**18. (3)** As the value of standard reduction potential increases, the strength of an oxidising agent also increases. The value of standard reduction potential is the highest for the reduction of $S_2O_8^{2-}$. Therefore, $S_2O_8^{2-}$ is the strongest oxidising agent.

**19. (3)** The overall cell reaction is given below :

$$Fe^{2+}(aq) + Ag^+(aq) \rightarrow Fe^{3+} (aq) + Ag(s)$$

The half cell reactions at cathode and anode are given below :

$$Fe^{2+} (aq) \rightarrow Fe^{3+} (aq) + e^- \quad E_{Fe^{2+}/Fe^{3+}}^o = mV$$

$$Ag^+(aq) + e^- \rightarrow Ag(s) \qquad E_{Ag^+/Ag}^o = xV$$

$$E_{cell}^o = (m + x) \text{ V} \qquad \qquad ...(1)$$

The value of $\Delta°G$ is calculated as shown below :

$$Fe^{2+}(aq) + 2e^- \rightarrow Fe(s) \qquad E_1^o = yV$$

$$\Delta_1^o G = -(2Fy) \qquad \qquad ...(2)$$

$$Fe^{3+}(aq) + 3e^- \rightarrow Fe(s) \qquad E_2^o = zV$$

$$\Delta_2^o G = -(2Fy) \qquad \qquad ...(3)$$

Subtract equation (3) from equation (2).

$$Fe^{2+}(aq) \rightarrow Fe^{3+}(aq) + e^- \quad E_3^o = mV$$

$$\Delta_3^o G = -(1Fm)$$

The value of $m$ is calculated as shown below :

$$\Delta_3^o G = \Delta_1^o G - \Delta_2^o G$$

$$-(1Fm) = -(2Fy) - (3Fz)$$

$$m = (2y - 3z) \qquad \qquad ...(4)$$

Substitute the value of equation (4) in equation (1).

$$E_{cell}^o = (x + 2y - 3z)V$$

**20. (1)** The formula to calculate gibbs free energy is shown below :

$$\Delta G° = -nFE°$$

$$= -2 \times 96000 \times (2)$$

$$= -3840000 \text{ J/mol}$$

$$= -384 \text{ kJ/mol}$$

**21. (1)** One faraday electricity is produced by 1 mol of one mole of electrons.

The number moles of electrons required to produce one mole of Ni is 2 mol.

Therefore, the number of mole of Ni that will deposited on cathode is calculated as shown below :

$$n = \frac{0.1}{2}$$

$$= 0.05$$

**22. (2)** Due to the decrease in the number of ions per milliter on dilution, the conductivity decreases. Therefore, S1 is incorrect.

Molar conductivity is calculated by the formula given below :

$$\lambda_m = \frac{1000 \times \kappa}{C}$$

Due to decrease in concentration, the value of C decreases more rapidly than $\kappa$, due to which the molar conductivity increases. Therefore, S2 is correct.

**23. (1)** The compounds NaCl and KCl dissociate completely in solution, that is, they are strong electrolytes. The conductance of $K^+$ (aq) is higher than of $Na^+$ (aq) due to lower hydration. Therefore, the correct graph is shown below :

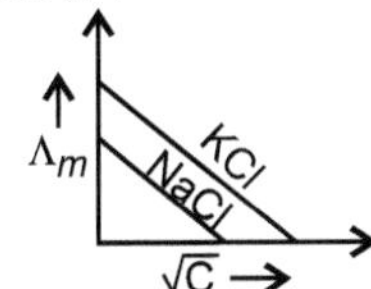


**24. (2)** The standard reduction potential of a species indicates the ease with which it can get reduce and oxides other species. Therefore, the order of increasing oxidising power is shown below :

$$Bi^{3+} < Ce^{4+} < Pb^{4+} < Co^{3+}$$

**25. (1)** The conductivity of an acidic solution increases with the degree of ionisation. The degree of ionisation increases with increase in acidic strength. The acidic strength of formic acid is higher than that of benzoic acid and acidic strength of benzoic acid is higher than that of acetic acid. Therefore, the correct order of electrical conductivity is shown below :

$$A > C > B$$

**26. (3)** The plot that provide the correct representation of micelle formation in the solution of sodium stearate is shown below :

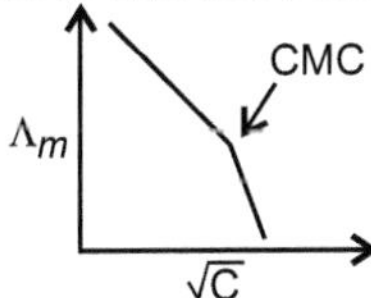


The molar conductivity increases with decrease in concentration. The peak oif the curve corresponds to critical micelle concentration, that is, the concentration at which micelle formation starts.

**27.** The reaction is given below :

$$Fe^{2+}(aq) + S^{2-}(aq) \rightarrow FeS(s)$$

It is given that the concentration of $Fe^{2+}$ (aq) and $S^{2-}$ (aq) are 0.06 M and 0.2 M respectively. It means that 0.06 mol $Fe^{2+}$ (aq) reacts with 0.2 mol $S^{2-}$ (aq). Consider that 0.03 mol $Fe^{2+}$ (aq) reacts with 0.1 mol $S^{2-}$ (aq).

$$Fe^{2+}(aq) + S^{2-}(aq) \rightarrow FeS(s)$$
$$\underset{0.03-x}{\overset{0.03\ M}{}} \qquad \underset{0.1-x}{\overset{0.1\ M}{}}$$

**28.** The reaction at anode is shown below :

$$Mg \rightarrow Mg^{2+} + 2e^-$$

The reaction at cathode is shown below :

$$Cu^{2+} + 2e^- \rightarrow Cu$$

The final equation is

$$Mg + Cu^{2+} \rightarrow Mg^{2+} + Cu$$

The Nernst equation with substituted values is shown below :

$$E = E^\circ - \frac{RT}{nF} \times 2.303 \log \frac{x}{1}$$

$$2.67 = 2.70 - \frac{300}{2 \times 11500} \times 2.303 \log \frac{x}{1}$$

$$x = 9.77$$

$$\simeq 10$$

**29.** The reaction at the anode is shown below :

$$A \rightarrow A^{n+} + ne^- \qquad \qquad ...(1)$$

The reaction at the cathode is shown below :

$$B^{2n+} + 2ne^- \rightarrow B \qquad \qquad ...(2)$$

Multiply equation (1) with a factor of 2 and then add both the equations.

$$2A \rightarrow 2A^{n+} + 2ne^-$$
$$B^{2n+} + 2ne^- \rightarrow B$$

The final equation is shown below.

$$2A + B^{2n+} \rightarrow 2A^{n+} + B$$

The Nernst equation with substituted values is shown below.

$$E = E^\ominus - \frac{RT}{2nF} \ln \frac{[A^{n+}]^2}{[B^{2n+}]}$$

$$E^\ominus = \frac{RT}{2nF} \ln 4$$

As, $\quad \Delta G^\ominus = -2nFE^\ominus$

$$= -2nF \frac{RT}{2nF} \ln 4$$

$$= -RT \ln 4$$

Also, $\quad \Delta G^\ominus = \Delta H^\ominus - T\Delta S^\ominus$

$$\Delta G^\ominus = 2\Delta G^\ominus - T\Delta S^\ominus$$

$$\Delta G^\ominus = T\Delta S^\ominus$$

Now, $\quad \Delta S^\ominus = \frac{\Delta G^\ominus}{T}$

$$= \frac{-RT \ln 4}{T}$$

$$= -8.3 \, J \, K^{-1} mol^{-1} \times 0.14$$

$$= -11.62 J \, K^{-1} \, mol^{-1}$$

**30. (3)** The balanced chemical equation for the combustion of diborane is,

$$B_2H_6 + 3O_2 \rightarrow B_2O_3 + 3H_2O$$

The number of moles of diborane is calculated as,

$$\text{Moles of } B_2H_6 = \frac{27.66\,g}{27.6\,g/mol}$$
$$= 1.00 \text{ mol}$$

Therefore, the number of moles of oxygen gas required in the reaction is 3.00 mol. The number of electrons transferred in the given reaction is four times of the number of moles of oxygen which is 12.

The time required for the complete combustion of diborane is calculated by the formula,

Number of coulombs = Current (A) × time (s)

$$12 \times 96500 = 100 \times t$$

formula, $$t = \frac{12 \times 96500}{100}$$
$$= 11580 \text{ s}$$
$$= 3.2 \text{ hr}$$

**31. (1)** The reduction taking place at cathode is,

$$2H^+ \text{(aq)} + 2e^- \rightarrow H_2(g)$$

At N.T.P.,

$$22.4 \text{ L of } H_2 = 1 \text{ mole of } H_2$$
$$112 \text{ ml of } H_2 = \frac{112}{22400} \times 1 \text{ mole of } H_2$$
$$= 0.005 \text{ mole of } H_2$$
$$\text{Moles} = \frac{I \times t}{96500 \times v.f.}$$
$$0.005 \text{ mol} = \frac{I \times 965s}{96500} \times \frac{1 \text{ mol } H_2}{2 \text{ mol } e^\ominus}$$
$$I = 1A$$

**32. (1)** It is given that 9.65 ampere was passed for 1.0 hour.

The number of moles of electrons passed is calculated by the formula.

$$\text{Moles} = \frac{I \times t}{96500}$$
$$= \frac{9.65 \times 3600}{96500}$$
$$= 0.36 \text{ moles}$$

The reaction for the formation of *p*-aminophenol is shown below.

$NO_2$ → (conc. $H_2SO_4$, 4[H]) → $NO_2$ → [Rearrangement] → $NO_2$ ... OH

It means 4 moles of electron will reduce 1 mole of nitrobenzene to *p*-aminophenol.

Thus, 0.36 moles will reduce 0.09 moles of nitrobenzene to *p*-aminophenol.

The molar mass of *p*-aminophenol is 109.14 g/mol.

Therefore, mass of *p*-aminophenol is,
$$= 109.14 \text{ g/mol} \times 0.09 \text{ mol}$$
$$= 9.81 \text{ g}$$

**33.** For the given monobasic weak electrolyte, the conductivity (κ) is calculated as,

$$\kappa = G(\text{Conductance}) \times \frac{l(\text{Length})}{a(\text{Area})}$$
$$= \frac{5 \times 10^7\,S \times 120\,cm}{1\,cm^2}$$
$$= 6 \times 10^{-5}\,S.cm^{-1}$$

The molar conductivity of the given solution is calculated as,

$$\Lambda_m^c = \kappa \times \frac{1000}{C}$$
$$= \frac{6 \times 10^{-5} \times 1000}{0.0015}$$
$$= 40$$

For the solution with pH 4 the value of hydrogen ion concentration will be $10^{-4}$. The degree of dissociation is calculated as,

$$[H^+] = \alpha C$$
$$\alpha = \frac{[H^+]}{C}$$
$$= \frac{10^{-4}}{0.0015}$$

For the given solution specific molar conductivity value is given and it is expressed as,

$$\Lambda_m^c = \frac{\lambda_m^c}{\alpha}$$
$$Z \times 10^2 S.cm^{-1} = \frac{40 \times 0.0015}{10^{-4}}$$
$$Z \times 10^2 S.cm^{-1} = 6 \times 10^2\,S.cm^{-1}$$
$$Z = 6$$

**34. (2)** For the given cell, half reactions are given as,

$$Zn \rightarrow Zn^{2+} + 2e^-$$
$$Cu^{2+} + 2e^- \rightarrow Cu$$

Overall reaction is given as,

$$Zn + Cu^{2+} \rightarrow Zn^{2+} + Cu$$

Cell potential for this reaction is calculated by the Nernst equation as,

$$E = E° - \frac{2.303RT}{nF} \log \frac{[Zn^{2+}]}{[Cu^{2+}]}$$
$$= 1.1 - \frac{2.303\,RT}{2F} \log(10)$$
$$= 1.1 - \frac{2.303RT}{2F}$$

The expression for ΔG is given as,

$$\Delta G = -nFE°$$
$$= -2F\left(1.1 - \frac{2.303RT}{2F}\right)$$
$$= 2.303RT - 2.2F$$

**35. (3)** When zinc metal reacts with aqueous sodium hydroxide, it produces hydrogen gas. Reaction is given as,
$$Zn + 2NaOH \rightarrow Na_2ZnO_2 + H_2 \text{ (gas)}$$

**36. (3)** The redox couple is a stronger reducing agent than $H^+/H_2$ couple when $E°$ (standard electrode potential) is negative and a positive $E°$ means that the redox couple is a weaker reducing agent than $H^+/H_2$ couple. Higher is the reduction potential weaker is the reducing agent. Therefore, among the given redox couples the strongest reducing agent is Cr with $E°_{Cr^{3+}/Cr} = -0.74$ V.

**37. (1)**
$$Fe^{2+} + 2e^- \rightarrow Fe \qquad E° = -0.47 \text{ V ...(1)}$$
$$Fe^{3+} + e^- \rightarrow Fe^{2+} \qquad E° = 0.77 \text{ V ...(2)}$$
By adding equation (1) and (2), the new equation obtained is shown as follows.
$$Fe^{2+} + 3e^- \rightarrow Fe$$
Thus, the Gibbs free energy for the above equations (1) is given as follows.
$$\Delta G° = -nFE°$$
$$= -2(-0.47)F \qquad ...(3)$$
$$= 0.94F$$
Thus, Gibbs free energy for the above equations (2) is given as follows.
$$\Delta G° = -nFE°$$
$$= -1(0.77)F \qquad ...(4)$$
$$= -0.77F$$
The addition of equation (3) and (4) gives
$$\Delta G° = +0.17 \text{ F}$$
Thus,
$$E°(Fe^{3+} \rightarrow Fe) = \frac{\Delta G°}{-nF}$$
$$= \frac{+0.17F}{-3F}$$
$$= -0.057 \text{ V}$$

**38. (3)** As $Ti^+$ possess negative electrode potential, that is $E° = -0.34$, thus it is not able to convert itself into T1 but in the case of $T1^{3+}$ it has positive electrode potential, that is, $E° = +1.26$, the transformation to T1 is possible. Therefore, $T1^+$ is more stable than $T1^{3+}$.

In the case of Al, $Al^{3+}$ with $E° = -1.66$ is more stable than $Al^+$ with $E° = +0.55$. Since the electrode potential of $T1^+$ is more negative than that of $Al^+$, $Ti^+$ is more stable than $Al^+$.

**39. (2)** The value of $E°$ is calculated by the formula,
$$E° = \text{Cell potential} + \frac{0.059}{3}$$
$$\log \frac{[\text{Reduced state}]}{[\text{Oxidised state}]^3}$$
Substitute the values of cell potential, [Reduction] and [Oxidation] in the above expression.

$$E° = 0.421 + \frac{0.059}{3} \log \frac{0.001}{(0.01)^3}$$
$$= 0.421 + \frac{0.059}{3} \log(10^3)$$
$$= 0.421 + 0.059$$
$$= 0.48$$

The value of $E°_{M^3/M}$ is calculated by the formula,

$$E°_{M^{3+}/M} = 0.8 - 0.480$$
$$= 0.32 \text{ Volt}$$

**40. (4)** The overall reaction takes place.
$$M^{4+} + H_2 \rightarrow M^{2+} + 2H^+$$
The Nernst equation is given below.
$$E_{cell} = E°_{cell} - \frac{0.059}{2} \log \left( \frac{[M^{2+}][H^+]}{[M^{4+}]P_{H_2}} \right)$$
$$0.092 = 0.1512 - \frac{0.059}{2} \log_{10}(10^x)$$
$$0.092 = 0.1512 - \frac{0.059}{2} x$$
$$x = 2$$
Thus, the value of $x$ is 2.

**41. (4)** If a block of copper metal is dropped into a beaker containing a solution of 1M $ZnSO_4$ then no reaction will take place because $E°_{Zn^{2+}/Zn} = -0.76$ V and $E°_{Cu^{2+}/Cu} = +0.34$V.

Thus, copper is not able to displace zinc from 1M $ZnSO_4$ solution.

**42. (4)** The correct statement is ``corrosion of iron can be minimized by forming an impermeable barrier at its surface.''

**43. (4)** Rusting of iron can be prevented by applying a coating of zinc and this process is known as galvanisation.

**44. (4)** For $M^+ \rightarrow M^{3+} + 2e^-$, the $E°$ is $-0.25$ V
The formula to calculate Gibbs free energy is
$$\Delta G° = -nFE°$$
$$= -2 \times 96500 \times -0.25$$
$$= 48250 \text{ J/mol}$$
$$= 48.25 \text{ kJ/mol}$$
The energy released for the conversion of $X \rightarrow Y$ is $DG° = -193$ kJ/mol.
Thus, number of moles $M^+$ oxidized is,
$$= \frac{193}{48.25}$$
$$= 4 \text{ moles}$$

**45. (2)** The deposition of copper takes place at cathode.

$$Cu^+(aq) + 2e^- \rightarrow Cu(s)$$

Here, two Faraday charge deposits one mole of copper. Therefore, the mass of copper that is deposited at cathode is 63.5 g.

**46. (4)** When the external voltage is less than 1.1 V and more than 1.1 V, then the flow of electrons is from anode to cathode in both the cases.

**47. (3)** The ions $Br^-$ and $I^-$ are expected to oxidize easily because these ions possess less value of reduction potential. The species with low reduction potential tends to lose electrons easily.

Consider the following reaction.

$$MnO_4^- + 8H^+ + 5e^- \rightarrow Mn^{2+} + 4H_2O$$

The value of E is calculated by the formula.

$$E = 1.51 - \frac{0.059}{5}\log\frac{[Mn^{2+}]}{[MnO_4^-][H^+]^8}$$

$$= 1.51 - \frac{0.059}{5} \times 8\log\frac{1}{[H^+]}$$

$$= 1.51 - \frac{0.059}{5} \times 8 \times 3$$

$$= 1.227 \text{ V}$$

Thus, $MnO_4^-$ oxidise only $Br^-$ and $I^-$ because the standard reduction value of $Cl^-$ is high than $MnO_4^-/Mn^{2+}$.

**48. (1)** The formula to calculate specific conductance is,

$$\kappa = \frac{1}{R} \times \frac{1}{A}$$

$$1.4 \text{ S m}^{-1} = \frac{1}{50\Omega} \times \frac{1}{A}$$

$$\frac{1}{A} = 1.4 \times 50 \text{ m}^{-1}$$

Therefore,

$$\kappa = \frac{1}{R} \times \frac{1}{A}$$

$$= \frac{1}{280}\Omega^{-1} \times 1.4 \times 50 \text{ m}^{-1}$$

$$= \frac{1}{4}\Omega^{-1}\text{m}^{-1}$$

Since, $1 \text{ M} = 10^{-3} \text{ mol/m}^3$, molar conductivity is calculated by the formula,

$$L_m = \frac{\kappa}{1000 \times M}$$

$$= \frac{1}{4 \times 1000 \times 0.5}$$

$$= 5 \times 10^{-4} \text{ S m}^{-2} \text{ mol}^{-1}$$

**49. (3)** NaCl is a strong electrolyte. Therefore, the correct relationship between $\lambda_C$ and $\lambda_\infty$ is given by Debye Huckel Onsagar equation,

$$\lambda_C = \lambda_\infty - (B)\sqrt{C}$$

**50. (2)** $H_2$ gas will be obtained at cathode during the electrolysis of ani aqueous solution of calcium salt. This is due to the fact that reduction potential of $H^+$ is higher than that of $Ca^+$.

**51. (1)**

$$Mn^{2+} + 2e^- \rightarrow Mn \qquad E° = -1.18 \text{ V}$$
$$2Mn^{2+} \rightarrow 2Mn^{3+} + 2e^- \qquad E° = -1.51 \text{ V}$$

The resultant equation will be,

$$3Mn^{2+} \rightarrow Mn + 2Mn^{3+}$$

The standard electrode potential $(E°)$ is calculated as,

$$E° = -1.18 \text{ V} + (-1.51 \text{ V})$$
$$= -2.69 \text{ V}$$

Negative $E°$ indicates that the reaction will not occur.

**52. (3)** The sequence of deposition of metals on applying potentials is C, B, D, A, because if the value of reduction potential is high then the rate of deposition is also higher.

**53. (3)**

$$\text{Work done, } W = \frac{E}{96500} \times It$$

Total number of moles

$$= \frac{It}{96500 \times (n\text{-factor})}$$

$$n\text{-factor} = \frac{720 \times 4}{965}$$

$$= +3$$

Thus, the value of X is + 3.

**54. (4)** The redox couple is a stronger reducing agent than $H^+/H_2$ couple, when $E°$ (standard electrode potential) is negative and a positive $E°$ means that the redox couple is a weaker reducing agent than $H^+/H_2$ couple. Higher is the reduction potential weaker is the reducing agent. Lower the reduction potential, higher will be the reducing power. Therefore, the correct order of reducing power is $Al < Fe^{2+} < Br^-$.

**55. (3)** The number of molecules of copper formed in the given electrolysis process is calculated as,

$$\text{Molecules of Cu} = \frac{6.35\text{g} \times N_A}{63.5\text{g}/\text{mol}}$$

$$= 0.1 N_A$$

$$= \frac{N_A}{10}$$

Since 2 electrons are required to form one copper molecule. Therefore, the number of electrons is double the number of molecules of copper. Hence, the number of electrons required in the given system is,

$$\text{Number of electrons} = 2 \times \frac{N_A}{10}$$

$$= \frac{N_A}{5}$$

**56. (4)** (P) The value of $E°$ for $(Fe^{3+}/Fe)$ is calculated as follows.

$$\Delta G°_{Fe^{3+}/Fe} = \Delta G°_{Fe^{3+}/Fe} + \Delta G°_{Fe^{2+}/Fe}$$

$$-3 \times FE°_{Fe^{3+}/Fe} = -1 \times FE°_{Fe^{3+}/Fe^{2+}}$$

$$+\left(-2 \times FE°_{Fe^{2+}/Fe}\right)$$

$$E°_{Fe^{3+}/Fe} = -0.04 \text{ V}$$

(Q) $O_2(g) + 2H_2O + 4e^- \rightarrow 4OH^-$ $\quad E° = 0.40$

$$2H_2O \rightarrow O_2(g) + 4H^+ + 4e^-$$
$$E° = -1.23 \text{ V}$$

Thus, the value of $E°$ for $(4H_2O \rightleftharpoons 4H^+ + 4OH^-)$ is calculated as follows.

$$E° = 0.40 \text{ V} - 1.23 \text{ V}$$
$$= -0.83 \text{ V}$$

(R) The value of $E°$ for $(Cu^{2+}/Cu)$ is calculated as follows.

$$\Delta G°_{Cu^{2+}/Cu} = \Delta G°_{Cu^{2+}/Cu} + \Delta G°_{Cu^+/Cu}$$

$$-2 \times FE°_{Cu^{2+}/Cu} = -1 \times Fe°_{Cu^{2+}/Cu^+}$$

$$+\left(-1 \times FE°_{Cu^+/Cu}\right)$$

$$E°_{Cu^{2+}/Cu} = -0.18 \text{ V}$$

(S) The value of $E°$ for $(Cr^{3+}/Cr^{2+})$ is calculated as follows.

$$\Delta G°_{Cr^{3+}/Cr^{2+}} = \Delta G°_{Cr^{3+}/Cr} + \Delta G°_{Cr/Cr^{2+}}$$

$$-1 \times FE°_{Cr^{3+}/Cr^{2+}} = -3 \times FE°_{Cr^{3+}/Cr}$$

$$+\left(-2 \times FE°_{Cr/Cr^{2+}}\right)$$

$$E°_{Fe^{3+}/Fe} = -0.4 \text{ V}$$

**57. (1)** (P)

$$(C_2H_5)_3N + CH_3COOH \rightarrow (C_2H_5)_3NH^+CH_3COO^-$$
$$\quad\; X \qquad\qquad Y$$

In the beginning, conductivity increases because of the formation of ions. Then, slowly it becomes constant because it is impossible for X to produce ions alone. Thus, it will match with (3).

(Q) $KI \, (0.1M) + AgNO_3 \rightarrow AgI^- \downarrow + KNO_3$
$$\qquad X \qquad\qquad Y$$

In this solution, the total number of ions remains constant till all $AgNO_3$ gets precipitated out in the form of AgI. Thus, this reaction leads to the increase in conductance because the number of ions also increases. Thus, it will match with (4).

(R) In this reaction, there is a decrease in the conductance initially because the total number of ions of hydroxyl ions decreases and total number of $H^+$ ions increases. Thus, it will match with (2).

(S) In this reaction, there is decrease in $H^+$ ions because of which conductivity decreases and after sometime conductivity increases due to increase in the concentration of hydroxyl ions. Thus, it will match with (1).

**58. (2)** The reaction occuring at the anode is shown below.

$$M \rightarrow M^{2+} (aq)_A + 2e^-$$

The reaction occuring at the cathode is shown below.

$$M^{2+} (aq)_C + 2e^- \rightarrow M$$

Add both the reactions.

$$M^{2+} (aq)_C \rightleftharpoons M^{2+} (aq)_A$$

Substitute these in Nernst equation,

$$E = E° - \frac{0.059}{n} \log \frac{[M^{2+}]_A}{[M^{2+}]_C}$$

$$0.059 = -\frac{0.059}{n} \log \frac{[M^{2+}]_A}{0.001}$$

$$\log \frac{0.001}{[M^{2+}]_A} = 2$$

$$[M^{2+}]_A = 10^{-5}$$

The dissociation of $MX_2$ occurs as shown below.

$$MX_2 \rightleftharpoons M^{2x} + 2X^-$$

The value of $K_{sp}$ is calculated as shown below.

$$K_{sp} = (s)(2s)^2$$
$$= 4s^3$$
$$= 4 \times (10^{-5})^3$$
$$= 4 \times 10^{-15}$$

**59. (4)** The value of $\Delta G$ is calculated as shown below.

$$\Delta G = -n FE$$
$$= -2 \times 96500 \times 0.059 \times 10^{-3} \text{ kJ.mol}^{-1}$$
$$= -11.387 \text{ kJ. mol}^{-1}$$
$$= -11.4 \text{ kJ.mol}^{-1}$$

**60. (2)** The metal rod should be made up of copper. Because, when copper rod is dipped in the aqueous solution of compound silver nitrate, solution turns light blue due to the formation of copper nitrate.

**61. (1)** The compound N should be silver nitrate because, when copper metal is dipped in the aqueous solution of silver nitrate, solution turns blue due to the formation of copper nitrate. The reaction is as follows :

$$2AgNO_3(N) + Cu(M) \rightarrow Cu(NO_3)_2$$
$$\text{(light blue)} + 2Ag$$

**62. (4)** For the given cell reaction, cell potential is calculated by the Nernst equation as,

$$E = E° - \frac{0.06}{n} \log \frac{[Fe^{2+}]^2}{Po_2[H^+]^4}$$

$$= 1.67 - \frac{0.06}{4} \log \frac{(10^{-3}M)^2}{0.1(10^{-3}M)^4}$$

$$= 1.67 - \frac{0.06}{4} \log(10^7)$$

$$\approx 1.57\,V$$

**63. (1, 2)** Intensive properties are those properties which do not depend on mass.

Resistance and heat are extensive properties. Molar conductivity and electromotive force do not depend upon mass.

Thus, they are intensive properties.

**64. (2)** The following reaction takes place.

$$M(s) + M^+_{(aq,\,1M)} \longrightarrow M^+(aq,\,0.5\,M) + M(s)$$

The Nernst equation is given below.

$$E_{cell} = E^o_{cell} - \frac{2.303RT}{nF} \log \frac{[M^+_c]}{[M^+_A]}$$

Substitute the values in the above equation.

$$E^o_{cell} = 0$$

$$E_{cell} = 0 - \frac{2.303RT}{1 \times F} \log \frac{[0.05]}{[1]}$$

$$= 0.077\,V$$

The value of $E_{cell}$ is positive.

Thus, $\Delta G = - nFE_{cell}$ is negative.

Thus, $E_{cell} > 0$ and $\Delta G < 0$

**65. (3)** The following equation is,

$$M(s) + M^+_{(aq,1M)} \to M^+(aq,\,0.5\,M) + M(s)$$

The Nernst equation is given below.

$$E_{cell} = E^o_{cell} - \frac{2.303RT}{nF} \log \frac{[M^+_c]}{[M^+_A]}$$

Substitute the value in the above equation.

$$E^o_{cell} = 0$$

$$E_{cell} = -\frac{2.303RT}{1 \times F} \log \frac{[0.0025]}{[1]}$$

$$= 140\,mV$$

**66. (1,2,4)** The metals having reduction potential lesser than that of the $NO_3^-$ can be oxidised by $NO_3^-$ in the aqueous solution. The reduction potential of vanadium, iron and mercury is less than that of nitrate ion. Therefore, they can be oxidixed by nitrate ion in the aqueous solution.

**67. (2)** The time required is calculated as,

$$t = \frac{\begin{array}{c}\text{number of electrons} \times \text{moles} \\ \times \text{ Faraday's constant}\end{array}}{\text{current}}$$

The electrolysis of dilute solution is,

$$2H_2O + 2e^- \to H_2 + 2OH^-$$

Substitute the number of electrons involved, moles of $H_2$, Faraday's constant and current in the above formula,

$$t = \frac{2 \times 0.01\ mol \times 96500\,C\,mol^{-1}}{10 \times 10^{-3}\,C\ sec^{-1}}$$

$$= 19.3 \times 10^4\ sec$$

**68. (2)** The decomposition of NaCl is,

$$NaCl(aq) \to Na^+(aq) + Cl^-(aq)$$

At anode $Cl_2$ gas is evolved.

$$2Cl^-(aq) \to Cl_2(g) + 2e^-$$

This means that there are two moles of $Cl^-$ in 500 mL that evolves one mole of $Cl_2$ gas at anode.

**69. (4)** When cathode is Hg electrode, it will form two moles of amalgam. The molar mass of $Na-Hg$ amalgam is 223 $g.mol^{-1}$. Thus, the weight of amalgam formed is,

$$m = 2 \times 223$$

$$= 446\ g$$

**70. (4)** The complete electrolysis requires 2 mol $e^-(n)$. The total charge required for complete electrolysis is calculated by the formula,

$$q = n \times F$$

Substitute the value of $n$ in above equation.

$$q = 2 \times 96500$$

$$= 193000\ C$$

**71. (3)** The standard reduction potential value of chlorine is greater than that of iodine. Therefore, chlorine can oxidise iodide ion.

**72. (1)** The formula to calculate $E^o_{cell}$ is,

$$E^o_{cell} = \frac{RT}{nF} \ln K$$

The above formula can be written as,

$$E^o_{cell} = \frac{RT}{nF} \ln K$$

$$(E^o_{red} + E^o_{oxi}) = \frac{RT}{nF} \ln K$$

Substitute all the values in the above formula.

$$(0.8 - 005) = \frac{1}{2} \frac{0.0592}{2.303} \ln K$$

$$\ln K = \frac{(0.8 - 0.05) \times 2 \times 2.303}{0.0592}$$

$$= 58.38$$

**73. (1)** The concentration of $H^+$ ion decreases on increasing the concentration of ammonia.

The formula to calculate Nernst equation is,

$$E = E° - \frac{RT}{nF}\ln\frac{[red]}{[oxd]}$$

Substitute all the values in the above formula.

$$= E° - \frac{0.0591}{2}\log\frac{[C_6H_{12}O_6]}{[C_6H_{12}O]}[H^+]^2$$

$$= E° - 0.0591\log[H^+]$$

$$= E° + 0.0591 \times \log[10^{-11}]$$

$$= E° + 0.65$$

Thus, anode is affected by change in pH.

**74. (4)** In the detection of aldehyde, if ammonia is not added in the reaction, then the salt of gluconic acid is formed due to which it is preferred to add ammonia. Ammonia does not affect the standard reduction potential of glucose electrode.

Therefore, the incorrect statement is (D).

**75. (a)** The cell reactions are,

$$Ag + \frac{1}{2}Cl_2 \rightarrow AgCl_2$$

$$Ag \rightarrow Ag^+ + e^-$$

$$\frac{1}{2}Cl_2 + e^- \rightarrow Cl^-$$

The cell representation is $Ag\,|\,Ag^+\,|\,AgCl\,|\,Cl^-\,|\,Cl_2, Pt$

The overall cell reaction can be written as,

$$Ag^+(aq) + Cl^-(aq) \rightarrow AgCl(s)$$

The value of $\Delta G°$ is calculated as,

$$\Delta G° = -109 - (-129 + 77)$$

$$= -57 = -1 \times F \times E°$$

$$-57\text{ kJ} = -1 \times 96500 \times E°$$

$$E° = \frac{57000}{96500} = 0.59\text{ V}$$

The value of $\log K_{sp}$ is calculated as follows.

$$-57 = -2.303\text{ RT}\log K_o$$

$$\log K_o = \frac{57 \times 1000}{2.303 \times 8.314 \times 298}$$

$$\log K_o = 9.98 \approx 10$$

$$K_o = 10^{10}$$

$$K_{sp} = \frac{1}{K_0} = \frac{1}{10^{10}}$$

$$K_{sp} = 10^{-10}$$

$$\log K_{sp} = -10$$

**(b)** The half reactions taking place in the given reaction are,

$$2Ag^+ + 2e^- \rightarrow 2Ag \qquad E° = 0.80\text{ V}$$

$$Zn \rightarrow Zn^{2+} + 2e^- \qquad E° = -0.77\text{ V}$$

$$2Ag^+(aq) + Zn(s) \rightarrow Zn^{2+}(aq) + 2Ag(s)$$

The value of $E°_{cell}$ is $0.80 - (0.77) = 1.57$ V

The number of moles of Zn is

$$= \frac{\text{Given mass}}{\text{Molar mass}}$$

$$= \frac{65.39 \times 10^{-2}}{65.39} = 10^{-3}$$

In a saturated solution, $[Ag^+]$ is $= \sqrt{10^{-10}}$

$$= 10^{-5}\text{ M}$$

The formula to calculate $E°_{cell}$ is given below.

$$E°_{cell} = \frac{RT}{nF}\ln\frac{[Zn^{2+}]}{[Ag^+]}$$

Rearrange the above equation.

$$\log\frac{[Zn^{2+}]}{[Ag^+]^2} = E°_{cell} \times \frac{nF}{RT}$$

$$\log\frac{[Zn^{2+}]}{[Ag^+]^2} = \frac{2 \times 1.57}{0.059} = 53.2$$

The value of equilibrium constant is very high. Therefore, the reaction almost goes to completion.

The number of moles of Ag precipitated is

$$= \frac{10^{-5}}{10} = 10^{-6}\text{ mol}$$

**76. (2)** The given half cell reaction for rusting of iron with their electrode potential value is,

$$2H^+ + \frac{1}{2}O_2 + 2e^- \rightarrow H_2O \qquad E° = +1.23\text{ V}$$

$$Fe^{2+} + 2e^- \rightarrow Fe_{(s)} \qquad E° = -0.44\text{ V}$$

The overall reaction of the given half cell is,

$$Fe_{(s)} + 2H^+ + \frac{1}{2}O_2 \rightarrow Fe^{2+} + H_2O$$

$$E° = 1.23 - (-0.44) = 1.67\text{ V}$$

The value of $n$ is 2.

The value of Faraday's constant, F is 1.67.

The formula to calculate $\Delta G°$ is given below.

$$\Delta G° = -nFE°_{cell}$$

Substitute the value of $n$, Faraday's constant in the above expression.

$$\Delta G° = -2 \times 96500 \times 1.67$$

$$= -322\text{ kJ}$$

Thus, the $\Delta G°$ kJ for the half cell reaction for rusting of iron is $-322$ kJ.

Hence, the correct option is (B).

**77.** The given reaction is,

$$Cu^{2+} + In^{2+} \rightleftharpoons Cu^+ + In^{3+}$$

The relationship between $\Delta G°$ and $E°_{cell}$ is given as,

$$\Delta G^\circ = -nFE^\circ_{cell}$$

Substitute all the values in the above formula.

$$\Delta G^\circ = -nFE^\circ_{cell}$$

$$-0.59\ F = -nFE^\circ_{cell}$$

$$E^\circ_{cell} = 0.59$$

The Nernst equation for cell reaction is as follows :

$$E_{cell} = E^\circ_{cell} - \frac{0.0591}{n}\log K_c$$

The value of $K_c$ is calculated as follows :

$$0.59 = \frac{0.0591}{1}\log K_c$$

$$K_c = \frac{0.5}{0.059}$$

$$= 10^{10}$$

**78. (2)** The reaction at the anode is shown below :

$$Zn \rightarrow Zn^{2+} + 2e^- \quad E^\circ = 0.76\ V$$

The reaction at the cathode is shown below :

$$Fe^{2+} + 2e^- \rightarrow Fe \quad E^\circ = -0.44\ V$$

The standard EMF is given as shown below :

$$E^\circ = (0.76 - 0.44)\ V$$

$$= 0.32\ V$$

The Nernst equation is given as shown below :

$$E = E^\circ - \frac{0.0591}{2}\log K$$

$$0.32 = 0.02955\ \log K$$

$$K = 10^{0.32/0.02955}$$

**79. (a)** N, the pH value of water will not be same at 25°C and 4°C because it depends upon $K_w$. The value of $K_w$ changes on increasing the value of temperature. Therefore, the value of pH changes with change in temperature.

**(b)** The given value of $\dfrac{2.203\ RT}{F}$ is 0.06. It is assumed that the emf of first cell is $x$ volt.

Therefore, emf of second cell is,

$$= (x + 0.03)\ volt$$

The reaction involved in this process is as follows :

$$Zn + Cu^{2+} \rightarrow Zn^{2+} + Cu$$

The Nernst equation for first cell reaction is as follows :

$$E_1 = E_1^\circ - \frac{2.303RT}{2F}\log\frac{[Zn^{2+}]}{[Cu^{2+}]_1} \qquad ...(1)$$

Similarly, the Nernst equation for second cell reaction is as follows :

$$E_2 = E_2^\circ - \frac{2.203RT}{2F}\log\frac{[Zn^{2+}]}{[Cu^{2+}]^2} \qquad ...(2)$$

From equation (1) and (2),

$$E_2 - E_1 = \frac{2.303RT}{2F}\left[\log\frac{[Zn^{2+}]}{[Cu^{2+}]_1} - \log\frac{[Zn^{2+}]}{[Cu^{2+}]_2}\right] \qquad ...(3)$$

Substitute all the values in the above equation.

$$0.03 = 0.03\left[\log\frac{[Zn^{2+}]}{[Cu^{2+}]_1} \times \log\frac{[Cu^{2+}]_2}{[Zn^{2+}]}\right]$$

$$1 = \log\frac{[Cu^{2+}]_2}{[Cu^{2+}]_1}$$

$$[Cu^{2+}]_1 = 0.05\ M$$

**80. (3)** The flow of electrons take place from cathode to anode through internal supply when ions generated during electrolysis migrate to oppositely charged electrodes. The loss of electron takes place at anode and gain of electron occurs at cathode, hence electrons flow from cathode to anode in electrolytic cell. This flow of electrons occurs through internal supply.

**81. (1)** The equation for oxidation of $Cl^-$ ion by $MnO_4^-$ is shown below :

$$2MnO_4^- + 16H^+ + 10Cl^- \rightarrow 2Mn^{2+} + 8H_2O + 5Cl_2\uparrow$$

The difference in electrode potential is calculated by the formula,

$$E^\circ_{cell} = 1.151\ V - 1.40\ V$$

$$= 0.11\ V$$

Thus, the value of $\Delta G^\circ$ will be negative because $E^\circ_{cell}$ is positive, which results in feasibility of above reaction. $MnO_4^-$ oxidises $Cl^-$ ions simultaneously during the oxidation of $Fe^{2+}$ ions.

●●

## QUESTIONS

1. The figure that is not a direct manifestation of the quantum nature of atoms is : **[2020, Main]**

(1) 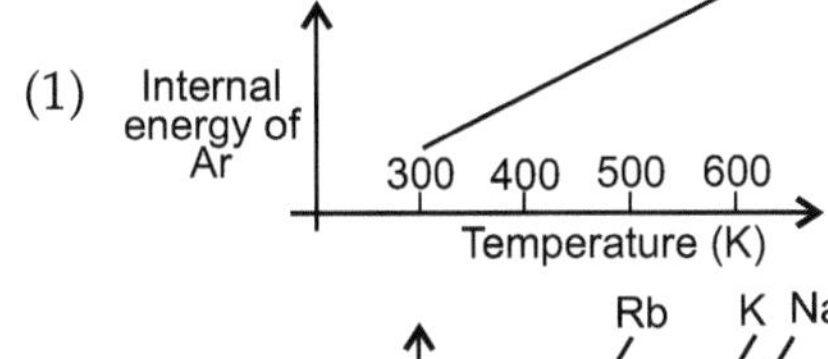


(2) 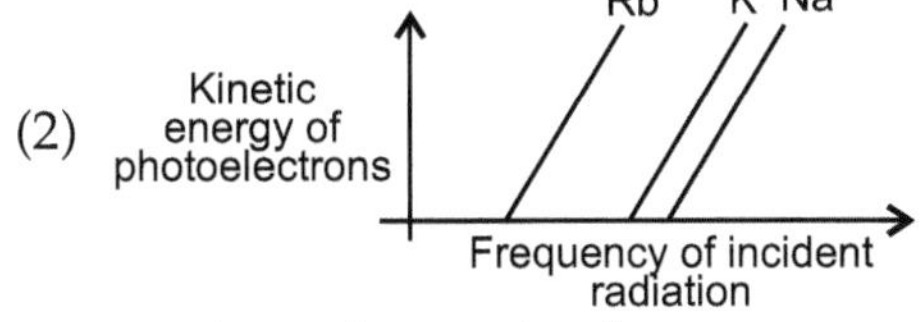


(3) 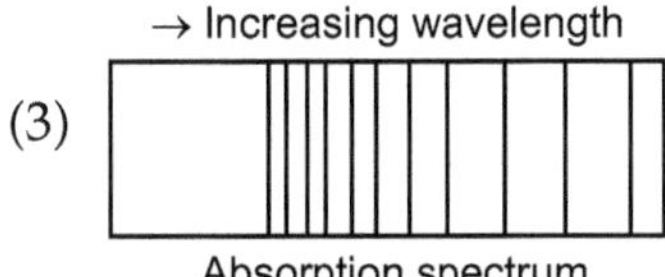


(4) 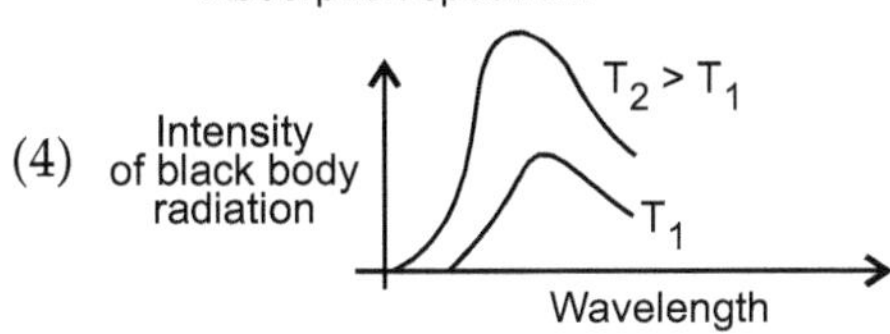


2. The results given in the below table were obtained during kinetic studies of the following reaction :

$$2A + B \rightarrow C + D$$

| Experi-ment | [A]/molL$^{-1}$ | [B]/molL$^{-1}$ | Initial rate/ molL$^{-1}$ min$^{-1}$ |
|---|---|---|---|
| I | 0.1 | 0.1 | $6.00 \times 10^{-3}$ |
| II | 0.1 | 0.2 | $2.40 \times 10^{-2}$ |
| III | 0.2 | 0.1 | $1.20 \times 10^{-2}$ |
| IV | X | 0.2 | $7.20 \times 10^{-2}$ |
| V | 0.3 | Y | $2.88 \times 10^{-1}$ |

X and Y in the given table are respectively : **[2020, Main]**

(1) 0.3, 0.4     (2) 0.4, 0.3
(3) 0.4, 0.4     (4) 0.3, 0.3

3. The work function of sodium metal is $4.41 \times 10^{-19}$ J. If the photons of wavelength 300 nm are incident on the metal, the kinetic energy of the ejected electrons will be ($h = 6.63 \times 10^{-34}$ Js; $c = 3 \times 10^8$ m/s) .............. $\times 10^{-21}$ J. **[2020, Main]**

4. It is true that : **[2020, Advanced]**
(1) A zero order reaction is a single step reaction
(2) A second order reaction is always a multistep reaction
(3) A first order reaction is always a single step reaction
(4) A zero order reaction is a multistep reaction

5. For the reaction $2A + 3B + \dfrac{3}{2}C \rightarrow 3P$, which statement is correct ? **[2020, Main]**

(1) $\dfrac{dn_A}{dt} = \dfrac{dn_B}{dt} = \dfrac{dn_C}{dt}$

(2) $\dfrac{dn_A}{dt} = \dfrac{2}{3}\dfrac{dn_B}{dt} = \dfrac{3}{4}\dfrac{dn_C}{dt}$

(3) $\dfrac{dn_A}{dt} = \dfrac{3}{2}\dfrac{dn_B}{dt} = \dfrac{3}{4}\dfrac{dn_C}{dt}$

(4) $\dfrac{dn_A}{dt} = \dfrac{2}{3}\dfrac{dn_B}{dt} = \dfrac{4}{3}\dfrac{dn_C}{dt}$

6. For the equilibrium $A \rightleftharpoons B$, the variation of the rate of the forward (a) and reverse (b) reaction with time is given by : **[2020, Main]**

(1) 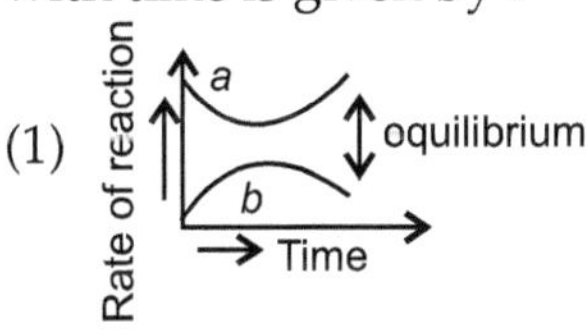


(2) 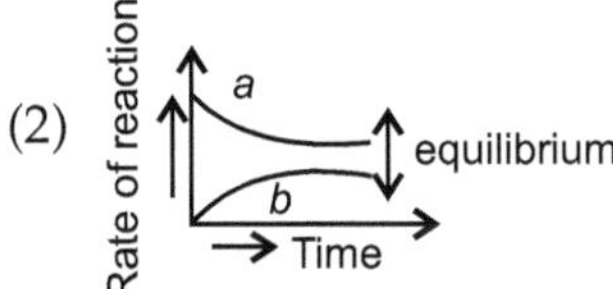


(3) 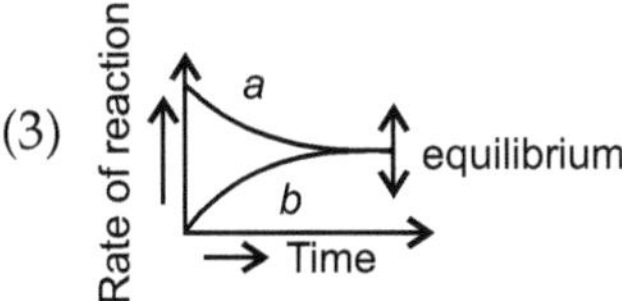


(4) 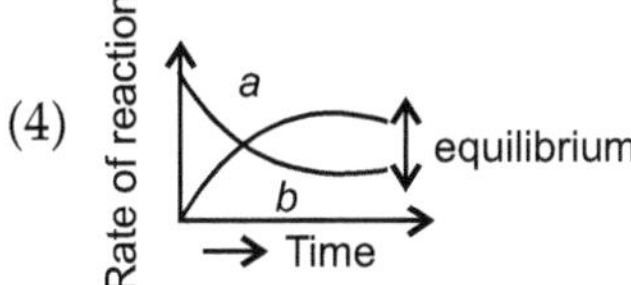


7. If 75% of a first order reaction was completed in 90 minutes, 60% of the same reaction would be completed in approximately (in minutes)........ .
(Take : log 2 = 0.30; log 2.5 = 0.40)

**[2020, Main]**

8. The rate of a reaction decreased by 3.555 times when the temperature was changed from 40°C

to 30°C. The activation energy (in kJ mol$^{-1}$) of the reaction is ................. .

Take; R = 8.314 J mol$^{-1}$ K$^{-1}$ ln 3.555 = 1.268

**[2020, Main]**

9. A flask contains a mixture of compounds A and B. Both compounds decompose by first-order kinetics. The half-lives for A and B are 300 s and 180 s, respectively. If the concentrations of A and B are equal initially, the time required for the concentration of A to be four times that of B (in S) : (Use ln 2 = 0.693) **[2020, Main]**

(1) 180            (2) 120

(3) 300            (4) 900

10. Consider the following reactions :

A → P1; B → P2; C → P3; D → P4

The order of the above reactions are $a$, $b$, $c$ and $d$ respectively. The following graph is obtained when log [rate] vs. log [conc] are plotted :

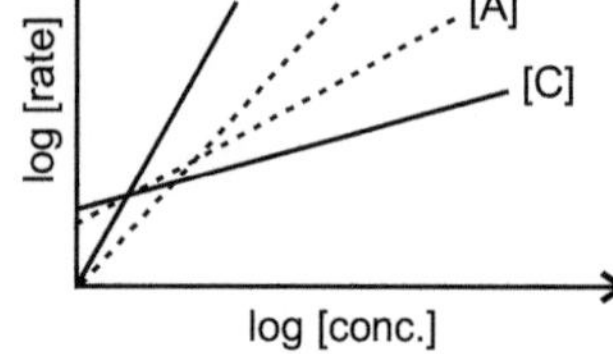


Among the following, the correct sequence for the order of the reactions is : **[2020, Main]**

(1) a > b > c > d      (2) c > a > b > d

(3) d > b > a > c      (4) d > a > b > c

11. The number of molecules with energy greater than the threshold energy for a reaction increases five fold by a rise of temperature from 27 °C to 42 °C. Its energy of activation in J/mol is ........... . (Take ln 5 = 1.6094; R = 8.314 J mol$^{-1}$ K$^{-1}$)

**[2020, Main]**

12. The rate constant ($k$) of a reaction is measured at different temperatures (T) and the data are plotted in the given figure. The activation energy of the reaction in kJ mol$^{-1}$ is :

(R is gas constant) **[2020, Main]**

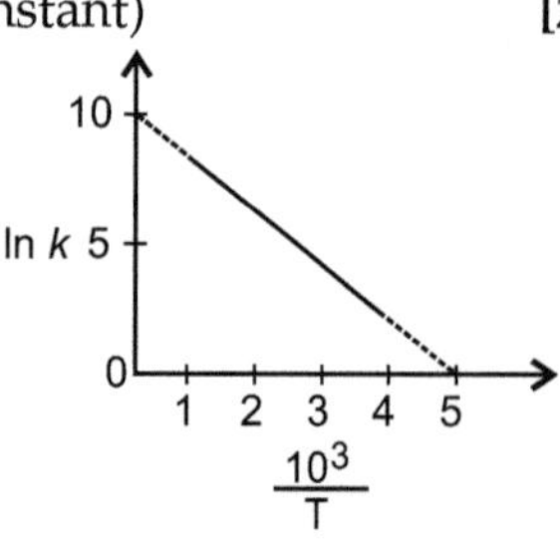


(1) 2R           (2) R

(3) 1/R         (4) 2/R

13. $^{238}_{92}$U is known to undergo radioactive decay to form $^{206}_{82}$Pb by emitting alpha and beta particles.

A rock initially contained $68 \times 10^{-6}$ g of $^{238}_{92}$U. If the number of alpha particles that it would emit

during its radioactive decay of $^{238}_{92}$U to $^{206}_{82}$Pb in three half-lives is Z × 10$^{18}$, then what is the value of Z ? **[2020, Advanced]**

14. In an experiment, $m$ grams of a compound X (gas/liquid/solid) taken in a container is loaded in a balance as shown in figure I below. In the presence of a magnetic field, the pan with X is either deflected upwards (figure II) or defleted downwards (figure III), depending on the compound X. Identify the correct statement(s)

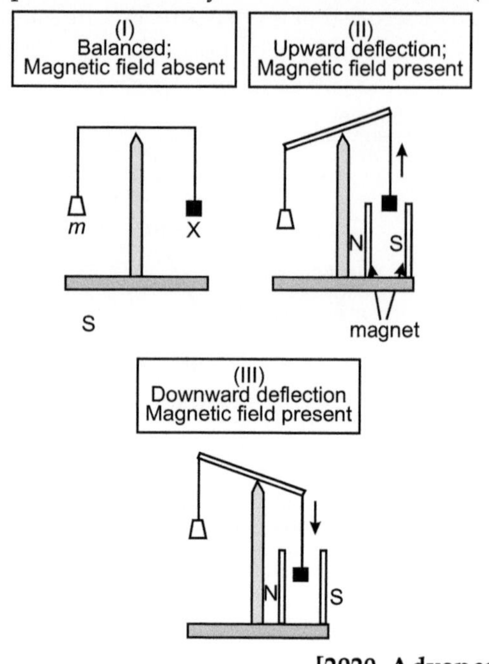


**[2020, Advanced]**

(1) If X is H$_2$O($l$), deflection of the pan is upwards

(2) If X is K$_4$Fe(CN)$_6$]($s$), deflection of the pan is upwards.

(3) If X is O$_2$ (g), deflection of the pan is downwards

(4) If X is C$_6$H$_6$($l$), deflection of the pan is downwards

15. Which of the following plots is(are) correct for the given reaction ?

([P]$_0$ is the initial concentration of P)

$$H_3C-\underset{\underset{CH_3}{|}}{\overset{\overset{CH_3}{|}}{C}}-Br + NaOH \longrightarrow H_3C-\underset{\underset{CH_3}{|}}{\overset{\overset{CH_3}{|}}{C}}-OH + NaBr$$

P                            Q

**[2020, Advanced]**

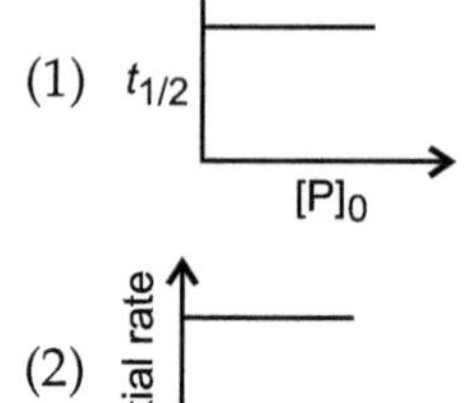

(3) 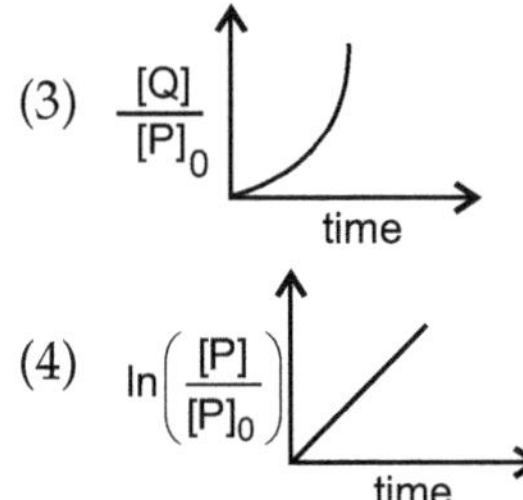

(4) (graph of $\ln\left(\dfrac{[P]}{[P]_0}\right)$ vs time)

**16.** Which among the following statement(s) is(are) true for the extraction of aluminium from bauxite ? **[2020, Advanced]**

(1) Hydrated $Al_2O_3$ precipitates, when $CO_2$ is bubbled through a solution of sodium aluminate

(2) Addition of $Na_3AlF_6$ lowers the melting point of alumina

(3) $CO_2$ is evolved at the anode during electrolysis

(4) The cathode is a steel vessel with a lining of carbon

**17.** A sample of milk splits after 60 min. at 300 K and after 40 min. at 400 K when the population of lactobacillus acidophilus in it doubles. The activation energy (in kJ/mol) for this process is closest to ............... . **[2020, Main]**

(Given, R = 8.3 J mol$^{-1}$ K$^{-1}$, $\ln\left(\dfrac{2}{3}\right) = 0.4$, $e = 4.0$)

**18.** The rate of a certain biochemical reaction at physiological temperature (T) occurs $10^6$ times faster with enzyme than without. The change in the activation energy upon adding enzyme is : **[2020, Main]**

(1) $-6RT$        (2) $+6RT$

(3) $+6(2.303)RT$      (4) $-6(2.303)RT$

**19.** The magnitude of work done by a gas that undergoes a reversible expansion along the path ABC shown in the figure is ...... **[2020, Main]**

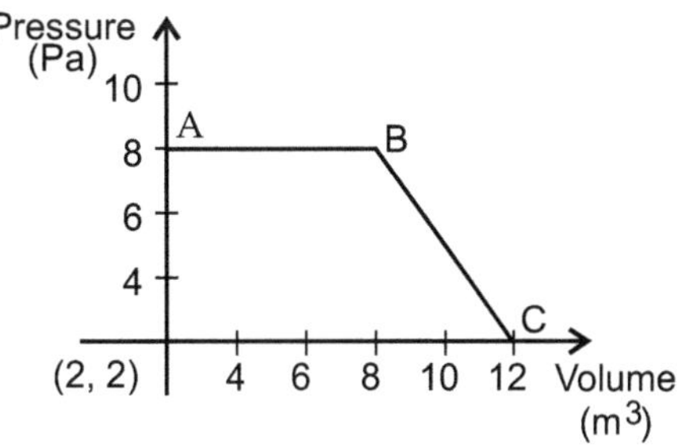

**20.** For the following reactions :

$$A \xrightarrow{700\ K} \text{Product}$$

$$A \xrightarrow[\text{catalyst}]{500\ K} \text{Product}$$

It was found that $E_a$ is decreased by 30 kJ/mol in the presence of a catalyst.

If the rate remains unchanged, the activation energy for catalysed reaction is (Assume pre exponential factor is same) : **[2020, Main]**

(1) 135 kJ/mol      (2) 105 kJ/mol

(3) 198 kJ/mol      (4) 75 kJ/mol

**21.** Consider the following plots of rate constant versus $\dfrac{1}{T}$ for four different reactions. Which of the following order is correct for the activation energies of these reactions ? **[2020, Main]**

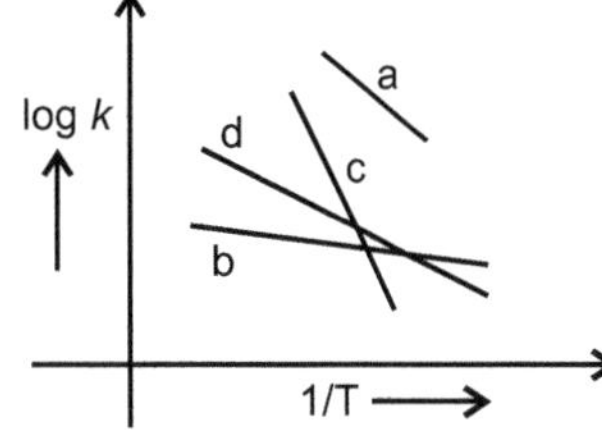

(1) $E_b > E_d > E_c > E_a$    (2) $E_a > E_c > E_d > E_b$

(3) $E_c > E_a > E_d > E_b$    (4) $E_b > E_a > E_d > E_c$

**22.** For the following reactions : **[2020, Main]**

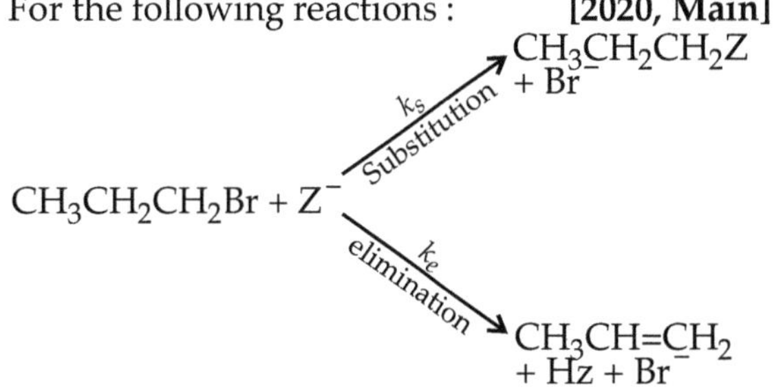

where,

$$Z^- = CH_3CH_2O^-\ (A)\ \text{or}\ H_3C-\overset{\displaystyle CH_3}{\underset{\displaystyle CH_3}{\overset{|}{\underset{|}{C}}}}-O^-\ (B),$$

$k_s$ and $k_e$ are respectively, the rate constants for substitution and elimination, and $\mu = \dfrac{k_s}{k_e}$, the correct option is .................... .

(1) $\mu_A > \mu_B$ and $k_e(A) > k_e(B)$
(2) $\mu_B > \mu_A$ and $k_e(A) > k_e(B)$
(3) $\mu_A > \mu_B$ and $k_e(B) > k_e(A)$
(4) $\mu_B > \mu_A$ and $k_e(B) > k_e(A)$

**23.** For the reaction $2A + B \rightarrow C$, the values of initial rate at different reactant concentrations are given in the table below. The rate law for the reaction is : **[2019, Main]**

| [A] (mol L$^{-1}$) | [B] (mol L$^{-1}$) | Initial Rate (mol L$^{-1}$s$^{-1}$) |
|---|---|---|
| 0.05 | 0.05 | 0.045 |
| 0.10 | 0.05 | 0.090 |
| 0.20 | 0.10 | 0.72 |

(1) Rate = $k[A][B]^2$    (2) Rate = $k[A]^2[B]^2$

(3) Rate = $k[A][B]$      (4) Rate = $k[A]^2[B]$

24. For a reaction scheme $A \xrightarrow{k_1} B \xrightarrow{k_2} C$, if the rate of formation of B is set to be zero then the concentration of B is given by : **[2019, Main]**

(1) $(k_1 - k_2)[A]$ 

(2) $k_1 k_2 [A]$

(3) $(k_1 + k_2)[A]$ 

(4) $\left(\dfrac{k_1}{k_2}\right)[A]$

25. The given plots represent the variation of the concentration of a reactant R with time for two different reactions (i) and (ii). The respective orders of the reactions are : **[2019, Main]**

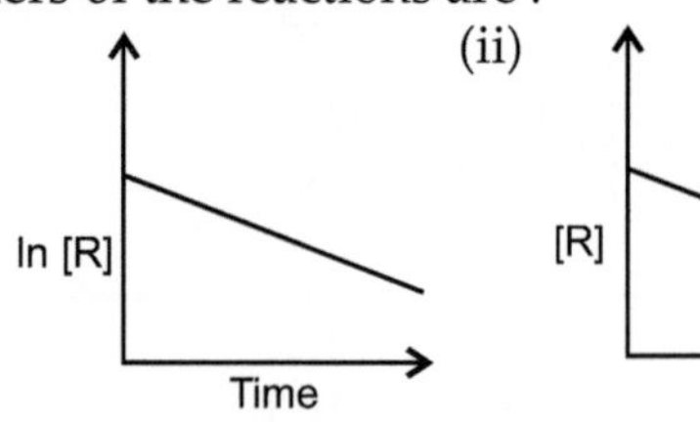

(1) 1, 0 

(2) 1, 1

(3) 0, 1 

(4) 0, 2

26. Consider the given plot of enthalpy of the following reaction between A and B.

$$A + B \rightarrow C + D.$$

Identify the incorrect statement. **[2019, Main]**

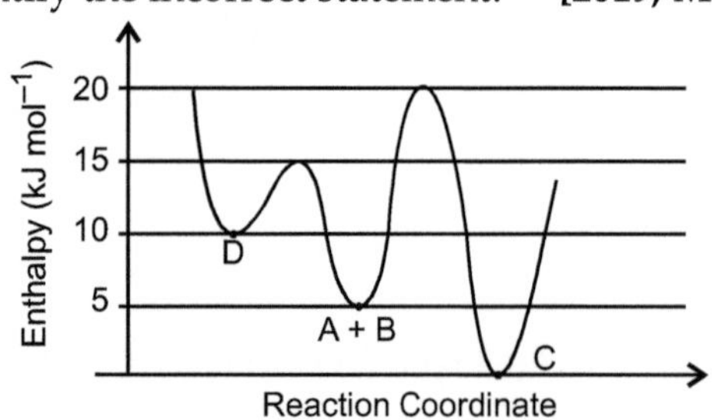

(1) Activation enthalpy to form C is 5 kJ mol$^{-1}$ less than that to form D.

(2) C is the thermodynamically stable product.

(3) D is kinetically stable product.

(4) Formation of A and B from C has highest enthalpy of activation.

27. A bacterial infection in an internal wound grows as $N'(t) = N_0 \exp(t)$, where the time t is in hours. A dose of antibiotic, taken orally, needs 1 hour to reach the wound. Once it reaches there, the bacterial population goes down as $\dfrac{dN}{dt} = -5N^2$.

What will be the plot of $\dfrac{N_0}{N}$ vs. t after 1 hour ?

**[2019, Main]**

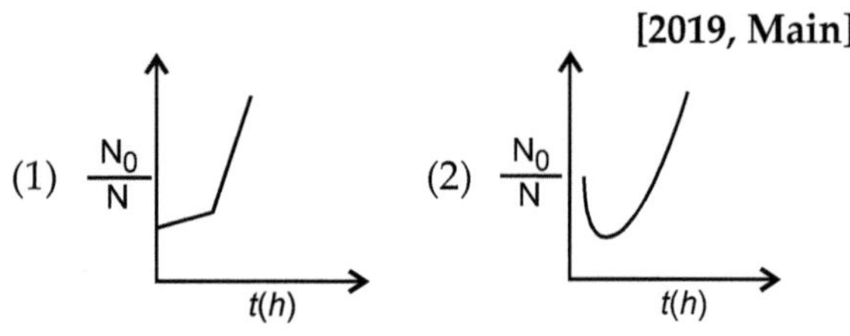

28. Points I, II and III in the following plot respectively correspond to

($V_{mp}$ : most probable velocity) **[2019, Main]**

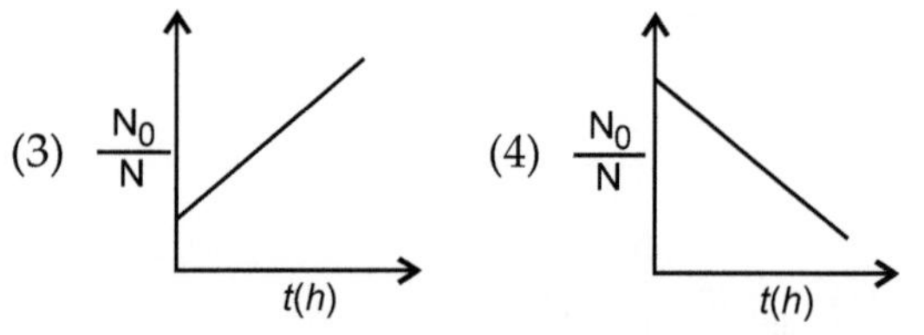

(1) $V_{mp}$ of $N_2$ (300 K); $V_{mp}$ of $O_2$ (400 K); $V_{mp}$ of $H_2$ (300 K)

(2) $V_{mp}$ of $O_2$ (400 K); $V_{mp}$ of $N_2$ (300 K); $V_{mp}$ of $H_2$ (300 K)

(3) $V_{mp}$ of $N_2$ (300 K); $V_{mp}$ of $H_2$ (300 K); $V_{mp}$ of $O_2$ (400 K)

(4) $V_{mp}$ of $H_2$ (300 K); $V_{mp}$ of $N_2$ (300 K); $V_{mp}$ of $O_2$ (400 K)

29. For the reaction of $H_2$ with $I_2$, the rate constant is $2.5 \times 10^{-4}$ dm$^3$ mol$^{-1}$ s$^{-1}$ at 327 °C and 1.0 dm$^3$ mol$^{-1}$ s$^{-1}$ at 527 °C. The activation energy for the reaction, in kJ mol$^{-1}$ is : **[2019, Main]** ($R = 8.314$ J K$^{-1}$ mol$^{-1}$)

(1) 166 

(2) 150

(3) 72 

(4) 59

30. In the following reaction; $xA \rightarrow yB$

$$\log_{10}\left[-\dfrac{d[A]}{dt}\right] = \log_{10}\left[\dfrac{d[B]}{dt}\right] + 0.3010$$

`A' and `B' respectively can be : **[2019, Main]**

(1) *n*-Butane and Iso-butane

(2) $C_2H_2$ and $C_6H_6$

(3) $C_2H_4$ and $C_4H_8$

(4) $N_2O_4$ and $NO_2$

31. $NO_2$ required for a reaction is produced by the decomposition of $N_2O_5$ in $CCl_4$ as per the equation,

$$2N_2O_5(g) \rightarrow 4NO_2(g) + O_2(g)$$

The initial concentration of $N_2O_5$ is 3.00 mol L$^{-1}$ and it is 2.75 mol L$^{-1}$ after 30 minutes. The rate of formation of $NO_2$ is : **[2019, Main]**

(1) $4.167 \times 10^{-3}$ mol L$^{-1}$ min$^{-1}$

(2) $1.667 \times 10^{-2}$ mol L$^{-1}$ min$^{-1}$

(3) $8.333 \times 10^{-3}$ mol L$^{-1}$ min$^{-1}$

(4) $2.083 \times 10^{-3}$ mol L$^{-1}$ min$^{-1}$

**32.** Which of the following statement(s) is(are) corect regarding the root mean square speed ($u_{rms}$) and average translational kinetic energy ($\varepsilon_{av}$) of a molecule in a gas at equilibrium ?

**[2019, Advanced]**

(1) $u_{rms}$ is doubled when its temperature is increased four times

(2) $\varepsilon_{av}$ is doubled when its temperature is increased four times

(3) $\varepsilon_{av}$ at a given temperature does not depend on its molecular mass

(4) $u_{rms}$ is inversely proportional to the square root of its molecular mass

**33.** Consider the kinetic data given in the following table for reaction $A + B + C \rightarrow$ Product.

| Experiment No. | [A] (mol dm⁻³) | [B] (mol (dm⁻³) | [C] (mol dm⁻³) | Rate of reaction (mol dm⁻³ s⁻¹) |
|---|---|---|---|---|
| 1 | 0.2 | 0.1 | 0.1 | $6.0 \times 10^{-5}$ |
| 2 | 0.2 | 0.2 | 0.1 | $6.0 \times 10^{-5}$ |
| 3 | 0.2 | 0.1 | 0.2 | $1.2 \times 10^{-4}$ |
| 4 | 0.3 | 0.1 | 0.1 | $9.0 \times 10^{-5}$ |

The rate of the reaction of [A] – 0.15 mol dm⁻³, [B] – 0.25 mol dm⁻³ and [C] – 0.15 mol dm⁻³ is found to be $Y \times 10^{-5}$ mol dm⁻³ s⁻¹. The value of Y is ............

**[2019, Advanced]**

**34.** The decomposition reaction $2N_2O_5(g) \rightarrow 2N_2O_4(g) + O_2(g)$ is started in a closed cylinder under isothermal isochoric condition at an initial pressure of 1 atm. After $Y \times 10^3$ s, the pressure inside the cylinder is found to be 1.45 atm. If the rate constant of the reaction is $5 \times 10^{-4}$ s⁻¹, assuming ideal gas behaviour, the value of Y is .......

**[2019, Advanced]**

**35.** For a first order reaction $A(g) \rightarrow 2B(g) + C(g)$ at constant volume and 300 K, the total pressure at the beginning ($t = 0$) and at time $t$ are $P_0$ and $P_t$, respectively. Initially, only A is present with concentration $[A]_0$ and $t_{1/3}$ is the time required for the partial pressure of A to reach $1/3^{rd}$ of its initial value. The correct options is/are :

(Assume that all these gases behave as ideal gases)

**[2018, Advanced]**

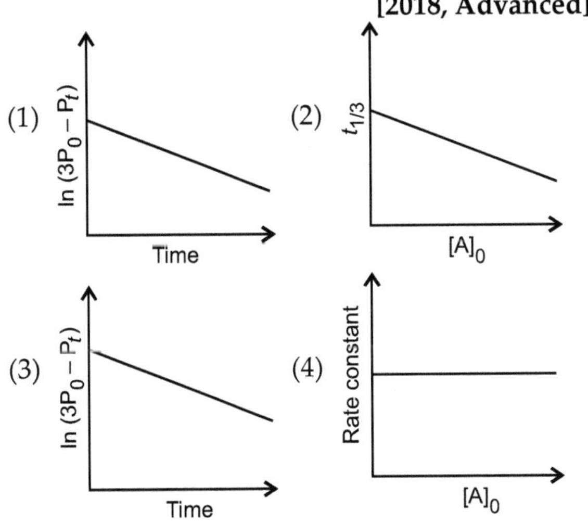

**36.** At 518°C, the rate of decomposition of a sample of gaseous acetaldehyde, intially at a pressure of 363 Torr, was 1.00 Torr s⁻¹ when 5% had reacted and 0.5 Torr s⁻¹ when 33% had reacted. The order of the reaction is :

**[2018, Main]**

(1) 2      (2) 3

(3) 1      (4) 0

**37.** For a first order reaction, $A \rightarrow P$, $t_{1/2}$ (half-life) is 10 days. The time required for $\frac{1}{4}^{th}$ conversion of A (in days) is :      **[2018, Main]**

($\ln 2 = 0.693$, $\ln 3 = 1.1$)

(1) 5      (2) 3.2

(3) 4.1      (4) 2.5

**38.** $N_2O_5$ decomposes to $NO_2$ and $O_2$ and follows first order kinetics. After 50 minutes, the pressure inside the vessel increases from 50 mmHg to 87.5 mmHg. The pressure of the gaseous mixture after 100 minutes at constant temperature will be :

**[2018, Main]**

(1) 175.0 mmHg      (2) 116.25 mmHg

(3) 136.25 mmHg      (4) 106.25 mmHg

**39.** If 50% of a reaction occurs in 100 second and 75% of the reaction occurs in 200 second, the order of this reaction is :      **[2018, Main]**

(1) Zero      (2) 1

(3) 2      (4) 3

**40.** In a bimolecular reaction, the steric factor P was experimentally determined tobe 4.5. The correct options among the following is/are :

**[2018, Main]**

(1) The activation energy of the reaction is unaffected by the value of the steric factor.

(2) Experimentally determined value of frequency factor is higher than that predicted by Arrhenius equation.

(3) Since $P = 4.5$, the reaction will not proceed unless an effective catalyst is used.

(4) The value of frequency factor predicted by Arrhenius equation is higher than that determined experimentally.

**41.** Two reactions $R_1$ and $R_2$ have identical pre-exponential factors. Activation energy of $R_1$ exceeds that of $R_2$ by 10 kJ mol⁻¹. If $k_1$ and $k_2$ are rate constants for reactions $R_1$ and $R_2$ respectively at 300 K, then $\ln(k_2/k_1)$ is equal to :

($R = 8.314$ J mole⁻¹ K⁻¹)      **[2017, Main]**

(1) 6      (2) 4

(3) 8      (4) 12

**42.** The rate of a reaction A doubles on increasing the temperature from 300 to 310 K. By how much, the temperature of reaction B should be increased from 300 K so that rate doubles if activation energy of the reaction B is twice to that of reaction A ? **[2017, Main]**

(1) 9.84 K      (2) 4.92 K

(3) 2.45 K      (4) 19.67 K

**43.** The rate of a reaction quadruples when the temperature changes from 300 to 310 K. The activation energy of this reaction is :

(Assume activation energy and pre-exponential factor are independent of temperature; $\ln 2$ = 0.693, R = 8.314 J mol$^{-1}$ K$^{-1}$) **[2017, Main]**

(1) 107.2 kJ mol$^{-1}$      (2) 53.6 kJ mol$^{-1}$

(3) 26.8 kJ mol$^{-1}$      (4) 414.4 kJ mol$^{-1}$

**44.** According to the Arrhenius equation :

**[2016, Main]**

(1) A high activation energy usually implies a fast reaction.

(2) Rate constant increases with increase in temperature. This is due to a greater number of collisions whose energy exceeds the activation energy.

(3) Higher the magnitude of activation energy, stronger is the temperature dependence of the rate constant.

(4) The pre-exponential factor is a measure of the rate at which collisions occur, irrespective of their energy.

**45.** The reaction of ozone with oxygen atoms in the presence of chlorine atoms can occur by a two step process shown below :

$$O_3(g) + Cl^{\bullet}(g) \rightarrow O_2(g) + ClO^{\bullet}(g) \quad ...(i)$$
$$k_i = 5.2 \times 10^9 \text{ L mol}^{-1} \text{ s}^{-1}$$
$$ClO^{\bullet}(g) + O^{\bullet}(g) \rightarrow O_2(g) + Cl^{\bullet}(g) \quad ...(ii)$$
$$k_{ii} = 2.6 \times 10^{10} \text{ L mol}^{-1} \text{ s}^{-1}$$

The closest rate constant for the overall reaction $O_3(g) + O^{\bullet}(g) \rightarrow 2O_2(g)$ is : **[2016, Main]**

(1) $5.2 \times 10^9$ L mol$^{-1}$ s$^{-1}$

(2) $2.6 \times 10^{10}$ L mol$^{-1}$ s$^{-1}$

(3) $3.1 \times 10^{10}$ L mol$^{-1}$ s$^{-1}$

(4) $1.4 \times 10^{20}$ L mol$^{-1}$ s$^{-1}$

**46.** The rate law for the reaction below is given by the expression $k[A][B]$

$$A + B \rightarrow \text{Product}$$

If the concentration of B is increased from 0.1 to 0.3 mole, keeping the value of A at 0.1 mole, the rate constant will be : **[2016, Main]**

(1) $k$      (2) $k/3$

(3) $3k$      (4) $9k$

**47.** Decomposition of $H_2O_2$ follows a first order reaction. In fifty minutes the concentration of $H_2O_2$ decreases from 0.5 to 0.125 M in one such decomposition. When the concentration of $H_2O_2$ reaches 0.05 M, the rate of formation of $O_2$ will be : **[2016, Main]**

(1) $6.93 \times 10^{-2}$ mol min$^{-1}$

(2) $6.93 \times 10^{-4}$ mol min$^{-1}$

(3) 2.66 L min$^{-1}$ at STP

(4) $1.34 \times 10^{-2}$ mol min$^{-1}$

**48.** Higher order (> 3) reactions are rare due to :

**[2015, Main]**

(1) Low probability of simultaneous collision of all the reacting species.

(2) Increase in entropy and activation energy as more molecules are involved.

(3) Shifting of equilibrium towards reactants due to elastic collisions.

(4) Loss of active species on collision.

**49.** Match the catalysts to the correct processes :

**[2015, Main]**

| Catalyst | Process |
|---|---|
| (A) $TiCl_3$ | (i) Wacker process |
| (B) $PdCl_2$ | (ii) Ziegler-Natta polymerisation |
| (C) $CuCl_2$ | (iii) Contact process |
| (D) $V_2O_5$ | (iv) Deacon's process |

| | (A) | (B) | (C) | (D) |
|---|---|---|---|---|
| (1) | (iii) | (ii) | (iv) | (i) |
| (2) | (ii) | (i) | (iv) | (iii) |
| (3) | (ii) | (iii) | (iv) | (i) |
| (4) | (iii) | (i) | (ii) | (iv) |

**50.** The reaction :

$$2N_2O_5(g) \rightarrow 4NO_2(g) + O_2(g)$$

follows first order kinetics. The pressure of a vessel containing only $N_2O_5$ was found to increase from 50 mm Hg to 87.5 mm Hg in 30 min. The pressure exerted by the gases after 60 min. will be (Assume temperature remains constant) :

**[2015, Main]**

(1) 106.25 mm Hg      (2) 116.25 mm Hg

(3) 125 mm Hg      (4) 150 mm Hg

**51.** $A + 2B \rightarrow C$, the rate equation for this reaction is given as

$$\text{Rate} = k[A][B]$$

If the concentration of A is kept the same but that of B is doubled what will happen to the rate itself ? **[2015, Main]**

(1) Halved      (2) The same

(3) Doubled      (4) Quadrupled

**52.** For the elementary reaction $M \rightarrow N$, the rate of disappearance of M increases by a factor of 8 upon doubling the concentration of M. The order of the reaction with respect to M is : **[2014, Advanced]**

(1) 4      (2) 3

(3) 2      (4) 1

**53.** For the non-stoichiometre reaction $2A + B \rightarrow C + D$, the following kinetic data were obtained in three separate experiments, all at 298 K.

| Initial Concenration (A) | Initial Concenration (B) | Initial rate of formation of C (mol L$^{-}$S$^{-}$) |
| --- | --- | --- |
| 0.1 M | 0.1 M | $1.2 \times 10^{-3}$ |
| 0.1 M | 0.2 M | $1.2 \times 10^{-3}$ |
| 0.2 M | 0.1 M | $2.4 \times 10^{-3}$ |

The rate law for the formation of C is :

[2014, Main]

(1) $\dfrac{dc}{dt} = k[A][B]$

(2) $\dfrac{dc}{dt} = k[A]^2[B]$

(3) $\dfrac{dc}{dt} = k[A][B]^2$

(4) $\dfrac{dc}{dt} = k[A]$

**54.** The half-life period of a first order reaction is 15 minutes. The amount of substance left after one hour will be : [2014, Main]

(1) $\dfrac{1}{4}$ of the original amount

(2) $\dfrac{1}{8}$ of the original amount

(3) $\dfrac{1}{16}$ of the original amount

(4) $\dfrac{1}{32}$ of the original amount

**55.** In the reaction of formation of sulphur trioxide by contact process $2SO_2 + O_2 \rightleftharpoons 2SO_3$ the rate of reaction was measured as $\dfrac{d[O_2]}{dt} = -2.5 \times 10^{-4}$ mol L$^{-1}$ s$^{-1}$. The rate of reaction in terms of $[SO_2]$ in mol L$^{-1}$s$^{-1}$ will be : [2014, Main]

(1) $-1.25 \times 10^{-4}$

(2) $-2.50 \times 10^{-4}$

(3) $-3.75 \times 10^{-4}$

(4) $-5.00 \times 10^{-4}$

**56.** For the reaction, $2N_2O_5 \rightarrow 4NO_2 + O_2$, the rate equation can be expressed in two ways $-\dfrac{d[N_2O_5]}{dt} = k[N_2O_5]$ and $+d[NO_2] = k'[N_2O_5]$.

$dt$ Here, $k$ and $k'$ are related as : [2014, Main]

(1) $k = k'$

(2) $2k = k'$

(3) $k = 2k'$

(4) $k = 4k'$

**57.** The rate coefficient ($k$) for a particular reaction is $1.3 \times 10^{-4}$ M$^{-1}$ s$^{-1}$ at 100°C, and $1.3 \times 10^{-3}$ M$^{-1}$ s$^{-1}$ at 150°c. What is the energy of activation ($E_A$) (in kJ) for this reaction ? (R = molar gas constant = 8.314 JK$^{-1}$ mol$^{-1}$) [2014, Main]

(1) 16

(2) 60

(3) 99

(4) 132

**58.** For the reaction,
$$3A + 2B \rightarrow C + D,$$
the differential rate law can be written as : [2014, Main]

(1) $3\dfrac{d[A]}{dt} = \dfrac{d[C]}{dt} = k[A]^n[B]^m$

(2) $-\dfrac{d[A]}{dt} = \dfrac{d[C]}{dt} = k[A]^n[B]^m$

(3) $+\dfrac{1}{3}\dfrac{d[A]}{dt} = \dfrac{d[C]}{dt} = k[A]^n[B]^m$

(4) $-\dfrac{1}{3}\dfrac{d[A]}{dt} = \dfrac{d[C]}{dt} = k[A]^n[B]^m$

**59.** In the reaction,
$$P + Q \rightarrow R + S$$
the time taken for 75% reaction of P is twice the time taken for 50% reaction of P. The concentration of Q varies with reaction time as shown in the figure. The overall order of the reaction is : [2013, Advanced]

(1) 2

(2) 3

(3) 0

(4) 1

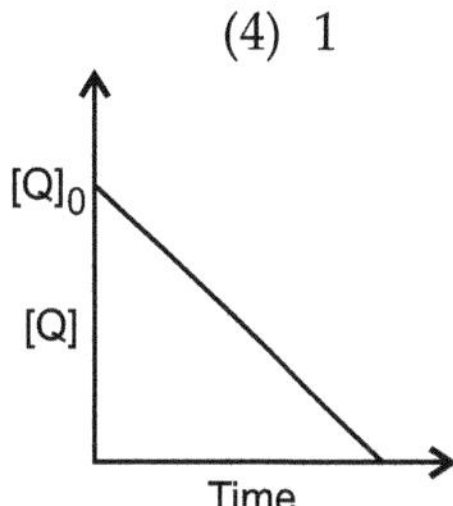


**60.** An organic compound undergoes first-order decomposition. The time taken for its decomposition to 1/8 and 1/10 of its initial concentration are $t_{1/8}$ and $t_{1/10}$ respectively. What is the value of $\dfrac{[t_{1/8}]}{[t_{1/10}]} \times 10$? (take $\log_{10} 2 = 0.3$)

[2012, Advanced]

**61.** For the first order reaction,
$$2N_2O_5(g) \rightarrow 4NO_2(g) + O_2(g)$$
[2011, Advanced]

(1) The concentration of the reactant decreases exponentially with time.

(2) The half-life of the reaction decreases with increasing temperature.

(3) The half-life of the reaction depends on the initial concentration of the reactants.

(4) The reaction proceeds to 99.6% completion in eight half-life duration.

**62.** Plots showing the variation of the rate constant ($k$) with temperature (T) are given below. The plot that follows Arrhenius equation is : [2010, Advanced]

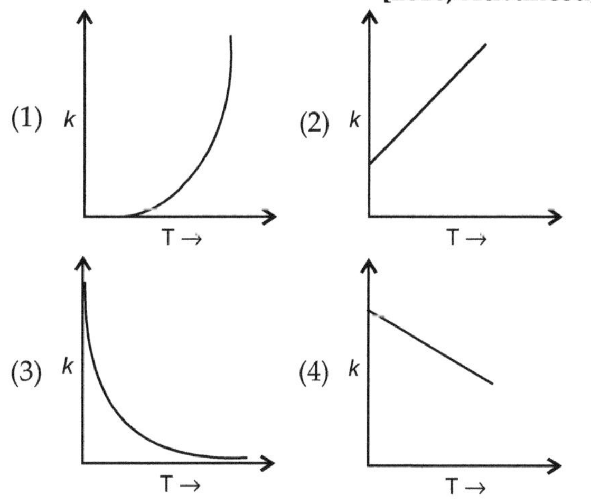

63. The concentration of R in the reaction $R \rightarrow P$ was measured as a function of time and the following data is obtained : **[2010, Advanced]**

| [R] molar | 1.0 | 0.75 | 0.40 | 0.10 |
|---|---|---|---|---|
| t[min.] | 0.0 | 0.05 | 0.12 | 0.18 |

The order of the reaction is :

64. For a first order reaction $A \rightarrow P$, the temperature (T) dependent rate constant $(k)$ was found to follow the equation $\log k = -(2000)\dfrac{1}{T} + 6.0$. The pre-exponential factor A and the activation energy $E_a$, respectively, are : **[2009, Advanced]**
    (1) $1.0 \times 10^6 \text{ s}^{-1}$ and $9.2 \text{ kJ mol}^{-1}$
    (2) $6.0 \text{ s}^{-1}$ and $16.6 \text{ kJ mol}^{-1}$
    (3) $1.0 \times 10^6 \text{ s}^{-1}$ and $16.6 \text{ kJ mol}^{-1}$
    (4) $1.0 \times 10^6 \text{ s}^{-1}$ and $38.3 \text{ kJ mol}^{-1}$

65. Under the same reaction conditions, initial concentration of $1.386 \text{ mol dm}^{-3}$ of a substance becomes half in 40 seconds and 20 seconds through first order and zero order kinetics, respectively. Ratio $\left(\dfrac{k_1}{k_0}\right)$ of the rate constants for first order $(k_1)$ and zero order $(k_0)$ of the reactions is : **[2008, Advanced]**
    (1) $0.5 \text{ mol}^{-1} \text{ dm}^3$  (2) $1.0 \text{ mol dm}^{-3}$
    (3) $1.5 \text{ mol dm}^{-3}$  (4) $2.0 \text{ mol}^{-1} \text{ dm}^3$

66. Consider a reaction $aG + bH \rightarrow$ Products. When concentration of both the reactants G and H is doubled, the rate increases by eight times. However, when concentration of G is doubled keeping the concentration of H fixed, the rate is doubled. The overall order of the reaction is : **[2007, Advanced]**
    (1) 0  (2) 1
    (3) 2  (4) 3

67. $2X_{(g)} \longrightarrow 2Y_{(g)} + 2Z_{(g)}$

| Time (in Min) | 0 | 100 | 200 |
|---|---|---|---|
| Partial pressure of X (in mm of Hg) | 800 | 400 | 200 |

Assuming ideal gas condition. Calculate : **[2005, Main]**
    (1) Order of reaction
    (2) Rate constant
    (3) Time taken for 75% completion of reaction
    (4) Total pressure when $P_x = 700$ mm

68. Which of the following statement is incorrect about order of reaction ? **[2005, Screening]**
    (1) Order of reaction is determined experimentally.
    (2) It is the sum of power of concentration terms in the rate law expression.
    (3) It does not necessarily depend on stoichiometric coefficients.
    (4) Order of the reaction can not have fractional value.

69. For the given reaction,
    $A + B \longrightarrow$ Products
    Following data were given : **[2004, Main]**

| Initial conc. (m / L) [A] | Initial conc. (m / L) [B] | Initial rate $[\text{mL}^{-1}\text{s}^{-1}]$ |
|---|---|---|
| 0.1 | 0.1 | 0.05 |
| 0.2 | 0.1 | 0.1 |
| 0.1 | 0.2 | 0.05 |

    (1) Write the rate equation
    (2) Calculate the rate constant.

70. (A) follows first order reaction. $(A) \longrightarrow$ product Concentration of A, changes from 0.1 M to 0.025 M in 40 minutes. Find the rate of reaction of A when concentration of A is 0.01 M : **[2004, Screening]**
    (1) $3.47 \times 10^{-4} \text{ M min}^{-1}$
    (2) $3.47 \times 10^{-5} \text{ M min}^{-1}$
    (3) $1.73 \times 10^{-4} \text{ M min}^{-1}$
    (4) $1.73 \times 10^{-5} \text{ M min}^{-1}$

71. In a first order reaction the concentration of reactant decreases from $800 \text{ mol/dm}^3$ to $50 \text{ mol/dm}^3$ is $2 \times 10^4$ sec. The rate constant of reaction in $\text{sec}^{-1}$ is : **[2003, Screening]**
    (1) $2 \times 10^4$  (2) $3.45 \times 10^{-5}$
    (3) $1.386 \times 10^{-4}$  (4) $2 \times 10^{-4}$

72. Consider the chemical reaction, $N_2(g) + 3H_2(g) \rightarrow 2NH_3(g)$. The rate of this reaction can be expressed in terms of time derivative of concentration of $N_2(g)$, $H_2(g)$ or $NH_3(g)$. Identify the correct relationship amongst the rate expressions. **[2002, Screening]**
    (1) $\text{Rate} = -d[N_2]/dt = -1/3\,d[H_2]/dt = 1/2\,d[NH_3]/dt$
    (2) $\text{Rate} = -d[N_2]/dt = -3\,d[H_2]/dt = 2\,d[NH_3]/dt$
    (3) $\text{Rate} = d[N_2]/dt = -1/3\,d[H_2]/dt = 1/2\,d[NH_3]/dt$
    (4) $\text{Rate} = -d[N_2]/dt = -d[H_2]/dt = d[NH_3]/dt$

## ANSWER KEY

| | | | | | | | | | |
|---|---|---|---|---|---|---|---|---|---|
| **1.** (1) | **2.** (1) | **3.** (*) | **4.** (4) | **5.** (4) | **6.** (3) | **7.** (*) | **8.** (*) | **9.** (4) | **10.** (3) |
| **11.** (*) | **12.** (1) | **13.** (*) | **14.** (1,2,3) | **15.** (1) | **16.** (1,2,3,4) | **17.** (*) | **18.** (4) | **19.** (*) | **20.** (4) |
| **21.** (3) | **22.** (3) | **23.** (1) | **24.** (4) | **25.** (1) | **26.** (1) | **27.** (3) | **28.** (1) | **29.** (1) | **30.** (3) |
| **31.** (2) | **32.** (1, 3, 4) | **33.** (*) | **34.** (*) | **35.** (1, 4) | **36.** (1) | **37.** (3) | **38.** (4) | **39.** (2) | **40.** (1, 2) |

| | | | | | | | | | |
|---|---|---|---|---|---|---|---|---|---|
| **41.** (2) | **42.** (2) | **43.** (1) | **44.**(2, 3, 4) | **45.** (4) | **46.** (1) | **47.** (2) | **48.** (1) | **49.** (2) | **50.** (1) |
| **51.** (3) | **52.** (2) | **53.** (4) | **54.** (3) | **55.** (4) | **56.** (2) | **57.** (2) | **58.** (4) | **59.** (4) | **60.** (*) |
| **61.** (1,2,4) | **62.** (1) | **63.** (*) | **64** (4) | **65.** (1) | **66.** (4) | **67.** (*) | **68.** (4) | **69.** (*) | **70.** (1) |
| **71.** (3) | **72.** (1) | | | | | | | | |

## ANSWERS WITH EXPLANATIONS

**1. (1)** Photoelectric effect (option 2), atomic spectrum (option 3) and Black body radiations (option 4) may be explained by quantum theory.

As on increasing temperature, all the values of internal energy becomes possible, it is not directly explained from quantum theory.

**2. (1)** From rate law

$$r = -\frac{1}{2}\frac{d[A]}{dt} = \frac{-d[B]}{dt}$$

$$= K[A]^x[B]^y$$

$$6 \times 10^{-3} = K(0.1)^x (0.1)^y \qquad ...(i)$$
$$2.4 \times 10^{-2} = K(0.1)^x (0.2)^y \qquad ...(ii)$$
$$1.2 \times 10^{-2} = K(0.2)^x (0.1)^y \qquad ...(iii)$$

$$(3) \div (1) \Rightarrow x = 1$$
$$(2) \div (3) \Rightarrow x = 2$$

So, other with respect to A = 1

Order with respect to B = 2

So, other with respect to A = 1

Order with respect to B = 2

$$(4) \div (3)$$

$$\left(\frac{x}{0.2}\right) \times \left(\frac{0.2}{0.1}\right)^2 = \frac{7.2 \times 10^{-2}}{1.2 \times 10^{-2}}$$

$$x = \frac{6 \times 0.2}{4}$$

$$x = 0.3 \text{ M}$$

$$(5) \div (4)$$

$$\left(\frac{y}{0.2}\right)^2 = \frac{2.88 \times 10^{-1}}{7.2 \times 10^{-2}}$$

$$y^2 = 4 \times 0.2^2$$

$$y = 0.4 \text{ M}$$

**3.**

$$E = W + K.E_{max}$$

$$K.E_{max} = E - W$$

$$= \frac{hc}{\lambda} - 4.41 \times 10^{-19}$$

$$= \frac{6.63 \times 10^{-34} \times 3 \times 10^8}{300 \times 10^{-9}} - 4.41 \times 10^{-19}$$

$$= 2.22 \times 10^{-19} \text{ J}$$

$$= 222 \times 10^{-21} \text{ J}$$

**4. (4)** Zero order reaction is multiple step reaction.

**5. (4)** For $aA + bB \rightarrow cC$;

$$\frac{-1}{a}\frac{d[A]}{dt} = \frac{-1}{b}\frac{d[B]}{dt} = \frac{1}{c}\frac{d[C]}{dt}$$

$$\therefore \quad \frac{-1}{2}\frac{d[A]}{dt} = \frac{-1}{3}\frac{d[B]}{dt}$$

$$= \frac{-2}{3}\frac{d[C]}{dt}$$

$$= \frac{1}{3}\frac{d[p]}{dt}$$

**6. (3)** at equilibrium

$$r_a = r_b$$

**7.**

$$t_{0.75} = 2 \times \frac{\ln 2}{k} = 90$$

$$k = \frac{\ln 2}{45} \text{ min}^{-1}$$

$$kt = \ln\frac{1}{1-0.6} = \ln 2.5$$

$$\frac{\ln 2}{45} \times t = \ln 2.5$$

$$t = 45 \times \frac{\log 2.5}{\log 2}$$

$$= 45 \times \frac{0.4}{0.3} = 60 \text{ min}$$

**8.**

$$\ln\left(\frac{K_{T_2}}{K_{T_1}}\right) = \frac{E_a}{R}\left[\frac{1}{T_1} - \frac{1}{T_2}\right]$$

$$T_1 = 303 \text{ K}; T_2 = 313 \text{ K}$$

$$\frac{K_{T_2}}{K_{T_1}} = 3.555$$

$$\ln(3.555) = \frac{E_a}{8.314}\left[\frac{1}{303} - \frac{1}{313}\right]$$

$$E_u = 99980.715$$

$$E_a = 99.98 \frac{\text{kJ}}{\text{mole}}$$

**9. (4)**

$$[A]_t = 4[B]_t$$

$$[A]_0 \, e^{-(\ln 2/300)t} = 4[B]_0 e^{(-\ln 2/180)t}$$

$$e^{\left(\frac{\ln 2}{180} - \frac{\ln 2}{300}\right)} = 4$$

$$\left(\frac{\ln 2}{180} - \frac{\ln 2}{300}\right)t = \ln 4$$

$$\left(\frac{1}{180} - \frac{1}{300}\right)t = 2$$

$$\Rightarrow \qquad t = \frac{2 \times 180 \times 300}{120}$$

$$= 900 \text{ sec.}$$

**10. (3)** $d > b > a > c.$

**11.** As per question $K_{T_2} = 5K_{T_1}$ as molecules activated are increased five times so $k$ will increases 5 times

Now

$$\ln\left(\frac{K_{T_2}}{K_{T_1}}\right) = \frac{Ea}{R}\left(\frac{1}{T_1} - \frac{1}{T_2}\right)$$

$$\ln 5 = \frac{Ea}{R}\left(\frac{15}{300 \times 315}\right)$$

So, $$E_a = \frac{1.6094 \times 8.314 \times 300 \times 315}{15}$$

$$E_a = 84297.47 \text{ Joules/mole}$$

**12. (1)** $$\text{Slope} = -\frac{E_a}{R}$$

$$-\frac{10}{5} = -\frac{E_a}{R}$$

$$E_a = 2R$$

**13.** Initial moles of $U^{238} = \dfrac{68 \times 10^{-6}}{238} = x$

Moles of $U^{238}$ decayed in three half-lives $= \dfrac{7}{8}x$

In decay from $U^{238}$ to $Pb^{206}$, each $U^{238}$ atom decays and produces 8 $\alpha$-particles and hence, total number of $\alpha$-particles emitted out

$$= \left(\frac{7}{8}x\right) \times 8 \times N_A$$

$$= 7 \times \frac{68 \times 10^{-6}}{238} \times 6.022 \times 10^{23}$$

$$= 1.204 \times 10^{18}$$

**14. (1,2,3)** Paramagnetic compound (X) are attracted towards magnetic field and the pan is deflected downwards.

While the Diamagnetic compound (X) are repelled by magnetic field and pan is deflected upward.

(1) $X \Rightarrow H_2O \to$ Diamagnetic (correct)

(2) $X \Rightarrow K_4[Fe(CN)_6](s) \to$ Diamagnetic (correct)

Here $Fe^{2+}$ + Strong field ligand $\to 3d^6 \Rightarrow [t_2g^6, eg^0]$

(3) $X \Rightarrow O_2 \to$ Paramagnetic (correct)

Here $O_2(g)$ is paramagnetic due to two-unpaired electrons present in $\pi^*$ (antibonding orbitals).

(4) $X \Rightarrow C_6H_6(l) \to$ Diamagnetic (Incorrect)

It is due to presence of 0 unpaired electrons.

**15. (1)**

$$\underset{\substack{|\\CH_3}}{\overset{\substack{CH_3\\|}}{CH_3 - C}} - Br + NaOH \xrightarrow[\text{(first order)}]{SN^1}$$

$$\underset{\substack{|\\CH_3}}{\overset{\substack{CH_3\\|}}{CH_3 - C}} - OH + NaBr$$

| | | |
|---|---|---|
| $t = 0$ | $P_0$ | $0$ |
| $t$ | $P$ | $P_0 - P$ |

$$\text{rate} = k[\text{$\nwarrow$Br}] \qquad \ln\frac{P_0}{P} = kt$$

$$t_{1/2} = \frac{0.693}{k} \qquad \ln\frac{P}{P_0} = -kt$$

$$\frac{[Q]}{[P]_0} = \frac{[P]_0 - [P]}{[P_0]} = 1 - \frac{[P]}{[P_0]} = 1 - e^{-kt}$$

**16. (1,2,3,4)**

(1) $2Na[Al(OH)_4]_{(aq.)} + CO_2 \to Na_2CO_3 + H_2O + 2Al(OH)_3(\downarrow)$ or $Al_2O_3.2H_2O(\text{ppt})$

(2) Function of $Na_3AlF_6$ is to lower the melting point of electrolyte.

(3) During electrolysis of $Al_2O_3$, the reactions at anode are :

$$[2Al^{3+}(l) + 3O^{2-}(l) \xrightarrow{\text{At anode}} O_2(\text{gas}) + 2e^-]$$

$$C(\text{graphite}) + O_2 \to CO(\uparrow) + CO_2(\uparrow)$$

(4) The steel vessel with a lining of carbon acts as cathode.

**17.** $$\ln\left(\frac{k_1}{k_2}\right) = \frac{E_a}{R}\left[\frac{1}{T_2} - \frac{1}{T_1}\right]$$

$$\ln\left(\frac{60}{40}\right) = \frac{E_a}{8.3}\left[\frac{1}{400} - \frac{1}{300}\right]$$

$$E = 0.4 \times 1200 \times 8.3$$

$$= 3.984 \text{ kJ/mole}$$

**18. (4)** We know that the,

Rate of reaction $(K) = Ae^{-E/RT}$ ...(a)

and, $10^6 K = Ae^{-E_c/RT}$ ...(b)

By dividing equation (b) by (a), we get

$$\frac{10^6.K}{K} = \frac{Ae^{-E_c/RT}}{Ae^{-E/RT}}$$

$$10^6 = e^{(E-E_c)/RT}$$

$$6.\ln 10 = (E - E_c)/RT$$

$$\frac{E-E_c}{RT} = 2.303 \times 6$$

$$E - E_c = 6 \times 2.303 \ RT$$

or $\quad \Delta E_a = E_c - E = -6 \times 2.303 \ RT$

**19.** Work done = Area covered by the diagram

$$= \tfrac{1}{2} \times (\text{sum of parallel sides}) \times \text{height}$$

$$= \tfrac{1}{2} \times (10 + 6) \times 6$$
$$= \tfrac{1}{2} \times 16 \times 6$$
$$= 48 \ J$$

**20. (4)** $\quad K_1 = Ae^{-\dfrac{E_a}{R \times 700}}$

$$K_2 = A \times e^{-\dfrac{(E_a - 30)}{R \times 500}}$$

For same rate

$$K_1 = K_2$$

$$e^{-\dfrac{E_a}{700R}} = e^{-\dfrac{(E_a - 30)}{R \times 500}}$$

$$\frac{E_a}{700R} = \frac{E_a - 30}{R \times 500}$$

$$5E_a = 7E_a - 210$$
$$210 = 2E_a$$
$$E_a = 105 \ kJ/mole$$
$$E_a - 30 = 75$$

**21. (3)** $\quad \log K = \dfrac{-E_a}{2.303 \ RT} + \log A$

According to Arrhenius equation plot of `log K'

Vs. $\dfrac{1}{T}$ is linear with.

$$\text{Slope} = \frac{-E_a}{2.303 \ R}$$

From plot we conclude slop in magnitude as

$$|\text{slope}| : c > a > d > b$$
(magnitude)

$$\therefore \quad E_c > E_a > E_d > E_b$$

**22. (3)** $\mu_A > \mu_B$ and $K_e(B) > K_e(A)$

$Z^- = CH_3 - CH_2 - O^-$ favours substitution over elimination $(K_S > K_e)$ whereas, in case of bulky base $(CH_3)_3CO^-$, elimination is favoured over substitution $(K_e > K_S)$.

**23. (1)** The rate can be expressed as shown below :

$$\text{Rate} = k[A]^x[B]^y$$

The values of concentrations of A and B can be substituted as shown below :

$$0.045 = k[0.05]^x[0.05]^y \quad ...(1)$$
$$0.045 = k[0.05]^x[0.05]^y \quad ...(2)$$

$$0.045 = k[0.05]^x[0.05]^y \quad ...(3)$$

Divide equation (1) by equation (2) :

$$\frac{0.045}{0.090} = \frac{k[0.05]^x[0.05]^y}{k[0.10]^x[0.05]^y}$$

$$\left(\frac{1}{2}\right)^1 = \left(\frac{1}{2}\right)^x$$

$$x = 1$$

Divide equation (2) by equation (3) :

$$\frac{0.090}{0.72} = \frac{k[0.10]^x[0.05]^y}{k[0.20]^x[0.10]^y}$$

$$\frac{1}{8} = \left(\frac{1}{2}\right)^1 \left(\frac{1}{2}\right)^y$$

$$y = 2$$

Therefore, the rate of the reaction is Rate $= k[A][B]^2$.

**24. (4)** The given reaction scheme is $A \xrightarrow{k_1} B \xrightarrow{k_2} C$.

It is given that the rate of formation is zero, i.e., $\dfrac{d[B]}{dt} = 0$

Therefore,

$$\frac{d[B]}{dt} = 0$$

$$k_1[A] - k_2[B] = 0$$

$$[B] = \frac{k_1}{k_2}[A]$$

**25. (1)** The rate law equation of zero order reaction is shown below :

$$[R] = [R]_0 - kt$$

The concentration of reactant decreases with time.

The rate law equation of first order reaction is shown below.

$$\ln[R] = \ln[R]_0 - kt$$

The value $\ln[R]$ decreases with time.

Therefore, the correct order of reaction for the given graphs is shown below :

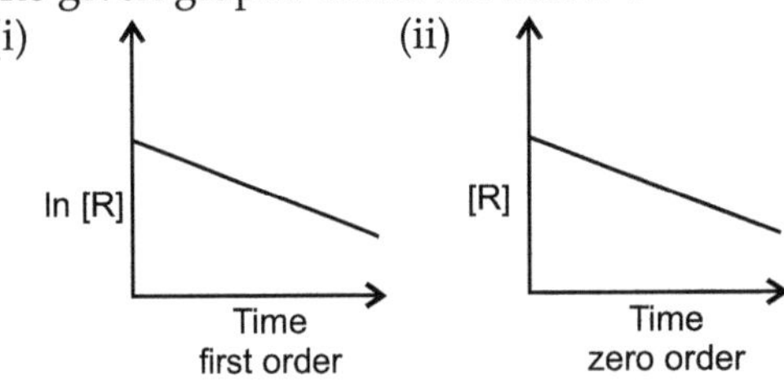


**26. (1)** The activation energy to form C is calculated as shown below :

$$E_A = 20 \ kJ/mol - 5 \ kJ/mol$$
$$= 15 \ kJ/mol$$

The activation energy to form D is calculated as shown below :

$$E_A = 15 \ kJ/mol - 5 \ kJ/mol$$
$$= 10 \ kJ/mol$$

The activation energy to form C is 5 kJ/mol more than the activation energy to form D. Therefore, the statement that activation enthalpy to form C is 5 kJ/mol less than the activation energy to form D is incorrect.

**27. (3)** From $t = 0$ to $t = 1$ h, $N' = N_0 e^t$. Therefore, at $t = 1$ h, $N' = eN_0$.

From $t = 1$ h onwards,

$$\frac{dN}{dT} = -5N^2$$

Integration of the above equation is shown below :

$$\int_{eN_o}^{N} \frac{dN}{N^2} = 5\int_{1}^{t} dT$$

$$\frac{1}{N} - \frac{1}{eN_o} = 5(t-1)$$

$$\frac{N_o}{N} - \frac{1}{e} = 5N_o(t-1)$$

$$\frac{N_o}{N} = 5N_o(t-1) + \frac{1}{e}$$

The above expression is rearranged as shown below :

$$\frac{N_o}{N} = 5N_o(t-1) + \frac{1}{e}$$

$$\frac{N_o}{N} = 5N_o t + \left(\frac{1}{e} - 5N_o\right)$$

The above expression follows the equation for a straight line, that is $y = mx + c$.

Therefore, the plot of $\dfrac{N_o}{N}$ versus time after one hour is shown below :

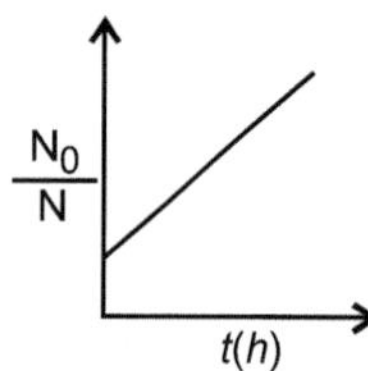

**28. (1)** The formula for most probable velocity is given below :

$$V_{mp} = \sqrt{\frac{2RT}{M}}$$

$$V_{mp} \propto \sqrt{\frac{T}{M}}$$

The values oif most probable velocity for $N_2$, $O_2$ and $H_2$ respectively are shown below :

$$\sqrt{\frac{300}{28}} < \sqrt{\frac{400}{32}} < \sqrt{\frac{300}{2}}$$

$V_{mp}$ $(N_2)$(300 K) $< V_{mp}$ $(O_2)$ (400 K) $< V_{mp}$ $(H_2)$ (300 K).

**29. (1)** The value of activation energy is calculated as shown below :

$$\log\frac{k_2}{k_1} = \frac{E_a}{2.303R}\left(\frac{1}{600} - \frac{1}{800}\right)$$

$$\log\frac{1}{2.5 \times 10^{-4}} = \frac{E_a}{2.303 \times 8.31}\left(\frac{200}{600 \times 800}\right)$$

$$E_a \approx 166 \,kJ/mol$$

**30. (3)** The given equation is shown below :

$$\log_{10}\left[-\frac{d[A]}{dt}\right] = \log_{10}\left[\frac{d[B]}{dt}\right] + 0.3010$$

$$\log_{10}\left[-\frac{d[A]}{dt}\right] = \log_{10}\left[\frac{d[B]}{dt}\right] + \log_{10} 2$$

$$\log_{10}\left[-\frac{d[A]}{dt}\right] = \log_{10}(2)\left[\frac{d[B]}{dt}\right]$$

The above equation can be written as shown below :

$$\left[-\frac{d[A]}{dt}\right] = (2)\left[\frac{d[B]}{dt}\right]$$

$$\frac{1}{2}\left[-\frac{d[A]}{dt}\right] = \left[\frac{d[B]}{dt}\right]$$

Therefore, the coefficient of reactant is 2 and product is 1.

The expected reaction is shown below :

$$2A \rightarrow B$$
$$2C_2H_4 \rightarrow C_4H_8$$

**31. (2)** The chemical reaction is shown below :

$$2N_2O_5(g) \rightarrow 4NO_2(g) + O_2(g)$$

The rate equation for the reaction is shown below :

$$\frac{1}{4}\frac{[\Delta[NO_2]}{\Delta t} = \frac{1}{2}\frac{\Delta[N_2O_5]}{\Delta t}$$

$$\frac{1}{4}\frac{\Delta[NO_2]}{\Delta t} = \frac{1}{2}\frac{(3.00 - 2.75)}{30}$$

$$\frac{\Delta[NO_2]}{\Delta t} = \frac{4}{2}\frac{(3.00 - 2.75)}{30}$$

$$= 1.667 \times 10^{-2} \,mol\,L^{-1}\,min^{-1}$$

The rate of formation of $NO_2$ is $1.667 \times 10^{-2}$

**32.(1, 3, 4)** The formula for $U_{rms}$ is shown below :

$$U_{rms} = \sqrt{\frac{3RT}{M}}$$

and $\quad U_{rms} \propto \dfrac{1}{\sqrt{M}}$

The formula for $e_{av}$ is shown below :

$$e_{av} = \frac{3}{2}RT$$

When the temperature is increased four times, the value of $U_{rms}$ is doubled. The $U_{rms}$ depends inversely on the square root of molar mass. The value of $e_{av}$ does not depend on the molecular mass.

**33.** Rate is given by the expression shown below :
$$\text{Rate} = k[A]^x[B]^y[C]^z$$
The rate expression for experiment (1) is shown below :
$$6 \times 10^{-5} = k[0.2]^x[0.1]^y[0.1]^z \quad ...(1)$$
The rate expression for experiment (2) is shown below :
$$6 \times 10^{-5} = k[0.2]^x[0.2]^y[0.1]^z \quad ...(2)$$
The rate expression for experiment (3) is shown below :
$$1.2 \times 10^{-4} = k[0.2]^x[0.1]^y[0.2]^z \quad ...(3)$$
The rate expression for experiment (4) is shown below :
$$9 \times 10^{-5} = k[0.3]^x[0.1]^y[0.1]^z \quad ...(4)$$
Divide equation (2) by equation (1).
$$\frac{6 \times 10^{-5}}{6 \times 10^{-5}} = \frac{k[0.2]^x[0.2]^y[0.1]^z}{k[0.2]^x[0.1]^y[0.1]^z}$$
$$y = 0$$
Divide equation (3) by equation (1).
$$\frac{1.2 \times 10^{-4}}{6 \times 10^{-5}} = \frac{k[0.2]^x[0.2]^y[0.1]^z}{k[0.2]^x[0.1]^y[0.1]^z}$$
$$z = 1$$
Divide equation (4) by equation (1).
$$\frac{9 \times 10^{-5}}{6 \times 10^{-5}} = \frac{k[0.3]^x[0.1]^y[0.2]^z}{k[0.2]^x[0.1]^y[0.1]^z}$$
$$x = 1$$
Substitute the values of $x$, $y$ and $z$ in equation (1).
$$\text{Rate} = k[0.2]^x[0.1]^y[0.1]^z$$
$$k = 3 \times 10^{-3}$$
The rate is calculated as shown below :
$$\text{Rate} = 3 \times 10^{-3} \times 0.15 \times 0.15$$
$$= 6.75 \times 10^{-5}$$
$$= Y \times 10^{-5}$$
Therefore, the value of Y is 6.75.

**34.** The final pressure are calculated as shown below :
$$2N_2O_5(g) \rightarrow 2N_2O_4(g) + O_2(g)$$

| $t = 0$ | $1$ | $-$ | $-$ |
| $t = t$ | $1 - 2P$ | $2P$ | $P$ |

The total pressure will be calculate as :
$$P_t = 1 - 2P + 2P + P$$
$$1.45 \text{ atm} = 1 + P$$
Rearrange above equation for the value of P
$$P = (1.45 - 1) \text{ atm}$$
$$= 0.45 \text{ atm}$$
The first order rate equation is shown below :
$$t = \frac{1}{2k}\ln\left(\frac{1}{1-2P}\right)$$
$$= \frac{1}{2(5 \times 10^{-4})}\ln\left(\frac{1}{1-2(0.45)}\right)$$
$$= 2.30 \times 10^3$$
Therefore, Y = 2.30.

**35. (1, 4)** The final pressure are calculated as shown below :

$$A \rightarrow 2B + C$$

| $t = 0$ | $P_0$ | $-$ | $-$ |
| $t = t$ | $P_0 - P$ | $2P$ | $P$ |

As,
$$P_t = P_0 - P + 2P + P$$
$$= P_0 + 2P$$
The first order of rate equation is shown below :
$$K = \frac{1}{t}\ln\left(\frac{P_0}{P_0 - P}\right)$$
$$= \frac{1}{t}\ln\left(\frac{P_0}{P_0 - \left(\frac{P_t - P_0}{2}\right)}\right)$$
$$kt = \ln 2P_0 - \ln(3P_0 - P_t)$$
or $\ln(3P_0 - P_t) = \ln 2P_0 - kt$

Graph between $\ln(3P_0 - P_t) = \ln 2P_0 - kt$

Graph between $\ln(3P_0 - P_t)$ Vs $t$ is a straight line with negative slope.
The graph obtained is shown below :

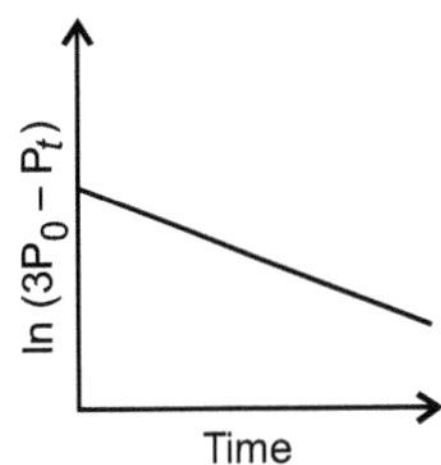


Hence, graph 1 is correct option

Also, as the rate constant is not dependent on the concentration, graph 4 is also correct.

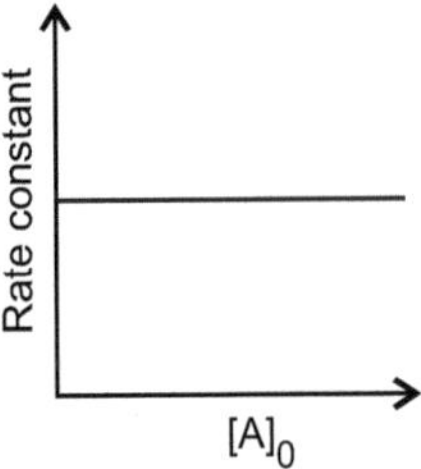


**36. (1)** The order of given reaction is calculated by the formula–
$$\frac{r_1}{r_2} = \left[\frac{[CH_3CHO]_1}{[CH_3CHO]_2}\right]^m$$

$$r_1 = 1 \text{ torr/sec}$$
when 5% reacted (95% unreacted)
$$r_2 = 0.5 \text{ torr/sec}$$
when 33% reacted (67% unreacted),
$$m = \text{order of reaction,}$$

$$\frac{1.00}{0.5} = \left[\frac{0.95}{0.67}\right]^m$$

$$2 = 1.14 = (\sqrt{2})^m$$

$$m = 2$$

Therefore, the given reaction is a second order reaction.

**37. (3)** The half life $t_{1/2} = 10$ days

The decay constant

$$k = \frac{0.693}{t_{1/2}}$$

$$= \frac{0.693}{10 \text{ days}}$$

$$= 0.0693 \text{ days}^{-1}$$

The time required for one-fourth conversion is :

$$t = \frac{2.303}{k}\log_{10}\frac{a}{a-x}$$

$$= \frac{2.303}{0.0693 \text{ day}^{-1}}\log_{10}\frac{1}{1-(1/4)}$$

$$= 4.1 \text{ days}$$

The time required for one-fourth conversion is 4.1 days.

**38. (4)** The decomposition of $N_2O_5$ is,

$$N_2O_5 \rightleftharpoons 2NO_2 + \frac{1}{2}O_2$$

| | | | |
|---|---|---|---|
| $t = 0$ : | 50 | 0 | 0 |
| $t = 50$ : | $50 - x$ | $2x$ | $\frac{x}{2}$ |
| $t = 100$ : | $50 - x_1$ | $2x_1$ | $\frac{x_1}{2}$ |

Therefore,

$$87.5 = 50 - x + 2x + \frac{x}{2}$$

$$87.5 = 50 + \frac{3x}{2}$$

$$\frac{3x}{2} = 37.5$$

$$x = 25$$

Thus,

$$50 - x = 25 \text{ and } 50 - x_1 = 12.5$$

Since, 50 min is the half life period and for 100 min,

$$50 - x_1 = 12.5$$

$$x_1 = 37.5 \text{ mm of Hg}$$

The total pressure at 100 min is,

$$= 50 - x_1 + 2x_1 + \frac{x_1}{2}$$

$$= 50 + \frac{3x_1}{2}$$

$$= 50 + 56.25$$

$$= 106.25 \text{ mm of Hg}$$

**39. (2)** Let the initial concentration of reactant is 1 M.

The concentration of reactant is reduced to 50% in the first 100 s.

$$= 1 \times \frac{50}{100}$$

$$= 0.5 \text{ M}$$

Similarly, in the next 100 s, the concentration of reactant is reduced to 25%.

$$= 1 \times \frac{25}{100}$$

$$= 0.025 \text{ M}$$

Thus, we can observe from the above calculation that after each 100s, the concentration of reactant is reduced to one half. As 100 seconds is the half-life period and is independent of reactant concentration. Hence, it is the first order reaction.

**40. (1, 2)** Given, $\rho = 4.5$

$$\therefore \qquad \rho > 1$$

We know, $\dfrac{K_{exp}}{K_{collision}} = \rho$

$$K_{exp} = \rho A e^{\frac{-E_a}{RT}}$$

$$A_{exp} = \rho A$$

$$\therefore \qquad A_{exp} > A$$

According to above equation, experimentaly determine value of frequency factor is higher than that predicted by Arrhenius equation. Therefore, option 2 is correct.

In this equation, $K_{exp} = \rho A e^{\frac{-E_a}{RT}}$

The value of $E_a$ is not changed, it means that the activation energy of the reaction is unaffected by the value of the steric factor. Hence, option 1 is correct.

**41. (2)** The rate constant for reaction is :

$$k_1 = Ae^{-E_{a_1}/RT}$$

The rate constant for reaction (2) is

$$k_2 = Ae^{-E_{a_2}/RT}$$

Therefore,

$$\frac{k_2}{k_1} = e^{\frac{1}{RT}(E_{a_1} - E_{a_2})}$$

$$\ln\frac{k_2}{k_1} = \frac{E_{a_1} - E_{a_2}}{RT}$$

$$\ln\frac{k_2}{k_1} = \frac{((E_{a_2}+10) - E_{a_2})\times 10^3}{RT}$$

$$\ln\frac{k_2}{k_1} = \frac{10\times 10^3}{8.314\times 300}$$

$$\ln\frac{k_2}{k_1} = 4$$

**42. (2)** For reaction A,

$$\log\frac{K_2}{K_1} = \frac{E_a}{2.303R}\left[\frac{1}{T_1} - \frac{1}{T_2}\right]$$

$$\log 2 = \frac{E_a}{2.303R}\left[\frac{1}{300} - \frac{1}{310}\right] \qquad ...(1)$$

For reaction B,

$$\log 2 = \frac{E_a}{2.303R}\left[\frac{1}{300} - \frac{1}{T_2}\right] \qquad ...(2)$$

Equate both the equations.

$$\frac{E_a}{2.303R}\left[\frac{1}{300} - \frac{1}{310}\right] = \frac{E_a}{2.303R}\left[\frac{1}{300} - \frac{1}{T_2}\right]$$

$$2\left[\frac{1}{300} - \frac{1}{T_2}\right] = \frac{310 - 300}{300\times 310}$$

$$T_2 = 304.92 \text{ K}$$

Thus, the change in temperature is shown as follows :

$$\Delta T = 304.92 \text{ K} - 300 \text{ K}$$
$$= 4.92 \text{ K}$$

**43. (1)** The rate of reaction quadruples on changing temperature.
The value of ln 2 is 0.693.
The activation energy is calculated by the formula,

$$\text{Rate of reaction} = e^{\frac{E_a}{R}\left(\frac{T_2 - T_1}{T_1\times T_2}\right)}$$

Rearrange the above expression.

$$\ln(\text{Rate of reaction}) = \frac{E_a}{R}\left(\frac{T_2 - T_1}{T_1\times T_2}\right)$$

$$E_a = \frac{\ln(\text{Rate of reaction})\times R \times T_1\times T_2}{\Delta T}$$

$$E_a = \frac{2\times (\ln 2)\times R\times T_1\times T_2}{\Delta T}$$

$$= \frac{2\times 0.693\times 8.314\times 300\times 310}{10}$$

$$= 107165.79 \text{ J.mol}^{-1}$$

$$= 107.165 \text{ KJ.mol}^{-1}$$

**44. (2, 3, 4)** (1) High activation energy usually implies a slow reaction.
So, statement A is incorrect.

**(2)** The Arrhenius equation is

$$k = Ae^{-E_a/RT}$$

The rate constant increases with increase in temperature because number of collision increases with increase in temperature.
So, statement 2 is correct.

**(3)**

$$k = Ae^{-E_a/RT}$$

$$\frac{dk}{dT} = A\frac{E_a}{RT}$$

$$\frac{dk}{dT} \propto E_a$$

If the magnitude of activation is higher; stronger is the temperature dependence of the rate constant.
So, statement 3 is correct.

**(4)** In the Arrhenius equation, frequency factor increases when number of collisions per unit volume increases. Thus, pre-exponential factor is the measure of the rate at which collisions occur.

So, statement 4 is correct.

**45. (4)** The addition of equation (i) and (ii) results in the following reaction.

$$O_3(g) + O\bullet(g) \rightarrow 2O_2(g)$$

Thus, the overall value of rate constant is,

$$K_{\text{overall}} = k_i \times k_{ii}$$

$$= 5.2\times 10^9 \times 2.6\times 10^{10}$$

$$= 1.325\times 10^{20}$$

$$\approx 1.4\times 10^{20} \text{ L mol}^{-1}\text{s}^{-1}$$

**46. (1)** On changing the concentration, the rate of reaction changes but rate constant remains same. Therefore, rate constant for the given reaction is $k$.

**47. (2)** The decomposition of $H_2O_2$ is shown below :

$$H_2O_2 \rightarrow H_2O = \frac{1}{2}O_2$$

The first order equation is shown below :

$$k = \frac{1}{t}\times 2.303\log\frac{A_0}{A}$$

$$= \frac{1}{50 \text{ min}}2.303\log\frac{0.5}{0.125}$$

$$= 0.0277 \text{ min}^{-1}$$

Rate of decomposition of $H_2O_2$
$$= 2 \times \text{Rate of formation of } O_2$$

$$= \frac{1}{2}\times k[H_2O_2]$$

$$= \frac{1}{2} \times 0.0277[0.05]$$

$$= 6.93 \times 10^{-4} \text{ mol min}^{-1}.$$

**48. (1)** There is low probability of simultaneous collision of all the reacting species. Thus, the higher order reactions (> 3) are rare.

**49. (2)** The catalyst $TiCl_3$ is used for Ziegler - Natta polymerization.

The catalyst $PdCl_2$ is used for the Wacker process. This process is an industrial process which allows the synthesis of ethanol from ethane in the presence of $PdCl_2$.

The catalyst $CuCl_2$ is used for Deacon's process. In this process, hydrogen chloride gas is oxidized by atmospheric oxygen in the presence of $CuCl_2$ catalyst at 723 K.

The catalyst $V_2O_5$ is used for the Contact process. It is an industrial method which is used for producing sulphuric acid in the presence of catalyst $V_2O_5$.

**50. (1)** The pressure of each gas at initial and final temperature is,

$$2N_2O_5(g) \rightarrow 4NO_2(g) + O_2(g)$$

| | | | |
|---|---|---|---|
| $t = 0$ | 50 | 0 | 0 |
| $t = 30$ min | $50 - 2x$ | $4x$ | $x$ |

The final pressure is 87.5 mm Hg.

The value of $x$ is,

$$3x = 87.5 - 50$$

$$x = \frac{37.5}{3}$$

$$= 12.5 \text{ mm Hg}$$

The pressure of $N_2O_5$ after 30 min is $= 50 - 25$

$$= 25 \text{ torr}$$

The pressure of $N_2O_5$ after two half lives (60 min) is $= \dfrac{50}{4} = 12.5$ torr

The decrease in pressure of $N_2O_5$ after two half lives (60 min) is $= 50 - 12.5$

$$= 37.5 \text{ torr}$$

The pressure of $NO_2$ is $= 2 \times 37.5$

$$= 75 \text{ torr}$$

The pressure of $O_2$ is $= \dfrac{37.5}{3}$

$$= 18.75 \text{ torr}$$

The total pressure exerted by solution is

$$P_T = 12.5 + 75 + 18.75$$

$$= 106.25 \text{ torr}$$

**51. (3)** The rate of reaction is first order with respect to B in the given reaction. Thus, the rate will be doubled on doubling concentration of B and same concentration of A.

**52. (2)** The given reaction is $M \rightarrow N$

The rate of the reaction is given by expression,

$$\text{Rate} = k[M]^n$$

On doubling the concentration of M, the rate of disappearance of M increases by a factor of 8. Therefore, the rate of the reaction becomes,

$$r_1 = k[M]^n \qquad \qquad ...(1)$$

$$8r_1 = k[2M]^n \qquad \qquad ...(2)$$

$$\frac{1}{8} = \left(\frac{1}{2}\right)^n$$

$$\left(\frac{1}{2}\right)^3 = \left(\frac{1}{2}\right)^n$$

$$n = 3$$

**53. (4)** The rate law equation for the formation of C is given as,

$$\frac{dC}{dT} = k[A]^x[B]^y$$

For first experiment,

$$1.2 \times 10^{-3} = k[0.1]^x[0.1]^y \qquad ...(1)$$

For second experiment,

$$1.2 \times 10^{-3} = k[0.1]^x[0.2]^y \qquad ...(2)$$

For third experiement,

$$2.4 \times 10^{-3} = k[0.2]^x[0.1]^y \qquad ...(3)$$

Divide equation (1) by (3) to calculate the value of $x$.

$$\frac{1.2 \times 10^{-3}}{2.4 \times 10^{-3}} = \frac{k[0.1]^x[0.1]^y}{k[0.2]^x[0.1]^y}$$

$$x = 1$$

Divide equation (1) by (2) to calculate the value of $y$.

$$\frac{1.2 \times 10^{-3}}{1.2 \times 10^{-3}} = \frac{k[0.1]^x[0.1]^y}{k[0.1]^x[0.2]^y}$$

$$1 = \left(\frac{1}{2}\right)^y$$

$$y = 0$$

Therefore,

$$\frac{dC}{dT} = k[A]^x[B]^y$$

$$\frac{dC}{dT} = k[A]^1[B]^0$$

$$\frac{dC}{dT} = k[A]^1$$

**54. (3)** For the given first order reaction, $t_{1/2} = 15$ min.

Thus, the total number of half-life is,

$$= \frac{60}{15}$$

$$= 4$$

The amount of substance left after one hour is,

$$= \frac{A_0}{(2)^n}$$

$$= \frac{A_0}{(2)^4}$$

$$= \frac{A_0}{16}$$

Thus, the amount of substance is 1/16 of the original amount.

**55. (4)** The rate of reaction in terms of $[SO_2]$ in mol $L^{-1}$ $s^{-1}$ is,

$$-\frac{1}{2}\frac{d}{dt}[SO_2] = -\frac{d}{dt}[O_2]$$

$$\frac{d}{dt}[SO_2] = -2 \times 2.5 \times 10^{-4} \text{ mol } L^{-1} s^{-1}$$

$$= -5 \times 10^{-4} \text{ mol } L^{-1} s^{-1}$$

**56. (2)** It is given that rate equation is expressed in two ways :

$$-\frac{d[N_2O_5]}{dt} = k[N_2O_5] \qquad \ldots(1)$$

$$\frac{d[NO_2]}{dt} = k'[N_2O_5] \qquad \ldots(2)$$

The rate equation is expressed as,

$$-\frac{d}{dt}[N_2O_5] = k'[N_2O_5]$$

For the given reaction,

$$-\frac{1}{2}\frac{d}{dt}[N_2O_5] = \frac{1}{4}k'[N_2O_5]$$

$$2k = k'$$

**57. (2)** The activation energy of the given reaction is calculated by the formula,

$$\ln\left(\frac{k_1}{k_2}\right) = \left(\frac{E_a}{R}\right)\left(\frac{1}{T_2} - \frac{1}{T_1}\right)$$

$$\ln\left(\frac{1.3 \times 10^{-4} M^{-1}s^{-1}}{1.3 \times 10^{-4} M^{-1}s^{-1}}\right) = \left(\frac{E_a}{8.314 \text{ J/mol.K}}\right)$$

$$\left(\frac{1}{423 \text{ K}} - \frac{1}{373 \text{ K}}\right)$$

$$E_a = -26235.5 \times \ln\left(\frac{1.3 \times 10^{-4} M^{-1}s^{-1}}{1.3 \times 10^{-3} M^{-1}s^{-1}}\right)$$

$$E_a = 60409 \text{ J/mol } (= 60.4 \text{ kJ/mol})$$

**58. (4)** Rate of the given reaction is expressed as,

$$\text{Rate} = -\frac{1}{3}\frac{d[A]}{dt} = -\frac{1}{2}\frac{d[B]}{dt}$$

$$= \frac{d[C]}{dt} = \frac{d[D]}{dt}$$

Also,

$$\text{Rate} = k[A]^n[B]^m$$

Compare both equations.

$$-\frac{1}{3}\frac{d[A]}{dt} = -\frac{1}{2}\frac{d[B]}{dt} = \frac{d[C]}{dt}$$

$$= \frac{d[D]}{dt} = k[A]^n[B]^m$$

$$-\frac{1}{3}\frac{d[A]}{dt} = \frac{d[C]}{dt} = k[A]^n[B]^m$$

**59. (4)** For P, if $t_{50\%} = x$

then $t_{75\%} = 2x$

This is true only for first order reaction. So, order with respect to P is 1.

Further the graph shows that concentration of Q decreases with time. So rate, with respect to Q, remains constant. Hence, it is zero order wrt Q.

So, overall order is $1 + 0 = 1$

**60.**

$$t = \frac{2.303}{k}\log\left(\frac{a}{a-x}\right)$$

For decomposition to 1/8 of its initial concentration

$$t_{1/8} = \frac{2.303}{k}\log\left(\frac{1}{1/8}\right) = \frac{2.08}{k}$$

For decomposition to 1/10 of its initial concentration

$$t_{1/10} = \frac{2.303}{k}\log\left(\frac{1}{1/10}\right) = \frac{2.303}{k}$$

Hence, $\dfrac{[t_{1/8}]}{[t_{1/10}]} \times 10 = \dfrac{\frac{2.08}{k}}{\frac{2.303}{k}} \times 10 = 9$

**61. (1,2,4)** For the given first order reaction, the integrated rate equation is given as,

$$[A] = [A]e^{-kt}$$

From the above equation, it is clear that as the concentration of reactant decreases, concentration of product increase. For first order reaction it always decreases exponentially with time and becomes zero at infinity.

Half-life for first order reaction is given as,

$$t_{1/2} = \frac{0.693}{k} \qquad \ldots(1)$$

From the above equation, it is clear that half-life is independent of concentration and it decreases as the temperature increases.

For the completion of 99.6% reaction, the time duration is calculated as,

$$t_{99.6} = \frac{2.303}{k} \log \frac{100}{100 - 99.6}$$

$$= \frac{2.303}{k}(2.4) \qquad ...(2)$$

Divide equation 2 by 1.

$$\frac{t_{99.6}}{t_{1/2}} = \frac{\dfrac{2.303}{k}(2.4)}{\dfrac{0.693}{k}}$$

$$= 7.976$$
$$\approx 8$$

**62. (1)** The Arrhenius equation is,

$$k = Ae^{-E_a/RT}$$

As the temperature increases, the rate constant of reaction increases exponentially.

**63.** The intetraged law for zero order reaction :

$$[R]_0 - [R]_t = kt$$

Substitute the value in the above equation.

$$1 - 0.75 = k(0.05)$$
$$k = 5$$
$$1 - 0.4 = k(0.2)$$
$$k = 5$$

The value of rate constant does not change with concentration. So, it is zero order reaction.

**64. (4)** The Arrhenius equation is,

$$\log k = -\frac{E_a}{2.303R} \frac{1}{T} + \log A \quad ...(1)$$

The given expression of rate constant is,

$$\ln k = -(2000)\frac{1}{T} + 6.0 \qquad ...(2)$$

The value of $E_a$ is calculated by comparing the equations (1) and (2)

$$\frac{E_a}{2.303R} = 2000$$

$$E_a = 2000 \times 2.303 \times 8.314 \text{ J/molK}$$
$$= 38294 \text{ J/mol}$$
$$= 38.29 \text{ JK/mol} \approx 383. \text{ kJ/mol}$$

The value of A is calculated as,

$$\log A = 6.0$$
$$A = \text{antilog } (6.0)$$
$$= 1.0 \times 10^6 \text{ s}^{-1}$$

**65. (1)** The relation between rate constant of first order reaction and half life is given as,

$$k_1 = \frac{0.693}{t_{1/2}}$$

Substitute $t_{1/2}$ = 40 s in the above equation.

$$k_1 = \frac{0.693}{40 \text{ s}}$$
$$= 0.017325 \text{ s}^{-1}$$

The relation between rate constant, initial concentration and half-life of zero order reaction is given as,

$$k_0 = \frac{A_0}{2t_{1/2}}$$

Substitute $A_0 = 1.386$ mol dm$^{-3}$ and $t_{1/2} = 20$ s in the above equation.

$$k_0 = \frac{1.386 \text{ mol dm}^{-3}}{2 \times 20 \text{ s}}$$
$$= 0.03465 \text{ mol dm}^{-3} \text{ s}^{-1}$$

The ratio of rate constant of first order and zero order is,

$$\frac{k_1}{k_0} = \frac{0.017325 \text{ s}^{-1}}{0.03465 \text{ mol dm}^{-3} \text{ s}^{-1}}$$
$$= 0.5 \text{ mol}^{-1} \text{ dm}^3$$

**66. (4)** The given reaction is,

$$aG + bH \rightarrow \text{Products}$$

Rate of the above reaction is $\propto [G]^a[H]^b$

When,

$a = 1, b = 2$

The overall order of reaction becomes 3.

**67. (a)** The given equation is,

$$2X_{(g)} \rightarrow 2Y_{(g)} + 2Z_{(g)}$$

The given data for time and partial pressure is given in the table below.

| Time (in Min) | 0 | 100 | 200 |
|---|---|---|---|
| Partial pressure of X (in mm of Hg) | 800 | 400 | 200 |

According to this given data, the value of $t_{1/2}$ of the X remains constant at 100 min.

Thus, the order of the reaction is first.

**(b)** The value of $t_{1/2}$ for the given first order reaction is 100 min.

The formula to calculate the rate constant, K is,

$$K = \frac{0.693}{t_{1/2}}$$

Substitute the value of $t_{1/2}$ in the above expression.

$$K = \frac{0.693}{100 \text{ min}}$$

$$= 6.93 \times 10^{-3} \text{ min}^{-1}$$

Thus, the value of rate constant for the given reaction is $6.93 \times 10^{-3}$ min$^{-1}$.

(c) The time taken by the reaction for 75% completion is calculated by $2t_{1/2}$. Thus, the time taken by the given reaction for 75% completion is $2 \times 100$ min = 200 min.

(d) According to the given reaction,

$$2X(g) \rightarrow 2Y(g) + 2Z(g)$$

Initial pressure $\quad 800 \qquad 0 \qquad 0$

At $\qquad\qquad 800 - x \qquad \dfrac{3}{2}x \qquad x$

time $t$

The given partial pressure is 700 mm.

Thus, according to the above given data, $800 - x$ is equal to 700 mm. Thus,

$$800 - x = 700$$

$$x = 100 \text{ mm}$$

If $x$ = 100 mm, then, $\dfrac{3}{2} \times 100$ = 150 mm.

Therefore, the total pressure is,

Total pressure = 700 mm + 100 mm + 150 mm

$$= 950 \text{ mm}$$

Thus, the total pressure is 950 mm.

**68. (4)** Generally, the order of reaction is predicted by the experimental ways. Thus, the value of order of reaction can be fractional in nature.

Thus, the statement given in option (4) is incorrect about the order of reaction.

**69. (1)** Let the order corresponding to A and B are $m$ and $n$.

Therefore,

$$\text{Rate} = K[A]^m[B]^n$$

Thus, for A,

$$0.05 = K[0.1]^m[0.1]^n$$

$$0.1 = K[0.2]^m[0.1]^n \qquad ...(1)$$

On solving equation (1),

$$2 = [2]^m$$

$$m = 1$$

Similarly, for B is,

$$0.05 = K[0.1]^m[0.1]^n$$

$$0.05 = K[0.1]^m[0.2]^n \qquad ...(2)$$

On solving equation (2),

$$1 = [2]^n$$

$$n = 0$$

The rate of reaction for the given reaction is,

$$\text{Rate} = K[A][B]^0$$

(2) The value of rate constant is,

$$\text{Rate} = K[A][B]^0$$

$$0.1 = K[0.2][0.1]^0$$

$$0.1 = K[0.2]$$

$$K = 0.5 \text{ sec}^{-1}$$

**70. (1)** The concentration of reactant changes from 0.1 M to 0.025 M in 40 minutes. Hence, half-life of the reaction is,

$$t_{1/2} = \frac{40}{2}$$

$$= 20 \text{ minutes}$$

The rate of reaction is,

$$r = k[A]$$

$$= \frac{0.693}{20} \times 0.01$$

$$= 3.47 \times 10^{-4} \text{ M min}^{-1}$$

**71. (3)** The rate of first order reaction is calculated by the formula,

$$K = \frac{2.303}{t} \log \frac{[A]_0}{[A]_1}$$

Substitute the values of $t$, $[A]_0$ and $[A]_1$ in the above formula.

$$K = \frac{2.303}{2 \times 10^4} \log \frac{800}{50}$$

$$= 1.386 \times 10^4 \text{ s}^{-1}$$

**72. (1)** The chemical reaction is shown below :

$$N_2(g) + 3H_2(g) \rightarrow 2NH_3(g)$$

The rate expression of above reaction in terms of time derivative of concentration of reactants and product is shown below.

$$\text{Rate} = \frac{-d[N_2]}{dt} = \frac{-1}{3}\frac{d[H_2]}{dt}$$

$$= \frac{1}{2}\frac{d[NH_3]}{dt}$$

The sign of reactants and product are negative and positive respectively because reactants are consumed during the reaction to form product.

●●

## ❓ QUESTIONS

1. Which of the following is used for the preparation of colloids ? **[2020, Main]**
   (1) Ostwald process
   (2) Van Arkel Method
   (3) Bredig's Arc Method
   (4) Mond Process

2. The mass of gas absorbed, $x$, per unit mass of adsorbate, $m$, was measured at various pressures, $p$. A graph between $\log \dfrac{x}{m}$ and $\log p$ gives a straight line with slope equal to 2 and the intercept equal to 0.4771. The value of $\dfrac{x}{m}$ at a pressure of 4 atm is : (Given $\log 3 = 0.4771$) **[2020, Main]**

3. Amongst the following statements regarding adsorption, those that are valid are : **[2020, Main]**
   (a) $\Delta H$ becomes less negative as adsorption proceeds
   (b) On a given adsorbent, ammonia is adsorbed more than nitrogen gas
   (c) On adsorption, the residual force acting along the surface of the adsorbent increases
   (d) With increase in temperature, the equilibrium concentration of adsorbate increases
   (1) (b) and (c)     (2) (a) and (b)
   (3) (d) and (a)     (4) (c) and (d)

4. Match the type of interaction in Column A with the distance dependence of their interaction energy in Column B : **[2020, Main]**

   | A | B |
   |---|---|
   | (I) Ion-ion | (a) $\dfrac{1}{r}$ |
   | (II) Dipole-dipole | (b) $\dfrac{1}{r^2}$ |
   | (III) London dispersion | (c) $\dfrac{1}{r^3}$ |
   | | (d) $\dfrac{1}{r^6}$ |

   (1) (I)-(a), (II)-(b), (III)-(c)
   (2) (I)-(a), (II)-(c), (III)-(d)
   (3) (I)-(a), (II)-(b), (III)-(d)
   (4) (I)-(b), (II)-(d), (III)-(c)

5. Tyndall effect of observed when : **[2020, Main]**
   (1) The diameter of dispersed particles is much smaller than the wavelength of light used
   (2) The diameter of dispersed particles is much larger than the wavelength of light used
   (3) The diameter of dispersed particles is similar to the wavelength of light used
   (4) The refractive index of dispersed phase is greater than that of the dispersion medium

6. Thermal power plants can lead to : **[2020, Main]**
   (1) Ozone layer depletion
   (2) Eutrophication
   (3) Acid rain
   (4) Blue baby syndrome

7. An ionic micelle is formed on the addition of : **[2020, Main]**
   (1) excess water to liquid
   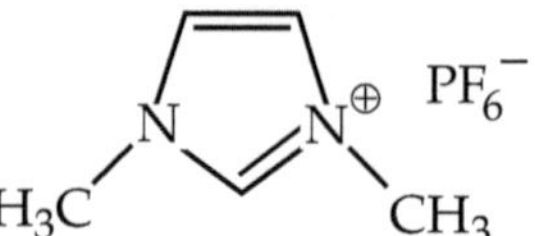
   (2) excess water to liquid
   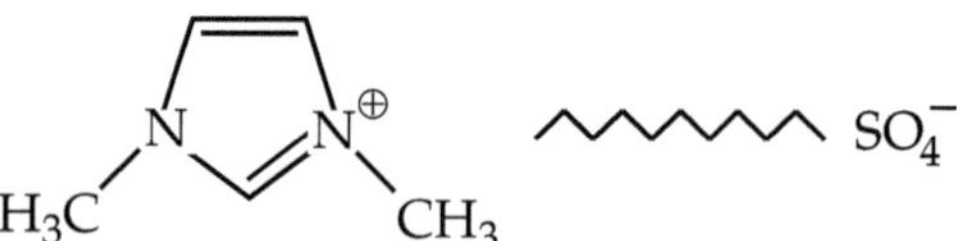
   (3) liquid diethyl ether to aqueous NaCl solution
   (4) sodium stearate to pure toluene

8. Match the following : **[2020, Main]**

   | | | | |
   |---|---|---|---|
   | (i) Foam | | (a) smoke |
   | (ii) Gel | | (b) cell fluid |
   | (iii) Aerosol | | (c) jellies |
   | (iv) Emulsion | | (d) rubber |
   | | | (e) froth |
   | | | (f) milk |

   (1) (i)-(b), (ii)-(c), (iii)-(e), (iv)-(d)
   (2) (i)-(d), (ii)-(b), (iii)-(e), (iv)-(f)
   (3) (i)-(e), (ii)-(c), (iii)-(a), (iv)-(f)
   (4) (i)-(d), (ii)-(b), (iii)-(a), (iv)-(e)

**9.** For Freundlich adsorption isotherm, a plot of log $(x/m)$ ($y$-axis) and log $p$ ($x$-axis) gives a straight line. The intercept and slope for the line is 0.4771 and 2, respectively. The mass of gas, adsorbed per gram of adsorbent if the initial pressure is 0.04 atm, is ............ $\times 10^{-4}$ g.

(log 3 = 0.4771) **[2020, Main]**

**10.** Identify the correct molecular picture showing that happens at the critical micellar concentration (CMC) of an aqueous solution of a surfactant (o polar head; ~ non-polar tail; • water).

**[2020, Main]**

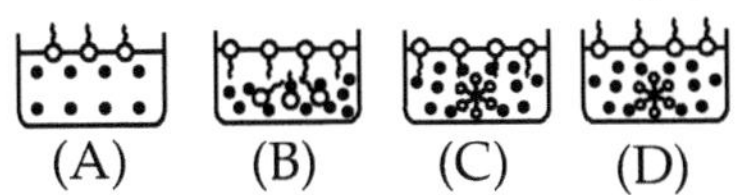

(A)  (B)  (C)  (D)

(1) (B)      (2) (A)

(3) (D)      (4) (C)

**11.** Kraft temperature is the temperature :

**[2020, Main]**

(1) below which the formation of micelles takes place

(2) below which the aqueous solution of detergents starts freezing

(3) above which the formation of micelles takes place

(4) above which the aqueous solution of detergents starts boiling

**12.** A sample of red ink (a colloidal suspension) is prepared by mixing eosin dye, egg white, HCHO and water. The component which ensures stability of the ink sample is : **[2020, Main]**

(1) HCHO     (2) Eosin dye

(3) Egg white    (4) Water

**13.** Adsorption of a gas follows Freundlich adsorption isotherm. If $x$ is the mass of the gas adsorbed on mass $m$ of the adsorbent, the correct plot of $\dfrac{x}{m}$ versus $p$ is : **[2020, Main]**

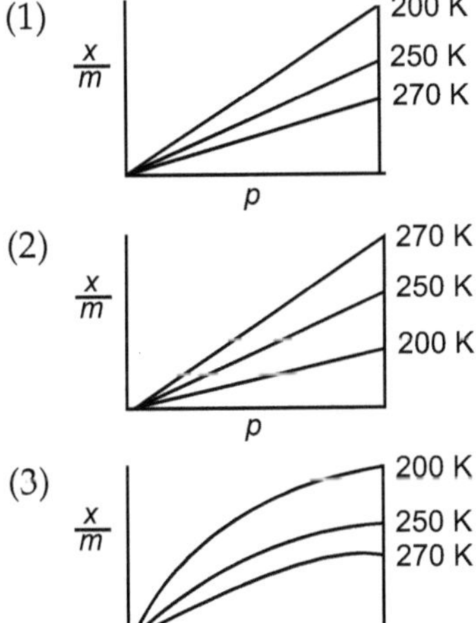

**14.** Consider the following reaction :

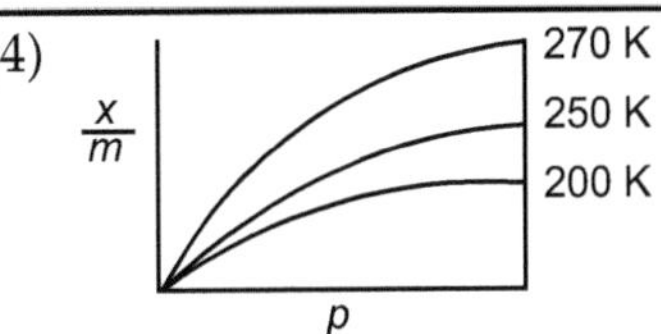

The product 'X' is used : **[2020, Main]**

(1) in acid base titration as an indicator

(2) in protein estimation as an alternative to ninydrin

(3) in laboratory test for phenols

(4) as food grade colourant

**15.** A mixture of gases $O_2$, $H_2$ and CO are taken in a losed vessel containing charcoal. The graph that represents the correct behaviour of pressure with time is : **[2020, Main]**

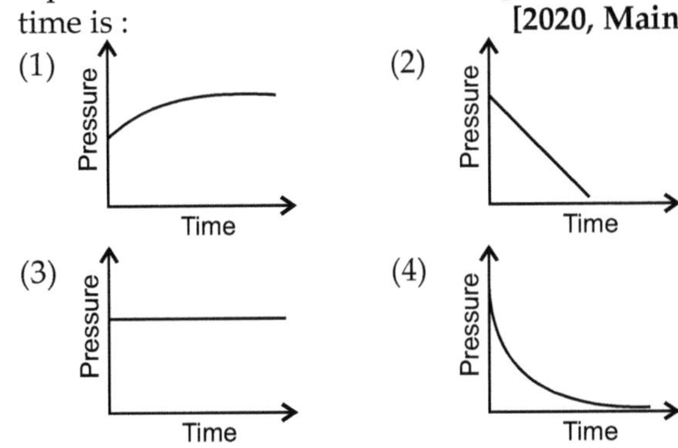

**16.** The flocculation value of HCl for arsenic sulphide sol. is 30 m mol $L^{-1}$. If $H_2SO_4$ is used for the flocculation of arsenic sulphide, the amount, in grams, of $H_2SO_4$ in 250 ml required for the above purpose is ............ **[2020, Main]**

(molecular mass of $H_2SO_4$ = 98 g/mol)

**17.** Adsorption of a gas follows Freundlich adsorption isotherm. $x$ is the mass of the gas adsorbed on mass $m$ of the adsorbent. The plot of $\log \dfrac{x}{m}$ versus log p is shown in the given graph. $\dfrac{x}{m}$ is proportional to : **[2019, Main]**

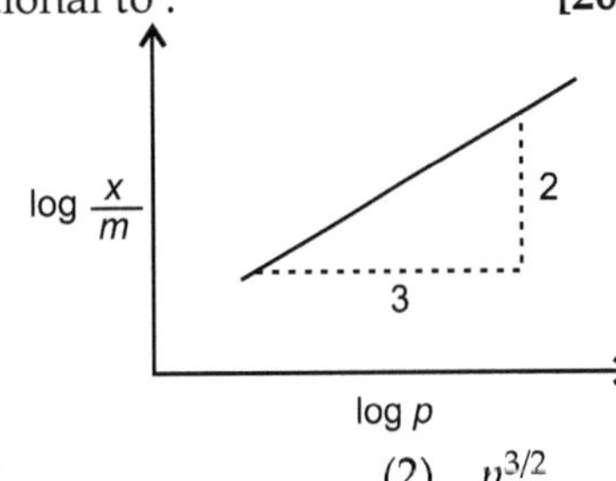

(1) $p^{2/3}$     (2) $p^{3/2}$

(3) $p^3$      (4) $p^2$

**18.** With respect to an i ore, Ellingham diagram helps to predict the feasibility of its : **[2019, Main]**

(1) Electrolysis

(2) Zone refining

(3) Vapour phase refining

(4) Thermal reduction

**19.** The aerosol is a kind of colloid in which :

**[2019, Main]**

(1) solid is dispersed in gas

(2) gas is dispersed in solid

(3) gas is dispersed in liquid

(4) liquid is dispersed in water

**20.** 10 mL of 1 mM surfactant solution forms a monolayer covering $0.24 \text{ cm}^2$ on a polar substrate. If the polar head is approximated as a cube, what is its edge length ? **[2019, Main]**

(1) 1.0 pm      (2) 2.0 pm

(3) 0.1 nm      (4) 2.0 nm

**21.** A gas undergoes physical adsorption on a surface and follows the given Freundlich adsorption isotherm equation

$$\frac{x}{m} = kp^{0.5}$$

Adsorption of the gas increases with :

**[2019, Main]**

(1) Decrease in $p$ and increase in T

(2) Decrease in $p$ and decrease in T

(3) Increase in $p$ and decrease in T

(4) Increase in $p$ and increase in T

**22.** The correct option among the following is :

**[2019, Main]**

(1) Colloidal medicines are more effective because they have small surface area.

(2) Addition of alum to water makes it unfit for drinking.

(3) Colloidal particles in lyophobic sols can be precipitated by electrophoresis.

(4) Brownian motion in colloidal solution is faster if the viscosity of the solution is very high.

**23.** Consider the following reactions : **[2019, Main]**

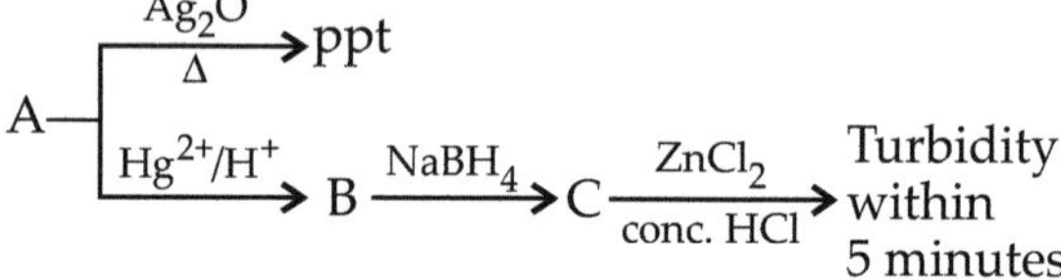

(1) $CH \equiv CH$

(2) $CH_3 - C \equiv C - CH_3$

(3) $CH_3 - C \equiv CH$

(4) $CH_2 = CH_2$

**24.** Among the following, the **INCORRECT** statement about colloids is : **[2019, Main]**

(1) They can scatter light.

(2) They are larger than small molecules and have high molar mass.

(3) The osmotic pressure of a colloidal solution is of higher order than the true solution at the same concentration.

(4) The range of diameters of colloidal particles is between 1 and 1000 nm.

**25.** Calamine, malachite, magnetite and cryolite, respectively, are : **[2019, Main]**

(1) $ZnSO_4$, $CuCO_3$, $Fe_2O_3$, $AlF_3$

(2) $ZnSO_4$, $Cu)OH)_2$, $Fe_3O_4$, $Na_3AlF_6$

(3) $ZnCO_3$, $CuCO_3.Cu(OH)_2$, $Fe_3O_4$, $Na_3AlF_6$

(4) $ZnCO_3$, $CuCO_3$, $Fe_2O_3$, $Na_3AlF_6$

**26.** If $x$ gram of gas is adsorbed by m gram of adsorbent at pressure P, the plot of $\log \dfrac{x}{m}$ versus $\log P$ is linear. The slope of the plot is : ($n$ and $k$ are constants and $n > 1$) **[2018, Main]**

(1) $2k$      (2) $\log k$

(3) $n$      (4) $\dfrac{1}{n}$

**27.** Which of the following statements about colloids is **False** ? **[2018, Main]**

(1) Freezing point of colloidal solution is lower than true solution at same concentration of a solute.

(2) Colloidal particles can pass through ordinary filter paper.

(3) When silver nitrate solution is added to potassium iodide solution, a negatively charged colloidal solution is formed.

(4) When excess of electrolyte is added to colloidal solution, colloidal particle will be precipitated.

**28.** Which one of the following is not a property of physical adsorption ? **[2018, Main]**

(1) Higher the pressure, more the adsorption

(2) Lower the temperature, more the adsorption

(3) Greater the surface area, more the adsorption

(4) Unilayer adsorption occurs

**29.** The correct statements about surface properties is/are : **[2017, Advanced]**

(1) Adsorption is accompanied by decrease in enthalpy and decrease in entropy of the system

(2) The critical temperatures of ethane and nitrogen are 563 K and 126 K, respectively. The adsorption of ethane will be more than that of nitrogen on same amount of activated charcoal at a given temperature

(3) Cloud is an emulsion type of colloid in which liquid is dispersed phase and gas is dispersion medium

(4) Brownian motion of colloidal particles does not depend on the size of the particles but depends on viscosity of the solution

**30.** The Tyndall effect is observed only when following conditions are satisfied : **[2017, Main]**

(a) The diameter of the dispersed particles is much smaller than the wavelength of the light used.

(b) The diameter of the dispersed particle is not much smaller than the wavelength of the light used.

(c) The refractive indices of the dispersed phase and dispersion medium are almost similar in magnitude.

(d) The refractive indices of the dispersed phase and dispersion medium differ greatly in magnitude.

(1) (a) and (c)　　　　(2) (b) and (c)
(3) (a) and (d)　　　　(4) (b) and (d)

**31.** Among the following, correct statement is : **[2017, Main]**
(1) Brownian movement is more pronounced for smaller particles than for bigger-particles.
(2) Sols of metal sulphides are lyophilic.
(3) Hardy Schulze law states that bigger the size of the ions, the greater is its coagulating power.
(4) One would expect charcoal to adsorb chlorine more than hydrogen sulphide.

**32.** Adsorption of a gas on surface follows Freundlich adsorption isotherm. Plot of $\log \dfrac{x}{m}$ versus $\log p$ gives a straight line with slope equal to 0.5, then  : ( $\dfrac{x}{m}$ is the mass of the gas adsorbed per gram of adsorbent) **[2017, Main]**
(1) Adsorption is independent of pressure.
(2) Adsorption is proportinal to the pressure.
(3) Adsorption is proportional to the square root of pressure.
(4) Adsorption is proportional to the square of pressure.

**33.** A particular adsorption process has the following characteristics : (i) It arises due to van der Waals forces and (ii) it is reversible. Identify the correct statement that describes the above adsorption process : **[2016, Main]**
(1) Enthalpy of adsorption is greater than 100 kJ mol$^{-1}$.
(2) Energy of activation is low.
(3) Adsorption is monolayer.
(4) Adsorption increases with increase in temperature.

**34.** The most appropriate method of making egg-albumin sol is : **[2016, Main]**
(1) Break an egg carefully and transfer the transparent part of the content to 100 mL of 5% w/V saline solution and stir well.
(2) Break an egg carefully and transfer only the yellow part of the content to 100 mL of 5% w/V saline solution and stir well.
(3) Keep the egg in boiling water for 10 minutes. After removing the shell, transfer the white part of the content to 100 mL of 5% w/V saline solution and homogenise with a mechanical shaker.
(4) Keep the egg in boiling water for 10 minutes. After removing the shell, transfer the yellow part of the content to 100 mL of 5% w/V saline solution and homogenise with a mechanical shaker.

**35.** Gold numbers of some colloids are : Gelatin : 0.005 – 0.01, Gum Arabic : 0.15 - 0.25; Oleate : 0.04 - 1.0; Starch : 15 - 25. Which among these is a better protective colloid ? **[2016, Main]**
(1) Gelatin　　　　(2) Gum Arabic
(3) Oleate　　　　(4) Starch

**36.** For a linear plot of log ($x/m$) versus log $p$ in a Freundlich adsorption isotherm, which of the following statements is correct ? ($k$ and $n$ are constants) **[2016, Main]**
(1) Both $k$ and $1/n$ appear in the slope term.
(2) $1/n$ appears as the intercept.
(3) Only $1/n$ appears as the slope.
(4) log ($1/n$) appears as the intercept.

**37.** Which of the following is an anionic detergent ? **[2016, Main]**
(1) Sodium stearate
(2) Sodium lauryl sulphate
(3) Cetyltrimethyl ammonium bromide
(4) Glyceryl oleate

**38.** When $O_2$ is adsorbed on a metallic surface, electron transfer occurs from the metal to $O_2$. The **True** statements regarding this adsorption is/are  : **[2015, Advanced]**
(1) $O_2$ is physisorbed
(2) heat is released
(3) occupancy of $\pi_{2p}^{*}$ of $O_2$ is increased
(4) bond length of $O_2$ is increased

**39.** 3 g of activated charcoal was added to 50 mL of acetic acid solution (0.06N) in a flask. After an hour it was filtered and the strength of the filtrate was found to be 0.042 N. The amount of acetic acid adsorbed (per gram of charcoal) is : **[2015, Main]**
(1) 18 mg　　　　(2) 36 mg
(3) 42 mg　　　　(4) 54 mg

**40.** The following statements relate to the adsorption of gases on a solid surface. Identify the **incorrect** statement among them : **[2015, Main]**
(1) Enthalpy of adsorption is negative
(2) Entropy of adsorption is negative
(3) On adsorption, the residual forces on the surface are increased
(4) On adsorption decrease in surface energy appears as heat

**41.** Methylene blue, from its aqueous solution, is adsorbed on activated charcoal at 25°C. For this process, the correct statement is :
**[2015, Advanced]**
(1) The adsorption requires activation at 25°C.
(2) The adsorption is accompanied by a decrease in enthalpy.
(3) The adsorption increases with increase of temperature.
(4) The adsorption is irreversible.

**42.** Choose the correct reason(s) for the stability of the **lyophobic** colloidal particles.
**[2012, Advanced]**

    (1) Preferential adsorption of ions on their surface from the solution

    (2) preferential adsorption of solvent on their surface from the solution

    (3) Attraction between different particles having opposite charges on their surface

    (4) Potential difference between the fixed layer and the diffused layer of opposite charges around the colloidal particles

**43.** The given graphs/data **I, II, III** and **IV** represent general trends observed for different physisorption and chemisorption processes under mild conditions of temperature and pressure. Which of the following choices about **I, II, III** and **IV** is/are correct ? **[2012, Advanced]**

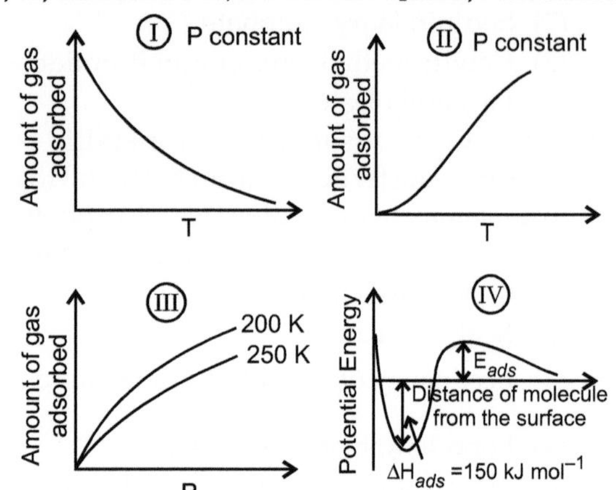



    (1) **I** is physisorption and **II** is chemisorption

    (2) **I** is physisorption and **III** is chemisorption

    (3) **IV** is chemisorption and **II** is chemisorption

    (4) **IV** is chemisorption and **III** is chemisorption

**44.** The correct statement(s) pertaining to the adsorption of a gas on a solid surface is/are :

**[2012, Advanced]**

    (1) Adsorption is always exothermic.

    (2) Physisorption may transform into chemisorption at high temperature.

    (3) Physisorption increases with increasing temperature but chemisorption decreases with increasing temperature.

    (4) Chemisorption is more exothermic than physisorption, however it is very slow due to higher enegy of activation.

**45.** Among the electrolytes $Na_2SO_4$, $CaCl_2$, $Al_2(SO_4)_3$ and $NH_4Cl$, the most effective coagulating agent for $Sb_2S_3$ sol is : **[2009, Advanced]**

    (1) $Na_2SO_4$      (2) $CaCl_2$

    (3) $Al_2(SO_4)_3$      (4) $NH_4Cl$

**46.** Among the following, the surfactant that will form micelles in aqueous solution at the loest molar concentration at ambient conditions is :

**[2008, Advanced]**

    (1) $CH_3(CH_2)_{15}N^+(CH_3)_3Br^-$

    (2) $CH_3(CH_2)_{11}OSO_3^-Na^+$

    (3) $CH_3(CH_2)_6COO^-Na^+$

    (4) $CH_3(CH_2)_{11}N^+(CH_3)_3Br^-$

**47.** **Statement-1 :** Micelles are formed by surfactant molecules above the critical micellar concentration (CMC).

**because**

**Statement-2 :** The conductivity of a solution having surfactant molecules decreases sharply at the CMC.

**[2007, Advanced]**

    (1) Statement-1 is True, Statement-2 is True; Statement-2 is a correct explanation for Statement-1

    (2) Statement-1 is True, Statement-2 is True; Statement-2 is not a correct explanation for Statement-1

    (3) Statement-1 is True, Statement-2 is False

    (4) Statement-1 is False, Statement-2 is True

**48.** Which of the following is correct for lyophilic sols ? **[2005, Screening]**

    (1) They are irreversible

    (2) They are formed by inorganic substances

    (3) They are readily coagulated by addition of electrolytes

    (4) They are self stablised

**49.** Spontaneous adsorption of a gas on solid surface is an exothermic process because :

**[2004, Screening]**

    (1) $\Delta H$ increases for system

    (2) $\Delta S$ increases for gas

    (3) $\Delta S$ decreases for gas

    (4) $\Delta G$ increases for gas

**50.** Rate of physiorption increases with :

**[2003, Screening]**

    (1) decrease in temperature

    (2) increase in temperature

    (3) decrease in pressure

    (4) decrease in surface area

## ANSWER KEY

| 1. (3) | 2. (*) | 3. (2) | 4. (2) | 5. (3) | 6. (3) | 7. (2) | 8. (3) | 9. (*) | 10. (3) |
|---|---|---|---|---|---|---|---|---|---|
| 11. (3) | 12. (3) | 13. (3) | 14. (1) | 15. (4) | 16. (*) | 17. (1) | 18. (4) | 19. (1) | 20. (1) |
| 21. (3) | 22. (3) | 23. (2) | 24. (3) | 25. (3) | 26. (4) | 27. (1) | 28. (4) | 29. (1,2) | 30. (4) |
| 31. (1) | 32. (3) | 33. (2) | 34. (1) | 35. (1) | 36. (3) | 37. (*) | 38. (2,3,4) | 39. (1) | 40. (3) |
| 41. (2) | 42. (1, 4) | 43. (1,3) | 44. (1,2,4) | 45. (3) | 46. (1) | 47. (2) | 48. (4) | 49. (3) | 50. (1) |

## ANSWERS WITH EXPLANATIONS

**1. (3)** Bredig's Arc method is used to form metal colloids.

**2.**
$$\frac{x}{m} = k\,p^x \qquad \qquad \text{...(i)}$$

$$\log \underbrace{\frac{x}{m}}_{y} = \underbrace{\log k}_{c} + \underbrace{x \log p}_{x}$$

$\Rightarrow$ Given $c = \log k = 0.4771$ or $k = 3$

slope $x = 2$

put in eq. (1) $\dfrac{x}{m} = 3 \times (4)^2 \Rightarrow 48$

**3. (2)** (a) Since adsorption is exothermic process, as adsorption proceeds number of active sites present over adsorbent decreases, so less heat is evolved.

(b) Since $NH_3$ has higher force of attraction on adsorbent due to its polar nature (high value of '$a$').

(c) As the adsorption increases, residual forces over surface decreases.

(d) Since process is exothermic, on increasing temperature it shift to backward direction, so concentration of adsorbate particle decreases.

**4. (2)**

| Type of interaction | Interaction Energy (E) |
|---|---|
| ion-ion | $E \propto \dfrac{1}{r}$ |
| dipole-dipole | $E \propto \dfrac{1}{r^3}$ |
| London dispersion | $E \propto \dfrac{1}{r^6}$ |

**5. (3)** The diameter of dispersed particles is similar to wavelength of light used.

**6. (3)** Thermal power plants lead to acid rain.

**7. (2)** Excess water to liquid

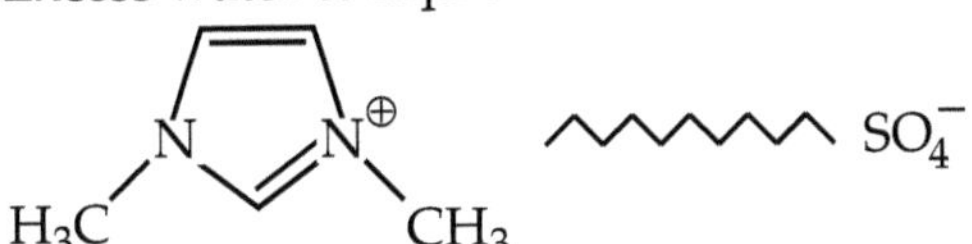

**8. (3)** (i) Foam—(e) Froth

(ii) Gel → (c) Jellies

(iii) Aerosol → (a) Smoke

(iv) Emulsion → (f) Milk

**9.**
$$\frac{x}{m} = KP^{1/n}$$

$$\log\left(\frac{x}{m}\right) = \frac{1}{n}\log P + \log K$$

$$\text{slope} = \frac{1}{n} = 2$$

$$\text{intercept} = \log K = 0.4771$$
$$K = 3$$

mass of gas adsorbed per gm of adsorbent

$$= \frac{x}{m}$$

$$\frac{x}{m} = 3 \times (0.04)^2 = 48 \times 10^{-4}$$

**10. (3)**

**11. (3)** Above which the formation of micelles takes place.

**12. (3)** Egg white.

**13. (3)** $\dfrac{x}{m} = K.P.^{1/n}$

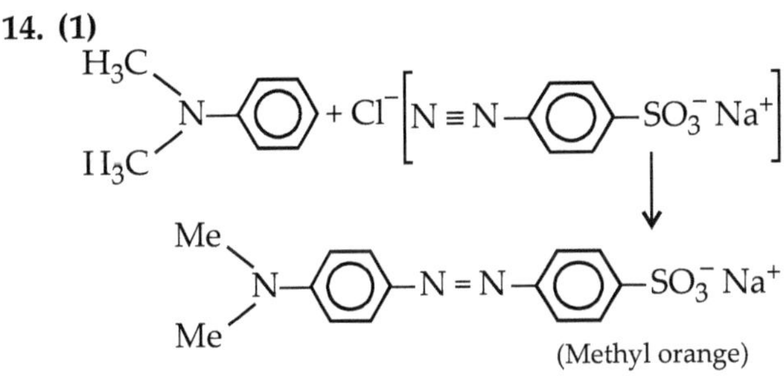


**14. (1)**



It is an acid base indicator.

**15. (4)** Adsorption of Gases will decreases.

**16.** 1 litre solution of 30 m mol of HCl is required.

For 1 litre solution of 1s m mol of $H_2SO_4$ is required.

250 ml of solution required :

$$\frac{15}{4} \times 10^{-3} \text{ (m mol) of } H_2SO_4 = 0.3675 \text{ gm.}$$

**17. (1)** The graph of $\log \dfrac{x}{m}$ versus $\log P$ is shown below :

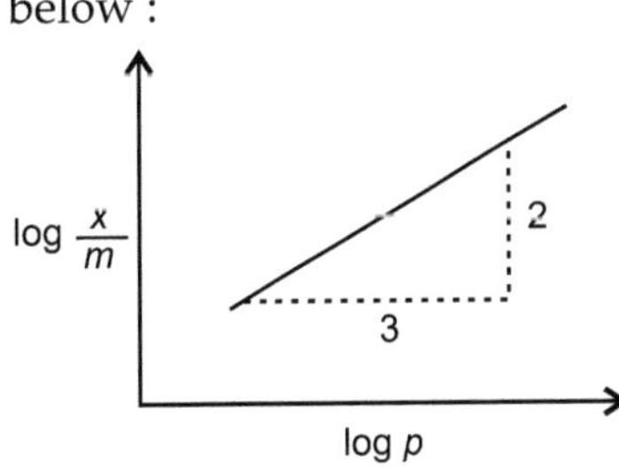

The relationship between amount of gas adsorbed on a unit mass of adsorbent and pressure is given below :

$$\frac{x}{m} = kP^{\frac{1}{n}}$$

Take logarithm on both sides of the above equation,

$$\log\frac{x}{m} = \log k + \frac{1}{n}\log P \qquad ...(1)$$

Compare the above equation with equation for a straight line, that is $y = mx + c$. Here, $m$ represents the slope of the graph. According to the equation (1), $\frac{1}{n}$ is the slope.

According to the graph, the value of slope is shown below :

$$\frac{1}{n} = \frac{2}{3}$$

Therefore,

$$\frac{x}{m} = kP^{\frac{2}{3}}$$

$$\frac{x}{m} \propto P^{\frac{2}{3}}$$

**18. (4)** Ellingham diagram is a plot of $\Delta G$ versus T. It helps to determine the appropriate reducing agent for the reduction of metal oxides. Therefore, it helps to predict the feasibility of the thermal reduction of an ore.

**19. (1)** The aerosol is colloid of solid or liquid dispersed in gas. For example smog and fog.

**20. (1)** The number of moles of surfactant is calculated as shown below :

$$n = MV$$

$$= (1\ mM)\left(\frac{1\ M}{10^3\ mM}\right)(10\ mL)\left(\frac{1\ L}{10^3\ mL}\right)$$

$$= (10^{-5}\ M.L)\left(\frac{1\ mol/L}{1\ M}\right)$$

$$= 10^{-5}\ mol$$

The number of molecules present in $10^{-5}$ mol is calculated as shown below :

$$N = nN_A$$

$$= (10^{-5}\ mol)(6.023 \times 10^{23}\ molecules/mol)$$

$$= 6.023 \times 10^{18}\ molecules$$

The surface area occupied by $6.023 \times 10^{18}$ molecules is calculated as shown below :

$$a^2 = \frac{0.24\ cm^2}{6.023 \times 10^{18}}$$

$$a^2 \approx 4 \times 10^{-20}\ cm^2$$

$$a = (4 \times 10^{-10}\ cm^2)^{1/2}$$

$$= 2 \times 10^{-10}\ cm$$

The value of edge length is converted into pm as shown below :

$$a = (2 \times 10^{-10}\ cm)\left(\frac{1\ pm}{10^{-10}\ cm}\right)$$

$$= 2\ pm$$

**21. (3)** The given equation is $\frac{x}{m} = kp^{0.5}$. The adsorption increases with increase in pressure. As physical adsorption is exothermic, adsorption increases with decrease in temperature.

**22. (3)** The colloidal particles that are present in lyophobic sols can be precipitated by the process of electrophoresis in which colloidal particles migrate to the oppositely charged electrodes and get precipitated. Brownian movement in a colloidal solution would be faster if the viscosity of the solution would be less. Colloidal medicines are more effective as they have large surface area. Addition to alum makes water fit for drinking.

**23. (2)** The process of conversion of a precipitate into colloidal solution by shaking is termed as peptisation.

**24. (3)** The colligative properties of colloids are smaller than that of true solution. Osmotic pressure is colligative properties. The osmotic pressure of a colloidal solution is less than that of true solutiohn at same concentration.

**25. (3)** Calamine is $ZnCO_3$, malachite is $CuCO_3$. $Cu(OH)_2$, magnetite is $Fe_3O_4$ and cryolite is $Na_3AlF_6$.

**26. (4)** According to Freundlich adsorption isotherm,

$$\frac{x}{m} = kP^{1/n}$$

$$\log_{10}\frac{x}{m} = \frac{1}{n}\log_{10}P + \log_{10}k$$

This is the equation of straight line of type,

$$y = mx + c$$

So, Slope is $\frac{1}{n}$.

**27. (1)** The statement that is wrong corresponding to colloids is freezing point of colloidal solution is lower than true solution at same concentration of a solute because instead of lower it remains same as that of true solution. The depression in freezing point depends upon the number of solute particles. It does not depend upon the shape and size of solute particles.

**28. (4)** The unilayer adsorption is not a property of physical adsorption. Physical adsorption depends upon the pressure and temperature.

Physical adsorption increases with increase in pressure and decreases with increase in temperature.

**29. (1,2)** In the process of adsorption, both enthalpy and entropy change should be negative. The extent of adsorption depends upon the critical temperature. Therefore, ethane will be adsorbed more than nitrogen. Cloud is an aerosol. It contains liquid droplets. It is not an emulsion. A random movement of microscopic particles is called Brownian motion. Therefore, it will depend upon the size of particles.

**30. (4)** The two conditions necessary for Tyndall effect are,

   (1) The size of the dispersed particle does not differ much more than the wavelength of the light used.

   (2) There is a significant difference in the refractive indices of dispersed phase and dispersion medium.

**31. (1)** The Brownian movement is the random movement of particles that are present in a solution (liquid or gas) and this movement is the result of the collision of the fast moving atoms in the liquid or gaseous state. Thus, only smaller particles are actually responsible for Brownian movement. Thus, the correct statement is that Brownian movement is more pronounced for smaller particles than for bigger-particles.

**32. (3)** The plot of $\log \dfrac{x}{m}$ versus $\log p$ gives straight line and slope is $0.5$.

The expression for Freundlich adsorption isotherm is shown below :

$$\log\left(\frac{x}{m}\right) = \log K + \frac{1}{n}\log P$$

$$= \log (K.P^{1/n})$$

The value of $n$ is 2. Thus,

$$\frac{x}{m} \propto p^{1/2}$$

**33. (2)** The adsorption which occurs because of van der Waals forces and is reversible in nature is also called as physisorption. The enthalpy of physisorption is always low. Physisorption will decrease with increase in temperature as shown below.

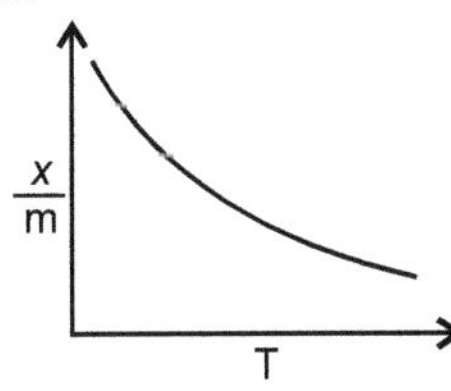

It requires less amount of activation energy. Thus, the energy of activation is low for physisorption.

**34. (1)** The most appropriate method of making an egg-albumin sol is breaking an egg and transferring its transparent part to 100 mL of 5% w/V saline solution. After that, stir well the solution. This method is only done with the transparent part of the egg because only its transparent part contains albumin.

**35. (1)** The relation between gold number and protective power is as follows :

$$\text{Gold number} \propto \frac{1}{\text{Protective power}}$$

Thus, gelatin is the better protective colloid from the given colloids.

**36. (3)** The equation corresponding to Freundlich adsorption isotherm is shown below.

$$\frac{x}{m} = kp^{1/n}$$

$$\log\frac{x}{m} = \log k + \frac{1}{n}\log p$$

The slope in the given equation is $1/n$.

**37. (2)** Sodium stearate is an anionic soap.
Sodium lauryl sulphate is an anionic detergent.
Cetyltrimethyl ammonium bromide is a cationic detergent.
Glyceryloleate is a non ionic detergent.

**38. (2,3,4)** Adsorption of oxygen on metal surface is an exothermic phenomenon. Hence, energy is released.
During transfer of electron from metal to $O_2$, electron occupies $\pi^{*}_{2p}$ orbital of $O_2$ as shown below.

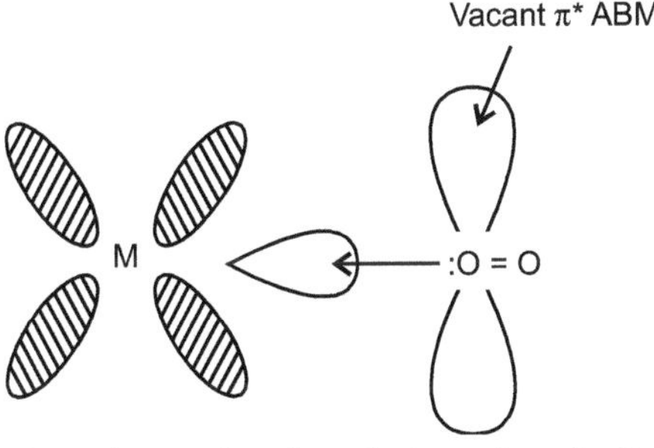


Therefore, the bond length of $O_2$ is increased.

**39. (1)** The amount of acetic acid adsorbed per gram of charcoal is calculated as,

Amount of $CH_3COOH$

$$= \frac{M_{CH_3COOH} \times n_{\text{adsorbed } CH_3COOH}}{3}$$

The number of moles of adsorbed acetic acid is calculated as,

$$= \frac{0.06 \times 50}{1000} - \frac{0.042 \times 50}{1000}$$

$$= 3 \times 10^{-3} - 2.1 \times 10^{-3}$$

$$= 0.9 \times 10^{-3}$$

Substitute this calculated value in above equation.

$$\text{Amount of } CH_3COOH = \frac{60 \times 0.9 \times 10^{-3}}{3}$$
$$= 18 \text{ mg}$$

**40. (3)** The residual forces on the surface, prior to the adsorption, is more. As adsorption takes place, the residual forces decrease.

**41. (2)** The adsorption of methylene blue on activated charcoal is an exothermic process.

During adsorption, energy is liberated due to attraction between adsorbate and adsorbent which results in decrease in enthalpy.

**42. (1, 4)** (1) Lyophobic colloidal particles are stable due to the adsorption of common ions from the solution.

(2) Preferential adsorption of ions occurs from the solution rather than solvent.

(3) They are stable due to repulsion between the ions rather than the attraction.

(4) The presence of oppositely charged particles around the colloidal particles leads to a decrease in the potential energy and thus increases their stability.

**43. (1, 3)** (1) In graph **(I)**, the amount of adsorption decreases with an increase in temperature; hence, it corresponds to physisorption while in graph **(II)**, the amount of adsorption increases with an increase in temperature; thus, it corresponds to chemisorption.

(2) In graph **(I)** and **(III)**, the amount of adsorption decreases with an increase in temperature; hence, it corresponds to physisorption.

(3) Graph **(IV)** represents the chemical bond formation and thus corresponds to chemisorption. In graph **(II)**, amount of adsorption increases with an increase in temperature and, thus, it corresponds to chemisorption.

(4) Graph **(IV)** represents the chemical bond formation and thus corresponds to chemisorption. In graph **(III)**, the amount of adsorption decreases with an increase in temperature; hence, it corresponds to physisorption.

**44. (1,2,4)** Adsorption of a gas on a solid surface results in decrease in free energy. Therefore, it is exothermic.

Physical adsorption takes place at lower temperature and decreases with increase of temperature. At the same time chemical adsorption increases with this decrease in physical adsorption. The example of this is adsorption of hydrogen gas on surface of nickel. This process is also known as activated adsorption.

Statement third is contradictory of second statement. Therefore, it is incorrect.

Chemisorption is accompanied with evolution of large amount of heat that is approximately 200-400 kJ/mol. Therefore, fourth statement is correct.

**45. (3)** According to the Hardy-Schulze rule, high charge density on cation results in the effective coagulation of the $Sb_2S_3$ (negative sol). The cation having highest charge density among the given electrolytes is aluminium. Therefore, the effective coagulating agent for $Sb_2S_3$ is $Al_2(SO_4)_3$.

**46. (1)** The critical micelle concentration of surfactant depends upon the molecular weight of hydrocarbon chain. As the molecular weight of hydrocarbon chain increases, molar concentration decreases. The molecular weight of $CH_3(CH_2)_{15}N^+(CH_3)_3Br^-$ is maximum, hence it forms micelles at lowest molar concentration.

**47. (2)** The formation of micelles depends on CMC (critical micelle concentration). Only above this concentration, formation of micelles take place.

Each micelle comprises at least hundred molecules. Therefore, at CMC the conductivity of the solution decreases sharply.

**48. (4)** Lyophilic sols are self stabilized because they possess the solvent loving nature.

Thus, the statement given in option (4) is correct about the lyophilic sols.

**49. (3)** As adsorption is spontaneous, it means Gibbs free energy change is also negative. The adsorption leads to a decrease in entropy and thus, $T\Delta S$ is also negative. This leads to a negative value of $\Delta H$ as $\Delta G = \Delta H - T\Delta S$.

**50. (1)** Physisorption is a process of adsorption of gas molecules on the solid surface. The rate of Physisorption increases with decrease in temperature because decrease in temperature increases the liquefaction ability of gases which favors the adsorption of gas molecules on solid results in the increase in the rate of adsorption.

# Classification of Elements and Periodicity in Properties

## QUESTIONS

1. The five successive ionization enthalpies of an element are 800, 2427, 3658, 25024 and 32824 kJ mol$^{-1}$. The number of valence electrons in the element is : **[2020, Main]**
   (1) 2          (2) 3
   (3) 4          (4) 5

2. In general, the property (magnitudes only) that shows an opposite trend in comparison to other properties across a period is : **[2020, Main]**
   (1) Electronegativity
   (2) Electron gain enthalpy
   (3) Ionization enthalpy
   (4) Atomic radius

3. Three elements X, Y and Z are in the 3$^{rd}$ period of the periodic table. The oxides of X, Y and Z, respectively, are basic, amphoteric and acidic. The correct order of the atomic numbers of X, Y and Z is : **[2020, Main]**
   (1) Z < Y < X          (2) X < Z < Y
   (3) X < Y < Z          (4) Y < X < Z

4. The oxidation states of transition metal atoms in $K_2Cr_2O_7$, $KMnO_4$ and $K_2FeO_4$, respectively, are $x$, $y$ and $z$. The sum of $x$, $y$ and $z$ is ..........

   **[2020, Main]**

5. The atomic number of the element unnilennium is : **[2020, Main]**
   (1) 119          (2) 108
   (3) 102          (4) 109

6. Among the statements (I-IV), the correct ones are : **[2020, Main]**
   (I) Be has smaller atomic radius compared to Mg
   (II) Be has higher ionization enthalpy than Al
   (III) Charge/radius ratio of Be is greater than that of Al
   (IV) Both Be and Al form mainly covalent compounds
   (1) (I), (II) and (IV)          (2) (II), (III) and (IV)
   (3) (I), (II) and (III)          (4) (I), (III) and (IV)

7. On heating, lead (II) nitrate gives a brown gas (A). The gas (A) on cooling changes to a colourless solid/liquid (B). (B) on heating with NO changes to a blue solid (C). The oxidation number of nitrogen in solid (C) is : **[2020, Main]**
   (1) +5          (2) +2
   (3) +4          (4) +3

8. The elements with atomic numbers 101 and 104 belong to, respectively : **[2020, Main]**
   (1) Group 11 and Group 4
   (2) Actinoids and Group 4
   (3) Actinoids and Group 6
   (4) Group 6 and Actinoids

9. The ionic radii of $O_2^-$, $F^-$, $Na^+$ and $Mg^{2+}$ are in the order : **[2020, Main]**
   (1) $F^- > O^{2-} > Na^+ > Mg^{2+}$
   (2) $Mg^{2+} > Na^+ > F^- > O^{2-}$
   (3) $O^{2-} > F^- > Mg^{2+} + Na^+$
   (4) $O^{2-} > F^- > Na^+ > Mg^{2+}$

10. A crystal is made up of metal ions '$M_1$' and '$M_2$' and oxide ions. Oxide ions form a ccp lattice structure. The cation '$M_1$' occupies 50% of octahedral voids and the cation '$M_2$' occupies 12.5% of tetrahedral voids of oxide lattice. The oxidation numbers of '$M_1$' and '$M_2$' are, respectively : **[2020, Main]**
    (1) +2, +4          (2) +3, +1
    (3) +1, +3          (4) +4, +2

11. The atomic number of Unnilunium is ........... .

    **[2020, Main]**

12. The lanthanoid that does NOT show +4 oxidation state is : **[2020, Main]**
    (1) Dy          (2) Eu
    (3) Ce          (4) Tb

13. Choose the correct statement(s) among the following : **[2020, Advanced]**
    (1) $SnCl_2.2H_2O$ is a reducing agent
    (2) $SnO_2$ reacts with KOH to form $K_2[Sn(OH)_6]$
    (3) A solution of $PbCl_2$ in HCl contains $Pb^{2+}$ and $Cl^-$ ions
    (4) The reaction of $Pb_3O_4$ with hot dilute nitric acid to give $PbO_2$ is a redox reaction

14. B has a smaller first ionization enthalpy than Be. Consider the following statements : **[2020, Main]**
    (I) It is easier to remove $2p$ electron than $2s$ electron
    (II) $2p$ electron of B is more shielded from the nucleus by the inner core of electrons than the $2s$ electrons of Be
    (III) $2s$ electron has more penetration power than $2p$ electron
    (IV) Atomic radius of B is more than Be
    (Atomic number B = 5, Be = 4)

The correct sttements are :

(1) (I), (II) and (III)  (2) (II), (III) and (IV)

(3) (I), (III) and (IV)  (4) (I), (II) and (IV)

**15.** The atomic radius of Ag is closest to : **[2020, Main]**

(1) Cu  (2) Hg

(3) Au  (4) Ni

**16.** The first ionization energy (in kJ/mol) of Na, Mg, Al and Si respectively, are : **[2020, Main]**

(1) 496, 737, 577, 786

(2) 786, 737, 577, 496

(3) 496, 577, 737, 786

(4) 496, 577, 786, 737

**17.** The third ionization enthalpy is minimum for : **[2020, Main]**

(1) Fe  (2) Ni

(3) Co  (4) Mn

**18.** The increasing order of the atomic radii of the following elements is : **[2020, Main]**

(a) C  (b) O

(c) F  (d) Cl

(e) Br

(1) (b) < (c) < (d) < (a) < (e)

(2) (a) < (b) < (c) < (d) < (e)

(3) (d) < (c) < (b) < (a) < (e)

(4) (c) < (b) < (a) < (d) < (e)

**19.** The IUPAC symbol for the element with atomic number 119 would be : **[2019, Main]**

(1) uue  (2) une

(3) unh  (4) unn

**20.** The element having greatest difference between its first and second ionisation energies, is : **[2019, Main]**

(1) Ca  (2) Sc

(3) Ba  (4) K

**21.** The isoelectronic set of ions is : **[2019, Main]**

(1) $N^{3-}$, $O^{2-}$, $F^-$ and $Na^+$

(2) $N^{3-}$, $Li^+$, $Mg^{2+}$ and $O^{2-}$

(3) $F^-$, $Li^+$, $Na^+$ and $Mg^{2+}$

(4) $Li^+$, $Na^+$, $O^{2-}$ and $F^-$

**22.** In comparison to boron, berylium has : **[2019, Main]**

(1) Lesser nuclear charge and lesser first ionisation enthalpy.

(2) Greater nuclear charge and lesser first ionisation enthalpy.

(3) Greater nuclear charge and greater first ionisation enthalpy.

(4) Lesser nuclear charge and greater first ionisation enthalpy.

**23.** Among the following, the energy of $2s$ orbital is lowest in : **[2019, Main]**

(1) K  (2) H

(3) Li  (4) Na

**24.** Which of the following compounds contain(s) no covalent bonds ? **[2018, Main]**

$KCl$, $PH_3$, $O_2$, $B_2H_6$, $H_2SO_4$

(1) $KCl$, $B_2H_6$, $PH_3$  (2) $KCl$, $H_2SO_4$

(3) $KCl$  (4) $KCl$, $B_2H_6$

**25.** For $Na^+$, $Mg^{2+}$, $F^-$ and $O^{2-}$; the correct order of increasing ionic radii is : **[2018, Main]**

(1) $O^{2-} < F^- < Na^+ < Mg^{2+}$

(2) $Na^+ < Mg^{2+} < F^- < O^{2-}$

(3) $Mg^{2+} < Na^+ < F^- < O^{2-}$

(4) $Mg^{2+} < O^{2-} < Na^+ < F^-$

**26.** The group having isoelectronic species is : **[2017, Main]**

(1) $O^{2-}$, $F^-$, Na, $Mg^{2+}$  (2) $O^-$, $F^-$, $Na^+$, $Mg^{2+}$

(3) $O^{2-}$, $F^-$, $Na^+$, $Mg^{2+}$  (4) $O^-$, $F^-$, Na, $Mg^+$

**27.** Consider the following ionisation enthalpies of two elements 'A' and 'B'. **[2017, Main]**

| Element | Ionisation enthalpy (kJ/mol) | | |
|---|---|---|---|
| | **1st** | **2nd** | **3rd** |
| A | 899 | 1757 | 14847 |
| B | 737 | 1450 | 7731 |

Which of the following statements is correct ?

(1) Both 'A' and 'B' belong to group-1 where 'B' comes below 'A'

(2) Both 'A' and 'B' belong to group-1 where 'A' comes below 'B'

(3) Both 'A' and 'B' belong to group-2 where 'B' comes below 'A'

(4) Both 'A' and 'B' belong to group-2 where 'A' comes below 'B'

**28.** The electronic configuration with the highest ionisation enthalpy is : **[2017, Main]**

(1) $[Ne]3s^23p^1$  (2) $[Ne]3s^23p^2$

(3) $[Ne]3s^23p^3$  (4) $[Ar]3d^{10}4s^24p^3$

**29.** The correct order of the stability of alkaline-earth metal sulphates in water is : **[2016, Main]**

(1) Mg < Ca < Sr > Ba  (2) Mg < Sr < Ca < Ba

(3) Mg > Sr > Ca > Ba  (4) Mg > Ca > Sr > Ba

**30.** Aqueous solution of which salt will not contain ions with the electronic configuration $1s^22s^22p^63s^23p^6$ ? **[2016, Main]**

(1) NaF  (2) NaCl

(3) KBr  (4) $CaI_2$

**31.** The following statements concern elements in the periodic table. Which of the following is true ? **[2016, Main]**

(1) All the elements in Group 17 are gases.

(2) The Group 13 elements are all metals.

(3) Elements of Group 16 have lower ionisation enthalpy values compared to those of Group 15 in the corresponding periods.

(4) For group 15 elements, the stability of + 5 oxidation state increases down the group.

**32.** Which of the following atoms has the highest first ionisation energy ? **[2016, Main]**

(1) Rb        (2) Na

(3) K        (4) Sc

**33.** The ionic radii (in Å) of $N^{3-}$, $O^{2-}$ and $F^-$ are respectively : **[2015, Main]**

(1) 1.36, 1.40 and 1.71   (2) 1.36, 1.71 and 1.40

(3) 1.71, 1.40 and 1.36   (4) 1.71, 1.36 and 1.40

**34.** Which one has the highest boiling point ? **[2015, Main]**

(1) He        (2) Ne

(3) Kr        (4) Xe

**35.** In the long form of the periodic table, the valence shell electronic configuration of $5s^2 5p^4$ corresponds to the elements present in : **[2015, Main]**

(1) Group 16 and period 6

(2) Group 17 and period 5

(3) Group 16 and period 5

(4) Group 17 and period 6

**36.** Which of the following series correctly represents relations between the elements from X to Y ? **[2014, Main]**

$X \rightarrow Y$

(1) $_3Li \rightarrow _{19}K$    Ionisation enthalpy increases

(2) $_9F \rightarrow _{35}Br$    Electron gain enthalpy with negative sign increases

(3) $_6C \rightarrow _{32}Ge$    Atomic radii increases

(4) $_{18}Ar \rightarrow _{54}Xe$    Noble character increases

**37.** Similarity in chemical properties of the atoms of elements in a group of the Periodic table is most closely related to : **[2014, Main]**

(1) Atomic numbers

(2) Atomic masses

(3) Number of principal energy levels

(4) Number of valence electrons

**38.** Which of the following arrangements represents the increasing order (smallest to largest) of ionic radii of the given species $O^{2-}$, $S^{2-}$, $N^{3-}$, $P^{3-}$ ? **[2014, Main]**

(1) $O^{2-} < N^{3-} < S^{2-} < P^{3-}$

(2) $O^{2-} < P^{3-} < N^{3-} < S^{2-}$

(3) $N^{3-} < O^{2-} < P^{3-} < S^{2-}$

(4) $N^{3-} < S^{2-} < O^{2-} < P^{3-}$

**39.** Which one of the following has largest ionic radius ? **[2014, Main]**

(1) $Li^+$        (2) $O_2^{2-}$

(3) $B^{3+}$        (4) $F^-$

**40.** Identify the correct order of acidic strenghts of $CO_2$, $CuO$, $CaO$, $H_2O$ : **[2002, Screening]**

(1) $CaO < CuO < H_2O < CO_2$

(2) $H_2O < CuO < CaO < CO_2$

(3) $CaO < H_2O < CuO < CO_2$

(4) $H_2O < CO_2 < CaO < CuO$

**41.** Identify the least stable ion amongst the following : **[2002, Screening]**

(1) $Li^-$        (2) $Be^-$

(3) $B^-$        (4) $C^-$

## ANSWER KEY

| 1. (2) | 2. (4) | 3. (3) | 4. (*) | 5. (4) | 6. (3) | 7. (4) | 8. (2) | 9. (4) | 10. (1) |
|---|---|---|---|---|---|---|---|---|---|
| 11. (*) | 12. (2) | 13. (1,2,3) | 14. (1) | 15. (3) | 16. (1) | 17. (1) | 18. (4) | 19. (1) | 20. (4) |
| 21. (1) | 22. (4) | 23. (1) | 24. (3) | 25. (3) | 26. (3) | 27. (3) | 28. (3) | 29. (4) | 30. (1) |
| 31. (3) | 32. (4) | 33. (3) | 34. (4) | 35. (3) | 36. (3) | 37. (4) | 38. (1) | 39. (2) | 40. (1) |
| 41. (2) | | | | | | | | | |

## ANSWERS WITH EXPLANATIONS

**1. (2)** Let suppose element $X \Rightarrow$

$$X_{(g)} \xrightarrow[800]{IE_1} X^+_{(g)} \xrightarrow[2427]{IE_2} X^{+2}_{(g)} \xrightarrow[3658]{IE_3}$$

$$X^{+3}_{(g)} \xrightarrow[25024]{IE_4} X^{+4}_{(g)} \xrightarrow[32824]{IE_5} X^{+5}_{(g)}$$

$X^{+3}$ has stable inert gas configuration as there is high jump after $IE_3$

So valence electrons are 3.

**2. (4)** In general across a period atomic radius decreases while ionisation enthalpy, electron gain enthalpy and electronegativity increases because effective nuclear charge ($Z_{eff}$) increases.

**3. (3)** When we are moving from left to right in a periodic table acidic character of oxides increases (as well as atomic number of atom increases)

$\therefore$      $X < Y < Z$    (acidic character)

        $X < Y < Z$    (atomic number)

**4.** $K_2Cr_2O_7$

$$2(+1) + 2x + 7(-2) = 0$$
$$x = +6$$

In $K_2Cr_2O_7$, Transition metal (Cr) present in +6 oxidation state.

$KMnO_4$

$$(+1) + y + 4(-2) = 0$$
$$x = +7$$

In $KMnO_4$, transition metal (Mn) present in +7 oxidation state

$K_2FeO_4$

$$2(+1) + z + 4(-2) = 0$$
$$x = +6$$

In $K_2FeO_4$, transition metal (Fe) present in +6 oxidation state

So,
$$x = +6$$
$$y = +7$$
$$z = +6$$
$$\overline{x + y + z = 19}$$

Therefore, the sum of $x$, $y$ and $z$ is 19.

**5. (4)** 1     0     9

un    nil    enn

Hence correct name → unnilennium

**6. (3)** I. $A_N$ : Be < Mg

II. IE : Be > Al

III. Charge/radius ratio of Be w less than that of Al

IV. Be, Al mainly form covalent compounds.

**7. (4)** $Pb(NO_3)_2 \xrightarrow{\Delta} PbO + 2NO_2 + \dfrac{1}{2}O_2(g)$
                                Brown
                                gas
                                (A)

$NO_2(g) \xrightarrow{\text{Cooling}} N_2O_4$
                                  (B)

$N_2O_4 + NO \xrightarrow{\Delta} N_2O_3$
                             Blue Solid
                               (C)

O.S. of nitrogen in $N_2O_3$ is + 3

$N_2O_3$ $2x + 3(-2) = 0$

$$x = +3$$

**8. (2)** Element with atomic number 101 and 104 belong to actinoids and group 4.

**9. (4)**

|  | $O^2$ | $F^-$ | $Na^+$ | $Mg^{2+}$ |
|---|---|---|---|---|
| $z$ | 8 | 9 | 11 | 12 |
| $e^-$ | 10 | 10 | 10 | 10 |
| $\dfrac{z}{e}$ | 0.8 | 0.9 | 1.1 | 1.2 |

as $\dfrac{z}{e}$ ratio increases size decreases.

Thus, correct ionic radii order is :
$$O^2 > F^- > Na^+ > Mg^{2+}$$

**10. (1)** $O^{-2}$ ions from ccp. $O_4$
                                ↓

                    (− 8 charge)

                $M_1$ = 50% of O.V.

$$\Rightarrow \quad \frac{50}{100} \times 4 = 2 : (M_1)_2$$

                $M_2$ = 12.5% of T.V.

$$\Rightarrow \quad \frac{12.5}{100} \times 8 = 1 : (M_2)_1$$

So formula is : $(M_1)_2 (M_2)_1 O_4$

This must be neutral. Both metals must have +8 charge in total.

From given options : $\begin{Bmatrix} \text{O. N. of } M_1 = +2 \\ M_2 = +4 \end{Bmatrix}$

**11.** The atomic number of Unnilunium is 101.

**12. (2)** The lanthanoid that does NOT show +4 oxidation state is Europium.

**13. (1,2) OR (1,2,3)**

(1) $SnCl_2.2H_2O$ is a reducing agent since $Sn^{2+}$ tends to convert into $Sn^{4+}$.

(2) $\underset{\text{(Amphoteric)}}{SnO_2} + \underset{\text{(Base)}}{2KOH_{(aq.)}} + 2H_2O$

$$\rightarrow K_2[Sn(OH)_6]$$

(3) First group cations ($Pb^{2+}$) form insoluble chloride with HCl that is $PbCl_2$ however it is slightly soluble in water and therefore lead +2 ion is never completely precipitated on adding hydrochloric acid in test sample of $Pb^{2+}$, rest of the $Pb^{2+}$ ions are quantitatively precipitated with $H_2S$ in acidic medium.

So that we can say that filtrate of first group contain solution of $PbCl_2$ in HCl which contains $Pb^{2+}$ and $Cl^-$.

However in the presence of conc. HCl or excess HCl it can produce $H_2[PbCl_4]$.

So, we can conclude A, B or A, B, C should be answers.

(4) $\underset{\substack{\text{(2PbO PbO}_2)\\\text{(mixture of oxides)}}}{Pb_3O_4} + 4HNO_3 \rightarrow PbO_2(\downarrow)$

It is not a redox reaction.

**14. (1)** Be $\Rightarrow 1s^2 2s^2$

B $\Rightarrow 1s^2 2s^2 2p^1$

B has a smaller size than Be.

It is easier to remove $2p$ electron than $2s$ electron due to less pentration effect of $2p$ than $2s$.

$2p$ electron of Boron is miore shielded from the nucleus by the inner core of electron than the $2s$ electron of Be.

B has a smaller size than Be.

**15. (3)** The atomic radius of Ag and Au is nearly same due to lanthanide contraction.

This phenomenon is associated with the intersection of the $4f$ orbitals which must be filled before $5d$ series of elements begin.

The filling of $4f$ orbital before $5d$ orbitals results in a regular decrease in radii of the elements. This is called as Lanthanoid Contraction.

From the given atoms Na, Mg, Al and Si and their electronic configuration, we can see that the atomic size of Si is maximum therefore, it has highest IE and Na has least but if we compare Mg and Al, Mg has higher IE than Al due more Zeff as compared to Al.

**16. (1)** Ionization energy is the amount of energy required to remove the outer shell electron of an atom.

Electronic configuration of Na = [Ne] $3s^1$

$$Mg = [Ne]\ 3s^2$$
$$Al = [Ne]\ 3s^2\ 3p^1$$
$$Si = [Ne]\ 3s^2\ 3p^2$$

As the size of an atom increases, the effective nuclear charge (Zeff) increases and ionization energy also increases.

**17. (1)** Electronic configuration of

$$_{25}Mn \qquad\qquad _{26}Fe$$
$$Mn = [Ar]3d^54s^1 \qquad Fe = [Ar]3d^64s^2$$
$$Mn^{2+} = [Ar]3d^54s^0 \qquad Fe^{3+} = [Ar]3d^54s^0$$

$$_{27}Co \qquad\qquad _{28}Ni$$
$$[Ar]3d^74s^2 \qquad [Ar]3d^84s^2$$
$$[Ar]3d^74s^0 \qquad [Ar]3d^84s^0$$

So, third ionisation energy is minimum for Fe.

**18. (4)** If the given elements are arranged according to their position in periodic table :

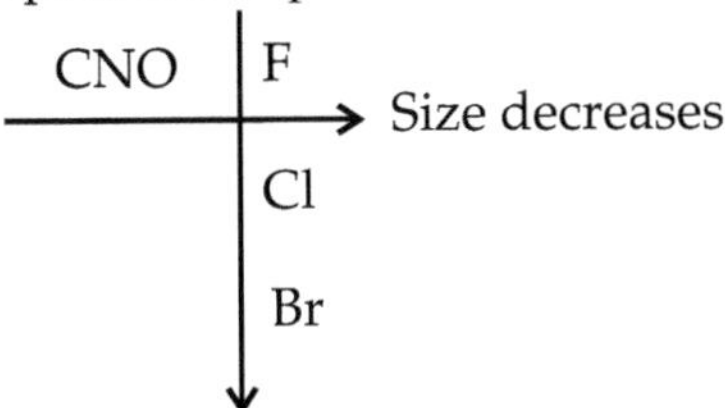


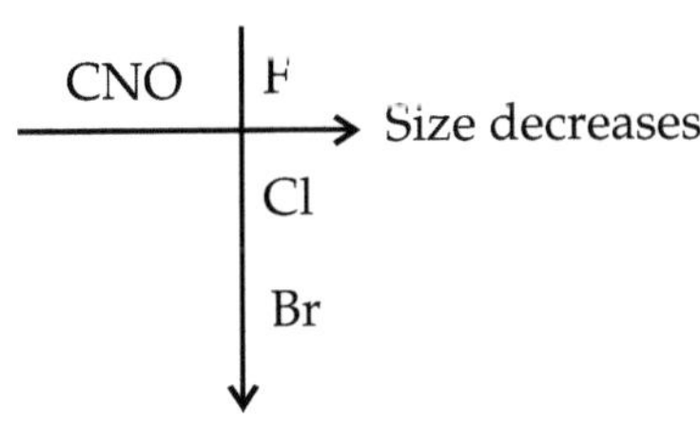


$$c < b < a < d < e$$

**19. (1)** The digits and the corresponding abbreviation is shown below :

| Digit | Abbreviation |
|---|---|
| 0 | n |
| 1 | u |
| 2 | b |
| 3 | t |
| 4 | q |
| 5 | p |
| 6 | h |
| 7 | s |
| 8 | o |
| 9 | e |

The IUPAC symbol for the element with atomic number 119 is uue.

**20. (4)** Calcium, barium and scandium belong to the second group of the periodic table. Potassium belong to first group of periodic table. The electronic configuration of potassium is $[Ar]4s^1$. The first ionisation energy of potassium is low as it can easily donate its valence electron in $4s^1$ to get noble gas configuration. The second ionisation energy of potassium is high as large amount of energy is required to remove electron from positively charged potassium with stable noble gas configuration. Therefore, the potassium (K) has greatest difference between its first and second ionisation energies.

**21. (1)** The number of electrons in $N^{3-}$, $O^{2-}$, $Mg^{2+}$ and Na+ is the same, i.e., 10. Therefore, these ions form an isoelectric set of ions.

**22. (4)** The atomic number of boron is higher than atomic number of beryllium. The size of the beryllium is higher than the size of boron. Therefore, the nuclear charge on beryllium is less than boron.

**23. (1)** The electronic configuration of H is $1s^1$.

The electronic configuration of Li is $1s^22s^1$.

The electronic configuration of Na is $1s^22s^22p^63s^1$.

The electronic configuration of K is $1s^22s^22p^63s^23p^64s^1$.

The force of attraction feel by $2s$ electrons in K is maximum. Therefore, the energy of $2s$ orbital is lowest in K.

**24. (3)** The difference in the electronegativity of potassium (group 1 element) and chlorine (group 17 element) is large due to which the bond formed between these two atoms by transfer of electrons. Thus, the compound contains only ionic bond. On the other hand, the electronegativity difference between corresponding atoms involved in bonding in $PH_3$, $O_2$, $B_2H_6$ and $H_2SO_4$ is less. Therefore, they are all covalent compounds.

**25. (3)** The given ions are iso-electronic species as they all contain 10 electrons.

In case of iso-electronic species, the ionic radius increases with increase in negative charge and decreases with increase in positive charge. Thus, the correct order for increasing ionic radii of the given species is,

$$Mg^{2+} < Na^+ < F^- < O^{2-}$$

**26. (3)** The ions $O^{2-}$, $F^-$, $Na^+$ and $Mg^{2+}$ are isoelectronic as they possess ten electrons each. Therefore, they are isoelectronic species.

**27. (3)** Generally, the ionization energy increases while going from left to right in the period and decreases from top to bottom while going down the group.

In the given table, the first ionization energy of A and B is greater as compared to the group-1 elements (Li = 520 kJ mol$^{-1}$ to Cs = 374 kJ mol$^{-1}$). It concludes that elements A and B belong to the group-2. For element B, all the values of ionization energies are low which shows that element B will come below A.

**28. (3)** The electronic configuration with the highest ionization enthalpy is $[Ne]3s^23p^3$ due to partially filled electronic configuration.

The electronic configuration, $[Ar]3d^{10}4s^24p^3$ also partially filled but it requires less ionization energy as compared to $[Ne]3s^23p^3$ due to more ionization energy of $P_3$ than $P_4$.

The order of ionization energy for orbitals, which present in different shells is shown below.

$$S_1 < P_1 < S_2 < P_2 < P_4 < P_3 < P_5 < P_6$$

**29. (4)** The solubility of alkaline-earth metals decreases down the group due to increase in size of atom and decrease in hydration enthalpy. Thus, the correct solubility order is,

$$Mg > Ca > Sr > Ba$$

**30. (1)** The ions present in compound are $Na^+$ and $F^-$.

The electronic configuration of $Na^+$ is $[He]2s^22p^6$.

The electronic configuration of $F^-$ is $[He]2s^22p^6$.

Thus, configuration of sodium and fluoride ion does not match with the configuration given in the question.

**31. (3)** The ionization energy of group 15 elements is higher than that of group 16 elements due to half-filled configuration of group 15 elements. This half-filled electronic configuration of group 15 elements gives them extra stability due to which their ionization energy increases.

**32. (4)** Ionization energy decreases down the group but it increases along the period on moving from left to right. Scandium belongs to group 3 while all the other given elements belong to group 1. Thus, scandium has the highest first ionization energy.

**33. (3)** The decreasing order of radius of given ions is,

$$N^{3-} > O^{2-} > F^-$$

Therefore, the possible values of ionic radii of given ions is,

$$N^{3-} = 1.71 \text{ Å}$$
$$O^{2-} = 1.40 \text{ Å}$$
$$F^- = 1.36 \text{ Å}$$

**34. (4)** The boiling point of Xe is highest amoing all as,

$$\text{Boiling Point} \propto \text{Molecular Mass}$$

As the size of atom increases from He to Rn, the Van der Waals force increases and the boiling point also increases.

**35. (3)** The electronic configuration $5s^25p^4$ indicates that element belongs to period 5 as principal quantum number is 5. The general electronic configuration $ns^2np^4$ corresponds to group 16.

**36. (3)** On moving down the group, atomic radii of element increases. This is due to the fact that atomic number increases down the group and a new shell is added.

**37. (4)** According to the Modern Periodic Law, the elements having an equal number of valence electrons in their valence shell show similarity in their chemical properties. Therefore, the similarity in the chemical properties of elements can be justified by the number of valence electrons in their outermost shell.

**38. (1)** The atomic radii of $O^{2-}$, $N^{3-}$ and $S^{2-}$ is smaller than that of $P^{3-}$ because the atomic radius of elements decreases along the period. The atomic radius of $O^{2-}$ is smaller than that of $N^{3-}$ because both the ions have an equal number of electrons but the number of protons is greater in $O^{2-}$ as compared to $N^{3-}$. Hence, the increasing order of atomic radii of the given elements is $O^{2-} < N^{3-} < S^{2-} < P^{3-}$.

**39. (2)** On moving from left to right in periodic table, ionic radii decreases and is more dependent on the number of electrons. $O_2^{2-}$ and $F^-$ are isoelectronic species. However, due to presence of one extra proton, the ionic radii of $O_2^{2-}$ is higher than that of $F^-$.

**40. (1)** Oxides of metals are basic in nature and oxides of non-metals are acidic in nature. Therefore, the order of increasing acidic strength is $CaO < CuO < H_2O < CO_2$.

**41. (2)** The electronic configuration of Be in ground state is $1s^2 2s^2$. The electronic configuration of $Be^-$ ion is $1s^2 2s^2 2p^1$. The fully filled configuration of Beryllium is lost on acceptance of an electron. So, it is unstable.

●●

## QUESTIONS

1. The oxidation states of iron atoms in compounds (A), (B) and (C), respectively, are $x$, $y$ and $z$. The sum of $x$, $y$ and $z$ is ........... . **[2020, Main]**

$$Na_4[Fe(CN)_5NOS)] \quad Na_4[FeO_4] \quad [Fe_2(CO)_9]$$
$$(A) \qquad\qquad (B) \qquad\quad (C)$$

2. Cast iron is used for the manufacture of : **[2020, Main]**
   (1) wrought iron and pig iron
   (2) wrought iron and steel
   (3) wrought iron, pig iron and steel
   (4) pig iron, scrap iron and steel

3. Among statement (a)-(d), the correct ones are : **[2020, Main]**
   (a) Lime stone is decomposed to CaO during the extraction of iron from its oxides
   (b) In the extraction of silver, silver is extracted as an anionic complex
   (c) Nickel is purified by Mond's process
   (d) Zr and Ti are purified by Van Arkel method
   (1) (c) and (d) only
   (2) (a), (c) and (d) only
   (3) (b), (c) and (d) only
   (4) (a), (b), (c) and (d)

4. The element that can be refined by distillation is : **[2020, Main]**
   (1) Nickel        (2) Zinc
   (3) Gallium       (4) Tin

5. Mischmetal is an alloy consisting mainly of : **[2020, Main]**
   (1) lanthanoid metals
   (2) actinoid metals
   (3) actinoid and transition metals
   (4) lanthanoid and actinoid metals

6. Dihydrogen of high purity ($> 99.95\%$) is obtained through : **[2020, Main]**
   (1) the electrolysis of warm $Ba(OH)_2$ solution using Ni electrodes.
   (2) the reaction of Zn with dilute HCl.
   (3) the electrolysis of brine solution.
   (4) the electrolysis of acidified water using Pt electrodes.

7. The INCORRECT statement is : **[2020, Main]**
   (1) Bronze is an alloy of copper and tin.

   (2) Brass is an alloy of copper and nickel.
   (3) Cast iron is used to manufacture wrought iron.
   (4) German silver is an alloy of zinc, copper and nickel.

8. The processes of calcination and roasting in metallurgical industries, respectively, can lead to : **[2020, Main]**
   (1) Global warming and acid rain
   (2) Photochemical smog and ozone layer depletion
   (3) Global warming and photochemical smog
   (4) Photochemical smog and global warming

9. Which of the following compounds will form the precipitate with aq. $AgNO_3$ solution most readily ? **[2020, Main]**

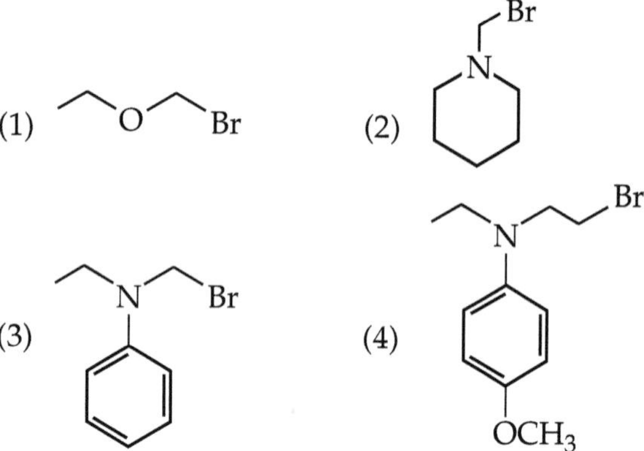

10. For the following Assertion and Reason, the correct option is : **[2020, Main]**
    **Assertion :** The pH of water increases with increase in temperature.
    **Reason :** The dissociation of water into $H^+$ and $OH^-$ is an exothermic reaction.
    (1) Both assertion and reason are true, but the reason is not the correct explanation for the assertion
    (2) Both assertion and reason are false
    (3) Assertion is not true, but reason is true
    (4) Both assertion and reason are true, and the reason is the corect explanation for the assertion

11. Among the reactions (a) - (d), the reaction(s) that does/do not occur in the blast furnace during the extraction of iron is/are : **[2020, Main]**
    (a) $CaO + SiO_2 \rightarrow CaSiO_3$

(b) $3Fe_2O_3 + CO \rightarrow 2Fe_3O_4 + CO_2$

(c) $FeO + SiO_2 \rightarrow FeSiO_3$

(d) $FeO \rightarrow Fe + \dfrac{1}{2}O_2$

(1) (c) and (d)    (2) (a) and (b)

(3) (d)    (4) (a)

12. Within each pair of elements F & Cl, S & Se and Li & Na, respectively, the elements that release more energy upon an electron gain are : **[2020, Main]**

(a) Cl, Se and Na    (2) Cl, S and Li

(c) F, S and Li    (4) F, Se and Na

13. The refining method used when the metal and the impurities have low and high melting temperatures, respectively, is : **[2020, Main]**

(a) vapour phase refining    (2) distillation

(c) liquation    (4) zone refining

14. The Mond process is used for the : **[2019, Main]**

(1) purification of Ni

(2) extraction of Mo

(3) purification of Zr and Ti

(4) extraction of Zn

15. The ore that contains the metal in the form of fluoride is : **[2019, Main]**

(1) cryolite    (2) malachite

(3) magnetite    (4) sphalerite

16. For the extraction of iron, haematite ore is used.

**Reason :** Haematite is a carbonate ore of iron.

**[2019, Main]**

(1) Only the reason is correct.

(2) Both the assertion and reason are correct, but the reason is not the correct explanation for the assertion.

(3) Both the assertion and reason are correct and the reason is the correct explanation for the assertion.

(4) Only the assertion is correct.

17. The one that is not a carbonate ore is :

**[2019, Main]**

(1) Malachite    (2) Calamine

(3) Siderite    (4) Bauxite

18. Match the refining methods (Column I) with metals (Column II).    **[2019, Main]**

| Column I<br>(Refining methods) | Column II<br>(Metals) |
|---|---|
| (I) Liquation | (a) Zr |
| (II) Zone Refining | (b) Ni |
| (III) Mond Process | (c) Sn |
| (IV) Van Arkel Method | (d) Ga |

(1) (I) - (c); (II) - (a); (III) - (b); (IV) - (d)

(2) (I) - (b); (II) - (c); (III) - (d); (IV) - (a)

(3) (I) - (c); (II) - (d); (III) - (b); (IV) - (a)

(4) (I) - (b); (II) - (d); (III) - (a); (IV) - (c)

19. The alloy used in the construction of aricrafts is :

**[2019, Main]**

(1) Mg – Al    (2) Mg – Zn

(3) Mg – Sn    (4) Mg – Mn

20. The correct statement is :    **[2019, Main]**

(1) aniline is a froth stabilizer

(2) zincite is a carbonate ore

(3) sodium cyanide cannot be used in the metallurgy of silver

(4) zone refining process is used for the refining of titanium

21. The idea of froth floatation method came from a person X and this method is related to the process Y of ores. X and Y, respectively are : **[2019, Main]**

(1) Fisher woman and concentration

(2) Washer woman and concentration

(3) Fisher man and reduction

(4) Washer man and reduction

22. The correct statement is :    **[2019, Main]**

(1) Leaching of bauxite using concentrated NaOH solution gives sodium aluminate and sodium silicate.

(2) The Hall-Heroult process is used for the production of aluminium and iron.

(3) Pig iron is obtained from cast iron.

(4) The blistered appearance of copper during the metallurgical process is due to the evolution of $CO_2$

23. The green colour produced in the borax bead test of a chromium(III) salt is due to : **[2019, Advanced]**

(1) $Cr(BO_2)_3$    (2) $Cr_2(B_4O_7)_3$

(3) $Cr_2O_3$    (4) $CrB$

24. In the leaching method, bauxite ore is digested with a concentrated solution of NaOH that produces 'X'. When $CO_2$ gas is passed through the aqueous solution of 'X', a hydrated compound 'Y' is precipitated. 'X' and 'Y' respectively are :

**[2018, Main]**

(1) $NaAlO_2$ and $Al_2(CO_3)_3.x\ H_2O$

(2) $Al(OH)_3$ and $Al_2O_3.x\ H_2O$

(3) $Na[Al(OH)_4]$ and $Al_2O_3.x\ H_2O$

(4) $Na[Al(OH)_4]$ and $Al_2(CO_3)_3.x\ H_2O$

25. Two compounds I and II are eluted by column chromatography (adsorption of I > II). Which one of following is a correct statement ? **[2018, Main]**

(1) I moves faster and has higher $R_f$ value than II

(2) II moves faster and has higher $R_f$ value than I

(3) I moves slower and has higher $R_f$ value than II

(4) II moves slower and has higher $R_f$ value than I

26. In the extraction of copper from its sulphide ore, metal is finally obtained by the oxidation of cuprous sulphide with :    **[2018, Main]**

(1) $Fe_2O_3$    (2) $Cu_2O$

(3) $SO_2$    (4) $CO$

27. Extraction of copper from copper pyrite ($CuFeS_2$) involves :    **[2018, Advanced]**

(1) Crushing followed by concentration of the ore by froth-flotation

(2) Removal of iron as slag

(3) Self-reduction step to produce 'blister copper' following evolution of $SO_2$

(4) Refining of 'blister copper' by carbon reduction

28. The plot shows the variation of $-\ln K_p$ versus temperature for the two reactions.

$$M(s) + \frac{1}{2}O_2(g) \rightarrow MO(s)$$

and

$$C(s) + \frac{1}{2}O_2(g) \rightarrow CO(s)$$

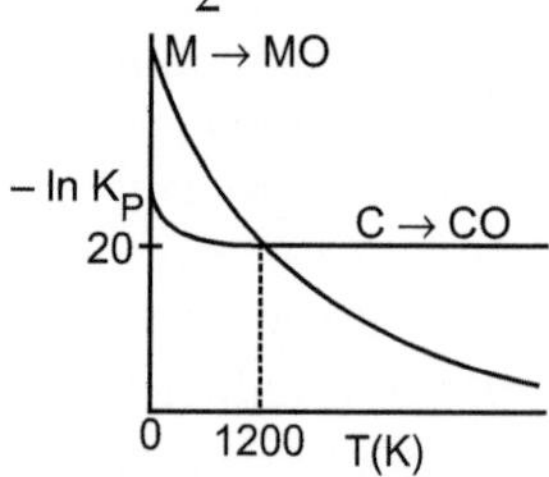


Identify the correct statement : **[2016, Main]**

(1) At T > 1200 K, carbon will reduce MO(s) to M(s)

(2) At T < 1200 K, the reaction

$$MO(s) + C(s) \rightarrow M(s) + CO(g)$$ is spontaneous

(3) At T < 1200 K, oxidation of carbon is unfavourable

(4) Oxidation of carbon is favourable at all temperatures

29. Extraction of copper by smelting uses silica as an additive to remove : **[2018, Main]**

(1) $Cu_2S$     (2) $FeO$

(3) $FeS$     (4) $Cu_2O$

30. Which one of the following ores is best concentrated by froth floatation method ?

**[2016, Main]**

(1) Magnetite     (2) Siderite

(3) Galena     (4) Malachite

31. Copper is purified by electrolytic refining of blister copper. The correct statements about this process is/are : **[2015, Advanced]**

(1) Impure Cu strip is used as cathode

(2) Acidified aqueous $CuSO_4$ is used as electrolyte

(3) Pure Cu deposits at cathode

(4) Impurities settle as anode-mud

32. Match the anionic species given in Column I that are present in the ores given in Column II.

**[2015, Advanced]**

| Column I | | Column II |
|---|---|---|
| (1) Carbonate | (P) | Siderite |
| (2) Sulphide | (Q) | Malachite |
| (3) Hydroxide | (R) | Bauxite |
| (4) Oxide | (S) | Calamine |
| | (T) | Argentite |

33. In the context of the Hall-Heroult process for the extraction of Al, which of the following statements is false ? **[2015, Main]**

(1) CO and $CO_2$ are produced in this process

(2) $Al_2O_3$ is mixed with $CaF_2$ which lowers the melting point of the mixture and brings conductivity

(3) $Al^{3+}$ is reduced at the cathode to form Al

(4) $Na_3AlF_6$ serves as the electrolyte

34. In the isolation of metals, calcination process usually results in : **[2015, Main]**

(1) Metal carbonate    (2) Metal oxide

(3) Metal sulphide    (4) Metal hydroxide

35. Calamine is an ore of : **[2015, Main]**

(1) Aluminium    (2) Copper

(3) Iron    (4) Zinc

36. Upon heating with $Cu_2S$, the reagents that give copper metal is/are : **[2014, Advanced]**

(1) $CuFeS_2$    (2) $CuO$

(3) $Cu_2O$    (4) $CuSO_4$

37. The form of iron obtained from blast furnace is :

**[2014, Main]**

(1) Steel    (2) Cast Iron

(3) Pig Iron    (4) Wrought Iron

38. Which one of the following ores is known as Malachite : **[2013, Advanced]**

(1) $Cu_2O$    (2) $Cu_2S$

(3) $CuFeS_2$    (4) $Cu(OH)_2.CuCO_3$

39. Sulfide ores are common for the metals :

**[2013, Advanced]**

(1) Ag, Cu and Pb    (2) Ag, Cu and Sn

(3) Ag, Mg and Pb    (4) Al, Cu and Pb

40. The carbon-based reduction method is NOT used for the extraction of : **[2013, Advanced]**

(1) Tin from $SnO_2$

(2) Iron from $Fe_2O_3$

(3) Aluminium from $Al_2O_3$

(4) Magnesium from $MgCO_3.CaCO_3$

41. In the cyanide extraction process of silver from argentite ore, the oxidising and reducing agents used are : **[2012, Advanced]**

(1) $O_2$ and CO respectively

(2) $O_2$ and Zn dust respectively

(3) $HNO_3$ and Zn dust respectively

(4) $HNO_3$ and CO respectively

42. Extraction of metal from the ore cassiterite involves : **[2012, Advanced]**

(1) Carbon reduction of an oxide ore

(2) Self-reduction of a sulphide ore

(3) Removal of copper impurity

(4) Removal of iron impurity

43. Oxidation states of the metal in the minerals haematite and magnetite, respectively, are :

**[2011, Advanced]**

(1) II, III in haematite and III in magnetite

(2) II, III in haematite and II in magnetite

(3) II in haematite and II, III in magnetite

(4) III in haematite and II, III in magnetite

**44.** Partial roasting of chalcopyrite produces :
**[2011, Advanced]**
(1) $Cu_2S$ and $FeO$     (2) $Cu_2O$ and $FeO$
(3) $CuS$ and $Fe_2O_3$     (4) $Cu_2O$ and $Fe_2O_3$

**45.** Iron is removed from chalcopyrite as :
**[2010, Advanced]**
(1) $FeO$     (2) $FeS$
(3) $Fe_2O_3$     (4) $FeSiO_3$

**46.** Match the conversions in Column I with the types of reactions given in Column II. Indicate your answer by darkening the appropriate bubbles of the 4 × 4 matrix given in the ORS.
**[2008, Advanced]**

| Column I | Column II |
|---|---|
| (A) $PbS \rightarrow PbO$ | (p) roasting |
| (B) $CaCO_3 \rightarrow CaO$ | (q) calcination |
| (C) $ZnS \rightarrow Zn$ | (r) carbon reduction |
| (D) $Cu_2S \rightarrow Cu$ | (s) self reduction |

**47.** Extraction of zinc from zinc blende is achieved by :
**[2007, Advanced]**
(1) Electrolytic reduction
(2) Roasting followed by reduction with carbon
(3) Roasting followed by reduction with another metal
(4) Roasting followed by self-reduction

**48.** Match the extraction processes listed in Column I with metals listed in Column II : **[2006, Main]**

| Column I | Column II |
|---|---|
| (A) Self reduction | (P) Lead |
| (B) Carbon reduction | (Q) Silver |
| (C) Complex formation and displacement by metal | (R) Copper |
| (D) Decomposition of iodide | (S) Boron |

**49.** Which of the following ore contains both Copper and Iron ?
**[2005, Screening]**
(1) Cuprite     (2) Chalcocite
(3) Chalcopyrite     (4) Malachite

**50.** $A_1$ and $A_2$ are two ores of metal M. $A_1$ on calcination gives black precipitate, $CO_2$ and water.
**[2004, Main]**

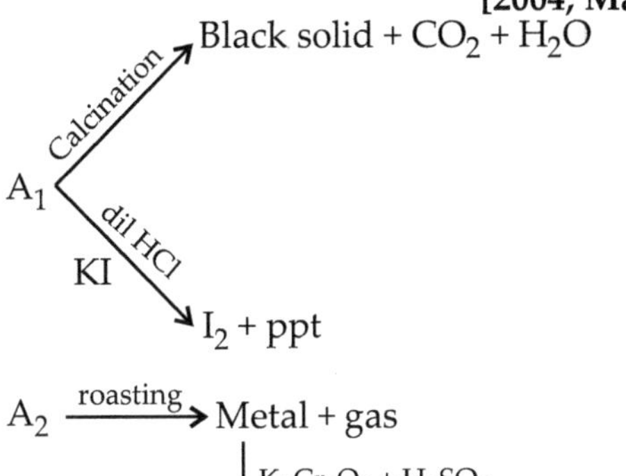


**51.** The methods chiefly used for the extraction of Lead and Tin from their ores are respectively :
**[2004, Screening]**
(1) Self reduction and carbon reduction
(2) Self reduction and electrolytic reduction
(3) Carbon reduction and self reduction
(4) Cyanide process and carbon reduction

**52.** Write down reactions involved in the extraction of Pb. What is the oxidation number of lead in litharge ? **[2003, Main]**

**53.** In the process of extraction of gold.
$$\text{Roasted gold ore} + CN^- + H_2O \xrightarrow{O_2} [X] + OH^-$$
$$[X] + Zn \rightarrow [Y] + Au \qquad \textbf{[2003, Screening]}$$
Identify the complexes [X] and [Y]
(1) $X = [Au(CN)_2]^-$ $Y = [Zn(CN)_4]^{2-}$
(2) $X = [Au(CN)_4]^{3-}$ $Y = [Zn(CN)_4]^{2-}$
(3) $X = [Au(CN)_2]^-$ $Y = [Zn(CN)_6]^{4-}$
(4) $X = [Au(CN)_4]^-$ $Y = [Zn(CN)_4]^{2-}$

**54.** Which of the following process is used in the extractive metallurgy of magnesium ?
**[2002, Screening]**
(1) Fused salt electrolysis
(2) Self reduction
(3) Aqueous solution electrolysis
(4) Thermite reduction

## ANSWER KEY

| | | | | | | | | | |
|---|---|---|---|---|---|---|---|---|---|
| **1.** (*) | **2.** (2) | **3.** (4) | **4.** (2) | **5.** (1) | **6.** (1) | **7.** (2) | **8.** (1) | **9.** (2) | **10.** (2) |
| **11.** (1) | **12.** (2) | **13.** (3) | **14.** (1) | **15.** (1) | **16.** (4) | **17.** (4) | **18.** (3) | **19.** (1) | **20.** (1) |
| **21.** (2) | **22.** (1) | **23.** (1,2,3) | **24.** (3) | **25.** (2) | **26.** (2) | **27.** (1,2,3) | **28.** (3) | **29.** (2) | **30.** (3) |
| **31.** (2,3,4) | **32.** (*) | **33.** (4) | **34.** (2) | **35.** (4) | **36.** (2,3,4) | **37.** (3) | **38.** (4) | **39.** (1) | **40.** (3,4) |
| **41.** (2) | **42.** (1,3,4) | **43.** (4) | **44.** (2) | **45.** (4) | **46.** (*) | **47.** (2) | **48.** (*) | **49.** (3) | **50.** (*) |
| **51.** (1) | **52.** (*) | **53.** (1) | **54.** (1) | | | | | | |

## ANSWERS WITH EXPLANATIONS

**1.** (A) $Na_4[\overset{x}{Fe}(CN)_5(NOS)]$

$(+1)4 + x + (-1)5 + (-1)1 = 0$

$x = +2$

(B) $Na_4[\overset{y}{Fe}O_4]$

$(+1)4 + y + (-2)4 = 0$

$y = +4$

(C)   $[\overset{z}{Fe}_2(CO)_9]$

$$2z + 0 \times 9 = 0$$
$$z = 0$$

so,    $(x + y + z) = +2 + 4 + 0$
$$= 6$$

**2. (2)** Cast iron is used for the manufacturing of wrought iron and steel.

**3. (4)**  (a) $CaCO_3 \xrightarrow{\Delta} CaO + CO_2$ {In Blast furnace}

lime stone

(b) Ag from cyanide complex $[Ag(CN)_2]^-$ during cyaride process

$$Ag/Ag_2S + CN^- \rightarrow [Ag(CN)_2]^-$$

(c) Ni is purified by mond's process.

(d) Zr and Ti are purified by van Arkel method

All (a), (b), (c), (d) are correct statements.

Thus, correct option is (4).

**4. (2)** Impure zinc is refined by distillation method.

**5. (1)** Alloys of lanthanides with Fe are called Misch metal, which consists of a lanthanoid metal (~95%) and iron (~5%) and traces of S, C, Ca and Al.

**6. (1)** High purity (>99.95%) dihydrogen is obtained by electrolysing warm aqueous barium hydroxide solution between nickel electrodes.

**7. (2)** Brass is an alloy of copper and nickel.

**8. (1)** Due to industrial process $SO_2$ gas is released which is responsible for acid rain and global warming.

**9. (2)** The rate of precipitate formation of Agx depends on stability of carbocation ($R^+$)

In the given question the four different carbocation formed by the given four options carbocation will be

|     (1)     |     (2)     |     (3)     |     (4)     |

As the most stable carbocation is (2), therefore

will form the precipitate with aq.

$AgNO_3$ solution most readily.

**10. (2)**  $H_2O(l) \rightleftharpoons H^+_{(aq)} + OH^-_{(aq)}$

For ionisation of $H_2O : DH > O$

$\Rightarrow$ ENDOTHERMIC

On temperature increase reaction shifts forward

$\Rightarrow$ both [$H^+$] and [$OH^-$] increase

$\Rightarrow$ pH & pOH decreases.

**11. (1)** In blast furnace (metallugy of iron) involved reactions are

(a)  $CaO + SiO_2 \rightarrow CaSiO_3$

(b)  $2Fe_2O_3 + CO \rightarrow 2Fe_3O_4 + CO_2$

**12. (2)** Cl, S and Li

Down the group electron affinity decrease due to increasing size. So, the electron affinity of S > Se and Li > Na so energy release will also be more. But, in case of F and Cl, there is exception, Cl > F. It is due to the small size of F atom where the incoming electron face high electron-electron repulsion. So, the energy release will be more in Cl.

**13. (3)** Metal with low melting point containing impurities of high melting point can be purified by liquation because liquation separation is based on differences in the melting point and density of alloy and on the low level of mutual solubility of the constituents.

**14. (1)** The Mond process is a method used for the purification of nickel. In this process, impure nickel is reacted with carboin monoxide to form volatile nickel tetracarbonyl. Further, nickel tetracarbonyl is decomposed to give pure nickel.

**15. (1)** The formula of cryolite is $Na_3AlF_6$.
The formula of magnetite is $Fe_3O_4$.
The formula of sphalerite is ZnS.
The formula of malachite is $Cu(OH)_2.CuCO_3$.
Therefore, cryolite is the ore that contain metal in the form of fluoride.

**16. (4)** Haematite is a ore of iron. Its chemical formula is $Fe_2O_3$. It is used in the extraction process of iron. Therefore, only the assertion is correct.

**17. (4)** The formula of bauxite is $AlO_x(OH)_{3-2x}$.
The formula of siderite is $FeCO_3$.
The formula of calamite is $ZnCO_3$.
The formula of malachite is $Cu(OH)_2.CuCO_3$.
Therefore, bauxite is the ore that do not contain carbonate ore.

**18. (3)** The metal Sn is refined using liquation, Ga is refined using zone refining, Ni is refined using Mond process and Zr is refined using Van Arkel method.

**19. (1)** An alloy of Mg–Al is used for the construction of aircrafts as they are light weight and are resistant to corrosion.

**20. (1)** Aniline is a froth stabilizer.

The formula of zincite is ZnO. Therefore, it is not a carbonate ore.

The metal titanium is not refined using the process of zone refining.

The compound sodium cyanide is uded in the metallurgy of silver to convert the impure silver into a cyanide complex.

**21. (2)** A washer woman discovered a method for concentration of sulphide ore. The process is termed as froth floatation method. Therefore, the correct option is washer woman and concentration.

**22. (1)** The leaching is a process in which an ore is dissolved in a liquid for the extraction process.

The leaching of bauxite involves its reaction with concentrated NaOH to from sodium aluminate and sodium silicate and $Fe_2O_3$ precipitate.

**23. (1,2,3)** The gold extraction process is shown below :
$$4Au(s) + 8CN^- + 2H_2O\ (aq) + O_2(g)$$
$$\rightarrow 4[Au(CN)_2]^-\ (aq) + 4OH^-(aq)$$
$$2[Au(CN)_2]^-\ (aq) + Zn(s)$$
$$\rightarrow [Zn(CN)_4]^{2-}\ (aq) + 2Au(s)$$
The correct combination are $Q = O_2$, $T = Zn$, $Z = [Zn(CN)_4]^{2-}$ and $R = [Au(CN)_2]^-$.

**24. (3)** The given reactions occur in the Bayer process as,
$$2Al_2O_3 + 2NaOH \rightarrow 2Na[Al(OH)_4]$$
$$2Na[Al(OH)_4] + CO_2 \rightarrow Al_2O_3.xH_2O$$
Therefore, X is $Na[Al(OH)_4]$ and Y is $Al_2O_3.xH_2O$.

**25. (2)** The principle of column chromatography is adsorption. The compound that has less adsorption towards stationary phase will go with the mobile phase and its $R_f$ will be more. The speed of compound is slow if its adsorption is more. The adsorption of compound I is more than that of II, hence it will move slower than II and its $R_f$ value will also be less than that of compound II.

**26. (2)** In the extraction of copper from its sulphide ore, metal is finally obtained by the oxidation of cuprous sulphide with $Cu_2O$ as shown below.
$$Cu_2S + 2Cu_2O \rightarrow 6Cu + SO_2$$

**27. (1,2,3)** The extraction of copper from copper pyrite is shown below.

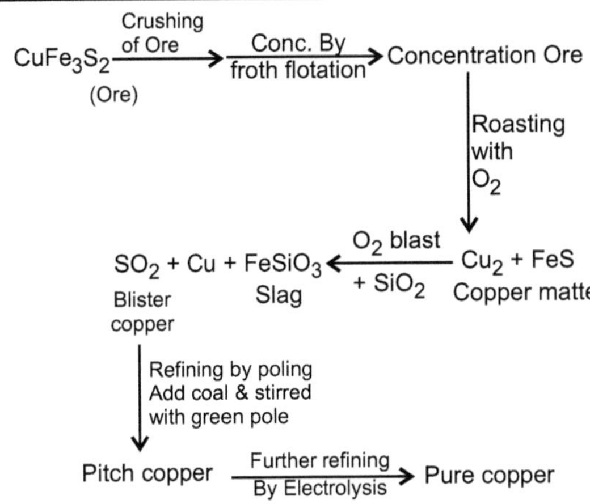


In the first step, the ore is crushed and then concentrated by froth floatation process. Then roasting is done which forms a mixture of $Cu_2S$ and FeS. Then $O_2$ blast takes place in the presence of $SiO_2$ and iron is removed as slag.

In self-reduction step, blister copper is produced followed by the evolution of $SO_2$.

Blister copper is further refined by electrolysis.

Refining of blister copper is not done by reduction with carbon.

Thus, correct statements are (1), (2) and (3).

**28. (3)** The diagram that is given by Ellingham is shown below.

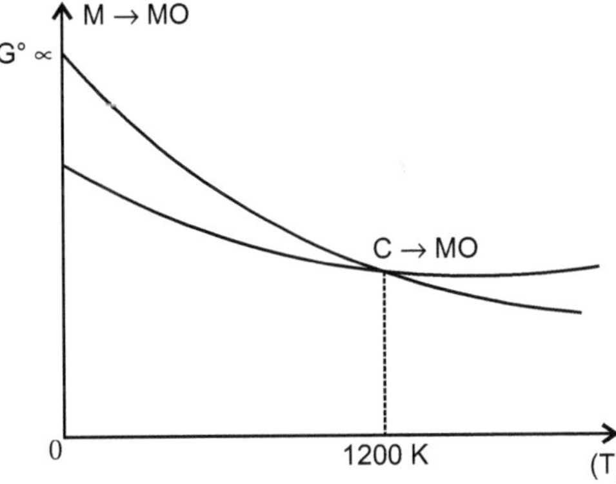


It is clearly seen in the graph that at T < 1200, carbon will reduce MO(s) to M(s).

Thus, the reaction $C(s) + MO(s) \rightarrow M(s) + CO(g)$ is spontaneous.

**29. (2)** The reaction involved in the smelting process is as follows :
$$FeO + SiO_2 \rightarrow FeSiO_3$$
In this process, $SiO_2$ is flux and FeO is gangue which results in the formation of $FeSiO_3$.

**30. (3)** Froth flotation process is used for sulphide ores. Only galena (PbS) is an ore of sulphide.

**31. (2,3,4)** In refining method of blister copper, at anode impure strip of copper is used, whereas at cathode pure copper is deposited and the acidified solution of $CuSO_4$ is used as electrolyte. Impurities settle as anode-mud.

**32.** (A)-(P), (Q), (S); (B)-(T); (C)-(Q), (R); (D)-(R)

    (A) Carbonate ion is present in the ore of siderite ($FeCO_3$), malachite ($CuCO_3.Cu(OH)_2$) and calamine ($ZnCO_3$).

    (B) Sulphide ion is present in the ore of argentite ($Ag_2S$).

    (C) Hydroxide ion is present in the ore of malachite ($CuCO_3.Cu(OH)_2$) and bauxite ($AlO_x(OH)_{3-2x}$).

    (D) Oxide ion is present in the ore of bauxite ($AlO_x(OH)_{3-2x}$).

**33.** **(4)** In the given process molten alumina ($Al_2O_3$) serves as an electrolyte.

**34.** **(2)** The decomposition of metal carbonates, metal hydroxides leads to the formation of metal oxide in the process of calcination.

**35.** **(4)** The formula of calamine is $ZnCO_3$. It is an ore of zinc.

**36.** **(2,3,4)** (A) No reaction occurs.

    (B) $Cu_2S + 2CuO \rightarrow 4Cu + SO_2\uparrow$

    (C) $Cu_2S + 2Cu_2O \rightarrow 6Cu + SO_2\uparrow$

    (D) $Cu_2S + CuSO_4 \rightarrow 3Cu + 2SO_2\uparrow$

**37.** **(3)** The form of iron that is obtained from the blast furnace is pig iron. Pig iron possesses 92-94% of iron and 3-5% of carbon.

**38.** **(4)** $Cu(OH)_2.CuCO_3$ ore is known Malachite.

**39.** **(1)** The chemical formula of sulfide ion is $S^{2-}$. The metal compounds containing sulfide ions are shown below.

$$Ag \rightarrow Ag_2S$$
$$Cu \rightarrow CuFeS_2$$
$$Pb \rightarrow PbS$$

**40.** **(3,4)** (A) The carbon-based reduction method is used to extract tin from $SnO_2$.

    (B) The carbon-based reduction method is used to extract iron from $Fe_2O_3$.

    (C) The carbon-based reduction method is not used to extract aluminium from $Al_2O_3$ because aluminium is extracted through electrolytic reduction.

    (D) The carbon-based reduction method is not used to extract magnesium from $MgCO_3.CaCO_3$ because magnesium is extracted through electrolytic reduction.

**41.** **(2)** The reaction involved in the given extraction process is shown below.

$$Ag_2S + 4NaCN \rightarrow 2Na[Ag(CN)_2] + Na_2S$$
$$4Na_2S + 2H_2O + 5O_2 \rightarrow 2Na_2SO_4 + 4NaOH + 2S$$
$$2Na[Ag(CN)_2] + Zn \rightarrow Na_2[Zn(CN)_4] + 2Ag\downarrow$$

Here oxygen acts as an oxidizing agent and zinc acts as a reducing agent.

**42.** **(1,3,4)** Cassiterite is an ore of tin metal. It is found in tin oxide ($SnO_2$) form. The extraction of metal from this ore involves carbon reduction, then removal of iron and copper impurity. Copper impurity is present in trace amount. The reaction for carbon reduction is given as,

$$SnO_2 + 2C \rightarrow 2CO + Sn$$

There is no sulfur atom is present. Therefore, self-reduction of sulphide ore is not possible.

**43.** **(4)** The molecular formula of hematite and magnetite are $Fe_2O_3$ and $Fe_3O_4$ respectively. The common name of magnetite is ferrous-ferric oxide. The formula is also expressed as, $FeO.FeO_2$. Oxidation state of iron in $Fe_2O_3$ is III. In $Fe_3O_4$ oxidation state of iron is II and III.

**44.** **(2)** The following reaction takes place in the partial roasting of chalcopyrite $CuFeS_2$.

$$2CuFeS_2 + O_2 \rightarrow Cu_2S + 2FeS + SO_2$$
$$2Cu_2S + 3O_2 \rightarrow Cu_2O + 2SO_2$$
$$2FeS + 3O_2 \rightarrow FeO + 2SO_2$$

The partial roasting of chalcopyrite $CuFeS_2$ produces $Cu_2O$ and $FeO$.

**45.** **(4)** Iron is removed from chalcopyrite by reacting it with $SiO_2$, which produces $FeSiO_3$ as slag.

$$FeO + SiO_2 \rightarrow FeSiO_3$$

**46.** (A)-(p); (B)-(aq); (C)-(p), (r); (D)-(p), (s)

    (A) The given reaction is an example of roasting.

    (B) The given process is an example of calcination.

    (C) At high temperature, ZnS converts into ZnO in the presence of air which on reduction with C converts into Zn.

    (D) At high temperature, $Cu_2S$ converts into $Cu_2O$ in the presence of air and on self reduction gives Cu.

**47.** **(2)** The first step for extraction of zinc from zinc blende (ZnS) is roasting.

$$2ZnS + 3O_2 (\text{excess}) \xrightarrow{9000°C} 2ZnO + 2SO_2$$

The second step is reduction of ZnO with carbon.

$$ZnO + C \rightarrow Zn + CO$$

Hence, the extraction of zinc from zinc blende is achieved by roasting of ZnS followed by reduction with carbon.

**48.** (A)-(p), (r); (B)-(p), (r); (C)-(q); (D)-(s)

Self reduction is the process in which extraction of less electropositive metal takes place without use of any reducing agent.

The reaction involved in the self reduction process for the extraction of lead is as follows :

$$2PbS + 3O_2 \rightarrow 2PbO + 2SO_2$$
$$2PbS + 2PbO \rightarrow 3Pb + SO_2$$

Similarly, the reaction involved in the self reduction process for the extraction of copper is as follows :

$$Cu_2S + 2Cu_2O \rightarrow SO_2 + 6Cu$$

Carbon reduction is the process in which oxides are heated with carbon to give the metal. Thus, carbon reduction involves the extraction of lead and copper from its ore.

The extraction of silver involves leaching of metal and the formation of complex ion by using cyanide ion.

The thermal decomposition of boron triiodide over red hot tungsten results in the formation of boron. The reaction involved in this process is as follows :

$$2BI_3 \rightarrow 2B + 3I_2$$

**49. (3)** Among the given ores, the ore that contains both copper and iron is chalcopyrite. The chemical formula of chalcopyrite, $CuFeS_2$. Hence, the correct option is (3).

**50.** The $A_1$ must be malachite because on calcination it gives black solid that is CuO. The confirmatory reaction involved in this process is as follows :

$$Cu(OH)_2 CuCO_3 \xrightarrow{\text{calcination}} 2CuO + CO_2 + H_2O$$

$$Cu(OH)_2 CuCO_3 \xrightarrow[KI]{HCl} Cu_2 I_2 + KCl + I_2$$

Thus, $A_1$ is $Cu(OH)_2 CuCO_3$.

The confirmatory reaction involved in the roasting process is as follows :

$$Cu_2S \xrightarrow[O_2]{\text{Roasting}} Cu_2O + SO_2$$

$$Cu_2S + Cu_2O \rightarrow Cu + SO_2$$

Sulphur dioxide gives green color when reacts with $K_2Cr_2O_7$ and $H_2SO_4$. The reaction involved in this process is as follows :

$$3SO_2 + K_2Cr_2O_7 + H_2SO_4 \rightarrow K_2SO_4 + Cr_2(SO_4)_2$$
$$+ 4H_2O$$

Thus, $A_2$ is $Cu_2S$.

**51. (1)** The extraction of lead occurs by self reduction as shown below :

$$PbS + 3O_2 \xrightarrow{\Delta} 2PbO + 2SO_2$$

$$PbS + 3PbO(s) \xrightarrow{\Delta} 3Pb + SO_2$$

The extraction of tin occurs by carbon reduction as shown below.

$$SnO_2 + C \xrightarrow{\Delta} Sn + CO_2$$

**52.** Galena is a mineral that consists of 86.6% lead. The chemical formula of galena is PbS.

The reactions involved in the extraction process of lead from galena are as follows :

$$2PbS + 3O_2 \rightarrow 2PbO + 2SO_2$$
$$PbS + 2O_2 \rightarrow 2PbSO_4$$
$$2PbO + PbS \rightarrow 3Pb + SO_2$$
$$PbSO_4 + PbS \rightarrow 2Pb + 2SO_2$$

The chemical formula of litharge is PbO. The oxidation number of Pb in PbO is + 2.

**53. (1)** The reaction for the extraction of gold is given below :

$$2Au + 4CN^- + H_2O + \frac{1}{2} O_2 \rightarrow 2[Au(CN)_2]^- + 2OH^-$$

$$2[Au(CN)_2]^- + Zn \rightarrow [Zn(CN)_4]^{2-} + 2Au$$

Thus, complexes [X] is $[Au(CN)_2]^-$ and complex [Y] is $[Zn(CN)_4]^{2-}$.

**54. (1)** The extractive metallurgy of magnesium is shown below :

$$MgCl_2 \rightarrow Mg^{2+} + 2Cl^-$$

The reaction at cathode is shown below :

$$Mg^{2+} + 2e^- \rightarrow Mg$$

The reaction at anode is shown below :

$$2Cl^- - 2e^- \rightarrow Cl_2 \uparrow$$

Thus, magnesium and chlorine gas is formed at cathode and anode respectively.

●●

## QUESTIONS

**1.** Which one of the following compounds possesses the most acidic hydrogen ?   **[2020, Main]**

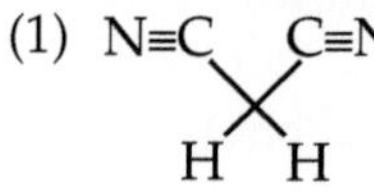

(2) $H_3C-C\equiv C-H$

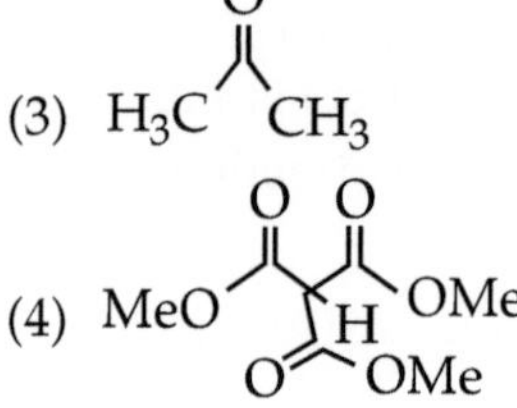

**2.** 5 g of zinc is treated separately with an excess of :

(a) dilute hydrochloric acid and

(b) aqueous sodium hydroxide

The ratio of the volumes of $H_2$ evolved in these two reactions is :   **[2020, Main]**

(1)  1 : 4          (2)  1 : 2

(3)  2 : 1          (4)  1 : 1

**3.** Hydrogen has three isotopes (A), (B) and (C). If the number of neutron(s) in (A), (B) and (C) respectively, are (x), (y) and (z), the sum of (x), (y) an (z) is :   **[2020, Main]**

(1)  4          (2)  3

(3)  2          (4)  1

**4.** Among statements (a)-(d), the correct ones are :   **[2020, Main]**

(a) Decomposition of hydrogen peroxide gives dioxygen

(b) Like hydrogen peroxide, compounds, such as $KClO_3$, $Pb(NO_3)_2$ and $NaNO_3$ when heated liberate dioxygen

(c) 2-Ethylanthraquinone is useful for the industrial preparation of hydrogen peroxide

(d) Hydrogen peroxide is used for the manufacture of sodium peroborate

(1)  (a), (b), (c) and (d)

(2)  (a), (b) and (c) only

(3)  (a), (c) and (d) only

(4)  (a) and (c) only

**5.** Hydrogen peroxide oxidises $[Fe(CN)_6]^{4-}$ to $[Fe(CN)_6]^{3-}$ in acidic medium but reduces $[Fe(CN)_6]^{3-}$ to $[Fe(CN)_6]^{4-}$ in alkaline medium. The other products formed are, respectively :   **[2018, Main]**

(1)  $(H_2O + O_2)$ and $H_2O$

(2)  $(H_2O + O_2)$ and $(H_2O + OH^-)$

(3)  $H_2O$ and $(H_2O + O_2)$

(4)  $H_2O$ and $(H_2O + OH^-)$

**6.** In which of the following reactions, hydrogen peroxide acts as an oxidising agent ?   **[2017, Main]**

(1)  $HOCl + H_2O_2 \rightarrow H_3O^+ + Cl^- + O_2$

(2)  $I_2 + H_2O_2 + 2OH^- \rightarrow 2I^- + 2H_2O + O_2$

(3)  $2MnO_4^- + 3H_2O_2 \rightarrow 2MnO_2 + 3O_2 + 2H_2O + 2OH^-$

(4)  $PbS + 4H_2O_2 \rightarrow PbSO_4 + 4H_2O$

**7.** Identify the incorrect statement regarding heavy water :   **[2016, Main]**

(1) It reacts with $Al_4C_3$ to produce $CD_4$ and $Al(OH)_3$

(2) It is used as a coolant in nuclear reactors

(3) It reacts with $CaC_2$ to produce $C_2D_2$ and $Ca(OD)_2$

(4) It reacts with $SO_3$ to form deuterated sulphuric acid $(D_2SO_4)$

**8.** From the following statements regarding $H_2O_2$, choose the **incorrect** statement :   **[2015, Main]**

(1) It can act only as an oxidising agent

(2) It decomposes on exposure to light

(3) It has to be stored in plastic or wax lined glass bottles in dark

(4) It has to be kept away from dust

**9.** Permanent hardness in water cannot be cured by :   **[2015, Main]**

(1) Boiling

(2) Ion exchange method

(3) Calgon's method

(4) Treatment with washing soda

**10.** Which physical property of dihydrogen is wrong ? **[2015, Main]**

(1) Colourless gas

(2) Odourless gas

(3) Tasteless gas

(4) Non-inflammable gas

**11.** Hydrogen peroxide in its reaction with $KIO_4$ and $NH_2OH$ respectively, is acting as a : **[2014, Main]**

(1) reducing agent, oxidising agent

(2) reducing agent, reducing agent

(3) oxidising agent, oxidising agent

(4) oxidising agent, reducing agent

**12.** In which of the following reactions of $H_2O_2$ acts as a reducing agent ? **[2014, Main]**

(a) $H_2O_2 + 2H^+ + 2e^- \rightarrow 2H_2O$

(b) $H_2O_2 - 2e^- \rightarrow O_2 + 2H^+$

(c) $H_2O_2 + 2e^- \rightarrow 2OH^-$

(d) $H_2O_2 + 2OH^- - 2e^- \rightarrow O_2 + 2H_2O$

(1) (a), (b)  (2) (c), (d)

(3) (a), (c)  (4) (b), (d)

**13.** Hydrogen peroxide acts both as an oxidising and as a reducing agent depending upon the nature of the reacting species. In which of the following cases $H_2O_2$ acts as a reducing agent in acid medium ? **[2014, Main]**

(1) $MnO_4^-$  (2) $Cr_2O_7^{2-}$

(3) $SO_3^{2-}$  (4) KI

**14.** The reagents used for softening the temporary hardness of water is/are : **[2010, Main]**

(1) $Ca_3(PO_4)_2$  (2) $Ca(OH)_2$

(3) $Na_2CO_3$  (4) NaOCl

**15.** Write balance equations for the reactions of the following compounds with water : **[2002, Main]**

(1) $Al_4C_3$  (2) $CaCN_2$

(3) $BF_3$  (4) $NCl_3$

(5) $XeF_4$

**16.** Polyphosphates are used as water softening agents because they : **[2002, Main]**

(1) form soluble complexes with anionic species

(2) precipitate anionic species

(3) form soluble complexes with cationic species

(4) precipitate cationic species

## ANSWER KEY

| | | | | | | | | | |
|---|---|---|---|---|---|---|---|---|---|
| **1.** (4) | **2.** (4) | **3.** (2) | **4.** (1) | **5.** (3) | **6.** (4) | **7.** (2) | **8.** (1) | **9.** (1) | **10.** (4) |
| **11.** (1) | **12.** (4) | **13.** (1) | **14.** (2, 3, 4) | **15.** (*) | **16.** (3) | | | | |

## ANSWERS WITH EXPLANATIONS

**1. (4)** 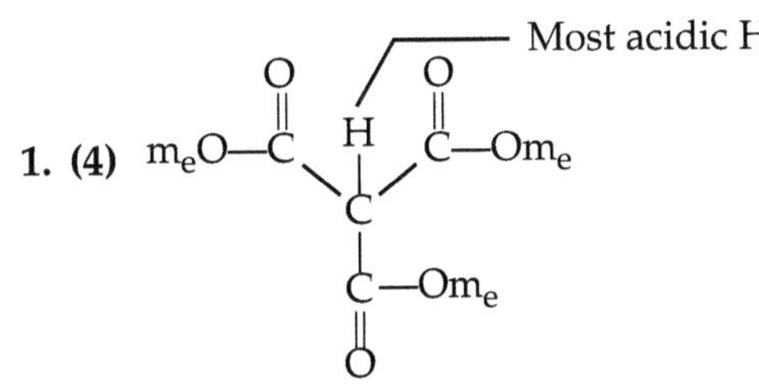


Due to presence of 3 (—R) groups.

**2. (4)** $Zn + 2HCl \longrightarrow ZnCl_2 + H_2$

$Zn + 2NaOH \longrightarrow Na_2ZnO_2 + H_2$

The ratio of the volume of $H_2$ is 1 : 1.

**3. (2)** Hydrogen has three isotopes

| Isotopes | Number of neutrons |
|---|---|
| Protium ($^1_1H$) | 0 |
| Deutrium ($^2_1H$) | 1 |
| Tritium ($^3_1H$) | 2 |

Hence the sum of neutrons are 3.

**4. (1)** (a), (b), (c) and (d).

**5. (3)** The reaction of hydrogen peroxide with $[Fe(CN)_6]^{4-}$ in acidic medium given as,

$[Fe(CN)_6]^{4-} + H_2O_2 + 2H^+ \rightarrow [Fe(CN)_6]^{3-} + 2H_2O$

The reaction of hydrogen peroxide with $[Fe(CN)_6]^{3-}$ in basic medium given as

$[Fe(CN)_6]^{3-} + H_2O_2 + 2OH^- \rightarrow [Fe(CN)_6]^{4-} + O_2 + 2H_2O$

**6. (4)** In the reaction, $PbS + 4H_2O_2 \rightarrow PbSO_4 + 4H_2O$, hydrogen peroxide undergoes reduction and thus behaves as an oxidising agent as shown below :

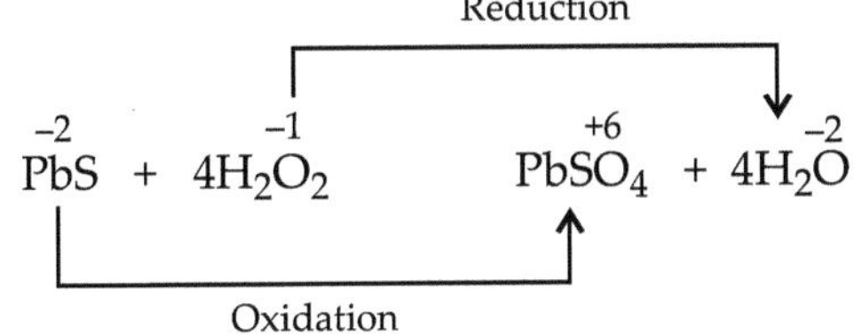


In this reaction, hydrogen peroxide oxidizes sulfur from − 2 oxidation state to + 6

**7. (2)** The statement that heavy water is used as a coolant in nuclear reactors is not true. As heavy water, that is $D_2O$, acts as a moderator that slows down the speed of neutrons in nuclear reactor, it cannot acts as a coolant.

**8. (1)** Hydrogen peroxide acts as an oxidizing as well as a reducing agent.

**9. (1)** The permanent hardness in water cannot be cured by boiling. It can be used to temporarily remove the hardness that is caused by the presence of $Ca^{2+}$ and $Mg^{2+}$ bicarbonates.

**10. (4)** Dihydrogen ($H_2$) is highly inflammable gas.

**11. (1)** The reaction of hydrogen peroxide with $KIO_4$ is,

$$\overset{-1}{H_2O_2} + K\overset{+7}{I}O_4 \rightarrow K\overset{+5}{I}O_3 + H_2O + \overset{0}{O_2}$$

Therefore, hydrogen peroxide acts as a reducing agent.

The reaction of hydrogen peroxide with $NH_2OH$ is,

$$\overset{-1}{H_2O_2} + \overset{-1}{N}H_2OH \rightarrow H_2\overset{-2}{O} + \overset{+3}{N_2O_3}$$

Therefore, hydrogen peroxide acts as an oxidising agent.

**12. (4)** (a) $\overset{-1}{H_2O_2} + 2H^+ + 2e^- \rightarrow 2H_2\overset{-2}{O}$

(b) $\overset{-1}{H_2O_2} - 2e^- \rightarrow \overset{0}{O_2} + 2H^+$

(c) $\overset{-1}{H_2O_2} + 2e^- \rightarrow 2\overset{-2}{O}H^-$

(d) $\overset{-1}{H_2O_2} + 2OH^- \rightarrow 2e^- \rightarrow \overset{0}{O_2} + 2H_2\overset{-2}{O}$

In reaction (b) and (d), $H_2O$ loses electrons. Therefore, it acts as a reducing agent in reaction (b) and (d).

**13. (1)** Hydrogen peroxide acts as a reducing agent in the reaction with permaganate ion in the acidic medium which is given as,

$$5H_2O_2 + 2MnO_4^- + 6H^+ \rightarrow 2Mn^{2+} + 8H_2O + 5O_2$$

**14. (2, 3, 4)** The temporary hardness in water can be removed by the addition of $Ca(OH)_2$ in water, by reacting hard water with washing soda and addition of $NaOCl$ in hard water. The reaction of calcium bicarbonate present in water with  is given below :

$$Ca(HCO_3)_2 + Ca(OH)_2 \rightarrow 2CaCO_3 + 2H_2O$$

The reaction of calcium bicarbonate present in water with washing soda is given below.

$$Ca(HCO_3)_2 + Na_2CO_3 \rightarrow CaCO_3 + 2NaHCO_3$$

The reaction of calcium bicarbonate present in water with  is given below.

$$2NaOCl + 2H_2O \rightarrow 2HOCl + 2NaOH$$

$$Ca(HCO_3)_2 + 2OH^- \rightarrow CaCO_3 + CO_3^{2-} + 2H_2O$$

In all the above reactions, insoluble calcium carbonate is precipitated out. Thus, water is filtered and temporary hardness is removed from water.

**15.** The balanced equation follows the law of conservation of mass. The unbalanced equation means that number of the atoms of elements present in the reactant is not equal to the product side.

(I) The balanced chemical equation for the reaction of $Al_4C_3$ with $H_2O$ is as follows :

$$Al_4C_3 + 12H_2O \rightarrow 4Al(OH)_3 + 3CH_4$$

(II) The balanced chemical equation for the reaction of $CaCN_2$ with  is as follows :

$$CaCN_2 + 5H_2O \rightarrow CaCO_3 + 2NH_4OH$$

(III) The balanced chemical equation for the reaction of  with  is as follows :

$$BF_3 + 3H_2O \rightarrow B(OH)_3 + 3HF$$

(IV) The balanced chemical equation for the reaction of  with  is as follows :

$$NCl_3 + 4H_2O \rightarrow NH_4OH + 3HOCl$$

(V) The balanced chemical equation for the reaction of $XeF_4$ with $H_2O$ is as follows :

$$XeF_4 + 6H_2O \rightarrow 2Xe + XeO_3 + 12HF + \frac{3}{2}O_2$$

**16. (3)** The reaction of polyphosphates with calcium present in hard water is expressed as

$$2Ca^{2+} + Na_2[Na_4(PO_3)_6] \rightarrow 4Na^+ + Na_2[Ca_2(PO_3)_6]$$

The product formed by the reaction $Na_2[Ca_2(PO_3)_6]$ is water soluble.

●●

## QUESTIONS

**1.** On heating compound (A) gives a gas (B) which is constituent of air. This gas when treated with $H_2$ in the presence of a catalyst gives another gas (C) which is basic in nature. (A) should not be :
**[2020, Main]**

(1) $(NH_4)_2Cr_2O_7$  (2) $Pb(NO_3)_2$
(3) $NaN_3$  (4) $NH_4NO_2$

**2.** The metal mainly used in devising photoelectric cells is : **[2020, Main]**

(1) Na  (2) Rb
(3) Li  (4) Cs

**3.** Two elements A and B have similar chemical properties. They don't form solid hydrogencarbonates, but react with nitrogen to form nitrides. A and B, respectively, are :
**[2020, Main]**

(1) Na and C  (2) Li and Mg
(3) Cs and Ba  (4) Na and Rb

**4.** On combustion Li, Na and K in excess of air, the major oxides formed, respectively, are :
**[2020, Main]**

(1) $Li_2O$, $Na_2O$ and $K_2O_2$
(2) $Li_2O$, $Na_2O_2$ and $K_2O$
(3) $Li_2O$, $Na_2O_2$ and $KO_2$
(4) $Li_2O_2$, $Na_2O_2$ and $K_2O_2$

**5.** Match the following compounds (Column-I) with their uses (Column-II) : **[2020, Main]**

| S. No. | Column - I | S. No. | Column - II |
|---|---|---|---|
| (I) | $Ca(OH)_2$ | (A) | casts of statues |
| (II) | $NaCl$ | (B) | white wash |
| (III) | $CaSO_4 \cdot \frac{1}{2}H_2O$ | (C) | antacid |
| (IV) | $CaCO_3$ | (D) | Washing soda preparation |

(1) (I)-(D), (II)-(A), (III)-(C), (IV)-(B)
(2) (I)-(B), (II)-(C), (III)-(D), (IV)-(A)
(3) (I)-(C), (II)-(D), (III)-(B), (IV)-(A)
(4) (I)-(B), (II)-(D), (III)-(A), (IV)-(C)

**6.** Which of the following liberates $O_2$ upon hydrolysis ? **[2020, Advanced]**

(1) $Pb_3O_4$  (2) $KO_2$
(3) $Na_2O_2$  (4) $Li_2O_2$

**7.** An alkaline earth metal 'M' readily forms water soluble sulphate and water insoluble hydroxide. Its oxide MO is very stable to heat and does not have rock-salt structure. M is : **[2020, Main]**

(1) Ca  (2) Be
(3) Mg  (4) Sr

**8.** The number of chiral centres in penicillin is ...... :
**[2020, Main]**

**9.** The first and second ionisation enthalpies of a metal are 496 and 4560 kJ $mol^{-1}$, respectively. How many moles of HCl and $H_2SO_4$, respectively, will be needed to react completely with 1 mole of the meal hydroxide ? **[2020, Main]**

(1) 1 and 0.5  (2) 2 and 0.5
(3) 1 and 1  (4) 1 and 2

**10.** Among the statements (a)-(d) the correct ones are : **[2020, Main]**

(a) Lithium has the highest hydration enthalpy among the alkali metals.
(b) Lithium chloride is insoluble in pyridine.
(c) Lithium cannot form ethynide upon its reaction with ethyne.
(d) Both lithium and magnesium react slowly with $H_2O$.

(1) (a), (b) and (d) only
(2) (b) and (c) only
(3) (a), (c) and (d) only
(4) (a) and (d) only

**11.** Oxidatio number of potassium in $K_2O$, $K_2O_2$ and $KO_2$, respectively, is : **[2020, Main]**

(1) $+1$, $+4$ and $+2$  (2) $+1$, $+2$ and $+4$
(3) $+1$, $+1$ and $+1$  (4) $+2$, $+1$ and $+\dfrac{1}{2}$

**12.** A metal (A) on heating in nitrogen gas gives compound B. B on treatment with $H_2O$ gives a colourless gas which when passed through $CuSO_4$ solution gives a dark blue-violet coloured solution. A and B respectively, are :
**[2020, Main]**

(1) Mg and $Mg_3N_2$  (2) Na and $NaNO_3$
(3) Mg and $Mg(NO_3)_2$  (4) Na and $Na_3N$

**13.** In the following reactions, products (A) and (B), respectively, are : **[2020, Main]**

$$NaOH + Cl_2 \rightarrow (A) + \text{side products}$$

(hot and conc.)

$$Ca(OH)_2 + Cl_2 \rightarrow (B) + \text{side products}$$
(dry)

(1) $NaClO_3$ and $Ca(ClO_3)_2$
(2) $NaOCl$ and $Ca(ClO_3)_2$
(3) $NaOCl$ and $Ca(OCl)_2$
(4) $NaClO_3$ and $Ca(OCl)_2$

**14.** The correct order of hydration enthalpies of alkali metal ions is : **[2019, Main]**
(1) $Li^+ > Na^+ > K^+ > Cs^+ > Rb^+$
(2) $Na^+ > Li^+ > K^+ > Rb^+ > Cs^+$
(3) $Na^+ > Li^+ > K^+ > Cs^+ > Rb^+$
(4) $Li^+ > Na^+ > K^+ > Rb^+ > Cs^+$

**15.** The covalent alkaline earth metal halide (X = Cl, Br, I) is : **[2019, Main]**
(1) $MgX_2$      (2) $CaX_2$
(3) $BeX_2$      (4) $SrX_2$

**16.** Magnesium powder burns in air to give : **[2019, Main]**
(1) $Mg(NO_3)_2$ and $Mg_3N_2$
(2) $MgO$ and $Mg_3N_2$
(3) $MgO$ only
(4) $MgO$ and $Mg(NO_3)_2$

**17.** The structurres of beryllium chloride in the solid state and vapour phase, respectively, are : **[2019, Main]**
(1) chain and chain
(2) dimeric and dimeric
(3) chain and dimeric
(4) dimeric and chain

**18.** A hydraged solid X on heating initially gives a monohydrated compound Y. Y upon heating above 373 K leads to an anhydrous white powder Z. X and Z, respectively, are : **[2019, Main]**
(1) Washing soda and soda ash.
(2) Baking soda and dead burnt plaster.
(3) Washing soda and dead burnt plaster.
(4) Baking soda and soda ash.

**19.** The correct sequence of thermal stability of the following carbonates is : **[2019, Main]**
(1) $BaCO_3 < CaCO_3 < SrCO_3 < MgCO_2$
(2) $MgCO_3 < CaCO_3 < SrCO_3 < BaCO_2$
(3) $MgCO_3 < SrCO_3 < CaCO_3 < BaCO_2$
(4) $BaCO_3 < SrCO_3 < CaCO_3 < MgCO_2$

**20.** The **INCORRECT** statement is : **[2019, Main]**
(1) Lithium is the strongest reducing agent among the alkali metals.
(2) Lithium is least reactive with water among the alkali metals.

(3) $LiNO_3$ decomposes on heating to give $LiNO_2$ and $O_2$.
(4) $LiCl$ crystallisers from aqueous solution is $LiCl.2H_2O$.

**21.** Both lithium and magnesium display several similar properties due to the diagonal relationship; however, the one which is incorrect, is : **[2017, Main]**
(1) Both form nitrides
(2) Nitrates of both Li and Mg yield $NO_2$ and $O_2$ on heating
(3) Both form basic carbonates
(4) Both form soluble bicarbonates

**22.** The commercial name for calcium oxide is : **[2016, Main]**
(1) Milk of lime      (2) Slaked lime
(3) Limestone      (4) Quick lime

**23.** Which one of the following alkaline earth metal sulphates has its hydration enthalpy greater than its lattice enthalpy ? **[2015, Main]**
(1) $CaSO_4$      (2) $BeSO_4$
(3) $BaSO_4$      (4) $SrSO_4$

**24.** The correct order of thermal stability of hydroxides is : **[2015, Main]**
(1) $Ba(OH)_2 < Sr(OH)_2 < Ca(OH)_2 < Mg(OH)_2$
(2) $Ba(OH)_2 < CA(OH)_2 < Sr(OH)_2 < Mg(OH)_2$
(3) $Mg(OH)_2 < Ca(OH)_2 < Sr(OH)_2 < Ba(OH)_2$
(4) $Mg(OH)_2 < Sr(OH)_2 < Ca(OH)_2 < Ba(OH)_2$

**25.** Which of the alkaline earth metal halides given below is essentially covalent in nature ? **[2015, Main]**
(1) $MgCl_2$      (2) $BeCl_2$
(3) $SrCl_2$      (4) $CaCl_2$

**26.** Amongst the following, the total number of compounds whose aqueous solution turns red litmus paper blue is : **[2010, Advanced]**

$KCN \quad K_2SO_4 \quad (NH_4)_2C_2O_4 \quad NaCl \quad Zn(NO_3)_2$
$FeCl_3 \quad K_2CO_3 \quad NH_4NO_3 \quad LiCN$

**27.** The compounds formed upon combustion of sodium metal in excess air is/are : **[2009, Advanced]**
(1) $Na_2O_2$      (2) $Na_2O$
(3) $NaO_2$      (4) $NaOH$

**28.** A sodium salt of an unknown anion when treated with $MgCl_2$ gives white precipitate only on boiling. The anion is : **[2004, Screening]**
(1) $SO_4^{2-}$      (2) $HCO_3^-$
(3) $CO_3^{2-}$      (4) $NO_3^-$

## ANSWER KEY

| 1. (2) | 2. (4) | 3. (2) | 4. (3) | 5. (4) | 6. (2) | 7. (2) | 8. (*) | 9. (1) | 10. (3) |
|---|---|---|---|---|---|---|---|---|---|
| 11. (3) | 12. (1) | 13. (4) | 14. (4) | 15. (3) | 16. (2) | 17. (3) | 18. (1) | 19. (2) | 20. (3) |
| 21. (3) | 22. (4) | 23. (2) | 24. (3) | 25. (2) | 26. (3) | 27. (1, 2) | 28. (2) | | |

# ANSWERS WITH EXPLANATIONS

**1. (2)**

$$\textcircled{A} \xrightarrow{\Delta} \textcircled{B}$$

Compound        Gas

$\downarrow$ +H$_2$ catalyst  (Haber's process)

$$\textcircled{C}$$

Basic gas (C) must be ammonia ($NH_3$).
It means (B) gas should be $N_2$ which is formed by heating of compound (A).

(1) $(NH_4)_2Cr_2O_7 \xrightarrow{\Delta} N_2\uparrow + Cr_2O_3 + 4H_2O\uparrow$

(2) $Pb(NO_3)_2 \xrightarrow{\Delta} PbO + 2NO_2\uparrow + \dfrac{1}{2}O_2\uparrow$

(3) $2NaN_3 \xrightarrow{\Delta} 2Na + 3N_2\uparrow$

(4) $NH_4NO_2 \xrightarrow{\Delta} N_2\uparrow + 2H_2O\uparrow$

So, (A) should not be $Pb(NO_3)_2$.

**2. (4)** Cs used in photoelectric cell as it has least ionisation energy.

**3. (2)** Both Li and Mg form nitride when reacts directly with nitrogen.
The hydrogen carbonate of both Li and Mg does not exist in solid state.
All alkali metal hydrogen carbonate exist in solid state except $LiHCO_3$.

**4. (3)**      $Li + O_2 \rightarrow Li_2O$ (Major oxides)

        excess

      $Na + O_2 \rightarrow Na_2O_2$ (Major oxides)

      $K + O_2 \rightarrow KO_2$ (Major oxides)

**5. (4)** (I) $Ca(OH)_2$ is used in white wash.

(II) NaCl is used in preparation of washing soda

$2NH_3 + H_2O + CO_2 \rightarrow (NH_4)_2CO_3$
$(NH_4)_2CO_3 + H_2O + CO_2 \rightarrow 2NH_4HCO_3$
$NH_4HCO_3 + NaCl \rightarrow NH_4Cl + NaHCO_3(s)$
$2NaHCO_3 \xrightarrow{\Delta} Na_2CO_3 + CO_2 + H_2O$

(III) $CaSO_4 \cdot \dfrac{1}{2}H_2O$ (Plaster of Paris) is used

for making casts of statues.

(IV) $CaCO_3$ is used as an antacid.

**6. (2)** (1) $Pb_3O_4$ is insoluble in water or do not react with water.

(2) $2KO_2 + 2H_2O \rightarrow 2KOH + H_2O_2 + O_{2(g)}\uparrow$

(3) $Na_2O_2 + 2H_2O \rightarrow 2NaOH + H_2O_2$

(4) $Li_2O_2 + 2H_2O \rightarrow 2LiOH + H_2O_2$

**7. (2)** [Be]

$BeSO_4$ is water soluble

$Be(OH)_2$ is water insoluble

$BeO$ is stable to heat

**8.** The structure of penicillin is

$$R-\overset{\overset{\textstyle O}{\|}}{C}-HN \cdots$$

*Chiral center = 3

**9. (1)** IE valus indicate, that the metal belongs to I$^{st}$ group since second IE is very high

($\because$ only one valence electron)

Metal hydroxide will be of type, MOH.

$$MOH + HCl \rightarrow MCl + H_2O$$

$$\underset{\text{(1 mol)}}{MOH} + \underset{(\frac{1}{2}\text{ mol})}{\dfrac{1}{2}H_2SO_4} \rightarrow \dfrac{1}{2}M_2SO_4 + H_2O$$

So one mole of HCl required to react with one mole MOH.

So $\dfrac{1}{2}$ mole of $H_2SO_4$ required to react with one mole MOH.

**10. (3)** Lithium has highest hydration enthalpy among alkali metals due to its small size.
LiCl is soluble in pyridine because LiCl have more covalent character.
Li does not form ethynide with ethyne.
Both Li and Mg reacts slowly with $H_2O$.

**11. (3)** Potassium has an oxidation of +1 (only) in combined state.

**12. (1)**

$$3Mg + N_2 \xrightarrow{\Delta} \underset{(B)}{Mg_3N_2} \xrightarrow{6H_2O} 3Mg(OH)_2 + \underset{\substack{\text{colourless} \\ \text{gas}}}{2NH_3}$$

(A)

$$CuSO_4 + 4NH_3 \longrightarrow \underset{\text{deep blue solution}}{[Cu(NH_3)_4]SO_4}$$

**13. (4)** $6NaOH + 3Cl_2 \rightarrow 5NaCl + NaClO_3 + 3H_2O$
$2Ca(OH)_2 + Cl_2 \rightarrow Ca(OCl)_2 + CaCl_2 + H_2O$

**14. (4)** The hydration enthalpy of an ion is directly proportional to the charge density of the ion. The charge density is the ratio of charge and the size of the ion. On moving down the group 1 of the periodic table, the charge remains the same, whereas, the size of the ion decreases. The leads to decrease in the value of charge density and hence, the hydration enthalpy also decreases down the group. Therefore, the correct order of hydration enthalpies of the alkali metal ions is $Li^+ > Na^+ > O\, K^+ > Rb^+ > Cs^+$.

**15. (3)** Generally, alkaline earth metal halides are ionic in nature. Due to small size and high ionisation enthalpy of Be, $BeX_2$ is covalent in nature.

**16. (2)** The atmospheric air contains nitrogen and oxygen gas. The reaction of magnesium metal with atmospheric oxygen and nitrogen is shown below :

$$Mg + N_2 + O_2 \rightarrow MgO + Mg_3N_2$$

**17. (3)** The structure of beryllium chloride in the solid state and vapour phase are shown below :

Solid State
(Chain)

Vapour State
(Dimeric)

The structure of beryllium chloride in the solid state and vapour phase are polymeric chain and dimeric molecules.

**18. (1)** The completed reaction is given below :

$$Na_2CO_3.10H_2O(s) \xrightarrow{\Delta} Na_2CO_3.H_2O$$

washing soda (X)       (Y)

$$\xrightarrow[\Delta]{T > 373\,K} Na_2CO_3$$

soda ash (Z)

Therefore, X and Z are washing soda and soda ash respectively.

**19. (2)** The electropositivity of the alkaline earth increases on going down the group. Therefore, the ionic character carbonate of alkaline earth metal increase down the group. Thermal stability of carbonate of alkaline earth metal increases on going down the group. Therefore, the correct order of thermal stability of the carbonate is shown below :

$$MgCO_3 < CaCO_3 < SrCO_3 < BaCO_3$$

**20. (3)** The decomposition reaction of $LiNO_3$ is shown below :

$$2LiNO_3 \xrightarrow{\Delta} Li_2O + 2NO_2 + \frac{1}{2}O_2$$

Therefore, the statement that $LiNO_3$ decomposes to give $LiNO_2$ and $O_2$ is incorrect.

**21. (3)** In lithium and magnesium, basic carbonates are only formed by magnesium. For example, $3MgCO_3.Mg(OH)_2.3H_2O$. Lithium does not form basic carbonates.

**22. (4)** The chemical formula of calcium oxide is CaO. The commercial name for calcium oxide is quick lime.

**23. (2)** Beryllium sulphate ($BaSO_4$) has hydration enthalpy greater than that of its lattice enthalpy.

**24. (3)** The thermal stability of hydroxides increases as the size of cation increases. The increasing order of atomic size of group 2 elements is $Mg < Ca < Sr < Ba$. Hence, the order of thermal stability of hydroxide is $Mg(OH)_2 < Ca(OH)_2 < Sr(OH)_2 < Ba(OH)_2$.

**25. (2)** Beryllium chloride forms covalent bond due to more polarization. It results in permanent displacement of electrons. Thus, $BeCl_2$ prefers to share electrons rather than accepting or donating electrons.

**26. (3)** Those solutions which are basic in nature turn red litmus paper to blue. KCN, $K_2CO_3$ and LiCN are basic in nature. So, their aqueous solutions will turn red litmus paper to blue.

**27. (1, 2)** The reaction of sodium metal with excess of air leads to the formation of sodium peroxide and sodium oxide because sodium metal does not form superoxide. Therefore, the products obtained in the reaction of sodium metal with excess of air is $Na_2O_2$ and $Na_2O$.

**28. (2)** A soluble bicarbonate salt of magnesium is generated in the reaction of $NaHCO_3$ with $MgCl_2$.

$$MgCl_2 + 2NaHCO_3 \rightarrow Mg(HCO_3)_2 + 2NaCl$$

The magnesium salt form white precipitate on heating.

$$Mg(HCO_3)_2 \xrightarrow{\Delta} MgCO_3 \downarrow + H_2O + CO_2$$

●●

# Chapter 18

# The *p*-Block Elements

## QUESTIONS

**1.** In a molecule of pyrophosphoric acid, the number of P–OH, P = O and P–O–P bonds/ moiety(ies) respectively are : **[2020, Main]**
(1) 3, 3 and 3
(2) 2, 4 and 1
(3) 4, 2 and 0
(4) 4, 2 and 1

**2.** Reaction of an inorganic sulphite X with dilute $H_2SO_4$ generates compound Y. Reaction of Y with NaOH gives X. Further, the reaction of X with Y and water affords compound Z. Y and Z, respectively, are : **[2020, Main]**
(1) S and $Na_2SO_3$
(2) $SO_2$ and $NaHSO_3$
(3) $SO_3$ and $NaHSO_3$
(4) $SO_2$ and $Na_2SO_3$

**3.** The reaction of NO with $N_2O_4$ at 250 K gives : **[2020, Main]**
(1) $N_2O_5$
(2) $NO_2$
(3) $N_2O$
(4) $N_2O_3$

**4.** The equation that represents the water-gas shift reaction is : **[2020, Main]**

(1) $CO(g) + H_2O(g) \xrightarrow[\text{Catalyst}]{673K} CO_2(g) + H_2(g)$

(2) $CH_4(g) + H_2O(g) \xrightarrow[\text{Ni}]{1270K} CO(g) + 3H_2(g)$

(3) $C(s) + H_2O(g) \xrightarrow{1270K} CO(g) + H_2(g)$

(4) $2C(s) + O_2(g) + 4N_2(g) \xrightarrow{1273K} 2CO(g) + 4N_2(g)$

**5.** The correct statement with respect to dinitrogen is : **[2020, Main]**
(1) liquid dinitrogen is not used in cryosurgery
(2) it can be used as an inert diluent for reactive chemicals
(3) it can combine with dioxygen at 25°C
(4) $N_2$ is paramagnetic in nature

**6.** Among the sulphates of alkaline earth metals, the solubilities of $BeSO_4$ and $MgSO_4$ in water, respectively, are : **[2020, Main]**
(1) high and high
(2) poor and poor
(3) high and poor
(4) poor and high

**7.** The number of Cl = O bonds in perchloric acid is, "...............". **[2020, Main]**

**8.** Boron and silicon of very high purity can be obtained through : **[2020, Main]**
(1) vapour phase refining
(2) electrolytic refining
(3) liquation
(4) zone refining

**9.** Reaction of ammonia with excess $Cl_2$ gives : **[2020, Main]**
(1) $NH_4Cl$ and $N_2$
(2) $NCl_3$ and $NH_4Cl$
(3) $NH_4Cl$ and HCl
(4) $NCl_3$ and HCl

**10.** With respect to hypochlorite, chlorate and perchlorate ions, choose the correct statement(s). **[2020, Main]**
(1) The hypochlorite ion is the strongest conjugate base
(2) The molecular shape of only chlorate ion is influenced by the lone pair of electrons of Cl
(3) The hypochlorite and chlorate ions disproportionate to give rise to identical set of ions
(4) The hypochlorite ion oxidizes the sulfite ion

**11.** The major aromatic product C in the following reaction sequence will be : **[2020, Main]**

$$\text{(benzopyran)} \xrightarrow[\Delta]{\substack{\text{HBr} \\ \text{(excess)}}} \text{(A)} \xrightarrow[\text{(ii) H}^+]{\text{(i) KOH (Alc.)}} \text{B} \xrightarrow[\text{Zn/H}_3\text{O}^+]{O_3} \text{C}$$

(1) 2-(hydroxymethyl)phenol with $CO_2H$ (OH and $CO_2H$)
(2) (OH and CHO)
(3) (Br and CHO)
(4) (Br and $CO_2H$)

**12.** The major product of the following reaction is : **[2020, Main]**

$$\text{CH}_3\text{-C}_6\text{H}_3(\text{OH})(\text{NO}_2) \xrightarrow{\text{conc. HNO}_3 + \text{conc. H}_2\text{SO}_4}$$

**[2020, Main]**

(1) [structure: phenol ring with $OH$ at top, $H_3C$ at position 2, $O_2N$ and $NO_2$ at positions 3 and 5]

(2) [structure: phenol ring with $OH$ at top, $H_3C$, two $NO_2$ groups]

(3) [structure: phenol ring with $OH$ at top, $H_3C$, two $NO_2$ groups]

(4) [structure: phenol ring with $OH$ at top, $H_3C$, three $NO_2$ groups]

**13.** Two compounds A and B with same molecular formula ($C_3H_6O$) undergo Grignard's reaction with methylmagnesium bromide to give products C and D. products C and D show following chemical tests. **[2020, Main]**

| Test | C | D |
|---|---|---|
| Ceric ammonium nitrate Test | Positive | Positive |
| Lucas Test | Turbidity obtained after five minutes | Turbidity obtained immediately |
| Iodoform Test | Positive | Negative |

C and D respectively are :

(1) $C = H_3C-\underset{\underset{CH_3}{|}}{\overset{\overset{CH_3}{|}}{C}}-OH$;

  $D = H_3C-CH_2-\underset{\underset{OH}{|}}{CH}-CH_3$

(2) $C = H_3C-CH_2-CH_2-CH_2-OH$;

  $D = H_3C-\underset{\underset{CH_3}{|}}{\overset{\overset{CH_3}{|}}{C}}-OH$

(3) $C = H_3C-CH_2-\underset{\underset{OH}{|}}{CH}-CH_3$;

  $D = H_3C-\underset{\underset{CH_3}{|}}{\overset{\overset{CH_3}{|}}{C}}-OH$

(4) $C = H_3C-CH_2-CH_2-CH_2-OH$;

  $D = H_3C-CH_2-\underset{\underset{OH}{|}}{CH}-CH_3$

**14.** An organic compound 'A' ($C_9H_{10}O$) when treated with conc. HI undergoes cleavage to yield compounds 'B' and 'C'. 'B' gives yellow precipitate with $AgNO_3$ where as 'C' tautomerizes to 'D'. 'D' gives positive iodoform test. 'A' could be : **[2020, Main]**

(1) $C_6H_5-O-CH=CH-CH_3$

(2) $C_6H_5-CH_2-O-CH=CH_2$

(3) $C_6H_5-O-CH_2-CH=CH_2$

(4) $H_3C-C_6H_4-O-CH=CH_2$

**15.** The compound A in the following reaction is :

$A \xrightarrow[\text{(ii) Conc. } H_2SO_4/\Delta]{\text{(i) } CH_3MgBr/H_2O}$

$B \xrightarrow[\text{(ii) } Zn/H_2O]{\text{(i) } O_3} C + D$

$C \xrightarrow[\text{(ii) } \Delta]{\text{(i) Conc. KOH}} C_6H_5-COO^-K^+ + C_6H_5-CH_2OH$

$D \xrightarrow[\Delta]{Ba(OH)_2} H_3C-\underset{\underset{CH_3}{|}}{C}=CH-\overset{\overset{O}{||}}{C}-CH_3$

**[2020, Main]**

(1) $C_6H_5-\overset{\overset{O}{||}}{C}-CH\overset{CH_3}{\underset{CH_3}{<}}$

(2) $C_6H_5-\overset{\overset{O}{||}}{C}-CH_2CH_3$

(3) $C_6H_5-CH_2-\overset{\overset{O}{||}}{C}-CH_3$

(4) $C_6H_5-\overset{\overset{O}{||}}{C}-CH_3$

**16.** When neopentyl alcohol is heated with an acid, it slowly converted into an $85:15$ mixture of alkenes A and B, respectively. What are these alkenes ? **[2020, Main]**

(1) [structures: $H_3C$ and $H_3C$ on a double-bonded carbon with $CH_3$; and a second alkene with $CH_2$]

(2) 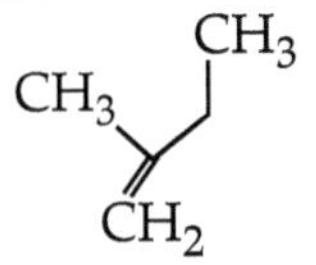 — structures: 2-ethyl-3-methylbut-1-ene and isopropyl-vinyl compound (and)

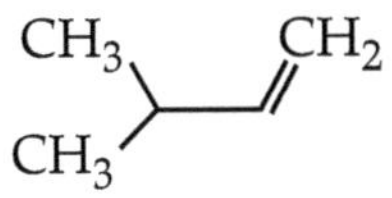

(3) 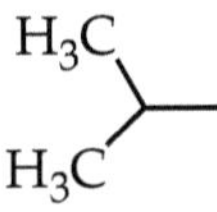 — structures (and)

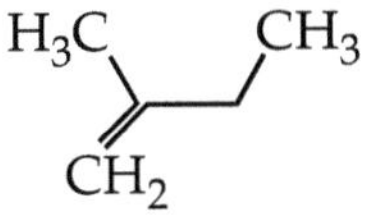

(4) 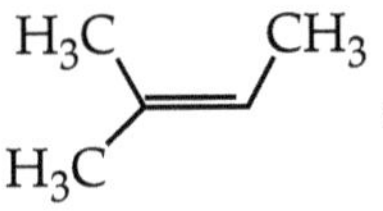 — structures (and)

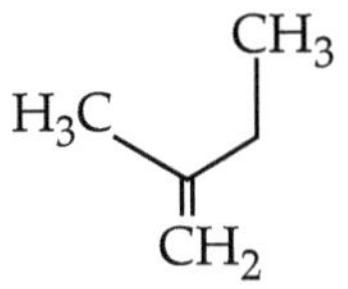

**17.** [P] on treatment with $Br_2/FeBr_3$ in $CCl_4$ produced a single isomer $C_8H_7O_2Br$ while heating [P] with sodalime gave toluene. **[2020, Main]**
The compound [P] is :

(1) 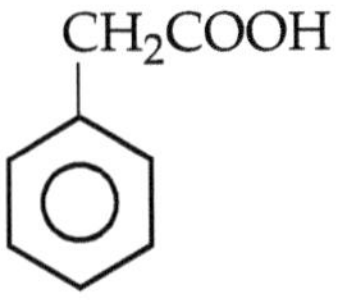 $CH_2COOH$ attached to benzene ring

(2) 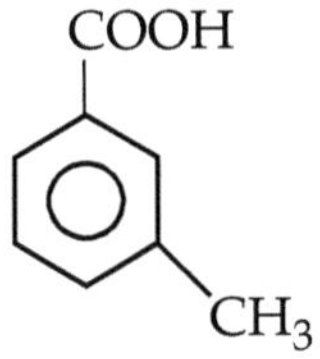 benzene ring with $COOH$ and $CH_3$ (meta)

(3) benzene ring with $COOH$ and $CH_3$ (ortho)

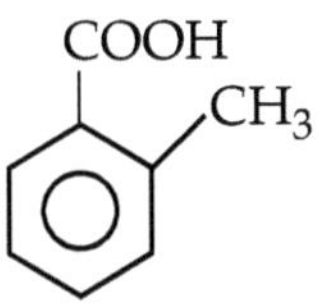

(4) 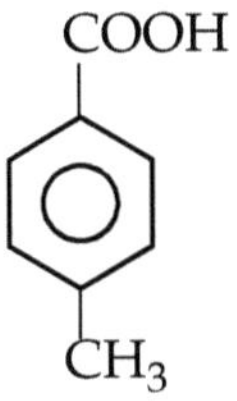 benzene ring with $COOH$ and $CH_3$ (para)

**18.** A solution of phenol in chloroform when treated with aqueous NaOH gives compound P as a major product. The mass percentage of carbon in P is ................ . (to the nearest integer)
(Atomic mass : C = 12; H = 1; O = 16)
**[2020, Main]**

**19.** In the following reaction sequence the major products A and B are :

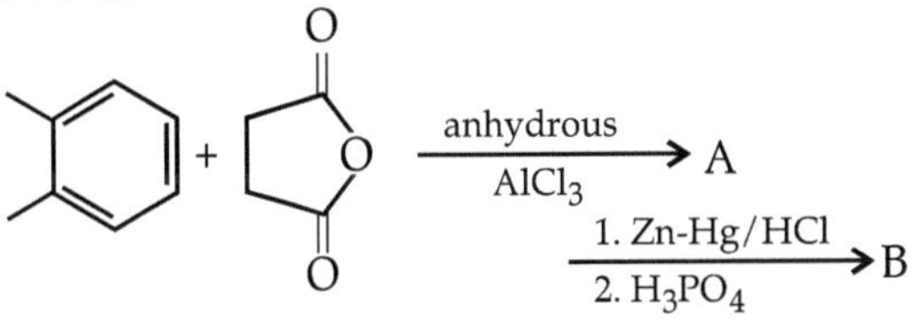

xylene $+$ succinic anhydride $\xrightarrow[\text{AlCl}_3]{\text{anhydrous}}$ A $\xrightarrow[\text{2. H}_3\text{PO}_4]{\text{1. Zn-Hg/HCl}}$ B

**[2020, Main]**

(1) A = ... ; B = ...

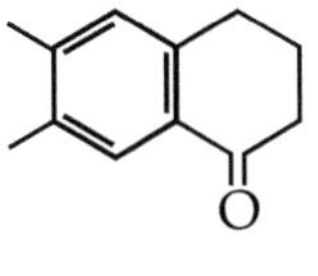

(2) A 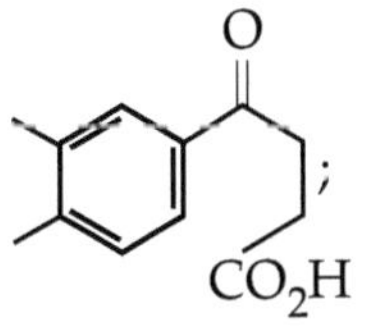 = ... ; B = ...

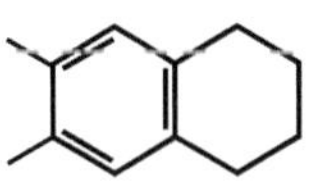

(3) A 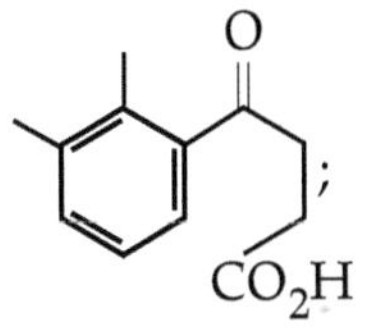 = ... ; B = ...

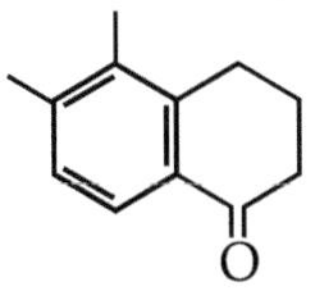

(4) A = aryl ketone with $CO_2H$ ; B = methylnaphthalenone

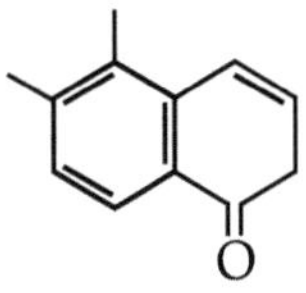

**20.** Which of the following derivatives of alcohols is unstable in an aqueous base ? **[2020, Main]**

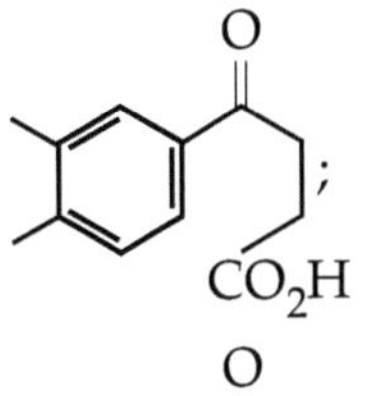

(1) $RO\text{—}CMe_3$

(2) 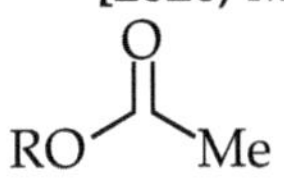 $RO$ with formate (RO–CHO–Me)

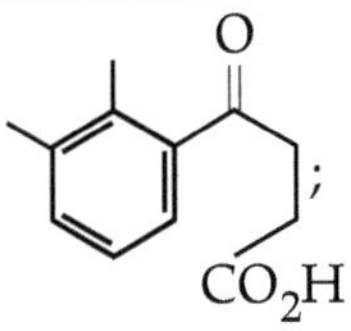

(3) 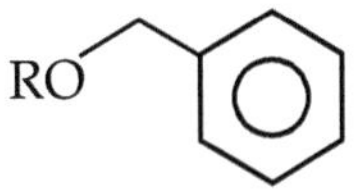 $RO$ attached to benzyl (benzene ring)

(4) 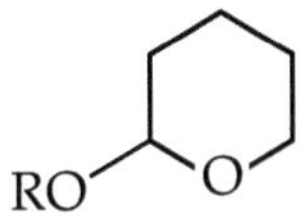 $RO$ attached to tetrahydropyran ring

**21.** The major product obtained from the following reaction is :

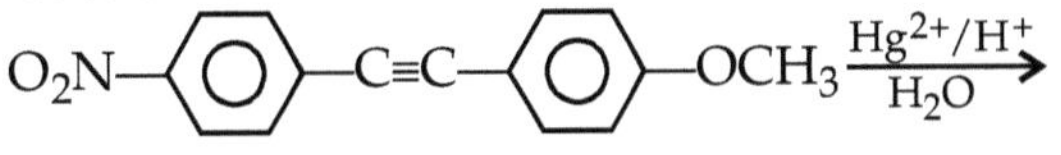

$O_2N$—⟨benzene⟩—$C\equiv C$—⟨benzene⟩—$OCH_3 \xrightarrow[\text{H}_2\text{O}]{\text{Hg}^{2+}/\text{H}^+}$

**[2020, Main]**

(1) 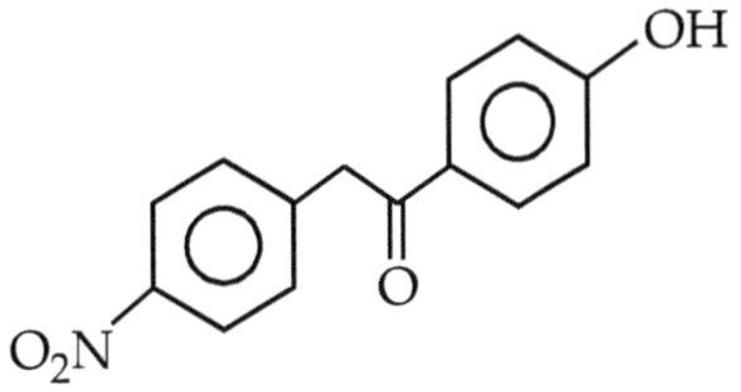 structure with OH, $O_2N$, ketone

(2) 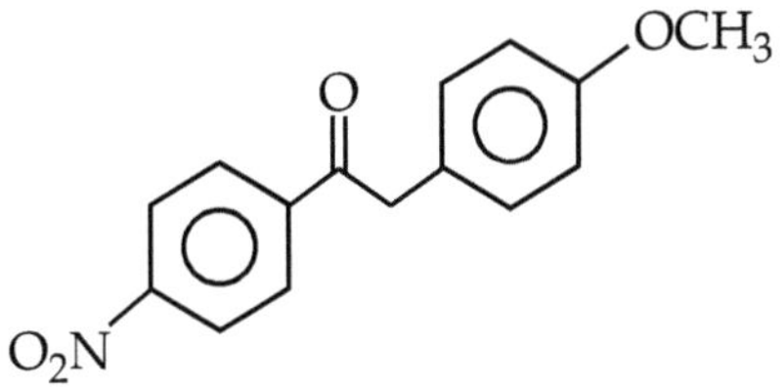 structure with $OCH_3$, $O_2N$, ketone

(3) structure with $OCH_3$, $O_2N$, ketone

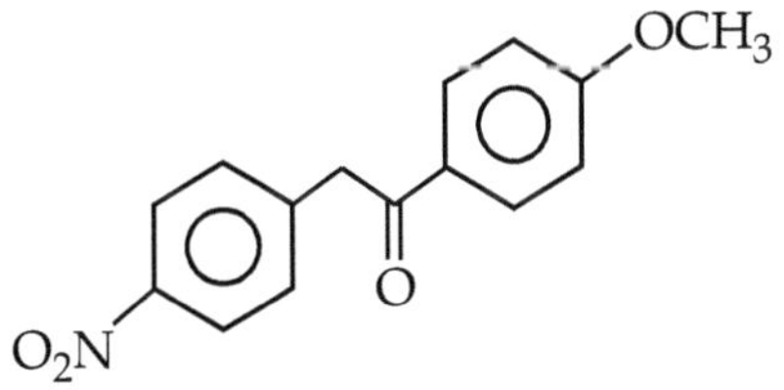

(4) 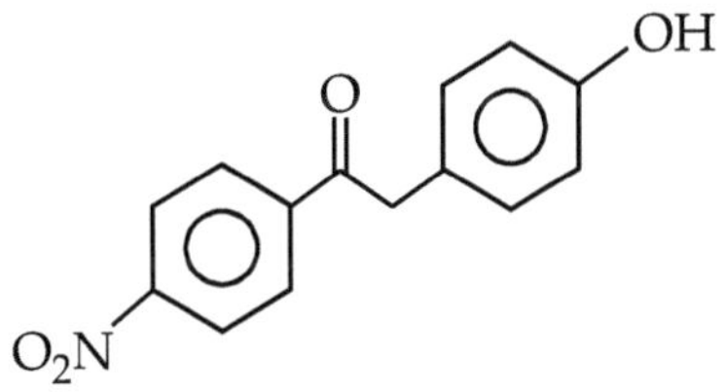 structure with OH, $O_2N$, ketone

**22.** The major product [C] of the following reaction sequence will be :

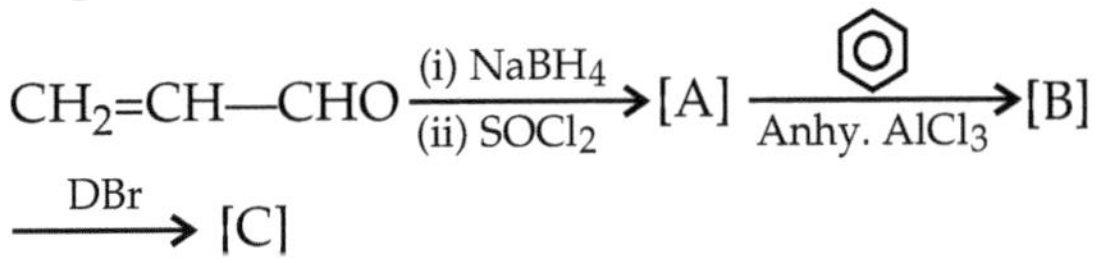

$CH_2{=}CH{-}CHO \xrightarrow[\text{(ii) SOCl}_2]{\text{(i) NaBH}_4} [A] \xrightarrow[\text{Anhy. AlCl}_3]{\text{benzene}} [B] \xrightarrow{\text{DBr}} [C]$

**[2020, Main]**

(1) 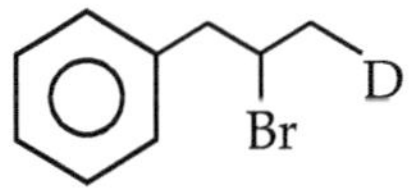 benzene ring with $CH_2CHBr$–$CH_2D$

(2) 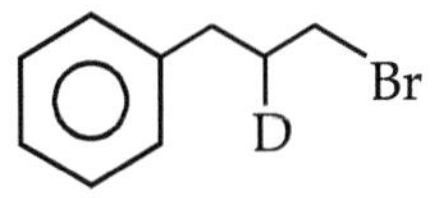 benzene ring with $CH_2CHD$–$CH_2Br$

**(3)** 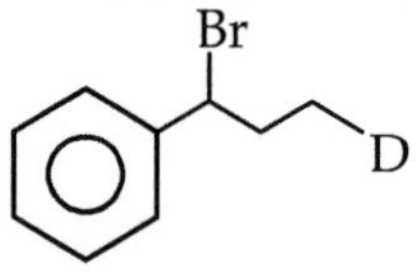 [structure: phenyl–CH(Br)–CH$_2$–CH$_2$D]

**(4)** 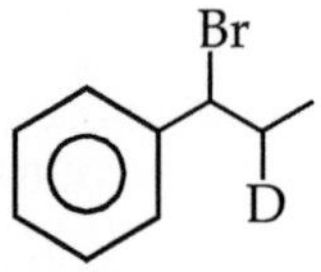 [structure: phenyl–CH(Br)–CH(CH$_3$)–D]

**23.** The Kjeldahl method of Nitrogen estimation fails for which of the following reaction products ?

**[2020, Main]**

**(a)** 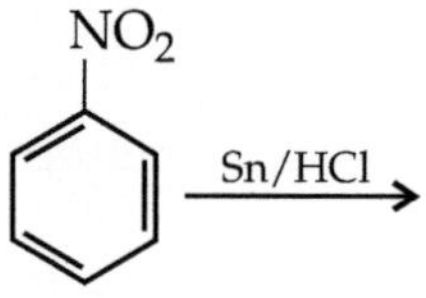 [nitrobenzene, NO$_2$] $\xrightarrow{\text{Sn/HCl}}$

**(b)** 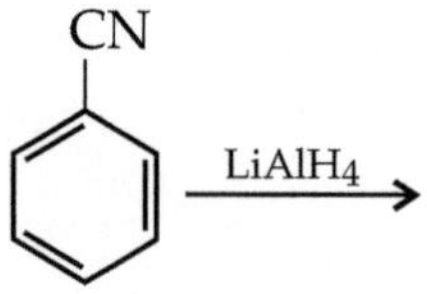 [benzonitrile, CN] $\xrightarrow{\text{LiAlH}_4}$

**(c)** 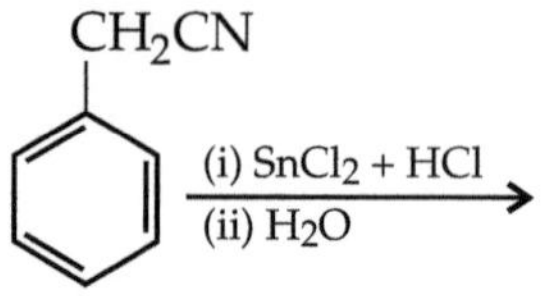 [CH$_2$CN on benzene] $\xrightarrow[\text{(ii) H}_2\text{O}]{\text{(i) SnCl}_2 + \text{HCl}}$

**(d)** 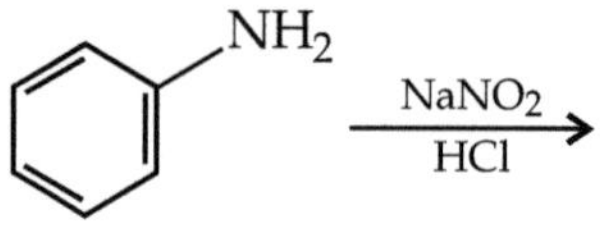 [aniline, NH$_2$] $\xrightarrow[\text{HCl}]{\text{NaNO}_2}$

**(1)** (a) and (d)  
**(2)** (c) and (d)  
**(3)** (a), (c) and (d)  
**(4)** (b) and (c)

**24.** Which of the following compounds can be prepared in good yield by Gabriel phthalimide synthesis ? **[2020, Main]**

**(1)** 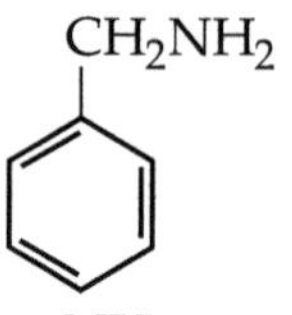 [benzene–CH$_2$NH$_2$]

**(2)** [benzene–NH$_2$]

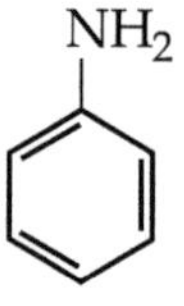

**(3)** 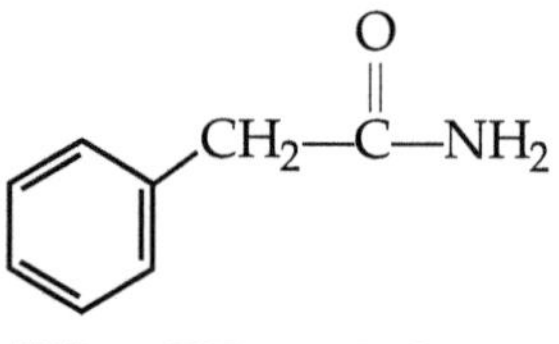 [benzene–CH$_2$–C(=O)–NH$_2$]

**(4)** $CH_3-CH_2-NHCH_3$

**25.** The major product of the following reaction is :

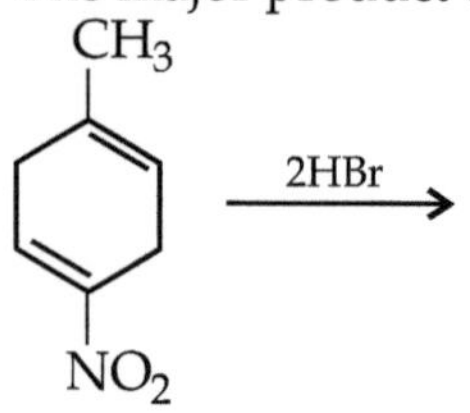

[4-methyl-nitrobenzene: CH$_3$ top, NO$_2$ bottom] $\xrightarrow{\text{2HBr}}$

**[2020, Main]**

**(1)** 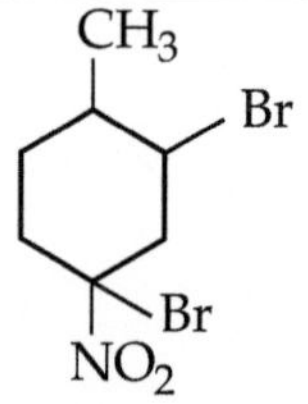 [cyclohexane: CH$_3$ top, Br, Br bottom with NO$_2$]

**(2)** [cyclohexane: Br, CH$_3$ top, Br, NO$_2$ bottom]

**(3)** [cyclohexane: H$_3$C, Br top, Br, NO$_2$ bottom]

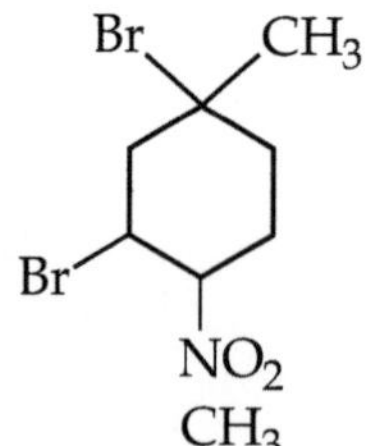

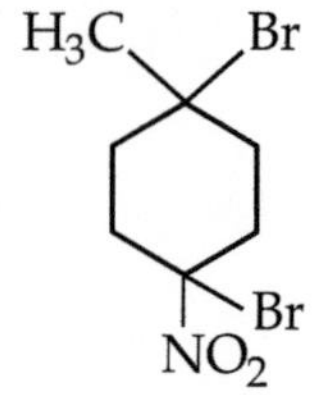

**(4)** 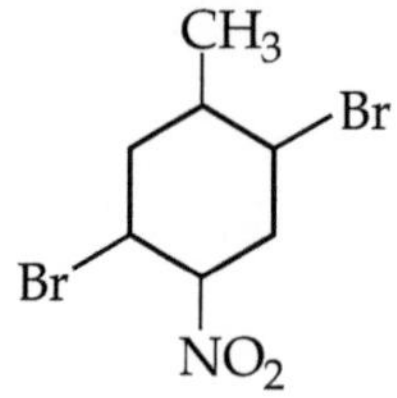 [cyclohexane: CH$_3$ top, Br, Br, NO$_2$ bottom]

**26.** In the following reaction sequence, [C] is :

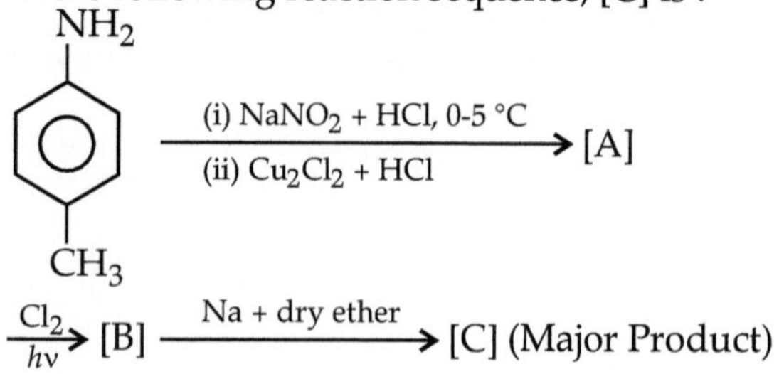

[p-toluidine: NH$_2$ top, CH$_3$ bottom] $\xrightarrow[\text{(ii) Cu}_2\text{Cl}_2 + \text{HCl}}]{\text{(i) NaNO}_2 + \text{HCl, 0-5 °C}}$ [A]

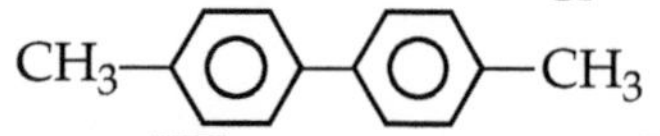

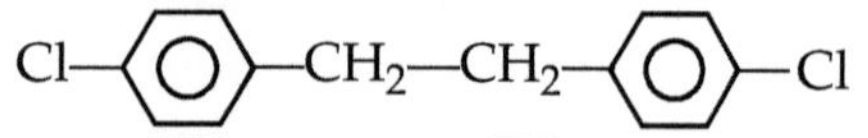

$\xrightarrow[hv]{\text{Cl}_2}$ [B] $\xrightarrow{\text{Na + dry ether}}$ [C] (Major Product)

**[2020, Main]**

**(1)** 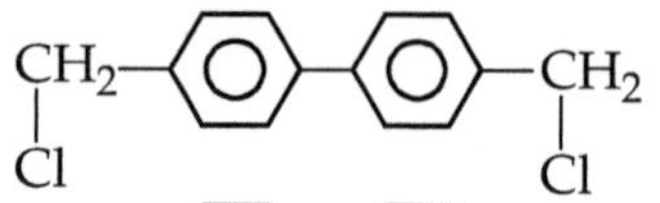 ClCH$_2$–C$_6$H$_4$–C$_6$H$_4$–CH$_2$Cl (biphenyl)

**(2)** CH$_3$–C$_6$H$_4$–C$_6$H$_4$–CH$_3$ (biphenyl)

**(3)** Cl–C$_6$H$_4$–CH$_2$–CH$_2$–C$_6$H$_4$–Cl

**(4)** Cl–C$_6$H$_4$–CH$_2$–C$_6$H$_4$–CH$_2$–Cl

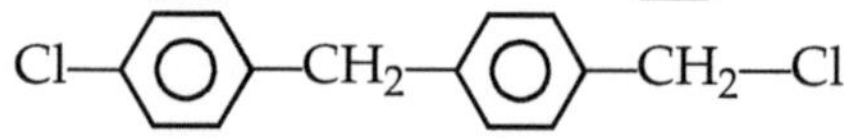

**27.** The final major product of the following reaction is :

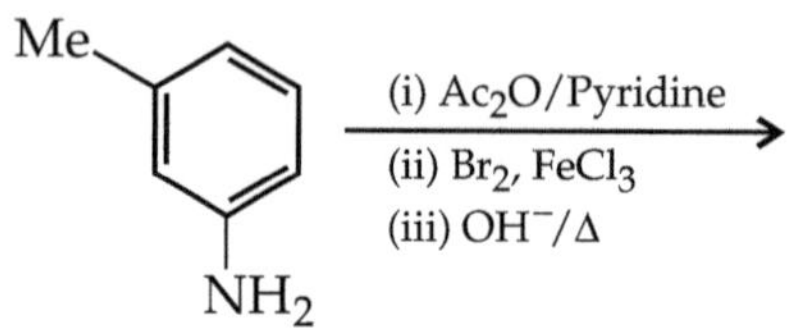

[m-toluidine: Me, NH$_2$] $\xrightarrow[\text{(iii) OH}^-/\Delta]{\substack{\text{(i) Ac}_2\text{O/Pyridine} \\ \text{(ii) Br}_2, \text{FeCl}_3}}$

**[2020, Main]**

**(1)** 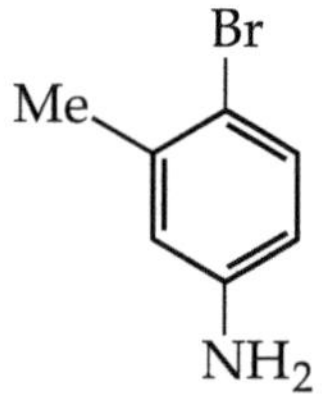 [benzene ring: Me, Br, NH$_2$]

**(2)** [benzene ring: Me, Br, NH$_2$]

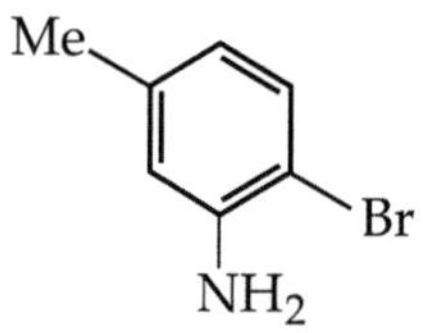

**(3)** 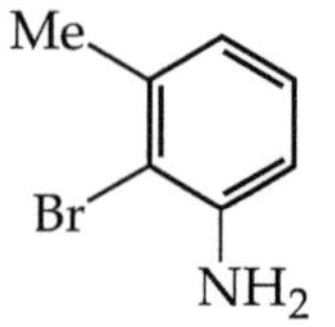 [benzene ring: Me, Br, NH$_2$]

**(4)** 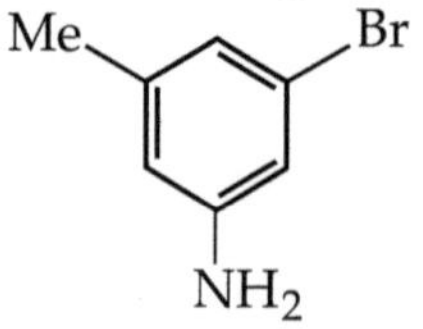 [benzene ring: Me, Br, NH$_2$]

**28.** White phosphorus on reaction with concentrated NaOH solution in an inert atmosphere of $CO_2$ gives phosphine and compound (X). (X) on acdification with HCl gives compound (Y). The basicity of compound (Y) is : **[2020, Main]**

**(1)** 4  
**(2)** 1  
**(3)** 2  
**(4)** 3

**29.** For the following Assertion and Reason, the correct option is : **[2020, Main]**

**Assertion :** For hydrogenation reactions, the catalytic activity increases from Group 5 to Group 11 metals with maximum activity shown by Group 7-9 elements.

**Reason :** The reactants are most strongly adsorbed on group 7-9 elements.

(1) Both assertion and reason are true but the reason is but the correct explanation for the assertion.

(2) Both assertion and reason for false.

(3) Both assertion and reason are true and the reason is the correct explanation for the assertion.

(4) The assertion is true, but the reason is false.

**30.** The number of bionds between sulphur and oxygen atoms in $S_2O_8^{2-}$ and the number of bonds between sulphur and sulphur atoms in rhombic sulphur, respectively, are : **[2020, Main]**

(1) 4 and 8      (2) 4 and 6

(3) 8 and 8      (4) 8 and 6

**31.** The electron gain enthalpy (in kJ/mol) of fluorine, chlorine, bromine and iodine, respectively are : **[2020, Main]**

(1) – 333, – 349, – 325 and – 296

(2) – 296, – 325, – 333 and – 349

(3) – 333, – 325, – 349 and – 296

(4) – 349, – 333, – 325 and – 296

**32.** The acidic, basic and amphoteric oxides, respectively, are : **[2020, Main]**

(1) $MgO, Cl_2O, Al_2O_3$

(2) $Cl_2O, CaO, P_4P_{10}$

(3) $Na_2O, SO_3, Al_2O_3$

(4) $N_2O_3, Li_2O, Al_2O_3$

**33.** $C_{60}$, an allotrope of carbon contains : **[2019, Main]**

(1) 12 hexagons and 20 pentagons.

(2) 18 hexagons and 14 pentagons.

(3) 16 hexagons and 16 pentagons.

(4) 20 hexagons and 12 pentagons.

**34.** The correct statements among I to III regarding group 13 element oxides are, **[2019, Main]**

(I) Boron trioxide is acidic.

(II) Oxides of aluminium and gallium are amphoteric.

(III) Oxides of indium and thallium are basic.

(1) (I) and (II) only      (2) (I), (II) and (III)

(2) (I) and (III) only      (4) (II) and (III) only

**35.** The correct order of catenation is : **[2019, Main]**

(1) $C > Sn > Si \approx Ge$    (2) $C > Si > Ge \approx Sn$

(3) $Si > Sn > C > Ge$    (4) $Ge > Sn > Si > C$

**36.** The basic structural unit of feldspar, zeolites, mica and asbestos is : **[2019, Main]**

(1) $(SiO_3)^{2-}$

(2) $SiO_2$

(3) $(SiO_4)^{4-}$

(4) $\begin{array}{c} R \\ | \\ -\!(Si\!-\!O)_n\!- \ (R = Me) \\ | \\ R \end{array}$

**37.** The correct name of the following polymer is : **[2019, Main]**

(1) Polyisobutane      (2) Polytert-butylene

(3) Polyisoprene      (4) Polyisobutylene

**38.** The C – C bond length is maximum in : **[2019, Main]**

(1) graphite      (2) $C_{70}$

(3) $C_{60}$      (4) diamond

**39.** The correct statement about $ICl_5$ and $ICl_4^-$ is : **[2019, Main]**

(1) both are isostructural.

(2) $ICl_5$ is trigonal bipyramidal and $ICl_4^-$ is tetrahedral.

(3) $ICl_5$ is square pyramidal and $ICl_4^-$ is tetrahedral.

(4) $ICl_5$ is square pyramidal and $ICl_4^-$ is square planar.

**40.** The correct order of the oxidation states of nitrogen in $NO$, $N_2O$, $NO_2$ and $N_2O_3$ is : **[2019, Main]**

(1) $NO_2 < NO < N_2O_3 < N_2O$

(2) $NO_2 < N_2O_3 < NO < N_2O$

(3) $N_2O < N_2O_3 < NO < NO_2$

(4) $N_2O < NO < N_2O_3 < NO_2$

**41.** The oxoacid of sulphur that does not contain bond between sulphur atoms is : **[2019, Main]**

(1) $H_2S_4O_6$      (2) $H_2S_2O_3$

(3) $H_2S_2O_7$      (4) $H_2S_2O_4$

**42.** The noble gas that does NOT occur in the atmosphere is : **[2019, Main]**

(1) He      (2) Kr

(3) Ne      (4) Ra

**43.** The group number, number of valence electrons, and valency of an element with atomic number 15, respectively, are : **[2019, Main]**

(1) 16, 5 and 2      (2) 15, 5 and 3

(3) 16, 6 and 3      (4) 15, 6 and 2

**44.** The green colour produced in the borax bead test of a chromium (III) salt is due to : **[2019, Main]**

(1) $Cr(BO_2)_3$      (2) $Cr_2(B_4O_7)_3$

(3) $Cr_2O_3$      (4) $CrB$

**45.** Fusion of $MnO_2$ with KOH in presence of $O_2$ produces a salt W. Alkaline solution of W upon electrolytic oxidation yields another salt X. The manganese containing ions present in W and X, respectively, are Y and Z. Correct statement(s) is(are) : **[2019, Main]**

(1) In aqueous acidic solution, Y undergoes disproportionation reaction to give Z and $MnO_2$

(2) Both Y and Z are coloured and have tetrahedral shape

(3) Y is diamagnetic in nature while Z is paramagnetic

(4) In both Y and Z, $\pi$-bonding occurs between $p$-orbitals of oxygen and $d$-orbitals of manganese.

**46.** Among $B_2H_6$, $B_3N_3H_6$, $N_2O_3$, $N_2O_4$, $H_2S_2O_3$ and $H_2S_2O_6$, the total number of molecules containing covalent bond between two atoms of the same kind is ...........

**47.** At 143 K, the reaction of $XeF_4$ with $O_2F_2$ products a xenon compound Y. The total number of lone pair(s) of electrons present on the whole molecule of Y is. **[2019, Main]**

**48.** With reference to *aqua regia,* choose the correct option(s) : **[2019, Main]**

(1) *Aqua regia* is prepared by mixing conc. HCl and conc. $HNO_3$ in 3 : 1 (*v/v*) ratio

(2) Reaction of gold with *aqua regia* produces an anion having Au in +3 oxidation state

(3) Reaction of gold with *aqua regia* produces $NO_2$ in the absence of air

(4) The yellow colour of *aqua regia* is due to the presence of NOCl and $Cl_2$

**49.** When metal 'M' is treated with NaOH, a white gelatinous precipitate 'X' is obtained, which is soluble in excess of NaOH. Compound 'X' when heated strongly gives an oxide which is used in chromatography as an adsorbent. The metal 'M' is : **[2018, Main]**

(1) Zn                (2) Ca

(3) Al                (4) Fe

**50.** The correct order of electron affinity is : **[2018, Main]**

(1) $F > Cl > O$      (2) $F > O > Cl$

(3) $Cl > F > O$      (4) $O > F > Cl$

**51.** In graphite and diamond, the percentage of $p$-characters of the hybrid orbitals in hybridisation are respectively : **[2018, Main]**

(1) 33 and 25       (2) 33 and 75

(3) 50 and 75       (4) 67 and 75

**52.** A group 13 element 'X' reacts with chlorine gas to produce a compound $XCl_3$. $XCl_3$ is electron deficient and easily reacts with $NH_3$ to form $Cl_3X \leftarrow NH_3$ adduct; however, $XCl_3$ does not dimerize. X is : **[2018, Main]**

(1) B                (2) Al

(3) Ga              (4) In

**53.** The compounds which generates $N_2$ gas upon thermal decomposition below 300°C is/are : **[2018, Advanced]**

(1) $NH_4NO_3$       (2) $(NH_4)_2Cr_2O_7$

(3) $Ba(N_3)_2$        (4) $Mg_3N_2$

**54.** Based on the compounds of group 15 elements, the correct statements is/are : **[2018, Advanced]**

(1) $Bi_2O_5$ is more basic than $N_2O_5$

(2) $NF_3$ is more covalent than $BiF_3$

(3) $PH_3$ boils at lower temperature than $NH_3$

(4) The N–N single bond is stronger than the P–P single bond

**55.** The total number of compounds having at least one bridging oxo group among the molecules given below is ................ . **[2018, Advanced]**

$N_2O_3$, $N_2O_5$, $P_4O_6$, $P_4O_7$, $H_4P_2O_5$, $H_5P_3P_{10}$, $H_2S_2O_3$, $H_2S_2O_5$

**56.** Total number of lone pair of electrons in $I_3^-$ ion is : **[2018, Main]**

(1) 3                (2) 6

(3) 9                (4) 12

**57.** The compound that does not produce is : **[2018, Main]**

(1) $Ba(N_3)_2$       (2) $(NH_4)_2Cr_2O_7$

(3) $NH_4NO_2$       (4) $(NH_4)_2SO_4$

**58.** For per gram of reactant, the maximum quantity of $N_2$ gas is produced in which of the following thermal decomposition reactions ? **[2018, Main]**

(Given : Atomic wt. – Cr = 52 u, Ba = 137 u)

(1) $(NH_4)_2Cr_2O_7(s) \rightarrow N_2(g) + 4H_2O(g) + Cr_2O_3(s)$

(2) $2NH_4NO_3(s) \rightarrow 2N_2(g) + 4H_2O(g) + O_2(g)$

(3) $Ba(N_3)_2(s) \rightarrow Ba(s) + 3N_2(g)$

(4) $2NH_3(g) \rightarrow N_2(g) + 3H_2(g)$

**59.** The number of P – O bonds in $P_4O_6$ is : **[2018, Main]**

(1) 6                (2) 9

(3) 12               (4) 18

**60.** In $XeO_3F_2$, the number of bond pairs, $\pi$-bonds and lone pairs on Xe atom respectively are : **[2018, Main]**

(1) 5, 2, 0           (2) 4, 2, 2

(3) 5, 3, 0           (4) 4, 4, 0

**61.** Identify the pair in which the geometry of the species is T-shape and square pyramidal, respectively : **[2018, Main]**

(1) $ClF_2$ and $IO_4^-$     (2) $ICl_2^-$ and $ICl_5$

(3) $XeOF_2$ and $XeOF_4$   (4) $IO_3^-$ and $IO_2F_2^-$

**62.** Xenon hexafluoride on partial hydrolysis produces compounds 'X' and 'Y'. Compounds 'X' and 'Y' and the oxidation state of Xe are respectively : **[2018, Main]**

(1) $XeO_2$ (+ 4) and $XeO_3$ (+ 6)

(2) $XeOF_4$ (+ 6) and $XeO_3$ (+ 6)

(3) $XeO_2F_2$ (+ 6) and $XeO_2$ (+ 4)

(4) $XeOF_4$ (+ 6) and $XeO_2F_6$ (+ 6)

**63.** Among the oxides of nitrogen : $N_2O_3$, $N_2O_4$ and $N_2O_5$; the molecules having nitrogen-nitrogen bond is/are : **[2018, Main]**
(1) Only $N_2O_5$
(2) $N_2O_3$ and $N_2O_5$
(3) $N_2O_4$ and $N_2O_5$
(4) $N_2O_3$ and $N_2O_4$

**64.** The correct statements about the oxoacids, $HClO_4$ and $HClO$, is/are : **[2017, Advanced]**
(1) The central atom in both $HClO_4$ and $HClO$ is $sp^3$ hybridised
(2) $HClO_4$ is more acidic than $HClO$ because of the resonance stablisation of its anion
(3) $HClO_4$ is formed in the reaction between $Cl_2$ and $H_2O$
(4) The conjugate base of $HClO_4$ is weaker base than $H_2O$

**65.** The order of the oxidation state of the phosphorus atom in $H_3PO_2$, $H_3PO_4$, $H_3PO_3$ and $H_4P_2O_6$ is : **[2017, Advanced]**
(1) $H_3PO_3 > H_3PO_2 > H_3PO_4 > H_4P_2O_6$
(2) $H_3PO_4 > H_3PO_2 > H_3PO_3 > H_4P_2O_6$
(3) $H_3PO_4 > H_4P_2O_6 > H_3PO_3 > H_3PO_2$
(4) $H_3PO_2 > H_3PO_3 > H_4P_2O_6 > H_3PO_4$

**Paragraph for Question 66 and 67**

Upon heating $KClO_3$ in the presence of catalytic amount of $MnO_2$, a gas **W** is formed. Excess amount of **W** reacts with white phosphorus to give **X**. The reaction of **X** with pure $HNO_3$ gives **Y** and **Z**.

**66.** W and X are, respectively : **[2017, Advanced]**
(1) $O_3$ and $P_4O_6$
(2) $O_2$ and $P_4O_6$
(3) $O_2$ and $P_4O_{10}$
(4) $O_3$ and $P_4O_{10}$

**67.** Y and Z are, respectively : **[2017, Advanced]**
(1) $N_2O_3$ and $H_3PO_4$
(2) $N_2O_5$ and $HPO_3$
(3) $N_2O_4$ and $HPO_3$
(4) $N_2O_4$ and $H_3PO_4$

**68.** Which of the following reactions is an example of a redox reaction ? **[2017, Advanced]**
(1) $XeF_6 + H_2O \rightarrow XeOF_4 + 2HF$
(2) $XeF_6 + 2H_2O \rightarrow XeO_2F_2 + 4HF$
(3) $XeF_4 + O_2F_2 \rightarrow XeF_6 + O_2$
(4) $XeF_2 + PF_5 \rightarrow [XeF]^+ + PF_6^-$

**69.** The products obtained when chlorine gas reacts with cold and dilute aqueous NaOH are : **[2017, Main]**
(1) $Cl^-$ and $ClO^-$
(2) $Cl^-$ and $ClO_2^-$
(3) $ClO^-$ and $ClO_3^-$
(4) $ClO_2^-$ and $ClO_3^-$

**70.** The number of S = O and S – OH bonds present in peroxodisulphuric acid and pyrosulphuric acid respectively are : **[2017, Main]**
(1) (2 and 2) and (2 and 2)
(2) (2 and 4) and (2 and 4)
(3) (4 and 2) and (2 and 4)
(4) (4 and 2) and (4 and 2)

**71.** $XeF_6$ on partial hydrolysis with water produces a compound 'X'. The same compound 'X' is formed when $XeF_6$ reacts with silica. The compound 'X' is : **[2017, Main]**
(1) $XeF_2$
(2) $XeF_4$
(3) $XeOF_4$
(4) $XeO_3$

**72.** The number of P – OH bonds and the oxidation state of phosphorus atom in pyrophosphoric acid ($H_4P_2O_7$) respectively are : **[2017, Main]**
(1) four and four
(2) five and four
(3) five and five
(4) four and five

**73.** The correct sequence of decreasing number of $\pi$-bonds in the structures of $H_2SO_3$, $H_2SO_4$ and $H_2S_2O_7$ is : **[2017, Main]**
(1) $H_2SO_3 > H_2SO_4 > H_2S_2O_7$
(2) $H_2SO_4 > H_2S_2O_7 > H_2SO_3$
(3) $H_2S_2O_7 > H_2SO_4 > H_2SO_3$
(4) $H_2S_2O_7 > H_2SO_3 > H_2SO_4$

**74.** Among the following, the correct statements is/are : **[2017, Advanced]**
(1) $Al(CH_3)_3$ has the three-centre two electron bonds in its dimeric structure
(2) $BH_3$ has the three-centre two-electron bond in its dimeric structure
(3) $AlCl_3$ has the three-centre two-electron bonds in its dimeric structure
(4) The Lewis acidity of $BCl_3$ is greater than that of $AlCl_3$

**75.** The options with only amphoteric oxides is/are : **[2017, Advanced]**
(1) $Cr_2O_3$, BeO, SnO, $SnO_2$
(2) $Cr_2O_3$, CrO, SnO, PbO
(3) NO, $B_2O_3$, PbO, $SnO_2$
(4) ZnO, $Al_2O_3$, PbO, $PbO_2$

**76.** In the following reactions, ZnO is respectively acting as a/an : **[2017, Main]**
(a) $ZnO + Na_2O \rightarrow Na_2ZnO_2$
(b) $ZnO + CO_2 \rightarrow ZnCO_3$
(1) Acid and acid
(2) Acid and base
(3) Base and acid
(4) Base and base

**77.** Which one of the following is an oxide ? **[2017, Main]**
(1) $KO_2$
(2) $BaO_2$
(3) $SiO_2$
(4) $CsO_2$

**78.** The increasing order of atomic radii of the following Group 13 element is : **[2016, Advanced]**
(1) $Al < Ga < In < Tl$
(2) $Ga < Al < In < Tl$
(3) $Al < In < Ga < Tl$
(4) $Al < Ga < Tl < In$

**79.** The crystalline form of borax has : **[2016, Advanced]**
(1) tetranuclear $[B_4O_5(OH)_4]^{2-}$
(2) all boron atoms in the same plane
(3) equal number of $sp^2$ and $sp^3$ hybridised boron atoms
(4) one terminal hydroxide per boron atom

**80.** Match the items in **Column I** with its main use listed in **Column II** : **[2016, Main]**

| Column I | Column II |
| --- | --- |
| (A) Silica gel | (i) Transistor |
| (B) Silicon | (ii) Ion-exchanger |
| (C) Silicone | (iii) Drying agent |
| (D) Silicate | (iv) Sealant |

(1)  (A)-(iii), (B)-(i), (C)-(iv), (D)-(ii)

(2)  (A)-(iv), (B)-(i), (C)-(ii), (D)-(iii)

(3)  (A)-(ii), (B)-(iv), (C)-(i), (D)-(iii)

(4)  (A)-(ii), (B)-(i), (C)-(iv), (D)-(iii)

81. Identify the reaction which does not liberate hydrogen : **[2016, Main]**

(1)  Reaction of zinc with aqueous alkali

(2)  Electrolysis of acidified water using Pt electrodes

(3)  Allowing a solution of sodium in liquid ammonia to stand

(4)  Reaction of lithium hydride with $B_2H_6$

82. **Assertion** : Among the carbon allotropes, diamond is an insulator, whereas, graphite is a good conductor of electricity

**Reason** : Hybridisation of carbon in diamond and graphite are $sp^3$ and $sp^2$, respectively. **[2016, Main]**

(1)  Both assertion and reason are correct and the reason is the correct explanation for the assertion

(2)  Both assertion and reason are correct but the reason is not the correct explanation for the assertion

(3)  Assertion is incorrect statement, but the reason is correct

(4)  Both assertion and reason are incorect

83. The nitrogen containing compound produce in the reaction of $HNO_3$ and $P_4O_{10}$ : **[2016, Advanced]**

(1)  can also be prepared by reaction of $P_4$ and $HNO_3$

(2)  is diamagnetic

(3)  contains one N–N bond

(4)  reacts with Na metal producing a brown gas

84. The non-metal that does not exhibit positive oxidation state is : **[2016, Main]**

(1)  Oxygen  (2)  Iodine

(3)  Chlorine  (4)  Fluorine

85. The group of molecules having identical shape is : **[2016, Main]**

(1)  $SF_4$, $XeF_4$, $CCl_4$  (2)  $ClF_3$, $XeOF_2$, $XeF_3^+$

(3)  $BF_3$, $PCl_3$, $XeO_3$  (4)  $PCl_5$, $IF_5$, $XeO_2F_2$

86. Identify the incorrect statement : **[2016, Main]**

(1)  $S_2$ is paramagnetic like oxygen

(2)  Rhombic and monoclinic sulphur have $S_8$ molecules

(3)  $S_8$ ring has a crown shape

(4)  The S-S-S bond angles in the $S_8$ and $S_6$ rings are the same

87. The species in which the N atom is in a state of $sp$ hybridisation is : **[2016, Main]**

(1)  $NO_2^+$  (2)  $NO_2^-$

(3)  $NO_3^-$  (4)  $NO_2$

88. The reaction of zinc with dilute and concentrated nitric acid, respectively, produces : **[2016, Main]**

(1)  $N_2O$ and $NO_2$  (2)  $NO_2$ and $NO$

(3)  $NO$ and $N_2O$  (4)  $NO_2$ and $N_2O$

89. The pair in which phosphorous atoms have a formal oxidation state of $+3$ is : **[2016, Main]**

(1)  Orthophosphorous and pyrophosphorous acids

(2)  Pyrophosphorous and hypophosphoric acids

(3)  Orthophosphorous and hypophosphoric acids

(4)  Pyrophosphorous and pyrophosphoric acids

90. Which among the following is the most reactive ? **[2015, Main]**

(1)  $Cl_2$  (2)  $Br_2$

(3)  $I_2$  (4)  $ICl$

91. **Assertion** : Nitrogen and Oxygen are the main components in the atmosphere but these do not react to form oxides of nitrogen.

**Reason** : The reaction between nitrogen and oxygen requires high temperature. **[2015, Main]**

(1)  Both assertion and reason are correct, and the reason is the correct explanation for the assertion

(2)  Both assertion and reason are correct, but the reason is not the correct explanation for the assertion

(3)  The assertion is incorrect, but the reason is correct

(4)  Both the assertion and reason are incorrect

92. The least number of oxyacids are formed by : **[2015, Main]**

(1)  Nitrogen  (2)  Sulphur

(3)  Fluorine  (4)  Chlorine

93. The geometry of $XeOF_4$ by VSEPR theory is : **[2015, Main]**

(1)  trigonal bipyramidal  (2)  square pyramidal

(3)  octahedral  (4)  pentagonal planar

94. Which of the following compounds has a P – P bond ? **[2015, Main]**

(1)  $H_4P_2O_5$  (2)  $H_4P_2O_6$

(3)  $H_4P_2O_7$  (4)  $(HPO_3)_3$

95. Chlorine water on standing loses its colour and forms : **[2015, Main]**

(1)  HCl only  (2)  $HOCl$ and $HOCl_2$

(3)  HCl and HOCl  (4)  HCl and $HClO_2$

96. Three moles of $B_2H_6$ are completely reacted with methanol. The number of moles of boron containing product formed is. **[2015, Advanced]**

**97.** The correct statements for orthoboric acid is/are : **[2014, Advanced]**

(1) It behaves as a weak acid in water due to self ionisation

(2) Acidity of its aqueous solution increases upon addition of ethylene glycol

(3) It has a three dimensional structure due to hydrogen bonding

(4) It is a weak electrolyte in water

**98.** In the following sets of reactants which two sets best exhibit the amphoteric character of $Al_2O_3.xH_2O$ ? **[2014, Main]**

Set 1 : $Al_2O_3.xH_2O(s)$ and $OH^-(aq)$
Set 2 : $Al_2O_3.xH_2O(s)$ and $H_2O(l)$
Set 3 : $Al_2O_3.xH_2O(s)$ and $H^+(aq)$
Set 4 : $Al_2O_3.xH_2O(s)$ and $NH_3(aq)$

(1) 1 and 2      (2) 1 and 3
(3) 2 and 4      (4) 3 and 4

**99.** Which of these statements is **not** true ? **[2014, Main]**

(1) $NO^+$ is not isoelectronic with $O_2$

(2) B is always covalent in its compounds

(3) In aqueous solution, the $Tl^+$ ion is much more stable than Tl (III)

(4) $LiAlH_4$ is a versatile reducing agent in organic synthesis

**100.** Example of a three-dimensional silicate is : **[2014, Main]**

(1) Zeolites      (2) Ultramarines
(3) Feldspars      (4) Beryls

**101.** The pairs of reagents that yield paramagnetic species is/are : **[2014, Main]**

(1) Na and excess of $NH_3$

(2) K and excess of $O_2$

(3) Cu and dilute $HNO_3$

(4) $O_2$ and 2-ethylanthraquinol

**102.** Among $PbS$, $CuS$, $HgS$, $MnS$, $Ag_2S$, $NiS$, $CoS$, $Bi_2S_3$ and $SnS_2$, the total number of **BLACK** coloured sulfides is. **[2014, Main]**

**103.** The product formed in the reaction of $SOCl_2$ with white phosphorous is : **[2014, Advanced]**

(1) $PCl_3$      (2) $SO_2Cl_2$
(3) $SCl_2$      (4) $POCl_3$

**104.** Under ambient conditions, the total number of gases released as products in the final step of the reaction scheme shown below is : **[2014, Advanced]**

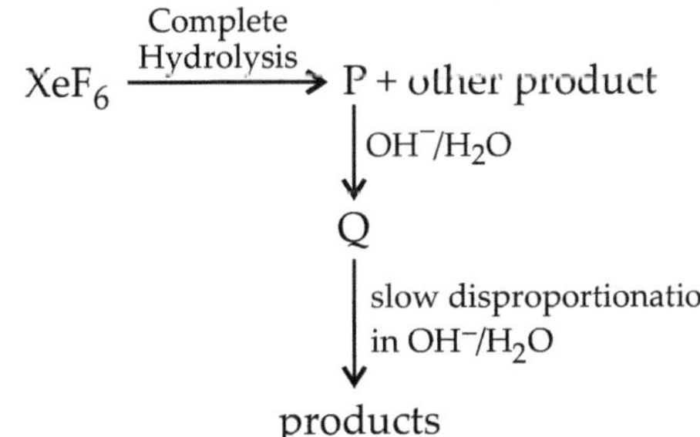



(1) 0      (2) 1
(3) 2      (4) 3

**105.** Among the following oxoacids, the correct decreasing order of acid strength is : **[2014, Main]**

(1) $HOCl > HClO_2 > HClO_3 > HClO_4$

(2) $HClO_4 > HOCl > HClO_2 > HClO_3$

(3) $HClO_4 > HClO_3 > HClO_2 > HOCl$

(4) $HClO_2 > HClO_4 > HClO_3 > HOCl$

**106.** Which one of the following properties is **not** shown by NO ? **[2014, Main]**

(1) It is diamagnetic in gaseous state

(2) It is a neutral oxide

(3) It combines with oxygen to form nitrogen dioxide

(4) It's bond order is 2.5

**107.** The gas evolved on heating $CaF_2$ and $SiO_2$ with concentrated $H_2SO_4$, on hydrolysis gives a white gelatinous precipitate. The precipitate is : **[2014, Main]**

(1) hydrofluosilicic acid

(2) silica gel

(3) silicic acid

(4) calciumfluorosilicate

**108.** Which of the following statments about the depletion of ozone layer is correct ? **[2014, Main]**

(1) The problem of ozone depletion is less serious at poles because $NO_2$ solidifies and is not available for consuming $ClO^•$

(2) The problem of ozone depletion is more serious at poles because ice crystals in the clouds over poles act as catalyst for photochemical reactions involving the decomposition of ozone by $Cl^•$ and $ClO^•$ radicals

(3) Ferons, chlorofluorocarbons, are inert chemically, they do not react with ozone in stratosphere.

(4) Oxides of nitrogen also do not react with ozone in stratosphere

**109.** Shapes of certain interhalogen compounds are stated below. Which one of them is **not** correctly stated ? **[2014, Main]**

(1) $IF_7$ : pentagonal bipyramid

(2) $BrF_5$ : trigonal bipyramid

(3) $BrF_3$ : planat T-shaped

(4) $ICl_3$ : planar dimeric

**110.** Which of the following xenon-OXO compounds may not be obtained by hydrolysis of xenon fluorides ? **[2014, Main]**

(1) $XeO_2F_2$      (2) $XeOF_4$
(3) $XeO_3$      (4) $XeO_4$

**111.** Concentrated nitric acid, upon long standing, turns yellow-brown due to the following of :

**[2014, Advanced]**

(1) NO  
(2) $NO_2$  
(3) $N_2O$  
(4) $N_2O_4$

**112.** The correct statements about $O_3$ is/are :

**[2013, Advanced]**

(1) O-O bond lenghts are equal  
(2) Thermal decomposition of $O_3$ is endothermic  
(3) $O_3$ is diamagnetic in nature  
(4) $O_3$ has a bent structure

**Paragraph for Question 113 and 114**

The reactions of $Cl_2$ gas with cold-dilute and hot-concentrated NaOH in water give sodium salts of two (different) oxoacids of chlorine, **P** and **Q**, respectively. The $Cl_2$ gas reacts with $SO_2$ gas, in presence of charcoal, to give a product **R**. **R** reacts with white phosphorus to give a compound **S**. On hydrolysis, **S** gives an oxoacid of phosphorus, **T**.

**113.** **P** and **Q**, respectively, are the sodium salts of :

**[2013, Advanced]**

(1) hypochlorus and chloric acids  
(2) hypochlorus and chlorus acids  
(3) chloric and perchloric acids  
(4) chloric and hypochlorus acids

**114.** **R, S** and **T** respectively, are : **[2013, Advanced]**

(1) $SO_2Cl_2$, $PCl_5$ and $H_3PO_4$  
(2) $SO_2Cl_2$, $PCl_3$ and $H_3PO_3$  
(3) $SOCl_2$, $PCl_3$ and $H_3PO_2$  
(4) $SOCl_2$, $PCl_5$ and $H_3PO_4$

**115.** The unbalanced chemical reactions given in List I shows missing reagent or conditon (?) which are provided in List II. Match List I with List II and select the correct answer using the code given below the lists : **[2013, Advanced]**

| List I | | List II |
|---|---|---|
| P. $PbO_2 + H_2SO_4 \xrightarrow{?} PbSO_4$ $+ O_2 +$ other product | | 1. NO |
| Q. $Na_2S_2O_3 + H_2O \xrightarrow{?} + NaHSO_4$ $+$ other product | | 2. $I_2$ |
| R. $N_2H_4 \xrightarrow{?} N_2 +$ other product | | 3. Warm |
| S. $XeF_2 \xrightarrow{?} Xe +$ other product | | 4. $Cl_2$ |

**Codes :**

| | P | Q | R | S |
|---|---|---|---|---|
| (1) | 4 | 2 | 3 | 1 |
| (2) | 3 | 2 | 1 | 4 |
| (3) | 1 | 4 | 2 | 3 |
| (4) | 3 | 4 | 2 | 1 |

**116.** Which of the following hydrogen halides reacts with $AgNO_3$(aq) to give a precipitate that dissolves in $Na_2S_2O_3$(aq) ? **[2012, Advanced]**

(1) HCl  
(2) HF  
(3) HBr  
(4) HI

**117.** The reaction of white phosphorus with aqueous NaOH gives phosphine along with another phosphorus containing compound. The reaction type; the oxidation states of phosphorus in phosphine and the other product are respectively :

**[2012, Advanced]**

(1) redox reaction; $-3$ and $-5$  
(2) redox reaction; $+3$ and $+5$  
(3) disproportionation reaction; $-3$ and $+5$  
(4) disproportionation reaction; $-3$ and $+3$

**118.** The shape of $XeO_2F_2$ molecule is :

**[2012, Advanced]**

(1) trigonal bipyramidal  (2) square planar  
(3) tetrahedral  (4) see-saw

**Paragraph for Question 119**

Bleacing powder and bleach solution are produced on a large scale and used in several house-hold products. The effectiveness of bealch solution is often measured by iodometry.

**119.** Bleaching powder contains a salt of an oxoacid as one of its components. The anhydride of that oxoacid is : **[2012, Advanced]**

(1) $Cl_2O$  
(2) $Cl_2O_7$  
(3) $ClO_2$  
(4) $Cl_2O_6$

**120.** With respect to graphite and diamond, which of the statements given below is/are correct ?

**[2012, Advanced]**

(1) Graphite is harder than diamond  
(2) Graphite has higher electrical conductivity than diamond  
(3) Graphite has higher thermal conductivity than diamond  
(4) Graphite has higher C-C bond order than diamond

**121.** Extra pure $N_2$ can be obtained by heating :

**[2011, Advanced]**

(1) $NH_3$ with CuO  (2) $NH_4NO_3$  
(3) $(NH_4)_2Cr_2O_7$  (4) $Ba(N_3)_2$

**122.** Among the following, the number of compounds that can react with $PCl_5$ to give $POCl_3$ is $O_2$, $CO_2$, $SO_2$, $H_2O$, $H_2SO_4$, $P_4O_{10}$. **[2011, Advanced]**

**123.** The value of n in the molecular formula $Be_nAl_2Si_6O_{18}$ is. **[2010, Advanced]**

**124.** All the compounds listed in **Column I** react with water. Match the result of the respective reactions with the appropriate options listed in **Column II**.

**[2010, Advanced]**

| Column I | Column II |
|---|---|
| (1) $(CH_3)_2SiCl_2$ | (p) Hydrogen halide formation |
| (2) $XeF_4$ | (q) Redox reaction |
| (3) $Cl_2$ | (r) Reacts with glass |
| (4) $VCl_5$ | (s) Polymerisation |
| | (t) $O_2$ formation |

**125.** The reaction of $P_4$ with **X** leads selectively to $P_4O_6$. The **X** is : **[2009, Advanced]**

(1) Dry $O_2$
(2) A mixture of $O_2$ and $N_2$
(3) Moist $O_2$
(4) $O_2$ in the presence of aqueous NaOH

**126.** The nitrogen oxides that contains N-N bonds is/are : **[2009, Advanced]**

(1) $N_2O$      (2) $N_2O_3$
(3) $N_2O_4$      (4) $N_2O_5$

**127.** Match each of the reactions given in **Column I** with the corresponding products given in **Column II.** **[2009, Advanced]**

| Column I | Column II |
|---|---|
| (1) $Cu + dil\ HNO_3$ | (p) NO |
| (2) $Cu + conc\ HNO_3$ | (q) $NO_2$ |
| (3) $Zn + dil\ HNO_3$ | (r) $N_2O$ |
| (4) $Zn + conc\ HNO_3$ | (s) $Cu(NO_3)_2$ |
| | (t) $Zn(NO_3)_2$ |

**128.** In the reaction
$$2X + B_2H_6 \rightarrow [BH_2(X)_2]^+ [BH_4]^-$$
the amines **X** is/are : **[2009, Advanced]**

(1) $NH_3$      (2) $CH_3NH_2$
(3) $(CH_3)_2NH$      (4) $(CH_3)_3N$

**129. Statement-1 :** $Pb^{4+}$ compounds are stronger oxidising agents than $Sn^{4+}$ compounds

**and**

**Statement-2 :** The higher oxidation states for the group 14 elements are more stable for the heavier members of the group due to 'inert pair effect' **[2008, Advanced]**

(1) **Statement-1** is True, **Statement-2** is True; **Statement-2** is a correct explanation for **Statement-1**
(2) **Statement-1** is True, **Statement-2** is True; **Statement-2** is **NOT** a correct explanation for **Statement-1**
(3) **Statement-1** is True, **Statement-2** is False
(4) **Statement-1** is False, **Statement-2** is True

**130.** A solution of colourless salt **H** on boiling with excess NaOH produces a non-flammable gas. The gas evolution ceases after sometime. Upon addition of Zn dust to the same solution, the gas evolution restarts. The colourless salts **H** is/are : **[2008, Advanced]**

(1) $NH_4NO_3$      (2) $NH_4NO_2$
(3) $NH_4Cl$      (4) $(NH_4)_2SO_4$

**Paragraph for Question 131 to 133**

There are some deposits of nitrates and phosphates in earth's crust. Nitrates are more soluble in water. Nitrates are difficult to reduce under the laboratory conditions but microbes do it easily. Ammonia forms large number of complexes with transition metal ions. Hybridisation easily explains the ease of sigma donation capability of $NH_3$ and $PH_3$. Phosphine is a flammable gas and is prepared from white phosphorous.

**131.** Among the following, the correct statement is : **[2008, Advanced]**

(1) Phosphates have no biological significance in humans
(2) Between nitrates and phosphates, phosphates are less abundant in earth's crust
(3) Between nitrates and phosphates, nitrates are less abundant in earth's crust
(4) Oxidation of nitrates is possible in soil

**132.** Among the following, the correct statement is : **[2008, Advanced]**

(1) Between $NH_3$ and $PH_3$, $NH_3$ is a better electron donor because the lone pair of electrons occupies spherical 's' orbital and is less directional
(2) Between $NH_3$ and $PH_3$, $PH_3$ is a better electron donor because the lone pair of electrons occupies $sp^3$ orbital and is more directional
(3) Between $NH_3$ and $PH_3$, $NH_3$ is a better electron donor because the lone pair of electrons occupies $sp^3$ orbital and is more directional
(4) Between $NH_3$ and $PH_3$, $PH_3$ is a better electron donor because the lone pair of electrons occupies spherical 's' orbital and is less directional

**133.** White phosphorus on reaction with NaOH gives $PH_3$ as one of the products. This is a : **[2008, Advanced]**

(1) dimerisation reaction
(2) disproportionation reaction
(3) condensation reaction
(4) precipitation reaction

**134. Statement-1 :** In water, orthoboric acid behaves as a weak monobasic acid

because

**Statement-2 :** In water, orthoboric acid acts as a proton donor. **[2007, Advanced]**

(1) **Statement-1** is True, **Statement-2** is True; **Statement-2** is a correct explanation for **Statement-1**
(2) **Statement-1** is True, **Statement-2** is True; **Statement-2** is **NOT** a correct explanation for **Statement-1**
(3) **Statement-1** is True, **Statement-2** is False
(4) **Statement-1** is False, **Statement-2** is True

**135.** The percentage of $p$-character in the orbitals forming P-P bonds in $P_4$ is : **[2007, Advanced]**

(1) 25      (2) 33
(3) 50      (4) 75

**136.** Argon is uded in arc welding because of its : **[2007, Advanced]**

(1) low reactivity with metal
(2) ability to lower the melting point of metal
(3) flammability
(4) high calorific value

**137.** The structure of $XeO_3$ is :     [2007, **Advanced**]
(1) linear      (2) planar
(3) pyramidal      (4) T-shaped

**138.** $XeF_4$ and $XeF_6$ are expected to be :
         [2007, **Advanced**]
(1) oxidising      (2) reducing
(3) unreactive      (4) strongly basic

**139.** $MgSO_4$ on reaction with $NH_4OH$ and $Na_2HPO_4$ forms a white crystalline precipitate. What is its formula ?      [2006, **Main**]
(1) $Mg(NH_4)PO_4$      (2) $Mg_3(PO_4)_2$
(3) $MgCl_2.MgSO_4$      (4) $MgSO_4$

**140.** $B(OH)_3 + NaOH \rightleftharpoons NaBO_2 + Na[B(OH)_4] + H_2O$
How can this reaction is made to proceed in forward direction ?      [2006, **Main**]
(1) addition of cis 1, 2 diol
(2) addition of borax
(3) addition of trans 1, 2 diol
(4) addition of $Na_2HPO_4$

**141.** Match the following :      [2006, **Main**]

| **Column I** | | **Column II** |
|---|---|---|
| (A) $Bi^{3+} \rightarrow (BiO)^+$ | (P) | Heat |
| (B) $[AlO_2]^- \rightarrow Al(OH)_3$ | (Q) | Hydrolysis |
| (C) $SiO_4^{4-} \rightarrow Si_2O_7^{6-}$ | (R) | Acidification |
| (D) $(B_4O_7^{2-}) \rightarrow [B(OH)_3]$ | (S) | Dilution by water |

**142.** Which of the following isomers of phosphorus in theromodynamically most stable ?
         [2005, **Screening**]
(1) Red      (2) White
(3) Black      (4) Yellow

**143.** A metal nitrate gives black ppt. with KI and on adding excess of KI it gives orange colour. It is :
         [2005, **Screening**]
(1) $Hg^{+2}$      (2) $Bi^{+3}$
(3) $Sn^{+2}$      (4) $Pb^{+2}$

**144.** A pale blue liquid which obtained by equi molar mixture of two gases at $-30°C$ is :
         [2005, **Screening**]
(1) $N_2O$      (2) $N_2O_3$
(3) $N_2O_4$      (4) $N_2O_5$

**145.** Which gas is evolved when $PbO_2$ is treated with conc. $HNO_3$ ?      [2005, **Screening**]
(1) $NO_2$      (2) $O_2$
(3) $N_2$      (4) $N_2O$

**146.** Which of the following contains maximum number of lone pairs on the central atom ?
         [2005, **Screening**]
(1) $ClO_3^-$      (2) $XeF_4$
(3) $SF_4$      (4) $I_3^-$

**147.** Which of the following has $-O-O-$ linkage :
         [2004, **Screening**]
(1) $H_2S_2O_6$      (2) $H_2S_2O_8$
(3) $H_2S_2O_3$      (4) $H_2S_4O_6$

**148.** Number of lone pairs in $XeOF_4$ is/are :
         [2004, **Screening**]

(1) 0      (2) 1
(3) 2      (4) 3

**149.** Which silicates is formed from $[SiO_4]^{4-}$, tetrahedral units of sharing 3 oxygen atoms ?
         [2005, **Screening**]
(1) Sheet silicates
(2) Pyro silicates
(3) Linear chain silicates
(4) 3 dimensional silicates

**150.** $H_3BO_3$ is :      [2003, **Screening**]
(1) Monobasic and weak Lewis acid
(2) Monobasic and weak Bronsted acid
(3) Monobasic and strong Lewis acid
(4) Tribasic and weak Bronsted acid

**151.** $(Me)_2SiCl_2$ on hydrolysis will produce :
         [2003, **Screening**]
1) $(Me)_2Si(OH)_2$      (2) $(Me)_2Si = O$
(3) $-[-O-(Me)_2Si-O-]_n-$      (4) $Me_2SiCl(OH)$

**152.** For $H_3PO_3$ and $H_3PO_4$, the correct choice is :
         [2003, **Screening**]
(1) $H_3PO_3$ is dibasic and reducing
(2) $H_3PO_3$ is dibasic and non-reducing
(3) $H_3PO_4$ is tribasic and reducing
(4) $H_3PO_3$ is tribasic and non-reducing

**153.** Anhydrous ferric chloride is prepared by :
         [2002, **Screening**]
(1) heating hydrated ferric chloride at a high temperature in a stream of air
(2) heat metallic iron in a stream of dry chlorine gas
(3) reaction of metallic iron with hydrochloric acid
(4) reaction of metallic iron with hydrochloric acid

**154.** A gas 'X' is passed through water to form a saturated solution. The aqueous solution on treatment with silver nitrate gives a white precipitate. The saturated aqueous solution also dissolves magnesium ribbon with evolution of a colourless gas 'Y'. Identify 'X' and 'Y'.
         [2002, **Screening**]
(1) $X = CO_2, Y = Cl_2$      (2) $X = Cl_2, Y = CO_2$
(3) $X = Cl_2, Y = H_2$      (4) $X = H_2, Y = Cl_2$

**155.** How is boron obtained from borax ? Give chemical equations with reaction conditons. Write the structure of $B_2H_6$ and its reaction with HCl.
         [2002, **Main**]

**156.** An aqueous solution of substance gives a white precipitate on treatment with dilute hydrochloric acid, which dissolves on heating. When hydrogen sulfide is passed through the hot acidic solution, a black precipitate is obtained. The substance is a :
         [2002, **Screening**]
(1) $Hg_2^{2+}$ salt      (2) $Cu^{2+}$ salt
(3) $Ag^+$ salt      (4) $Pb^{2+}$

## ANSWER KEY

| | | | | | | | | | |
|---|---|---|---|---|---|---|---|---|---|
| **1.** (4) | **2.** (2) | **3.** (4) | **4.** (1) | **5.** (2) | **6.** (1) | **7.** (*) | **8.** (4) | **9.** (4) | **10.** (1,2,4) |
| **11.** (2) | **12.** (3) | **13.** (3) | **14.** (2) | **15.** (3) | **16.** (4) | **17.** (4) | **18.** (*) | **19.** (1) | **20.** (2) |
| **21.** (3) | **22.** (3) | **23.** (2) | **24.** (1) | **25.** (2) | **26.** (3) | **27.** (1) | **28.** (2) | **29.** (4) | **30.** (3) |
| **31.** (1) | **32.** (4) | **33.** (1) | **34.** (2) | **35.** (2) | **36.** (3) | **37.** (1) | **38.** (4) | **39.** (4) | **40.** (2) |
| **41.** (3) | **42.** (4) | **43.** (2) | **44.** (1) | **45.** (1,2,4) | **46.** (4) | **47.** (*) | **48.** (1,2,4) | **49.** (3) | **50.** (3) |
| **51.** (4) | **52.** (1) | **53.** (2) | **54.** (2) | **55.** (*) | **56.** (3) | **57.** (4) | **58.** (4) | **59.** (3) | **60.** (3) |
| **61.** (3) | **62.** (4) | **63.** (4) | **64.** (1,2,4) | **65.** (3) | **66.** (3) | **67.** (2) | **68.** (3) | **69.** (1) | **70.** (4) |
| **71.** (3) | **72.** (4) | **73.** (3) | **74.** (1,2,3,4) | **75.** (1,4) | **76.** (2) | **77.** (3) | **78.** (2) | **79.** (1,3,4) | **80.** (1) |
| **81.** (4) | **82.** (1) | **83.** (2,4) | **84.** (4) | **85.** (2) | **86.** (4) | **87.** (1) | **88.** (1) | **89.** (1) | **90.** (4) |
| **91.** (1) | **92.** (3) | **93.** (2) | **94.** (2) | **95.** (3) | **96.** (*) | **97.** (2, 4) | **98.** (2) | **99.** (2) | **100.** (1,2,3) |
| **101.** (1,2,3) | **102.** (*) | **103.** (1) | **104.** (3) | **105.** (3) | **106.** (1) | **107.** (1) | **108.** (2) | **109.** (2) | **110.** (4) |
| **111.** (2) | **112.** (1,3,4) | **113.** (1) | **114.** (1) | **115.** (4) | **116.** (1,3,4) | **117.** (3) | **118.** (4) | **119.** (1) | **120.** (2,4) |
| **121.** (4) | **122.** (*) | **123.** (3) | **124.** (*) | **125.** (2) | **126.** (1,2,3) | **127.** (*) | **128.** (1,2,3) | **129.** (3) | **130.** (1,2) |
| **131.** (3) | **132.** (3) | **133.** (2) | **134.** (3) | **135.** (4) | **136.** (1) | **137.** (3) | **138.** (1) | **139.** (1) | **140.** (1) |
| **141.** (*) | **142.** (3) | **143.** (2) | **144.** (2) | **145.** (2) | **146.** (4) | **147.** (2) | **148.** (2) | **149.** (1) | **150.** (1) |
| **151.** (3) | **152.** (1) | **153.** (2) | **154.** (3) | **155.** (*) | **156.** (4) | | | | |

## ANSWERS WITH EXPLANATIONS

**1. (4)** Pyrophosphoric acid.

$$HO-\underset{OH}{\overset{O}{\underset{\|}{P}}}-O-\underset{OH}{\overset{O}{\underset{\|}{P}}}-OH$$

P—OH linkages = 4
P = O linikages = 2
P–O–P linkages = 1

**2. (2)**

$$Na_2SO_3 \underset{(X)}{\xrightarrow{dil.\ H_2SO_4}} \underset{(Y)}{SO_2} \xrightarrow{NaOH} \underset{(X)}{Na_2SO_3}$$

$$\downarrow \begin{array}{c} SO_2 \\ + \\ H_2O \end{array}$$

$$\underset{(Z)}{NaHSO_3}$$

**3. (4)** $2NO + N_2O_4 \xrightarrow{250K} \underset{blue\ solid}{2N_2O_3}$

**4. (1)** (1) Water gas shift reaction

$$CO_{(g)} + H_2O_{(g)} \xrightarrow[catalyst]{673K} CO_{2(g)} + H_{2(g)}$$

(2) Water gas is produced by this reaction.

$$CH_{4(g)} + H_2O_{(g)} \xrightarrow[Ni]{1270K} CO_{(g)} + 3H_{2(g)}$$

(3) Water gas is produced by this reaction.

$$C_{(s)} + H_2O_{(g)} \xrightarrow{1270K} CO_{(g)} + H_{2(g)}$$

(4) Producer gas is produced by this reaction.

$$2C_{(s)} + O_{2(g)} + 4N_{2(g)} \xrightarrow{1270K} 2CO_{(g)} + 4N_{2(g)}$$

**5. (2)** It can be used as an inert diluent for reactive chemicals.

**6. (1)** high and high.

**7.** 3.00.

**8. (4)** "Boron" and "Silicon" of very high purity can be obtained through : zone refining method only.
While other methods are used for other metals/elements i.e.,
(i) Vapour phase refining
(ii) Electrolytic refining
(iii) Liquation etc.

**9. (4)** $NH_3 + \underset{excess}{3Cl_2} \longrightarrow NCl_3 + 3HCl$

**10. (1,2,4)**
Hypochlorite ion : $ClO^-$
Chlorate ion : $ClO_3^-$
Per chlorate ion : $ClO_4^-$
(A) Acidic order : $H\overset{+1}{Cl}O < H\overset{+5}{Cl}O_3 < H\overset{+7}{Cl}O_4$

Conjugate base order : $ClO^- > ClO_3^- > ClO_4^-$
(B) Hypochlorite ion ($ClO^-$) :

$:\ddot{Cl} - \ddot{O}:$      Linear shape

Chlorate ion ($ClO_3^-$) :

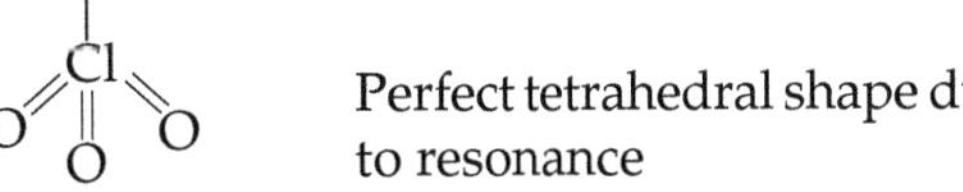

Trigonal pyramidal shape

Perchlorate ion ($ClO_4^-$) :

Perfect tetrahedral shape due to resonance

In chlorate ion bond angle changes due to presence of lone pair on chlorine atom. While hypochlorite ion is linear and perchlorate ion is tetrahedral and there is no effect of lone pair on hypochlorite ion.

(C) Disproportionation reaction of :

(i) hypochlorite ion : $3ClO^- \rightarrow 2Cl^- + ClO_3^-$

(ii) Chlorate ion : $4ClO_3^- \rightarrow 3ClO_4^- + Cl^-$ ✓

(D) $ClO^- + SO_3^{2-} \rightarrow SO_4^{2-} + Cl^-$

**11. (2)**

$\xrightarrow[\Delta]{\text{HBr (excess),}}$

$\xrightarrow[\text{(ii) } H^+]{\text{(i) KOH (Alc.)}}$

$\xrightarrow[\text{Zn}/H_3O^+]{O_3}$

**12. (3)**

More donating group

$\xrightarrow{\text{Conc. } HNO_3/H_2SO_4}$

(Major)

[Minor due to crowding]

**13. (3)** $CH_3-CH_2-\overset{\overset{\displaystyle O}{\|}}{C}-H$ (A) $\xrightarrow{CH_3MgBr}$

$CH_3-CH_2-\overset{\overset{\displaystyle OH}{|}}{C}H-CH_3$

2° Alcohol

(C)

CAN test for alcohol : ✓

Iodoform test : ✓

$CH_3-\overset{\overset{\displaystyle O}{\|}}{C}-CH_3$ (B) $\xrightarrow{CH_3MgBr}$ $CH_3-\overset{\overset{\displaystyle OH}{|}}{\underset{\underset{\displaystyle CH_3}{|}}{C}}-CH_3$

3° Alcohol

CAN test for alcohol : ✓

Lucas test : Immediately

Iodoform test : ✗

**14. (2)**

$\bigcirc-CH_2-O-CH=CH_2 \xrightarrow{\text{Conc. HI}}$

$C_9H_{10}O$

[A]

$\bigcirc-CH_2-\overset{\overset{\displaystyle H}{|}}{O}^{\oplus}-CH=CH_2$

Cleavage of ether by $SN_1$

$\bigcirc-\overset{\oplus}{C}H_2 \quad + \quad HO-CH=CH_2$

AgI↓ $\xleftarrow{AgNO_3}$ $\bigcirc-CH_2-I$

Yellow ppt     [B]

Tauto

$H-\overset{\overset{\displaystyle O}{\|}}{C}=CH_3$

[D]

Iodoform test

**15. (3)**

$\xrightarrow{\text{(1) } CH_3MgBr/H_2O}$

(A)

$\xrightarrow{H_2SO_4/\Delta}$

(B)

$\xleftarrow{O_3/Zn}$

$\overset{\overset{\displaystyle O}{\|}}{C}=O + Ph-C-H$

(D)     (C)

$Ph-\overset{\overset{\displaystyle O}{\|}}{C}-H \xrightarrow[\text{NaOH (cannizaro)}]{\text{Conc.}} Ph-COOK+Ph-CH_2OH$

$\xrightarrow[\text{Aldol}]{OH^-/\Delta}$

**16. (4)**

(A)

$\xleftarrow{-H^+}$

(B)

$\xrightarrow{-H^+}$

**17. (4)**

$\xrightarrow[Br_2/FeBr_3]{Br_2}$

(Only single product)

Sodalime $\Delta$

**18.**

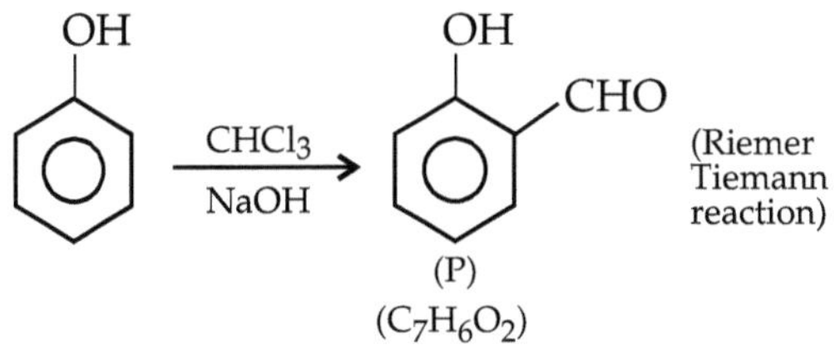

(Riemer Tiemann reaction)

(P)
$(C_7H_6O_2)$

Molecular weight of $C_7H_6O_2 = 122$

$$\%C = \frac{12 \times 7 \times 100}{122} = 68.85 \approx 69$$

**19. (1)**

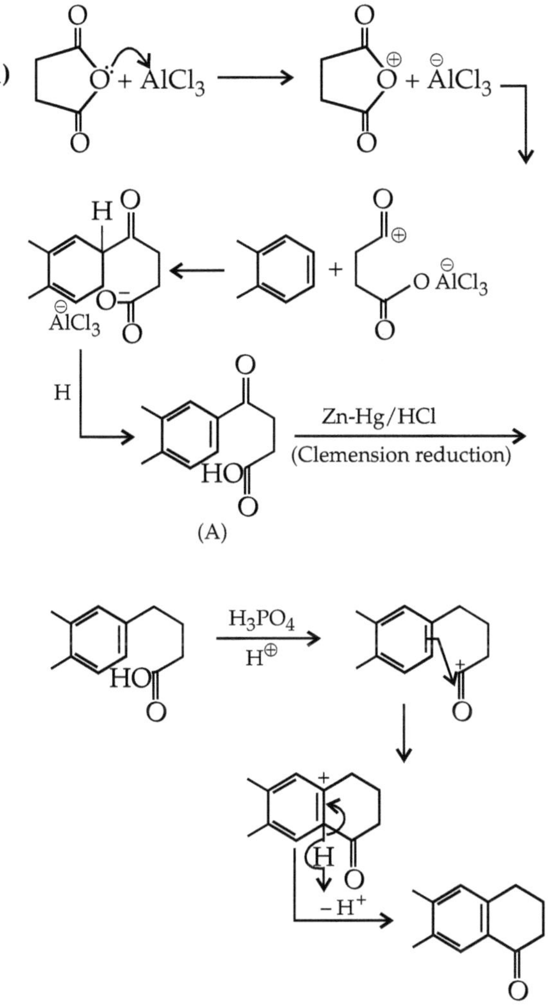

$\overset{\ominus}{O}\,AlCl_3$

Zn-Hg/HCl
(Clemension reduction)

(A)

$\xrightarrow[H^{\oplus}]{H_3PO_4}$

$-H^+$

**20. (2)** $R-O-\underset{O}{\overset{O}{C}}-CH_3 \xrightarrow{\overset{\ominus}{OH}/H_2O} R-O-\underset{O}{\overset{OH}{C}}-CH_3$

(ester)

$CH_3-\underset{O}{\overset{O}{C}}-OH + \overset{\ominus}{O}R$

(Base)
(Acid)

$CH_3-\underset{O}{\overset{O}{C}}-\overset{\ominus}{O} + R{-}OH$

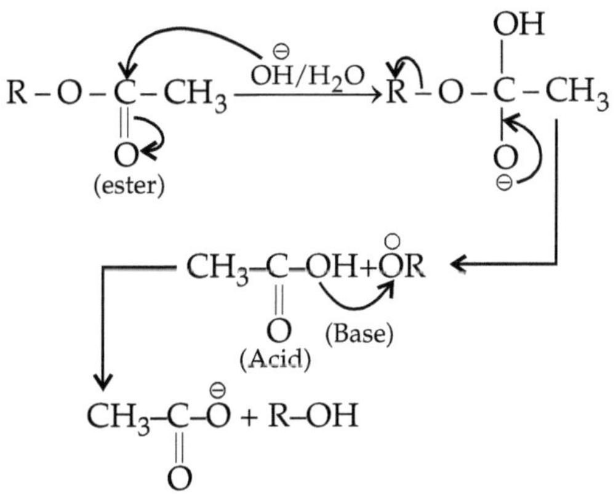

It is a hydrolysis of ester in basic medium.

**21. (3)**

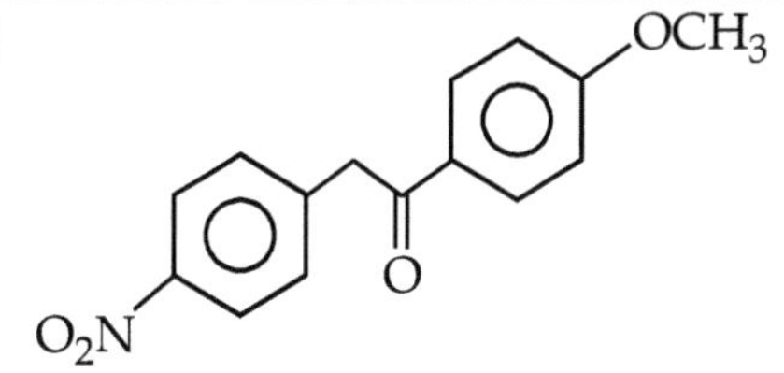

$O_2N$ ... $OCH_3$

**22. (3)** $CH_2{=}CH{-}\underset{O}{\overset{O}{C}}{-}H \xrightarrow[\text{(ii) } SOCl_2]{\text{(i) } NaBH_4} CH_2{=}CH{-}CH_2{-}Cl$

(A)

$+ AlCl_3$

$CH_2{-}CH{=}CH_2$

DBr

$\underset{Br}{\overset{}{C}}H{-}CH_2{-}\underset{D}{\overset{}{C}}H_2$

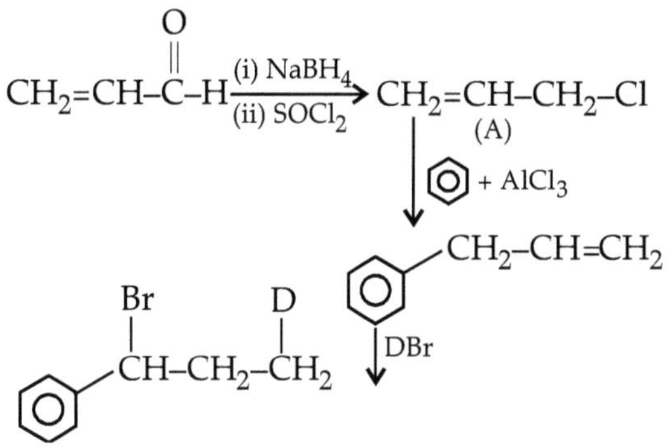

**23. (2)** Diazo compounds and inorganic nitrogen cannot be estimated by Kjeldahl method.

$CH_2{-}C{\equiv}N$

$\xrightarrow[\text{(ii) } H_2O]{\text{(i) } SnCl_2 + HCl}$

$\underset{O}{\overset{O}{C}}{-}H$  Not estimated by Kjeldahl method

$NH_2$

$\xrightarrow[+ HCl]{NaNO_2}$

$N{\equiv}N$  Not estimated by Kjeldahl method

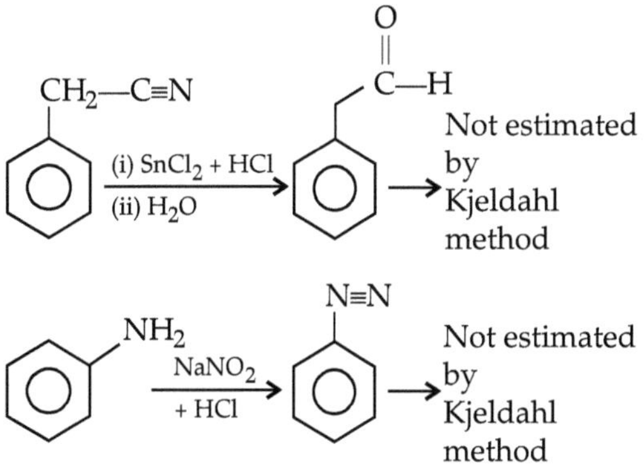

**24. (1)** Gabriel phthalimide synthesis is used for preparation of 1° Aliphatic amine

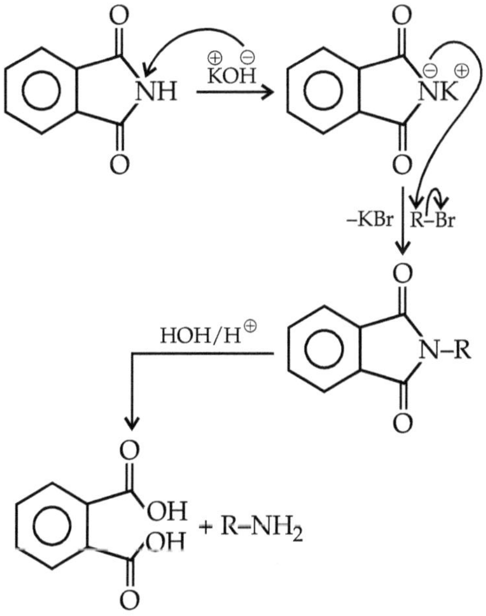

$NH \xrightarrow[]{\overset{\oplus}{K}\overset{\ominus}{OH}} \overset{\ominus}{N}\overset{\oplus}{K}$

$-KBr$  R–Br

N–R

$\xrightarrow{HOH/H^{\oplus}}$

$\underset{O}{\overset{O}{C}}{-}OH$ ... $OH$  $+ R{-}NH_2$

Here  $R{-}Br = $  (benzyl bromide, $CH_2{-}Br$)

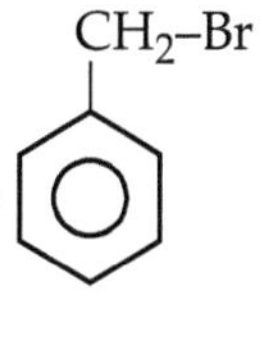

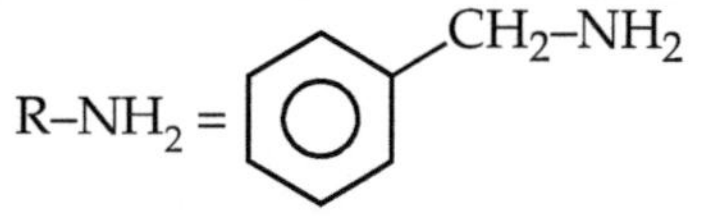

**25. (2)**

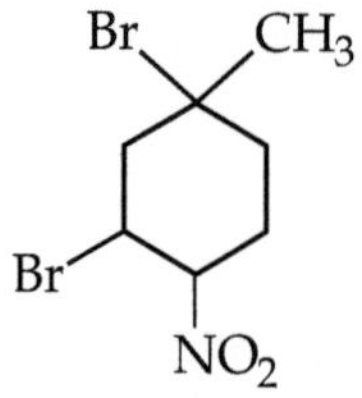

**26. (3)**

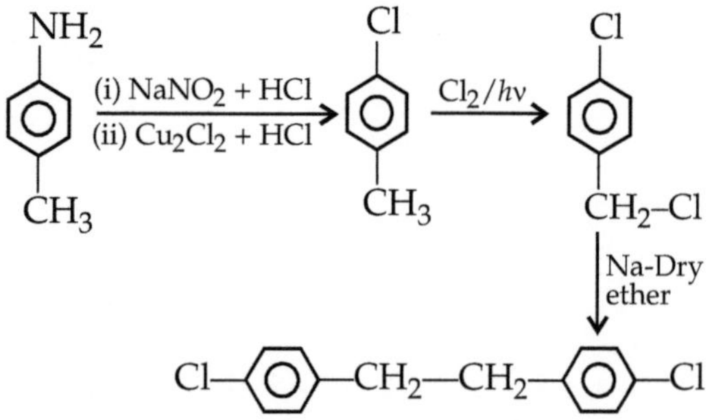

**27. (1)**

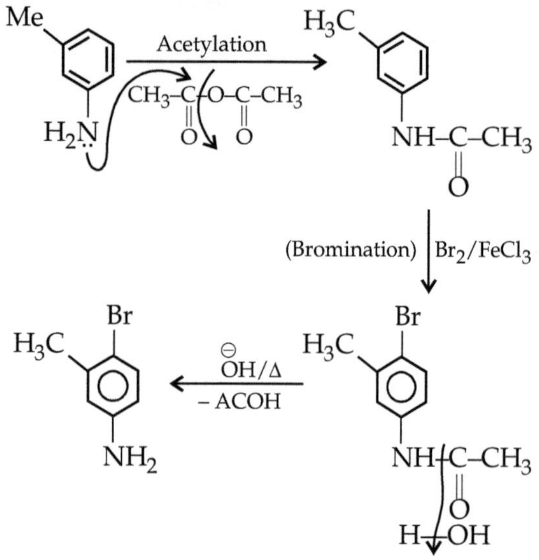

**28. (2)**

$$P_4 + 3NaOH + 3H_2 \longrightarrow \underset{(X)}{3NaH_2PO_2} + PH_3$$

$$NaH_2PO_2 + HCl \longrightarrow NaCl + \underset{(Y)}{H_3PO_2}$$

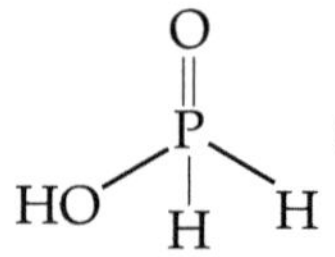

(mono basic acid)

**29. (4)** The assertion is true, but the reason is false.

**30. (3)** $S_2O_8^{2-}$ :

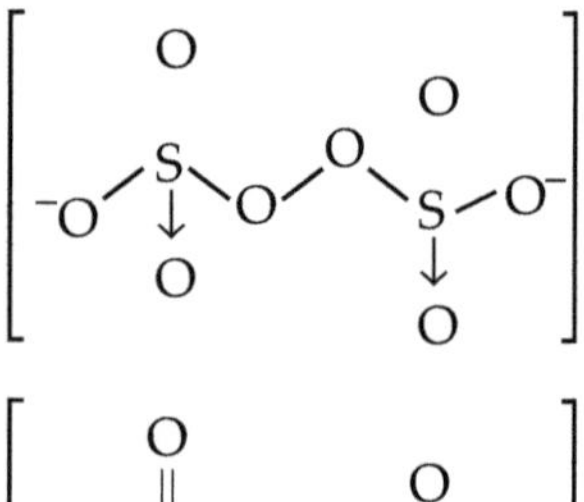

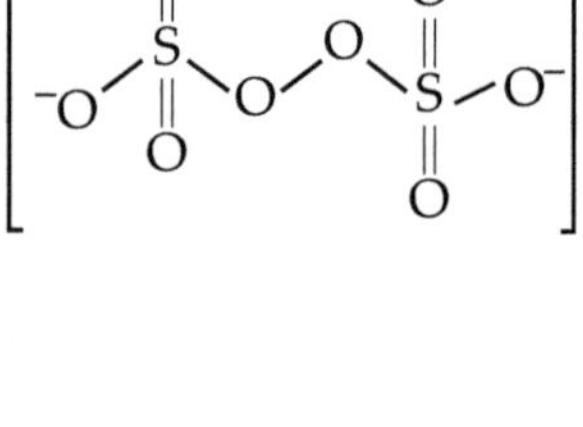

8 bonds are present between sulphur and oxygen. (It is best answer in given options)

**Rhombic sulphur :**

($S_8$)

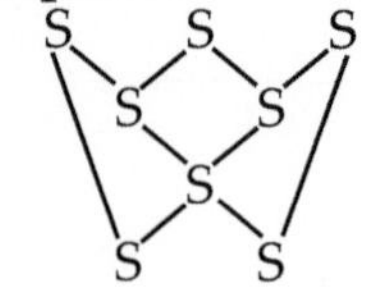

8 bonds are present between sulphur and sulphur atoms.

**31. (1)** Order of electron gain enthalpy (magnitude) is :

$$Cl < F > Br > I$$

**32. (4)**  1.  MgO Basic
     $Cl_2O$ Acidic
     $Al_2O_3$ amphoteric
2.  $Cl_2O$ Acidic
     CaO Basic
     $P_4O_{10}$ Acidic
3.  $Na_2O$ Basic
     $SO_3$ Acidic
     $Al_2O_3$ amphoteric
4.  $N_2O_3$ Acidic
     $Li_2O$ Basic
     $Al_2O_3$ amphoteric

**33. (1)** The carbon allotrope ($C_{60}$) contains 20 hexagoans and 12 pentagons.

**34. (2)** The acidic character of metal oxides of group 13 decreases down the group.

The boron trioxide is a acidic compound. The oxides of aluminium and gallium are amphoteric in nature. The oxides of indium and thallium are basic in nature.

**35. (2)** The tendency of an atom to form bonds with the same atom is known as catenation. The bond strength decreases on moving down a group, therefore, the tendency to undergo catenation decreases. Hence, the correct order of catenation is $C > Si > Ge \approx Sn$.

**36. (3)** Fledespar, zeolites, mica and asbestos are silicates.

They all contain a basic unit of silicate that is $(SiO_4)^{4-}$.

**37. (1)** The structure of $(SiH_3)_3N$ and $(CH_3)_3N$ is shown below :

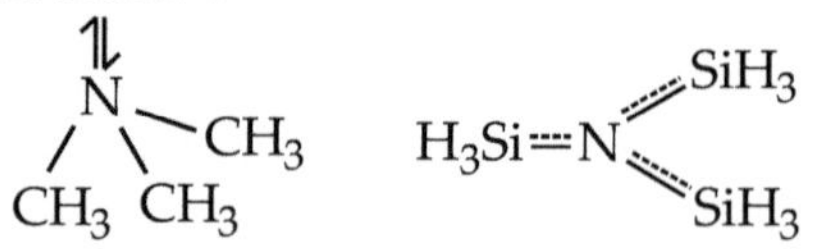

The compound $(SiH_3)_3N$ has planar structure. The structure of $(SiH_3)_3N$ indicates that lone pair of nitrogen are not available from donation. Therefore, $(SiH_3)_3N$ is less basic than $(CH_3)_3N$.

**38. (4)** The graphite, $C_{60}$ ad $C_{70}$ have double bonds between carbon atoms. The diamonds does not have double bond between carbon atoms. Therefore, the diamond have maximum $C-C$ bond length.

**39. (1)** The steric number of $ICl_5$ is calculated as shown below :

Steric number

$$= \frac{1}{2} \times \left( \begin{array}{l} \text{valence } e^- + \text{monovalent atoms} + \\ \text{positive charge} + \text{negative charge} \end{array} \right)$$

$$= \frac{1}{2} \times (7 + 5 + 0 + 0)$$

$$= 6$$

The steric number of $ICl_5$ is 6, that is, the hybridisation is $sp^3d^2$.

The steric number of $ICl_4^-$ is calculated as shown below :

Steric number

$$= \frac{1}{2} \times \left( \begin{array}{l} \text{valence } e^- + \text{monovalent atoms} + \\ \text{positive charge} + \text{negative charge} \end{array} \right)$$

$$= \frac{1}{2} \times (7 + 4 + 0 + 1)$$

$$= 6$$

The steric number oif $ICl_4^-$ is 6, that is, the hybridisation is $sp^3d^2$.

The structures of $ICl_5$ and $ICl_4^-$ are shown below :

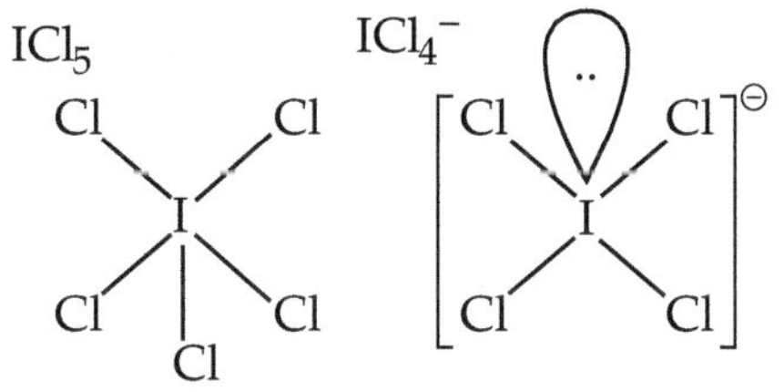

Therefore, the structures of $ICl_5$ and $ICl_4^-$ are square pyramidal and square planar respectively.

**40. (2)** The oxidation number nitrogen in $NO_2$ is 4.

The oxidation number nitrogen in $N_2O_3$ is +3.

The oxidation number nitrogen in $NO$ is +2.

The oxidation number nitrogen in $N_2O$ is +1.

Therefore, the correct order of increasing oxidation number of nitrogen is shown below :

$$NO_2 < N_2O_3 < NO < N_2O$$

**41. (3)** The structures of the given oxoacids are shown below :

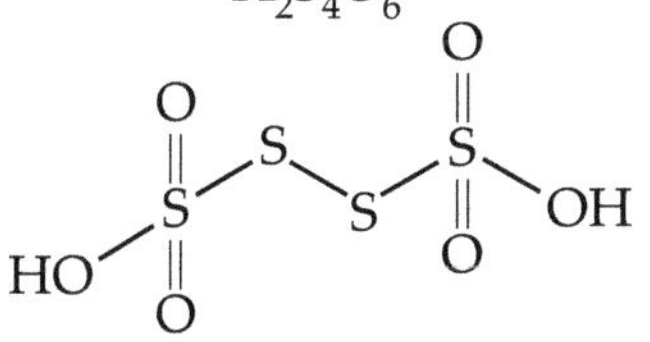

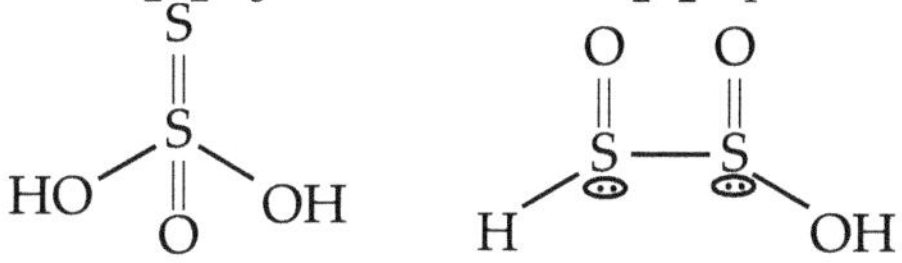

The compound that does not contain bond between sulphur atoms is $H_2S_2O_7$.

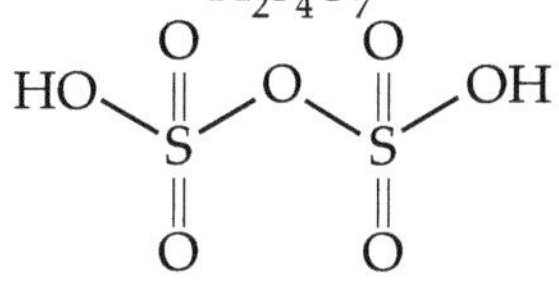

**42. (4)** The element Ra is an alkaline earth metal and not a noble gas.

**43. (2)** Phosphorus has atomic number 15.

Phosphorus belong to the group 15.

The electronic configuration of the phosphorous atom is $[Ne]3s^23p^3$.

The number of valence electron in phosphorus is 5.

The number of electrons needed by phosphorous to complete its octet are 3. Therefore, the valency of phosphorus is 3.

**44. (1)** The reactions for borax bead test are given below :

$$\text{Chromium (III) salt} \xrightarrow{\Delta} Cr_2O_3$$

$$\text{Borax} \xrightarrow{\Delta} B_2O_3 + NaBO_2$$

$$2C_2O_3 + 6B_2O_3 \longrightarrow 4Cr(BO_2)_3$$

Therefore, $Cr(BO_2)_3$ is formed.

**45. (1,2,4)** The reactions are given below :

$$MnO_2 + 2KOH + \frac{1}{2}O_2 \xrightarrow{\Delta} K_2MnO_4(W)$$

$$+ H_2O$$

$$K_2MnO_4 \rightleftharpoons 2K^+ + MnO_4^{2-}(Y)$$

The electrolytic oxidation of W is shown below :

$$K_2MnO_4 + H_2O \xrightarrow[\text{Redox}]{\text{Electrolytic}} H_2 + KOH$$

$$+ KMnO_4(X)$$

The anion of X is $MNO_4^- (Z)$.

The electrolytic oxidation of Y is shown below :

$$MnO_4^{2-}(Y) \xrightarrow[\text{Oxidation}]{\text{Electrolytic}} MnO_4^-(Z) + e^-$$

The disproportionation reaction of Y is shown below :

$$3MnO_4^{2-} + 4H^+ \longrightarrow 2MnO_4^-(Z) + MnO_2$$

$$+ 2H_2O$$

Both $MnO_4^{2-}$ and $MnO_4^-$ are coloured and have tetrahedral shape. The $\pi$ bonding occurs between the $p$ orbital of oxygen and the $d$ orbital of manganese in both these compounds. The structures of $MnO_4^{2-}$ and $MnO_4^-$ are shown below :

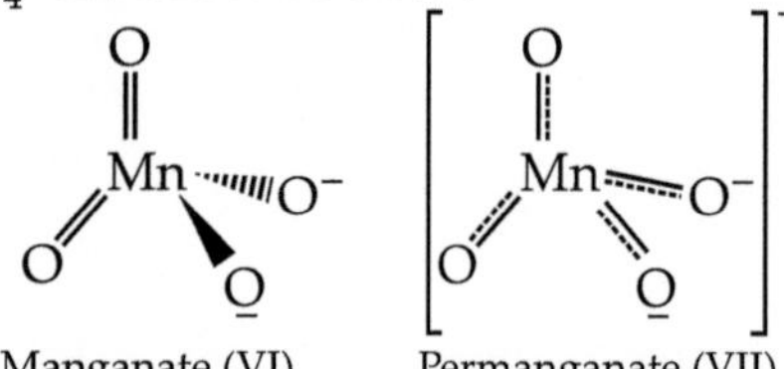

Manganate (VI)      Permanganate (VII)

**46. (4)** Among the given molecules, the total number of molecules containing covalent bond between two atoms of the same kind is 4. They are shown below :

$$N \equiv N \longrightarrow O$$

$$O_2N - NO_2$$

$$HO - \overset{\overset{O}{\|}}{\underset{\underset{O}{\|}}{S}} - OH$$

$$HO - \overset{\overset{S}{\|}}{\underset{\underset{O}{\|}}{S}} - O - \overset{\overset{S}{\|}}{\underset{\underset{O}{\|}}{S}} - OH$$

**47.** The reaction of $XeF_4$ and $O_2F_2$ is shown below :

$$\underset{(Y)}{XeF_4 + O_2F_2 \longrightarrow XeF_6 + O_2}$$

The molecule Y is $XeF_6$. It has three lone pair of electrons on each atom of F and one lone pair is present on the Xe atom. Therefore, the total number of lone pair of electrons in the compound $XeF_6$ is 19.

**48. (1,2,4)** The aqua regia is good oxidising agent, made up with $3 : 1$(v/v) ratio of concentrated HCl and concentrated $HNO_3$. It decomposes to produce NOCl and $Cl_2$, due to this it is yellow in colour. The reaction of gold with aqua regia is shown below :

$$Au + HNO_3 + 4HCl \rightarrow AuCl_4^- + H_3O^+ + NO + H_2O$$

**49. (3)** Alumina is used as adsorbent in the chromatography which is formed by heating aluminium hydrogen (X). Aluminium hydroxide is soluble in the excess of sodium hydroxide and formed by the reaction of aluminium with water in the presence of sodium hydroxide. The reactions involved are shown below.

$$Al + 3H_2O \xrightarrow{\text{NaOH}} \underset{(x)}{Al(OH)_3} \downarrow + 3/2H_{2(g)}$$

white gelatinous ppt.

$$\downarrow$$

soluble in excess of NaOH<br>and Form $Na[Al(OH)_4]$

$$2Al(OH)_3 \xrightarrow{\Delta} Al_2O_3 + 3H_2O$$

used as<br>absorbent in chromatography

Hence, the unknown metal **M** is aluminium.

**50. (3)** Generally, the value of electron affinity decreases on moving down the group. However, the electron affinity of chlorine is more than that of fluorine because less energy is released during addition of electron in $2p$ orbital of fluorine due to its small size. The electron affinity of oxygen is less than those of chlorine and fluorine.

**51. (4)** The hybridization of diamond is $sp^3$. It contains one $s$-orbital and three $p$-orbitals. The total orbitals are four.
The hybridization of graphite is $sp^2$. It contains one $s$-orbital and two $p$-orbitals. The total orbitals are three.
The formula to calculate the % of $p$-character is,

$$\%p\text{-characters} = \frac{p\text{-orbitals}}{\text{total orbitals}}$$

Therefore,
The percentage of p-characters in graphite is
$$\frac{2}{3} \times 100 = 67\%.$$

The percentage of p-characters in diamond is
$$\frac{3}{4} \times 100 = 75\%.$$

**52. (1)** Among the given elements, boron is highly electron deficient. It reacts with chlorine in the following manner,

$$B + Cl_2 \rightarrow BCl_3$$

In this compound, dimerization is not possible due to $p\pi\text{-}p\pi$ back bonding. This bonding is shown as,

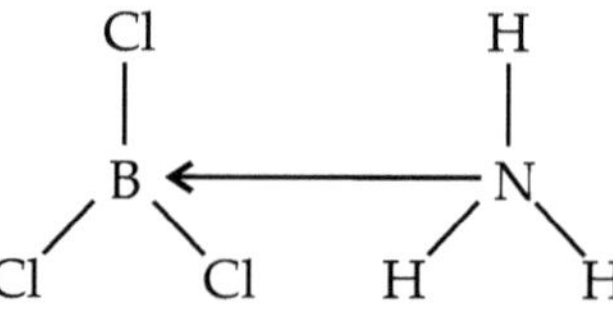

Here, lone pair present on ammonia involves in back bonding.

**53. (2)** Decomposition of given species below 300 °C is shown below :

$$NH_4NO_3 \xrightarrow{\Delta} N_2O + H_2O$$

$$(NH_4)_2Cr_2O_7 \xrightarrow{\Delta} N_2 + Cr_2O_3 + H_2O$$

$$Ba(N_3)_2 \xrightarrow{\Delta} Ba + N_2$$

The compound $Mg_3N_2$ does not undergo decomposition.

**54. (2) (1)** The compound $Bi_2O_5$ is metallic oxide and thus is basic while the compound $N_2O_5$ is non-metallic oxide and, thus is acidic.

(2) All the elements in $NH_3$ are non-metals but in $BiF_3$, bismuth is metallic. Thus, the covalent character of $NF_3$ is greater than $BiF_3$.

(3) Due to the presence of hydrogen bonding in $NH_3$ it has higher boiling point than $PH_3$.

(4) Lone pair-lone pair repulsion is more in dinitrogen due to its small size and, thus N–N bond is weak.

**55.** The structures for given compounds is shown below :

$N_2O_3 =$ O=N–N ⇌ N–O–N

$N_2O_5 =$ N–N

$H_5P_3O_{10} =$ HO–P–O–P–O–P–OH

$H_2S_2O_3 =$ HO–S—OH

$H_2S_2O_5 =$ HO–S–S–OH

$H_4P_2O_5 =$

$P_4O_6 =$

$P_4O_7 =$

The compounds containing A–O–A or A=O are known as oxo compounds. Thus, the compounds containing at least one oxo group among the molecules is six.

**56. (3)** The Lewis structure of $I_3^-$ is,

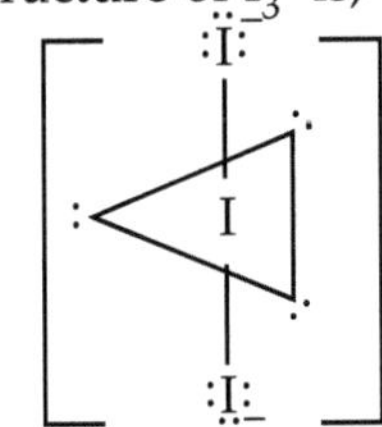

The total number of lone pair of electrons in $I_3^-$ is 9.

**57. (4)** The thermal decomposition of $Ba(N_3)_2$ is,

$$Ba(N_3)_2 \xrightarrow{\Delta} Ba + 3N_2$$

The thermal decomposition of $(NH_4)_2 Cr_2O_7$ is,

$$(NH_4)_2 Cr_2O_7 \xrightarrow{\Delta} Cr_2O_3 + N_2 + 4H_2O$$

The thermal decomposition of $NH_4NO_2$ is,

$$NH_4NO_2 \xrightarrow{\Delta} N_2 + 2H_2O$$

The thermal decomposition of $(NH_4)_2SO_4$ is,

$$(NH_4)_2 SO_4 \xrightarrow{\Delta} H_2SO_4 + 2NH_3$$

Hence, nitrogen gas is not produced in the thermal decomposition of $(NH_4)_2SO_4$.

**58. (4)** (1) Molar mass of $(NH_4)_2Cr_2O_7$ = 252 g/mol. One mole of $(NH_4)_2 Cr_2O_7$ will give one mole of $N_2$.

So, $\dfrac{1g}{252 g/mol}$ moles of $(NH_4)_2 Cr_2O_7$ will give,

$$1 \times \frac{1}{252 g/mol} \text{moles of } N_2$$

$$= 0.0039 \text{ moles of } N_2$$

(2) Molar mass of $NH_4NO_3$ = 80 g/mol. One mole of $NH_4NO_3$ will give one mole of $N_2$.

So, $\dfrac{1g}{80 g/mol}$ moles of $NH_4NO_3$ will give,

$$1 \times \frac{1g}{80 g/mol} \text{moles of } N_2$$

$$= 0.0125 \text{ moles of } N_2$$

(3) Molar mass of $Ba(N_3)_2$ = 221 g/mol. One mole of $Ba(N_3)_2$ will give three moles of $N_2$.

So, $\dfrac{1g}{221 g/mol}$ moles of $Ba(N_3)_2$ will give,

$$3 \times \frac{1g}{221 g/mol} \text{moles of } N_2$$

$$= 0.014 \text{ moles of } N_2$$

(4) Molar mass of $NH_3$ = 17 g/mol, One mole of $NH_3$ will give one mole of $N_2$.

So, $\dfrac{1g}{17 g/mol}$ moles of $NH_3$ will give,

$$\frac{1g}{2 \times 17 g/mol} \text{moles of } N_2$$

$$= 0.0294 \text{ moles of } N_2$$

So, the maximum quantity of $N_2$ will be produced in the following reaction,

$$2NH_3(g) \rightarrow N_2(g) + 3H_2(g)$$

**59. (3)** The structure of $P_4O_6$ is given below.

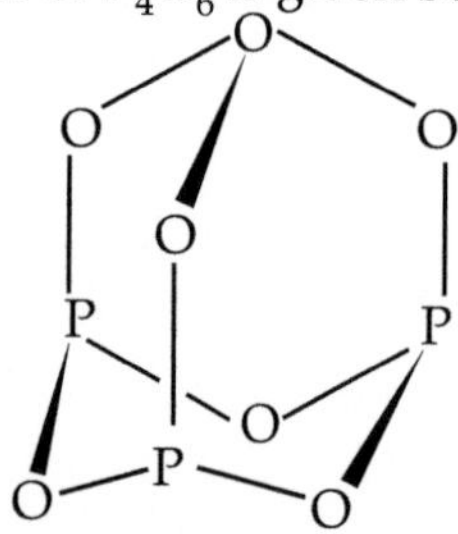

There are total 12 P – O bonds in $P_4O_6$.

**60. (3)** The structure of $XeO_3F_2$ is,

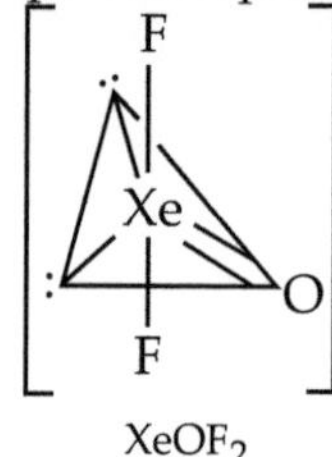

The structure of $XeO_3F_2$ shows that Xe atom has 5 bond pairs, $3\pi$-bonds and 0 lone pair.

**61. (3)** In the given pair, $XeOF_2$ and $IO_2F_2^-$ have T-shape and square-pyramidal geometry.

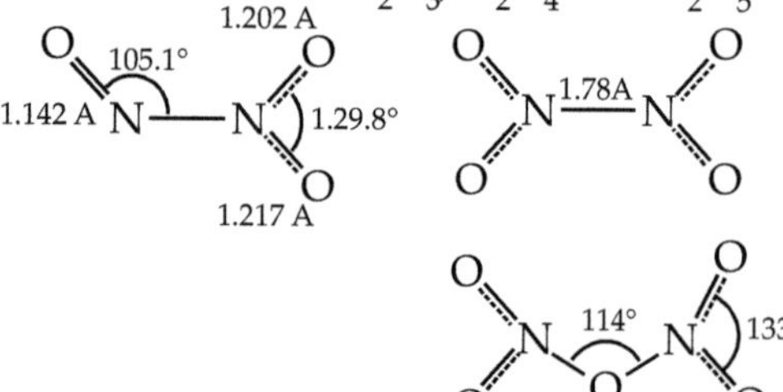

$XeOF_2$
T-shape

$XeOF_4$
Square-pyramidal

**62. (4)** The partial hydrolysis reaction of xenon hexafluoride is shown below.

$$XeF_6 + H_2O \xrightarrow{\text{Partial hydrolysis}} \overset{+6}{Xe}OF_4$$
$$\text{(X)}$$

$$XeF_6 + H_2O \xrightarrow{\text{Partial hydrolysis}} \overset{+6}{Xe}O_2F_2$$
$$\text{(Y)}$$

Compound X is $XeOF_4$ in which the oxidation state of xenon is $+6$.

Compound Y is $XeO_2F_2$ in which the oxidation state of xenon is $+6$.

**63. (4)** The structures of $N_2O_3$, $N_2O_4$ and $N_2O_5$ are,

From the structures, it is clear that $N_2O_3$ and $N_2O_4$ contains N – N bond.

**64. (1,2,4)** The structures of the given oxoacid are as follows,

In both the structures central atom is "$sp^3$" hybridized.

$HClO_4$ is more acidic because after donating its proton, it is stabilized by four resonating structures which are as follows,

There is no such stabilization in $ClO^-$.

$HClO_4$ is formed as,

$$NaClO_4 + HCl \rightarrow NaCl + HClO_4$$

Conjugate base of $HClO_4$ is $ClO_4^-$ and it is weaker than water, because $HClO_4$ is a strong acid than water. Conjugate base of strong acid is always weak. The reaction for this is given as,

$$HClO_4 + H_2O \rightarrow ClO_4^- + H_3O^+$$

**65. (3)** The oxidation state of phosphorus in all the given species is given as,

$$H_3PO_4 = +5$$
$$H_2P_2O_6 = +4$$
$$H_3PO_3 = +3$$
$$H_3PO_2 = +1$$

Therefore, the order of oxidation is,

$$H_3PO_4 > H_4P_2O_6 > H_3PO_3 > H_3PO_2$$

**66. (3)** The reaction for the given is as follows :

$$2KClO_3 \xrightarrow{MnO_2} 2KCl + 3O_2 \, (W)$$

$$P_4 + 5O_2 \longrightarrow P_4O_{10} (X)$$

**67. (2)** The reaction for the given condition is as follows :

$$P_4O_{10} \equiv P_2O_5$$
$$P_2O_5 + 2HNO_3 \rightarrow N_2O_5 (Y) + 2HPO_3 (Z)$$

**68. (3)** The redox reaction is shown below :

$$\overset{+4}{Xe}F_4 + \overset{+1}{O_2}F_2 \rightarrow \overset{+6}{Xe}F_6 + \overset{0}{O_2}$$

In this reaction, XE is oxidized and oxygen is reduced.

**69. (1)** The reaction of chlorine gas with cold and dilute aqueous NaOH is,

$$Cl_2 + 2NaOH \rightarrow NaCl + NaOCl + H_2O$$

Dissociation of sodium chloride (NaCl) is shown below :

$$NaCl \rightarrow Na^+ + Cl^-$$

Dissociation of sodium hypochlorite (NaOCl) is shown below :

$$NaOCl \rightarrow Na^+ + ClO^-$$

**70. (4)** The total number of S = O and S—OH bonds in peroxodisulphuric acid, $H_2S_2O_8$, are 4 and 2 respectively as shown below :

$$HO—\overset{\overset{O}{\|}}{\underset{\underset{O}{\|}}{S}}—O—O—\overset{\overset{O}{\|}}{\underset{\underset{O}{\|}}{S}}—OH$$

The total number of S = O and S – OH bonds in pyrosulphuric acid, $H_2S_2O_7$ are 4 and 2 respectively as shown below :

$$HO—\overset{\overset{O}{\|}}{\underset{\underset{O}{\|}}{S}}\underset{O}{\diagdown\diagup}\overset{\overset{O}{\|}}{\underset{\underset{O}{\|}}{S}}—OH$$

**71. (3)** The partial hydrolysis of $XeF_6$ with water is shown below :

$$XeF_6 + H_2O \rightarrow XeOF_4 + 2HF$$

The reaction of $XeF_6$ with silica is shown below.

$$2XeF_6 + SiO_2 \rightarrow 2XeOF_4 + SiF_4$$

Thus, both reactions result in the formation of same product.

**72. (4)** The structure of $H_4P_2O_7$ is shown below :

$$\underset{HO}{\overset{\overset{O}{\|}}{}}\underset{\underset{OH}{|}}{P}—O—\underset{\underset{OH}{|}}{\overset{\overset{O}{\|}}{P}}\overset{}{OH}$$

Thus, the number of P–OH bonds in pyro-phosphoric acid is four.

The oxidation number of phosphorous in pyrophosphoric acid is calculated as,

$$4(\text{charge of H}) + 2(\text{charge of P}) + 7(\text{charge of O}) = 0$$
$$+ 4 + 2x \times 7(-2) = 0$$
$$+4 + 2x - 14 = 0$$
$$x = 5$$

**73. (3)** The structures of $H_2S_2O_7$, $H_2SO_4$ ad $H_2SO_3$ are shown below.

$$H_2S_2O_7 = HO—\overset{\overset{O}{\|}}{\underset{\underset{O}{\|}}{S}}—O—\overset{\overset{O}{\|}}{\underset{\underset{O}{\|}}{S}}—OH$$

$$H_2SO_4 = HO—\overset{\overset{O}{\|}}{\underset{\underset{O}{\|}}{S}}—OH$$

$$H—\overset{\overset{:O:}{\|}}{\underset{}{\ddot{O}}}—S—\ddot{O}—H$$

The numbers of p-bonds in $H_2S_2O_7$, $H_2SO_4$ and $H_2SO_3$ are 4, 2 and 1 respectively.

**74. (1,2,3,4)** Both $Al(CH_3)_3$ and $BH_3$ exists in dimeric forms. $Al(CH_3)_3$ has 2 three centre-two electron bonds in dimeric structure.

$BH_3$ also has 2 three centre-two electron bonds in dimeric structure.

$AlCl_3$ has 2 three centre-four electron bonds in dimeric structure.

The Lewis acidity decreases down the group. Therefore, Lewis acidity of $AlCl_3$ is greater than $BCl_3$.

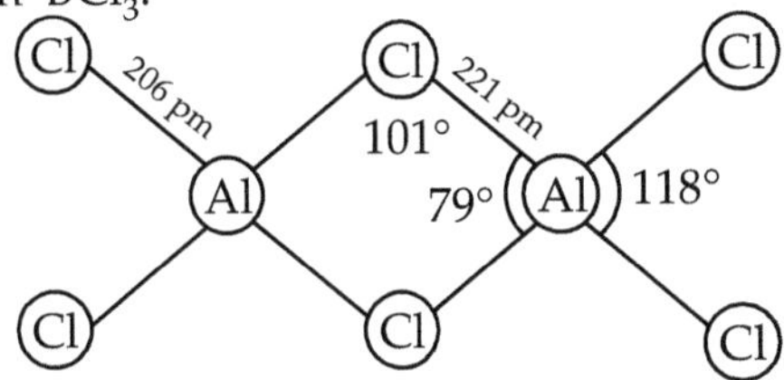


**75. (1,4)** Amphoteric oxides are those oxides which react with acids as well as bases. In all the given oxides, three oxides are not amphoteric. These are NO, CrO, $B_2O_3$. Other than these all are amphoteric.

NO is a neutral oxide.

CrO is a basic oxide.

$B_2O_3$ is an acidic oxide.

**76. (2)** In the reaction,

$$ZnO + Na_2O \rightarrow Na_2ZnO_2$$

Zinc oxide is an amphoteric oxide. In this reaction, $Na_2O$ is a basic oxide that reacts with an acidic oxide ZnO to form $Na_2ZnO_2$ salt. Therefore, ZnO acts as acidic oxide.

In the reaction,

$$ZnO + CO_2 \rightarrow ZnCO_3$$

Here, ZnO acts as basic oxide because $CO_2$ is an acidic oxide.

**77. (3)** The compound, $SiO_2$ is an oxide because oxidation number of oxygen in this compound is –2.

**78. (2)** The radius of Ga is less than that of Al due to poor shielding of nuclear charge by $3d\ e^-$.

In and T1 follow regular trend as radius increases on moving down the group.

So, correct order of atomic radii of following group 13 elements is,

$$Ga < Al < In < T1$$

**79. (1,3,4)** The structure of borax $Na_2[B_4O_5(OH)_4]$. $8H_2O$ is given below :

Structure of Borax

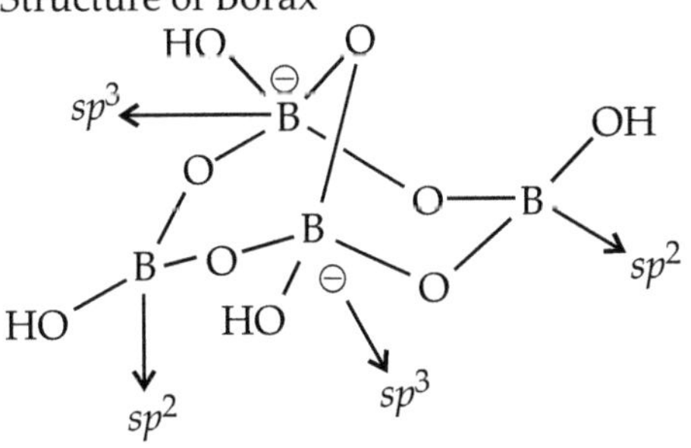

(A) Boron has tetrahedral unit $[B_4O_5(OH)_4]^{2-}$.

(B) Only two boron atoms are in same plane.

(C) Two boron atoms are $sp^2$ hybridized and two boron atoms are $sp^3$ hybridized.

(D) There is one terminal hydroxide per Boron atoms.

Thus, statement (1), (3) and (4) are correct regarding structure of borax.

**80. (1)** Silica gel is used as a drying agent. Silicon has its usage in transistors. Silicone is a sealant and silicates are used as zeolites in ion exchangers.

**81. (4)** The reaction of lithium hydride with $B_2H_6$ is as follows.

$$2LiH + B_2H_6 \rightarrow 2Li[BH_4]$$

The above reaction shows that the liberation of hydrogen gas is not possible.

**82. (1)** Carbon atom in diamond is bonded through a covalent bond to four other carbon atoms in a tetrahedral manner. The hybridization of carbon atom in diamond is $sp^3$. In diamond, carbon utilizes its unpaired electrons in the formation of bond. Therefore, it is a bad conductor of electricity.

Carbon atom in graphite is bonded through a covalent bond to three other carbon atoms to give trigonal geometry. The hybridization of carbon atom in graphite is $sp^2$. In graphite, carbon utilizes its three unpaired electrons in the formation of bond. Therefore, it is a good conductor of electricity

**83. (2,4)** (1) The nitrogen containing compound produced in the reaction of $HNO_3$ and $P_4O_{10}$ is shown in the reaction below.

$$HNO_3 + P_4O_{10} \rightarrow 2N_2O_5 + 4HPO_3$$

The reaction of $P_4$ and $HNO_3$ is shown below :

So, same nitrogen containing compound, $N_2O_5$ which was produced in the reaction of $HNO_3$ and $P_4O_{10}$, is not formed by the reaction of $P_4$ and $HNO_3$. So, statement (1) is incorrect.

(2) $N_2O_5$ formed by the reaction of $HNO_3$ and $P_4O_{10}$ is diamagnetic in nature. So, statement (2) is correct.

(3) The structure of $N_2O_5$ formed by the reaction of $HNO_3$ and $P_4O_{10}$ is given below :

$$O = N-O-N = O$$
$$\downarrow \qquad \downarrow$$
$$O \qquad O$$

Thus structure does not one bond. So, statement (3) is incorrect.

(D) The reaction of $N_2O_5$ with sodium metal is given below :

$$N_2O_5 + Na \rightarrow NaNO_3 + NO_2$$

In the above reaction, brown gas of $NO_2$ is formed.

So, statement (4) is correct.

**84. (4)** The non-metal that does not exhibit positive oxidation state is fluorine because it is the most electronegative element of the periodic table. Therefore, it always exhibits $-1$ oxidation state in all of its compounds.

**85. (2)** The group of molecules that have identical shape is $ClF_3$, $XeOF_2$, $XeF_3^+$ as shown below. These molecules have $sp^3d$ hybridisation with two lone pairs of electrons. Thus, they all have T-shaped structure.

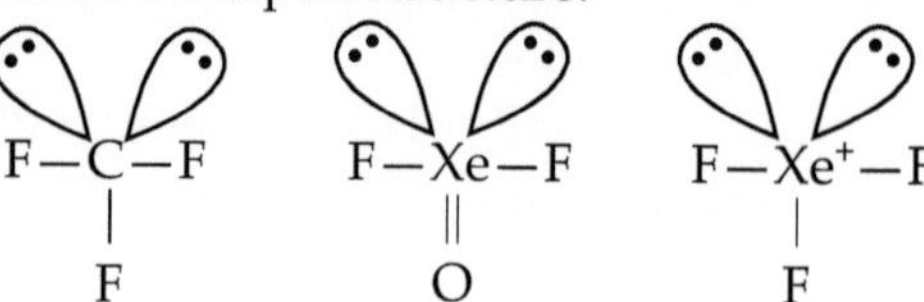

**86. (4)** The incorrect statement is "The $S-S-S$ bond angle in the $S_8$ and $S_6$ and rings are the same."

The bond length in $S_6$ and $S_8$ molecule is same but bond angles are different. The $S_8$ molecule has a puckered ring with crown conformation, whereas $S_6$ a molecule has a chair conformation as shown below.

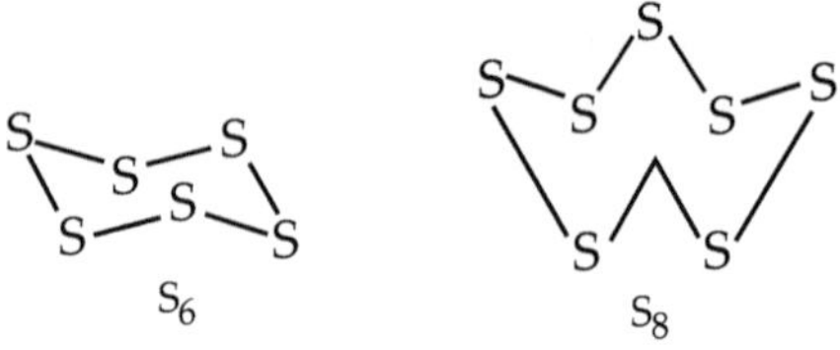

**87. (1)** The structures of given species are shown below.

The hybridisation is $sp$, $sp^2$, $sp^2$, $sp^2$ respectively.

**88. (1)** The reaction of zinc with dilute and concentrated nitric acid is shown below :

$$4Zn + 10HNO_3(dil) \rightarrow 4Zn(NO_3)_2 + 5H_2O + N_2O$$

$$Zn + 4HNO_3(conc) \rightarrow Zn(NO_3)_2 + 2H_2O + NO_2$$

**89. (1)** The oxidation state of phosphorus in orthophosphorus acid ($H_3PO_3$) is $+3$.

The oxidation state of phosphorus in pyrophosphorus acid is ($H_4P_2O_5$) is $+3$.

The oxidation state of phosphorus in hypophosphoric acid is ($H_4P_2O_6$) is $+4$.

**90. (4)** ICl is a weakly bonded interhalogen compound. These type of compounds are more reactive than that of their diatomic form ($I_2$, $Br_2$, $Cl_2$).

**91. (1)** Both nitrogen and oxygen are the main components of atmosphere. The reaction between these two components occurs at higher temperature, that is, around 3000 °C. During thunderstorm nitrogen forms its oxide.

$$N_2 + O_2 \rightarrow 2NO$$

**92. (3)** The least number of oxyacids are formed by Fluorine, because it cannot show multiple oxidation states.

**93. (2)** The structure of $XeOF_4$ is,

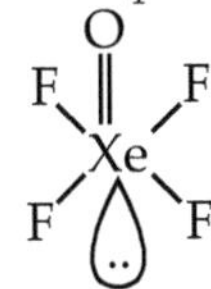

It consists of five atoms bonded to central atom and one lone pair of electron. The arrangement of atoms is octahedral but the geometry of compound is square pyramidal.

**94. (2)** The compound $H_4P_2O_6$ has a P–P bond as shown below.

$$\begin{array}{c} \quad O \quad\quad O \\ \quad \| \quad\quad \| \\ HO-O-P-OH \\ \quad\quad | \quad | \\ \quad\quad OH \;\; OH \end{array}$$

**95. (3)** Chlorine water on standing loses its color due to formation of HCl and HOCl as shown below :

$$Cl_2 + H_2O \rightarrow HCl + HOCl$$

**96.** The balanced chemical reaction of $B_2H_6$ with methanol is given below.

$$3B_2H_6 + 18MeOH \rightarrow 6B(OMe)_3 + 18H_2$$

Thus, the number of moles of boron formed in the product is 6.

**97. (2, 4)** (1) The reaction of boric acid in water is shown below.

$$H_3BO_3 + 2H_2O \rightarrow B(OH)_4^- + H_3O^+$$

It acts as a Lewis acid as it accepts from $H_2O$.

(2) It is more acidic because it does not form chelate complex on addition of ethylene glycol.

(3) Due to hydrogen bonding it has two dimensional structure.

(4) It is a weak monobasic acid and a weak electrolyte in water.

**98. (2)** The amphoteric species can act both as acid and base. Thus, the set-1 shows the basic nature of $Al_2O_3.xH_2O(s)$ that forms $Al(OH)_4^-$ in the solution. The set-3 shows the acidic nature of $Al_2O_3.xH_2O(s)$ that forms $Al^{3+}$ and $H_2O$ in the solution.

**99. (2)** Boron is covalent as well as ionic in its compounds.

**100. (1,2,3)** Zeolites, ultramarines and feldspars come in the class of three-dimensional silicates.

**101. (1,2,3)** (1) $Na + (a+b)NH_3$ (excess)

$$\rightarrow [Na(NH_3)_a]^+ + b\, e^-$$

The complex $[Na(NH_3)_a]^+$ is blue in color and the resulting species is paramagnetic in nature.

(2) $K + O_2$ (excess) $\rightarrow K^+O_2^-$

$K^+O_2^-$ is paramagnetic.

(3) $3Cu + 8HNO_3(dil) \rightarrow 3Cu(NO_3)_2$
$$+ 4H_2O + 2NO$$

NO is paramagnetic.

(4) $O_2$ + 2-ethylanthraquinol form diamagnetic $H_2O_2$.

**102.** The black coloured sulfides are PbS, CuS, HgS, $Ag_2S$, NiS, CoS and $Bi_2S_3$.

**103. (1)** The reaction of $SOCl_2$ with white phosphorous ($P_4$) is

$$P_4 + 8SOCl_2 \rightarrow 4PCl_3 + 4SO_2 + 2S_2Cl_2$$

**104. (3)** The complete reaction is shown below.

$XeF_6 + 3H_2O$(complete hydrolysis)
$$\rightarrow XeO_3 + 3H_2F_2$$

$XeO_3 + OH^- \rightarrow HXeO_4^-$

$2HXeO_4^- + 2OH^- \rightarrow XeO_6^{4-} + Xe(g) + 2H_2O$
$$+ O_2(g)$$

The total number of gases released as products in the final step of the reaction is two, that is, Xe(g) and $O_2(g)$.

**105. (3)** Acidic strength of oxoacids increases with increase in the oxidation number of central atom. Therefore, the correct decreasing order of acid strength is,

$$\overset{+7}{HClO_4} > \overset{+5}{HClO_3} > \overset{+3}{HClO_2} > \overset{+1}{HOCl}$$

**106. (1)** **NO** is paramagnetic due to presence of one unpaired electron.

$$\cdot\ddot{N} = \ddot{O}\,:$$

**107. (1)** The complete reactions for the heating of $CaF_2$ and $SiO_2$ with concentrated $H_2SO_4$ are as follows :

$$CaF_2 + H_2SO_4 \rightarrow H_2F_2 + Ca(HSO_4)_2$$
$$SiO_2 + 2H_2F_2 \rightarrow SiF_4 + 2H_2O$$
$$SiF_4 + H_2O \rightarrow H_2[SiF_6]$$

Thus, the precipitate is of hydrofluosilicic acid, $H_2[SiF_6]$.

**108. (2)** The problem of ozone depletion is highest at poles because ice crystals in the clouds over poles act as catalyst for various photochemcial reactions. These reactions involve decomposiiton of ozone by $Cl^*$ and $ClO^*$ radicals. These radicals undergo various catalytic cycles which are responsible in destroying the ozone layer

**109. (2)** The shape of interhalogen compound $BrF^5$ is square pyramidal with one lone pair of electrons.

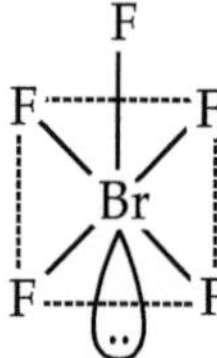

**110. (4)** The reactions of xenon fluoride with water are given below :
The oxidation state of xenon in $XeO_4$ is $+8$.
$$XeF_6 + H_2O \rightarrow XeOF_4 + 2HF$$
$$XeF_6 + 2H_2O \rightarrow XeO_2F_2 + 4HF$$
$$XeF_6 + 3H_2O \rightarrow XeO_3 + 6HF$$

**111. (2)** The reaction of concentrated nitric acid, upon long standing is shown below :
$$4HNO_3 \rightarrow 4NO_2 + 2H_2O + O_2$$
The above reaction shows that nitric acid upon long standing produces nitrogen dioxide, water and oxygen. Nitrogen dioxide $(NO_2)$ is yellow colored gas, due to which concentrated nitric acid turns yellow.

**112. (1,3,4)** (1) The bond lengths of $O - O$ bond in ozone are equal as shown below :

$$\overset{\oplus}{O}\ 1.278\ Å$$
$$(-)O\ \overset{116.8°}{\diagdown}\ O(-)$$

    (2) Thermal decomposition of Ozone $(O_3)$ is exothermic not endothermic because on decomposition, oxygen atom is formed which is more stable than ozone. The more stable oxygen will have lower energy as compared to ozone. Thus, the thermal decomposition will be exothermic.

    (3) It is correct that Ozone $(O_3)$ is diamagnetic in nature because all the electrons in ozone are paired.

    (4) Ozone $(O_3)$ has the bent structure because of the presence of a pair of valence electron at the upper part of the structure. This pair of electron suppresses the whole structure to become bent as shown below :

**113. (1)** P and Q are the sodium salts of hypochlorus acid and chloric acid respectively as shown below.

$$Cl_2 + 2NaOH \xrightarrow{Cold} NaOCl(P) + NaCl + H_2O$$
$$3Cl_2 + 6NaOH \xrightarrow{Hot} NaClO_3(Q) + 5NaCl + 3H_2O$$

**114. (1)** R, S and T are $SO_2Cl_2$, $PCl_5$ and $H_3PO_4$ respectively as shown below.
$$SO_2 + Cl_2 \xrightarrow{Charcoal, catalyst} SO_2Cl_2(R)$$
$$10SO_2Cl_2 + P_4 \xrightarrow{Cold} 4PCl_5(S) + 10SO_2$$
$$PCl_5 + 4H_2O \xrightarrow{Cold} H_3PO_4(T) + 5HCl$$

**115. (4)** The correct reagents or conditions of the given reactions are shown as follows.
(P) $2PbO_2 + 2H_2SO_4 \xrightarrow{Warm} 2PbSO_4 + 2H_2O + O_2$
(Q) $Na_2S_2O_3 + 5H_2O + 4Cl_2 \rightarrow 2NaHSO_4 + 8HCl$
(R) $N_2H_4 + 2I_2 \rightarrow N_2 + 4HI$
(S) $XeF_2 + 2NO \rightarrow Xe + 2NOF$

**116. (1,3,4)** The reaction of $AgNO_3$ with different given halides is shown below.
$$AgNO_3 + HCl \rightarrow AgCl \downarrow + HNO_3$$
$$AgNO_3 + HI \rightarrow AgI \downarrow + HNO_3$$
$$AgNO_3 + HBr \rightarrow AgBr \downarrow + HNO_3$$
$$AgNO_3 + HF \rightarrow AgF + HNO_3$$

First three halides form precipitate that dissolves in $Na_2S_2O_3$ (aq) and forms complex $Na_3[Ag(S_2O_3)_2]$. The last reaction does not form precipitate.

**117. (3)** The reaction corresponding to the given statement is shown below.
$$P_4(white) + 3NaOH + 3H_2O \rightarrow PH_3 + 3NaH_2PO_2$$
The salt $NaH_2PO_2$ undergoes the following changes in heting :
$$4NaH_2PO_2 \longrightarrow Na_4P_2O_7 + 2PH_3 + H_2O$$
$$\underset{+1}{\phantom{4NaH_2PO_2}}\quad\underset{+5}{\phantom{Na_4P_2O_7}}\quad\underset{+3}{\phantom{2PH_3}}$$
The oxidation state of phosphorus in $P_4$ (white) is zero and it is $-3$ in $PH_3$ that is phosphine. The oxidation state of phosphorus in is $NaH_2PO_2$ is $+1$. It is a disproportionation reaction.

**118. (4)** The structure of $XeO_2F_2$ is shown below :

The geometry of given compound is trigonal pyramidal. The presence of lone pair leads to see-saw shape.

**119. (1)** The formula of bleaching powder is $CaOCl_2$. This can also be written as $Ca(OCl)Cl$. The anion is $OCl^-$ that belongs to HOCl. The formation of anhydride of HOCl is shown below :
$$2HOCl \xrightarrow{\Delta} H_2O + Cl_2O$$

**120. (2, 4)** (A)  Diamond is harder than graphite.

(B)  Graphite is conductive due to the presence of one free valency while there is no free valency of carbon in diamond.

(C)  Thermal vibrations occurs in the case of diamond due to its compact structure and are thus responsible for its thermal conduction. Thus, thermal conductivity of diamond is more than thermal conductivity of graphite.

(D)  Double bond is present in case of graphite. Thus, its bond order is higher than diamond.

**121. (4)** Extra pure nitrogen gas ($N_2$) can be obtained by heating barium azide. The heating reaction is given as,

$$Ba(N_3)_2 \xrightarrow{\Delta} Ba + 3N_2$$

On heating, the compound of barium azide, metallic barium is also liberated.

**122.** Among the following compounds, the number of compounds that can react with $PCl_5$ to give $POCl_3$ is five. The reactions are given as,

$$PCl_5 + H_2O \rightarrow POCl_3 + 2HCl$$
$$6PCl_5 + P_4O_{10} \rightarrow 10POCl_3$$
$$PCl_5 + H_2SO_4 \rightarrow POCl_3 + SO_2Cl_2 + H_2O$$
$$PCl_5 + SO_2 \rightarrow POCl_3 + SOCl_2$$
$$2PCl_5 + O_2 \rightarrow 2POCl_3 + 2Cl_2$$

With carbon dioxide, there will be no reaction.

**123. (3)** According to charge balance in molecule,

Total cationic charge + Total anionic charge = 0
$$2n + 2(+3) + 6(+4) + 18(-2) = 0$$
$$2n + 6 + 24 - 36 = 0$$
$$2n = 36 - 30$$
$$n = 3$$

Thus, to balance charge in a molecule, beryllium should contain three atoms.

**124.** (A) : P and S; (B) : p, q, r, t; (C) : p and q; (D) = p

(1)  The $(CH_3)_2SiCl_2$ reacts with water to give hydrochloric acid and $(CH_3)_2Si(OH)_2$. $(CH_3)_2Si(OH)_2$ undergoes polymerization reaction.

$$(CH_3)_2SiCl_2 + H_2O \rightarrow (CH_3)_2Si(OH)_2 + HCl$$

$$\begin{array}{ccccccc} & CH_3 & & CH_3 & & CH_3 & \\ & | & & | & & | & \\ -O- & Si & -O_3- & Si & -O- & Si & -O- \text{ (polymer)} \\ & | & & | & & | & \\ & CH_3 & & CH_3 & & CH_3 & \end{array}$$

So, (1) matches with option (p) and (s).

(2)  The reaction of $XeF_4$ with water is given below.

$$3XeF_4 + 6H_2O \rightarrow XeO_3 + 2Xe + \frac{3}{2}O_2 + 12HF$$
$$SiO_2(\text{glass}) + 4HF \rightarrow SiF_4 + 2H_2O$$
$$SiF_4 + 2HF \rightarrow H_2[SiF_6]$$

In the following reaction, $XeF_4$ reacts with water to give hydrofluoric acid. Then glass reacts with HF to give $SiF_4$. Then $SiF_4$ reacts with hydrofluoric acid to give soluble $H_2[SiF_6]$.

So, (2) matches with option (p), (q), (r) and (s).

(3)  The reaction of $Cl_2$ with water is given below.

$$Cl_2 + H_2O \rightarrow HCl + HOCl$$

So, hydrochloric acid will be formed. This is an example of redox reaction.

So, (3) matches with option (p) and (q).

(4)  The reaction of $VCl_5$ with water is given below.

$$VCl_5 + 7H_2O \rightarrow [V(H_2O_6)]^{3+} + 3Cl^- + HCl + HOCl$$

So, hydrochloric acid will be formed.

Thus, (4) matches with option (p).

**125. (2)** The reaction of $P_4$ with oxygen in the presence of nitrogen gas selectively leads to the formation of $P_4O_6$ because nitrogen gas prevents the system to undergo further oxidation.

The balanced chemical equation for the given reaction is,

$$P_4 + 3O_2 \xrightarrow{N_2} P_4O_6$$

**126. (1,2,3)** The structures of the given nitrogen oxides are shown below :

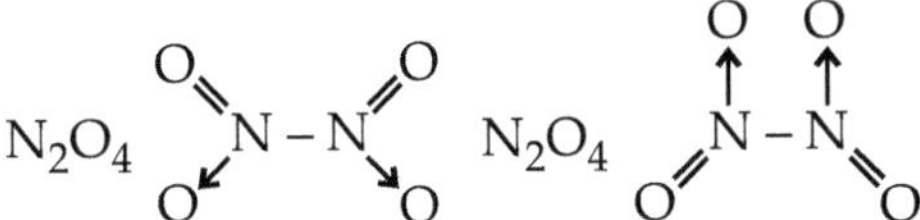

$$N_2O \quad N \equiv N \rightarrow O$$

$N_2O_3$, $N_2O_4$ structures shown with N–N bonds.

Hence, the nitrogen oxides that contain N – N bond is $N_2O$, $N_2O_3$ and $N_2O_4$.

**127.** (A)-(p), (s); (B)-(q), (s); (C)-(r), (t); (D)-(q), (t)

The reaction of copper with dilute nitric acid is,

$$3Cu + 8HNO_3 \rightarrow 3Cu(NO_3)_2 + 4H_2O + 2NO$$

Products NO and $Cu(NO_3)_2$ is formed in the given reaction. Therefore, the options (p) and (s) is correct for reaction (1).

The reaction of copper with concentrated nitric acid is,

$$Cu + 4HNO_3 \rightarrow Cu(NO_3)_2 + 2H_2O + 2NO_2$$

Products $NO_2$ and $Cu(NO_3)_2$ is formed in the given reaction. Therefore, the options (q) and (s) is correct for reaction (2).

The reaction of zinc with dilute nitric acid is,

$$4Zn + 10HNO_3 \rightarrow 4Zn(NO_3)_2 + 5H_2O + N_2O$$

Products $N_2O$ and $Zn(NO_3)_2$ is formed in the given reaction. Therefore, the options (r) and (t) is correct for reaction (3).

The reaction of zinc with concentrated nitric acid is,

$$Zn + 4HNO_3 \rightarrow Zn(NO_3)_2 + 2H_2O + 2NO_2$$

Products $NO_2$ and $Zn(NO_3)_2$ is formed in the given reaction. Therefore, the options (q) and (t) is correct for reaction (4).

**128. (1,2,3)** Tertiary amines do not reacts with diborane to form $[BH_2(X)_2]^+$ and $[BH_4]^+$ ions because presence of larger number of alkyl groups increases the steric hindrance and reaction does not occurs. Therefore, the amines which reacts in the given reaction are $NH_3$, $CH_3NH_2$ and $(CH_3)_2NH$.

**129. (3)** The + 4 oxidation state of Pb is not stable as compared to +4 oxidation state of Sn. As a result, it accepts two electrons and acts as an oxidizing agent.

On moving down the group in group 14, the stability of higher oxidation states decreases due to inert pair effect.

**130. (1,2)** Ammonium nitrite $(NH_4NO_2)$ and ammonium nitrate $(NH_4NO_3)$ on reaction with sodium hydroxide gives ammonia $(NH_3)$ gas along with sodium nitrite and sodium nitrate, respectively, which on further reaction with Zinc gives ammonia gas.

$$NH_4NO_3 + NaOH \rightarrow NH_3 + NaNO_3 + H_2O$$

$$7NaOH + NaNO_3 + 4Zn \rightarrow 4Na_2ZnO_2 + NH_3 + 2H_2O$$

$$NH_4NO_2 + NaOH \rightarrow NH_3 + NaNO_2 + H_2O$$

$$5NaOH + NaNO_2 + 3Zn \rightarrow 3Na_2ZnO_2 + NH_3 + H_2O$$

**131. (3)** Nitrates, as compared to phosphates, are less available in earth's crust as their solubility in water is more.

**132. (3)** The ability of donation of electrons is more in $NH_3$ than in $PH_3$ because the size of nitrogen is smaller than phosphorous. The hybridization of nitrogen in $NH_3$ is $sp^3$ and is more directional. The hybridization of $PH_3$ is not well defined.

**133. (2)** The reaction between white phosphorous and NaOH is expressed as,

$$P_4 + 3NaOH + 3H_2O \rightarrow PH_3 + 3NaH_2PO_2$$

In the above reaction, oxidation and reduction of phosphorous takes place simultaneously to form sodium hypophosphite and phosphine respectively. Hence, the reaction is a disproportionation reaction.

**134. (3)** The orthoboric acid $(H_3BO_3)$ is a weak Lewis acid (monobasic). Therefore, instead of donation of proton it accepts $^-OH$ from water.

**135. (4)** The structure of $P_4$ is,

$$\begin{array}{c} \ddot{P} \\ :P\!\!-\!\!\!\diamond\!\!-\!\!P: \\ \ddot{P} \end{array}$$

Each phosphorous atom in the above structure is $sp^3$ hybridized. Thus, it contains 75% p character.

**136. (1)** Argon is an inert gas. It does not react or shows very low reactivity with metals at high tempearture. Therefore, it is used in arc welding.

**137. (3)** The structure of $XeO_3$ is pyramidal.

$$\begin{array}{c} Xe \\ O^{\diagup} \, \| \, ^{\diagdown} O \\ O \end{array}$$

**138. (1)** Both $XeF_4$ and $XeF_6$ exhibit oxidizing nature.

$$6XeF_4 + 12H_2O \rightarrow 4Xe + 2XeO_3 + 24HF + 3O_2$$

$$XeF_6 + 3H_2O \rightarrow XeO_3 + 6HF$$

**139. (1)** The reaction that takes place between $MgSO_4$, $NH_4OH$ and $Na_2HPO_4$ is shown below.

$$MgSO_4 + NH_4Cl + Na_3PO_4 \rightarrow Mg(NH_4)PO_4 + Na_2SO_4 + NaCl$$

Thus, the white precipitate formed is $Mg(NH_4)PO_4$.

**140. (1)** The given reaction is,

$$B(OH)_2 + NaOH \rightarrow NaBO_2 + Na[B(OH)_4] + H_2O$$

The reaction is taking place between boric acid and sodium hydroxide, where boric acid is a weak acid. Boric acid does not react with sodium hydroxide in a definite manner. Therefore, addition of cis-1, 2 diol converts boric acid into strong monobasic acid due to the formation of chelated complex. Thus, by the addition of cis-1, 2 diol, reaction proceeds in the forward direction.

**141.** The reaction involved in the formation of $BiO_3^-$ is as follows :

$$Bi^{3+} + 3H_2O \rightarrow BiO_3^-$$

The conversion of $Al(OH)_3$ to $[AlO_2]^-$ involves acidification.

The conversion of $Si_2O_7^{6-}$ to $SiO_4^{4-}$ takes place in the presence of heat.

The conversion of boric acid to $(B_4O_7^{2-})$ is as follows :

$$4H_3BO_3 + 2NaOH \rightarrow Na_2B_4O_7 + 7H_2O$$

The above reaction involves acidification and hydrolysis to give a titration curve.

**142. (3)** The isomer of phosphorus that is thermodynamically most stable is black phosphorus because this phosphorus possess the layered structure. Black phosphorus is made up heating white phosphorus at high temperature and pressure.

Thus, the correct option is (C).

**143. (2)** The metal nitrate that gives black precipitate on reaction with potassium iodide and gives orange color on excess addition of potassium iodide is $Bi^{3+}$.

The reaction of $Bi^{3+}$ with potassium iodide is given as follows :

$$Bi^{3+} + KI \rightarrow \underset{\text{Black}}{BiI_3}$$

The reaction of $Bi^{3+}$ with excess of potassium iodide is given as follows :

$$Bi^{3+} + KI \rightarrow \underset{\text{Orange}}{K[BiI_4]}$$

Thus, the correct option is (2).

**144. (2)** The reaction between the equimolar mixture of nitric oxide and nitrogen dioxide at $-30°C$ forms nitrogen trioxide. The color of nitrogen trioxide is pale blue. The chemical reaction for the same is given below :

$$NO + NO_2 \xrightarrow{-30°C} N_2O_3$$

Hence, the correct option is (2).

**145. (2)** The reaction of $PbO_2$ with concentrated nitric acid is,

$$PbO_2 + 2HNO_3 \rightarrow Pb(NO_3)_3 + H_2O + \frac{1}{2}O_2$$

Thus, the gas that is evolved after the reaction of $PbO_2$ with concentrated nitric acid is oxygen, $O_2$.

Hence, the correct option is (2).

**146. (4)** Among the given compounds, $I_3^-$ possesses three lone pairs of electrons on the central atom as shown below :

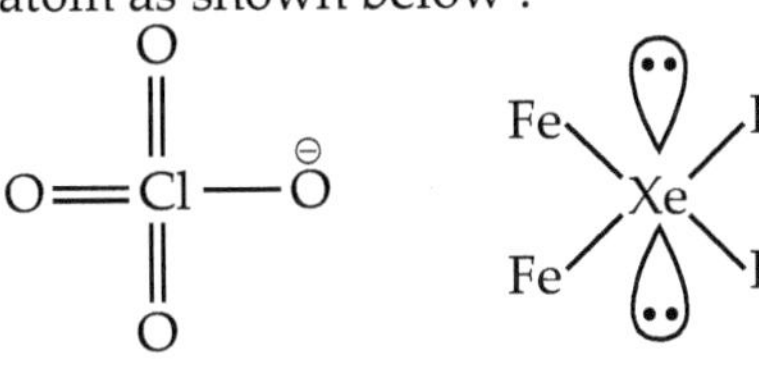

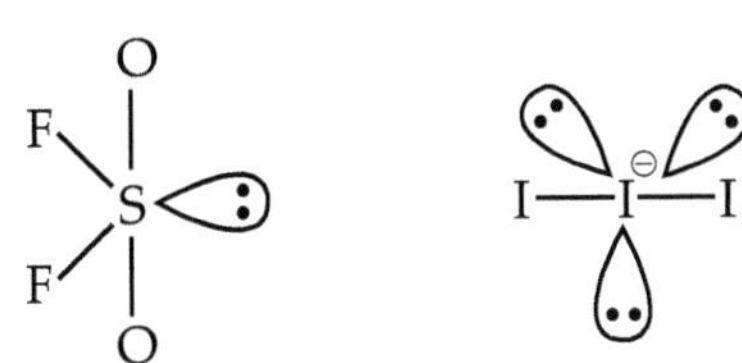

Thus, $I_3^-$ possesses the maximum number of lone pairs of electrons on the central atom.

Hence, the correct option is (4).

**147. (2)** The structural representation of $H_2S_2O_8$ is,

$$\underset{\overset{\displaystyle\|}{O}}{\overset{\overset{\displaystyle O}{\|}}{HO-S}}-O-O-\underset{\overset{\displaystyle\|}{O}}{\overset{\overset{\displaystyle O}{\|}}{S}}-OH$$

The structure of $H_2S_2O_8$ shows that it contains $-O-O-$ linkage.

**148. (2)** The structure of $XeOF_4$ is,

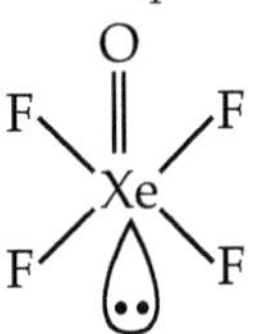

It consists of five atoms bonded to the central atom and oine lone pair oif electrons.

**149. (1)** The sheet silicates are formed from $[SiO_4]^{4-}$, tetrahedral units by sharing three oxygen atoms as shown below.

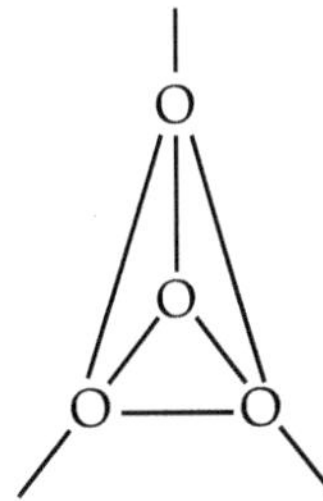

Hence, the correct option is (A).

**150. (1)** $H_3BO_3$ is a weak monobasic acid because octet of boron in $H_3BO_3$ is incomplete. Thus, it accepts a pair of electrons. There is no $d$-orbital of suitable energy in boron atom. So, it can accommodate only one additional electron pair in its outermost shell. Therefore, it is a weak monobasic Lewis acid.

**151. (3)** When $(Me)_2SiCl_2$ undergoes hydrolysis it gives $(Me_2)Si(OH)_2$. The hydrolysis of $(Me_2)Si(OH)_2$ will foom $Me_2Si = O$, because size of silicon is large as compare to oxygen and is unable to form pi-bond. Thus, the product formed is polymeric in nature as shown below :

$$\underset{\overset{\displaystyle|}{CH_3}}{\overset{\overset{\displaystyle CH_3}{|}}{Cl-Si-Cl}} \xrightarrow{H_2O} \underset{\overset{\displaystyle|}{CH_3}}{\overset{\overset{\displaystyle CH_3}{|}}{HO-Si-OH}} \longrightarrow$$

$$H-O-\left(\underset{\overset{\displaystyle|}{CH_3}}{\overset{\overset{\displaystyle CH_3}{|}}{Si}}-O-\underset{\overset{\displaystyle|}{CH_3}}{\overset{\overset{\displaystyle CH_3}{|}}{Si}}\right)_n-O-H$$

$$\downarrow \; Me_3SiCl, H_2O$$

$$\underset{Me}{\overset{Me}{Me}}{\diagdown}Si-O\left(\underset{\overset{\displaystyle|}{CH_3}}{\overset{\overset{\displaystyle CH_3}{|}}{Si}}-O-\underset{\overset{\displaystyle|}{CH_3}}{\overset{\overset{\displaystyle CH_3}{|}}{Si}}\right)_n O-Si\overset{Me}{\underset{Me}{\diagup}}$$

**152. (1)** The structure of $H_3PO_3$ is,

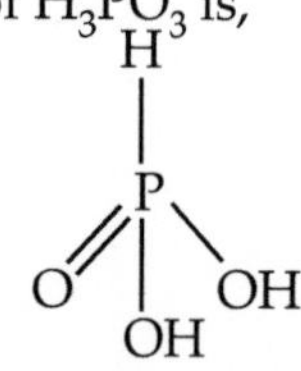

The compound $H_3PO_3$ contains two hydroxyl groups and one $P - H$. It is dibasic in nature due to the presence of two hydroxyl group and is reducing in nature due to the presence of one $P - H$ bond. Hence, the option (1) is correct out of the given options.

**153. (2)** The chemical reaction for preparation of anhydrous ferric chloride is shown below :

$$2Fe + 3Cl_2 \rightarrow 2FeCl_3$$

**154. (3)** The reaction that takes place when chlorine gas is passed through water is,

$$Cl_2 + H_2O \rightarrow HOCl + HCl$$

On reaction with $AgNO_3$, white precipitates are obtained due to the formation of AgCl.

The reaction of aqueous solution with magnesium ribbon is,

$$2HCl + Mg \rightarrow MgCl_2 + H_2\uparrow$$

**155.** The chemical formula of borax is $Na_2B_4O7.10H_2O$. The first step in the extraction of boron is the reaction of borax with concnetrated HCl. The chemical reaction involved in this process is as follows :

$$Na_2B_4O_7.10H_2O + 2HCl \rightarrow 2NaCl + 4H_3BO_3 + 5H_2O$$

The next step is the heating of $H_3BO_3$. This results in the formation of boric anhydride. The reaction involved in this process is as follows :

$$2H_3BO_3 \xrightarrow{\Delta} B_2O_3 + 3H_2O$$

The next step is the reaction of boric anhydride with potassium is as follows:

$$B_2O_3 + 6K \rightarrow 2B + 3K_2O$$

The structure of $B_2H_6$ is shown below.

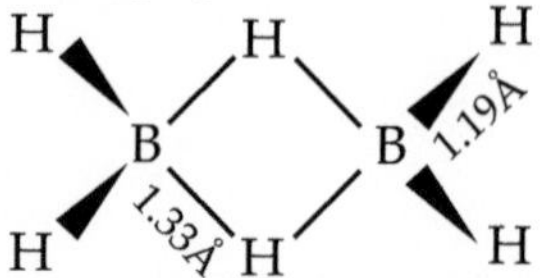

The reaction of $B_2H_6$ with HCl is as follows :

$$B_2H_6 + HCl \rightarrow B_2H_5Cl + H_2$$

**156. (4)** The reaction of formation of black ppt. is shown below :

$$Pb^{2+} + 2HCl + \underset{\text{White ppt.}}{PbCl_2} \downarrow \xrightarrow{H_2S} \underset{\text{Black ppt.}}{PbS} \downarrow$$

●●

# The *d*- and *f*-Block Elements

## QUESTIONS

1. In the sixth period, the orbitals that are filled are : **[2020, Main]**
   (1) $6s, 5f, 6d, 6p$
   (2) $6s, 6p, 6d, 6f$
   (3) $6s, 5d, 5f, 6p$
   (4) $6s, 4f, 5d, 6p$

2. Aqua regia is used for dissolving noble metals (Au, Pt, etc). The gas evolved in this process is : **[2020, Main]**
   (1) $N_2$
   (2) $N_2O_3$
   (3) $NO$
   (4) $N_2O_5$

3. A colourless aqueous solution contains nitrates of two metals, X and Y. When it was added to an aqueous solution of NaCl, a white precipitate was formed. This precipitate was found to be partly soluble in hot water to give a residue P and a solution Q. The residue P was soluble in aq. $NH_3$ and also in excess sodium thiosulphate. The hot solution Q gave a yellow precipitate with KI. The metals X and Y, respectively, are : **[2020, Main]**
   (1) Ag and Pb
   (2) Ag and Cd
   (3) Cd and Pb
   (4) Cd and Zn

4. The electronic configurations of bivalent europium and trivalent cerium are
   (atomic number :Xe = 54, Ce = 58, Eu = 63) **[2020, Main]**
   (1) $[Xe]\,4f^4$ and $[Xe]\,4f^9$
   (2) $[Xe]\,4f^7$ and $[Xe]\,4f^1$
   (3) $[Xe]\,4f^7\,6s^2$ and $[Xe]\,4f^2 6s^2$
   (4) $[Xe]rf^2$ and $[Xe]4f^7$

5. The correct order of the spin-only magnetic moments of the following complexes is : **[2020, Main]**
   (I) $[Cr[H_2O]_6]Br_2$
   (2) $Na_4[Fe(CN)_6]$
   (3) $Na_3[Fe(C_2O_4)_3]\ (\Delta_0 > P)$
   (4) $(Et_4N)_2\,[CoCl_4]$
   (1) (III) > (I) > (II) > (IV)
   (2) (I) > (IV) > (III) > (II)
   (3) (II) ≈ (I) > (IV) > (III)
   (4) (III) > (I) > (IV) > (II)

6. The lanthanide ion that would show colour is : **[2010, Main]**
   (1) $Gd^{3+}$
   (2) $Sm^{3+}$
   (3) $La^{3+}$
   (4) $Lu^{3+}$

7. Match the catalysts (Column I) with products (Column II). **[2019, Main]**

   | Column I | Column II |
   |---|---|
   | Catalyst | Product |
   | (A) $V_2O_5$ | (i) Polyethylene |
   | (B) $TiCl_4/Al(Me)_3$ | (ii) ethanal |
   | (C) $PdCl_2$ | (iii) $H_2SO_4$ |
   | (D) Iron Oxide | (iv) $NH_3$ |

   (1) (A)-(iii); (B)-(iv); (C)-(i); (D)-(ii)
   (2) (A)-(ii); (B)-(iii); (C)-(i); (D)-(iv)
   (3) (A)-(iii); (B)-(i); (C)-(ii); (D)-(iv)
   (4) (A)-(iv); (B)-(iii); (C)-(ii); (D)-(i)

8. The maximum number of possible oxidation states of actinoides are shown by : **[2019, Main]**
   (1) nobelium (No) and lawrencium (Lr)
   (2) actinium (Ac) and throium (Th)
   (3) berkelium (Bk) and californium (Cf)
   (4) neptunium (Np) and plutonium (Pu)

9. The highest possible oxidation states of uranium and plutonium, respectively, are : **[2019, Main]**
   (1) 6 and 7
   (2) 6 and 4
   (3) 7 and 6
   (4) 4 and 6

10. The correct order of the first ionisation enthalpies is : **[2019, Main]**
    (1) Ti < Mn < Zn < Ni
    (2) Ti < Mn < Ni < Zn
    (3) Mn < Ti < Zn < Ni
    (4) Zn < Ni < Mn < Ti

11. Thermal decomposition of a Mn compound (X) at 513 K results in compound Y, $MnO_2$ and a gaseous product. $MnO_2$ reacts with NaCl and concentrated $H_2SO_4$ to give a pungent gas Z, X, Y and Z respectively, are : **[2019, Main]**
    (1) $K_3MnO_4$, $K_2MnO_4$ and $Cl_2$
    (2) $K_2MnO_4$, $KMnO_4$ and $SO_2$
    (3) $KMnO_4$, $K_2MnO_4$ and $Cl_2$
    (4) $K_2MnO_4$, $KMnO_4$ and $Cl_2$

12. The pair that has similar atomic radii is : **[2019, Main]**
    (1) Mn and Re
    (2) Ti and Hf
    (3) Sc and Ni
    (4) Mo and W

13. Consider the following reactgions (unbalanced)
    $Zn + hot\ conc.\ H_2SO_4 \rightarrow G + R - X$
    $Zn + conc.\ NaOH \rightarrow T + G$
    $G - H_2S + NH_4OH \rightarrow Z\ (a\ precipitate) + X + Y$
    Choose the correct option(s) : **[2019, Main]**

(1) **Z** is dirty white in colour

(2) The oxidation state of Zn in T is + 1

(3) **R** is a V-shaped molecule

(4) Bond order of **Q** is 1 in its ground state

**14.** Among the species given below, the total number of diamagnetic species is .........

H atom, $NO_2$ monomer, $O_2^-$ (superoxide), dimeric sulphur in vapour phase, $Mn_3O_4$, $(NH_4)_2[FeCl_4]$, $(NH_4)_2[NiCl_4]$, $K_2MnO_4$, $K_2CrO_4$. **[2018, Advanced]**

**15.** The correct options to distinguish nitrate salts of $Mn^{2+}$ and $Cu^{2+}$ taken separately is/are :

**[2018, Advanced]**

(1) $Mn^{2+}$ shows the characteristics green colour in the flame test

(2) Only $Cu^{2+}$ shows the formation of precipitate by passing $H_2S$ in acidic medium

(3) Only $Mn^{2+}$ shows the formation of precipitate by passing $H_2S$ in faintly basic medium

(4) $Cu^{2+}/Cu$ has higher reduction potential than $Mn^{2+}/Mn$ (measured under similar conditons)

**16.** To measure the quantity of $MnCl_2$ dissolved in an aqueous solution, it was completely converted to $KMnO_4$ using the reaction,

$$MnCl_2 + K_2S_2O_8 + H_2O \rightarrow KMnO_4 + H_2SO_4 + HCl$$

(equation not balanced).

Few drops of concentrated HCl were added to this solution and gently warmed. Further, oxalic acid (225 mg) was added in portions till the colour of the permanganate ion disappeared. The quantity of $MnCl_2$ (in mg) present in the initial solution is...... **[2018, Advanced]**

(Atomic weights in g $mol^{-1}$ : Mn = 55, Cl = 35.5)

**17.** The correct order of spin-only magnetic moments among the following is :

(Atomic number : Mn = 25, Co = 27, Ni = 28, Zn = 30) **[2018, Main]**

(1) $[ZnCl_4]^{2-} > [NiCl_4]^{2-} > [CoCl_4]^{2-} > [MnCl_4]^{2-}$

(2) $[CoCl_4]^{2-} > [MnCl_4]^{2-} > [NiCl_4]^{2-} > [ZnCl_4]^{2-}$

(3) $[NiCl_4]^{2-} > [CoCl_4]^{2-} > [MnCl_4]^{2-} > [ZnCl_4]^{2-}$

(4) $[MnCl_4]^{2-} > [CoCl_4]^{2-} > [NiCl_4]^{2-} > [ZnCl_4]^{2-}$

**18.** When $XO_2$ is fused with an alkali metal hydroxide in presence of an oxidising agent such as $KNO_3$; a dark green product is formed which disproportionates in acidic solution to afford a dark purple solution. X is : **[2018, Main]**

(1) Ti  (2) V

(3) Cr  (4) Mn

**19.** Sodium salt of an organic acid `X' produces effervescence with conc. $H_2SO_4$. `X' reacts with the acidified aqueous $CaCl_2$ solution to give a white precipitate which decolourises acidic solution of $KMnO_4$. `X' is : **[2017, Main]**

(1) $CH_3COONa$  (2) $Na_2C_2O_4$

(3) $C_6H_5COONa$  (4) $HCOONa$

**20.** The pair of compounds having metals in their highest oxidation state is : **[2017, Main]**

(1) $MnO_2$ and $CrO_2Cl_2$

(2) $[NiCl_4]^{2-}$ and $[CoCl_4]^{2-}$

(3) $[Fe(CN)_6]^{3-}$ and $[Cu(CN)_4]^{2-}$

(4) $[FeCl_4]^-$ and $Co_2O_3$

**21.** A solution containing a group-IV cation gives a precipitate on passing $H_2S$. A solution of this precipitate in dil. HCl produces a white precipitate with NaOH solution and bluish-white precipitate with basic potassium ferrocyanide. The cation is : **[2017, Main]**

(1) $Co^{2+}$  (2) $Ni^{2+}$

(3) $Mn^{2+}$  (4) $Zn^{2+}$

**22.** Which of the following ions does not liberate hydrogen gas on reaction with dilute acids ? **[2017, Main]**

(1) $Ti^{2+}$  (2) $V^{2+}$

(3) $Cr^{2+}$  (4) $Mn^{2+}$

**23.** Which one of the following species is stable in aqueous solution ? **[2016, Main]**

(1) $Cr^{2+}$  (2) $Cu^+$

(3) $MnO_4^{3-}$  (4) $MnO_4^{2-}$

**24.** Which of the following compounds is metallic and ferromagnetic ? **[2016, Main]**

(1) $TiO_2$  (2) $CrO_2$

(3) $VO_2$  (4) $MnO_2$

**25.** The correct statments about $Cr^{2+}$ and $Mn^{3+}$ is/are :

[Atomic numbers of Cr = 24 and Mn = 25]

**[2015, Advanced]**

(1) $Cr^{2+}$ is a reducing agent

(2) $Mn^{3+}$ is an oxidising agent

(3) Both $Cr^{2+}$ and $Mn^{3+}$ exhibit $d^4$ electronic configuration

(4) When $Cr^{2+}$ is used as a reducing agent, the chromium ion attains $d^5$ electronic congiruation

**26.** The pairs of ions where BOTH the ions are precipitated upon passing $H_2S$ gas in presence of dilute HCl, is/are : **[2015, Advanced]**

(1) $Ba^{2+}$, $Zn^{2+}$  (2) $Bi^{3+}$, $Fe^{3+}$

(3) $Cu^{2+}$, $Pb^{2+}$  (4) $Hg^{2+}$, $Bi^{3+}$

**27.** The colour of $KMnO_4$ is due to : **[2015, Main]**

(1) M → L charge transfer transition

(2) $d$–$d$ transition

(3) L → M charge transfer transition

(4) $\sigma - \sigma^*$ transition

**28.** The cation that will not be precipitated by $H_2S$ in the presence of dil HCl is : **[2015, Main]**

(1) $Cu^{2+}$  (2) $Pb^{2+}$

(3) $As^{2+}$  (4) $Co^{2+}$

**29.** Which of the following statements is false ? **[2015, Main]**

(1) $CrO_4^{2-}$ is tetrahedral in shape

(2) $Cr_2O_7^{2-}$ has a Cr – O – Cr bond

(3) $Na_2Cr_2O_7$ is a primary standard in volumetry

(4) $Na_2Cr_2O_7$ is less soluble than $K_2Cr_2O_7$

**30.** A pink coloured salt turns blue on heating. The presence of which cation is most likely ? **[2015, Main]**

(1) $Cu^{2+}$  (2) $Fe^{2+}$

(3) $Zn^{2+}$  (4) $Co^{2+}$

**31.** Which series of reactions correctly represents chemical relations related to iron and its compound ? **[2014, Main]**

(1) $Fe \xrightarrow{\text{dil } H_2SO_4} FeSO_4 \xrightarrow{H_2SO_4, O_2}$

$Fe_2(SO_4)_3 \xrightarrow{\text{heat}} Fe$

(2) $Fe \xrightarrow{O_2, \text{heat}} FeO \xrightarrow{\text{dil } H_2SO_4}$

$FeSO_4 \xrightarrow{\text{heat}} Fe$

(3) $Fe \xrightarrow{Cl_2, \text{het}} FeCl_3 \xrightarrow{\text{heat, air}}$

$FeCl_2 \xrightarrow{Zn} Fe$

(4) $Fe \xrightarrow{O_2, \text{heat}} Fe_3O_4 \xrightarrow{CO, 600°C}$

$FeO \xrightarrow{CO, 700°C} Fe$

**32.** Chloro compound of Vanadium has only spin magnetic moment of 1.73 BM. This Vanadium chloride has the formula : **[2014, Main]** (at. no. of V = 23)

(1) $VCl_2$      (2) $VCl_4$
(3) $VCl_3$      (4) $VCl_5$

**33.** Which of the following is not formed when $H_2S$ reacts with acidic $K_2Cr_2O_7$ solution ? **[2014, Main]**

(1) $CrSO_4$      (2) $Cr_2(SO_4)_3$
(3) $K_2SO_4$      (4) $S$

**34.** Which one of the following exhibits the largest number of oxidation states ? **[2014, Main]**

(1) Ti (22)      (2) V (23)
(3) Cr (24)      (4) Mn (25)

**35.** Copper becomes green when exposed to moist air for a long period. This is due to : **[2014, Main]**

(1) the formation of a layer of cupric oxide on the surface of copper.
(2) the formation of a layer of basic carbonate of copper on the surface of copper
(3) the formation of a layer of cupric hyroxide on the surface of copper
(4) the formation of basic copper sulphate layer on the surface of the metal

**36.** Upon treatment with ammoniacal $H_2S$, the metal ion that precipitates as a sulfide is : **[2013, Advanced]**

(1) Fe(III)      (2) Al(III)
(3) Mg(II)      (4) Zn(II)

**Paragraph for Questions 37 and 38**

A aqueous solution of a mixture of two inorganic salts, when treated with dilute HCl, gave a precipitate (**P**) and a filtrate (**Q**). The precipitate **P** was found to dissolve in hot water. The filtrate (**Q**) remained unchanged, when treated with $H_2S$ in a silute mineral acid medium. However, it gave a precipitate (**R**) with $H_2S$ in an ammoniacal medium. The precipitate **R** gave a coloured solution (**S**), when treated with $H_2O_2$ in an aqueouse NaOH medium.

**37.** The precipitate P contains : **[2013, Advanced]**

(1) $Pb^{2+}$      (2) $Hg_2^{2+}$
(3) $Ag^+$      (4) $Hg^{2+}$

**38.** The coloured solution S contains : **[2013, Advanced]**

(1) $Fe_2(SO_4)_3$      (2) $CuSO_4$
(3) $ZnSO_4$      (4) $Na_2CrO_4$

**39.** The colour of light absorbed by an aqueous solution of $CuSO_4$ is : **[2012, Advanced]**

(1) orange-red      (2) blue-green
(3) yellow      (4) violet

**40.** Passing $H_2S$ gas into a mixture of $Mn^{2+}$, $Ni^{2+}$, $Cu^{2+}$ and $Hg^{2+}$ ions in an acidified aqueous solution precipitates : **[2011, Advanced]**

(1) CuS and HgS      (2) MnS and CuS
(3) MnS and NiS      (4) NiS and HgS

**41.** Reduction of the metal centre in aqueous permanganate ion involves : **[2011, Advanced]**

(1) 3 electrons in neutral medium
(2) 5 electrons in neutral medium
(3) 3 electrons in alkaline medim
(4) 5 electrons in acidic medium

**42.** The oxidation number of Mn in the product of alkaline oxidative fusion of $MnO_2$ is : **[2009, Advanced]**

**43.** Among the following, the coloured compound is : **[2008, Advanced]**

(1) CuCl      (2) $K_3[Cu(CN)_4]$
(3) $CuF_2$      (4) $[Cu(CH_3CN)_4]BF_4$

**44.** Consider a titration of potassium dichromate solution with acidified Mohr's salt solution using diphenylamine as indicator. The number of moles of Mohr's salt required per mole of dichromate is : **[2007, Advanced]**

(1) 3      (2) 4
(3) 5      (4) 6

**45.** While $Fe^{3+}$ is stable, $Mn^{3+}$ is not stable in acid solution because : **[2007, Advanced]**

(1) $O_2$ oxidises $Mn^{2+}$ to $Mn^{3+}$
(2) $O_2$ oxidises both $Mn^{2+}$ to $Mn^{3+}$ and $Fe^{2+}$ to $Fe^{3+}$
(3) $Fe^{3+}$ oxidises $H_2O$ to $O_2$
(4) $Mn^{3+}$ oxidises $H_2O$ to $O_2$

**46.** Write balanced chemical equation for developing a black and white photograhic film. Also give reason why the solution of sodium thiosulphate on acidification turns milky white and give balanced equation of this reaction. **[2005, Main]**

**47.** Which of the following pair is expected to exhibit same colour in solution ? **[2005, Main]**

(1) $VOCl_2$; $FeCl_2$      (2) $CuCl_2$; $VOCl_2$

(3) $MnCl_2$; $FeCl_2$      (4) $FeCl_2$; $CuCl_2$

**48.** Which of the following will not be oxidised by $O_3$ ? **[2005, Screening]**

(1) KI      (2) $FeSO_4$

(3) $KMnO_4$      (4) $K_2MnO_4$

**49.** $(NH_4)_2Cr_2O_7$ on heating gives a gas which is also given by : **[2004, Screening]**

(1) Heating $NH_4NO_2$      (2) Heating $NH_4NO_3$

(3) $Mg_3N_2 + H_2O$      (4) $Na(comp.) + H_2O_2$

**50.** The pair of compounds having metals in their highest oxidation state is : **[2004, Screening]**

(1) $MnO_2$, $FeCl_3$      (2) $[MnO_4]^-$, $CrO_2Cl_2$

(3) $[Fe(CN)_6]^{3-}$, $[Co(CN)_3$   (4) $[NiCl_4]^{2-}$, $[CoCl_4]^-$

**51.** When $I^-$ is oxidised by $MnO_4^-$ in alkaline medium, $I^-$ converts into : **[2004, Screening]**

(1) $IO_3^-$      (2) $I_2$

(3) $IO_4^-$      (4) $IO^-$

**52.** A mixture consists A (yellow solid) and B (colourless solid) which gives lilac colour in flame.

**[2003, Main]**

(a) Mixture gives black precipitate C on passing $H_2S_4$

(b) C is soluble in aqua-regia and on evaporation on aqua-regia and adding $SnCl_2$ gives greyish black precipitate D.

The salt solution with $NH_4OH$ gives a brown precipitate.

(1) The sodium extract of the salt with $CCl_4/FeCl_3$ gives a violet layer

(2) The sodium extract gives yellow precipitate with $AgNO_3$ solution which is insoluble in $NH_3$

Identify A and B, and the precipitates C and D.

**53.** $[X] + H_2SO_4$ [Y] a colourless gas with irritating smell

$[Y] + K_2Cr_2O_7 + H_2SO_4$ green solution

$[X]$ and $[Y]$ is : **[2003, Screening]**

(1) $SO_3^{2-}$, $SO_2$      (2) $Cl^-$, $HCl$

(3) $S^{2-}$, $H_2S$      (4) $CO_3^{2-}$, $CO_2$

**54.** When $MnO_2$ is fused with KOH, a coloured compound is formed, the product and its colour is : **[2003, Screening]**

(1) $K_2MnO_4$, purple green

(2) $KMnO_4$, purple

(3) $Mn_2O_3$, brown

(4) $Mn_3O_4$ black

**55.** When a white crystalline compound X is heated with $K_2Cr_2O7$ and concentrated $H_2SO_4$, a reddish brown gas A is evolved. On passing A into caustic soda solution, a yellow coloured solution of B is obtained Neutrailizing the solution B with acetic acid and on subsequent addition of lead acetate, a yellow precipitate C is obtained. When X is heated with NaOH solutiohn, a colourless gas is evolved and on pasing this gas into $K_2K_2HgI_4$ solutio, a reddish brown precipitate D is formed, Identity A, B, C, D and X. Write the equations of reactions involved. **[2002, Main]**

## ANSWER KEY

| 1. | (4) | 2. | (3) | 3. | (1) | 4. | (2) | 5. | (2) | 6. | (2) | 7. | (3) | 8. | (4) | 9. | (1) | 10. | (2) |
|---|---|---|---|---|---|---|---|---|---|---|---|---|---|---|---|---|---|---|---|
| 11. | (3) | 12. | (4) | 13. | (1) | 14. | (1) | 15. | (2,4) | 16. | (*) | 17. | (4) | 18. | (4) | 19. | (*) | 20. | (1) |
| 21. | (4) | 22. | (4) | 23. | (4) | 24. | (2) | 25. | (1,2,3) | 26. | (3,4) | 27. | (3) | 28. | (4) | 29. | (4) | 30. | (4) |
| 31. | (4) | 32. | (2) | 33. | (1) | 34. | (4) | 35. | (2) | 36. | (4) | 37. | (1) | 38. | (4) | 39. | (1) | 40. | (1) |
| 41. | (1,3,4) | 42. | (*) | 43. | (3) | 44. | (4) | 45. | (4) | 46. | (*) | 47. | (2) | 48. | (3) | 49. | (1) | 50. | (2) |
| 51. | (1) | 52. | (*) | 53. | (1) | 54. | (1) | 55. | (*) | | | | | | | | | | |

## ANSWERS WITH EXPLANATIONS

**1. (4)** As per $(n + l)$ rule in $6^{th}$ period, order of orbitals, filling is $6s, 4f, 5d, 6p$.

**2. (3)** The gas evolved is NO, as shown in reaction below :

$$Au + HNO_3 + 4HCl \rightarrow HAuCl_4 + NO\uparrow + 2H_2O$$

**3. (1)** X : Ag      P : AgCl

Y : PB      Q : $PbCl_2$

$$\begin{array}{c} AgNO_3 \\ + \\ Pb(NO_3)_2 \end{array} \xrightarrow{+ \text{ NaCl}} \underset{\text{white ppt}}{AgCl\downarrow} + \underset{\text{white ppt}}{PbCl_2\downarrow}$$

Aqueous suspension is heated and then filtered

Residue      Filtrate

$\underset{\text{white ppt}}{AgCl^-\downarrow (P)}$      $\underset{\text{Hot solution}}{PbCl_2 (Q)}$

$AgCl + 2NH_3$ solution $\rightarrow [Ag(NH_3)_2]Cl$

(P)   (excess)      clear solution

$AgCl + 2Na_2S_2O_3$ solution $\rightarrow Na_3[Ag(S_2O_3)_2]$

(P)   (excess)      clear solution

     + NaCl

$\underset{\text{Hot solution}}{PbCl_2} + 2KI \rightarrow \underset{\text{(yellow ppt)}}{PbI_2\downarrow} + 2KCl$

(Q)

**4. (2)** $Eu_{63} \Rightarrow [X] 4f^7 5d^0 6s^2$

$Eu^{2\oplus} \Rightarrow [Xe] 4f^7$

$Ce38 \Rightarrow [Xe] 4f^1 5d^1 6s^2$

$Ce^{2\oplus} \Rightarrow [Xe] 4f^1$

**5. (2)** I.   $[Cr(H_2O)_6]^{2+}$

$Cr^{+2} \Rightarrow [Ar] 3d^4$

$H_2O \rightarrow$ Weak field ligand

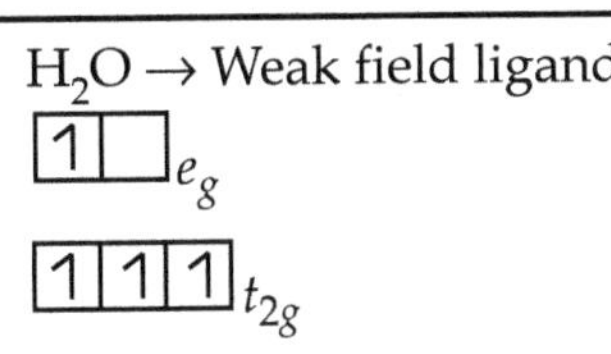

Unpaired $e^- = 4$

Magnetic moment $= \sqrt{24}$ BM

$\qquad\qquad = 4.89$ BM

II. $[Fe(CN)_6]^4$

$Fe^{2+} \Rightarrow [Ar] 3d^6$

$CN^- \rightarrow$ Strong field ligand

Unpaired $e^- = 0$

Magnetic moment $= 0$ BM

$\qquad\qquad = 0$ BM

III. $[Fe(C_2O_4)_3]^{3-}$

$Fe^{2+} \Rightarrow [Ar] 3d^5$

As $\Delta_0 > P$

Unpaired $e^- = 1$

Magnetic moment $= \sqrt{3}$ BM

$\qquad\qquad = 1.73$ BM

IV. $(Et_4N)^+[CoCl_4]^{2-}$

$Co^{+2}$ Þ $[Ar]3d^7$

$[CoCl_4]^{-2} =$

Unpaired electrons $= 3$

Magnetic moment $= \sqrt{15}$ BM

$\qquad\qquad = 3.87$ BM

Hence order of magnetic moment is

$I > IV > III > II$

**6. (2)** The electronic configuration of $Sm^{3+}$ is $[Xe]4f^5$. It contains five electrons in its outermost $f$ orbital. Therefore, $Sm^{3+}$ shows colour. In case of $La^{3+}$ and $Lu^{3+}$, there are completely filled outermost shells and in the case of $Gd^{3+}$, the outermost $f$ orbital is half filled. Therefore, $La^{3+}$, $Lu^{3+}$ and $Gd^{3+}$ are colourless.

**7. (3)** (A) Vanadium pentoxide $(V_2O_5)$ is used as catalyst in contact process for sulfuric acid $(H_2SO_4)$ synthesis.

(B) Zeigleer Natta salt $(TiCl_4/Al(Me)_3)$ is used as catalyst in polymerisation process of ethene.

(C) Palladium chloride $(PdCl_2)$ is used as catalsyt in Wacker process of ethanal synthesis.

(D) Iron oxide is used as catalyst in Haber's process of $NH_3$ synthesis.

**8. (4)** The oxidation states shown by plutonium are 3+, 4+, 5+, 6+ and 7+.

The oxidation states shown by neptunium are 3+, 4+, 5+, 6+ and 7+.

The oxidation states shown by berkelium are 3+ and 4+.

The oxidation states shown by californium are 3+, 4+ and 2+.

The oxidation states shown by nobelium are 2 + and 3+.

The oxidation states shown by lawrencium is 3+.

The oxidation states shown by actinium is 3+.

The oxidation states shown by thorium are 3+ and 4+.

Therefore, the maximum number of oxidation stated shown by plutonium and neptunium.

**9. (1)** The highest oxidation state of U and Pu is +6 and +7 respectively.

**10. (2)** The electronic configuration of the elements is given below :

$$Ti: [Ar]3d^24s^2$$
$$Mn: [Ar]3d^54s^2$$
$$Ni: [Ar]3d^84s^2$$
$$Zn: [Ar]3d^{10}4s^2$$

As the atomic number increases, it becomes difficult to remove the last electron and hence, the ionisation enthalpy increases. Therefore, the correct order of ionisation enthalpies is Ti $< Mn < Ni < Zn$.

**11. (3)** The complete reactio sequence is shown below :

$$2KMnO_4 \xrightarrow[\Delta]{513\,K} K_2MnO_4 + MnO_2 + O_2$$

$$MO_2 + 4NaCl + 4H_2SO_4 \rightarrow MnCl_2 + NaHSO_4 + 2H_2O + Cl_2$$

Therefore, the compound X, compound Y and gas Z are $KMnO_4$, $K_2MnO_4$ and $Cl_2$ respectively.

**12. (4)** The size of lanthanoid elements is almost same because of the lanthanoid contraction. The element Mo and W are langhanoid elements. Therefore, the element Mo and W will have similar atomic radii.

**13. (1,2,3)** The complete balanced reactions are shown below :

$Zn + 2H_2SO_4$ (Hot and conc.)

$$\rightarrow ZnSO_4 + SO_2 + 2H_2O$$

$Zn + 2NaOH$ (conc.) $\rightarrow Na_2ZnO_2 + H_2$

$ZnSO_4 + H_2S + 2NH_4OH \rightarrow ZnS\downarrow$

$$+ 2H_2O + (NH_4)_2SO_4$$

The correct statements are shown below :

- Hydrogen gas (Q) has bond 1.

- The colour of ZnS (Z) is dirty white.
- The structure of $SO_2$ (R) is V-shape.

**14. (1)** Hydrogen atom has one electron. Thus, it is paramagnetic.

The given species $NO_2$ monomer has an odd electron. Thus, it is paramagnetic.

The given species $O_2^-$ superoxide has one unpaired electron in its $\pi^*$. Thus, it is paramagnetic.

The given species $S_2$ has two unpaired electrons in its $\pi^*$. Thus, it is paramagnetic.

The given species $Mn_3O_4$ exists as $2Mn^{+2}O$. $Mn^{+4}O_2$. Thus, it is paramagnetic.

In the given species $(NH_4)2[FeCl_4]$, iron exists in + 2 oxidation state. Thus, it is paramagnetic.

In the given species $(NH_4)_2[NiCl_4]$, nickel exists in +2 oxidation state. Thus, it is paramagnetic.

In the given species $K_2MnO_4$, manganese exists in +6 oxidation state. Thus, it is paramagnetic.

In the given species $K_2CrO_4$, manganese exists in +6 oxidation state. Thus, it is diamagnetic.

**15. (2,4)** (1) Both the ions $Mn^{2+}$ and $Cu^{2+}$ impart green colour to the flame and thus, these cannot be distinguished.

(2) $Cu^{2+}$ belongs to group (II) and thus, on passing $H_2S$ through acidic medium it forms precipitate of CuS.

(3) Both the ions $Mn^{2+}$ and $Cu^{2+}$ on passing $H_2S$ through basic medium forms precipitate.

(4) The value of standard reduction potential for $Cu^{2+}$ is greater than that of $Mn^{2+}$ on the basis of electrochemical series.

**16.** The given reactions are shown below :
$$2MnCl_2 + 5K_2S_2O_8 + 8H_2O \rightarrow 2KMnO_4 + 4K_2SO_4$$
$$+ 6H_2SO_4 + 4HCl$$
$$2KMnO_4 + 5H_2C_2O_4 + 3H_2SO_4 \rightarrow K_2SO_4 + 2MnSO_4$$
$$+ 8H_2O + 10CO_2$$

Number of millimoles of oxalic acid $= \dfrac{225}{90}$
$$= 2.5$$

Millimoles of $KMnO_4$ that react with oxalic acid = 1
Millimoles of $MnCl_2$ that are required initially = 1
Mass of $MnCl_2$ that is required initially = $1 \times 126$ mg
$$= 126 \text{ mg}$$

**17. (4)** The spin-only magnetic moment is calculated by,

$$\mu = \sqrt{n(n+2)}$$

The number of unpaired electrons present in is $Zn^{2+}$ is 0.

The number of unpaired electrons present in is $Ni^{2+}$ is 2.

The number of unpaired electrons present in is $Co^{2+}$ is 3.

The number of unpaired electrons present in is $Mn^{2+}$ is 5.

Hence, the correct order is
$$[MnCl_4]^{2-} > [CoCl_4]^{2-} > [NiCl_4]^{2-} > [ZnCl_4]^{2-}.$$

**18. (4)** For the given reaction condition, the chemical equation is written as,
$$MnO_2 + KOH \rightarrow K_2MnO_4 \text{ (green)}$$
$$\xrightarrow{\text{acidic solution}} KMnO_4 \text{ (purple)}$$

Other than manganese, no other metal undergoes disproportionation reaction.

**19.** An organic acid X whose sodium salt produces effervesence with conc. $H_2SO_4$ and the complete reaction scheme is shown below.
$$\underset{(X)}{Na_2C_2O_4} + H_2SO_4 \text{ (conc.)} \rightarrow Na_2SO_4 + \underset{\text{Oxalic acid}}{H_2C_2O_4}$$

$$H_2C_2O_4 \xrightarrow[\Delta, -H_2O]{\text{Conc. } H_2SO_4} CO\uparrow + CO_2^-$$
$$\text{(effervescence)}$$

$$\underset{(X)}{Na_2C_2O_4} + CaCl_2 \rightarrow \underset{\text{white ppt.}}{CaC_2O_4\downarrow} + 2NaCl$$

$$2MnO_4^- + 5C_2O_4^{2-} + 16H^+ \rightarrow 2Mn^{2+} + 10CO_2$$
$$+ 8H_2O$$

**20. (1)** The compounds that are present in their highest oxidation states are $MnO_2$ in which manganese has +4 oxidation state and $CrO_2Cl_2$, in which chromium has +6 oxidation state.

**21. (4)** The complete reactions given by the group-IV cation in the presence of HCl are shown as follows.

$$\left.\begin{array}{c} ZnS \\ MnS \end{array}\right\} \xrightarrow{HCl} \begin{array}{c} ZnCl_2 \\ MnCl_2 \end{array}$$

$$\left.\begin{array}{c} CoS \\ NiS \end{array}\right\} \xrightarrow{HCl} \text{No reaction}$$

$$ZnS \xrightarrow{HCl} ZnCl_2 \xrightarrow{NaOH} \underset{\text{White ppt}}{Zn(OH)_2}$$
$$\downarrow K_4[Fe(CN)_6]$$
$$\underset{\text{bluish white ppt}}{Zn_2[Fe(CN)_6]}$$

Thus, the cation of group-IV is $Zn^{2+}$.

**22. (4)** The reactivity of metal ion with acid depends upon its position in electrochemical series. The reactivity of these metals with an acid increases in the following order.
$$Mn^{2+} < Cr^{2+} < V^{2+} \text{ and } Ti^{2+}$$

**23. (4)** The species that is stable in aqueous solution is $MnO_4^{2-}$, because it undergoes disproportionation in neutral and acidic solutions as shown below :

$$3MnO_4^{2-} + 4H^+ \rightarrow 2MnO_4^{2-} + MnO_2 + 2H_2O$$

In $MnO_4^{2-}$, manganese is present in oxidation state which is highly stable.

**24. (2)** The compound that is metallic and ferro-magnetic is $CrO_2$.

**25. (1,2,3)** The correct statements for $Cr^{3+}$ and $Mn^{3+}$ are :

(A) $Cr^{2+}$is a reducing agent because it attain $3d^3$ electronic configuration which is more stable. Thus, it acts as a reducing agent.

(B) The electronic configuration of $Mn^{3+}$ is $3d^4$ and it is an oxidizing agent because $Mn^{2+}$ is more stable.

(C) The electronic configuration of Cr is $[Ar]4s^13d^5$. When chromium looses two electrons from their outermost shell $Cr^{2+}$ ion is formed. Thus, the electronic configuration changes from $[Ar]4s^13d^5$ to $[Ar]4s^03d^{4.}$. Similarly, the electronic configuration of $Mn^{3+}$ is $[Ar]4s^03d^4$. Therefore, $Cr^{2+}$ and $Mn^{3+}$ exhibits $d^4$ electronic configuration.

**26. (3,4)** The concentration of sulfide will be very low when $H_2S$ is added in presence of HCl. So the ions that will give ppt on reaction with $H_2S$ in presence of dil. HCl is $Cu^{2+}$, $Pb^{2+}$, $Hg^{2+}$ and $Bi^{3+}$.

The reaction of given ions with hydrogen sulfide is as shown below :

$$Cu^{2+} + H_2S \xrightarrow{\text{dil. HCl}} CuS\downarrow + 2H^+$$

$$Pb^{2+} + H_2S \xrightarrow{\text{dil. HCl}} PbS\downarrow + 2H^+$$

$$Hg^{2+} + H_2S \xrightarrow{\text{dil. HCl}} HgS\downarrow + 2H^+$$

$$Bi^{3+} + H_2S \xrightarrow{\text{dil. HCl}} Bi_2S_3\downarrow + 2H^+$$

$$Zn^{2+} + H_2S \rightarrow ZnS \xrightarrow{\text{dil. HCl}} ZnCl_2$$
$$\text{(soluble)} + H_2S\uparrow$$

$$Fe^{3+} + H_2S \rightarrow Fe^{2+} + 2H^+ + S\downarrow$$

**27. (3)** The colour of potassium permanganate ($KMnO_4$) arises due to $L \rightarrow M$ charge transfer transition.

**28. (4)** Out of the given cations, $Co^{2+}$ belongs to group IV and is not precipitated in the presence of HCl. It is precipitated by $H_2S$ in the presence of $NH_4OH$ to CoS (black precipitates).

**29. (4)** The compound,$Na_2Cr_2O_7$ is more soluble than $K_2Cr_2O_7$ due to small size of sodium.

**30. (4)** $Zn^{2+}$ salts are white in color due to the absence of unpaired electrons in $d$-orbital, whereas $Fe^{2+}$ and $Cu^{2+}$ ions generally shows pale green and blue color respectively. Thus, $Co^{2+}$ forms pink color in aqueous solution

**31. (4)** In reaction (1), $FeSO_4$ cannot be converted into Fe on reaction with $H_2SO_4$ in the presence of $O_2$. $FeSO_4$ will give oxide(s).

In reaction (2), $FeSO_4$ cannot be converted into Fe on heating. It will give oxide(s).

In reaction (3), $FeCl_3$ will not be reduced to $FeCl_2$.

Therefore, reaction (4) correctly represents the chemical reactions related to iron and its compound.

**32. (2)** The given value of magnetic moment is 1.73 BM that shows that vanadium just have only unpaired electron in this valence shell. Thus, in case of $VCl_4$, vanadium possesses +4 oxidation state. The electronic configuration of $V^{4+}$ is $[Ar]3d^1$.

Hence, the formula is $VCl_4$.

**33. (1)** The compound that is not formed in the reaction of $H_2S$ with acidic $K_2Cr_2O_7$ solution is $CrSO_4$ as shown below.

$$K_2Cr_2O_7 + H_2S \rightarrow Cr_2(SO_4)_3 + S + K_2SO_4$$
$$+ H_2O$$

**34. (4)** The number of oxidation states exhibited by an element depends upon the number of unpaired electrons present in the $d$-orbital. Since, manganese has five unpaired electrons in the d orbital that is larger than that of titanium, vanadium, and chromium. Therefore, manganese exhibits the largest number of oxidation states among the given compounds

**35. (2)** When copper metal is exposed to air for a longer time, it reacts with carbon dioxide, water, and oxygen to form copper carbonate and copper hydroxide. The color of copper changes to green due to the formation of copper carbonate (green color).

The chemical equation involved in the reaction of copper with moist air is,

$$2Cu + H_2O + CO_2 + O_2 \rightarrow CuCO_3 + Cu(OH)_2$$

**36. (4)** The charge of sulphur in $H_2S$ is +2. Zinc with +2 charge reacts with $S^{2-}$ to form insoluble ZnS due to stability of a compound. The sulphide of zinc is more common as compared to rest of ions because $Al^{3+}$, $Mg^{2+}$ and $Fe^{3+}$ preferred to form hydroxides rather than sulphides.

**37. (1)** The precipitate P contains $Pb^{2+}$ as shown below :

$$Pb^{2+} + 2HCl \rightarrow PbCl_2 \xrightarrow{\text{Hot water}} \text{Soluble}$$

**38. (4)** The coloured solution S contains $Na_2CrO_4$ as shown below :

$$Cr^{3+} \xrightarrow[\text{ammonical medium}]{H_2S} Cr(OH)_3$$

$$Cr(OH)_3 \xrightarrow[H_2O_2]{NaOH} Na_2CrO_4$$

**39. (1)** The colour of aqueous solution of $CuSO_4$ is blue. Its complementary colour is orange-red.

**40. (1)** On passing hydrogen sulfide gas into a mixture of $Mn^{2+}$, $Ni^{2+}$, $Cu^{2+}$ and $Hg^{2+}$ ions in acidified aqueous solution, precipitates of Cu and Hg are observed. These are copper monosulfide and mercuric sulfide.

**41. (1,3,4)** Reduction of the metal centre in aqueous permanganate ion in acidic medium is shown as,

$$MnO_4^- + 8H^+ + 5e^- \rightarrow Mn^{2+} + 4H_2O$$

In neutral and alkaline medium reduction is given as,

$$MnO_4^- + 2H_2O + 3e^- \rightarrow MnO_2 + 4OH^-$$

From the above reactions, it is clear that in neutral and alkaline medium three electrons are involved. In acidic medium, five electrons are involved

**42.** The balanced chemical equation for the alkaline oxidative fusion of $MnO_2$ is,

$$2MnO_2 + 4KOH + O_2 \rightarrow 2K_2MnO_4 + 2H_2O$$

The oxidation number of manganese in $K_2MnO_4$ is 6.

**43. (3)** The oxidation state of Copper in $CuF_2$ is +2. Hence, its electronic configuration is $[Ar]3d^9$. It contains an unpaired electron which imparts blue color to the compound in crystalline form.

**44. (4)** The balanced equation for the titration of potassium dichromate solution with acidified Mohr's salt is,

$$Cr_2O_7^{2-} + 6Fe^{2+} + 14H^+ \rightarrow 2Cr^{3+} + 6Fe^{3+} + 7H_2O$$

Thus, six moles of Mohr's salt is required for each mole of dichromate.

**45. (4)** $Mn^{3+}$ ion can oxidize water into oxygen. This is due to spontaneous reaction of $Mn^{3+}$ ion with water.

$$2Mn^{3+} (aq) + 2H_2O(l) \rightarrow MnO_2(s) + Mn^{2+}(aq) + 4H^+(aq)$$

**46.** The balanced chemical equation that is involved during the development of a photographic film is as follows.

$$2AgBr + \underset{\substack{\text{Hydroquinone} \\ \text{(developer)}}}{C_6H_4(OH)_2} \rightarrow \underset{\substack{\text{black silver} \\ \text{particles}}}{2Ag} + 2HBr + C_6H_4O_2$$

$$2AgBr + 2Na_2S_2O_3 \rightarrow Na_3[Ag(S_2O_3)_2] + NaBr$$

Sensitive   Hypo
unexposed  solution
emulsion

The acidification of sodium thiosulphate results in the precipitation of colloidal sulphur which turns the solution milky. The corresponding reaction is given below.

$$Na_2S_2O_3 + 2H^+ \rightarrow 2Na^+ + H_2SO_4 + \underset{\substack{\text{colloidal} \\ \text{sulphur}}}{S \downarrow}$$

**47. (2)** Among the given pair, the pair that possesses the same color in the solution is $CuCl_2$ and $VOCl_2$. The reason of possessing same color by $CuCl_2$ and $VOCl_2$ is that the ions $Cu^{2+}$ and $V^{4+}$ contains only one unpaired electron in their valence shell.

Thus, the correct option is (2).

**48. (3)** The compound that cannot be oxidized by ozone is potassium permanganate, $KMnO_4$ because in $KMNO_4$, manganese is present in its highest oxidation state that is $Mn^{6+}$. Thus, it is not possible for any oxidizing agent to oxidize $KMnO_4$ in the highest oxidation state of manganese.

Thus, the correct option is (3)

**49. (1)** The heating of $(NH_4)_2\ Cr_2O_7$ is shown below :

$$(NH_4)_2Cr_2O_7 \xrightarrow{\Delta} N_2 \uparrow + Cr_2O_3 + 4H_2O$$

The heating of $NH_4NO_2$ is shown below :

$$NH_4NO_2 \xrightarrow{\Delta} N_2 \uparrow + 2H_2O$$

**50. (2)** The oxidation state of Mn is +7 in $[MnO_4]^-$ and oxidation state of Cr is +6 in $CrO_2Cl_2$.

**51. (1)** The reaction of $KMnO_4$ in alkaline medium is expressed as,

$$2KMnO_4 + 2KOH \rightarrow 2K_2MnO_4 + H_2O + O$$

$$2K_2MnO_4 + 2H_2O \rightarrow 2MnO_2 + 4KOH + 2O$$

$$2K_2MnO_4 + H_2 \xrightarrow{\text{alkaline}}$$

$$2MnO_2 + 2KOH + 3[O]$$

$$KI + [O] \rightarrow KIO_3$$

$$2KMnO_4 + KI + H_2O \rightarrow 2KOH + 2MnO_2 + KIO_3$$

**52. (a)** It is given that a mixture of A and B gives lilac color in the flame. During flame test, potassium ions give lilac color.

Therefore, compound A is **KI** and compound B is **HgI_2**.

The reaction involved on passing $H_2S$ in the given mixture is as follows :

$$HgI_2 + H_2S \rightarrow HgS + 2HI$$

Therefore, the compound C is $HgI_2$.

**(b)** It is given that the compound C is soluble in aqua-regia and on adding $SnCl_2$ gives grayish black precipitate D.

The reaction involved in this process is,

$$HgI_2 \xrightarrow{\text{aqua-regia}} HgCl_2$$

$$HgCl_2 + SnCl_2 \longrightarrow Hg\downarrow + SnCl_4$$

**53. (1)** The species $SO_3^{2-}$ reacts with sulfuric acid to form $SO_2$ gas which is a colorless gas having irritating smell.

$$\underset{(X)}{SO_3^{2-}} + H_2SO_4 \rightarrow \underset{(Y)}{SO_2} + H_2O + SO_4^{2-}$$

Sulfur dioxide gas reacts with potassium dichromate and sulfuric acid to form green color solution.

$$3SO_2 + K_2Cr_2O_7 + H_2SO_4 \rightarrow K_2SO_4 + Cr_2(SO_4)_3 + H_2O$$

Hence, the species X is $SO_3^{2-}$ and the species Y is $SO_2$.

**54. (1)** The reaction of manganese dioxide with potassium hydroxide leads to the formation of $K_2MnO_4$ as a product which is purple green in color.

$$2MnO_2 + 2KOH + O_2 \rightarrow 2K_2MnO_4 + 2H_2O$$

Hence, the formula and color of the product formed in the given reaction is $K_2MnO_4$ and purple green respectively.

**55.** It is given that on heating compound X with $K_2Cr_2O_7$ and conc. $H_2SO_4$, a reddish brown gas A is evolved. The chemical reactions involved in this process are given below :

$$NH_4Cl + K_2Cr_2O_7 + 3H_2SO_4 \rightarrow K_2SO_4$$
$$+ (NH_4)_2SO_4 + 2CrO_2Cl_2\uparrow + 3H_2O$$

Thus, compound X is $NH_4Cl$ and A is $CrO_2Cl_2$.

The reaction involved in the formation of compound B and C is shown below :

$$CrO_2Cl_2 + 4NaOH \rightarrow 2NaCl + Na_2CrO_4 + 2H_2O$$
$$Na_2CrO_4 + (CH_3COO)_2Pb \rightarrow PbCrO_4$$
$$+ CH_3COONa$$

Thus, compound B is $Na_2CrO_4$ and C is $PbCrO_4$.

The reaction involved in the formation of compound D is shown below :

$$NH_4Cl + 2K_2HgI_4 + KOH \rightarrow$$

$$\underset{(X)}{} \quad Hg \underset{Hg}{\overset{NH_2}{\diagdown}} O$$

Brown ppt

$$+ 7KI + KCl + H_2O$$

●●

## ⌨ QUESTIONS

**1.** For octahedral Mn(II) and tetrahedral Ni(II) complexes, consider the following statements: **[2020, Main]**

(I)   Both the complexes can be high spin.

(II)  Ni(II) complex can very rarely be low spin.

(III) With strong field ligands, Mn(II) complexes can be low spin.

(IV) Aqueous solution of Mn(II) ions is yellow in colour.

The correct statements are :

(1) (I), (III) and (IV) only

(2) (II), (III) and (IV) only

(3) (I), (II) and (III) only

(4) (I) and (II) only

**2.** Consider that a $d^6$ metal ion ($M^{2+}$) forms a complex with aqua ligands and the spin only magnetic moment of the complex is 4.90 BM. The geometry and the crystal field stablization energy of the complex is : **[2020, Main]**

(1) tetrahedral and $-1.6\,\Delta_t + 1P$

(2) tetrahedral and $-0.6\,\Delta_t$

(3) octahedral and $-1.6\,\Delta_0$

(4) octahedral and $-2.4\,\Delta_0 + 2P$

**3.** Simplified absorption spectra of three complexes [(i), (ii) and (iii)] of $M^{n+}$ ion are provided below; their $\lambda_{max}$ values are marked as A, B and C respectively. The correct match between the complexes and their $\lambda_{max}$ values is :

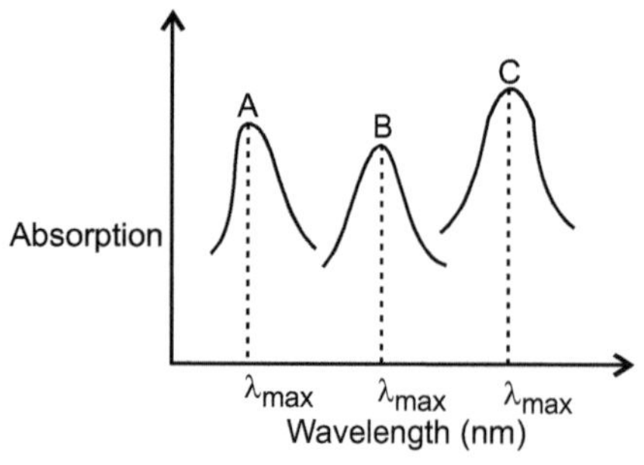


**[2020, Main]**

(i)   $[M(NCS)_6]^{(-6+n)}$     (ii)  $[MF_6]^{(-6+n)}$

(iii) $[M(NH_3)_6]^{n+}$

(1) A-(ii), (B)-(i), C-(iii)

(2) A-(iii), B-(i), C-(ii)

(3) A-(ii), B-(iii), C-(i)

(4) A-(i), B-(ii), C-(iii)

**4.** The one that is not expected to show isomerism is : **[2020, Main]**

(1) $[Ni(NH_3)_4(H_2O)_2]^{2+}$   (2) $[Ni(NH_3)_2Cl_2]$

(3) $[Pt(NH_3)_2Cl_2]$     (4) $[Ni(en)_3]^{2+}$

**5.** The complex that can show optical activity is : **[2020, Main]**

(1) trans-$[Fe(NH_3)_2(CN)_4]^-$

(2) cis-$[Fe(NH_3)_2(CN)_4]^-$

(3) cis-$[CrCl_2(ox)_2]^{3-}$ (ox = oxalate)

(4) trans-$[Cr(Cl_2)(ox)_2]^{3-}$

**6.** The electronic spectrum of $[Ti(H_2O)_6]^{3+}$ shows a single broad peak with a maximum at 20,300 cm$^{-1}$. The crystal field stabilization energy (CFSE) of the complex ion, in kJ mol$^{-1}$, is : **[2020, Main]**

(1) 242.5     (2) 83.7

(3) 145.5     (4) 97

**7.** The $d$-electron configuration of $[Ru(en)_3]Cl_2$ and $[Fe(H_2O)_6]Cl_2$, respectively are : **[2020, Main]**

(1) $t_{2g}^4 e_g^2$ and $t_{2g}^6 e_g^0$   (2) $t_{2g}^6 e_g^0$ and $t_{2g}^6 e_g^0$

(3) $t_{2g}^6 e_g^0$ and $t_{2g}^4 e_g^2$   (4) $t_{2g}^4 e_g^2$ and $t_{2g}^4 e_g^2$

**8.** The incorrect statement is : **[2020, Main]**

(1) In manganate and permanganate ions, the $\pi$-bonding takes place by overlap of $p$-orbitals of oxygen and $d$-orbitals of manganese

(2) Manganate ion is green in colour and permanganate ion in purple in colour

(3) Manganate and permanganate ions are paramagnetic

(4) Manganate and permanganate ions are tetrahedral

**9.** The number of isomers possible for $[Pt(en)(NO_2)_2]$ is : **[2020, Main]**

(1) 3     (2) 2

(3) 1     (4) 4

**10.** The pair in which both the species have the same magnetic moment (spin only) is : **[2020, Main]**

(1) $[Mn(H_2O)_6]^{2+}$ and $[Cr(H_2O)]^{2+}$

(2) $[Cr(H_2O)_6]^{2+}$ and $[CoCl_4]^{2-}$

(3) $[Cr(H_2O)_6]^{2+}$ and $[Fe(H_2O)_6]^{2+}$

(4) $[Co(OH)_4]^{2-}$ and $[Fe(NH_3)_6]^{2+}$

**11.** For a $d^4$ metal ion in an octahedral field, the correct electronic configuration is :

**[2020, Main]**

(1) $t_{2g}^4 e_g^0$ when $\Delta_0 < P$

(2) $e_g^2 t_{2g}^2$ when $\Delta_0 < P$

(3) $t_{2g}^3 e_g^1$ when $\Delta_0 < P$

(4) $t_{2g}^3 e_g^1$ when $\Delta_0 > P$

**12.** The values of the crystal field stabilization energies for a high spin $d^6$ metal ion in octahedral and tetrahedral fields, respectively, are :

**[2020, Main]**

(1) $-0.4\,\Delta_0$ and $-0.27\,\Delta_t$

(2) $-1.6\,\Delta_0$ and $-0.4\,\Delta_t$

(3) $-0.4\,\Delta_0$ and $-0.6\,\Delta_t$

(4) $-2.4\,\Delta_0$ and $-0.6\,\Delta_t$

**13.** The total number of coordination sites in ethylene di amine tetraacetate (EDTA$^{4-}$) is ........... .

**[2020, Main]**

**14.** The species that has a spin only magnetic moment of 5.9 BM, is : **[2020, Main]**

(1) $[Ni(CO)_4](T_d)$

(2) $[MnBr_4]^{2-}(T_d)$

(3) $[NiCl_4]^{2-}(T_d)$

(4) $[Ni(CN)_4]^{2-}$ (square planar)

**15.** Which of the following compounds shows geometrical isomerism : **[2020, Main]**

(1) 2-methylpent-2-ene

(2) 4-methylpent-1-ene

(3) 4-methylpent-2-ene

(4) 2-methylpent-1-ene

**16.** The crystal field stabilization energy (CFSE) of $[CoF_3(H_2O)_3]$ ($\Delta_0 < P$) is : **[2020, Main]**

(1) $-0.8\,\Delta_0$ 　　(2) $-0.4\,\Delta_0 + P$

(3) $-0.8\,\Delta_0 + 2P$ 　　(4) $-0.4\,\Delta_0$

**17.** The one that can exhibit highest paramagnetic behaviour among the following is :

**[2020, Main]**

(1) $[Pd(gly)_2]$

(2) $[Ti(NH_3)_6]^{3+}$

(3) $[Co(OX)_2(OH)_2]^-$ $(\Delta_0 > P)$

(4) $[Fe(en)(bpy)(NH_3)_2]^{2+}$

**18.** Consider the complex ions,

*trans*-$[Co(en)_2Cl_2]^+$ (A) and *cis*-$[Co(en)_2Cl_2]^+$ (B). The correct statement regarding them is :

**[2020, Main]**

(1) both (A) and (B) can be optically active

(2) both (A) and (B) cannot be optically active

(3) (A) can be optically active, but (B) cannot be optically active

(4) (A) cannot be optically active, but (B) can be optically active

**19.** The major product formed in the following reaction is :

$$CH_3CH = CHCH(CH_3)_2 \xrightarrow{HBR}$$ **[2020, Main]**

(1) $CH_3\,CH_2\,CH_2\,C(Br)\,(CH_3)_2$

(2) $Br(CH_2)_3\,CH(CH_3)_2$

(3) $CH_3\,CH_2\,CH(Br)\,CH(CH_3)_2$

(4) $CH_3\,CH(Br)\,CH_2\,CH(CH_3)_2$

**20.** Choose the correct statement(s) among the following : **[2020, Main]**

(1) $[FeCl_4]^-$ has tetrahedral geometry

(2) $[Co(en)(NH_3)_2Cl_2]^+$ has 2 geometrical isomers

(3) $[FeCl_4]^-$ has higher spin-only magnetic moment than $[Co(en)(NH_3)_2Cl_2]^+$

(4) The cobalt ion in $[Co(en)(NH_3)_2Cl_2]^+$ has $sp^3d^2$ hybridization

**21.** An acidified solution of potassium chromate was layered with an equal volume of amyl alcohol. When it was shaken after the addition of 1 mL of 3% $H_2O_2$, a blue alcohol layer was obtained. The blue colour is due to the formation of a chromium (VI) compound 'X'. What is the number of oxygen atoms bonded to chromium through only single bonds in a molecule of X ? **[2020, Advanced]**

**22.** Amond (a)–(d) the complexes that can display geometrical isomerism are : **[2020, Main]**

(a) $[Pt(NH_3)_3Cl]^+$ 　　(b) $[Pt(NH_3)Cl_5]^-$

(c) $[Pt(NH_3)_2Cl(NO_2)]$ 　　(d) $[Pt(NH_3)_4ClBr]^{2+}$

(1) (d) and (a) 　　(2) (a) and (b)

(3) (b) and (c) 　　(4) (c) and (d)

**23.** The correct order of the calculated spin-only magnetic moments of complexes (A) to (D) is :

**[2020, Main]**

(A) $Ni(CO)_4$ 　　(B) $[Ni(H_2O)_6]Cl_2$

(C) $Na_2[Ni(CN)_4]$ 　　(D) $PdCl_2(PPh_3)_2$

(1) (A) $\approx$ (C) $\approx$ (D) < (B)

(2) (A) $\approx$ (C) < (B) $\approx$ (D)

(3) (C) < (D) < (B) < (A)

(4) (C) $\approx$ (D) < (B) < (A)

**24.** Complexes ($ML_5$) of metals Ni and Fe have ideal square pyramidal and trigonal bipyramidal geometries, respectively. The sum of the 90°, 120° and 180° L-M L angles in the two complexes is ............... . **[2020, Main]**

**25.** The theory that can completely/properly explain the nature of bonding in $[Ni(CO)_4]$ is :

**[2020, Main]**

(1) Werner's theory

(2) Crystal field theory

(3) Valence bond theory

(4) Molecular orbital theory

**26.** The IUPAC name of the complex $[Pt(NH_3)_2Cl(NH_2CH_3)]Cl$ is : **[2020, Main]**

    (1) Diammine (methanamine) chlorido platinum (II) chloride

    (2) Bisammine (methanamine) chlorido platinum (II) chloride

    (3) Diamminechlorido (aminomethane) platinum (II) chloride

    (4) Diamminechlorido (methanamine) platinum (II) chloride

**27.** The complex that can show fac-and mer-isomers is : **[2020, Main]**

    (1) $[Pt(NH_3)_2Cl_2]$     (2) $[Co(NH_3)_4Cl_2]^+$

    (3) $[Co(NH_3)_3(NO_2)_3]$     (4) $[CoCl_2(en)_2]$

**28.** The major products A and B in the following reactions are : **[2020, Main]**

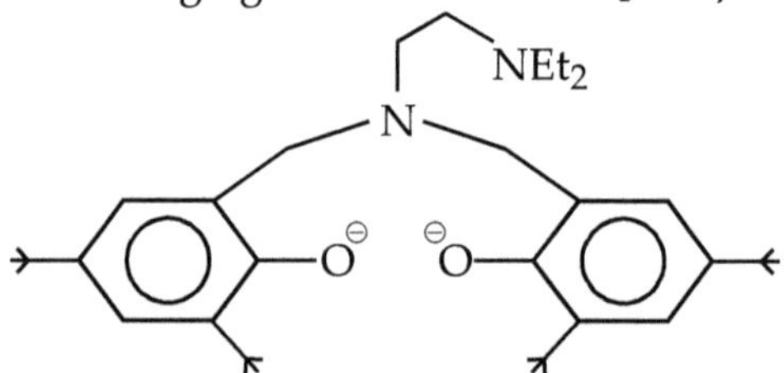

    (1) A = ... and B = ...

    (2) A = ... and B = ...

    (3) A = ... and B = ...

    (4) A = ... and B = ...

**29.** A chemist has 4 samples of artificial sweetner A, B, C and D. To identify these samples, he performed certain experiments and noted the following observations : **[2020, Main]**

    (i) A and D both form blue-violet colour with nihydrin.

    (ii) Lassaigne extract of C gives positive $AgNO_3$ test and negative $Fe_4[Fe(CN)_6]_3$ test

    (iii) Lassaigne extract of B and D gives positive sodium nitroprusside test

Based on these observations which option is correct ?

    (1) A : Aspartame : B : Saccharin : C : Sucralose : D : Alitame

    (2) A : Alitame : B : Saccharin : C : Aspartame : D : Sucralose

    (3) A : Saccharin : B : Alitame : C : Sucralose : D : Aspartame

    (4) A : Aspartame : B : Alitame : C : Saccharin : D : Sucralose

**30.** The isomer(s) of $[Co(NH_3)_4Cl_2]$ that has/have a Cl–Co–Cl angle of 90°, is/are : **[2020, Main]**

    (1) meridional and trans

    (2) cis and trans

    (3) trans only

    (4) cis only

**31.** $[Pd(F)(Cl)(Br)(I)]^{2-}$ has $n$ number of geometrical isomers. Then, the spin-only magnetic moment and crystal field stablisation energy [CFSE] of $[Fe(CN)_6]^{n-6}$, respectively are : **[2020, Main]**

[Note : Ignore and pairing energy]

    (1) 2.84 BM and $-1.6\,\Delta_0$

    (2) 1.73 BM and $-2.0\,\Delta_0$

    (3) 0 BM and $-2.4\,\Delta_0$

    (4) 5.92 BM and 0

**32.** The number of possible optical isomers for the complexes $MA_2B_2$ with $sp^3$ and $dsp^2$ hybridized metal atom, respectively, is : **[2020, Main]**

Note : A and B are unidentate neutral and unidentate monoanionic ligands, respectively.

    (1) 0 and 1     (2) 0 and 0

    (3) 2 and 2     (4) 0 and 2

**33.** Among the statements (a)-(d), the incorrect ones are : **[2020, Main]**

    (a) Octahedral Co(III) complexes with strong field ligands have very high magnetic moments

    (b) When $D_0 < P$, the $d$-electron configuration of Co(III) in an octahedral complex is $t_{eg}^4 e_g^2$

    (c) Wavelength of light absorbed by $[Co(en)_3]^{3+}$ is lower than that of $[CoF_6]^{3-}$

    (d) If the $\Delta_0$ for an octahedral complex of Co(III) is 18,000 cm$^{-1}$, the $\Delta_t$ for its tetrahedral complex with the same ligand will be 16,000 cm$^{-1}$

    (1) (b) and (c) only     (2) (a) and (b) only

    (3) (a) and (d) only     (4) (c) and (d) only

**34.** The correct order of the spin-only magnetic moment of metal ions in the following low-spin complexes, $[V(CN)_6]^{4-}$, $[Fe(CN)_6]^{4-}$, $[Ru(NH_3)_6]^{3+}$ and $[Cr(NH_3)_6]^{2+}$, is : **[2019, Main]**

    (1) $Cr^{2+} > Ru^{3+} > Fe^{2+} > V^{2+}$

    (2) $V^{2+} > Cr^{2+} > Ru^{3+} > Fe^{2+}$

    (3) $V^{2+} > Ru^{3+} > Cr^{2+} > Fe^{2+}$

    (4) $Cr^{2+} > V^{2+} > Ru^{3+} > Fe^{2+}$

**35.** The following ligand is : **[2019, Main]**



    (1) hexadentate     (2) tetradentate

    (3) bidentate     (4) tridentate

**36.** The compound that inhibits the growth of tumors is : **[2019, Main]**

    (1) $trans$-$[Pt(Cl)_2(NH_3)_2]$

    (2) $cis$-$[Pd(Cl)_2(NH_3)_2]$

    (3) $cis$-$[Pt(Cl)_2(NH_3)_2]$

    (4) $trans$-$[Pd(Cl)_2(NH_3)_2]$

**37.** The calculated spin-only magnetic moments (BM) of the anionic and cationic species of $[Fe(H_2O)_6]_2$ and $[Fe(CN)_6]$, respectively are : **[2019, Main]**

(1) 0 and 4.9      (2) 2.84 and 5.92

(3) 4.9 and 0      (4) 0 and 5.92

**38.** The number of water molecule(s) not coordinated to copper ion directly in $CuSO_4.5H_2O$ is :

**[2019, Main]**

(1) 2      (2) 3

(3) 1      (4) 4

**39.** The one that will show optical activity is :

(en = ethane-1,2-diamine)      **[2019, Main]**

(1) 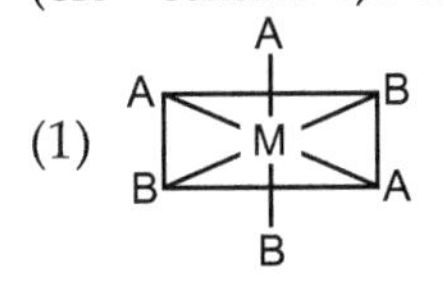      (2) 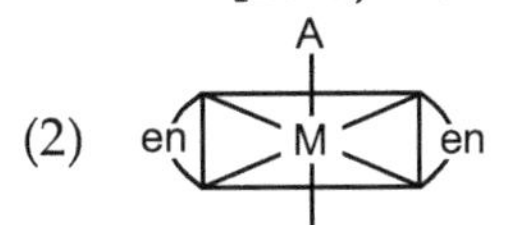

(3) 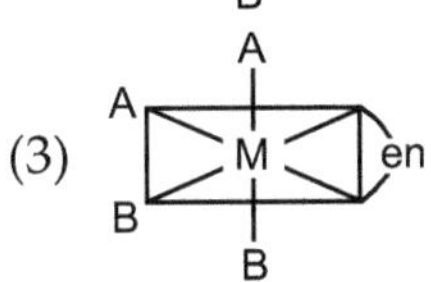      (4) 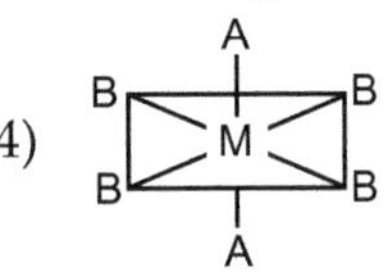

**40.** The degenerate orbitals of $[Cr(H_2O)_6]^{3+}$ are :

**[2019, Main]**

(1) $d_{xz}$ and $d_{yz}$      (2) $d_{yz}$ and $d_{z^2}$

(3) $d_{z^2}$ and $d_{xz}$      (4) $d_{x^2-y^2}$ and $d_{xy}$

**41.** The correct statements among I to III are :

**[2019, Main]**

(I) Valence bond theory cannot explain the colour exhibited by transition metal complexes.

(II) Valence bnd they can predict quantitatively are magnetic properties of transition metal complexes.

(III) Valence bond theory cannot distinguish ligands as weak and strong field ones.

(1) (II) and (III) only      (2) (I), (II) and (III)

(3) (I) and (III) only      (4) (I) and (II) only

**42.** The maximum possible denticities of a ligand given below towards a common transition and iner-transition metal ion, respectively, are :

**[2019, Main]**

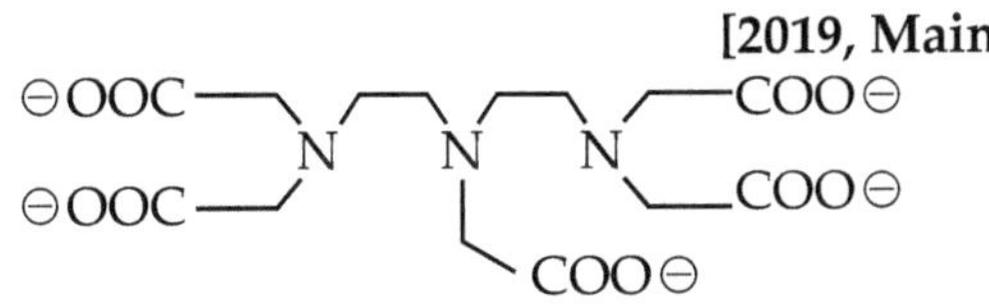

(1) 8 and 6      (2) 6 and 8

(3) 6 and 8      (4) 8 and 8

**43.** The species that can have a *trans*-isomer is :

(en = ethane, 1, 2-diamine, ox = oxalate)

(1) $[Zn(en)Cl_2]$      (2) $[Pt(en)Cl_2]$

(3) $[Cr(en)_2(ox)]^+$      (4) $[Pt(en)_2Cl_2]^{2+}$

**44.** Consider the hydrated ions of $Ti^{2+}$, $V^{2+}$, $Ti^{3+}$ and $Sc^{3+}$. The correct order of their spin-only magnetic moments is : **[2019, Main]**

(1) $V^{2+} < Ti^{2+} < Ti^{3+} < Sc^{3+}$

(2) $Sc^{3+} < Ti^{3+} < Ti^{2+} < V^{2+}$

(3) $Ti^{3+} < Ti^{2+} < Sc^{3+} < V^{2+}$

(4) $Sc^{3+} < Ti^{3+} < V^{2+} < Ti^{2+}$

**45.** Three complexes,

$[CoCl(NH_3)_5]^{2+}$ (I),

$[Co(NH_3)_5H_2O]^{3+}$ (II) and

$[Co(NH_3)_6]^{3+}$ (III)

absorb light in the visible region. The correct order of the wavelength of light absorbed by them is :

(1) (III) > (I) > (II)      (2) (III) > (II) > (I)

(3) (II) > (I) > (III)      (4) (I) > (II) > (III)

**46.** The crystal field of stablisation energy (CFSE) of $[Fe(H_2O)_6]Cl_2$ and $K_2[NiCl_4]$, respectively are :

**[2019, Main]**

(1) $-0.6\,\Delta_o$ and $-0.8\Delta_t$      (2) $-0.4\,\Delta_o$ and $-0.8\Delta_t$

(3) $-2.4\,\Delta_o$ and $-1.2\Delta_t$      (4) $-0.4\,\Delta_o$ and $-1.2\Delta_t$

**47.** The INCORRECT statement is :      **[2019, Main]**

(1) the gemstone, ruby, has $Cr^{3+}$ ions occupying the octahedral sites of beryl.

(2) the spin-only magnetic moment of $[Ni(NH_3)_4(H_2O)_2]^{2+}$ is 2.83 BM.

(3) the colour of $[CoCl(NH_3)_5]^{2+}$ is violet as it absorbs the yellow light.

(4) the spin-only magnetic moments of $[Fe(H_2O)_6]^{2+}$ and $[Cr(H_2O)_6]^{2+}$ are nearly similar.

**48.** The complex ion that will lose its crystal field stabilisation energy upon oxidation of its metal to + 3 state is :      **[2019, Main]**

(Phen = 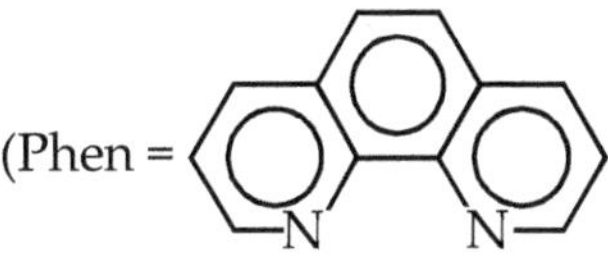

and

ignore pairing energy)

(1) $[Co(phen)_3]^{2+}$      (2) $[Ni(phen)_3]^{2+}$

(3) $[Zn(phen)_3]^{2+}$      (4) $[Fe(phen)_3]^{2+}$

**49.** Complete removal of both the axial ligands (along the $z$-axis) from an octahedral complex leads to which of the following splitting patterns ? (relative orbital energies not on scale).

**[2019, Main]**

(1) $E$
— $d_{x^2-y^2}$
— $d_{xy}$
— $d_{z^2}$
= $d_{xz}, d_{yz}$

(2) $E$
— $d_{z^2}$
— $d_{x^2-y^2}$
= $d_{xz}, d_{yz}$
— $d_{xy}$

**50.** The compound used in the treatment of lead poisoning is :      **[2019, Main]**

(1) D-penicillamine      (2) desferrioxime B

(3) *Cis*-platin      (4) EDTA

**51.** The coordination numbers of Co and Al in $[Co(Cl)(en)_2]Cl$ and $K_3[Al(C_2O_4)_3]$, respectively, are : (en = ethane-1, 2-diamine)

(1) 5 and 3      (2) 3 and 3

(3) 6 and 6      (4) 5 and 6

**52.** Total number of *cis* N–Mn–Cl bond angles (that is, Mn–N and Mn–Cl bonds in *cis* positions) present in a molecule of *cis*-$[Mn(en)_2Cl_2]$ complex is ....... (*en*–$NH_2CH_2CH_2NH_2$)      **[2019, Advanced]**

**53.** A tin chloride Q undergoes the following reactions (not balanced)

$$Q + Cl \rightarrow X$$
$$Q + Me_2N \rightarrow Y$$
$$Q + CuCl_2 \rightarrow Z + CuCl$$

X is a monoanium having pyramidal geometry. Both Y and Z are neutral compounds. Choose the correct option(s) : **[2019, Advanced]**

(1) The central atom in X is $sp^3$ hybridised

(2) There is a coordinate boind in Y

(3) The oxidation state of the central atom in Z is $+2$

(4) The central atom in Z has one lone pair of electrons

**54.** The correct statements regarding the binary transition metal carbonyl compounds is/are :

**[2018, Advanced]**

(Atomic numbers : Fe = 26, Ni = 28)

(1) Total number of valence shell electrons at metal centre in $Fe(CO)_5$ or $Ni(CO)_4$ is 16

(2) These are predominantly low spin in nature

(3) Metal-carboin bond strengthens when the oxidation state of the metal is lowered

(4) The carbonyl C–O boind weakens when the oxidation state of the metal is increased

**55.** The correct options regarding the complex $[Co(en)(NH_3)_3(H_2O)]^{3+}$ **[2018, Advanced]**

(en = $H_2NCH_2CH_2NH_2$) is/are :

(1) It has two geometrical isomers

(2) It will have three geometrical isomers if bidentate 'en' is replaced by two cyanide ligands

(3) It is paramagnetic

(4) It absorbs light at longer wavelength as compared to $[Co(en)(NH_3)_4]^{3+}$

**56.** Match each set of hybrid orbitals from List-I with complexes given in List-II. **[2018, Advanced]**

| List-I | | List-II |
|---|---|---|
| P. | $dsp^2$ | 1. | $[FeF_6]^{4-}$ |
| Q. | $sp^2$ | 2. | $[Ti(H_2O)_3Cl_3]$ |
| R. | $sp^3d^2$ | 3. | $[Cr(NH_3)_6]^{3+}$ |
| S. | $d^2sp^3$ | 4. | $[FeCl_4]^{2-}$ |
| | | 5. | $Ni(CO)_4$ |
| | | 6. | $[Ni(CN)_4]^{2-}$ |

The correct option is :

(1) P → 5; Q → 4, 6; R → 2, 3; S → 1

(2) P → 5, 6; Q → 4, R → 3; S → 1, 2

(3) P → 6; Q → 4, 5; R → 1; S → 2, 3

(4) P → 4, 6; Q → 5, 6; R → 1, 2; S → 3

**57.** The recommended concentration of fluoride ion in drinking water is up to 1 ppm as fluoride ion is required to make teeth enamel harder by converting $[3Ca_3(PO_4)_2.Ca(OH)_2]$ to :

**[2018, Main]**

(1) $[CaF_2]$

(2) $[3(CaF_2).Ca(OH)_2]$

(3) $[3Ca_3(PO_4)_2.CaF_2]$

(4) $[3\{Ca(OH)_2\}.CaF_2]$

**58.** The oxidation states of Cr in $[Cr(H_2O)_6]Cl_3$, $[Cr(C_6H_6)_2]$ and $K_2[Cr(CN)_2(O)_2(NH_3)]$ respectively are : **[2018, Main]**

(1) $+3, +4$ and $+6$    (2) $+3, +2$ and $+4$

(3) $+3, 0$ and $+6$    (4) $+3, 0,$ and $+4$

**59.** Consider the following reaction and statements :

**[2018, Main]**

$$[Co(NH_3)_4Br_2]^+ + Br^- \rightarrow [Co(NH_3)_3Br_3] + NH_3$$

(I) Two isomers are produced if the reactant complex ion is a *cis*-isomer

(II) Two isomers are produced if the reactant complex ion is a *trans*-isomer

(III) Only one isomer is produced if the reactant complex ion is a *trans*-isomer

(IV) Only one isomer is produced if the reactant complex ion is a *cis*-isomer

The correct statements are :

(1) (I) and (II)    (2) (I) and (III)

(3) (III) and (IV)    (4) (II) and (IV)

**60.** The total number of possible isomers for square-planar $[Pt(Cl)(NO_2)(NO_3)(SCN)]^{2-}$ is :

**[2018, Main]**

(1) 8    (2) 12

(3) 16    (4) 24

**61.** The correct combination is : **[2018, Main]**

(1) $[Ni(CN)_4]^{2-}$-tetrahedral; $[Ni(CO)_4]$-paramagnetic

(2) $[NiCl_4]^{2-}$-paramagnetic; $[Ni(CO)_4]$-tetrahderal

(3) $[Ni(Cl)_4]^{2-}$-square-planar; $[Ni(CN)_4]^{2-}$-paramagnetic

(4) $[NiCl_4]^{2-}$-diamagnetic; $[Ni(CO)_4]$-square-planar

**62.** In Wilkinson's catalyst, the hybridisation of central metal ion and its shape are respectively :

**[2018, Main]**

(1) $sp^3d$, trigonal bipyramidal

(2) $sp^3$, tetrahedral

(3) $dsp^2$, square planar

(4) $d^2sp^3$, octahedral

**63.** Which of the following complexes will show geometrical isomerism ? **[2018, Main]**

(1) aquachlorobis (ethylenediamine) cobalt(II) chloride

(2) pentaaquachlorochromium(III) chloride

(3) potassium amminetrichloroplatinate(II)

(4) potassium tris(oxalato)chromate(III)

**64.** In a complexometric titration of metal ion with ligand M(Metal ion) + L(Ligand) → C(Complex) end point is estimated spectrophoto-metrically (through light absorption). If 'M' and 'C' do not absorb light and only 'L' absorbs, then the titration plot between absorbed light (A) versus volume of ligand 'L' (V) would look like : **[2018, Main]**

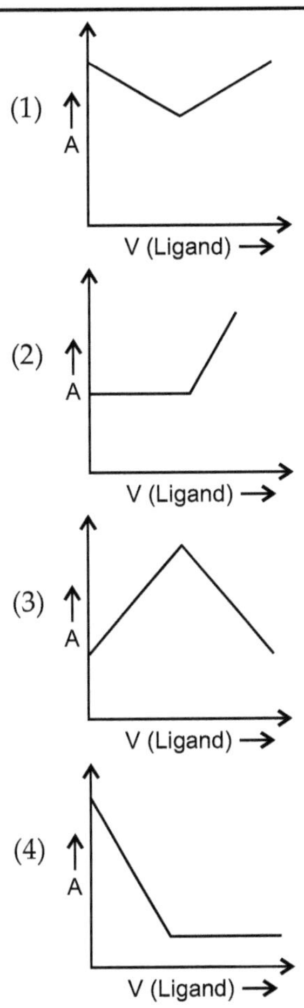

(1) $A$ — V (Ligand) →

(2) $A$ — V (Ligand) →

(3) $A$ — V (Ligand) →

(4) $A$ — V (Ligand) →

**65.** Addition of excess aqueous ammonia to a pink coloured aqueous solution of $MCl.6H_2O$ (X) and $NH_4Cl$ gives an octahedral complex Y in the presence of air. In aqueous solution, complex Y behaves as 1 : 3 electrolyte. The reaction of X with excess HCl at room temperature results in the formation of a blue coloured complex Z. The calculated spin only magnetic moment of X and Z is 3.87 B.M., whereas it zero for complex Y. Among the following options, which statements is/are correct ? **[2017, Advanced]**
(1) Addition of silver nitrate to Y gives only two equivalents of silver chloride
(2) The hybridisation of the central metal ion in Y is $d^2sp^3$
(3) Z is a tetrahedral complex
(4) When X and Z are in equilibrium at 0°C, the colour of the solution is pink

**66.** The sum of the number of lone pairs of electrons on each central atom in the following species is :
$[TeBr_6]^{2-}$, $[BrF_2]^+$, $SNF_3$ and $[XeF_3]^-$
(Atomic numebrs : N = 7, F = 9, S = 16, Br = 35, Te = 52, Xe = 54) **[2017, Advanced]**

**67.** On treatment of 100 mL of 0.1 M solution of $CoCl_3.6H_2O$ with excess $AgNO_3$; $1.2 \times 10^{22}$ ions are precipitated. The complex is : **[2017, Main]**
(1) $[Co(H_2O)_6]Cl_3$
(2) $[Co(H_2O)_5Cl]Cl_2.H_2O$
(3) $[Co(H_2O)_4Cl_2]Cl.2H_2O$
(4) $[Co(H_2O)_3Cl_3].3H_2O$

**68.** A metal 'M' reacts with nitrogen gas to afford '$M_3N$'. '$M_3N$' on heating at high temperature gives back 'M' and on reaction with water produces a gas 'B'. Gas 'B' reacts with aqueous solution of $CuSO_4$ to form a deep blue compound. 'M' and 'B' respectively are : **[2017, Main]**
(1) Li and $NH_3$
(2) Ba and $N_2$
(3) Na and $NH_3$
(4) Al and $N_2$

**69.** $[Co_2(CO)_8]$ displays : **[2017, Main]**
(1) one Co – Co bond, six terminal CO and two bridging CO
(2) one Co – Co bond, four terminal CO and four bridging CO
(3) no Co – Co bond, six terminal CO and two bridging CO
(4) no Co – Co bond, four terminal CO and four bridging CO

**70.** Among $[Ni(CO)_4]$, $[NiCl_4]^{2-}$, $[Co(NH_3)_4 Cl_2]Cl$, $Na_3[COF_6]$, $Na_2O_2$ and $CsO_2$, the total number of paramagnetic compounds is : **[2016, Advanced]**
(1) 2
(2) 3
(3) 4
(4) 5

**71.** The number of geometric isomers possible for the complex $[CoL_2Cl_2]^-$ ($L = H_2NCH_2CH_2O^-$) is. **[2016, Advanced]**

**72.** In the following reaction sequence in aqueous solution, the species X, Y and Z, respectively, are : **[2016, Advanced]**

$$S_2O_3^{2-} \xrightarrow{Ag^+} \underset{\substack{\text{clear}\\ \text{precipitate}}}{X} \xrightarrow{Ag^+} \underset{\substack{\text{white}\\ \text{precipitate}}}{Y}$$

$$\xrightarrow{\text{with time}} \underset{\substack{\text{black}\\ \text{precipitate}}}{Z}$$

(1) $[Ag(S_2O_3)_2]^{3-}$, $Ag_2S_2O_3$, $Ag_2S$
(2) $[Ag(S_2O_3)_3]^{5-}$, $Ag_2SO_3$, $Ag_2S$
(3) $[Ag(S_2O_3)_2]^{3-}$, $Ag_2S_2O_3$, Ag
(4) $[Ag(SO_3)_3]^{3-}$, $Ag_2SO_4$, Ag

**73.** The geometries of the ammonia complexes of $Ni^{2+}$, $Pt^{2+}$ and $Zn^{2+}$, respectively, are : **[2016, Advanced]**
(1) octahedral, square planar and tetrahedral
(2) square planar, octahedral and tetrahedral
(3) tetrahedral, square planar and octahedral
(4) octahedral, tetrahedral and square planar

**74.** Which one of the following complexes will consume more equivalents of aqueous solution of $Ag(NO_3)$ ? **[2016, Main]**
(1) $Na_3[CrCl_6]$
(2) $[Cr(H_2O)_5Cl]Cl_2$
(3) $[Cr(H_2O)_6]Cl_3$
(4) $Na_2[CrCl_5(H_2O)]$

**75.** Identify the correct trend given below :
(Atomic No. = Ti : 22, Cr : 24 and Mo : 42) **[2016, Main]**
(1) $\Delta_0$ of $[Cr(H_2O)_6]^{2+} > [Mo(H_2O_6]^{2+}$ and $\Delta_0$ of $[Ti(H_2O_6]^{3+} > [Ti(H_2O)_6]^{2+}$

(2) $\Delta_0$ of $[Cr(H_2O)_6]^{2+} > [Mo(H_2O_6]^{2+}$ and $\Delta_0$ of $[Ti(H_2O_6)]^{3+} < [Ti(H_2O)_6]^{2+}$

(3) $\Delta_0$ of $[Cr(H_2O)_6]^{2+} < [Mo(H_2O_6]^{2+}$ and $\Delta_0$ of $[Ti(H_2O_6)]^{3+} < [Ti(H_2O)_6]^{2+}$

(4) $\Delta_0$ of $[Cr(H_2O)_6]^{2+} < [Mo(H_2O)_6]^{2+}$ and $\Delta_0$ of $[Ti(H_2O)_6]^{3+} < [Ti(H_2O)_6]^{2+}$

**76.** Which of the following is an example of homoleptic complex ? **[2016, Main]**

(1) $[Co(NH_3)_6]Cl_3$

(2) $[Pt(NH_3)_2Cl_2]$

(3) $[Co(NH_3)_4Cl_2]$

(4) $[Co(NH_3)_5Cl]Cl_2$

**77.** The transition metal ions responsible for colour in ruby and emerald are, respectively : **[2016, Main]**

(1) $Cr^{3+}$ and $Co^{3+}$ 　　(2) $Co^{3+}$ and $Cr^{3+}$

(3) $Cr^{3+}$ and $Co^{3+}$ 　　(4) $Cr^{3+}$ and $Cr^{3+}$

**78.** The pair having the same magnetic moment is : [At. No. : Cr = 24, Mn = 25, Fe = 26, Co = 27] **[2016, Main]**

(1) $[Cr(H_2O)_6]^{2+}$ and $[CoCl_4]^{2-}$

(2) $[Cr(H_2O)_6]^{2+}$ and $[Fe(H_2O)_6]^{2+}$

(3) $[Mn(H_2O)_6]^{2+}$ and $[Cr(H_2O)_6]^{2+}$

(4) $[CoCl_4]^{2-}$ and $[Fe(H_2O)_6]^{2+}$

**79.** Which one of the following complexes shows optical isomerism ? **[2016, Main]**

(1) $[Co(NH_3)_3Cl_3]$

(2) $cis[Co(en)_2Cl_2]Cl$

(3) $trans[Co(en)_2Cl_2]Cl$

(4) $[Co(NH_3)_4Cl_2]Cl$

(en = ethylenediamine)

**80.** For the octahedral complexes of $Fe^{3+}$ in $SCN^-$ (thiocyanato-S) and in $CN^-$ ligand environments, the difference between the spin-only magnetic moments in Bohr magnetons (when approximated to the nearest integer) is : [Atomic number of Fe = 26] **[2015, Advanced]**

**81.** In the complex acetylbromidodicarbonylbis (triethylphosphine)iron(II), the number of Fe–C bonds is. **[2015, Advanced]**

**82.** Among the complex ions, $[Co(NH_2\text{-}CH_2\text{-}CH_2\text{-}NH_2)_2Cl_2]^+$, $[CrCl_2(C_2O_4)_2]^{3-}$, $[Fe(H_2O)_4(OH)_2]^+$, $[Fe(NH_3)_2(CN)_4]^-$, $[Co)NH_2\text{-}CH_2\text{-}CH_2\text{-}NH_2)_2$ $(NH_3)Cl]^{2+}$ and $[Co(NH_3)_4(H_2O)Cl]^{2+}$, the number of complex ions that shows *cis-trans* isomerism is. **[2015, Advanced]**

**83.** In dilute aqueous $H_2SO_4$, the complex diaquodioxalatoferrate(II) is oxidsed by $MnO_4^-$. For this reaction, the ratio of the rate of change of $[H^+]$ to the rate of change of $[MnO_4^-]$ is. **[2015, Advanced]**

**84.** The number of geometric isomers that can exist for square planar $[Pt(Cl)(py)(NH_3)(NH_2OH)]^+$ is (*py* = pyridine) : **[2015, Main]**

(1) 2 　　　　(2) 3

(3) 4 　　　　(4) 6

**85.** Which of the following compounds is not coloured yellow ? **[2015, Main]**

(1) $Zn_2[Fe(CN)_6]$ 　　(2) $K_3[Co(NO_2)_6]$

(3) $(NH_4)_3[As(Mo_3O_{10})_4]$ (4) $BaCrO_4$

**86.** An aqueous solution of a salt X turns blood red on treatment with $SCN^-$ and blue on treatment with $K_4[Fe(CN)_6]$. X also gives a positive chromyl chloride test. The salt X is : **[2015, Main]**

(1) $CuCl_2$ 　　　　(2) $FeCl_3$

(3) $Cu(NO_3)_2$ 　　(4) $Fe(NO_3)_3$

**87.** Which molecule/ion among the following cannot act as a ligand in complex compounds ? **[2015, Main]**

(1) CO 　　　　(2) $CN^-$

(3) $CH_4$ 　　　　(4) $Br^-$

**88.** The correct statement on the isomerism associated with the following complex ions **[2015, Main]**

(a) $[Ni(H_2O)_5NH_3]^{2+}$

(b) $[Ni(H_2O)_4(NH_3)_2]^{2+}$ and

(c) $[Ni(H_2O)_3(NH_3)_3]^{2+}$ is :

(1) (a) and (b) show only geometrical optical isomerism

(2) (a) and (b) show geometrical and optical isomerism

(3) (b) and (c) show geometrical and optical isomerism

(4) (b) and (c) show only geometrical isomerism

**89.** When concentrated HCl is added to an aqueous solution of $CoCl_2$, its colour changes from reddish pink to deep blue. Which complex ion gives blue colour in this reaction ? **[2015, Main]**

(1) $[CoCl_6]^{4-}$ 　　(2) $[CoCl_6]^{3-}$

(3) $[CoCl_4]^{2-}$ 　　(4) $[Co(H_2O)_6]^{2+}$

**90.** Which of the following complex ions has electrons that are symmetrically filled in both $t_{2g}$ and $e_g$ orbitals ? **[2015, Main]**

(1) $[CoF_6]^{3-}$ 　　(2) $[Co(NH_3)_6]^{2+}$

(3) $[Mn(CN)_6]^{4-}$ 　　(4) $[FeF_6]^{3-}$

**91.** A list of species having the formula $XZ_4$ is given below. **[2014, Advanced]**

$XeF_4$, $SF_4$, $SiF_4$, $BF_4^-$, $BrF_4^-$ $[Cu(NH_3)_4]^{2+}$, $[FeCl_4]^{2-}$, $[CoCl_4]^{2-}$ and $[PtCl_4]^{2-}$.

Defining shape on the basis of the location of X and Z atoms, the total number of species having a square planar shape is.

**92.** M1, Q and R, respectively are : **[2014, Advanced]**

(1) $Zn^{2+}$, KCN and HCl

(2) $Ni^{2+}$, HCl and KCN

(3) $Cd^{2+}$, KCN and HCl

(4) $Co^{2+}$, HCl, and KCN

**93.** Reagent S is : **[2014, Advanced]**

(1) $K_4[Fe(CN)_6]$ 　　(2) $Na_2HPO_4$

(3) $K_2CrO_4$ 　　　　(4) KOH

**94.** Match each coordination compound in List-I with an appropriate pair of characteristics from List-II and select the correct answer using the code given below the lists. **[2014, Advanced]**

{en = $H_2NCH_2CH_2NH_2$; atomic numbers: Ti = 22; Cr = 24; Co = 27; Pt = 78}

| List-I | List-II |
|---|---|
| P. $[Cr(NH_3)_4Cl_2]Cl$ | 1. Paramagnetic and exhibits ionisation isomerism |
| Q. $[Ti(H_2O)_5Cl](NO_3)_2$ | 2. Diamagnetic and exhibits cis-trans isomerism |
| R. $[Pt(en)(NH_3)Cl]NO_3$ | 3. Paramagnetic and exhibits cis-trans isomerism |
| S. $[Co(NH_3)_4(NO_3)_2]NO_3$ | 4. Diamagnetic and exhibits ionisation isomerism |

|  | P | Q | R | S |
|---|---|---|---|---|
| (1) | 4 | 2 | 3 | 1 |
| (2) | 3 | 1 | 4 | 2 |
| (3) | 2 | 1 | 3 | 4 |
| (4) | 1 | 3 | 4 | 2 |

**95.** The octahedral complex of a metal ion $M^{3+}$ with four monodentate ligands $L_1$, $L_2$, $L_3$ and $L_4$ absorb wavelengths in the region of red, green, yellow and blue, respectively. The increasing order of ligand strength of the four length is : **[2014, Main]**

(1) $L_4 < L_3 < L_2 < L_1$  (2) $L_1 < L_3 < L_2 < L_4$
(3) $L_3 < L_2 < L_4 < L_1$  (4) $L_1 < L_2 < L_4 < L_3$

**96.** The equation which is balanced and represents the correct products is : **[2014, Main]**

(1) $Li_2O + 2KCl \rightarrow 2LiCl + K_2O$
(2) $[CoCl(NH_3)_5]^+ + 5H^+ \rightarrow Co^{2+} + 5NH_4^+ + Cl^-$
(3) $[Mg(H_2O_6)]^{2-} + (EDTA)^{4-} \xrightarrow{\text{excess NaOH}}$
$[Mg(EDTA)^{2+} + 6H_2O$
(4) $CuSO_4 + 4KCN \rightarrow K_2[Cu(CN)_4] + K_2SO_4$

**97.** An octahderal complex of $Co^{3+}$ is diamagnetic. The hybridisation involved in the formation of the complex is : **[2014, Main]**

(1) $sp^3d^2$  (2) $dsp^2$
(3) $d^2sp^3$  (4) $dsp^3d$

**98.** The correct statement about the magnetic properties of $[Fc(CN)_6]^{3-}$ and $[FeF_6]^{3-}$ is : (Z = 26) **[2014, Main]**

(1) both are paramagnetic
(2) both are diamagnetic
(3) $[Fe(CN)_6]^{3-}$ is diamagnetic, $[FeF_6]^{3-}$ is paramagnetic
(4) $[Fe(CN)_6]^{3-}$ is paramagnetic, $[FeF_6]^{3-}$ is diamagnetic

**99.** Which of the following name formula combinations is not correct ? **[2014, Main]**

| | Formula | Name |
|---|---|---|
| (1) | $K_2[Pt(CH)_4]$ | Potassium tetracyanoplatinate(II) |
| (2) | $[Mn(CN)_5]^{2-}$ | Pentacyanomagnate(II) ion |
| (3) | $K[Cr(NH_3)_2Cl_4]$ | Potassium diammine tetrachlorochromate(III) |
| (4) | $[Co(NH_3)_4(H_2O)I]SO_4$ | Tetraammine aquaiodo cobalt(III) sulphate |

**100.** Consider the coordination compound, $[Co(NH_3)_6]Cl_3$. In the formation of this complex, the species whcih acts as the Lewis acid is : **[2014, Main]**

(1) $[Co(NH_3)_6]^{3+}$  (2) $Cl^-$
(3) $Co^{3+}$  (4) $NH_3$

**101.** Among the following species the one which causes the highest CFSE, $\Delta_0$ as a ligand is : **[2014, Main]**

(1) $CN^-$  (2) $NH_3$
(3) $F^-$  (4) $CO$

**102.** Which one of the following complexes will most likely absorb visible light ? **[2014, Main]**

(At nos. Sc =21, Ti = 22, V = 23, Zn = 30)

(1) $[Sc(H_2O)_6]^{3+}$  (2) $[Ti(NH_3)_6]^{4+}$
(3) $[V(NH_3)_6]^{3+}$  (4) $[Zn(NH_3)_6]^{2+}$

**103.** An octahedral complex with molecular composition $M.5NH_3.Cl.SO_4$ has two isomers, A and B. The solution of A gives a white precipitae with $AgNO_3$ solution and the solution of B gives white precipitate with $BaCl_2$ solution. The type of isomerism exhibited by the complex is : **[2014, Main]**

(1) Linkage isomerism
(2) Ionisation isomerism
(3) Coordinate isomerism
(4) Geometrical isomerism

**104.** Nickel(Z = 28) combines with a uninegative monodenate ligand toi form a diamagnetic complex $[NiL_4]^{2-}$. The hybridisation involved and the number of unpaired electrons present in the complex are respectively : **[2014, Main]**

(1) $sp^3$, two  (2) $dsp^2$, zero
(3) $dsp^2$, one  (4) $sp^3$, zero

**105.** Consider the following complex ions, P, Q and R. $P = [FeF_6]^{3-}$, $Q = [V(H_2O)_6]^{2+}$ and $R = [Fe(H_2O)_6]^{2+}$. The correct order of the complex ions, according to their spin-only magnetic moment values (in B.M.) is : **[2013, Advanced]**

(1) $R < Q < P$  (2) $Q < R < P$
(3) $R < P < Q$  (4) $Q < P < R$

**106.** The pairs of coordination complexes/ions exhibiting the same kind of isomerism is/are : **[2013, Advanced]**

   (1) $[Cr(NH_3)_5Cl]Cl_2$ and $[Cr(NH_3)_4Cl_2]Cl$

   (2) $[Co(NH_3)_4Cl_2]^+$ and $[Pt(NH_3)_2(H_2O)Cl]^+$

   (3) $[CoBr_2Cl_2]^{2-}$ and $[PtBr_2Cl_2]^{2-}$

   (4) $[Pt(NH_3)_3(NO_3)]Cl$ and $[Pt(NH_3)_3Cl]Br$

**107.** EDTA$^{4-}$ is ethylenediaminetetraacetate ion. The total number of N–Co–O bond angles in $[Co(EDTA)]^{1-}$ complex ion is. **[2013, Advanced]**

**108.** As per IUPAC nomenclature, the name of the complex $[Co(H_2O)_4(NH_3)_2]Cl_3$ is : **[2012, Advanced]**

   (1) Tetraaquadiaminecobalt(III) chloride

   (2) Tetraaquadiamminecobalt(III) chloride

   (3) Diaminetetraaquacobalt(III) chloride

   (4) Diamminetetraaquacobalt(III) chloride

**109.** $NiCl_2\{P(C_2H_5)_2(C_6H_5)\}_2$ exhibits temperature dependent magnetic behaviour (paramagnetic/diamagnetic). The coordination geometries of $Ni^{2+}$ in the paramagnetic and diamagnetic states are respectively : **[2012, Advanced]**

   (1) tetrahedral and tetrahedral

   (2) square planar and square planar

   (3) tetrahedral and square planar

   (4) square planar and tetrahedral

**110.** Geometrical shapes of the complexes formed by the reaction of $Ni^{2+}$ with $Cl^-$, $CN^-$ and $H_2O$, respectively, are : **[2011, Advanced]**

   (1) octahedral, tetrahderal and square planar

   (2) tetrahderal, square planar and octahedral

   (3) square planar, tetrahedral and octahedral

   (4) octahedral, square planar and octahedral

**111.** The final solution contains : **[2011, Advanced]**

   (1) $[Pb(NH_3)_4]^{2+}$ and $[CoCl_4]^{2-}$

   (2) $[Al(NH_3)_4]^{3+}$ and $[Cu(NH_3)_4]^{2+}$

   (3) $[Ag(NH_3)_2]^+$ and $[Cu(NH_3)_4]^{2+}$

   (4) $[Ag(NH_3)_2]^+$ and $[Ni(NH_3)_6]^{2+}$

**112.** Among the following complexes (K–P), $K_3[Fe(CN)_6]$ (K), $[Co(NH_3)_6]Cl_3$ (L), $Na_3[Co(oxalate)_3]$ (M), $(NI(H_2O)_6]Cl_2$ (N), $K_2[Pt(CN)_4]$ (O) and $[Zn(H_2O)_6]$ $(NO_3)_2$ (P) **[2011, Advanced]**

   (1) K, L, M, N       (2) K, M, O, P

   (3) L, M, O, P       (4) L, M, N, O

**113.** The correct structure of ethylenediaminetetra-acetic acid (EDTA) is : **[2010, Advanced]**

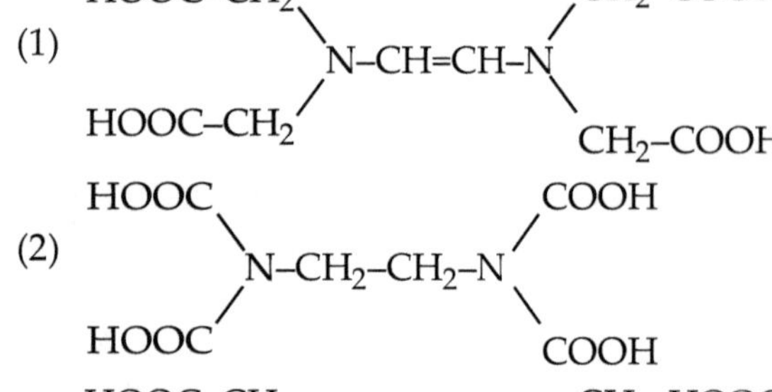

**114.** The ionisation isomer of $[Cr(H_2O)_4Cl(NO_2)]Cl$ is : **[2010, Advanced]**

   (1) $[Cr(H_2O)_4(O_2N)]Cl_2$

   (2) $[Cr(H_2O)_4Cl_2](NO_2)$

   (3) $[Cr(H_2O)_4Cl(ONO)]Cl$

   (4) $[Cr(H_2O)_4Cl_2(NO_2)].H_2O$

**115.** The complex showing a spin-only magnetic moment of 2.82 B.M. is : **[2010, Advanced]**

   (1) $Ni(CO)_4$       (2) $[NiCl_4]^{2-}$

   (3) $Ni(PPh_3)_4$       (4) $[Ni(CN)_4]^{2-}$

**116.** The compounds that exhibits geometrical isomerism is/are : **[2009, Advanced]**

   (1) $[Pt(en)Cl_2]$       (2) $[Pt(en)_2]Cl_2$

   (3) $[Pt(en)_2Cl_2]Cl_2$       (4) $[Pt(NH_3)_2Cl_2]$

**117.** The spin only magnetic moment value (in Bohr magneton units) of $Cr(CO)_6$ is : **[2009, Advanced]**

   (1) 0       (2) 2.84

   (3) 4.90       (4) 5.92

**118.** The number of water molecules directly bonded to the metal centre in $CuSO_4.5H_2O$ is. **[2008, Advanced]**

**119.** Native silver metal forms a water soluble complex with a dilute aqueous solution of NaCN in the presence of : **[2008, Advanced]**

   (1) nitrogen       (2) oxygen

   (3) carbon dioxide       (4) argon

**120.** Both $[Ni(CO)_4]$ and $[Ni(CN)_4]^{2-}$ are diamagnetic. The hybridisations of nickel in these complexes, respectively, are : **[2008, Advanced]**

   (1) $sp^3, sp^3$       (2) $sp^3, dsp^2$

   (3) $dsp^2, sp^3$       (4) $dsp^2, dsp^2$

**121.** The IUPAC name of $[Ni(NH_3)_4] [NiCl_4]$ is : **[2008, Advanced]**

   (1) Tetrachloronickel(II)-tetraamminenickel(II)

   (2) Tetraachloronickel(II)-tetrachloronickel(II)

   (3) Tetraamminenickel(II)-tetrachloro-nickelate(II)

   (4) Tetrachloronickel(II)-tetraammine-nickelete(0)

**122. Statement-1 :** $[Fe(H_2O_5NO]SO_4$ is paramagnetic. and

**Statement-2 :** The Fe in $[Fe(H_2O)_5NO]SO_4$ has three unpaired electrons. **[2008, Advanced]**

   (1) Statement-1 is True, Statement-2 is True, Statement-2 is a correct explanation for Statement-1

(2) Statement-1 is True, Statement-2 is True, Statement-2 is NOT a correct explanation for Statement-1

(3) Statement-1 is True, Statement-2 is False

(4) Statement-1 is False, Statement-2 is True

**123. Statement-1 :** The geometrical isomers oif the complex $[M(NH_3)_4Cl_2]$ are optically inactive.

and

**Statement-2 :** Both geometrical isomers oif the complex $[M(NH_3)_4Cl_2]$ possess axis of symmetry.
**[2008, Advanced]**

(1) Statement-1 is True, Statement-2 is True, Statement-2 is a correct explanation for Statement-1

(2) Statement-1 is True, Statement-2 is True, Statement-2 is NOT a correct explanation for Statement-1

(3) Statement-1 is True, Statement-2 is False

(4) Statement-1 is False, Statement-2 is True

**124.** Match the complexes in Column I with their properties listed in Column II. Indicate your answer by darkening the appropriate bubbles of the 4 × 4 matrix given in the ORS.
**[2007, Advanced]**

| Column I | | Column II |
|---|---|---|
| (1) $[Co(NH_3)_4(H_2O)_2]Cl_2$ | (p) | geometrical isomers |
| (2) $[Pt(NH_3)_2Cl_2]$ | (q) | paramagnetic |
| (3) $[Co(H_2O)_5Cl]Cl$ | (r) | diamagnetic |
| (4) $[Ni(H_2O)_6]Cl_2$ | (s) | metal ion with +2 oxiation state |

**125.** Among the following metal carbonyls, the C–O bond order is lowest in :
**[2007, Advanced]**

(1) $[Mn(CO)_6]^+$  (2) $[Fe(CO)_5]$

(3) $[Cr(CO)_6]$  (4) $[V(CO)_6]^-$

**126.** A solution when diluted with $H_2O$ and boiled, it gives a white precipitate. On addition of excess $NH_4Cl/NH_4OH$, the volume of precipitate decreases leaving behind a white gelatinous precipitate. Identify the precipitate which dissolves in $NH_4OH/NH_4Cl$.
**[2006, Main]**

(1) $Zn(OH)_2$  (2) $Al(OH)_3$

(3) $Mg(OH)_2$  (4) $Ca(OH)_2$

**127.** $CuSO_4$ decolourises on addition of KNC, the product is :
**[2006, Main]**

(1) $[Cu(CN)_4]^{2-}$

(2) $Cu^{2+}$ get reduced to form $[Cu(CN)_4]^{3-}$

(3) $Cu(CN)_2$

(4) CuCN

**128.** If the bond length of CO bond in carbon monoxide is 1.128 Å, then what is the value of CO bond length in $Fe(CO)_5$ ?
**[2006, Main]**

(1) 1.15 Å  (2) 1.128 Å

(3) 1.72 Å  (4) 1.118 Å

**129.** The IUPAC name of A and B are :  **[2006, Main]**

(1) Potassium tetracyanonickelate(II), potassium tetrachloronickelate(II)

(2) Tetracyanopotassiumnickelate(II), tetera-chloropotassiumnickelate(II)

(3) Tetracyanornickel (II), tetrachloronickel(II)

(4) Potassium tetracyanonickel (II), potassium tetrachloronickel (II)

**130.** Predict the magnetic nature of A and B :
**[2006, Main]**

(1) Both are diamagnetic

(2) A is diamagnetic and B is paramagnetic with one unpaired electron

(3) A is diamagnetic and B is paramagnetic with two unpaired electrons

(4) Both are paramagnetic

**131.** The hybridisation of A and B are :  **[2006, Main]**

(1) $dsp^2, sp^3$  (2) $sp^3, sp^3$

(3) $dsp^2, dsp^2$  (4) $sp^3d^2, d^2sp^3$

**132.** $Fe^{3+} \xrightarrow{SCN^-\text{excess})}$ blood red (A) $\xrightarrow{F^-(\text{excess})}$ colourless (B)

Identify A and B.  **[2005, Main]**

(a) Write IUPAC name of A and B

(b) Find out spin only magnetic moment of B.

**133.**

(B) $\xleftarrow{\text{Moist air}}$ $MCl_4$
(white fumes having pungent smell)  (M = transitionelement colourless)

$\xrightarrow{Zn}$ (A) (purple colour)

Identify A and B.  **[2005, Main]**

(a) Write IUPAC name of A and B

(b) Find out spin only magnetic moment of B.

**134.** Which type of isomerism is shown by $Co(NH_3)_4Br_2Cl$ ?  **[2005, Screening]**

(1) Geometrical and Ionisation

(2) Optical and Ionisation

(3) Geometrical and Optical

(4) Geometrical only

**135.** $NiCl_2$ in the presence of dimethyl glyoxime (DMG) gives a complex which precipitates in the presence of $NH_4OH$, giving a bright red colour.
**[2004, Screening]**

(1) Draw its structure & show H-bonding

(2) Give oxidation state of Ni & its hybridisation

(3) Predict wether it is paramagnetic or diamagnetic

**136.** The compound having tetrahedral geometry is :
**[2004, Screening]**

(1) $[Ni(CN)_4]^{2-}$  (2) $[Pd(CN)_4]^{2-}$

(3) $[PdCl_4]^{2-}$  (4) $[NiCl_4]^{2-}$

**137.** Spin only magnetic moment of the compound $Hg[Co(SCN)_4]$ is : **[2004, Screening]**

(1) $\sqrt{3}$

(2) $\sqrt{15}$

(3) $\sqrt{24}$

(4) $\sqrt{8}$

**138.** Write the IUPAC nomenclature of the given complex along with its hybridisatio and structure. $K_2[Cr(NO)(NH_3)(CN)_4]$, $\mu = 1.73$ BM

**[2003, Main]**

**139.** Mixture X = 0.02 mol of $[Co(NH_3)_5SO_4]Br$ and 0.02 mol of $[Co(NH_3)_5Br]SO_4$ was prepared in 2 litre of solution.

1 litre of mixture X + excess $AgNO_3 \longrightarrow$ Y.

1 litre of mixture X + excess $BaCl_2 \longrightarrow$ Z.

No. of moles of Y and Z are : **[2003, Screening]**

(1) 0.01, 0.01

(2) 0.02, 0.01

(3) 0.01, 0.02

(4) 0.02, 0.02

**140.** Deduce the structures of $[NiCl_4]^{2-}$ and $[NI(CN)_4]^{2-}$ considering the hybridisation of the metal ion. Calculate the magnetic moment (spin only) of the species. **[2002, Main]**

## ANSWER KEY

| 1. (3) | 2. (2) | 3. (2) | 4. (2) | 5. (3) | 6. (4) | 7. (3) | 8. (3) | 9. (1) | 10. (3) |
|---|---|---|---|---|---|---|---|---|---|
| 11. (3) | 12. (3) | 13. (*) | 14. (2) | 15. (3) | 16. (4) | 17. (3) | 18. (4) | 19. (4) | 20. (1,3) |
| 21. (4) | 22. (4) | 23. (1) | 24. (*) | 25. (4) | 26. (4) | 27. (3) | 28. (1) | 29. (1) | 30. (4) |
| 31. (2) | 32. (2) | 33. (3) | 34. (2) | 35. (2) | 36. (3) | 37. (3) | 38. (3) | 39. (3) | 40. (1) |
| 41. (3) | 42. (2) | 43. (4) | 44. (2) | 45. (4) | 46. (2) | 47. (1) | 48. (4) | 49. (1) | 50. (4) |
| 51. (4) | 52. (*) | 53. (1,2) | 54. (2, 3) | 55. (1, 2, 4) | 56. (3) | 57. (3) | 58. (3) | 59. (2) | 60. (2) |
| 61. (2) | 62. (3) | 63. (1) | 64. (2) | 65. (2, 3, 4) | 66. (*) | 67. (2) | 68. (1) | 69. (1) | 70. (2) |
| 71. (*) | 72. (1) | 73. (1) | 74. (3) | 75. (4) | 76. (1) | 77. (4) | 78. (2) | 79. (2) | 80. (4) |
| 81. (3) | 82. (*) | 83. (*) | 84. (2) | 85. (1) | 86. (2) | 87. (3) | 88. (4) | 89. (3) | 90. (4) |
| 91. (4) | 92. (2) | 93. (4) | 94. (2) | 95. (2) | 96. (2) | 97. (3) | 98. (1) | 99. (2) | 100. (3) |
| 101. (4) | 102. (3) | 103. (2) | 104. (2) | 105. (3) | 106. (2, 4) | 107. (*) | 108. (4) | 109. (3) | 110. (2) |
| 111. (3) | 112. (3) | 113. (3) | 114. (2) | 115. (2) | 116. (3, 4) | 117. (1) | 118. (4) | 119. (2) | 120. (2) |
| 121. (3) | 122. (1) | 123. (2) | 124. (*) | 125. (4) | 126. (1) | 127. (4) | 128. (1) | 129. (1) | 130. (2) |
| 131. (1) | 132. (*) | 133. (*) | 134. (1) | 135. (*) | 136. (4) | 137. (2) | 138. (*) | 139. (1) | 140. (*) |

## ANSWERS WITH EXPLANATIONS

**1. (3)** (I) Under weak field ligand, octahderal Mn(II) and tetrahedral Ni(II) both the complexes are high spin complex.

(II) Tetrahedral Ni(II) complex can very rarely be low spin because square planar (under strong ligand) complexes of Ni(II) are low spin complexes.

(III) With strong field ligands Mn(II) complexes can be low spin because they have less number of unpaired electron (unpaired electron = 1)

While with weak field ligands Mn(II) complexes can be high spin because they have more number of unpaired electron (unpaired electron = 5)

(IV) Aqueous solution of Mn(II) ions is pink in colour.

**2. (2)** If spin only magnetic moment of the complex is 4.90 BM, it means number of unpaired electrons should be 4.

(A) In octahedral complex : $[M(H_2O)_6]^{2+}$

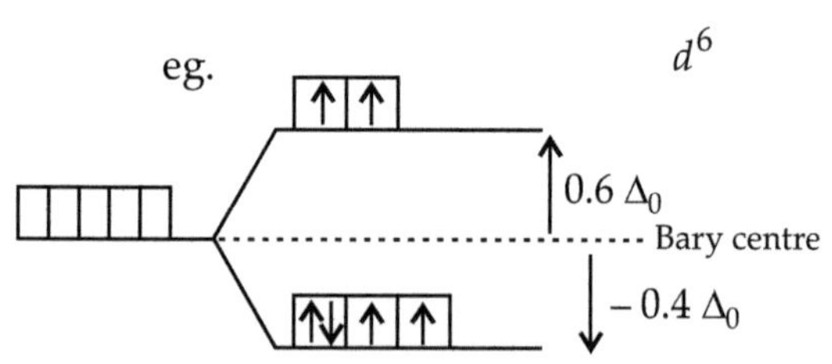


C.F.S.E. $= (-0.4\,\Delta_0) \times 4 + (+0.6\,\Delta_0) \times 2 + 0 \times P$

$= -0.4\,\Delta_0$

(B) In tetrahedral complex : $[M(H_2O)_4]^{2+}$

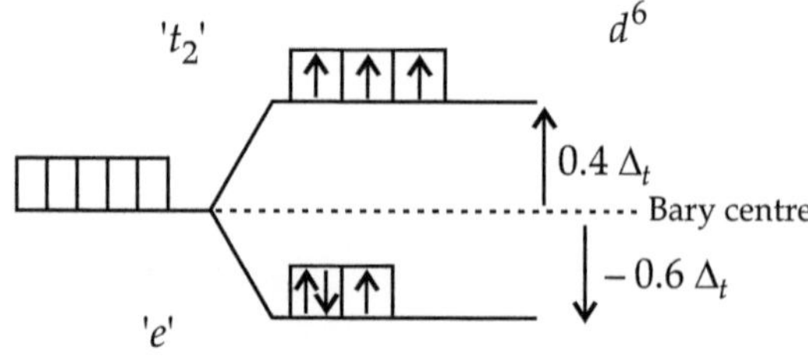


C.F.S.E. $= (-0.6\,\Delta_t) \times 3 + (+0.4\,\Delta_t) \times 3 + 0 \times P$

$= -0.6\,\Delta_t$

**3. (2)** Strength of ligand $F^- < NCS^- < NH_3$

$$[MF_6]^{(-6+n)} \quad [M(NCS)]^{(-6+n)} \quad [M(NH_3)_6]^{n+}$$
$$\text{(ii)} \qquad\qquad \text{(i)} \qquad\qquad\quad \text{(iii)}$$

$$\xrightarrow{\hspace{4cm}} \Delta_{Oh}\uparrow$$

$$\xrightarrow{\hspace{4cm}} \lambda_{max}\downarrow$$

As given in graph : $A < B < C$ ($\lambda_{max}$)

$\therefore$ Correct matching is A-(iii), B-(i), C-(ii).

**4. (2)** $[Ni(NH_3)_2Cl_2]$ is tetrahedral complex, therefore does not show geometrical and optical isomerism.

$[Ni(NH_3)_2Cl_2$ does not show structural isomerism.

$[Ni(NH_3)_4(H_2O)_2]^{2+}$ & $[Pt(NH_3)_2Cl_2]$ show geometrical isomerism.

$[Ni(en)_3]^{2+}$ show optical isomerism.

**5. (3)** (1)

$$\begin{bmatrix} \begin{array}{c} NH_3 \\ NC\diagdown \mid \diagup CN \\ \text{----}Fe\diagdown\text{----} \\ NC\diagup \mid \diagdown CN \\ NH_3 \end{array} \end{bmatrix}^- \quad \text{optically inactive}$$

(2)

$$\begin{bmatrix} \begin{array}{c} NH_3 \\ NC\diagdown \mid \diagup NH_3 \\ Fe \\ NC\diagup \mid \diagdown CN \\ CN \end{array} \end{bmatrix}^- \quad \text{optically inactive}$$

(3)

$$\begin{bmatrix} \begin{array}{c} Cl \\ \mid \quad Cl \\ OX\diagdown Cr\diagup \\ \diagdown OX \end{array} \end{bmatrix}^{3-} \quad \text{optically active}$$

(4)

$$\begin{bmatrix} \begin{array}{c} Cl \\ \mid \\ OX\diagdown Cr\diagup OX \\ \mid \\ Cl \end{array} \end{bmatrix}^{3-} \quad \text{optically inactive}$$

**6. (4)** $\qquad CFSE = 0.4\,\Delta_0$

$$= 0.4 \times \frac{20300}{83.7}$$

$$= 97 \text{ kJ/mol}$$

**7. (3)** $[Ru(en)_3]Cl_2 \qquad R_u \Rightarrow 4d$ series

$\qquad\qquad\qquad$ en $\Rightarrow$ chelating ligand

CN = 6, octahedral splitting

$\qquad$ hence laye splitting of $d$-subshell

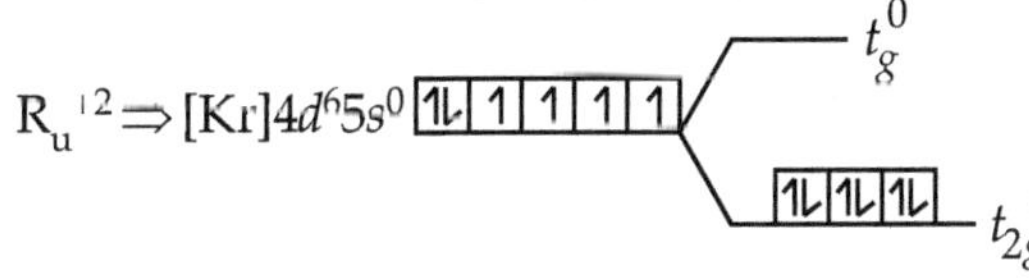

$R_u{}^{+2} \Rightarrow [Kr]4d^6 5s^0$

$[Fe(H_2O)_6Cl_2 \Rightarrow H_2O \Rightarrow$ Weak filled ligand

$\qquad\qquad Fe^{+2} \Rightarrow [Ar]\,3d^6 4s^0$

$\qquad\qquad$ less splitting

CN = 6 octahedral splitting

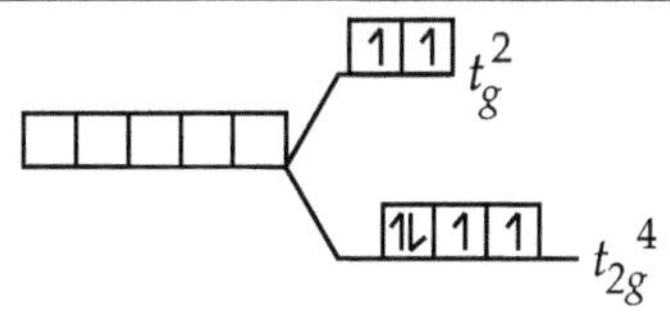

**8. (3)** Option (1) Manganate $\Rightarrow MNO_4^{2-}$,

Permanganate $\Rightarrow MnO_4^-$

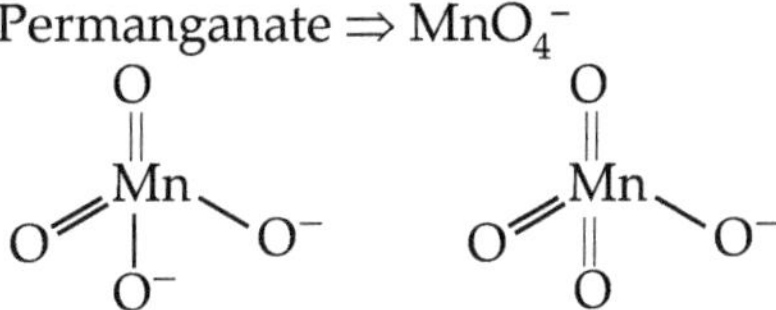

hybridisation $\qquad$ hybridisation

of Mn $\Rightarrow d^3 s \qquad$ of Mn $\Rightarrow d^3 s$

Mn $\Rightarrow$ $\boxed{1\,1\,1\,1\,1}$ $\quad$ $\boxed{1\!\!\downarrow}$

$\qquad\qquad 3d^5 \qquad\qquad 4s^2$

After excitation

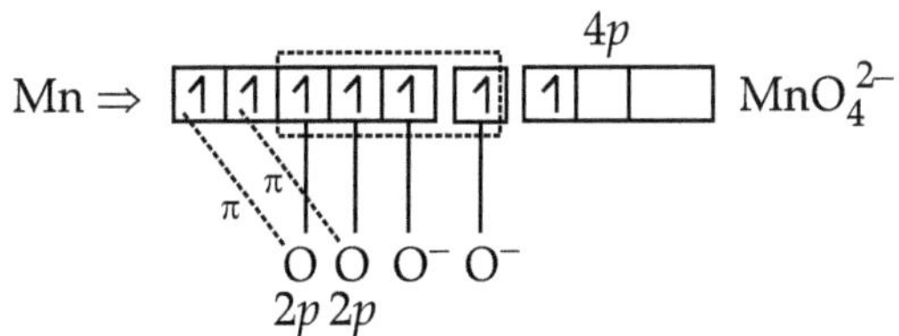

$2 \times 2p_\pi - 3d_{\pi\sigma}$

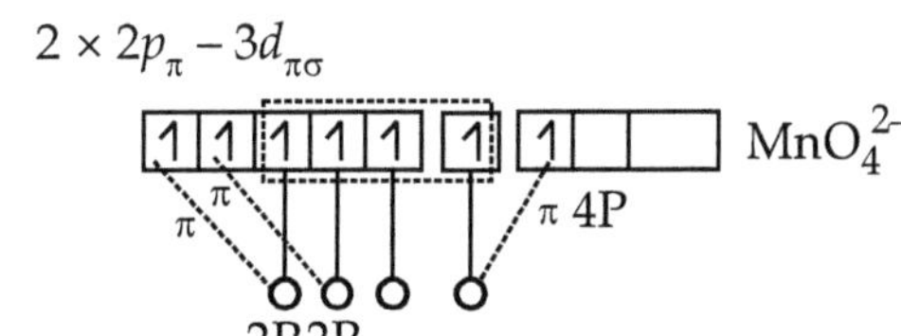

$2 \times 2P_\pi - 3d_\pi$

$1 \times 2P_\pi - 4P_\pi$

(2) $MnO_4^{2-} \Rightarrow$ green

$\qquad MnO_4^- \Rightarrow$ purple/violet

(3) Manganate contains 1 unpaired electron, hence it is paramagnetic, where as permanganetic contains no unpaired electrons hence it is diamagnetic.

(4) Both have $d^3 s$ hybridisation hence both have tetrahedral geometry.

**9. (1)** $[Pt(en)(NO_2)_2] \Rightarrow$ does not show G.I. as well as optical isomerism.

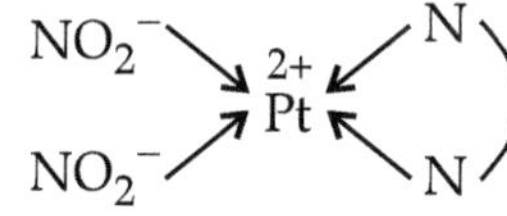

This complex will have three linkage isomers as follows :

$[Pt\,(en)\,(NO_2)_2]$ I

$[Pt\,(en)\,(NO_2)(ONO)]$ II

$[Pt\,(cn)\,(ONO)_2]$ III

**10. (3)**

| Complex | $e^-$ configuration | no. of unpaired $e^-$ |
|---|---|---|
| $[Mn(H_2O)_6]^{2+}$ | $\boxed{1\,1\,1}\,eg$ | 5 |
| WFL | $\boxed{1\,1\,1\,1}\,t2g$ | |
| $[Cr(H_2O)_6]^{2+}$ | $\boxed{1\,1}\,eg$ | 4 |
| WFL | $\boxed{1\,1\,1\,1}$ | |
| $[COCl_4]^{2-}$ | $\boxed{1\,1\,1\,1}\,t_2$ | 3 |

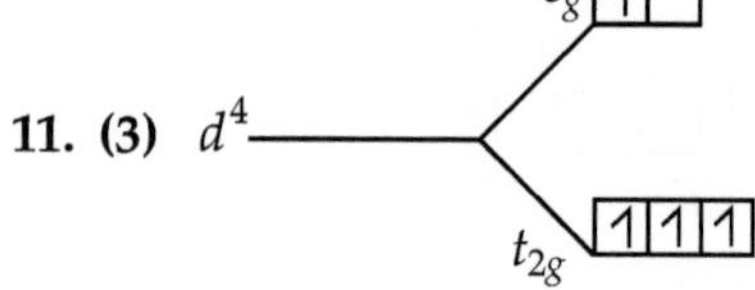

Tetrahedral    $e$

$[Fe(H_2O)_6]^{2+}$    $e_g$    4

WFL    $t_{2g}$

$[Co(OH)_4]^{2-}$    $t_2$    3

WFL    $e$

Tetrahedral    4

$[Fe(NH_3)_6]^{2+}$

Thus complex $[Cr(H_2O)_6]^{2+}$ and $[Fe(H_2O)_6]^{2+}$ have same no. of unpaired $e^-$ and hence same magnetic moment (spin only).

**11. (3)** $d^4$

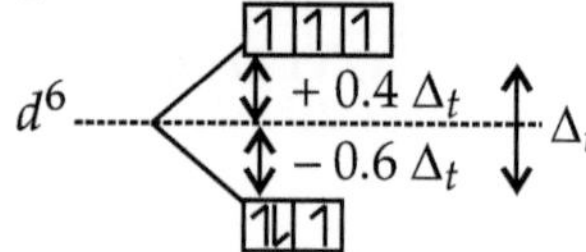

back pairing is not possible because pairing energy $> \Delta_O$.

**12. (3)** For high spin octahedral field

$d^6$    $+ 0.6\,\Delta_0$    $\Delta_0$    $- 0.4\,\Delta_0$

CFSE = $(4)(-0.4\,\Delta_0) + 2(0.6\,\Delta_0) = -0.4\,\Delta_0$

For high spin tetrahedral field

$d^6$    $+ 0.4\,\Delta_t$    $\Delta_t$    $- 0.6\,\Delta_t$

CFSE = $3(-0.6\,\Delta_t) + 3(0.4\,\Delta_t) = -0.6\,\Delta_t$

**13.** EDTA$^{4-}$ is hexadentate ligand, so its donation sites are six.

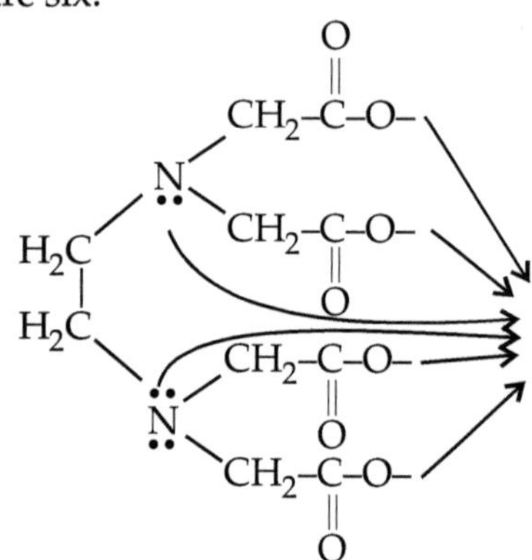

**14. (2)** $[MnBr_4]^{2-}$ $(T_d)$.

**15. (3)** 4-methylpent-2-ene.

**16. (4)** $[CoF_3(H_2O)_3]$    $\Delta_0 < P$

Means all ligands behaves as weak field ligands

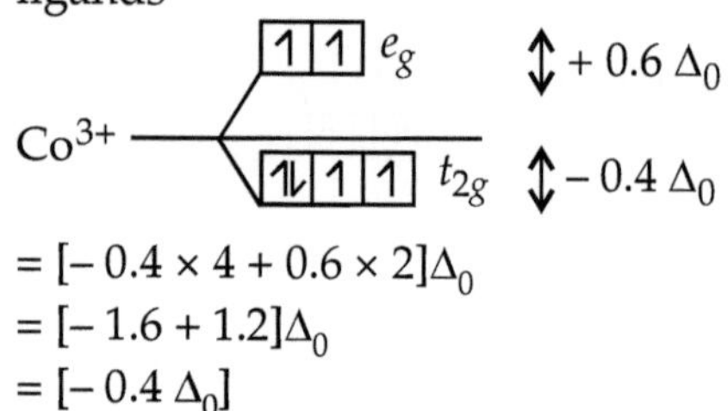

Co$^{3+}$    $e_g$    $+0.6\,\Delta_0$    $t_{2g}$    $-0.4\,\Delta_0$

$= [-0.4 \times 4 + 0.6 \times 2]\Delta_0$

$= [-1.6 + 1.2]\Delta_0$

$= [-0.4\,\Delta_0]$

**17. (3)** $[Co(OX)_2(OH)_2]^-$    $\Delta_0 > P$ [S.F.L.]

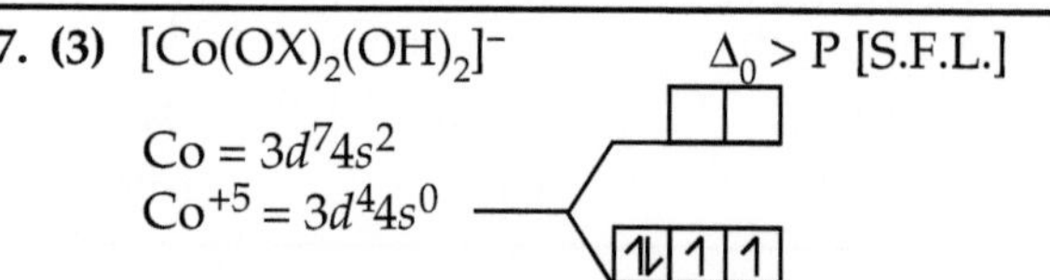

Co = $3d^7 4s^2$

Co$^{+5}$ = $3d^4 4s^0$

It has highest number of unpaired $e^-$s, so it is most paramagnetic.

**18. (4)** (A) *trans*-$[Co(en)_2Cl_2]^+$

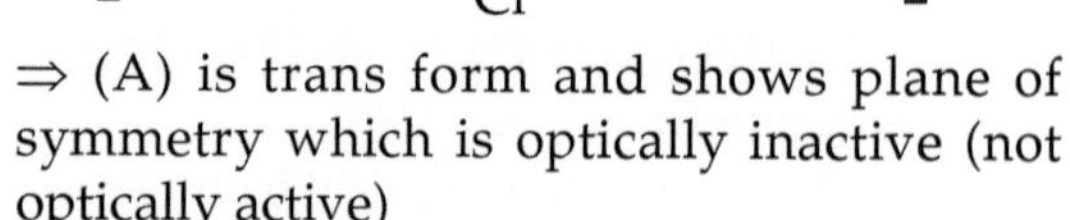


$\Rightarrow$ (A) is trans form and shows plane of symmetry which is optically inactive (not optically active)

(B) *cis*-$[Co(en)_2Cl_2]^+$

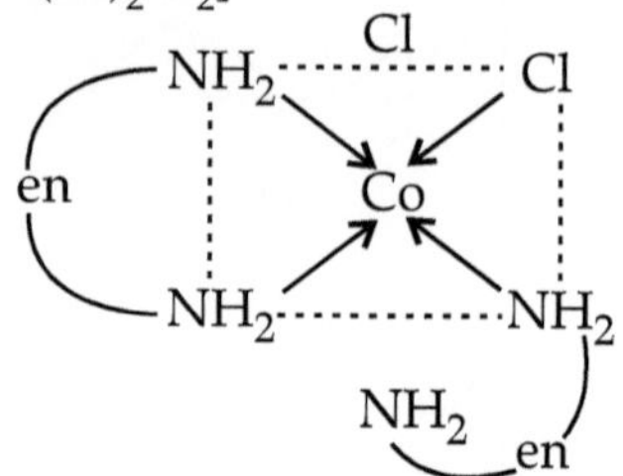


$\Rightarrow$ (B) is cis form and does not shows plane of symmetry, hence it is optically active.

**19. (4)** $CH_3-CH=CH-CH-CH_3$

From HBr $\Big|$ H$^+$ CH$_3$

$CH_3-\overset{\oplus}{C}H-CH-CH-CH_3$   H   CH$_3$

$\Big|$ Br$^-$

$CH_3-\overset{\oplus}{C}H-CH_2-CH-CH_3$   Br   CH$_3$

Addition of HBr according to M.R.

**20. (1,3)** (A) $[FeCl_4]^-$

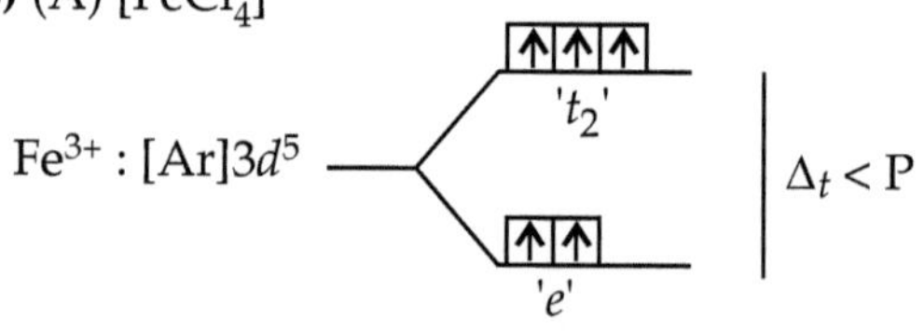

Fe$^{3+}$ : [Ar]$3d^5$    '$t_2$'    '$e$'    $\Delta_t < P$

$[FeCl_4]^-$ is $sp^3$ hybridised and has tetrahedral geometry with 5 unpaired electrons.

(B) $[Co(en)(NH_3)_2Cl_2]^+$ has three geometrical isomers.

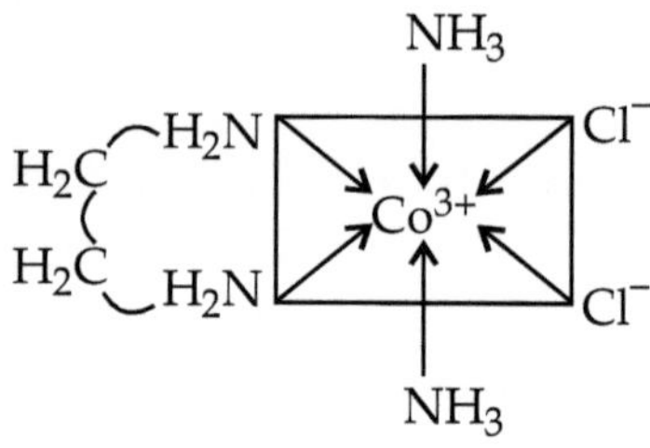

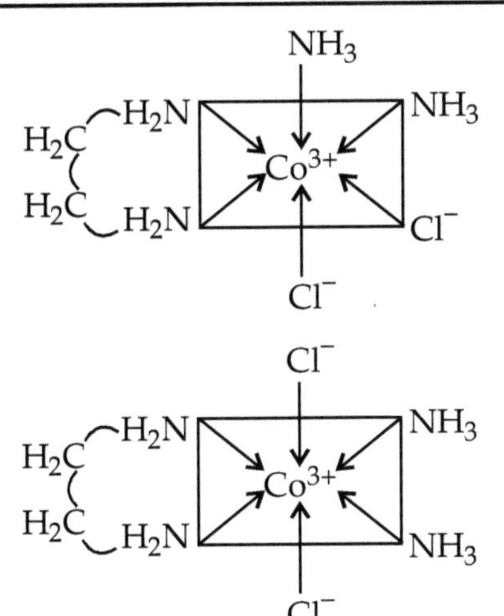

(C) $[FeCl_4]^-$

$Fe^{3+} : [Ar]3d^5$    $\Delta_t < P$

Number of unpaired electrons $(n) = 5$

Spin only magnetic moment $= \sqrt{n(n+2)}$ B.M.

$$= 5.92 \text{ B.M.}$$

$[Co(en)(NH_3)_2Cl_2]^+$

$Co^{3+} : [Ar]3d^6$    $\Delta_o > P$

Number of unpaired electrons $(n) = 0$

Spin only magnetic moment $= \sqrt{n(n+2)}$ B.M.

$$= 0$$

(D) $[Co(en)(NH_3)_2Cl_2]^+$

$Co^{3+} : [Ar]3d^6$    $\Delta_o > P$

$[Co(en)(NH_3)_2Cl_2]^+$ is $d^2sp^3$ hybridised and has octahedral geometry with 0 unpaired electron.

**21.** $K_2CrO_4 + H_2O_2 \xrightarrow[\text{(In acidic medium)}]{\text{Amyl alcohol}} CrO_5$
(X)
(Blue liquid)

Here the structure of $CrO_5$ is :

Here, single bonded O-atoms with Cr is = 04

**22. (4)** $[Pt(NH_3)_3Cl]^+$ and $[Pb(NH_3)Cl_5]^-$ does not show geometrical isomerism

**23. (1)**

| | |
|---|---|
| $[Ni(CO)_4]$ | $\mu_m = 0$ B. M. |
| $[Ni(H_2O)_6]Cl_2$ | $\mu_m = 2.8$ B. M. |
| $Na_2[Ni(CN)_4]$ | $\mu_m = 0$ B. M. |
| $[PdCl_2(CN)_4]$ | $\mu_m = 0$ B. M. |

$A \approx C \approx D \approx B$

**24.** 20.

**25. (4)** In complex $[Ni(CO)_4]$ decrease in Ni–C bond length and increase in C–O bond length as well as it's magnetic property is explained by MOT.

**26. (4)**

**27. (3)** $[Ma_3b_3]$ type complex shows fac and mer isomerism.

$[Co(NH_3)_3(NO_2)_3]$

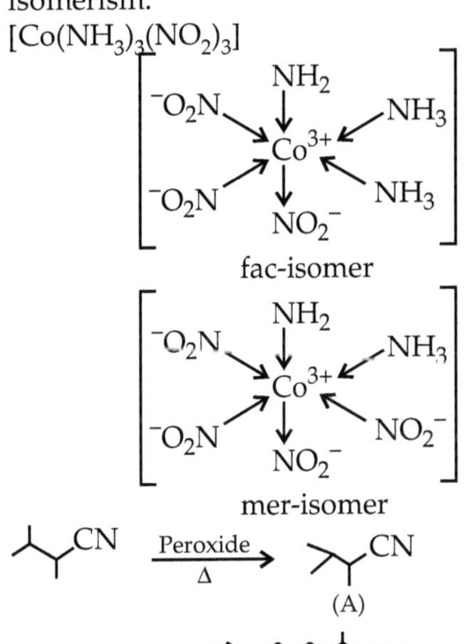

fac-isomer

mer-isomer

**28. (1)**

**29. (1)** (i) Blue violet colour with Nihydrine → amino acid derivative. So it cannot be saccharide or sucraloe.

(ii) Lassaigne extract give +ve test with $AgNO_3$. So Cl is present, –ve test with $Fe_4[Fe(CN)_6]_3$ means N is absent. So it can't be Aspartame or Saccharine or Alitame, so C is sucralose.

(iii) Lassaigne solution B and D given +ve sodium nitroprusside test, so it is having S, so it is Saccharine and Alitame.

(A) Aspartame

(B) Saccharine

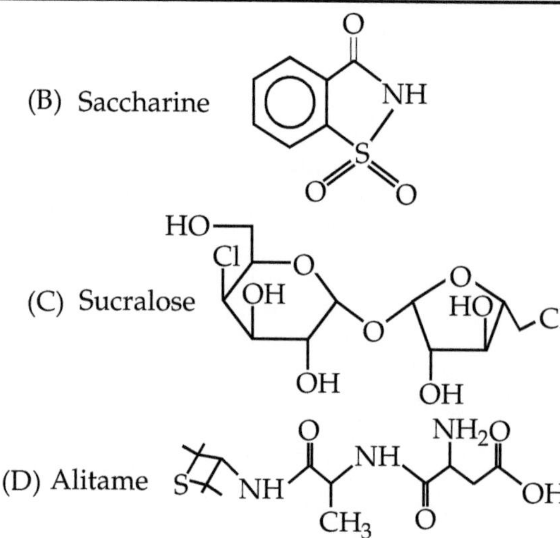

(C) Sucralose

(D) Alitame

**30. (4)** $[Co(NH_3)_4Cl_2]$ has 2 geometrical isomers

trans       cis

cis isoimer has Cl–Co–Cl angle of $90°$.

**31. (2)** 1.73 BM and $-2.0\,\Delta_0$.

**32. (2)** As in $MA_2B_2$ tetrahedral structure which is $sp^3$ hybridised, the central metal is not chiral hence, it does not show optical isomers.

In the case of square planar that is $dsp^2$ hybridised, two geometrical isomers will form but not optical isomers.

**33. (3)** Strong field ligands have high pairing energy.

For strong field ligand :

$$\Delta_0 = \Delta_t \times 1.125$$
$$\frac{18000}{1.125} = \Delta_t$$
$$16000 = \Delta_t$$

**34. (2)** All the given compounds form low spin complexes. Therefore, pairing of electrons takes place in the complexes. The configuration of $d$ orbital and the number of unpaired electrons in the given complexes are shown below :

| Complex | Configuration of $d$ orbital | Number of unpaired electrons |
|---|---|---|
| $[V(CN)_6]^{4-}$ | $t_{2g}^3 e_g^0$ | 3 |
| $[Cr(NH_3)_6]^{2+}$ | $t_{2g}^4 e_g^0$ | 2 |
| $[Ru(NH_3)_6]^{3+}$ | $t_{2g}^5 e_g^0$ | 1 |
| $[Fe(CN)_6]^{4-}$ | $t_{2g}^6 e_g^0$ | 0 |

Therefore, the correct order of spin-only magnetic moment of metal ions is shown below :

$$V^{2+} > Cr^{2+} > Ru^{3+} > Fe^{2+}$$

**35. (2)** The given ligand can ligate through both the nitrogen and the oxygen atoms. Therefore, it is a tetradentate ligand.

**36. (3)** The compound *cis*-$[Pt(Cl)_2(NH_3)_2]$ has been used in chemotherapy as this compound inhibits the growth of tumors.

**37. (3)** The electronic configuration of Fe in $[Fe(H_2O)_6]^{2+}$ is $t_{2g}^4 e_g^2$. It contains four unpaired electrons. The spin-only magnetic moment is $= \sqrt{n(n+2)} = \sqrt{4(4+2)} = 4.9$ B.M. The electronic configuration of Fe in $[Fe(CN)_6]$ is $t_{2g}^6 e_g^0$. It does not contain any unpaired electrons. The spin-only magnetic moment is $= \sqrt{n(n+2)} = \sqrt{0(0+2)} = 0$ B.M.

**38. (3)** The structure of the compound, $CuSO_4.5H_2O$, is shown below :

One water molecule is not directly coordinated to copper ion.

**39. (3)** The compound (3) do not have any plane of symmetry therefore, it will show optical activity. The structure of compound (3) is shown below :

The rest of the compounds do not have any plane of symmetry. Therefore, they will not show optical activity.

**40. (1)** The electronic configuration of chromium atom is $[Ar]3d^5 4s^1$.

The electronic configuration of $Cr^{3+}$ ion is $[Ar]3d^3 4s^0$.

The three valence electron of $Cr^{3+}$ ion will be present in $d_{xy}$, $d_{yz}$ and $d_{xz}$ orbitals.

The empty orbital will be $d_{x^2-y^2}$ and $d_{z^2}$. The set of orbitals that has same energy are $t_{2g}$ ($d_{xy}$, $d_{yz}$ and $d_{xz}$) and $e_g$ ($d_{x^2-y^2}$ and $d_{z^2}$).

Therefore, degenerated orbital among the options are $d_{yz}$ and $d_{xz}$.

**41. (3)** The some limitation of valence bond theory are listed below :

- The colour imparted by transition metal complexes cannot be explained with valence bond theory.

- The classification of ligands as weak and strong field ligands is not explained by valence bond theory.

The magnetic properties of transition metal complexes can be explained with valence bond theory.

**42. (2)** The maximum coordination number possible for transition metals is 6.

The inner transition metal can have more than 6 coordination number.

Therefore, the maximum possible denticities of the given ligand for any transition metal and inner-transition metal ion is 6 and 8 respectively.

**43. (4)** The structures of the given compounds are shown below :

(1) $\mathrm{Cl}\!\!>\!\!\mathrm{Pt}\!\!<\!\!en$ (with $\mathrm{Cl}$)

(2) $\left[\mathrm{Ox}\!>\!\mathrm{Cr}\!<\!\!\begin{array}{c}en\\en\end{array}\right]^{+}$

(3) $\mathrm{Cl}\!\!>\!\!\mathrm{Zn}\!\!<\!\!\begin{array}{c}en\\ \mathrm{Cl}\end{array}$

(4) $\left[en\!>\!\mathrm{Pt}\!<\!en\right]^{+2}$ (with $\mathrm{Cl}$, $\mathrm{Cl}$) $\quad\left[\begin{array}{c}\mathrm{Cl}\\ \mathrm{Cl}\end{array}\!\!>\!\!\mathrm{Pt}\!<\!\!\begin{array}{c}en\\en\end{array}\right]$

In compound (1) and (2), as the bidentate ligands coordinates at 90° in a square planar complex, no trains isomer would be possible. In compound (3), due to $sp^3$ hybridisation, no trains isomer would be possible. In compound (4), both *cis* and *trans* isomer are possible.

**44. (2)** The electronic configuration of $\mathrm{Ti}^{2+}$ is $[\mathrm{Ar}]3d^2$. The number of unpaired electrons is 2.
The spin-only magnetic moment is $= \sqrt{n(n+2)}$

$= \sqrt{2(2+2)} = 2.83$ B.M.

The electronic configuration of $\mathrm{Ti}^{3+}$ is $[\mathrm{Ar}]3d^1$. The number of unpaired electrons is 1.

The spin-only magnetic moment is $= \sqrt{n(n+2)}$

$= \sqrt{1(1+2)} = 1.73$ B.M.

The electronic configuration of $\mathrm{V}^{2+}$ is $[\mathrm{Ar}]3d^3$. The number of unpaired electrons is 3.

The spin-only magnetic moment is $= \sqrt{n(n+2)}$

$= \sqrt{3(3+2)} = 3.87$ B.M.

The electronic configuration of $\mathrm{Sc}^{3+}$ is $[\mathrm{Ar}]3d^0$. The number of unpaired electrons is 0.

The spin-only magnetic moment is $= \sqrt{n(n+2)}$

$= \sqrt{0(0+2)} = 0$ B.M.

Therefore, the correct order of spin-only magnetic moment is $\mathrm{Sc}^{3+} < \mathrm{Ti}^{3+} < \mathrm{Ti}^{2+} < \mathrm{V}^{2+}$.

**45. (4)** The light having least wavelength and highest energy would be absorbed by the compound that has a strong field ligand. The compound $[\mathrm{CoCl(NH_3)_5}]^{2+}$ has the weakest field ligand and therefore, light having the least energy and the highest wavelength would be absorbed. The compound $[\mathrm{Co(NH_3)_6}]^{3+}$ has the strongest field ligand and therefore, light having the highest energy and the lowest wavelength would be absorbed.

**46. (2)** Consider the compound $[\mathrm{Fe(H_2O)_6}]\mathrm{Cl_2}$. The central metal atom Fe is in +2 oxidation state. The electronic configuration is $(t_{2g})^4(e_g)^2$. The crystal field splitting energy is calculated as shown below :

$$\text{C.F.S.E.} = 4 \times (-0.4\,\Delta_o) + 2 \times (-0.6\,\Delta_o)$$
$$= -0.4\,\Delta_o$$

Consider the compound $\mathrm{K_2[NiCl_4]}$. The central metal atom Ni is in +2 oxidation state. The electronic configuration is $(e_g)^4(t_{2g})^4$. The crystal field splitting energy is calculated as shown below :

$$\text{C.F.S.E.} = 4 \times (-0.6\,\Delta_t) + 4 \times (0.4\,\Delta_t)$$
$$= -0.8\,\Delta_t$$

**47. (1)** In the compound $[\mathrm{Fe(H_2O)_6}]^{2+}$, the central atom has + 2 oxidation state and contains four unpaired electrons. In the compound $[\mathrm{Cr(H_2O)_6}]^{2+}$, the central atom has +2 oxidation state and contains four unpaired electrons.

In the compound $[\mathrm{Ni(NH_3)_4(H_2O)}]^{2+}$, the central atom has + 2 oxidation state and contains two unpaired electrons. The spin-only magnetic moment is $= \sqrt{n(n+2)}$

$= \sqrt{2(2+2)} - 2.83$ B.M.

The compound $[\mathrm{Ni(NH_3)_4(H_2O)_2}]^{2+}$ absorbs yellow light and is violet in colour, as violet is the complimentary colour of yellow.

The $\mathrm{Cr}^{3+}$ ions, in ruby gemstone, occupy the octahedral sites of $\mathrm{Al_2O_3}$.

**48. (4)** The electronic configuration of $\mathrm{Fe}^{2+}$ is $[\mathrm{Ar}]3d^6$.
The electronic configuration of $\mathrm{Fe}^{3+}$ is $[\mathrm{Ar}]3d^5$.
The electronic configuration of $\mathrm{Co}^{2+}$ is $[\mathrm{Ar}]3d^7$.
The electronic configuration of $\mathrm{Ni}^{2+}$ is $[\mathrm{Ar}]3d^8$.
The electronic configuration of $\mathrm{Ni}^{3+}$ is $[\mathrm{Ar}]3d^7$.
The electronic configuration of $\mathrm{Zn}^{2+}$ is $[\mathrm{Ar}]3d^{10}$.
The electronic configuration of $\mathrm{Zn}^{3+}$ is $[\mathrm{Ar}]3d^9$.
When electron is removed from the $t_{2g}$ level, the crystal field stabilisation energy of the complex get reduced.

| Ion | Configuration of $t_{2g}$ | Configuration of $e_g$ |
| --- | --- | --- |
| $\mathrm{Fe}^{2+}$ | $t_{2g}^{\ 6}$ | $e_g^{\ 0}$ |
| $\mathrm{Fe}^{3+}$ | $t_{2g}^{\ 5}$ | $e_g^{\ 0}$ |
| $\mathrm{Co}^{2+}$ | $t_{2g}^{\ 6}$ | $e_g^{\ 1}$ |
| $\mathrm{Co}^{2+}$ | $t_{2g}^{\ 6}$ | $e_g^{\ 0}$ |

| Ni$^{2+}$ | $t_{2g}^{6}$ | $e_{g}^{2}$ |
|---|---|---|
| Ni$^{2+}$ | $t_{2g}^{6}$ | $e_{g}^{1}$ |
| Zn$^{2+}$ | $t_{2g}^{6}$ | $e_{g}^{4}$ |
| Zn$^{3+}$ | $t_{2g}^{6}$ | $e_{g}^{3}$ |

Therefore, the complex that will lose its crystal field stablisation energy is [Fe(phen)$_3$]$^{2+}$.

**49. (1)** When ligands from $z$-axis are removed in complex, the $z$-axis component of the metal ion get stabilised. The stabilisation process is shown below :

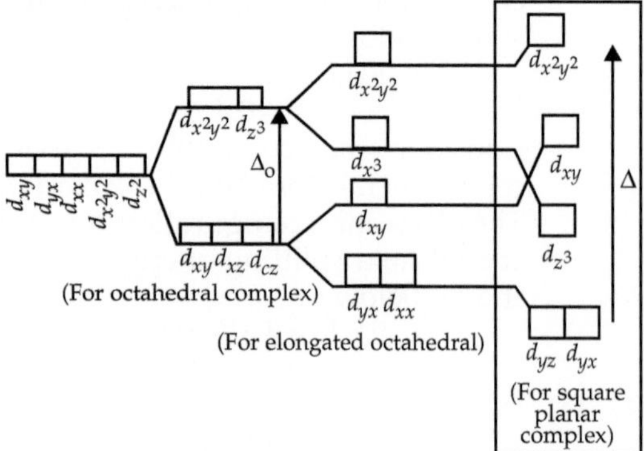

Therefore, the correct representation is shown below.

$$E \left\{ \begin{array}{l} — d_{x^2-y^2} \\ — d_{xy} \\ — d_{z^2} \\ = d_{xz},\ d_{yz} \end{array} \right.$$

**50. (4)** EDTA forms a complex with lead ion. The structure of EDTA and lead complex is shown below :

Therefore, EDTA can be used to treatment of lead poisoning.

**51. (4)** The oxalate ion (C$_2$O$_3^{2-}$) and ethane-1, 2-diamine are bidentate ligands. Therefore, the coordination number of Co in [Co(Cl)(en)$_2$] Cl and Al in K$_3$[Al(C$_2$O$_4$)$_3$] are 5 and 6 respectively.

**52.** The structure of *cis*-[Mn(*en*)$_2$Cl$_2$] is shown below :

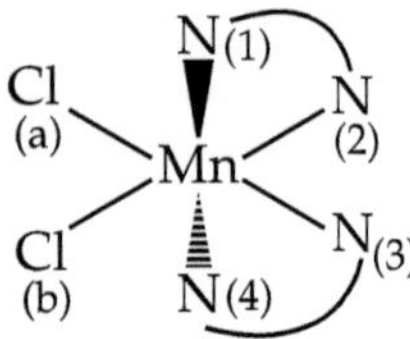

The different type of cis bond angles are N(1) – Mn – Cl(a), N(2) – Mn – Cl(a), N(4) – Mn – Cl(a), N(1) – Mn – Cl(b), N(3) – Mn – Cl(b), and N(4) – Mn – Cl(b).

Therefore, the number of *cis* N – Mn – Cl bonds are 6.

**53. (1,2)** The first reaction is shown below :
$$\underset{Q}{SnCl_2} + Cl^- \rightarrow \underset{X}{SnCl_2^-}$$

The second reaction is shown below :
$$\underset{Q}{SnCl_2} + Me_2N \rightarrow \underset{Y}{SnCl_2.NMe_3}$$

The Third reaction is shown below :
$$\underset{Q}{SnCl_2} + 2CuCl_2 \rightarrow \underset{Z}{SnCl_2} + 2CuCl$$

**54. (2, 3)** (1) Total number of valence electrons in Fe(CO)$_5$ and Ni(CO)$_4$ is 18.

(2) Carbonyl group is a strong field ligand. Therefore, the complexes are low spin in nature.

(3) The lower oxidation state of metal means it has high electron density. Thus, it leads to an increased back bonding. Therefore, the strength of M – C bond increases.

(4) Increased oxidation state of metal decreases back bonding and thus it leads to an increased strength of C – O bond

**55. (1, 2, 4)** (A) The structures of isomers formed are shown below :

Thus, it has two geometrical isomers.

(B) The structures of isomers formed are shown below :

Thus, it has three geometrical isomers.

(C) Cobalt is present in + 3 oxidation state. It is $d^6$ in configuration and as it is attached to strong field ligand. Thus, it is diamagnetic.

(D) Ammonia is a strong ligand in comparison to water. Therefore, CFSE is lower in the former case and thus, it will absorb light of longer wavelength.

**56. (3)** The hybridisation of $[FeF_6]^{4-}$ is shown below :

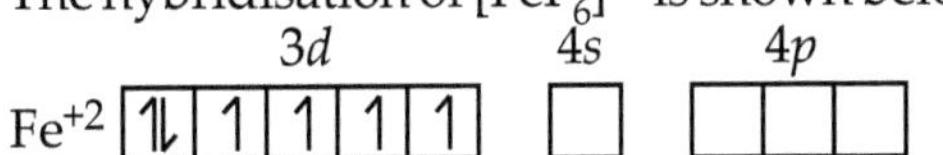

As $F^-$ is a weak ligand; therefore, no pairing occurs. Thus, hybridisation is $sp^3d^2$.

The hybridisation of $[Ti(H_2O)_3Cl_3]$ is shown below :

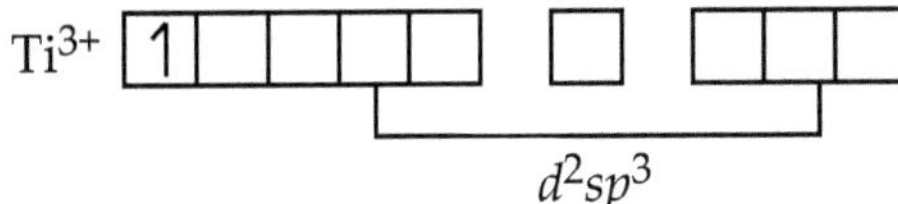

As $Cl^-$ and water are weak ligands therefore, no pairing occurs. Thus, hybridisationis $d^2sp^3$.

The hybridisation of $[Cr(NH_3)_6]^{3+}$ is shown below :

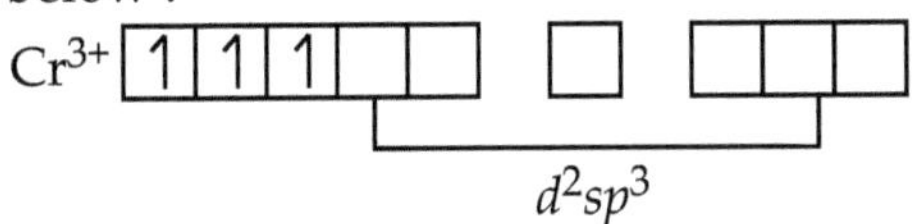

As six ligands are attached, it means six vacant orbitals are required. Thus, pairing will not occur. The, hybridisations $d^2sp^3$.

The hybridisation of $[FeCl_4]^{2-}$ is shown below :

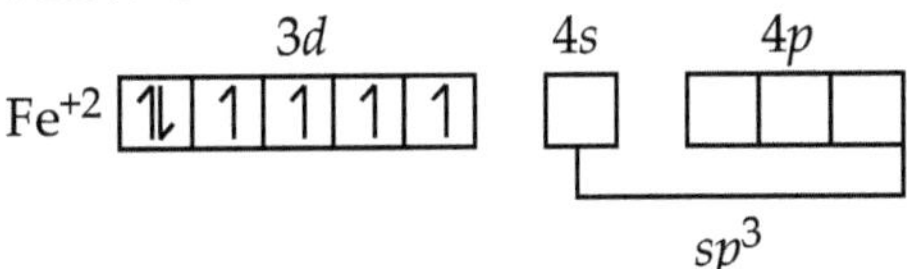

As $Cl^-$ is a weak ligand; therefore, no pairing occurs. Thus, hybridisationis $sp^3$.

The hybridisation of $NICO_4$ is shown below :

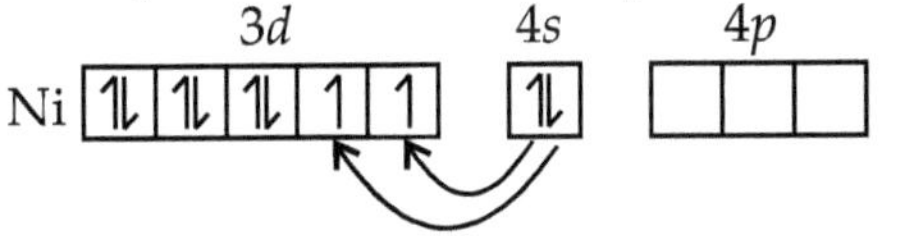

As CO is a strong ligand; therefore, pairing occurs. Thus, hybridisations $sp^3$.

The hybridisation of $[Ni(CN)_4]^{2-}$ is shown below :

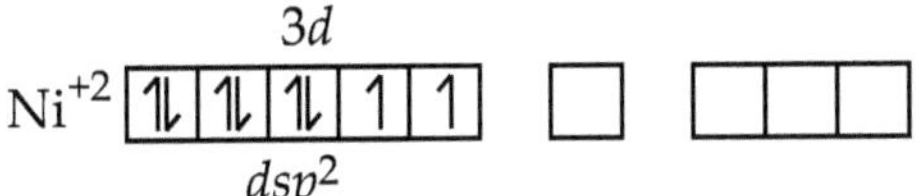

As CN is a strong ligand; therefore, pairing occurs. Thus, hybridisationis $dsp^2$.

**57. (3)** The reaction of fluoride ions with $[3Ca_3(PO_4)_2 Ca(OH)_2]$ is,

$$[3Ca_3(PO_4)_2Ca(OH)_2] + 2F^-$$
$$\rightarrow [3Ca_3(PO_4)_2CaF_2] + 2OH^-$$

The complex $[3Ca_3(PO_4)_2CaF_2]$ formed in the above reaction makes the teeth enamel harder.

**58. (3)** The oxidation state of chromium in $[Cr(H_2O)_6]Cl_3$ is calculated as,

$$x + 0 + 3(-1) = 0$$
$$x = +3$$

The oxidation state of chromium in $[Cr(C_6H_6)_2]$ is calculated as,

$$x + 2(0) = 0$$
$$x = 0$$

The oxidation state of chromium in $K_2[Cr(CN)_2(O)_2(O)_2(NH_3)]$ is calculated as,

$$x + 2(-1) + (-1) + 2(-2) + 0 = 0$$
$$x - 8 = -2$$
$$x = +6$$

**59. (2)** The reaction of *cis* and *trans* isomers with bromide ions is shown as,

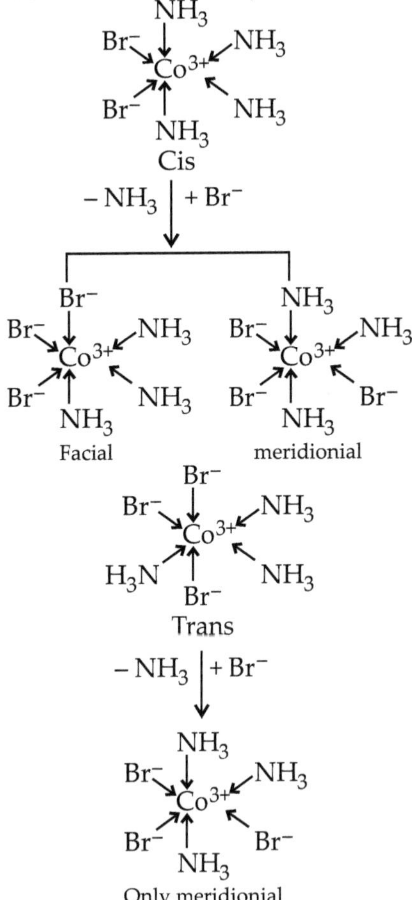

Since, the reaction of *cis* isomer with bromide ions leads to the formation of two isomers. Therefore, the statement (I) is correct and statement (IV) is incorrect.

Since, the reaction of trans isomer with bromide ions leads to the formation of only one isomer. Therefore, the statement (II) is incorrect and the statement (III) is correct.

**60. (2)** Coordination complex with general formula MABCD shows three isomers. However, $NO_2$ and SCN are ambidentate ligands. Hence, the total number of isomer shown by this complex is $= 3 \times 4$.
$$= 12$$

**61. (2)** The complex $[Ni(Cl)_4]^{2-}$ has tetrahedral geometry with $sp^3$ hybridisation and contains two unpaired electron. Therefore, it is paramagnetic in nature.

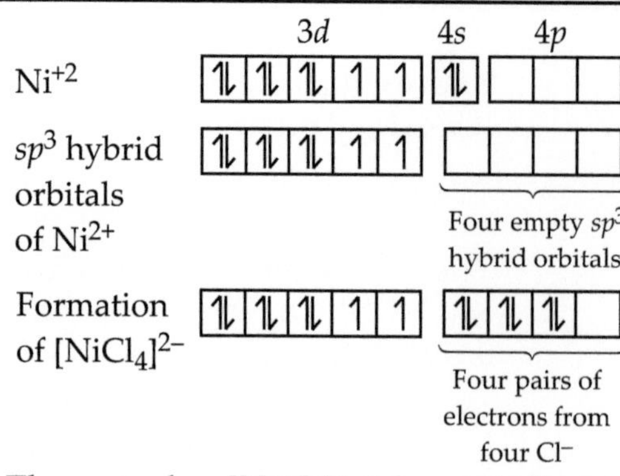

The complex $[Ni(CO)_4]$ has tetrahedral geometry with $sp^3$ hybridisation. Carbonyl is a strong field ligand.

Outer electronic configuration of Ni atom in ground state.

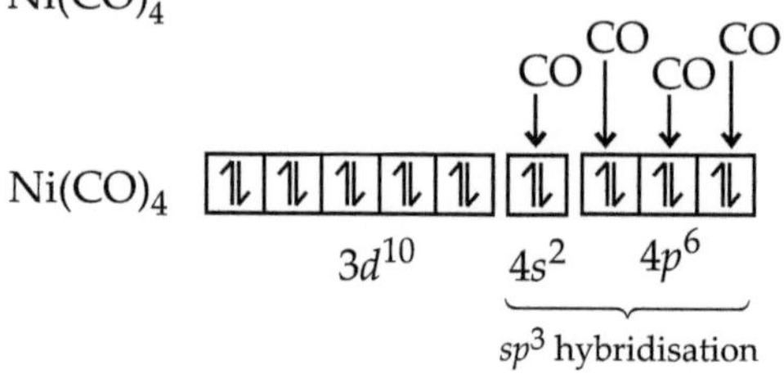

Outer electronic configuration of Ni atom in $Ni(CO)_4$

Tetrahedral

**62. (3)** The hybridisation of central metal ion in Wilkinson catalyst, $RhCl(PPh_3)_3$ is $dsp^2$. Its geometry is square planar.

**63. (1)** Aquachlorobis(ethylenediamine) cobalt(II) chloride exhibits geometrical isomerism as shown below.

trans        cis

aquachlorobis (ethylenediamine) cobalt(II) chloride.

**64. (2)** Metal first reacts with ligand compound and forms complex. In this process absorbed light is remains constant. In the given condition, metal and complex will not absorb light. When complex formation is completed, the concentration of ligand increases. Then ligand will absorb light.

**65. (2, 3, 4)** For the given conditions, the reaction is given as,

$$(\text{pink}) \ X \xrightarrow[\text{+ air}]{NH_3 \text{ excess}} Y \ (\text{octahedral})$$

Room-T $\Big|$ HCl excess     (aqueous solution)

Z (blue)        1:3 electrolyte

According to the given condition, central metal should be cobalt. Therefore, the complex X will be $[Co(H_2O)_6]Cl_2$. In excess ammonia it will give octahedral complex of $[Co(NH_3)_6]Cl$. Its aqueous solution contains 1:3 electrolyte.

In excess HCl blue coloured compound Z is obtained. This compound will have the formula $[CoCl_4]^{2-}$. It is ``$sp^3$'' hybridized. Therefore, its structure is tetrahedral.

Compound X and Z are in equilibrium at 0°C. The reaction is given as,

$$[CoCl_4]^{2-} + 6H_2O \rightleftharpoons [Co(H_2O)_6]^{2+} + 4Cl^-$$

When ice is added to the solution, the equilibrium shifts right. Therefore, pink colour remains predominant.

**66.** In $[TeBr_6]^{2-}$ the number of lone pairs on central atom is 1.

In $[BrF_2]^+$ the number of lone pairs on central atom is 2.

In $[SnF_3]$ the number of lone pairs on central atom is 0.

In $[XeF_3]^-$ the number of lone pairs on central atom is 3.

Therefore, total number of lone pairs on all the species is six.

**67. (2)** The moles of complex is calculated by the formula,

Molex of complex

$$= \frac{\text{Molarity} \times \text{Volume (mL)}}{1000}$$

$$= \frac{0.1 \times 100}{1000}$$

$$= 0.01 \ mol$$

The moles of ions precipitated with excess of $AgNO_3$ is,

$$= \frac{1.2 \times 10^{22}}{6.022 \times 10^{23}}$$

$$= 0.02 \ mol$$

The number of chloride ions present in the ionisation sphere is calculated as,

$$\frac{\text{Moles of ions precipitated with excess } AgNO_3}{\text{Moles of complex}} = \frac{0.02}{0.01} = 2$$

Therefore, two chloride ions are present in ionisation sphere. Hence, the complex is $[Co(H_2O)_5Cl]Cl_2 \cdot H_2O$.

**68. (1)** The compound M and B are Li and $NH_3$ respectively. The complete reaction of compound M and B are as follows :

$$Li(s) + N_2(g) \rightarrow 2Li_3N(s)$$
$$Li_3N + 3H_2O \rightarrow 3LiOH + NH_3$$
$$CuSO_4 + 4NH_3 \rightarrow [Cu(NH_3)_4]SO_4$$

The complex $[Cu(NH_3)_4]SO_4$ shows deep blue colour.

**69. (1)** The structure of $[Co_2(CO)_8]$ is shown below :

$$OC \underset{OC}{\overset{OC}{—}} Co \underset{OC}{\overset{OC}{—}} Co \underset{CO}{\overset{CO}{—}} CO$$

Thus, the above structure displayes one Co–Co bond, six terminal CO and two bridging CO bonds.

**70. (2)** The number of unpaired electrons in following compounds is given below :

| Compound | Hybridisation | Number of unpaired electron |
|---|---|---|
| $[Ni(CO)_4]$ | $3d^{10}$, $sp^3$ | 0 |
| $[Ni(Cl)_4]^{2-}$ | $3d^8$, $sp^3$ | 2 |
| $[CO(NH_3)_4Cl_2]Cl$ | $3d^6$, $d^2sp^3$ | 0 |
| $Na_3[CoF_6]$ | $3d^6$, $sp^3d^2$ | 4 |
| $Na_2O_2$ | hybridisation of $O_2^{2-}$ | 0 |
| $CsO_2$ | hybridisation of $O_2^{-1}$ | 1 |

$CsO_2$, $Na_3[CoF_6]$ and $[Ni(Cl)_4]^{2-}$ are paramagnetic.

So, number of paramagnetic compounds is three.

**71.** In $[CoL_2Cl_2]^-$, $L = H_2NCH_2CH_2O^-$ is a didentate ligand.

So, possible geometrical isomers of $[CoL_2Cl_2]^-$ are given below :

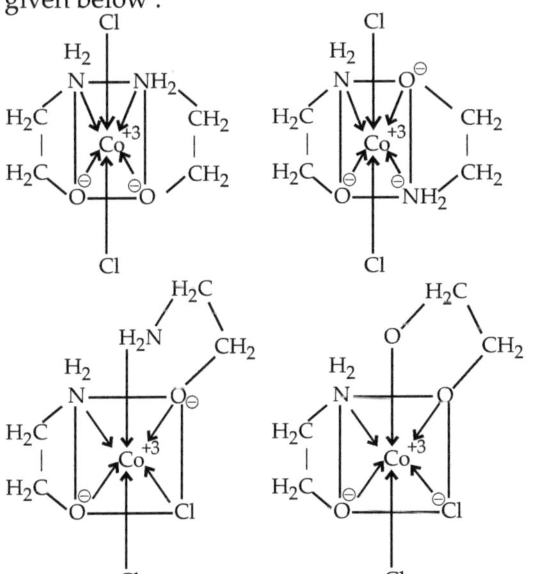

So, total five geometrical isomers are possible for $[CoL_2Cl_2]^-$.

**72. (1)** The following reaction is given below :

$$Ag^+ + S_2O_3^{2+} \rightarrow \underset{(X)}{[Ag(S_2O_3)_2]^{3-}} \xrightarrow{Ag^+}$$

$$\underset{\text{White ppt. (Y)}}{Ag_2S_2O_3(\downarrow)} \xrightarrow{\text{(With time)}} \underset{\text{Black (Z)}}{Ag_2S(\downarrow)}$$

In the following reaction, silver ion reacts with $S_2O_3^{2-}$ to give compond X $[Ag(S_2O_3)_2]^{2-}$. Then this compound reacts with silver ions to give white precipitate of compound Y $Ag_2S_2O_3$. This compound Y reacts further with silver ions to give black precipitate of compound Z $Ag_2S$.

**73. (1)** $Ni^{2+}$ with ammonia show coordination number 6. It will form $[Ni(NH_3)_6]^{2+}$ and the geometry of complex is octahedral.

$Pt^{2+}$ with ammonia show coordination number 4. It will form $[Pt(NH_3)_4]^{2+}$ and the geometry of complex is square planar.

$Zn^{2+}$ with ammonia show coordination number 4. It will form $[Zn(NH_3)_4]^{2+}$ and the geometry of complex is tetrahedral.

**74. (3)** The complex that gives higher number of chlorine ions in the solution will consume more equivalents of aqueous solution of $Ag(NO_3)$. Thus, the complex, $[Cr(H_2O)_6]Cl_3$ will consume more equivalents of aqueous solution of $Ag(NO_3)$.

**75. (4)** As, $\Delta_0 \propto$ CFSE (Crytsal field stabilisation energy)

Thus, $\Delta_0$ of $[Cr(H_2O)_6]^{2+} < \Delta_0$ of $[Mo(H_2O)_6]^{2+}$ because in this case $\Delta_0$ is dependent upon the $Z_{eff}$. In this case $Z_{eff}$ of $4d$ series is greater than $3d$ series.

The stability of the complex is inversely proportional to the size of the cations. Thus, $\Delta_0$ of $[Ti(H_2O)_6]^{3+} < \Delta_0$ of $[Ti(H_2O)_6]^{2+}$.

**76. (1)** Homoleptic complexes are those complexes that contain only one type of ligand bound to central metal atom. Therefore, the complex $[Co(NH_3)_6]Cl_3$ is a homoleptic complex that has six ammonia ligands bound to the central metal atom cobalt.

**77. (4)** The transition metal ions that are responsible for colour in ruby and emerabld is $Cr^{3+}$.

Aluminium oxide is also known as ruby. It contains of chromium ions. Each aluminium and chromium ion is surrounded by six oxide ions in an octahderal manner. Emerald is composed of beryllium aluminium silicate in which chromium ions is surrounded by six silicate ions. Thus, in both the cases, chromium is responsible for colour.

**78. (2)** In all the given complexes weak field ligands are attached to the central metal atom.

Magnetic moment is related to the number of unpaired electrons present in the central metal atom. The number of unpaired electrons present in different given species are shown below :

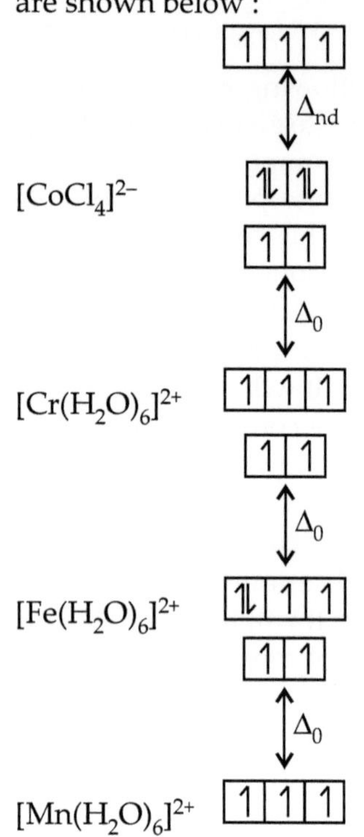

**79. (2)** The structure of $cis[Co(en)_2Cl_2]Cl$ is shown below :

It is optically active. The mirror image is non superimposable.

**80. (4)** The complex formed by $Fe^{3+}$ with the given ligands are $[Fe(SCN)_6]^{3-}$ and $[Fe(CN)_6]^{3-}$. In both the complex, the electronic configuration of $Fe^{3+}$ will be $[Ar]4s^03d^5$.

$CN^-$ is a strong field ligand due to which pairing is possible in $[Fe(CN)_6]^{3-}$, whereas $SCN^-$ is a weak field ligand so pairing is not possible in $[Fe(SCN)_6]^{3-}$ complex as given below :

$Fe^{3+}$ in $[Fe(SCN)_6]^{3-}$ = ⬛⬛⬛⬛⬛ $3d$
$[d^5$ configuration (High spin)]

$Fe^{3+}$ in $[Fe(CN)_6]^{3-}$ = ⬛⬛⬛⬜⬜
$[d^5$ configuration (Low spin)]

The number of unpaired electrons in first case is 5, whereas in second case the number of unpaired electrons is 1.

The formula to calculate spin only magnetic moment is

$$\mu = \sqrt{n(n+2)}$$

The spin-only magnetic moment for $[Fe(CN)_6]^{3-}$ is $\sqrt{3}$ BM and for $[Fe(SCN)_6]^{3-}$ is $\sqrt{35}$ BM.

The difference in spin only magnetic moment is

$$= \sqrt{35} - \sqrt{3}$$
$$= 4$$

**81. (3)** The structure of acetylbromidodicarbonylbis (triethylphosphine) iron(II) complex is shown below :

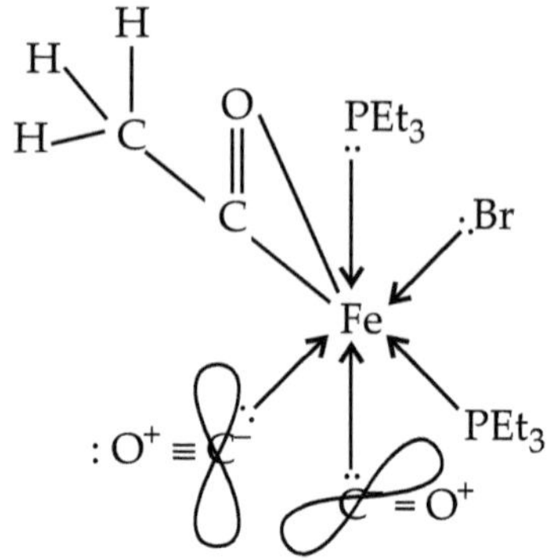

Thus, the number of Fe – C bond is 3.

**82.** All the complexes will show cis-rans isomerism.

$$[Co(NH_2-CH_2-\overset{H_2}{C}-NH_2)_2Cl_2]^+$$

$[CrCl_2(C_2O_4)_2]^{3-}$

$[Fe(H_2O)_4(OH)_2]^-$

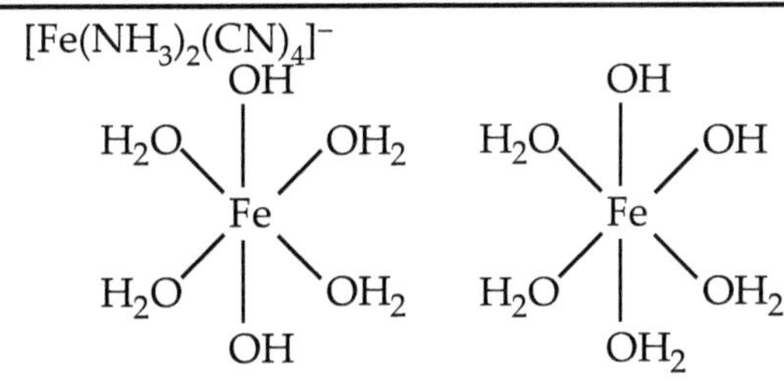

$[Fe(NH_3)_2(CN)_4]^-$

$[Co(NH_2-CH_2-\overset{H_2}{C}-NH_2)_2(NH_3)Cl]^{2+}$

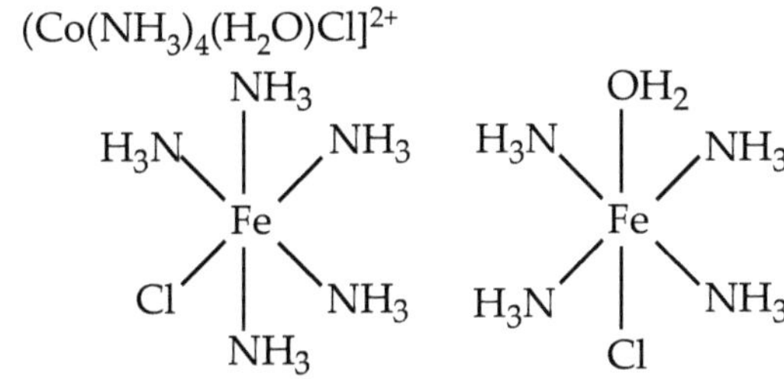

$(Co(NH_3)_4(H_2O)Cl]^{2+}$

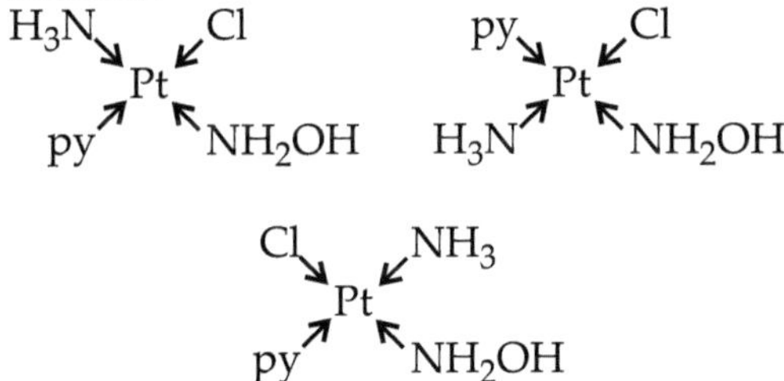

83. The given reaction is
$$[Fe(C_2O_4)(H_2O)]^{2-} + MnO_4^{2-} + 8H^+$$
$$\rightarrow Mn^{2+} + Fe^{3+} + 4CO_2 + 6H_2O$$
So the ratio of rate of change of $[H^+]$ to that of rate of change of $[MnO_4^-]$ is $\dfrac{8}{1} = 8$.

84. **(2)** The given complex is a square planar complex of type [MABCD]. These types of complexes exhibit three possible geometrical isomers.

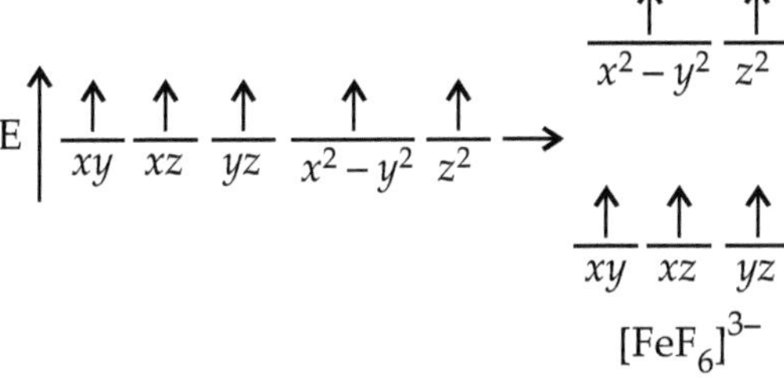

85. **(1)** $Zn_2[Fe(CN)_6]$ is not a yellow colour compound. It is whitish blue coloured compound.

86. **(2)** Iron in +3 oxidation state on reaction with $SCN^-$ leads to the formation of $Fe(SCN)_6$ which is red in colour.
$$FeCl_3 + 3SCN^- \rightarrow [Fe(SCN)_3 + 3Cl^-$$
Iron on reaction with $K_4[Fe(CN)_6]$ undergoes displacement reaction,
$$Fe^{3+} + K_4[Fe(CN)_6] \rightarrow Fe(CN)_6]_3 \text{ (blue)}$$
Chromyl chloride test is given by the compounds that contain chlorine in their molecular structure.
$$2FeCl_3 + 3H_2SO_4 \rightarrow Fe_2(SO_4)_3 + 6HCl$$



$$K_2Cr_2O_7 + 2H_2SO_4 \rightarrow 2KHSO_4 + 2CrO_3 + H_2O$$
$$CrO_3 + 3HCl \rightarrow CrO_2Cl_2 + H_2O$$
$$CrO_2Cl_2 + 4NaOH \rightarrow Na_2CrO_4 + 2NaCl$$
$$+ 2H_2O$$

87. **(3)** Methane cannot act as a ligand in complex compounds as it does not contain lone pair of electrons.

88. **(4)** The geometrical isomerism is shown by $[Ni(H_2O)_4(NH_3)_2]^{2+}$ and $[Ni(H_2O)_3(NH_3)_3]^{2+}$. However, they are optically inactive because octahedral complexes show optical activity when there are two or three bidentate ligands.

89. **(3)** When concentrated HCl is added to an aqueous solution of $CoCl_2$, formation of blue coloured complex $[CoCl_4]^{2-}$ takes place.

90. **(4)** The complex ion, $[FeF_6]^{3-}$ is high spin complex due to which $t_{2g}$ and $e_g$ orbitals are symmetrically filled.
In $[FeF_6]^{3-}$ complex Fe has +3 charge, which leads to five unpaired electrons in $d$-orbital.

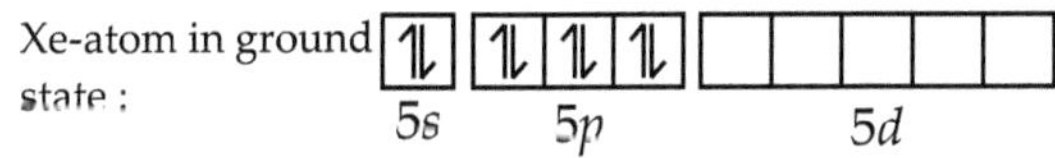

91. **(4)** $XeF_4$, $BF_4^-$, $[Cu(NH_3)_4]^{2+}$ and $[PtCl_4]^{2-}$.

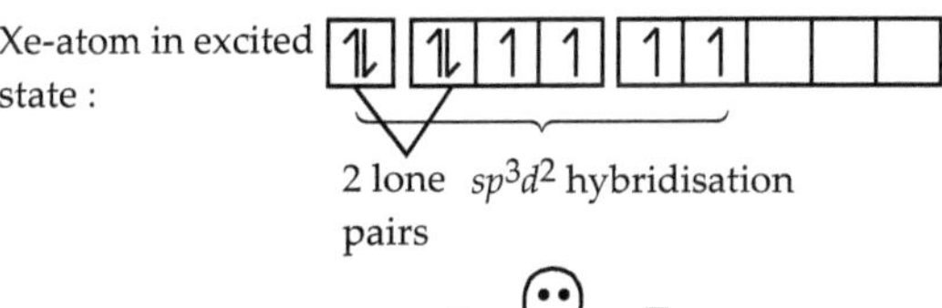

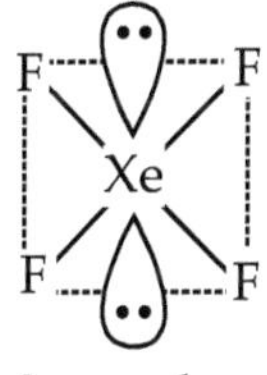

Square planar

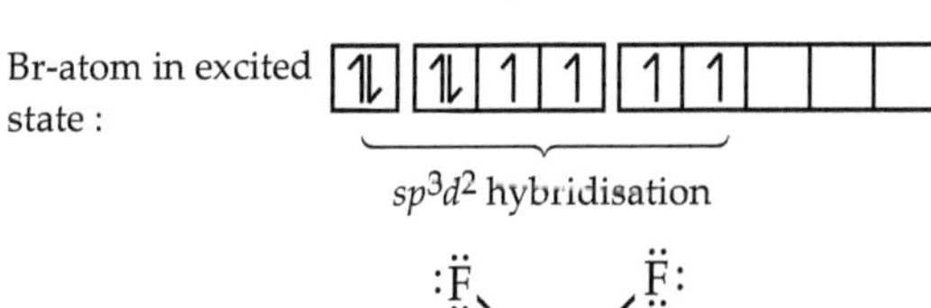

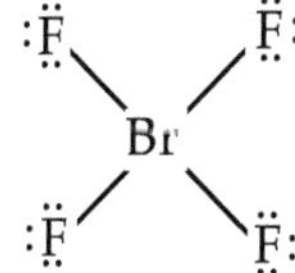

Square planar

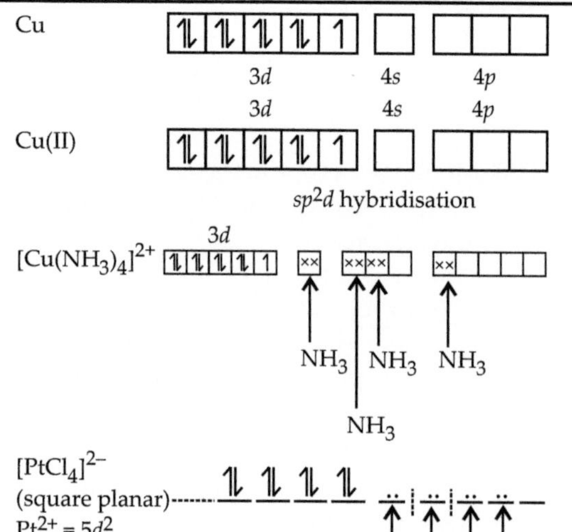

92. **(2)** The complete reaction for the identification of M1, Q and R is shown below :

$$[Ni(Cl)_4]^{2-} \xleftarrow[\text{excess}]{\text{HCl}} Ni^{2+} \xrightarrow[\text{excess}]{\text{KCN}} [Ni(CN)_4]^{2-}$$

The complex $[Ni(Cl)_4]^{2-}$ has tetrahedral geometry with $sp^3$ hybridisation.

The complex $[Ni(CN)_4]^{2-}$ has square planar geometry with $dsp^2$ hybridisation.

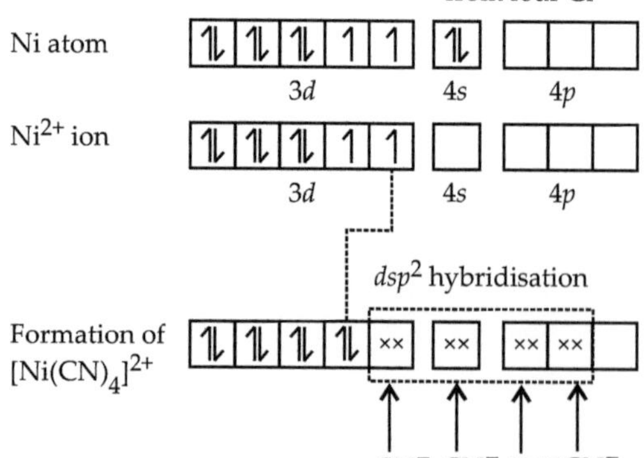

93. **(4)** The complete reaction for the identification of M2, Q and R is shown below :

$$[Zn(Cl)_4]^{2-} \xleftarrow[\text{excess}]{\text{HCl}} Zn^{2+} \xrightarrow[\text{excess}]{\text{KCN}} K_2Zn(CN)_4$$

The complex $[Zn(Cl)_4]^{2-}$ has tetrahedral geometry.

The complex $K_2Zn(CN)_4$ has tetrahedral geometry.

Therefore, M2 is $Zn^{2+}$. The complete reaction is shown below.

$$Zn^{2+} + OH^- \rightarrow Zn(OH)_2 \xrightarrow{OH^-} [Zn(OH)_4]^{2-}$$
$$\text{(soluble)}$$

The white precipitate of $Zn(OH)_2$ is formed. The reagent S is KOH.

94. **(2)** (P) $[Cr(NH_3)_4Cl_2]Cl$

In the given complex, Cr is in + 1 oxidation state. Its electronic configuration is $3d^5$. The structure of the given complex is shown as :

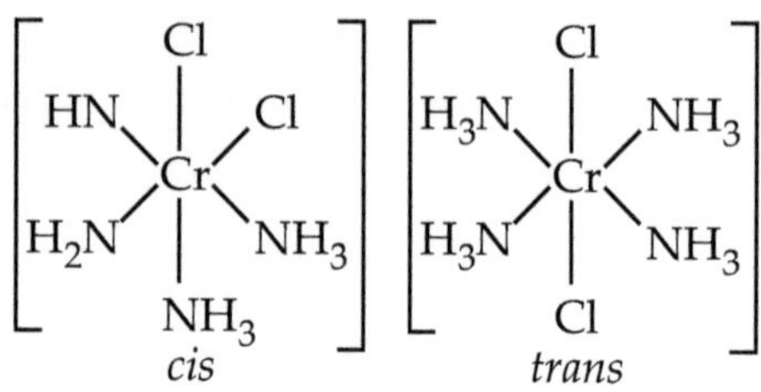

Therefore, it is paramagnetic and exhibits *cis-trans* isomerism.

(Q) $[Ti(H_2O)_5Cl](NO_3)_2$

In the given complex, $NO_3$ is an ambidentate ligand and Ti is in +3 oxidation state.

Its electronic configuration is $3d^1$ as shown below :

$$3d^1 \;\boxed{\boxed{\uparrow}\ \square\ \square\ \square\ \square}$$

Therefore, it is paramagnetic and exhibits ionisation isomerism.

(R) $[Pt(en)(NH_3)Cl]NO_3$

In the given complex, $NO_3$ is an ambidentate ligand that results in the pairing of electrons and Pt is in +2 oxidation state. Its electronic configuration is $5d^8$ as shown below :

$$5d^8 \;\boxed{\boxed{\uparrow\downarrow}\boxed{\uparrow\downarrow}\boxed{\uparrow\downarrow}\boxed{\uparrow\downarrow}\ \square}$$

Therefore, it is diamagnetic and exhibits ionisation isomerism.

(S) $[Co(NH_3)_4(NO_3)_2]NO_3$

In the given complex, $NH_3$ is a strong field ligand that results in the pairing of electrons and Co is in +3 oxidation state. Its electronic configuration is $3d^6$. The structure of the given complex is shown as,

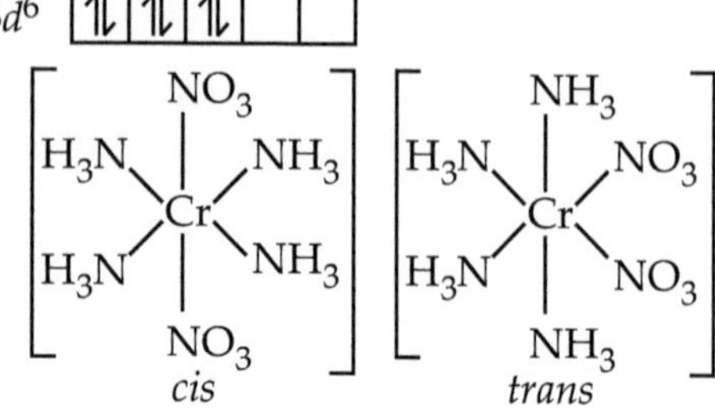

Therefore, it is diamagnetic and exhibits *cis-trans* isomerism.

95. **(2)** Stronger the ligand, higher will be the absorption frequency of complex. According to VIBGYOR, the correct decreasing order of wavelength is,

$$\lambda_{red} > \lambda_{yellow} > \lambda_{green} > \lambda_{blue}$$

Energy and wavelength are inversely related. Therefore, the increasing order of ligand strength of the four ligands is,

$$L_1 < L_3 < L_2 < L_4$$

96. **(2)** Reaction given in equation (1) is not feasible in forward direction due to the formation of unstable compound $K_2O$.

Charge is not balanced in equation (3). The product formed in equation (4), $K_2[Cu(CN)_4]$ is not correct. Therefore, the equation (2) is balanced and represents the correct products.

97. **(3)** The electronic configuration of $Co^{3+}$ is $[Ar]3d^6$. $Co^{3+}$ is diamagnetic in nature, it means there is no unpaired electron present in the $d$-orbital of cobalt. Therefore, the hybridisation involved in the formation of the complex of $Co^{3+}$ must be $d^2sp^3$ (inner orbital complex) as shown below :

$Co^{3+}$ : $4s^0 3d^6$ diamagnetic

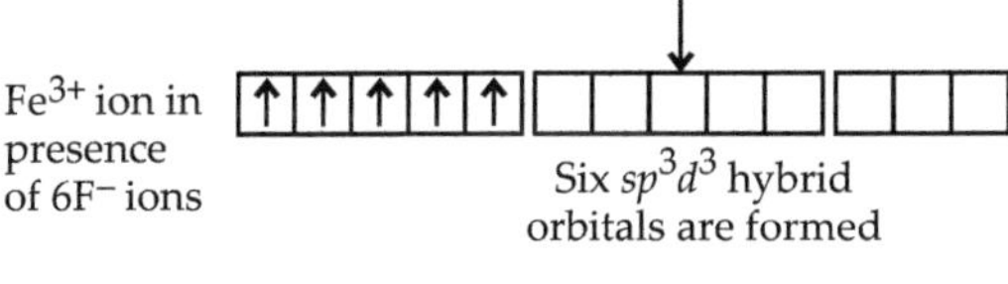

$d^2sp^3$ hybridisation

98. **(1)** Fluorine is a weak field ligand due to which pairing of electrons is not possible. The distribution of electrons in the orbitals is shown below :

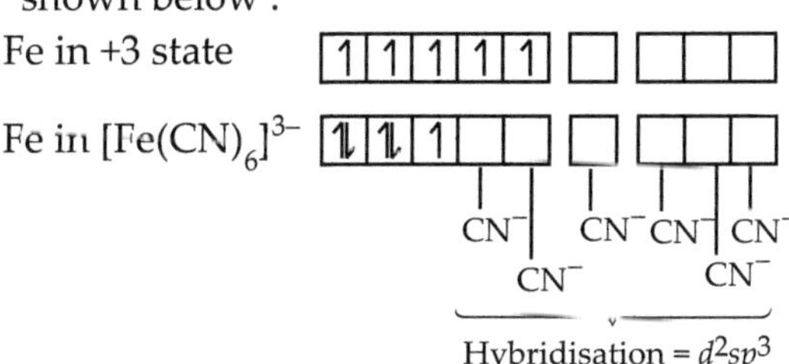

Cyanide is a strong field ligand due to which pairing of electrons is possible. The distribution of electrons in the orbitals is shown below :

Fe in +3 state

Fe in $[Fe(CN)_6]^{3-}$

Hybridisation = $d^2sp^3$

Both the complex consists of unpaired electrons. Therefore, both are paramagnetic in nature.

99. **(2)** The correct IUPAC name of $[Mn(CN)_5]^{2-}$ is Pentacyanomagnate(III) ion.

100. **(3)** During the formation of $[Co(NH_3)_6]Cl_3$ complex, the species which will act as the Lewis acid is $Co^{3+}$. It will accept lone pair of electrons from ammine ($NH_3$) ligands.

101. **(4)** The crystal field splitting energy of ligand depends upon the strength of ligands. The ligands having higher strength cause splitting of molecular orbitals results in the high crystal field splitting energy. Since the strength of CO ligand is higher than that of the $CN^-$, $NH_3$ and $F^-$. Therefore, CO causes highest crystal field splitting energy out of the given ligands.

102. **(3)** The electronic configuration of central metal ions in the given complexes is given below :

$Sc^{3+} = 1s^2 2s^2 2p^6 3s^2 3p^6$

$Ti^{4+} = 1s^2 2s^2 2p^6 3s^2 3p^6$

$V^{3+} = 1s^2 2s^2 2p^6 3s^2 3p^6 4s^2$

$Sc^{3+} = 1s^2 2s^2 2p^6 3s^2 3p^6 3d^{10}$

The central metal ion present in the complex $[V(NH_3)_6]^{3+}$ has its valence electrons in the $4s$ orbital that can easily excite to the $3d$ orbital and can absorb visible light, but in case of other complexes, the central metal ion has fully filled electronic configuration. Therefore, the complex $[V(NH_3)_6]^{3+}$ is most likely to absorb visible light among the given complexes.

103. **(2)** The given complex exhibits ionisation isomerism.

A : $[M(NH_3)_5SO_4]Cl(aq) + AgNO_3(aq)$
$\rightarrow [M.(NH_3)_5SO_4]NO_3(aq) + AgCl(s)\downarrow$

B : $[M(NH_3)_5Cl]SO_4(aq) + BaCl_2(aq)$
$\rightarrow [M.(NH_3)_5Cl]Cl_2(aq) + BaSO_4(s)\downarrow$

104. **(2)** An example of such ion that fulfils the given criteria is $[Ni(CN)_4]^{2-}$. This ion is diamagnetic with zero unpaired electrons. The hybridisation involved in $[NI(CN)_4]^{2-}$ ion is

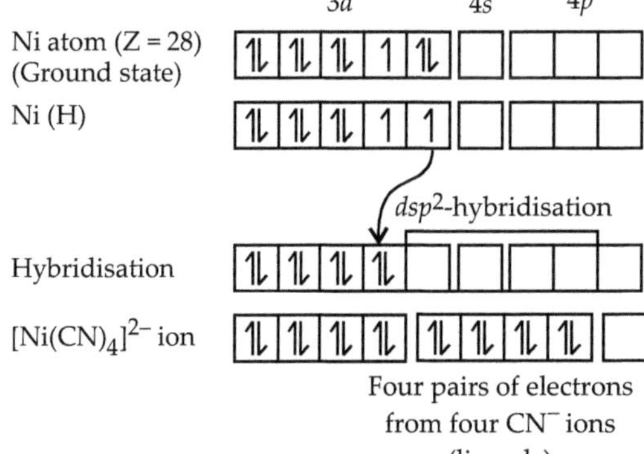

Four pairs of electrons
from four $CN^-$ ions
(ligands)

105. **(3)** The spin-only magnetic value depends upon the number of unpaired electrons. The complex ion with more number of unpaired electrons would have more spin-only magnetic moment value.

The number of unpaired electrons in P, Q and R is 5, 3 and 4 respectively. Thus, the correct order of spin-only magnetic moment values is $Q < R < P$.

**106. (2, 4)** The compounds $[Co(NH_3)_4Cl_2]^+$ and $[Pt(NH_3)_2(H_2O)Cl]^+$ will show geometrical isomerism, whereas the compounds $[Pt(NH_3)_3(NO_3)Cl$ and $[Pt(NH_3)_3Cl]Br$ will show ionisation isomerism.

The pairs of option (1) and option (3) show different type of isomerism.

**107.** The structure of $[Co(EDTA)]^{1-}$ complex is shown below :

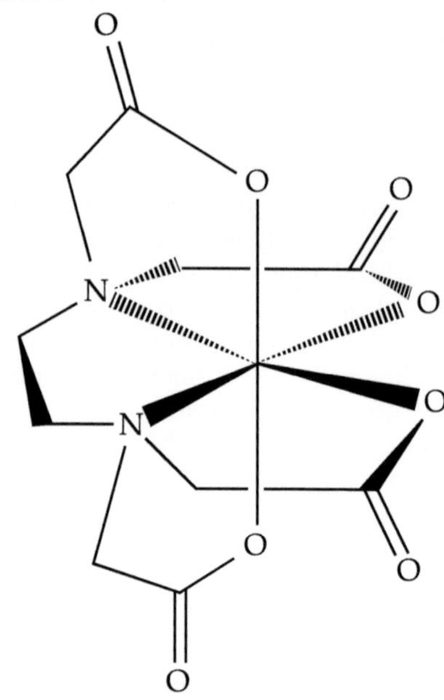

The above structure of complex shows that total number of N – Co – O bonds is 8.

**108. (3)** The central metal atom is cobalt. The ligands are aqua and ammine. The counter ion is chloride ion. The oxidation state of cobalt is + 3. Thus, the nomenclature of given compound is Diamminetetraaquacobalt(III) chloride.

**109. (3)** The electronic configuration of $Ni^{+2}$ in paramagnetic form is shown below :

| 3d | 4s | 4p |
|---|---|---|

It has hybridisation of $sp^3$ and thus, its coordination geometry is tetrahedral.
The electronic configuration of $Ni^{+2}$ in diamagnetic form is shown below :

| 3d | 4s | 4p |
|---|---|---|

It has hybridisation of $dsp^2$ and thus, its coordination geometry is square planar.

**110. (2)** Generally nickel forms stable complexes in (+2) oxidation state. Therefore, the complex of nickel with $Cl^-$ and $CN^-$ should be $[Ni(Cl)_4]^{2-}$ and $[Ni(CN)_4]^{2-}$. Chlorie ion is

a weak field ligand whereas; cyanide ion is a strong field ligand. In $[Ni(Cl)_4]^{2-}$ the hybridisation pattern observed is $sp^3$ and in $[Ni(Cl)_4]^{2-}$ it is $dsp^2$. Therefore, the shape of $[Ni(Cl)_4]^{2-}$ is tetrahedral and $[Ni(Cl)_4]^{2-}$ is square planar.

In case of water, the complex will be $[Ni(H_2O)_6]^{2+}$. Due to weak field nature of water ligand is hybridisation pattern is $sp^3d^2$. Therefore, the shape of $[Ni(H_2O)_6]^{2+}$ is octahedral.

**111. (3)** The final solution should contains the complex compounds $[Ag(NH_3)_2]^+$ and $[Cu(NH_3)_4]^{2+}$. This is shown by the following reaction

$$2AgNO_3(N) + Cu(M) \rightarrow Cu(NO_3)_2$$
$$\text{(light blue)} + 2Ag$$
$$AgNO_3 + NaCl \rightarrow AgCl \text{ (white ppt)}$$
$$+ NaNO_3$$
$$Cu^{2+} + 4NH_3 \rightarrow [Cu(NH_3)_4]^{2+}$$
$$AgCl + 2NH_3 \rightarrow [Ag(NH_3)_2]^+ Cl^-$$

**112. (3)** The complexes $[Co.(NH_3)_6]Cl_3$, $Na_3[Co.(oxalate)_3]$, $K_2[Pt.(CN)_4]$ and $[Zn.(H_2O)_6](NO_3)_2$ are diamagnetic in nature due to absence of unpaired electrons in central atom.

**113. (3)** Ethylenediaminetetraacetic acid (EDTA) is a hexadentate ligand. In its structure, four carboxyl groups and two nitrogen atoms interact with $M^+$ ion.

Thus, the correct structure of ethylenediaminetetraacetic acid (EDTA) is (C).

**114. (2)** Ionization isomers are those isomers that are obtained by interchanging of ions that are present inside and outside of coordination sphere.

In $[Cr(H_2O)_4Cl_2](NO_2)$, chloride ion $Cl^-$ is replaced by $NO_2^-$ in ionisation sphere.

**115. (2)** In $[NiCl_4]^{2-}$, the oxidation state of Ni is + 2. The electronic configuration of Ni is $3d^84s^2$
In $Ni^{2+} = 3d^8$
The electronic configuration of $Ni^{2+}$ is shown below.

| 3d | 4s | 4p |
|---|---|---|

In $[NICl_4]^{2-}$, Cl is weak field ligand. So it will not cause pairing of electrons.
So, number of unpaired electrons ($n$) in $[NiCl_4]^{2-}$ is 2.
The spin-only magnetic moment of $[NiCl_4]^{2-}$ is,

$$\mu = \sqrt{n(n+2)}$$
$$= \sqrt{2(2+2)}$$
$$= \sqrt{8}$$
$$= 2.82 \, B.M.$$

Thus, $[NiCl_4]^{2-}$ shows 2.82 B.M. spin-only magnetic moment.

**116.** **(3, 4)** The complex $[Pt(en)Cl_2]$ contains one bidendate ligand and two chloro ligands. The complex $[Pt(en)_2]Cl_2$ contains two bidendate ligands inside the complex ions. Therefore, they do not exhibit geometrical isomerism.

The geometrical isomers of $[Pt(en)_2Cl_2]$ $Cl_2$ and $[Pt(NH_3)_2Cl_2]$ are shown below :

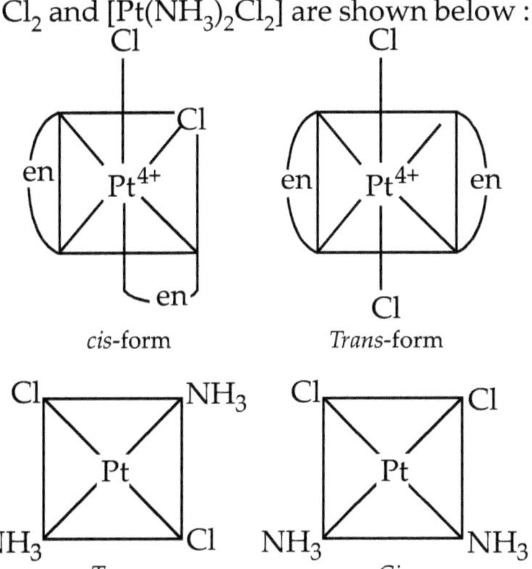

cis-form          Trans-form

*Trans*          *Cis*

**117.** **(1)** The electronic configuration of chromium is $[Ar]3d^5 4s^1$.

Chromium contains six unpaired electrons which become paired up in the presence of CO (strong field ligand) due to which the resulting complex contains only paired electrons. The spin only magnetic moment of diamagnetic complexes is zero. Hence, the spin only magnetic moment of $[Cr(CO)_6$ is zero.

**118.** **(4)** The compound $CuSO_4.5H_2O$ actually exists in the form of coordination complex $[Cu(H_2O)_4]SO_4.H_2O$ in which four water molecules are present inside the coordination complex and one water molecule is present outside the complex ion. Therefore, four water molecules are directly boned to the central metal atom in the given compound.

**119.** **(2)** Silver on reaction with aqueous solution of sodium cyanide in the presence of air gives sodium argentocyanide which is used in the electroplating of a metal.

$$4Ag + 8NaCN + 2H_2O + O_2 \rightarrow 4Na[Ag(CN)_2] + 4NaOH$$

**120.** **(2)** The oxidation state of Nickel in $[Ni(CO)_4]$ and $[Ni(CN)_4]^{2-}$ is 0 and +2, respectively. The electronic configuration of Ni and $Ni^{2+}$ in the presence of CO and CN is $[Ar]3d^{10}4s^0$ and $[Ar]3d^8 4s^0$ respectively. Hence, the hybridisation of nickel in $[Ni(CO)_4]$ and $[Ni(CN)_4]^{2-}$ is $sp^3$ and $dsp^2$ respectively.

**121.** **(3)** The oxidation state of nickel in $[Ni(NH_3)_4]$ and $[NiCl_4]$ is + 2. Hence, the IUPAC name is Tetraamminenickel(II)tetrachloronickelate(II).

**122.** **(1)** The oxidation state of iron in $[Fe(H_2O)_5NO]$ $SO_4$ is +1. The electronic configuration of $Fe^+$ is $[Ar]3d^6 4s^1$. The electron present in $4s$ orbital goes to $3d$ orbital in the presence of $NO^+$. So, the total unpaired electron are 3. Hence, the compound is paramagnetic.

**123.** **(2)** The geometrical isomers of complex $[M(NH_3)_4Cl_2]$ are,

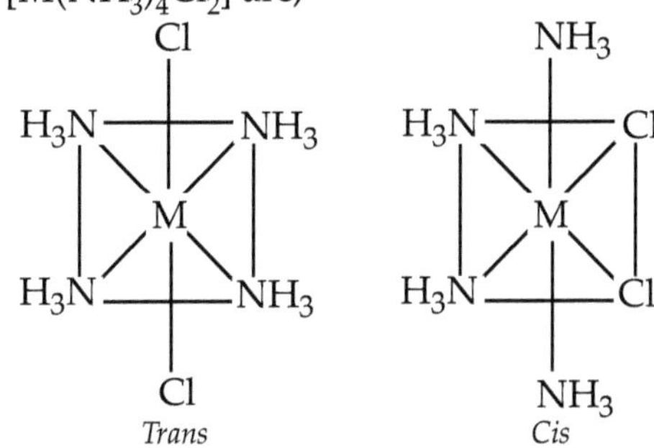

*Trans*          *Cis*

Both geometrical isomers have axis of symmetry. Octahedral complexes are optically active when they posses two or three bidentate ligands.

**124.** (1) (p), (q), (s); (2) (p), (r), (s); (3) (q), (s); (4) (q), (s)

(1)

Trans          Cis

$Co^{2+} = 3d^7$ (Paramagnetic)

(2)

(cis)          (trans)

(3)

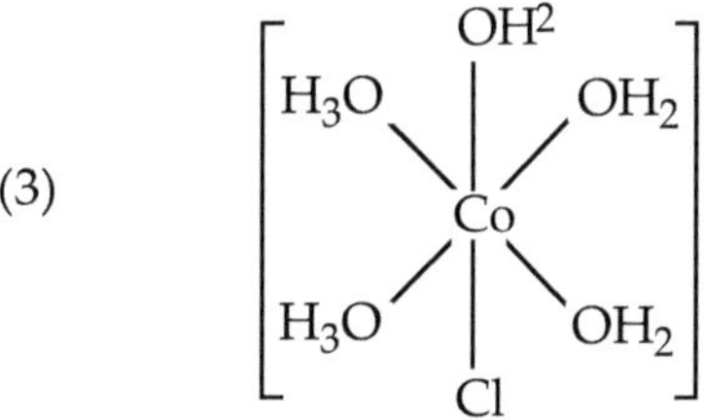

$Co^{2+} = 3d^7$ (Paramagnetic)

(4)

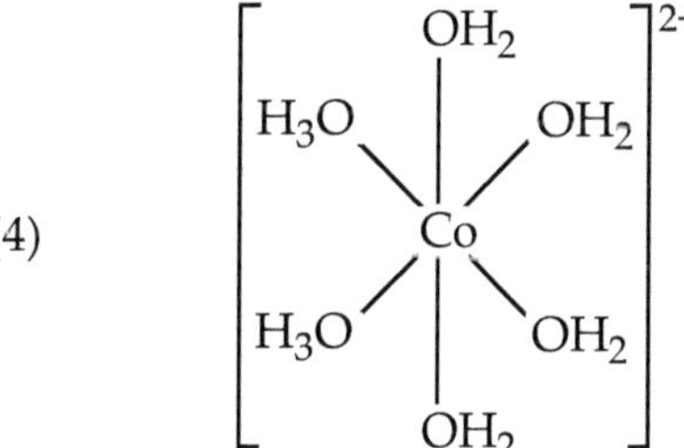

$Ni^{2+} = 3d^8$ (Weak field ligand, paramagnetic)

**125. (4)** In $[V(CO)_6]^-$ the electronic configuration of $V^-$ ion is $[Ar]3d^6$. Thus, it has filled $d$-orbitals for back bonding (M – CO). Stronger the M – CO bond, weaker is the C – O bond or bond order.

**126. (1)** It is given that a solution on dilution with water results in the formation of white precipitate. The volume of precipitate decreases when excess of $NH_4Cl/NH_4OH$ is added leaving behind a white gelatinous precipitate. This takes place due to the formation of tetraammine zinc complex.

The reaction takes place in this process is as follows :

$$Zn^{2+} + 2NH_4OH \rightarrow Zn(OH)_2 + 2NH_4^+$$
$$Zn(OH)_2 + 4NH_4^+ \rightarrow [Zn(NH_3)_4]^{2+} + 2H_2O + 2H^+$$

The tetraammine zinc complex formed is $[Zn(NH_3)_4]^{2+}$.

**127. (4)** It is given that the copper sulphate solution gets decolourised on addition of KCN.

The reaction of copper sulpahte with KCN is as follows :

$$CuSO4 + KCN \rightarrow Cu(CN)_2 + K_2SO_4$$
$$2Cu(CN)_2 \rightleftharpoons 2CuCN + (CN)_2$$

Therefore, the product formed is CuCN.

**128. (1)** The given bond length of carbon monoxide is 1.128 Å.

The bond order of carbon monoxide decreases due to synergic bonding between Fe and CO. Thus, bond length increases. Synergic bonding is a process in which donation of electrons takes place from the filled pi orbitals to an empty orbital of the metal. Hence, the nearby value is 1.15 Å.

**129. (1)** The complex (A) formed for the given reaction is,

$$NiCl_2 + \xrightarrow[\text{excess}]{KCN} K_2Ni(CN)_4$$

The complex (A) formed is $K_2Ni(CN)_4$. The IUPAC name of $K_2Ni(CN)_4$ is potassium tetracyanonickelate (II).

The complex (B) formed for the given reaction is,

$$NiCl_2 + \xrightarrow[\text{excess}]{KCN} K_2Ni(Cl)_4$$

The complex (A) formed is $K_2Ni(CN)_4$. The IUPAC name of $K_2Ni(CN)_4$ is potassium tetrachloronickelate(II).

**130. (2)** Chlorine is a weak field ligand due to which it is unable to pair up the electrons, whereas cyanide is a strong field ligand and have the ability to pair up the electrons. Thus, complex (A) $[K_2Ni(CN)_4]$ is diamagnetic, whereas complex (B) $K_2Ni(Cl)_4$ is paramagnetic with two unpaired electrons

**131. (1)** The electronic configuration of Ni is $[Ar]3d^84s^2$. The electronic configuration is $Ni^{2+}$ is $[Ar]3d^8$.

Chlorine is a weak field ligand due to which it is unable to pair up the electrons. Therefore, distribution of electrons in $3d$ orbitals is shown below :

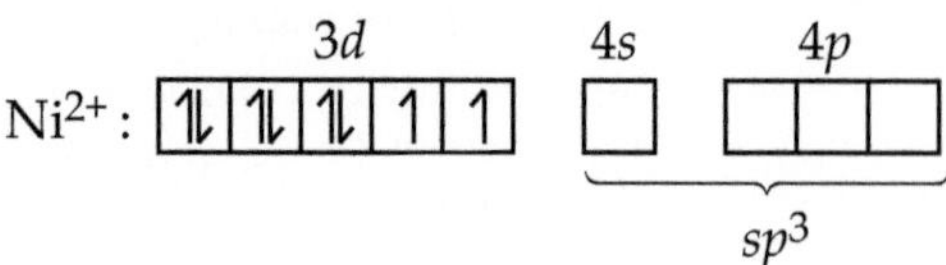

Thus, the hybridisation of complex (A) is $sp^3$. Cyanide is a strong ligand and has the ability to pair up the electrons. Therefore, distribution of electrons in $3d$ orbitals is shown below :

Thus, the hybridisation of complex (B) is $dsp^2$.

**132.** The compounds A and B are given below :

$$Fe^{3+} \xrightarrow{SCN^- \text{ (excess)}} [Fe(SCN)(H_2O)_5]^{2+}$$
(A) blood red
$$\xrightarrow{F^- \text{ (excess)}} [FeF_6]^{3-}$$
(B) colourless

(a) The IUPAC name of 1 and 2 are pentaaquathiocyanato iron (III) ion and hexafluoroferrate(III) ion respectively.

(b) The spin only magnetic moment of B is calculated as follows :

$$\text{Magnetic moment} = \sqrt{n(n+2)}$$
$$= \sqrt{35}$$
$$= 5.92 \text{ B.M.}$$

**133.** The metal M is Titanium and the compound $MCl_4$ is $TiCl_4$. The compound A is $[Ti(H_2O)_6]^{3+}$ and B is $TiO_2$. In the compound , titanium is present in oxidation state. Since in this oxidation state there are no d electrons, the compound is colourless. The complex is purple in colour due to the presence of $d$-$d$ transition of one electron present in the  metal ion

**134. (1)** The given compound, $[Co(NH_3)_4(Br)_2]Cl$ is able to show both geometrical and ionisation isomers a.

The ionisation isomers of $[Co(NH_3)_4(Br)_2]Cl$ are shown by the following reactions.

$$[Co(NH_3)_4(Br)_2]Cl \rightleftharpoons [Co(NH_3)_4(Br)_2]^{2+} + 2Cl^-$$

$$[Co(NH_3)_4(Br)_2]Cl \rightleftharpoons [Co(NH_3)_4BrCl]^+ + Br^-$$

The possible geometrical isomers of $[Co(NH_3)_4(Br)_2]Cl$ are shown as follows :

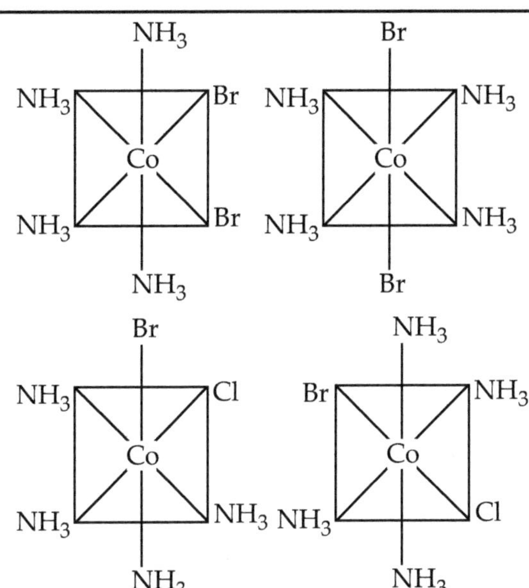

Thus, the correct option is (1).

**135.** (a) The structure of the complex is shown below :

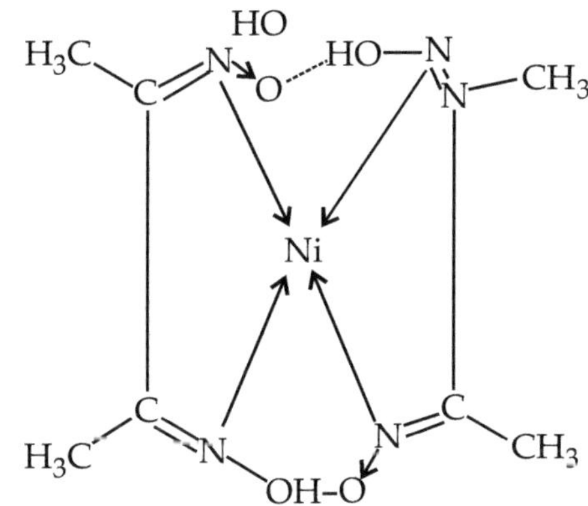

The structure of the complex is shown below.

(b) The oxidation state of nickel in this compound is + 2. The hybridization of this compound is $dsp^2$.

(c) The distribution of electrons in the $3d$ orbitals of $Ni^{2+}$ is shown below :

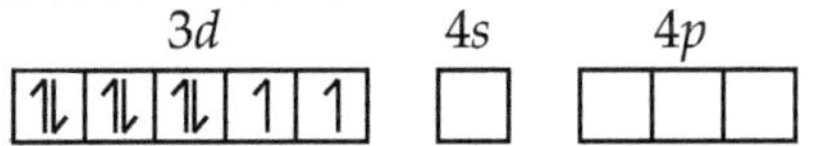

The hybridization of the given complex is $dsp^2$ and this only possible when electrons of $3d$ orbitals rearrange themselves as shown below :

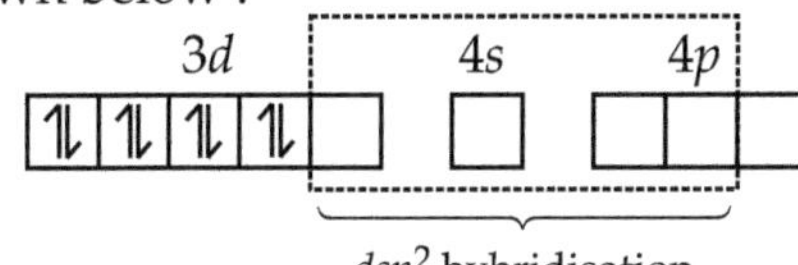

Thus, it is diamagnetic in nature.

**136.** (4) The oxidation state of nickel is + 2.

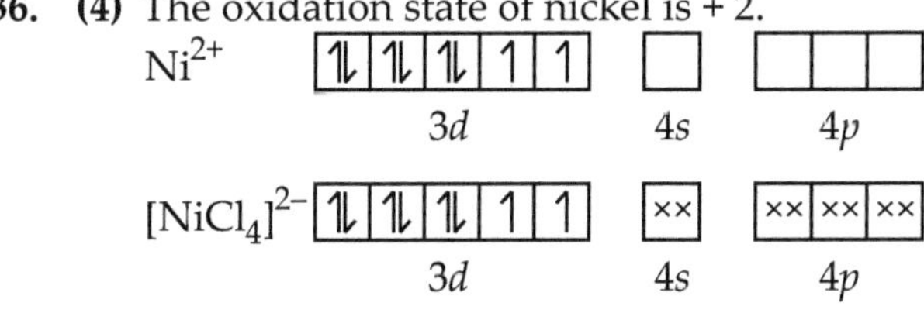

Therefore, its hybridisation is $sp^3$ and the given complex is tetrahedral.

**137.** (2) In the given complex cobalt is present in +2 oxidation state.

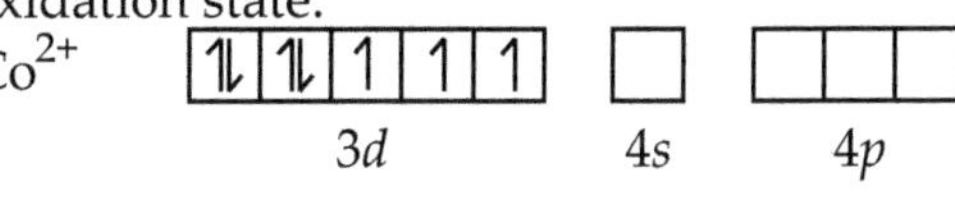

The spin only magnetic moment $= \sqrt{n(n+2)}$

$$= \sqrt{3(3+2)}$$

$$= \sqrt{15}$$

**138.** The given complex is $[K_2[Cr(NO)(NH_3)(CN)_4]$. The IUPAC name of the given complex is Potassium amminetetracyanonitrosonium chromate(I).

The electronic configuration of chromium is $[Ar]3d^54s^1$. Therefore, the electronic configuration of $Cr^+$ is $[Ar]3d^5$.

The distribution of electrons in $3d$ orbital is shown below.

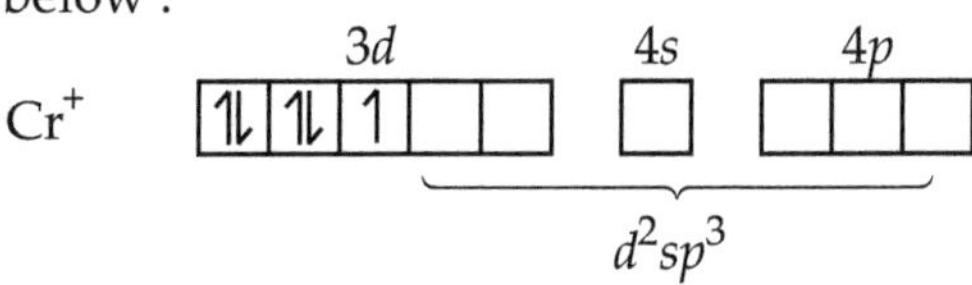

Cyanide is a strong field ligand and has the ability to pair up the electrons. Therefore, distribution of electrons in $3d$ orbitals is shown below :

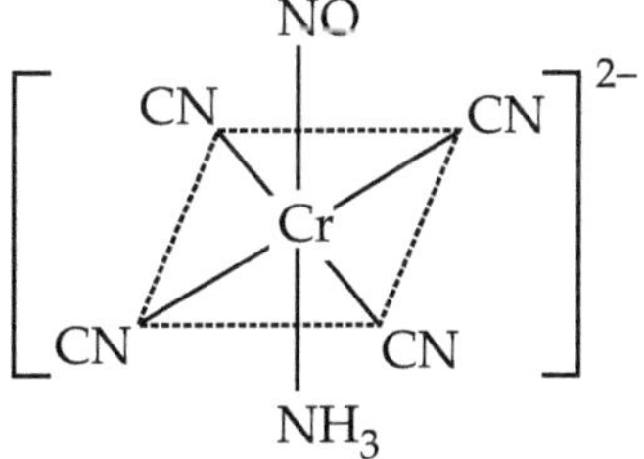

Thus, the hybridisation of given complex is $d^2sp^3$. The shape of given complex is octahedral. The structure of given complex is shown below.

$$\begin{bmatrix} & & NO & & \\ CN & \cdots & | & \cdots & CN \\ & & Cr & & \\ CN & \cdots & | & \cdots & CN \\ & & NH_3 & & \end{bmatrix}^{2-}$$

**139.** (1) The reaction for the formation of AgBr is,

$$Ag^+ + Br^- \rightarrow AgBr$$

The reaction for the formation of $BaSO_4$ is,

$$Ba^{2+} + SO_4^{2-} \rightarrow BaSO_4$$

Thus, the number of moles of Y and Z are 0.01.

**140.** The atomic number of nickel is 28. The electronic configuration of nickel is $[Ar]3d^84s^2$. The oxidation state of nickel in $[NiCl_4]^{2-}$ and $[Ni(CN)_4]^{2-}$ is +2. Thus, the electronic configuration of $Ni^{2+}$ is $[Ar]3d^8$. Chlorine is a weak field ligand, whereas $CN^-$ is a strong field ligand. Therefore, the pairing of electrons is possible in case of $[Ni(CN)_4]^{2-}$.

The distribution of electrons in $3d$ orbitals for both the cases is shown below.

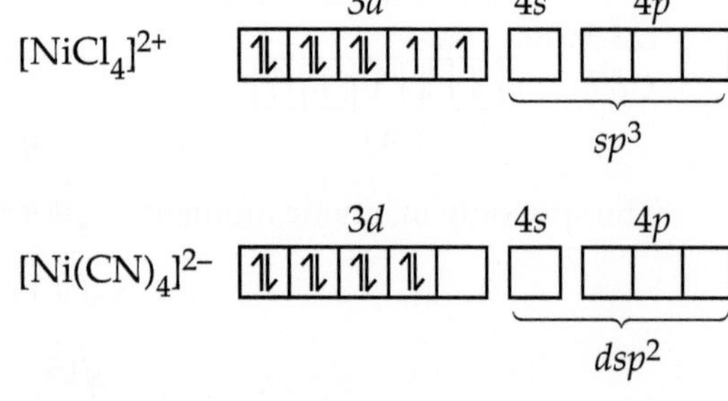

$[NiCl_4]^{2+}$ — $sp^3$

$[Ni(CN)_4]^{2-}$ — $dsp^2$

Therefore, the geometry of $[NiCl_4]^{2-}$ is tetrahedral, whereas the geometry of $[Ni(CN)_4]^{2-}$ is square planar.

In case of $[Ni(CN)_4]^{2-}$, the number of unpaired electron is zero. Therefore, the magneic moment for this complex is 0 B.M.

In case of $[NiCl_4]^{2-}$, the number of unpaired electrons are two. Therefore, the magnetic moment for this complex is,

$$= \sqrt{n(n+2)}$$
$$= \sqrt{2(2+2)}$$
$$= \sqrt{8}$$
$$= 2\sqrt{2} \text{ B.M.}$$

## ⌨ QUESTIONS

1. The statement that is not true about ozone is : **[2020, Main]**
   (1) in the stratosphere, it forms a protective shield against UV radiation
   (2) it is a toxic gas and its reaction with NO gives $NO_2$
   (3) in the atmosphere, it is depleted by CFCs
   (4) in the stratosphere, CFCs release chlorine free radicals (Cl) which reacts with $O_3$ to give chlorine dioxide radicals

2. The incorrect statement(s) among (a)-(d) regarding acid rain is (are) : **[2020, Main]**
   (a) It can corrode water pipes
   (b) It can damage structures made up of stone
   (c) It cannot cause respiratory ailments in animals
   (d) It is not harmful for trees
   (1) (c) and (d)     (2) (a), (b) and (d)
   (3) (c) only     (4) (a), (c) and (d)

3. The condition that indicates a polluted environment is : **[2020, Main]**
   (1) BOD value of 5 ppm
   (2) eutrophication
   (3) 0.03% of $CO_2$ in the atmosphere
   (4) pH of rain water to be 5.6

4. The presence of soluble fluoride ion upto 1 ppm concentration in drinking water is : **[2020, Main]**
   (1) harmful to bones     (2) harmful for teeth
   (3) safe for teeth     (4) harmful to skin

5. The one that is NOT suitable for the removal of permanent hardness of water is : **[2020, Main]**
   (1) Treatment with sodium carbonate
   (2) Calgon's method
   (3) Clark's method
   (4) Ion-exchange method

6. Among the gases (a) - (e), the gases that cause greenhouse effect are : **[2020, Main]**
   (a) $CO_2$     (b) $H_2O$
   (c) CFCs     (d) $O_2$
   (e) $O_3$
   (1) (a), (b), (c) and (d)     (2) (a), (c), (d) and (e)
   (3) (a) and (d)     (4) (a), (b), (c) and (e)

7. When gypsum is heated to 383 K, it forms : **[2020, Main]**
   (1) Dead burnt plaster
   (2) Anhydrous $CaSO_4$
   (3) $CaSO_4.5H_2O$
   (4) $CaSO_4.0.5H_2O$

8. Which of the wrong with respect toour responsibility as a human being to protect our environment ? **[2019, Main]**
   (1) Restricting the use of vehicles,
   (2) Avoiding the use of floodlighted facilities.
   (3) Setting up compost tin in gardens.
   (4) Using plastic bags.

9. **Assertion :** Ozone is destroyed by CFCs in the upper stratosphere.
   **Reason :** Ozone holes increase the amount of UV radiation reaching the earth. **[2019, Main]**
   (1) Assertion and reason are incorrect.
   (2) Assertion and reason are both correct, and the reason is the correct explanation for the assertion.
   (3) Assertion and reason are correct, but the reason is not the explanation for the assertion.
   (4) Assertion is false, but the reason is correct.
   (1) 5 ppm     (2) 0.05 ppm
   (3) 0.5 ppm     (4) 3 ppm

10. Excessive release of $CO_2$ into the atmosphere results in : **[2019, Main]**
    (1) global warming
    (2) polar vortex
    (3) formation of smog
    (4) depletion of ozone

11. The layer of atmosphere between 10 km to 50 km above the sea level is called as : **[2019, Main]**
    (1) troposhere     (2) thermosphere
    (3) stratosphere     (4) mesosphere

12. The regions of the atmosphere, where clouds form and where we live, respectively, are : **[2019, Main]**
    (1) Troposphere and Stratosphere
    (2) Stratosphere and Troposphere
    (3) Troposphere and Troposphere
    (4) Stratosphere and Stratosphere

13. Air pollution that occurs in sunlight is : **[2019, Main]**
    (1) reducing smog     (2) acid rain
    (3) oxidising smog     (4) FOG

**14.** The correct set of species responsible for the photochemical smog is : **[2019, Main]**
(1) $N_2$, $NO_2$ and hydrocarbons
(2) $CO_2$, $NO_2$, $SO_2$ and hydrocarbons
(3) $NO$, $NO_2$, $O_3$ and hydrocarbons
(4) $N_2$, $O_2$, $O_3$ and hydrocarbons

**15.** The primary pollutant that leads to photochemical smog is : **[2019, Main]**
(1) acrolein
(2) nitrogen oxides
(3) ozone
(4) sulphur dioxide

**16.** Biochemical Oxygen Demand (BOD) value can be a measure of water pollution caused by the organic matter. Which of the following statements is correct ? **[2018, Main]**
(1) Aerobic bacteria decrease the BOD value
(2) Anaerobic bacteria increase the BOD value
(3) Clean water has BOD value higher than 10 ppm.
(4) Polluted water has BOD value higher than 10 ppm

**17.** A water sample has ppm level concentration of following anions,
$$F^- = 10;\ SO_4^{2-} = 100;\ NO_3^- = 50$$
The anion/anions that make/makes the water sample unsuitable for drinking is/are : **[2017, Main]**
(1) Only $F^-$
(2) Only $SO_4^{2-}$
(3) Only $NO_3^-$
(4) Both $SO_4^{2-}$ and $NO_3^-$

**18.** Identify the pollutant gases largely responsible for the discoloured and lusterless nature of marble of the Taj Mahal. **[2017, Main]**
(1) $O_3$ and $CO_2$
(2) $CO_2$ and $NO_2$
(3) $SO_2$ and $NO_2$
(4) $SO_2$ and $O_3$

**19.** Which of the following is a set of green house gases ? **[2017, Main]**
(1) $CH_4$, $O_3$, $N_2$, $SO_2$
(2) $O_3$, $N_2$, $CO_2$, $NO_2$
(3) $O_3$, $NO_2$, $SO_2$, $Cl_2$
(4) $CO_2$, $CH_4$, $N_2O$, $O_2$

**20.** BOD stands for : **[2016, Main]**
(1) Biological Oxygen Demand
(2) Bacterial Oxidation Demand
(3) Biochemical Oxygen Demand
(4) Biochemical Oxidation Demand

**21.** Which one of the following substances used in dry cleaning, is a better strategy to control environmental pollution ? **[2016, Main]**
(1) Tetrachloroethylene
(2) Carbon dioxide
(3) Sulphur dioxide
(4) Nitrogen dioxide

**22.** The concentration of fluoride, lead, nitrate and iron in a water sample from an underground lake was found to be 1000 ppb, 40 ppb, 100 ppm and 0.2 ppm, respectively. This water is unsuitable for drinking due to high concentration of : **[2016, Main]**
(1) Fluoride
(2) Lead
(3) Nitrate
(4) Iron

**23.** Photochemical smog consists of excessive amount of X, in addition to aldehydes, ketones, peroxy acetyl nitrile (PAN), and so forth. **X** is : **[2015, Main]**
(1) $CH_4$
(2) $CO$
(3) $CO_2$
(4) $O_3$

**24.** Addition of phosphate fertilisers to water bodies causes : **[2015, Main]**
(1) enhanced growth of algae
(2) increase in amount of dissolved oxygen in water
(3) deposition of calcium phosphate
(4) increase in fish population

**25.** Chlorobenzene reacts with trichloro acetaldehyde in the presence of $H_2SO_4$. **[2014, Main]**

$$\text{C}_6\text{H}_5\text{Cl} + H-\overset{\overset{O}{\|}}{C}-CCl_3 \xrightarrow{H_2SO_4}$$

The major product formed is :

(1) $Cl-C_6H_4-\underset{Cl}{\overset{Cl}{\underset{|}{\overset{|}{C}}}}-C_6H_4-Cl$

(2) $Cl-C_6H_4-\underset{CH_2Cl}{\overset{Cl}{\underset{|}{\overset{|}{C}}}}-C_6H_4-Cl$

(3) $Cl-C_6H_4-\underset{CCl_3}{\overset{|}{CH}}-C_6H_4-Cl$

(4) $Cl-C_6H_4-\underset{Cl}{\overset{|}{CH}}-C_6H_4-Cl$

**26.** Global warming is due to increase of : **[2014, Main]**
(1) methane and nitrous oxide in atmosphere
(2) methane and $CO_2$ in atmosphere
(3) methane and $O_3$ in atmosphere
(4) methane and CO in atmosphere

## ANSWER KEY

| | | | | | | | | | |
|---|---|---|---|---|---|---|---|---|---|
| **1.** (4) | **2.** (2) | **3.** (2) | **4.** (3) | **5.** (3) | **6.** (4) | **7.** (4) | **8.** (4) | **9.** (3) | **10.** (4) |
| **11.** (1) | **12.** (3) | **13.** (3) | **14.** (3) | **15.** (3) | **16.** (4) | **17.** (1) | **18.** (3) | **19.** (4) | **20.** (3) |
| **21.** (2) | **22.** (3) | **23.** (4) | **24.** (1) | **25.** (3) | **26.** (2) | | | | |

## ANSWERS WITH EXPLANATIONS

**1. (4)** In the stratosphere, CFCs release chlorine free radical ($\dot{C}l$).

$$CF_2Cl_2(g) \xrightarrow{UV} \dot{C}l(g) + \dot{C}F_2Cl(g)$$

which react with $O_3$ to give chlorine oxide ($\dot{C}l\dot{O}$) radical not chlorine dioxide ($\dot{C}lO_2$) radical.

$$\dot{C}l(g) + O_3(g) \rightarrow Cl\dot{O}(g) + O_2(g)$$

**2. (1)** (1) Acid rain coorodes water pipes resulting in the leaching of heavy metals such as iron, lead and copper into the drinking water.

(2) Acid rain damages buildings and other structures made of stone or metal.

(3) Acid rain causes respiratory ailments in human beings and animals. Therefore, option 3 is incorrect .

(4) Acid rain is harmful for agriculture, trees and plants as it wasshes down the nutrients needed for its growth. Therefore, option 4 is incorrect.

**3. (2)** In Eutrophication nutrient enriched water bodies support a dense plant population, which kills animal life by depriving it of oxygen and results in subsequent loss of biodiversity. If indicates polluted environment.

**4. (3)** Safe for teeth.

**5. (3)** Temporary hardness of water is removed by clark method and boiling. While permanent hardness of water is removed by treatment with sodium carbonate ($Na_2CO_3$), calgons method and ion-exchange method.

**6. (4)** $CO_2$, $H_2O$, CFCs and $O_3$ are green house gases.

**7. (4)**
$$\underset{\text{Gypsum}}{CaSO_4.2H_2O} \xrightarrow{393\ K} \underset{\text{Plaster of paris}}{CaSO_4.\frac{1}{2}H_2O} + \frac{3}{2}H_2O$$

**8. (4)** Plastic is a polymer which is non-biodegradable. The use of plastic bags is harmful for the environment. The burning of plastic releases toxic substances in the atmosphere. It can also seep into the soil and cause soil pollution and groundwater pollution. Therefore, using plastic bags is wrong with respect to an individual's responsibility as a human being to protect the environment.

**9. (3)** With the increased use of CFCs, the ozone layer in the upper stratosphere is getting depleted at a faster rate. Due to the depletion of ozone layer, harmful UV radiations from the sun enter the earth's atmosphere. Therefore, both the assertion and the reason

are correct, but the reason is not the correct explanation for the assertion.

**10. (4)** The maximum prescribd concentration of copper in drinking water is 3 ppm.

**11. (1)** The green house gases are carboin dioxide, methane, nitrous oxide and ozone. Carbon dioxide is a major contributor in a green house effect. The green house gases cause global warming.

**12. (3)** Stratosphere is the layer of atmosphere that present between 10 km to 50 km above sea level.

**13. (3)** The lowest layer of the atmosphere is the troposphere. All the forms of life and most of the cloud formation exist in the troposphere.

**14. (3)** The photochemical smog in the presence of sunlight contains oxidising agent in high concentration. Therefore, it is called oxidizing smog.

**15. (3)** Photochemical smog consists of aldehydes, nitrogen oxides, peroxyacyl nitrates and tropospheric ozone.

Therefore, the correct set of optin of NO, $NO_2$, $O_3$ and hydrocarbons.

**16. (4)** Polluted water has BOD value higher than 10 ppm and clean water has BOD value less than 5 ppm.

Thus, statement 4 is correct.

**17. (1)** The given concentration of $F^-$ anion is 10 ppm. But the acceptable concentration of $F^-$ anion is up to 1 ppm in drinking water. Therefore, excess concentration of $F^-$ anion results in the decay of bones. Thus, it make water sample unsuitable for drinking.

**18. (3)** The pollutant gases that are responsible for the discolored and lusterless nature of marble of the Taj mahal are **$SO_2$** and **$NO_2$**.

**19. (4)** The green house gases are carbon dioxide, methane, nitrous oxide and ozone. Carbon dioxide is a major contributor in a green house effect. The sources of these gases can be natural or man-made.

**20. (3)** The full form of **BOD** is Biochemical Oxygen demand.

**21. (2)** The use of carbon dioxide in dry cleaning is a better strategy to control environmental pollution because it does not increase environmental pollution. On the other hand, the substances such as tetrachloroethylene, sulfur dioxide and nitrogen dioxide are environmental pollutant due to which their use in dry cleaning is not a better strategy. Hence, the substance which can be used in dry cleaning to control environmental pollution is carbon dioxide.

**22. (3)** The maximum allowed concentration of given ions is shown below.

| Ions | Maximum concentration |
| --- | --- |
| Fluoride | 1.5 ppm |
| Lead | 50 ppb |
| Nitrate | 50 ppb |
| Iron | 0.2 ppm |

The water is unsuitable due to high concentration of nitrate.

**23. (4)** Photochemical smog consists of aldehydes, nitrogen oxides, peroxyacyl nitrates and tropospheric ozone.

**24. (1)** Addition of phosphate fertilisers to water bodies result in the excess formation of algae, which ultimately affects animals live in water bodies by decreasing the amount of dissolved oxygen in water.

**25. (3)** Chlorobenzene reacts with Trichloroacetaldehyde in the presence of $H_2SO_4$ to form DDT as major product.

**26. (2)** Global warming is caused due to the increase in the amount of methane and carbon dioxide gas in the atmosphere. The increase in the amount of these gases warms the earth's atmosphere which results in the global warming.

●●

# Chapter 22

# Organic Chemistry–Some Basic Principles and Techniques

## ⌕ QUESTIONS

**1.** The principle of column chromatography is : **[2019, Main]**
(1) Gravitational force
(2) Capillary action.
(3) Differential absorptin of the substances on the solid phase.
(4) Differential adsorption of the substances on the solid phase.

**2.** In chromatography, which of the following statements is INCORRECT for $R_f$ ? **[2019, Main]**
(1) $R_f$ value depends on the type of chromatography.
(2) The value of $R_f$ can not be more than one.
(3) Higher $R_f$ value means higher adsorption
(4) $R_f$ value is dependent on the mobile phase.

**3.** The IUPAC name for the following compound is : **[2019, Main]**

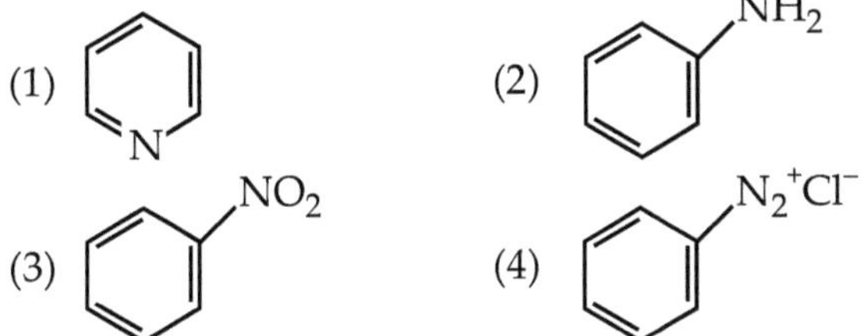

(1) 3-methyl-4-(3-methylprop-1-enyl)-1-heptyne
(2) 3, 5-dimethyl-4-propylhept-6-en-1-yne
(3) 3-methyl-4-(1-methylprop-2-ynyl)-1-heptene
(4) 3, 5-dimethyl-4-propylhept-1-en-6-yne

**4.** Which of the following compounds will be suitable for Kjeldahl's method for nitrogen estimation ? **[2018, Main]**

(1) — pyridine    (2) — aniline (NH₂)
(3) — nitrobenzene (NO₂)    (4) — benzenediazonium chloride ($N_2^+Cl^-$)

**5.** The IUPAC name of the following compound is : **[2018, Main]**

(1) 4-methyl-3-ethylhex-4-ene
(2) 3-ethyl-4-methylhex-4-ene
(3) 4-ethyl-3methylhex-2-ene
(4) 4, 4-diethyl-3-methylbut-2-ene

**6.** The correct match between items of **List-I** and **List-II** is : **[2018, Main]**

| List-I | List-II |
|---|---|
| (A) Coloured impurity | (P) Steam distillation |
| (B) Mixture of *o*-nitrophenol and *p*-nitrophenol | (Q) Fractional distillation |
| (C) Crude Naphtha | (R) Charcoal treatment |
| (D) Mixture of glycerol and sugars | (S) Distillation under reduced pressure |

| | (A) | (B) | (C) | (D) |
|---|---|---|---|---|
| (1) | (R) | (S) | (P) | (Q) |
| (2) | (R) | (P) | (S) | (Q) |
| (3) | (R) | (P) | (Q) | (S) |
| (4) | (P) | (S) | (R) | (Q) |

**7.** Which of the following statements is not true about partition chromatography ? **[2017, Main]**
(1) Mobile phase can be a gas.
(2) Stationary phase is a finely divided solid adsorbent.
(3) Separation depends upon equilibration of solute between a mobile and a stationary phase.
(4) Paper chromatography is an example of partition chromatography.

**8.** Sodium extract is heated with concentrated $HNO_3$ before testing for halogens because : **[2016, Main]**
(1) Silver halides are totally insoluble in nitric acid.
(2) $Ag_2S$ and $AgCN$ are soluble in acidic medium.
(3) $S^{2-}$ and $CN^-$, if present, are decomposed by conc. $HNO_3$ and hence do not interfere in the test.
(4) Ag reacts faster with halides in acidic medium.

**9.** 1.4 g of an organic compound was digested according to Kjeldahl's method and the ammonia evolved was absorbed in 60 mL of $\dfrac{M}{10}$ $H_2SO_4$ solution. The excess sulphuric acid required 20 mL of $\dfrac{M}{10}$ NaOH solution for neutralisation. The percentage of nitrogen in the compound is : **[2015, Main]**

(1)  3       (2)  5

(3)  10      (4)  24

**10.** Match the organic compounds in column-I with the Lassaigne's test results in column-II appropriately : **[2015, Main]**

| Column-I | | Column-II |
|---|---|---|
| (A) Aniline | (i) | Red colour with $FeCl_3$ |
| (B) Benzene sulfonic acid | (ii) | Violet colour with sodium nitro-prusside |
| (C) Thiourea | (iii) | Blue colour with hot and acidic solution of $FeSO_4$ |

|  | A | B | C |
|---|---|---|---|
| (1) | (ii) | (i) | (iii) |
| (2) | (iii) | (ii) | (i) |
| (3) | (ii) | (iii) | (i) |
| (4) | (iii) | (i) | (ii) |

**11.** The total numbers of stable conformers with non-zero dipole moment for the following compound is/are : **[2014, Advanced]**

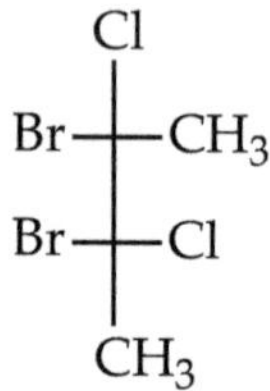

**12.** For the estimation of nitrogen, 1.4 g of an organic compound was digested by Kjeldahl method and the evolved ammonia was absorbed in 60 mL of $\dfrac{M}{10}$ sulphuric acid. The unreacted acid required 20 mL of $\dfrac{M}{10}$ sodium hydroxide for complete neutralisation. The percentage of nitrogen in the compound is : **[2014, Main]**

(1)  6%      (2)  10%

(3)  3%      (4)  5%

**13.** For which of the following molecule significant $\mu \neq 0$ ? **[2014, Main]**

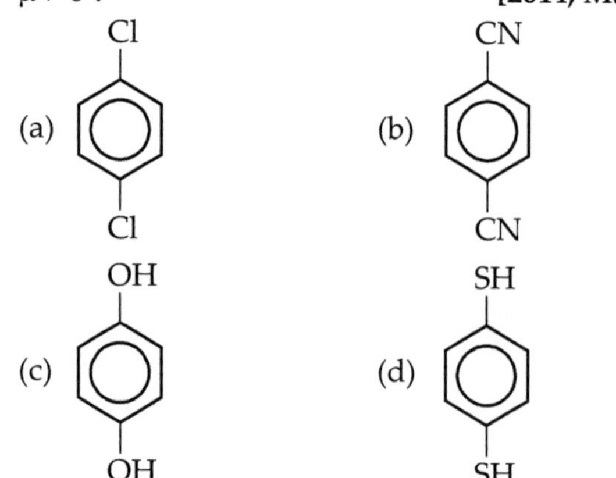

(1)  Only (a)      (2)  (a) and (b)

(3)  Only (c)      (4)  (c) and (d)

**14.** The correct IUPAC name of the following compound

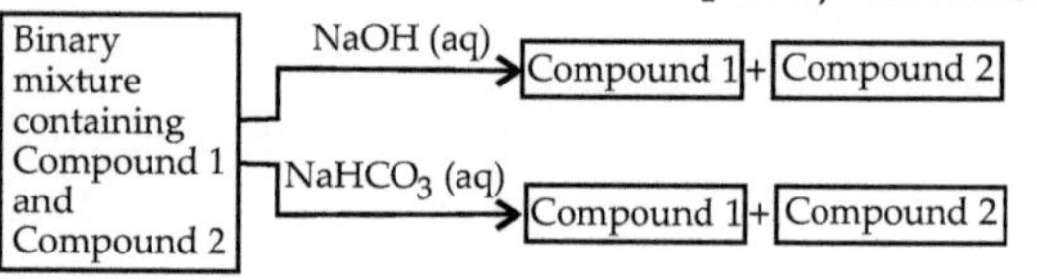

is : **[2014, Main]**

(1)  4-methyl-3-ethylhexane

(2)  3-ethyl-4-methylhexane

(3)  3, 4-ethylmethylhexane

(4)  4-ethyl-3-methylhexane

**15.** The compound that does not liberate $CO_2$, on treatment with aqueous sodium bicarbonate solution, is : **[2013, Advanced]**

(1)  Benzoic acid

(2)  Benzenesulphonic acid

(3)  Salicylic acid

(4)  Carbolic acid (Phenol)

**16.** Identify the binary mixtures that can be separated into individual compounds, by differential extraction, as shown in the given scheme. **[2012, Advanced]**

| Binary mixture containing Compound 1 and Compound 2 | NaOH (aq) → | Compound 1 + Compound 2 |
|---|---|---|
|  | $NaHCO_3$ (aq) → | Compound 1 + Compound 2 |

(1)  $C_6H_5OH$ and $C_6H_5COOH$

(2)  $C_6H_5COOH$ and $C_6H_5CH_2OH$

(3)  $C_6H_5CH_2OH$ and $C_6H_5OH$

(4)  $C_6H_5CH_2OH$ and $C_6H_5CH_2COOH$

**17.** The compound Y is : **[2009, Advanced]**

(1)  $MgCl_2$      (2)  $FeCl_2$

(3)  $FeCl_3$      (4)  $ZnCl_2$

**18.** The compound Z is : **[2009, Advanced]**

(1)  $Mg_2[Fe(CN)_6]$      (2)  $Fe[Fe(CN)_6]$

(3)  $Fe_4[Fe(CN)_6]_3$      (4)  $K_2Zn_3[Fe(CN)_6]_2$

**19.** Match the compounds in Column I with their characteristic tests/reactions given in Column II. Indicate your answer by darkening the appropriate bubbles of the 4 × 4 matrix given in the ORS. **[2008, Advanced]**

| Column I | Column II |
|---|---|
| (1) $H_2\overset{\oplus}{N}-\overset{\ominus}{NH_3}Cl$ | (p) sodium fusion extract of the compound gives Prussian blue colour with $FeSO_4$ |
| (2) $HO-\langle\ \rangle-\underset{COOH}{\overset{\overset{\oplus}{NH_3}\overset{\ominus}{I}}{}}$ | (q) gives positive $FeCl_3$ test |
| (3) $HO-\langle\ \rangle-\overset{\oplus}{NH_3}\overset{\ominus}{Cl}$ | (r) gives white precipitate with $AgNO_3$ |

(4) $O_2N$—〈〉—$NH$-$\overset{\oplus}{N}H_3\overset{\ominus}{Br}$ (s) reacts with aldehydes to form the corresponding hydrazone derivative

with $NO_2$ substituent.

**20.** Among the following, the least stable resonance structure is :  [2007, Advanced]

(1)  (2)

(3)  (4)

**21.** Sodium fusion extract, obtained from aniline, on treatment with iron(II) sulphate and $H_2SO_4$ in presence of air gives a Prussian blue precipitate. The blue colour is due to the formaiton of :

[2007, Advanced]

(1)  $Fe_4[Fe(CN)_6]_3$ (2)  $Fe_3[Fe(CN)_6]_2$
(3)  $Fe_4[Fe(CN)_6]_2$ (4)  $Fe_3[Fe(CN)_6]_3$

**22.** For 1-methoxy-1, 3-butadiene, which of the following resonating structure is the least stable ?

[2005, Screening]

(1)  $\overset{\ominus}{H_2C}-\overset{\oplus}{CH}-CH = CH - O - CH_3$

(2)  $\overset{\ominus}{H_2C}-CH = CH - CH = \overset{\oplus}{O} - CH_3$

(3)  $H_2C = \overset{\oplus}{CH}-\overset{\ominus}{CH}- CH - O - CH_3$

(4)  $H_2C = CH - \overset{\ominus}{CH}- CH = \overset{\oplus}{O} - CH_3$

## ANSWER KEY

| 1. (4) | 2. (3) | 3. (4) | 4. (2) | 5. (3) | 6. (3) | 7. (2) | 8. (3) | 9. (3) | 10. (2) |
|---|---|---|---|---|---|---|---|---|---|
| 11. (3) | 12. (2) | 13. (4) | 14. (2) | 15. (4) | 16. (2, 4) | 17. (3) | 18. (2) | 19. (*) | 20. (1) |
| 21. (1) | 22. (3) | | | | | | | | |

## ANSWERS WITH EXPLANATIONS

**1. (4)** Column chromatography is a technique of separation of organic compounds due to differential adsorption of substances on the solid phase.

**2. (3)** Higher $R_f$ value indicates that the distance travelled by the component is more, that is, the adsorption is less. Therefore, the statement that ``Higher $R_f$ value means higher adsorption'' is incorrect.

**3. (4)** The numbering priories will be given to the alkene. The longest chain is the seven carbon chain. The structure of the compound is shown below :

3, 5-dimethyl-4-propylhept-1-en-6-yne

**4. (2)** Kjedahl's test is used for the estimation of nitrogen from the compounds containing ammonia or ammonium group. The compound which contains amino group out of the given compounds is aniline. Therefore, aniline is suitable for kjedahl's method of nitrogen estimation.

**5. (3)** The parent chain consists of six carbon atoms with a double bond present on second carbon atom, $C_2$. Therefore, the root name is hex-2-ene. Methyl and ethyl groups are attached to $C_3$ and $C_4$ respectively. Therefore, the IUPAC name for the given compound is 4-ethyl-3-methylhex-2-ene.

**6. (3)** (A) Charcoal treatment is used to remove coloured impurity through adsorption process.

(B) Steam distillation is used to separate $o$-nitrophenol and $p$-nitrophenol. Due to the presence of intramolecular hydrogen bonding, $o$-nitrophenol is steam volatile and $p$-nitrophenol is non-volatile.

(C) Fractional distillation is used to separate crude naphtha. Crude naphtha is an inflammable hydrocarbon mixture.

(D) Distillation under reduced pressure is used to separate mixture of glycerol and sugars.

Therefore, the correct match is (A)-(R), (B)-(P), (C)-(Q), (D)-(S).

**7. (2)** The technique that is used to separate the components of the mixture is known as partition chromatography. In this technique, the components get distributed into two phases like liquid-liquid phase or liquid-gas phase but the two phases cannot be solid-gas.

Thus, it is not possible that the stationary phase is a finely divided solid adsorbent in partition chromatography.

**8. (3)** The function of nitric acid is to decompose sodium cyanide or sodium sulphide that is formed during the fusion process and thus, they will not further interfere in testing.

**9. (3)** The percentage of nitrogen present in an organic compound is given as,

$$\% \text{ of N} = \frac{1.4 \times \text{milli equivalents of acid consumed}}{\text{mass of oganic compound}}$$

The milli equivalent of acid consumed is,

Milli equivalents of acid consumed

$$= \left(60 \times \frac{1}{10} \times 2\right) - \left(20 \times \frac{1}{10} \times 1\right)$$

$$= 10$$

Hence, the percentage of nitrogen present in an organic compound is,

$$\% \text{ of N} = \frac{1.4 \times 10}{1.4}$$
$$= 10\%$$

**10. (2)** Aniline reacts with hot and acidic solution of $FeSO_4$ to form blue colour. In Lassaigne's test, sulphur from benzene sulphonic acid reacts with sodium nitroprusside to form violet coloured compound. Thiourea in the presence of $FeCl_3$ produces red colour.

**11. (3)** The total number of stable conformers with non-zero dipole moment of the given compound is three.

**12. (2)** The percentage of nitrogen is calculated as,

$$\%N = \frac{1.4 \times \text{Milli equivalents of acid consumed}}{\text{Mass of organic compound}}$$

Milli equivalents of acid consumed is calculated as,

$M_{eq}$ of acid consumed

$$= \left(60 \times \frac{1}{10} \times 2\right) - \left(20 \times \frac{1}{10} \times 1\right)$$

$$= 10$$

$$\%N = \frac{1.4 \times \text{Milli equivalents of acid consumed}}{\text{Mass of organic compound}}$$

$$= \frac{1.4 \times 10}{1.4}$$

$$= 10\%$$

**13. (4)** Infinite conformations are possible in molecule (c) and (d). Therefore, their dipole moment is non zero.

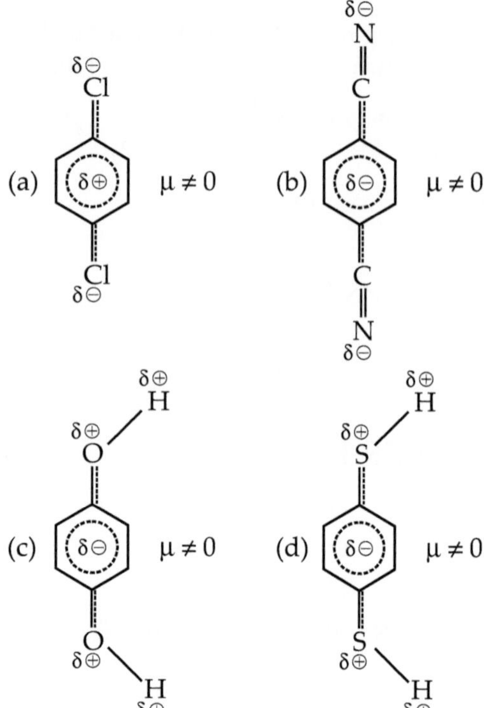

Compound (a) and (b) will have zero net dipole moment.

**14. (2)** The IUPAC names of given compound is 3-ethyl-4-methylhexane.

**15. (4)** Sodium bicarbonate test is used to detect organic compounds that comprises carboxyl group.

Benzoic acid, benzenesulphonic acid and salicylic acid contain carboxyl group, whereas this group is absent in carbolic acid (phenol).

**16. (2, 4)** (1) Both the given compounds are soluble in sodium hydroxide and thus it is not possible to separate them. Benzoic acid is soluble in $NaHCO_3$ but phenol is not soluble in it. Thus, they can be separated by $NaHCO_3$ only.

(2) Benzoic acid is soluble in both the given solutions but benzyl alcohol is insoluble in them. Thus, these two compounds are easily separated by given solutions.

(3) Benzyl alcohol and phenol is neither soluble in NaOH or $NaHCO_3$. Thus, it is not possible to separate them.

(4) The given phenyl acetic acid is soluble in NaOH as well as $NaHCO_3$ but benzyl alcohol is insoluble in both of them. Thus, they can be separated.

**17. (3)** The reaction of $FeCl_3$ with potassium hexacyanoferrate(II) produces intense blue colour precipitate due to the formation of iron hexacyanoferrate(II) and potassium chloride which is shown below :

$$4FeCl_3 + 3K_4[\overset{II}{Fe}(CN)_6] \rightarrow Fe_4[Fe(CN)_6]_3$$
$$\underset{\text{Intense blue}}{} + 2KCl$$

Hence, the compound Y is $FeCl_3$.

**18. (2)** The reaction of $FeCl_3$ with potassium hexacyanoferrate(III) produces brown colour solution due to the formation of iron hexacyanoferrate(III) complex which is shown below :

$$FeCl_3 + K_3[Fe(CN)_6] \rightarrow Fe[Fe(CN)_6] + KCl$$
$$\underset{\text{Brown colouration}}{}$$

Hence, the compound Z is $Fe[Fe(CN)_6]$.

**19.** (1) (r), (s); (2) (p), (q); (3) (p), (q), (r); (4) (p), (s)

(1) The reaction between $H_2N - NH_3^+Cl^-$ and $AgNO_3$ leads to the formation of white precipitate of AgCl and form corresponding hydrazone on reaction with aldehyde.

$$H_2N - NH_3^+Cl^- + RHC = O \rightarrow RHC$$
$$= N - NH_2 + HCl + H_2O$$

(2) The compound given in (2), on reaction with $FeSO_4$, gives blue colour due to the formation of ferric ferrocyanide. It gives positive $FeCl_3$ test due to presence of hydroxyl group.

(3) The compound given in (3), on reaction with $FeSO_4$, gives blue colour due to the formation of ferric ferrocyanide. It gives positive $FeCl_3$ test due to presence of hydroxyl group. On reaction with $AgNO_3$ it leads to the formation of white precipitates of AgCl.

(4) The compound given in (4) on reaction with $FeSO_4$ gives blue colour due to formation of ferric ferrocyanide and on reaction with aldehyde, it form corresponding hydrazone.

**20. (1)** The least stable resonance structure is,

It is due to repulsion between positive charges placed at nitrogen and its adjacent carbon.

**21. (1)** The blue colour arises due to the formation of Prussian blue precipitate. The formula of Prussian blue is $Fe_4[Fe(CN)_6]_3$.

**22. (3)** The structure of 1-methoxy-1, 3-butadiene is shown below :

$$H_2C = \underset{H}{C} - CH = \underset{H}{C} - \ddot{O} - CH_3$$

Among the given resonating structures, the least stable resonating structure for 1-methoxy-1, 3-butadiene is given as follows :

$$H_2C = \underset{H}{C} - \overset{\oplus H}{C} - \overset{\ominus H}{C} - O - CH_3$$

In the above resonace structure, the movement of pi electrons takes place in the opposite direction from the electrons of oxygen present in the methoxy group. Thus, the above shown structure is the least stable resonating structure for 1-methoxy-1, 3-butadiene.

Thus, the correct option is (3).

●●

# Hydrocarbons

## ▶ QUESTIONS

1. The ratio of the mass percentages of 'C & H' and 'C & O' of a saturated acyclic organic compound 'X' are 4 : 1 and 3 : 4 respectively. Then, the moles of oxygen gas required for complete combustion of two moles of organic compound 'X' is ........... .

**[2020, Main]**

2. Which of the following compounds produces an optically inactive compound on hydrogenation ?

**[2020, Main]**

3. The mechanism of $S_N^1$ reaction is given as :

$$R-X \rightarrow \underset{\substack{\text{Ion} \\ \text{pair}}}{R^{\oplus}X^{\ominus}} \rightarrow \underset{\substack{\text{Solvent} \\ \text{separated ion} \\ \text{pair}}}{R^{\oplus} \parallel X^{\ominus}} \xrightarrow{Y^{\ominus}} R-Y+X^{\ominus}$$

A student writes general characteristics based on the given mechanism as : **[2020, Main]**

(a) The reaction is favoured by weak nucleophiles

(b) $R^{\oplus}$ would be easily formed if the substituents are bulky

(c) The reaction is accompained by recemization

(d) The reaction is favoured by non-polar solvents

Which observations are correct ?

(1) b and d      (2) a and c

(3) a, b and c      (4) a and b

4. The total number of monohalogenated organic products in the following (including stereoisomers) reaction is ............. .

$$\underset{\substack{\text{(simplest optically} \\ \text{active alkene)}}}{A} \xrightarrow[\text{(ii) } X_2/\Delta]{\text{(i) } H_2/Ni/\Delta}$$

**[2020, Main]**

5. The decreasing order of reactivity of the following organic molecules towards $AgNO_3$ solution is :

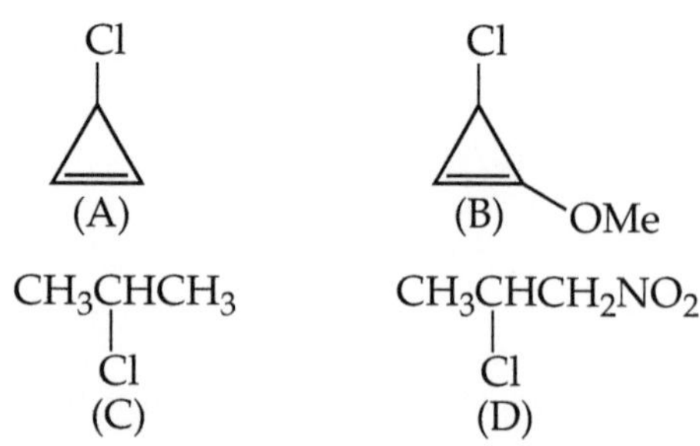

**[2020, Main]**

(1) (A) > (B) > (D) > (C)
(2) (A) > (B) > (C) > (D)
(3) (C) > (D) > (A) > (B)
(4) (B) > (A) > (C) > (D)

6. The increasing order of the acidity of the α-hydrogen of the following compounds is :

**[2020, Main]**

(1) (C) < (A) < (B) < (D)
(2) (B) < (C) < (A) < (D)
(3) (A) < (C) < (D) < (B)
(4) (D) < (C) < (A) < (B)

7. The major product [R] in the following sequence of reactions is :

$$HC\equiv CH \xrightarrow[\text{(ii) } H_3C]{\text{(i) } LiNH_2/ether} [P]$$

$$\xrightarrow[\text{(ii) } NaBH_4]{\text{(i) } HgSO_4/H_2SO_4/ether} [Q] \xrightarrow[\Delta]{\text{Conc. } H_2SO_4} [R]$$

**[2020, Main]**

**8.** Consider the following reactions :

(i) $Glucose + ROH \xrightarrow{dry\ HCl} Acetal$

$\xrightarrow[(CH_3CO)_2O]{x\ eq.\ of}$ acetyl derivative

(ii) $Glucose \xrightarrow{Ni/H_2} A \xrightarrow[(CH_3CO)_2O]{y\ eq.\ of}$ acetyl derivative

(iii) $Glucose \xrightarrow[(CH_3CO)_2O]{z\ eq.\ of}$ acetyl derivative

**[2020, Main]**

'$x$', '$y$' and '$z$' in these reactions are respectively.

(1) 5, 6 and 5
(2) 4, 5 and 5
(3) 5, 4 and 5
(4) 4, 6 and 5

**9.** The major product obtained from $E_2$-elimination of 3-bromo-2-fluoropentane is : **[2020, Main]**

(1) $CH_3CH_2-\overset{\overset{\displaystyle Br}{|}}{C}H-CH=CH_2$

(2) $CH_3-CH_2-\overset{\overset{\displaystyle Br}{|}}{C}=CH-CH_3$

(3) $CH_3-CH=CH-\overset{\overset{\displaystyle F}{|}}{C}H-CH_3$

(4) $CH_3CH_2CH=\overset{\underset{\displaystyle CH_3}{|}}{C}-F$

**10.** The major product in the following reaction is :

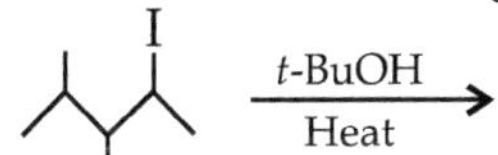

$\xrightarrow[Heat]{t\text{-BuOH}}$

**[2020, Main]**

(1) 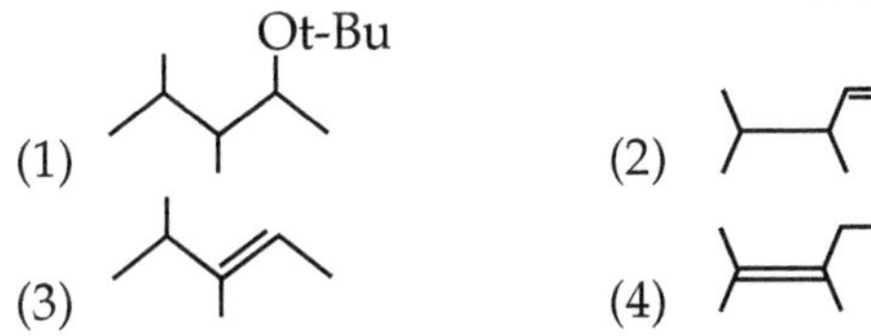 Ot-Bu

(2)

(3)

(4)

**11.** An organic compound (A) (molecular formula $C_6H_{12}O_2$) was hydrolysed with dil. $H_2SO_4$ to give a carboxylic acid (B) and an alcohol (C). 'C' give white turbidity immediately when treated with anhydrous $ZnCl_2$ and conc. HCl. The organic compound (A) is : **[2020, Main]**

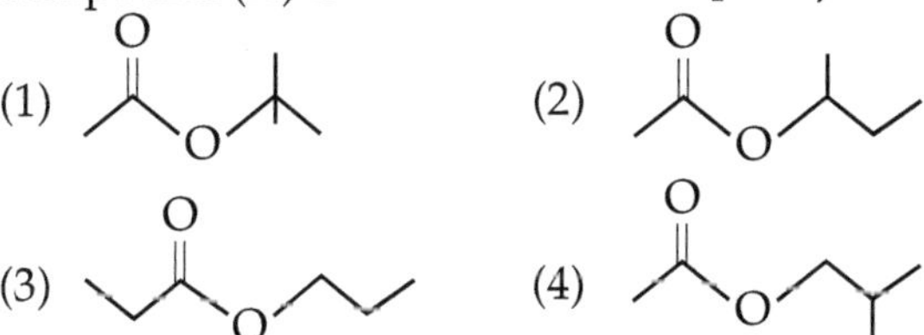

**12.** Match the following : **[2020, Main]**

| Test/Method | Reagent |
|---|---|
| (i) Lucas Test | (a) $C_6H_5SO_2Cl/aq.KOH$ |
| (ii) Dumas method | (b) $HNO_3/AgNO_3$ |
| (iii) Kjeldahl's method | (c) $CuO/CO_2$ |
| (iv) Hinsberg Test | (d) Conc. HCl and $ZnCl_2$ |
| | (e) $H_2SO_4$ |

(1) (i)-(d), (ii)-(c), (iii)-(e), (iv)-(a)
(2) (i)-(b), (ii)-(d), (iii)-(e), (iv)-(a)
(3) (i)-(d), (ii)-(c), (iii)-(b), (iv)-(e)
(4) (i)-(b), (ii)-(a), (iii)-(c), (iv)-(d)

**13.** The increasing order of the boiling points of the major products A, B and C of the following reactions will be : **[2020, Main]**

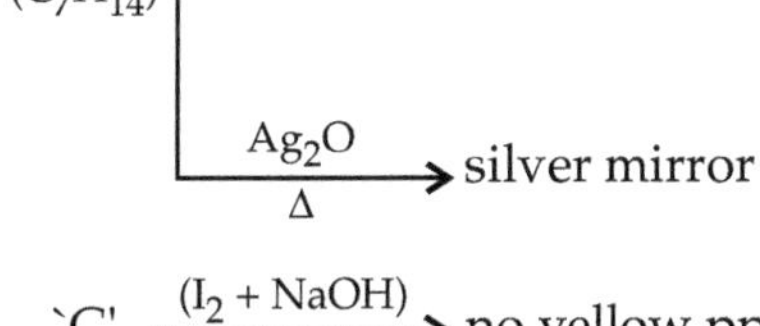

(a) $\diagup\diagup + HBr \xrightarrow{(C_6H_5\overset{\overset{\displaystyle O}{||}}{C})_2} A$

(b) $\diagup= + HBr \longrightarrow B$

(c) $\diagup\diagup + HBr \longrightarrow C$

(1) $C < A < B$
(2) $B < C < A$
(3) $A < B < C$
(4) $A < C < B$

**14.** The most appropriate reagent for conversion of $C_2H_5CN$ into $CH_3CH_2CH_2NH_2$ is : **[2020, Main]**

(1) $Na(CN)BH_3$
(2) $LiAlH_4$
(3) $NaBH_4$
(4) $CaH_2$

**15.** The minimum number of moles of $O_2$ required for complete combustion of 1 mole of propane and 2 moles of butane is ............ . **[2020, Main]**

**16.** Consider the following reactions :

'A' is : **[2020, Main]**

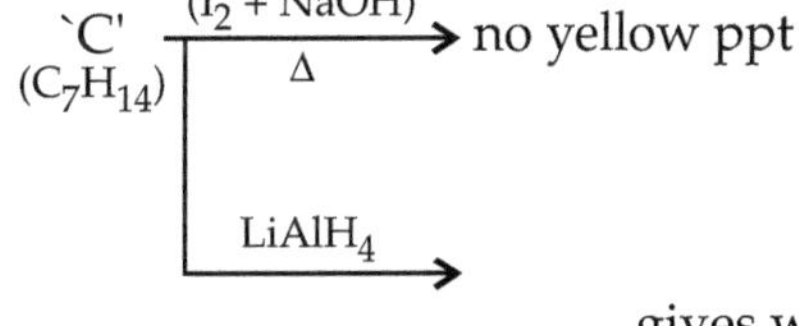

$\underset{(C_7H_{14})}{`A'} \xrightarrow{ozonolysis} `B' + `C'$

$\underset{(C_7H_{14})}{`B'} \xrightarrow[\Delta]{(I_2 + NaOH)}$ yellow ppt

$\xrightarrow[\Delta]{Ag_2O}$ silver mirror

$\underset{(C_7H_{14})}{`C'} \xrightarrow[\Delta]{(I_2 + NaOH)}$ no yellow ppt

$\xrightarrow{LiAlH_4}$

$`D' \xrightarrow[conc.\ HCl]{Anhydrous\ ZnCl_2}$ gives white turbidity within 5 minutes

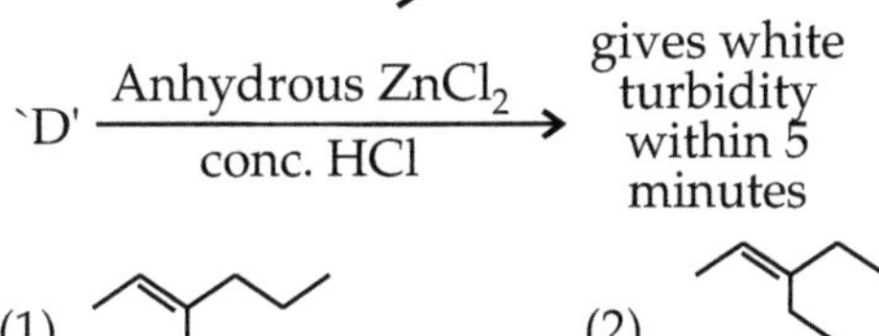

(1)

(2)

(3)

(4)

**17.** The major product [B] in the following reactions is : **[2020, Main]**

$CH_3-CH_2-\overset{\overset{\displaystyle CH_3}{|}}{C}H-CH_2-OCH_2-CH_3$

$\xrightarrow[Heat]{HI} [A]\ alcohol \xrightarrow[\Delta]{H_2SO_4} [B]$

(1) $CH_3-CH_2-\overset{\overset{\displaystyle CH_3}{|}}{C}=CH_2$

(2) $CH_3-CH_2-CH=CH-CH_3$

(3) $CH_2=CH_2$

(4) $CH_3-CH=\overset{\overset{\displaystyle CH_3}{|}}{C}-CH_3$

**18.** Consider the following reactions

$$A \xrightarrow[\text{(ii) }H_3O^+]{\text{(i) }CH_3MgBr} B \xrightarrow[573\,K]{Cu} \text{2-methyl 2 butene}$$

The mass percentage of carbon in A is ........... .

**[2020, Main]**

**19.** The major product of the following reaction is :

**[2019, Main]**

$$CH_3C \equiv CH \xrightarrow[\text{(ii) DI}]{\text{(i) DCI (1 equiv.)}}$$

(1) $CH_3CD(I)CHD(Cl)$

(2) $CH_3CD(Cl)CHD(I)$

(3) $CH_3CD_2CH(Cl)(I)$

(4) $CH_3C(I)(Cl)CHD_2$

**20.** At 300 K and 1 atmospheric pressure, 10 mL of a hydrocarbon required 55 mL of $O_2$ for complete combustion, and 40 mL of $CO_2$ is formed. The formula of the hydocarbon is :　**[2019, Main]**

(1) $C_4H_{10}$ (2) $C_4H_6$

(3) $C_4H_7Cl$ (4) $C_4H_8$

**21.** Which of these factors does not govern the stability of a conformation in acyclic compounds ?

**[2019, Main]**

(1) Steric interactions

(2) Torsional strain

(3) Electrostatic forces of interaction

(4) Angle strain

**22.** But-2-ene on reaction with alkaline $KMnO_4$ at elevated temperature followed by acidification will give :　**[2019, Main]**

(1) $CH_3-\underset{\underset{\displaystyle OH}{|}}{CH}-\underset{\underset{\displaystyle OH}{|}}{CH}-CH_3$

(2) one molecule of $CH_3CHO$ and one molecule of $CH_3COOH$

(3) 2 molecules of $CH_3COOH$

(4) 2 molecules of $CH_3CHO$

**23.** In the following skew conformation of ethane, $H'-C-C-H'$ dihedral angle is :　**[2019, Main]**

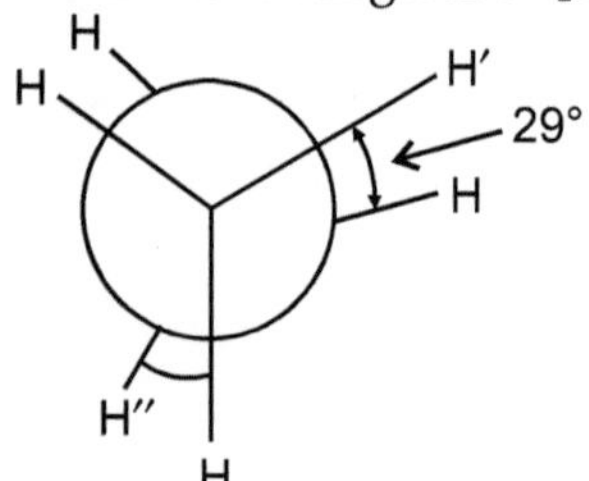

(1) 58° (2) 149°

(3) 151° (4) 120°

**24.** 25 g of unknown hydrocarbon upon burning produces 88 g of $CO_2$ and 9 g of $H_2O$. This unknown hydrocarbon contains :　**[2019, Main]**

(1) 20 g of carbon and 5 g of hydrogen

(2) 22 g of carbon and 3 g of hydrogen

(3) 24 g of carbon and 1 g of hydrogen

(4) 18 g of carbon and 7 g of hydrogen

**25.** Consider the following reactions :

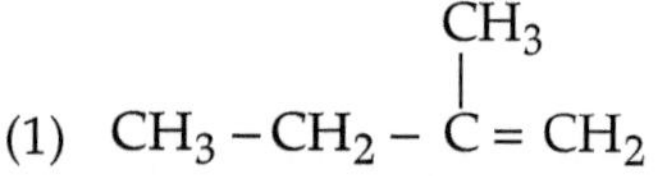

'A' is :　**[2019, Main]**

(1) $CH \equiv CH$

(2) $CH_3-C \equiv C-CH_3$

(3) $CH_3-C \equiv CH$

(4) $CH_2 = CH_2$

**26.** The synonym for water gas when used in the production of methanol is :　**[2019, Main]**

(1) natural gas (2) fuel gas

(3) laughing gas (4) syn gas

**27.** The correct statements among (a) to (d) are :

**[2019, Main]**

(a) saline hydrides produce $H_2$ gas when reacted with $H_2O$

(b) reaction of $LiAlH_4$ with $BF_3$ leads to $B_2H_6$

(c) $PH_3$ and $CH_4$ are electron - rich and electron - precise hydrides, respectively

(d) HF and $CH_4$ are called as molecular hydrides

(1) (a), (b), (c) and (d)

(2) (c) and (d) only

(3) (a), (c) and (d) only

(4) (a), (b) and (c) only

**28.** The metal that gives hydrogen gas upon treatment with both acid as well as base is :

**[2019, Main]**

(1) magnesium (2) mercury

(3) zinc (4) iron

**29.** The temporary hardness of a water sample is due to compound X. Boiling this sample converts X to compound Y. X and Y, respectively, are :

**[2019, Main]**

(1) $Mg(HCO_3)_2$ and $Mg(OH)_2$

(2) $Ca(HCO_3)_2$ and $Ca(OH)_2$

(3) $Mg(HCO_3)_2$ and $MgCO_3$

(4) $Ca(HCO_3)_2$ and $CaO$

**30.** For the given compound **X**, the total number of optically active stereoisomers is ........ .

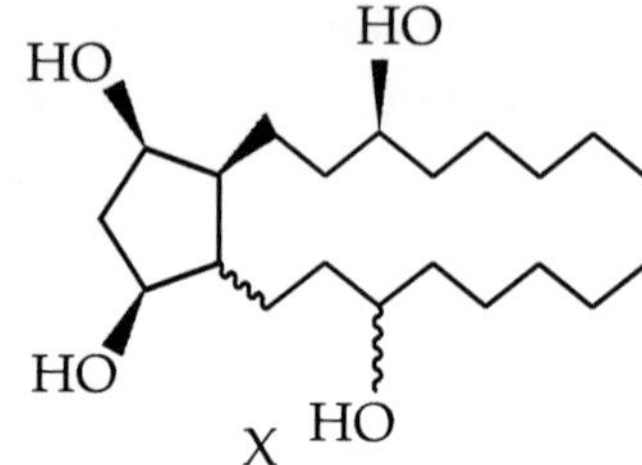

- This type of bond indicates that the configuration at the specific carbon and the geometry of the double bond is fixed

~ This type of bond indicates that the configuration at the specific carbon and the geometry of the double bond is **NOT** fixed    [**2018, Advanced**]

**31.** The *trans*-alkenes are formed by the reduction of alkynes with :    [**2018, Main**]
(1) $H_2$-Pd-C, $BaSO_4$    (2) $NaBH_4$
(3) Na/liq. $NH_3$    (4) Sn-HCl

**32.** When 2-butyne is treated with $H_2$/Lindlar's catalyst, compound X is produced as the major product and when treated with Na/liq. $NH_3$ it produces Y as the major product. Which of the following statements is correct ?    [**2018, Main**]
(1) X will have higher dipole moment and higher boiling point than Y
(2) Y will have higher dipole moment and higher boiling point than X
(3) X will have lower dipole moment and lower boiling point than Y
(4) X will have higher dipole moment and lower boiling point than X

**33.** The correct statements for the following addition reaction is/are :    [**2017, Advanced**]

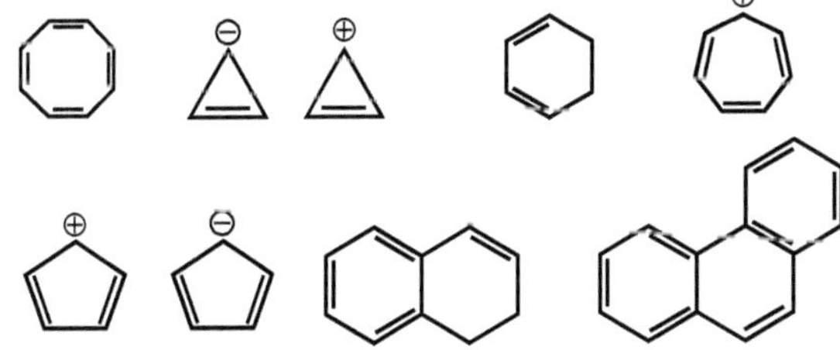

(1) **O** and **P** are identical molecules
(2) (**M** and **O**) and (**N** and **P**) are two pairs oif diastereomers
(3) (**M** and **O**) and (**N** and **P**) are two pairs of enantiomers
(4) Bromination proceeds through *trans*-addition in both the reactions

**34.** Among the following, the number of aromatic compound(s) is :    [**2017, Advanced**]

but not haloform reaction, whereas **S** undergoes haloform reaction but not Cannizzaro reaction.

(i) $\mathbf{P} \xrightarrow[\text{(ii) Zn/H}_2\text{O}]{\text{(i) O}_3\text{/CH}_2\text{Cl}_2} \mathbf{Q}$ $(C_8H_8O)$

(ii) $\mathbf{R} \xrightarrow[\text{(ii) Zn/H}_2\text{O}]{\text{(i) O}_3\text{/CH}_2\text{Cl}_2} \mathbf{S}$ $(C_8H_8O)$

The options with suitable combination of **P** and **R**, respectively, is/are :    [**2017, Advanced**]

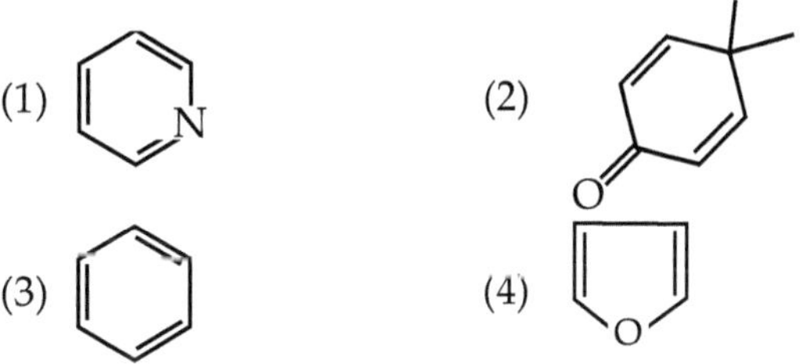

**36.** Which of the following molecules is least resonance stabilised ?    [**2017, Main**]

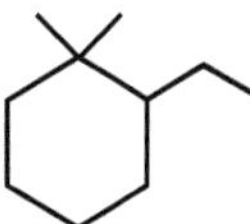

**37.** Methyl-pent-2-ene on reaction with HBr in presence of peroxide forms an addition product. The number of possible stereoisomers for the product is :    [**2017, Main**]
(1) Two    (2) Four
(3) Six    (4) Zero

**38.** The IUPAC name of the following compound is :    [**2017, Main**]

(1) 1, 1-Dimethyl-2-ethylcyclohexane
(2) 2-Ethyl-1, 1-dimethylcyclohexane
(3) 1-Ethyl-2, 2-dimethylcyclohexane
(4) 2, 2-Dimethyl-1-ethylcyclohexane

**39.** Which of the following compounds is most reactive to an aqueous solution of sodium carbonate ?    [**2017, Main**]

**35.** Compounds **P** and **R** upon ozonolysis produce **Q** and **S**, respectively. The molecular formula of **Q** and **S** is $C_8H_8O$. **Q** undergoes Cannizzaro reaction

**40.** In the following structure, the double bonds are marked as I, II, III and IV

Geometrical isomerism is not possible at sites :

**[2017, Main]**

(1) III

(2) I

(3) I and III

(4) III and IV

**41.** Among the following, reactions which gives/give *tert*-butyl benzene as the major product is/are :

**[2016, Advanced]**

(1) 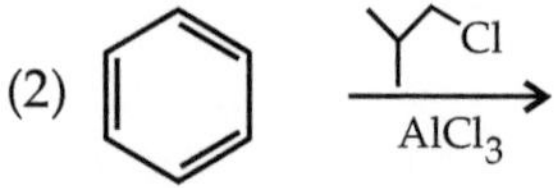

(2) 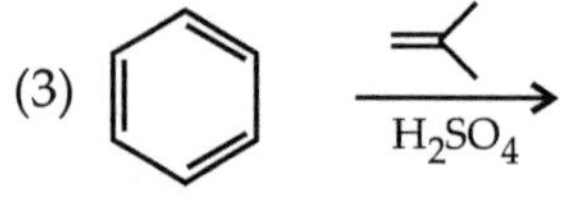

(3) (benzene) $\xrightarrow{\text{H}_2\text{SO}_4}$ (isobutylene)

(4) (benzene) $\xrightarrow{\text{BF}_3\text{OeT}_2}$ (isobutyl alcohol)

**42.** The hydrocarbon with seven carbon atoms containing a neopentyl and a vinyl group is :

**[2016, Main]**

(1) 2, 2-dimethyl-4-pentene

(2) Isopropyl-2-butene

(3) 4, 4-dimethylpentene

(4) 2, 2-dimethyl-3-pentene

**43.** The ``N'' which does not contribute to the basicity for the compound is :  **[2016, Main]**

(1) N7

(2) N9

(3) N1

(4) N3

**44.** The reaction of propene with HOCl ($Cl_2 + H_2O$) proceeds through the intermediate :

**[2016, Main]**

(1) $CH_3 - CH^+ - CH_2 - OH$

(2) $CH_3 - CH^+ - CH_2 - Cl$

(3) $CH_3 - CH(OH) - CH_2^+$

(4) $CH_3 - CHCl - CH_2^+$

**45.** Compounds that on hydrogenation produces optically inactive compound(s) is/are :

**[2016, Main]**

**46.** In the following reaction, the major product is :

**[2015, Advanced]**

**47.** In the following reactions, the product **S** is :

**[2015, Advanced]**

**48.** The major product **U** in the following reactions is :  **[2015, Advanced]**

(1) 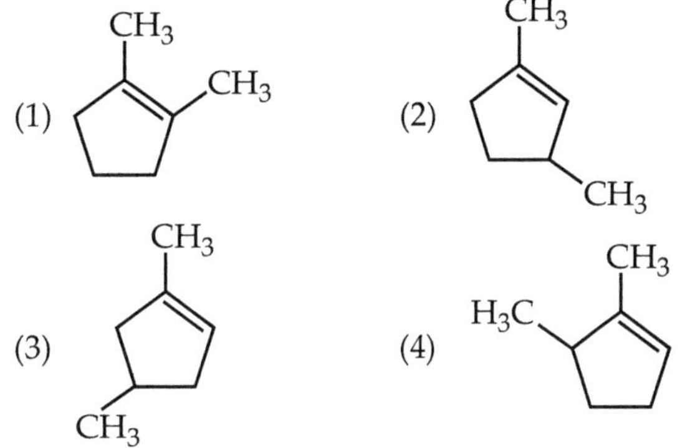

(2)

(3)

(4)

**Paragraph for Question 49**

In the following reactions

$$C_8H_6 \xrightarrow[\text{H}_2]{\text{Pd-BaSO}_4} C_8H_8 \xrightarrow[\text{(ii) H}_2\text{O}_2\text{,NaOH,H}_2\text{O}]{\text{(i) B}_2\text{H}_6} X$$

$$\downarrow \begin{array}{c} \text{H}_2\text{O} \\ \text{HgSO}_4\text{, H}_2\text{SO}_4 \end{array}$$

$$C_8H_8O \xrightarrow[\text{(ii) H}^+\text{, heat}]{\text{(i) EtMgBr, H}_2\text{O}} Y$$

**49.** Compound **X** is : **[2015, Advanced]**

(1)

(2)

(3)

(4)

**50.** The major compound **Y** is : **[2015, Advanced]**

(1)

(2)

(3)

(4)

**51.** Which of the following compounds will exhibit geometrical isomerism ? **[2015, Advanced]**

(1) 1-Phenyl-2-butene

(2) 3-Phenyl-1-butene

(3) 2-Phenyl-1-butene

(4) 1, 1-Diphenyl-1-propane

**52.** Which compound would give 5-keto-2-methyl hexanal upon ozonolysis ? **[2015, Main]**

(1)

(2)

(3)

(4)

**53.** The optically inactive compound from the following is : **[2015, Main]**

(1) 2-chloropropanal

(2) 2-chloropentane

(3) 2-chlorobutane

(4) 2-chloro-2-methylbutane

**54.** 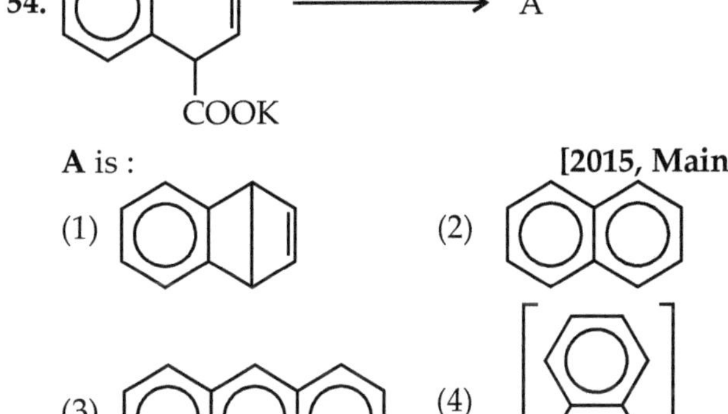

**A** is : **[2015, Main]**

(1)

(2)

(3)

(4)

**55.** A compound **A** with molecular formula $C_{10}H_{13}Cl$ gives a white precipitate on adding silver nitrate solution. **A** on reacting with alcoholic KOH gives compound **B** as the main product. **B** on ozonolysis gives **C** and **D**. **C** gives Cannizaro reaction but not aldol condensation. **D** gives aldol condensation but not Cannizaro reaction. A is : **[2015, Main]**

(1) $C_6H_5 - CH_2 - \underset{\underset{\text{Cl}}{|}}{\overset{\overset{\text{CH}_3}{|}}{C}} - CH_3$

(2) $C_6H_5 - CH_2 - CH_2 - \underset{\underset{\text{Cl}}{|}}{CH} - CH_3$

(3) $C_6H_5 - CH_2 - CH_2 - CH_2 - CH_2 - Cl$

(4)

**56.** The number of structural isomers for $C_6H_{14}$ is :
**[2015, Main]**
(1) 3         (2) 4
(3) 5         (4) 6

**57.** What is the major product expected from the following reaction ?

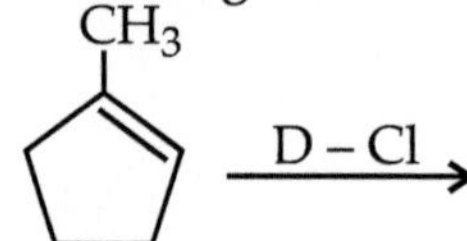

Where D is an isotope of Hydrogen.
**[2015, Main]**

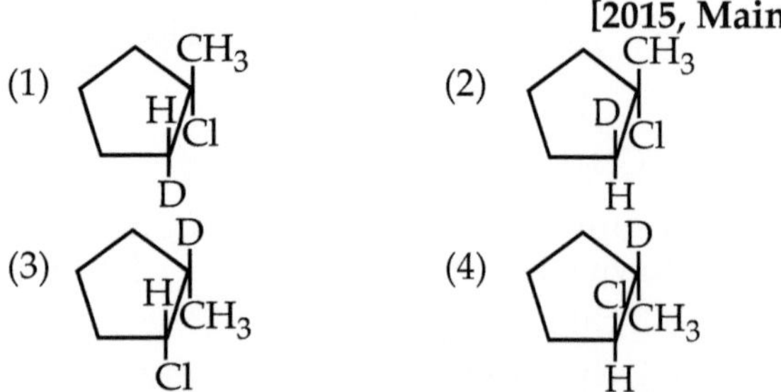

**58.** Isomers of hexane, based on their branching, can be divided into three distinct classes as shown in the figure. **[2014, Advanced]**

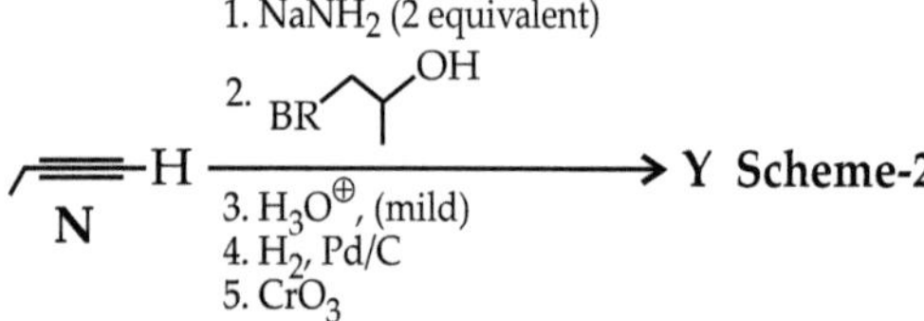

The correct order of their boiling point is :
(1) $I > II > III$      (2) $III > II > I$
(3) $II > III > I$      (4) $III > I > II$

**Paragraph for Question 59**

Schemes **1 and 2** describes sequential transformation of alkynes **M** and **N**. Consider only the **major products** formed in each step for the schemes.

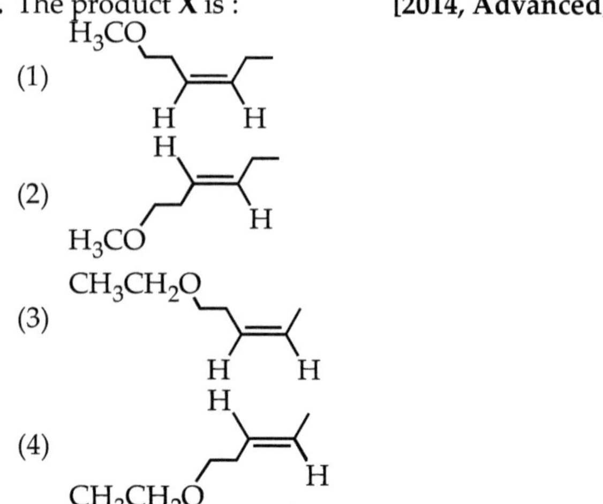

**59.** The product **X** is : **[2014, Advanced]**

(1)

(2)

(3)

(4)

**60.** The major organic compound formed by the reaction of 1, 1, 1-trichloroethane with silver powder is : **[2014, Main]**
(1) Acetylene      (2) Ethene
(3) 2-Butyne      (4) 2-Butene

**61.** In the hydroboration-oxidation reaction of propene with diborane, $H_2O_2$ and NaOH, the organic compound formed is : **[2014, Main]**
(1) $CH_3CH_2OH$    (2) $CH_3CHOHCH_3$
(3) $CH_3CH_2CH_2OH$    (4) $(CH_3)_3COH$

**62.** In which of the following pairs A is more stable than B ? **[2014, Main]**

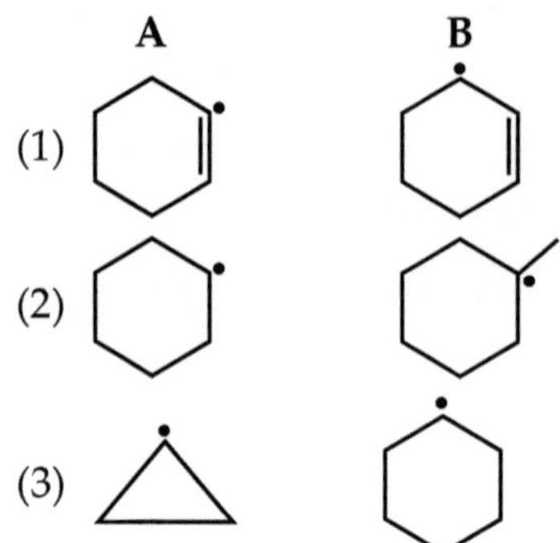

(4) $Ph_3C^{\bullet}, (CH_3)_3C^{\bullet}$

**63.** The reagent needed for converting

$$Ph-C\equiv C-Ph \longrightarrow \underset{H}{\overset{Ph}{}}C=C\underset{Ph}{\overset{H}{}}$$

is : **[2014, Main]**
(1) Cat. Hydrogenation    (2) $H_2$/Lindlar Cat.
(3) $Li/NH_3$      (4) $LiAlH_4$

**64.** The gas liberated by the electrolysis of Dipotassium succinate solution is : **[2014, Main]**
(1) Ethane      (2) Ethyne
(3) Ethene      (4) Propene

**65.** $C_6H_5-CH_2-CH=CH_2$ on mercuration demercuration produces the major product : **[2014, Main]**

(1) $C_6H_5-CH_2-CH(OH)-CH_3$

(2) $C_6H_5-CH_2-CH_2-CH_2-OH$

(3) $C_6H_5-CH_2-CH(OH)-CH_2(OH)$

(4) $C_6H_5-CH_2COOH$

**66.** In the presence of peroxide, HCl and HI do not give anti-Markownikoff's addition to alkenes because : **[2014, Main]**
(1) One of the steps is endothermic in HCl and HI
(2) Both HCl and HI are strong acids
(3) HCl is oxidising and the HI is reducing
(4) All the steps are exothermic in HCl and HI

**67.** Which of the following molecules has two sigma($\sigma$) and two pi($\pi$) bonds ?  **[2014, Main]**
(1) $C_2H_4$
(2) $N_2F_2$
(3) $C_2H_2Cl_2$
(4) HCN

**Paragraph for Question 68**

**P** and **Q** are isomers of dicarboxylic acid $C_4H_4O_4$. Both decolorise $Br_2/H_2O$. On heating, **P** forms the cyclic anhydride.

Upon treatment with dilute alkaline $KMnO_4$, **P** as well as **Q** as could produce one or more than one from **S, T** and **U**.

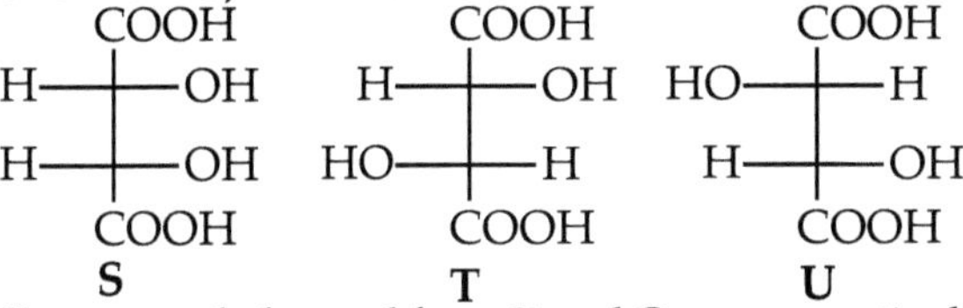

**68.** Compounds formed from **P** and **Q** are respectively **[2013, Advanced]**
(1) Optically active **S** and optically active pair (**T, U**)
(2) Optically inactive **S** and optically inactive pair (**T, U**)
(3) Optically active pair (**T, U**) and optically active **S**
(4) Optically inactive pair (**T, U**) and optically inactive **S**

**69.** Match the chemical conversions in **List I** with the appropriate reagents in **List II** and select the correct answer using the code given below this lists :  **[2013, Advanced]**

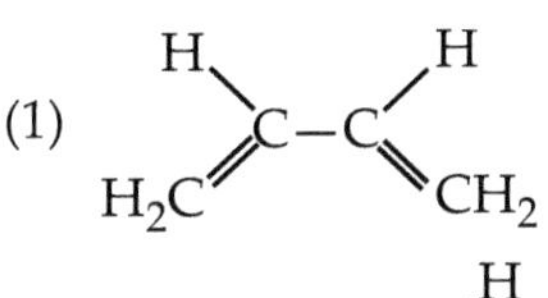

|  List I  |  List II  |
|---|---|
| (P) $\rangle$—Cl $\rightarrow$ $\rangle$= | 1. (i) $Hg(OAc)_2$; (ii) $NaBH_4$ |
| (Q) $\rangle$—ONa $\rightarrow$ $\rangle$—OEt | 2. NaOEt |
| (R) | 3. Et-Br |
| (S) | 4. (i) $BH_3$; (ii) $H_2O_2/NaOH$ |

**Codes :**

|  | P | Q | R | S |
|---|---|---|---|---|
| (1) | 2 | 3 | 1 | 4 |
| (2) | 3 | 2 | 1 | 4 |
| (3) | 2 | 3 | 4 | 1 |
| (4) | 3 | 2 | 4 | 1 |

**70.** The number of optically active products obtained from the complete ozonolysis of the given compound is :  **[2012, Advanced]**

$$CH_3-CH=CH-\overset{CH_3}{\underset{H}{C}}-CH=CH-\overset{H}{\underset{CH_3}{C}}-CH=CH-CH_3$$

(1) 0
(2) 1
(3) 2
(4) 4

**71.** Which of the following molecules, in pure form, is/are **unstable** at room temperature ?  **[2012, Advanced]**

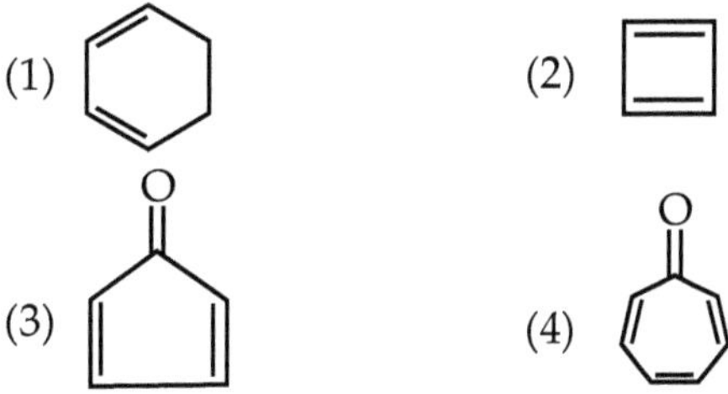

**72.** Amongst the given options, the compounds in which all the atoms are in one plane in all the possible conformations (if any) is/are :  **[2011, Advanced]**

(1) $\overset{H}{\underset{H_2C}{\diagdown}}C-C\overset{H}{\underset{CH_2}{\diagup}}$

(2) $H-C\equiv C-C\overset{H}{\underset{CH_2}{\diagdown}}$

(3) $H_2C = C = O$

(4) $H_2C = C = CH_2$

**Paragraph for Question 73 and 74**

An acyclic hydrocarbon **P**, having molecular formula $C_6H_{10}$, gave acetone as the only organic product through the following sequence of reactions, in which **Q** is an intermediate organic compound.

$$\underset{(C_6H_{10})}{P} \xrightarrow[\substack{\text{(ii) } NaBH_4/ethanol \\ \text{(iii) dil. acid}}]{\text{(i) dil. } H_2SO_4/HgSO_4} Q \xrightarrow[\substack{\text{(ii) } O_3 \\ \text{(iii) } Zn/H_2O}]{\substack{\text{(i) conc. } H_2SO_4 \\ \text{(catalytic amount)} \\ (-H_2O)}} 2 \begin{array}{c} O \\ \| \\ C \\ H_3C \quad CH_3 \end{array}$$

**73.** The structure of compound **P** is :  **[2011, Advanced]**
(1) $CH_3CH_2CH_2CH_2-C\equiv C-H$
(2) $H_3CH_2C-C\equiv C-CH_2CH_3$
(3) $\overset{H_3C}{\underset{H_3C}{\diagdown}}H-C-C\equiv C-CH_3$
(4) $\overset{H_3C}{\underset{H_3C}{\diagup}}H_3C-C-C\equiv C-H$

**74.** The structure of the compound **Q** is :
(1) $\overset{H_3C}{\underset{H_3C}{\diagdown}}H-\overset{OH}{\underset{H}{C}-C}-CH_2CH_3$

(2) 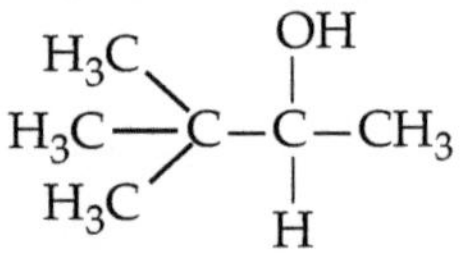

(3) 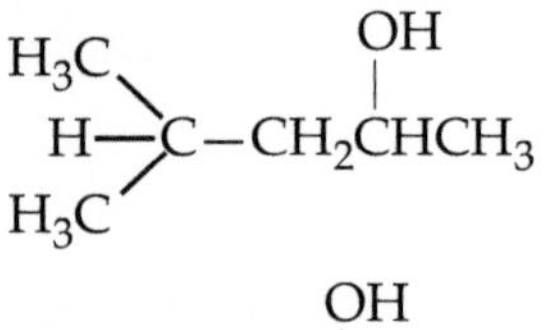

(4) 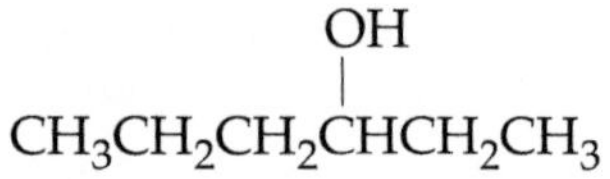

**75.** The total number of alkenes possible by dehydrobromination of 3-bromo-3-cyclopentylhexane using alcoholic KOH is : **[2011, Advanced]**

**76.** The total number of contributing structures showing hyperconjugation (involving C–H bonds) for the following carbocation is : **[2011, Advanced]**

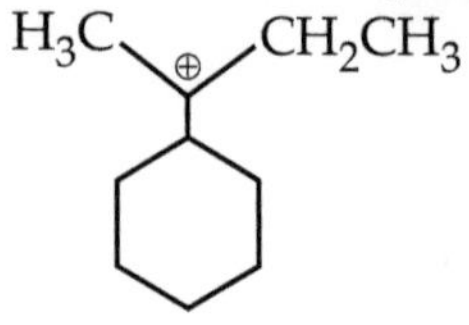

**77.** The synthesis of 3-octyne is achieved by adding a bromoalkane into a mixture of sodium amide and an alkyne. The bromoalkane and alkyne respectively are : **[2010, Advanced]**
(1) $BrCH_2CH_2CH_2CH_2CH_3$ and $CH_3CH_2C \equiv CH$
(2) $BrCH_2CH_2CH_3$ and $CH_3CH_2CH_2C \equiv CH$
(3) $BrCH_2CH_2CH_2CH_2CH_3$ and $CH_3C \equiv CH$
(4) $BrCH_2CH_2CH_2CH_3$ and $CH_3CH_2C \equiv CH$

**78.** In the Newman projection or 2, 2-dimethylbutane **X** and **Y** can respectively be : **[2010, Advanced]**

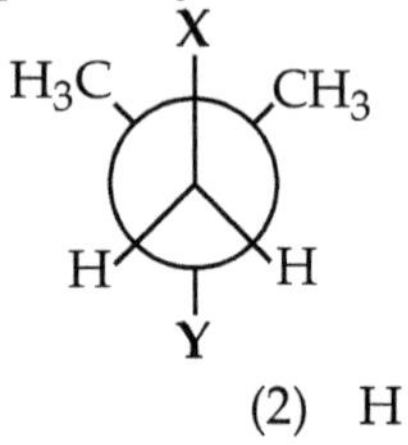

(1) H and H (2) H and $C_2H_5$
(3) $C_2H_5$ and H (4) $CH_3$ and $CH_3$

**79.** The total number of cyclic isomers possible for a hydrocarbon with the molecular formula $C_4H_6$ is.

**80.** The correct statements about the compound $H_3C(HO)HC{-}CH = CH{-}CH(OH)CH_3$ (**X**) is/are : **[2009, Advanced]**
(1) The total number of stereoisomers possible for **X** is 6
(2) The total number of diastereomers possible for **X** is 3
(3) If the stereochemistry about the double bond in **X** is *trans*, the number of enantiomers possible for X is 4
(4) If the stereochemistry about the double bond in **X** is *cis*, the number of enantiomers possible for **X** is 2

**81.** In the following carbocation, H/$CH_3$ that is most likely to migrate to the positively charged carbon is : **[2009, Advanced]**

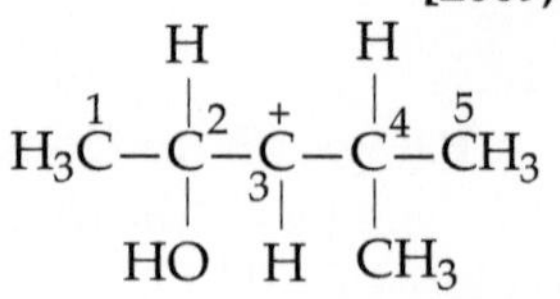

(1) $CH_3$ at C-4 (2) H at C-4
(3) $CH_3$ at C-2 (4) H at C-2

**82.** The total number of cyclic structural as well as stereo isomers possible for a compound with the molecular formula $C_5H_{10}$ is. **[2009, Advanced]**

**83.** Hyperconjugation involves overlap of the following orbitals : **[2008, Advanced]**
(1) $\sigma - \sigma$ (2) $\sigma - p$
(3) $p - p$ (4) $\pi - \pi$

**84.** One Indian and four American men and their wives are to be seated randomly around a circular table. Then the conditional probability that the Indian man is seated adjacent to his wife given that each American man is seated adjacent to his wife is : **[2007, Advanced]**
(1) $\frac{1}{2}$ (2) $\frac{1}{3}$
(3) $\frac{2}{5}$ (4) $\frac{1}{5}$

**85.** Monomer A of a polymer on ozonolysis yields two moles of HCHO and one mole of $CH_3COCHO$. **[2005, Main]**
(a) Deduce the structure of A.
(b) Write the structure of ``all *cis*''–form of polymer of compound A

**86.** $\mu_{obs} = \Sigma \mu_i x_i$
Where, $\mu_i$ is the dipole moment of stable conformer and $x_i$ is the mole fraction of that conformer. **[2005, Main]**
(a) Write stable conformer for $Z - CH_2 - CH_2 - Z$ in Newman's projection.
If $m_{solution}$ = 1.0 D and the mole fraction of anti form = 0.82, find $\mu_{Gouche.}$
(b) Write most stable mevso conformer of
CHDY
|
CHDY
If (i) Y = $CH_3$ about $C_2 - C_3$ rotation and
(ii) Y = OH about $C_1 - C_2$ rotation.

**87.** (a) Draw Newmann's projection for the less stable staggered form of butane. **[2007, Main]**
(b) Relatively less stability of the staggered form is due to
(i) Torsional strain.
(ii) Vander Waal's strain
(iii) Combination of the above two.

**88.** 7-bromo-1, 3, 5-cycloheptatriene exists as ionic species in aqueous solution while 5-bromo-1,3 cyclopentadiene doesn't ionise even in presence of $Ag^+$ (aq), Explain.

**89.** 2-hexyne gives trans-2-hexene on treatment with

**[2004, Screening]**

(1)  $Li/NH_3$          (2)  $Pd/BaSO_4$

(3)  $LiAlH_4$          (4)  $Pt/H_2$

**90.** Identify **X**, **Y** and **Z** in the following synthetic scheme and write their structures.

$$CH_3CH_2C = C - H \xrightarrow[\text{(ii) } CH_3CH_2Br]{\text{(i) } NaNH_2}$$

$$X \xrightarrow{H_2/Pd-BaSO_4} Y \xrightarrow{\text{alkaline } KMnO_4} Z$$

is the compound **Z** optically active ? Justify your answer. **[2002, Main]**

**91.** A biologically active compound, Bombykol $(C_{14}H_{30}O)$ is obtained from a natural source. The structure of the compound is determined by the following reactions. **[2002, Main]**

(a) On hydrogenation, Mombykol gives a compound A, $C_{14}H_{34}O$, which reacts with acetic anhydride to give an ester

(b) Bombykol also reacts with acetic anhydride to give another ester, which on oxidative ozonolysis $(O_3/H_2O_2)$ gives a mixture of butanoic acid, oxalic acid and 10-acetoxy decanioc acid

Determine the number of double bonds in Bombykol. Write the structures of compound A and Bombykol. How many geometrical isomers are possible for Bombykol ?

**92.** The nodal plane in the $\pi$-bond of ethene is located in : **[2002, Screening]**

(1)  the molecular plane

(2)  a plane parallel to the molecular plane

(3)  a plane perpendicular to the molecule plane which bisects the carbon-carbon $\sigma$-bond at right angle

(4)  a plane perpendicular to the molecular plane which contains the carbon-carbon $\sigma$-bond

**93.** Identify the reagent from the following list which can easily distinguish between 1-butyne and 2-butyne. **[2002, Screening]**

(1)  bromine, $CCl_4$

(2)  $H_2$, Lindlar catalyst

(3)  dilute $H_2SO_4$, $HgSO_4$

(4)  ammoniacal $Cu_2Cl_2$ solution

**94.** Which of the following hydrocarbons has the lowest dipole moment ? **[2002, Screening]**

(1)
$$\begin{array}{cc} H_3C & CH_3 \\ \diagdown & \diagup \\ C = C \\ \diagup & \diagdown \\ H & H \end{array}$$

(2)  $CH_3C \equiv CCH_3$

(3)  $CH_3CH_2C \equiv CH$

(4)  $CH_2 = CH - C \equiv CH$

## ANSWER KEY

|  |  |  |  |  |  |  |  |  |  |
|---|---|---|---|---|---|---|---|---|---|
| **1.** (*) | **2.** (2) | **3.** (3) | **4.** (*) | **5.** (2) | **6.** (4) | **7.** (2) | **8.** (4) | **9.** (4) | **10.** (4) |
| **11.** (1) | **12.** (1) | **13.** (1) | **14.** (2) | **15.** (*) | **16.** (2) | **17.** (4) | **18.** (*) | **19.** (4) | **20.** (2) |
| **21.** (4) | **22.** (3) | **23.** (2) | **24.** (3) | **25.** (3) | **26.** (4) | **27.** (1) | **28.** (3) | **29.** (1) | **30.** (*) |
| **31.** (3) | **32.** (1) | **33.** (2, 4) | **34.** (*) | **35.** (1, 2) | **36.** (2) | **37.** (2) | **38.** (2) | **39.** (3) | **40.** (2) |
| **41.** (2,3,4) | **42.** (3) | **43.** (2) | **44.** (2) | **45.** (2,4) | **46.** (4) | **47.** (1) | **48.** (2) | **49.** (3) | **50.** (4) |
| **51.** (1) | **52.** (2) | **53.** (4) | **54.** (2) | **55.** (1) | **56.** (3) | **57.** (1,2) | **58.** (2) | **59.** (1) | **60.** (3) |
| **61.** (3) | **62.** (4) | **63.** (3) | **64.** (3) | **65.** (1) | **66.** (1) | **67.** (4) | **68.** (2) | **69.** (1) | **70.** (1) |
| **71.** (2, 3) | **72.** (2, 3) | **73.** (4) | **74.** (4) | **75.** (*) | **76.** (*) | **77.** (4) | **78.** (2, 4) | **79.** (*) | **80.** (1, 4) |
| **81.** (4) | **82.** (*) | **83.** (2) | **84.** (3) | **85.** (*) | **86.** (*) | **87.** (*) | **88.** (*) | **89.** (1) | **90.** (*) |
| **91.** (*) | **92.** (1) | **93.** (4) | **94.** (2) |  |  |  |  |  |  |

## ANSWERS WITH EXPLANATIONS

**1.** $C : H = 4 : 1$

$C : O = 3 : 4$

Mass ratio

$C : H : O = 12 : 3 : 16$

Mole ratio

$C : H : O = 1 : 3 : 1$

Empirical formula = $CH_3O$

Molecular formula = $C_2H_6O_2$

(saturated acyclic organic compound)

$$C_2H_6O_2 + \frac{5}{2}O_2 \longrightarrow 2CO_2 + 3H_2O$$

$\underset{\text{2 mole}}{\phantom{C_2H_6O_2}} \quad \underset{\text{5 mole}}{\phantom{\frac{5}{2}O_2}}$

Moles of $O_2$ required = 5 moles

**2.** (2) 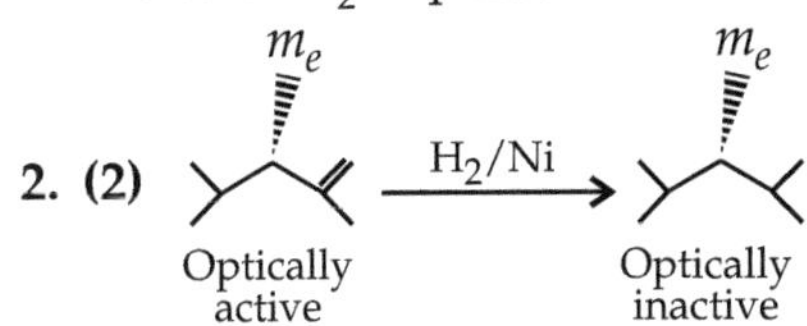

**3. (2)** $S_N^1$ favours

(a) The reaction is favoured by weak nucleophiles

(b) $R^\oplus$ would be easily formed if the substituents are bulky

(c) The reaction is accompained by recemization.

**4.**

$$\text{(alkene)} \xrightarrow{\text{Ni/H}_2} \text{(alkane, m}_e\text{)} \xrightarrow[hv]{Cl_2}$$

Simplest

O.A. Alkene

(Cl structures — 2, 4, 1, 1)

**Alternative Method :**

Str. of Tri peptide

$$\underset{\substack{|\\CH_2\\|\\O=C\\|\\OH}}{H_2N-CH}-\overset{O}{\overset{||}{C}}-\underset{\substack{|\\CH_2\\|\\CH_2\\|\\C=O\\|\\OH}}{NH-CH}-\overset{O}{\overset{||}{C}}-\underset{\substack{|\\(CH_2)_4\\|\\NH_2}}{NH-CH}-\overset{O}{\overset{||}{C}}-OH$$

**5. (2)**

(A), (B) OMe

$\downarrow$ AgNO$_3$   $\downarrow$ AgNO$_3$

$\oplus$ Aromatic

$\oplus$ Aromatic + OMe increase stability

$$CH_3-\underset{\substack{|\\Cl}}{CH}-CH_3 \xrightarrow{AgNO_3} CH_3-\overset{\oplus}{CH}-CH_3$$
(2° Cation) (C)

$$CH_3-\underset{\substack{|\\Cl}}{CH}-CH_2-NO_2 \xrightarrow{AgNO_3} CH_3-\overset{\oplus}{CH}-CH_2-NO_2$$
2° Cation and (–I of NO$_2$) (D)

$\therefore$ Stability Cation B > A > C > D.

**6. (4)** $D < C < A < B$

More cross conjugation / Cross conjugation

least stable anion (Least Acidic)

most stable Anion (more Acidic)

$$Ph-\overset{O}{\overset{||}{C}}-\overset{\ominus}{CH}-\overset{O}{\overset{||}{C}}-Ph$$

**7. (2)**

$$CH\equiv CH \xrightarrow[\text{(ii)}]{\text{(i) LiNH}_2/\text{ether}} CH_3-CH-C\equiv CH$$

$\downarrow$ (i) HgSO$_4$/H$_2$SO$_4$  (ii) NaBH$_4$

(alcohol with OH, CH$_3$, CH)

$\downarrow$ $H^+/\Delta$

$$CH_3 \underset{\substack{||\\C\\/\ \backslash\\CH_3\ \ CH_3}}{} CH_2-CH_3$$
(major)

Now : (i) HgSO$_4$/dil. H$_2$SO$_4$

(ii) NaBH$_4$

convert triple bond into ketone which is reduced by NaBH$_4$ and convert it into alcohol.

**8. (4)** (i) Glucose + dry HCl $\xrightarrow{ROH}$ Acetal

$$\xrightarrow[\text{(CH}_3\text{CO)}_2\text{O}]{x\,Eq} \text{acetyl derivative}$$

(ii) Glucose $\xrightarrow{\text{Ni/H}_2}$ A $\xrightarrow[\text{(CH}_3\text{CO)}_2\text{O}]{y\,Eq}$ Acetyl derivative

(iii) Glucose $\xrightarrow[\text{(CH}_3\text{CO)}_2\text{O}]{z\,Eq}$ Acetyl derivative

due to presence of –OH group in Glucose the reaction is

$$R-OH + CH_3-\overset{O}{\overset{||}{C}}-O-\overset{O}{\overset{||}{C}}-CH_3 \rightarrow R-O-\overset{O}{\overset{||}{C}}-CH_3$$
Acetyl derivative

so for (i)

**11. (1)**



**12. (1)**

| | Test | Correct reagent |
|---|---|---|
| (i) | Lucas test | conc. HCl + $ZnCl_2$ |
| (ii) | Dumas method | $CuO/CO_2$ |
| (iii) | Kjeldahl's method | $H_2SO_4$ |
| (iv) | Hinsberg Test | $C_6H_5SO_2Cl$ + aq. KOH |

**13. (1)** (a)



(b)



(c)



$$B.P. \propto \frac{1}{Branching} \quad \therefore a > c > b \text{ (order of B.P.)}$$

**14. (2)**

$$CH_3-CH_2-C\equiv N \xrightarrow{?} CH_3-CH_2-CH_2-NH_2$$

$$CH_3-CH_2-C\equiv N \xrightarrow{LiAlH_4} CH_3-CH_2-CH_2-NH_2$$

**15.**

$$\underset{\text{1 mole}}{C_3H_8} + \underset{\text{5 mole}}{SO_2} \rightarrow 3CO_2 + 4H_2O$$

For 1 mole propane combustion 5 mole $O_2$ required.

$$C_4H_{10} + \frac{13}{2}O_2 \rightarrow 4CO_2 + 5H_2O$$

1 mole          6.5 mole

2 mole          13 mole

For 2 moles of butane 13 mole of $O_2$ is required
total moles = 13 + 5 = 18.

**17. (4)**

**16. (2)**



---

**(ii)**

$$\underset{\overset{|}{CH=O}}{\overset{}{}}\begin{matrix}CH=O\\(CH-OH)_4\\CH_2-OH\end{matrix} \xrightarrow[H_2]{Ni} \begin{matrix}CH_2-OH\\(CH-OH)_4\\CH_2-OH\end{matrix} \xrightarrow[Ac_2O]{6 Eq.} \begin{matrix}CH_2-OAc\\(CH_2-OAc)_4\\CH_2-OAc\end{matrix}$$

**(iii)**



**9. (4)**



**10. (4)**

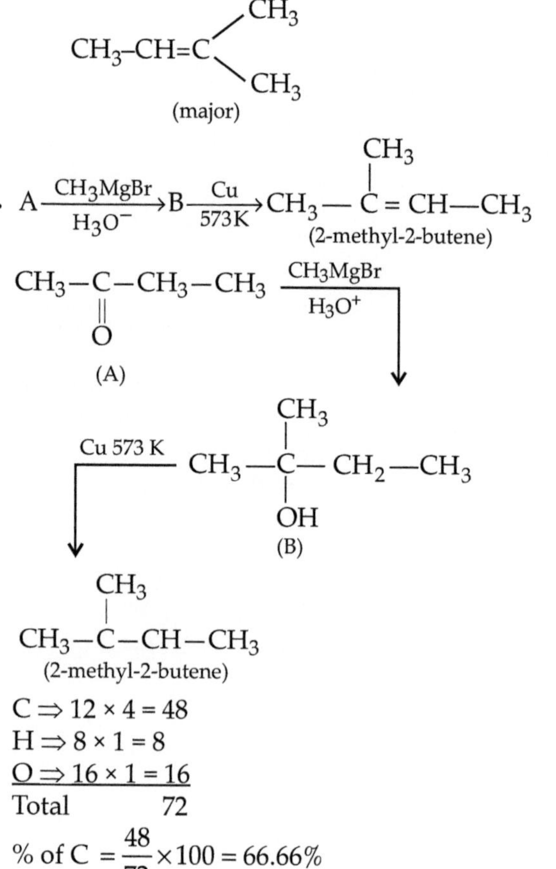

18.

$$A \xrightarrow[H_3O^-]{CH_3MgBr} B \xrightarrow[573K]{Cu} CH_3 - \underset{\underset{CH_3}{|}}{C} = CH - CH_3$$
(2-methyl-2-butene)

$C \Rightarrow 12 \times 4 = 48$
$H \Rightarrow 8 \times 1 = 8$
$O \Rightarrow 16 \times 1 = 16$
Total $\qquad 72$

% of C $= \dfrac{48}{72} \times 100 = 66.66\%$

19. **(4)** The electronegative part of DCl attacks the more substituted carbon of starting material and electropositive will attack the less substituted carbon atom of starting material to form $CH_3C(Cl)=CHD$. The electronegative part of DI attacks the more substituted carbon atom of $CH_3C(Cl) = CHD$ and electropositive will attack the less substituted carbon atom iof $CH_3C(Cl) = CHD$ to form $CH_3C(I)(Cl)CHD_2$. The complete reaction is shown below :

$$CH_2 - C = CH \xrightarrow{DCl} CH_3 - \underset{\underset{Cl}{|}}{C} = CHD$$

$$\downarrow DI$$

$$CH_3 - \underset{\underset{Cl}{|}}{C} = CHD_2$$

20. **(2)** The general equation for the combustion oif a hydrocarbion is given below :

$$\underset{10}{C_xH_y} + \underset{\left(x+\frac{y}{4}\right)}{\left(x+\frac{y}{4}\right)O_2} \longrightarrow \underset{10x}{xCO_2} + \frac{y}{2}H_2O$$

According to the above equation,

$$10\left(x + \frac{y}{4}\right) = 55 \qquad \qquad ...(1)$$

$$10x = 40$$
$$x = 4 \qquad \qquad ...(2)$$

Substitute equation (2) in equation (1).

$$10\left(x + \frac{y}{4}\right) = 55$$

$$10\left(4 + \frac{y}{4}\right) = 55$$

$$y = 6$$

Therefore, the formula of the hydrocarbon is $C_4H_6$.

21. **(4)** In acyclic compounds, the factor that does niot govern the stability of a conformation is angle strain. This is because rotation of C – C bond in acyclic compounds does niot lead to angle strain.

22. **(3)** Potassium permanganate is good oxidising agent it oxidises alkene in carboxylic acid in acidic condition.

The reaction mechanism is shown below :

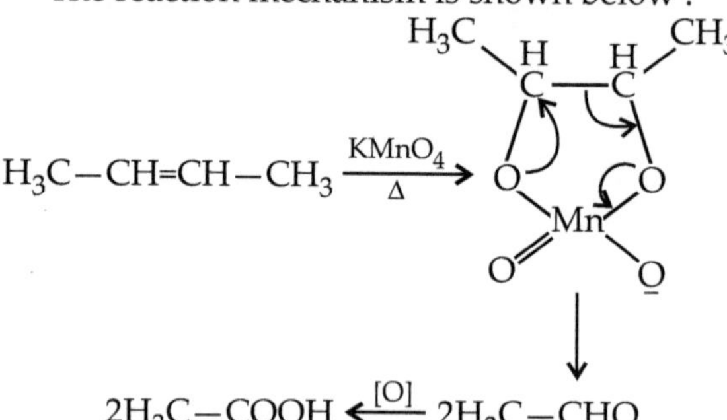

$$2H_3C - COOH \xleftarrow{[O]} 2H_3C - CHO$$

23. **(2)** The skew conformation of ethane is shown below :

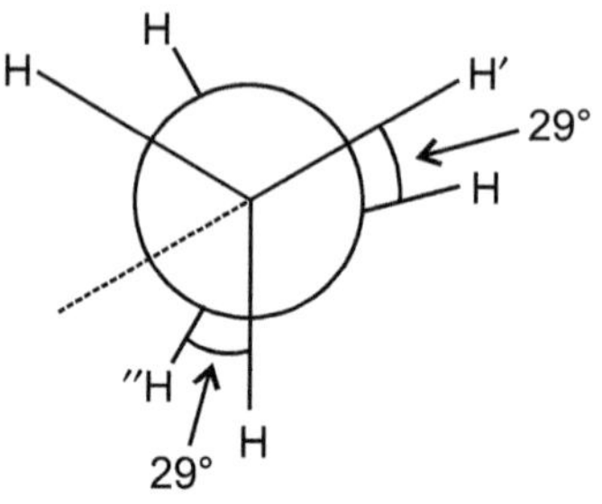


The calculation of dihedral angle H'—C—C—H' is shown below :

$$\theta = 120° + 29°$$
$$= 149°$$

24. **(3)** The number of moles of $CO_2$ is calcualted as shown below :

$$n_{CO_2} = \frac{88\text{ g}}{44\text{ g/mol}}$$
$$= 2\text{ mol}$$

The number of moles of $H_2O$ is calculated as shown below :

$$n_{H_2O} = \frac{9\text{ g}}{18\text{ g/mol}}$$
$$= 0.5\text{ mol}$$

The general equation for the combustion of a hydrocarbon is given below :

$$C_xH_y + \left(x+\frac{x}{4}\right)O_2 \rightarrow xCO_2 + \frac{y}{2}H_2O$$

$$\left(\frac{25}{M}\right) \qquad\qquad \left(\frac{25}{M}\right)x \qquad \left(\frac{25}{M}\right)\left(\frac{y}{2}\right)$$

$$= 2 \qquad\qquad = 0.5$$

According to the above equation, the expression formed for $CO_2$.

$$x\left(\frac{25}{M}\right) = 2$$

$$x = \frac{2M}{25} \qquad\qquad ...(1)$$

The expression formed for $H_2O$.

$$\left(\frac{25}{M}\right)\left(\frac{y}{2}\right) = 0.5$$

$$y = \frac{M}{25} \qquad\qquad ...(2)$$

The relation between $x$ and $y$ from equation (1) and (2),

$$x = 2y$$

Therefore, the formula of the hydrocarbon is $C_{2y}H_y$.

The expected ratio of molar mass of carbon and hydrogen in the hydrocarbon is calculated as shown below :

$$C : H = 2(12\ g) : 1\ g$$

$$C : H = 24 : 1$$

Therefore, the unknown hydrocarbon has 24 g of carbon and 1 g hydrogen.

**25. (3)** The complete reaction sequence is shown below :

$$CH_3-C \equiv CH \xrightarrow[\Delta]{Ag_2O} CH_3-C \equiv C-Ag \downarrow$$
(terminal alkyne)        (ppt)

$$CH_3-C \equiv CH \xrightarrow[\text{dil. } H_2SO_4]{Hg^{2+}} CH_3-\underset{\underset{}{OH}}{\overset{}{C}}=CH_2$$
(terminal alkyne)   (Kucherov reaction)

$$CH_3-\overset{\overset{O}{\|}}{C}-CH_3$$

$$\downarrow NaBH_4$$

$$CH_3-\underset{\underset{}{OH}}{CH}-CH_3$$

$$\downarrow \begin{array}{l}\text{Conc. HCl}\\ + ZnCl_2\end{array}$$

Turbidity within 5 min.
(Lucas Reagent Test)

Therefore, the compound A is $CH_3-C \equiv CH$.

**26. (4)** The synonym for water gas is syn gas because this gas is used to produce methanol.

**27. (1)** The equation for the reaction of saline hydrides with water is shown below :

$$\underset{\text{Saline hydride}}{MH} + H_2O \rightarrow MOH + H_2$$

Therefore, statement (a) is correct.

The equation for the reaction of $LiAlH_4$ with $BF_3$ is shown below :

Therefore, statement (b) is correct.

The compound $PH_3$ contains P atom which contains lone pair of electrons. Hence, it is an electron rich hydride. The compound $CH_4$ contains C atom which is neither electron deficient nor electron rich, that is, it is electron precise. Therefore, statement (c) is correct.

The compounds HF and $CH_4$ are called molecular hydrides because they possess covalent character. Therefore, statement (d) is correct.

**28. (3)** Zinc metal has amphoteric nature is reacts both with acid and base to hydrogen gas.

The reaction zinc metal acid is shown below :

$$Zn + 2HCl \rightarrow ZnCl_2 + H_2\uparrow$$

The reaction of zinc metal with base is shown below :

$$Zn + 2NaOH \rightarrow Na_2ZnO_2 + H_2\uparrow$$

**29. (1)** The temporary hardness of water is due to carbonate and bicarbonate of $Mg^{2+}$ and $Ca^{2+}$. The decomposition reaction of $Mg(HCO_3)_2$ is shown below :

$$Mg(HCO_3)_2(aq) \xrightarrow{Boil} Mg(OH)_2(s) + 2CO_2(g)$$

The decomposition reaction of $Ca(HCO_3)_2$ is shown below :

$$Ca(HCO_3)_2(aq) \xrightarrow{Boil} CaCO_3(s) + H_2O(l) + CO_2(g)$$

Therefore, the correct combination is

$$Y = Mg(HCO_3)_2 \text{ and } X = Mg(OH)_2.$$

**30.** Solid wedge represents the configuration and geometry is fixed. Dashed wedge shows that the configuration and geometry at the specified carbon is not fixed.

The number of stereocentres is three.

The number of stereoisomers is $2^n = 2^3$

$$= 8$$

There also occurs the formation of one meso compound. Hence, the total number of optically active stereoisomers is $8 - 1 = 7$.

**31. (3)** The reduction of alkynes with sodium in liquid ammonia is known as birch reduction which leads to the formation of trans alkene as a product. The reduction of alkynes with sodium in liquid ammonia is,

$$\equiv\!\!\!\equiv \xrightarrow{\text{Na/liq NH}_3} \diagdown\!=\!\!\diagup$$

**32. (1)** The net dipole moment of *trans* compounds is less than those of *cis* compounds because the groups present *trans* to each other cancel out the effect of each other but in *cis* compounds net dipole moment is not zero.

Due to the presence of net dipole moment, dipole-dipole interactions between *cis* compounds exist; as a result the boiling point of *cis* compounds is more than those of *trans* compounds.

$$CH_3C \equiv C-CH_3 \xrightarrow[\text{Lindlar catalyst}]{H_2} \quad \text{cis alkene (X)}$$

$$H_3C-C \equiv C-CH_3 \xrightarrow[\text{Liq. NH}_3]{Na} \quad \text{Trans alkene (Y)}$$

**33. (2, 4)** Both the given reactants are isomeric compounds. First reactant is *trans* alkene. Its bromination in the presence of chloroform solvent is given as,

trans-2-butene

M and N are same
(meso-2, 3-Dibromobutane)

Two products are obtained in the above reaction. Both these products are meso compounds. Due to the presence of plane of symmetry and two chiral centre both the product compounds are meso.

Second reactant is *cis*-alkene and its bromination in the presence of chloroform solvent is given as,

cis-2-butene

*cis*-bromonium ion

(rac-2, 3-Dibromobutane)

Here, also two products are obtained. Both these are enantiomers due to the presence of non-superimposable mirror images of each other. Therefore, **O** and **P** are non-identical molecules.

Bromination proceeds through *trans*-addition in both the reactions.

(**M** and **O**) and (**N** and **P**) cannot be enantiomers because, these are diastereomeric pairs.

**34.** The species which follow Huckel's rule are always aromatic. All the species are classified as,

Non-aromatic    Anti-aromatic    Non-aromatic

Anti-aromatic    Aromatic    Aromatic

Aromatic    Aromatic    Aromatic

**35. (1, 2)** The required chemical reactions are shown below :

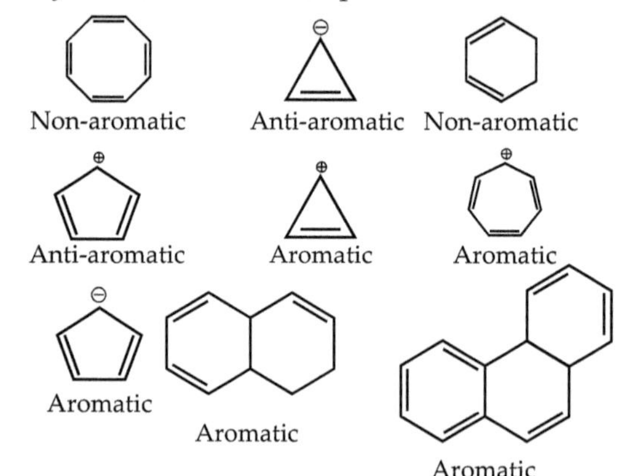

Q($C_8H_8O$)

Undergoes Cannizzaro but not haloform

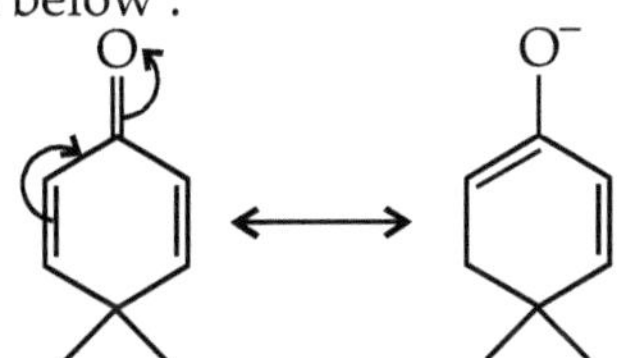

Undergoes Cannizzaro but not haloform

Undergoes Haloform but not Cannizzaro

Undergoes Haloform but not Cannizzaro

From all the above reactions, it is clear that only options 1 and 2 follows the reaction condition as given in the question.

**36. (2)** The least resonance stabilized molecule is shown below :

The other molecules are aromatic in nature. Therefore, they are highly resonance stabilized.

**37. (2)** The reaction of 3-Methyl-pent-2-ene with HBr in the presence of peroxide is,

3-methylpent-2-ene

Product X

The product X contains two chiral centers marked by asterisk. It is unsymmetrical. Therefore, the total stereoisomers are calculated as,

$$(2)^n = (2)^2 = 4.$$

**38. (2)** The IUPAC name of the following compound is 2-Ethyl-1, 1-dimethylcylohexane

**39. (3)** The following compound is most reactive due to formation of aromatic anion. It indicates that compound is highly acidic. The formation of aromatic anion is shown below :

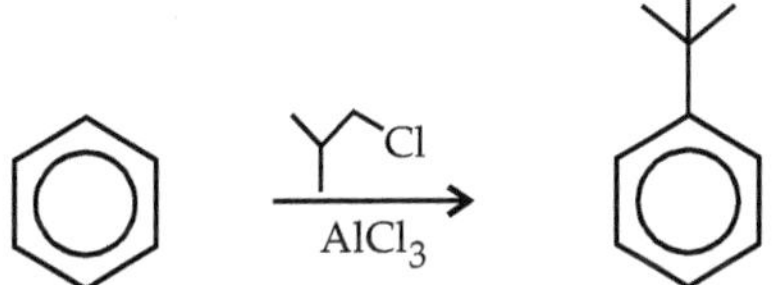

$(4n + 2)$pi electron system

The reaction of compound with aqueous solution of sodium carbonate is shown below :

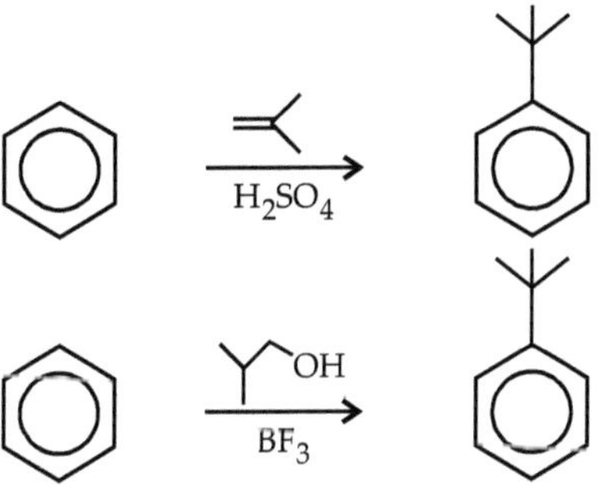

**40. (2)** The structure with marked double bonds is shown below :

The geometrical isomerism is not possible at double bond (I) due to the presence of same alkyl groups at $sp^2$ hybridized carbon atom.

**41. (2,3,4)** The reactions which gives *tert*-butyl benzene as the major product is/are,

via rearrangement of carbocation

via rearrangement of carbocation

Thus options (2), (3) and (4) are correct.

**42. (3)** The compound that contains 7 carbon atoms possessing a neopentyl and a vinyl group is 4, 4-dimethylpentene as shown below :

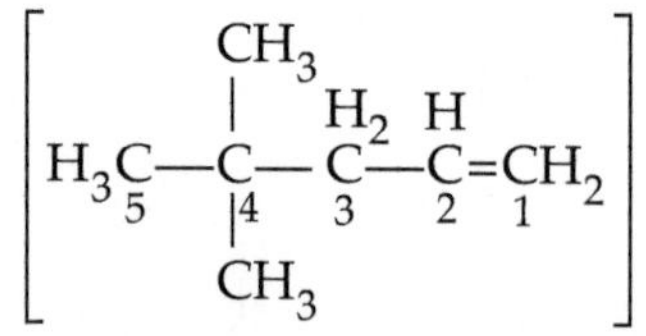

$$\left[\ \underset{\overset{|}{CH_3}}{\overset{\overset{CH_3}{|}}{H_3\underset{5}{C}-\underset{4}{C}-\underset{3}{\overset{H_2}{C}}-\underset{2}{\overset{H}{C}}=\underset{1}{CH_2}}}\ \right]$$

**43. (2)** Lone pair of nitrogen number 9 is involved in the resonance and is thus involved in aromaticity also.

**44. (2)** The given reaction is shown below :

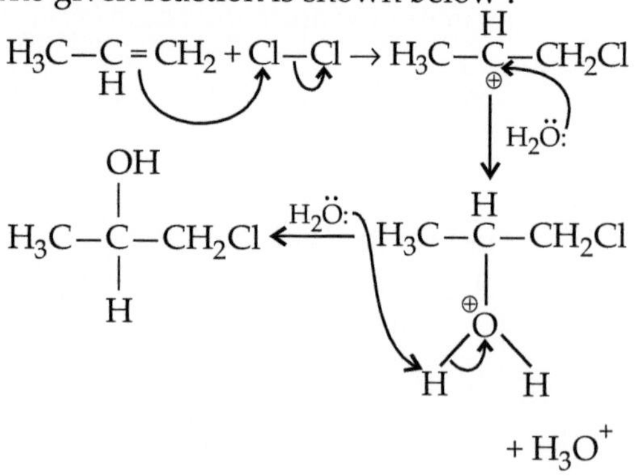

$$H_3C-\overset{H}{\underset{H}{C}}=CH_2 + Cl{-}Cl \rightarrow H_3C-\overset{\oplus}{C}-CH_2Cl$$

$$\xrightarrow{H_2\ddot{O}:} H_3C-\overset{H}{\underset{\overset{|}{\overset{\oplus}{O}}}{C}}-CH_2Cl$$

$$\xrightarrow{H_2\ddot{O}:} \underset{H}{\overset{OH}{\underset{|}{H_3C-C-CH_2Cl}}}$$

$$+ H_3O^+$$

**45. (2,4)** The compounds that on hydrogenation produces optically inactive compounds are shown below :

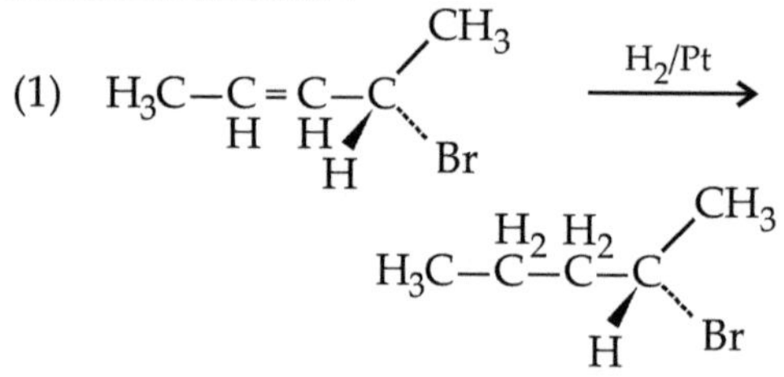

(1) $H_3C-\overset{H}{C}=\overset{H}{C}-\overset{CH_3}{\underset{H}{C}}Br \xrightarrow{H_2/Pt}$

$H_3C-\overset{H_2}{C}-\overset{H_2}{C}-\overset{CH_3}{\underset{H}{C}}Br$

Optically active

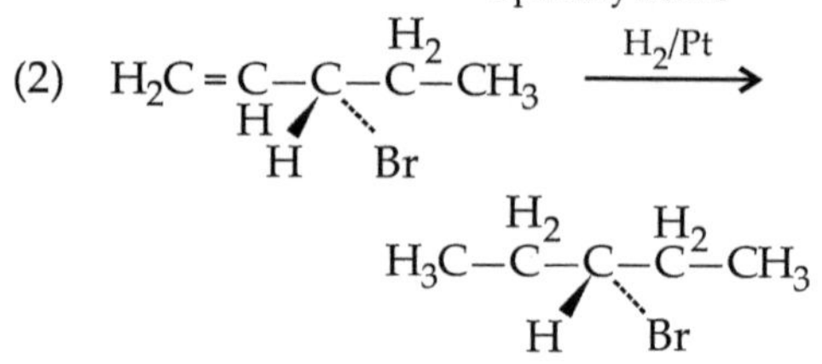

(2) $H_2C=\overset{H}{C}-\overset{H}{\underset{Br}{C}}-\overset{H_2}{C}-CH_3 \xrightarrow{H_2/Pt}$

$H_3C-\overset{H_2}{C}-\overset{H}{\underset{Br}{C}}-\overset{H_2}{C}-CH_3$

Optically inactive

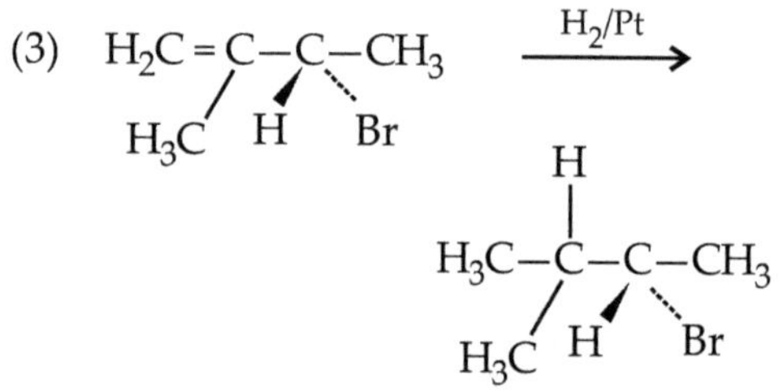

(3) $H_2C=\overset{H_3C}{\underset{}{C}}-\overset{H}{\underset{Br}{C}}-CH_3 \xrightarrow{H_2/Pt}$

$H_3C-\overset{H}{\underset{H_3C}{C}}-\overset{H}{\underset{Br}{C}}-CH_3$

Optically active

(4) $H_2C=\overset{H}{\underset{H}{C}}-\overset{H_2}{\underset{Br}{C}}-CH_3 \xrightarrow{H_2/Pt}$

$H_3C-\overset{H_2}{C}-\overset{H}{\underset{Br}{C}}-\overset{H_2}{C}-CH_3$

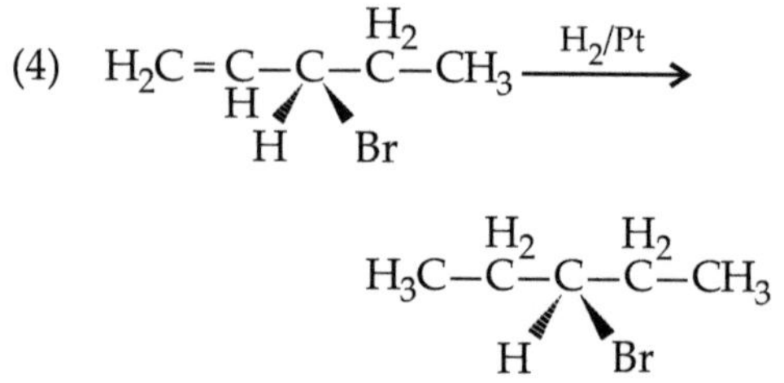

Optically Active

Thus, only 2 and 4 give optically inactive compounds.

**46. (4)** The mechanism for the formation of major product is shown below :

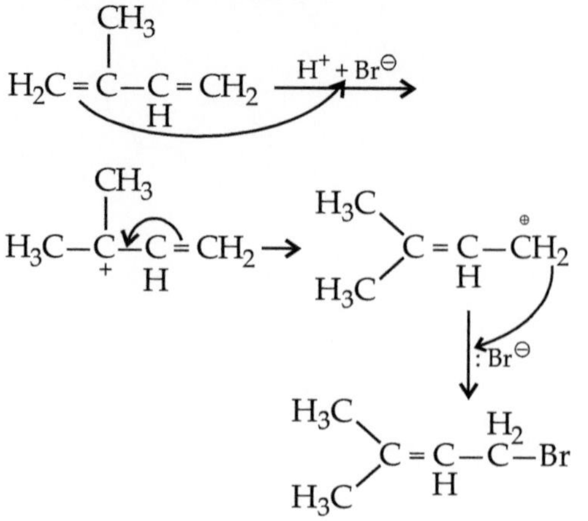

$$H_2C=\overset{\overset{CH_3}{|}}{C}-\overset{H}{C}=CH_2 \xrightarrow{H^+ + Br^{\ominus}}$$

$$H_3C-\overset{CH_3}{\underset{+}{C}}\overset{H}{C}=CH_2 \rightarrow \overset{H_3C}{\underset{H_3C}{C}}=\overset{\oplus}{C}-CH_2 \downarrow :Br^{\ominus}$$

$$\overset{H_3C}{\underset{H_3C}{C}}=\overset{H}{C}-\overset{H_2}{C}-Br$$

Thus, the major product formed is shown below.

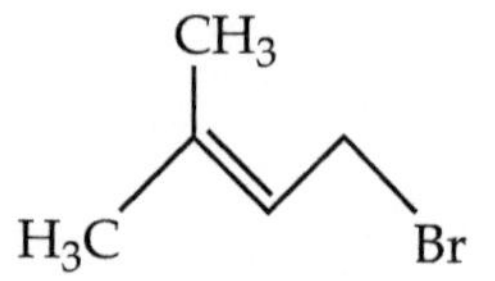

$$\overset{CH_3}{\underset{H_3C}{}} \diagup \diagdown Br$$

**47. (1)** The first step is the ozonolysis of alkene and the second step is the reaction of product R with $NH_3$ to give the final product S.

The mechanism for the formation of R is shown below :

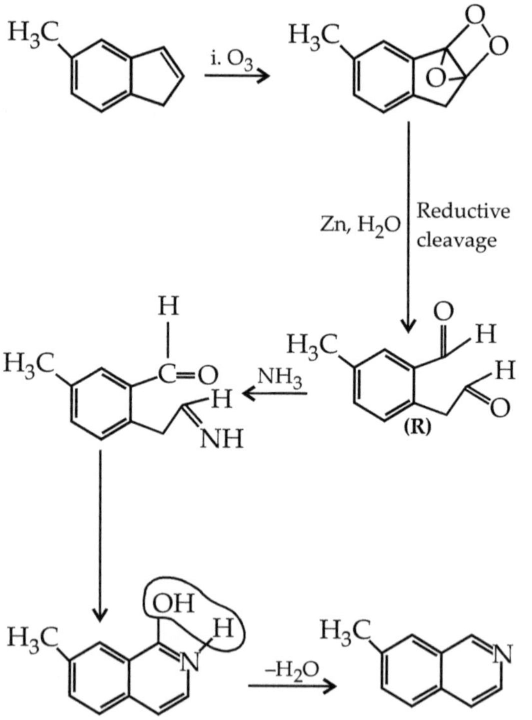

$$\xrightarrow{i.\ O_3}$$

$$\xrightarrow[\text{cleavage}]{Zn,\ H_2O\ \ \text{Reductive}} \quad (R)$$

$$\xleftarrow{NH_3}$$

$$\xrightarrow{-H_2O}$$

Thus, the product S is shown below :

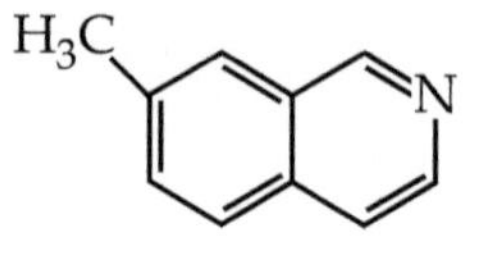

**48. (2)** The reaction for the formation of **U** is shown below :

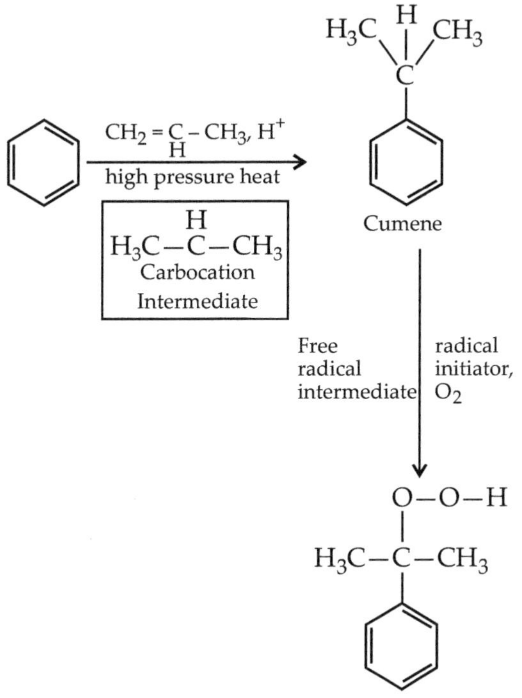

$CH_2=\underset{H}{C}-CH_3,\ H^+$ / high pressure heat

$\underset{\text{Carbocation Intermediate}}{H_3C-\overset{H}{\underset{}{C}}-CH_3}$

Cumene

Free radical intermediate | radical initiator, $O_2$

$\underset{\text{[Cumene hydroperoxide]}}{H_3C-\overset{O-O-H}{\underset{}{C}}-CH_3}$

Thus, the product **U** is shown below :

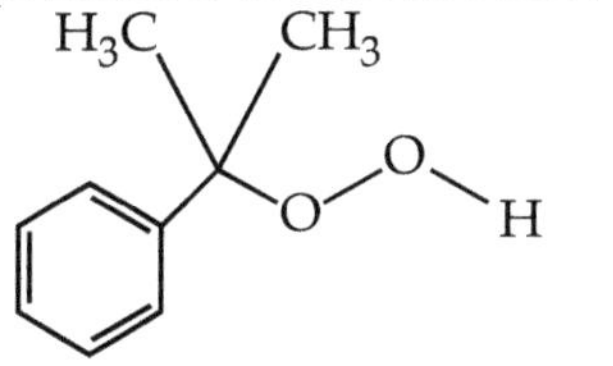

**49. (3)** Pd/BaSO$_4$ is Lindar catalyst which is used for the reduction of alkyne to give alkene. The second reaction is the hydroboration of alkene to give alcohol.

The formation of compound **X** is shown below :

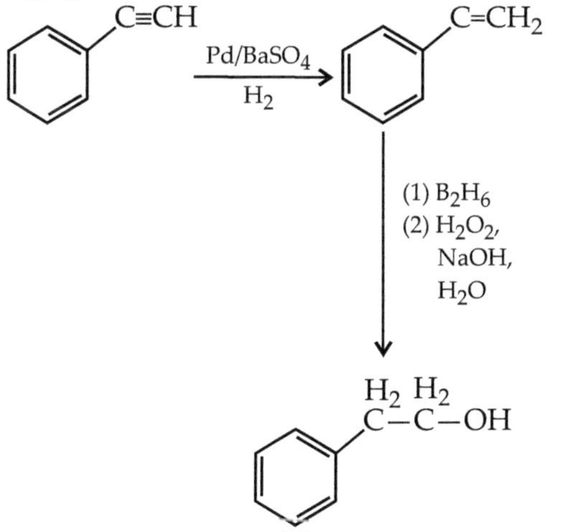

$Ph-C\equiv CH \xrightarrow[\ H_2\ ]{\ Pd/BaSO_4\ } Ph-C=CH_2$

(1) $B_2H_6$
(2) $H_2O_2$, NaOH, $H_2O$

$\underset{(X)}{Ph-\overset{H_2}{\underset{}{C}}-\overset{H_2}{\underset{}{C}}-OH}$

**50. (4)** The first step is the oxymercuration-demercuration of alkynes to yield ketone through tautomerisation of enol. The second step is the Grignard reaction to convert ketone into alcohol. The last step involved formation of alkene.

The compound formed **Y** is shown below :

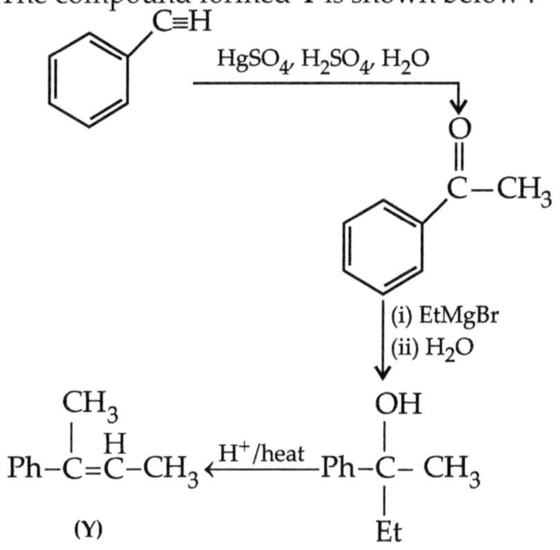

Ph–C≡H $\xrightarrow{HgSO_4,\ H_2SO_4,\ H_2O}$ Ph–C(=O)–CH$_3$

(i) EtMgBr
(ii) H$_2$O

$\underset{Et}{Ph-\overset{OH}{\underset{}{C}}-CH_3} \xrightarrow{H^+/heat} \underset{(Y)}{Ph-\overset{CH_3}{\underset{H}{C=C}}-CH_3}$

**51. (1)** 1-Phenyl-2-butene exhibits geometrical isomerism.

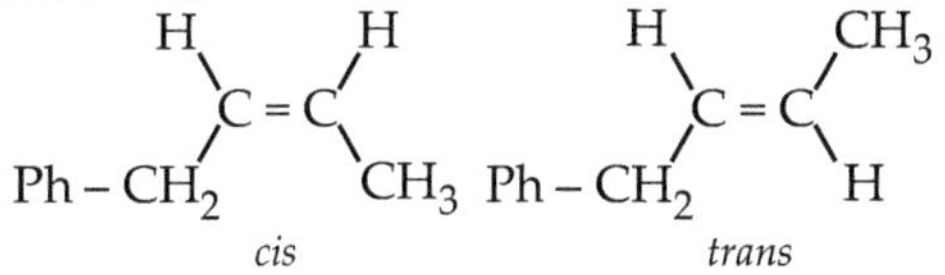

*cis*     *trans*

**52. (2)** On ozonolysis, compound (2) gives desired product.

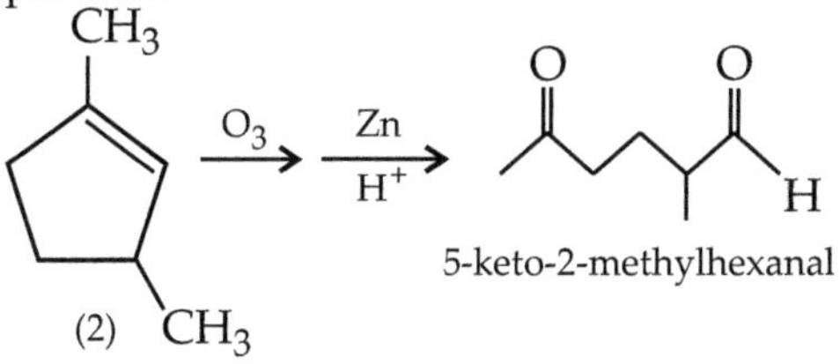

(2) $\xrightarrow[H^+]{O_3,\ Zn}$ 5-keto-2-methylhexanal

**53. (4)** The compound 2-chloro-2-methylbutane is optically inactive because carbon atom in this compound is not chiral. The second carbon atom is attached to two methyl groups.

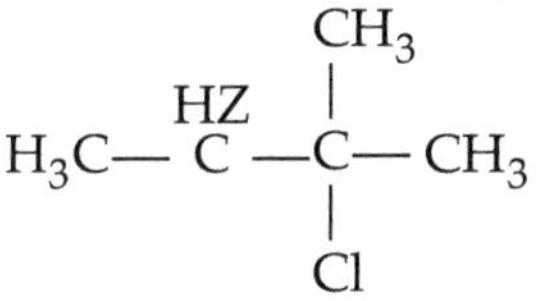

$H_3C-\overset{HZ}{\underset{Cl}{C}}-\overset{CH_3}{\underset{}{C}}-CH_3$

**54. (2)** The electrolysis of given compound leads to the formation of naphthalene.

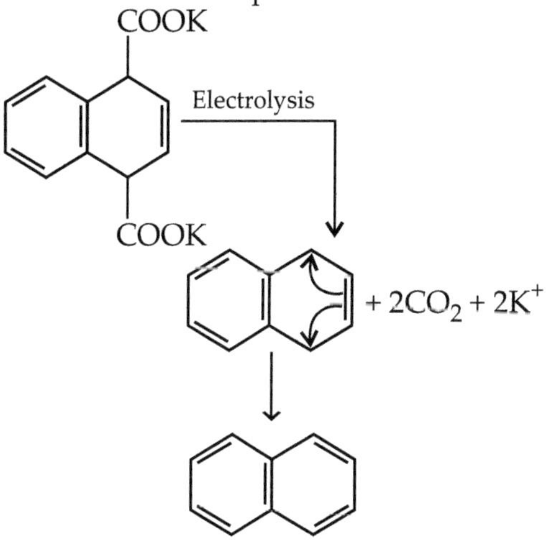

Electrolysis $\longrightarrow$ $+\ 2CO_2 + 2K^+$

**55. (1)** Chlorine atom attached to tertiary carbon atom gives white precipitates of AgCl on reaction with $AgNO_3$.

On reaction with alcoholic KOH, it gives alkene by losing HCl.

$$C_6H_5-\underset{\underset{Cl}{|}}{\overset{\overset{H_2}{|}}{C}}-\underset{\underset{CH_3}{|}}{\overset{\overset{CH_3}{|}}{C}} \xrightarrow{alc.\ KOH} C_6H_5-\underset{\underset{H}{|}}{C}=\underset{\underset{\underset{(B)}{CH_3}}{|}}{C}-CH_3$$

↓ Ozonolysis

$$\underset{(C)}{C_6H_5CHO}+\underset{(D)}{H_3C-\overset{\overset{O}{\|}}{C}-CH_3} \leftarrow C_6H_5-\underset{}{\overset{}{C}}\underset{O\ \ O}{\overset{}{\underset{O}{}}}\overset{CH_3}{\underset{CH_3}{C}}\overset{H_2}{}$$

**56. (3)** The structural isomers of $C_6H_{14}$ is shown below :

**57. (1,2)** The major product expected from the given reaction is shown below :

**58. (2)** The boiling point of alkanes decreases on increasing the branching. Therefore, isomer (III) is *n*-hexane and has highest boiling point. Isomer (I) contains maximum branching so, it has the least boiling point.

**59. (1)** The complete reaction for the formation of product **X** is,

$$HO-\overset{\overset{H_2}{|}}{C}-\overset{\overset{H_2}{|}}{C}-C\equiv CH \xrightarrow{NaNH_2}$$

$$HO-\overset{\overset{H_2}{|}}{C}-\overset{\overset{H_2}{|}}{C}-C\equiv C^-Na^+ \xrightarrow{CH_3CH_2I}$$

$$HO-\overset{\overset{H_2}{|}}{C}-\overset{\overset{H_2}{|}}{C}-C=C-\overset{\overset{H_2}{|}}{C}-CH_3 \xrightarrow{CH_3I}$$

$$H_3C-O-\overset{\overset{H_2}{|}}{C}-\overset{\overset{H_2}{|}}{C}-\overset{\overset{H}{|}}{C}=\overset{\overset{H}{|}}{C}-\overset{\overset{H_2}{|}}{C}-CH_3$$

$$\xrightarrow[catalyst]{H_2/Lindlar's} H_3COCH_2-CH_2\ \ \underset{\underset{X}{}}{H_2C-CH_3}$$

**60. (3)** The major organic compound formed by the reaction is 2-butyne.

$$H_3C-\underset{\underset{Cl}{|}}{\overset{\overset{Cl}{|}}{C}}-Cl\ +6Ag\ \ Cl-\underset{\underset{Cl}{|}}{\overset{\overset{Cl}{|}}{C}}-CH_3$$

↓

$$\underset{\text{2-butyne}}{H_3C-C\equiv C-CH_3}\ +6AgCl\downarrow$$

**61. (3)** The hydroboration-oxidation reaction of propene to give 1-propanol is shown below :

$$CH_3CH=CH_2 \xrightarrow[H_2O_2/OH^-]{B_2H_6/THF} CH_3CH_2CH_2OH$$

**62. (4)** In case of A-$Ph_3C$ and B-$(CH_3)_3C$, A is more stable than B due to the resonance effect in compound, $Ph_3C$. The resonance effect does not takes place in $(CH_3)_3C$.

**63. (3)** In the given conversion, alkyne is converted into a *trans* alkene. The reagent required for this conversion is $Li/NH_3$. It is used for hydrogenation of alkyne. *Trans* alkene is obtained with the help of this reagent.

**64. (3)** Succinate anion is produced during the electrolysis of dipotassium succinate. The ionisation reaction is shown below :

$$\underset{\underset{CH_2COOK}{|}}{CH_2COOK} \xrightarrow{ionisation} \underset{\underset{CH_2COO^-}{|}}{CH_2COO^-}+2K^+$$

$$2H_2O \underset{}{\overset{ionisation}{\rightleftharpoons}} 2OH^-+2H^+$$

The half-cell reaction taking place at anode is,

$$\underset{\underset{CH_2COO^-}{|}}{CH_2COO^-}+2e^- \longrightarrow \underset{unstable}{\left[\underset{\underset{CH_2COO}{|}}{CH_2COO}\right]}$$

$$\longrightarrow \underset{\underset{CH_2}{\|}}{CH_2}+2CO_2$$

The half-cell reaction taking place at cathode is,

$$2H^++2e^-\rightarrow H_2$$

Therefore, the gas liberated by the electrolysis of dipotassium succinate solution is ethene.

**65. (1)** The mechanism involved in the mercuration-demercuration of the given compound is shown below :

$$Ph-CH_2-CH=CH_2 \rightarrow Ph-CH_2-\overset{\oplus}{CH}-CH_2-$$

OAc

$$\underset{\text{Non-classical carbocation}}{Ph-CH_2-\overset{}{CH}-CH_2} \overset{}{\underset{\overset{Hg}{\oplus}}{}}$$

↓ $H_2\ddot{O}$

$$\underset{\underset{OH}{|}}{Ph-CH_2-CH-CH_3} \xleftarrow{NaBH_4} \underset{\underset{OH}{|}}{\overset{\overset{HgOAc}{|}}{Ph-CH_2-CH-CH_2}}$$

The mercuration-demercuration reaction of the given compound involves the formation of cyclic carbocation intermediate. This cyclic carbocation intermediate cannot undergo rearrangement because, it is a type of non-classical carbocation.

**66. (1)** The steps involved in the antimarkovnikov addition of hydrogen chloride and hydrogen iodide on alkenes in the presence of peroxide are endothermic in nature due to which the antimarkovnikov addition of hydrogen chloride and hydrogen iodide is not favorable.

**67. (4)** The structure of HCN is,

$$H-C \equiv N$$

There are two sigma bonds and two pi bonds in the structure of HCN.

**68. (2)** The compounds formed from **P** and **Q** are optically inactive **S** and optically inactive pair (**T**, **U**) respectively.

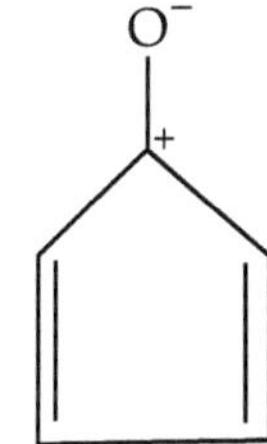

**69. (1)** The correct reagents of the given reactions are shown as follows :

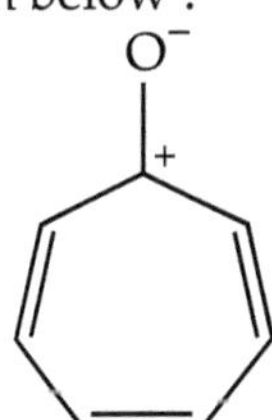

**70. (1)** The products formed by ozonolysis of given compound are shown below :

All the compounds that are formed do not contain any chiral centre and are thus optically inactive.

**71. (2, 3)** (1) The given structure contains $sp^3$ hybridized carbon atoms. Thus, it is non-aromatic.

(2) The given structure follows $4n\pi$ rule. It is antiaromatic and is therefore unstable at room temperature.

(3) The given structure follows $4n\pi$ rule as shown below :

It is antiaromatic and is therefore unstable at room temperature.

(4) The given structure follows $(4n + 2)\pi$ rule as shown below :

It is aromatic as it contains $6\pi$ electrons. Therefore, it is stable at room temperature.

**72. (2, 3)** In 1, 3-butadiene, conformations along carbon-carbon single bond will not lie in the same plane.

In forth compound that is allene also, conformations will not lie in the same plane. In this molecule, central carbon is "$sp$" hybridized and terminal carbon atoms are "$sp^2$" hybridized. All the four hydrogen atoms do not exist in same plane.

In second and third compound, all the confirmations lie in the same plane.

**73. (4)** The compound **P** is acyclic hydrocarbon with the molecular formula $C_6H_{10}$. It undergoes acid catalyzed oxidation followed by reduction to give compound **Q**, therefore, compound **P** is 3, 3-dimethylpropyne. The structure of this compound is,

$$H_3C-\underset{\underset{H_3C}{|}}{\overset{\overset{H_3C}{|}}{C}}-C\equiv C-H$$

The complete reaction is given as,

$$CH_3-\underset{\underset{CH_3}{|}}{\overset{\overset{CH_3}{|}}{C}}-C\equiv C-H \xrightarrow{\text{dil } H_2SO_4/HgSO_4}$$

$$\xrightarrow[\text{(2) dilute acid}]{\text{(1) NaNH}_2/\text{ethanol}} CH_3-\underset{\underset{CH_3}{|}}{\overset{\overset{CH_3}{|}}{C}}-\overset{\overset{O}{||}}{C}-CH_3$$

$$CH_3-\underset{\underset{CH_3}{|}}{\overset{\overset{CH_3}{|}}{C}}-\overset{\overset{OH}{|}}{C}-CH_3 \xrightarrow[\text{(catalylic amount)}]{\text{conc. } H_2SO_4}$$
(Q)

$$CH_3-\underset{\underset{CH_3}{|}}{\overset{\overset{CH_3}{|}}{\underset{\oplus}{C}}}-CH-CH_3 \leftarrow CH_3-\underset{\underset{CH_3}{|}}{\overset{\overset{CH_3}{|}}{C}}-CH-CH_3$$

$$CH_3-\underset{\underset{CH_3}{|}}{\overset{\overset{CH_3}{|}}{C}}=C-CH_3 \xrightarrow[\text{(2) Zn/H}_2O]{\text{(1) O}_3} 2CH_3\overset{\overset{CH_3}{|}}{C}=O$$

**74. (2)** The compound **Q** undergoes $S_N1$ reaction which is followed by dehydration process. Further the process of ozonolysis occurs and acetone is formed. The complete reaction is given in above part. Therefore, the compound **Q** is 3, 3-dimethylbutan-2-ol.

**75.** Total number of possible alkenes by dehydrobromination of 3-Bromo-3-cyclopentylhexane using alcoholic KOH is given as,

$$H_3C-CH_2-CH_2-C=CH-CH_3$$
(E & Z)

$$H_3C-CH_2-CH_2=C-CH_2-CH_3$$
(E & Z)

$$H_3C-H_2C-CH_2-C-CH_2-CH_3$$
(only 1)

Compound one and two are present in two isomeric forms. It means total four alkenes are present. Third compound is present in monomeric form. Therefore, total five alkenes are present.

**76.** The given compound contains total six alpha hydrogens. Therefore, total number of contributing structures showing hyperconjugation structures will be six.

**77. (4)** The reaction mixture of sodium amide and but-1-yne is given below :

$$CH_3CH_2C\equiv CH + NaNH_2 \rightarrow$$
$$CH_3CH_2C\equiv C^-Na^+$$

Further reaction with bromobutane gives 3-octyne.

$$CH_3CH_2C\equiv C^-Na^+ + BrCH_2CH_2CH_2CH_3 \rightarrow$$
$$CH_3CH_2C\equiv CCH_2CH_2CH_2CH_3 + NaBr$$

**78. (2, 4)** The structure of 2-dimethylbutane is given below :

$$\overset{1}{H_3C}-\underset{\underset{CH_3}{|}}{\overset{\overset{CH_3}{|}}{\overset{2}{C}}}-\overset{3}{\underset{H_2}{C}}-\overset{4}{CH_3}$$

The Newman projection for $C_2 - C_3$ bond is given below :

In the $C_2 - C_3$ bond, X is $CH_3$ and Y is $CH_3$. The Newman projection for $C_1 - C_2$ bond is given below :

In the $C_1 - C_2$ bond, X is H and Y is $C_2H_5$.

**79.** There are five cyclic isomers possible for hydrocarbon with molecular formula $C_4H_6$.

The structures of cyclic isomers are given below :

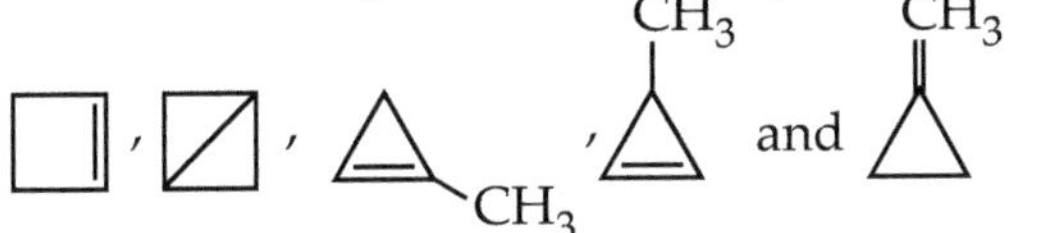

**80. (1, 4)** The stereoisomers possible for the given compound are shown below :

Stereoisomers of *cis* form :

$$\begin{array}{ccc}
CH_3 & CH_3 & CH_3 \\
| & | & | \\
H-C-OH & H-C-OH & HO-C-OH \\
| & | & | \\
C-H & C-H & C-H \\
|| & || & || \\
C-H & C-H & C-H \\
| & | & | \\
H-C-OH & HO-C-H & H-C-OH \\
| & | & | \\
CH_3 & CH_3 & CH_3
\end{array}$$

Stereoisomers of *trans* form :

$$\begin{array}{ccc}
CH_3 & CH_3 & CH_3 \\
| & | & | \\
H-C-OH & H-C-OH & OH-C-H \\
| & | & | \\
H-C & H-C & H-C \\
|| & || & || \\
C-H & C-H & C-H \\
| & | & | \\
H-C-OH & OH-C-H & H-C-OH \\
| & | & | \\
CH_3 & CH_3 & CH_3
\end{array}$$

In case of both cis and trans form of the given compound, two enantiomers exists.

Four pairs of diastereoisomers are possible for the given compound.

**81. (4)** The migration of hydrogen atom from C–2 to C–3 involves the shifting of carbocation to the carbon atom containing hydroxyl group which stabilizes the carbocation by donating lone pairs of oxygen. The hydroxyl group in conjugation provides extra stability to the compound. Therefore, the shifting of hydrogen atom is favorable.

$$\overset{1}{H_3C}-\overset{H}{\underset{OH}{\overset{|}{\underset{|}{C}}}}-\overset{H}{\underset{H}{\overset{\oplus}{\underset{|}{C_3}}}}-\overset{5}{\underset{CH_3}{\overset{|}{C}}}-CH_3 \quad \xrightarrow{\text{H+ shift from } C_2 \text{ to } C_3}$$

$$\overset{1}{H_3C}-\overset{\oplus}{\underset{OH}{\overset{|}{C_2}}}-\overset{3}{CH_2}-\overset{4}{\underset{CH_3}{\overset{|}{CH}}}-\overset{5}{CH_3}$$

**82.** The cyclic isomers of $C_5H_{10}$ are shown below :

The cyclic isomers for the given compound are 5. Out of these five isomers, 3 *cis-trans* isomers and one optical isomer is also possible for third structure. Therefore, the total number of isomers possible for the given compound is 7.

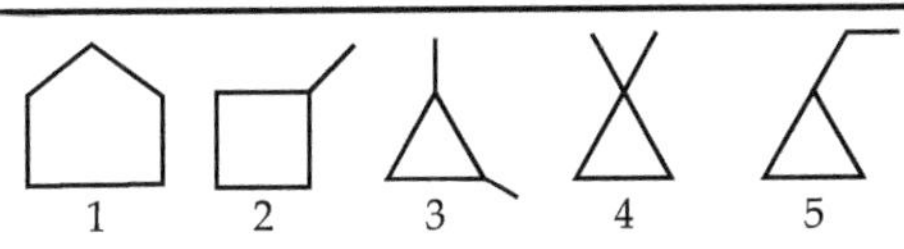

**83. (2)** Hyperconjugation involves the interaction of sigma orbital (in which electrons are present) with the neighbouring p-orbital, which is empty, to generate a stable structure.

**84. (3)** The number of structural isomers for $C_6H_{14}$ is five.

$$H_3C-\overset{H_2}{C}-\overset{H_2}{C}-\overset{H_2}{C}-\overset{H_2}{C}-CH_3$$

$$H_3C-\overset{H}{\underset{CH_3}{\overset{|}{C}}}-\overset{H_2}{C}-\overset{H_2}{C}-CH_3$$

$$H_3C-\overset{H_2}{C}-\overset{H}{\underset{CH_3}{\overset{|}{C}}}-\overset{H_2}{C}-CH_3$$

$$H_3C-\overset{H}{\underset{CH_3}{\overset{|}{C}}}-\overset{H}{\underset{CH_3}{\overset{|}{C}}}-CH_3$$

$$H_3C-\overset{CH_3}{\underset{CH_3}{\overset{|}{\underset{|}{C}}}}-\overset{H_2}{C}-CH_3$$

**85. (a)** The reactions in which cleavage of double or triple bonds, in saturated compounds, takes place using ozone, is known as ozonolysis reaction. It is given that two moles of HCHO and one mole of $CH_3COCHO$ is produced by the ozonolysis of monomer A. Therefore, the structure of monomer A and its reaction with ozone is given below :

**(b)** The *cis* isomer is a geometrical isomer in which same groups are present on the same side of the double bond. The structure of "all *cis*"- form of polymer of compound A is shown below :

**86. (a)** The stable conformer of $Z-CH_2-CH_2-Z$ in Newmann's projection is shown below :

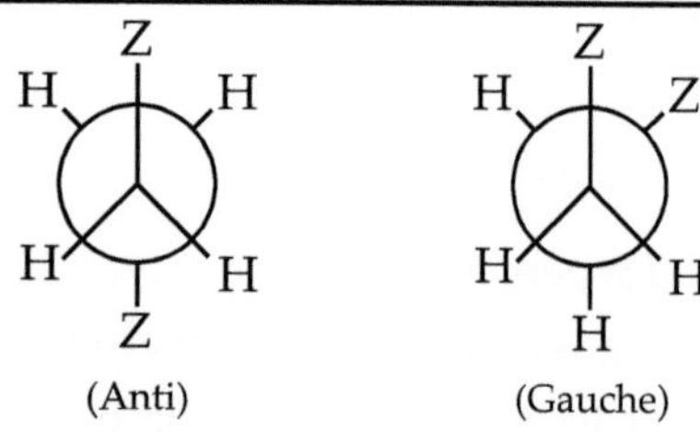

(Anti)　　　　(Gauche)

It is given that the mole fraction of the anti form is 0.82 and the mole fraction of the Gauche form is 0.18. The value of $\mu_{obs}$ is 1 and the value of $\mu_{anti}$ is 0.

$$1 = (\mu_{anti} \times 0.82) + (\mu_{gauche} \times 0.18)$$

Therefore,

$$1 = (\mu_{gauche} \times 0.18)$$

$$\mu_{gauche} = \frac{1}{0.18} = 5.55 \text{ D}$$

(b) (i) The most stable meso conformer is shown below :

(ii) The most stable meso conformer is shown below :

**87.** (a) Newmann projections are drawn to visualize the different conformations of a compound around C – C bond. In Newmann projection the circle represents the back carbon and the dot represents the front carbon.

The Newmann's projection for the less stable staggered form of butane is shown below :

(b) Relatively less stability of the staggered form is due to Van der Waal's strain because the distance between the group is minimum from each other therefore, the repulsive forces between them are high.

**88.** The intermediate formed in case of 7-bromo-1,3,5-cycloheptatriene is aromatic (stable) in nature and follows Huckel rule, whereas, the intermediate

formed in case of 5-bromo-1, 3 cylopentadiene is antiaromatic (unstable) in nature and does not follows Huckel rule. Thus, due to this reason 7-bromo-1,3,5-cycloheptatriene exists as ionic species in aqueous solution while 5-bromo-1,3 cylopentadiene does not ionise even in presence of $Ag^+$ (aq) solution.

**89. (1)** The conversion of 2-hexyne to trans-2-hexene takes place with the treatment of $Li/NH_3$.

**90.** The complete synthetic scheme for identification of **X, Y** and **Z** is shown below :

$$CH_3-CH_2-C\equiv CH \xrightarrow{NaNH_2}$$

$$CH_3-CH_2-C\equiv C \, Na^+ \; CH_3-CH_2-Br \rightarrow$$

$$CH_3-CH_2-C\equiv C-CH_2-CH_3 \xrightarrow[BaSO_4]{H_2/Pd}$$
$$(X)$$

Compound **Z** is a meso compound because it consists of plane of symmetry. Thus, it is a optically inactive compound. The structure of compound **Z** is shown below :

**91.** The structure of bombykol is,

$$CH_3-CH_2-CH_2-CH=CH-CH= CH$$
$$|$$
$$(CH_2)_8$$
$$|$$
$$CH_2-OH$$

The number of double bond present in bombykol is two.

The product(A) formed by the hydrogenation of bombykol is $CH_3-(CH_2)_{14}-CH_2-OH$.

The geometrical isomers possible for bombykol are given below :

CH$_2$–CH–CH$_2$–CH=CH, (CH$_2$)$_8$–CH$_2$–OH

$$\underset{\underset{(Cis)}{H \qquad H}}{C=C}$$

CH$_3$–(CH$_2$)$_2$, H

$$\underset{\underset{(Trans)}{H \qquad CH=CH-(CH_2)_8-CH_2-OH}}{C=C}$$

CH$_2$–CH$_2$–CH$_2$–CH = CH, H

$$\underset{\underset{(Trans)}{H \qquad (CH_2)_8-CH_2-OH}}{C=C}$$

**92. (1)** The $\pi$-bond formation takes place by the sideways overlap of p-orbital of two carbon atoms. The molecular plane is deficient of $\pi$-electron density, hence nodal plane is located in molecular plane.

**93. (4)** Ammoniacal $Cu_2Cl_2$ solution reacts with terminal alkynes. It does not show reaction with internal alkyne. Out of the given compounds, 2-butyne is an internal alkyne.

**94. (2)** The given compound $CH_3C \equiv CCH_3$ is linear and same group is attached to both the carbon atoms, hence, the compound is symmetrical. Therefore, the dipole moment of $CH_3C \equiv CCH_3$ is lowest.

●●

# Chapter 24 | Haloalkanes and Haloarenes

## QUESTIONS

**1.** In Carius method of estimation of halogen, 0.172 g of an organic compound showed presence of 0.08g of bromine. Which of these is the correct structure of the compound : **[2020, Main]**

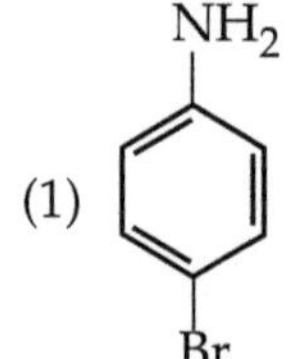

(1) $\text{NH}_2$ — $\text{C}_6\text{H}_4$ — $\text{Br}$ (para)

(2) $H_3C-CH_2-Br$

(3) $\text{Br}$ , $\text{NH}_2$ , $\text{Br}$ substituted benzene

(4) $H_3C-Br$

**2.** Which of the following compounds will show retention in configuration on nucleophic substitution by $OH^-$ ion ? **[2020, Main]**

(1) $CH_3-\underset{\overset{|}{C_2H_5}}{CH}-CH_2Br$

(2) $CH_3-\underset{\overset{|}{C_6H_5}}{CH}-Br$

(3) $CH_3-\underset{\overset{|}{CH_3}}{CH}-Br$

(4) $CH_3-\underset{\overset{|}{C_6H_{13}}}{\overset{\overset{\displaystyle Br}{|}}{C}}-H$

**3.** The major product in the following reaction is :

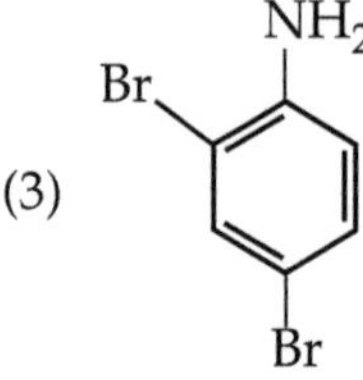

$\xrightarrow[\text{Heat}]{H_3O^+}$

**[2020, Main]**

(1) methylcyclohexadiene structure ($H_3C$, $CH_3$)

(2) $H_3C$ — C(OH)($CH_3$) cyclopentane

(3) dimethylcyclohexene ($CH_3$, $CH_3$)

(4) cyclopentene with $CH(CH_3)_2$ substituent

**4.** Among the following compounds, geometrical isomerism is exhibited by : **[2020, Main]**

(1) 4-chloro-1-methylenecyclohexane ($CH_2$, $Cl$)

(2) $CHCl$=cyclohexane with $CH_3$

(3) $CHCl$=cyclohexane

(4) $CHCl$=cyclohexane with two $CH_3$ ($H_3C$, $CH_3$)

**5.** In the reaction scheme shown below Q, R and S are the major products. **[2020, Advanced]**

$$P \xrightarrow{\text{AlCl}_3} Q$$

$$\xrightarrow[\text{(ii) H}_3\text{PO}_4]{\text{(i) Zn-Hg/HCl}} R \xrightarrow[\text{(iii) H}_2\text{SO}_4/\Delta]{\begin{array}{l}\text{(i) CH}_3\text{MgBr}\\\text{(ii) H}_3\text{O}^+\end{array}} S$$

The correct structure of

(1) S is ...

(2) Q is ...

(3) R is 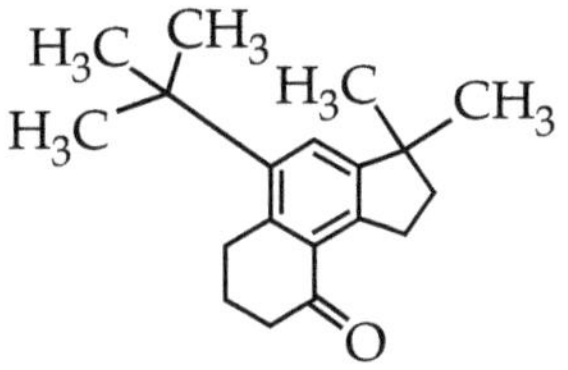

(4) S is 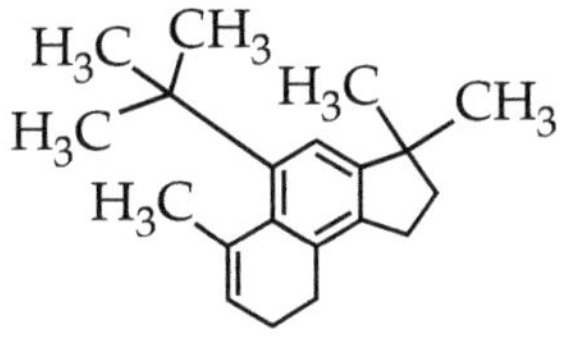

**6.** An unsaturated hydrocarbon X absorbs two hydrogen molecules on catalytic hydrogenation, and also gives following reaction :

$$X \xrightarrow[Zn/H_2O]{O_3} A \xrightarrow{[Ag(NH_3)_2]^+}$$

B (3-oxo-hexanedicarboxylic acid)

X will be : **[2020, Main]**

(1) 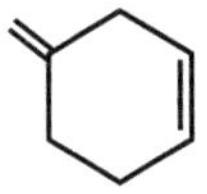 (2) 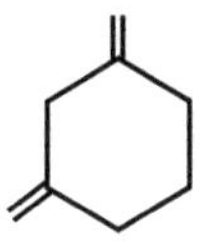

(3) 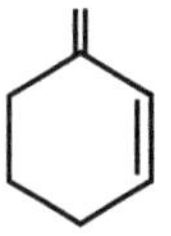 (4) 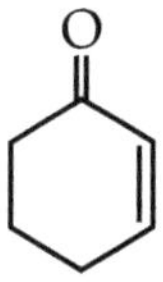

**7.** The major product [B] in the following sequence of reactions is : **[2020, Main]**

$$CH_3-C(CH(CH_3)_2)=CH-CH_2CH_3 \xrightarrow[(ii)\ H_2O_2,OH^-]{(i)\ B_2H_6} [A] \xrightarrow[\Delta]{dil.\ H_2SO_4} [B]$$

(1) $CH_3-C(=C(CH_3)_2)-CH_2CH_2CH_3$

(2) $CH_2=C(CH(CH_3)_2)-CH_2CH_2CH_3$

(3) $CH_3-CH(CH(CH_3)_2)-CH=CH-CH_3$

(4) $CH_3-C(CH(CH_3)_2)=CH-CH_2CH_3$

**8.** In the following sequence of reactions the maximum number of atoms present in molecule 'C' in one plane is ............. . **[2020, Main]**

$$A \xrightarrow[Cu\ tube]{Red\ hot} B \xrightarrow[Anhydrouns\ AlCl_3]{CH_3Cl(1.eq.)} C$$

(A is a lowest molecualr weight alkyne)

**9.** Which of the following reactions will not produce a racemic product ? **[2020, Main]**

(1) $CH_3-C(CH_3)(H)-CH=CH_2 \xrightarrow{HCl}$

(2) $CH_3-C(=O)CH_2CH_3 \xrightarrow{HCN}$

(3) 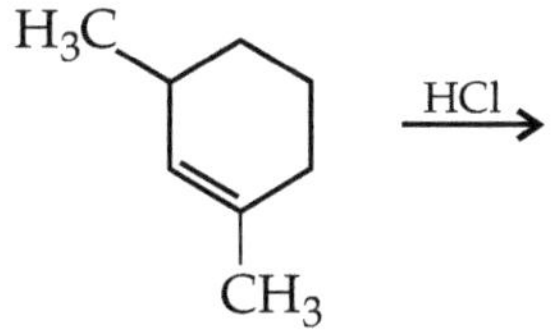

(4) $CH_3CH_2CH=CH_2 \xrightarrow{HBr}$

**10.** The correct order of heat of combustion for following alkadienes is : **[2020, Main]**

(a) 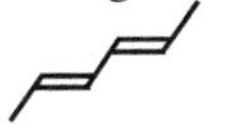 (b) 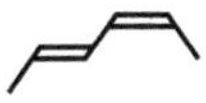

(c) 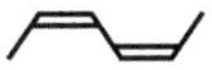

(1) (a) < (b) < (c) (2) (b) < (c) < (a)

(3) (c) < (b) < (a) (4) (a) < (c) < (b)

**11.** The major product (Y) in the following reactions is : **[2020, Main]**

$$CH_3-CH(CH_3)-C\equiv CH \xrightarrow[H_2O]{HgSO_4,H_2SO_4} X \xrightarrow[(ii)Conc.H_2SO_4/\Delta]{(i)C_2H_5MgBr,H_2O} Y$$

(1) $H_3C-C(=CH_2)-CH(C_2H_4)-CH_3$

(2) $CH_3-CH(CH_3)-C(CH_3)=CH-CH_3$

(3) $CH_3-C(CH_3)=C(CH_2CH_3)-CH_3$

(4) $CH_3-CH(CH_3)-C(CH_2CH_3)=CH_2$

**12.** The decreasing order of reactivity towards dehydrohalogenation ($E_1$) reaction of the following compounds is : **[2020, Main]**

(a) 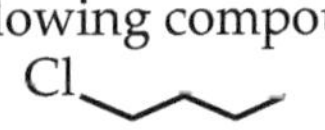 (b) 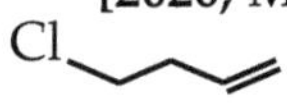

(c) 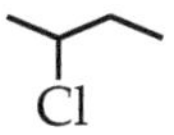 (d) 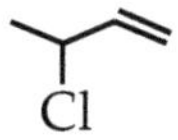

(1) B > D > A > C (2) B > D > C > A

(3) D > B > C > A (4) B > A > D > C

**13.** 1-methyl ethylene oxide when treated with an excess of HBr produces : **[2020, Main]**

(1) 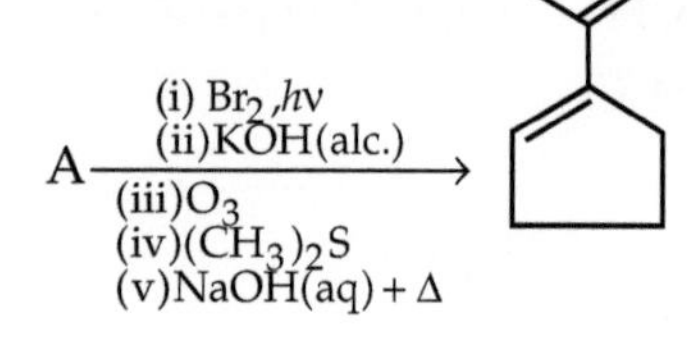

(2)

(3)

(4)

**14.** In the following reaction A is : **[2020, Main]**

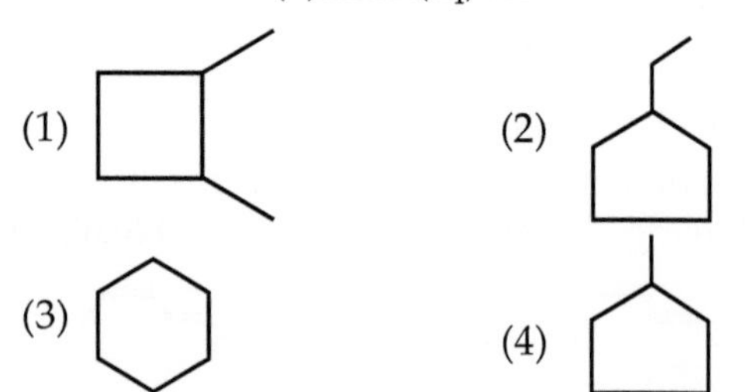

$$A \xrightarrow[\substack{(iii)O_3 \\ (iv)(CH_3)_2S \\ (v)NaOH(aq)+\Delta}]{\substack{(i)\,Br_2,h\nu \\ (ii)KOH(alc.)}}$$

(1)

(2)

(3)

(4)

**15.** The correct order of stability for the following alkoxides is : **[2020, Main]**

**(A)**    **(B)**    **(C)**

(1) (C) > (A) > (B)    (2) (C) > (B) > (A)
(3) (B) > (A) > (C)    (4) (B) > (C) > (A)

**16.** Consider the following reactions : **[2020, Main]**

(a) benzene + chlorobenzene $\xrightarrow{\text{anhyd. AlCl}_3}$ biphenyl

(b) benzene $+ Cl_2$ (excess) $\xrightarrow[\text{dark}]{\text{anhyd. AlCl}_3}$ hexachlorocyclohexane

(c) benzene $+ CH_2 = CH—Cl \xrightarrow[\text{dark}]{\text{anhyd. AlCl}_3}$ styrene

(d) benzene $+ CH_2 = CH—CH_2Cl \xrightarrow[\text{dark}]{\text{anhyd. AlCl}_3}$ allylbenzene

(1) (a) and (d)    (2) (b) and (d)
(3) (b), (c) and (d)    (4) (a) and (b)

**17.** Polysubstitution is a major drawback in : **[2019, Main]**

(1) Friedel Craft's alkylation
(2) Reimer Tiemann reaction
(3) Acetylation of aniline
(4) Friedel Craft's acylation

**18.** Which one of the following alkenes when treated with HCl yields majorly an anti Markovnikov product ? **[2019, Main]**

(1) $CH_3O – CH = CH_2$
(2) $Cl – CH = CH_2$
(3) $H_2N – CN = CH_2$
(4) $F_3C – CH = CH_2$

**19.** Increasing order of reactivity of the following compounds of $S_N1$ substitution is : **[2019, Main]**

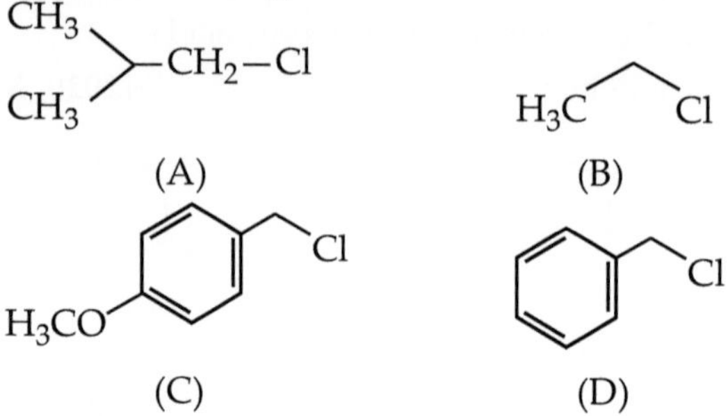

(1) (B) < (C) < (D) < (A)
(2) (B) < (C) < (A) < (D)
(3) (B) < (A) < (D) < (C)
(4) (A) < (B) < (D) < (C)

**20.** Which of the following potential energy (PE) diagrams represents the $S_N1$ reaction ? **[2019, Main]**

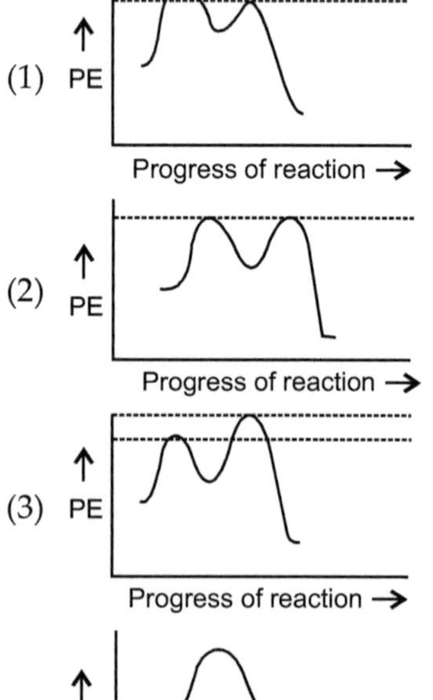

**21.** Increasing rate of $S_N1$ reaction in the following compounds is : **[2019, Main]**

(A)

MeO — (B)

H₃C — (C)

H₃CO — (D)

(1) (A) < (B) < (C) < (D)
(2) (B) < (A) < (C) < (D)
(3) (B) < (A) < (D) < (C)
(4) (A) < (B) < (D) < (C)

**22.** The major product of the following reaction is : **[2019, Main]**

$$CH_3 - \overset{\overset{\displaystyle CH_3}{|}}{\underset{\underset{\displaystyle H}{|}}{C}} - \overset{\overset{\displaystyle}{}}{\underset{\underset{\displaystyle Br}{|}}{CH}}CH_3 \xrightarrow{CH_3OH}$$

(1) $CH_3 - \overset{\overset{\displaystyle CH_3}{|}}{\underset{\underset{\displaystyle H}{|}}{C}} - CH=CH_2$

(2) $CH_3 - \overset{\overset{\displaystyle CH_3}{|}}{C} = CHCH_3$

(3) $CH - \overset{\overset{\displaystyle CH_3}{|}}{\underset{\underset{\displaystyle OCH_3}{|}}{C}} - CH_2CH_3$

(4) $CH - \overset{\overset{\displaystyle CH_3}{|}}{\underset{\underset{\displaystyle H}{|}}{C}} - \overset{}{\underset{\underset{\displaystyle OCH_3}{|}}{CH}}CH_3$

**23.** The increasing order of the reactivity of the following compounds towards electrophilic aromatic substitution reaction is : **[2019, Main]**

Cl — (I)    CH₃ — (II)    COCH₃ — (III)

(1) II < I < III      (2) III < II < I
(3) III < I < II      (4) I < III < II

**24.** The increasing order of nucleophilicity of the following nucleophilies of : **[2019, Main]**

(a) $CH_3CO_2^{\ominus}$     (b) $H_2O$

(c) $CH_3SO_3^{\ominus}$     (d) $\overset{\ominus}{OH}$

(1) (a) < (d) < (c) < (b)     (2) (b) < (c) < (d) < (a)
(3) (d) < (a) < (c) < (b)     (4) (b) < (c) < (a) < (d)

**25.** The major product of the following addition reaction is : **[2019, Main]**

$$H_3C - CH = CH_2 \xrightarrow{Cl_2, H_2O}$$

(1) $CH_3 - \underset{\underset{\displaystyle OH}{|}}{CH} - \underset{\underset{\displaystyle OH}{|}}{CH_2}$

(2) $H_3C - \underset{\underset{\displaystyle OH}{|}}{CH} - \underset{\underset{\displaystyle Cl}{|}}{CH_2}$

(3) $H_3C-\triangleleft O$

(4) $H_3C - \overset{\overset{\displaystyle O}{\|}}{C} - CH_3$

**26.** Which one of the following is likely to give a precipitate with $AgNO_3$ solution ? **[2019, Main]**

(1) $CH_2 = CH - Cl$     (2) $CCl_4$
(3) $CHCl_3$             (4) $(CH_3)_3CCl$

**27.** Heating of 2-chloro-1-phenylbutane with EtOK/ EtOH gives X as the major product. Reaction of X with $Hg(OAc)_2/H_2O$ followed by $NaBH_4$ gives Y as the major product. Y is : **[2019, Main]**

(1) Ph⌃⌄⌃⌄ with OH

(2) Ph⌃⌄ with OH

(3) Ph⌃⌄⌃ with OH

(4) Ph⌃⌄⌃⌄

**28.** An 'Assertion' and a 'Reason' are given below. Choose the correct answer from the following options :

**Assertion (A) :** Vinyl halides to not undergo nucleophilic substitution easily.

**Reason (R) :** Even though the intermediate carbocation is stabilized by loosely held π-electrons, the cleavage is difficult because of strong bonding. **[2019, Main]**

(1) Both (A) and (R) are wrong statements.
(2) Both (A) and (R) are correct statements and (R) is the correct explanation of (A).
(3) Both (A) and (R) are correct statements but (R) is not the correct explanation of (A).
(4) (A) is a correct statement but (R) is a wrong statement.

**29.** Choose the correct option(s) for the following set of reactions

$$C_6H_{10}O \xrightarrow[\text{(ii)}H_2O]{\text{(i)}MeMgBr} Q \xrightarrow{\text{conc.HCl}} S \text{ (major)}$$

$$\downarrow 20\% \; H_3PO_3, 360 \; K$$

$$T \text{ (major)} \xrightarrow[\text{(ii)}Br_2, h\nu]{\text{(i)}H_2, Ni} R \text{ (major)} \xrightarrow[\Delta]{\text{HBr, benzoyl peroxide}} U \text{ (major)}$$

**[2019, Advanced]**

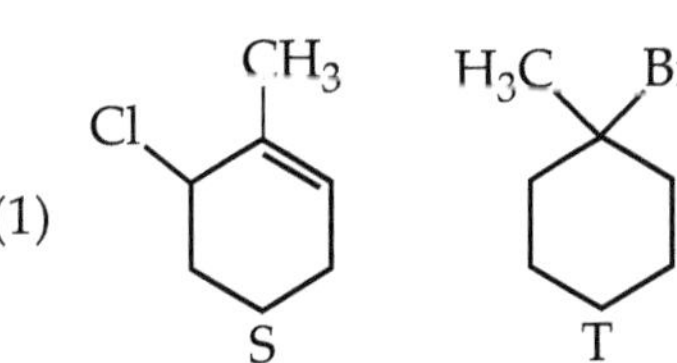


(1)

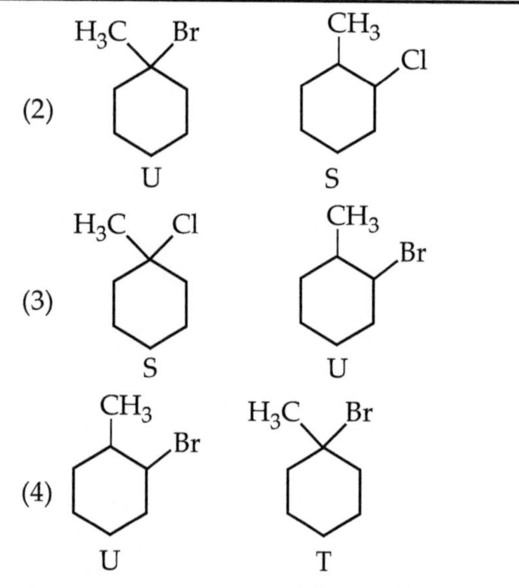

**(2)** U

**(3)** S

**(4)** U

(with structures labelled S, U, T)

**30.** Choose the correct option(s) that give(s) an aromatic compound as the major product :

**[2019, Advanced]**

(1) $H_3C$—CHBr—CH$_2$Br
(i) alc. KOH
(ii) NaNH$_2$
(iii) red hot iron tube, 873 K

(2) (cyclopentadiene) $\xrightarrow{\text{NaOMe}}$

(3) (cyclobutane) $\xrightarrow{\text{NaOEt}}$

(4) (cyclohexane) + Cl$_2$ (excess) $\xrightarrow{\text{UV, 500 K}}$

**31.** **List-I** contains reactions and **List-II** contains major products. **[2018, Advanced]**

**List-I**

P. (Me)$_3$C–ONa + (Me)$_2$CH–Br $\longrightarrow$

Q. (Me)$_3$C–OMe + HBr $\longrightarrow$

R. (Me)$_3$C–Br + NaOMe $\longrightarrow$

S. (Me)$_3$C–ONa + MeBr $\longrightarrow$

**List-II**

1. (Me)$_2$CH–OH

2. (Me)$_3$C–Br

3. (Me)$_3$C–OMe

4. (Me)$_2$C=CH$_2$

5. (Me)$_3$C–O–C(Me)$_3$

Match each reaction in **List-I** with one or more products in **List-II** and choose the correct option.

(1) P → 1, 5; Q → 2; R → 3; S → 4
(2) P → 1, 4; Q → 2; R → 4; S → 3
(3) P → 1, 4; Q → 1, 2; R → 3, 4; S → 4
(4) P → 4, 5; Q → 4; R → 4; S → 3, 4

**32.** The major product of the following reaction is :

**[2018, Main]**

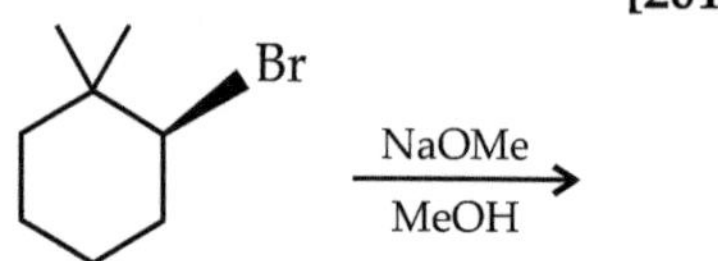

$\xrightarrow[\text{MeOH}]{\text{NaOMe}}$

**(1)** (cyclohexane with two methyl groups and OMe, wedge)

**(2)** (cyclohexene with gem-dimethyl)

**(3)** (cyclohexene with methyl)

**(4)** (cyclohexane with gem-dimethyl and OMe, wedge)

**33.** The major product formed in the following reaction is : **[2018, Main]**

(cyclopentane with NO$_2$, Cl, Cl, CH$_3$) $\xrightarrow[\text{Heat}]{\text{NaOCH}_3 \text{ (1 eq.)}}$

**(1)** (cyclopentene NO$_2$, Cl, CH$_3$)

**(2)** (cyclopentene NO$_2$, Cl, CH$_3$)

**(3)** (cyclopentene NO$_2$, Cl, CH$_3$)

**(4)** (cyclopentene NO$_2$, Cl, CH$_3$)

**34.** Which of the following will most readily give the dehydrohalogenation product ? **[2018, Main]**

**(1)** CH$_2$=C(Br)–CH=CH–CH$_3$

**(2)** (bromocyclohexane, aromatic)

**(3)** (1-bromocyclohexene)

**(4)** CH$_2$=CH–C(Br)=CH–Ph

**35.** The major product of the following reaction is :

**[2018, Main]**

(Ph–CH=CHCH$_3$) $\xrightarrow{\text{HBr}}$

**(1)** Ph–CHBr–CH$_2$CH$_3$

**(2)** Ph–CH$_2$–CHBr–CH$_3$

**(3)** Ph–CH$_2$CH$_2$CH$_2$Br

**(4)** Br–C$_6$H$_4$–CH=CH–CH$_3$

**36.** The most polar compound among the following is : **[2018, Main]**

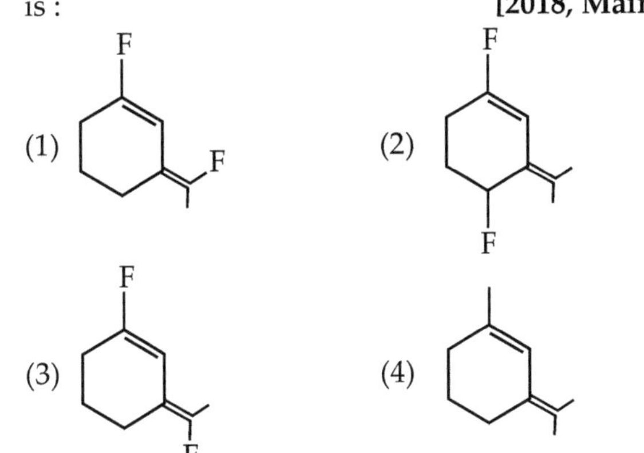

**37.** The major product of the following reaction is : **[2018, Main]**

(1) (2) (3) (4)

**38.** The IUPAC names of the following compound is/are : **[2017, Advanced]**

$$H_3C—\hspace{-4pt}\bigcirc\hspace{-4pt}—Cl$$

(1) 1-chloro-4-methylbenzene
(2) 4-chlorotoluene
(3) 4-methylchlorobenzene
(4) 1-methyl-4-chlorobenzene

**Columns of the following table**

Columns 1, 2 and 3 contain starting materials, reaction conditions, and type of reactions, respectively.

| Column I | Column 2 | Column 3 |
|---|---|---|
| (I) Toluene | (i) $NaOH/Br_2$ | (P) Condensation |
| (II) Acetophenone | (ii) $Br_2/h\nu$ | (Q) Carboxylation |
| (III) Benzaldehyde | (iii) $(CH_3CO)_2O/CH_3COOK$ | (R) Substitution |
| (IV) Phenol | (iv) $NaOH/CO_2$ | (S) Haloform |

**39.** The only CORRECT combination in which the reaction proceeds through radical mechanism is : **[2017, Advanced]**
(1) (III) (ii) (P)     (2) (IV) (i) (Q)
(3) (II) (iii) (R)     (4) (I) (ii) (R)

**40.** For the following compounds, the correct statements with respect to nucleophilic substitution reactions is/are : **[2017, Advanced]**

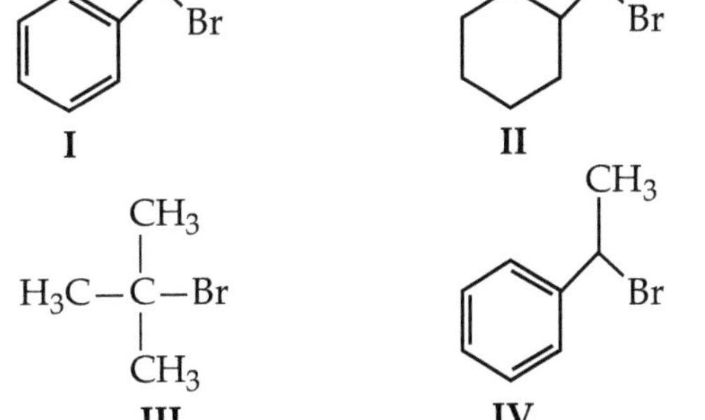

(1) **I** and **III** follow $S_N1$ mechanism
(2) **I** and **II** follow $S_N2$ mechanism
(3) Compound **IV** undergoes inversion of configuration
(4) The order of reactivity for **I, III** and **IV** is : **IV > I > III**

**41.** Which of the following, upon treatment with *tert*-BuONa followed by addition of bromine water, fails to decolourise the colour of bromine ? **[2017, Main]**

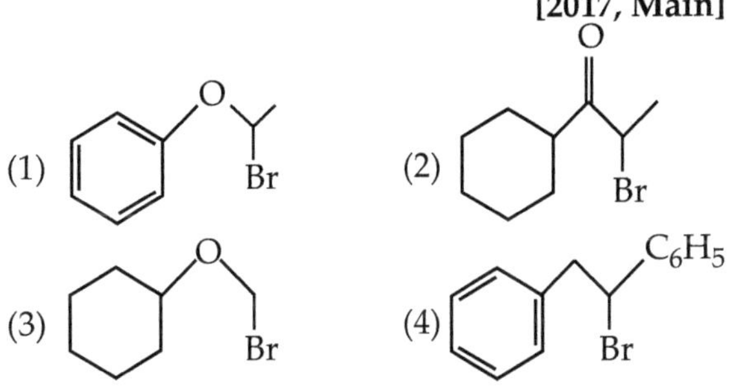

**42.** The increasing order of the reactivity of the following halides for the $S_N1$ reaction is : **[2017, Main]**

I. $CH_3CHCH_2CH_3$
   |
   Cl

II. $CH_3CH_2CH_2Cl$
III. $p\text{-}H_3CO—C_6H_4—CH_2Cl$
(1) (I) < (III) < (II)     (2) (II) < (III) < (I)
(3) (III) < (II) < (I)     (4) (II) < (I) < (III)

**43.** The major product obtained in the following reaction is : **[2017, Main]**

(1) $(+)C_6H_5CH(O^tBu)CH_2C_6H_5$
(2) $(-)C_6H_5CH(O^tBu)CH_2C_6H_5$
(3) $(\pm)C_6H_5CH(O^tBu)CH_2C_6H_5$
(4) $C_6H_5CH = CHC_6H_5$

**44.** Which of the following compounds will not undergo Friedel Craft's reaction with benzene ? **[2017, Main]**

(1) $CH_2=CH-COCl$     (2) $CH_2=CH-CH_2Cl$

(3) $CH_2=CH-CH_2Cl$     (4) $CH_2=C(CH_3)-COCl$

**45.** The major product of the following reaction is :

$$CH_3CHCH_2CHCH_2CH_3 \xrightarrow[\text{heat}]{KOH,\ CH_3OH}$$
$$\underset{Br}{|}\qquad\underset{Br}{|}$$

**[2017, Main]**

(1) $CH_2=CHCH_2CH=CHCH_3$
(2) $CH_2=CHCH=CHCH_2CH_3$
(3) $CH_3CH=C=CHCH_2CH_3$
(4) $CH_3CH=CH-CH=CHCH_3$

**46.** The major product of the following reaction is :

**[2017, Main]**

$$C_6H_5CH_2-\underset{\underset{Br}{|}}{\overset{\overset{CH_3}{|}}{C}}-CH_2-CH_3 \xrightarrow[C_2H_5OH]{C_2H_5ONa}$$

(1) $C_6H_5CH_2-\underset{\underset{OC_2H_5}{|}}{\overset{\overset{CH_3}{|}}{C}}-CH_2CH_3$

(2) $C_6H_5CH=\underset{\underset{CH_3}{|}}{C}-CH_2CH_3$

(3) $C_6H_5CH_2-\underset{\underset{CH_3}{|}}{C}=CHCH_3$

(4) $C_6H_5CH_2-\underset{\underset{CH_2CH_3}{|}}{C}=CH_2$

**47.** The major product of the following reaction is :

**[2017, Main]**

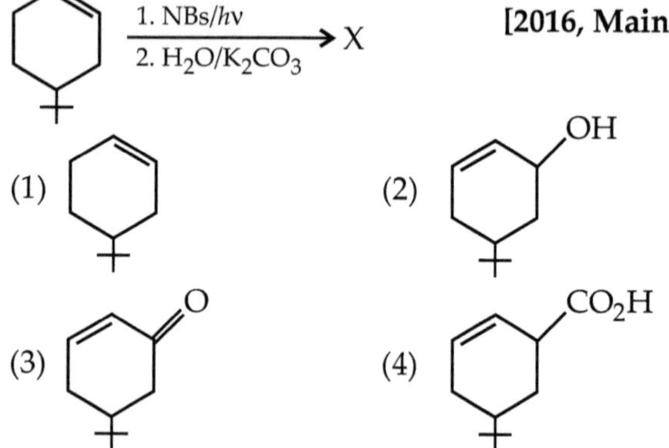

**48.** In the following monobromination reaction, the number of possible chiral products is :

**[2016, Advanced]**

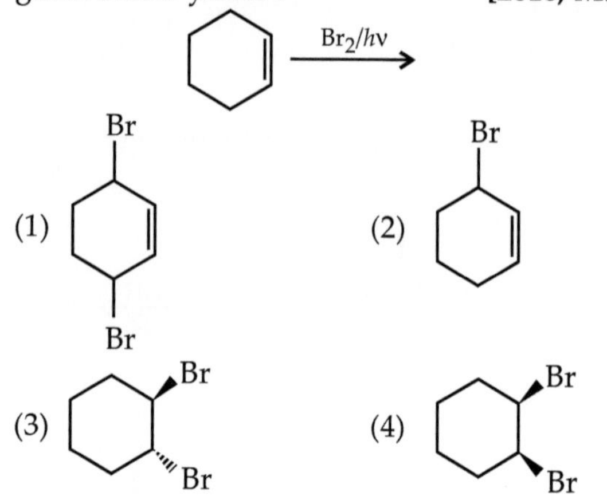

**49.** Bromination of cyclohexene under conditions given below yields : **[2016, Main]**

**50.** Which of the following reagents is **not** suitable for the elimination reaction ? **[2016, Main]**

(1) $NaOH/H_2O$     (2) $NaOEt/EtOH$
(3) $NaOH/H_2O\text{-EtOH}$     (4) $NaI$

**51.** The product of the reaction given below is :

$$\xrightarrow[\text{2. } H_2O/K_2CO_3]{\text{1. NBs/}h\nu} X$$

**[2016, Main]**

**52.** 2-chloro-2-methylpentane on reaction with sodium methoxide in methanol yields :

**[2016, Main]**

(a) $C_2H_5CH_2\underset{\underset{CH_3}{|}}{\overset{\overset{CH_3}{|}}{C}}-OCH_3$

(b) $C_2H_5CH_2\underset{\underset{CH_3}{|}}{C}-CH_2$

(c) $C_2H_5CH = C - CH_3$
    $\quad\quad\quad\quad\quad |$
    $\quad\quad\quad\quad CH_3$

(1) All of these      (2) (a) and (c)

(3) (c) only      (4) (a) and (b)

**53.** The synthesis of alkyl fluorides is best accomplished by :    **[2015, Main]**

(1) Free radical fluorination

(2) Sandmeyer's reaction

(3) Finkelstein reaction

(4) Swarts reaction

**54.** In $S_N2$ reactions, the correct order of reactivity for the following compounds :    **[2014, Main]**
$CH_3Cl$, $CH_3CH_2Cl$, $(CH_3)_2CHCl$ and $(CH_3)_3CCl$
is :

(1) $CH_3Cl > (CH_3)_2CHCl > CH_3CH_2Cl > (CH_3)_3CCl$

(2) $CH_3Cl > CH_3CH_2Cl > (CH_3)_2CHCl > (CH_3)_3CCl$

(3) $CH_3CH_2Cl > CH_3Cl > (CH_3)_2CHCl > (CH_3)_3CCl$

(4) $(CH_3)_2CHCl > CH_3CH_2Cl > CH_3Cl > (CH_3)_3CCl$

**55.** For the compounds
$CH_3Cl$, $CH_3Br$, $CH_3I$ and $CH_3F$,
the correct order of increasing C-halogen bond length is :    **[2014, Main]**

(1) $CH_3F < CH_3Cl < CH_3Br < CH_3I$

(2) $CH_3F < CH_3Br < CH_3Cl < CH_3I$

(3) $CH_3F < CH_3I < CH_3Br < CH_3Cl$

(4) $CH_3Cl < CH_3Br < CH_3F < CH_3I$

**56.** In a nucleophilic substitution reaction :

$$R - Br + Cl^- \xrightarrow{DMF} R - Cl + Br^-,$$

Which one of the following undergoes complete inversion of configuration ?    **[2014, Main]**

(1) $C_6H_5CHC_6H_5Br$

(2) $C_6H_5CH_2Br$

(3) $C_6H_5CHCH_3Br$

(4) $C_6H_5CCH_3C_6H_5Br$

**57.** The major product obtained in the photo catalysed bromination of 2-methylbutane is : **[2014, Main]**

(1) 1-bromo-2-methylbutane

(2) 1-bromo-3-methylbutane

(3) 2-bromo-3-methylbutane

(4) 2-bromo-2-methylbutane

**58.** KI in acetone, undergoes $S_N2$ reaction with each of **P, Q, R** and **S**. The rates of the reaction vary as :

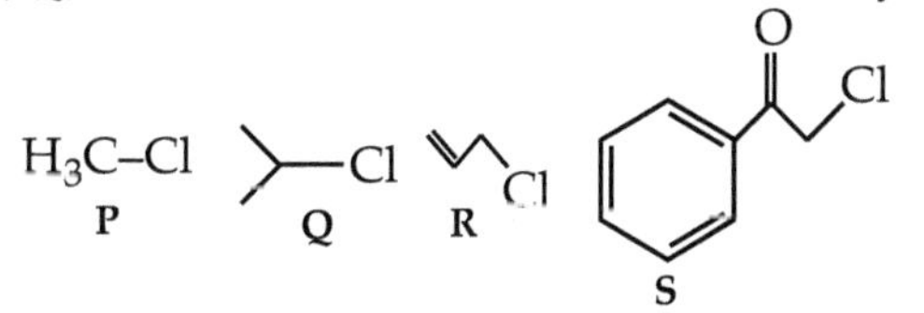

**[2013, Advanced]**

(1) $P > Q > R > S$      (2) $S > P > R > Q$

(3) $P > R > Q > S$      (4) $R > P > S > Q$

**59.** Among P, Q, R and S, the aromatic compounds is/are :    **[2013, Advanced]**

(1) P      (2) Q

(3) R      (4) S

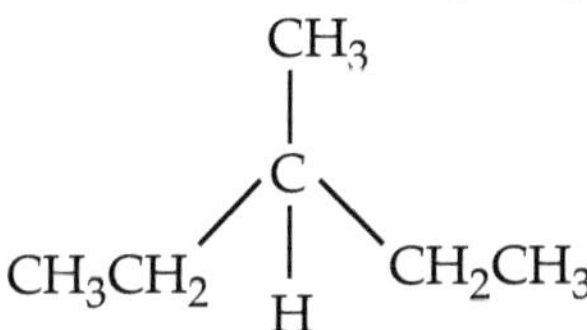

**60.** Which of the given statements about **N, O, P** and **Q** with respect to M is/are correct ?

**[2012, Advanced]**

(1) **M** and **N** are non-mirror image stereoisomers

(2) **M** and **O** are identical

(3) **M** and **P** are enantiomers

(4) **M** and **Q** are identical

**61.** The maximum number of isomers (including stereoisomers) that are possible on mono-chlorination of the following compound, is :

**[2011, Advanced]

**62.** The correct statements about the compound given below is/are : **[2008, Advanced]**

$$H_3C \overset{\overset{\displaystyle Cl \;\; H}{|}}{\underset{\underset{\displaystyle Cl \;\; H}{|}}{C-C}} CH_3$$

(1) The compound is optically active

(2) The compound possesses centre of symmetry

(3) The compound possesses plane of symmetry

(4) The compound possesses axis of symmetry

**63. Statement-1 :** Bromobenzene upon reaction with $Br_2/Fe$ gives 1, 4-dibromobenzene as the major product.

**and**

**Statement-2 :** In bromobenzene, the inductive effect of the bromo group is more dominant than the mesomeric effect in directing the incoming electrophile **[2008, Advanced]**

(1) Statement-1 is True, Statement-2 is True; Statement-2 is a correct explanation for Statement-1

(2) Statement-1- is True, Statement-2 is True; Statement-2 is NOT a correct explanation for Statement-1

(3) Statement-1 is True, Statement-2 is False

(4) Statement-1 is False, Statement-2 is True

**64.** The reagents for the following conversion,

$$\underset{\underset{\displaystyle Br}{}}{\overset{\overset{\displaystyle Br}{}}{\diagdown \diagup \diagdown}} \xrightarrow{\;?\;} H - \!\!\!\equiv\!\!\! - H$$

is/are : **[2007, Advanced]**

(1) alcoholic KOH

(2) alcoholic KOH followed by $NaNH_2$

(3) aqueous KOH followed by $NaNH_2$

(4) $Zn/CH_3OH$

**65.** The number of stereoisomers obtained by bromination of *trans*-2-butene is :

**[2007, Advanced]**

(1) 1        (2) 2

(3) 3        (4) 4

**66. Statement-1 :** Molecules that are not superimposable on their mirror images are chiral.

**because**

**Statement-2 :** All chiral molecules have chiral centres. **[2007, Advanced]**

(1) Statement-1 is True, Statement-2 is True; Statement-2 is a correct explanation for Statement-1

(2) Statement-1- is True, Statement-2 is True; Statement-2 is NOT a correct explanation for Statement-1

(3) Statement-1 is True, Statement-2 is False

(4) Statement-1 is False, Statement-2 is True

**67.** $CH_3-CH = CH_2 + NOCl \rightarrow P$

Identify the adduct. **[2006, Main]**

(1) $\underset{\underset{\displaystyle Cl \quad NO}{|\quad\;\;|}}{CH_3-CH-CH_2}$    (2) $\underset{\underset{\displaystyle NO \quad Cl}{|\quad\;\;|}}{CH_3-CH-CH_2}$

(3) $\underset{\underset{\displaystyle Cl}{|}}{\overset{\overset{\displaystyle NO}{|}}{CH_3-CH_2-CH}}$    (4) $\underset{\underset{\displaystyle Cl}{|}}{\overset{}{CH_2}}-\underset{\underset{\displaystyle NO}{|}}{CH_2}-\underset{\underset{\displaystyle Cl}{|}}{CH_2}$

**68.** $H_3C\overset{\overset{\displaystyle CH_3}{|}}{\underset{\underset{\displaystyle CH_3}{|}}{C}} \xrightarrow{Cl_2,\, h\nu} N$ (isomeric products)

$C_5H_{11}Cl \xrightarrow{\text{Fractional distillation}} M$ (isomeric products)

What are N and M ? **[2006, Main]**

(1) 6, 6        (2) 6, 4

(3) 4, 4        (4) 3, 3

**69.** Match the following : **[2006, Main]**

| Column I | Column II |
|---|---|
| (A) $CH_3-CHBr-CD_3$ on treatment with alc. KOH gives $CH_2{=}CH{-}CD_3$ as a major product | (P) E1 reaction |
| (B) $Ph-CHBr-CH_3$ reacts faster than $Ph\text{-}CHBr\text{-}CD_3$ | (Q) E2 reaction |
| (C) $Ph\text{-}CH_2\text{-}CH_2Br$ on treatment with $C_2H_5OD/$ $C_2H_5O^-$ gives $Ph\text{-}CD{=}CH_2$ as the major product | (R) E1 cb reaction |
| (D) $PhCH_2CH_2Br$ and $PhCD_2CH_2Br$ react with same rate | (S) First order reaction |

**70.** Give reasons : **[2005, Main]**

(1) (i) $\underset{}{\overset{\overset{\displaystyle H_3C \quad Br}{\diagup \;\; \diagdown}}{\bigodot}}CH_3 \xrightarrow{C_2H_5OH(aq)}$ acidic solution

(ii) $Br-\underset{}{\bigodot}-\overset{\overset{\displaystyle CH_3}{|}}{\underset{\underset{\displaystyle CH_3}{|}}{C}} \xrightarrow{C_2H_5OH(aq)}$ neutral

(2) (i) $\underset{\underset{\displaystyle O_2N \qquad CH_3}{}}{\overset{\overset{\displaystyle F}{}}{\bigodot}} \xrightarrow{NaOH(aq)} F^-$ (liberated)

(ii) 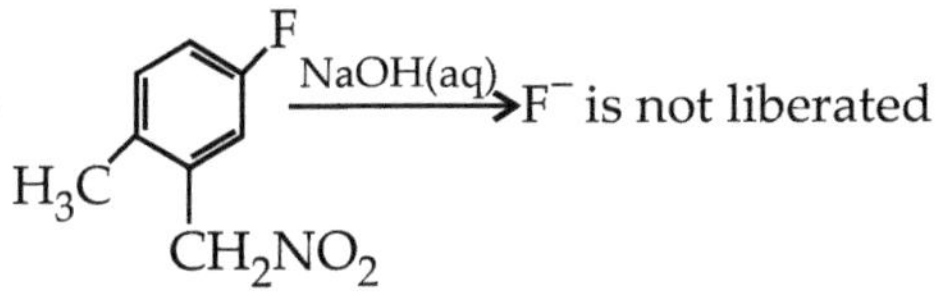 [structure: toluene with F, $CH_3$, $CH_2NO_2$ substituents] $\xrightarrow{\text{NaOH(aq)}}$ $F^-$ is not liberated

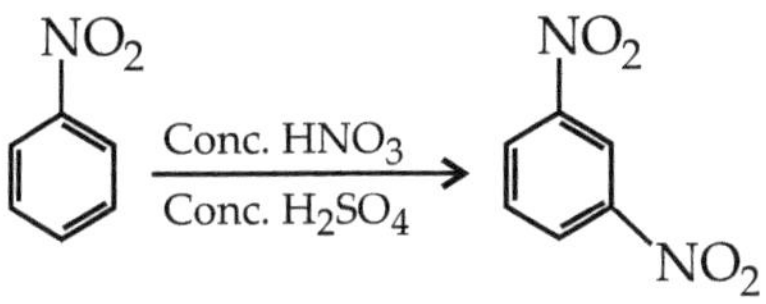

(3) (i) 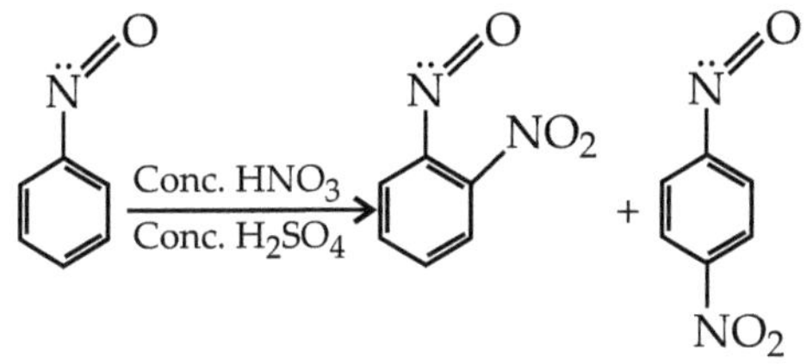 [nitrosobenzene] $\xrightarrow[\text{Conc. H}_2\text{SO}_4]{\text{Conc. HNO}_3}$ [nitroso compound with $NO_2$] + [nitroso compound with $NO_2$]

(ii) [nitrobenzene] $\xrightarrow[\text{Conc. H}_2\text{SO}_4]{\text{Conc. HNO}_3}$ [m-dinitrobenzene]

(4) [polycyclic structure] $\xrightarrow[\text{3 mole of H}_2]{\text{Pd/C}}$ [polycyclic product]

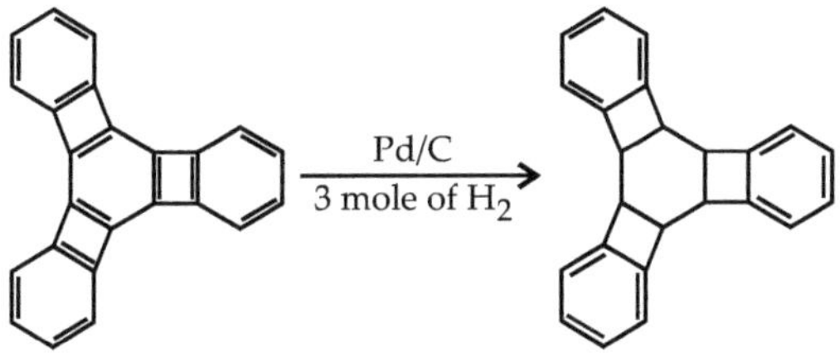

is formed but not [polycyclic structure]

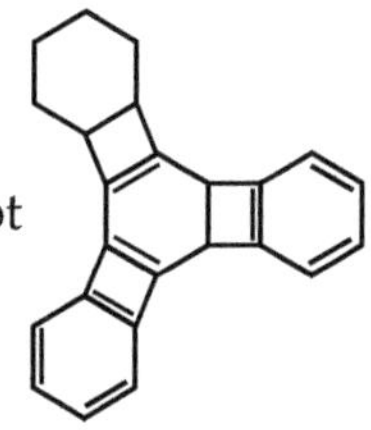

**71.** 1-bromo-3-chlorocyclobutane when treated with two equivalents of Na, in the presence of ether which of the following will be formed ?

**[2005, Screening]**

(1) 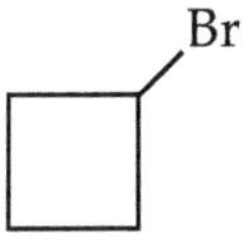 [cyclobutane with Br]
(2) 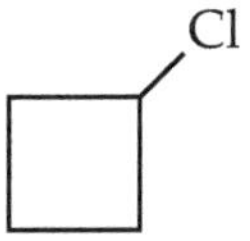 [cyclobutane with Cl]
(3) [cyclobutane]
(4)  [bicyclobutane]

**72.** 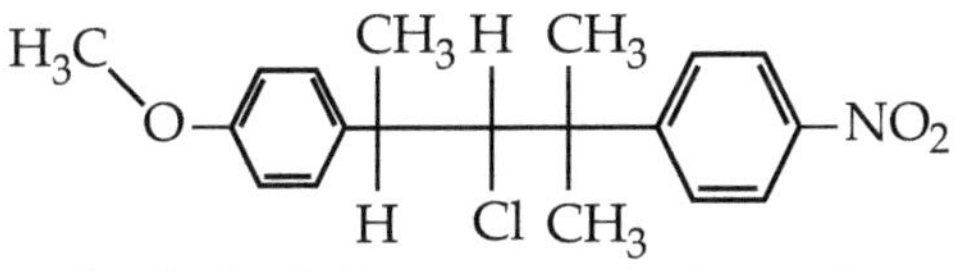 $H_3C$—O—[benzene]—C($CH_3$)(H)—C(H)(Cl)—C($CH_3$)($CH_3$)—[benzene]—$NO_2$

on hydrolysis in aqueous acetone gives,

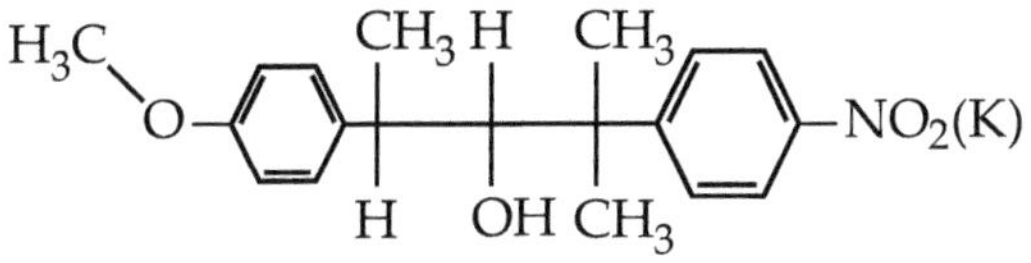

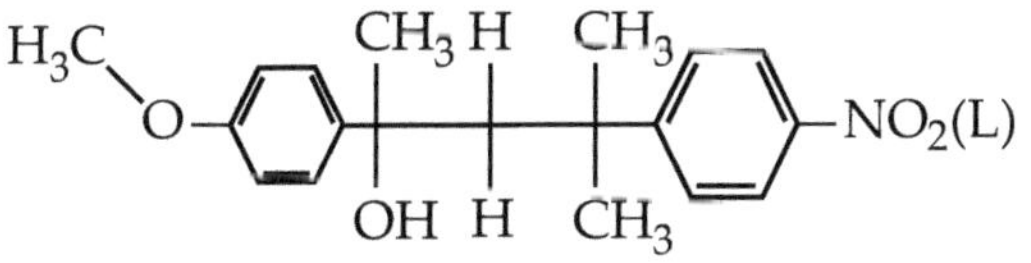

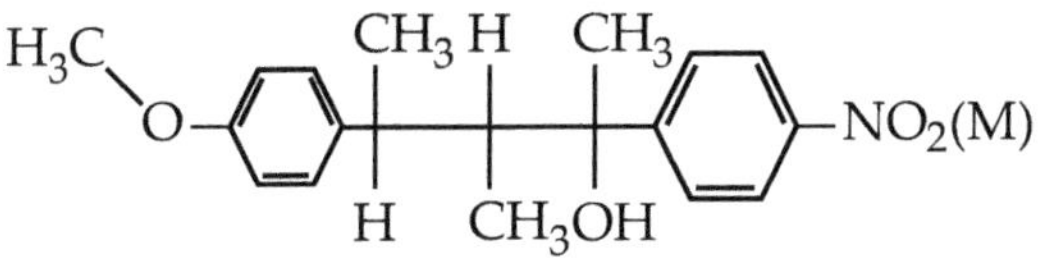

$H_3C$—O—[benzene]—C($CH_3$)(H)—C(H)(OH)—C($CH_3$)($CH_3$)—[benzene]—$NO_2$(K)

$H_3C$—O—[benzene]—C($CH_3$)(OH)—C(H)(H)—C($CH_3$)($CH_3$)—[benzene]—$NO_2$(L)

$H_3C$—O—[benzene]—C($CH_3$)(H)—C(H)($CH_3OH$)—C($CH_3$)—[benzene]—$NO_2$(M)

It mainly gives : **[2005, Screening]**
(1) K and L  (2) Only K
(3) L and M  (4) Only M

**73.** How many chiral compounds are possible on mono chlorination of 2-methyl butane ?

**[2004, Screening]**
(1) 2  (2) 4
(3) 6  (4) 8

**74.** Among the following, the molecule with the highest dipole moment is : **[2003, Screening]**
(1) $CH_3Cl$  (2) $CH_2Cl_2$
(3) $CHCl_3$  (4) $CCl_4$

**75.** 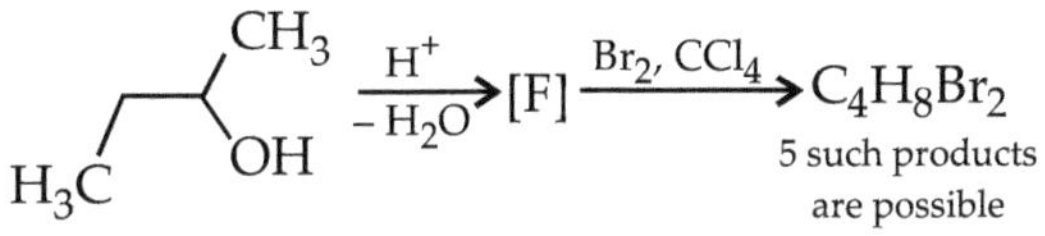 $H_3C$—CH(OH)—CH($CH_3$) $\xrightarrow[-\text{H}_2\text{O}]{\text{H}^+}$ [F] $\xrightarrow{\text{Br}_2,\ \text{CCl}_4}$ $C_4H_8Br_2$ (5 such products are possible)

How many structures of F is possible ?

**[2003, Screening]**
(1) 2  (2) 5
(3) 6  (4) 3

**76.** An enantiomerically pure acid is treated with racemic mixture of an alcohol having one chiral carbon. The ester formed will be :

**[2003, Screening]**
(1) Optically active mixture
(2) Pure enantiomer
(3) Meso compound
(4) Racemic mixture

**77.** Which of the following compounds exhibits stereoisomerism ? **[2002, Screening]**
(1) 2-methylbutene-1
(2) 3-methylbutyne-1
(3) 3-methylbutanoic acid
(4) 2-methylbutanoic acid

**78.** Consider the following reaction :

$$H_3C-\underset{D}{CH}-\underset{CH_3}{CH}-CH_3 + Br \longrightarrow \text{`X'} + HBr$$

Identify the structure of the major product `X'

**[2002, Screening]**

(1) $H_3C-\underset{D}{CH}-\underset{CH_3}{CH}-CH_2$

(2) $H_3C-\underset{D}{CH}-\underset{CH_3}{C}-CH_3$

(3) $H_3C-\underset{D}{C}-\underset{CH_3}{CH}-CH_3$

(4) $H_3C-CH-CH-CH_3$
  $\quad\quad\quad\;\; |$
  $\quad\quad\quad CH_3$

**79.** Identify the set of reagent/reaction conditions `X' and `Y' in the following set of transformations :
[2002, Screening]

$CH_3-CH_2-CH_2Br \xrightarrow{X} \text{Product} \xrightarrow{Y}$

$\quad\quad\quad\quad CH_3-CH-CH_3$
$\quad\quad\quad\quad\quad\quad\;\; |$
$\quad\quad\quad\quad\quad\quad\; Br$

(1) X = dilute aqueous NaOH, 20°C; Y = HBr/acetic acid, 20°C
(2) X = concentrated alcoholic NaOH, 80°C; Y = HBr/acetic acid, 20°C

(3) X = dilute aqueous NaOH, 20°C, 20°C' Y = Br₂/CHCl₃, 0°C
(4) X = concentrated alcoholic NaOH, 80°C; Y = Br₂/CHCl₃, 0°C

**80.** Identify the correct order of reactivity in electrophilic substitution reactions of the following compounds :
[2002, Screening]

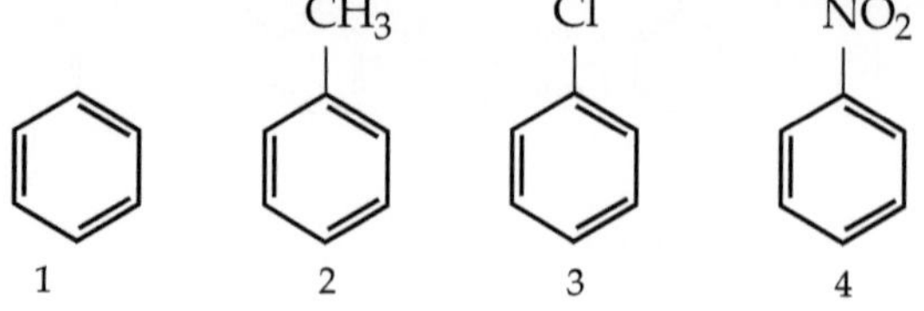


(1) 1 > 2 > 3 > 4
(2) 4 > 3 > 2 > 1
(3) 2 > 1 > 3 > 4
(4) 2 > 3 > 1 > 4

## ANSWER KEY

| | | | | | | | | | |
|---|---|---|---|---|---|---|---|---|---|
| **1.** (1) | **2.** (1) | **3.** (3) | **4.** (3) | **5.** (2,4) | **6.** (1) | **7.** (1) | **8.** 13 | **9.** (1) | **10.** (1) |
| **11.** (3) | **12.** (3) | **13.** (4) | **14.** (3) | **15.** (2) | **16.** (2) | **17.** (1) | **18.** (4) | **19.** (3) | **20.** (1) |
| **21.** (2) | **22.** (3) | **23.** (3) | **24.** (4) | **25.** (2) | **26.** (4) | **27.** (3) | **28.** (4) | **29.** (3, 4) | **30.** (1, 2) |
| **31.** (2) | **32.** (2) | **33.** (4) | **34.** (4) | **35.** (1) | **36.** (1) | **37.** (1) | **38.** (1,2,3) | **39.** (4) | **40.** (1,2,3,4) |
| **41.** (3) | **42.** (4) | **43.** (4) | **44.** (2) | **45.** (4) | **46.** (2) | **47.** (2) | **48.** (*) | **49.** (2) | **50.** (4) |
| **51.** (2) | **52.** (1) | **53.** (4) | **54.** (2) | **55.** (1) | **56.** (2) | **57.** (4) | **58.** (2) | **59.** (1,2,3,4) | **60.** (1,2,3) |
| **61.** (*) | **62.** (1) | **63.** (*) | **64.** (2) | **65.** (1) | **66.** (3) | **67.** (1) | **68.** (2) | **69.** (*) | **70.** (*) |
| **71.** (4) | **72.** (1) | **73.** (2) | **74.** (1) | **75.** (1) | **76.** (1) | **77.** (4) | **78.** (2) | **79.** (2) | **80.** (3) |

## ANSWERS WITH EXPLANATIONS

**1. (1)** In Carius method,

Mass of organic compound = 0.172 gm
Mass of bromine = 0.08 gm

Hence % of Bromine $= \dfrac{0.08}{0.172} \times 100$

$\quad\quad\quad\quad\quad = 46.51\%$

(1) (NH₃ / Br on benzene ring) $C_6H_6NBr$ $\left[\% Br = \dfrac{80}{172} \times 100\right]$

$\quad\quad\quad\quad = 46.51\%$

(2) $CH_3CH_2Br$ $C_2H_5Br$ $\% \, Br = \dfrac{80}{109} \times 100$

$\quad\quad\quad\quad = 73.33\%$

(3) (benzene ring with NH₂ and two Br) $C_6H_5NBr_2$

(4) $CH_3Br$

**2. (1)** (1)

$CH_3-\overset{*}{C}H-CH_2-Br \xrightarrow[S_N2]{\overline{O}H} CH_3-\overset{*}{C}H-CH_2OH$
$\quad\quad |\quad\quad\quad\quad\quad\quad\quad\quad\quad\quad |$
$\quad\quad Et\quad\quad\quad\quad\quad\quad\quad\quad\quad\quad Et$

(2) $CH_3-CH-Br \xrightarrow[S_N2]{\overline{O}H} Ph-CH-OH$
$\quad\quad\quad |\quad\quad\quad\quad\quad\quad\quad\quad |$
$\quad\quad\quad Ph\quad\quad\quad\quad\quad\quad\quad CH_3$

(3) $\text{>}-Br \xrightarrow[S_N2]{\overline{O}H} \text{>}-OH$

(4) $CH_3-CH-Br \xrightarrow[S_N2]{\overline{O}H} CH_3-CH-OH$
$\quad\quad\quad |\quad\quad\quad\quad\quad\quad\quad\quad\quad |$
$\quad\quad\quad C_6H_{13}\quad\quad\quad\quad\quad\quad C_6H_3$

**3. (3)** (cyclopentane ring with $H_3C$ and $CH=CH_2$) $\xrightarrow[\text{Heat}]{H_3O^+}$ (protonated intermediate $CH_3$, $\overset{\oplus}{C}H-CH_3$) $\xrightarrow{\text{ring expansion}}$ (cyclohexyl cation with $CH_3$ groups) $\xrightarrow[-H^+]{\Delta}$ (cyclohexene with two $CH_3$, **major**)

**4. (2)** (1) (cyclohexane ring with $CH_2$ and Cl) Does not show geometrical isomerism

(2) 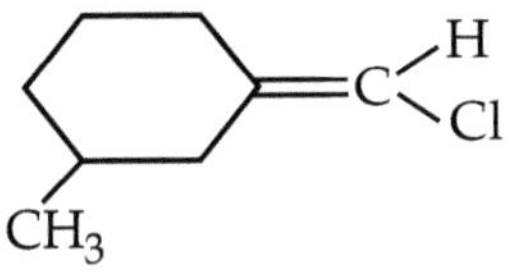 $\begin{array}{c}\text{Shows geometrical}\\\text{isomerism}\end{array}$ (structure with $C=CHCl$, $CH_3$-substituted cyclohexane)

(3) $\begin{array}{c}\text{Does not show}\\\text{geometrical}\\\text{isomerism}\end{array}$ (cyclohexylidene $=C<^H_{Cl}$)

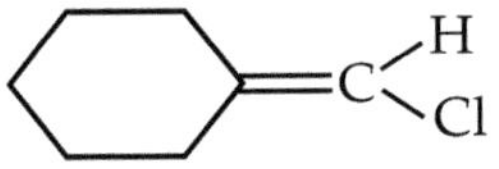

(4) 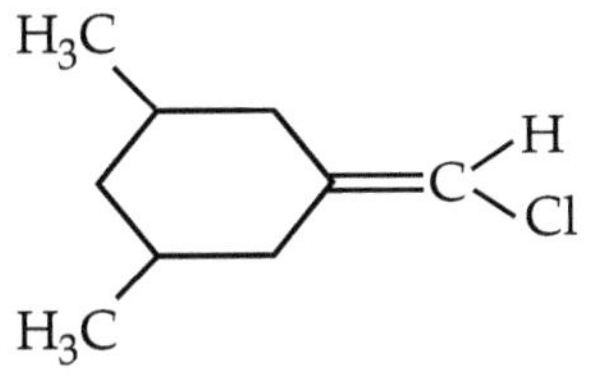 $\begin{array}{c}\text{Does not show}\\\text{geometrical}\\\text{isomerism}\end{array}$ (dimethyl cyclohexylidene $=C<^H_{Cl}$, with two $H_3C$ groups)

**5. (2,4)**

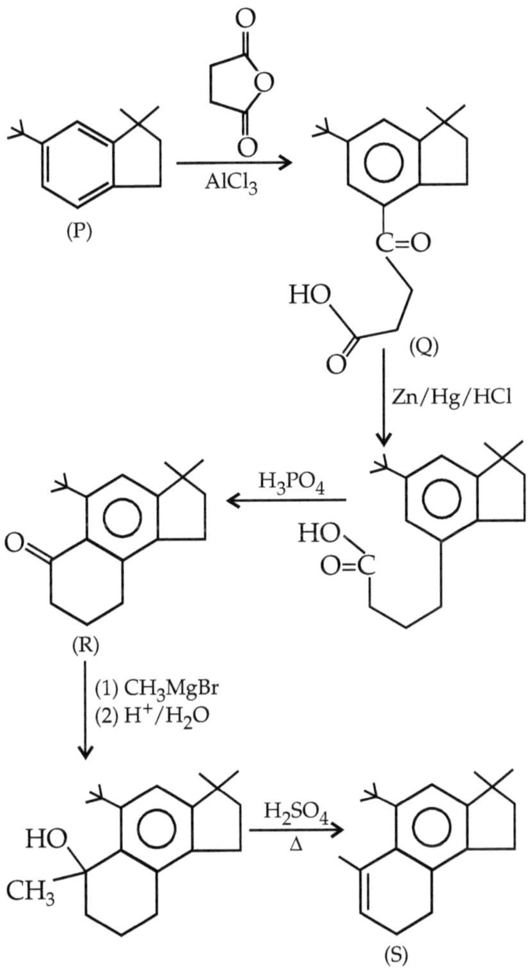

(P) $\xrightarrow[\text{AlCl}_3]{\text{(succinic anhydride)}}$ (Q)

(Q) $\xrightarrow{\text{Zn/Hg/HCl}}$ (intermediate, $HO-O=C$ chain)

$\xrightarrow{\text{H}_3\text{PO}_4}$ (R)

(R) $\xrightarrow[\text{(2) H}^+/\text{H}_2\text{O}]{\text{(1) CH}_3\text{MgBr}}$ (tertiary alcohol, $HO$, $CH_3$)

$\xrightarrow[\Delta]{\text{H}_2\text{SO}_4}$ (S)

**6. (1)** (methylene cyclohexadiene, positions 1–6) $\xrightarrow{\text{O}_3/\text{Zn}/\text{H}_2\text{O}}$ dialdehyde (positions 6,5,4,3,2,1 with $H$ and $O$)

$+\ H_2C=O \xrightarrow{\text{Ag(NH}_3)_2^+}$ $HO$–... diacid product (positions 6,5,4,3,2,1, $OH$)

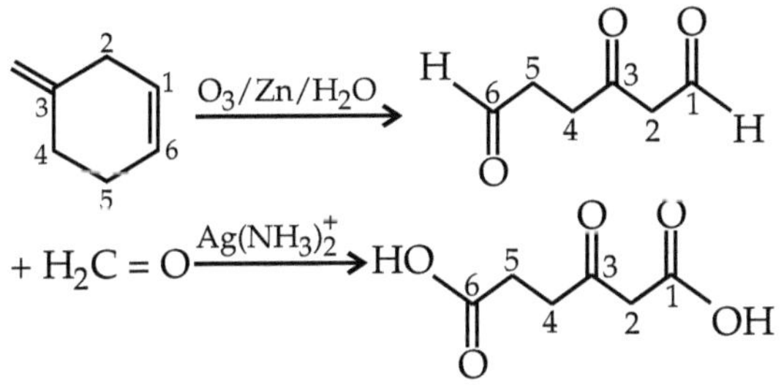

**7. (1)** $CH_3-\underset{\underset{CH(CH_3)_2}{|}}{C}=CH-CH_2-CH_3 \xrightarrow[\text{(ii) H}_2\text{O}_2/\text{OH}^-]{\text{(i) B}_2\text{H}_6}$

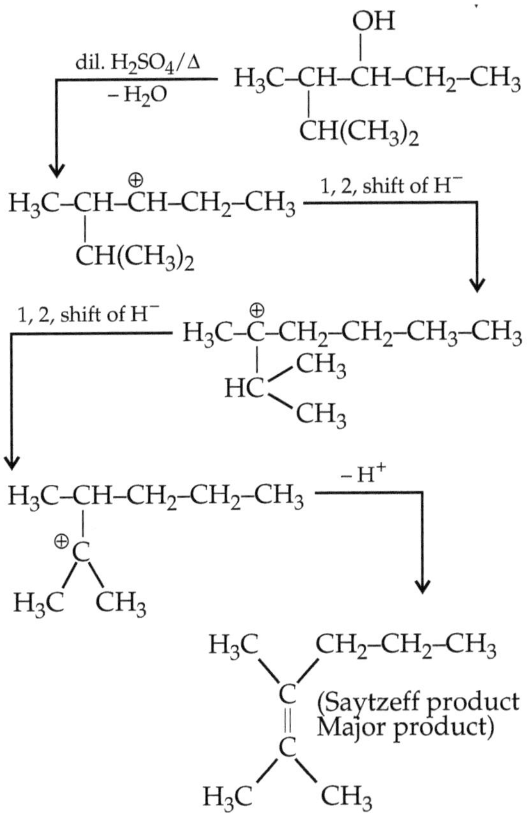

$\xrightarrow[-\text{H}_2\text{O}]{\text{dil. H}_2\text{SO}_4/\Delta}$ $H_3C-\underset{\underset{CH(CH_3)_2}{|}}{\overset{\overset{OH}{|}}{CH}}-CH-CH_2-CH_3$

$\downarrow$

$H_3C-\overset{\oplus}{CH}-\underset{\underset{CH(CH_3)_2}{|}}{CH}-CH_2-CH_3 \xrightarrow{1,2,\text{ shift of H}^-}$

$\xrightarrow{1,2,\text{ shift of H}^-} H_3C-\underset{\underset{\underset{CH_3}{|}}{\overset{|}{HC}-CH_3}}{\overset{\oplus}{C}}-CH_2-CH_2-CH_3-CH_3$

$\downarrow$

$H_3C-CH-CH_2-CH_2-CH_3$ with $\overset{\oplus}{C}$ ($H_3C$, $CH_3$) $\xrightarrow{-H^+}$

$\underset{H_3C}{\overset{H_3C}{>}}C=C\underset{CH_3}{\overset{CH_2-CH_2-CH_3}{<}}$ (Saytzeff product, Major product)

**8.** $(H-C\equiv C-H) \xrightarrow[\text{Cu-tube}]{\text{Red Hot}}$ (benzene)

$\xrightarrow[\text{Anhydrous AlCl}_3]{\text{CH}_3-\text{Cl (1 eq)}}$ (toluene, $H-\overset{H}{\underset{C_6H_5}{C}}-H$)

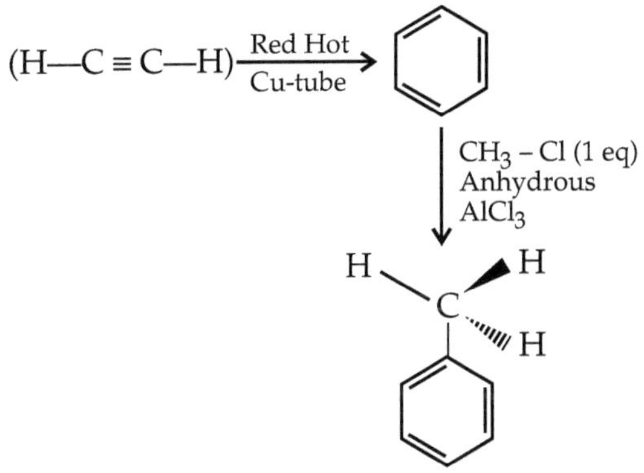

Total 13 atom are present in same plane (7 carbon and 6 hydrogen atoms.)

**9. (1)** $CH_3-\underset{\underset{CH_3}{|}}{CH}-CH=CH_2 + \overset{\oplus}{H} + \overset{\ominus}{Cl} \longrightarrow$

$\xrightarrow{\text{H-shift}} CH_3-\underset{\underset{CH_3}{|}}{CH}-\overset{\oplus}{CH}-CH_3$

$CH_3-\underset{\oplus}{C}-CH_2-CH_3$ with $CH_3$ $\xrightarrow{Cl^{\ominus}}$

$CH_3-\underset{\underset{Cl}{|}}{\overset{\overset{CH_3}{|}}{C}}-CH_2-CH_3$

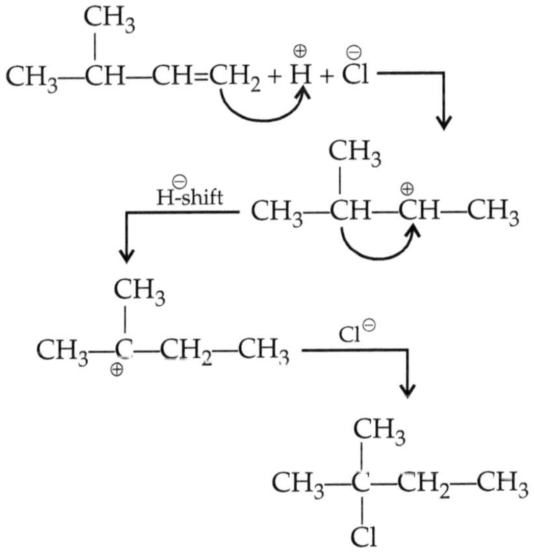

(No chiral centre, so no racemisation possible)

**10. (1)**

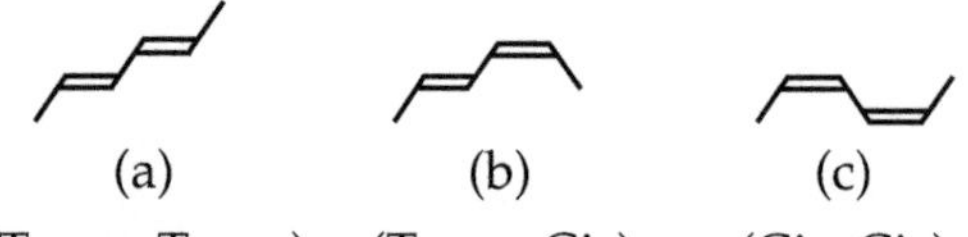

(a)       (b)       (c)

(Trans. Trans)  (Trans, Cis)  (Cis, Cis)

$\therefore$ Generally trans is more stable then cis form.

Heat of combustion (HOC) $\propto \dfrac{1}{\text{Stability}}$

Stability : a > b > c

HOC : c > b > a

**11. (3)**

$$CH_3-\underset{\underset{CH_3}{|}}{CH}-C\equiv CH \xrightarrow[H_2O]{HgSO_4,\ H_2SO_4} (X)$$

$$\downarrow \begin{array}{l}\text{(i) } C_2H_5MgBr,\ H_2O \\ \text{(ii) Conc. } H_2SO_4/\Delta\end{array}$$

$$(Y)$$

$$\therefore CH_3-\underset{\underset{CH_3}{|}}{CH}-C\equiv CH \xrightarrow[H_2O]{HgSO_4,\ H_2SO_4}$$

(Kucherov's Reaction)

$$\xrightarrow[\substack{\text{(Nucleophilic addition}\\ \text{reaction)}}]{C_2H_5\,MgBr,\ H_2O}$$

$$CH_3-\underset{\underset{CH_3}{|}}{CH}-\overset{\overset{O}{||}}{C}-CH_3$$

$$(X)$$

$$\xrightarrow{H^+/\Delta}$$

$$CH_3-\underset{\underset{CH_3}{|}}{CH}-\underset{\underset{CH_2-CH_3}{|}}{C}-CH_3$$

Major
(Saytzeff alkene)

$$CH_3-\underset{\underset{CH_3}{|}}{CH}-\underset{\underset{CH_2-CH_3}{|}}{\overset{\overset{OH}{|}}{C}}-CH_3$$

**12. (3)** Reactivity D > B > C > A

Carbocation formed from D is most stable.

Carbocation formed from A is least stable.

**13. (4)**

$$CH_3-\underset{O}{\overset{\diagup \diagdown}{CH-CH_2}} \xrightarrow{HBr} CH_3-\underset{\overset{+}{\underset{|}{O}}\atop H}{\overset{\diagup \diagdown}{CH-CH_2}}$$

$$\xrightarrow[\text{(2) HBr}]{\text{(1) Br}^-} CH_3-\underset{\underset{Br}{|}}{\overset{\overset{Br}{|}}{CH}}-CH_2$$

**14. (3)**

$$\xleftarrow[\substack{\text{(Intramolecular}\\ \text{aldol)}}]{NaOH/\Delta}$$

$$\uparrow O_3/(CH_3)_2S$$

$$\xrightarrow[hv]{Br_2} \xrightarrow[\Delta]{\text{Alc. KOH}}$$

**15. (2)** (C) < (B) < (A).

**16. (2)** Vinyl halides and Aryl halides to not give Friedel craft reaction due to partial double boind character.

**17. (1)** In the Friedal Craft's alkylation reaction, an alkyl group is substituted in the place of a hydrogen atom in the compound. This leads to the formation of an activated product and therefore, polysubstitution takes place.

**18. (4)** The alkene that yields majorly an anti-Markovnikov's product when treated with HCl is $F_3C-CH=CH_2$. This is due to the fact that $F_3C$ is highly electron withdrawing in nature. The corresponding reaction is shown below :

$$CF_3-CH=CH_2 \xrightarrow{HCl} CF_3-\underset{\overset{|}{\underset{}{}}}{\overset{\overset{H}{|}}{CH}}-\overset{\oplus}{CH_2}$$

$$\downarrow$$

$$CF_3-\underset{\underset{}{}}{\overset{\overset{H}{|}}{CH}}-\underset{\underset{}{}}{\overset{\overset{Cl}{|}}{CH_2}}$$

**19. (3)** The order reactivity of a compound of $S_N1$ reaction depends on the ease of molecule to from a stable carbocation. The carbocation formed by compound (C) is stabilized by +I effect and resonance effect. The carbocation formed by compound (D) is stabilized by resonance effect. The carbocation formed by compound (A) is more stable than the carbocation formed by compound (B) as tertiary carbocation is more stable than primary carbocation. The order of stability of the carbocation is shown below :

(B) < (A) < (D) < (C)

Therefore, the order of reactivity of the given compound is shown below :

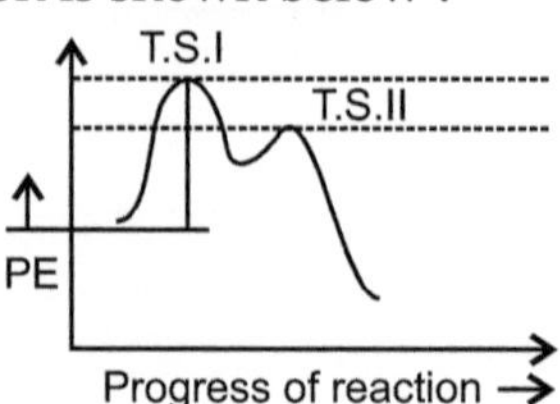


**20. (1)** The reaction mechanism of $S_N1$ contains two steps. The first step is the rate determining step. The activation energy of the first step is higher than the activation energy of second step. The correct potential energy diagram of $S_N1$ reaction is shown below :

T.S.I    T.S.II

PE

Progress of reaction →

**21. (2)** The rate of $S_N1$ reaction increases as the stability of the carbocation formed increases. The correct order of stability is shown below :

The structure D is highly stable due to positive mesomeric effect, the structure C is comparatively less stable than structure D due to high hyperconjugation effect and the structure B is the least stable due to negative inductive effect.

**22. (3)** The mechanism of the given reaction is shown below :

The above reaction proceeds via $S_N1$ mechanism due to the presence of polar protic solvent. Hydride shift takes place so that the formation of more stable tertiary carbocation takes place. Further, solvolysis takes place to obtain the final product.

**23. (3)** The rate of electrophilic substitution reaction increases when an electron donating group is attached to a benzene ring and decreases when an electron withdrawing group is attached to a benzene ring. Therefore, the correct order of electrophilic aromatic substitution is III < I < II.

**24. (4)** As the tendency of oxygen to donate lone pair of electrons decreases, the nucleophilicity also decreases. Therefore, the order of nucleophilicity is shown below :

$$^-OH > H_3C-\overset{O}{\underset{O}{C}}-O^- > H_3C-\overset{O}{\underset{O}{C}}-O^- > H_2O$$

Charged ion, neutral system

**25. (2)** The chlorine atom prefers to get attached to a less substituted carbon atom. The hydroxyl-group of water will get attached to more substituted carbon atom.
The complete reaction sequence is shown below :

**26. (4)** The stability order of carboncation is $1° < 2° < 3°$. The compound $(CH_3)_3CCl$ will form a stable $3°$ carbocation. Therefore, it is most likely to give precipitate with silver nitrate.
The corresponding chemical reaction is shown below :

$$CH_3-\overset{CH_3}{\underset{CH_3}{C}}-Cl + AgNO_3 \rightarrow (CH_3)_3C^{\oplus} + AgCl_{(a)}$$
(white ppt)

**27. (3)** The starting material undergoes elimination follow up by oxymercuration reaction.
The completed chemical reaction sequence is shown below :

**28. (4)** Vinyl halide ($CH_2 = CH = Cl$) forms highly unstable carbocation $\left(CH_2 = \overset{\oplus}{CH}\right)$ due to which it does not undergoes nucleophilic substitution reaction.
Therefore, the statement (A) is correct and statement (R) is wrong.

**29. (3, 4)** The completed reactions are shown below :

Therefore, U is 1-bromo-2-methylcyclohexane, S is 1-chloro-1-methylcyclohexane and T is 1-bromo-1-methylcyclohexane.

**30. (1, 2)** The complete chemical reactions are shown below :

(1)

$$CH_3-C\equiv CH \xrightarrow{\text{Red hot iron tube 873 K}}$$

(2)

(Aromatic ion)

(3)

(Substitution product)
(Non aromatic)

+

(Elimination product) → Dimerise → (Non aromatic)

(4)

(Non aromatic)

Therefore, the reactions that gives an aromatic compound are (1) and (2).

**31. (2)** The product formed in reaction (P) is shown below :

The product formed in reaction (Q) is shown below :

$$CH_3-\underset{CH_3}{\overset{CH_3}{C}}-O-CH_3 + HBr \rightarrow \underset{H_3C}{\overset{H_3C}{>}}\!\!<\!\!\underset{Br}{\overset{CH_3}{}} + MeOH$$

The product formed in reaction (R) is shown below :

$$\xrightarrow[E_2]{MeO^-Na^+}$$

The product formed in reaction (S) is shown below :

$$\underset{H_3C}{\overset{H_3C}{>}}\!\!<\!\!\underset{ONa}{\overset{CH_3}{}} + MeBr \xrightarrow{S_N2} \underset{H_3C}{\overset{H_3C}{>}}\!\!<\!\!\underset{OMe}{\overset{CH_3}{}}$$

**32. (2)** The reaction of halo compounds with sodium methoxide and methanol proceeds through $E_2$ elimination. Methoxide ion in the presence of methanol leads to the dehydrohalogenation which results in the formation of alkene.

$$\xrightarrow[\underset{(E_2 \text{ mechanism})}{MeOH}]{\overset{\ominus}{OMe}} + NaBr + MeOH$$

Hence, the major product formed in the given reaction corresponds to the organic compound given in the option (2).

**33. (4)** On addition of strong base, alkyl halide shows elimination reaction. The C–Cl bond, near which an electron withdrawing group is present, is easily broken.

$$\xrightarrow[\Delta]{NaOCH_3}$$

**34. (4)** In this case, dehydrohalogenation reaction takes place through E1cb and compound (4) forms the most stable carbanion. Therefore, it readily forms dehydrohalogenation product.

**35. (1)** In the given reaction, alkene undergoes $S_N2$ reaction.

$$\xrightarrow{HBr}$$

This is a single step reaction. In the first part of the reaction, a benzylic carbocation is generated, and in the second step, it undergoes bromination. A brominated product is generated.

**36. (1)** The polarity of the compound depends upon the direction of dipole moment. In the first structure, the dipole moment is not subtractive. In the rest of the compound, the dipole moment is subtractive in nature.

**37. (1)** As $S_N2$ reaction is given, it means inversion of configuration occurs at the carbon where, bromine is attached.

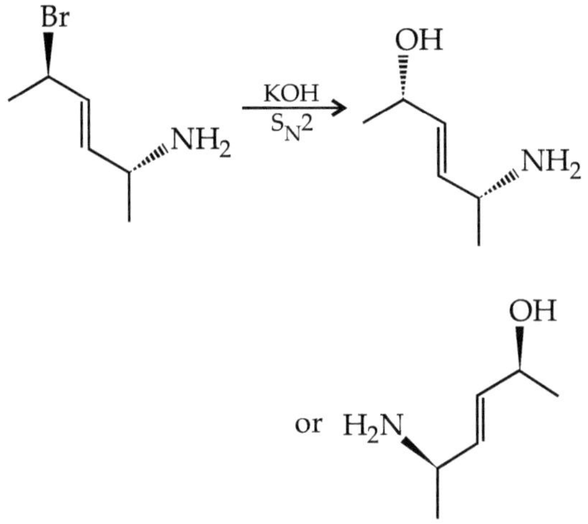

**38. (1,2,3)** The IUPAC name of the given compound is 1–Chloro–4-methylbenzene.

It contains a benzene ring with a methyl group. Therefore, this compound is also called 4-Chlorotoluene. The structure is given as,

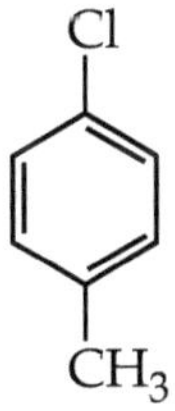

The name of this compound cannot be 4-Methylchlorobenzene because first priority is to be given to that group which alphabetically comes first.

The name of this compound cannot be 1-methyl-4-chlorobenzene because first priority is to be given to that group which has high molecular mass.

**39. (4)** The only correct combination in which the reaction proceeds through radical mechanism is (4). It is given as,

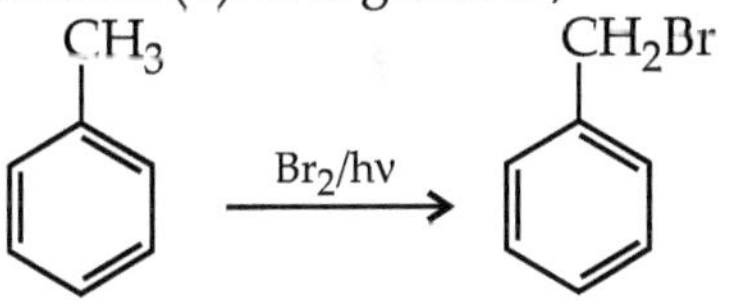

Free radical substitution

In the above reaction, bromination of toluene occurs via free radical mechanism and free radical substitution takes place.

**40. (1,2,3,4)** Compound I is a primary halide. It will undergo $S_N2$ reaction.
Compound II is also a primary halide. It will also undergo $S_N2$ reaction.
Compound III is a tertiary halide. It will also undergo $S_N1$ reaction. But compound I may also undergo $S_N1$ reaction due to the formation of stable carbocation.
Compound IV alkyl halide is chiral. Therefore, it will give inverted product via both the $S_N2$ and $S_N1$ reaction. These are given as,

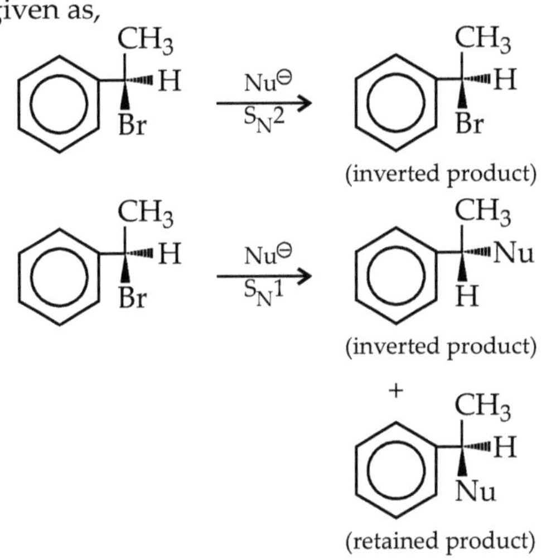

(inverted product)

(inverted product)

(retained product)

The order of reactivity is as follows,
$$IV > I > III$$

**41. (3)** The reaction is,

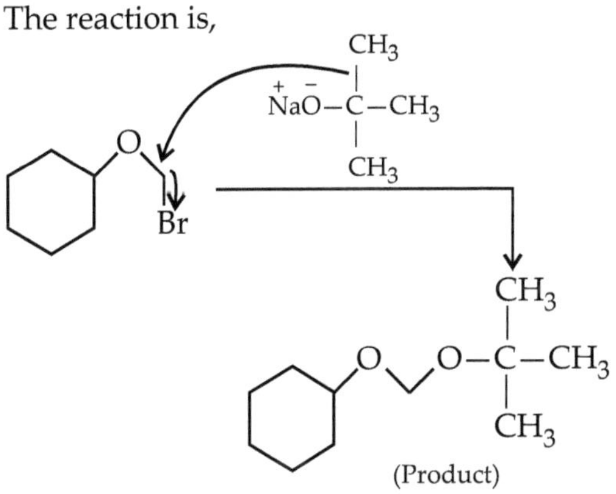

(Product)

The product formed does not possess C = C bond. Therefore, it will not undergo bromine water test.

**42. (4)** The rate of $S_N1$ reaction is directly proportional to the stability of carbocation. The carbocations of the given halides are shown below :

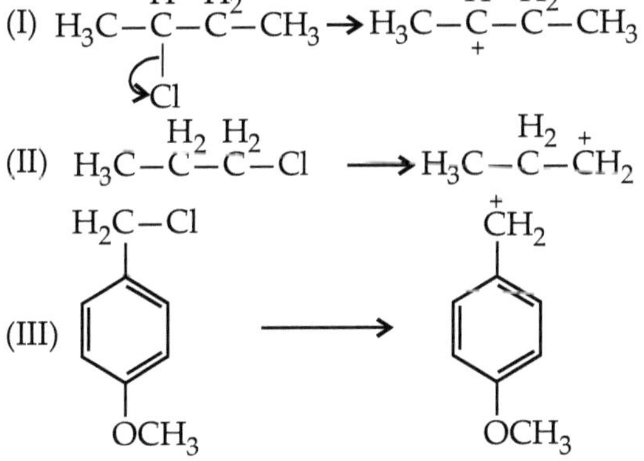

(I)

(II)

(III)

**43. (4)** The complete reaction is shown below :

$$C_6H_5\text{-CHBr-CH(H)-}C_6H_5 \xrightarrow[\Delta\ (E\text{-}2)]{t\text{-BuOK}} C_6H_5\text{-CH=CH-}C_6H_5$$

Hence, the major product is $C_6H_5CH = CHC_6H_5$.

**44. (2)** In the compound, $\diagup\hspace{-6pt}\diagdown\text{Cl}$, the formation of carbocation is not possible. Thus, this compound will not undergo Friedel Craft's reaction as shown below :

$$\diagup\hspace{-6pt}\diagdown\text{Cl} \xrightarrow{AlCl_3} \diagup\hspace{-6pt}\diagdown\overset{\oplus}{\text{Cl}}-\overset{\ominus}{\text{AlCl}_3} \to \diagup\hspace{-6pt}\diagdown\overset{\oplus}{\ } \text{ (less stable)}$$

**45. (4)** The major product of the given reaction is shown as follows :

$$H_3C-\overset{H}{\underset{Br}{C}}-\overset{H_2}{C}-\overset{H}{\underset{Br}{C}}-CH_2-CH_3$$

$$\xrightarrow[E2]{KOH,\ CH_3OH\ D} H_3C-C\overset{H}{=}\overset{}{C}-\overset{H}{\underset{H}{C}}-CH_3$$

(Saytzeff product)

**46. (2)** The major product of the given reaction is shown as follows :

$$C_2H_5O^{\ominus}$$

More acidic

$$C_6H_5-\overset{H}{\underset{(-\,I\ effect)}{C}}-\overset{CH_3}{\underset{H}{\underset{\searrow Br}{C}}}-\overset{H}{\underset{(+\,I\ effect)}{C}}-CH_3$$

$$\Big\downarrow \begin{array}{l} C_2H_5ONa \\ C_2H_5OH \end{array}$$

$$C_6H_5-\overset{CH_3}{\underset{H}{C}}=C-\overset{H_2}{C}-CH_3$$

**47. (2)** The major product of the given reaction is shown below :

$$Br_2 \xrightarrow{h\nu} 2\overset{..}{Br}$$

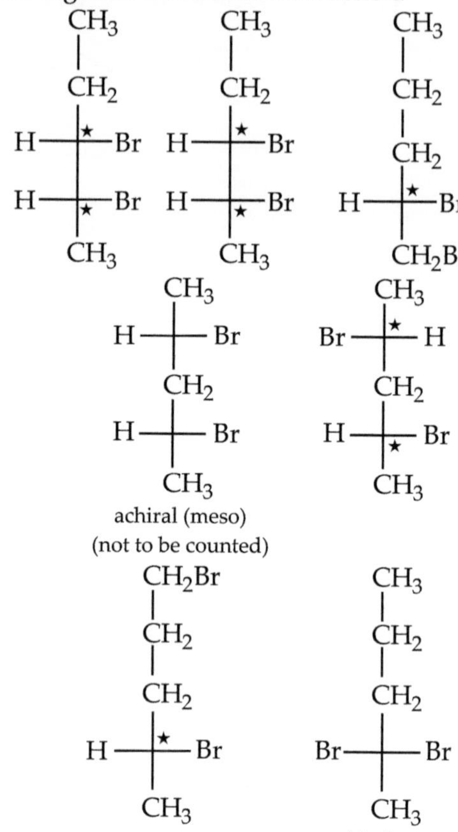

The above mechanism shows that bromine in the presence of light is converted into free radical, which abstracts hydrogen atom from the reactant to form stable intermediate followed by addition of bromine.

**48.** The possible chiral products are shown for the following monobromination reaction.

achiral (meso)
(not to be counted)

no chiral centre

Five chiral products and two achiral products are formed in the following monobromination reaction.

**49. (2)** The mechanism for the given reaction is shown below :

The given reaction undergoes free radical substitution.

The product formed by the bromination of cyclohexene in the presence of light is shown below :

**50. (4)** The given conversion is not carried out in the presence of NaI. The reaction of bromopropane with NaI, yields iodopropane.

$$CH_3CH_2CH_2Br + NaI \rightarrow CH_3CH_2CH_2I$$

**51. (2)** Bromination occurs at allylic position when NBS is used. The given reaction is shown below :

**52. (1)** Methoxide ion acts as a strong nucleophile in methanol and thus leads to elimination product but sideways substitution products are also possible.

**53. (4)** Swarts reaction is the best route to accomplish the synthesis of alkyl fluorides.

$$R-Cl + AgF \xrightarrow{\Delta} R-F + AgCl$$

**54. (2)** In $S_N2$ reactions, reactivity of alkyl halides decreases with increase in steric hindrance. The reactivity order of alkyl halides is,

$$CH_3-X > 1°\,R-X > 2°\,R-X > 3°\,R-X$$

Therefore, the correct order of reactivity of given compounds is,

$$CH_3Cl > CH_3CH_2Cl > (CH_3)_2CHCl$$
$$> (CH_3)_3CCl$$

**55. (1)** The correct increasing order for the bond length of C-halogen bond is as follows :

$$CH_3F < CH_3Cl < CH_3Br < CH_3I$$

As the atomic radii of halogens from fluorine to iodine increases, thus, the bond length of C-halogen bond also increases.

**56. (2)** In the given nucleophilic substitution reaction, the compound that undergoes complete inversion of configuration is $C_6H_5CH_2Br$ as shown below.

Inverted product

**57. (4)** The photocatalyzed bromination of 2-methylbutane proceeds via free radical mechanism. Since the stability of tertiary free radical is greater than that of primary and secondary radical, the major product obtained in the given reaction corresponds to that of tertiary free radical.

2-Bromo-2 methyl butane

Hence, the major product formed in the given reaction is 2-bromo-2-methylbutane.

**58. (2)** Among **P, Q, R** and **S**, **Q** is least stable due to more steric hindrance. The compound **R** is less reactive as compared to **S** and **P** due to unstable transition state.

Out of **S** and **P**, the transition state of **S** is more stable due to presence of carbonyl group. Carbonyl group increases the positive charge on carbon atom, which results in increase of nucleophilic attack.

Thus, reactivity order is,

**59. (1,2,3,4)** The formation of product **P** is shown below :

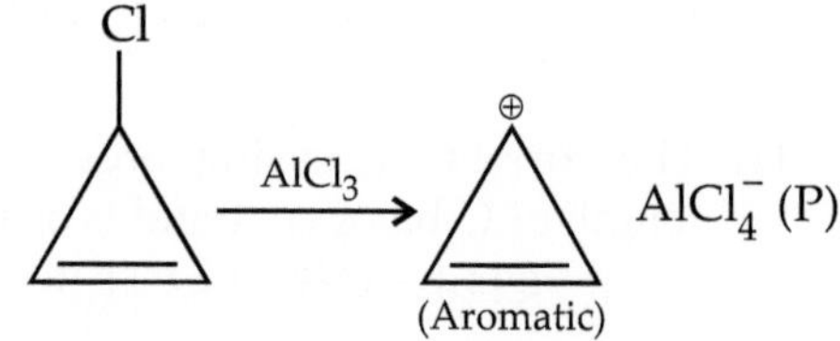

$$\xrightarrow{AlCl_3}$$ (Aromatic) $AlCl_4^-$ (P)

The formation of product **Q** is shown below :

$$\xrightarrow{NaH} \quad Na^+ \quad + H_2\uparrow$$

(aromatic)(Q)

The formation of product **R** is shown below :

$$+ NH_3 \rightarrow \quad \rightarrow$$

(R) Aromatic

The formation of product **S** is shown below.

$$\xrightarrow{HCl}$$

(S) Aromatic

All the products formed in above reactions are aromatic.

**60. (1,2,3)** (1) The Fischer projection is shown below.

**M** and **N**

They are diastereomers as they are not mirror images and are non superimposable.

(2) The Fischer projection is shown below :

**M** and **O**

Thus, they are identical.

(3) The Fischer projection is shown below :

**M** and **P**

Thus, they are mirror images that are non superimposable. Thus, they are enantiomers.

(4) The Fischer projection is shown below :

M and Q

They are diastereomers as they are not mirror images and are non superimposable.

**61.** Eight isomers are possible on monochlorination of the given compound as shown below :

$$CH_3CH_2 - \overset{CH_3}{\underset{H}{\overset{|}{\underset{|}{C^*}}}} - CH_2CH_2Cl \quad \text{Enantiomeric pair} = 2$$

$$CH_3CH_2 - \overset{CH_3}{\underset{H}{\overset{|}{\underset{|}{C^*}}}} - \overset{*}{C}HCH_3 \quad \text{Two Enantiomeric pairs} = 4$$

$$CH_3CH_2 - \overset{CH_3}{\underset{Cl}{\overset{|}{\underset{|}{C}}}} - CH_2CH_3 \quad 1$$

$$CH_3CH_2 - \overset{CH_2Cl}{\underset{H}{\overset{|}{\underset{|}{C^*}}}} - CH_2CH_3 \quad 1$$

$$\text{Total} = 2 + 4 + 1 + 1 = 8$$

**62. (1)** The given reaction involves the nucleophilic substitution of alkyl halide by $S_N2$ mechanism. Halides are good leaving groups and they can undergo substitution reaction. However, alkyl halides are more reactive towards substitution reaction than aryl halides because the bond between carbon atom of aromatic ring and halide has some double bond character due to resonance. As a result, it is not easy to break the bond between carbon atom of aromatic ring and halide. The solvent used in the reaction is dimethylformamide which favors the reaction through $S_N2$ mechanism.

**63. (1)** The compound is optically active as each carbon atom is bonded with four different groups which is a necessary condition to show optical activity.

(2) The compound does not possess center of symmetry.

(3) The compound does not possess plane of symmetry.

(4) The compound contains axis of symmetry ($C_2$) which is perpendicular to C—C bond.

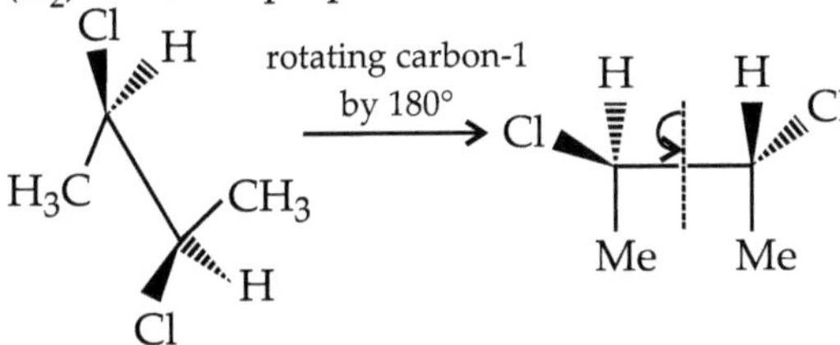

**64. (2)** The given compound (ethylene dibromide) is a gem dihalide. On reaction with alcoholic KOH in first step it gives a vinyl halide. However, the use of alcoholic KOH in second step gives poor yield as vinyl halide is less reactive towards it. To get better yield in the second step $NaNH_2$ is used instead of alcoholic KOH.

Ethylene dibromide
(Gem dihalide)

Vinyl halide

**65. (1)** Bromination of *trans*-2-butene gives respective meso product, through anti addition. Thus, there is only one stereoisomer.

trans-2-butene

a meso compound
perspective formula

plane of symmetry

**66. (3)** Chiral molecules possess non superimposable mirror images. The substituted biphenyls are chiral but do not possess chiral centre.

**67. (1)** The given reaction is,
$$CH_3 - CH = CH_2 + NOCl \rightarrow P$$
The mechanism for the formation of P is shown below :

The addition of $NO^+Cl^-$ follows markonikoff's rule. Therefore, the adduct formed is shown below :

**68. (2)** The given reaction is,
$$(CH_3)_2 - CH - CH_2 - CH_3 \xrightarrow{Cl_2}$$
$$\text{isomeric products } C_5H_{11}Cl \xrightarrow[\text{Distillation}]{\text{Fraction}} (F)$$
The number of N products formed is shown below :

(I) $d, l$    (II) $d,l$

(III)    (IV)

The first and second compound contains a chiral carbon. Thus, d and l isomers are possible for these compounds. Therefore, the number of isomeric products formed is six.

The physical properties of enantiomers are same due to which they cannot be separated by fractional distillation. Therefore, the number of M products formed is 4.

(A-Q); (B-Q); (C-R, S); (D-P, S)

**69.** It is given that the reaction of $CH_3 - CHBr - CD_3$ with alc. KOH results in the formation of $CH_2 = CH - CD_3$ as a major product. The given reaction involves two step mechanisms.

Ph – CHBr – CH$_3$ reacts faster than Ph – CHBr – CD$_3$ due to E$_2$ reaction.

The reaction of Ph – CH$_2$ – CH$_2$Br with C$_2$H$_5$OD/ C$_2$H$_5$O$^-$ results in the formation of Ph – Cd = CH$_2$ as a major product. The given reaction involves El$_{cb}$ mechanisms.

It is given that PhCH$_2$CH$_2$Br and PhCD$_2$CH$_2$Br reacts with same rate. Thus, it is a first order reaction and involves one step mechanisms.

**70. (a) (i)** The given incomplete reaction is,

$$H_3C \underset{CH_3}{\overset{Br}{\underset{|}{\overset{|}{C}}}}(C_6H_5) \xrightarrow{C_2H_5OH \ (aq)} \text{acidic solution}$$

The complete reaction is,

$$C_6H_5-\underset{CH_3}{\overset{CH_3}{\underset{|}{\overset{|}{C}}}}-Br \xrightarrow{C_2H_5OH(aq)}$$

$$C_6H_5-\underset{CH_3}{\overset{CH_3}{\underset{|}{\overset{|}{C}}}}-OC_2H_5 + HBr \text{ (acid)}$$

In this reaction, bromine gets eliminated to form an ether and hydrogen bromide acid.

**(ii)** The given incomplete reaction is,

$$Br-\bigcirc-\underset{CH_3}{\overset{CH_3}{\underset{|}{\overset{|}{CH}}}} \xrightarrow{C_2H_5OH \ (aq)} \text{neutral}$$

The complete reaction is,

$$\underset{Br}{\bigcirc}-\underset{\underset{CH_3}{|}}{\overset{CH_3}{CH}} \xrightarrow{NaOH(aq)} \text{No reaction}$$

The above reaction does not take place due to the presence of highly substituted group on the benzene ring. This highly substituted group creates hindrance in the reaction of sodium hydroxide.

**(b) (i)** The given incomplete reaction is,

$$\underset{O_2N}{\overset{F}{\bigcirc}}_{CH_3} \xrightarrow{NaOH(aq)} \text{F liberated}$$

The complete reaction is,

$$\underset{O_2N}{\overset{F}{\bigcirc}}_{CH_3} \xrightarrow{NaOH(aq)} \underset{O_2N}{\overset{OH}{\bigcirc}}_{CH_3}$$

$$+ \ F^- \text{ is liberated}$$

The above reaction takes place through biomolecular elimination reaction in which base eliminates the halide to form an alcohol. The rate of this reaction is high because of the presence of electron withdrawing nitro groups.

**(ii)** The complete reaction is,

$$\underset{CH_2NO_2}{\overset{F}{\bigcirc}} \xrightarrow{NaOH(aq)} + F^- \text{ is not liberated}$$

This reaction is not possible through biomolecular elimination due to presence of electron donating group.

**(c) (i)** The given reaction is,

$$\underset{}{\overset{\ddot{N}=O}{\bigcirc}} \xrightarrow[\text{Conc. H}_2SO_4]{\text{Conc. HNO}_3} \underset{}{\overset{\ddot{N}=O}{\bigcirc}}_{NO_2} + \underset{NO_2}{\overset{\ddot{N}=O}{\bigcirc}}$$

This reaction is nitration reaction that takes place smoothly. The addition of nitro group takes place at ortho and para positions due to the presence of nitric oxide which is an ortho and para directing group.

**(ii)** The given reaction is,

$$\underset{}{\overset{NO_2}{\bigcirc}} \xrightarrow[\text{Conc. H}_2SO_4]{\text{Conc. HNO}_3} \underset{NO_2}{\overset{NO_2}{\bigcirc}}$$

This reaction is nitration reaction that takes place smoothly. The addition of nitro group takes place at meta position only due to the presence of another nitro group which is a meta directing group.

**(d)** The given reaction is,

$$\xrightarrow[\text{3 mole of H}_2]{Pd/C}$$

In the above reaction, the reduction of the central ring takes place with the help of Pd/C. Due to the reduction, the present three and four membered ring becomes stable. But if the reduction of terminal ring takes place only one ring will become stable. Thus, the preferred product is shown above.

**71. (4)** The reaction that takes place 1-bromo-3-chlorocyclobutane and 2 equivalents of sodium in the presence of ether is as follows :

$$\underset{Cl}{\overset{Br}{\square}} \xrightarrow[\text{ether}]{2 \ Na} \boxtimes$$

The above reaction of 1-bromo-3-chlorocyclobutane with 2 equivalents of sodium in the presence of ether is the example of intramolecular Wurtz reaction. In this reaction, two alkyl halides forms an alkane with the loss of sodium chloride followed by the loss of sodium bromide.

Thus, the correct option is (4).

**72. (1)** In the hydrolysis reaction of the given nitro compound in the aqueous solution of acetone both the products K and L will be formed because both the substitution reactions, $S_N1$ and $S_N2$ can take place in the aqueous solution of acetone. The complete reaction is as follows :

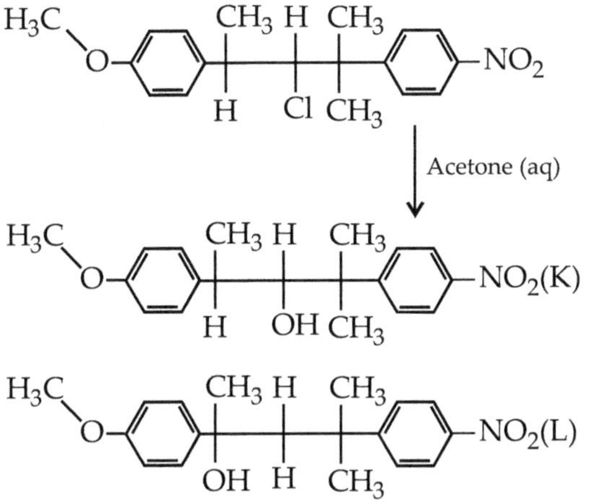

Thus, the correct option is (1).

**73. (2)** Four chiral compounds are possible by monochlorination of 2-methyl butane.

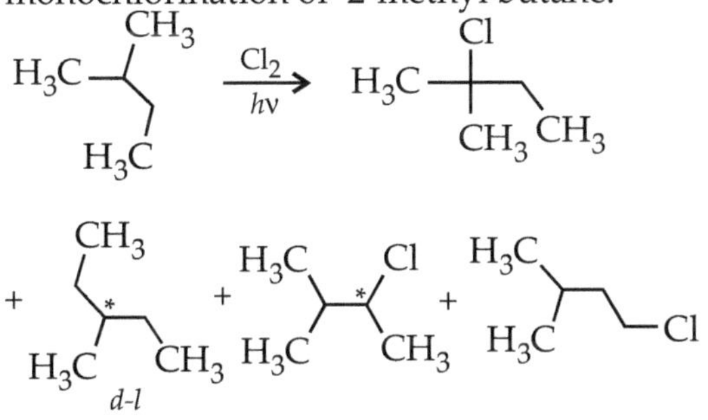

**74. (1)** The resultant dipole moment of the compound $CH_3Cl$ is highest because the dipole moment coming from three $C - H$ adds up in the dipole moment of $C - Cl$ but in case of $CHCl_3$, the dipole moment coming from two $C - Cl$ becomes cancelled out and in case of $CH_2Cl_2$, dipole moment of

two $C - H$ adds up in the bond moment of $C - Cl^+$ bonds. Therefore, the dipole moment of the compound $CH_3Cl$ is highest among the given compounds.

**75. (1)** The possible structures of F are cis and trans as shown below :

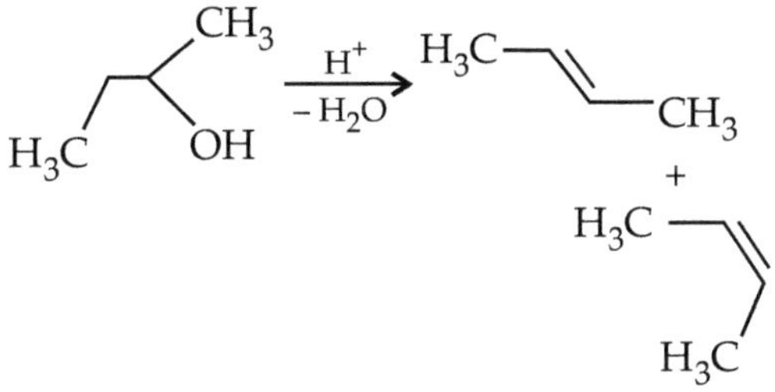

**76. (1)** The mixture formed will be optically active because the optically active acid will react with d and l form of alcohol present in the racemic mixture to give two types of isomeric esters. Each configuration of the chiral centre of acid will remain the same. So the mixture will be optically active.

**77. (4)** One chiral carbon atom is present in 2-methylbutanoic acid. Hence, it shows stereoisomerism.

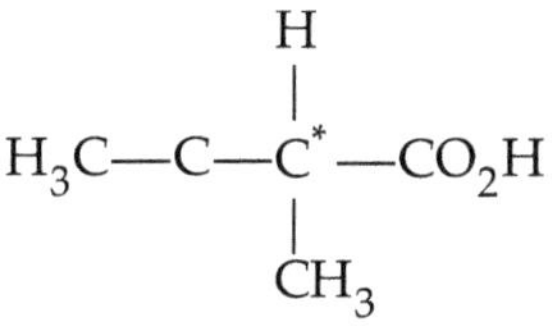

**78. (2)** The reactivity of bromine is very less but its selectivity is very high. It forms most stable free radical, that is, tertiary than primary or secondary. Hence, the major product formed from the reaction is tertiary radical.

**79. (2)** The first reaction is the dehydrobromination of alkyl halide by concentrated alcoholic NaOH at 80°C. The second reaction is the addition of HBr on alkene according to Markovnikoff's rule.

**80. (3)** The reactivity of benzene ring towards electrophilic substitution reaction is more if electron donating group is attached to it. Alkyl group $CH_3$ is electron donating group and shows $+ I$ and $+ M$ effect. The $- I$ effect of chlorine is more than $+ M$ effect, hence it deactivates the ring. Nitro group is an electron withdrawing group, it deactivates the benzene ring most.

●●

## ?☑ QUESTIONS

**1.** Consider the following reaction :

$$\xrightarrow[\text{anhydride}]{\text{Chromic}} \text{'P'}$$

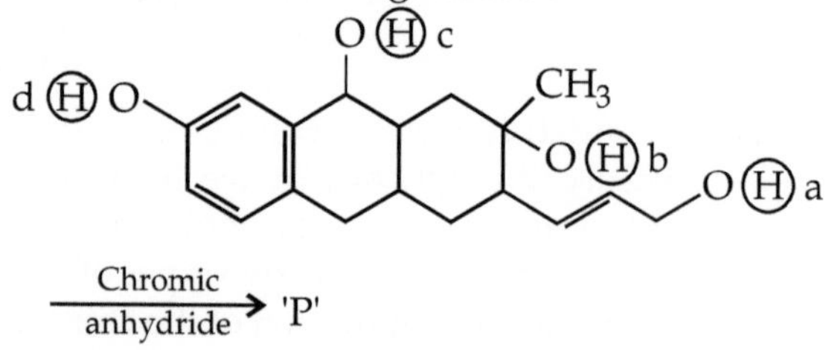

The product 'P' gives positive ceric ammonium nitrate test. This is because of the presence of which of these –OH group(s) ?

**[2020, Main]**

(1) (c) and (d)  
(2) (b) only  
(3) (d) only  
(4) (b) and (d)

**2.** The IUPAC name of the following compound is :

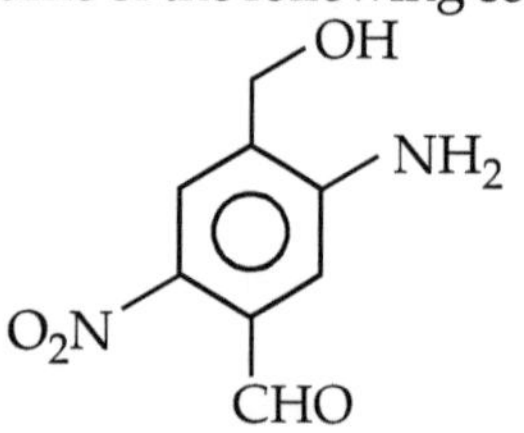

**[2020, Main]**

(1) 3-amino-4-hydroxymethyl-5-nitrobenzal-dehyde

(2) 2-nitro-4-hydroxymethyl-5-amino-benzaldehyde

(3) 4-amino-2-formyl-5-hydroxymethylnitro-benzene

(4) 5-amino-4-hydroxymethyl-2-nitrobenzalde-hyde

**3.** A solution of *m*-chloroaniline, *m*-chlorophenol and *m*-chlorobenzoic acid in ethyl acetate was initially extracted with a saturated solution of $NaHCO_3$ to give fraction A. The left over organic phase was extracted with dilute NaOH solution to give fraction B, The final organic layer was labelled as fraction C. Fractions A, B and C contain respectively : **[2020, Main]**

(1) *m*-chlorobenzoic acid, *m*-chloroaniline and *m*-chlorophenol

(2) *m*-chloroaniline, *m*-chlorobenzoic acid and *m*-chlorophenol

(3) *m*-chlorobenzoic acid, *m*-chlorophenol *m*-chloroaniline

(4) *m*-chlorophenol, *m*-chlorobenzoic acid and *m*-chloroaniline

**4.** Among the compounds A and B with molecular formula $C_9H_{18}O_3$, A is having higher boiling point then B. The possible structures of A and B are : **[2020, Main]**

(1) 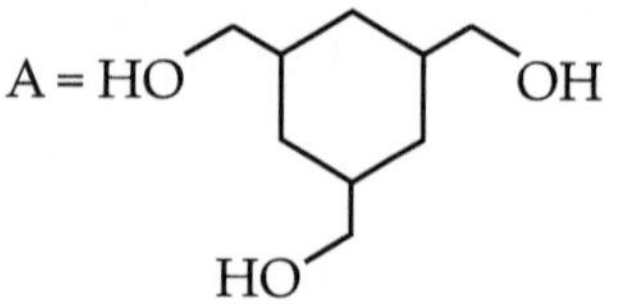 $A = HO$ ... $OH$ ; $B = H_3CO$ ... $OCH_3$

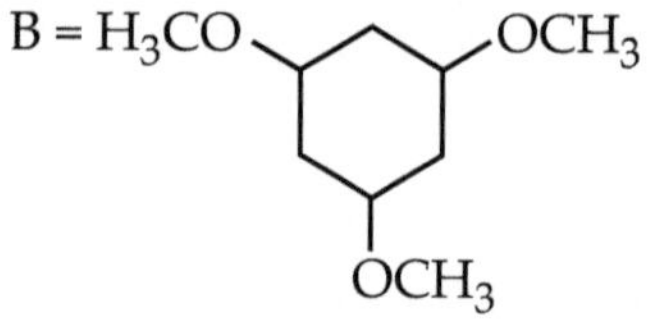

(2) $A = H_3CO$ ... $OCH_3$ ; $B = HO$ ... $OH$

(3) $A = H_3CO$ ... $OCH_3$ ; $B = HO$ ... $OH$

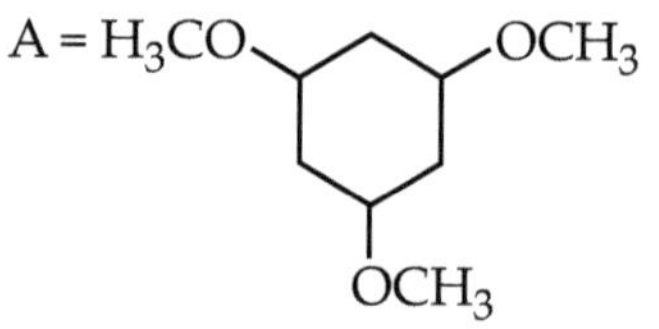

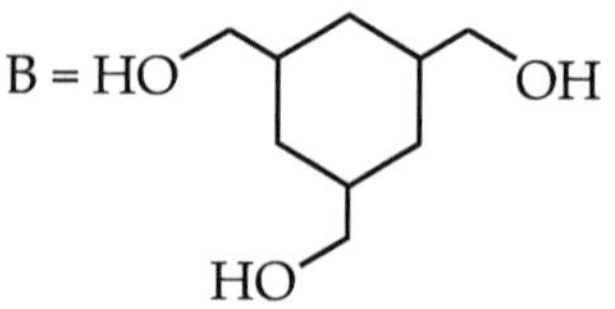

(4) 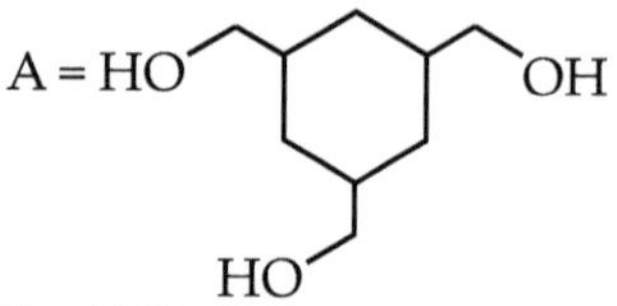 $A = HO$ ... $OH$ ; $B = HO$ ... $OH$

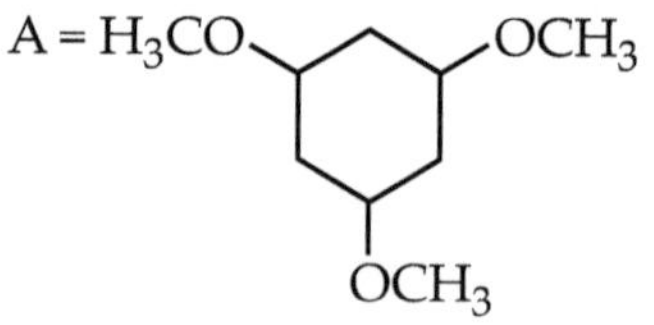

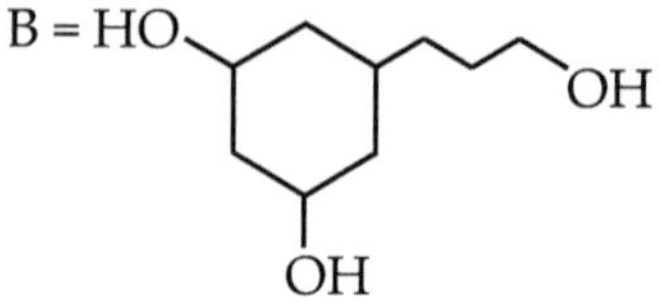

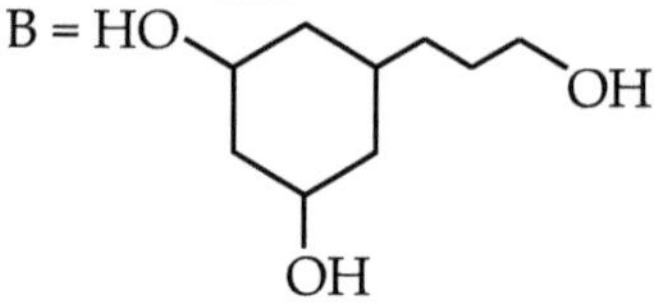

**5.** The major product in the following reaction is :

**[2020, Main]**

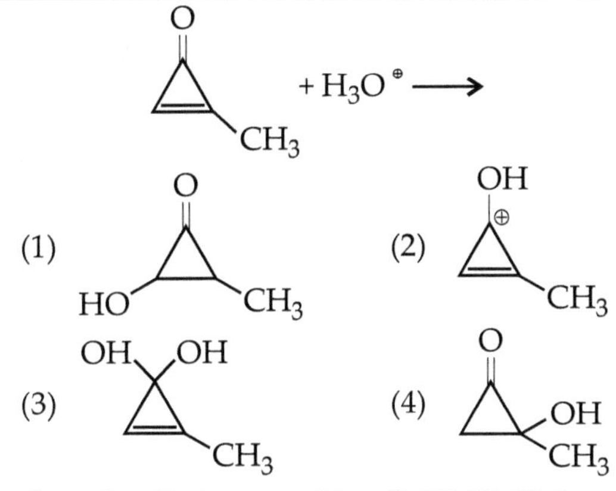

(1)  (2)

(3)  (4)

**6.** Complex X of composition $Cr(H_2O)_6Cl_n$ has a spin only magnetic moment of 3.83 BM. It reacts with $AgNO_3$ and shows geometrical isomerism. The IUPAC nomenclature of X is : **[2020, Main]**
   (1) Tetraaquadichlorido chromium (III) chloride dihydrate
   (2) Hexaaqua chromium (III) chloride
   (3) Dichloridotetraaqua chromium (IV) chloride dihydrate
   (4) Tetraaquadichlorido chromium (IV) chloride dihydrate

**7.** The mass percentage of nitrogen in histamine is ............ . **[2020, Main]**

**8.** Arrange the following compounds in increasing order of C–OH bond length :
   methanol, phenol, $p$-ethoxyphenol **[2020, Main]**
   (1) phenol < methanol < $p$-ethoxyphenol
   (2) phenol < $p$-ethoxyphenol < methanol
   (3) methanol < $p$-ethoxyphenol < phenol
   (4) methanol < phenol < $p$-ethoxyphenol

**9.** The major product of the following reaction is : **[2020, Main]**

(1)

(2)

(3)

(4)

**10.** In the following reaction sequence, structures of A and B, respectively will be : **[2020, Main]**

(1)

(2)

(3)

(4)

**11.** In organic compound `X' showing the following solubility profile is : **[2019, Main]**

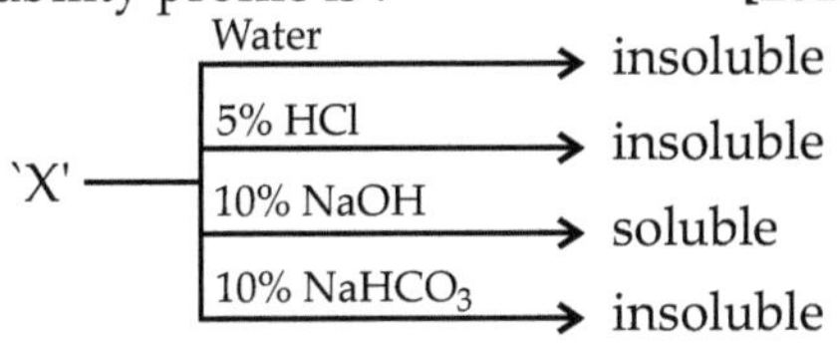

(1) $o$-Toluidine  (2) Oleic acid
(3) $m$-Cresol  (4) Benzamide

**12.** The major product of the following reaction is : **[2019, Main]**

(1)

(2)

(3)

(4)

**13.** Diborane $(B_2H_6)$ reacts independently with $O_2$ and $H_2O$ to produce, respectively : **[2019, Main]**

  (1) $B_2O_3$ and $H_3BO_3$
  (2) $B_2O_3$ and $[BH_4]^-$
  (3) $H_3BO_3$ and $B_2O_3$
  (4) $HBO_2$ and $H_3BO_3$

**14.** Which of the following compounds will show the maximum `enol' content ? **[2019, Main]**
  (1) $CH_3COCH_2COOC_2H_5$
  (2) $CH_3COCH_2COCH_3$
  (3) $CH_3COCH_3$
  (4) $CH_3COCH_2CONH_2$

**15.** The increasing order of reactivity of the following compounds towards aromatic electrophilic substitution reaction is : **[2019, Main]**

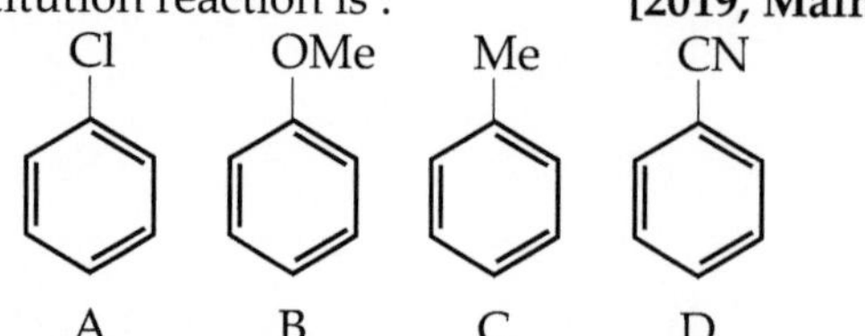

  A    B    C    D
  (1) $D < A < C < B$    (2) $B < C < A < D$
  (3) $A < B < C < D$    (4) $D < B < A < C$

**16.** The organic compound that gives following qualitative analysis is : **[2019, Main]**

| Test | Inference |
| --- | --- |
| (a) Dil. HCl | Insoluble |
| (b) NaOH solution | soluble |
| (c) $Br_2$/water | Decolourization |

  (1) [phenol with OH]    (2) [aniline with NH₂]
  (3) [cyclohexylamine with NH₂]    (4) [cyclohexanol with OH]

**17.** The major product of the following reaction is : **[2019, Main]**

[3-hydroxymethyl cyclohexanone] → 1. $PBr_3$ → 2. KOH (alc.)

  (1) [structure with OH]    (2) [structure with OH and HO]
  (3) [cyclohexenone]    (4) [cyclohexenone]

**18.** *p*-Hydroxybenzophenone upon reaction with bromine in carbon tetrachloride gives : **[2019, Main]**

  (1) [structure with Br, O, HO]
  (2) [structure with Br, O, Br, HO]

  (3) [structure with O, HO, Br]
  (4) [structure with O, HO, Br]

**19.** The major product of the following reaction is : **[2019, Main]**

[aromatic compound with OMe, NC, O-isopropyl] → HI (excess), $\Delta$

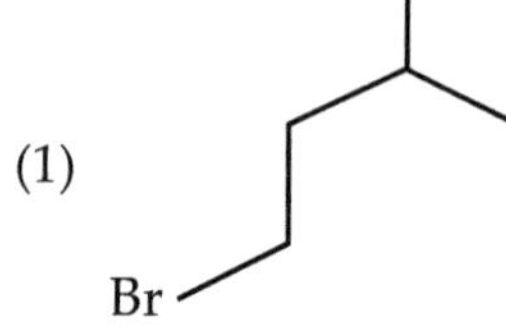
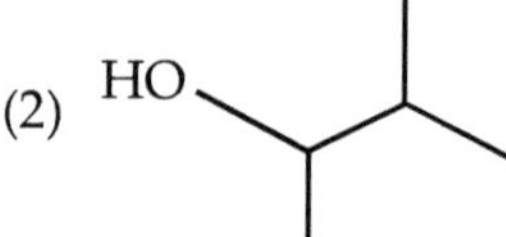

  (1) [structure with OH, NC, OH]    (2) [structure with I, NC, OH]
  (3) [structure with OH, NC, I]    (4) [structure with I, NC, I]

**20.** The major product `Y' in the following reaction is : **[2019, Main]**

[Cl substituted alkane] → EtONa, Heat → X → HBr → Y

  (1) [Br structure]
  (2) [HO structure]
  (3) [Br structure]
  (4) [Br structure]

**21.** What will be the major product when *m*-cresol is reacted with propargyl bromide ($HC \equiv C - CH_2Br$) in presence of $K_2CO_3$ in acetone ? **[2019, Main]**

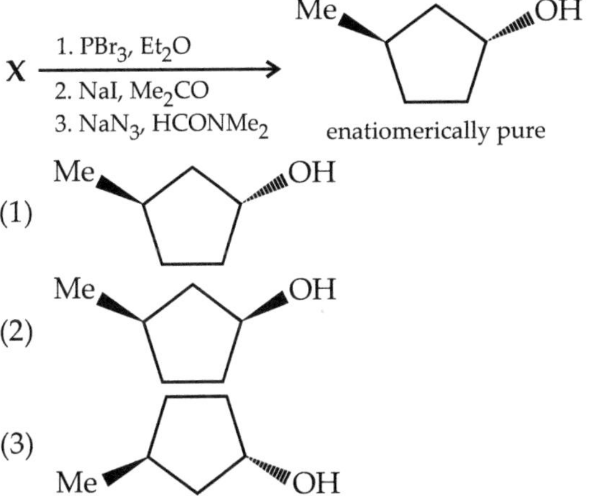

(1) — (2) — (3) — (4)

**22.** Total number of hydroxyl groups present in molecule of the major product **P** is **[2019, Main]**

$$\xrightarrow[\text{(ii) dil. KMnO}_4 \text{ (excess), 273 K}]{\text{(i) H}_2\text{, Pd-BaSO}_4\text{, quinoline}} \mathbf{P}$$

**23.** Total number of isomers, considering both structural and stereoisomers, of cyclic ethers with the molecular formula $C_4H_8O$ is ........

**[2019, Main]**

**24.** In the following reaction sequence, the correct structure(s) of X is/are : **[2018, Advanced]**

$$\mathbf{X} \xrightarrow[\substack{\text{2. NaI, Me}_2\text{CO} \\ \text{3. NaN}_3\text{, HCONMe}_2}]{\text{1. PBr}_3\text{, Et}_2\text{O}}$$

enatiomerically pure

(1)

(2)

(3)

(4)

**25.** The desired product **X** can be prepared by reacting the major product of the reactions in List-I with one or more appropriate reagents in List-II.

(given, order of migratory aptitude: aryl > alkyl > hydrogen) **[2018, Advanced]**

**List-I**      **List-II**

**P.** $+ H_2SO_4$    1. $I_2$, NaOH

**Q.** $+ HNO_2$    2. $[Ag(NH_3)_2]OH$

           3. Fehling solution

**R.** $+ H_2SO_4$    4. HCHO, NaOH

**S.** $+ AgNO_3$    5. NaOBr

The correct option is :

(1) P → 1; Q → 2, 3; R → 1, 4; S → 2, 4

(2) P → 1, 5; Q → 3, 4; R → 4, 5; S → 3

(3) P → 1, 5; Q → 3, 4; R → 5; S → 2, 4

(4) P → 1, 5; Q → 2, 3; R → 1, 5; S → 2, 3

**26.** Phenol on treatment with $CO_2$ in the presence of NaOH followed by acidification produces compound X as the major product. X on treatment with $(CH_3CO)_2O$ in the presence of catalytic amount of $H_2SO_4$ produces : **[2018, Main]**

(1)      (2)

(3)      (4)

**27.** Phenol reacts with methyl chloroformate in the presence of NaOH to form product A. A reacts with $Br_2$ to form product B. A and B are respectively. **[2018, Main]**

(1)

(2)

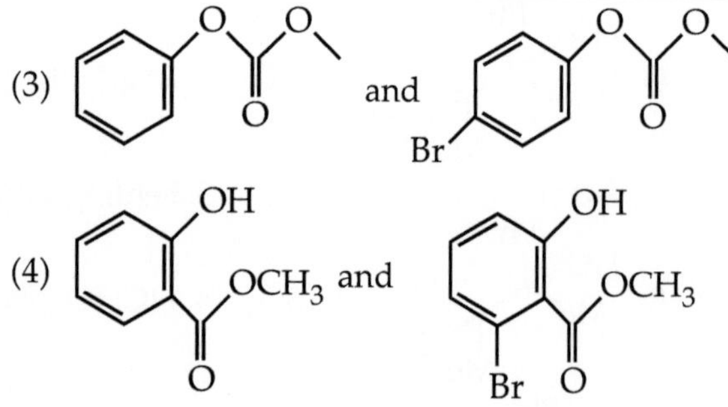

(3) and

(4) and

**28.** The major product formed in the following reaction is : **[2018, Main]**

(1)

(2)

(3)

(4)

**29.** On treatment of the following compound with a strong acid, the most susceptible site for bond cleavage is : **[2018, Main]**

(1) C1 – O2

(2) O2 – C3

(3) C4 – O5

(4) O5 – C6

**30.** The total number of optically active compounds formed on the following reaction is : **[2018, Main]**

(1) Two

(2) Four

(3) Six

(4) Zero

**31.** The major product formed in the following reaction is : **[2018, Main]**

(1)

**32.** The major product of the following reaction is : **[2017, Main]**

(1)

(2)

(3)

(4)

**33.** The increasing order of the boiling points for the following compounds is : **[2017, Main]**

$$\underset{\text{(I)}}{C_2H_5OH} \quad \underset{\text{(II)}}{C_2H_5Cl} \quad \underset{\text{(III)}}{C_2H_5CH_3} \quad \underset{\text{(IV)}}{C_2H_5OCH_3}$$

(1) (III) < (IV) < (II) < (I)

(2) (IV) < (III) < (I) < (II)

(3) (II) < (III) < (IV) < (I)

(4) (III) < (II) < (I) < (IV)

**34.** In the following reaction sequence : **[2017, Main]**

$$\underset{(C_3H_6Cl_2)}{I} \xrightarrow{KOH\ (aq)} II \xrightarrow[\text{(ii) } H_2O/H^+]{\text{(i) } CH_3MgBr} III$$

$$\xrightarrow{\text{Anhy. ZnCl}_2 + \text{Con. HCl}} \text{gives turbidity immediately}$$

The compound I is :

(1) $\underset{\displaystyle \overset{|}{Cl} \quad \overset{|}{Cl}}{CH_2 - CH - CH_3}$

(2) $\underset{\displaystyle \overset{|}{Cl} \qquad \overset{|}{Cl}}{CH_2 - CH_2 - CH_2}$

(3) $Cl-\underset{\underset{Cl}{|}}{CH}-CH_2-CH_3$

(4) $CH_3-\underset{\underset{Cl}{|}}{\overset{\overset{Cl}{|}}{C}}-CH_3$

**35.** The gas evolved on heating $CH_3MgBr$ in methanol is : **[2016, Main]**
(1) HBr      (2) Methane
(3) Ethane     (4) Propane

**36.** The number of resonance structures for **N** is :
**[2015, Advanced]**

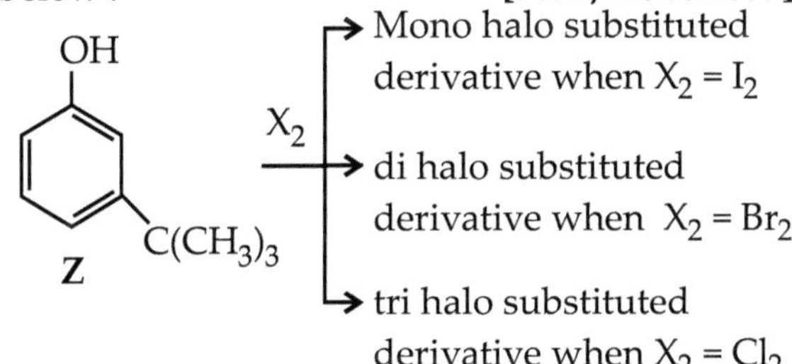

**37.** The number of hydroxyl group(s) in **Q** is :
**[2015, Advanced]**

**38.** The correct combination of names for isomeric alcohols with molecular formula $C_4H_{10}O$ is/are :
**[2014, Advanced]**
(1) *tert*-butanol and 2-methylpropan-2-ol
(2) *tert*-butanol and 1, 1-dimethylethan-1-ol
(3) *n*-butanol and butan-1-ol
(4) isobutyl alcohol and 2-methylpropan-1-ol

**39.** The reactivity of compound **Z** with different halogens under appropriate conditions is given below : **[2014, Advanced]**

→ Mono halo substituted derivative when $X_2 = I_2$
→ di halo substituted derivative when $X_2 = Br_2$
→ tri halo substituted derivative when $X_2 = Cl_2$

The observed pattern of electrophilic substitution can be explained by :
(1) the steric effect of the halogen
(2) the steric effect of the *tert*-butyl group
(3) the electronic effect of the phenolic group
(4) the electronic effect of the *tert*-butyl group

**40.** The acidic hydrolysis of ether (X) shown below is fastest when **[2014, Advanced]**

**[X]**

(1) one phenyl group is replaced by a methyl group
(2) one phenyl group is replaced by a *para*-methoxyphenyl group
(3) two phenyl group is replaced by two *para*-methoxyphenyl groups
(4) no structural change is made to **X**

**41.** The most suitable reagent for the conversion of $R-CH_2-OH \rightarrow R-CHO$ is : **[2014, Main]**
(1) $KMnO_4$
(2) $K_2Cr_2O_7$
(3) $CrO_3$
(4) PCC (Pyridinium Chlorochromate)

**42.** Allyl phenyl ether can be prepared by heating : **[2014, Main]**
(1) $C_6H_5Br + CH_2 = CH - CH_2 - ONa$
(2) $CH_2 = CH - CH_2 - Br + C_6H_5ONa$
(3) $C_6H_5 - CH = CH - Br + CH_3 - ONa$
(4) $CH_2 = CH - Br + C_6H_5 - CH_2 - ONa$

**43.** The following reaction

is known as : **[2014, Main]**
(1) Perkin reaction
(2) Gattermann-Koch Formylation
(3) Kolbe's reaction
(4) Gattermann reaction

**44.** Which one of the following statements is not correct ? **[2014, Main]**
(1) Alcohols are weaker acids than water
(2) Acid strength of alcohols decreases in the following order
$RCH_2OH > R_2CHOH > R_3COH$
(3) Carbon-oxygen bond length in methanol, $CH_3OH$ is shorter than that of $C - O$ bond length in phenol
(4) The bond angle C    H in methanol is 108.9°

**45.** In the Victor-Meyer's test, the colour given by 1°, 2° and 3° alcohols are respectively : **[2014, Main]**
(1) Red, colourless, blue
(2) Red, blue, colourless
(3) Colourless, red, blue
(4) Red, blue, violet

**46.** Which one of the following substituents at *para*-position is most effective in stabilizing the phenoxide ion ? **[2014, Main]**
(1) $-CH_3$      (2) $-OCH_3$
(3) $-COCH_3$    (4) $-CH_2OH$

**47.** Williamson synthesis of ether is an example of : **[2014, Main]**
(1) Nucleophilic addition

    (2)  Electrophilic addition
    (3)  Electrophilic substitution
    (4)  Nucleophilic substitution

**48.** In the following reaction, the product(s) formed is(are) : **[2013, Advanced]**

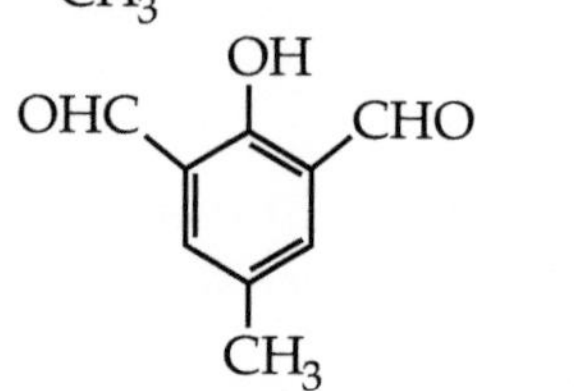

P, Q, R, S structures:

**P**, **Q**, **R**, **S**

(1) **P** (major)  (2) **Q** (minor)
(3) **R** (minor)  (4) **S** (major)

**49.** The major products(s) of the following reaction is(are) : **[2013, Advanced]**

**P**, **Q**, **R**, **S**

(1) **P**  (2) **Q**
(3) **R**  (4) **S**

**50.** The major product of the following reaction is : **[2011, Advanced]**

$$\text{(tetrahydropyran)} \xrightarrow[\text{H}^{\oplus}\text{ (anhydrous)}]{\text{RCH}_2\text{OH}}$$

(1)  a hemiacetal  (2)  an acetal
(3)  an ether  (4)  an ester

**51.** In the reaction $C_6H_5$—$OCH_3 \xrightarrow{\text{HBr}}$ the products are : **[2010, Advanced]**

(1) $Br$—$\langle\rangle$—$OCH_3$ and $H_2$

(2) $\langle\rangle$—$Br$ and $CH_3Br$

(3) $\langle\rangle$—$Br$ and $CH_3OH$

(4) $\langle\rangle$—$OH$ and $CH_3Br$

**52.** In the reaction (phenol) $\xrightarrow{\text{NaOH(aq)/Br}_2}$ the intermediate(s) is(are) : **[2010, Advanced]**

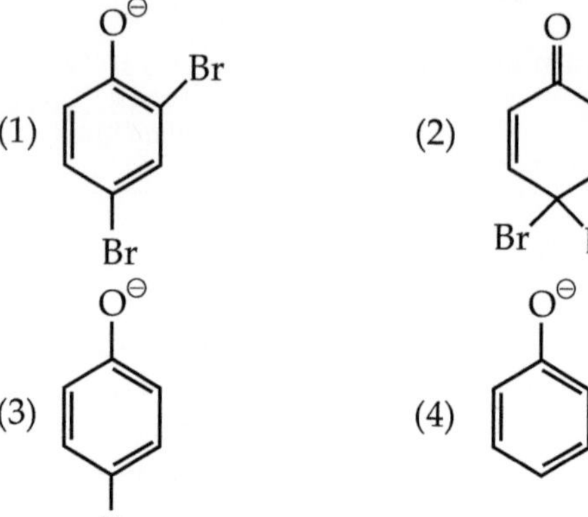

**53.** Amongst the following, the total number of compounds soluble in aqueous NaOH is : **[2010, Advanced]**

(1) $N,N$-dimethylaniline

cyclohexane-COOH

(2) 2-ethoxybenzyl alcohol ($OCH_2CH_3$, $CH_2OH$)

phenol (OH)

(3) nitrobenzene ($NO_2$)

$N,N$-dimethyl-4-aminophenol (OH, $N(CH_3)_2$)

(4) 1,2-diethylbenzene ($CH_2CH_3$, $CH_2CH_3$)

naphthalene-COOH

**54.** The IUPAC name of the following compound is : **[2009, Advanced]**

(1) 4-Bromo-3-cyanophenol
(2) 2-Bromo-5-hydroxybenzonitrile
(3) 2-Cyano-4-hydroxybromobenzene
(4) 6-Bromo-3-hydroxybenzonitrile

**55.** The correct stability order for the following species is : **[2008, Advanced]**

(I)    (II)    (III)    (IV)

(1) (II) > (IV) > (I) > (III)
(2) (I) > (II) > (III) > (IV)
(3) (II) > (I) > (IV) > (III)
(4) (I) > (III) > (II) > (IV)

**Paragraph Question** — A tertiary alcohol **H** upon acid catalysed dehydration gives a product **I**. Ozonolysis of **I** leads to compounds **J** and **K**. Compound **J** upon reaction with KOH gives benzyl alcohol and a compound **L**, whereas **K** on reaction with KOH gives only **M**.

$$M = \underset{Ph}{\overset{H_3C}{\diagdown}}C=\underset{H}{\overset{O}{\diagup Ph}}$$

**56.** The structure of compound **I** is : **[2008, Advanced]**

(1) $\underset{H}{\overset{Ph}{\diagdown}}C=\underset{Ph}{\overset{CH_3}{\diagup}}$   (2) $\underset{H}{\overset{H_3C}{\diagdown}}C=\underset{Ph}{\overset{Ph}{\diagup}}$

(3) $\underset{H}{\overset{Ph}{\diagdown}}C=\underset{CH_2Ph}{\overset{CH_3}{\diagup}}$   (4) $\underset{Ph}{\overset{H_3C}{\diagdown}}C=\underset{H}{\overset{CH_3}{\diagup}}$

**Paragraph for Question 57 to 59**

Reimer-Tiemann reaction introduces an aldehyde group, on to the aromatic ring of phenol, *ortho* to the hydroxyl group. This reaction involves electrophilic aromatic substitution. This is a general method for the synthesis of substituted salicyladehydes as depicted below.

**57.** Which one of the following reagents in used in the above reaction ? **[2007, Advanced]**

(1) aq. NaOH +CH$_3$Cl
(2) aq. NaOH + CH$_2$Cl$_2$
(3) aq. NaOH + CHCl$_3$
(4) aq. NaOH + CCl$_4$

**58.** The electrophile in this reaction is :

**[2007, Advanced]**

(1) :CHCl          (2) $^+$CHCl$_2$
(3) :CCl$_2$          (4) ·CCl$_3$

**59.** The structure of the intermediate **I** is :

**[2007, Advanced]**

(1)          (2)

(3)          (4)

**60.** When benzene sulfonic acid and p-nitrophenol are treated with NaHCO$_3$, the gases released respectively are : **[2006, Advanced]**

(1) SO$_2$, NO$_2$          (2) SO$_2$, NO
(3) SO$_2$, CO$_2$          (4) CO$_2$, CO$_2$

**61.** (I)    1, 2-dihydroxy benzene
(II)    1, 3-dihydroxy benzene
(III)    1, 4-dihydroxy benzene
(IV)    Hydroxy benenze

The increasing order of boiling points of above mentioned alcohols is : **[2006, Advanced]**

(1) I < II < III < IV          (2) I < II < IV < III
(3) IV < I < II < III          (4) IV < II < I < III

**62.** $\bigcirc$ + Cl – CH$_2$CH$_2$ – CH$_3$ $\xrightarrow{AlCl_3}$ P $\xrightarrow[\text{(ii) } H_2O^+]{\text{(i) } O_2/\Delta}$

Q + Phenol

The major products P and Q are : **[2006, Main]**

(1) [benzene ring with isopropyl group] and CH$_3$CH$_2$ClIO

(2) [benzene ring with isopropyl group] and CH$_3$COCH$_3$

(3) [isopropylbenzene structure] and $CH_3COCH_3$

(4) [isopropenylbenzene structure] and $CH_3CH_2CHO$

**63.** [1-methylcyclopentanol structure] $\xrightarrow{H^+/\Delta}$ X $\xrightarrow[\text{2. Zn/CH}_3\text{COOH}]{\text{1. O}_3}$ X $\xrightarrow{NaOH}$ [cyclopentenone structure]

Identify X and Y. **[2005, Main]**

**64.** When Phenyl Magnesium Bromide reacts with tert. butanol, which of the following is formed ? **[2005, Screening]**

(1) Tert. butyl methyl ether
(2) Benzene
(3) Tert. butyl benzene
(4) Phenol

**65.** Cyclohexene is best prepared from cyclohexanol by which of the following : **[2005, Screening]**

(1) conc. $H_3PO_4$     (2) conc. $HCl/ZnCl_2$
(3) conc. HCl        (4) conc. HBr

**66.** 2-phenyl propene on acidic hydration gives : **[2004, Screening]**

(1) 2-phenyl-2-propanol
(2) 2-phenyl-1-propanol
(3) 3-phenyl-1-propanol
(4) 1-phenyl-2-propanol

**67.** Which one is more soluble in diethyl ether anhydrous $AlCl_3$ or hydrous $AlCl_3$ ? Explain in terms of bonding. **[2003, Main]**

**68.** A racemic mixture of (±) 2-phenyl propanoic acid on esterification with (+) 2-butanol gives two estersn. Mention the stereochemistry of the two esters produced. **[2003, Main]**

**69.** Convert **[2003, Main]**

(a) [phenol with COOH structure] $\rightarrow$ [benzoic acid with methyl, COOH structure] (In not more than 3 steps)

(b) [phenol structure] $\rightarrow$ Aspirin

**70.** [benzene structure] $+ C_2H_5I \xrightarrow[\text{Anhydrous (C}_2\text{H}_5\text{OH)}]{O^-C_2H_5}$ **[2003, Screening]**

(1) $C_6H_5OC_2H_5$     (2) $C_2H_5OC_2H_5$
(3) $C_6H_5OC_6H_5$     (4) $C_6H_5I$

**71.** Ethyl ester $\xrightarrow[\text{excess}]{CH_3MgBr}$ P. The product P will be : **[2003, Screening]**

(1) [structure: H3C, CH3, H3C, OH]
(2) [structure: H3C, C2H5, H5C2, OH]
(3) [structure: H5C2, C2H5, H5C2, OH]
(4) [structure: H5C2, C2H5, H7C3, OH]

## ANSWER KEY

| | | | | | | | | | |
|---|---|---|---|---|---|---|---|---|---|
| 1. (2) | 2. (4) | 3. (3) | 4. (1) | 5. (2) | 6. (1) | 7. (*) | 8. (2) | 9. (2) | 10. (1) |
| 11. (3) | 12. (4) | 13. (1) | 14. (2) | 15. (1) | 16. (1) | 17. (3) | 18. (2) | 19. (3) | 20. (3) |
| 21. (1) | 22. (*) | 23. (*) | 24. (2) | 25. (4) | 26. (1) | 27. (3) | 28. (4) | 29. (2) | 30. (1) |
| 31. (3) | 32. (1) | 33. (1) | 34. (4) | 35. (2) | 36. (*) | 37. (4) | 38. (1,3,4) | 39. (1,2,3) | 40. (3) |
| 41. (4) | 42. (2) | 43. (4) | 44. (3) | 45. (2) | 46. (3) | 47. (4) | 48. (2, 4) | 49. (2) | 50. (2) |
| 51. (4) | 52. (1, 3) | 53. (4) | 54. (2) | 55. (4) | 56. (1) | 57. (3) | 58. (3) | 59. (2) | 60. (4) |
| 61. (3) | 62. (3) | 63. (*) | 64. (2) | 65. (1) | 66. (1) | 67. (*) | 68. (*) | 69. (1) | 70. (2) |
| 71. (1) | | | | | | | | | |

## ANSWERS WITH EXPLANATIONS

**1. (2)** Compound $\xrightarrow[\text{anhydride}]{\text{Chromic}}$ [complex fused ring structure with O, OH, O, H groups]

**2. (4)** [benzene ring structure with OH, NH2, O2N, CHO substituents numbered 1-6]

5-amino-4-hydroxymethyl-2-nitrobenzalde-hyde.

**3. (3)** [three benzene ring structures: one with NH2 and Cl, one with OH and Cl, one with COOH and Cl]

[structure: $O = C - OH$ on benzene ring] $\xrightarrow{NaHCO_3}$ [structure: $O = C - O^-Na^+$ on benzene ring with Cl]

Fraction-A

$+ H_2CO_3 \rightarrow H_2O + CO_2$

**Fraction-B**

**Fraction-C**

**4. (1)** Alcohol has more boiling point than ether (due to hydrogen bonding).

So,

has more boiling point than

**5. (2)**

(Aromtic stable product)

**6. (1)** $Cr(H_2O)_6Cl_n$

If magnetic moment is 3.83 BM then it contain three unpaired electrons. It means chromium in +3 oxidation state has molecular formula $Cr(H_2O)_6Cl_3$

∴ This formula have following isomers :

(a) $[Cr(H_2O)_6]Cl_3$ : react with $AgNO_3$ but does not show geometrical isomerism.

(b) $[Cr(H_2O)_5Cl]Cl_2.H_2O$ react with $AgNO_3$ but does not show geometrical isomerism.

(c) $[Cr(H_2O)_4Cl_2]Cl.2H_2O$ react with $AgNO_3$ and show geometrical isomerism.

(d) $[Cr(H_2O)_3Cl_3].3H_2O$ does not react with $AgNO_3$ and show geometrical isomerism.

$[Cr(H_2O)_4Cl_2]Cl.2H_2O$ react with $AgNO_3$ and show geometrical isomerism and it's IUPAC nomenclature is Tetraaquadichlorido chromium (III) Chloride dihydrate.

**7.**

Molecular Formula of histamine is $C_5H_9N_3$

Molecular mass of Histamine is 111

Now, mass % of nitrogen $= \left(\dfrac{42}{111}\right) \times 100$

$= 37.84\%$

**8. (2)** $H_3C - OH$ (100% single bond)

↔ C–OH bond has partial double bond character

↔ C–OH bond has some double bond character but double bond character is less)

(+M)

$CH_3OH >$ (*p*-ethoxyphenol) >

**9. (2)**

Terpineol

**10. (1)**

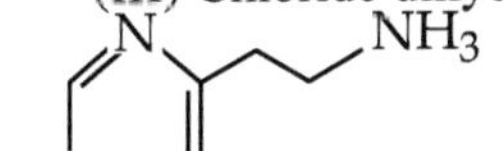

**11. (3)** The compound *m*-cresol is insoluble in water, insoluble in 5% HCl, soluble in 10% NaOH to form sodium-4-methylphenolate and insoluble in 10% $NaHCO_3$. The compound Oleic acid is also soluble in 10% $NaHCO_3$. The compounds benzamide and *o*-toluidine are also available in both 10% $NaCHCO_3$ and 10% NaOH.

**12. (4)** The reagent $NaBH_4$ acts as a reducing agent. The mechanism of the reaction is shown below. It attacks the acarbonyl carbon of the compound to form the sodium salt of the compound. The lone pair of electrons on the oxygen atom attack the adjacent carbon atom to form an epoxide along with the release of NaBr.

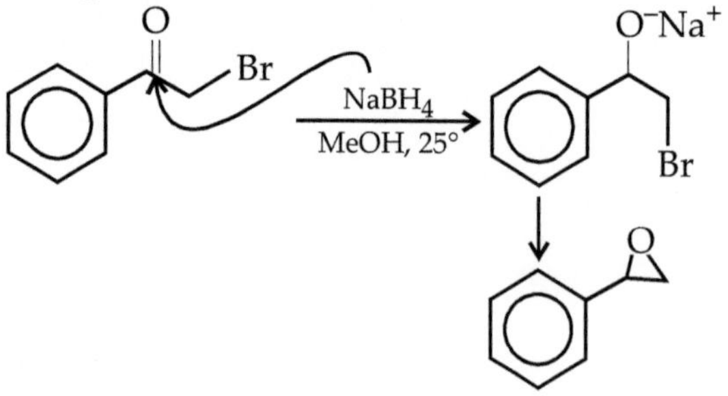

**13. (1)** The reaction of $B_2H_6$ with water produces boric acid as shown below :
$$B_2H_6 + 3\,H_2O \rightarrow 2H_3BO_3 + 3H_2$$
The reaction of $B_2H_6$ with oxygen produces boron trioxide as shown below :
$$B_2H_6 + 3O_2 \rightarrow B_2O_3 + 3H_2O$$

**14. (2)** The keto-enolo tautomerisation reaction is given below :

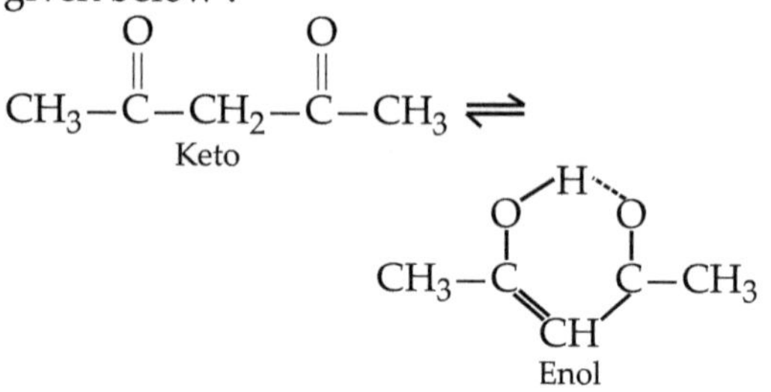

In the compound $CH_3COCH_2COCH_3$, intra-molecular hydrogen bonding and resonance stabilization leads to maximum enol content of the compound.

**15. (1)** The reactivity of electrophilic substitution increases with increase in electron density on the aromatic ring. The methoxy group is electron donating group. The chloro and nitrile group is electron withdrawing group. The electron withdrawing tendency of nitrile group is higher than chloro. The order of increasing electron density of the ring is shown below.

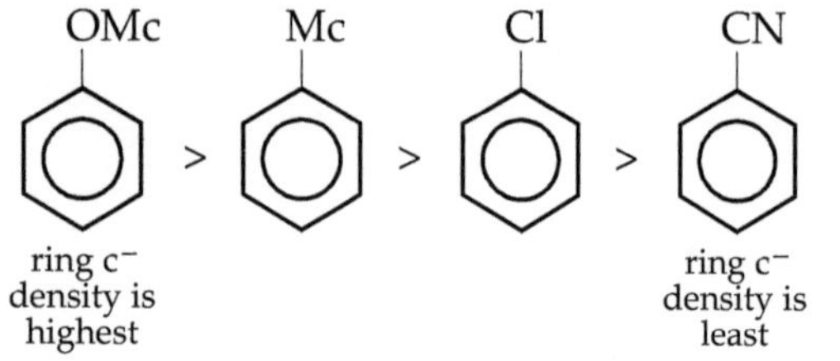

Therefore, the order of reactivity of the compounds is D < A < C < B.

**16. (1)** Phenol is ani acidic organic compound. Phenol is insoluble in dilute HCl acid. Phenol is soluble in NaOH because it forms a soluble phenoxide ion. The structure of sodium phenoxide is shown below :

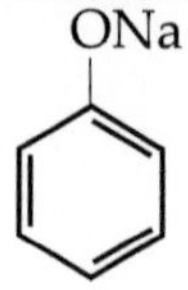

Phenol decolourizes the bromine as it reacts with it to form 2, 4, 6-tribromophenol. The chemical reaction is shown below :

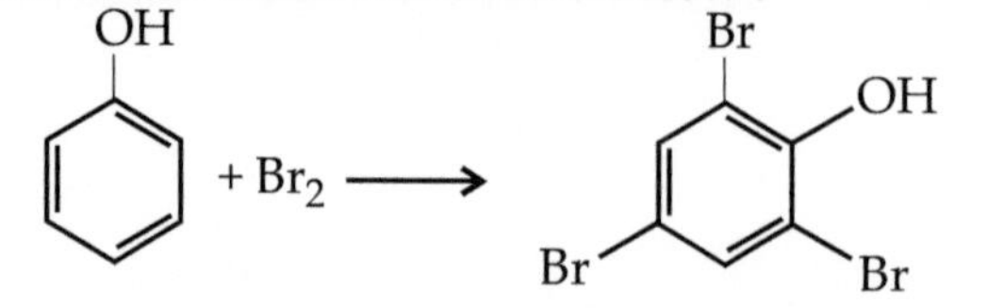

**17. (3)** Nucleophilic substitution reaction occurs between the given starting material and $PBr_3$ to form bromine substituted compound, the bromine substituted compound undergoes elimination reaction with alcoholic potassium hydroxide.
The completed chemical reaction is shown below :

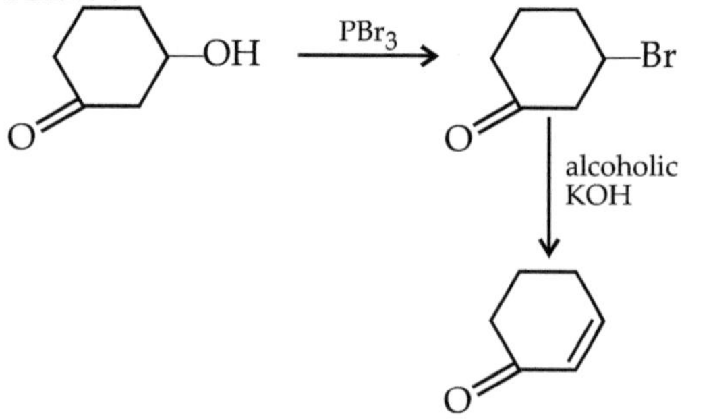

**18. (2)** The phenol group of the starting material is an electron donating group and it prefer the addition of bromo-group on its ortho position.
The complete chemical reaction is shown below :

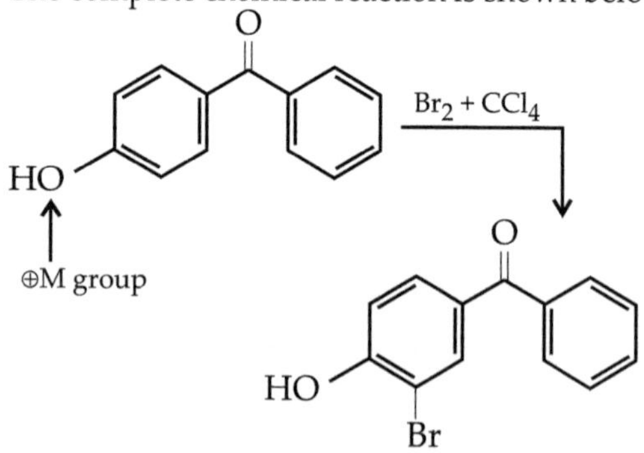

**19. (3)** The completed reaction is given below :

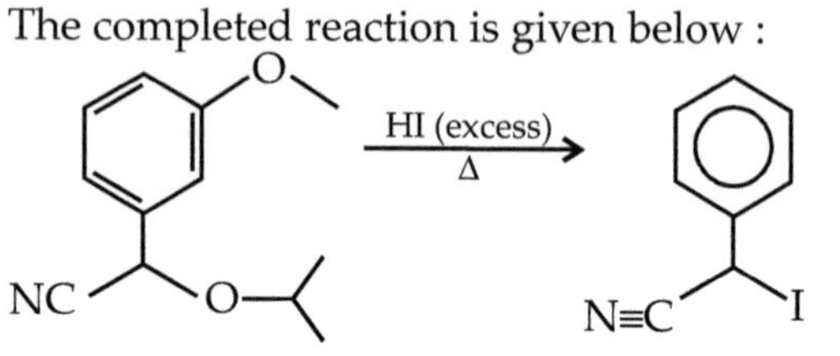

The benzylic O that has –CN attached to it, reacts with HI by $S_N2$ mechanism tio form the final product.

**20. (3)** The completed reaction is given below :

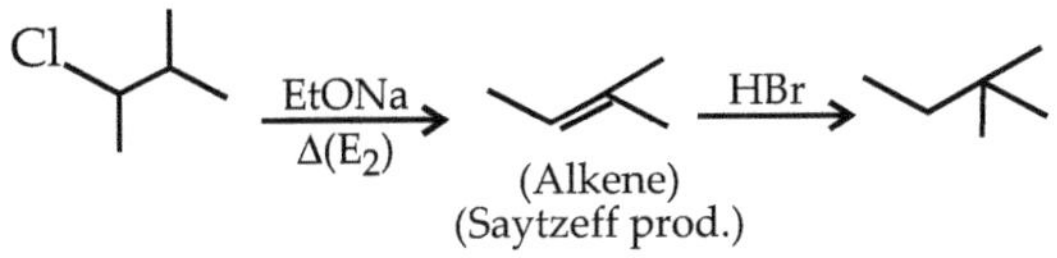

The final product is formed according to Saytzeff's rule, that is, more substituted product is formed.

**21. (1)** The propargyl bromide undergoes nucleophilic substitution reaction with m-cresol to give the product.

The complete reaction sequence is shown below :

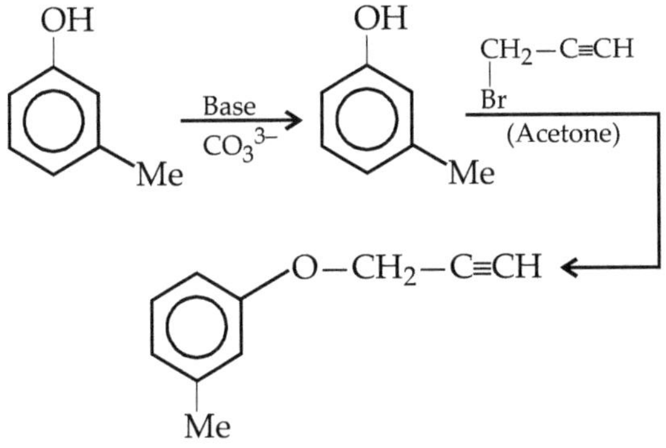

**22.** The starting material undergoes reduction follow up by oxidation to from resultant compound. The complete chemical reaction is shown below :

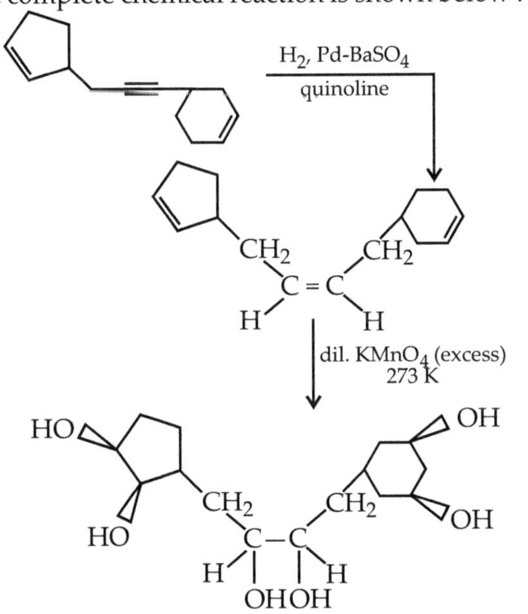

The number of hydroxyl group in the major product is 6.

**23.** All the possible isomers of ethers with molecular formula $C_4H_8O$ are shown below :

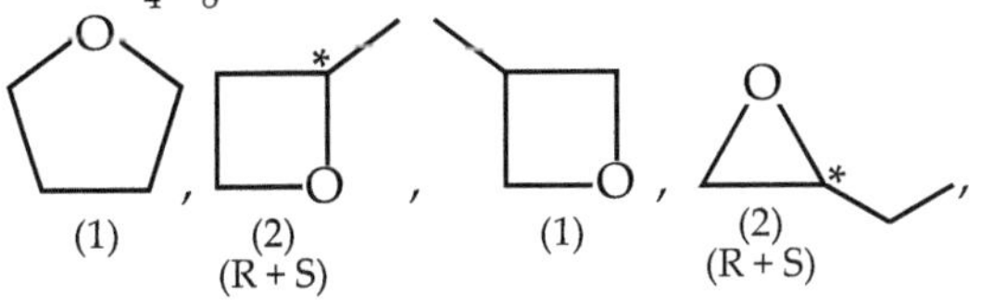

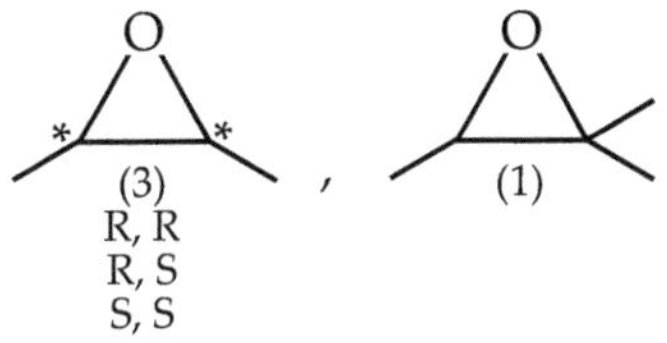

Therefore, the number of isomers are ethers with molecular formula $C_4H_8O$ is 10.

**24. (2)** The correct sequence of reaction is shown below :

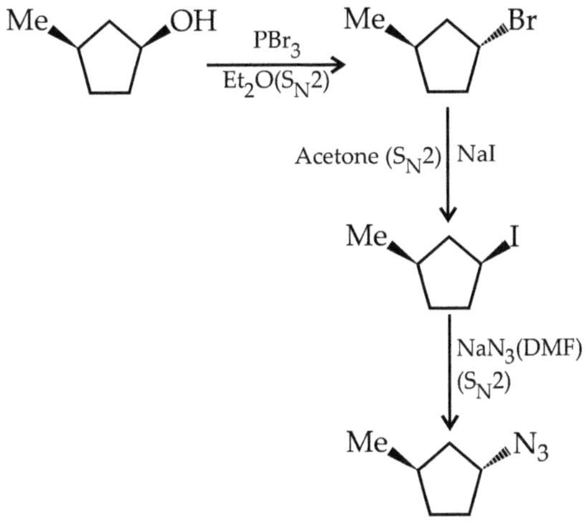

**25. (4)** (P) The final product is given as shown below :

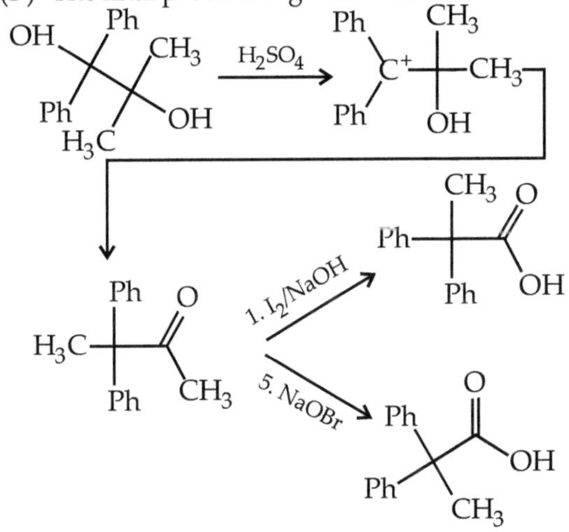

(Q) The final product is given as shown below :

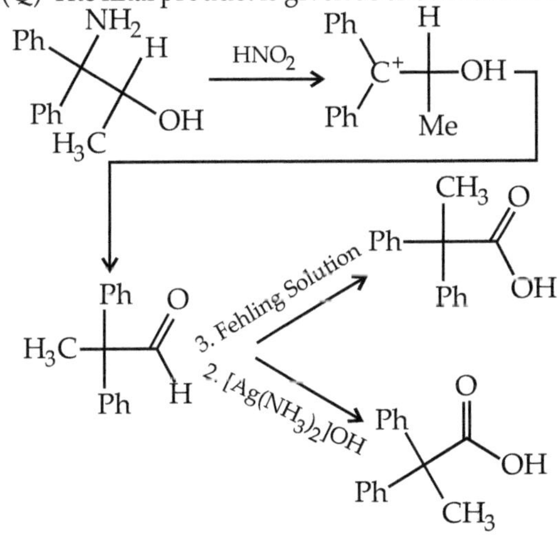

(R) The final product is given as shown below :

$$\text{(pinacol structure)} \xrightarrow{H_2SO_4} \text{(carbocation intermediate)}$$

$$\xrightarrow{1.\ I_2/NaOH} \quad \xrightarrow{5.\ NaOBr}$$

(S) The final product is given as shown below :

$$\text{(bromo structure)} \xrightarrow{AgNO_3} \text{(carbocation intermediate)}$$

$$\xrightarrow{2.\ [Ag(NH_3)_2]OH} \quad \xrightarrow{3.\ Fehling\ Solution}$$

**26. (1)** The reaction of phenol with carbon dioxide in the presence of sodium hydroxide followed by acidification leads to the formation of salicylic acid (X). The reaction of salicylic acid with acetic anhydride and small amount of sulfuric acid results in the formation of aspirin.

$$\text{Phenol} \xrightarrow[\text{(ii) acidification}]{\text{(i) } CO_2,\ NaOH} \text{Salicylic acid (X)}$$

$$\text{(X)} + (CH_3CO)_2O + \text{conc. } H_2SO_4 \longrightarrow \text{Aspirin}$$

**27. (3)** Phenol reacts with methyl chloroformate in the presence of sodium hydroxide as shown below :

$$\text{Phenol} + Cl-\overset{\overset{\displaystyle O}{\|}}{C}-O-Me + NaOH \longrightarrow$$

Methylchloroformate

The product formed in the above reaction contains ortho-para directing group on the benzene ring which leads to the formation of para-substituted product on reaction with bromine.

$$\text{(A) (o/p directing)} + Br_2 \longrightarrow \text{(B)} + HBr$$

Hence, A and B corresponds to the organic compounds given in the option (3).

**28. (4)** Ether on reaction with hydrogen iodide and heat undergo nucleophilic substitution reaction. Since, tertiary carbocation if more stable as compared to the arylic carbocation. Therefore, in the given reaction substitution occurs at the tertiary position.

The mechanism involved in the given reaction is shown below :

$$\xrightarrow[\substack{-\ Et\text{-}I \\ (S_N2)}]{HI/\Delta} \xrightarrow[\substack{-\ CH_3OH \\ S_N1}]{} $$

Hence, the major product formed in the given reaction corresponds to the organic compound given in option (4).

**29. (2)** The cleavage of ether with strong acid is expressed as,

$$R-O-R' \xrightarrow{HX} RX + R'OH$$

The carbon atom with positive charge is stabilized by hyperconjugating structures after cleavage.

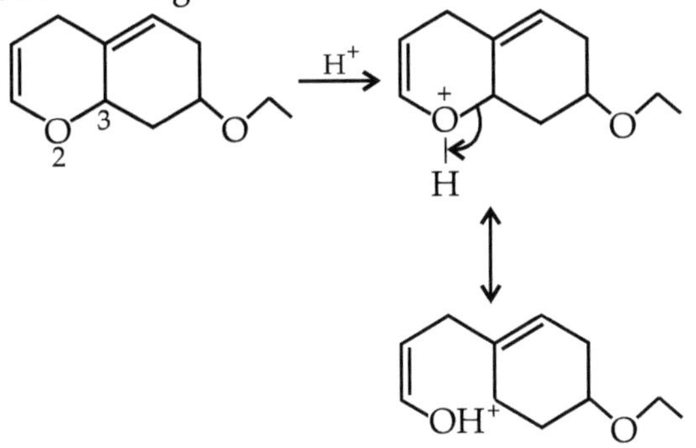

**30. (1)** Cleavage of ether group takes place on addition of HBr. The product formed undergoes tautomerism and gives chiral carbon center. The compound that has chiral carbon center shows two possible non-superimposable mirror images.

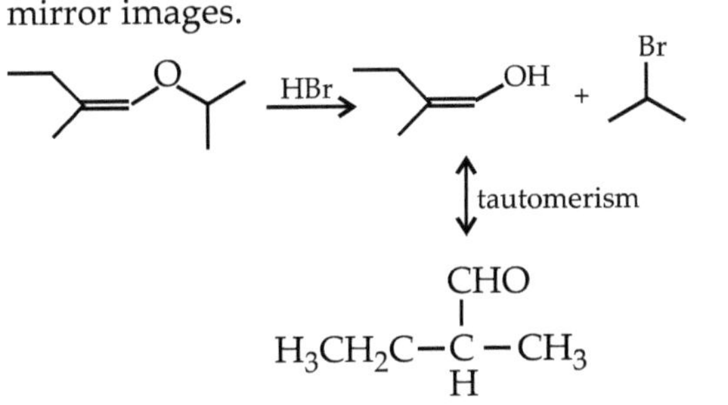

**31. (3)** Primary and secondary alcohols on reaction with Pyridiniumchlorochromate leads to the formation of corresponding aldehyde and ketone.

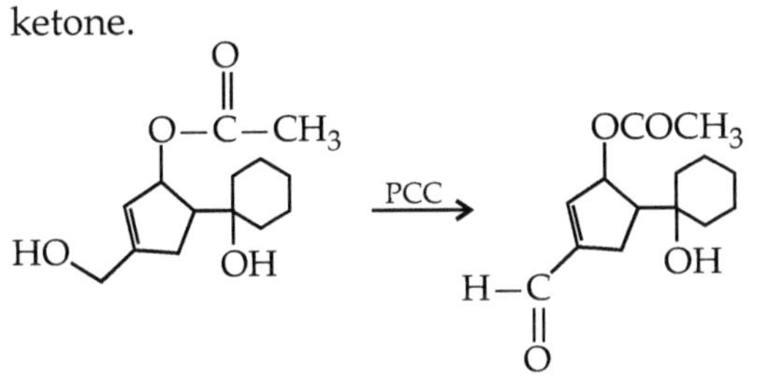

**32. (1)** The major product of the given reaction is shown as follows :

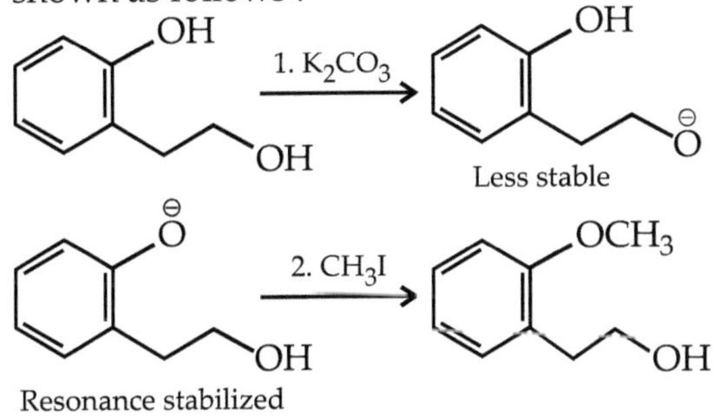

**33. (1)** Ethanol has highest boiling point due to – OH group. These groups aid in formation of strong hydrogen bonding. Ethyl chloride has higher boiling point than ethyl methyl ether due to presence of polar atom attaches

to alkyl group, which leads to strong inter-molecular interactions.

The boiling point of propane is less as compared to ethyl methyl ether because the structure of ethyl methyl ether resembles with structure of water and it has two $C - O$ bonds.

**34. (4)** The complete reaction sequence is shown below :

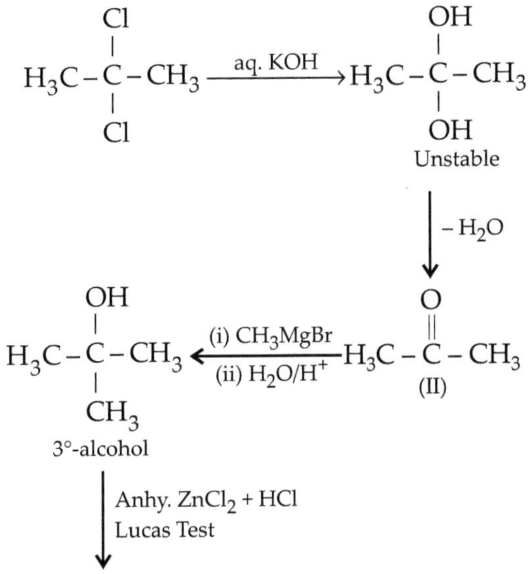

Gives turbidity instantly

Thus, the compound (I) is

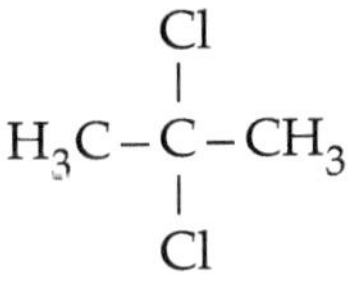

**35. (2)** The gas that is evolved on heating $CH_3MgBr$ is methane as shown below :

$$CH_3MgBr + CH_3OH \rightarrow (CH_3O)\, MgBr + CH_4\ (gas)$$

**36.** The reaction for the formation of **N** is shown below :

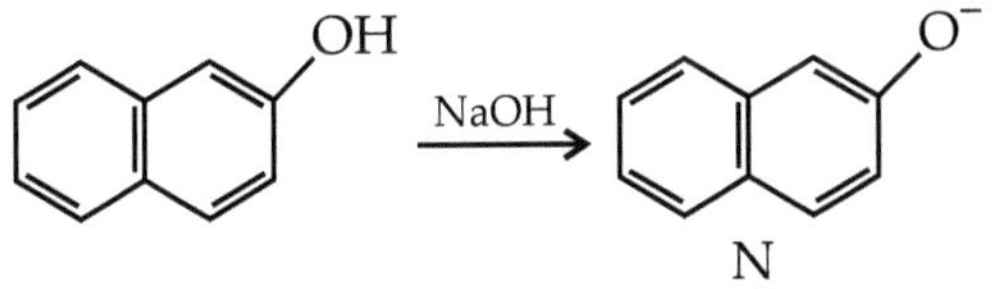

The possible resonance structure for **N** is shown below :

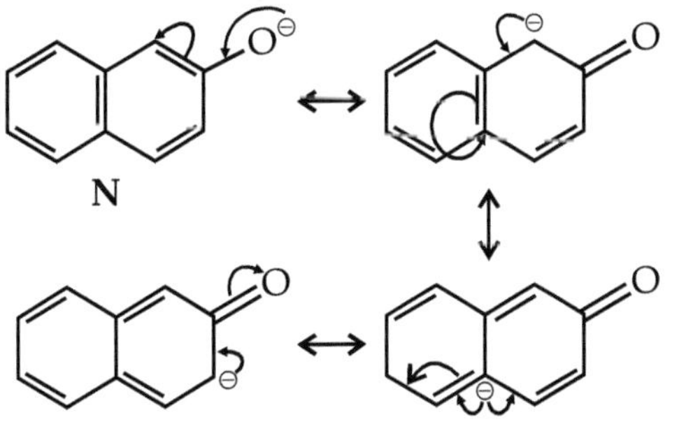

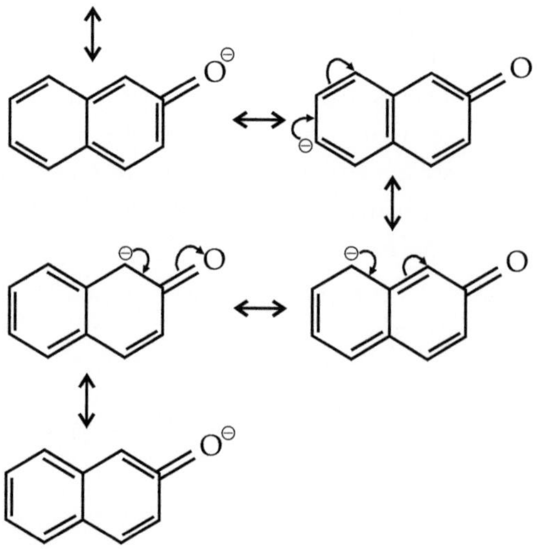

Thus, the possible resonance structure for **N** is 9.

**37. (4)** The first step in the reaction is the dehydration of alcohol and the second step is the formation of syndiol rearrangement as shown below :

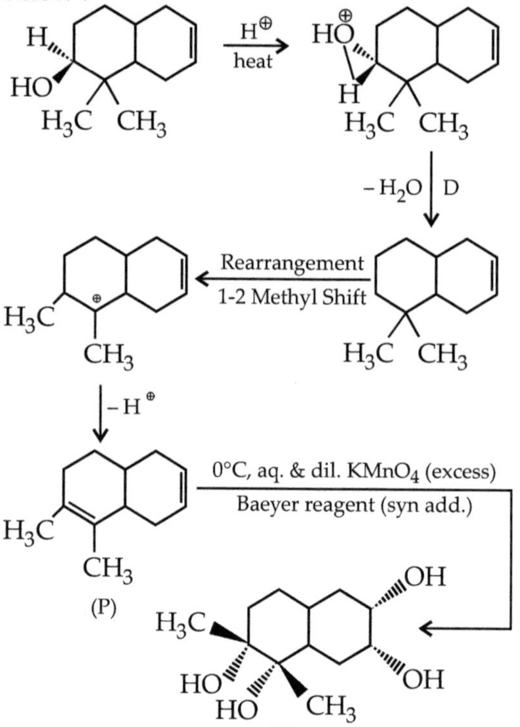

Therefore, the total number of hydroxyl groups in **Q** is 4.

**38. (1)** The structures of *tert*-butanol and 2-methylpropan-2-ol are,

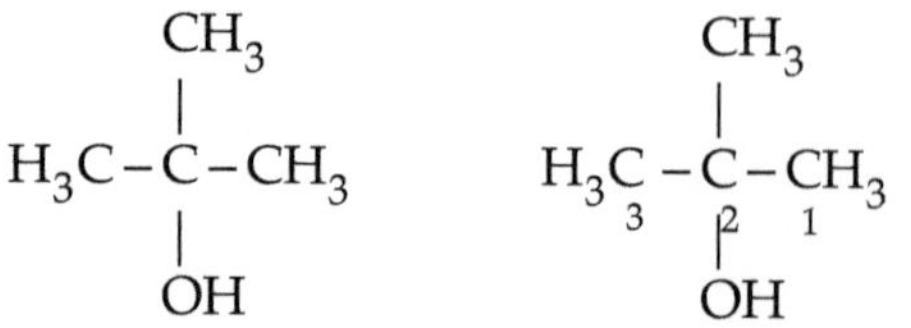

*tert*-butanol    2-methylpropan-2-ol

From the above structures, it is clear that they are isomers of each other.

**(2)** The structures of *tert*-butanol and 1, 1-dimethyl-ethan-1-ol are,

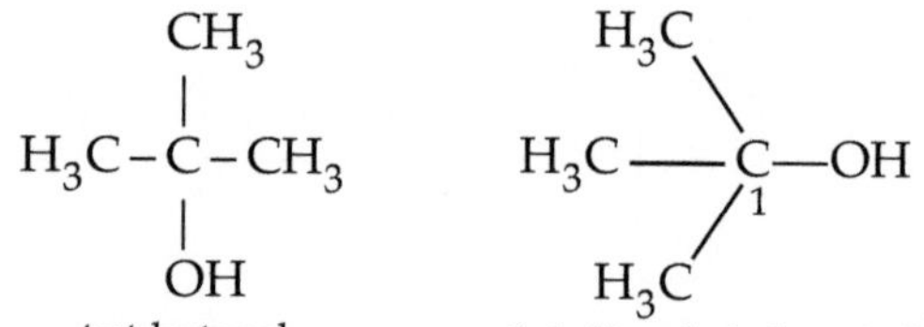

*tert*-butanol    1, 1-dimethylethan-1-ol

From the above structures, it is clear that they are not isomers of each other.

**(3)** The structures of *n*-butanol and butan-1-ol are,

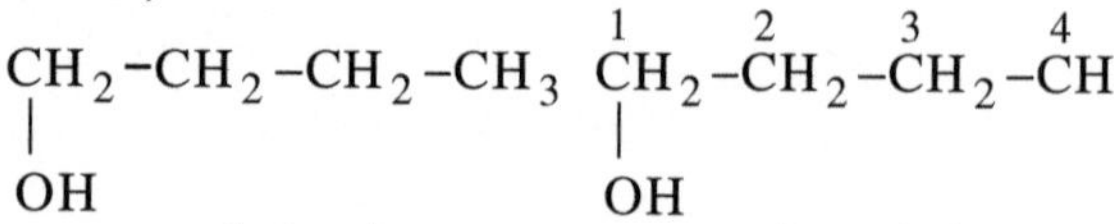

*n*-butanol    butan-1-ol

From the above structures, it is clear that they are isomers of each other.

**(4)** The structures of isobutyl alcohol 2-methylpropan-1-ol are,

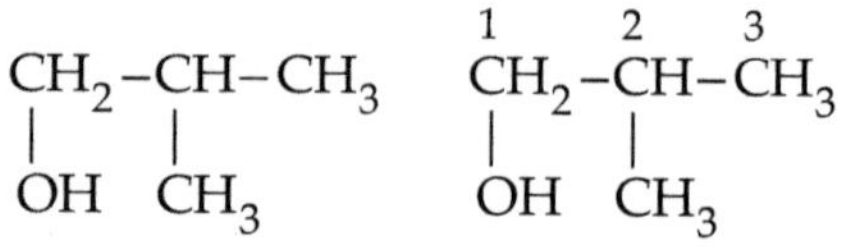

Isobutyl alcohol    2-methylpropan-1-ol

From the above structures, it is clear that they are isomers of each other.

**39. (1,2,3)**

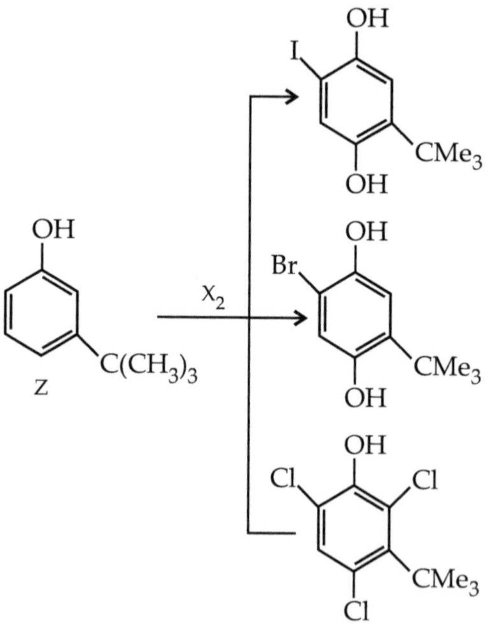

In I, Br and Cl, I is large in size and creates more steric repulsion. Also, steric effect of *tert*-butyl group and electronic effect of phenolic group is present. Therefore, I atom attacks at only $C_2$ position and does not attack at $C_4$ and $C_6$ positions due to more steric repulsion.

**40. (3)** When the replacement of two phenyl groups takes place by two *para*-methoxyphenyl groups, the acidic hydrolysis of ether [X] becomes fastest because methoxy ($-OCH_3$) is an electron donating group that stabilize the carbocation.

**41. (4)** PCC is the most suitable reagent for the conversion of $RCH_2OH$ to $RCHO$. It acts as a selective oxidising agent which converts alcohol into aldehyde or ketone. Other reagents can convert $RCHO$ into $RCOOH$.

**42. (2)** The preparation of allyl phenyl ether is as follows :

$$C_6H_5\overset{\ominus}{O}\overset{\oplus}{Na} + H_2C = \underset{H}{C} - CH_2 - Br \rightarrow$$

$$C_6H_5O - CH_2 - \underset{H}{C} = CH_2$$

Allyl phenyl ether

**43. (4)** The given reaction is Gattermann reaction. In this reaction, phenol reacts with HCl and HCN in the presence of catalyst such as $AlCl_3$ or anhydrous $ZnCl_2$ to form salicylaldehyde.

$$\text{(phenol)} + HCl + HCN \xrightarrow[ZnCl_2]{Anhyd.} \text{(salicylaldehyde)}$$

**44. (3)** In phenol, lone pair of electrons on oxygen is present in conjugation with benzene ring. This conjugation is absent in methanol. Therefore, $C-O$ bond length in phenol is less than $C-O$ bond length in methanol.

(Methanol: $C-O$ = 142 pm)  (Phenol: $C-O$ = 136 pm)

**45. (2)** Primary alcohols gives blood red color solution of nitrolic acid in sodium hydroxide in the Victor Meyer's test which is shown below :

1° Alcohol

$$RCH_2OH \xrightarrow[Red\ P + I_2]{Conc.\ HI\ or} RCH_2I \xrightarrow{AgNO_2} RCH_2NO_2$$

$$\xrightarrow[HNO_2]{(NaNO_2 + H_2SO_4)\ or}$$

$$R - \underset{\underset{N\ OH}{\|}}{C} - NO_2$$

Nitrolic acid

$$\downarrow NaOH$$

Blood Red colour

Secondary alcohols gives a blue color solution of pseudonitrol in sodium hydroxide in the Victor Meyer's test which is shown below :

$$R_2CHOH \xrightarrow[Red\ P + I_2]{Conc.\ HI\ or} R_2CHI \xrightarrow{AgNO_2} R_2CHNO_2$$

$$\xrightarrow[HNO_2]{(NaNO_2 + H_2SO_4)\ or}$$

$$R_2\underset{\underset{NO}{\|}}{C} - NO_2$$

Pseudonitrol

$$\downarrow NaOH$$

Blue colour

Tertiary alcohols form a colorless solution at the end of Victor Meyer's test which is shown below :

$$R_3C{-}OH \xrightarrow[Red\ P + I_2]{Conc.\ HI\ or} R_2C - I \xrightarrow{AgNO_2} R_3C - NO_2$$

$$\xrightarrow[HNO_2]{(NaNO_2 + H_2SO_4)\ or}$$

No reaction

$$\downarrow NaOH$$

colourless

**46. (3)** The $-COCH_3$ group is an electron withdrawing group which can stabilize the phenoxide ion.

**47. (4)** Williamson synthesis of ether is an example of nucleophilic substitution reaction.

$$RO^-Na^+ + R' - X \rightarrow RO - R' + NaX$$

**48. (2, 4)**

(p-cresol) $\xrightarrow[\bar{O}H]{CHCl_2}$ (Minor) + (Major)

$$CHCl_3 + \bar{O}H \longrightarrow :CCl_2 + H_2O + Cl^-$$

The complete mechanism of the given reaction is shown as follows :

$$\text{(p-cresol)} + \bar{O}H \longrightarrow \text{(phenoxide)} + H_2O$$

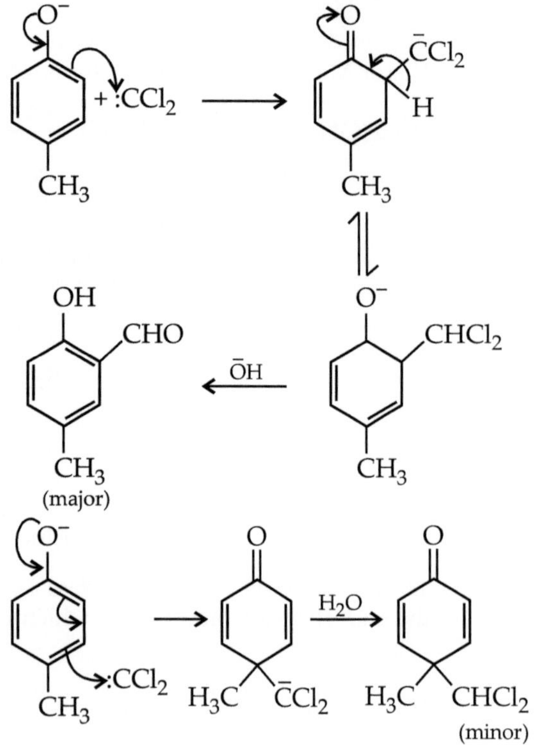

**49. (2)**

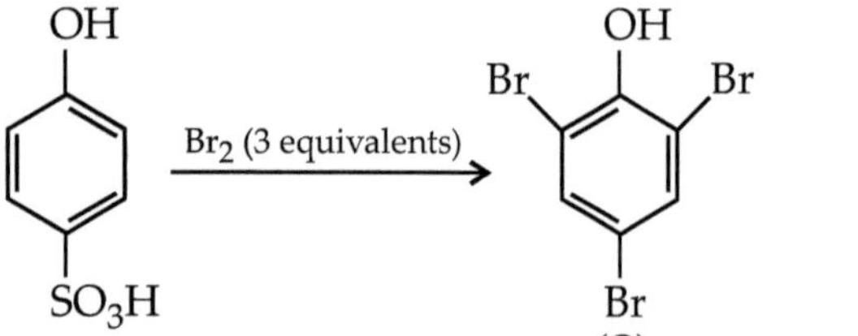

In the given reaction, bromination of the given compound occurs at the ortho and para position to the OH group after the removal of $SO_3H$ group.

**50. (2)** In the given reaction, hydrolysis of cyclic acetal takes place. The complete reaction is given as,

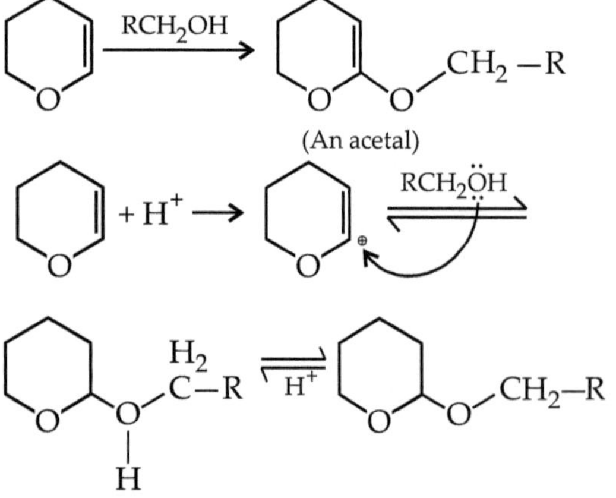

(An acetal)

**51. (4)** The following reaction gives phenol and methylbromide is given below :

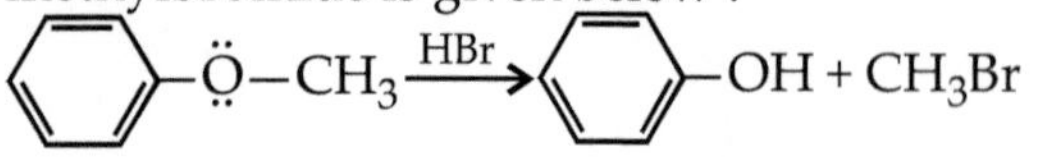

In the following reaction, $O-CH_3$ is a weaker bond than $O-C_6H_5$ because hybridization of carbon of phenyl group is $sp^2$. So this bond is more stable than $O-CH_3$. Thus, attack of HBr will lead to breaking of $O-CH_3$ bond to form bromomethane and phenol.

**52. (1,3)** The following reactions take place.

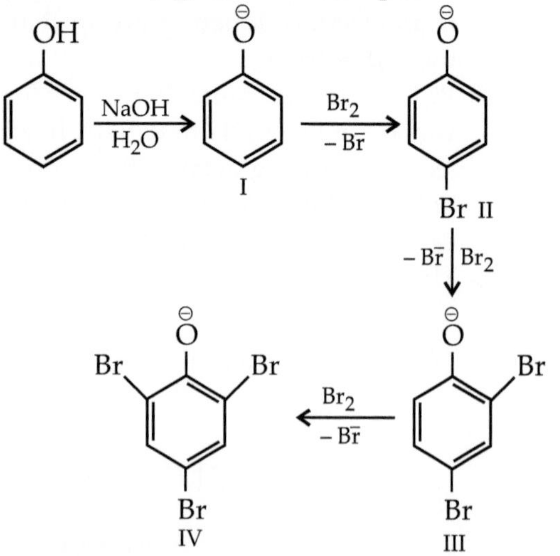

In the above equations, phenol is ortho-para directing. The intermediates formed are (I), (II) and (III) as shown in figure.
So, the correct options are 1 and 3.

**53. (4)** Phenol and carboxylic acids are soluble in aqueous NaOH.

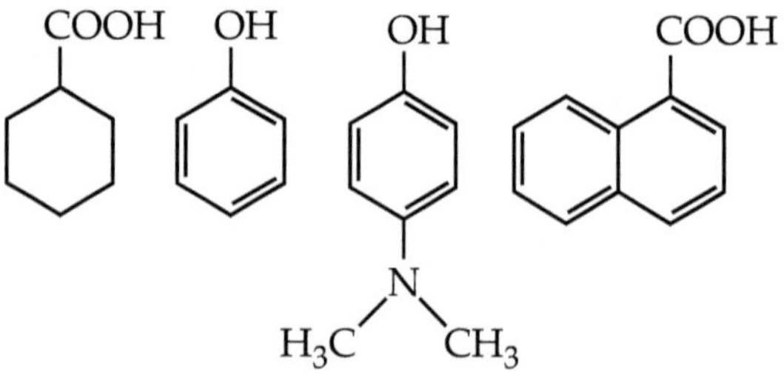

So, there are total four compounds that are soluble in aqueous NaOH.

**54. (2)** The order of priority of functional groups present in the given compound is $CN > Br > OH$. Therefore, the numbering of aromatic carbon chain starts from CN, bromide group will get second position and hydroxyl group will get fifth position. Hence, the IUPAC name of the given compound is 2-bromo-5-hydroxybenzonitrile.

**55. (4)** The stability of carbocation depends upon the number of hyperconjugative structures and resonance structures. The carbocation is more stable when resonance and hyperconjugative structures are more. Structure (I) is most stable as it has resonance structure and has six alpha hydrogen atoms.

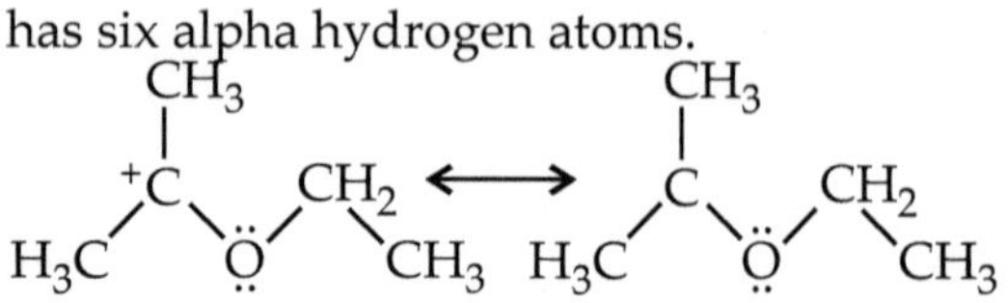

Structure (III) is resonance stabilized and has three alpha hydrogen atoms.

$$H_3C-\overset{H}{\underset{\oplus}{C}}-O-CH\overset{CH_3}{\underset{CH_3}{<}} \quad\longleftrightarrow\quad$$

$$H_3C-CH=\overset{\oplus}{O}-HC\overset{CH_3}{\underset{CH_3}{<}}$$

Structure (II) is not resonance stabilized and but, it has five alpha hydrogen atoms.

$$H_3C-\overset{H}{\underset{\oplus}{C}}-\overset{H_2}{O}-CH\overset{CH_3}{\underset{CH_3}{<}}$$

Structure (IV) is least stable as it has two alpha hydrogen atoms.

$$H_3C-\overset{\oplus}{C}-\overset{H_2}{C}-CH\overset{CH_3}{\underset{CH_3}{<}}$$

Hence, the stability order is  (I) > (III) > (II) > (IV).

**56. (1)** The dehydration reaction of H is expressed as,

$$\underset{\underset{H_2C-Ph}{|}}{\overset{\overset{OH}{|}}{Ph-C-CH_3}} \xrightarrow[-H_2O]{H^+} \underset{(I)}{\overset{\overset{CH_3}{|}}{Ph-C=CH-Ph}}$$

**57. (3)** In Reimer-Tiemann reaction, mixture of aq. NaOH + $CHCl_3$ is used as they give dichlorocarbene which acts as an electrophile.

$$\overset{\ominus}{OH}_{aq}+CHCl_3 \rightleftharpoons \overset{\ominus}{CCl_3}+H_2O$$

$$\overset{\ominus}{CCl_3} \longrightarrow \overset{\ominus}{Cl}+:CCl_2$$
$$\text{dichlorocarbene}$$

**58. (3)** In Reimer-Tiemann reaction, dichlorocarbene acts as an electrophile.

**59. (2)** The electrophilic attack of dichlorocarbene on phenoxide ion gives an intermediate.

$$+\;:CCl_2 \longrightarrow$$

**60. (4)** The reaction for the dissociation of $NaHCO_3$ is as follows :

$$NaHCO_3 \rightarrow Na^+ + HCO_3^-$$

The dissociation of sodium hydrogen carbonate results in the formation of $HCO_3^-$ (a salt of carbonic acid). Carbonic acid is a weak acid than benzene sulphonic acid and para nitrophenol.

Therefore, the reaction that takes place between benzene sulfonic acid and  $NaHCO_3$ is shown below :

$$+\;NaHCO_3 \longrightarrow +\;CO_2+H_2O$$

Similarly, the reaction that takes place between para-nitrophenol with $NaHCO_3$ is shown below.

$$+\;NaHCO_3 \longrightarrow +\;CO_2+H_2O$$

Thus, the gas evolved in the both cases is carbon dioxide ($CO_2$).

**61. (3)** Boiling point of a compound depends upon the molar mass. Generally, compound that contains large molar mass boils at high temperature. Therefore, hydroxy benzene will have least boiling point. In 1, 2-dihydroxy benzene, intramolecular hydogen bonding is present, whereas compound (III) exhibit intermolcular hydrogen bonding.

Therefore, the increasing order of boiling points of the given alcohols is,
$$IV < I < II < III$$

**62. (3)** The given reaction undergoes cumene hydroperoxide rearrangement. In this rearrangement, formation of acetone and phenol takes place.

The mechanism for the formation of product **P** and **Q** are shown below :

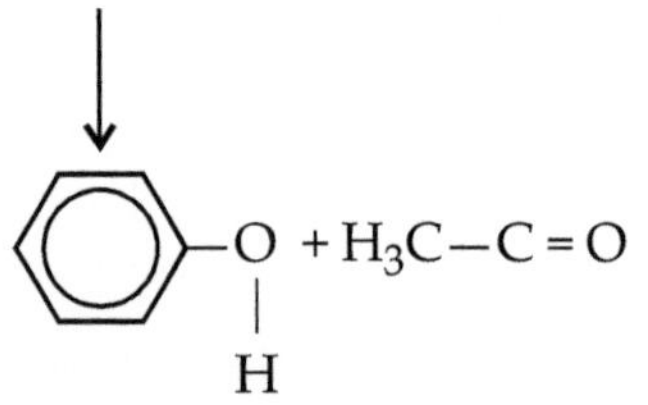

Therefore, the major product **P** and **Q** are,

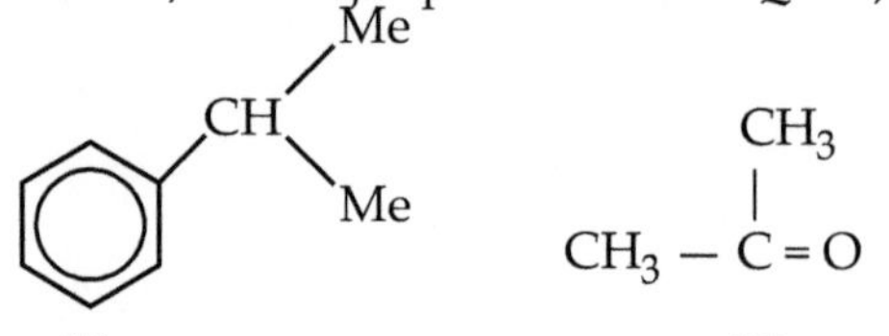

**(P)**

**(Q)**

**63.** The products **X** and **Y** have been shown in the conversion given below.

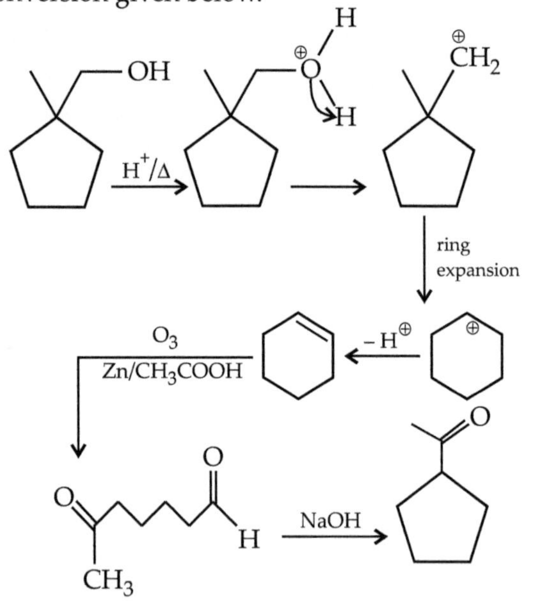

$$\xrightarrow{H^+/\Delta}$$

ring expansion

$$\xrightarrow[Zn/CH_3COOH]{O_3}$$

$$\xrightarrow{NaOH}$$

**64. (2)** The reaction that takes place between phenyl magnesium bromide and tertiary butanol is as follows :

$$C_6H_5MgBr + Me_3COH \rightarrow C_6H_6 + Me_3COMgBr$$

Thus, the reaction of phenyl magnesium bromide which is Grignard reagent with tertiary butanol forms benzene.

Thus, the correct option is (2).

**65. (1)** The reaction for the formation of cyclohexene with the help of cyclohexanol is as follows :

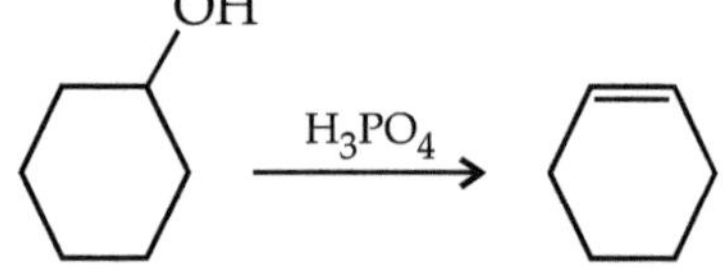

$$\xrightarrow{H_3PO_4}$$

In the above reaction, cyclohexanol reacts with concentrated phosphoric acid ($H_3PO_4$) to produce cyclohexene. In this reaction, conc. $H_3PO_4$ behaves like a dehydrating agent and results in the loss of water molecule from cyclohexanol. The loss of water molecule from cyclohexanol results in the formation

of an alkene that is cyclohexene. Thus, cyclohexene is best prepared by the reaction of cyclohexanol with conc. $H_3PO_4$.

Thus, the correct option is (1).

**66. (1)** The mechanism involved in the given reaction is shown below :

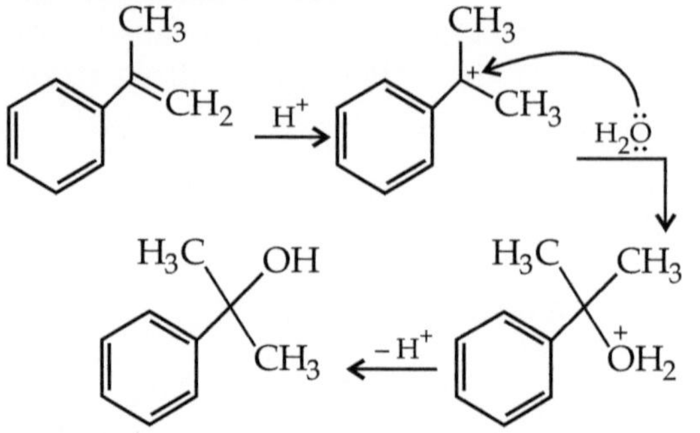

**67.** Anhydrous $AlCl_3$ is a good lewis acid. Thus, it is an electron deficient molecule due to which diethyl ether can donate its electron to anhydrous $AlCl_3$. In case of hydrous $AlCl_3$, water molecules are present which make it poor lewis acid. Therefore, anhydrous $AlCl_3$ is more soluble in diethyl ether.

**68.** The product formed by the reaction of 2-phenyl propanoic acid with 2-butanol is shown below :

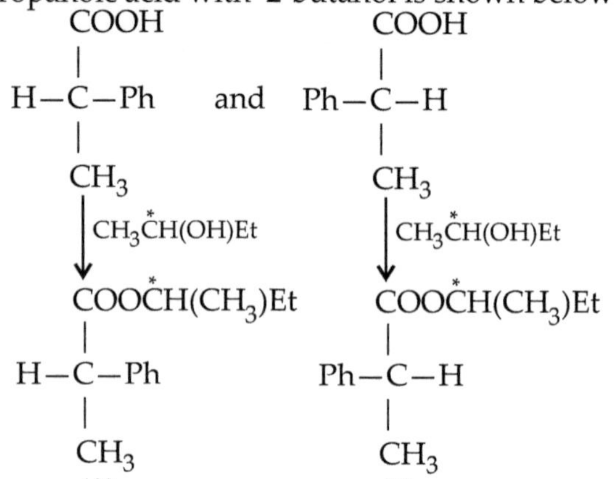

**(A)**          and          **(B)**

Both (1) and (2) are diastereomers. The two compounds which are neither super-imposable nor mirror images to each other are known as diastereomers.

**69. (1) (a)** The conversion of benzoic acid to fluorobenzoic acid is shown below :

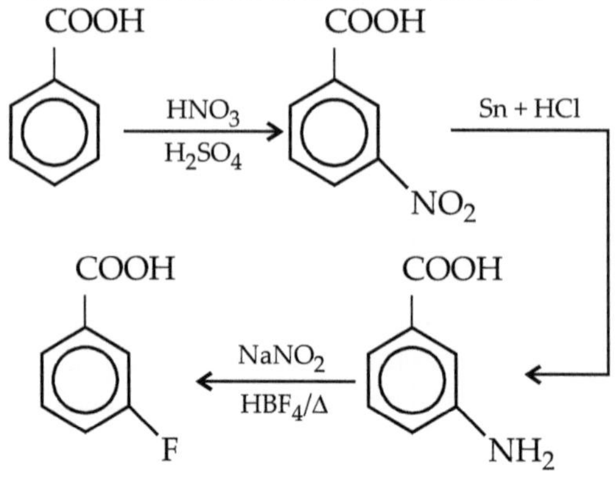

$$\xrightarrow[H_2SO_4]{HNO_3}$$

$$\xrightarrow{Sn + HCl}$$

$$\xleftarrow[HBF_4/\Delta]{NaNO_2}$$

**(b)** The conversion of phenol to aspirin is shown below :

$$\underset{\text{OH}}{\text{C}_6\text{H}_5} \xrightarrow[-\text{H}_2\text{O}]{\text{NaOH}} \underset{\text{O}^-\text{Na}^+}{\text{C}_6\text{H}_5} \xrightarrow[\text{(ii) H}^+]{\text{(i) CO}_2\,(140°\text{C, 6atm})} \text{(salicylic acid)} \xrightarrow{(\text{CH}_3\text{CO})_2\text{O}} \text{(aspirin)}$$

**70. (2)** The reaction of phenol with ethyl iodide in the presence of sodium ethoxide and anhydrous methanol results in the nucleophilic substitution in the ethyl iodide but not in the phenoxide ion because the electron density on the oxygen atom of ethoxide ion is more as compared to the oxygen atom in phenoxide ion due to which the nucleophilic attack of ethoxide ion is favorable. The reaction of eth-

oxide ion with ethyl iodide is shown below.

$$\text{H}_3\text{C}-\text{O}^- + \text{H}_3\text{C}-\text{CH}_2-\text{I} \longrightarrow \text{H}_3\text{C}-\text{O}-\text{CH}_2\text{CH}_3 + \text{:I}^-$$

Hence, the product formed in the given reaction is ethyl ethanoate.

**71. (1)** Ethyl ester reacts with Grignard reagent to give alcohol product.

The reaction for the formation of P is shown below :

$$R-\underset{\text{OC}_2\text{H}_5}{\overset{\text{O}}{\text{C}}} + \text{CH}_2\text{MgBr} \longrightarrow R-\underset{\text{CH}_3}{\overset{\text{O}^-\;\text{OC}_2\text{H}_5}{\text{C}}}$$

$$\xrightarrow{} \text{C}_3\text{H}_3\text{O}^- + R-\underset{\text{CH}_3}{\overset{\text{O}}{\text{C}}}$$

$$\xrightarrow{\text{CH}_3\text{MgX}} R-\underset{\text{CH}_3}{\overset{\text{XMgO}\;\;\text{CH}_3}{\text{C}}} \xrightarrow{\text{HCH/H}^+} R-\underset{\text{CH}_3}{\overset{\text{HO}\;\;\text{CH}_3}{\text{C}}}$$

Chapter

# |26| Aldehydes, Ketones and Carboxylic Acids

## QUESTIONS

1. The increasing order of the following compounds towards HCN addition is : **[2020, Main]**

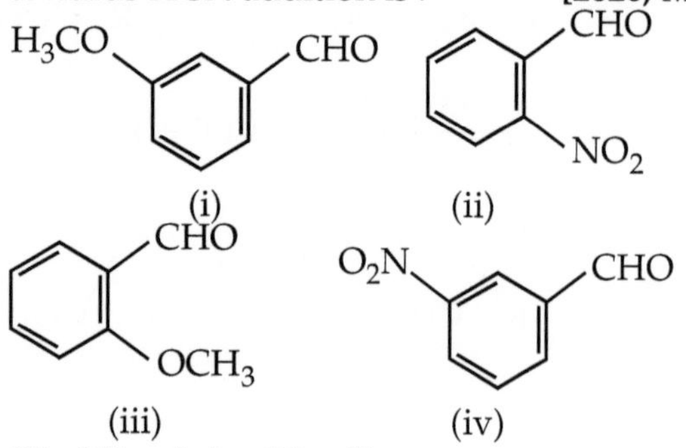

(1) (iii) < (iv) < (ii) < (i)
(2) (iii) < (iv) < (i) < (ii)
(3) (iii) < (i) < (iv) < (ii)
(4) (i) < (iii) < (iv) < (ii)

2. An organic compound [A], molecular formula $C_{10}H_{20}O_2$ was hydrolyzed with dilute sulphuric acid to give a carboxylic acid [B] and alcohol [C]. Oxidation of [C] with $CrO_3-H_2SO_4$ produced [B]. Which of the following structures are not possible for [A] ? **[2020, Main]**

(1) $(CH_3)_3-C-COOCH_2C(CH_3)_3$
(2) $CH_3CH_2CH_2COOCH_2CH_2CH_2CH_3$
(3) $CH_3-CH_2-CH(CH_3)-OCOCH_2CH(CH_3)-CH_2CH_3$
(4) $CH_3-CH_2-CH(CH_3)-COOCH_2-CH(CH_3)-CH_2CH_3$

3. The major products of the following reaction are :

$$CH_3-CH(CH_3)-CH(OSO_2CH_3)-CH_3 \xrightarrow[\text{(ii) } O_3/H_2O_2]{\text{(i) } KO^tBu/\Delta}$$

**[2020, Main]**

(1) 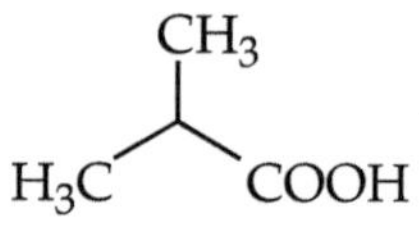 + HCOOH

(2) 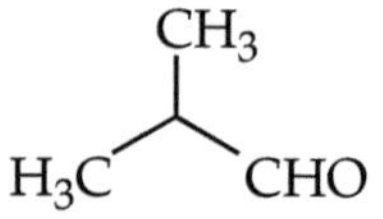 + HCHO

(3) 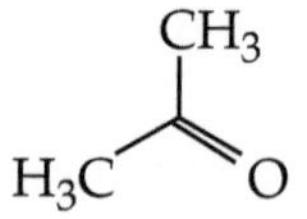 + $CH_3CHO$

(4) 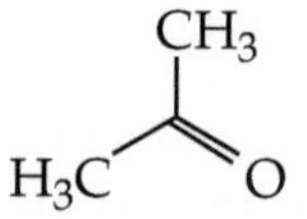 + $CH_3COOH$

4. Consider the following reaction :

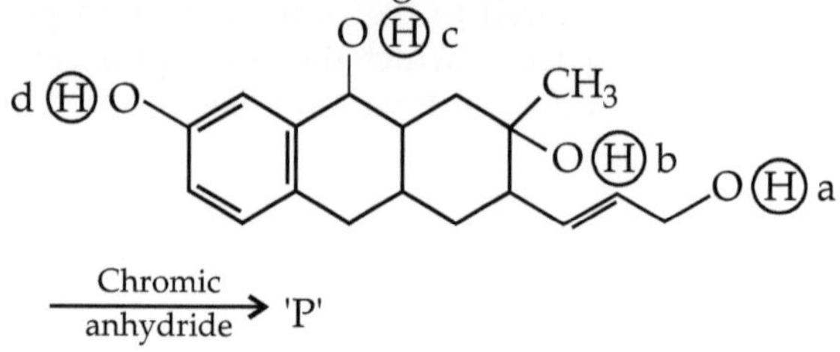

The product 'P' gives positive ceric ammonium nitrate test. This is because of the presence of which of these –OH group(s) ?

**[2020, Main]**

(1) (c) and (d) (2) (b) only
(3) (d) only (4) (b) and (d)

5. The major product of the following reaction is :

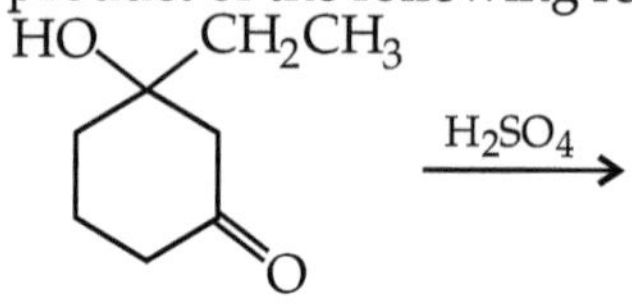

**[2020, Main]**

(1) 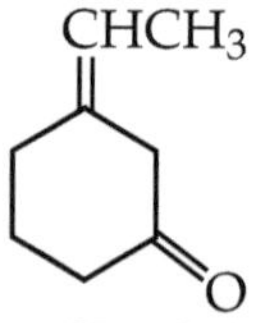

(2) 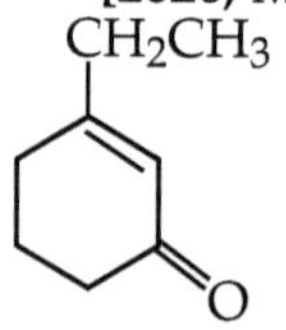

(3) 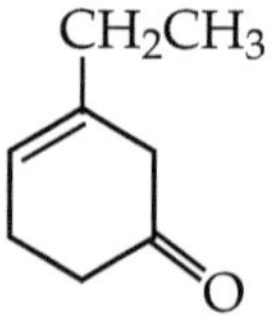

(4) 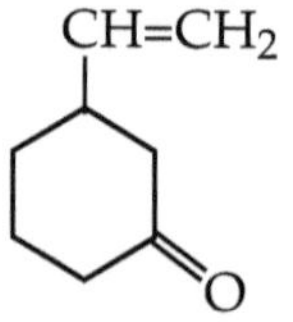

6. With respect to the compounds I-V, choose the correct statement(s). **[2020, Advanced]**

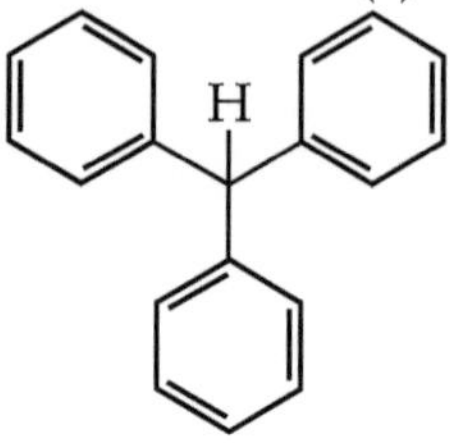

I

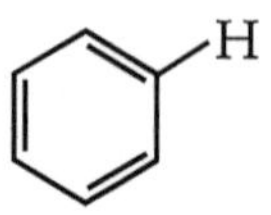

II

H–$CH_3$

III

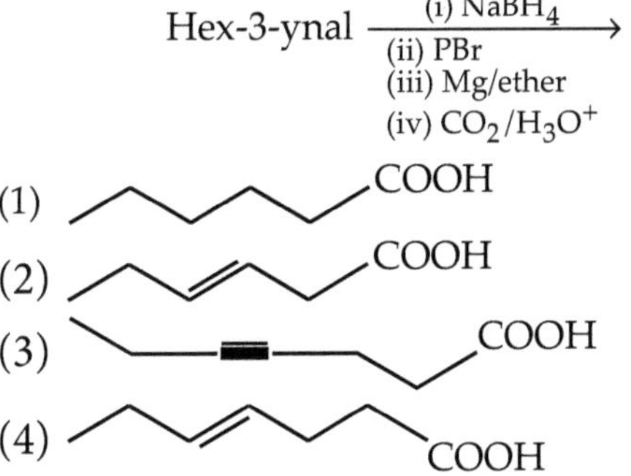

IV       V

(1) The acidity of compound I is due to delocalization in the conjugate base

(2) The conjugate base of compound IV is aromatic

(3) Compound II becomes more acidic, when it has a $-NO_2$ substitutent

(4) The acidity of compounds follows the order I > IV > V > II > III

**7.** The increasing order of the reactivity of the following compound in nucleophilic addition reaction is : **[2020, Main]**

Propanal, Benzaldehyde, Propanone, Butanone

(1) Butanone < Propanone < Benzaldehyde < Propanal

(2) Benzaldehyde < Butanone < Propanone < Propanal

(3) Propanal < Propanone < Butanone < Benzaldehyde

(4) Benzaldehyde < Propanal < Propanone < Butanone

**8.** Identify (A) in the following reaction sequence : **[2020, Main]**

(A) $\xrightarrow[\substack{\text{(ii) } H^+/H_2O/H_3O^+ \\ \text{(iii) Conc. } H_2SO_4/\Delta}]{\text{(i) } CH_3MgBr}$ (B) $\xrightarrow{O_3/Zn, H_2O}$

Gives positive iodoform test

(1)

(2)

(3)

(4)

**9.** What is the product of following reaction ?
**[2020, Main]**

Hex-3-ynal $\xrightarrow[\substack{\text{(ii) PBr} \\ \text{(iii) Mg/ether} \\ \text{(iv) CO}_2/H_3O^+}]{\text{(i) NaBH}_4}$ ?

(1)    COOH

(2)    COOH

(3)    COOH

(4)    COOH

**10.** The correct match between Item-I (starting material) and Item-II (reagent) for the preparation of benzaldehyde is : **[2020, Main]**

| Item-I | Item-II |
|---|---|
| (I) Benzene | (P) HCl and $SnCl_2$, $H_3O^+$ |
| (II) Benzonitrile | (Q) $H_2$, Pd-BaSO$_4$, S and quinoline |
| (III) Benzoyl Chloride | (R) CO, HCl and $AlCl_3$ |

(1) (I)-(Q), (II)-(R) and (III)-(P)

(2) (I)-(R), (II)-(Q) and (III)-(P)

(3) (I)-(R), (II)-(P) and (III)-(Q)

(4) (I)-(P), (II)-(Q) and (III)-(R)

**11.** The reactions leading to the formation of 1, 3, 5-trimethylbenzene is (are) : **[2018, Advanced]**

(1) $\xrightarrow[\Delta]{\text{Conc. } H_2SO_4}$

(2) Me ≡ H $\xrightarrow[873 \text{ K}]{\text{heated iron tube}}$

(3) $\xrightarrow[\substack{\text{2. } H_3O^+ \\ \text{3. sodalime, } \Delta}]{\text{1. Br}_2, \text{ NaOH}}$

(4) $\xrightarrow{\text{Zn/Hg, HCl}}$

**Paragraph for Question 12 and 13**

Treatment of benzene with CO/HCl in the presence of anhydrous $AlCl_3$/CuCl followed by reaction with $Ac_2O$/NaOAc gives compound X as the major product. Compound X upon reaction with $Br_2$/$Na_2CO_3$, followed by heating at 473 K with moist KOH furnishes Y as the major product. Reaction of X with $H_2$/Pd-C, followed by $H_3PO_4$ treatment gives Z as the major product.

**12.** The compound Y is : **[2018, Advanced]**

(1)    COBr

(2)    OH, Br

(3)    (4)

**13.** The compound Z is :     **[2018, Advanced]**

(1)    (2)

(3)    (4)

### Paragraph for Question 14

A organic acid P ($C_{11}H_{12}O_2$) can easily be oxidised to a dibasic acid which reacts with ethyleneglycol to produce a polymer dacron. Upon ozonolysis, P gives an aliphatic ketone as one of the products. P undergoes the following reaction sequences to furnish R *via* Q. The compound P also undergoes another set of reactions to produce S.

$$S \xleftarrow[\substack{4.\ CHCl_3/KOH,\ \Delta \\ 5.\ H_2/Pd\text{-}C}]{\substack{1.\ H_2/Pd\text{-}C \\ 2.\ NH_3/\Delta \\ 3.\ Br_2/NaOH}} P \xrightarrow[\substack{3.\ MeMgBr,\ CdCl_2 \\ 4.\ NaBH_4}]{\substack{1.\ H_2/Pd\text{-}C \\ 2.\ SOCl_2}} Q \xrightarrow[\substack{3.\ CO_2\ (dry\ ice) \\ 4.\ H_3O^+}]{\substack{1.\ HCl \\ 2.\ Mg/Et_2O}} R$$

**14.** The compound R is :     **[2018, Advanced]**

(1)    (2)

(3)    (4)

**15.** The increasing order of the acidity of the following carboxylic acids is :     **[2018, Main]**

I    II    III    IV

(1) I < III < II < IV    (2) IV < II < III < I
(3) II < IV < III < I    (4) III < II < IV < I

**16.** The main reduction product of the following compound with $NaBH_4$ in methanol is :     **[2018, Main]**

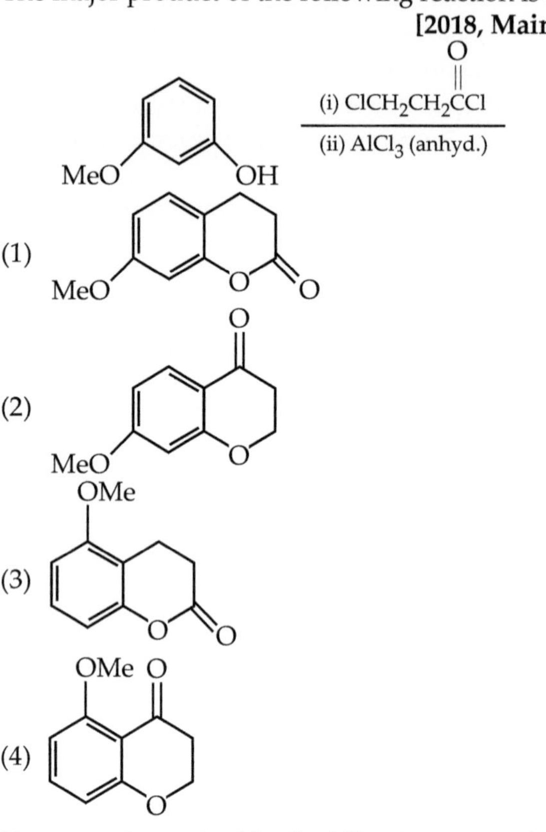

(1)    (2)

(3)    (4)

**17.** The major product of the following reaction is :     **[2018, Main]**

$$\xrightarrow[\text{(ii) } AlCl_3\ (anhyd.)]{\text{(i) } ClCH_2CH_2\overset{O}{\overset{\|}{C}}Cl}$$

(1)    (2)

(3)    (4)

**18.** The reagents required for the following conversion are :     **[2018, Main]**

(1) (i) $B_2H_6$     (ii) $SnCl_2/HCl$
     (iii) $H_3O^+$
(2) (i) $LiAlH_4$     (ii) $H_3O^+$
(3) (i) $B_2H_6$     (ii) DIBAL-H
     (iii) $H_3O^+$
(4) (i) $NaBH_4$     (ii) Raney Ni, $H_2$
     (iii) $H_3O^+$

**19.** Which of the following compounds will most readily be dehydrated to give alkene under acidic condition ?     **[2018, Main]**

(1) 1-Pentanol
(2) 4-Hydroxypentan-2-one
(3) 3-Hydroxypentan-2-one
(4) 2-Hydroxycyclopentanone

**20.** The major product B formed in the following reaction sequence is : **[2018, Main]**

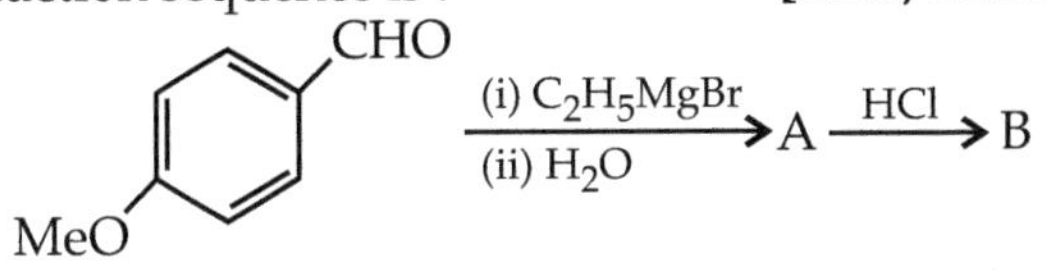


(1) 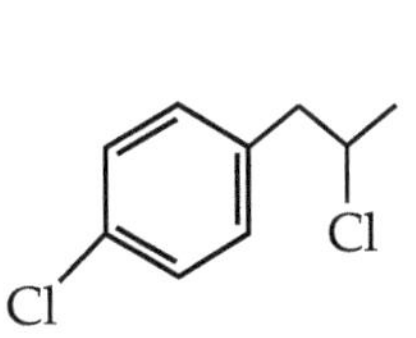

(2) 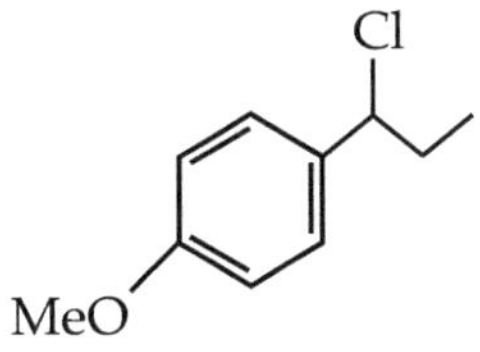

(3) 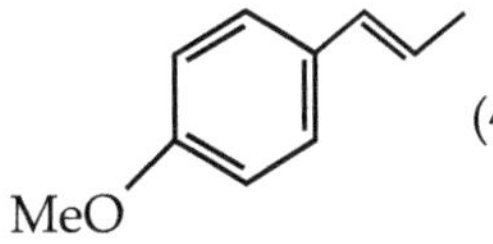

(4) 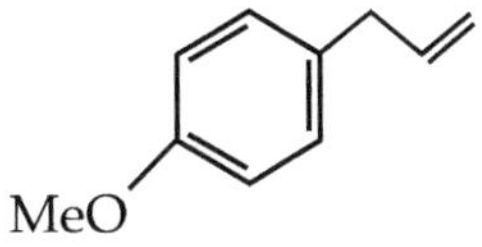


**21.** The major product of the following reaction is : **[2018, Main]**

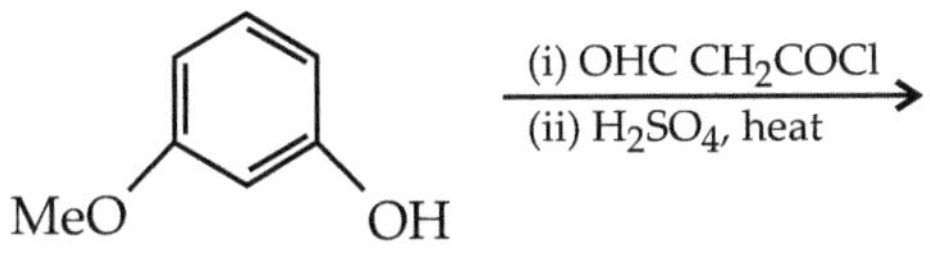


(1) 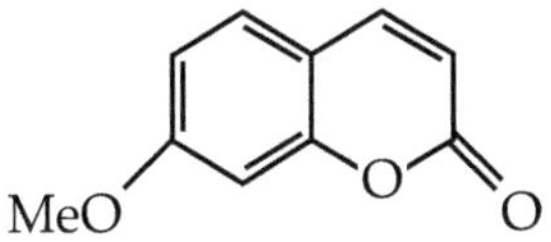

(2) 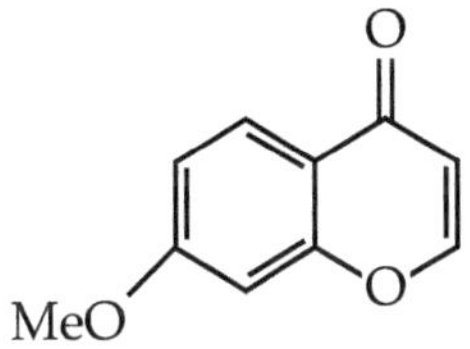

(3) 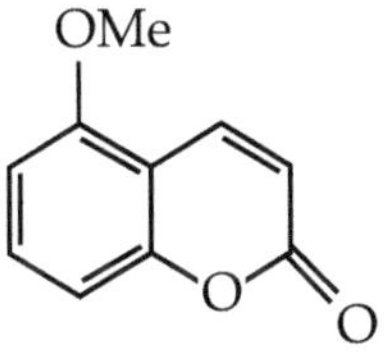

(4) 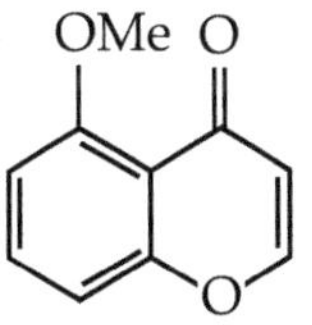


**Answer Q. 22 and Q. 23 by appropriately matching the information given in three columns of the following table.**

Columns 1, 2 and 3 contain starting materials, reaction conditions and type of reactions, respectively.

| Column 1 | Column 2 | Column 3 |
|---|---|---|
| (I) Toluene | (i) $NaOH/Br_2$ | (P) Condensation |
| (II) Acetophenone | (ii) $Br_2$/hv | (Q) Carboxylation |
| (III) Benzaldehyde | (ii) $(CH_3CO)_2O/CH_3COOK$ | (R) Substitution |
| (IV) Phenol | $NaOH/CO_2$ | (S) Haloform |

**22.** For the synthesis of benzoic acid, the only CORRECT combination is : **[2017, Advanced]**

(1) (II) (i) (S)
(2) (IV) (ii) (P)
(3) (I) (iv) (Q)
(4) (III) (iv) (R)

**23.** The only CORRECT combination that gives two different carboxylic acids is : **[2017, Advanced]**

(1) (II) (iv) (R)
(2) (IV) (iii) (Q)
(3) (III) (iii) (P)
(4) (I) (i) (S)

**Paragraph for Question 24 and 25**

The reaction of compound P with $CH_3MgBr$ (excess) in $(C_2H_5)_2O$ followed by addition of $H_2O$ gives Q. The compound Q on treatment with $H_2SO_4$ at 0°C gives R. The reaction of R with $CH_3COCl$ in the presence of anhydrous $AlCl_3$ in $CH_2Cl_2$ followed by treatment with $H_2O$ produces compound S. [Et in compound P is ethyl group]

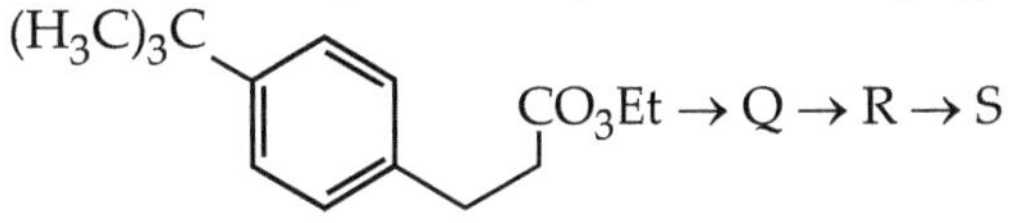


P

**24.** The product S is : **[2017, Advanced]**

(1) 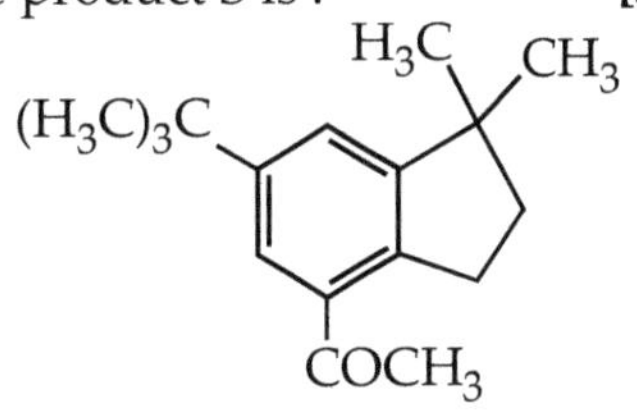

(2) 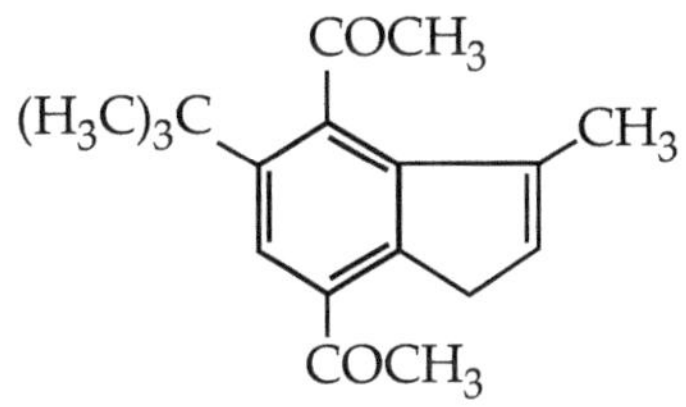

(3) 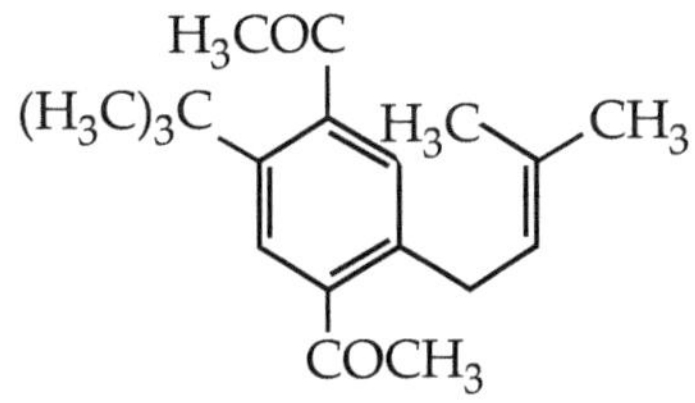

(4) 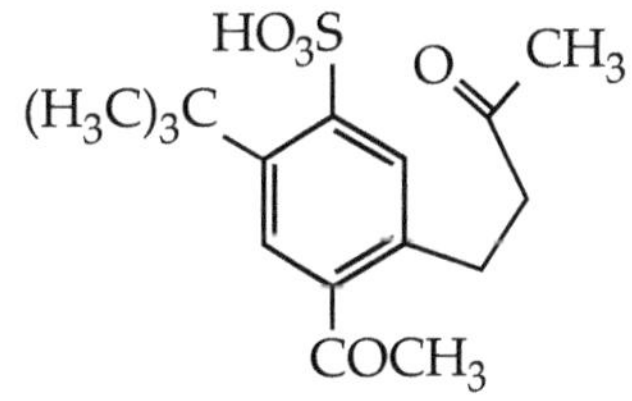


**25.** The reactions, Q to R and R to S, are : **[2017, Advanced]**

(1) Dehydration and Friedel-Crafts acylation
(2) Aromatic sulfonation and Friedel-Crafts acylation

(3) Friedel-Crafts alkylation, dehydration and Friedel-Crafts acylation

(4) Friedel-Crafts alkylation and Friedel-Crafts acylation

**26.** The correct sequence of reagents for the following conversion will be : **[2017, Main]**

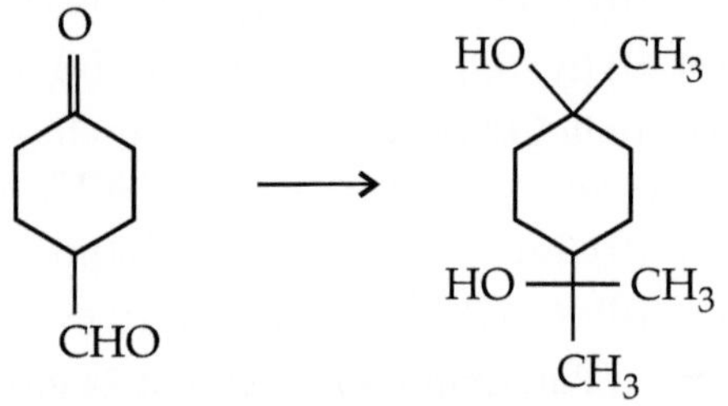


(1) $CH_3MgBr$, $[Ag(NH_3)_2]^+OH^-$, $H^+/CH_3OH$

(2) $[Ag(NH_3)_2]^+OH^-$, $CH_3MgBr$, $H^+/CH_3OH$

(3) $[Ag(NH_3)_2]^+OH^-$, $H^+/CH_3OH$, $CH_3MgBr$

(4) $CH_3MgBr$, $H^+/CH_3OH$, $[Ag(NH_3)_2]^+OH^-$

**27.** The major product obtained in the following reaction is : **[2017, Main]**

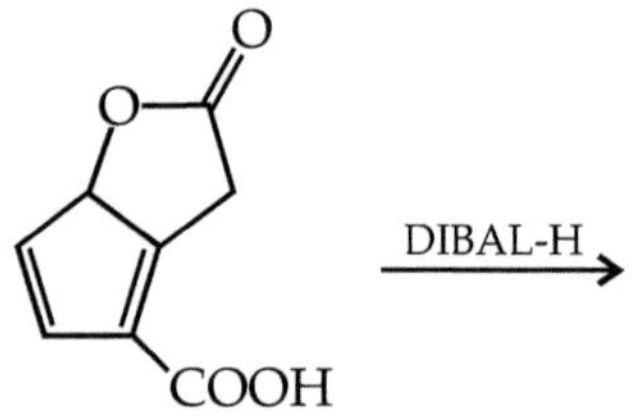


(1) 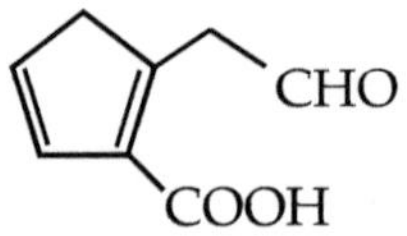


(2) 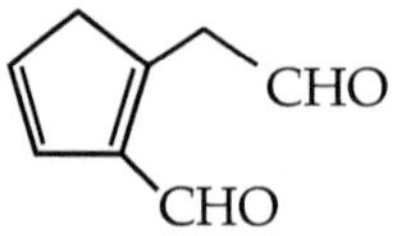


(3) 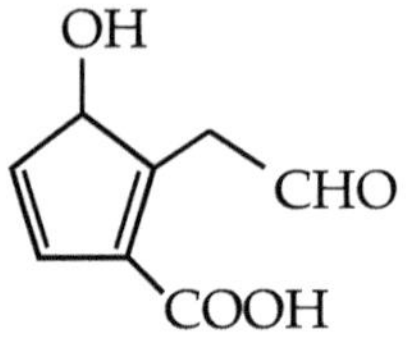


(4) 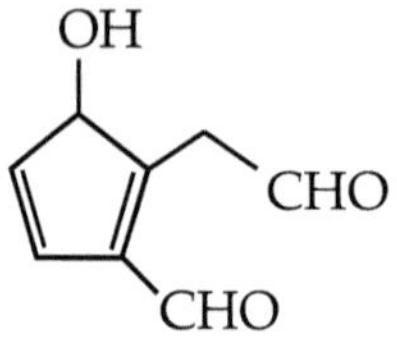


**28.** Tha major product expected from the following reaction is : **[2017, Main]**

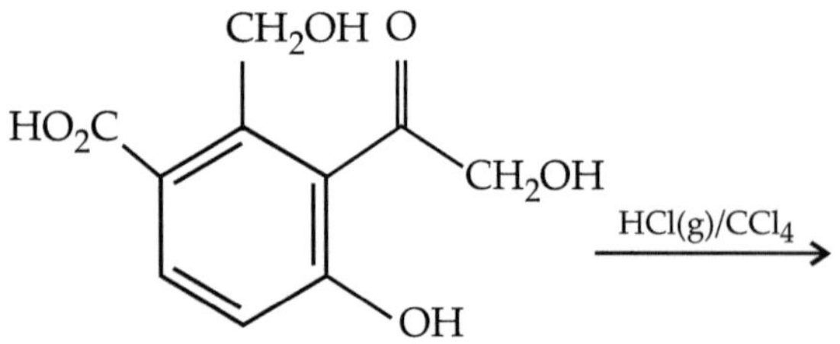


(1) 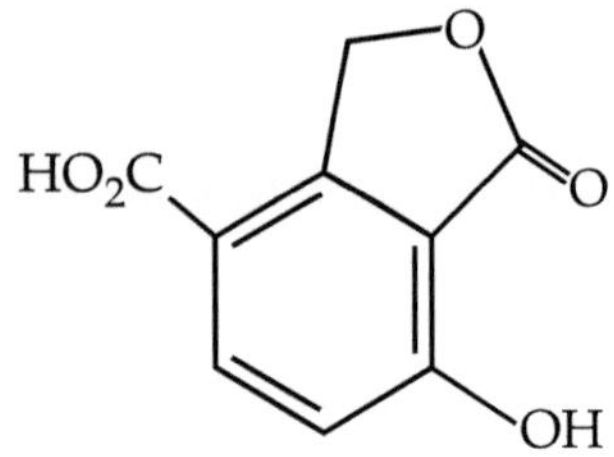


(2) 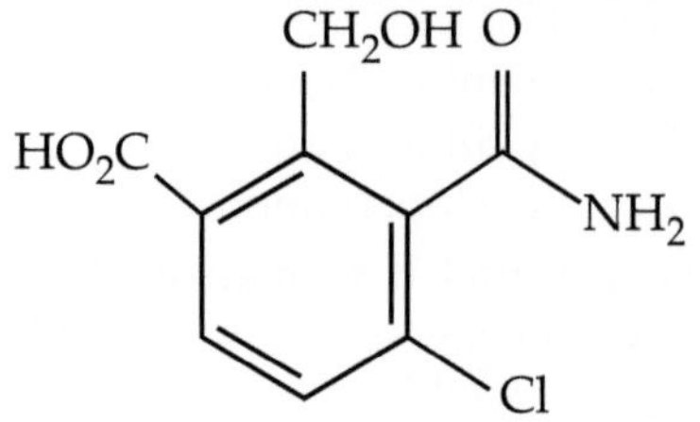


(3) 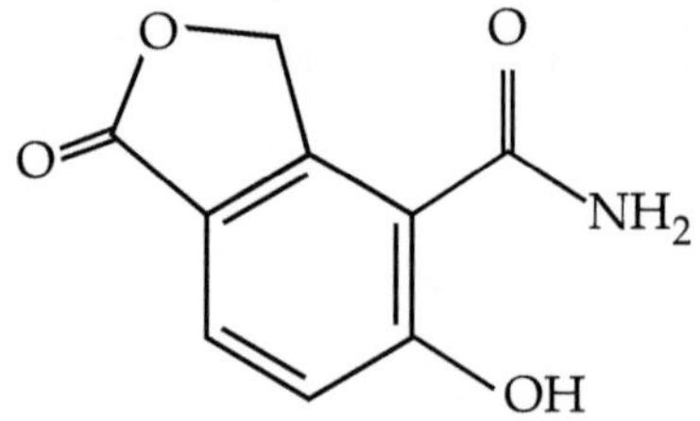


(4) 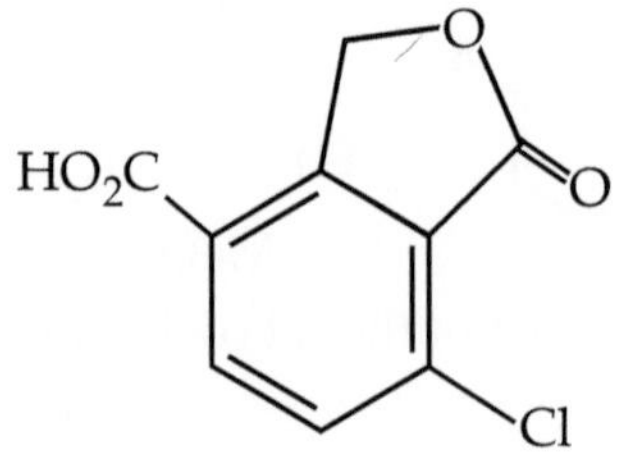


**29.** A compound of molecular formula $C_8H_8O_2$ reacts with actophenone to form a single cross-aldol product in the presence of base. The same compound on reaction with conc. NaOH forms benzyl alcohol as one of the products. The structure of the compound is : **[2017, Main]**

(1) 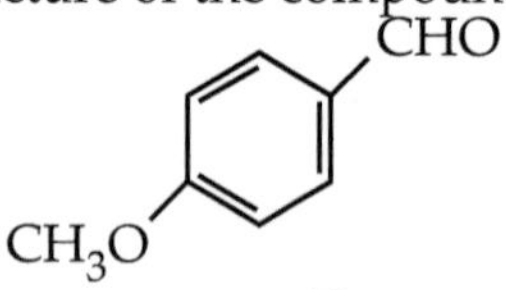


(2) 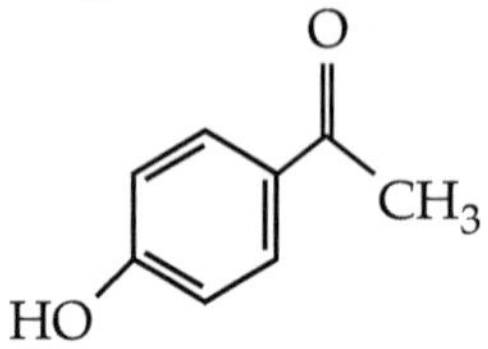


(3) 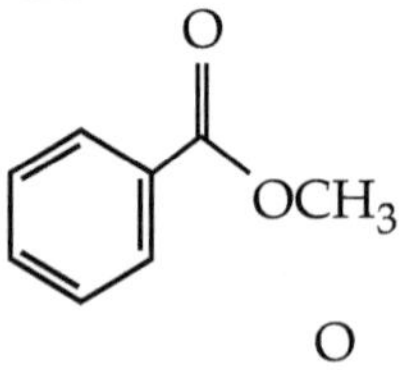


(4) 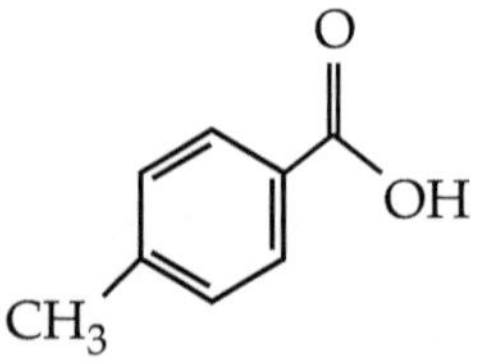


**30.** Which of the following compounds will show highest dipole moment ? **[2017, Main]**

(I) 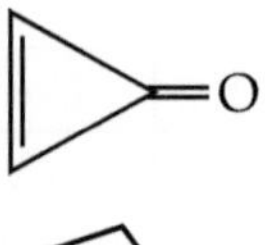


(II) 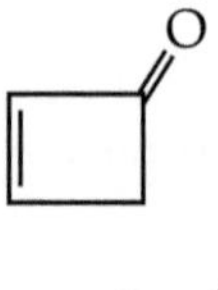


(III) 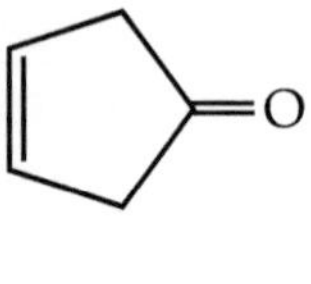


(IV) 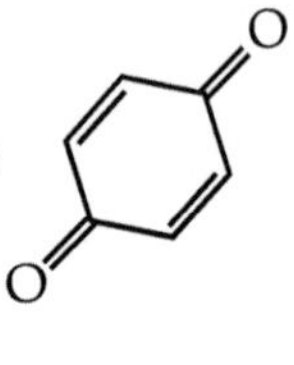

(1) (I)      (2) (II)
(3) (III)     (4) (IV)

**31.** Positive Tollen's test is observed for :

**[2016, Advanced]**

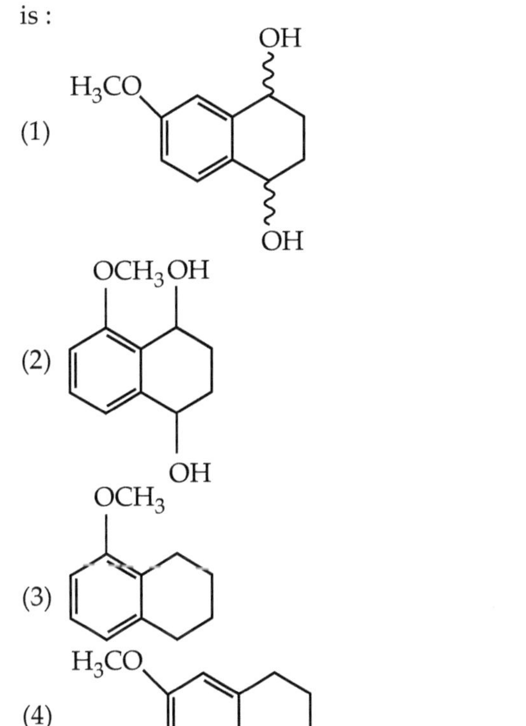

(1)    (2)    (3)    (4)

**32.** The correct statements about the following reaction sequence is/are :    **[2016, Advanced]**

Cumene $(C_9H_{12})$ $\xrightarrow[\text{(ii)}\,H_3O^+]{\text{(i)}\,O_2}$ P

$\xrightarrow{CHCl_3/NaOH}$ Q (major) + R (minor)

Q $\xrightarrow[PhCH_2Br]{NaOH}$ S

(1) R is steam volatile
(2) Q gives dark violet coloration with 1% aqueous $FeCl_3$ solution
(3) S gives yellow precipitate with 2, 4-dinitrophenylhydrazine
(4) S gives dark violet coloration with 1% aqueous $FeCl_3$ solution

**33.** The major product of the following reaction sequence is :    **[2016, Advanced]**

$\xrightarrow[\text{(ii) HCHO/H}^+\text{ (catalytic amount)}]{\text{(i) HCHO (excess)/NaOH, heat}}$

(1)    (2)    (3)    (4)

**34.** Reagents which can be used to bring about the following transformation is/are : **[2016, Advanced]**

(1) $LiAlH_4$ in $(C_2H_5)_2O$
(2) $BH_3$ in THF
(3) $NaBH_4$ in $C_2H_5OH$
(4) Raney $Ni/H_2$ in THF

**35.** Bouveault-Blanc reduction reaction involves :

**[2016, Main]**

(1) Reduction of an acyl halide with $H_2/Pd$
(2) Reduction of an ester with $Na/C_2H_5OH$
(3) Reduction of a carbonyl compound with Na/Hg and HCl
(4) Reduction of an anhydride with $LiAlH_4$

**36.** Consider the reaction sequence below :

**[2016, Main]**

$\xrightarrow[AlCl_3]{\text{Succinic anhydride}}$ A $\xrightarrow[\text{reduction}]{\text{Clemmenson's}}$ X

is :

(1)    (2)    (3)    (4)

**37.** The correct statement about the synthesis of erythritol $C_4H_{10}O_4$ used in the preparation of PETN is : **[2016, Main]**
(1) The synthesis requires four aldol condensations between methanol and ethanol
(2) The synthesis requires two aldol condensations and two Cannizzaro reactions
(3) The synthesis requires three aldol condensations and one Cannizzaro reaction
(4) Alpha hydrogens of ethanol and methanol are involved in this reaction

**38.** The absolute configuration of    **[2016, Main]**

is :
(1) (2R, 2S)      (2) (2S, 2R)
(3) (2S, 3S)      (4) (2R, 3R)

**39.** The total number of stereoisomers that can exist for M is : **[2015, Advanced]**

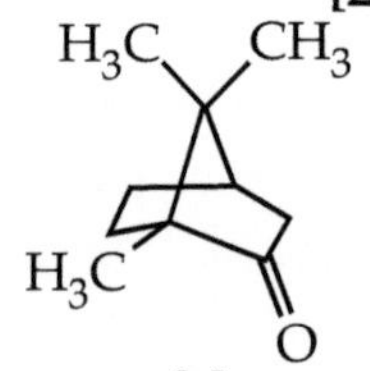

**40.** The major product of the following reaction is : **[2015, Advanced]**

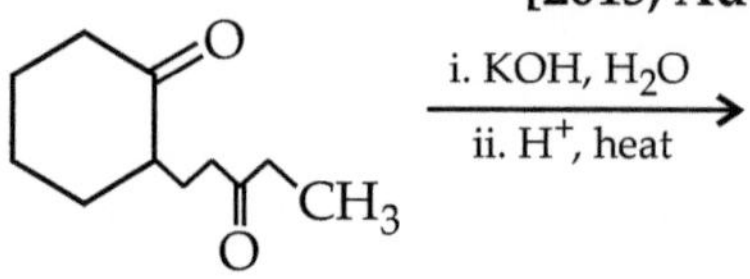

i. KOH, $H_2O$
ii. $H^+$, heat

(1)

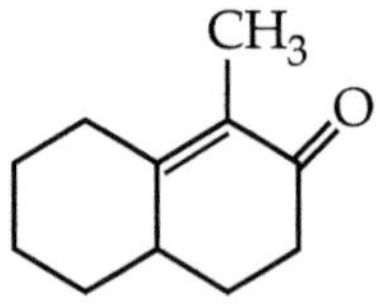

(2)

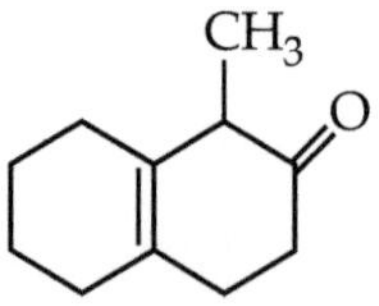

(3)

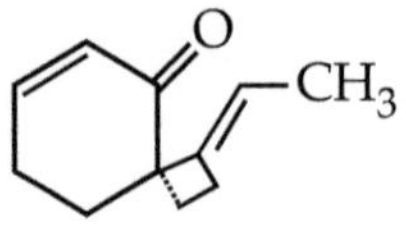

(4)

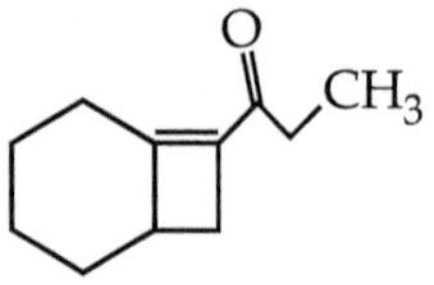

**41.** Among the following, the number of reactions that produces benzaldehyde is : **[2015, Advanced]**

(1) 
CO, HCl / Anhydrous $AlCl_3$/CuCl

(2) 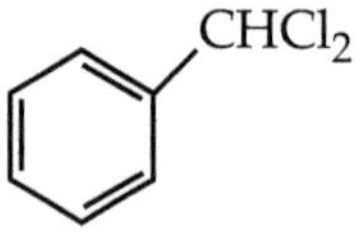 $CHCl_2$
$H_3O$ / 100°C

(3) 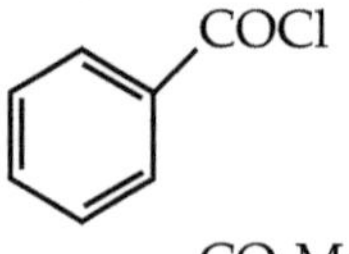 COCl
$H_2$ / Pd-BaSO$_4$

(4) 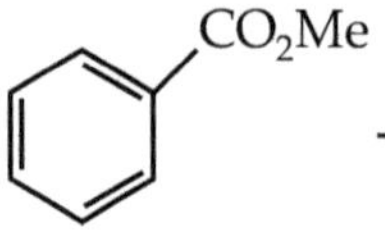 $CO_2Me$
DIBAL-H / Toluene, – 78°C / $H_2O$

**42.** In the following sequence of reactions : **[2015, Main]**

$$\text{Toluene} \xrightarrow{KMnO_4} A \xrightarrow{SOCl_2} B \xrightarrow[BaSO_4]{H_2/Pd} C,$$

the product C is :
(1) $C_6H_5COOH$
(2) $C_6H_5CH_3$
(3) $C_6H_5CH_2OH$
(4) $C_6H_5CHO$

**43.** In the presence of a small amount of phosphorous, aliphatic carboxylic acids react with chlorine or bromine to yield a compound in which α-hydrogen has been replaced by halogen. This reaction is known as : **[2015, Main]**
(1) Wolf-Kischner reaction
(2) Etard reaction
(3) Hell-Volhard-Zelinsky reaction
(4) Rosenmund reaction

**44.** Which of the following pairs of compounds are positional isomers ? **[2015, Main]**

(1) $CH_3 - CH_2 - CH_2 - CH_2 - CHO$

and $CH_3 - CH_2 - CH_2 - \overset{\overset{O}{||}}{C} - CH_3$

(2) $CH_3 - CH_2 - CH_2 - \overset{\overset{||}{O}}{C} - CH_3$ and

$CH_3 - \underset{\underset{CH_3}{|}}{CH} - CH_2 - CHO$

(3) $CH_3 - CH_2 - CH_2 - \overset{\overset{||}{O}}{C} - CH_3$ and

$CH_3 - CH_2 - \overset{\overset{||}{O}}{C} - CH_2 - CH_3$

(4) $CH_3 - CH_2 - \overset{\overset{||}{O}}{C} - CH_2 - CH_3$ and

$\underset{CH_3}{\overset{CH_3}{>}} CH - CH_2 - CHO$

**45.** In the reaction sequence **[2015, Main]**
$$2CH_3CHO \xrightarrow{OH^-} A \xrightarrow{\Delta} B;$$
the product B is :
(1) $CH_3 - CH_2 - CH_2 - CH_2 - OH$
(2) $CH_3 - CH = CH - CHO$
(3) $CH_3 - \overset{\overset{O}{||}}{C} - CH_3$
(4) $CH_3 - CH_2 - CH_2 - CH_3$

**46.** Consider all possible isomeric ketones, including stereoisomers, of MW = 100. All these isomers are independently reacted with $NaBH_4$ (**Note :** stereoisomers are also reacted separately). The total number of ketones that will give a racemic products is/are......... **[2014, Advanced]**

**47.** The major product in the following reaction is : **[2014, Advanced]**

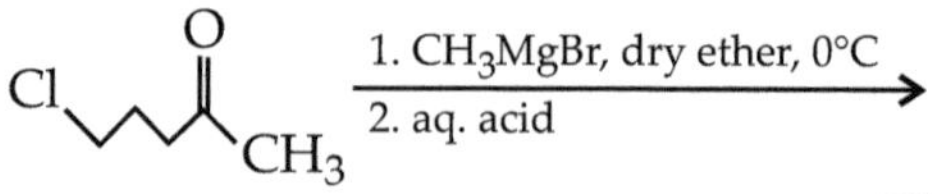

1. 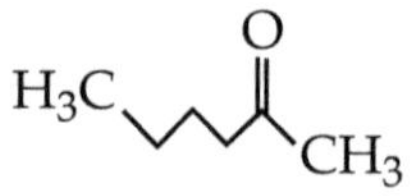 $CH_3MgBr$, dry ether, 0°C
2. aq. acid

(1)

(2)

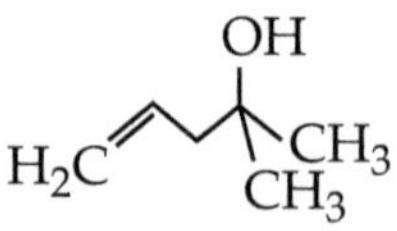

(3)

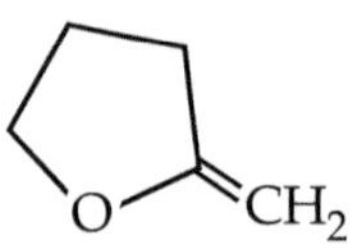

(4)

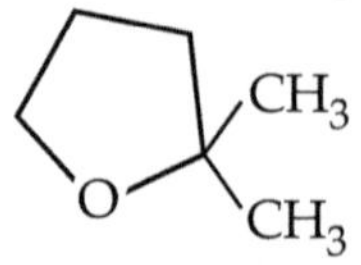

**48.** The correct statement with respect to product Y is : **[2014, Advanced]**
(1) It gives a positive Tollens test and is a functional isomer of X
(2) It gives a positive Tollens test and is a

geometrical isomer of X

(3) It gives a positive iodoform test and is a functional isomer of X

(4) It gives a positive iodoform test and is a geometrical isomer of X

**49.** Different possible thermal decomposition pathways for peroxyesters are shown below. Match each pathway from List I with an appropriate structure from List II and select the correct answer using the code given below the lists.

**[2014, Advanced]**

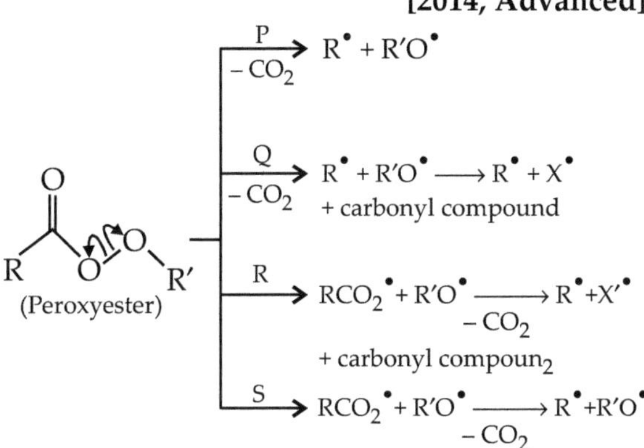

**List-I**

P. Pathway P

Q. Pathway Q

R. Pathway R

S. Pathway S

**List-II**

$C_6H_5CH_2$—O—O—COCH$_3$ (structure 1)

$C_6H_5CH_2$—O—O—C(CH$_3$)$_2$CH$_2$C$_6$H$_5$ (structure 2)

$C_6H_5$—CO—O—O—CH$_3$ (structure 3)

$C_6H_5$—CO—O—O—C(CH$_3$)$_2$C$_6$H$_5$ (structure 4)

**Codes :**

| | P | Q | R | S |
|---|---|---|---|---|
| (1) | 1 | 3 | 4 | 2 |
| (2) | 2 | 4 | 3 | 1 |
| (3) | 4 | 1 | 2 | 3 |
| (4) | 3 | 2 | 1 | 4 |

**50.** Sodium phenoxide when heated with $CO_2$ under pressure at 125°C yields a product which on acetylation produces C.

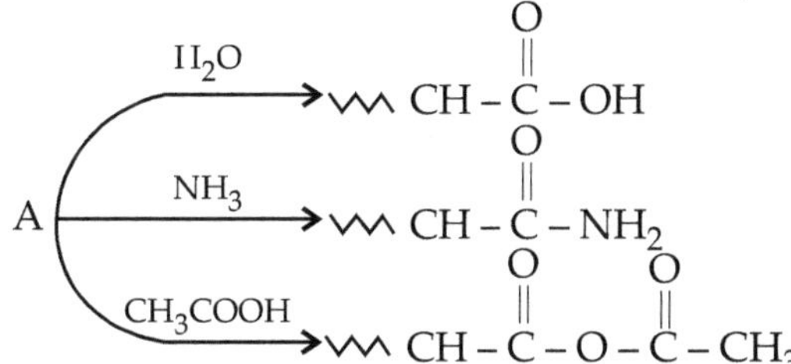

The major product C would be : **[2014, Main]**

(1) structure with O COCH$_3$ and COOH on benzene ring

(2) structure with OH, COOH and COCH$_3$ on benzene ring

(3) structure with OH and COOCH$_3$ on benzene ring

(4) structure with O COCH$_3$ and COOH on benzene ring

**51.** In the reaction,
$$CH_3COOH \xrightarrow{\text{LiAlH}_4} A \xrightarrow{\text{PCl}_5} B \xrightarrow{\text{Alc.KOH}} C,$$
the product C is : **[2014, Main]**
(1) Acetaldehyde
(2) Acetylene
(3) Ethylene
(4) Acetyl chloride

**52.** Which one of the following reactions will not result in the formation of carbon-carbon bond ?

**[2014, Main]**

(1) Reimer-Tiemann reaction
(2) Friedel Craft's acylation
(3) Wurtz reaction
(4) Cannizzaro reaction

**53.** Which is the major product formed when acetone is heated with iodine and potassium hydroxide ?

**[2014, Main]**

(1) Iodoacetone
(2) Acetic acid
(3) Iodoform
(4) Acetophenone

**54.** An oganic compound A, $C_5H_8O$; reacts with $H_2O$, $NH_3$ and $CH_3COOH$ as described below :

**[2014, Main]**

A:
- $H_2O$ → CH–CO–OH
- $NH_3$ → CH–CO–NH$_2$
- $CH_3COOH$ → CH–CO–O–CO–CH$_3$

A is :

(1) $CH_3CH=C(CH_3)-CHO$

(2) $CH_2=CHCH(CH_3)-CHO$

(3) $CH_3-CH_2-C(CH_3)=C=O$

(4) $CH_3-CH_2-C(CH_2H)-C=O$

**55.** Tischenko reaction is a modification of :

**[2014, Main]**

(1) Aldol condensation
(2) Claisen condensation
(3) Cannizzaro reaction
(4) Pinalol-pinacolene reaction

**56.** Which one of the followng acids does not exhibit optical isomerism ? **[2014, Main]**
(1) Lactic acid (2) Tartaric acid
(3) Maleic acid (4) $\alpha$-amino acids

**57.** Phthalic acid reacts with resorcinol in the presence of concentrated $H_2SO_4$ to give : **[2014, Main]**
(1) Phenolphthalein (2) Alizarin
(3) Coumarin (4) Fluorescein

**58.** The major product formed when 1, 1, 1-trichloro-propane is treated with aqueous potassium hydroxide is : **[2014, Main]**
(1) Propyne (2) 1-Propanol
(3) 2-Propanal (4) Propionic acid

**59.** Which one of the following compounds will not be soluble in sodium bicarbonate ? **[2014, Main]**
(1) 2, 4, 6-Trinitrophenol
(2) Benzoic acid
(3) $o$-Nitrophenol
(4) Benzene sulphonic acid

**60.** Among the following organic acids, the acid present in rancid butter is : **[2014, Main]**
(1) Pyruvic acid (2) Lactic acid
(3) Butyric acid (4) Acetic acid

**61.** The total number of carboxylic acid groups in the product P is : **[2013, Advanced]**

$$\xrightarrow[\begin{array}{c}\text{2. }O_3\\\text{3. }H_2O_2\end{array}]{\text{1. }H_3O^+,\ \Delta} P$$

**62.** After completion of the reactions (I and II), the organic compounds in the reaction mixtures is/are : **[2013, Advanced]**

Reaction I : $H_3C-CO-CH_3 \xrightarrow[\text{aqueous/NaOH}]{Br_2\ (1.0\ \text{mol})}$

Reaction II : $H_3C-CO-CH_3 \xrightarrow[\text{CH}_3\text{COOH}]{Br_2\ (1.0\ \text{mol})}$

$H_3C-CO-CH_2Br$   $H_3C-CO-CBr_3$   $Br_3C-CO-CBr_3$
P       Q       R

$BrH_2C-CO-CH_2Br$   $H_3C-CO-ONa$   $CHBr_3$
S       T       U

(1) Reaction I : P and Reaction II : P
(2) Reaction I : U acetone and Reaction II : Q, acetone
(3) Reaction I : T, U, acetone and Reaction II : P
(4) Reaction I : R, acetone and Reaction II : S, acetone

**63.** In the following reaction sequences V and W are, respectively : **[2013, Advanced]**

$$Q\ A \xrightarrow[\Delta]{H_2/Ni} V$$

$$\bigcirc + V \xrightarrow{AlCl_3\ \text{(anhydrous)}} \xrightarrow[\text{2.}H_3PO_4]{\text{1/ Zn-Hg/HCl}} W$$

(1) [structure] V and [structure] W
(2) [structure with $CH_2OH$, $CH_2OH$] V and [structure] W
(3) [structure] V and [structure] W
(4) $HOH_2C{-}{\cdots}{-}CH_2OH$ V and [structure] $CH_2OH$ W

**64.** The number of aldol reactions that occurs in the given transformation is **[2012, Advanced]**

$$CH_3CHO + 4HCHO \xrightarrow{\text{conc. aq. NaOH}} \begin{array}{c} OH\ \ OH \\ \square \\ HO\ \ \ OH\end{array}$$

(1) 1 (2) 2
(3) 3 (4) 4

**65.** The carboxyl functional group ($-COOH$) is present in : **[2012, Advanced]**
(1) picric acid (2) barbituric acid
(3) ascorbic acid (4) aspirin

**66.** The compound that undergoes decarboxylation most readily under mild condition is :
**[2012, Advanced]**
(1) [cyclohexane with COOH, $CH_2COOH$]
(2) [cyclohexane with COOH, O]
(3) [cyclohexane with COOH, COOH]
(4) [cyclohexane with $CH_2COOH$, O]

**67.** The major product H of the given reaction sequence is : **[2012, Advanced]**

$$CH_3-CH_2-CO-CH_3 \xrightarrow{^{\ominus}CN} G \xrightarrow[\text{Heat}]{95\%\ H_2SO_4} H$$

(1) $CH_3-CH=C-COOH$
$\qquad\qquad\quad |$
$\qquad\qquad\ CH_3$

(2) $CH_3-CH=\underset{\underset{CH_3}{|}}{C}-CN$

(3) $CH_3-CH_2-\underset{\underset{CH_3}{|}}{\overset{\overset{OH}{|}}{C}}-COOH$

(4) $CH_3-CH=\underset{\underset{CH_3}{|}}{C}-CO-NH_2$

**68.** The compound I is :  **[2012, Advanced]**

(1) 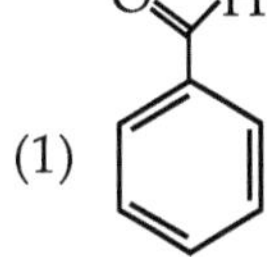

(2) 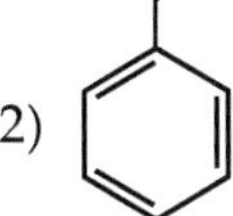

(3) 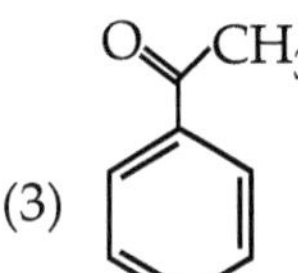

(4) 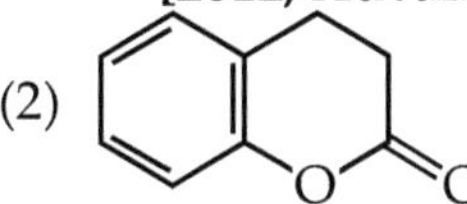

**69.** The compound K is :  **[2012, Advanced]**

(1) (2)

(3) (4)

**70.** With reference to the scheme given, which of the given statements about T, U, V and W is/are correct ?  **[2012, Advanced]**

$V \xleftarrow{CrO_3/H^\oplus} U \xrightarrow{\text{excess } (CH_3CO)_2O} W$

(1) T is soluble in hot aqueous NaOH
(2) U is optically active
(3) Molecular formula for W is $C_{10}H_{18}O_4$
(4) V gives effervescence on treatment with aqueous $NaHCO_3$

**71.** Among the following compounds the most acidic is :  **[2011, Advanced]**
(1) *p*-nitrophenol
(2) *p*-hydroxybenzoic acid
(3) *o*-hydroxybenzoic acid
(4) *p*-toluic acid

**72.** Match the reactions in column I with appropriate types of steps/reactive intermediate involved in these reactions as given in column II.  **[2011, Advanced]**

**Column I**

(1) $\xrightarrow{\text{aq NaOH}}$

(2) $\xrightarrow{CH_3MgI}$

(3) $\xrightarrow{H_2SO_4}$

(4) $\xrightarrow{H_2SO_4}$

**Column II**
(p) Nucleophilic substitution
(q) Electrophilic substitution
(r) Dehydration
(s) Nucleophilic addition
(t) Carbanion

**73.** In the scheme given below, the total number of intramolecular aldol condensation products formed from 'Y' is :  **[2010, Advanced]**

$\xrightarrow[\text{2. Zn, H}_2\text{O}]{1.\,O_3} Y \xrightarrow[\text{2. heat}]{1.\,\text{NaOH(aq)}}$

**74.** The compounds P, Q and R.  **[2010, Advanced]**

P   Q   S

were separately subjected to nitration using $HNO_3/H_2SO_4$ mixture. The major product formed in each case respectively, is

(1)

(2)

(3)

(4)

**Paragraph for Question 75, 76 and 77**

Two aliphatic aldehdes P and Q react in the presence of aqueous $K_2CO_3$ to give compound R, which upon treatment with HCN provides compound S. On acidification and heating, S gives the product shown below :

(structure: $H_3C$ and $OH$ substituted γ-butyrolactone with two $H_3C$ groups)

**75.** The compounds P and Q respectively are : **[2010, Advanced]**

(1) $CH_3$–$CH$($CH_3$)–$CHO$ and $H_3C$–$CHO$

(2) $CH_3$–$CH$($CH_3$)–$CHO$ and $H$–$CHO$ ($HCHO$)

(3) $H_3C$–$CH$($CH_3$)–$CH_2$–$CHO$ and $H_3C$–$CHO$

(4) $H_3C$–$CH$($CH_3$)–$CH_2$–$CHO$ and $H$–$CHO$ ($HCHO$)

**76.** The compound R is : **[2010, Advanced]**

(1) $(H_3C)_2C(CH_2OH)$–$CHO$

(2) $(H_3C)_2C$–$CHO$ with $CH(CH_3)$–$OH$ branch

(3) $CH_3$–$CH$–$CH(CH_2OH)$–$CHO$ branch structure

(4) $CH_3$–$CH$–$CH(CH_2$–$H_3C$–$OH)$–$CHO$

**77.** The compound S is : **[2010, Advanced]**

(1) $CH_3$–$CH$–$CH(CH_2CN)$–$CHO$

(2) $(H_3C)_2C(CH_2CN)$–$CHO$

(3) $CH_3$–$CH$–$CH(CH_2OH)$–$CH(CN)$–$OH$

(4) $(H_3C)_2C(CH_2OH)$–$CH(CN)$–$OH$

**78.** The correct activity order of the following is : **[2009, Advanced]**

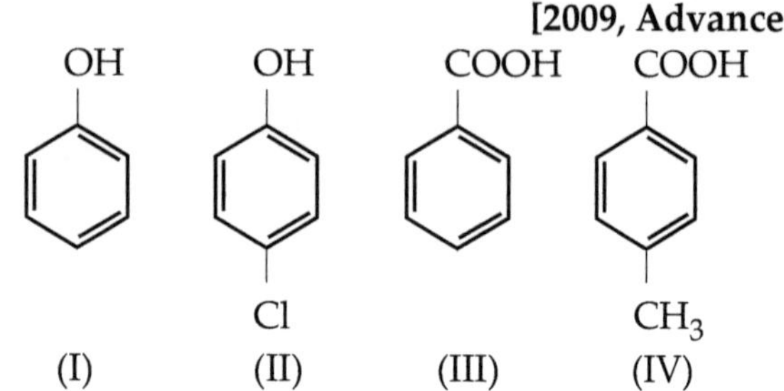

(I) phenol $OH$  (II) phenol with $Cl$ (para)  (III) $COOH$ benzene  (IV) $COOH$ with $CH_3$ (para)

(1) (III) > (IV) > (II) > (I)  (2) (IV) > (III) > (I) > (II)

(3) (III) > (II) > (I) > (IV)  (4) (II) > (III) > (IV) > (I)

**Paragraph for Question 79, 80 and 81**

A carbonyl compound P, which gives positive iodoform test, undergoes reaction with MeMgBr followed by dehydration to give an olefin Q. Ozonolysis of Q leads to a dicarbonyl compound R, which undergoes intramolecular aldol reaction to give predominantly S.

$$P \xrightarrow[\substack{2.\,H^+,\,H_2O \\ 3.\,H_2SO_4,\,D}]{1.\,MeMgBr} Q \xrightarrow[2.\,Zn,\,H_2O]{1.\,O_3} R \xrightarrow[2.\,\Delta]{1.\,OH^-} S$$

**79.** The structure of the carbonyl compound P is : **[2009, Advanced]**

(1) (phenyl–CH=CH–CO–Me)  (2) (phenyl–CH=C(Me)–CO–Me)

(3) [structure] (4) [structure]

**80.** The structures of the products Q and R, respectively, are : **[2009, Advanced]**

(1) [structures]

(2) [structures]

(3) [structures]

(4) [structures]

**81.** The structure of the product S is : **[2009, Advanced]**

(1) [structure] (2) [structure]

(3) [structure] (4) [structure]

**82.** Match each of the compounds given in Column I with the reactions, that they can undergo, given in Column II. **[2009, Advanced]**

**Column I**

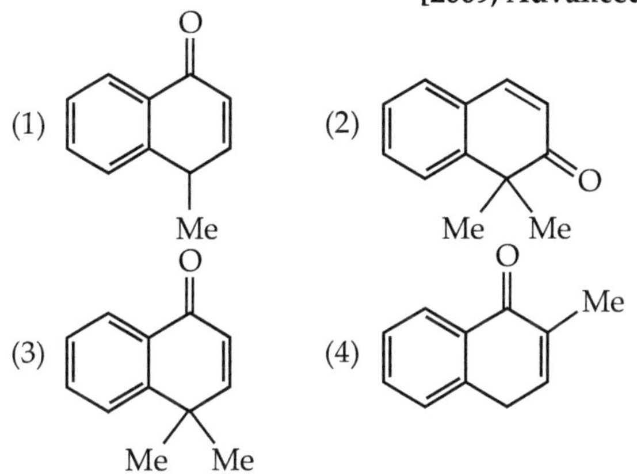

**Column II**

(1) [structure]    (p) Nucleophilic substitution

(2) [structure]    (q) Elimination

(3) [structure]    (r) Nucleophilic addition

(4) [structure with Br and NO₂]

     (s) Esterification with acetic anhydride

     (t) Dehydrogenation

**83.** The correct statements concerning the structures E, F and G is/are : **[2008, Advanced]**

(E)    (F)    (G)

(1) E, F and G are resonance structures
(2) E, F and E, G are tautomers
(3) F and G are geometrical isomers
(4) F and G are diastereomers

**Paragraph for Question 84, 85 and 86**

In the following reaction sequence, products I, J and L are formed. K represents a ragent.

$$\text{Hex-3-ynal} \xrightarrow[\text{2. PBr}_3]{\text{1. NaBH}_4} I \xrightarrow[\substack{\text{2 CO}_2\\ \text{3. H}_3\text{O}^+}]{\text{1. Mg/ether}} J \xrightarrow{K}$$

[structure] $\xrightarrow[\substack{\text{P/BaSO}_4\\ \text{quinoline}}]{\text{H}_2}$ L

**84.** The structure of the product I is : **[2008, Advanced]**

(1) [structure] (2) [structure]

(3) [structure] (4) [structure]

**85.** The structures of compound J and K, respectively, are : **[2008, Advanced]**

(1) [structure] and $SOCl_2$

(2) [structure] and $SO_2Cl_2$

(3) [structure] and $SOCl_2$

(4) [structure] and $CH_3SO_2Cl$

**86.** The structure of product L is : **[2008, Advanced]**

(1) [structure] (2) [structure]

(3) [structure] (4) [structure]

**87.** In the following reaction sequence, the correct structures of E, F and G are : **[2008, Advanced]**

[structure] $\xrightarrow{\text{Heat}}$ E $\xrightarrow[\text{NaOH}]{I_2}$ [F] + [G]

(* implies $^{13}$C labelled carbon)

(1) E = [structure]   F = [structure]   G = CHI₃

(2) $E =$ Ph-CO-CH$_3$ (C*)   $F =$ Ph-CO-O$^\ominus$Na$^\oplus$   $G = CHI_3$

(3) $E =$ Ph(*)-CO-CH$_3$(*)   $F =$ Ph(*)-CO-O$^\ominus$Na$^\oplus$   $G = \overset{*}{C}HI_3$

(4) $E =$ Ph(*)-CO-CH$_3$(*)   $F =$ Ph(*)-CO-O$^\ominus$Na$^\oplus$(*)   $G = \overset{*}{C}HI_3$

**88.** Compound H is formed by the reaction of :

**[2008, Advanced]**

(1) $Ph-CO-CH_3$ + PhMgBr

(2) $Ph-CO-CH_3$ + PhCH$_2$MgBr

(3) $Ph-CO-H$ + PhCH$_2$MgBr

(4) $Ph-CO-H$ + $Ph-C(Me)-MgBr$

**89.** The structures of compounds J, K and L respectively, are : **[2008, Advanced]**

(1) $PhCOCH_3$, $PhCH_2COCH_3$ and $PhCH_2COO^-K^-$

(2) $PhCHO$, $PhCH_2CHO$ and $PhCOO^-K^+$

(3) $PhCOCH_3$, $PhCH_2CHO$ and $CH_3COO^-K^+$

(4) $PhCHO$, $PHCOCH_3$ and $PhCOO^-K^+$

**90. Statement-1 :** $p$-Hydroxybenzoic acid has a lower boiling point than $o$-hydroxybenzoic acid.

**because**

**Statement-2 :** $o$-Hydroxybenzoic acid has intramolecular hydrogen bonding.

**[2007, Advanced]**

(1) Statement-1 is True, Statement-2 is True; Statement-2 is a correct explanation for Statement-1

(2) Statement-1 is True, Statement-2 is True; Statement-2 is a NOT a correct explanation for Statement-1

(3) Statement-1 is True, Statement-2 is False

(4) Statement-1 is False, Statement-2 is True

**91.** Cyclohexene on ozonolysis followed by reaction with zinc dust and water gives compound E. Compound E on further treatment with aqueous KOH yields compound F. Compound F is :

**[2007, Advanced]**

(1) cyclopentene—CHO   (2) cyclopentene—CHO

(3) cyclopentene—COOH   (4) cyclohexane(CO$_2$H)(CO$_2$H)

**92.** Match the compounds/ions in Column I with their properties/reactions in Column II. Indicate your answer by darkening the appropriate bubbles of the 4 × 4 matrix given in the ORS.

**[2007, Advanced]**

| Column I | Column II |
|---|---|
| (1) $C_6H_5CHO$ | (p) gives precipitate with 2, 4-dinitrophenylhydrazine |
| (2) $CH_3C \equiv CH$ | (q) gives precipitate with $AgNO_3$ |
| (3) $CH^-$ | (r) is a nucleophile |
| (4) $I^-$ | (s) is involved in cyano-hydrin formation |

**93.** The IUPAC name of $C_6H_5COCl$ is :

**[2006, Main]**

(1) Benzoyl chloride

(2) Benzene chloro ketone

(3) Benzene carbonyl chloride

(4) Chloro phenyl ketone

**94.** Which of the following reactants on reaction with conc. NaOH followed by acidification gives the following lactone as the only product ?

**[2006, Main]**

(1) benzene–COCH$_3$ / benzene–COOH (ortho)

(2) benzene–COOH / benzene–CHO (ortho)

(3) benzene–CHO / benzene–CHO (ortho)

(4) benzene–COOH / benzene–COOH (ortho)

**95.** The smallest ketone and its next homologue are reacted with $NH_2OH$ to form oxime.

**[2006, Main]**

(1) Two different oximes are formed

(2) Three different oximes are formed

(3) Both the oximes are optically active

(4) All oximes are optically active

**96.** MeO–benzene–CHO $+ X \xrightarrow{CH_3COONa}$ MeO–benzene–CH=CH–COOH

What is X ?   **[2005, Screening]**

(1) $CH_3COOH$   (2) $BrCH_2, COOH$

(3) $(CH_3CO)_2O$   (4) $CHO-COOH$

**97.** But-2-one can be converted to propanoic acid by which of the following : **[2005, Screening]**

(1) $NaOH$, $NaI/H^+$   (2) Fehling solution

(3) $NaOH$, $I_2/H^+$   (4) Tollen's reagent

**98.** Which of the following is obtained when 4-Methylbenzensulphonic acid is hydrolysed with excess of sodium acetate ?**[2005, Screening]**

(1)  $CH_3$—⬡—$COO^- \overset{+}{Na}$

(2)  $CH_3$—⬡ $+ SO_3$

(3)  $CH_3$—⬡—$\overset{-}{S}O_3 \overset{+}{Na} + CH_3COOH$

(4)  $CH_3$—⬡—$SO_3Na + CH_3COOH$
(Weak acid)
(Strong acid)

**99.** An organic compound 'P' having the molecular formula $C_5H_{10}O$ is treated with dil $H_2SO_4$ gives two compounds, Q & R both gives positive iodoform test. The reaction of $C_5H_{10}O$ with dil $H_2SO_4$ gives reaction $10^{15}$ times faster then ethylene. Identify organic compound Q & R. Give the reason for the extra stability of P.  **[2004, Main]**

**100.** The order of reactivity of Phenyl Magnesium Bromide with the following compounds is :

**[2004, Screening]**

$H_3C \overset{O}{\underset{}{C}} CH_3$   $H_3C \overset{O}{\underset{}{C}} H$   $Ph \overset{O}{\underset{}{C}} Ph$
(I)          (II)          (III)

(1)  (II) > (III) > (I)

(2)  (I) > (III) > (II)

(3)  (II) > (I) > (III)

(4)  All react with the same rate

**101.**

$p$-$NH_2$—⬡—COOH  and

$p$-OH—⬡—COOH both all give efferves-

ences of $CO_2$ with $NaHCO_3$

$p$-$NH_2$—⬡—$\overset{-}{COO}$ will give positive azo

dye test

$p$-OH—⬡—COOH  will  give  positive

lebemann nitroso test  **[2003, Main]**

**102.**

**[2003, Main]**

**103. (a)** $H_3C$⟍⟍$CH_2 \longleftrightarrow H_3C$⟍⟍$CH_3$

**(b)**  (A) ⇌ (B)

(A) →$KMnO_4$→ Metaextermic acid  **[2003, Main]**

**104.**  →$\text{2 moles NaNH}_2$→

The product A will be : **[2003, Screening]**

(1) 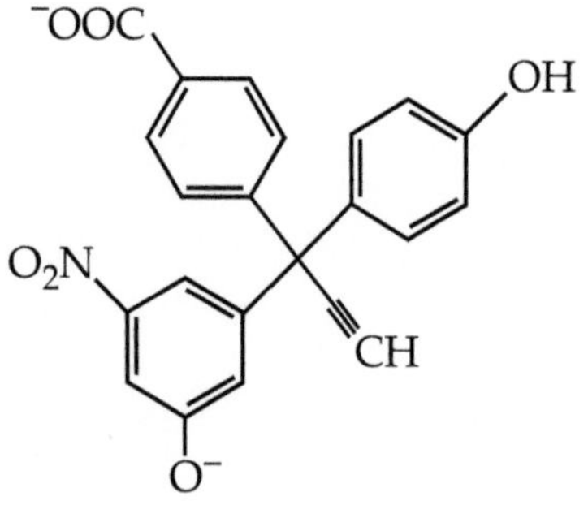 [structure: $^-OOC$-substituted benzene ring attached to central carbon bearing a para-OH phenyl, a $CH$, and a benzene ring with $O_2N$ and $O^-$ substituents]

(2) 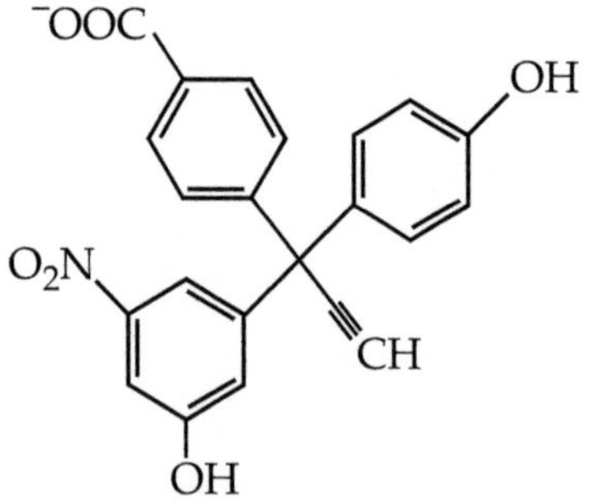 [structure: $^-OOC$-substituted benzene ring attached to central carbon bearing a para-OH phenyl, a $CH$, and a benzene ring with $O_2N$ and $OH$ substituents]

(3) 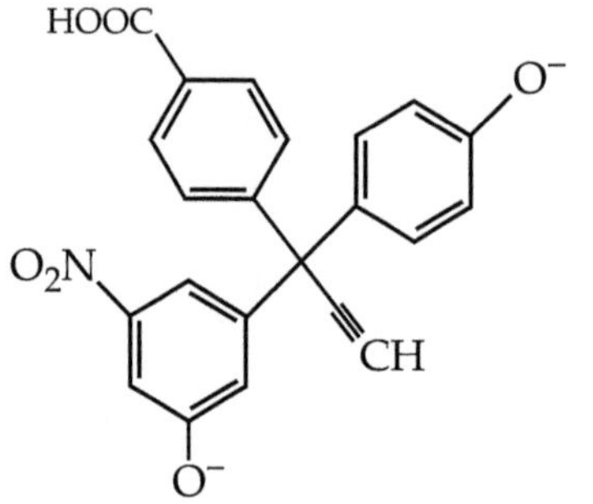 [structure: $HOOC$-substituted benzene ring attached to central carbon bearing a para-$O^-$ phenyl, a $CH$, and a benzene ring with $O_2N$ and $O^-$ substituents]

(4) 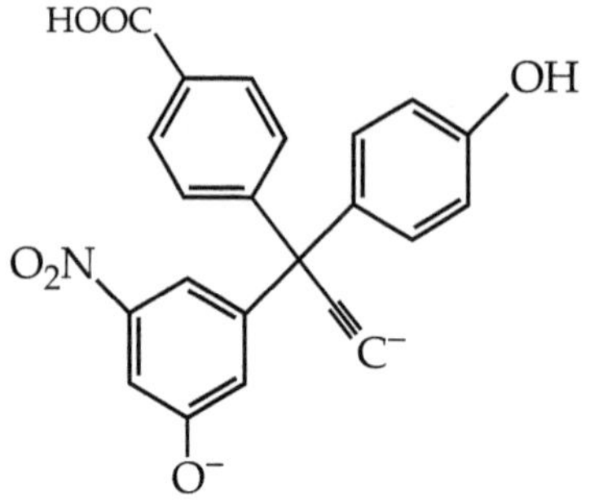 [structure: $HOOC$-substituted benzene ring attached to central carbon bearing a para-OH phenyl, a $C^-$, and a benzene ring with $O_2N$ and $O^-$ substituents]

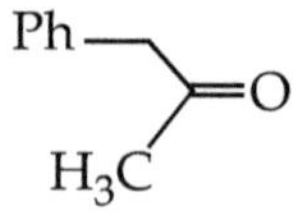

**105.** The product of acid hydrolysis of P and Q can be distinguished by **[2003, Screening]**

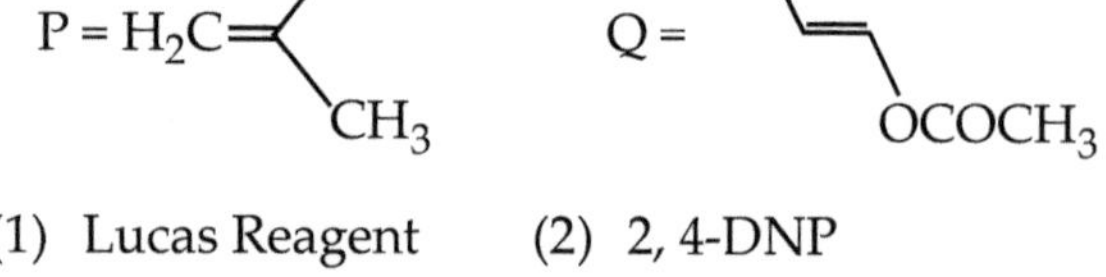

$$P = H_2C = \overset{OCOCH_3}{\underset{CH_3}{C}} \qquad Q = \overset{H_2C}{\diagdown}\!\!-\!\!OCOCH_3$$

(1) Lucas Reagent   (2) 2, 4-DNP

(3) Fehling's solution   (4) $NaHSO_3$

**106.** 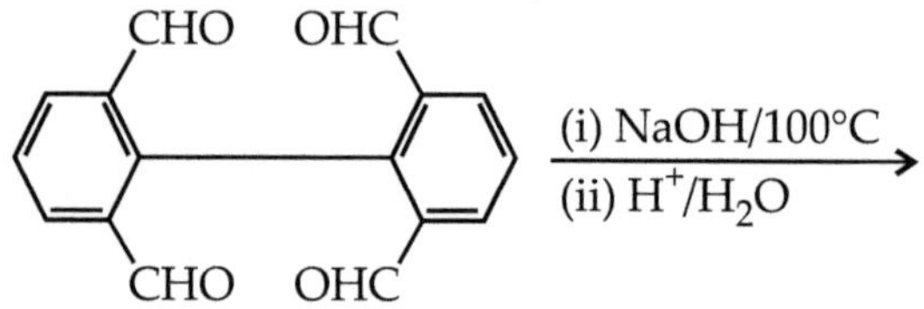 [structure: biphenyl with two CHO (OHC) groups on each ring]

$$\xrightarrow[\text{(ii) } H^+/H_2O]{\text{(i) NaOH/100°C}}$$

Major Product is :   **[2003, Screening]**

(1) 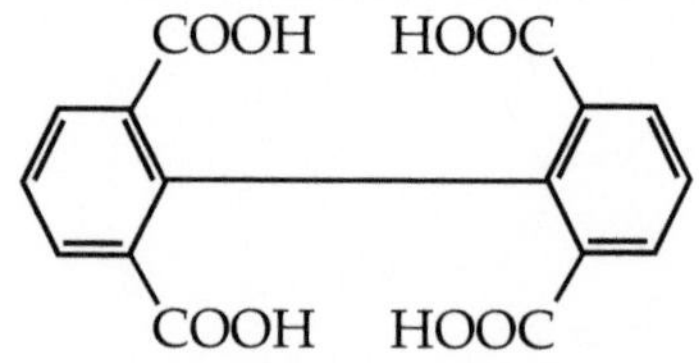 [structure: biphenyl with COOH (HOOC) groups]

(2) 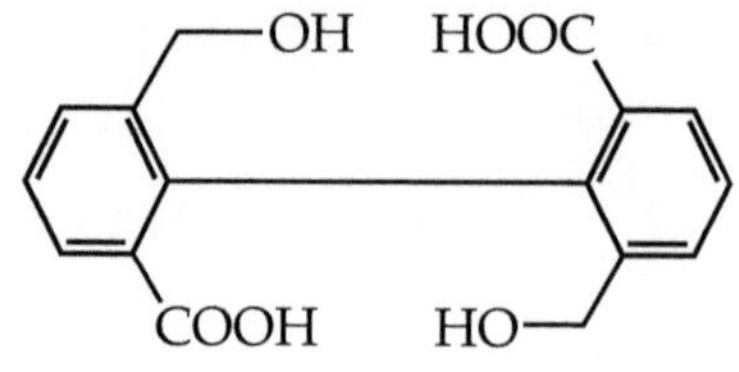 [structure: biphenyl with CH$_2$OH (—OH) and HOOC/COOH and HO— groups]

(3) 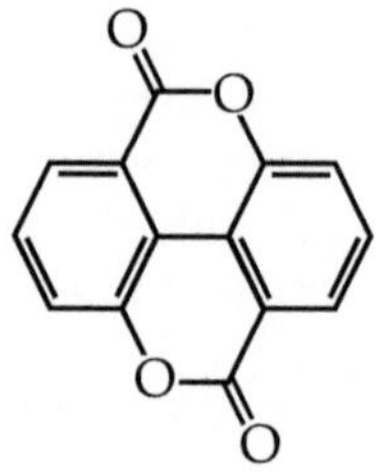 [structure: fused lactone (double anhydride/lactone ring) structure]

(4) 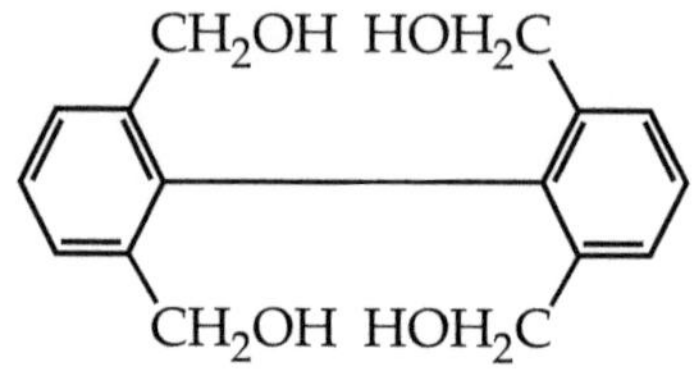 [structure: biphenyl with CH$_2$OH (HOH$_2$C) groups on each ring]

**107.** $Ph - C \equiv C - CH_3 \xrightarrow{Hg^{2+}/H^+} A.$ A is :

**[2003, Screening]**

(1) 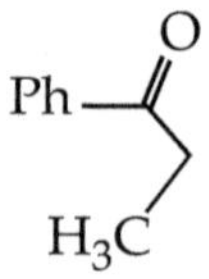 $Ph - \overset{O}{\underset{H_3C}{C}}\!\!<$  (2) $Ph - \underset{H_3C}{C} = O$

(3) 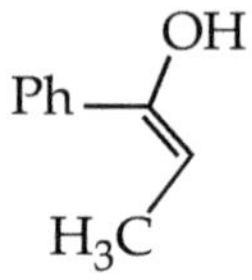 $Ph - \overset{OH}{\underset{H_3C}{C}} =$  (4) 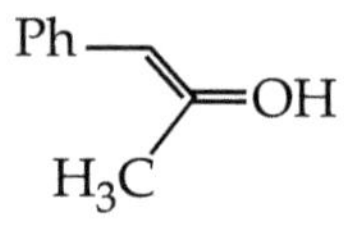 $Ph - \underset{H_3C}{C} = OH$

**108.** Five isomeric para-disubtituted aromatic compounds A to E with molecular formula $C_6H_6O_2$ were given for identification. Based on the following observations, give structures of the compounds. **[2002, Main]**

(1) Both A and B form a silver mirror with Tollen's reagent; also B gives a positive test with $FeCl_3$ solution

(2) C gives positive Iodoform test

(3) D is readily extracted in aqueous $NaHCO_3$ solution

(4) E on acid hydrolysis gives 1, 4-dihydroxybenzene

**109.** Write structures of the product A, B, C, D and E in the following scheme.

$$\text{(4-Chlorophenyl)-CO-CH}_2\text{CH}_2\text{CH}_3 \xrightarrow{\text{Cl}_2/\text{FeCl}_3} A$$

$$C \xleftarrow{\text{HNO}_3/\text{H}_2\text{SO}_4} B \xleftarrow{\text{Na-Hg/HCl}}$$

$$\xrightarrow[\text{CH}_2=\text{CHCH}_2\text{O-Na}^+]{} D \xrightarrow{\text{H}_2/\text{Pd/C}} E$$

**[2002, Main]**

**110.** Identify the correct order of boiling points of the following compounds :

$CH_3CH_2CH_2CH_2OH$, $CH_3CH_2CH_2CHO$,

$CH_3CH_2CH_2COOH$ **[2002, Screening]**

(1) $1 > 2 > 3$       (2) $3 > 1 > 2$

(3) $1 > 3 > 2$       (4) $3 > 2 > 1$

**111.** Compound 'A' (molecular formula $C_3H_8O$) is treated with acidified potassium dichromate to form a product 'B' (molecular formula $C_3H_6O$). 'B' forms a shining silver mirror on warming with ammoniacal silver nitrate. 'B' when treated with an aqueous solution of $H_2NCONHNH_2.HCl$ and sodium acetate gives a product 'C'. Identify the structure of 'C'.

(1) $CH_3CH_2CH = NNHCONH_2$

(2) $CH_3 - \underset{\underset{CH_3}{|}}{C} = NNHCONH_2$

(3) $CH_3 - \underset{\underset{CH_3}{|}}{C} = NCONHNH_2$

(4) $CH_3CH_2CH = NCONHNH_2$

# ANSWER KEY

| | | | | | | | | | |
|---|---|---|---|---|---|---|---|---|---|
| **1.** (3) | **2.** (3) | **3.** (1) | **4.** (2) | **5.** (2) | **6.** (1,2,3) | **7.** (1) | **8.** (4) | **9.** (3) | **10.** (3) |
| **11.** (1,3,4) | **12.** (3) | **13.** (1) | **14.** (1) | **15.** (4) | **16.** (3) | **17.** (2) | **18.** (1) | **19.** (2) | **20.** (2) |
| **21.** (1) | **22.** (1) | **23.** (3) | **24.** (1) | **25.** (4) | **26.** (3) | **27.** (4) | **28.** (3) | **29.** (1) | **30.** (1) |
| **31.** (1,2,3) | **32.** (2,3) | **33.** (1) | **34.** (3,4) | **35.** (2) | **36.** (4) | **37.** (3) | **38.** (2) | **39.** (2) | **40.** (1) |
| **41.** (4) | **42.** (4) | **43.** (3) | **44.** (3) | **45.** (2) | **46.** (5) | **47.** (4) | **48.** (3) | **49.** (1) | **50.** (1) |
| **51.** (3) | **52.** (4) | **53.** (3) | **54.** (3) | **55.** (3) | **56.** (3) | **57.** (4) | **58.** (4) | **59.** (3) | **60.** (3) |
| **61.** (2) | **62.** (3) | **63.** (1) | **64.** (3) | **65.** (4) | **66.** (2) | **67.** (1) | **68.** (1) | **69.** (3) | **70.**(1,3,4) |
| **71.** (3) | **72.** (*) | **73.** (1) | **74.** (3) | **75.** (2) | **76.** (1) | **77.** (4) | **78.** (1) | **79.** (2) | **80.** (*) |
| **81.** (2) | **82.** (*) | **83.** (2,3,4) | **84.** (4) | **85.** (1) | **86.** (3) | **87.** (3) | **88.** (*) | **89.** (4) | **90.** (4) |
| **91.** (1) | **92.** (*) | **93.** (3) | **94.** (3) | **95.** (2) | **96.** (3) | **97.** (3) | **98.** (3) | **99.** (*) | **100.** (3) |
| **101.** (*) | **102.** (*) | **103.** (*) | **104.** (1) | **105.** (3) | **106.** (2) | **107.** (1) | **108.** (*) | **109.** (*) | **110.** (2) |
| **111.** (1) | | | | | | | | | |

# ANSWERS WITH EXPLANATIONS

**1. (3)** Greater the electrophilicity on $-\overset{\overset{\textstyle O}{\|}}{C}-$ group greater the reactivity in nucleophilic addition.

(o-OCH$_3$ benzaldehyde, +R, +I) < (m-OCH$_3$ benzaldehyde, −I)

(m-NO$_2$ benzaldehyde, −I only) < (o-NO$_2$ benzaldehyde, −R, −I)

(iii) < (i) < (iv) < (ii)

**2. (3)** (1)

$$\underset{m_e}{\overset{m_e}{\underset{m_e}{>}}}C - \overset{\overset{\textstyle O}{\|}}{C} + O - CH_2 - C\underset{m_e}{\overset{m_e}{<}}_{m_e} \quad \xrightarrow{H^+/H_2O}$$
(A)

$$HO - CH_2 - \quad \xleftarrow{\overset{KMnO_4}{+}} \quad \underset{(B)}{>\overset{\overset{\textstyle O}{\|}}{C} - OH}$$
(C)

(2) $\sim\sim\overset{\overset{\textstyle O}{\|}}{C} - O - CH_2 - CH_2 - CH_3$

Total 8 'C' → so molecular formula not matched.

(3) $m_e - CH_2 - \underset{\underset{m_e}{|}}{CH} - O - \overset{\overset{\textstyle O}{\|}}{C} - CH_2 - \underset{}{CH} - Et \quad \xrightarrow{H^+/H_2O}$

$$m_e - CH_2 - \underset{\underset{m_e}{|}}{CH} - OH + \overset{\overset{\textstyle O}{\|}}{C} - CH_2 - \underset{\underset{Et}{|}}{CH}$$
$$\underset{HO}{}$$

not inter convertible by oxidation

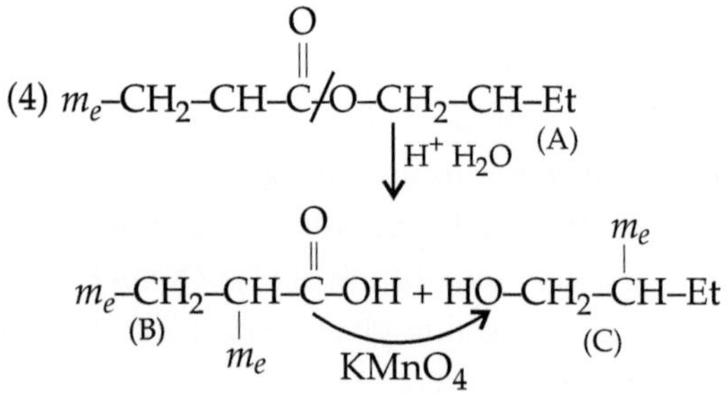

**(4)** $m_e$–CH$_2$–CH–C$\overset{\overset{O}{\|}}{/}$O–CH$_2$–CH–Et

$\downarrow$ H$^+$ H$_2$O  **(A)**

$m_e$–CH$_2$–CH–C–OH + HO–CH$_2$–CH–Et
**(B)** $m_e$    **(C)** $m_e$

KMnO$_4$

**3. (1)**

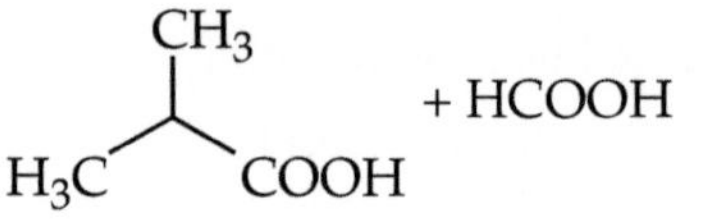

$$\text{(CH}_3\text{)}_2\text{CH–COOH} + \text{HCOOH}$$

**4. (2)** Compound $\xrightarrow[\text{anhydride}]{\text{Chromic}}$

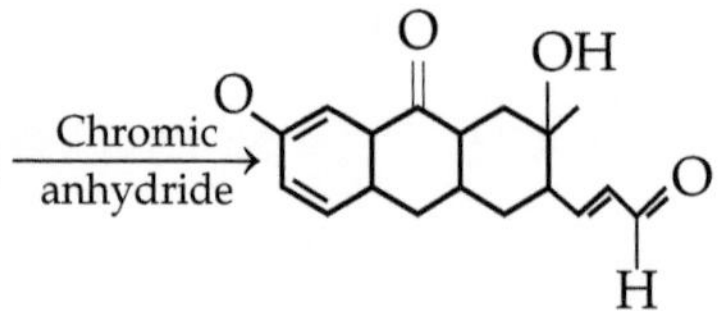

**5. (2)**

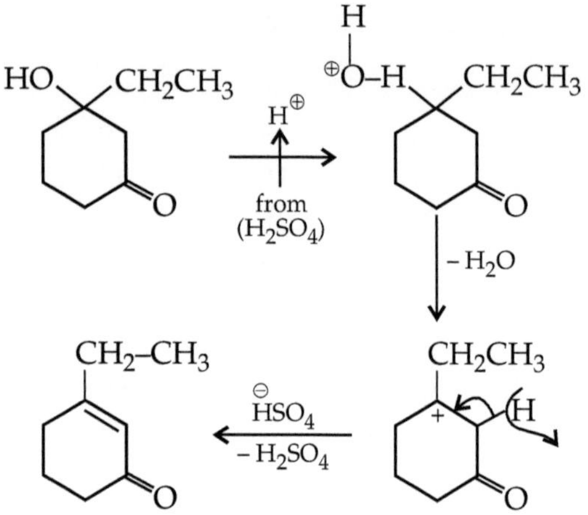

$\xrightarrow[\text{from (H}_2\text{SO}_4\text{)}]{\text{H}^\oplus}$

$\downarrow$ –H$_2$O

$\xleftarrow[\text{– H}_2\text{SO}_4]{\overset{\ominus}{\text{HSO}_4}}$

**6. (1,2,3)**

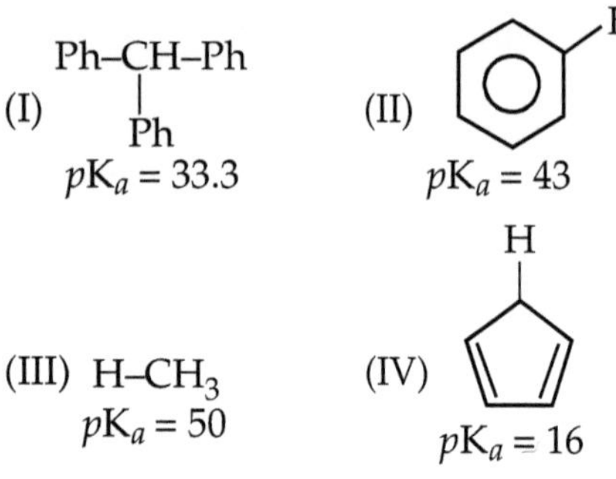

(I) Ph–CH–Ph
       |
       Ph
$pK_a = 33.3$

(II) $pK_a = 43$

(III) H–CH$_3$
$pK_a = 50$

(IV) $pK_a = 16$

(V) CH≡CH
$pK_a = 25$

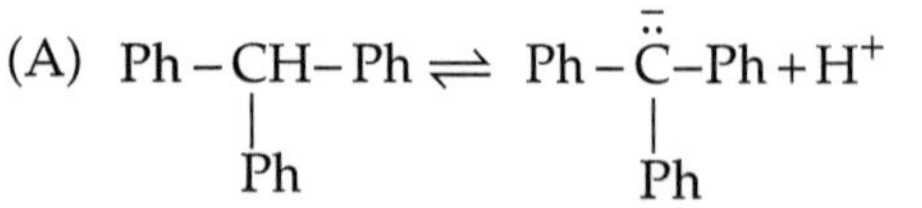

(A) Ph–CH–Ph $\rightleftharpoons$ Ph–$\overset{..}{\text{C}}$–Ph + H$^+$
        |                        |
        Ph                      Ph
(Resonance stabilised)

(B) $\rightleftharpoons$ + H$^+$
Aromatic

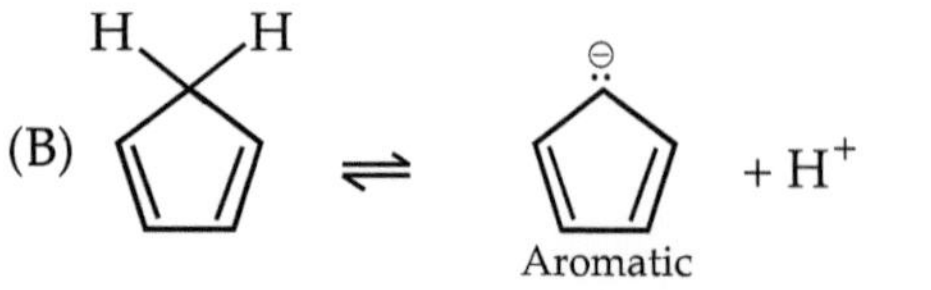

(C) –NO$_2$ is –I group (electron withdrawing group). It increases acid strength.

(D) Acid strength order : IV > V > I > II > III

**7. (1)** Reactivity order of various carbonyl compounds → Aldehydes > Ketones

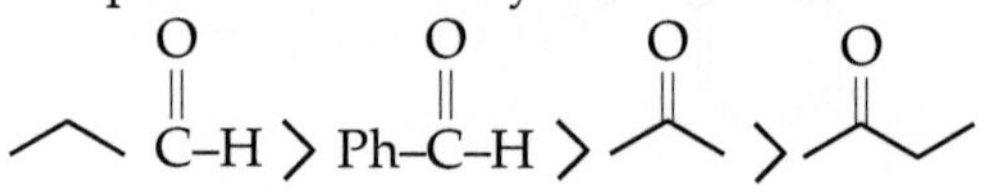

$$\text{CH}_3\text{CH}_2\text{–C–H} > \text{Ph–C–H} > \text{CH}_3\text{–C–CH}_3 > \text{CH}_3\text{CH}_2\text{–C–CH}_2\text{CH}_3$$

**8. (4)**

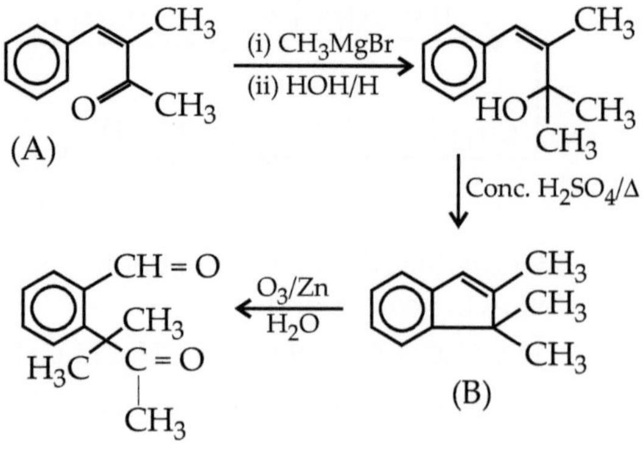

(A) $\xrightarrow[\text{(ii) HOH/H}]{\text{(i) CH}_3\text{MgBr}}$

$\downarrow$ Conc. H$_2$SO$_4$/$\Delta$

(B) $\xleftarrow[\text{H}_2\text{O}]{\text{O}_3\text{/Zn}}$

**9. (3)** CH$_3$ – CH$_2$ – C ≡ C – CH$_2$ – C$\overset{\overset{O}{\|}}{\underset{H}{}}$ $\xrightarrow{\text{NaBH}_4}$

CH$_3$ – CH$_2$ – C ≡ C – CH$_2$ – CH$_2$ – OH

$\downarrow$ PBr$_3$

CH$_3$ – CH$_2$ – C ≡ C – CH$_2$ – CH$_2$ – Br

$\xleftarrow{\text{Mg/ether}}$

CH$_3$ – CH$_2$ – C ≡ C – CH$_2$ – CH$_2$ – MgBr $\xrightarrow[\text{(2) H}_3\text{O}]{\text{(1) CO}_2}$

CH$_3$ – CH$_2$ – C ≡ C – CH$_2$ – CH$_2$ – C – OH

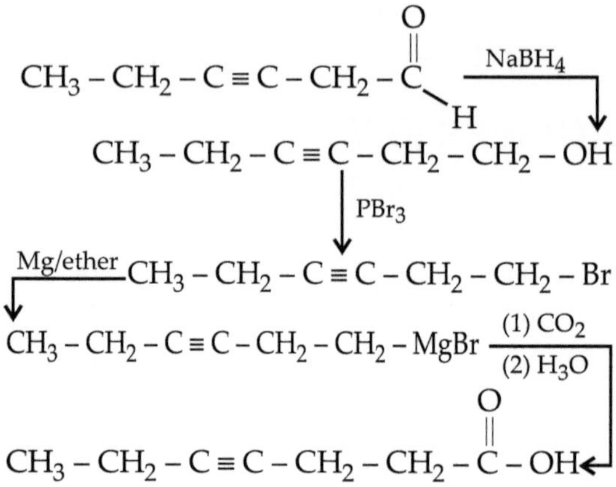

**10. (3)**

(i) $\xrightarrow[\text{AlCl}_3]{\text{CO, HCl}}$

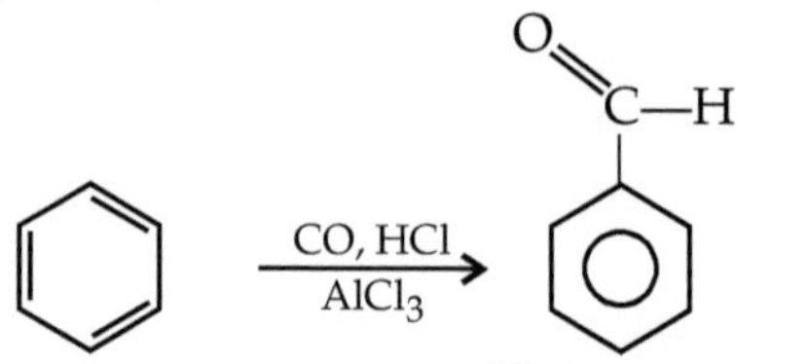

(Gattermann koch reaction)

(ii) $\xrightarrow{\text{(i) SnCl}_2\text{, HCl}}$ Imine $\xrightarrow{\text{H}_3\text{O}^\oplus}$

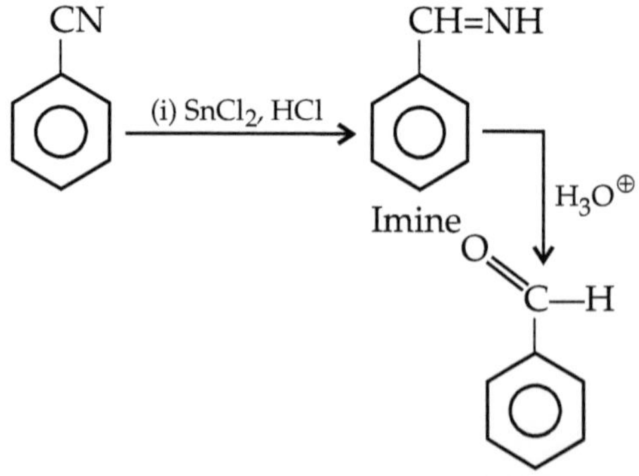

(Stephen reduction)

(iii) $\xrightarrow[\substack{\text{BaSO}_4\text{, S,} \\ \text{Quinoline}}]{\text{H}_2\text{, Pd}}$

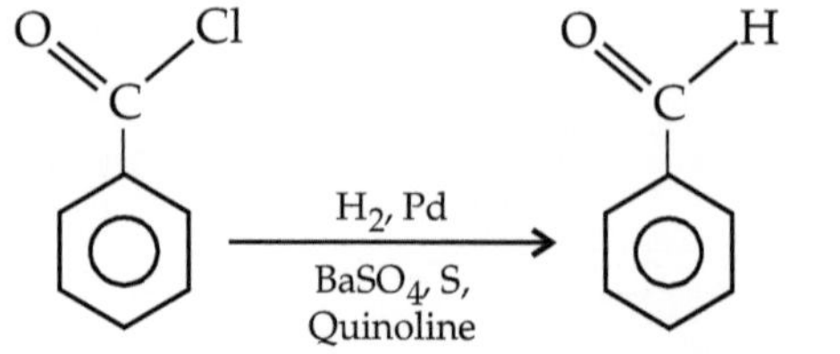

(Rosenmund reduction)

**11. (1,3,4)**

(1) $H_3C-CO-CH_3$ $\xrightarrow[\text{Heat}]{\text{conc. } H_2SO_4}$ (1,3,5-trimethylbenzene)

(2) $H_3C-C\equiv C-H$ $\xrightarrow[873 \text{ K}]{\text{Heated Iron tube}}$ (1,3,5-trimethylbenzene)

(3) (1,3,5-triacetylbenzene) $\xrightarrow[\text{3. sodalime, D}]{\text{1. } Br_2, \text{ NaOH} \quad \text{2. } H_3O}$ (benzene)

(4) (benzene-1,3,5-tricarbaldehyde) $\xrightarrow{\text{Zn, Hg/HCl}}$ (1,3,5-trimethylbenzene)

**12. (3)** The correct sequence for the formation of Y is shown below :

Benzene $\xrightarrow[AlCl_3/CuCl]{CO/HCl}$ (Benzaldehyde, CHO) $\xrightarrow{Ac_2O/NaOAc}$

$$\underset{H}{\overset{HC=C-COOH}{\big|}} \text{(X)} \xrightarrow{Br_2/Na_2CO_3}$$

$$\underset{\text{COONa}}{\overset{\text{OH Br}}{\underset{}{HC-CH}}}$$

$\xrightarrow[473 \text{ K}]{\text{moist KOH}}$ $C\equiv CH$ attached to benzene ring (Y)

**13. (1)** The correct sequence for the formation of Z is shown below :

$$\underset{H}{\overset{HC=C-COOH}{\big|}} \text{(phenyl)} \xrightarrow{8H_2/Pd\text{-}C} \overset{H_2}{\underset{}{H_2C-C-COOH}} \text{(cyclohexyl)}$$

$\xrightarrow{\Delta}$ (indanone) $H_2C-CH_2$ with $C=O$

**14. (1)** The correct sequence for the formation of R is shown below :

$\text{Ar-COOH}$ $\xrightarrow{H_2/Pd\text{-}C}$ $\text{Ar-COOH}$ $\xrightarrow{SOCl_2}$ $\text{Ar-COCl}$ $\xrightarrow[\text{COCl}_2]{\text{MeMgBr,}}$ $\text{Ar-CO-Me}$ $\xrightarrow{NaBH_4}$

$\underset{H}{\overset{CH_3}{Ar-C-OH}}$ $\xrightarrow{HCl}$ $\text{Ar-CHCl-CH}_3$ $\xrightarrow{Mg, Et_2O}$ $\text{Ar-MgCl}$ $\xrightarrow[\text{2. } H_3O^+]{\text{1. } CO_2 \text{ (dry ice)}}$ $\text{Ar-COOH}$

**15. (4)** Nitro group shows negative inductive and mesomericeffect, hence the removal of hydrogen from carboxylic group becomes easier. The OH and Cl group shows negative inductive effect but due to more electronegativity of chlorine, it shows more negative inductive effect than OH, hence the removal of hydrogen is easier in IV than in III. Hydroxyl group shows mesomeric effect more than negative inductive effect so removal of hydrogen is easier in II than in III.

**16. (3)** Sodium borohydride ($NaBH_4$) is a reducing agent. It reduces carbonyl group of ketone to secondary alcohol. The complete reaction is shown below :

(cyclohexene ring with C=O and $NMe_2$) $\xrightarrow[\text{2. Methanol}]{\text{1. } NaBH_3}$ (reduced product with $NMe_2$)

**17. (2)** The complete reaction is shown below :

(3-methoxyphenol, MeO···OH) $\xrightarrow[\text{(ii) } AlCl_3 \text{ (anhyd.)}]{\text{(i) } ClCH_3CH_3CCl}$ (chromanone, MeO substituted)

**18. (1)** The complete reaction is shown below :

$$\xrightarrow{B_2H_6}$$

$$\xrightarrow{SnCl_2/HCl}$$

$$\xleftarrow{H_3O^+}$$

Therefore, reagents require for the above conversion are.

**19. (2)** In the given compounds, 4-Hydroxypentane-2-one will be most readily dehydrated to give the conjugated base. Its structure is given as :

**20. (2)** The correct reaction series is shown below :

$$\xrightarrow[\text{(ii) } H_2O]{\text{(i) } C_2H_5MgBr}$$

$$\xleftarrow[S_N1]{HCl}$$

The first step involves the reaction of given compound wih Grignard reagent and then it undergoes hydrolysis. The product undergoes $S_N1$ reaction.

**21. (1)** The mechanism involves in the given reaction is shown below :

$$H-\overset{O}{\overset{\|}{C}}-CH_2-\overset{O}{\overset{\|}{C}}-Cl$$

The first step involves the attack of hydroxyl group over the acyl group. Then, the formation of hydroxyl-substituted lactone takes place that on heating leads to dehydration.

**22. (1)** For the synthesis of benzoic acid, the only correct option is A. It is given as :

$$\xrightarrow{NaOH/Br_2} \quad + CHBr_3$$

Acetophenone reacts with bromine in the presence of alkali and sodium benzoate and bromoform. This reaction is known as haloform reaction.

**23. (3)** The only correct combination that gives two different carboxylic acids is (3). Benzaldehyde reacts in the following manner :

$$\xrightarrow{(CH_3CO)_2O,\ CH_3COOK}$$

$$\xrightarrow{H_3O^+}$$

$$H-\overset{OH}{\underset{}{C}}-CH_2-\overset{O}{\overset{\|}{C}}-O-\overset{O}{\overset{\|}{C}}-CH_3$$

Perkin condensation (P)

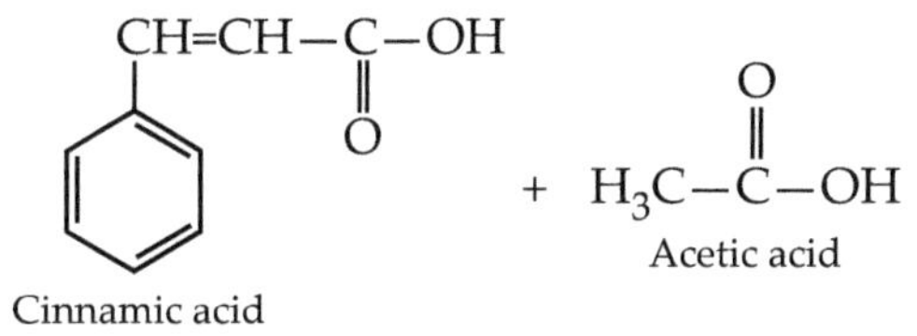

Cinnamic acid

$+$ H$_3$C–C–OH
Acetic acid

In the above reaction, two carboxlic acids are formed which are cinnamic acid and acetic acid.

**24. (1)** For the given reaction condition, the compound S will be

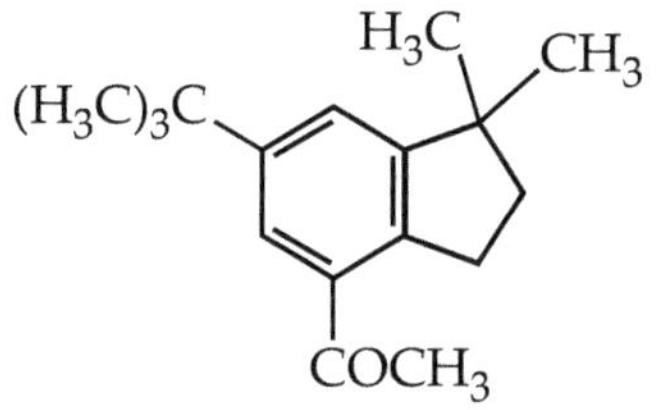

The complete reaction is given in the next part.

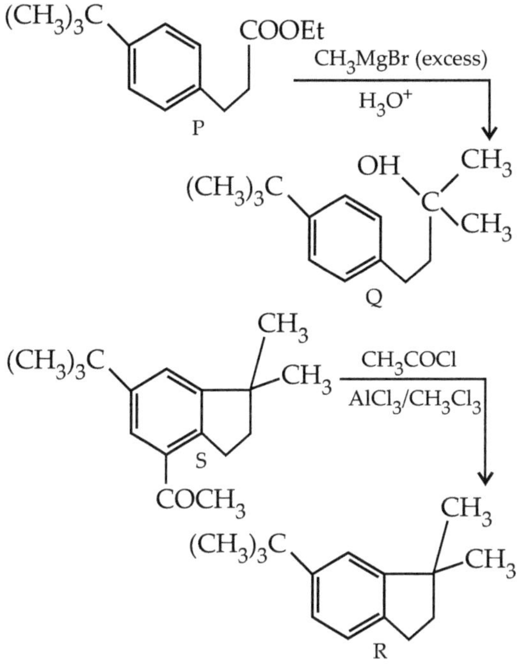

**25. (4)** The complete reaction is given as follows :

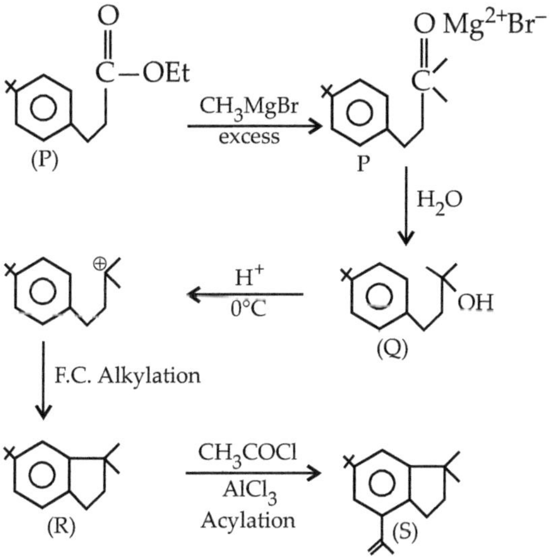

**26. (3)** The complete reaction is shown below :

Esterification CH$_3$OH/H$^+$

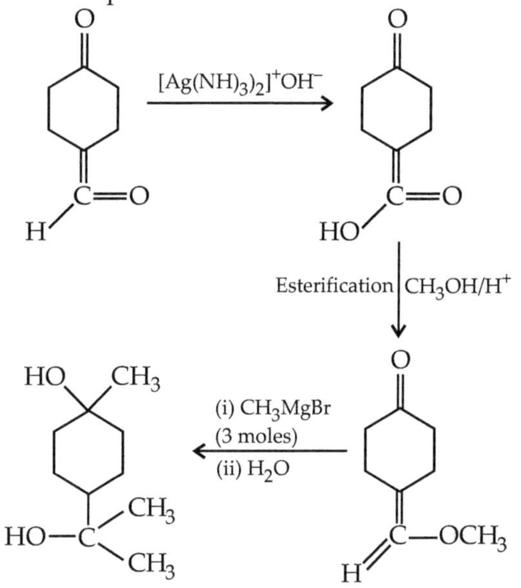

Therefore, the correct sequence of reagent is :

[Ag(NH$_3$)$_2$]$^+$ OH$^-$, H$^+$/CH$_3$OH, CH$_3$MgBr.

**27. (4)** The complere reaction is shown below :

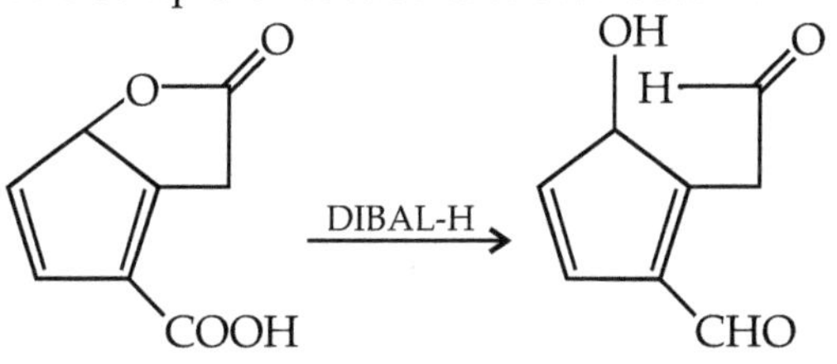

Major product

The reagent DIBAL-H reduces the esters and carboxylic acid groups of reactants into aldehydes.

**28. (3)** The major product of the given reaction is shown as follows :

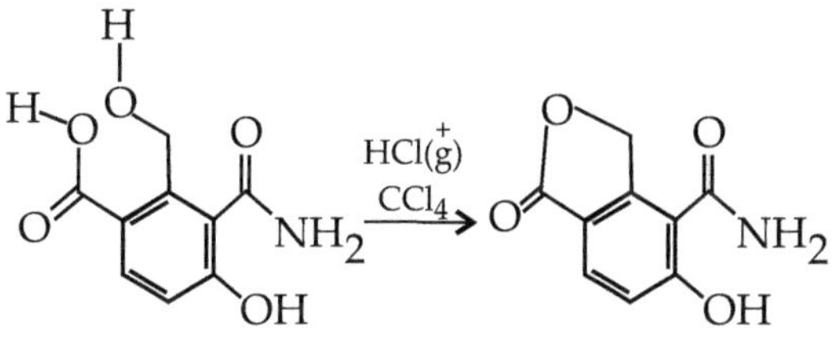

The mechanism for the same is given below :

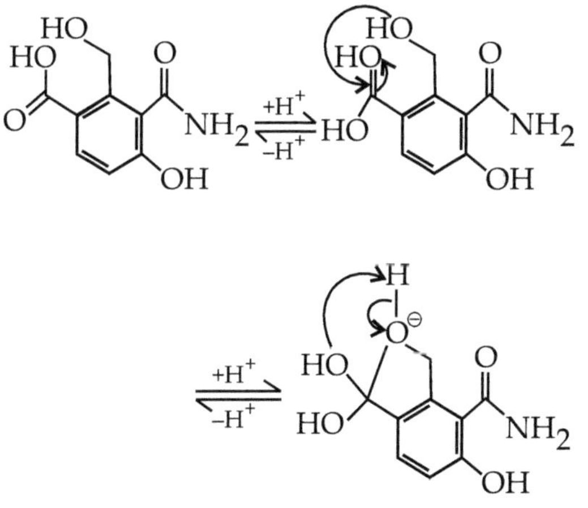

**29. (1)** The structure of the compound is :

The required chemical reactions are shown below :

$(C_8H_8O_2)$ + $H_3\overset{O}{\overset{||}{C}}-CH_3$ Acetophenone

↓ Aldol condensation base

↓ Cannizzaro reaction Conc. NaOH

**30. (1)** The compound (I) will have highest dipole moment due to formation of zwitter ions as shown below :

Exist in Zwitter ion

**31. (1,2,3)** Aldehydes and α-hydroxyketones show positive Tollen's test.

$\xrightarrow[\text{Reagent}]{\text{Tollen's}}$ Silver mirror ↓

$\xrightarrow[\text{Reagent}]{\text{Tollen's}}$ Silver mirror ↓

$\xrightarrow[\text{Reagent}]{\text{Tollen's}}$ Silver mirror ↓

So, compounds given in options (A), (B) and (C) will give positive Tollen's test.

**32. (2,3)** The following sequences of reactions take place.

$\xrightarrow[\text{(ii) } H_2O^+]{\text{(i) } O_2}$ P $\xrightarrow{CHCl_3/NaOH}$

Q (major)

+

R (minor)

$\xrightarrow[\text{PhCH}_2\text{Br}]{\text{NaOH}}$ S

Q is steam volatile not R.
Q and R both show positive test with aqueous solution of  solution.
Q, R and S show positive test with -dinitrophenyl hydrazine.
Thus, the correct statements regarding following reactions are (B) and (C).

**33. (1)** The following reaction takes place.

$\xrightarrow[\text{Cross aldol}]{HCHO/OH^\ominus}$

$\xrightarrow[\text{Cross Cannizaro}]{HCHO/OH^\ominus}$ + HCOOH

↓ Nucleophilic addition | $HCHOH/H^\oplus$

First cross aldol reaction takes place in the presence of base, then cross cannizarro reaction takes place. After that nucleophilic addition will take place.
Thus, the major product is formed.

**34. (3,4)** NaBH$_4$ in ethanol and raney nickel or hydrogen in THF will not react with ester, acid or epoxide in an organic compound. Thus, NaBH$_4$ in ethanol and raney nickel or hydrogen in THF are used as reagents to bring about following conversion.

**35. (2)** The Bouveault-Blanc reduction reaction involves the reduction of an ester by using sodium dissolved in ethyl alcohol.

**36. (4)** The following sequence of reaction is given below :

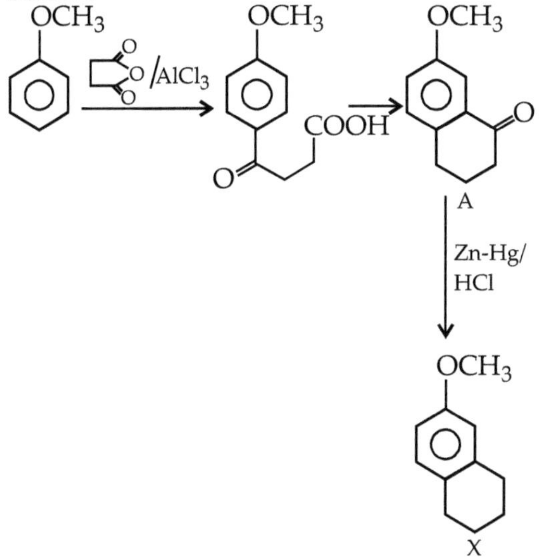

**37. (3)** The synthesis of erythritol (C(CH$_2$OH)$_2$) involves first three aldol reactions between formaldehyde and acetaldehyde and then one Cannizzaro reaction with formaldehyde. It is expressed as,

$$3HCHO + CH_3CHO \xrightarrow[\text{three aldol reactions}]{\text{NaOH}}$$

$$\left[ HOH_2C - \overset{\overset{\displaystyle CH_2OH}{|}}{\underset{\underset{\displaystyle CH_2OH}{|}}{C}} - CHO \right] \xrightarrow[\text{Cannizzaro reaction}]{\text{HCHO}}$$

$$HOH_2C - \overset{\overset{\displaystyle CH_2OH}{|}}{\underset{\underset{\displaystyle CH_2OH}{|}}{C}} - CH_2OH + HCO_2H$$

**38. (2)** The configuration is assigned as shown below :

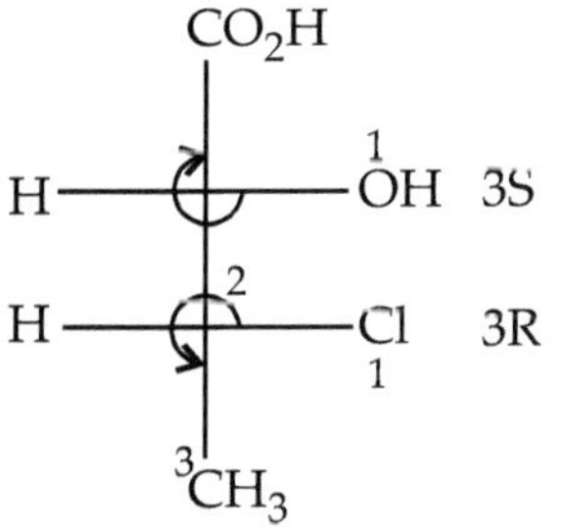

**39. (2)** The given structure contains two possible chiral centres as shown below :

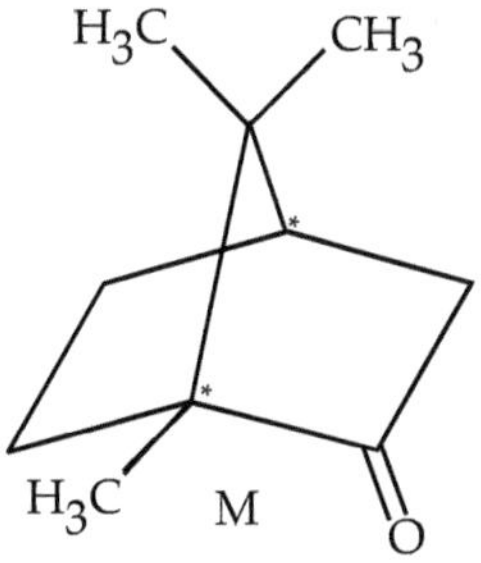

The bridged atom does not allow orientation in opposite manner. Thus, the possible stereoisomer of the given compound is 2.

**40. (1)** The mechanism for the formation of major product is shown below :

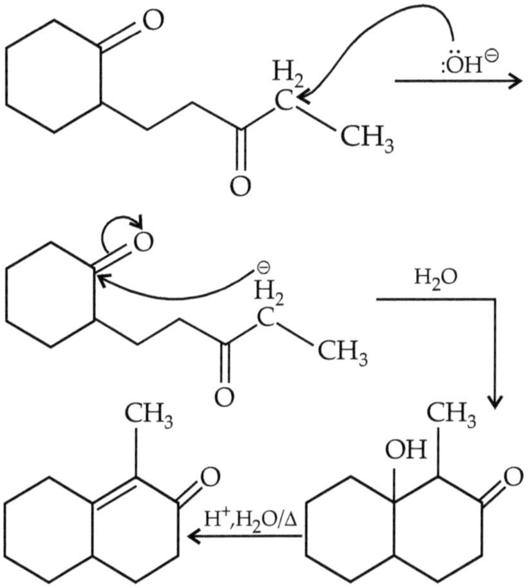

Thus, the major product formed is shown below.

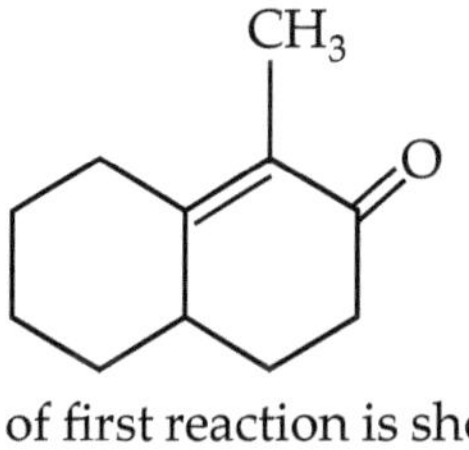

**41. (4)** The product of first reaction is shown below :

$$\text{(Benzene)} + CO + HCl \xrightarrow[\text{CuCl}]{\text{Anhydrous AlCl}_3} \text{Benzaldehyde}$$

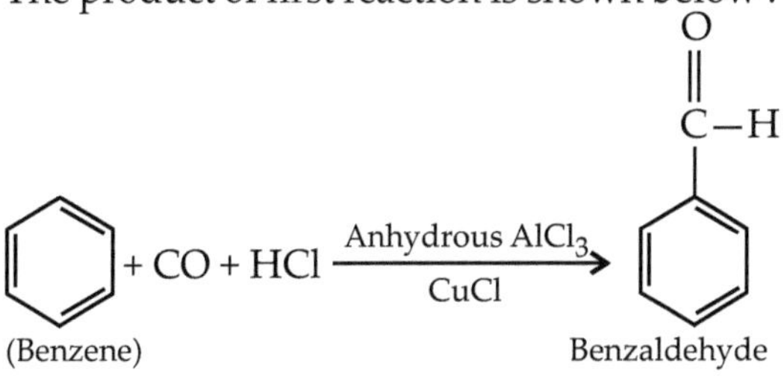

The product of second reaction is shown below :

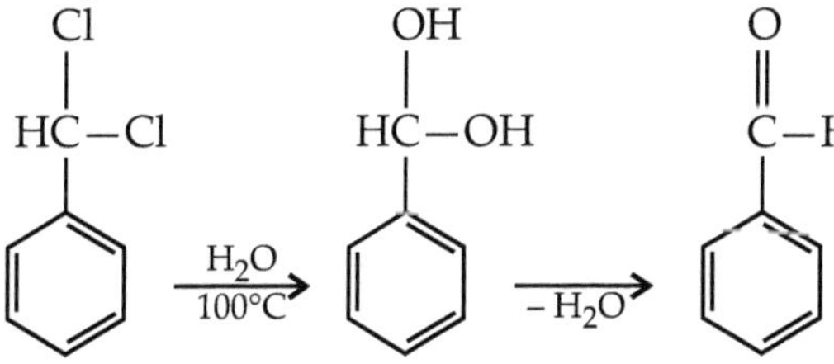

The product of third reaction is shown below :

Benzoyal chloride $\xrightarrow[\text{Pd-BaSO}_4]{\text{Lindlar catalyst H}_2}$ Benzaldehyde

[Rosenmund reduction]

The product of fourth reaction is shown below :

$$C_6H_5\text{-C(=O)-O-Me} \xrightarrow[\substack{\text{Toluene, }-78°C \\ \text{H}_2\text{O restrictive} \\ \text{reduction}}]{\text{DIBAL-H}} \text{Benzaldehyde}$$

Thus, all the given reaction produces benzaldehyde

**42. (4)** The product C is $C_6H_5CHO$ and obtained as follows :

$$\underset{A}{\text{C}_6\text{H}_5\text{-CH}_3} \xrightarrow{\text{KMnO}_4} \underset{A}{\text{COOH}} \xrightarrow{\text{SOCl}_2} \underset{B}{\text{COCl}} \xrightarrow{\text{SOCl}_2} \underset{C}{\text{CHO}}$$

**43. (3)** The reaction that corresponds to the given statement is Hell-Volhard-Zelinsky reaction.

$$RCH_2COOH \xrightarrow[\text{(ii) H}_2\text{O}]{\text{(i) X}_2,\text{P}} R\underset{X}{CH}COOH$$

**44. (3)** The pair with positional isomers is shown below :

$$CH_3-CH_2-CH_2-\underset{O}{\overset{\|}{C}}-CH_3$$

and

$$CH_3-CH_2-\underset{O}{\overset{\|}{C}}-\overset{H_2}{C}-CH_3$$

The names of both compounds are pentane-2-one and pentane-3-one. Both the compounds differ from each other due to position of –C=O group.

**45. (2)** The formation of product is shown below :

$$H_3C-\underset{H}{\overset{|}{C}}H-CHO \xrightarrow[-H_2O]{-OH} H_2\overset{\ominus}{C}-CHO \xrightarrow{H_3C-\overset{\|}{C}-H}$$

$$H_3C-\underset{H}{\overset{|}{\underset{O^-}{C}}}-\overset{H_2}{C}-CHO$$

$$\downarrow H_2O$$

$$H_3C-\underset{A}{\overset{\boxed{OH\ H}}{C-C}}-CHO \xrightarrow[-H_2O]{\Delta} H_3C-C=C-CHO$$

In this reaction, the product is formed by aldol condensation reaction.

**46. (5)** Reactions of ketone with a molecular weight 100 with $NaBH_4$ are shown below :

(1) $CH_3-\overset{}{C}-CH_2-CH_2-CH_2-CH_3 \xrightarrow{NaBH_4}$

$$CH_3-\underset{OH}{\overset{*H}{\overset{|}{C}}}-CH_2-CH_2-CH_2-CH_3$$

Racemic mixture

(2) $CH_3-\underset{O}{\overset{\|}{C}}-CH_2-\underset{CH_3}{\overset{|}{C}}H-CH_3 \xrightarrow{NaBH_4}$

$$CH_3-\underset{OH}{\overset{*H}{\overset{|}{C}}}-CH_2-\underset{CH_3}{\overset{|}{C}}H-CH_3$$

Racemic mixture

(3) $CH_3-\underset{O}{\overset{\|}{C}}-\underset{CH_3}{\overset{CH_3}{\overset{|}{\underset{|}{C}}}}-CH_3 \longrightarrow$

$$CH_3-\underset{OH}{\overset{*H}{\overset{|}{C}}}-\underset{CH_3}{\overset{CH_2-CH_3}{\overset{|}{\underset{|}{C}}}}-CH_3$$

Racemic mixture

(4) $CH_3-\underset{OH}{\overset{\|}{C}}-\underset{H}{\overset{CH_2-CH_3}{\overset{|}{C}}}-CH_3 \longrightarrow$

+&-both gives distereomers

$$CH_3-\underset{OH}{\overset{*H}{\overset{|}{C}}}-\underset{*H}{\overset{CH_2-CH_3}{\overset{|}{C}}}-CH_3$$

(5) $CH_3-CH_2-\underset{O}{\overset{\|}{C}}-CH_2-CH_2-CH_3 \longrightarrow$

$$CH_3-CH_2-\underset{OH}{\overset{*H}{\overset{|}{C}}}-CH_2-CH_2-CH_3$$

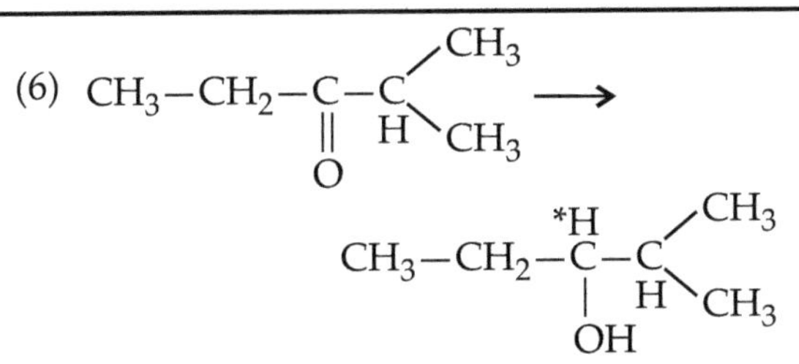

(6) $CH_3-CH_2-\overset{\underset{\displaystyle \|}{O}}{C}-\overset{\overset{\displaystyle CH_3}{|}}{\underset{\underset{\displaystyle CH_3}{|}}{\overset{H}{C}}} \longrightarrow$

$CH_3-CH_2-\overset{\overset{\displaystyle *H}{|}}{\underset{\underset{\displaystyle OH}{|}}{C}}-\overset{\overset{\displaystyle CH_3}{\diagup}}{\underset{\underset{\displaystyle CH_3}{}}{\overset{H}{C}}}$

Racemic mixture

**47. (4)** The complete reaction is :

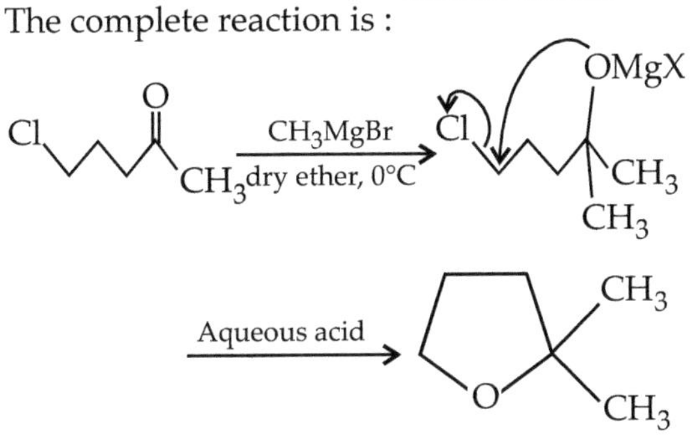

$$\xrightarrow[\text{dry ether, 0°C}]{CH_3MgBr}$$

$$\xrightarrow{\text{Aqueous acid}}$$

The final product of the reaction is 2, 2-Dimethyltetrahydrofuran.

**48. (3)** The complete reaction for the formation of product Y is :

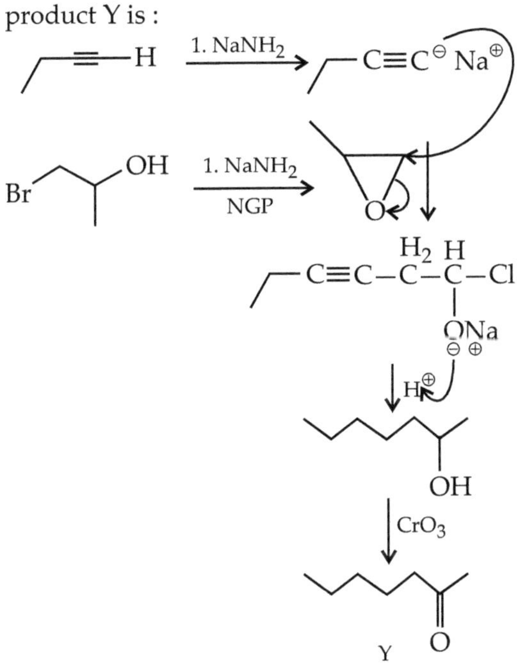

$$\xrightarrow{\text{1. NaNH}_2}$$

$$\xrightarrow[\text{NGP}]{\text{1. NaNH}_2}$$

$$\downarrow H^{\oplus}$$

$$\downarrow CrO_3$$

The product Y gives positive iodoform test because it possesses   group and it is a functional isomer of product X.

**49. (1)** The complete reaction scheme is shown below :

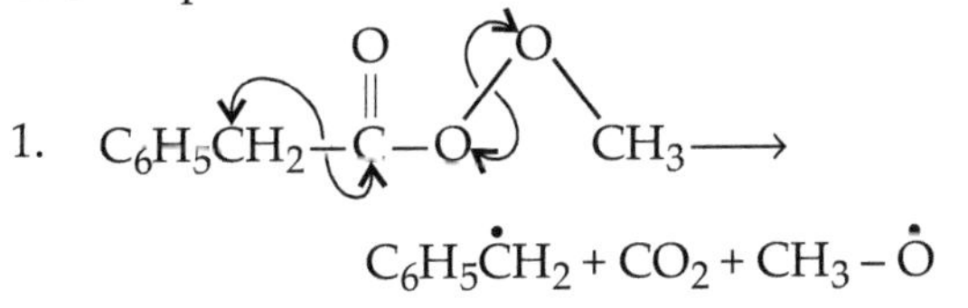

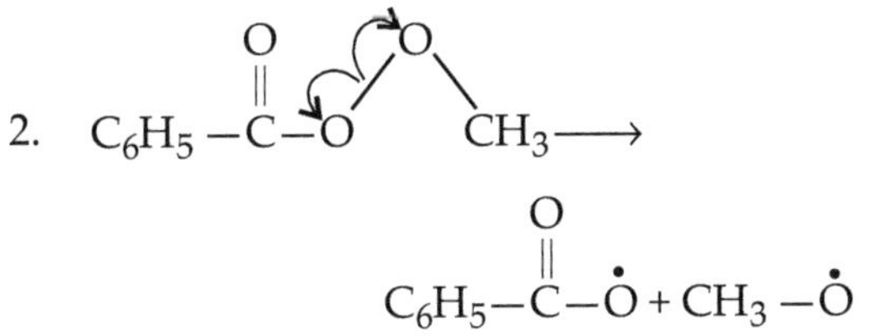

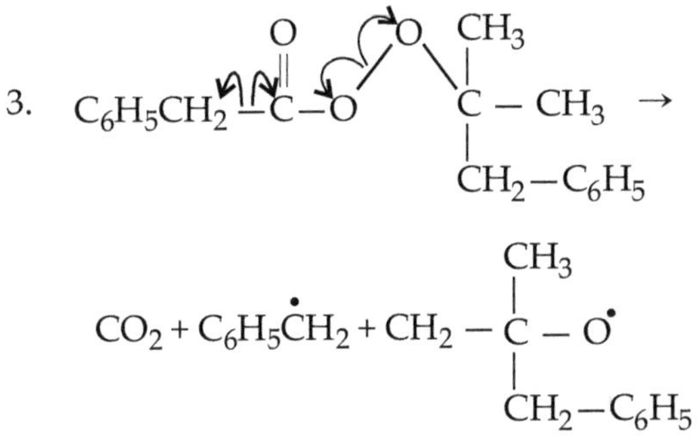

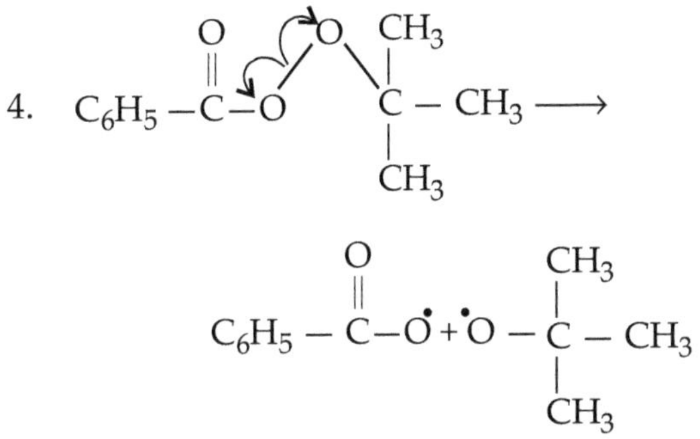

1.   $C_6H_5\overset{\bullet}{C}H_2 + CO_2 + CH_3-\overset{\bullet}{O}$

2.   $C_6H_5-\overset{\underset{\displaystyle \|}{O}}{C}-O \qquad CH_3 \longrightarrow$

$$C_6H_5-\overset{\underset{\displaystyle \|}{O}}{C}-\overset{\bullet}{O} + CH_3-\overset{\bullet}{O}$$

3.   $C_6H_5CH_2-\overset{\underset{\displaystyle \|}{O}}{C}-O \qquad \overset{\overset{\displaystyle CH_3}{|}}{\underset{\underset{\displaystyle CH_2-C_6H_5}{|}}{C}}-CH_3 \longrightarrow$

$$CO_2 + C_6H_5\overset{\bullet}{C}H_2 + CH_2-\overset{\overset{\displaystyle CH_3}{|}}{\underset{\underset{\displaystyle CH_2-C_6H_5}{|}}{C}}-\overset{\bullet}{O}$$

4.   $C_6H_5-\overset{\underset{\displaystyle \|}{O}}{C}-O \qquad \overset{\overset{\displaystyle CH_3}{|}}{\underset{\underset{\displaystyle CH_3}{|}}{C}}-CH_3 \longrightarrow$

$$C_6H_5-\overset{\underset{\displaystyle \|}{O}}{C}-\overset{\bullet}{O} + \overset{\bullet}{O}-\overset{\overset{\displaystyle CH_3}{|}}{\underset{\underset{\displaystyle CH_3}{|}}{C}}-CH_3$$

Therefore, the correct match is shown below :
$P = 1 \quad Q = 3 \quad R = 4 \quad S = 2$

**50. (1)** The major product C is aspirin.

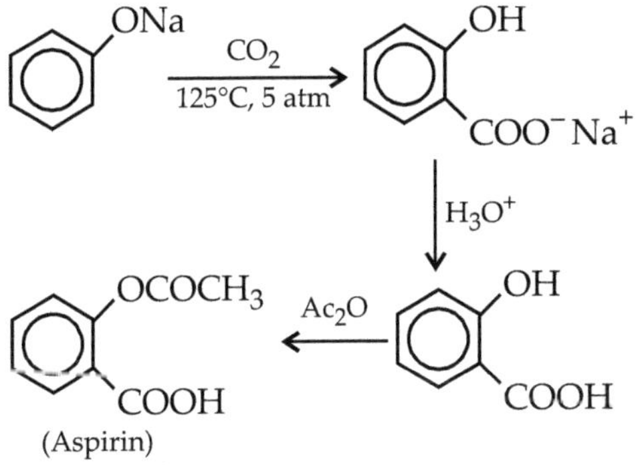

$$\xrightarrow[\text{125°C, 5 atm}]{CO_2}$$

$$\downarrow H_3O^+$$

$$\xleftarrow{Ac_2O}$$

(Aspirin)

Sodium phenoxide when heated with $CO_2$ under pressure at 125°C, the product formed is salicylic acid. It gives product C (aspirin) on acetylation.

**51. (3)** Reduction of acetic acid by  $LiAlH_4$ gives ethanol (A). It reacts with $PCl_5$ to form ethyl chloride (B) Ethyl chloride reacts with alcoholic KOH to give ethylene.

$$CH_3COOH \xrightarrow{LiAlH_4} CH_3CH_2OH \xrightarrow{PCl_3}$$

$$H_2C = CH_2 \xleftarrow{\text{alc. KOH}} CH_3CH_2Cl \leftarrow$$
(ethylene)

**52. (4)** In cannizzaro reaction, there will be no formation of C—C bond as shown below :

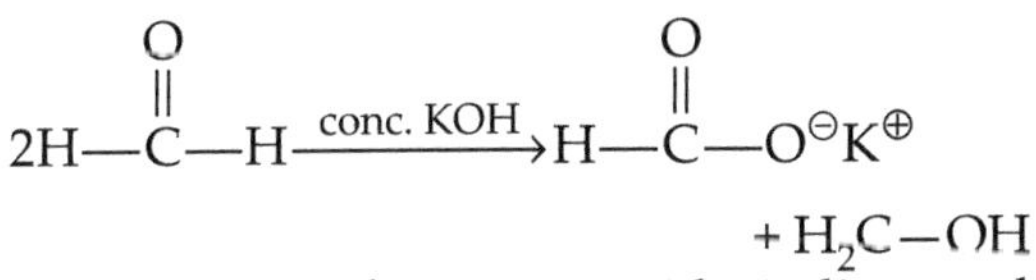

$$2H-\overset{\underset{\displaystyle \|}{O}}{C}-H \xrightarrow{\text{conc. KOH}} H-\overset{\underset{\displaystyle \|}{O}}{C}-O^{\ominus}K^{\oplus}$$

$$+ H_2C-OH$$

**53. (3)** The heating of acetone with iodine and potassium hydroxide forms iodoform. The reaction for the same is as follows :

$$H_3C-\overset{\overset{O}{\|}}{C}-CH_3 \xrightarrow[\text{Iodoform reaction}]{I_2+KOH}$$

$$CHI_3 + H_3C-\overset{\overset{O}{\|}}{C}-O^{\ominus}K^{\oplus}$$

**54. (3)** Organic compound A is :

$$H_3C-\overset{H_2}{\underset{\underset{CH_3}{|}}{C}}-C=C=O$$

Reaction of compound A with $H_2O$ is shown below :

$$H_3C-\overset{H_2}{\underset{\underset{CH_3}{|}}{C}}-C=C=O+H_2O\longrightarrow$$

$$H_3C-\overset{H_2}{\underset{\underset{CH_3}{|}}{C}}-\overset{H}{\underset{}{C}}-\overset{\overset{O}{\|}}{C}-OH$$

Reaction of compound A with $NH_3$ is shown below :

$$H_3C-\overset{H_2}{\underset{\underset{CH_3}{|}}{C}}-C=C=O \longrightarrow H_3C-\overset{H_2}{\underset{\underset{CH_3}{|}}{C}}-\overset{H}{\underset{}{C}}-C-O^-$$

$$\downarrow NH_3$$

$$H_3C-\overset{H_2}{\underset{\underset{CH_3\ CH_3}{|\quad\ |}}{C}}-C=C-OH$$

$$\Updownarrow$$

$$H_3C-\overset{H_2}{\underset{\underset{CH_3}{|}}{C}}-\overset{H}{\underset{}{C}}=\overset{\overset{O}{\|}}{C}-NH_2$$

Reaction of compound A with $CH_3COOH$ is shown below :

$$H_3C-\overset{H_2}{\underset{\underset{CH_3}{|}}{C}}-C=C=O \xrightarrow{CH_3COOH}$$

$$H_3C-\overset{H_2}{\underset{\underset{CH_3}{|}}{C}}-\overset{H}{\underset{}{C}}-\overset{\overset{O}{\|}}{C}-O-\overset{\overset{O}{\|}}{C}-NH_2$$

**55. (3)** Tischenko reaction is a modification of Cannizzaro reaction. In this reaction, disproportionation reaction of an aldehyde with no alpha hydrogen atom takes place in the presence of an alkoxide to produce an ester.

$$2 \overset{O}{\underset{H}{\|}}\phantom{ph} \xrightarrow[\text{50-60}°, 4\ hr]{C_6H_5CH_2ONa} \phantom{ph} 90\%$$

**56. (3)** The structure of maleic acid is

$$\overset{H}{\underset{H}{}}C=C\overset{COOH}{\underset{COOH}{}}$$

Maleic acid exhibits only geometrical isomerism because only cis and trans arrangement is possible in its structure due to the presence of two groups at each carbon atom. Therefore, the compound which does not exhibit optical isomerism is maleic acid.

**57. (4)** The reaction of phthalic acid with resorcinol leads to the formation of fluorescein which is shown below :

Phthalic acid + 2 Resorcinol $\xrightarrow{\text{conc. }H_2SO_4}$ Fluorescein

**58. (4)** Propionic acid is formed 1, 1, 1-trichloro-propane is treated with aqueous KOH.

$$CH_3-CH_2-\overset{\overset{Cl}{|}}{\underset{\underset{Cl}{|}}{C}}-Cl + \xrightarrow[-3\ KCl]{KOH\ (aq)} CH_3-CH_2-\overset{OH}{\underset{OH}{C}}-OH$$

$$\downarrow H_2O$$

$$CH_3-CH_2-\overset{\overset{O}{\|}}{C}-OH$$

**59. (3)** Weak acids are not soluble in weak bases. O-Nitorgen is a weak acid and sodium bicarbonate is a weak base.

**60. (3)** Butyric acid is present in rancid butter.

**61. (2)** The formation of product P by using given reactant and reagents is shown below :

$$\xrightarrow{H_3O^+} \quad \overset{COOH}{\underset{COOH}{}}$$

$$\downarrow -2CO_2$$

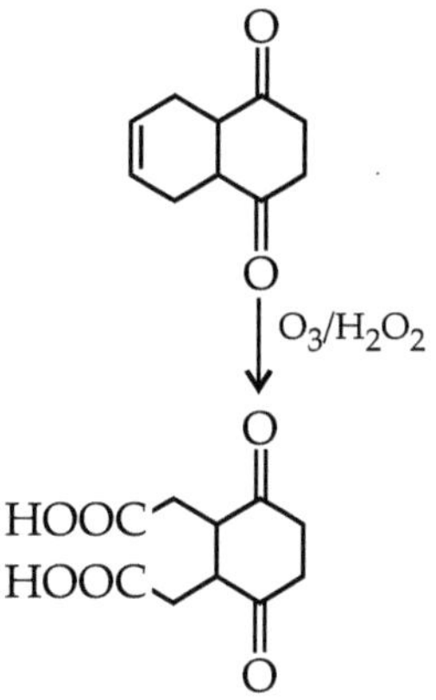

The above reaction shows that product contains two carboxylic acid groups (–COOH).

**62. (3)** According to the limiting reagent, the mechanisms of the complete reactions I and II are shown below.

Reaction I :

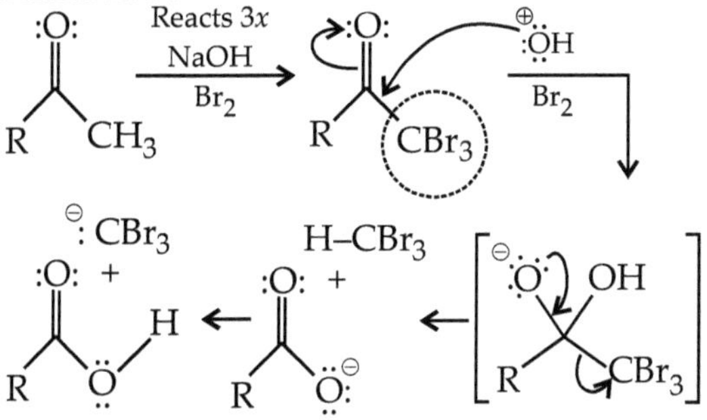

Where, R is acetone.

Reaction II :

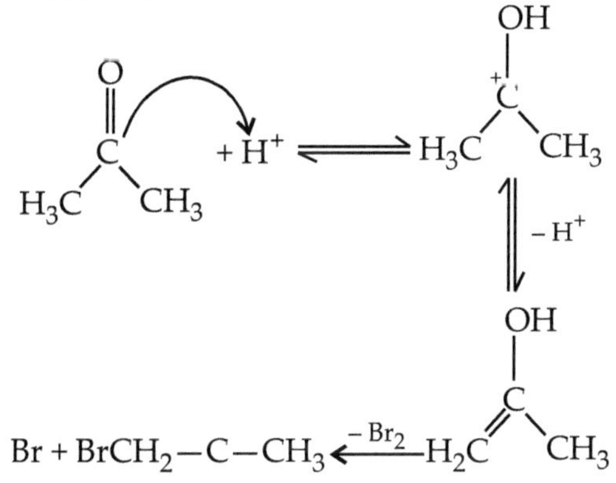

**63. (1)** The complete reaction showing products V and W are given as follows :

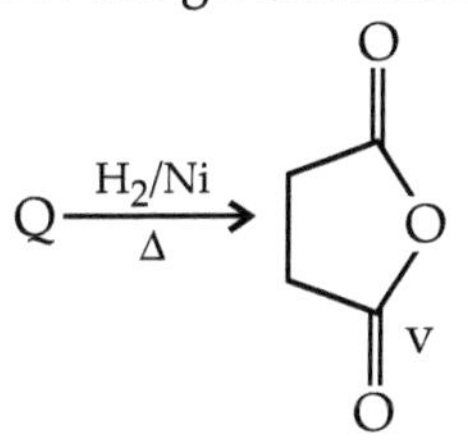

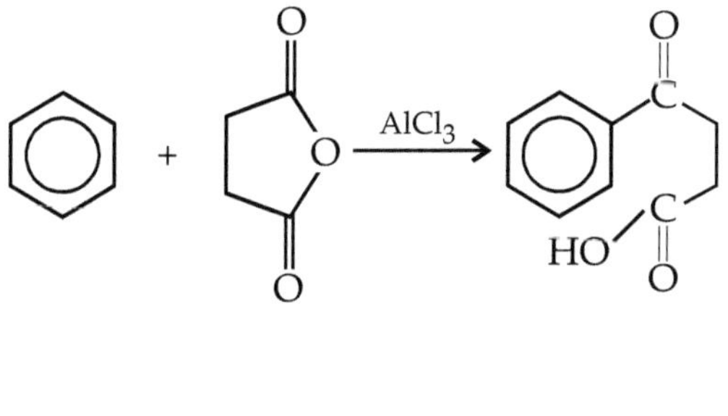

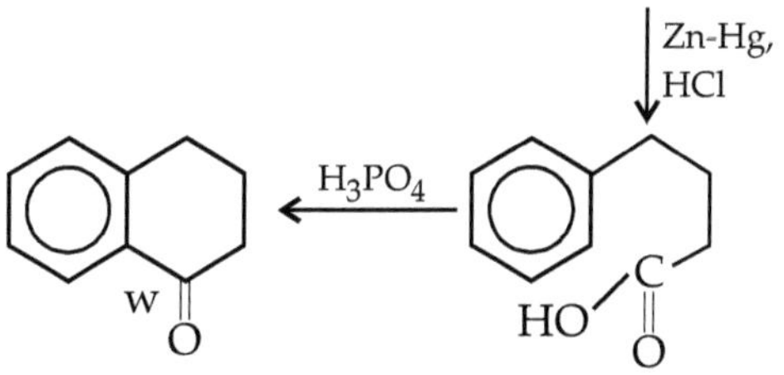

**64. (3)** The aldol condensation reaction taking place in the given conversion is shown below.

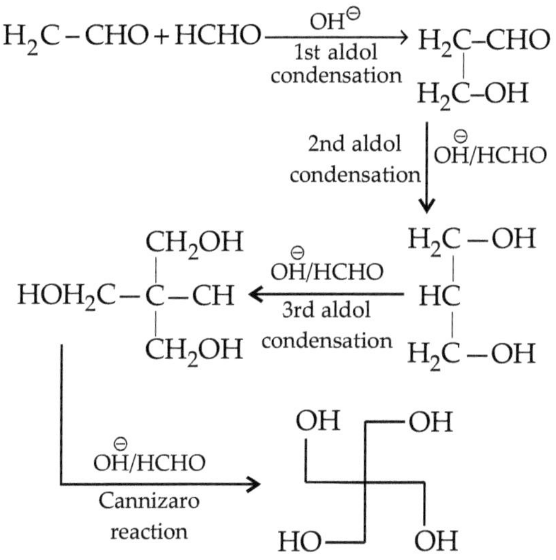

After third Aldol condensation there is no alpha hydrogen left. So at last Cannizaro reaction will take place.

**65. (4)** The structures of given compounds are shown below :

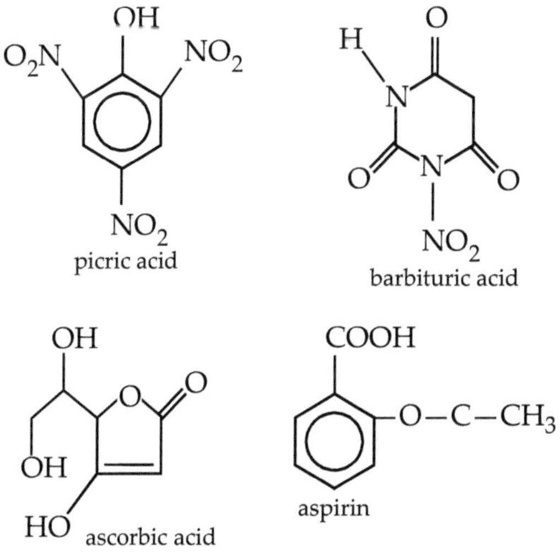

picric acid

barbituric acid

ascorbic acid

aspirin

Thus, only aspirin has –COOH group.

**66. (2)** The $\beta$ keto acids undergo decarboxylation very easily as the beta carbon acquires negative charge and gets stabilized.

**67. (1)** The steps involved in the given reaction are shown below :

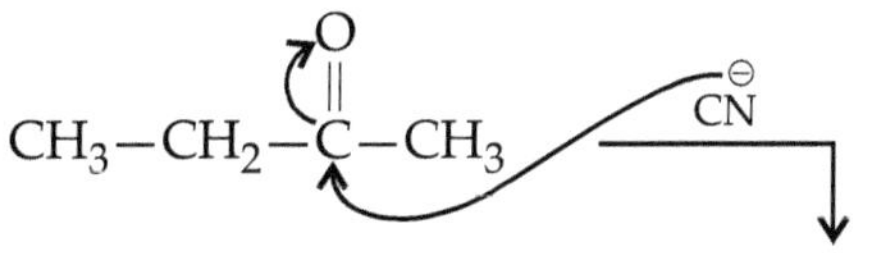

$$CH_3-CH_2-C-CH_3$$

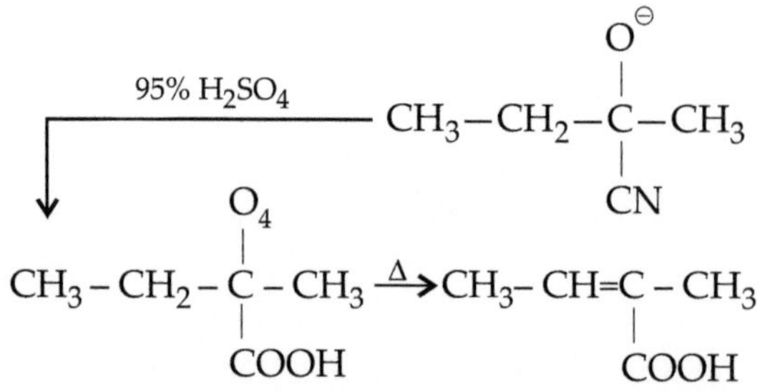

$$\xrightarrow{95\%\ H_2SO_4}\quad CH_3-CH_2-\overset{\overset{\displaystyle O^{\ominus}}{|}}{\underset{\underset{\displaystyle CN}{|}}{C}}-CH_3$$

$$CH_3-CH_2-\overset{\overset{\displaystyle O_4}{|}}{\underset{\underset{\displaystyle COOH}{|}}{C}}-CH_3 \xrightarrow{\Delta} CH_3-CH=\overset{\underset{\underset{\displaystyle COOH}{|}}{}}{C}-CH_3$$

**68. (1)** Effervescence formation occurs when carbon dioxide is released, it means decarboxylation has occurred. The Baeyer's test shows presence of unsaturation. Aldehyde undergoes Perkin condensation under the given conditions and forms α, β unsaturated aromatic acid. The first step of the reaction is shown below.

(structure I: benzaldehyde CHO) $\xrightarrow[\text{CH}_3\text{COONa}]{(CH_3CO)_2O}$ (structure J: $CH_2$–$CH_2$–COOH substituted benzene)

I → J

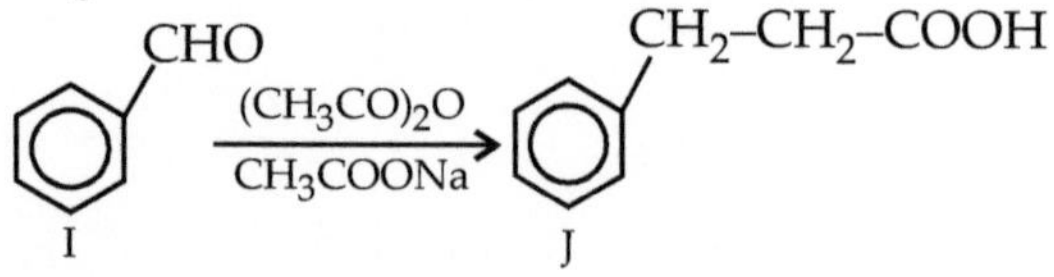

**69. (3)** The correct sequence of reaction is shown below :

(structure I: benzaldehyde CHO) $\xrightarrow[\text{CHCOONa}]{(CH_3CO)_2O}$ (structure J: CH–CH–COOH substituted benzene)

I → J

$\xrightarrow{H_2\text{-Pd/C}}$ (CH$_2$–CH$_2$–COOH substituted benzene) $\xrightarrow{SOCl_2}$ ($CH_2$–$CH_2$–C–Cl with =O, substituted benzene)

$\xleftarrow{AlCl_3}$ (compound K, indanone) O

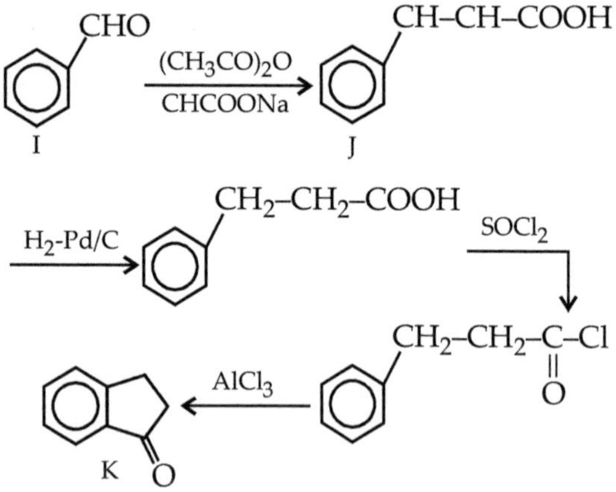

The compound K is formed by Friedel-Crafts acylation reaction at last.

**70. (1,3,4)**

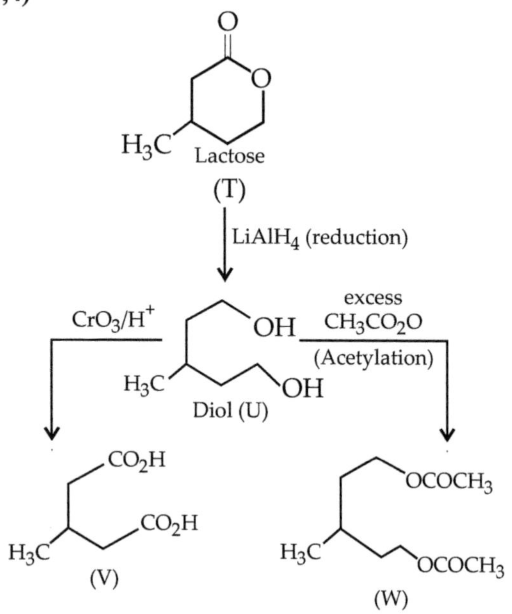

(structure T: lactone with H$_3$C, labelled Lactose)
(T)

$\downarrow$ LiAlH$_4$ (reduction)

$\xrightarrow{\text{excess}}$ (Diol U with OH, OH, H$_3$C) $\xrightarrow[\text{(Acetylation)}]{CH_3CO_2O}$

$\xrightarrow{CrO_3/H^+}$

(V: H$_3$C, CO$_2$H, CO$_2$H)
(V)

(W: H$_3$C, OCOCH$_3$, OCOCH$_3$)
(W)

**(A)** Lactones are soluble in hot aqueous sodium hydroxide.

**(B)** The final product U does not have any chiral centre and is thus optically inactive.

**(C)** Molecular formula of the product W is $C_{10}H_{18}O_4$.

**(D)** The product V is a diacid and is thus soluble in aqueous NaHCO$_3$.

**71. (3)** In all the given compounds, $o$-hydroxybenzoic acid is most acidic. This is due to the presence of strong intramolecular hydrogen bonding. After the removal of proton, carboxylate ion is stabilized by hydrogen bonding.

**72.** (A)-r, s, t, (B)-p, s, (C)-r, s, (D)-q, r

The mechanism for first reaction is given as,

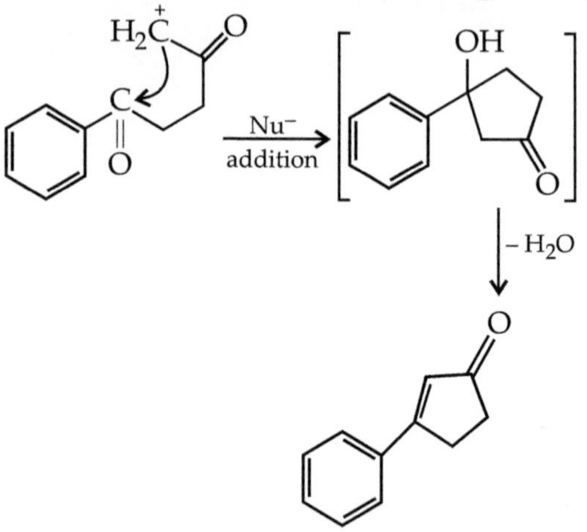

(mechanism structures: H$_2$C$^+$ with O, phenyl C=O $\xrightarrow[\text{addition}]{Nu^-}$ cyclopentanone intermediate with OH, phenyl) $\xrightarrow{-H_2O}$ (phenyl cyclopentenone)

Therefore, it is a nucleophilic addition reaction. In this reaction, carbanion is generated and dehydration takes place.

The mechanism for second reaction is given as,

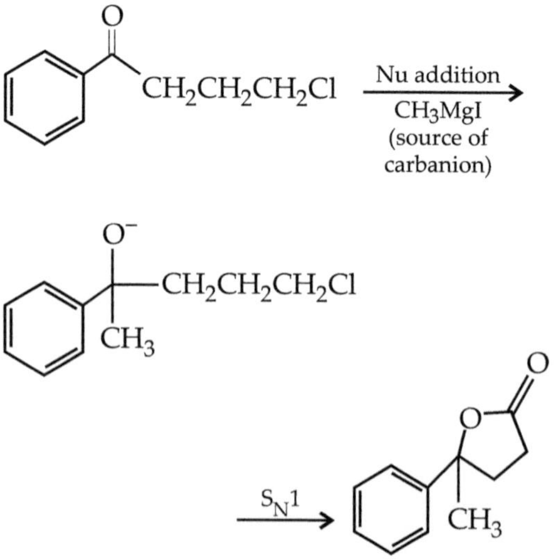

(phenyl ketone with CH$_2$CH$_2$CH$_2$Cl) $\xrightarrow[\substack{CH_3MgI \\ \text{(source of} \\ \text{carbanion)}}]{\text{Nu addition}}$

(alkoxide intermediate: O$^-$, phenyl, CH$_3$, CH$_2$CH$_2$CH$_2$Cl) $\xrightarrow{S_N1}$ (lactone with phenyl, CH$_3$, =O)

Here, nucleophilic addition takes place but in second step nucleophilic substitution also occurs.

The mechanism for third reaction is given as,

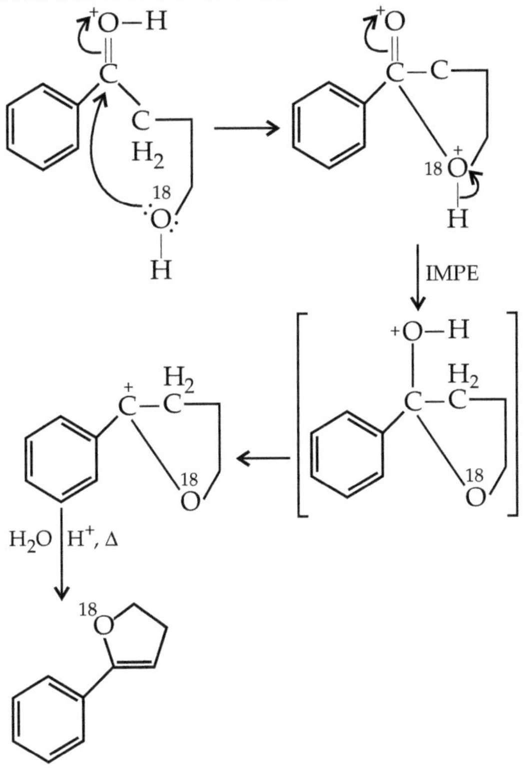

Here, nucleophilic addition takes place along with the process of dehydration.

The mechanism for fourth reaction is given as,

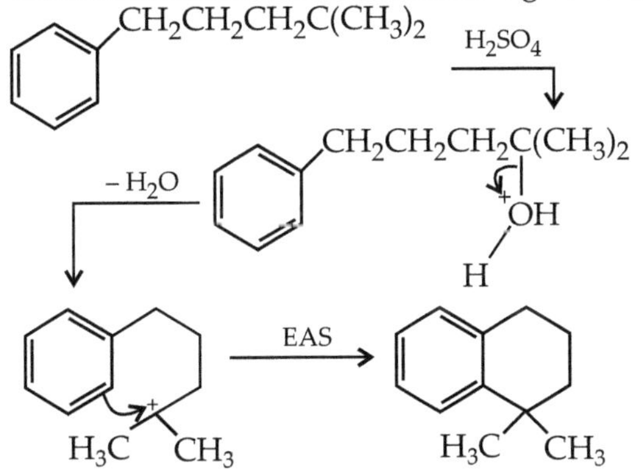

Here, dehydration takes place with electrophilic addition.

**73. (1)** The following reaction is given below :

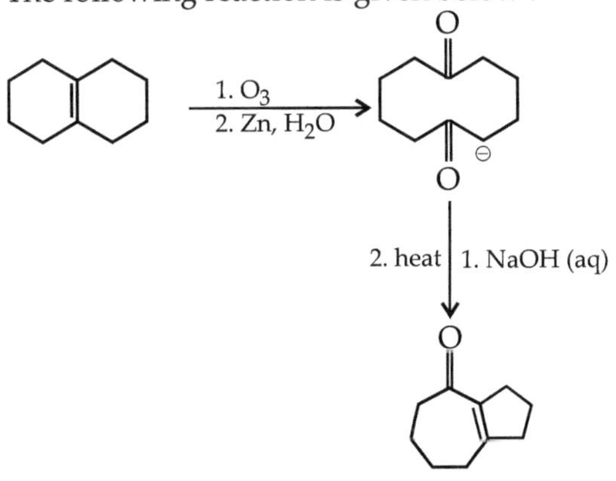

In the following reaction, only one intermolecular aldol condensation product, that is, $\alpha$, $\beta$ unsaturated compound is obtained from product Y.

**74. (3)** The nitration of compound P is shown below :

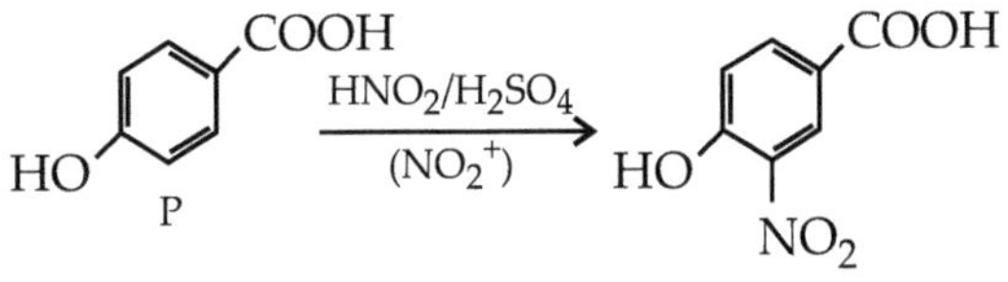

**Figure 4**

In compound P,  group is orthopara directing.

The nitration of compound Q is shown below.

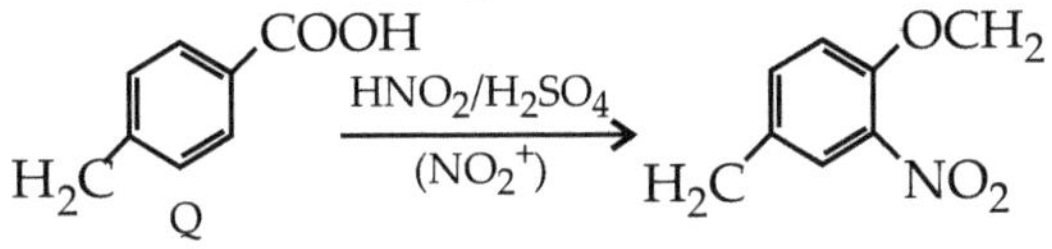

**Figure 5**

In compound Q,  group is a strong activator.

The nitration of compound S is shown below.

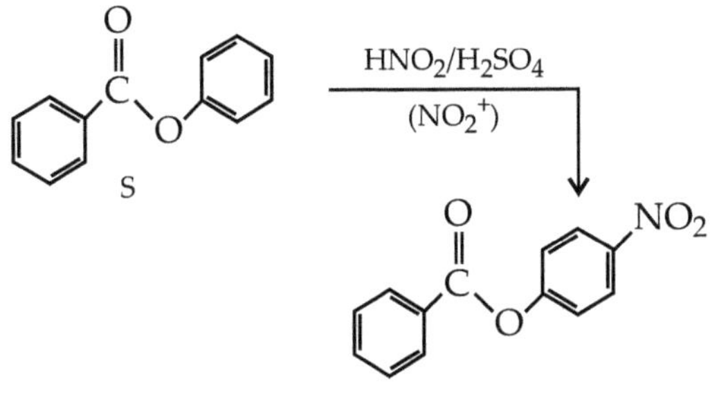

**Figure 6**

The substitution will take place in the activated ring at the least crowded para position.

**75. (2)** The following reactions are shown below :

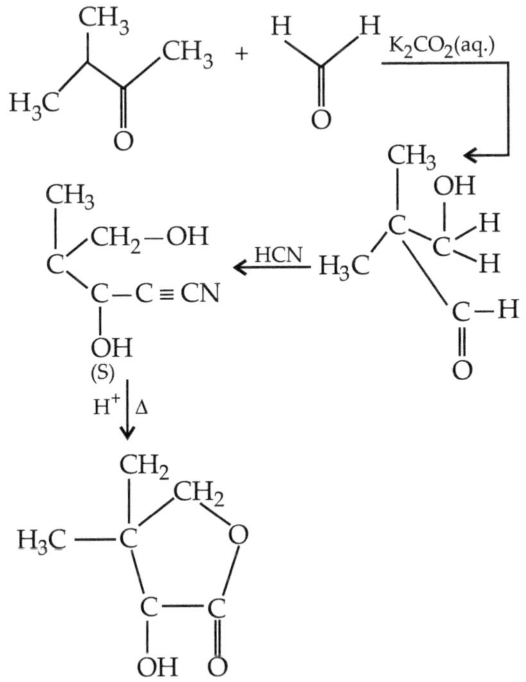

(Given product)

**76. (1)** The compound P and Q reacts in the presence of   to give compound R.

The structure of R is :

$$H_3C-CH(CH_3)-C(=O)- \quad + \quad -C(=O)- \quad \xrightarrow[\text{(cross aldol)}]{\text{aq. } K_2CO_3}$$

(P)    (Q)

(R)

**77. (4)** The compound P and Q reacts in the presence of $K_2CO_3$ to give compound R.

Compound R reacts with to give compound S

$$H_3C-CH(CH_3)-C(=O)- \quad + \quad -C(=O)- \quad \xrightarrow[\text{(cross aldol)}]{\text{aq. } K_2CO_3}$$

(P)    (Q)

(S)  $\xleftarrow{\text{HCN}}$  (R)

**78. (1)** The acidic strength of alcohols is less than that of carboxylic acids because carboxylate ion is stabilized by resonance. Therefore, acidic strength of compound (III) and (IV) is more than that of compound (I) and (II).

The acidic strength of aromatic compounds decreases with increase in electron withdrawing nature of the substituents attached to it. Therefore, para-chlorophenol is more acidic than phenol and para-methylbenzoic acid is less acidic than benzoic acid.

Therefore, the correct order of acidic strength of the given compound is (III) > (IV) > (II) > (I).

**79. (2)** The compound P gives positive iodoform test means one methyl group is attached to the carbonyl carbon. Therefore, the compound given in option (C) and (D) are not present in this reaction.

The hydrolysis of the olefin Q leads to the formation of dicarbonyl compound which undergoes intra molecular aldol condensation

reaction due to the formation of carbanion on the methyl group boned to the carbonyl carbon.

The reactions involved in the given conversion are shown below :

$$\xrightarrow[\text{(ii) } H^+]{\text{(i) } CH_3MgBr}$$

$$\Big\downarrow H^+/\Delta$$

(Q)   $\longleftarrow$

$$\Big\downarrow O_3/Zn/H_2O$$

(R)   $\xrightarrow{OH^-}$

$$\Big\downarrow$$

(S)   $\xleftarrow{\Delta}$

Hence, the compound P corresponds to the organic compound given in the option (B).

**80.** The carbonyl compounds react with Grignard reagent followed by hydrolysis to form alcohol which on dehydration leads to the formation of olefin. The ozonolysis of olefin leads to the formation of dicarbonyl product. The conversion of the compound P to Q and R is shown below.

$$\xrightarrow[\text{(ii) } H^+]{\text{(i) } CH_3MgBr}$$

$$\Big\downarrow H^+/\Delta$$

(Q)   $\longleftarrow$

$$\Big\downarrow O_3/Zn/H_2O$$

(R)

Hence, the compound Q and R corresponds to the organic compounds given in option (A).

**81. (2)** The intramolecular condensation in the compound R results in the formation of S which is shown below :

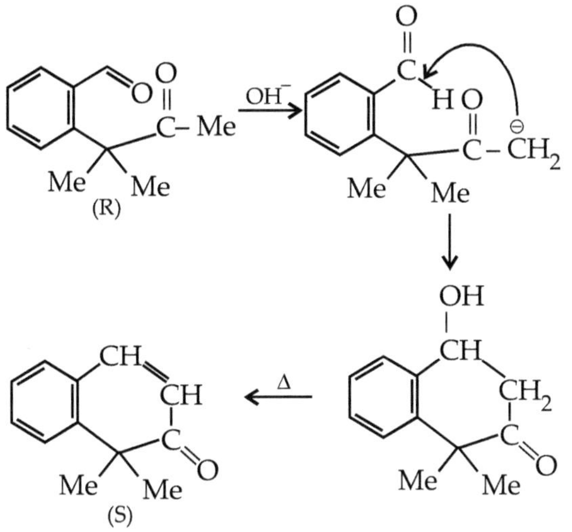

Hence, the compound S corresponds to the organic compound given in option (B).

**82.** ((A)-(p), (q), (t); (B)-(p), (s), (t); (C)-(r), (s); and (D)-(p)).

The compound given in option (A) contains one bromine group on a heterocyclic ring and the heterocyclic ring is connected to an aromatic ring. Therefore, this compound can undergo nucleophilic substitution, elimination and dehydrogenation reaction. Hence, (p), (q) and (t) are correct for (A).

The compound given in option (B) is benzyl alcohol which undergoes nucleophilic substitution, esterification with acetic anhydride and dehydrogenation reactions. Hence, (p), (s) and (t) are correct for (B).

The compound given in option (C) contains aldehyde and alcoholic group at ortho position on the benzene ring. Therefore, it can undergo esterification and nucleophilic addition reactions. Hence, (r) and (s) is correct for (C).

The compound given in the option (D) contains nitro group and alcohol group at ortho position on the benzene ring. Therefore, this compound can undergo only nucleophilic substitution reaction. Hence, (p) is correct for (D).

**83. (2,3,4)** (A) The structure E, F and G are not resonance structures because structure F and G are the same. Only the position of and is different.

(B) Structures E, F and structures E, G are tautomers as it involves conversion of hydroxyl group to keto group due

to the presence of adjacent double bond.

(C) In compound F, the groups with higher priority are on the same side of the double bond whereas in structure G, the groups with higher priority are on the opposite side of the double bond. So, F and G are geometrical isomers.

(D) Structure F and G are diastereomers because they are non-superimposable mirror images of each other.

**84. (4)** Protonation of Hex-3-ynal takes place on reaction with $NaBH_4$ and the aldehyde group gets converted into alcohol. The hydroxyl group of alcohol gets replaced by on reaction with $PBr_3$.

$$CH_3CH_2C \equiv CCH_2CHO \xrightarrow[\text{2.PBr}_3]{\text{1.NaBH}_4} CH_3CH_2C$$

$$\equiv CCH_2CH_2Br$$

**85. (1)** The product obtained by the reaction of $NaBH_4$ and $PBr_3$ with hex-3-ynal gets converted into $CH_3CH_2C \equiv CCH_2CH_2COOH$. And on further reaction with $SOCl_2$ form $CH_3CH_2C \equiv CCH_2CH_2COCl$.

**86. (3)** Acid chloride on reaction with $H_2$, $Pd/BaSO_4$ reduces to aldehyde and it reduces alkyne to cis-alkene.

$$CH_3CH_2C \equiv CCH_2CH_2COCl \xrightarrow[\substack{\text{Pd/BaSO}_4\\ \text{quinoline}}]{H_2}$$

$$CH_3CH_2CH \equiv CHCH_2CH_2CHO$$

**87. (3)** The correct sequence of reaction is expressed as,

$$\overset{O}{\overset{||}{Ph-C}}-\overset{O}{\overset{||}{\underset{*}{C}}}-\overset{O}{\overset{||}{C}}-OH \xrightarrow{H_2, \Delta} \overset{O}{\overset{||}{Ph-C}}-\underset{(E)}{CH_3} + CO_2$$

$$\overset{O}{\overset{||}{Ph-C}}-\underset{*}{CH_3} \xrightarrow[\text{NaOH}]{I_2} \overset{O}{\overset{||}{Ph-C}}-COONa + CHI_3$$
$$\qquad\qquad\quad (F)\quad\quad\quad (G)$$

**88.** The tertiary alcohol H is formed by the following reaction :

$$\overset{O}{\overset{||}{Ph-C}}-CH_3 + CH_3 + PhCH_2MgBr \longrightarrow$$

$$\overset{OH}{\overset{|}{Ph-\underset{|}{C}-CH_3}}$$
$$\underset{H_2C-Ph}{}$$

**89. (4)** The ozonolysis of I that leads to the formation of J and K is :

$$Ph-\underset{\underset{Ph}{|}}{\overset{\overset{CH_3}{|}}{C}}=CH \xrightarrow[H_2O/Zn]{O_3} Ph-\underset{(K)}{\overset{\overset{CH_3}{|}}{C}}=O + \underset{(J)}{Ph-CHO}$$

$$\underset{J}{\underset{\underset{}{\text{benzaldehyde}}}{}} \xrightarrow{KOH} \text{(benzyl alcohol)} + \text{(potassium benzoate, L)}$$

**90. (4)** Intramolecular hydrogen bonding stabilizes *o*-hydroxybenzoic acid. The existence of stronger intermolecular hydrogen bonding in *p*-hydroxybenzoic acid causes greater boiling point of *p*-hydroxybenzoic acid.

*o*-Hydroxybenzoic acid    *p*-Hydroxybenzoic acid

**91. (1)** Cyclohexene on reductive ozonolysis (ozonolysis followed by reaction with zinc dust) gives adipaldehyde as compound E, which on Aldol condensation gives desired compound F.

$$\text{(cyclohexene)} \xrightarrow[Zn]{O_3, H_2O} \underset{(E)}{\text{(adipaldehyde)}} \xrightarrow[\substack{\text{(aldol} \\ \text{condensation)}}]{KOH} \underset{(F)}{\text{(cyclopentene carbaldehyde)}}$$

**92.** (A)- (p), (s); (B)- (q); (C)- (q), (r), (s); (D)- (q), (r); (A)

$$PhCHO + O_2N-\underset{\overset{|}{NO_2}}{\text{C}_6\text{H}_3}-\overset{\overset{H}{|}}{N}-NH_2 \longrightarrow$$

$$PhHC=N-\overset{\overset{H}{|}}{N}-\underset{ppt.}{\text{C}_6\text{H}_3(NO_2)}-NO_2$$

$$PhCHOH + Ag_2O \xrightarrow{NH_3} PhCO\bar{O} + \underset{\text{White ppt}}{Ag \downarrow}$$

$$PhCHO \xrightarrow{KCN} Ph-\underset{\underset{H}{|}}{\overset{\overset{CN}{|}}{C}}-\bar{O}$$

**(B)** Silver nitrate gives white precipitate with $CH_3C \equiv CH$.

$$CH_3C \equiv CH \xrightarrow{AgNO_3} \underset{\text{White ppt.}}{CH_3-C \neq C^- Ag^+ \downarrow}$$

**(C)** $CN^-$ is a nucleophile, gives precipitate with silver nitrate and participates in cyanohydrin formation.

$$PhCHO \xrightarrow{KCN} Ph-\underset{\underset{H}{|}}{\overset{\overset{CN}{|}}{C}}-\bar{O}$$

$$AgNO_3 + CN^- \longrightarrow AgCN \downarrow$$

**(D)** Iodide ion is a nucleophile and gives precipitate with silver nitrate.

$$I^- + AgNO_3 \rightarrow AgI \downarrow + NO_3^-$$

**93. (3)** The structure of $C_6H_5COCl$ is shown below :

The given structure shows that the compound consists of one benzene ring. The functional group present in the given compound is $-COCl$. The name of the functional group is carbonyl chloride. Therefore, the suffix used for acid chloride is –oyl chloride.

Thus, the IUPAC name of $C_6H_5COCl$ is benzene carbonyl chloride.

**94. (3)** The reaction that shows the formation of lactone as a product is shown below :

$$\text{(benzene-1,2-dicarbaldehyde)} \xrightarrow[\substack{\text{Intramolecular} \\ \text{cannizzaro}}]{OH^-} \text{(2-(hydroxymethyl)benzoate)} \xrightarrow{H^+}$$

Thus, the reactant used for the formation of lactone only as a product is,

**95. (2)** The lowest molecular weight ketone is Me $-$ CO $-$ Me and the next higher homologue is $MeCH_2 - CO - Me$.

The reaction of both the ketone with hydroxyl amine is shown below :

$$Me_2C=O + NH_2OH \xrightarrow{H^+} \text{(I)}$$

$$Me_2C=O + NH_2OH \xrightarrow{H^+} \text{(II)}$$

(III)

Therefore, the three different oximes are obtained.

**96. (3)** The complete reaction is as follows :

$$P-MeO-C_6H_5-CHO + (AcO)_2O$$

$$O-MeO-C_6H_5-CHO + (AcO)_2O$$

$$\xrightarrow{CH_3COONa} P-MeO \text{ (Ph, COOH)}$$

The above reaction of para-methoxybenzaldehyde with acetic anhydride in the presence of sodium acetate forms an acid possessing a double bond.

Thus, the correct option is (C).

**97. (3)** The conversion of but-2-one to propanoic acid is takes place as follows :

$$H_3C-CO-CH_3 \xrightarrow[H^+]{NaOH,\ I_2} H_3C-COOH$$

The reaction of but-2-one with sodium hydroxide in the presence of iodine and ions forms propanoic acid. This reaction is the example of iodoform test. In iodoform reaction, a ketone and aldehyde reacts with a base in the presence of iodine to form an acid.

Thus, the correct option is (C).

**98. (3)** The hydroxylation reaction of 4-methyl-benzene-sulphuric acid with excess of sodium sulfate is,

$$H_3C-C_6H_4-SO_3H + CH_3COONa \longrightarrow$$
(Strong acid)

$$H_3C-C_6H_4-SO_3Na + CH_3COONa$$
(Weak acid)

In the above reaction, sodium acetate is a base which abstracts the proton from 4-methylbenzenesulfonic acid to form a salt as the desired product. Acetic acid is also formed as the side product in the above acid-base reaction.

Hence, the correct option is (C).

**99.** The given molecular formula is $C_5H_{10}O$. The degree of unsaturation is one. It is given that the compound on treating with dilute acid gives positive iodoform test. This indicate that these compounds contain either $R-CO-$ group. Therefore, the reaction that shows the formation of Q and R product is shown below.

$$\xrightarrow{H^+}$$

P is stabilized by resonance

Highly stable carbocation $\downarrow H_2O$

$$C_2H_5OH + H_3C-CO$$

**100. (3)** The inductive effect of ketones is greater than that of aldehydes; thus, the carbonyl carbon is more electron deficient in comparison to ketones. Hence, the reactivity of aldehydes is more than ketones. Therefore, (II) is the most reactive towards attack by phenyl magnesium bromide. Aryl group has $+ R$ effect while methyl group has $+ I$ effect, but due to steric hindrance in (III), its reactivity is the least. Therefore, the correct order is (II) > (I) > (III).

**101.** The separation of a mixture containing para hydroxyl benzoic acid and para amino benzoic acid is shown below.

$$\text{(OH, COOH)} \text{ and } \text{(NH}_2\text{, COOH)}$$

$$NO_3^+Cl^- \qquad OH \xrightarrow[\text{Evaporation}]{\Delta} OH$$

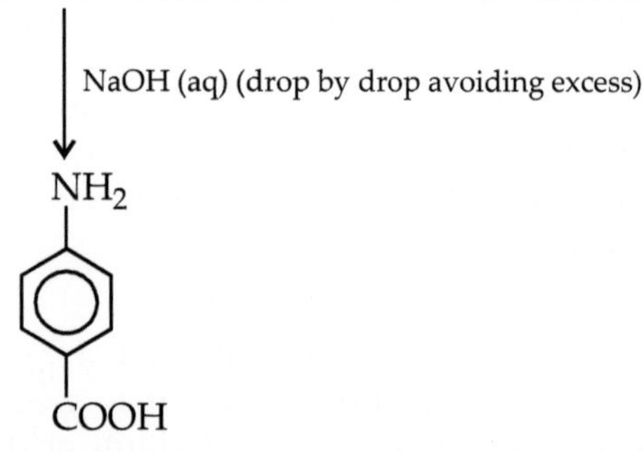



The confirmatory test for the presence of phenolic group and primary amine is shown below.



Similarly, the confirmatory test for carboxylic acid is as follows :

$$-COOH \xrightarrow{NaHCO_3} CO_2 \uparrow \xrightarrow[\text{lime water}]{\text{with efferevence}}$$

Milky solution

**102.** The given reaction is as follows :

$$A(C_6H_{12}) \xrightarrow{HCl} B(C_6H_{13}Cl) + C(C_6H_{13}Cl)$$

The compound A contains six carbon atoms and twelve hydrogen atoms. The structure of compound A is shown below.

$$H_2C = \underset{\underset{H}{|}}{C} - \underset{\underset{CH_3}{|}}{\overset{\overset{CH_3}{|}}{C}} - CH_3$$

The reaction of compound A with HCl is shown below.

$$H_2C = \underset{\underset{H}{|}}{C} - \underset{\underset{CH_3}{|}}{\overset{\overset{CH_3}{|}}{C}} - CH_3 \xrightarrow{HCl} H_3C - \underset{\underset{CH_3}{|}}{\overset{\overset{CH_3}{|}}{C}} - \underset{\underset{CH_3}{|}}{\overset{\overset{Cl}{|}}{C}} - CH_3$$

(B)

$$+ H_3C - \underset{\underset{H}{|}}{\overset{\overset{Cl}{|}}{C}} - \underset{\underset{CH_3}{|}}{\overset{\overset{CH_3}{|}}{C}} - CH_3$$

(C)

Therefore, structure B and C is :

$$CH_3 - \underset{\underset{CH_3}{|}}{\overset{\overset{CH_3 \quad Cl}{| \quad |}}{CH}} - C - CH_3 \qquad CH_3 - \underset{\underset{CH_3}{|}}{\overset{\overset{Cl \quad CH_3}{| \quad |}}{CH}} - C - CH_3$$

(B)  (C)

The reaction of compound B with alc. KOH is shown below.

$$H_3C - \underset{\underset{H}{|}}{\overset{\overset{CH_3 \quad Cl}{| \quad |}}{C}} - \underset{\underset{CH_3}{|}}{C} - CH_3 \xrightarrow{\text{Alcoholic KOH}}$$

(B)

$$H_3C - \underset{\underset{CH_3}{|}}{C} = C - CH_3 \quad \overset{CH_3}{|}$$

(D)

Therefore, the compound D is :

$$H_3C - \underset{\underset{CH_3}{|}}{\overset{\overset{CH_3}{|}}{C}} = C - CH_3$$

(D)

The product formed by the ozonolysis of compound D is shown below.

$$H_3C - \underset{\underset{CH_3}{|}}{\overset{\overset{CH_3}{|}}{C}} = C - CH_3 \xrightarrow{\text{Ozonolysis}} H_3C - \overset{\overset{O}{||}}{C} - CH_3$$

(D)  (E)

Therefore, the compound E is :

$$H_3C - \overset{\overset{O}{||}}{C} - CH_3$$

The product formed by the ozonolysis of compound A is shown below.

$$H_3C = \underset{\underset{CH_3}{|}}{\overset{\overset{CH_3}{|}}{\underset{H}{C}}} - C - CH_3 \xrightarrow{\text{Ozonolysis}}$$

$$H_3C - \underset{\underset{CH_3}{|}}{\overset{\overset{CH_3}{|}}{C}} - CHO + HCHO$$

(F)

Therefore, the compound F and G is :

$$CH_3 - \underset{\underset{CH_3}{|}}{\overset{\overset{CH_3}{|}}{C}} - CHO \qquad HCHO$$

(F)  (G)

**103. (a)** The given structure is shown below :

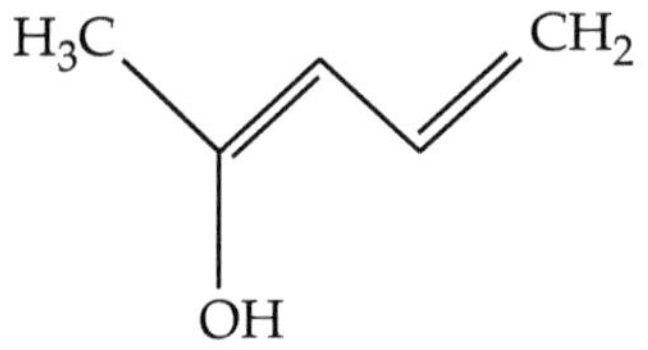

The resonating structures of the given compound are shown below :

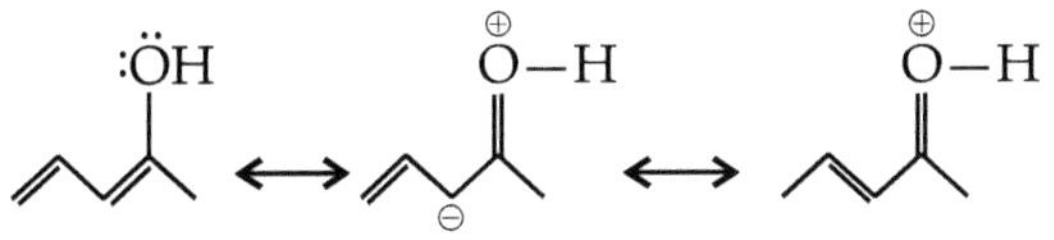

**(b)** The reaction that shows the oxidation of given compound with $KMNO_4$ is shown below :

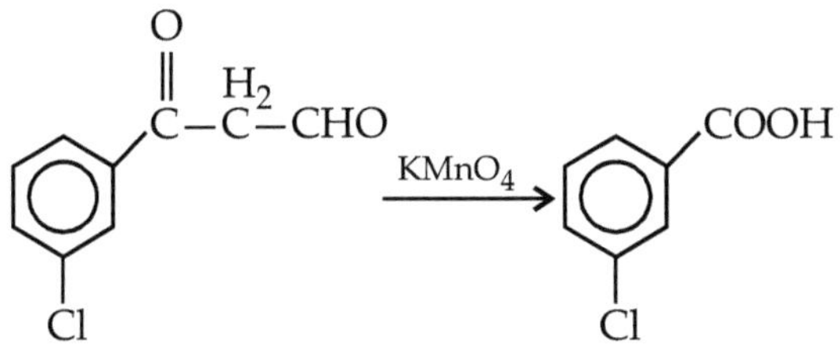

The given molecular formula is $C_9H_7O_2Cl$. The enolic and keto form of the given compound is shown below :

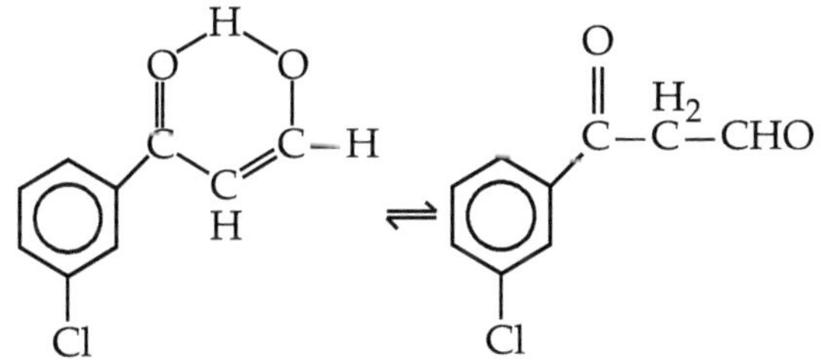

(A) (B)

$C_9H_7O_2Cl$

**104. (1)** The reaction of acidic compounds with $NaNH_2$ leads to the abstraction of acidic hydrogen. The hydrogen atom which is most acidic in nature out of all the hydrogen ions present in the compound will be abstracted on reaction with $NaNH_2$. The decreasing order of acidic strength of the hydrogen atoms present in the given compounds is,

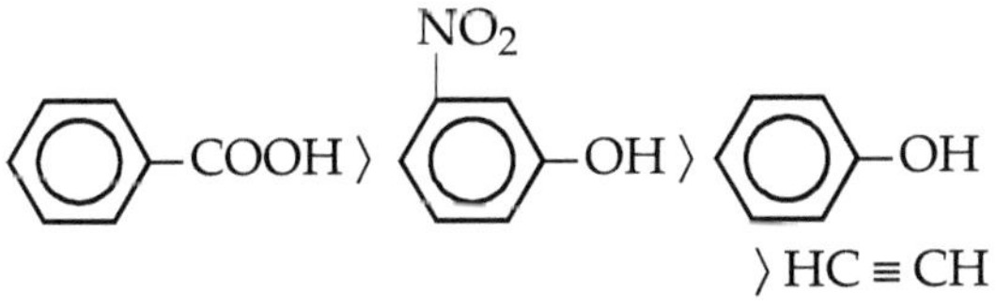

Therefore, two moles of abstract two hydrogen ions from the two most acidic groups present in the given compound.

Hence, the product obtained in the given reaction is

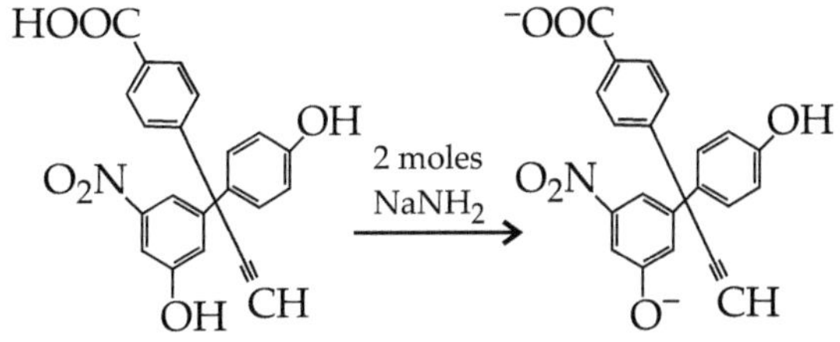

**105. (3)** The compound P on hydrolysis leads to the formation of aldehyde and the compound Q on hydrolysis results in the formation of ketone. These two products of hydrolysis are shown below :

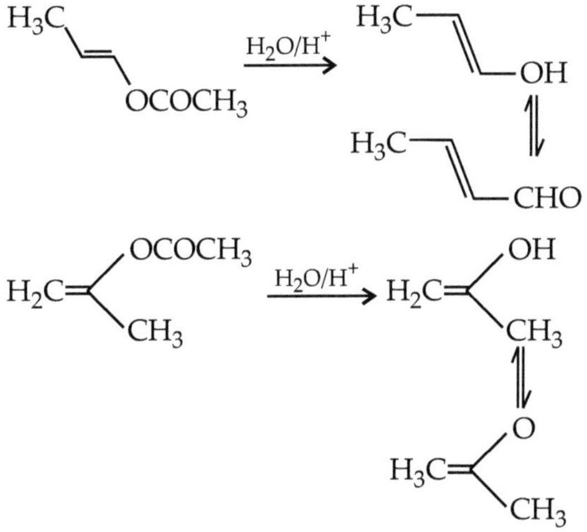

Aldehydes and ketones can be distinguished by using Fehling's solution. Therefore, the compounds formed by acid hydrolysis of P and Q can be distinguished by using Fehling's solution.

**106. (2)** The given compound undergoes intramolecular cannizzaro reaction followed by acid work-up to form the major product.

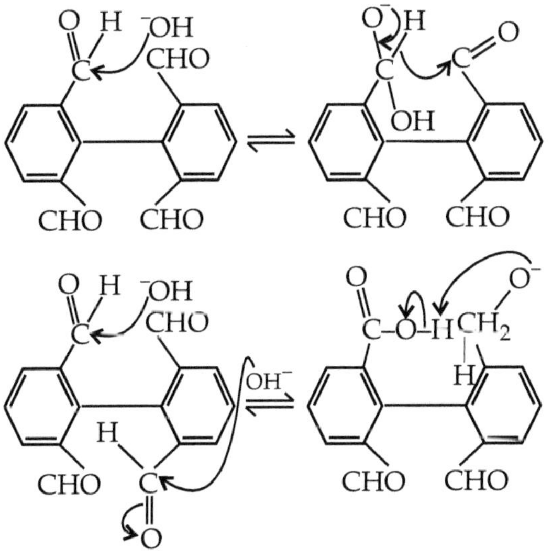

The cannizaro reaction results in the formation of carboxylic acid salt and alcohol which on hydrolysis leads to the formation of product

**107. (1)** The reaction mechanism for the formation of product A is shown below.

$$C_6H_5-C\equiv C-CH_3 \xrightarrow{Hg^{2+}} C_6H_5-C=C-CH_3$$

with $Hg^+$ bridging

$$C_6H_5-\underset{OH}{C}=CH-CH_3$$

(Ketoenol tautomerism)

$$C_6H_5-C-CH-CH_3$$

Thus, the product A formed is shown below :

(structure: Ph attached to C=O, then CH with $H_3C$)

**108. (i)** The given molecular formula is $C_8H_8O_2$. It is given that the compound A and B on treating tollens reagent gives a silver mirror and compound B gives a positive test with $FeCl_3$ solution. Therefore, the structure of A and B is shown below :

$A =$ (benzene ring with $CH_2OH$ and $OHC$ substituents)

$B =$ (benzene ring with $CH_2CHO$ and $HO$ substituents)

**(ii)** It is given that the compound C gives positive iodoform test. This indicate that the compound contain   group. Ths structure of C is shown below :

$C =$ (benzene ring with $HO$ and $\overset{O}{\overset{\|}{C}}-CH_3$ substituents)

**(iii)** The structure of D is shown below :

$D =$ (benzene ring with $CH_3$ and $CO_2H$ substituents)

**(iv)** The structure of E is shown below :

$E =$ ($CH_2=CH-O$ attached to benzene ring with $O-H$)

**109.** The complete synthetic scheme for identification of product A, B, C, D, and E is shown below :

(benzene ring with Cl and $\overset{O}{\overset{\|}{C}}-CH_2CH_2CH_3$) $\xrightarrow{Cl_2/FeCl_2}$

(benzene ring with two Cl and $\overset{O}{\overset{\|}{C}}-CH_2CH_2CH_3$) (A) $\xrightarrow{Ne-Hg/HCl}$

(benzene ring with two Cl and $CH_2CH_2CH_2CH_3$) (B) $\longrightarrow$

(benzene ring with $NO_2$, two Cl and $CH_2CH_2CH_2CH_3$) (C) $\xrightarrow{CH_2=CH-CH_2O-Na^+}$

(benzene ring with $NO_2$, Cl, $O-CH_2-CH_2=CH_2$ and $CH_2CH_2CH_2CH_3$) (E) $\xrightarrow{H_2/Pd/C}$

**110. (2)** The boiling point of carboxylic acids is more than that of alcohols and aldehydes because molecules are strongly bonded to each other through hydrogen bonding and dipole-dipole interactions. Alcohol has more boiling point than aldehydes due to the presence of hydrogen bonding among them.

**111. (1)** The name of compound A is propan-1-ol, which on reaction with potassium dichromate forms aldehyde. Aldehyde on reaction with aqueous solution of $H_2NCONHNH_2.HCl$ and sodium acetate form hydrazone.

$$CH_3CH_2CH_2OH \rightarrow CH_3CH_2CHO$$
$$CH_3CH_2CHO + H_2NCONHNH_2.HCl$$
$$\rightarrow CH_3CH_2CH = NNHCONH_2$$

# Nitrogen Containing Compounds

## ❓ QUESTIONS

**1.** Three isomers A, B and C (mol. formula $C_8H_{11}N$) give the following results :

$$A \text{ and } C \xrightarrow{\text{Diazotization}} P + Q$$

$$\xrightarrow[\substack{\text{(ii) oxidation} \\ (KMnO_4 + H^+)}]{\text{(i) Hydrolysis}} \begin{array}{l} R(\text{product of A}) \\ + \\ S \ (\text{product of C}) \end{array}$$

R has lower boiling point than S

$$B \xrightarrow{C_6H_5SO_2Cl} \text{alkali-insoluble product}$$

A, B and C respectively are : **[2020, Main]**

(1) 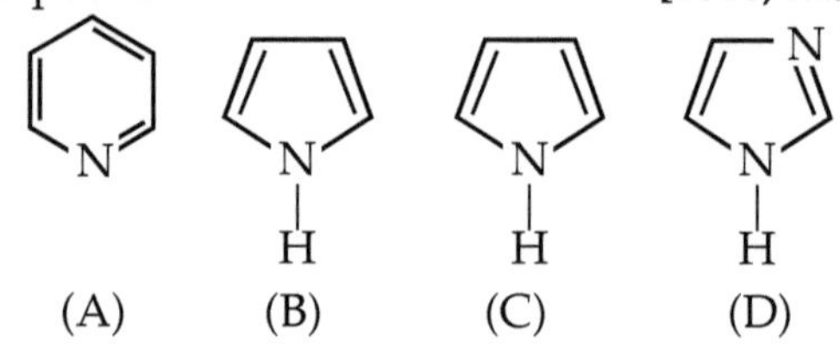

(2)

(3)

(4)

**2.** The decreasing order of reactivity of the following compounds towards nucleophilic substitution $(S_N^2)$ is : **[2020, Main]**

(I)
(II)
(III)
(IV)

(1) (IV) > (II) > (III) > (I)
(2) (II) > (III) > (IV) > (I)
(3) (II) > (III) > (I) > (IV)
(4) (III) > (II) > (IV) > (I)

**3.** The number of chiral centres present in [B] is ..... .

$$\xrightarrow[\text{(ii) } H_3O^-]{\text{(i) } C_2H_5MgBr} [A]$$

$$\xrightarrow[\text{(ii) } H_2O]{\text{(i) } CH_3MgBr} [B]$$

**4.** The increasing order of basicity of the following compounds is : **[2020, Main]**

(A)          (B)          (C)          (D)

(1) (A) < (B) < (C) < (D)
(2) (B) < (A) < (C) < (D)
(3) (D) < (A) < (B) < (C)
(4) (B) < (A) < (D) < (C)

**5.** The number of chiral carbon(s) present in peptide, Ile-Arg-Pro, is ........... . **[2020, Main]**

**6.** Kjeldahl's method cannot be used to estimate nitrogen for which of the following compounds ? **[2020, Main]**

(1) $C_6H_5NO_2$         (2) $C_6H_5NH_2$

(3) $CH_3CH_2-C\equiv N$         (4) $NH_2-\overset{\overset{O}{\|}}{C}-NH_2$

**7.** The major product Z obtained in the following reaction scheme is : **[2020, Main]**

$$\xrightarrow[273-278K]{NaNO_2/HCl} X \xrightarrow{Cu_2Br_2} Y \xrightarrow[H_2SO_4]{HNO_3} Z$$

(1)          (2)

(3)          (4)

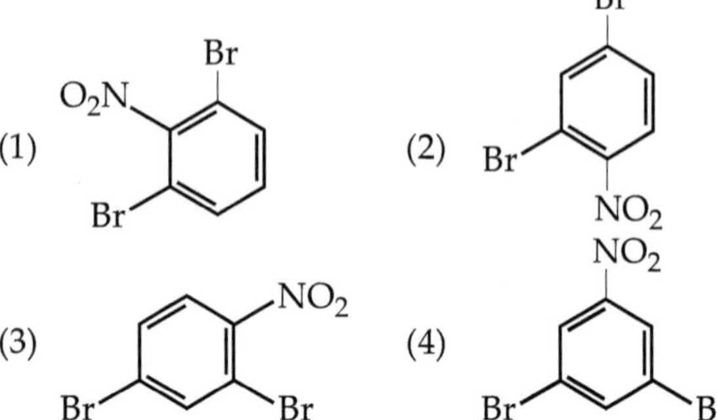

**8.** The most suitable reagent for the given conversion is : **[2020, Main]**

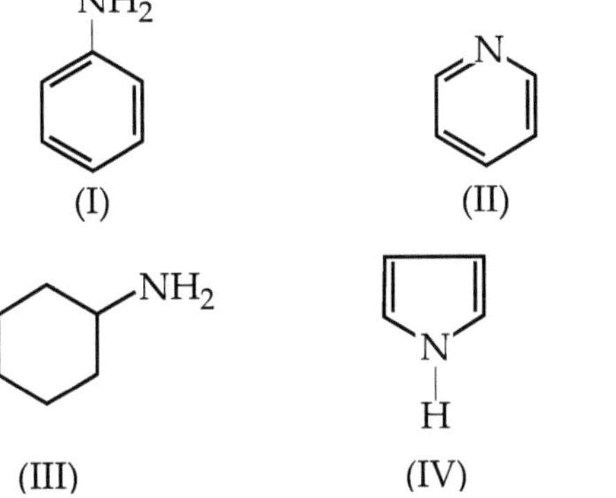

(1)  LiAlH$_4$     (2)  NaBH$_4$
(3)  H$_2$/Pd     (4)  B$_2$H$_6$

**9.** The decreasing order of basicity of the following amines is : **[2020, Main]**

(1)  (I) > (III) > (IV) > (II)
(2)  (III) > (I) > (II) > (IV)
(3)  (III) > (II) > (I) > (IV)
(4)  (II) > (III) > (IV) > (I)

**10.** The reaction of H$_3$N$_3$B$_3$Cl$_3$ (A) with LiBH$_4$ in tetrahydrofuran gives inorganic benzene (B). Further, the reaction (A) with (C) leads to H$_3$N$_3$B$_3$ (Me)$_3$. Compounds (B) and (C) respectively, are : **[2020, Main]**
(1)  Boron nitride and MeBr
(2)  Borazine and MeMgBr
(3)  Borazine and MeBr
(4)  Diborane and MeMgBr

**11.** In the following reaction sequence, the major product B is : **[2020, Main]**

**12.** In the following compounds, the decreasing order of basic strength will be : **[2019, Main]**
(1)  C$_2$H$_5$NH$_2$ > NH$_3$ > (C$_2$H$_5$)$_2$NH
(2)  (C$_2$H$_5$)$_2$NH > NH$_3$ > C$_2$H$_5$NH$_2$
(3)  (C$_2$H$_5$)$_2$NH > C$_2$H$_5$NH$_2$ > NH$_3$
(4)  NH$_3$ > C$_2$H$_5$NH$_2$ > (C$_2$H$_5$)$_2$NH

**13.** Which of the following amines can be prepared by Gabriel phthalimide reaction ? **[2019, Main]**
(1)  *n*-butylamine     (2)  triethylamine
(3)  *t*-butylamine     (4)  neo-pentylamine

**14.** Coupling of benzene diazonium chloride with 1-naphthol in alkaline medium will give : **[2019, Main]**

**15.** The major product in the following reaction is : **[2019, Main]**

**(1)** 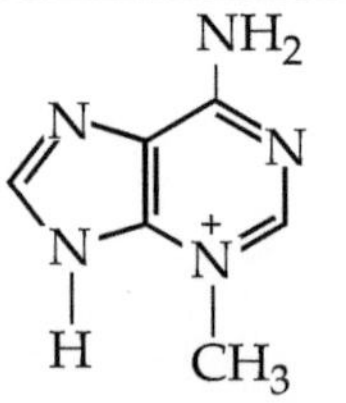 [structure: adenine-like purine with NH$_2$, N–H, N$^+$–CH$_3$]

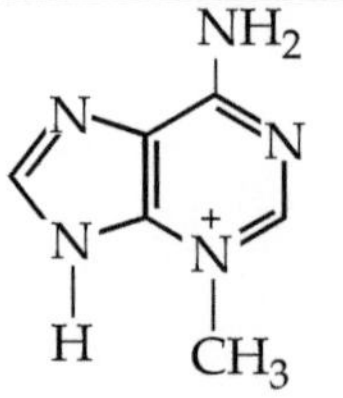

**(2)** [structure: adenine-like purine with NH$_2$, N–H, N$^+$–CH$_3$]

**(3)** [structure: purine with NHCH$_3$, N–H]

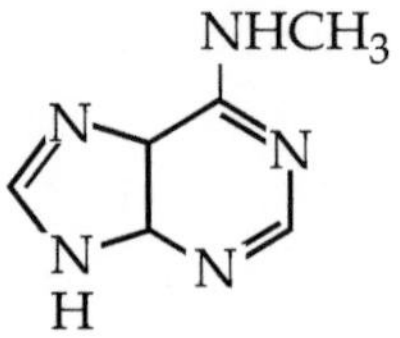

**(4)** 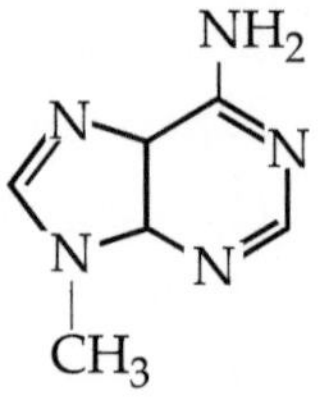 [structure: dihydropurine with NH$_2$, N–CH$_3$]

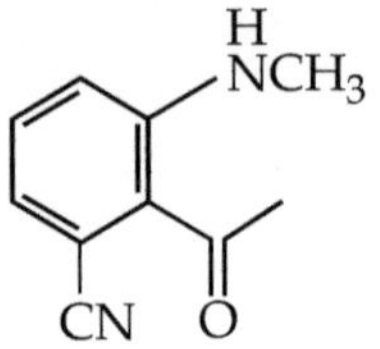

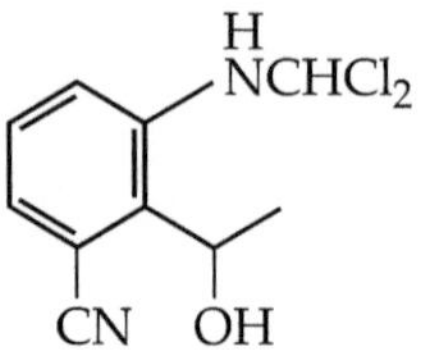

**16.** The major product obtained in the following reaction is : **[2019, Main]**

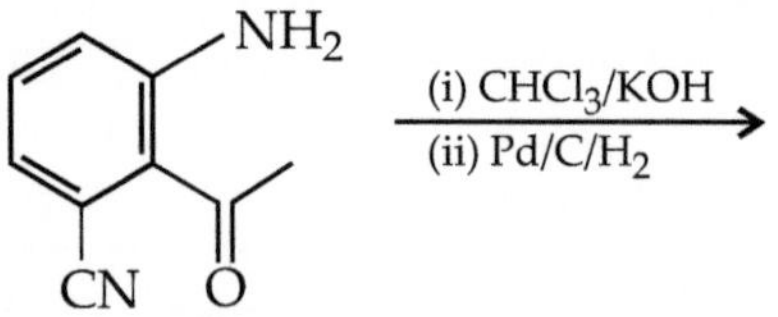

[structure: benzene with NH$_2$, C(=O)CH$_3$, CN]

$$\xrightarrow[\text{(ii) Pd/C/H}_2]{\text{(i) CHCl}_3\text{/KOH}}$$

**(1)** [structure: benzene with NHCH$_3$ (H), C(=O)CH$_3$, CN]

**(2)** [structure: benzene with NCHCl$_2$ (H), CH(OH)CH$_3$, CN]

**(3)** [structure: benzene with NCH$_3$ (H), CH(OH)CH$_3$, CN]

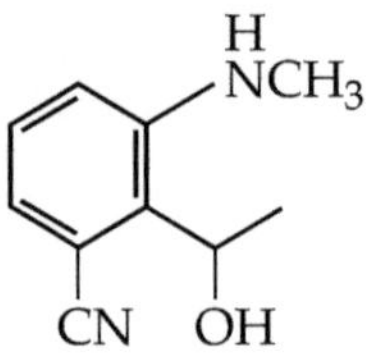

**(4)** 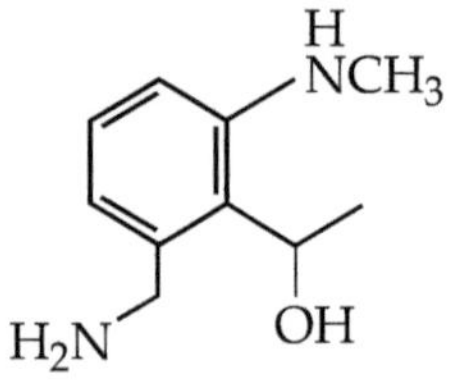 [structure: benzene with NCH$_3$ (H), CH(OH)CH$_3$, H$_2$N]

**17.** Aniline dissolved in dilute HCl is reacted with sodium nitrite at 0°C. This solution was added dropwise to a solution containing equimolar mixture of aniline and phenol in dil. HCl. The structure of the major product is : **[2019, Main]**

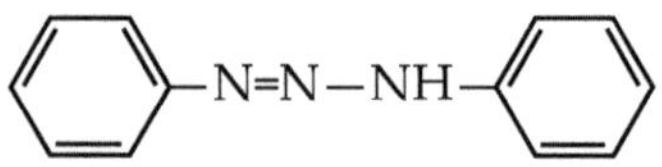

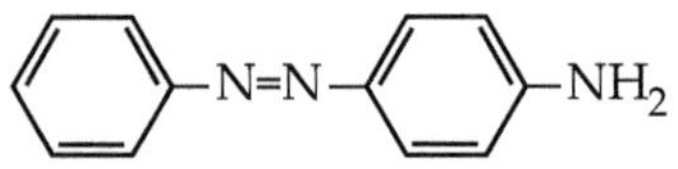

**(1)** 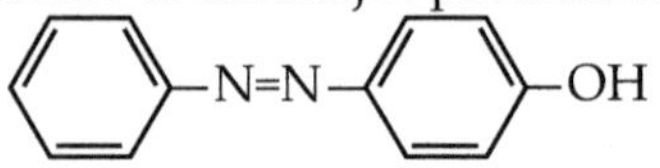 [structure: Ph–N=N–C$_6$H$_4$–OH]

**(2)** [structure: Ph–N=N–NH–Ph]

**(3)** [structure: Ph–N=N–C$_6$H$_4$–NH$_2$]

**(4)** [structure: Ph–N=N–O–Ph]

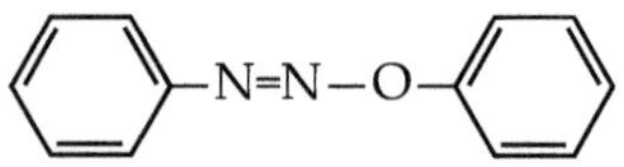

**18.** The correct IUPAC name of the following compound is : **[2019, Main]**

[structure: benzene with NO$_2$, Cl, CH$_3$]

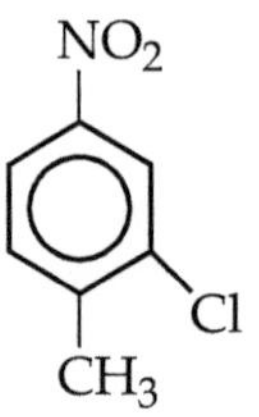

**(1)** 5-chloro-4-methyl-1-nitrobenzene

**(2)** 2-chloro-1-methyl-1-4-nitrobenzene

**(3)** 3-chloro-4-methyl-1-nitrobenzene

**(4)** 2-methyl-5-nitro-1-chlorobenzene

**19.** Hinsberg's reagent is : **[2019, Main]**

**(1)** $C_6H_5COCl$    **(2)** $SOCl_2$

**(3)** $C_6H_5SO_2Cl$    **(4)** $(COCl)_2$

**20.** The major products A and B for the following reactions are respectively : **[2019, Main]**

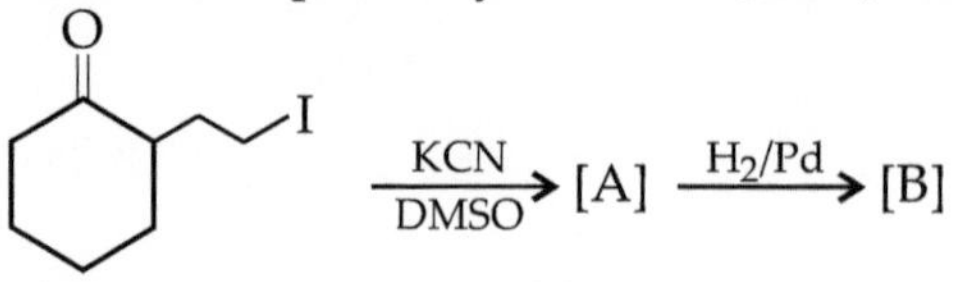

[structure: cyclohexanone with CH$_2$CH$_2$I side chain]

$$\xrightarrow[\text{DMSO}]{\text{KCN}} \text{[A]} \xrightarrow{\text{H}_2\text{/Pd}} \text{[B]}$$

**(1)** 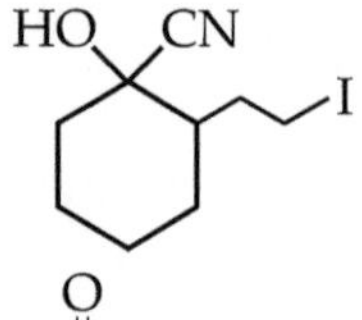 [structure: HO, CN cyclohexane with CH$_2$CH$_2$I] ; [structure: HO, CH$_2$–NH$_2$ cyclohexane with CH$_2$CH$_2$I]

**(2)** [structure: cyclohexanone with CH$_2$CH$_2$CN] ; [structure: cyclohexanone with CH$_2$CH$_2$CH$_2$NH$_2$]

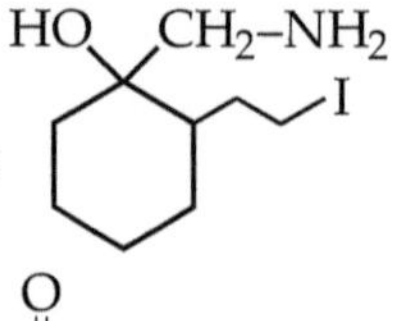

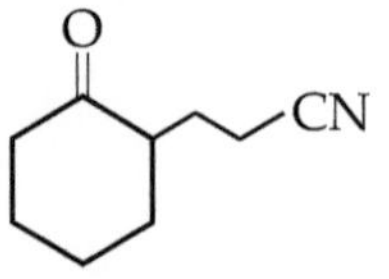

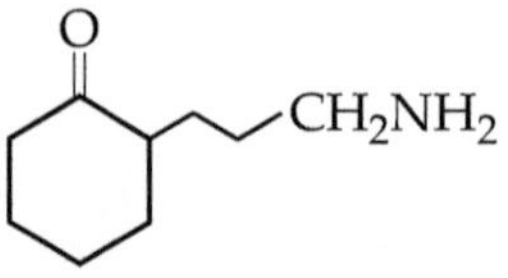

**(3)** 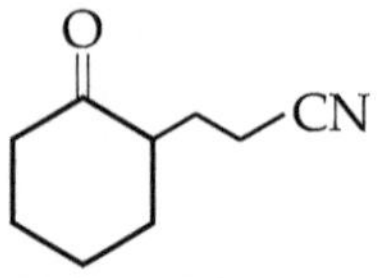 [structure: cyclohexanone with CH$_2$CH$_2$CN] ; [structure: cyclohexanol (OH) with CH$_2$CH$_2$CH$_2$NH$_2$]

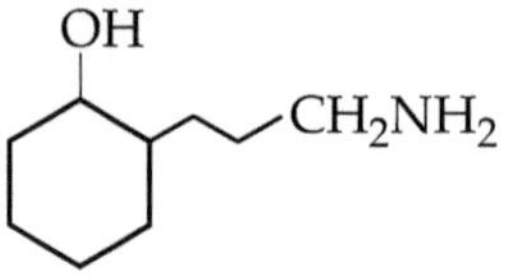

**(4)** 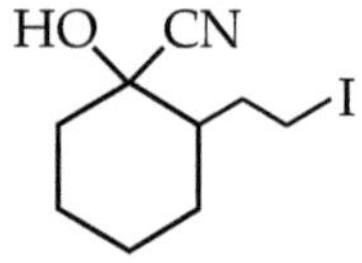 [structure: HO, CN cyclohexane with CH$_2$CH$_2$I] ; [structure: HO, CH$_2$–NH$_2$ cyclohexane with CH$_2$CH$_2$H]

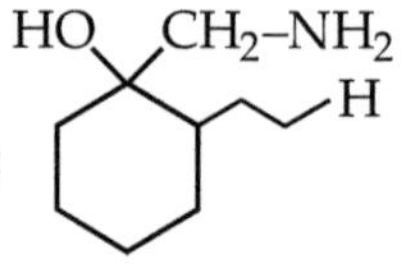

**21.** Ethylamine ($C_2H_5NH_2$) can be obtained from N-ethylphthalimide on treatment with : **[2019, Main]**

**(1)** $NH_2NH_2$    **(2)** $CaH_2$

**(3)** $NaBH_4$    **(4)** $H_2O$

**22.** Which of the following is NOT a correct method of the preparation of benzylamine from cyanobenzene ? **[2019, Main]**

**(1)** $H_2$/Ni

**(2)** (i) $LiAlH_4$    (ii) $H_3O^+$

**(3)** (i) $SnCl_2$ + HCl (gas)    (ii) $NaBH_4$

**(4)** (i) $HCl/H_2O$    (ii) $NaBH_4$

**23.** The increasing order of the $pK_b$ of the following compound is : **[2019, Main]**

**(A)** 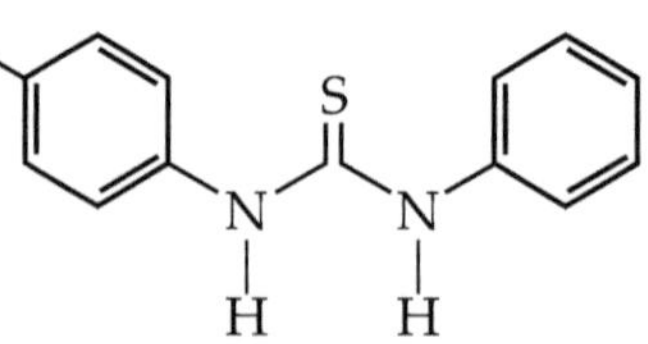 [structure: 4-fluorophenyl–NH–C(=S)–NH–phenyl (thiourea)]

**(B)** [structure: 4-methoxyphenyl–NH–C(=S)–NH–phenyl (thiourea)]

**(C)** [structure: 4-nitrophenyl–NH–C(=S)–NH–phenyl (thiourea)]

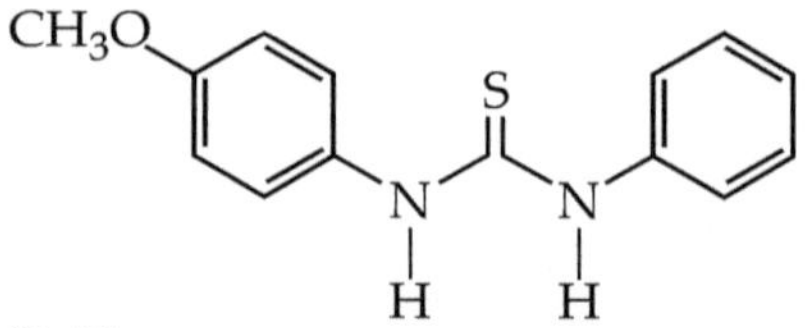

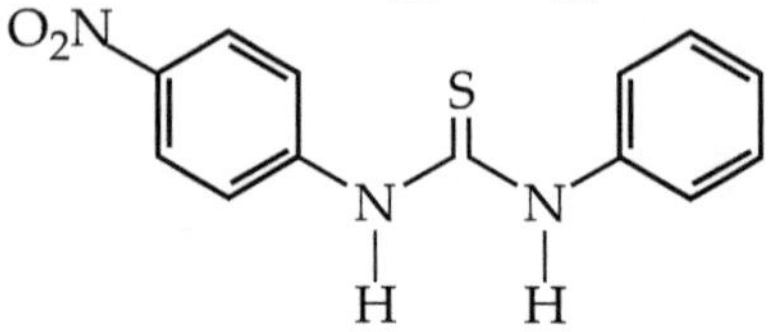

(D) 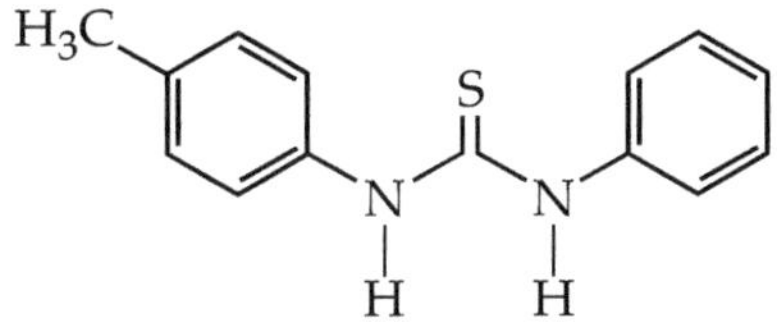

(1) (A) < (C) < (D) < (B)
(2) (C) < (A) < (D) < (B)
(3) (B) < (D) < (A) < (C)
(4) (B) < (D) < (C) < (A)

**24.** Benzene diazonium chloride on reaction with aniline in the presence of dilute hydrochloric acid gives : **[2019, Main]**

(1) 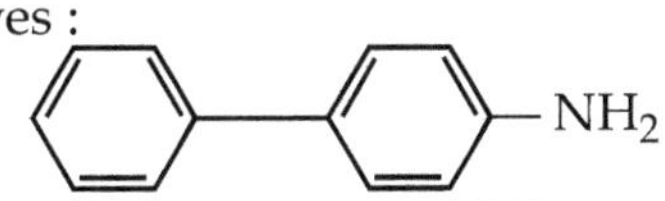

(2) 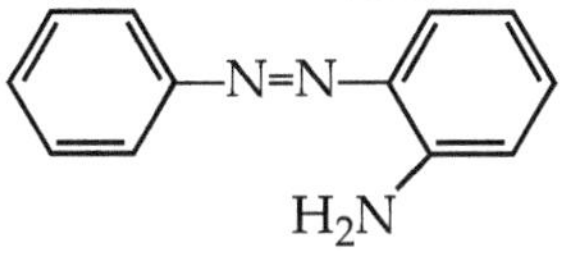

(3) 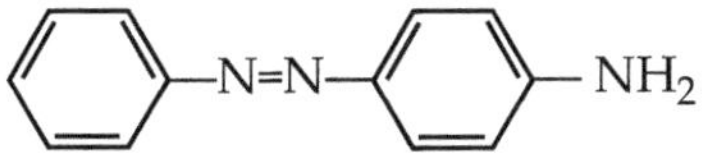

(4) 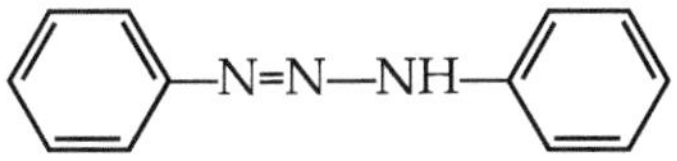

**25.** List-I includes starting materials and reagents of selected chemical reactions. List-II gives structures of compound that may be formed as intermediate products and/or final products from the reactions of List-I. **[2019, Main]**

**List-I** **List-II**

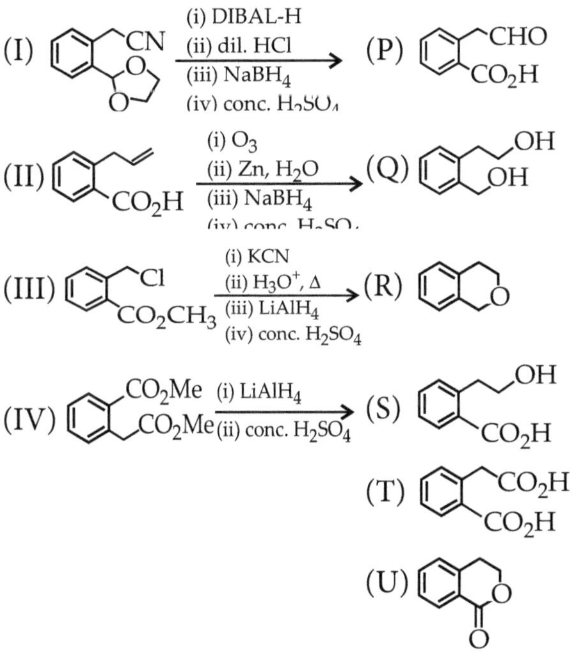
(I)
CN
(i) DIBAL-H
(ii) dil. HCl
(iii) NaBH$_4$
(iv) conc. H$_2$SO$_4$
(P)
CHO
CO$_2$H
(II)
CO$_2$H
(i) O$_3$
(ii) Zn, H$_2$O
(iii) NaBH$_4$
(Q)
OH
OH
(III)
Cl
CO$_2$CH$_3$
(i) KCN
(ii) H$_3$O$^+$, Δ
(iii) LiAlH$_4$
(iv) conc. H$_2$SO$_4$
(R)
O
(IV)
CO$_2$Me
CO$_2$Me
(i) LiAlH$_4$
(ii) conc. H$_2$SO$_4$
(S)
OH
CO$_2$H
(T)
CO$_2$H
CO$_2$H
(U)
O
O

Which of the following options has correct combination considering List-I and List-II ?

(1) (III), (S), (R) (2) (IV), (Q), (U)
(3) (III), (T), (U) (4) (IV), (Q), (R)

### Paragraph for Question 26

An organic acid **P** ($C_{11}H_{12}O_2$) can easily be oxidised to a dibasic acid which reacts with ethyleneglycol to produce a polymer dacron. Upon ozonolysis, **P** gives an aliphatic ketone as one of the products. **P** undergoes the following reaction sequences to furnish **R** *via* **Q**. The compound **P** also undergoes another set of reactions to produce **S**.

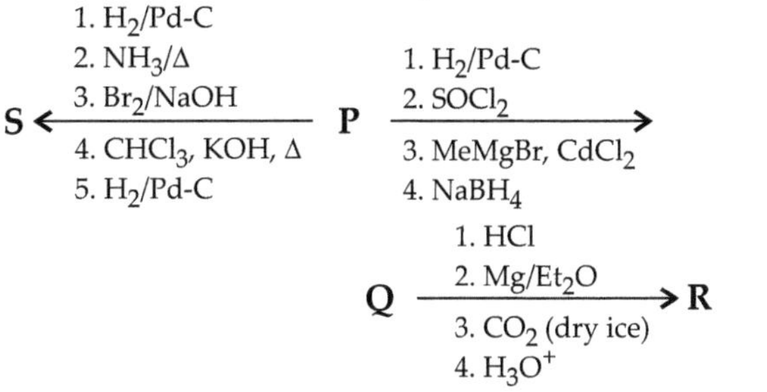
S
1. H$_2$/Pd-C
2. NH$_3$/Δ
3. Br$_2$/NaOH
4. CHCl$_3$, KOH, Δ
5. H$_2$/Pd-C
P
1. H$_2$/Pd-C
2. SOCl$_2$
3. MeMgBr, CdCl$_2$
4. NaBH$_4$
Q
1. HCl
2. Mg/Et$_2$O
3. CO$_2$ (dry ice)
4. H$_3$O$^+$
R

**26.** The compound **S** is : **[2018, Advanced]**

(1) 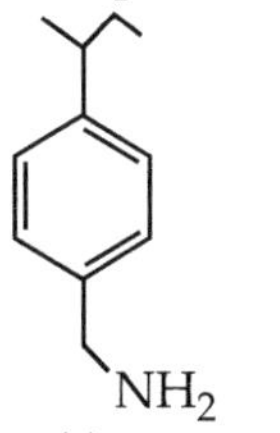
(a)

(2) 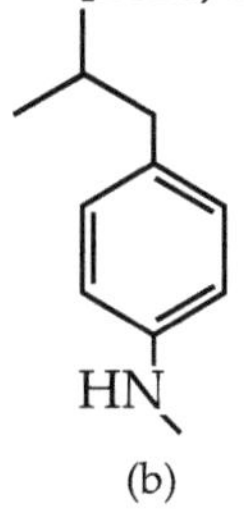
(b)

(3) 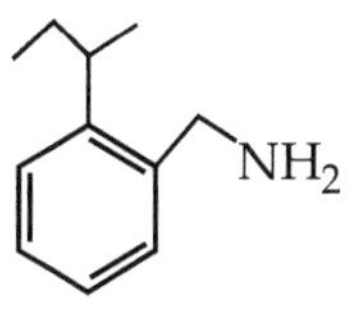
(c)

(4) 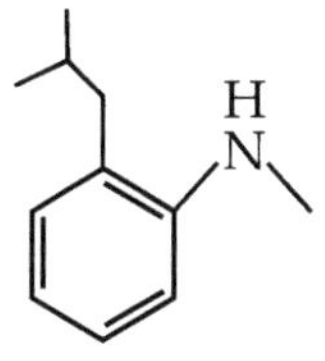
(d)

**27.** Aniline reacts with mixed acid (conc. $HNO_3$ and conc. $H_2SO_4$) at 288 K to give P(51%), Q(47%) and R(2%). The major products of the following reaction sequence is/are : **[2018, Advanced]**

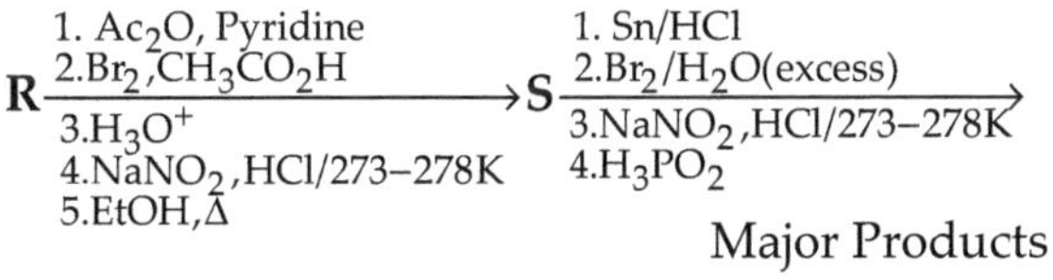
R
1. Ac$_2$O, Pyridine
2.Br$_2$,CH$_3$CO$_2$H
3.H$_3$O$^+$
4.NaNO$_2$,HCl/273–278K
5.EtOH,Δ
S
1. Sn/HCl
2.Br$_2$/H$_2$O(excess)
3.NaNO$_2$,HCl/273–278K
4.H$_3$PO$_2$

Major Products

(1) 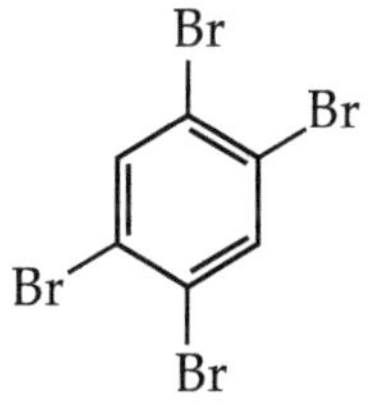

(2) 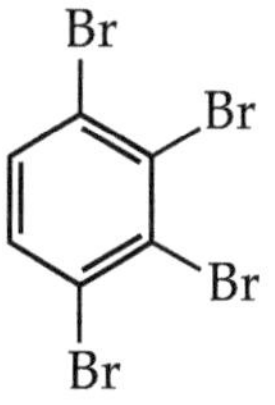

(3) 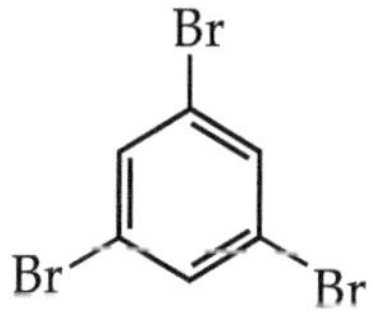

(4) 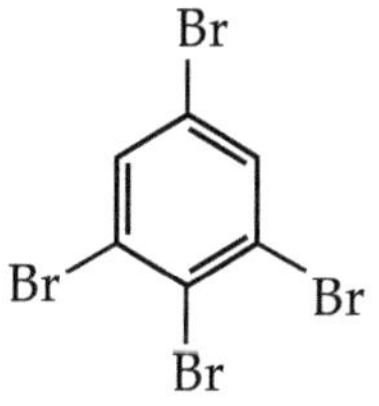

**28.** In the following reaction sequence, the amount of **D** (in g) formed from 10 moles of acetophenone is ......... . **[2018, Advanced]**

Atomic weights in g mol$^{-1}$ : H = 1, C = 12, N = 14, O = 16, Br = 80. The yield (%) corresponding to the product in each step is given in the parenthesis)

$$\text{[PhCOCH}_3\text{]} \xrightarrow[\text{H}_3\text{O}^+]{\text{NaOBr}} \textbf{A} \text{ (60\%)} \xrightarrow{\text{NH}_3, \Delta} \textbf{B} \text{ (50\%)} \xrightarrow{\text{Br}_2/\text{KOH}} \textbf{C} \text{ (50\%)}$$

$$\xrightarrow[\text{AcOH}]{\text{Br}_2 \text{ (3 equiv)}} \textbf{D} \text{ (100\%)}$$

**29.** The increasing order of basicity of the following compounds is : **[2018, Main]**

(a) (allyl-CH$_2$NH$_2$)     (b) (propenyl =NH)

(c) (CH$_3$C(NH$_2$)=NH)     (d) (CH$_3$CH$_2$NHCH$_3$)

(1) (a) < (b) < (c) < (d)     (2) (b) < (a) < (c) < (d)
(3) (b) < (a) < (d) < (c)     (4) (d) < (b) < (a) < (c)

**30.** The increasing order of diazotisation of the following compounds is : **[2018, Main]**

(a) (1-aminocyclohexane carboxylic acid, NH$_2$, COOH)

(b) (aniline, NH$_2$)

(c) (3-aminophenyl acetate, H$_3$C–C(=O)–O–C$_6$H$_4$–NH$_2$)

(d) (2-aminoacetophenone, COCH$_3$, NH$_2$)

(1) (a) < (b) < (c) < (d)     (2) (a) < (d) < (b) < (c)
(3) (a) < (d) < (c) < (b)     (4) (d) < (c) < (b) < (a)

**31.** The increasing order of nitration of the following compounds is : **[2018, Main]**

(a) NH$_2$     (b) Cl     (c) OCH$_3$     (d) CH$_3$

(1) (b) < (a) < (c) < (d)     (2) (a) < (b) < (c) < (d)
(3) (b) < (a) < (d) < (c)     (4) (a) < (b) < (d) < (c)

**32.** Which of the following will not exist in zwitter ionic form at pH = 7 ? **[2018, Main]**

(1) (cyclohexane with NH$_2$ and COOH)

(2) (cyclohexane with NH$_2$ and SO$_3$H)

(3) (2-aminobenzenesulfonic acid, NH$_2$, SO$_3$H)

(4) (N-acetyl amino acid, CH$_3$CO–NH–CH–CO$_2$H)

**33.** Products A and B formed in the following reactions are respectively : **[2018, Main]**

$$\overset{\oplus}{\text{NH}_3}\text{CH}_3\text{CO}\overset{\ominus}{\text{O}}$$
(4-aminobenzenesulfonic acid acetate salt, SO$_3$H) + HNO$_2 \longrightarrow \textbf{A} \xrightarrow{\text{C}_6\text{H}_5\text{NH}_2} \textbf{B}$

(1) (N=N–COCH$_3$, SO$_3$H) and (N=N–C$_6$H$_5$, SO$_3$H)

(2) (N=N–COCH$_3$, SO$_3$H) and HO$_3$S–(C$_6$H$_4$)–N(H)–(C$_6$H$_4$)–NH$_2$

(3) (N=N–O–C(=O)CH$_3$, SO$_3$H) and (N=N–N(H)–C$_6$H$_5$, SO$_3$H)

(4) (N=N–O–C(=O)CH$_3$, SO$_3$H) and (N=N–(C$_6$H$_4$)–NH$_2$, SO$_3$H)

**34.** The major product of the following reaction is : **[2017, Advanced]**

(2-aminobiphenyl-3'-ol, OH, NH$_2$) $\xrightarrow[\text{(ii) aq. NaOH}]{\text{(i) NaNO}_2\text{, HCl, 0°C}}$

(1) (biphenyl with OH and Cl)

(2) (biphenyl with O$^-$Na$^+$ and N$_2$Cl)

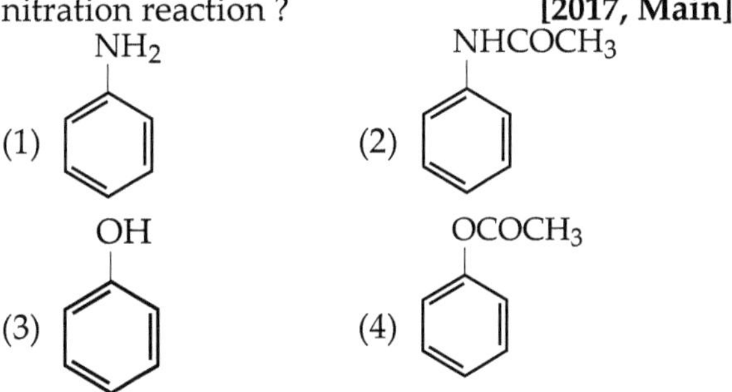

(3)

(4)

**35.** The order of basicity among the following compounds is : **[2017, Advanced]**

(1) II > I > IV > III  (2) IV > II > III > I
(3) IV > I > II > III  (4) I > IV > III > II

**36.** Which of the following compounds will form significant amount of meta product during mono-nitration reaction ? **[2017, Main]**

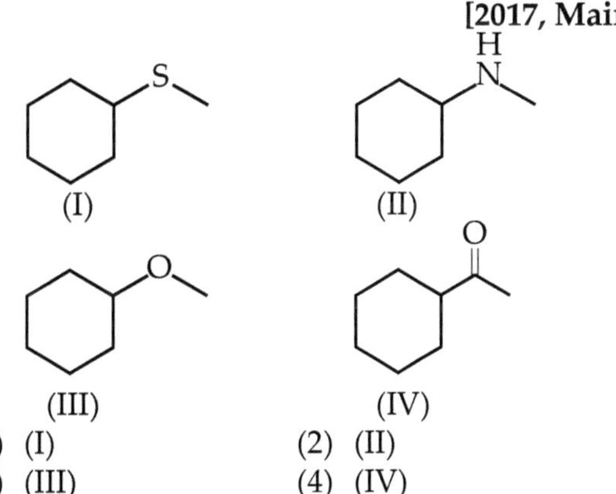

**37.** A mixture containing the following four compounds is extracted with 1M HCl. The compound that goes to aqueous layer is : **[2017, Main]**

(I)   (II)

(III)   (IV)

(1) (I)  (2) (II)
(3) (III)  (4) (IV)

**38.** Among the following compounds, the increasing order of their basic strength is : **[2017, Main]**

(I)   (II)

(III)   (IV)

(1) (I) < (II) < (IV) < (III)
(2) (I) < (II) < (III) < (IV)

(3) (II) < (I) < (IV) < (III)
(4) (II) < (I) < (III) < (IV)

**39.** The products of the following reaction sequence is/are : **[2016, Advanced]**

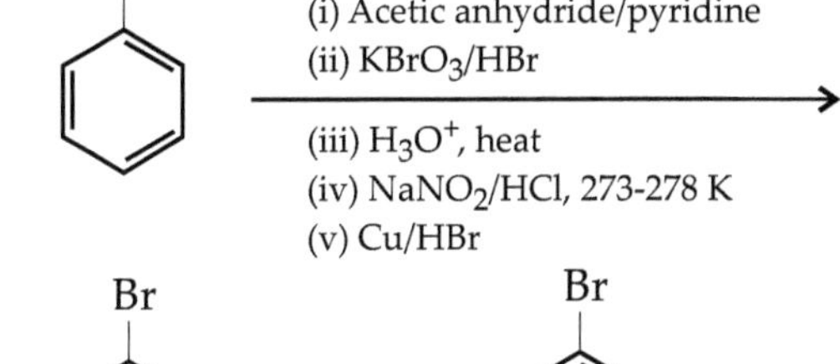

(i) Acetic anhydride/pyridine
(ii) $KBrO_3/HBr$
(iii) $H_3O^+$, heat
(iv) $NaNO_2/HCl$, 273-278 K
(v) $Cu/HBr$

(1)   (2)

(3)   (4)

**Paragraph for Question 40 and 41**

Treatment of compound **O** with $KMnO_4/H^+$ gave **P**, which on heating with ammonia gave **Q**. The compound **Q** on treatment with $Br_2/NaOH$ produced **R**. On strong heating, **Q** gave **S**, which on further treatment with ethyl 2-bromopropanoate in the presence of KOH followed by acidification, gave a compound **T**.

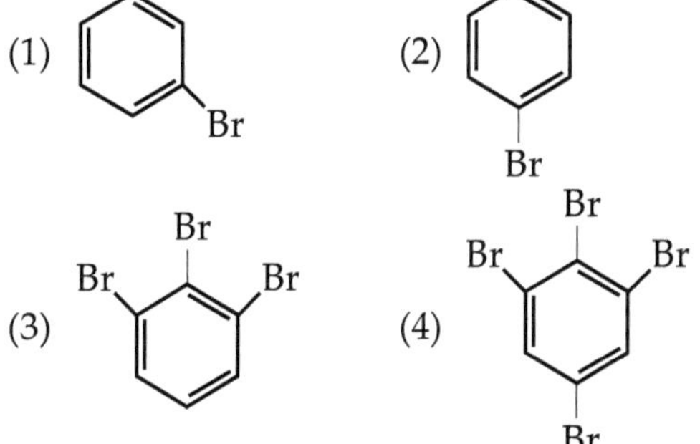

(O)

**40.** The compound **R** is : **[2016, Advanced]**

(1)   (2)

(3)   (4)

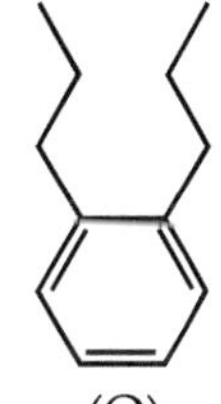

**41.** The compound **T** is : **[2016, Advanced]**
(1) Glycine  (2) Alanine
(3) Valine  (4) Serine

**42.** The test to distinguish primary, secondary and tertiary amines is : **[2016, Main]**
(1) Carbylamine reaction
(2) $C_6H_5SO_2Cl$
(3) Sandmeyer's reaction
(4) Mustard oil test

**43.** Fluorination of an aromatic ring is easily accomplished by treating a diazonium salt with $HBF_4$. Which of the following conditions is correct about this reaction ? **[2016, Main]**
(1) Only heat
(2) $NaNO_2/Cu$
(3) $Cu_2O/H_2O$
(4) $NaF/Cu$

**44.** In the Hofmann bromamide degradation reaction, the number of moles of NaOH and $Br_2$ used per mole of amine produced are : **[2016, Main]**
(1) One mole of NaOH and one mole of $Br_2$.
(2) Four moles of NaOH and two mole of $Br_2$.
(3) Two moles of NaOH and two moles of $Br_2$.
(4) Four mole of NaOH and one mole of $Br_2$.

**45.** In the following reactions, the major product $\overset{\circ}{W}$ is :
**[2015, Advanced]**

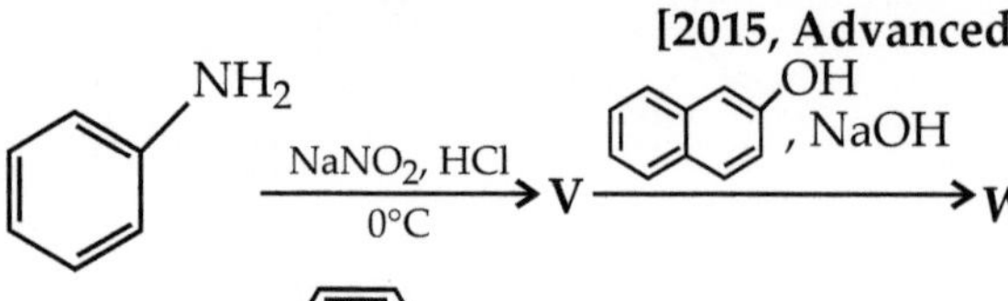

(1)

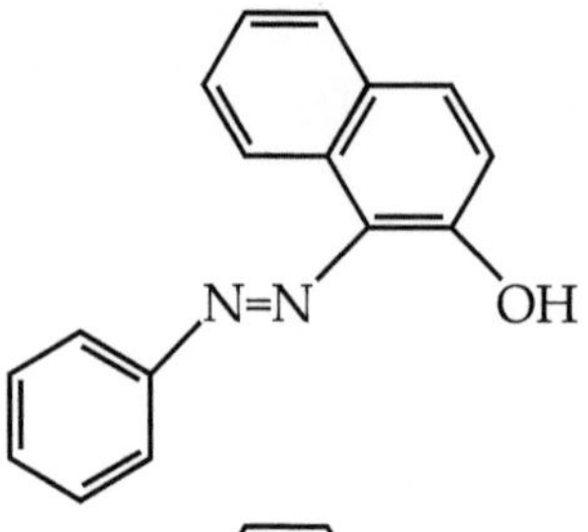

(2)

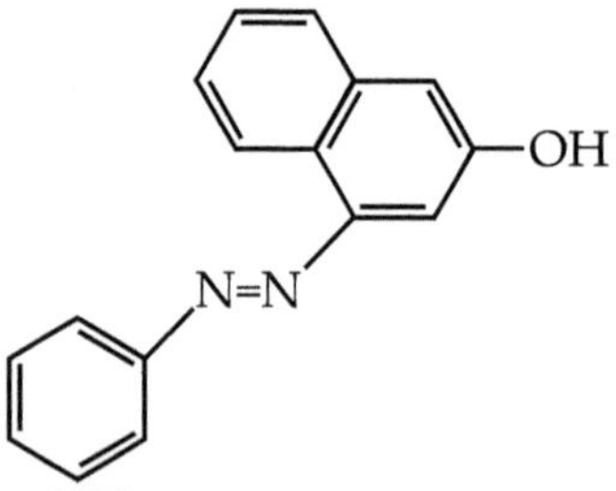

(3)

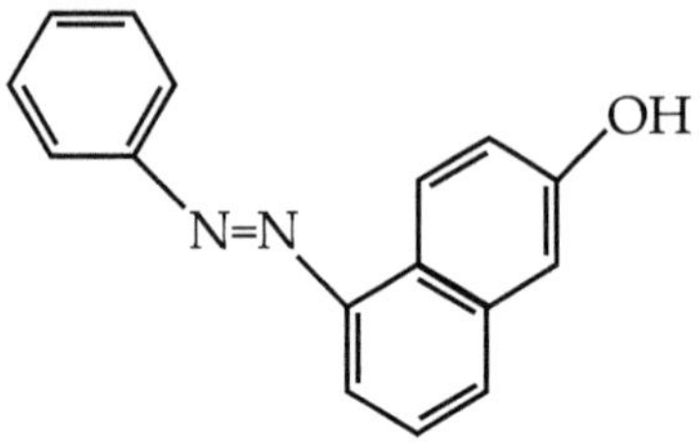

(4)

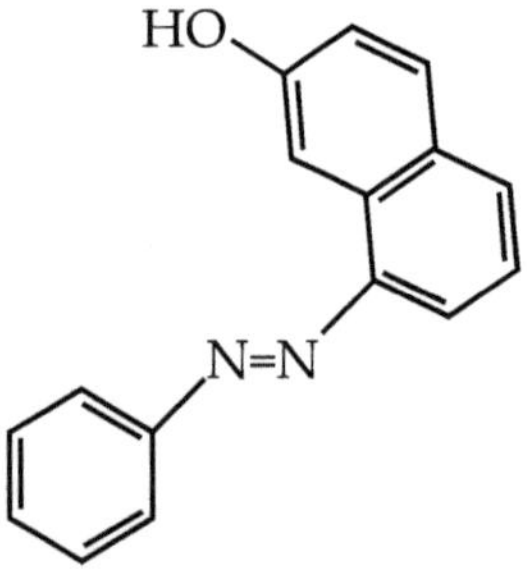

**46.** In the reaction the product E is :

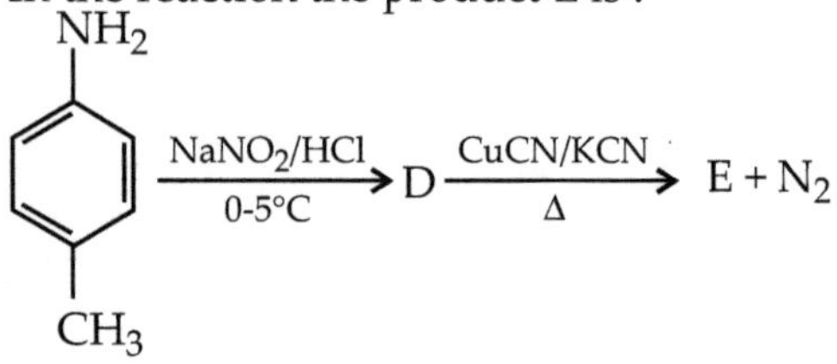

the product E is : **[2015, Main]**

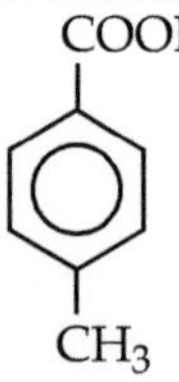

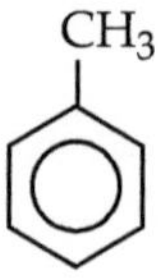

**47.** Arrange the following amines in the order of increasing basicity : **[2015, Main]**

(1)

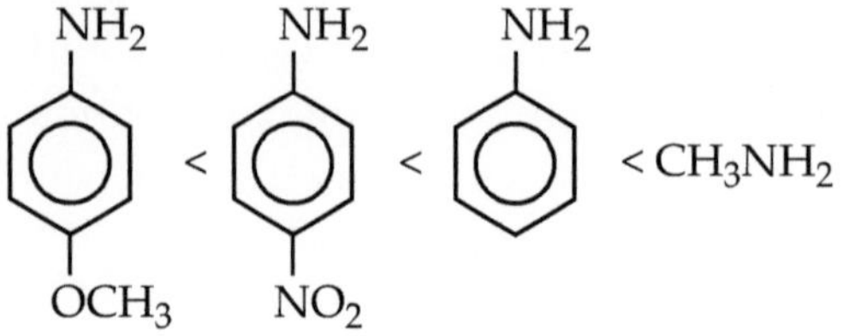

(2)

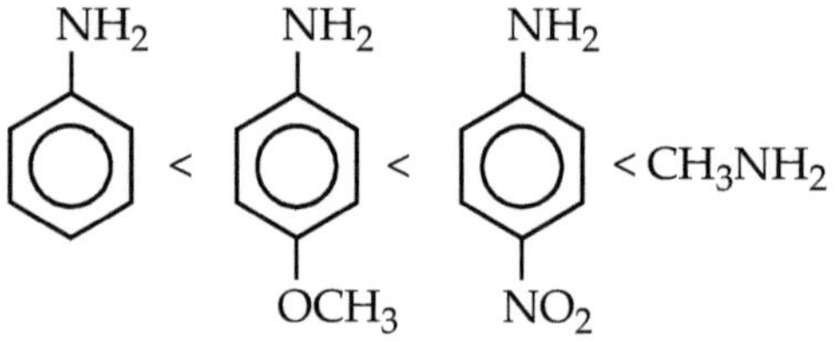

(3)

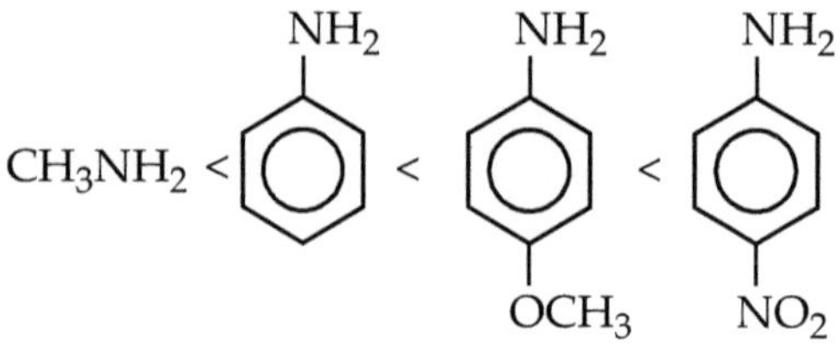

(4)

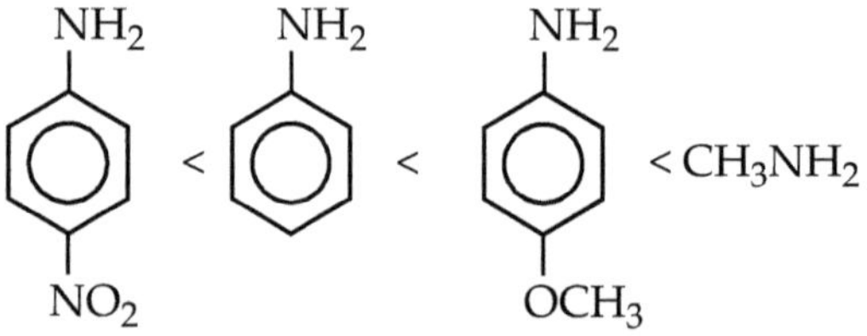

**48.** Which compound exibits maximum dipole moment among the following ? **[2015, Main]**

(1)

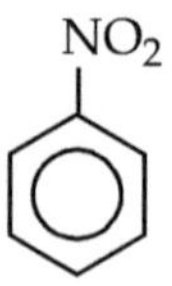

(2)

(3)

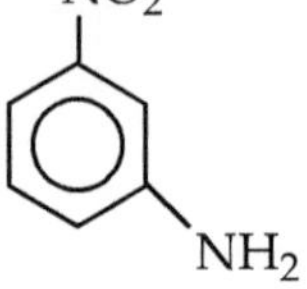

(4)

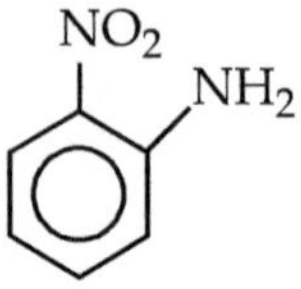

**49.** In the reaction shown below, the major products formed is/are : **[2014, Advanced]**

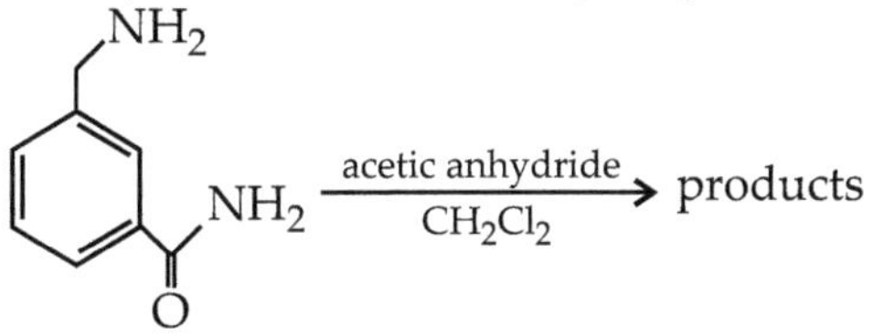

(1) 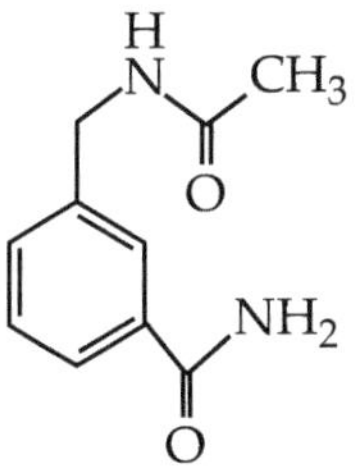 + $CH_3COOH$

(2) 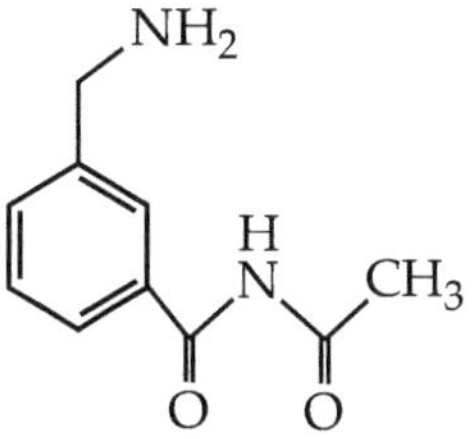 + $CH_3COOH$

(3) 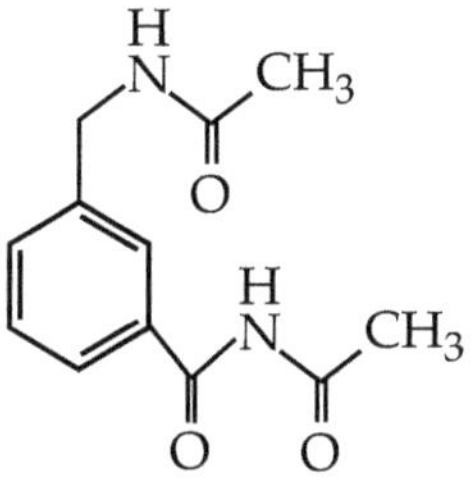 + $H_2O$

(4) 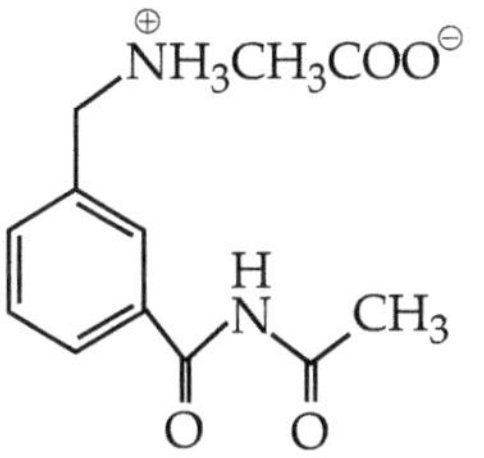

**50.** For the identification of β-naphthol using dye test, it is necessary to use : **[2014, Advanced]**

(1) dichloromethane solution of β-naphthol.

(2) acidic solution of β-naphthol.

(3) neutral solution of β-naphthol.

(4) alkaline solution of β-naphthol.

**51.** Match the four starting materials (**P, Q, R, S**) given in List I with the corresponding reaction schemes (**I, II, III, IV**) provided in **List II** and select the correct answer using the code given below the lists : **[2014, Advanced]**

| **List-I** | **List-II** |
|---|---|
| **(P)** $H-\equiv-H$ | **1. Scheme I**<br>(i) $KMnO_4$, $HO^\ominus$, heat<br>(ii) $H^\oplus$, $H_2O$ (iii) $SOCl_2$<br>(iv) $NH_3$<br>? ⟶ $C_7H_6N_2O_3$ |
| **(Q)** 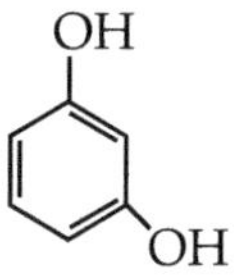 | **2. Scheme II**<br>(i) Sn/HCl (ii) $CH_3COCl$<br>(iii) conc. $H_2SO_4$ (iv) $HNO_3$<br>(v) dil. $H_2SO_4$, heat<br>(vi) $HO^\ominus$<br>? ⟶ $C_6H_6N_2O_2$ |
| **(R)** 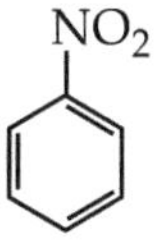 | **3. Scheme III**<br>(i) red hot iron, 873 K<br>(ii) fuming $HNO_3$, $H_2SO_4$, heat<br>(iii) $H_2S.NH_3$ (iv) $NaNO_2$, $H_2SO_4$ (v) hydrolysis<br>? ⟶ $C_6H_5NO_3$ |
| **(S)** 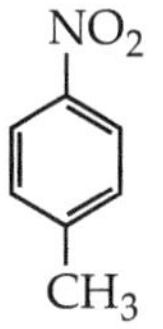 | **4. Scheme IV**<br>(i) conc. $H_2SO_4$, 60°C<br>(ii) conc. $HNO_3$, conc. $H_2SO_4$<br>(iii) dil. $H_2SO_4$, heat<br>? ⟶ $C_6H_5NO_4$ |

**Codes :**

| | P | Q | R | S |
|---|---|---|---|---|
| (1) | 1 | 4 | 2 | 3 |
| (2) | 3 | 1 | 4 | 2 |
| (3) | 3 | 4 | 2 | 1 |
| (4) | 4 | 1 | 3 | 2 |

**52.** On heating an aliphatic primary amine with chloroform and ethanolic potassium hydroxide, the organic compound formed is : **[2014, Main]**

(1) an alkanol (2) an alkanediol

(3) an alkyl cyanide (4) an alkyl isocyanide

**53.** Considering the basic strength of amines in aqueous solution, which one has the smallest $_pK_b$ value ? **[2014, Main]**

(1) $(CH_3)_2NH$ (2) $CH_3NH_2$

(3) $(CH_3)_3N$ (4) $C_6H_5NH_2$

**54.** The major product of the reaction is :

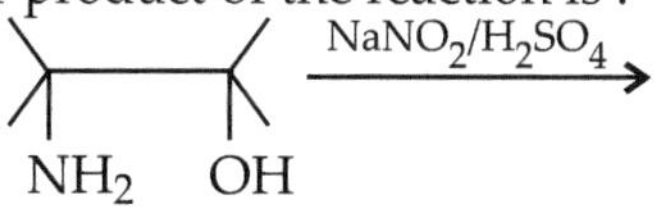

is : **[2014, Main]**

(1) 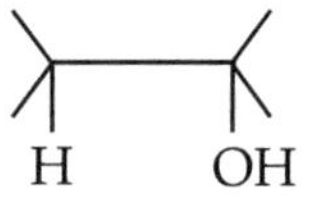 (2) 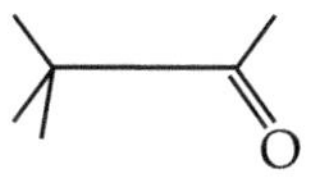

(3) 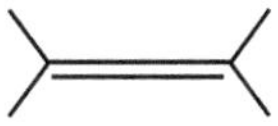 (4) 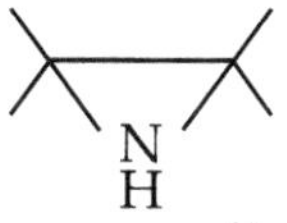

**55.** Complete reduction of benzene-diazonium chloride with Zn/HCl gives : **[2014, Main]**

(1) Aniline (2) Phenylhydrazine

(3) Azobenzene (4) Hydrazobenzene

**56.** Conversion of benzene diazonium chloride to chloro benzene is an example of which of the following reactions ? **[2014, Main]**

(1) Claisen (2) Friedel-craft

(3) Sandmeyer (4) Wurtz

**57.** The final product formed when Methyl amine is treated with $NaNO_2$ and HCl is : **[2014, Main]**

(1) Diazomethane (2) Methylalcohol

(3) Methylcyanide (4) Nitromethane

**58.** In a set of reactions *p*-nitrotoluene yielded a product E

$$\text{(p-nitrotoluene)} \xrightarrow[\text{FeBr}_3]{\text{Br}_2} B \xrightarrow[\text{HCl}]{\text{Sn/HCl}} C \xrightarrow[\text{HCl}]{\text{NaNO}_2} D \xrightarrow[\text{HBr}]{\text{CuBr}} E$$

The product E would be : **[2014, Main]**

(1) 3,5-dibromo-4-methyl (Br at 2,6 positions, Br at 4)

(2) 2-bromo-4-bromo toluene

(3) 2,3-dibromotoluene

(4) 4-bromo benzyl bromide ($CH_2Br$)

**59.** The major product of the following reaction is : **[2011, Advanced]**

phthalimide $\xrightarrow{\text{(i) KOH}}$ $\xrightarrow{\text{(ii) Br-C}_6\text{H}_4\text{-CH}_2\text{Cl}}$

(1) phthalimide $N-CH_2-C_6H_4-Br$

(2) phthalimide $N-C_6H_4-CH_2Cl$

(3) isoindole $O-CH_2-C_6H_4-Br$

(4) isoindole $O-C_6H_4-CH_2Cl$

**60.** Amongst the compounds given the one that would form a brilliant coloured dye on treatment with NaNO$_2$ in dil. HCl followed by addition to an alkaline solution of β-naphthol is : **[2011, Advanced]**

(1) $C_6H_5-N(CH_3)_2$

(2) $C_6H_5-NHCH_3$

(3) 4-methyl aniline ($H_3C-C_6H_4-NH_2$)

(4) $C_6H_5-CH_2NH_2$

**61.** In the reaction $H_3C-C_6H_4-C(=O)NH_2$

$$\xrightarrow[\text{(2) } C_6H_5-C(=O)Cl]{\text{(1) NaOH/Br}_2} T$$

the structure of the product T is : **[2010, Advanced]**

(1) $H_3C-C_6H_4-C(=O)-O-C(=O)-C_6H_5$

(2) $C_6H_5-NH-C(=O)-C_6H_4-CH_3$

(3) $H_3C-C_6H_4-NH-C(=O)-C_6H_5$

(4) $H_3C-C_6H_4-C(=O)-NH-C(=O)-C_6H_5$

**62.** Match the reactions in Column I with appropriate options in Column II. **[2010, Advanced]**

| Column I | Column II |
|---|---|
| (1) $C_6H_5-N_2Cl + C_6H_5-OH \xrightarrow[\text{0°C}]{\text{NaOH/H}_2\text{O}}$ $C_6H_5-N=N-C_6H_4-OH$ | (p) Racemic mixture |
| (2) $H_3C-\underset{CH_3}{\underset{\|}{C}}(OH)-\underset{CH_3}{\underset{\|}{C}}(OH)-CH_3 \xrightarrow{H_2SO_4}$ $H_3C-C(=O)-C(CH_3)_2-CH_3$ | (q) Addition reaction |

(3) [structure: acetophenone] $\xrightarrow[\text{2. H}_3\text{O}^+]{\text{1. LiAlH}_4}$ (r) Substitution reaction

[structure: 1-phenylethanol with OH, CH, CH₃]

(4) $HS-\langle\rangle-Cl \xrightarrow{\text{Base}} \langle S \rangle$ (s) Coupling reaction

(t) Carbocation intermediate

### Paragraph for Question 63

*p*-Amino-N, N-dimethylaniline is added to a strongly acidic solution of **X**. The resulting solution is treated with a few drops of aqueous solution of **Y** to yield blue coloration due to the formation of methylene blue. Treatment of the aqueous solution of **Y** with the reagent potassium hexacyanoferate(II) leads to the formation of an intense blue precipitate. The precipitate dissolves on excess addition of the reagent. Similarly, treatmet of the solution **Y** with the solution of potassium hexacyanoferrate (III) leads to a brown coloration due to the formation of **Z**.

**63.** The compound **X** is : **[2009, Advanced]**

(1) $NaNO_3$      (2) $NaCl$

(3) $Na_2SO_4$      (4) $Na_2S$

**64.** Match each of the compounds in **Column I** with its characteristic reactions in **Column II**.

**[2009, Advanced]**

| Column I | | Column II |
|---|---|---|
| (1) $CH_3CH_2CH_2CN$ | (p) | Reduction with Pd–C/H₂ |
| (2) $CH_3CH_2OCOCH_3$ | (q) | Reduction with SnCl₂/HCl |
| (3) $CH_3-CH=CH$<br>$-CH_2OH$ | (r) | Development of foul smell on treatment with chloroform and alcoholic KOH |
| (4) $CH_3CH_2CH_2CH_2$<br>$NH_2$ | (s) | Reduction with disobutylaluminium hydride (DIBAL-H) |
| | (t) | Alkaline hydrolysis |

**65.** The correct stability order of the following resonance structures is : **[2009, Advanced]**

$H_2C=\overset{+}{N}=\overset{-}{N}$       $H_2\overset{+}{C}-N=\overset{-}{N}$

   (I)                (II)

$H_2\overset{-}{C}=\overset{+}{N}\equiv N$       $H_2\overset{-}{C}-N\equiv\overset{+}{N}$

  (III)               (IV)

(1) (I) > (II) > (IV) > (III)

(2) (I) > (III) > (II) > (IV)

(3) (II) > (I) > (III) > (IV)

(4) (III) > (I) > (IV) > (II)

**66. Statement-1 :** Aniline on reaction with NaNO₂/HCl at 0°C followed by coupling with β-naphthol gives a dark blue coloured precipitate.

**and**

**Statement-2 :** The colour of the compound formed in the reaction of aniline with NaNO₂/HCl at 0°C followed by coupling with β-naphthol is due to the extended conjugation. **[2008, Advanced]**

(1) Statement-1 is True, Statement-2 is True; Statement-2 is a correct explanantion for Statement-1

(2) Statement-1 is True, Statement-2 is True; Statement-2 is **NOT** a correct explanantion for Statement-1

(3) Statement-1 is True, Statement-2 is False

(4) Statement-1 is False, Statement-2 is True

**67.** In the following reaction

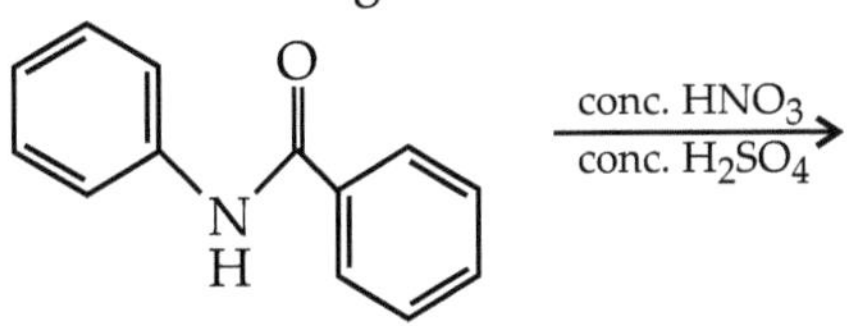

the structure of the major product 'X' is : **[2007, Advanced]**

(1)

(2)

(3)

(4)

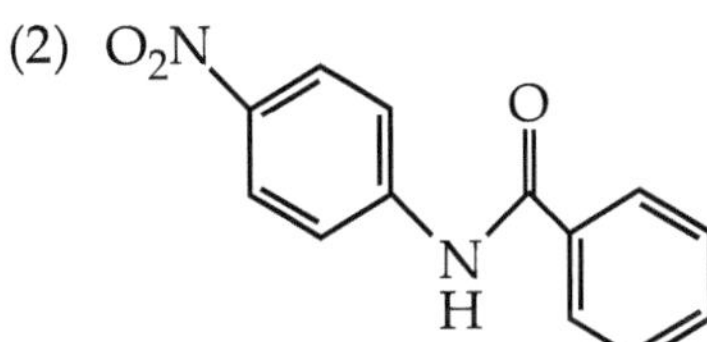

**68.** $CH_3NH_2 + CHCl_3 + KOH \rightarrow$ Nitrogen containing compound $+ KCl + H_2O$. Nitrogen containing compound is : **[2006, Main]**

(1) $CH_3-C\equiv N$      (2) $CH_3-NH-CH_3$

(3) $CH_3-\overset{-}{N}=\overset{+}{C}$      (4) $CH_3\overset{+}{N}\equiv\overset{-}{C}$

## Paragraph for Question 69 to 70

$RCONH_2$ is converted into $RNH_2$ by means by Hofmanin bromamide degradation.

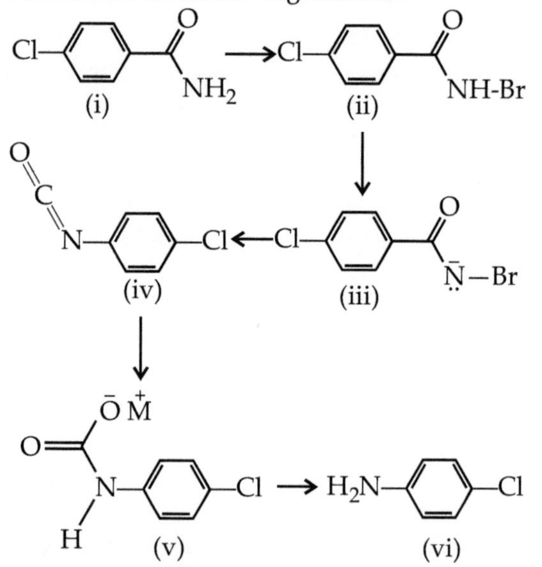

In this reaction, RCONHBr is formed from which this reaction has derived its name. Electron donating group at phenyl activates the reaction. Hofmann degradation reaction is an intramolecular reaction.

**69.** How can the conversion of (i) to (ii) be brought about ? **[2006, Main]**

(1) KBr
(2) $KBr + CH_3ONa$
(3) $KBr + KOH$
(4) $Br_2 + KOH$

**70.** Which is the rate determining step in Hofmann bromamide degradation ? **[2006, Main]**

(1) Formation of (i)
(2) Formation of (ii)
(3) Formation of (iii)
(4) Formation of (iv)

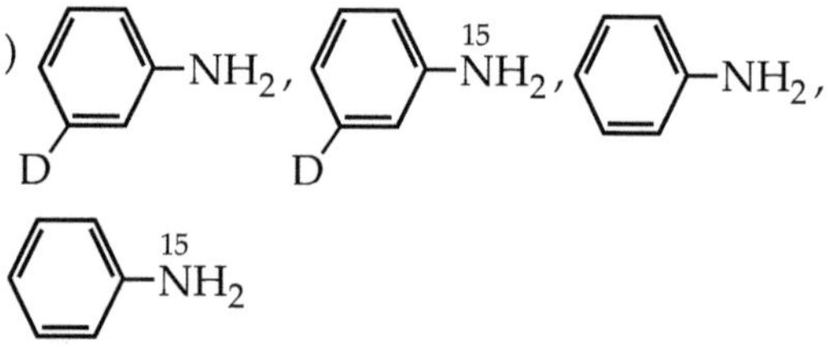

**71.** What are the constituent amines formed when the mixture of (i) and (ii) undergoes Hofmann bromamide degradation ? **[2006, Main]**

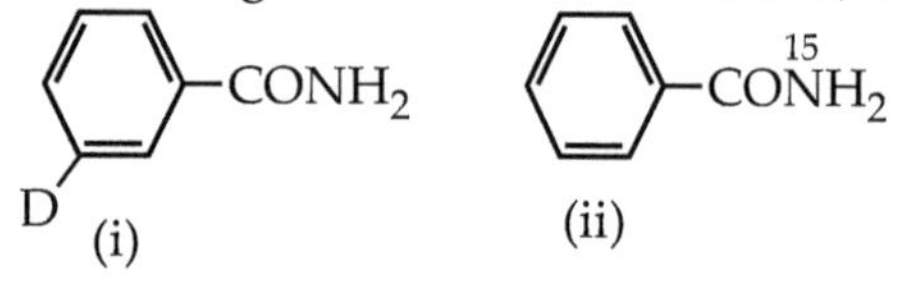

**72.** $C_5H_{13}N$ (Optically active) $\xrightarrow[-N_2]{NaNO_2, HCl}$ Y (Tertiary alcohol + other products)

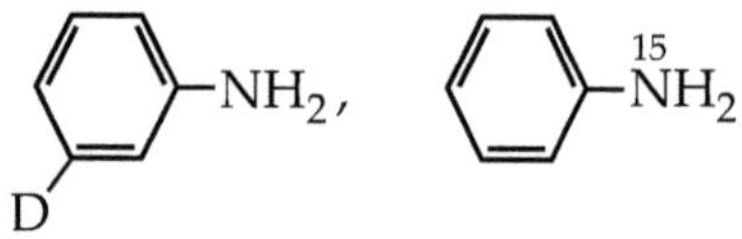

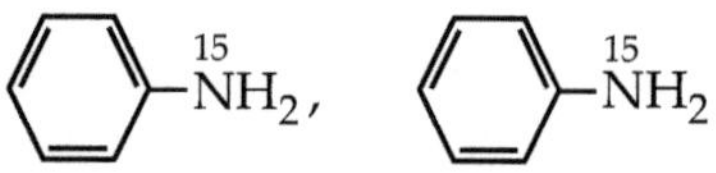

Find X and Y. Is Y optically active ? Write the intermediate steps. **[2005, Main]**

**73.** (Brown fumes and pungent smell) B $\xleftarrow{NaBr+MnO_2}$

A $\xrightarrow{conc.\ HNO_3}$ C (intermediate) $\longrightarrow$ D (Explosive product).

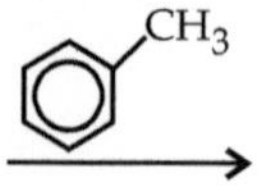

Find A, B, C and D. Also write equations A to B and A to C. **[2005, Main]**

**74.** Which of the following is more acidic and why ? **[2004, Main]**

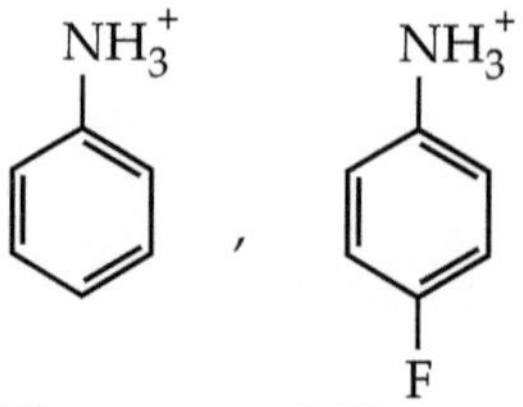

**75.** Convert [nitrobenzene] to [3-nitrophenol] in not more than four steps. Also, mention the temp and reaction condition. **[2004, Main]**

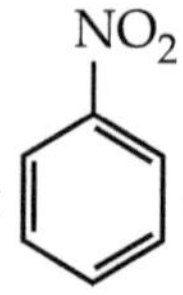

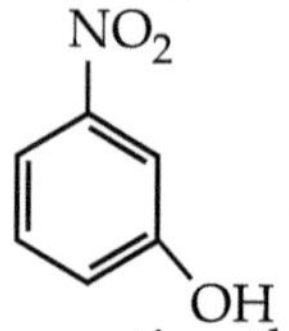

**76.** [benzyl chloride] $\xrightarrow[DMF]{KCN}$ (A) $\xrightarrow[C_6H_5CHO/\Delta]{C_2H_5ONa/C_2H_5OH}$ (B) $\xrightarrow[\Delta]{H_3O^+}$ (C) $\xrightarrow[CH_3NH_2]{SOCl_2}$ (D)

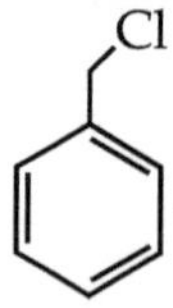

Identify A to D. **[2004, Main]**

**77.** $C_2$ is rotated anticlockwise 120° about $C_2$–$C_3$ bond. The resulting conformer is : **[2004, Screening]**

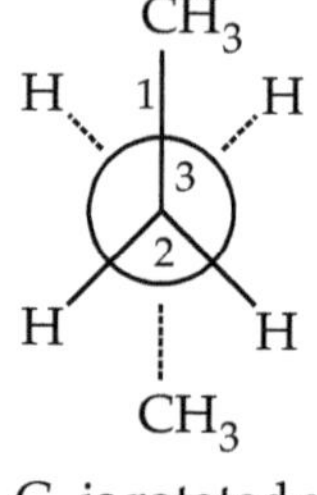

(1) Partially eclipsed
(2) Eclipsed
(3) Gauche
(4) Staggered

**78.** Benzamide on treatment with $POCl_3$ gives : **[2004, Screening]**

(1) Aniline
(2) Benzonitrile
(3) Chlorobenzene
(4) Benzyl amine

**79.** [naphthalene imide compound] $\xrightarrow{Fe/Br_2}$

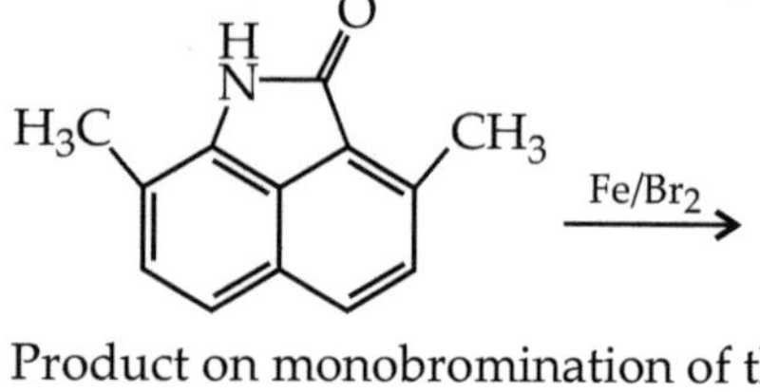

Product on monobromination of this compound is : **[2004, Screening]**

(1) 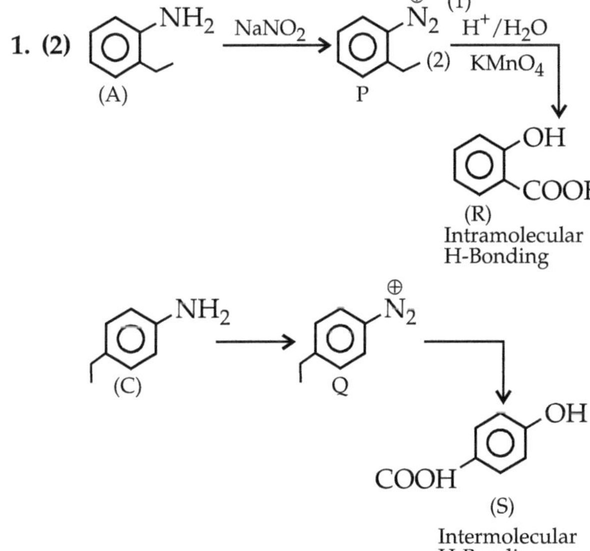

(2)

(3)

(4)

**80.** F—⟨benzene⟩—$NO_2$ $\xrightarrow[\text{DMF, }\Delta]{(CH_3)_2NH}$ (A) $\xrightarrow[\substack{0°\text{-}5°C \\ (ii)\ H_2/Ni}]{(i)\ NaNO_2/HCl}$ (B).

B is :   **[2003, Screening]**

(1) $H_2N$—⟨benzene⟩—$N\begin{smallmatrix}CH_3\\CH_3\end{smallmatrix}$

(2) $H_2N$—⟨benzene⟩—$NH_2$

(3) $O_2N$—⟨benzene⟩—$NH_2$

(4) $O_2N$—⟨benzene⟩—$N\begin{smallmatrix}CH_3\\ \end{smallmatrix}$

## ANSWER KEY

| | | | | | | | | | |
|---|---|---|---|---|---|---|---|---|---|
| **1.** (2) | **2.** (2) | **3.** (4) | **4.** (4) | **5.** (*) | **6.** (1) | **7.** (2) | **8.** (4) | **9.** (3) | **10.** (2) |
| **11.** (1) | **12.** (3) | **13.** (1) | **14.** (3) | **15.** (4) | **16.** (4) | **17.** (3) | **18.** (2) | **19.** (3) | **20.** (3) |
| **21.** (1) | **22.** (4) | **23.** (3) | **24.** (3) | **25.** (4) | **26.** (2) | **27.** (4) | **28.** 495 g | **29.** (3) | **30.** (2) |
| **31.** (4) | **32.** (4) | **33.** (4) | **34.** (3) | **35.** (3) | **36.** (1) | **37.** (2) | **38.** (4) | **39.** (2) | **40.** (1) |
| **41.** (2) | **42.** (2) | **43.** (1) | **44.** (4) | **45.** (1) | **46.** (3) | **47.** (4) | **48.** (2) | **49.** (1) | **50.** (4) |
| **51.** (3) | **52.** (4) | **53.** (1) | **54.** (2) | **55.** (1) | **56.** (3) | **57.** (2) | **58.** (2) | **59.** (1) | **60.** (3) |

**61.** (3)   **62.** (1) : r and s; (2) : t; (3) : p and q; (4) : r   **63.** (4)

**64.** (1)-(p), (q), (s) and (t); (2)-(s) and (t); (3)-(p): and (4)-(r).

| | | | | | | | | |
|---|---|---|---|---|---|---|---|---|
| **65.** (2) | **66.** (4) | **67.** (2) | **68.** (4) | **69.** (4) | **70.** (4) | **71.** (2) | **72.** (*) | **73.** (*) |

**74.** (*)   **75.** (*)   **76.** (*)   **77.** (3)   **78.** (2)   **79.** (2)   **80.** (1)

## ANSWERS WITH EXPLANATIONS

**1. (2)**

$Ph–CH_2–NH–Me \xrightarrow{Ph–SO_2Cl}$ Ph–S–N(Me)(CH₂–Ph)

Solid sulphonamide (not soluble in Aq.) NaOH

**2. (2)**

**3. (4)**

$$\text{(cyclohexyl)}\underset{\overset{|}{CH_3}}{CH}-C\equiv N \xrightarrow[\text{(ii) } H_3O^+]{\text{(i) } C_2H_5MgBr}$$

$$\xrightarrow[\text{(ii) } H_2O]{\text{(i) } CH_3MgBr} \quad \text{(cyclohexyl)}\underset{\overset{|}{CH_3}}{CH}-\overset{\overset{O}{\|}}{C}-C_2H_5$$

$$\text{(cyclohexyl)}\,\overset{*}{CH}-\overset{\overset{OH}{|}}{\overset{*}{C}}-C_2H_5$$
with $CH_3$ $CH_3$ and starred carbons.

**4. (4)**

(A) pyridine — $sp^2$ (Localised cone pair)

(B) pyrrole — lone pair involve in aromaticity ⇓ Weakest base (least Basic)

(C) $sp^3$ most basic

(D) imidazole — less Basic then (c) due to $\ominus I$ effect of $II^{nd}$ Nitrogen

**5. 4.**

**6. (1)** The Kjeldahl method is not applicable to nitro or diazo groups present in the ring, as nitrogen atom can not be converted to ammonium sulphate under the reaction conditions. Hence, this method is not applicable for nitrobenzene $C_6H_5NO_2$.

**7. (2)**

$$\underset{\underset{Br}{}}{C_6H_4-NH_2} \xrightarrow[\text{273–278K}]{NaNO_2/HCl} \underset{\underset{Br}{}}{C_6H_4-\overset{+}{N_2}Cl^-}$$
(Diazotisation) → (*m*-Bromo benzene diazonium chloride)

$$\xrightarrow[\text{reaction}]{Cu_2Br_2 \text{ Sand Mayer's}} \text{1,3-dibromobenzene (Br, Br)}$$

$$\xrightarrow[\text{(Nitration)}]{\underset{H_2SO_4}{HNO_3}} \text{(product with } NO_2, NH_2, Br\text{)}$$

**8. (4)**

decalin derivative with substituents $CONH_2$, $\overset{\overset{O}{\|}}{C}-CH_3$, $HO_2C$, $CN$ $\longrightarrow$

decalin derivative with substituents $CONH_2$, $COCH_3$, $HOH_2C$, $CN$

Most suitable reagent for given conversion is $B_2H_6$ (electrophilic reducing agent)

**9. (3)** Basicity is directly proportional to electron pair intensity on nitrogen.

Refer image (III), there is no resonance and +I effect from both sides. Therefore, it is most basic.

Refer image (II), nitrogen do not involve in resonance. Therefore, it is more basic.

Refer image (I), nitrogen lone pair is involved in resonance and it is less available for donation. Therefore, it is less basic.

Refer image (IV), aromatic nitrogen lone pair is participating in aromaticity. It is less available for donation. Therefore, it is least basic.

III > II > I > IV (Basicity order)

**10. (2)** $H_3N_3B_3Cl_3 + 3LiBH_4 \xrightarrow[\text{(T.H.F.)}]{\text{In tetrahydrofurene}}$

$$\underset{\text{(B)}}{N_3B_3H_6} + 3LiCl + 3BH_3 \cdot THF$$

Inorganic Benzene (Borazene)

$$\underset{\text{(A)}}{H_3N_3B_3Cl_3} + 3CH_3MgBr \xrightarrow{Q} \underset{\text{(C)}}{H_3N_3B_3(CH_3)_3}$$
$$+ 3MgBrCl$$

**11. (1)**

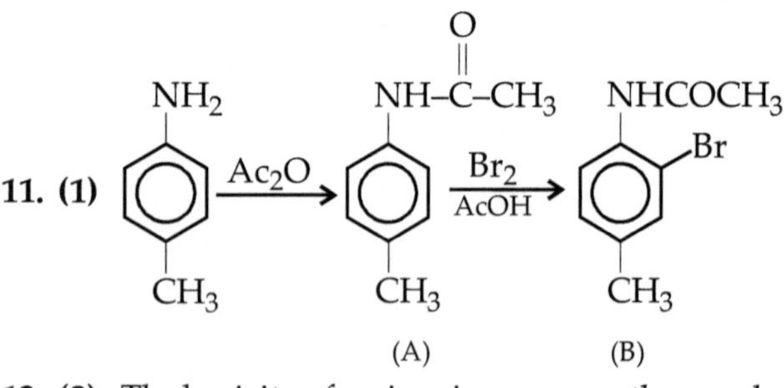

$$\underset{\underset{CH_3}{}}{C_6H_4-NH_2} \xrightarrow{Ac_2O} \underset{\underset{CH_3}{}}{C_6H_4-NH-\overset{\overset{O}{\|}}{C}-CH_3} \xrightarrow[\text{AcOH}]{Br_2} \underset{\underset{CH_3}{}}{C_6H_3-NHCOCH_3, Br}$$
(A) (B)

**12. (3)** The basicity of amines increases as the number of alkyl groups attached to the nitrogen atom increases. This is because electron donating alkyl groups increase the electron density on nitrogen atom and make the non bonding electrons on nitrogen atom more available for donation. Therefore, the decresing order of basic strength is given below.

$$(C_2H_5)_2NH > C_2H_5NH_2 > NH_3$$

**13. (1)** The Gabriel phthalimide reaction is used for the preparation of primary amines. Therefore, this reaction can be used for the preparation of *n*-butylamine, as it is a primary amine. The general reaction of Gabriel phthalimide synthesis is shown below :

$$\text{phthalimide-NH} \xrightarrow[\text{2. R}-X]{\text{1. KOH}} \text{phthalimide-N}-R$$
(1° halide)

$$R-NH_2 + \underset{\text{COOH}}{\overset{\text{COOH}}{\bigcirc}} \xrightarrow{H_3O^+}$$

In the above reaction, R represents a primary alkyl group.

**14. (3)** The product that is formed when 1-naphthol reacts with benzene diazonium chloride in alkaline medium is as follows :

α-naphthol
(1-naphthol)

orange red dye

**15. (4)** The complete reaction is shown below :

$$+ CH_3I \xrightarrow{\text{Base}}$$

Aromaticity is lost in both the rings as one double bond is missing.

**16. (4)** The complete reaction is shown below :

$$\xrightarrow[\substack{\text{Carbylamine}\\ \text{reaction}}]{CHCl_3/KOH}$$

$$\downarrow Pd/C/H_2$$

The given compound undergoes carbylamines reaction to form isocyanide. It further undergoes reduction to form the final product.

**17. (3)** The formation of diazonium salt from aromatic amines takes place using sodium nitrite and hydrochloric acid at low temperatures. This process is known as diazotisation. The diazonium salts can be converted to phenol by treatment with water. The reaction between aniline and phenol in the presence of sodium nitrite and dilute HCl is shown below :

$$\xrightarrow[0°C]{NaNO_2 + HCl}$$

in acidic medium

(C−N coupled product)

**18. (2)** The structure of the compound is shown below :

The IUPAC name of the compound is 2-chloro-1-methyl-4-nitrobenzene.

**19. (3)** Hinsberg's reagent is used to distinguish amines as primary, secondary and tertiary amines. The structrue of Hinsberg reagent is shown below :

The chemical formula of Hinsberg reagent is $C_6H_5SO_2Cl$.

**20. (3)** The iodo-group of the starting material is substituted by the –CN to form compound [A]. The compound [A] undergoes reduction reaction to produce compound [B]. The complete reaction sequence is shown below :

$$\xrightarrow[S_N2]{KCN, DMSO}$$

$$\downarrow \text{Reduction} \quad H_2/Pd$$

$$CH_2-NH_2$$

**21. (1)** The completed reaction is shown below :

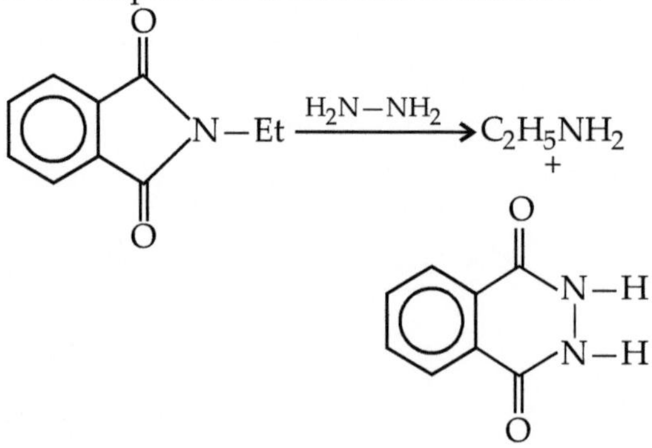

The reagent used is hydrazine ($NH_2NH_2$).

**22. (4)** The complete reactions are shown below :

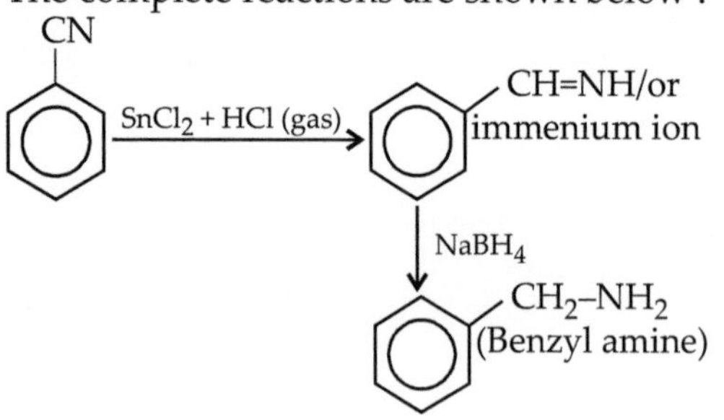

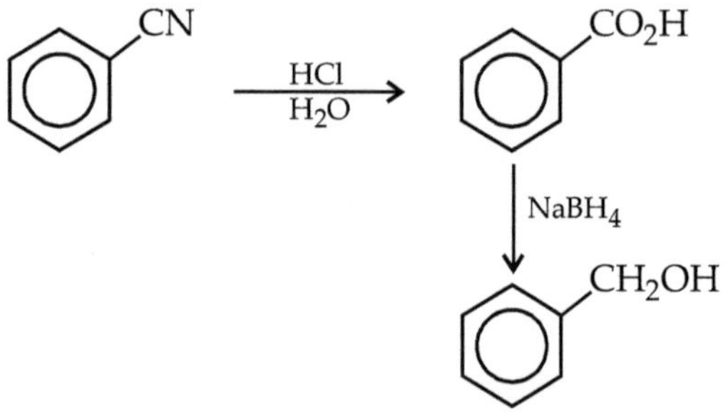

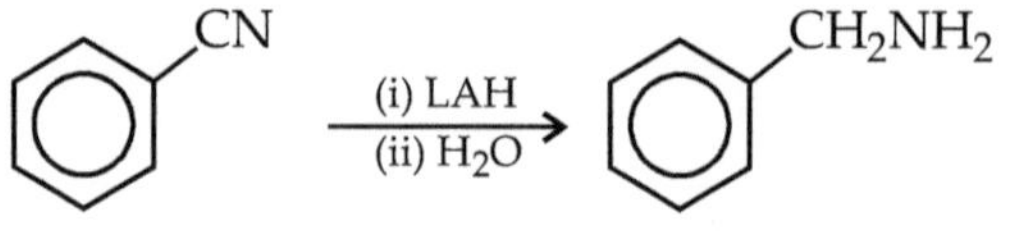

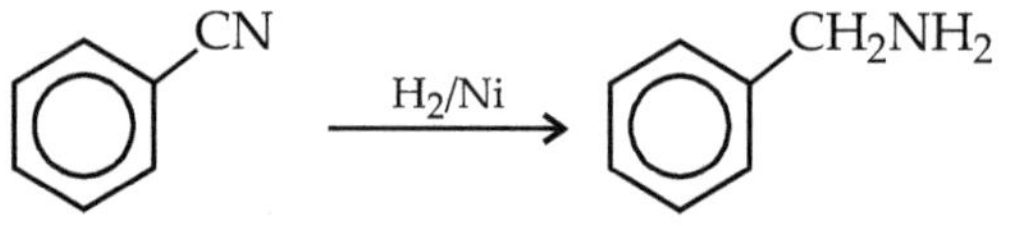

$$\text{(benzyl amine)}$$

Therefore, $HCl/H_2O$ and $NaBH_4$ is not a correct method for the preparation of benzylamine from cyanobenzene.

**23. (3)** The structure of given compounds are shown below :

(A)

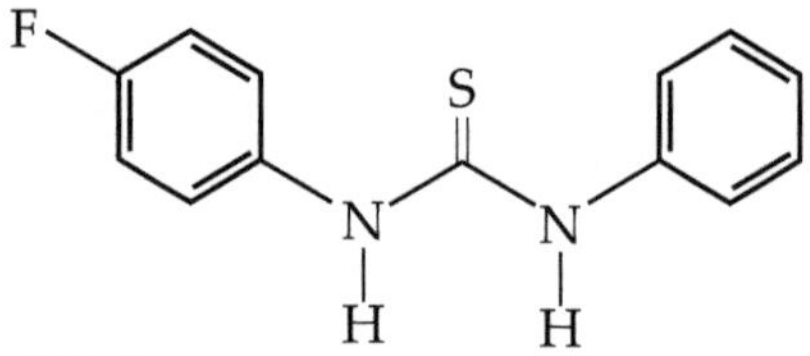

(B)

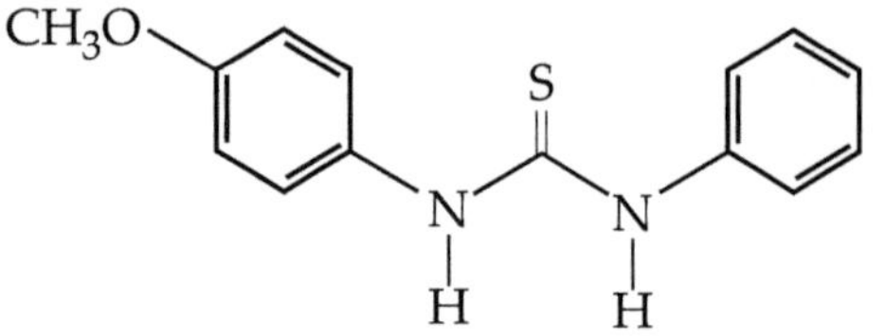

(C)

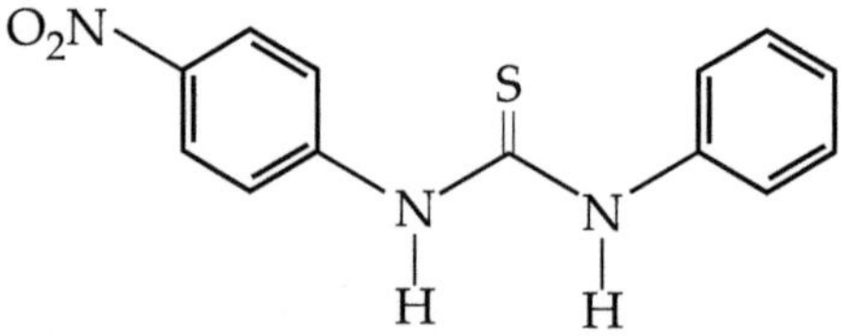

(D)

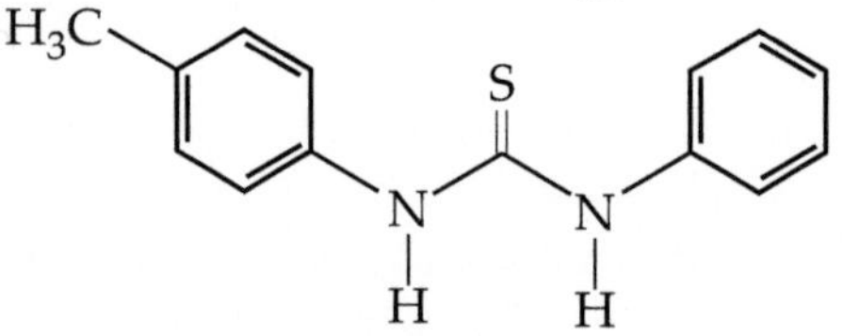

Basicity of a compound is inversely proportional to the value of $pK_a$.

The compound (C) is very basic due to the presence of electron withdrawing $-NO_2$ group. The compound (A) is less basic than the compound (C). Similarly, compound (D) is less basic than compound (A). The compound (B) is slightly basic due to the presence of electron releasing $-OCH_3$ group. The increasing order of value of $pK_a$ is shown below :

$$(B) < (D) < (A) < (C)$$

**24. (3)** The reaction between benzene diazonium chloride and aniline in the presence of dilute HCl is shown below :

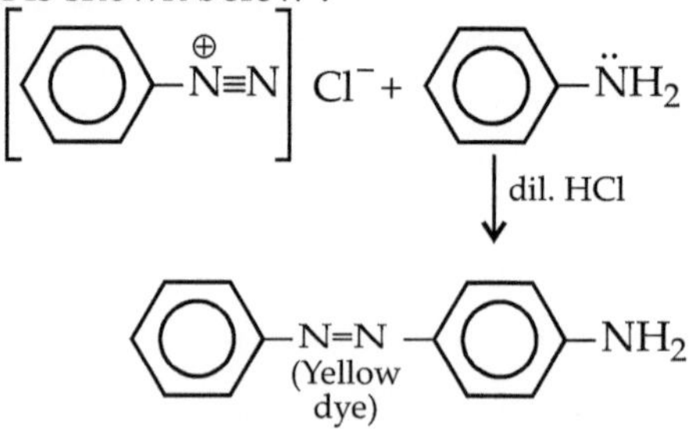

**25. (4)** The reaction for scheme 1 is shown below :

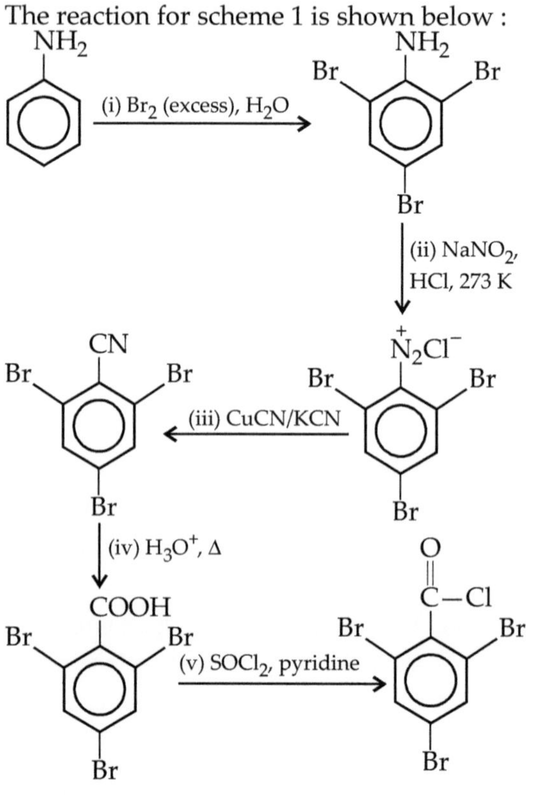

The reaction for scheme 2 is shown below :

$$\text{Benzene} \xrightarrow[\text{H}_2\text{SO}_4 + \text{SO}_3]{\text{(i) Oleum}} \text{C}_6\text{H}_5\text{SO}_3\text{H} \xrightarrow[\text{(iii) H}^\oplus]{\text{(ii) NaOH, }\Delta} \text{Phenol}$$

Phenol $\xrightarrow{\text{(vi) Br}_2,\ \text{CS}_2,\ 273\ \text{K}}$ o-bromophenol + p-bromophenol (Major)

The reaction for scheme 3 is shown below :

4-bromophenol $\xrightarrow{\text{(i) NaOH}}$ sodium 4-bromophenoxide

2,4,6-tribromobenzoyl chloride (Q) → ester (T)

Therefore, the total number of Br atoms in a molecule of T is 4.

**26. (2)** The correct sequence for the formation of S is shown below :

$$\text{isopropenyl-C}_6\text{H}_4\text{-COOH} \xrightarrow{\text{H}_2/\text{Pd-C}} \text{isopropyl-C}_6\text{H}_4\text{-COOH}$$

$$\xrightarrow{\text{NH}_3/\Delta} \text{isopropyl-C}_6\text{H}_4\text{-CONH}_2 \xrightarrow{\text{Br}_2/\text{NaOH}} \text{isopropyl-C}_6\text{H}_4\text{-NH}_2$$

$$\xrightarrow[\text{KOH}]{\text{CHCl}_3,\ \Delta} \text{isopropyl-C}_6\text{H}_4\text{-NC} \xrightarrow{\text{H}_2/\text{Pd-C}} \text{isopropyl-C}_6\text{H}_4\text{-N}\overset{\text{H}}{-}\text{CH}_3$$

**27. (4)** The correct reaction sequence is shown below :

Aniline $\xrightarrow[\text{conc. H}_2\text{SO}_4]{\text{conc. HNO}_3}$ p-nitroaniline (P) 51% + m-nitroaniline (Q) 47% + o-nitroaniline (R) 2%

$$\text{(R)} \xrightarrow{\text{Ac}_2\text{O, Pyridine}} \text{acetanilide derivative} \xrightarrow[\text{CH}_3\text{COOH}]{\text{Br}_2}$$

$$\xrightarrow{\text{H}_3\text{O}^+} \text{4-bromo-2-nitroaniline} \xrightarrow[\text{273-278 K}]{\text{NaNO}_2/\text{HCl}} \text{diazonium salt } (\text{N}_2^+\text{Cl}^-) \xrightarrow[\Delta]{\text{EtOH}} \text{(S)}$$

$$\text{(S)} \xrightarrow{\text{Sn, HCl}} \text{3-bromoaniline} \xrightarrow[\text{H}_2\text{O (excess)}]{\text{Br}_2} \text{2,4,6-tribromoaniline}$$

$$\text{2,4,6-tribromoaniline} \xrightarrow{\text{NaNO}_2,\ \text{HCl}} \text{diazonium salt} \xrightarrow{\text{H}_3\text{PO}_2} \text{1,3,5-tribromobenzene}$$

**28.** The correct sequence of reaction is shown below :

$$\text{Acetophenone (10 moles)} \xrightarrow[\text{H}_3\text{O}^+]{\text{NaOBr}} \text{COOH (A) (60\%)} \xrightarrow[\Delta]{\text{NH}_2} \text{CONH}_2 \text{ (B) (50\%)}$$

$$\text{B} \xrightarrow{\Delta \mid \text{Br}_2\text{KOH}}$$

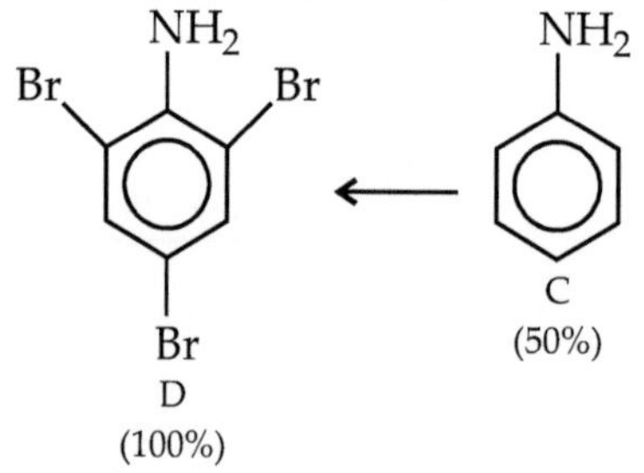

Thus, the moles of D formed

$$= 10 \times \frac{60}{100} \times \frac{50}{100} \times \frac{50}{100} = 1.5$$

Molar mass of tribromoaniline is 330 g/mol.

Mass of D formed = 1.5 mol × 330 g/mol

$$= 495 \text{ g}$$

**29. (3)** The basicity of amine groups depends upon the electron density present on the amine group. More is the electron density, more is the availability of electrons and higher will be the basicity of amine.

The amine group present in the compound (a) and (d) is $sp^3$ hybridized which has more electron density as compared to the amine group in compound (b) in which nitrogen atom is $sp^2$ hybridized. Therefore, the compound (b) is less basic than compound (a) and (d).

The amine group in compound (d) is bonded to two electropositive alkyl groups and the amine group in compound (a) is bonded to only one electropositive alkyl group. Therefore, the basicity of compound (d) is more than that of compound (a).

The compound (c) contains double bond at allylic position of one amine group and at vinylic position to second amine group. In this compound the electron density on amine group is highest due to resonance stabilization. Therefore, this compound is most basic among the given compounds.

Hence, the correct order of basicity of the given compounds is (b) < (a) < (d) < (c).

**30. (2)** Aromatic diazonium salts are more stable than aliphatic diazonium salts. Electron donating substituents increases electron density on benzene ring, hence, they increase the stability of diazonium salts.

On the other hand, electron withdrawing substituents decreases electron density on benzene ring. They decrease the stability of diazonium salts. $-COCH_3$ group is electron withdrawing and hence, (d) is less stable than (b). Although $-O-COCH_3$ is electron donating substituent, but it is present in meta position. Hence, it will not have significant effect on stability. The increasing order of diazotisation is (a)<(d)<(b)<(c).

**31. (4)** In the given compounds, methoxybenzene (anisole) undergoes faster nitration because oxygen is an electronegative group that increases the electron density and stabilizes the transition state. Then, toluene contains methyl group which is an electron donating group and shows inductive as well as resonance effect. Aniline is least reactive towards nitration due to the formation of anilinium ion. Therefore, the increasing order of nitration is (a) < (b) < (d) < (c).

**32. (4)** The compound in option (4) will not exist in zwitter ionic form at pH = 7 because nitrogen atom is in the form of an amide group. Hence, at pH 7, amide N will not be protonated.

**33. (4)** The steps involved in the given reaction are shown below :

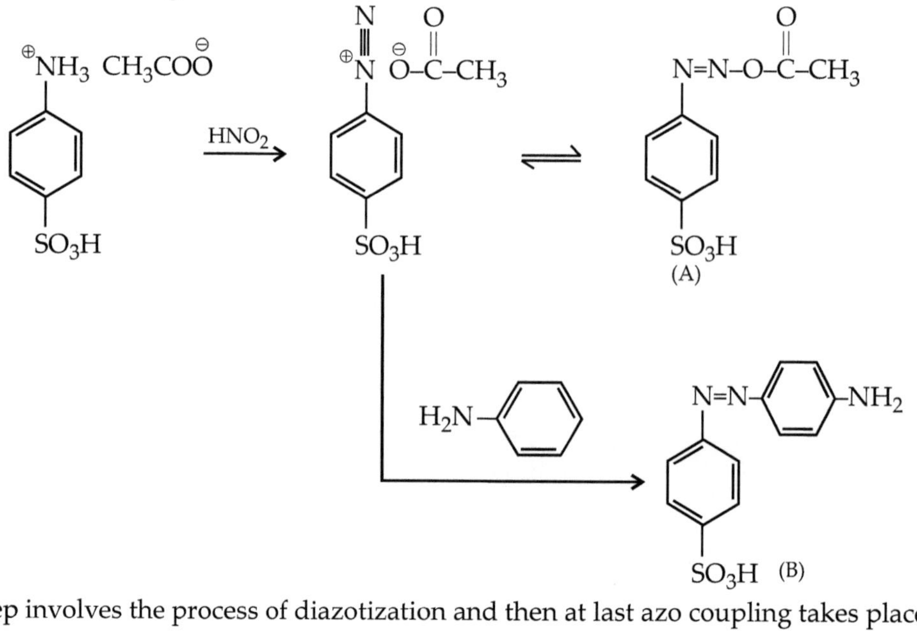

The first step involves the process of diazotization and then at last azo coupling takes place.

**34. (3)** The major product for the given reaction is expressed as :

The first step is diazotization of the aromatic amine followed by azo coupling which occurs at a position para to phenolic –OH group due to a combination of steric and electronic factors.

**35. (3)** In structure IV, lone pair of one nitrogen atom is in conjugation with the double bond. Therefore, it has total three canonical forms. As a result, it will be most basic in nature.

In structure I, one electron donating group is present at the doubly bonded carbon. Here also conjugation of double bond with nitrogen is present. Therefore, it has two canonical forms. As a result it will be less basic than the IV but more basic than II and III.

In II and III compounds, III will be least basic due to the involvement of lone pair in the ring. Due to which ring tends to aromaticity. Hence, the correct order of basicity is as follows :

**36. (1)** During mono-nitration, aniline will form significant amount of *meta* product. This is because in acidic medium, $Ph-NH_2$ will be protonated to form $Ph-NH_3^+$. $-NH_3^+$ group is meta directing.

**37. (2)** The compound (II) will go to the aqueous layer because if the given mixture is shaken with 1M HCl then the amine group present in compound (II) gets protonated that will result in the formation of the cation, $RNH_2^+$. This formed cation is not readily soluble in organic solvent. Thus, this cation gets dissolved in water due to the presence of charge on it.

**38. (4)** The increasing order of basic strength is shown below :

The compounds (I) and (II) are less basic because in these compounds lone pairs of nitrogen atom participated in conjugation. Primary amine is more basic than tertiary amine due to presence of steric hindrance in primary amine.

**39. (2)** The following sequence of reactions is given below to give the main product :

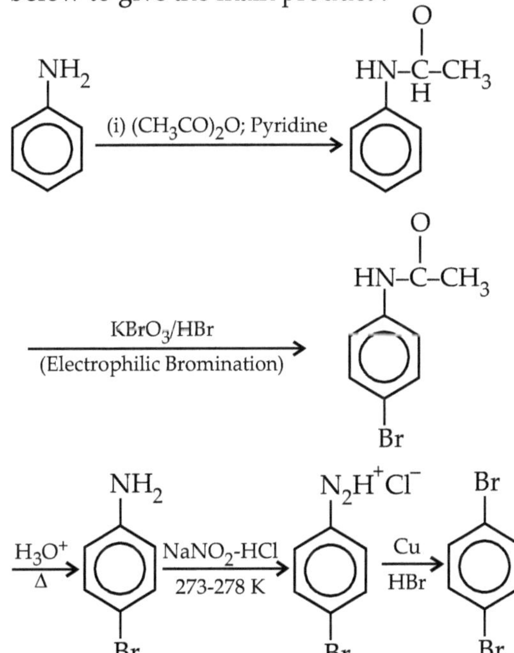

The product obtained is 1, 4-dibromobenzene.

**40. (1)** The following compounds will form in the reactions :

Compound O reacts with $KMnO_4/H^+$ to give compound P. Then Compound P reacts with ammonia to give compound Q which reacts with $Br_2/NaOH$ to give compound R.

Hence, the option which represents the correct structure of compound R is option (1).

**41. (2)** In the above reaction sequence compound Q on strong heating gives compound S. Compound S further reacts with ethyl-2-bromopropanoate in the presence of KOH followed by acidification to give compound T, alanine.

**42. (2)** The compound, benzene sulphonyl chloride, $C_6H_5SO_2Cl$ is used to distinguish between the primary, secondary and tertiary amines. This reaction is known as Hinsberg reaction. In this reaction, primary amines on reaction with $C_6H_5SO_2Cl$ forms water soluble sulfonamide salt whereas tertiary amines form water soluble sulfonate salts.

**43. (1)** The reaction for the fluorination of an aromatic ring is shown below :

This reaction is also known as Balz Schiemann's reaction. It takes place in the presence of heat. Thus, the condition that is correct for the given reaction is (1).

**44. (4)** In Hofmann Bromamide degradation reaction 4 moles of NaOH and one mole of $Br_2$ is required during the production of one mole of amine.

$$R-\overset{\overset{O}{\|}}{C}-NH_2 + Br_2 + 4NaOH \rightarrow$$

$$R-NH_2 + Na_2CO_3 + 2NaBr + 2H_2O$$

**45. (1)** The mechanism for the formation of W is shown below :

$$NaNO_2 + HCl \longrightarrow OH-N=O + NaCl$$

(Attacking species)
[Nitrosonium ion]

Benzene Diazonium chloride (BDC)

(coupling reaction)

Thus, the product W i.e., (E)-1(phenyldiazenyl) naphthalen-2-ol is shown below :

**46. (3)** The product E is obtained as follows :

**47. (4)** Aliphatic amines are more basic than aromatic amines thus methylamine is most basic.

The basic character of aromatic amines increases when group attached to them is electron donating group and decreases if the group attached to them is electron withdrawing group. Thus, $p$-methoxyaniline is more basic than aniline which is further more basic than p-nitroaniline.

**48. (2)** Dipole moment = (Distance between opposite charges, $d$) X (charge, $q$)

$$\mu = q \times d$$

The above structure exhibits maximum dipole moment because greater the distance between the opposite charges higher the dipole.

Due to the resonance the greater charge separation occurs between charges due to linearity.

**49. (1)**

Here, acylation reaction takes place. The reactant contains aliphatic amine group which is a strong nucleophile and amide group, a weak nucleophile. Acylation reaction proceeds through strong nucleophilic part of aliphatic amine.

**50. (4)** An alkaline solution of β-naphthol converts –OH to O⁻ which reacts with azo compound (benzene diazonium chloride) to form azo dye.

2-Naphtholaniline dye
(orange-red dye)

**51. (3)** The complete reaction scheme is shown below :

(P) $3CH \equiv CH \xrightarrow[\text{iron 873K}]{\text{red hot}}$ benzene $\xrightarrow[\text{H}_2\text{SO}_4]{\text{fuming HNO}_3,}$ nitrobenzene $\xrightarrow[\text{(selective reduction)}]{\text{H}_2\text{S NH}_2}$ m-nitroaniline

m-nitroaniline $\xrightarrow[\text{H}_2\text{SO}_4]{\text{NaNO}_2}$ $N_2^+HSO_4^-$ (m-nitro) $\xrightarrow{\text{Hydrolysis}}$ m-nitrophenol

(Q) resorcinol $\xrightarrow[60°C]{\text{conc. H}_2\text{SO}_4}$ $\xrightarrow{}$ (nitration) $\xrightarrow[\Delta]{\text{dil. H}_2\text{SO}_4}$

(R) nitrobenzene $\xrightarrow{\text{Sn/HCl}}$ aniline $\xrightarrow{\text{CH}_3\text{COCl}}$ acetanilide $\xrightarrow{\text{conc. H}_2\text{SO}_4}$ p-acetamidobenzenesulphonic acid $\xrightarrow{\text{HNO}_3}$ $\xrightarrow[\Delta]{\text{dil. H}_2\text{SO}_4}$ $\xrightarrow{\text{OH}^-}$

(S) p-nitrotoluene $\xrightarrow[-\text{OH}/\Delta]{\text{KMnO}_4}$ $\xrightarrow{\text{H}_3\text{O}^+}$ p-nitrobenzoic acid $\xrightarrow{\text{SOCl}_2}$ p-nitrobenzoyl chloride $\xrightarrow{\text{NH}_3}$ p-nitrobenzamide

Therefore, the correct match is shown below :
P = 3    Q = 4    R = 2    S = 1

**52. (4)** In carbylamine reaction, aliphatic primary amine reacts with chloroform and ethanolic potassium hydroxide to give alkyl isocyanide.

$$RCH_2NH_2 \xrightarrow[C_2H_5OH]{(CHCl_3+KOH)} RN \equiv C$$

**53. (1)** Basicity of aliphatic amines is greater than aromatic amines. In aqueous solution, the order of basic strength of amines is :

$(CH_3)_2NH > CH_3NH_2 > (CH_3)_3N > C_6H_5NH_2$

Stronger the base, smaller will be its $pK_b$ value. Therefore, $(CH_3)_2NH$ will have the smallest value of $pK_b$.

**54. (2)** The major product of the given reaction is as follows :

**55. (1)** Complete reduction of benzene-diazonium chloride with Zn/HCl results in the formation of aniline.

**56. (3)** Sandmeyer reaction involves the reaction of benzene diazonium salts with the solution of copper halide, and hydrochloric acid leads to the formation of halogen substituted benzene. The conversion of benzene diazonium salt to chlorobenzene is shown below :

**57. (2)** Methyl alcohol is formed when methylamine is treated with $NaNO_2$ and HCl.

$$NaNO_2 + HCl \rightarrow HNO_2 + NaCl$$
$$CH_3NH_2 + HNO_2 \rightarrow CH_3OH + H_2O + N_2\uparrow$$
Methylalcohol

**58. (2)** The bromination of given compound yields B which on reduction yields C. The diazotization of C yields D which on reaction with Cu(I) salt gives desired product.

**59. (1)** The complete chemical reaction is represented as,

In this reaction, nucleophilic attack will occur at benzylic position. This is due to the reason that at phenylic position (bromine side), partial double bond character is present.

**60. (3)** Reaction of aniline with sodium nitrate in dilute hydrochloric acid followed by the addition of beta naphtholgive orange dye. The reaction is given as :

Orange coloured dye

**61. (3)** The following reaction is shown below :

First Hofmann bromide reaction will take place in the presence of $NaOH/Br_2$, thenbenzoylation takes place to give the product.

**62. (1)** (1) : r and s; (2) : t; (3) : p and q; (4) : r

(1) The following mechanism takes place :

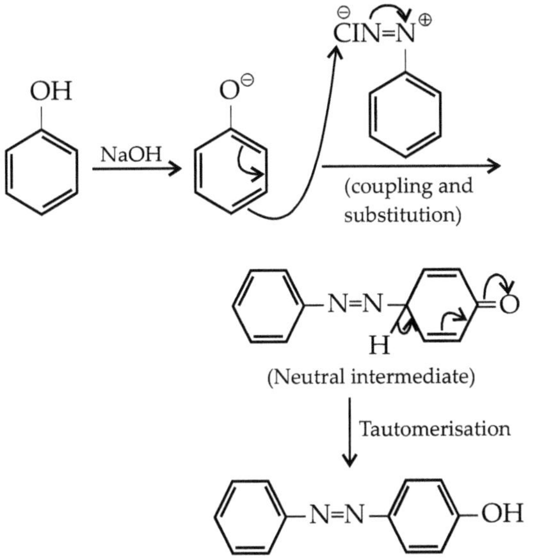

First phenol reacts with NaOH to form phenoxide ion, then $C_6H_5N_2Cl$ couple with phenoxide ion to form intermediate and then structure undergoes tautomerisation to give the final product.

So, substitution reaction and coupling reaction will take place.

So, (1) matches with options (r) and (s).

(2) The following mechanism takes place :

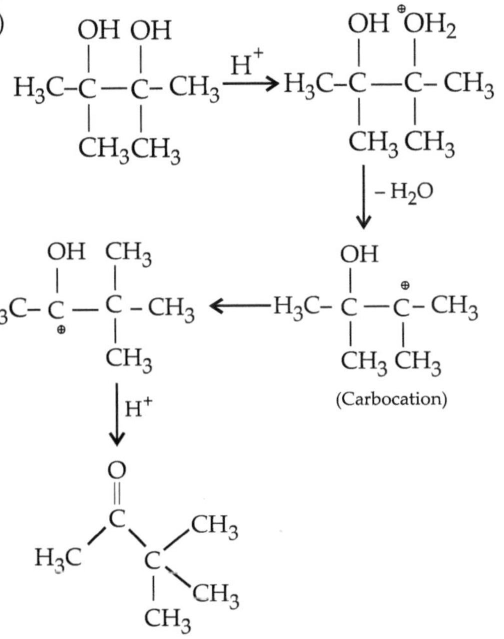

In the following reaction, the hydroxide ion from alcohol will attack $H^+$. There is a loss of water molecule to form carbocation as intermediate.

So, (2) matches with option (t).

(3) The following mechanism takes place :

(racemic mixture)

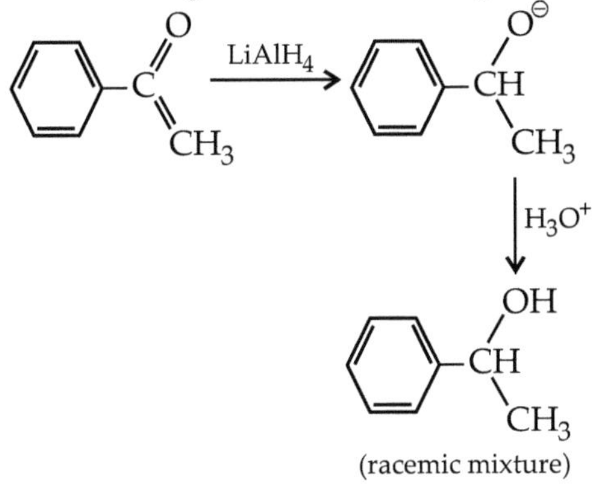

In the following reaction, both enantiomers will be formed. Thus racemic mixture is obtained. This reaction is an example of addition reaction of carbonyl compounds.

So, (3) matches with option (p) and (q).

(4) The following mechanism takes place :

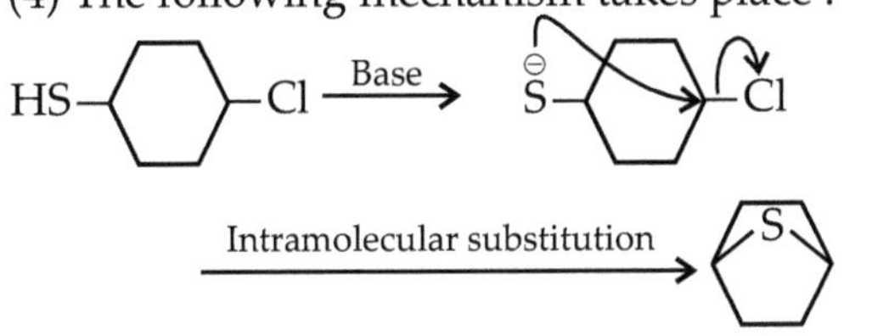

In the following reaction, nucleophilic substitution will take place.

So, (4) matches with option (r)

**63. (4)** The strongly acidic solution of $Na_2S$ reacts with *p*-amino-N, N-dimethylaniline and $Fe^{3+}$ ions leads to the formation of blue colour solution. This blue colour is due to the presence of methylene blue. The chemical equations involving the given reactions are shown below :

$$Na_2S + 2H^+ \rightarrow H_2S + 2Na^+$$
$$(X)$$

$+ H_2S + \quad + 6Fe_3^+ \rightarrow 6Fe_2^+$
$$(Y)$$

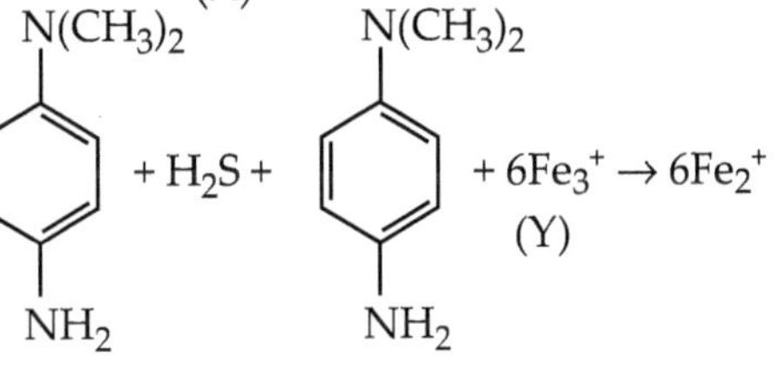

$$+ NH_4^+ + 4H_4^+ + \text{Methylene Blue}$$

Hence, the compound X is $Na_2S$.

**64.** (1)-(p), (q), (s) and (t); (2)-(s) and (t); (3)-(p): and (4)-(r).

The characteristic reactions of cyanide group are given below.

Reduction with $Pd–C/H_2$ :
$$CH_3CH_2CH_2CN \xrightarrow{Pd\text{-}C/H_2} CH_3CH_2CH_2CH_2NH_2$$

Reduction with $SnCl_2/HCl$ :
$$CH_3CH_2CH_2CN \xrightarrow{SnCl_2/HCl} CH_3CH_2CH_2CHO$$

Reduction with DIBAL-H :
$$CH_3CH_2CH_2CN \xrightarrow{DIBAL\text{-}H} CH_3CH_2CH_2CHO$$

Alkaline hydrolysis :
$$CH_3CH_2CH_2CN + H_2O + NaOH \rightarrow CH_3COONa + NH_3$$
Since, the reaction of organic compounds with chloroform and alcoholic is not a characteristic reaction of cyanide group. Therefore, the option (r) is incorrect for (1).

Esters react with DIBAL-H to form aldehyde which is given as,

$$CH_3CH_2OCOCH_3 \xrightarrow{\text{DIBAL-H}} CH_3CH_2CH_2OH$$

Alkaline hydrolysis of ester is,
$$CH_3CH_2OCOCH_3 + NaOH \rightarrow CH_3COONa + CH_3CH_2OH$$

Since, the reduction with $SnCl_2/HCl$, $Pd-C/H_2$ and the reaction involving foul smell are not the characteristic reactions of ester. Hence, the option (p), (q) and (r) are incorrect for (2). Alcohols and alkenes both groups undergo reduction in the presence of $Pd-C/H_2$.

$$CH_3CH{=}CHCH_2OH \xrightarrow{Pd-C/H_2} CH_3CH_2CH_2CH_3$$

Since, the reactions given in other options are not the characteristic reactions of alcohol. Therefore, they are incorrect for alcohols. Primary amines react with chloroform and alcoholic KOH to form isocyanides which are foul smelling substances.

$$CH_3CH_2CH_2CH_2NH_2 \xrightarrow[\text{KOH}]{\text{CHCl}_3}$$
$$CH_3CH_2CH_2CH_2N^+ \equiv C^-$$

Since, the reactions given in other options are not characteristic reactions of amines. Therefore, they are incorrect.

**65. (2)** The stability of structure (I) and (III) is higher than that of (II) and (IV) because oppositely charged atoms are present at greater distance in the structure (II) and (IV) as compared to the structures (I) and (III).

The structure (I) is more stable than (III) because carbon atom (electropositive) contains negative charge in structure (III) which is not stable. The structure (II) is more stable than that of structure (IV).

Hence, the order of stability of resonance structures is (I) > (III) > (II) > (IV).

**66. (4)** The product obtained by the reaction of aniline with $NaNO_2/HCl$ is Benzene diazoniumchloride ($C_6H_5N_2{}^+Cl^-$), which on coupling with β-naphthol give red precipitates. The colour of the precipitate is due to extension of conjugate double bonds.

**67. (2)** The – NHCOAr group is electron releasing group. It directs incoming electrophile ($NO_2$) at ortho and para positions. However, due to steric hindrance the major product (X) of given reaction is formed at para position as shown below :

**68. (4)** The given reaction is
$$CH_3NH_2 + CHCl_3 + KOH \rightarrow P + KCl + H_2O$$
Where,
P is the nitrogen contiating compound.
The given reaction is a carbylamine reaction in which primary amine reacts with chloroform in the presence of strong base to form isocynaide product. The reaction in this process is as follows :
$$CH_3NH_2 + CHCl_3 + KOH$$
$$\rightarrow CH_3 \overset{+}{N} \equiv \overset{-}{C} + KCl + H_2O$$

**69. (4)** The given reaction is an example of Hofmann bromamide degradation. In the Hofmann bromamide degradation, degradation of amide takes place which results in the formation of primary amine. The reaction takes place in the presence of strong base. The attack of base on amide results in the formation of anion. This anion reacts with bromine to give N-bromamide. Thus, the reagents for the conversion of (i) to (ii) are KOH and $Br_2$.

**70. (4)** In the Hoffmann bromamide degradation, degradation of amide takes place which results in the formation of primary amine. The reaction takes place in the presence of strong base. The attack of base on amide results in the formation of anion. This anion reacts with bromine to give N-bromamide. The next step is the deprotonation of N-bromamide which results in the formation of bromamide anion. The bromamide anion undergoes rearrangement in which methyl group migrates to nitrogen. In this step, elimination of bromine takes place to give isocyanate. The formation of isocyanate is a rate determining step.

**71. (2)** In the Hoffmann bromamide degradation, degradation of amide takes place which results in the formation of primary amine.

Thus, the products formed when given mixture undergo Hoffmann bromamide degradation is shown below :

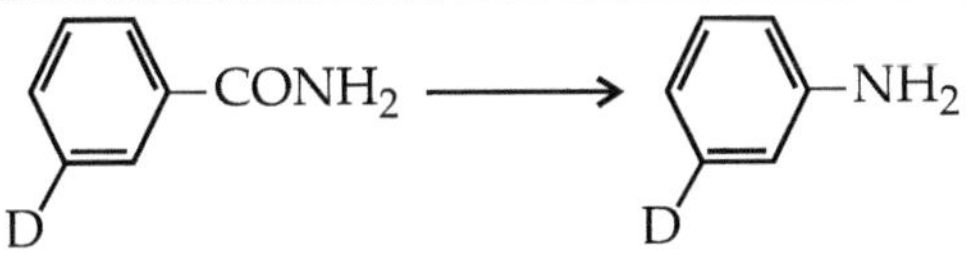

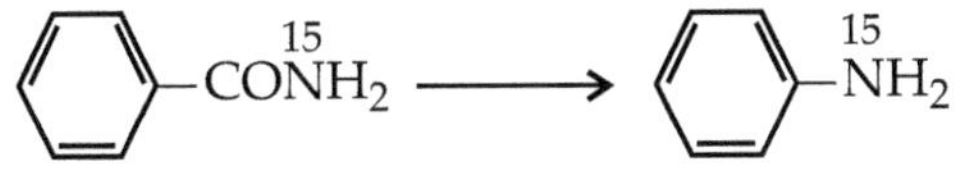

$$\text{(3-D-phenyl)}CONH_2 \longrightarrow \text{(3-D-phenyl)}NH_2$$

$$\text{(phenyl)}C^{15}ONH_2 \longrightarrow \text{(phenyl)}N^{15}H_2$$

**72.** The given incomplete reaction is,

$$\underset{(X)}{C_5H_{13}N} \xrightarrow[-N_2]{NaNO_2,\,HCl} Y$$

The complete reaction is,

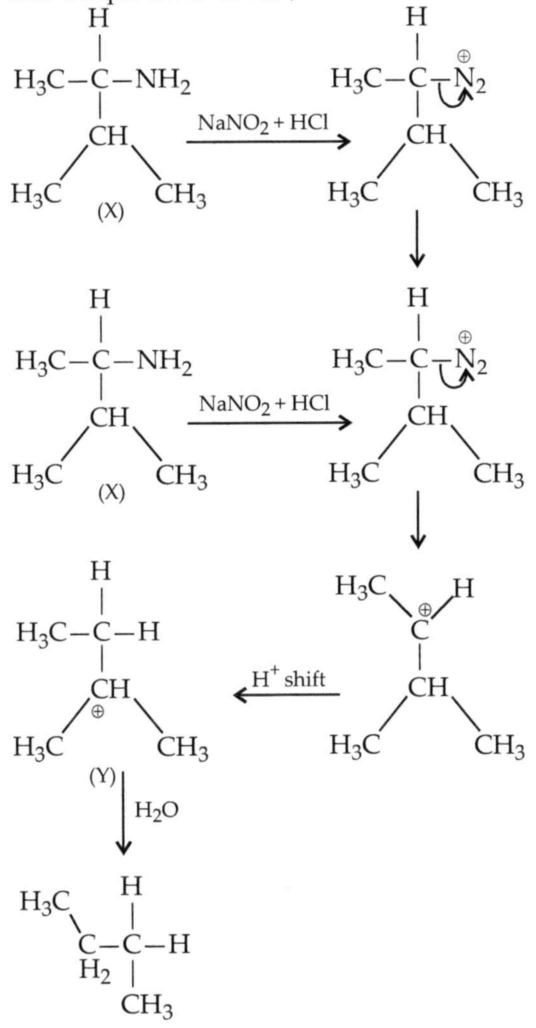

$$\underset{(X)}{\overset{\overset{\displaystyle H}{|}}{H_3C-\underset{\underset{\displaystyle H_3C}{|}}{\overset{\displaystyle CH}{C}}-NH_2}} \xrightarrow{NaNO_2 + HCl} H_3C-\overset{\oplus}{C}-\overset{\oplus}{N_2}$$

$$\underset{(X)}{H_3C-C-NH_2} \xrightarrow{NaNO_2 + HCl} H_3C-\overset{\oplus}{C}-\overset{\oplus}{N_2}$$

$$H_3C-\overset{H}{\underset{}{C}}-H \xleftarrow{H^+ \text{ shift}} \overset{H_3C}{\underset{H_3C}{}}\overset{\oplus}{C}\overset{H}{}$$

$$\underset{(Y)}{} \xdownarrow{H_2O}$$

$$\underset{H_2}{H_3C}\overset{H}{\underset{|}{C}}-\overset{|}{C}-H \quad CH_3$$

Thus, in the above reaction the amine compound reacts with sodium nitrate in the presence of hydrochloric acid to form an optically inactive compound (Y). This compound Y is a tertiary alcohol.

**73.** The compound A is $H_2SO_4$, B is $Br_2$, C is $NO_2^+$ and D is shown below :

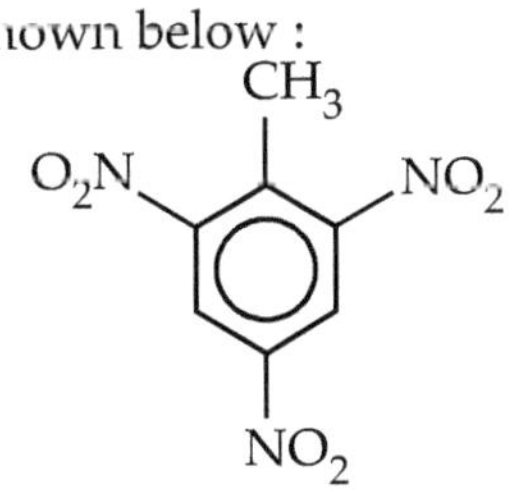

$$\text{(2,4,6-trinitrotoluene)}\quad O_2N-\text{ring}(CH_3)(NO_2)-NO_2$$

The reactions involved are given below :

$$\underset{(A)}{2H_2SO_4} + 2NaBr + MnO_2 \rightarrow \underset{(B)}{Br_2} + Na_2SO_4 + MnSO_4 + 2H_2O$$

$$\underset{(A)}{H_2SO_4} + HNO_3 \rightarrow HSO_4^- + \underset{(C)}{NO_2^+} + H_2O$$

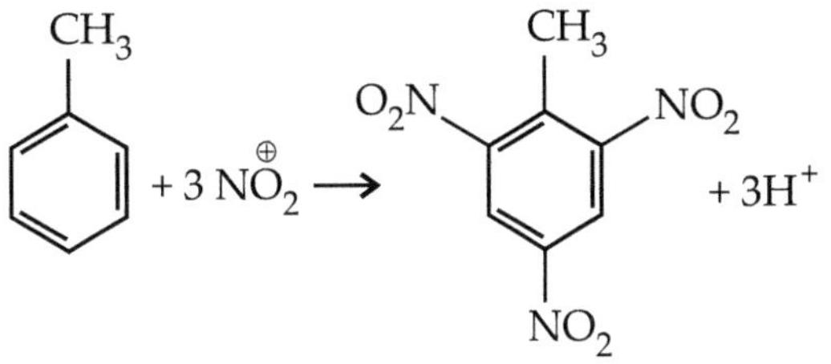

$$\text{(toluene)} + 3\,\overset{\oplus}{NO_2} \rightarrow \underset{(D)\,(Explosive)}{O_2N-\text{ring}(CH_3)(NO_2)(NO_2)} + 3H^+$$

**74.** The compound that is more acidic from the given compounds is shown below :

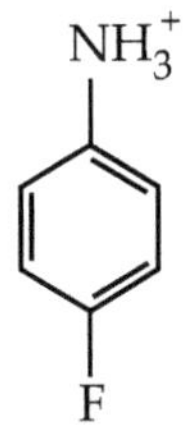

$$\text{(4-fluoroanilinium, } NH_3^+ \text{ ring } F)$$

Due to the negative inductive effect of fluorine the given compound is more acidic.

**75.** The conversion nitrobenzene to metanitro phenol is shown below :

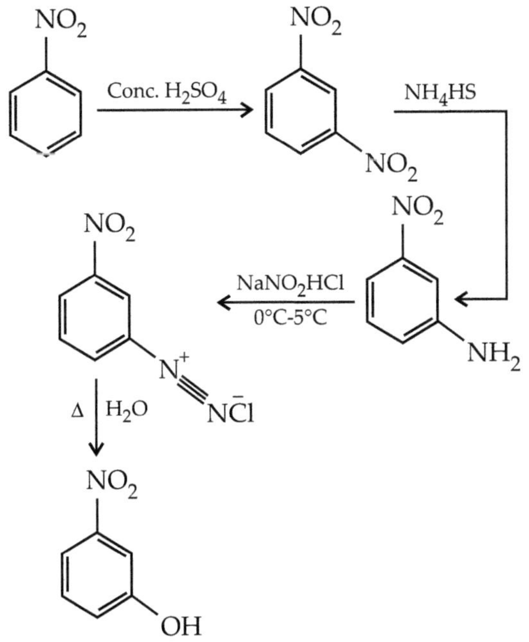

$$\text{(nitrobenzene)} \xrightarrow{Conc.\ H_2SO_4} \text{(1,3-dinitrobenzene)} \xrightarrow{NH_4HS} \text{(3-nitroaniline)}$$

$$\xrightarrow[0°C\text{-}5°C]{NaNO_2HCl} \text{(3-nitrobenzenediazonium chloride, } \overset{+}{N}=N\ \bar{C}l) \xrightarrow[\Delta]{H_2O} \text{(3-nitrophenol, } NO_2 \text{ ring } OH)$$

**76.** The products formed by using chlorobenzene as a starting material is shown below :

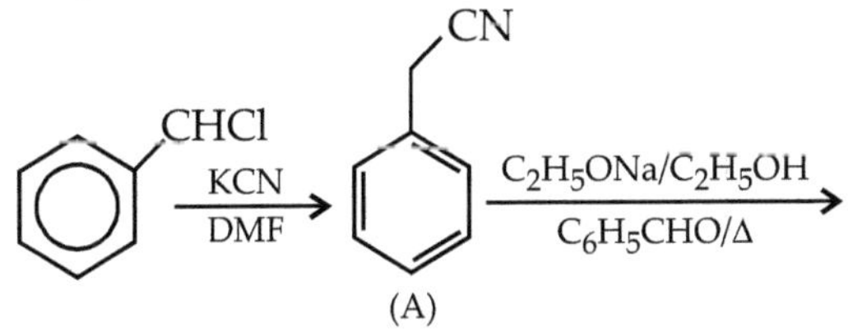

$$\text{(benzyl chloride, } CHCl) \xrightarrow[DMF]{KCN} \underset{(A)}{\text{(phenylacetonitrile, } CH_2CN)} \xrightarrow[C_6H_5CHO/\Delta]{C_2H_5ONa/C_2H_5OH}$$

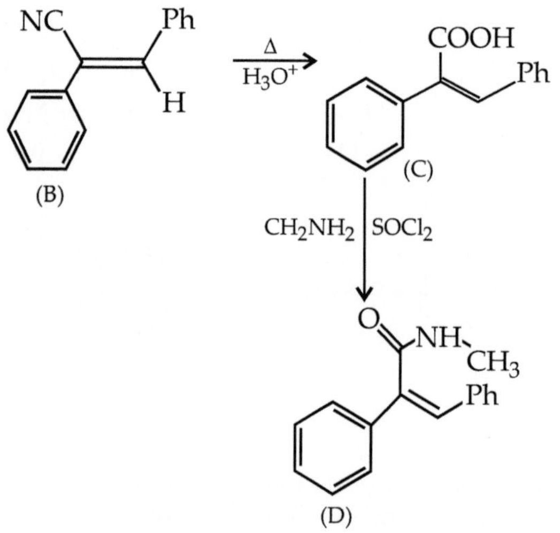

**77. (3)** The rotation by 120° angle is shown below :

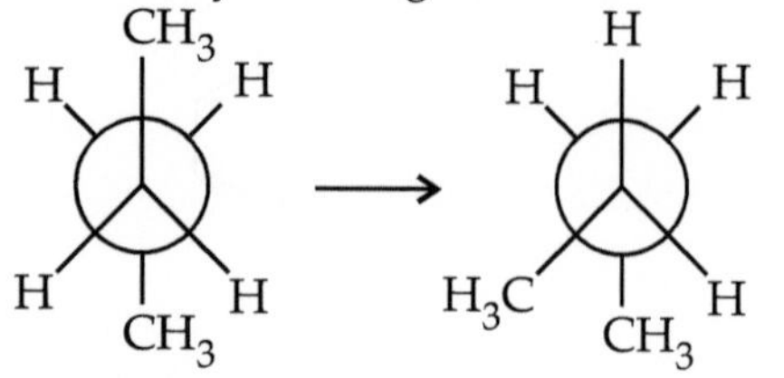

Hence, gauche conformation is obtained.

**78. (2)** The mechanism corresponding to the given reaction is shown below :

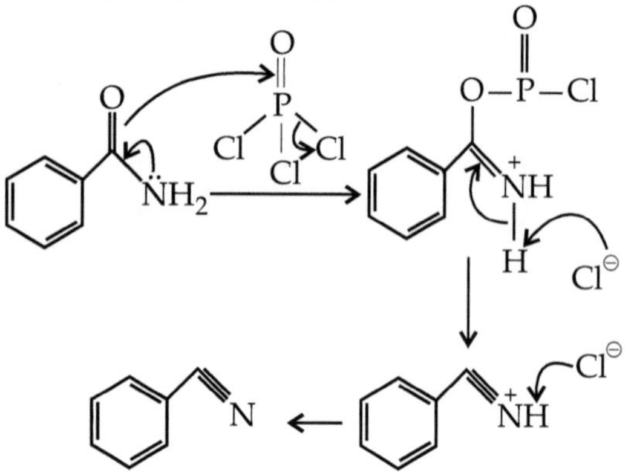

**79. (2)** An electrophile is generated in the given reaction and it will attack over the benzene ring with high electron density. Due to the presence of – NH group, the ring on the left hand side is substituted. As the ortho position is already occupied; therefore, the electrophile will attack at the para position.

**80. (1)** The reaction of para-fluoronitrobenzene with $(CH_3)_2NH$ is a type of nucleophilic aromatic substitution reaction. In this step, fluoride group is substituted by dimethyl amine group. The product formed in step 1 undergoes reduction with $NaNO_2/HCl$ which results in the conversion of nitro group to amine group.

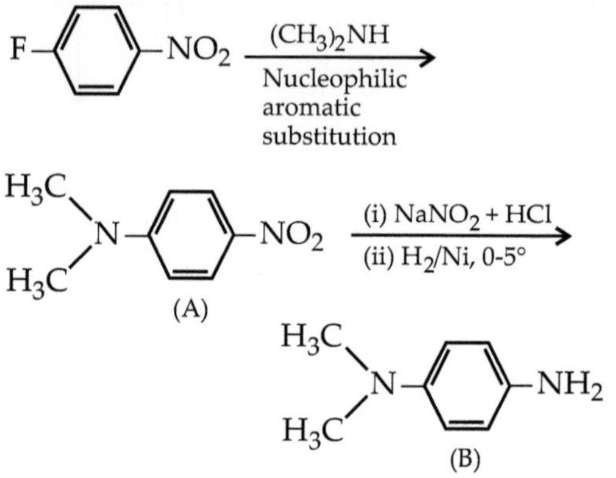

# |28| Polymers

## QUESTIONS

**1.** Newmann projections P, Q, R and S are shown below :

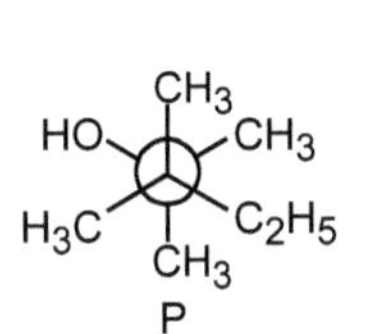

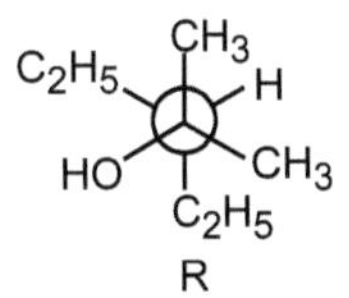

Which one of the following options represents identical molecules ? **[2020, Advanced]**

(1) P and Q
(2) Q and S
(3) Q and R
(4) R and S

**2.** The correct match between Item-I and Item-II :

| Item-I | | Item-II |
|---|---|---|
| (a) | Natural rubber | (I) 1, 3-butadiene + styrene |
| (b) | Neoprene | (II) 1, 3-butadiene + acrylonitrile |
| (c) | Buna-N | (III) Chloroprene |
| (d) | Buna-S | (IV) Isoprene |

**[2020, Main]**

(1) (a) - (III), (b) - (IV), (c) - (I), (d) - (II)
(2) (a) - (IV), (b) - (III), (c) - (II), (d) - (I)
(3) (a) - (IV), (b) - (III), (c) - (I), (d) - (II)
(4) (a) - (III), (b) - (IV), (c) - (II), (d) - (I)

**3.** Consider the Assertion and Reason given below.

**Assertion (A) :** Ethene polymerized in the presence of Ziegler Natta Catalyst at high temperature and pressure is used to make buckets and dustbins.

**Reason (R) :** High density polymers are closely packed and are chemically inert. Choose the correct answer from the following :

**[2020, Main]**

(1) (A) is correct but (R) is wrong
(2) (A) and (R) both are wrong
(3) Both (A) and (R) are correct and (R) is the correct explanation of (A)
(4) Both (A) and (R) are correct but (R) is not the correct explanation of (A)

**4.** Which one of the following polymers is not obtained by condensation polymerisation ?

**[2020, Main]**

(1) Buna-N
(2) Bakelite
(3) Nylon 6
(4) Nylon 6, 6

**5.** Which polymer has 'chiral' monomers(s) ?

**[2020, Main]**

(1) Buna-N
(2) Nylon 6,6
(3) Neoprene
(4) PHBV

**6.** The following ligand is : **[2019, Main]**

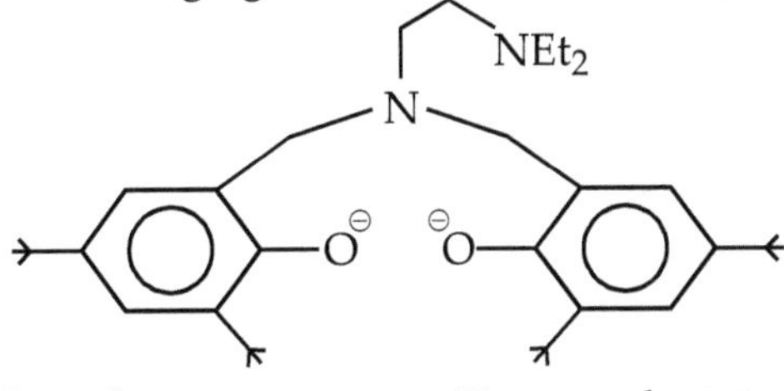

(1) hexadentate
(2) tetradentate
(3) bidentate
(4) tridentate

**7.** The major product of the following reaction is : **[2019, Main]**

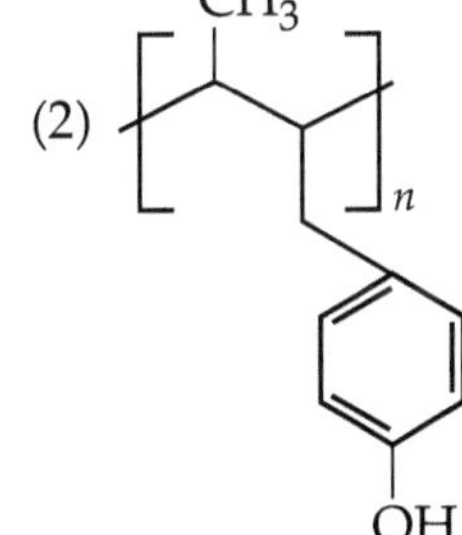

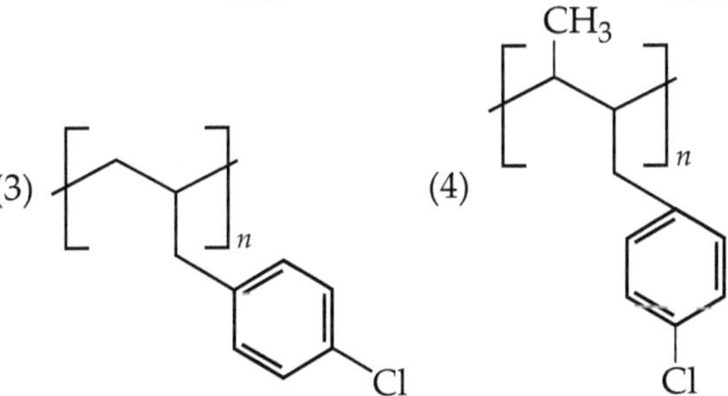

**8.** Which of the following compounds is a constitutent of the polymer $+HN - C - NH - CH_2 +_n$ ?

**[2019, Main]**

(1) N-Methyl urea
(2) Formaldehyde
(3) Methylamine
(4) Ammonia

**9.** Which of the following is a condensation polymer ? **[2019, Main]**

(1) Buna-S      (2) Neoprene
(3) Teflon      (4) Nylon 6, 6

**10.** The correct match betweeen item -I and Item -II is : **[2019, Main]**

|   | Item-I |   | Item-II |
|---|---|---|---|
| (a) | High density polythene | (I) | Peroxide catalyst |
| (b) | Polyacrylonitrile | (II) | Condensation at high temperature and pressure |
| (c) | Novolac | (III) | Ziegler-Natta Catalyst |
| (d) | Nylon 6 | (IV) | Acid or base catalyst |

(1) (a) → (IV), (b) → (II), (c) → (I), (d) → (III)
(2) (a) → (II), (b) → (IV), (c) → (I), (d) → (III)
(3) (a) → (III), (b) → (I), (c) → (II), (d) → (IV)
(4) (a) → (III), (b) → (I), (c) → (IV), (d) → (II)

**11.** Which of the following is a thermosetting polymer ? **[2019, Main]**

(1) Bakelite      (2) Buna-N
(3) Nylon 6      (4) PVC

**12.** The correct name of the following polymer is : **[2019, Main]**

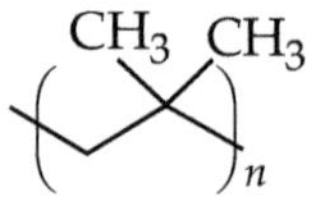

$$\left(\!\!-\!\!\overset{\displaystyle CH_3\ \ CH_3}{\underset{}{C}}\!\!-\!\!\right)_{\!n}$$

(1) Polyisobutane      (2) Polytert-butylene
(3) Polyisoprene      (4) Polyisobutylene

**13.** List-I includes starting materials and reagents of selected chemical reactions. List-II gives structures of compound that may be formed as intermediate products and/or final products from the reactions of List-I. **[2019, Main]**

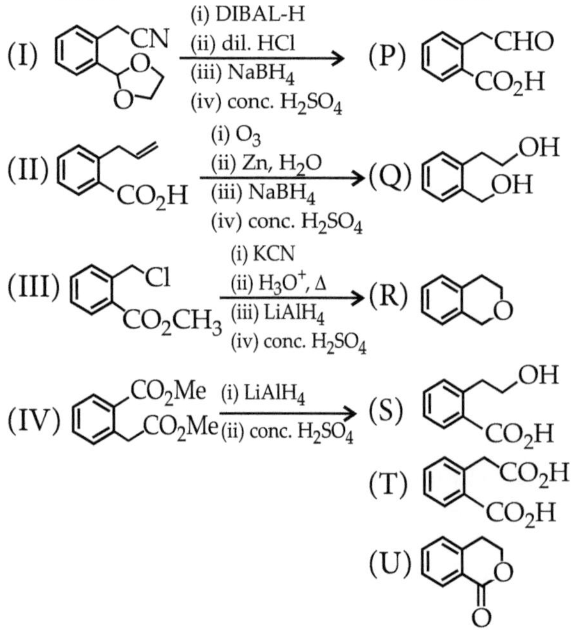

**List-I**

(I) benzene ring with CH₂CN and 1,3-dioxolane substituents
(i) DIBAL-H (ii) dil. HCl (iii) NaBH₄ (iv) conc. H₂SO₄

(II) benzene ring with allyl and CO₂H substituents
(i) O₃ (ii) Zn, H₂O (iii) NaBH₄ (iv) conc. H₂SO₄

(III) benzene ring with CH₂Cl and CO₂CH₃ substituents
(i) KCN (ii) H₃O⁺, Δ (iii) LiAlH₄ (iv) conc. H₂SO₄

(IV) benzene ring with CH₂CO₂Me and CO₂Me substituents
(i) LiAlH₄ (ii) conc. H₂SO₄

**List-II**

(P) benzene ring with CH₂CHO and CO₂H
(Q) benzene ring with CH₂CH₂OH and CH₂OH
(R) isochroman (benzo-fused oxygen heterocycle)
(S) benzene ring with CH₂CH₂OH and CO₂H
(T) benzene ring with CH₂CO₂H and CO₂H
(U) isochroman-1-one (benzo-fused lactone)

Which of the following options has correct combination considering List-I and List-II ?

(1) (III), (S), (R)      (2) (IV), (Q), (U)
(3) (III), (T), (U)      (4) (IV), (Q), (R)

**14.** Which of the following statement is not true ? **[2018, Main]**

(1) Step growth polymerisation requires a bifunctional monomer.
(2) Nylon 6 is an example of step-growth polymerisation
(3) Chain growth polymerisation includes both homopolymerisation and copolymerisation
(4) Chain growth polymerisation involves homopolymerisation only

**15.** The copolymer formed by addition polymerisation of styrene and acrylonitrile in the presence of peroxide is : **[2018, Main]**

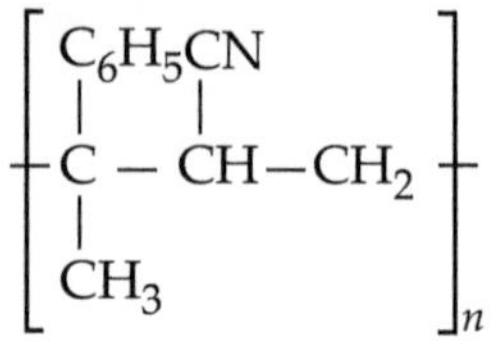

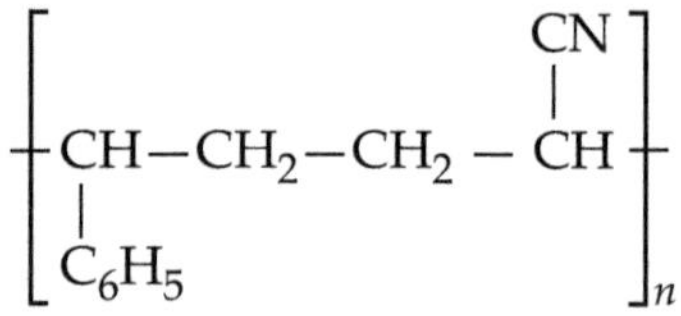

$$(1)\quad \left[\!-CH_2-\overset{C_6H_5}{\underset{}{CH}}-\overset{CN}{\underset{}{CH}}-CH_2-\right]_n$$

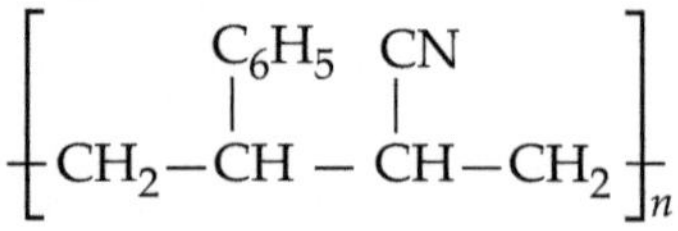

$$(2)\quad \left[\!-\overset{C_6H_5CN}{\underset{CH_3}{C}}-CH-CH_2-\right]_n$$

$$(3)\quad \left[\!-\overset{}{\underset{C_6H_5}{CH}}-CH_2-CH_2-\overset{CN}{\underset{}{CH}}-\right]_n$$

$$(4)\quad \left[\!-CH_2-\overset{}{\underset{C_6H_5}{CH}}-CH_2-\overset{}{\underset{CN}{CH}}-\right]_n$$

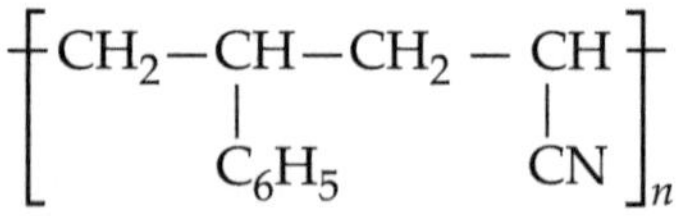

**16.** The formation of which of the following polymers involves hydrolysis reaction ? **[2017, Main]**

(1) Nylon 6, 6      (2) Terylene
(3) Nylon 6      (4) Bakelite

**17.** Which of the following is a biodegradable polymer ? **[2017, Main]**

$$(1)\quad \left[\!-HN-(CH_2)_5CONH-CH_6-\overset{O}{\overset{\|}{C}}-\right]_n$$

$$(2)\quad \left[\!-HN-(CH_2)_5-\overset{O}{\overset{\|}{C}}-\right]_n$$

$$(3)\quad \left[\!-HN-(CH_2)_6NHCO-(CH_2)_4-\overset{O}{\overset{\|}{C}}-\right]_n$$

$$(4)\quad \left[\!-\overset{O}{\overset{\|}{C}}-C_6H_4-COO-(CH_2)_2-O-\right]_n$$

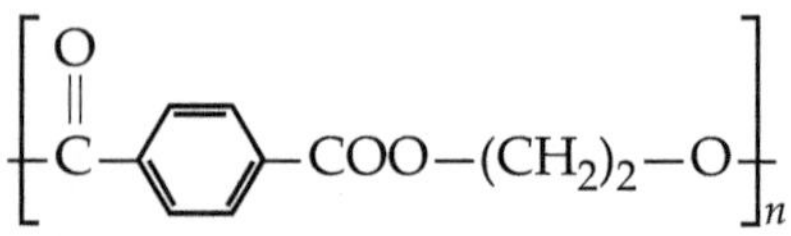

**18.** On complete hydrogenation, natural rubber produces : **[2016, Main]**

(1) ethylene-propylene copolymer
(2) vulcanised rubber
(3) polypropylene
(4) polybutylene

**19.** Which of the following polymers is synthesized using a free radical polymerisation technique ?
**[2016, Main]**
(1) Teflon  (2) Terylene
(3) Melamine polymer  (4) Nylon 6, 6

**20.** Which of the following statements about low density polythene is **FALSE** ? **[2015, Advanced]**
(1) Its synthesis requires high pressure
(2) It is a poor conductor of electricity
(3) Its synthesis requires dioxygen or a peroxide initiator as a catalyst
(4) It is used in the manufacture of buckets, dust-bins etc.

**21.** Under hydrolytic conditions, the compounds used for preparation of linear polymer and for chain termination, respectively, are :
**[2015, Main]**
(1) $CH_3SiCl_3$ and $Si(CH_3)_4$
(2) $(CH_3)_2SiCl_2$ and $(CH_3)_3SiCl$
(3) $(CH_3)_2SiCl_2$ and $CH_3SiCl_3$
(4) $SiCl_4$ and $(CH_3)_3SiCl$

**22.** Which polymer is used in the manufacture of paints and lacquers ? **[2015, Main]**
(1) Bakelite  (2) Glyptal
(3) Polypropene  (4) Polyvinylchloride

**23.** Match the polymers in **column-A** with their main uses in **column-B** and choose the correct answer :

| Column-A | | Column-B |
|---|---|---|
| (A) Polystyrene | (i) | Paints and lacquers |
| (B) Glyptal | (ii) | Rain coats |
| (C) Polyvinyl Cloride | (iii) | Manufacture of toys |
| (D) Bakelite | (iv) | Computer discs |

**[2015, Main]**
(1) (A)-(ii), (B)-(i), C-(iii), (D)-(iv)
(2) (A)-(iii), (B)-(i), C-(ii), (D)-(iv)
(3) (A)-(ii), (B)-(iv), C-(iii), (D)-(i)
(4) (A)-(iii), (B)-(iv), C-(ii), (D)-(i)

**24.** Which one of the following structures represents the neoprene polymer ? **[2014, Main]**

(1) $\left[ CH_2 - \underset{\underset{Cl}{|}}{C} = CH - CH_2 \right]_n$

(2) $\left[ CH_2 - \underset{\underset{CN}{|}}{CH} \right]_n$

(3) $\left[ CH_2 - \underset{\underset{Cl}{|}}{CH} \right]_n$

(4) $\left[ CH_2 - \underset{\underset{C_6H_5}{|}}{CH_2} \right]_n$

**25.** Which one is classified as a condensation polymer ? **[2014, Main]**
(1) Dacron  (2) Neoprene
(3) Teflon  (4) Acrylonitrile

**26.** Structure of some important polymers are given. Which one represents Buna-S ? **[2014, Main]**

(1) $\left[ CH_2 - \underset{\underset{CH_2}{|}}{C} = CH - CH_2 \right]_n$

(2) $\left[ CH_2 - CH = CH - CH_2 - \underset{\underset{C_6H_5}{|}}{CH} - CH_2 \right]_n$

(3) $\left[ CH_2 - CH = CH - CH_2 - \underset{\underset{CN}{|}}{CH} - CH_2 \right]_n$

(4) $\left[ CH_2 - \underset{\underset{Cl}{|}}{C} = CH - CH_2 \right]_n$

**27.** Which one of the following class of compounds is obtained by polymerisation of acetylene ? **[2014, Main]**
(1) Poly-yne  (2) Poly-ene
(3) Poly-ester  (4) Poly-amide

**28.** Which one of the following is an example of thermosetting polymers ?
(1) Neoprene  (2) Buna-N
(3) Nylon 6, 6  (4) Bakelite

**29.** The total number of lone-pairs of electrons in melamine is. **[2013, Advanced]**

**30.** The correct functional group X and the reagent/reaction conditions Y in the following scheme are

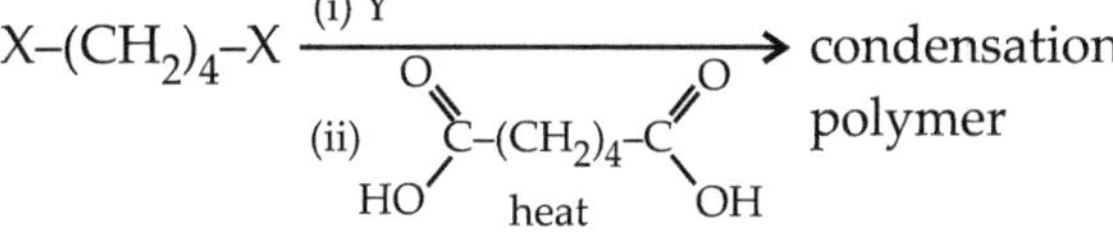

**[2011, Advanced]**
(1) $X = COOCH_3$, $Y = H_2/Ni/heat$
(2) $X = CONH_2$, $Y = H_2/Ni/heat$
(3) $X = CONH_2$, $Y = Br_2/NaOH$
(4) $X = CN$, $Y = H_2/Ni/heat$

**31.** Among cellulose, poly(vinyl chloride), nylon and natural rubber, the polymer in which the intermolecular force of attraction is weakest is :
**[2009, Advanced]**
(1) Nylon
(2) Poly(vinyl chloride)
(3) Cellulose
(4) Natural Rubber

**32.** Match the chemical substances in Column I with type of polymers/type of bonds in Column II. Indicate your answer by darkening the appropriate bubbles of the 4 × 4 matrix given in the ORS. **[2007, Advanced]**

| Column I | | Column II |
|---|---|---|
| (1) cellulose | (p) | natural polymer |
| (2) nylon-6, 6 | (q) | synthetic polymer |
| (3) protein | (r) | amide linkage |
| (4) sucrose | (s) | glycoside linkage |

**33.** Write down the heterogeneous catalyst involved in the polymerisation of ethylene. **[2003, Main]**

## ANSWER KEY

| | | | | | | | | | |
|---|---|---|---|---|---|---|---|---|---|
| **1.** (3) | **2.** (1) | **3.** (3) | **4.** (1) | **5.** (4) | **6.** (3) | **7.** (4) | **8.** (2) | **9.** (4) | **10.** (4) |
| **11.** (1) | **12.** (4) | **13.** (2, 3) | **14.** (4) | **15.** (4) | **16.** (3) | **17.** (1) | **18.** (1) | **19.** (1) | **20.** (4) |
| **21.** (2) | **22.** (2) | **23.** (2) | **24.** (1) | **25.** (1) | **26.** (2) | **27.** (2) | **28.** (4) | **29.** (*) | |
| **30.** (1,2,3,4) | | **31.** (4) | **32.** (*) | **33.** (*) | | | | | |

## ANSWERS WITH EXPLANATIONS

**1. (3)** P.

2, 3, 3-trimethyl pentan-2-ol

Q.

3-ethyl-2-methyl pentan-2-ol

R.

3-ethyl-2-methyl pentan-2-ol

S. (2)

3-ethyl-2-methyl pentan-3-ol

Q and R is same.

**2. (1)** (a)- (IV), (b)- (III), (c)-(II), (d)-(I)

(a) $n\text{CH}_2=\text{C}-\text{CH}=\text{CH}_2 \longrightarrow$ Poly cis-isoprene (Natural rubber), with $\text{CH}_3$ group — isoprene

(IV)

(b) $n\text{CH}_2=\text{C}-\text{CH}=\text{CH}_2 \rightarrow (-\text{CH}_2-\text{C}=\text{CH}-\text{CH}_2-)_n$, with Cl — Chloroprene → Neoprene

(III)

(c) $n\text{CH}_2 = \text{CH} - \text{CH} = \text{CH}_2 + n\text{CH}_2 = \text{CH}$ (with CN, Acrylonitrile), 1, 3 buta diene

$[-\text{CH}_2 - \text{CH} = \text{CH} - \text{CH}_2 - \text{CH}_2 - \text{CH}]_n$ (with CN)

Buna-N

(II)

(d) $\text{CH}_2=\text{CH}-\text{CH}=\text{CH}_2 + \text{CH}_2=\text{CH}-$ 1,3-buta diene, with styrene

$\{\text{CH}_2-\text{CH}=\text{CH}-\text{CH}_2-\text{CH}_2-\text{CH}\}_n$

Buna-S

(I)

**3. (3)** Both (A) and (R) are correct and (R) is the correcrt explanation of (A).

From ziegler - Natta catalyst high density polymers is produced, which is closely packed and are chemically inert, therefore, it is used to make backet and dustbins.

**4. (1)** Buna-N is an addition polymer which is obtained by co-polymerisation of 1,3-butadiene and acrylonitrile in the presence of a peroxide catalyst.

The reaction of formation of Buna-N is given below :

$n\text{H}_2\text{C}=\text{C}-\text{C}=\text{CH}_2 + n\text{H}_2\text{C}=\text{CH}$ (with H, H; and CN)

1,3-butadiene, acrylonitrile; Peroxide, Heat, Copolymerization

Buna-N

**5. (4)** PHBV : Poly β-hydroxy butyrate-co-β-hydroxy valerate

$\text{CH}_3 \text{CH CH}_2\text{COOH}$ (with OH)

(3-hydroxy butanoic acid)

+

$\text{CH}_3 - \text{CH}_2 - \text{CH} - \text{CH}_2 - \overset{\text{O}}{\overset{\|}{\text{C}}} - \text{OH}$ (with OH)

(3-hydroxy pentanoic acid)

**6. (3)** Nylon-6 is a polymer of caprolactam. The structure of nylon-6 is shown below :

$+\overset{\text{O}}{\overset{\|}{\text{C}}}-(\text{CH}_2)_5 - \overset{\text{H}}{\overset{|}{\text{N}}}\}_n$

**7. (4)** The starting material undergoes elimination reaction with alcoholic KOH. The resulted alkene than undergoes a free radical polymerisation to from a polymer. The corresponding reaction is shown below :

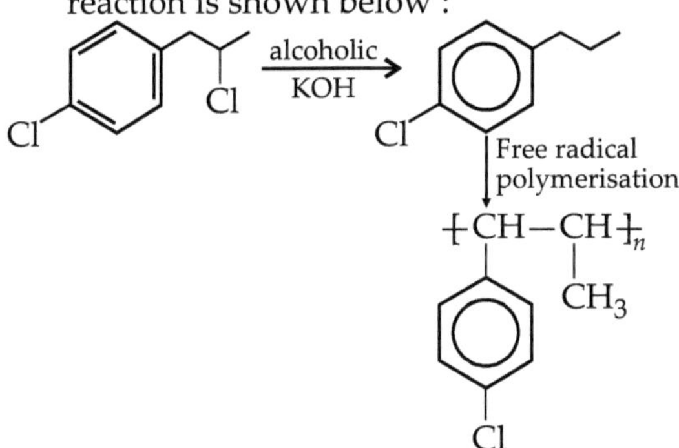

**8. (2)** The given polymer is urea-formaldehyde resin. Therefore, one of the constitutent of this polymer is formaldehyde. The synthesis reaction of the given polymer is shown below :

$$H_2N-\overset{\overset{\displaystyle O}{\|}}{C}-NH_2 + H-\overset{\overset{\displaystyle O}{\|}}{C}-H \longrightarrow$$

$$\left(\!NH-\overset{\overset{\displaystyle O}{\|}}{C}-NH-CH_2\!\right)_{\!n}$$

**9. (4)** The polymer nylon-6, 6 is formed by the condensation polymerisation of the monomers hexamethylene diamine and adipic acid.

**10. (4)** High density polythene is prepared by the use of Zeigler-Natta catalyst.
Polyacrylonitrile is prepared by the use of peroxide catalyst.
Novolac is prepared by the use of acid or base as catalyst.
Nylon-6 is prepared by condensation polymerisation at high temperature and pressure.

**11. (1)** Thermosetting polymers become brittle after heating. Bakelite is an example of thermosetting polymer.

**12. (4)** The expected structure of the monomer of the given polymer is shown below :

$$n\,H_2C\!\!=\!\!\overset{\displaystyle CH_3}{\underset{\displaystyle CH_3}{\big<}} \longrightarrow \left(\!\overset{H_3C\quad CH_3}{\bigwedge}\!\right)_{\!n}$$

Therefore, the name of the polymer is polyisobutylene.

**13. (2,3)** Natural rubber has cis alkene units init.
The structure of Nylon-6 is shown below :

$$\left[\!\overset{H}{\overset{|}{N}}-(CH_2)_5-\overset{\overset{\displaystyle O}{\|}}{C}\!\right]_{\!n}$$

Nylon-6 has amide linkages.
The reaction of formation of Teflon is shown below :

$$nF_2C = CF_2 \xrightarrow{\text{Persulphate}} \left(\!CF_2-CF_2\!\right)_{\!n}$$

The glycosidic linkage present in cellulose is β(1 → 4) linkage. The structure of cellulose is shown below :

**14. (4)** Chain growth polymerisation proceeds by the generation of active sites where the monomer gets attached. The attachment of monomer generates a new active site where another monomer gets attached. The process leads to the formation of polymer consisting of same monomers (homopolymerisation) or polymer of random monomers (copolymerisation)

**15. (4)** The formation of copolymer by addition polymerization of styrene and acrylonitrile is shown below :

**16. (3)** The formation of Nylon 6 involves the hydrolysis of its monomer, caprolactam. The hydrolysis reaction is shown below.

At the initial stage of the reaction, caprolactam is hydrolysed to form caproic acid. Caproic acid undergoes condensation to form Nylon 6.

**17. (1)** The formation of Nylon-2-Nylon-6 is shown below :

$$n\,H_2N - \underset{\text{Glycine}}{\overset{H_2}{C}} - COOH + n\,H_2N \left(\overset{H_2}{C}\right)_5 COOH \quad \text{Amino caproic acid}$$

$$\downarrow -H_2O$$

$$\left[\begin{array}{c} \underset{\|}{\overset{H_2}{C}} - \overset{H}{C} - N - \underset{\|}{\overset{H_2}{C}} - \overset{H}{C} - N \\ O \qquad\qquad O \end{array}\right]$$

Nylon-2-nylon-6

It is bio-degradable polymer becaus it disintegrates to form glycine and amino caproic acid. Hence, it does not cause harm to environment.

**18. (1)** The hydrogenation of natural rubber is shown below :

$$\text{Natural rubber} \xrightarrow{H_2/Ni} \text{(saturated polymer chain)}$$

$$\uparrow \text{Polymerisation}$$

$$\underset{\text{ethylene}}{CH_2 = CH_2} + \underset{\substack{H \\ \text{Propylene}}}{CH_2 = C - CH_3}$$

In the reaction, mixture of ethylene and propylene copolymers is produced.

**19. (1)** Teflon is synthesized by the free radical polymerization of tetrafluoroethylene. This polymerization is a type of vinyl polymerization and proceeds via free radical mechanism.

$$\underset{\text{Tetrafluoroethyelene}}{\overset{F}{\underset{F}{}}C = C\overset{F}{\underset{F}{}}} \xrightarrow[\text{vinyl polymerisation}]{\text{Free radical}} \underset{\text{Teflon}}{\left[\begin{array}{c} F \quad F \\ | \quad | \\ C - C \\ | \quad | \\ F \quad F \end{array}\right]_n}$$

Hence, the polymer which is synthesized using free radical polymerization out of the given polymers is Teflon.

**20. (4)** High density polyethene is used for the manufacturing of buckets, dustbin etc.

**21. (2)** Under hydrolytic conditions, the compound used for the preparation of linear polymer is $(CH_3)_2SiCl_2$ and for chain termination $(CH_3)_3SiCl$ is used.

$$\underset{CH_3}{\overset{CH_3}{Cl - Si - Cl}} \xrightarrow{H_2O} \underset{CH_3}{\overset{CH_3}{HO - Si - OH}}$$

$$\downarrow$$

$$H - O \left[\underset{CH_3}{\overset{CH_3}{Si}} - O - \underset{CH_3}{\overset{CH_3}{Si}}\right] O - H$$

$$\downarrow \text{Me}_3\text{SiCl, H}_2\text{O}$$

$$\underset{Me}{\overset{Me}{Me - Si}} - O \left[\underset{CH_3}{\overset{CH_3}{Si}} - O - \underset{CH_3}{\overset{CH_3}{Si}}\right]_n O - \underset{Me}{\overset{Me}{Si}} - Me$$

$(CH_3)_3SiCl_2$ can undergoes hydrolysis by sides. Thus, it form linear polymer, whereas $(CH_3)_3SiCl$ undergoes by only one side so it is used for chain termination.

**22. (2)** In manufacture of paints and lacquers, the Glyptal polymer is used.

**23. (2)** (A) Polystyrene is used in the manufacture of toys.

(B) Glyptal is used in paints and lacquers.

(C) Rains coat consists of Polyvinyl Chloride.

(D) Bakelite is used in computers discs.

**24. (1)** The structure of neoprene polymer is shown below.

$$\left[\underset{\substack{| \\ Cl}}{\overset{H_2}{C}} - C = C - \overset{H_2}{C}\right]_n$$

Neoprene polymer is also known as polychloroprene because it is madeup of monomer units of chloroprene

**25. (1)** Dacron is also called terylene. It is a condensation polymer of terepthalic acid and ethylene glycol. All other given polymers are addition polymers.

$$n\left(\underset{OH \quad OH}{\overset{CH_2 - CH_2}{|\qquad|}}\right) + n\left(HOOC - \bigcirc - COOH\right)$$

ethylene glycol        Terepthalic acid

$$\downarrow -n H_2O \text{ (Condensation)}$$

$$\left[-O - CH_2 - CH_2 - O - \underset{\|}{\overset{O}{C}} - \bigcirc - \underset{\|}{\overset{O}{C}} -\right]_n \text{(Dacron)}$$

**26. (2)** The polymerisation of Buna-S is as follows :

$$\underset{H \quad H}{H_2C = C - C = CH_2} + H_2C = CH$$

$$\bigcirc$$

Styrene

$$\downarrow \text{Polymerisation}$$

$$\left[\underset{H \quad H}{\overset{H_2}{C} - C = C - }\overset{H_2}{C} - \overset{H}{C} - \overset{H_2}{C}\right]_n$$

$$|$$
$$C_6H_5$$

Buna-S

Thus, the structure of Buna-S is represened by,

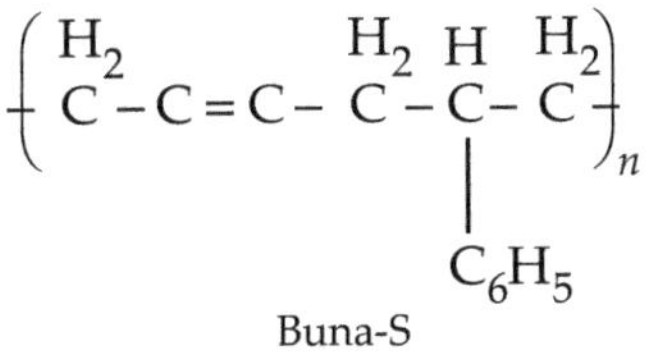

$$\left(\begin{array}{c} H_2 \\ C-C=C- \end{array}\begin{array}{c} H_2 \ H \ H_2 \\ C-C-C \\ | \\ C_6H_5 \end{array}\right)_n$$

Buna-S

**27. (2)** The compound that is obtained by the polymerisation of acetylene is poly-yne as shown below.

$$n\,HC \equiv CH \xrightarrow{\text{Polymerisation}} \left(C = C\right)_n$$
$$\text{yne} \qquad\qquad\qquad H \ \ H$$
$$\text{poly-yne}$$

**28. (4)** Bakelite is an example of thermosetting polymer.

**29.** The structure of melamine is shown below :

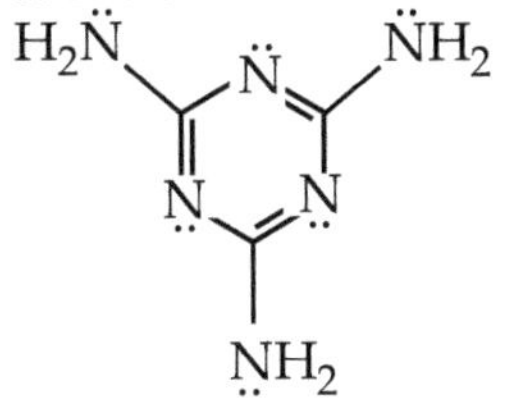

$$H_2\ddot{N} \quad\quad \ddot{N}H_2$$

The above structure shows that there are six nitrogen atoms in malamine and every nitrogen atom possesses lone-pairs of electrons.

**30. (1,2,3,4)** All the reaction involving the preparation of condensation polymers are given as

$$X-(CH_2)_4-X \xrightarrow[\text{(ii) HOOC-(CH}_2)_4-\text{COOH}]{\text{(i) y}}$$

Condensation polymer

$$H_3COOC-(CH_2)_4-COOCH_3 \xrightarrow[\Delta]{H_2/Ni}$$

$$OH-(CH_2)_6-OH \xrightarrow[\Delta]{HOOC-(CH_2)_4-COOH}$$
Hexane-1,6-diol

Condensation polyester

$$H_2NOC-(CH_2)_4-CONH_2 \xrightarrow[\Delta]{H_2/Ni}$$

$$H_2N-(CH_2)_6-NH_2 \xrightarrow[\Delta]{HOOC-(CH_2)_4-COOH}$$
Hexamathylene diamine

Condensation polyamide

$$H_2NOC-(CH_2)_4-CONH_2 \xrightarrow{Br_2/NaOH}$$

$$H_2N-(CH_2)_4-NH_2 \xrightarrow[\Delta]{HOOC-(CH_2)_4-COOH}$$
Tetramethylene diamine

Condensation polyamide

$$NC-(CH_2)_4-CN \xrightarrow{H_2/Ni}$$

$$H_2N-(CH_2)_6-NH_2 \xrightarrow[\Delta]{HOOC-(CH_2)_4-COOH}$$
Hexamethylene diamine

Condensation polyamide

**31. (4)** The forces of attractions present in the natural rubber are the van der Waals forces which are the weakest forces of attraction among the given polymers.

**32.** (1) (p), (s); (2) (q), (r); (3) (p), (r); (4) (s);

(1) Cellulose is a natural polymer.

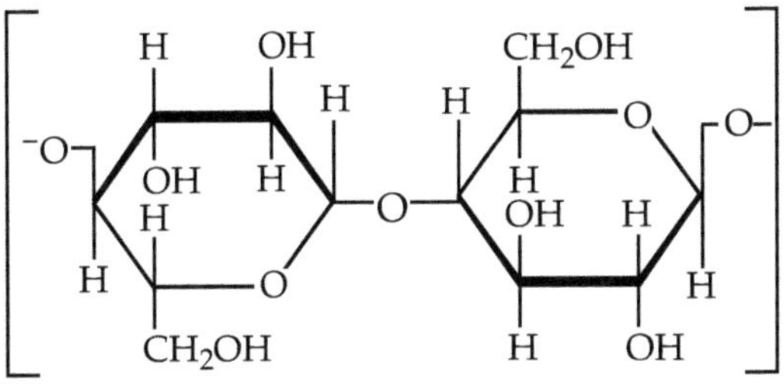

(Glycoside linkage)

(2) Nylon-6, 6 is a synthetic polymer.

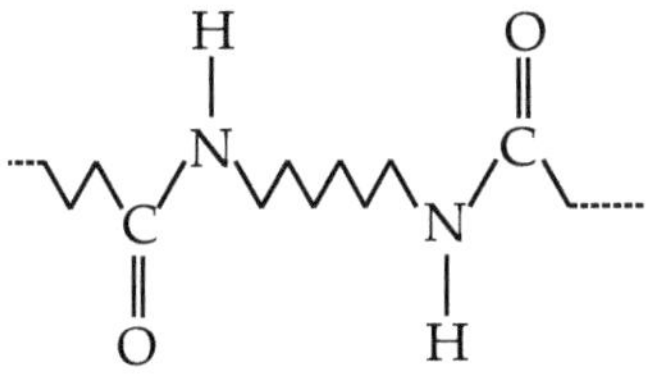

(Amide linkage)

(3) Protein is a natural polymer.

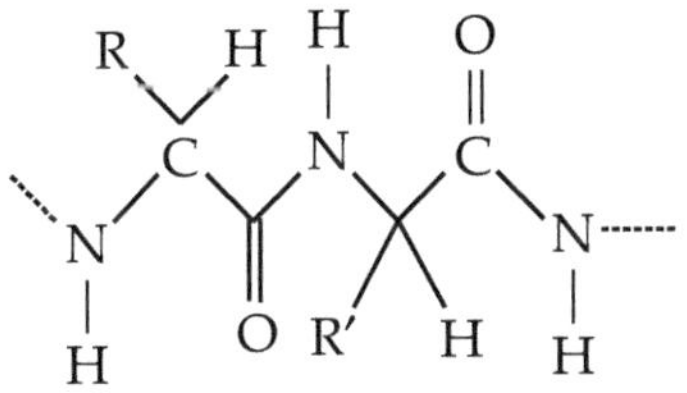

(Amide linkage)

(4) Sucrose has glycoside linkage.

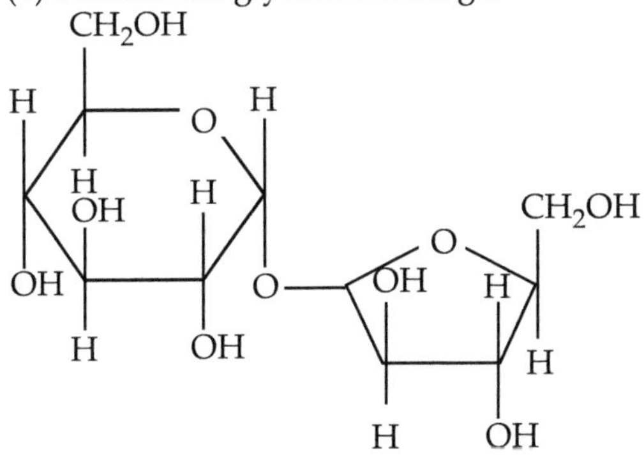

(Glycoside linkage)

**33.** Ziggler Natta catalyst is the heterogeneous catalyst that is involved in the polymerization of ethylene.

●●

## 🗨 QUESTIONS

**1.** The number of chiral carbons present in the molecule given below is ............. .

[2020, Main]

**2.** The Fischer projection of D-erythrose is shown below : [2020, Advanced]

$$CHO$$
H —— OH
H —— OH
$$CH_2OH$$

D-erythrose

D-Erythrose and its isomers are listed as P, Q, R and S in Column-I. Choose the correct relationship of P, Q, R and S with D-erythrose from Column II.

| Column-I | | Column-II |
|---|---|---|
| P. | | 1. Diastereomer |
| Q. | | 2. Identical |
| R. | | 3. Enantiomer |
| S. | | |

(1) $P \to 2, Q \to 3, R \to 2, S \to 2$
(2) $P \to 3, Q \to 1, R \to 1, S \to 2$
(3) $P \to 2, Q \to 1, R \to 1, S \to 3$
(4) $P \to 2, Q \to 3, R \to 3, S \to 1$

**3.** The number of $\,{>}C = O$ groups present in a tripeptide Asp – Glu – Lys is ........ . [2020, Main]

**4.** The correct observation in the following reactions is :

$$Sucrose \xrightarrow[\substack{Cleavage \\ (Hydrolysis)}]{Glycosidic\ bond} A + B \xrightarrow[reagent]{Seliwanoff's} ?$$

[2020, Main]

(1) Formation of blue colour
(2) Formation of violet colour
(3) Formation of red colour
(4) Gives no colour

**5.** The antifertility drug 'Novestrol' can react with : [2020, Main]

(1) $Br_2$/water; $ZnCl_2$/HCl; $FeCl_3$
(2) Alcoholic HCN; NaOCl; $ZnCl_2$/HCl
(3) $Br_2$/water; $ZnCl_2$/HCl; NaOCl
(4) $ZnCl_2$/HCl; $FeCl_3$; Alcoholic HCN

**6.** Which of the following will react with $CHCl_3$ + alc. KOH ? [2020, Main]

(1) Adenine and lysine
(2) Adenine and thymine
(3) Adenine and proline
(4) Thymine and proline

**7.** What are the functional groups present in the structure of maltose ? [2020, Main]

(1) One ketal and one hemiketal
(2) One acetal and one hemiacetal
(3) Two acetals
(4) One acetal and one ketal

**8.** Which one of the following statements not true ? [2020, Main]

(1) Lactose contains α-glycosidic linkage between $C_1$ of galactose and $C_4$ of glucose
(2) Lactose ($C_{11}H_{22}O_{11}$) is a disaccharide and it contains 8 hydroxyl groups
(3) On acid hydrolysis, lactose gives one molecule of D(+)-glucose and one molecule of D(+)-galactose
(4) Lactose is a reducing sugar and it gives Fehling's test

**9.** Which of the following is not an essential amino acid : [2020, Main]

(1) Valine          (2) Leucine
(3) Lysine          (4) Tryosine

**10.** The number of chiral carbons present in sucrose is ............. . [2020, Main]

**11.** The structure of a peptide is given below :

If the absolute values of the net charge of the peptide at pH = 2, pH = 6 and pH = 11 are $|z_1|$, $|z_2|$ and $|z_3|$, respectively, then what is $|z_1| + |z_2| + |z_3|$ ? **[2020, Advanced]**

12. A, B and C are three biomiolecules. The results of the tests performed on them are given below :

|   | Molisch's Test | Barfoed Test | Biuret Test |
|---|---|---|---|
| A | Positive | Negative | Negative |
| B | Positive | Positive | Negative |
| C | Negative | Negative | Positive |

A, B and C are respectively : **[2020, Main]**
(1) A = Glucose, B = Fructose, C = Albumin
(2) A = Lactose, B = Fructose, C = Alanine
(3) A = Lactose, B = Glucose, C = Alanine
(4) A = Lactose, B = Glucose, C = Albumin

13. Two momomers in maltose are : **[2020, Main]**
(1) α-D-glucose and β-D-glucose
(2) α-D-glucose and α-D-Fructose
(3) α-D-glucose and α-D-glucose
(4) α-D-glucose and α-D-galactose

14. The number of chiral centres present in threonine is ..................... . **[2020, Main]**

15. Maltose on treatment with dilute HCl gives : **[2019, Main]**
(1) D-Glucose and D-Fructose
(2) D-Fructose
(3) D-Galactose
(4) D-Glucose

16. Which of the following statements is not true about sucrose ? **[2019, Main]**
(1) It is a non reducing sugar
(2) The glycosidic linkage is present between $C_1$ or α-glucose and $C_1$ of β-fructose
(3) It is also named as invert sugar
(4) On hydrolysis, it produces glucose and fructose

17. The peptide that gives positive ceric ammonium nitrate and carbylamine tests is : **[2019, Main]**
(1) Ser - Lys      (2) Gln - Asp
(3) Lys - Asp      (4) Asp - Gln

18. Amylopectin is composed of : **[2019, Main]**
(1) α-D-glucose, $C_1 - C_4$ and $C_1 - C_6$ linkages
(2) β-D-glucose, $C_1 - C_4$ and $C_2 - C_6$ linkages
(3) β-D-glucose, $C_1 - C_4$ and $C_1 - C_6$ linkages
(4) α-D-glucose, $C_1 - C_4$ and $C_2 - C_6$ linkages

19. The number of stereo centers present in linear and cyclic structures of glucose are respectively : **[2019, Main]**
(1) 5 and 4      (2) 4 and 4
(3) 5 and 5      (4) 4 and 5

20. Glucose and Galactose are having identical configuration in all the positions except position. **[2019, Main]**
(1) C – 3      (2) C – 4
(3) C – 2      (4) C – 5

21. Which of the following statements is not true about RNA ? **[2019, Main]**
(1) It controls the synthesis of protein
(2) It has always double stranded α-helix structure
(3) It usually does not replicate
(4) It is present in the nucleus of the cell

22. Which of the given statements is INCORRECT about glycogen ? **[2019, Main]**
(1) It is a straight chain polymer similar to amylose.
(2) Only α-linkages are present in the molecule
(3) It is present in animal cells
(4) It is present in some yeast and fungi

23. The Fischer presentation of D-glucose is given below :

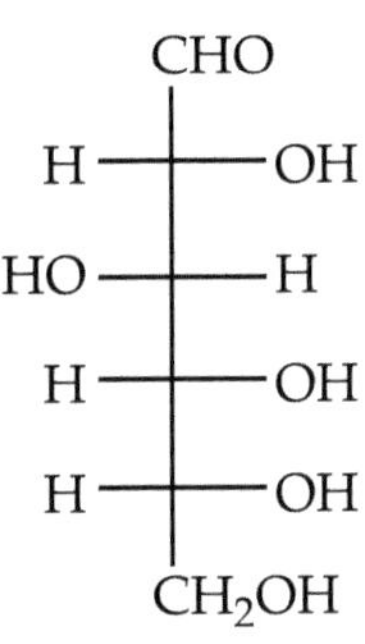

D-glucose

The correct structures of β-L-glucopyranose is/are : **[2018, Advanced]**

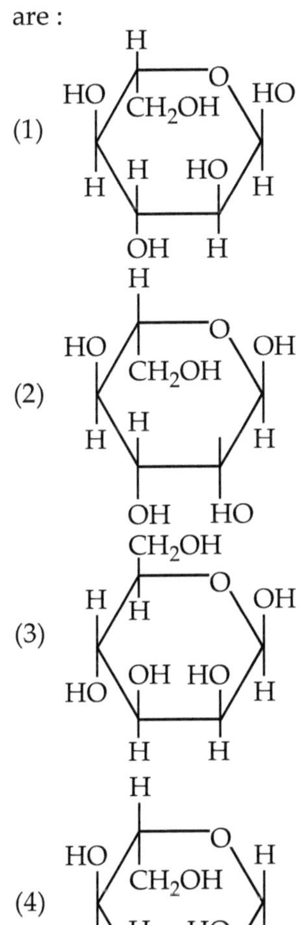

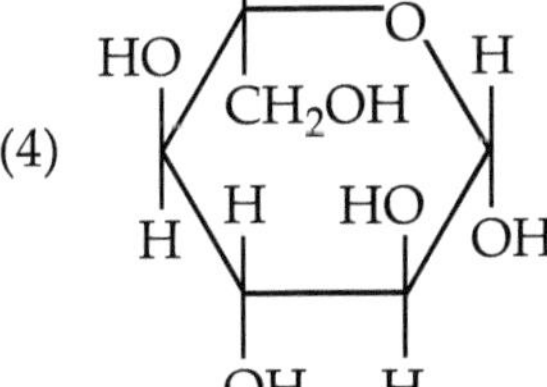

24. Glucose on prolonged heating with HI gives :

**[2018, Main]**

(1)  *n*-Hexane  (2)  1-Hexene
(3)  Hexanoic acid  (4)  6-iodohexanal

25. The dipeptide, Gln-Gly, on treatment with $CH_3COCl$ followed by aqueous work up gives :

**[2018, Main]**

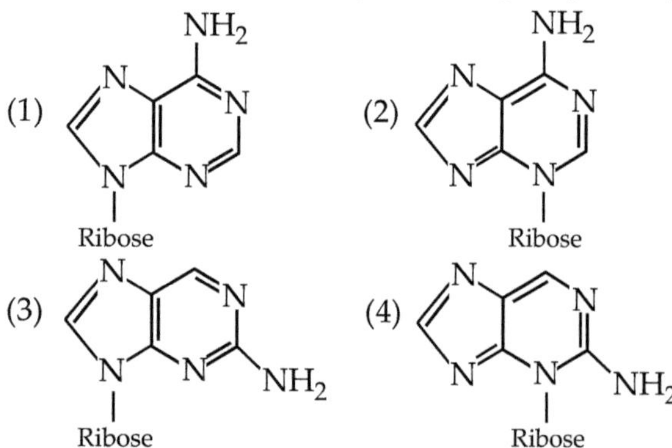

26. Which of the following is the correct structure of Adenosine ?  **[2018, Main]**

27. Among the following, the incorrect statement is :

**[2018, Main]**

(1)  Maltose and lactose has 1, 4-glycosidic linkage
(2)  Sucrose and amylose has 1, 2-glycosidic linkage
(3)  Cellulose and amylose has 1, 4-glycosidic linkage
(4)  Lactose contains β-D-galactose and β-D-glucose

28. Which of the following compounds will behave as a reducing sugar in an aqueous KOH solution ?

**[2017, Main]**

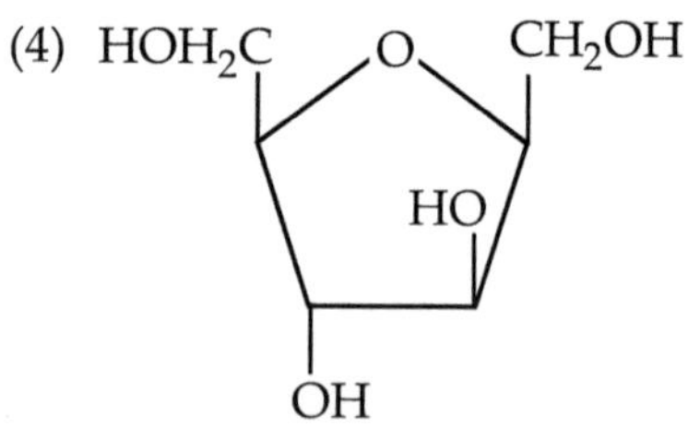

29. Among the following, the essential amino acid is :  **[2017, Main]**

(1)  Alanine  (2)  Valine
(3)  Aspartic acid  (4)  Serine

30. The incorrect statement among the following is :

**[2017, Main]**

(1)  α-D-glucose and β-D-glucose are anomers.
(2)  α-D-glucose and β-D-glucose are enantiomers.
(3)  Cellulose is a straight chain polysaccharide made up of only β-D-glucose units.
(4)  The penta acetate of glucose does not react with hydroxyl amine.

31. For 'invert sugar', the correct statements is/are :

**[2016, Advanced]**

(Given : specific rotatons of (+)-sucrose, (+)-maltose, L-(–)-glucose and L-(+)-fructose in aqueous solution are +66°, +140°, 52° and +92° respectively)

(1)  'invert sugar' is prepared by acid catalyzed hydrolysis of maltose
(2)  'invert sugar' is an equimolar mixture of D-(+)-glucose and D-(–)-fructose
(3)  specific rotation of 'invert sugar' is – 20°
(4)  on reaction with $Br_2$ water, 'invert sugar' forms saccharic acid as one of the product

**32. Assertion :** Rayon is a semisynthetic polymer whose properties are better than natural cotton.

**Reason :** Mechanical and aesthetic properties of cellulose can be improved by acetylation.

**[2016, Main]**

(1) Both assertion and reason are correct, and the reason is the correct explanation for the assertion.

(2) Both assertion and reason are correct, but the reason is not the correct explanation for the assertion.

(3) Assertion is incorrect statement, but the reason is correct.

(4) Both assertion and reason are incorrect.

**33.** Consider the following sequence for aspartic acid :

$$\underset{\underset{CH_2CO_2^+}{|}}{\overset{\overset{CO_2H}{|}}{H_2N-\!\!\!\!-H}} \underset{1.88}{\overset{pK_1}{\rightleftharpoons}} \underset{\underset{CH_2CO_2H}{|}}{\overset{\overset{CO_2^-}{|}}{H_3\overset{+}{N}-\!\!\!\!-H}}$$

$$\underset{3.65}{\overset{pK_R}{\rightleftharpoons}} \underset{\underset{CH_2CO_2^-}{|}}{\overset{\overset{CO_2^-}{|}}{H_3\overset{+}{N}-\!\!\!\!-H}} \underset{9.60}{\overset{pK_2}{\rightleftharpoons}} \underset{\underset{CH_2CO_2^-}{|}}{\overset{\overset{CO_2^-}{|}}{H_2N-\!\!\!\!-H}}$$

The $pI$ (isoelectric point) of aspartic acid is :

**[2016, Main]**

(1) 1.88        (2) 3.65

(3) 5.74        (4) 2.77

**34.** The artificial sweetener that has the highest sweetness value in comparison to cane sugar is :

**[2016, Main]**

(1) Aspartane        (2) Saccharin

(3) Sucralose        (4) Alitame

**35.** Observation of "Rhumann's purple" is a confirmatory test for the presence of :

**[2016, Main]**

(1) Reducing sugar        (2) Cupric ion

(3) Protein        (4) Starch

**36.** The structure of D-(+)-glucose is :

**[2015, Advanced]**

$$\begin{array}{c} CHO \\ H-\!\!\!\!-OH \\ HO-\!\!\!\!-H \\ H-\!\!\!\!-OH \\ H-\!\!\!\!-OH \\ CH_2OH \end{array}$$

The structure of L-(–)-glucose is :

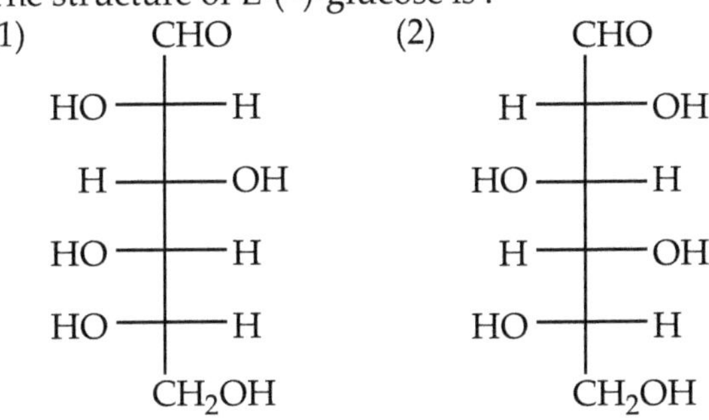

(1)
$$\begin{array}{c} CHO \\ HO-\!\!\!\!-H \\ H-\!\!\!\!-OH \\ HO-\!\!\!\!-H \\ HO-\!\!\!\!-H \\ CH_2OH \end{array}$$

(2)
$$\begin{array}{c} CHO \\ H-\!\!\!\!-OH \\ HO-\!\!\!\!-H \\ H-\!\!\!\!-OH \\ HO-\!\!\!\!-H \\ CH_2OH \end{array}$$

(3)
$$\begin{array}{c} CHO \\ HO-\!\!\!\!-H \\ HO-\!\!\!\!-H \\ H-\!\!\!\!-OH \\ HO-\!\!\!\!-H \\ CH_2OH \end{array}$$

(4)
$$\begin{array}{c} CHO \\ HO-\!\!\!\!-H \\ HO-\!\!\!\!-H \\ HO-\!\!\!\!-H \\ H-\!\!\!\!-OH \\ CH_2OH \end{array}$$

**37.** The major product of the reaction is :

**[2015, Advanced]**

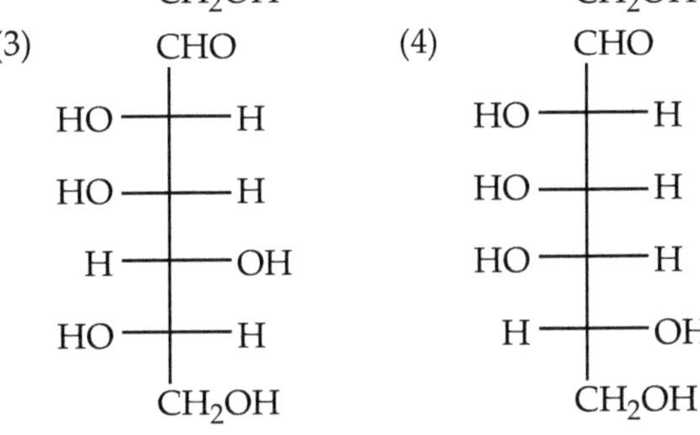


(1) H₃C  NH₂  CH₃OH

(2) H₃C  CO₂H  CH₃OH

(3) H₃C  CO₂H  CH₃OH

(4) H₃C  NH₂  CH₃OH

**38.** Which of the vitamins given below is water soluble ? **[2015, Main]**

(1) Vitamin C        (2) Vitamin D

(3) Vitamin E        (4) Vitamin K

**39.** Complete hydrolysis of starch gives :

**[2015, Main]**

(1) Glucose and fructose in equimolar amount

(2) Galactose and fructose in equimolar amount

(3) Glucose only

(4) Glucose and galactose in equimolar amount

**40.** Accumulation of which of the following molecules in the muscles occurs as a result of vigorous exercise ?        **[2015, Main]**

(1) Glucose        (2) Glycogen

(3) L-lactic acid        (4) Pyruvic acid

**41.** The total number of distinct naturally occurring amino acids obtained by complete acidic hydrolysis of the peptide shown below is :

**[2014, Advanced]**

**42.** Which one of the following bases is not present in DNA ? **[2014, Main]**

(1) Quinoline  (2) Adenine

(3) Cytosine  (4) Thymine

**43.** Which of the following will not show mutarotation ? **[2014, Main]**

(1) Maltose  (2) Lactose

(3) Glucose  (4) Sucrose

**44.** The reason for double helical structure of DNA is the operation of : **[2014, Main]**

(1) Electrostatic attractions

(2) Van der Waals forces

(3) Dipole-Dipole interactions

(4) Hydrogen bonding

**45.** A tetrapeptide has – COOH group on alanine. This produces glycine (Gly), valine (Val), phenyl alanine (Phe) and alanine (Ala), on complete hydrolysis. For this tetrapeptide, the number of possible sequences (primary structures) with – $NH_2$ group attached to a chiral center is :

**[2013, Advanced]**

**46.** The substituents $R_1$ and $R_2$ for nine peptides are listed in the table given below. How many of these peptides are positively charged at pH = 7.0 ? **[2012, Advanced]**

$$\overset{\oplus}{H_3}N-CH-CO-NH-CH-CO-NH-CH-CO$$

with substituents H, $R_1$, $R_2$

$$-NH-CH-COO^{\ominus}$$

with substituent H

| Peptide | $R_1$ | $R_2$ |
|---|---|---|
| I | H | H |
| II | H | $CH_3$ |
| III | $CH_2COOH$ | H |
| IV | $CH_2CONH_2$ | $(CH_2)_4NH_2$ |
| V | $CH_2CONH_2$ | $CH_2CONH_2$ |
| VI | $(CH_2)_4NH_2$ | $(CH_2)_4NH_2$ |
| VII | $CH_2COOH$ | $CH_2CONH_2$ |
| VIII | $CH_2OH$ | $(CH_2)_4NH_2$ |
| IX | $(CH_2)_4NH_2$ | $CH_3$ |

**47.** When the following aldohexose exists in its D-configuration, the total number of stereoisomers in its pyranose form is :

$$\begin{array}{c} CHO \\ | \\ CH_2 \\ | \\ CHOH \\ | \\ CHOH \\ | \\ CHOH \\ | \\ CH_2OH \end{array}$$

**48.** A decapeptide (Mol. Wt. 796) on complete hydrolysis gives glycine (Mol. Wt. 75), alanine and phenylalanine. Glycine contributes 47.0% to the total weight of the hydrolysed products. The number of glycine units present in the decapeptide is : **[2011, Advanced]**

**49.** The following carbohydrate is : **[2011, Advanced]**

(1) A ketohexose  (2) An aldohexose

(3) An α-furanose  (4) An α-pyranose

**50.** The correct statement about the following disaccharide is : **[2010, Advanced]**

(1) Ring (a) is pyranose with α-glycosidic link

(2) Ring (a) is furanose with α-glycosidic link

(3) Ring (b) is furanose with α-glycosidic link

(4) Ring (b) is pyranose with β-glycosidic link

**51.** The total number of basic groups in the following form of lysine is **[2010, Advanced]**

$$\overset{\oplus}{H_3}N-CH_2-CH_2-CH_2-CH_2-CH-C\overset{O}{\underset{O^{\ominus}}{\big\langle}}$$

with $H_2N$ substituent

**52.** The correct statements about the following sugars X and Y is/are : **[2009, Advanced]**

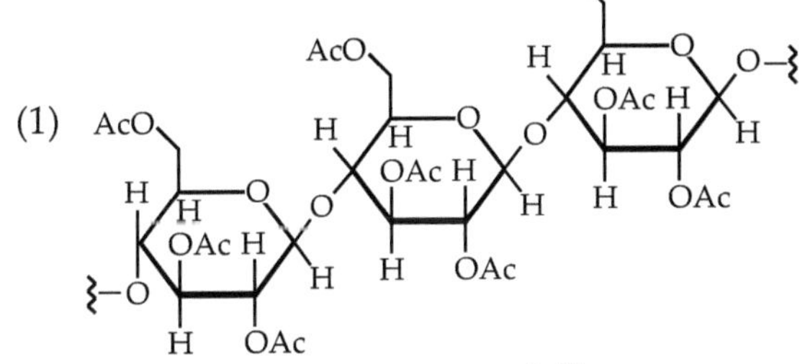

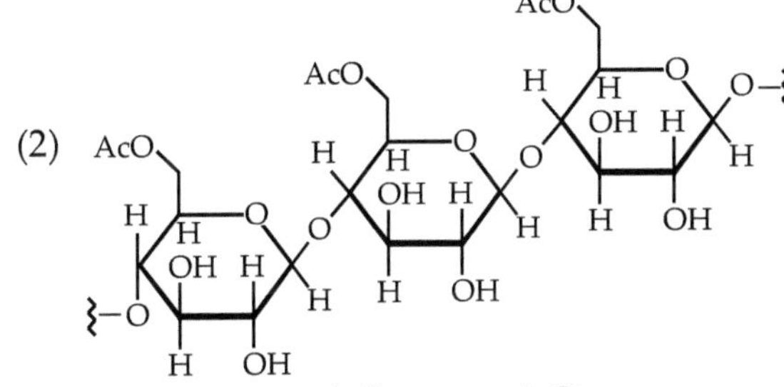

(1) X is a reducing sugar and Y is a non-reducing sugar
(2) X is a non-reducing sugar and Y is a reducing sugar
(3) The glucosidic linkages in X and Y are α and β, respectively
(4) The glucosidic linkages in X and Y are β and α, respectively

53. Cellulose upon acetylation with excess acetic anhydride/$H_2SO_4$ (catalytic) gives cellulose triacetate whose structure is : **[2008, Advanced]**

(1) 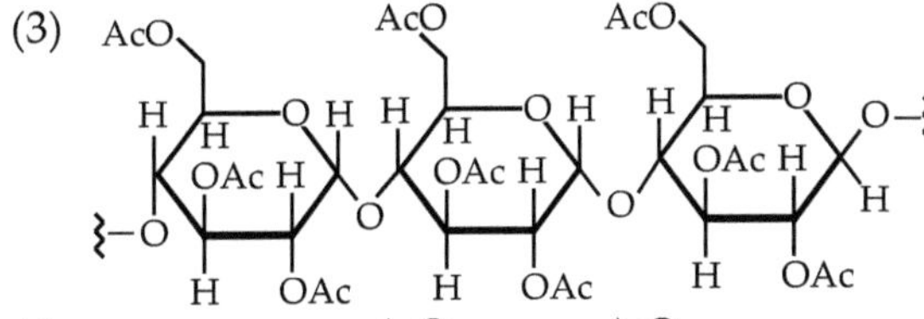

(2)

(3)

(4)

54. **Statement-1 :** Glucose gives a reddish-brown precipitate with Fehling's solution.
because

**Statement-2 :** Reaction of glucose with Fehling's solution gives CuO and gluconic acid.
**[2007, Advanced]**
(1) Statement-1 is True, Statement-2 is True; Statement-2 is a correct explanation for Statement-1
(2) Statement-1 is True, Statement-2 is True; Statement-2 is NOT a correct explanation for Statement-1
(3) Statement-1 is True, Statement-2 is False
(4) Statement-1 is False, Statement-2 is True

55. Which of the following disaccharide will not reduce Tollen's reagent ? **[2005, Main]**
(1) 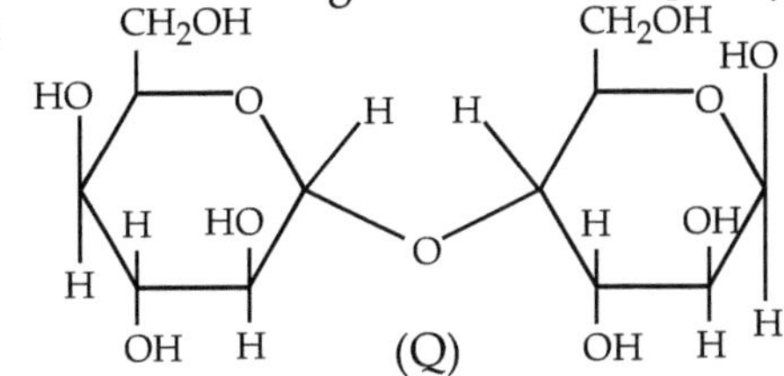

(2) 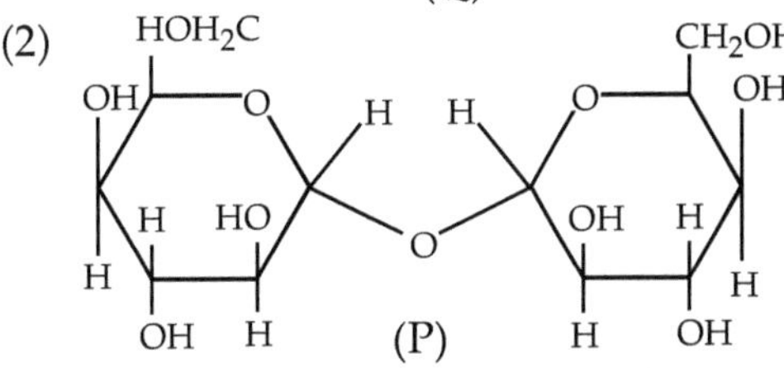

56. Two forms of D-glucopyranose, are called :
**[2005, Screening]**
(1) Enantiomers       (2) Anomers
(3) Epimers            (4) Diastereomers

57. The structure of D-glucose is as follows :

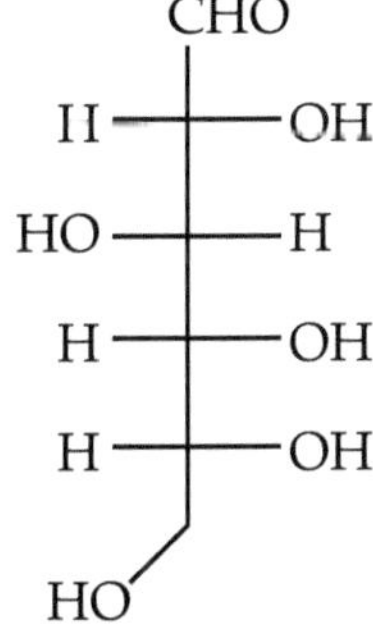

(1) Draw the structure of L-Glucose
(2) Give the reaction of L-Glucose with Tollens reagent. **[2004, Main]**

58. $H_3\overset{+}{N}$ ... $\overset{+}{N}H_3$

Arrange in order of increasing acidic strength :
**[2004, Advanced]**
(1) X > Z > Y        (2) Z < X > Y
(3) X > Y > Z        (4) Z > X > Y

59. Which of the following pairs give positive Tollen's test ? **[2004, Screening]**
(1) Glucose, sucrose
(2) Glucose, fructose
(3) Hexanal, acetophenone
(4) Fructose, sucrose

**60.** Following two amino acids lionise and glutamine from dipeptide linkage. What are two possible dipeptides ?  **[2003, Main]**

$$H_2N-CH_2CH_2CH_2CH_2-\underset{NH_2}{CH}-COOH \;+\; H_2N-CH_2CH_2-\underset{NH_2}{CH}-COOH$$

## ANSWER KEY

|     |        |     |        |     |        |     |       |     |       |     |       |     |       |     |       |     |       |     |       |
|-----|--------|-----|--------|-----|--------|-----|-------|-----|-------|-----|-------|-----|-------|-----|-------|-----|-------|-----|-------|
| 1.  | (*)    | 2.  | (3)    | 3.  | (*)    | 4.  | (3)   | 5.  | (1)   | 6.  | (1)   | 7.  | (2)   | 8.  | (1)   | 9.  | (4)   | 10. | (*)   |
| 11. | (*)    | 12. | (4)    | 13. | (3)    | 14. | (*)   | 15. | (4)   | 16. | (2)   | 17. | (1)   | 18. | (1)   | 19. | (4)   | 20. | (2)   |
| 21. | (2)    | 22. | (1)    | 23. | (4)    | 24. | (1)   | 25. | (3)   | 26. | (1)   | 27. | (2)   | 28. | (3)   | 29. | (2)   | 30. | (2)   |
| 31. | (2, 3) | 32. | (1)    | 33. | (4)    | 34. | (4)   | 35. | (3)   | 36. | (1)   | 37. | (3)   | 38. | (1)   | 39. | (3)   | 40. | (3)   |
| 41. | (*)    | 42. | (1)    | 43. | (4)    | 44. | (4)   | 45. | (*)   | 46. | (*)   | 47. | (*)   | 48. | (*)   | 49. | (2)   | 50. | (1)   |
| 51. | (*)    | 52. | (2, 3) | 53. | (1)    | 54. | (3)   | 55. | (2)   | 56. | (2)   | 57. | (*)   | 58. | (1)   | 59. | (2)   | 60. | (*)   |

## ANSWERS WITH EXPLANATIONS

**1.**

(structure of cinchona-type molecule with OH, CH, H₃C groups, quinoline ring, O-linked p-tolyl group)

**3.** Structure of Tri peptide Asp-Glu-Lys

$$H_2N-CH-\overset{O}{\overset{\|}{C}}-NH-CH-\overset{O}{\overset{\|}{C}}-NH-CH-\overset{O}{\overset{\|}{C}}-OH$$

with side chains:
- CH₂–C(=O)–OH
- CH₂–CH₂–C(=O)–OH
- (CH₂)₄–NH₂

**2. (3)**

```
      CHO
 H ---+--- OH
 H ---+--- OH
     CH2-OH
```
D-Erythrose

Compound P
```
      CHO
 H ---+--- OH
 H ---+--- OH
     CH2-OH
```
It is Identical    P-2

Compound Q
```
       CHO
 OH ---+--- H
  H ---+--- OH
     CH2-OH
```
It is Diastereomer    Q-1

Compound R
```
      CHO
 H ---+--- OH
 HO ---+--- H
     CH2-OH
```
It is Diastereomer    R-1

Compound S
```
       CHO
 HO ---+--- H
 HO ---+--- H
     CH2-OH
```
It is Enantiomer    S-3

P-2, Q-1, R-1, S-3

**4. (3)** Seliwanoff's test is used to distinguish aldoses from ketoses. On hydrolysis, ketoses are dehydrated more rapidly to give furfural derivatives and on condensation with seliwanoff reagent gives cherry red complex. Fructose and sucrose are two common sugars which give a positive test. Sucrose gives a positive test as it is a disaccharide consisting of fructose and glucose,.

$$\text{Sucrose} \xrightarrow{\text{Hydrolysis}} \underset{+}{\text{Glucose}} \xrightarrow[\text{reagent}]{\text{Seliwanoff's}}$$
Fructose → Cherry Red colour

**5. (1)**

(steroid structure with H₃C, C≡CH, H groups and HO-substituted aromatic ring)

Ethynylestradiol (novestrol)

The antifertility drug 'Novestrol" can react with $Br_2 + H_2O$ test, Lucas test with $ZnCl_2 + HCl$, $FeCl_3$ test of phenolic group.

**6. (1)** Both adenine and lysine both adenine have primary amine, therefore they react with $CHCl_3$ + alc. KOH.

(structure of Lysine with NH₂ groups)

Lysine

(structure of Adenine purine ring with NH₂)

Adenine

**7. (2)** The functional group present in maltose is one acetal and one hemiacetal.

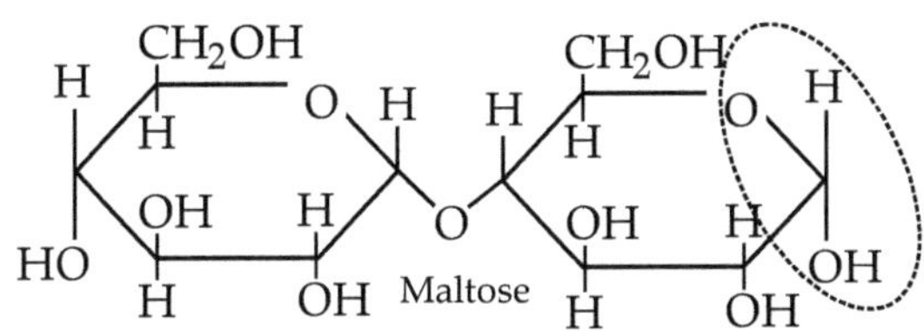

Maltose

Hemiacetal

**8. (1)**

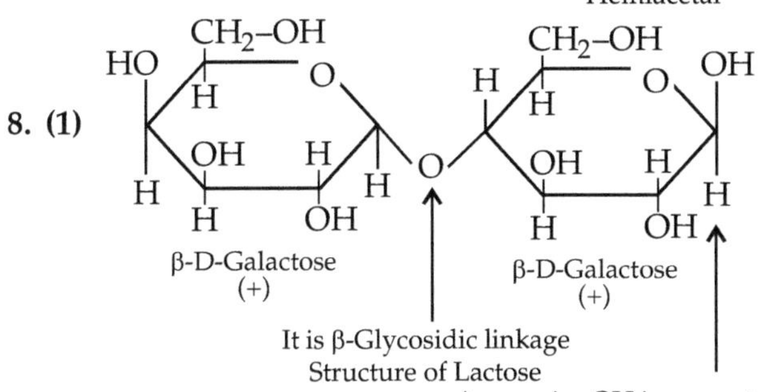

β-D-Galactose
(+)

β-D-Galactose
(+)

It is β-Glycosidic linkage
Structure of Lactose
Anomeric –OH is present
so it gives +ve Fehling Test

**9. (4)** Tyrosine is not an essential amino acid.

**10.** The total number of chiral carbon in sucrose is 9.

[α-D-Glucose]

[β-D-Fructose]

**11. (4)**

At pH = 2    $\overset{1}{NH_2}$ and $\overset{2}{NH_2}$ of Tyrosine and Lysine is +ve charged (+ 1 each) $+ 2 \, |z_1| = 2$

At pH = 6    $NH_2$ of Lysine (+1),

COOH (–1) of glutamic acid,

so because of dipolar ion exist $|z_2| = 0$

At pH = 11   COOH of Glutamic acid (– 1)

COOH of Lysine (– 1)

OH of phenol (– 1)

$|z_3| = 3$

$|z_1| + |z_2| + |z_3| = 5$

**12. (4)** Alanine does not show Biuret test because Biuret test is used for identification of peptide linkage and alanine is amino acid.

Albumine is protein having peptide linkage so it gives positive Biuret test.

Positive Barfoed test is shown by monosaccharide only. Positive Molisch's test is shown by glucose.

**13. (3)** Two mononers in maltose are α-D-glucose and α-D-glucose.

**14.** Structure of Threonine is :

S. 2-chiral center is present

**15. (4)** The reaction of maltose with HCl is shown below :

Maltose

$H_3O^+$

D-glucose

The reaction of maltose with HCl gives two molecules of D-glucose.

**16. (2)** In sucrose two monosaccharides are joined together by an oxide linkage which is formed by loss of water molecule. Such linkage through oxygen atom is called glycosidic linkage. As sucrose & fructose are involved in glycosidic bond formation, sucrose is non reducing sugar. The structure of sucrose is shown below :

As we can see from the structure of sucrose, the glycosidic linkage is present between C1 of α-glucose and $C_2$ of β-fructose.

Sucrose is non reducing sugar, i.e., it will not reduce Fehling's solution or Tollen's reagent. It does not form an oxime or an osazone, and does not undergo mutarotation. This indicates that hemiacetal group is not present in the rings.

**17. (1)** The carbylamine test is used to identify the amine group whereas the ceric ammonium nitrate test is used to identify the hydroxyl group.

The amino acid that contains two amine groups is lysine.

The amino acid that contains hydroxyl group is serine.

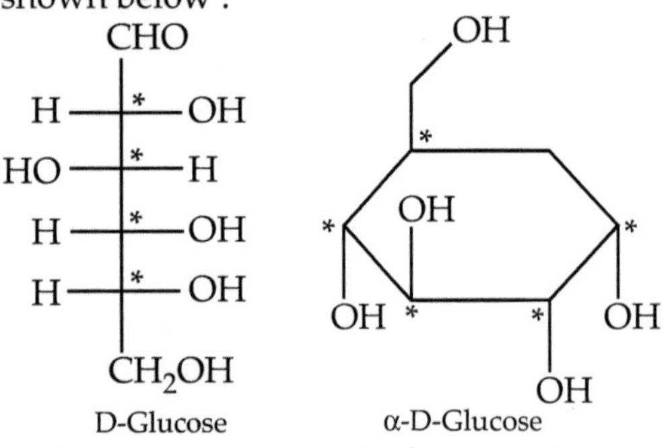


Serine has –OH group in its structure therefore, it gives positive ceric ammonium nitrate test and lysine had –NH$_2$ group in its structure therefore, it gives positive carbylamine test.

**18. (1)** The polymer amylopectin is composed of α-D-glucose units and the glucose units are linked by $C_1 - C_4$ and $C_1 - C_6$ linkages.

**19. (4)** The linear and cyclic structure of glucose is shown below :

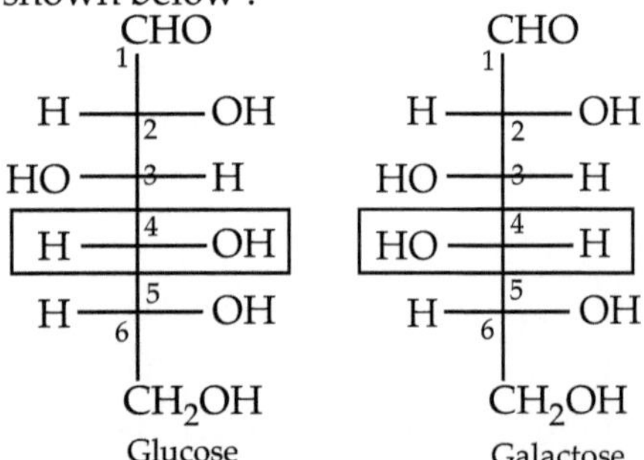


The number of stereocenters present in the linear and the cyclic structure of glucose are 4 and 5 respectively.

**20. (2)** The structure of glucose and galactose is shown below :



The configuration of glucose and galactose is different at C4 carbon atom.

**21. (2)** DNA molecule has double stranded α-helix structure and RNA has single strand structure. The statement that RNA has double stranded α-helix structure is not true.

**22. (1)** The polymeric chain of glycogen is similar to amylopectin, not amylose. Amylopectin is a branched chain polymer whereas amylose is straight chain polymer. Hence, statement 1 is incorrect about glycogen.

**23. (4)** The structure of β-L-glucopyranose is shown below :

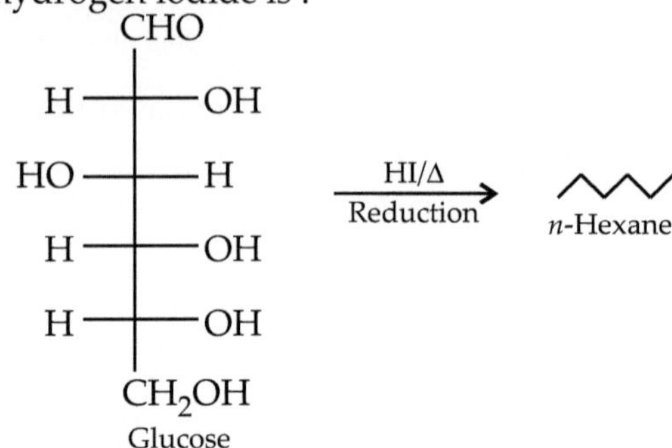


**24. (1)** Glucose undergoes reduction on heating with hydrogen iodide and results in the formation of n-hexane as product. The reaction involving prolong heating of glucose with hydrogen iodide is :



**25. (3)** The treatment of dipeptide Gln-Gly with CH$_3$COCl leads to the formation of peptide bond between these two. The reaction is expressed as :

$$H_2N-\overset{H}{\underset{CH_2CH_2-CONH_2}{\overset{|}{C}}}-COOH \quad + H_2N-CH_2COOH$$

gln         gly

$\downarrow$ CH$_3$COCl

$$CH_3-\overset{O}{\overset{||}{C}}-NH-CH\overset{CONH-CH_2COOH}{\underset{CH_2CH_2-C-NH_2}{}}$$

**26. (1)** Adenosine is a chemical with molecular formula $C_{10}H_{13}N_5O_4$. Its structure is shown below :

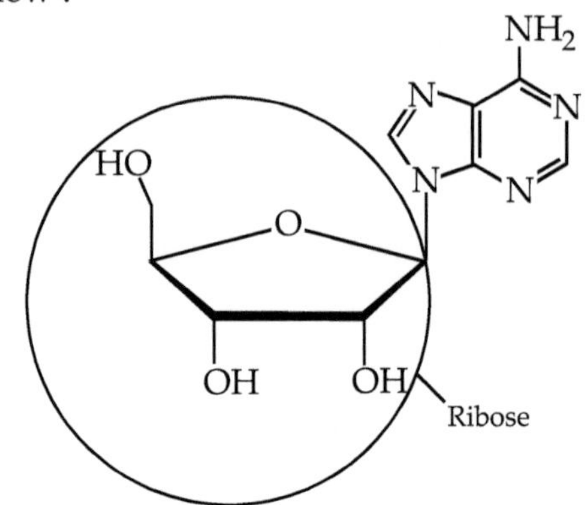

**27. (2)** Sucrose has 1, 2-glycosidic linkage, but amylose has 1, 4-glycosidic linkage.

**28. (3)** Reducing sugars possess free anomeric $-OH$ group. The sugar that behaves as a reducing sugar in an aqueous KOH solution is shown below :

$CH_3COOK +$

Free anomeric group

**29. (2)** Essential amino acids are those which are not synthesized in our body and are supplied to our body by some other sources. The nine essential amino acids are histidine, leucine, isoleucine, lysine, methionine, phenylalanine, threonine, tryptophan, and valine. Thus, valine comes under the category of essential amino acid.

**30. (2)** The compounds, α-D-glucose and β-D-glucose are anomers. They have same configuration at all chiral C atoms except first C atom.

α-D-glucose          β-D-glucose

anomers

**31. (2, 3)** The invert sugar is not prepared by the acid catalyzed hydrolysis of maltose.
Thus, option (A) is incorrect.
Invert sugar is an equimolar mixture of D-(+)-glucose and D-(−)-fructose.
Invert sugar is sucrose.
Thus, option (B) is correct.
Specific rotation is calculated as :
Average is taken considering that both monomers are present 1 mole each.

$$\alpha = \frac{+52° - 92°}{2}$$

$$= \frac{-40°}{2} = -20°$$

Thus option (C) is correct.

The reaction of invert sugar with bromine water does not form saccharic acid as one of the product.
Thus statement (D) is incorrect.

**32. (1)** In the given statements, both assertion and reason are correct, and reason is the correct explanation for the assertion because rayon is prepared by the acetylation of cellulose. Hence, both the statements complement each other completely.

**33. (4)** For the given sequence for aspartic acid, the isoelectric point ($pI$) of aspartic acid is calculated as follows :

$$pI = \frac{pK_1 + pK_2}{2}$$

$$= \frac{1.88 + 3.65}{2} = 2.77$$

**34. (4)** The artificial sweetner that has the highest sweetness value in comparision to cane sugar is alitame. Alitame is approximately two thousand times sweeter than sucrose and it is stable at higher temperature as well.

**35. (3)** The Ninhydrin test is used to detect the presence of α-amino acids. When the Ninhydrin (2,2-dihydroxyindane-1,3-dione) chemical react with these free amino acids, a product which is deep blue or purple in colour known as "Rhumann's purple" is produced.

nihydrin

purple coloured product

**36. (1)** L-(−)-glucose is the mirror image of D-(+)-glucose. The structures of D(+)-glucose and

L(–)-glucose differ in configuration at second, third, fourth and fifth Carbon atoms. Hence, option 1 is correct.

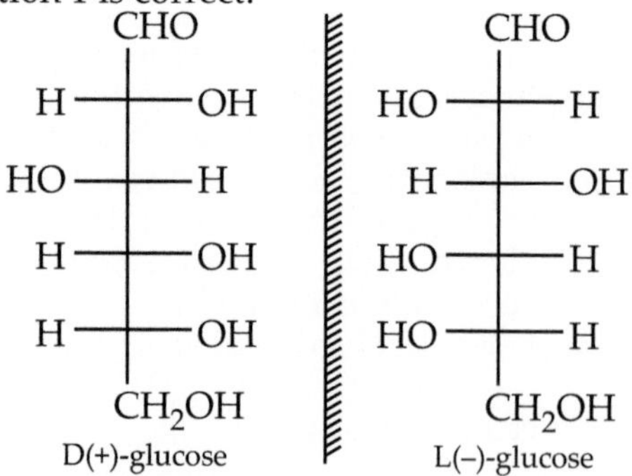

D(+)-glucose     L(–)-glucose

**37. (3)** The mechanism for the formation of major product is shown below.

The product of the given reaction is formed by diazotization of amino group.

Thus, the major product formed is shown below :

**38. (1)** Vitamin C is soluble in water.

**39. (3)** Starch is made up of number of glucose units bonded to each other through glycosidic linkage. On hydrolysis, starch leads to the formation of glucose.

**40. (3)** During the vigorous exercise, the formation of L-lactic acid occurs in muscles due to anaerobic respiration which is the degradation of carbohydrates in the absence of oxygen.

**41. (*)**

Amino acids are the organic molecules which consist of an acid, a base and an alkyl group which is different in every amino acid. The complete hydrolysis of the given peptide forms eight molecules of four types in which only glycine with molecular formula $NH_2 - CH_2 - COOH$ is naturally occurring amino acid.

Hence, the total number of distinct naturally occurring amino acids obtained by complete acidic hydrolysis of the peptide is 1.

**42. (1)** Adenine, cytosine and thymine are present in DNA. Quinoline is not present in DNA.

**43. (4)** Sucrose does not show mutarotation because the bond present in sucrose occurs between the anomeric carbons on glucose and fructose which eliminates the availability of alpha hydroxyl group. Because the hydroxyl group is not available, the ring cannot open and close and therefore sucrose does not undergo mutarotation.

**44. (4)** In DNA molecule, there are two polynucleotide chains which are twisted around a common axis but run in opposite directions to form a right handed helix. The two chains are joined together by specific hydrogen bonds which is the reason behind the helical structure of DNA.

**45. (*)** As the tetrapeptide comprises carboxylic acid group on alanine, it indicates that amino group of alanine is participitated in condensation reaction to eliminate water, which leads to formation of pepetide bond between two amino acids.

Chiral carbon is the α carbon atom present in every amino acid.

The possible sequences in tetrapeptide, when amino group attached to chiral carbon is shown below :

| V | G | P | | P | V | G |
|---|---|---|---|---|---|---|
| V | P | G | | P | G | V |

In the above sequences, V, G and P are valanine, glycine and phenyl, alanine respectively. The sequences show that number of possible sequences is 4.

46. **(*)** There are total 4 peptides from the given list which are positively charged at pH = 7.0. This is because the peptides that have isoelectric point greater than 7 exist in the form of cation in the solution with pH = 7 . It defines the basic nature of given polypeptide and thus, it must contain two or more than two amino groups. Hence, (IV), (VI), (VIII) and (IX) groups are the correct choices.

47. The pyranose form of given aldohexose is shown below :

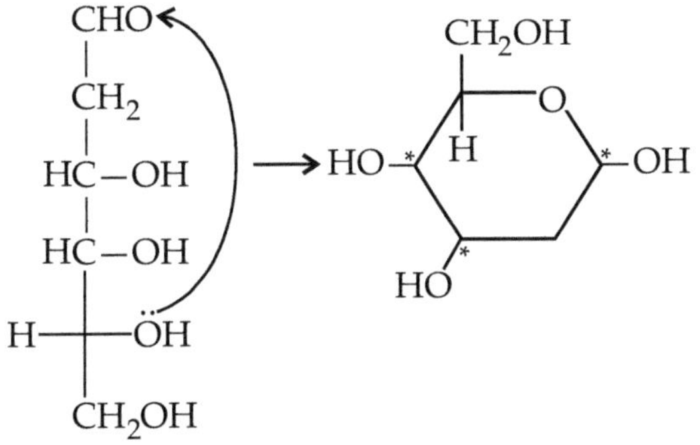

The number of chiral centres is three.

Hence, the total number of stereoisomers $= 2^n$

$$- 2^3$$
$$= 8$$

48. The number of water molecule needed for hydrolysis of peptides is always one unit less. Therefore, for decapeptide, nine water molecules are required for complete hydrolysis. The present number of glycine units is supposed to be "n". Total mass of decapeptide and nine water molecule is $796 + 9 \times 18 = 958$ g.

The numbers of glycine units are calculated as

$$958 \times 47\% = 75 \times n$$

$$958 \times \frac{47}{100} = 75 \times n$$

$$n = \frac{600.34}{100}$$

$$n \approx 6$$

49. **(2)** The given figure is heterocyclic in nature. It is a type of saccharide molecule. This structure is called pyranose due to the similarity with pyran. Therefore, it must be pyranose. But this is not an $\alpha$-pyranose. This is $\beta$-glucopyranose and it is a type of aldohexose. The structure is given as,

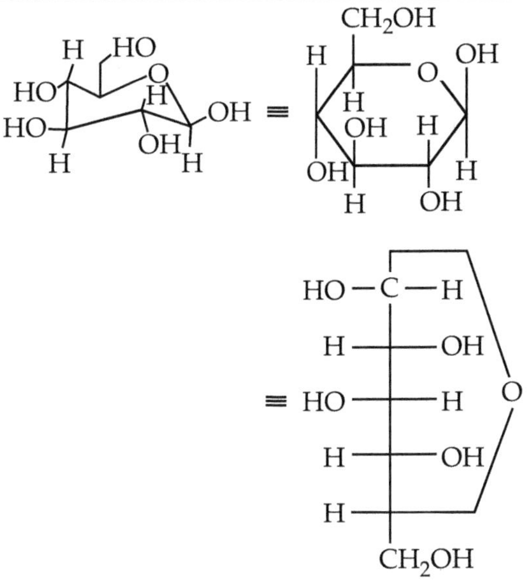

β-glucopyranose
(aldohexose)

50. **(1)** A cyclic organic compound with five carbon atoms and one oxygen atom in the chain is called pyranose. Therefore, ring (a) is pyranose because it contains five carbon atoms and one oxygen atom in cyclic ring and ring (b) is furanose because it is five membered ring that contains four carbon atoms and one oxygen atom in cyclic ring.
Ring (a) is pyranose with $\alpha$-glycosidic linkage and ring (b) is furanose with $\beta$-glycosidic linkage.

51. **(2)** There are two basic groups present in lysine that are $NH_2$ and $COO^-$.

52. **(2,3)** The sugar in which free aldehydic or ketonic group can be produced by opening the ring are known as the reducing sugars. The aldehydic group can be generated in the sugar (Y). Therefore, this is a reducing sugar but aldehydic or ketonic group cannot be generated in the sugar X. Therefore, sugar X is a non reducing sugar.
The sugar X is formed by the combination of $\alpha$-glucose and $\alpha$-fructose. Therefore, it exhibits $\alpha$-glycosidic linkages and the sugar Y is formed from $\beta$-glucose and $\beta$-fructose, therefore, it exhibits $\beta$ glycosidic linkages.

53. **(1)** The linkage present between each glucose unit in cellulose is $\beta$-1, 4-glycosidic linkage. On reaction with excess acetic anhydride, each hydroxyl group is replaced by acetoxy group and lead to the formation of cellulose triacetate.

54. **(3)** Reddish brown precipitates are formed when glucose is dissolved in Fehling solution.
$$C_6H_{12}O_6 + \text{Fehling solution } (2Cu^{2+} + 5OH^-)$$
$$\rightarrow C_6H_{11}O_7^- + Cu_2O + 3H_2O$$
Reddish brown ppt.

This is due to reduction of $Cu^{2+}$ by an aldehyde of glucose.

**55. (2)** The disaccharide P does not reduce Tollen's reagent. Both the rings of the disaccharide P are present in the acetyl form. Due to this, the disaccharide would not get hydrolysed in solution and hence, it does not reduce Tollen's reagent. On the other hand, one ring present in the disaccharide Q is in hemiacetal form. Due to this, hydrolysis of the disaccharide takes place in solution and hence, it can reduce Tollen's reagent.

**56. (2)** A compound that possesses a carbon atom which is attached with a hydroxyl group as well as with an alkoxy group is known as hemiacetal compound. In the cyclic form of hemiacetal compound, this carbon attached with a hydroxyl group as well as with an alkoxy group is known as anomeric carbon. The compound is called the anomer.

The cyclic form of glucose is called the D-glucopyranose. The structure of D-glucopyranose is shown as follows.

In D-glucopyranose, the carbon that is marked as 1 is the anomeric carbon of D-glucopyranose which contains both hydroxyl group and alkoxy group in the cyclic form of hemiacetal compound. Thus, the two forms of D-glucopyranose are anomers of each other and are known as $\alpha$ and $\beta$-anomers.

Thus, the correct option is (B).

**57. (1)** The structure of L-glucose is formed by changing the position of OH and H at the second last carbon of the given D-glucose as shown below :

**(2)** The reaction of L-glucose with tollens reagent is shown below :

From the given reaction it is clear that the oxidation of CHO to –COOH takes place.

**58. (1)** The value of acid dissociation constant of carboxylic group is less than that of amines, hence, its acidic strength is more. The acid dissociation constant value of $N^+H_3$ (y) is more than that of $N^+H_3$ (z) due to negative inductive effect of carboxylic group.

**59. (2)** Positive Tollen's test is given by compounds that contain aldehyde group or by $\alpha$-hydroxy ketones. Glucose and fructose contain aldehyde and $\alpha$-hydroxy ketones in their chemical structure, respectively.

**60.** The products formed by the reaction of the given amino acids are shown below.

## ❓ QUESTIONS

**1.** The mechanism of action of ''Terfenadine'' (Seldane) is : **[2020, Main]**
(1) Activates the histamine receptor
(2) Inhibits the secretion of histamine
(3) Inhibits the action of histamine receptor
(4) Helps in the secretion of histamine

**2.** Among the following compounds, geometrical isomerism is exhibited by : **[2020, Main]**

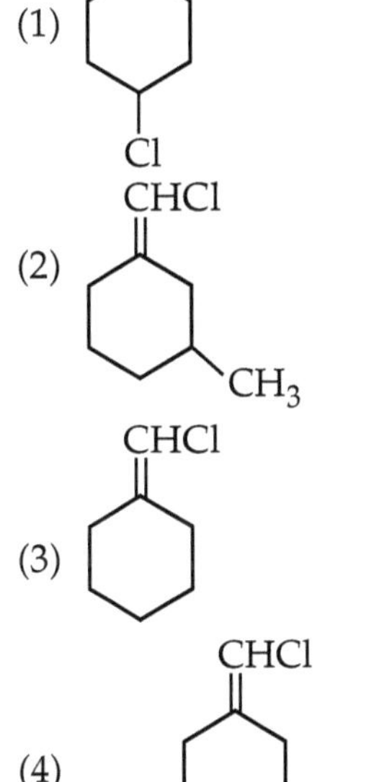

**3.** If you spill a chemical toilet cleaning liquid on your hand, your first aid would be :
**[2020, Main]**
(1) Aqueous $NH_3$    (2) Vinegar
(3) Aqueous $NaHCO_3$    (4) Aqueous NaOH

**4.** Match the following drugs with their therapeutic actions : **[2020, Main]**
(i) Ranitidine     (a) Antidepressant
(ii) Nardil     (b) Antibiotic
    (Phenelzine)
(iii) Chloramphenicol     (c) Antihistamine
(iv) Dimetane     (d) Antacid
    (Brompheniramine)     (e) Analgesic
(1) (i)-(a); (ii)-(c); (iii)-(b); (iv)-(e)
(2) (i)-(e); (ii)-(a); (iii)-(c); (iv)-(d)
(3) (i)-(d); (ii)-(a); (iii)-(b); (iv)-(c)
(4) (i)-(d); (ii)-(c); (iii)-(a); (iv)-(e)

**5.** If a person is suffering from the deficiency of nor-adrenaline, what kind of drug can be suggested ?
**[2020, Main]**
(1) Anti-inflammatory    (2) Analgesic
(3) Anti-histamine    (4) Anti-depressant

**6.** The following molecule acts as an :

$$\text{>N-(CH}_2)_2\text{-CH(C}_5\text{H}_4\text{N)(C}_6\text{H}_4\text{Br)}$$

(Brompheniramine)

**[2020, Main]**
(1) Antiseptic    (2) Anti-bacterial
(3) Anti-histamine    (4) Anti-depressant

**7.** The purest form of commercial iron is :
**[2020, Main]**
(1) Scrap iron and pig iron
(2) Wrought iron
(3) Cast iron
(4) Pig iron

**8.** Match the following : **[2020, Main]**
(i) Riboflavin     (a) Beriberi
(ii) Thiamine     (b) Scurvy
(iii) Pyridoxine     (c) Cheilosis
(iv) Ascorbic acid     (d) Convulsions
(1) (i)-(c), (ii)-(a), (iii)-(d), (iv)-(b)
(2) (i)-(c), (ii)-(d), (iii)-(a), (iv)-(b)
(3) (i)-(d), (ii)-(b), (iii)-(a), (iv)-(c)
(4) (i)-(a), (ii)-(d), (iii)-(c), (iv)-(b)

**9.** The number of chiral carbons in chloramphenicol is ................ . **[2020, Main]**

**10.** Biochemical Oxygen Demand (BOD) is the amount of oxygen required (in ppm) :
**[2020, Main]**
(1) By anaerobic bacteria to breakdown inorganic waste present in a water body.
(2) For the photochemical breakdown of waste present in $1\ m^3$ volume of a water body.
(3) By bacteria to break-down organic waste in a certain volume of a water sample.
(4) For sustaining life in a water body.

**11.** Consider the following reactions : **[2020, Main]**

$$NaCl + K_2Cr_2O_7 + H_2SO_4 \rightarrow (A) + \text{side products}$$
$$\text{(Conc.)}$$

$(A) + NaOH \rightarrow (B) + \text{Side products}$

$(B) + H_2SO_4 + H_2O_2 \rightarrow (C) + \text{Side produces}$

The sum of the total number of atoms in one molecule each of (A), (B) and (C) is ............ .

**12.** The number of $sp^2$ hybridised carbons present in ``Aspartame'' is ..................... .  **[2020, Main]**

**13.** Noradrenaline is a/an :  **[2019, Main]**
(1) Antacid
(2) Neurotransmitter
(3) Antidepressant
(4) Antihistamine

**14.** The predominant form of histamine present in human blood is ($pK_a$, Histidine = 6.0)

**[2018, Main]**

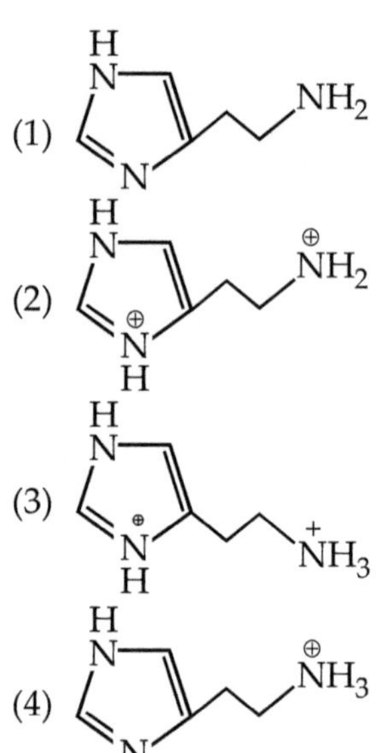

**15.** The correct match between items of List-I and List-II is :  **[2018, Main]**

| | List-I | | List-II |
|---|---|---|---|
| (A) | Phenelzine | (P) | Pyrimidine |
| (B) | Chloroxylenol | (Q) | Furan |
| (C) | Uracil | (R) | Hydrazine |
| (D) | Ranitidine | (S) | Phenol |

| | **(A)** | **(B)** | **(C)** | **(D)** |
|---|---|---|---|---|
| (1) | (R) | (S) | (P) | (Q) |
| (2) | (S) | (R) | (P) | (Q) |
| (3) | (S) | (R) | (Q) | (P) |
| (4) | (R) | (S) | (Q) | (P) |

**16.** The reason for ''drug induced poisoning'' is :
(1) Binding reversibly at the active site of the enzyme
(2) Bringing conformational change in the binding site of enzyme
(3) Binding irreversibly to the active site of the enzyme
(4) Binding at the allosteric sites of the enzyme

**17.** Which of the following is a bactericidal antibiotic ?
**[2016, Main]**
(1) Erythromycin
(2) Tetracycline
(3) Chloramphenicol
(4) Ofloxacin

**18.** Which of the following compounds is not an antacid ?  **[2015, Main]**
(1) Aluminium hydroxide
(2) Cimetidine
(3) Phenelzine
(4) Ranitidine

**19.** 

$$\underset{\text{OCOCH}_3}{\overset{\text{COOH}}{\bigcirc}}$$ is used as :  **[2015, Main]**

(1) Insecticide
(2) Antihistamine
(3) Analgesic
(4) Antacid

**20.** Which artificial sweetener contains chlorine ?
**[2015, Main]**
(1) Aspartame
(2) Saccharin
(3) Sucralose
(4) Alitame

**21.** Which one of the following is used as Antihistamine ?
**[2014, Main]**
(1) Omeprazole
(2) Chloranphenicol
(3) Diphenhydramine
(4) Norethindrone

**22.** Aminoglycosides are usually used as :
**[2014, Main]**
(1) Antibiotic
(2) Analgesic
(3) Hypnotic
(4) Antifertility

## ANSWER KEY

| | | | | | | | | | |
|---|---|---|---|---|---|---|---|---|---|
| **1.** (3) | **2.** (2) | **3.** (3) | **4.** (3) | **5.** (4) | **6.** (3) | **7.** (2) | **8.** (1) | **9.** (*) | **10.** (3) |
| **11.** (*) | **12.** (*) | **13.** (2) | **14.** (4) | **15.** (1) | **16.** (3) | **17.** (4) | **18.** (3) | **19.** (3) | **20.** (3) |
| **21.** (3) | **22.** (1) | | | | | | | | |

## ANSWERS WITH EXPLANATIONS

**1. (3)** Seldane is an antihistamine drugs, it inhibits the action of histamine receptor.

**2. (2)** (1) 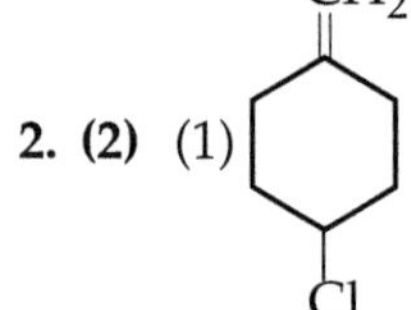 Not show GI

(2) Show GI

(3) Not show GI

(4) 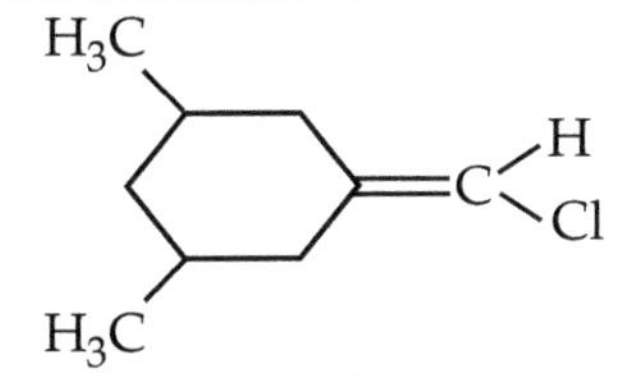 *(structure: 3,5-dimethylcyclohexylidene group with =C< bearing H and Cl)*    Show GI

3. **(3)** Toilet cleaning liquid has about 10.5% weight by volume HCl; therefore to neutralise its affect aqueous $NaHCO_3$ is used while NaOH is avoided for this purpose because its highly corosive in nature and can burn a person's body.

4. **(3)** Raniticline $\rightarrow$ Antacid
Nardil $\rightarrow$ Antidepressant
Chloramphenicol $\rightarrow$ Antibiotic
Dimetane $\rightarrow$ Antihistamine

5. **(4)** Anti depressant drug enhances the mood. As non adrenaline is neurotransmitter and if its level is low in body due to some reason then person suffers from depression and in that situation anti-depressant drug is required.

6. **(3)** Anti-histamine.

7. **(2)** Wrought iron is purest form commercial iron.

8. **(1)** (i) Riboflavin $\rightarrow$ (c) Cheilosis
(ii) Thiamine $\rightarrow$ (a) Beriberi
(iii) Pyridoxine $\rightarrow$ (d) Convulsions
(iv) Ascorbic acid $\rightarrow$ (b) Scurvy

9. 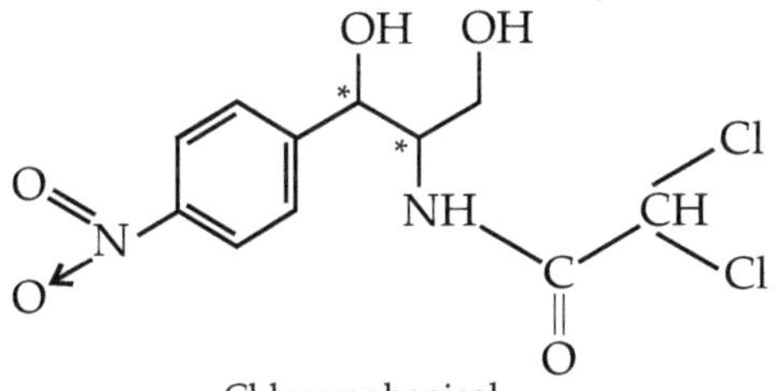 *(structure of Chloramphenicol)*

Chloramphenicol

10. **(3)** Biochemical Oxygen Demand (BOD) is amount of oxygen required by bacteria to break down organic waste in a certain volume of water sample.

11. **(4)** The sum of the total number of atoms in one molecule each of (A), (B) and (C) is :

$$NaCl \xrightarrow[H^+]{K_2Cr_2O_7} \underset{(A)}{CrO_2Cl_2} \xrightarrow{NaOH} \underset{(B)}{Na_2CrO_4}$$

$$\xrightarrow{H_2O_2/H^+} \underset{(C)}{CrO_5}$$

$CrO_2Cl_2 \rightarrow 5$
$Na_2CrO_4 \rightarrow 7$
$CrO_5 \rightarrow 6$
_______
18 atoms

12. The number of $sp^2$ hybridised carbons present in ``Aspartame'' is

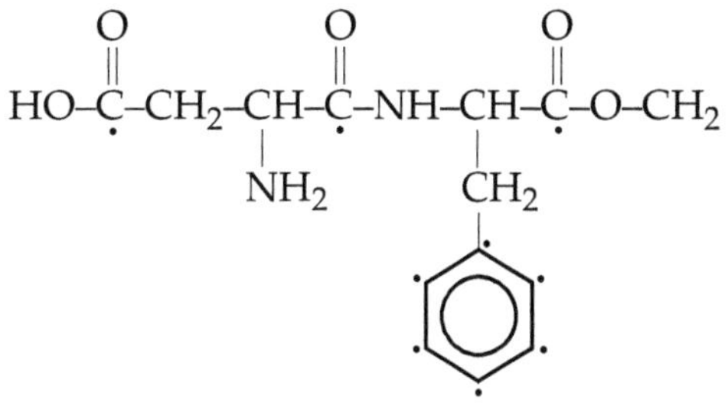

*(structure of Aspartame: HO–C(=O)–CH₂–CH(NH₂)–C(=O)–NH–CH(CH₂–C₆H₅)–C(=O)–O–CH₂)*

13. **(2)** Noradrenaline is a neurotransmitter. It belongs to catecholamine family and functions as chemical messengers in brain and body as a hormone to communicate with another cell.

14. **(4)** The structure of histamine in which amine group is protonated has value comparable to the pH value of blood. The structure of histamine that contains lone pair of electrons on nitrogen atom of amine group is more basic as compared to the blood. Therefore, the amine group of histamine is protonated in the human blood.
The predominant structure of histamine in the human blood is :

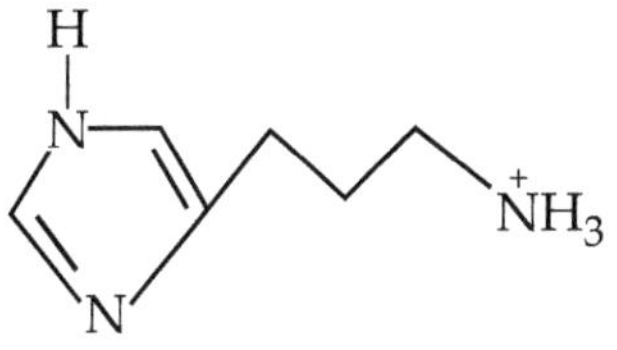

*(structure of protonated histamine with imidazole ring and $\overset{+}{N}H_3$)*

15. **(1)** Phenelzine contains hydrazine.
Chloroxylenol contains phenol.
Uracil is a pyrimidine base.
Ranitidine contains a furan ring.
Hydrazine is a compound with the formula, $N_2H_4$.
The structure of phenelzine is given as,

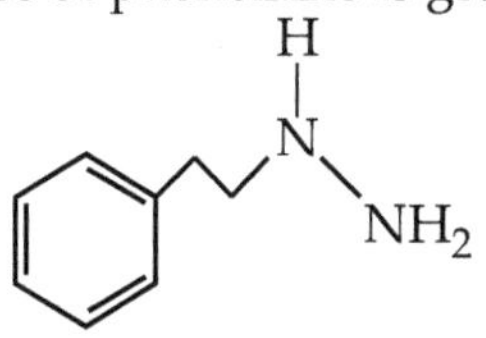

*(structure of phenelzine: benzyl–CH₂CH₂–NH–NH₂)*

In the above structure, substituted hydrazine is present.
The structure of chloroxylenol is given as,

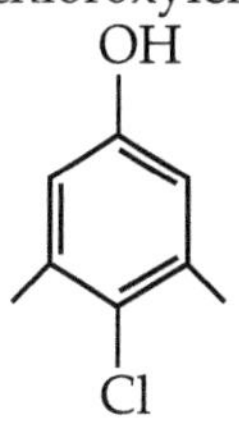

*(structure of chloroxylenol: phenol ring with OH, two CH₃ and Cl)*

From the above structure, it is clear that the phenol ring is present in chloroxylenol.
The structure of uracil is given as,

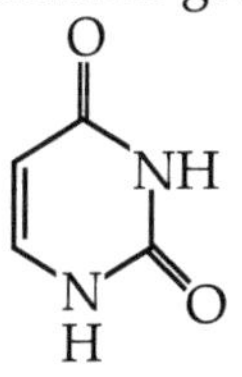

*(structure of uracil)*

From the above structure, it is clear that a pyrimidine ring is present in chloroxylenol.

**16. (3)** The process of enzyme inhibition may take place either reversibly or irreversibly. The irreversible inhibition allows the inhibitor to dissociate very slowly from its target enzyme. This process takes place either covalently or non-covalently. Thus, drug induced poisoning will bind irreversibly to the active site of the enzyme.

**17. (4)** Ofloxacin is a bactericidal antibiotic, whereas erythromycin, tetracycline and chloramphenicol are bacteriostatic antibiotic. Bactericidal antibiotics kill bacteria whereas bacteriostatic antibiotics are inhibits the growth of bacteria.

**18. (3)** Phenelzine is an antidepressant drug, not an antacid.

**19. (3)** The name of given compound is Acetyl salicylic acid or aspirin. It is used as an analgesic.

**20. (3)** The structure of artificial sweetener which contains chlorine is sucralose. Its structure is shown below :

**21. (3)** Diphenhydramine is used as antihistamine. It is trichloro derivative of sucrose and is 600 times sweeter than the cane sugar. It is used to treat common cold, allergy and hay fever.

**22. (1)** Aminoglycosides are a class of antibiotics due to which they are very useful as antibiotics. Therefore, the aminoglycosides are usually used as antibiotics.

●●

9 789390 278596

Printed by Libri Plureos GmbH in Hamburg,
Germany